Poetry Criticism

Guide to Thomson Gale Literary Criticism Series

For criticism on	Consult these Thomson Gale series
Authors now living or who died after December 31, 1999	*CONTEMPORARY LITERARY CRITICISM (CLC)*
Authors who died between 1900 and 1999	*TWENTIETH-CENTURY LITERARY CRITICISM (TCLC)*
Authors who died between 1800 and 1899	*NINETEENTH-CENTURY LITERATURE CRITICISM (NCLC)*
Authors who died between 1400 and 1799	*LITERATURE CRITICISM FROM 1400 TO 1800 (LC)* *SHAKESPEAREAN CRITICISM (SC)*
Authors who died before 1400	*CLASSICAL AND MEDIEVAL LITERATURE CRITICISM (CMLC)*
Authors of books for children and young adults	*CHILDREN'S LITERATURE REVIEW (CLR)*
Dramatists	*DRAMA CRITICISM (DC)*
Poets	*POETRY CRITICISM (PC)*
Short story writers	*SHORT STORY CRITICISM (SSC)*
Literary topics and movements	*HARLEM RENAISSANCE: A GALE CRITICAL COMPANION (HR)* *THE BEAT GENERATION: A GALE CRITICAL COMPANION (BG)* *FEMINISM IN LITERATURE: A GALE CRITICAL COMPANION (FL)* *GOTHIC LITERATURE: A GALE CRITICAL COMPANION (GL)*
Asian American writers of the last two hundred years	*ASIAN AMERICAN LITERATURE (AAL)*
Black writers of the past two hundred years	*BLACK LITERATURE CRITICISM (BLC)* *BLACK LITERATURE CRITICISM SUPPLEMENT (BLCS)*
Hispanic writers of the late nineteenth and twentieth centuries	*HISPANIC LITERATURE CRITICISM (HLC)* *HISPANIC LITERATURE CRITICISM SUPPLEMENT (HLCS)*
Native North American writers and orators of the eighteenth, nineteenth, and twentieth centuries	*NATIVE NORTH AMERICAN LITERATURE (NNAL)*
Major authors from the Renaissance to the present	*WORLD LITERATURE CRITICISM, 1500 TO THE PRESENT (WLC)* *WORLD LITERATURE CRITICISM SUPPLEMENT (WLCS)*

ISSN 1052-4851

Poetry Criticism

*Excerpts from Criticism of the Works
of the Most Significant and Widely
Studied Poets of World Literature*

Volume 71

Michelle Lee
Project Editor

THOMSON
★
GALE

Detroit • New York • San Francisco • New Haven, Conn. • Waterville, Maine • London • Munich

THOMSON

GALE

Poetry Criticism, Vol. 71

Project Editor
Michelle Lee

Editorial
Jessica Bomarito, Kathy D. Darrow, Jeffrey W. Hunter, Jelena O. Krstović, Thomas J. Schoenberg, Noah Schusterbauer, Lawrence J. Trudeau, Russel Whitaker

Data Capture
Frances Monroe, Gwen Tucker

Indexing Services
Laurie Andriot

Rights and Acquisitions
Margaret Abendroth, Margaret Chamberlain-Gaston, Edna Hedblad, and Shalice Shah-Caldwell

Imaging and Multimedia
Dean Dauphinais, Robert Duncan, Leitha Etheridge-Sims, Lezlie Light, Mike Logusz, Dan Newell, Christine O'Bryan, Kelly A. Quin, Denay Wilding, Robyn Young

Composition and Electronic Capture
Carolyn A. Roney

Manufacturing
Rhonda Dover

Associate Product Manager
Marc Cormier

LIBRARY OF CONGRESS CATALOG CARD NUMBER 91-118494

ISBN 0-7876-8705-7
ISSN 1052-4851

Printed in the United States of America
10 9 8 7 6 5 4 3 2 1

Contents

Preface

Poetry Criticism (*PC*) presents significant criticism of the world's greatest poets and provides supplementary biographical and bibliographical material to guide the interested reader to a greater understanding of the genre and its creators. Although major poets and literary movements are covered in such Thomson Gale Literary Criticism series as *Contemporary Literary Criticism* (*CLC*), *Twentieth-Century Literary Criticism* (*TCLC*), *Nineteenth-Century Literature Criticism* (*NCLC*), *Literature Criticism from 1400 to 1800* (*LC*), and *Classical and Medieval Literature Criticism* (*CMLC*), *PC* offers more focused attention on poetry than is possible in the broader, survey-oriented entries on writers in these Thomson Gale series. Students, teachers, librarians, and researchers will find that the generous excerpts and supplementary material provided by *PC* supply them with the vital information needed to write a term paper on poetic technique, to examine a poet's most prominent themes, or to lead a poetry discussion group.

Scope of the Series

PC is designed to serve as an introduction to major poets of all eras and nationalities. Since these authors have inspired a great deal of relevant critical material, *PC* is necessarily selective, and the editors have chosen the most important published criticism to aid readers and students in their research. Each author entry presents a historical survey of the critical response to that author's work. The length of an entry is intended to reflect the amount of critical attention the author has received from critics writing in English and from foreign critics in translation. Every attempt has been made to identify and include the most significant essays on each author's work. In order to provide these important critical pieces, the editors sometimes reprint essays that have appeared elsewhere in Thomson Gale's Literary Criticism Series. Such duplication, however, never exceeds twenty percent of a *PC* volume.

Organization of the Book

Each *PC* entry consists of the following elements:

- The **Author Heading** cites the name under which the author most commonly wrote, followed by birth and death dates. Also located here are any name variations under which an author wrote, including transliterated forms for authors whose native languages use nonroman alphabets. If the author wrote consistently under a pseudonym, the pseudonym will be listed in the author heading and the author's actual name given in parenthesis on the first line of the biographical and critical introduction. Uncertain birth or death dates are indicated by question marks. Single-work entries are preceded by the title of the work and its date of publication.

- The **Introduction** contains background information that introduces the reader to the author and the critical debates surrounding his or her work.

- A **Portrait of the Author** is included when available.

- The list of **Principal Works** is ordered chronologically by date of first publication and lists the most important works by the author. The first section comprises poetry collections and book-length poems. The second section gives information on other major works by the author. For foreign authors, the editors have provided original foreign-language publication information and have selected what are considered the best and most complete English-language editions of their works.

- Reprinted **Criticism** is arranged chronologically in each entry to provide a useful perspective on changes in critical evaluation over time. All individual titles of poems and poetry collections by the author featured in the entry are printed in boldface type. The critic's name and the date of composition or publication of the critical work are given at the beginning of each piece of criticism. Unsigned criticism is preceded by the title of the source in which it appeared. Footnotes are reprinted at the end of each essay or excerpt. In the case of excerpted criticism, only those footnotes that pertain to the excerpted texts are included.

- Critical essays are prefaced by brief **Annotations** explicating each piece.

- A complete **Bibliographical Citation** of the original essay or book precedes each piece of criticism.

- An annotated bibliography of **Further Reading** appears at the end of each entry and suggests resources for additional study. In some cases, significant essays for which the editors could not obtain reprint rights are included here. Boxed material following the further reading list provides references to other biographical and critical sources on the author in series published by Thomson Gale.

Cumulative Indexes

A **Cumulative Author Index** lists all of the authors that appear in a wide variety of reference sources published by Thomson Gale, including *PC*. A complete list of these sources is found facing the first page of the Author Index. The index also includes birth and death dates and cross references between pseudonyms and actual names.

A **Cumulative Nationality Index** lists all authors featured in *PC* by nationality, followed by the number of the *PC* volume in which their entry appears.

A **Cumulative Title Index** lists in alphabetical order all individual poems, book-length poems, and collection titles contained in the *PC* series. Titles of poetry collections and separately published poems are printed in italics, while titles of individual poems are printed in roman type with quotation marks. Each title is followed by the author's last name and corresponding volume and page numbers where commentary on the work is located. English-language translations of original foreign-language titles are cross-referenced to the foreign titles so that all references to discussion of a work are combined in one listing.

Citing *Poetry Criticism*

When citing criticism reprinted in the Literary Criticism Series, students should provide complete bibliographic information so that the cited essay can be located in the original print or electronic source. Students who quote directly from reprinted criticism may use any accepted bibliographic format, such as University of Chicago Press style or Modern Language Association (MLA) style. Both the MLA and the University of Chicago formats are acceptable and recognized as being the current standards for citations. It is important, however, to choose one format for all citations; do not mix the two formats within a list of citations.

The examples below follow recommendations for preparing a bibliography set forth in *The Chicago Manual of Style,* 14th ed. (Chicago: The University of Chicago Press, 1993); the first example pertains to material drawn from periodicals, the second to material reprinted from books:

Linkin, Harriet Kramer. "The Language of Speakers in *Songs of Innocence and of Experience.*" *Romanticism Past and Present* 10, no. 2 (summer 1986): 5-24. Reprinted in *Poetry Criticism.* Vol. 63, edited by Michelle Lee, 79-88. Detroit: Thomson Gale, 2005.

Glen, Heather. "Blake's Criticism of Moral Thinking in *Songs of Innocence and of Experience.*" In *Interpreting Blake,* edited by Michael Phillips, 32-69. Cambridge: Cambridge University Press, 1978. Reprinted in *Poetry Criticism.* Vol. 63, edited by Michelle Lee, 34-51. Detroit: Thomson Gale, 2005.

Suggestions are Welcome

Readers who wish to suggest new features, topics, or authors to appear in future volumes, or who have other suggestions or comments are cordially invited to call, write, or fax the Associate Product Manager:

Associate Product Manager, Literary Criticism Series
Thomson Gale
27500 Drake Road
Farmington Hills, MI 48331-3535
1-800-347-4253 (GALE)
Fax: 248-699-8054

Acknowledgments

The editors wish to thank the copyright holders of the criticism included in this volume and the permissions managers of many book and magazine publishing companies for assisting us in securing reproduction rights. Following is a list of the copyright holders who have granted us permission to reproduce material in this volume of *PC*. Every effort has been made to trace copyright, but if omissions have been made, please let us know.

COPYRIGHTED MATERIAL IN *PC*, VOLUME 71, WAS REPRODUCED FROM THE FOLLOWING PERIODICALS:

Atlantic Monthly, v. 295, January-February, 2005 for "A Nice Bloody Fool" by Christopher Hitchens. Copyright © 2005 by *Atlantic Monthly*. Reproduced by permission of the author.—*College English*, v. 27, February, 1966. Copyright © 1966 by the National Council of Teachers of English. Reproduced by permission of the publisher.—*Contemporary Literature*, v. 12, autumn, 1971. Copyright © 1971 by the Board of Regents of the University of Wisconsin System. Reproduced by permission.—*Durham University Journal*, v. 36, June, 1975. Reproduced by permission.—*Explicator*, v. 24, November, 1965; v. 27, winter, 1989; v. 49, summer, 1991; v. 54, spring, 1996; v. 62, fall, 2003. Copyright © 1965, 1989, 1991, 1996, 2003 by the Helen Dwight Reid Educational Foundation. All reproduced with permission of the Helen Dwight Reid Educational Foundation, published by Heldref Publications, 1319 18th Street, NW, Washington, DC 20036-1802.—*Field*, v. 41, fall, 1989. Copyright © 1989 by Oberlin College Press. Reproduced by permission.—*Iowa Review*, v. 5, spring, 1974 for "World's Guest—William Stafford" by John Lauber. Reproduced by permission of the Literary Estate of the author.—*Journal of European Studies*, v. 32, 2002. Copyright © 2002 by Richard Sadler Ltd. Reproduced by permission of Sage Publications, Thousand Oaks, London and New Delhi.—*Kansas Quarterly*, v. 2, spring, 1970 for "Problems with Landscapes in Early Stafford Poems" by Richard Hugo. Copyright © 1970 by the *Kansas Quarterly*. Reproduced by permission of the publisher and the author.—*Language and Style*, v. 17, winter, 1984 for "Frost's 'The Road Not Taken': Text-Structure and Poetic Theory" by Thomas Elwood Hart. Copyright © 1984 by E. L. Epstein. All rights revert to authors. Reproduced by permission of the author.—*MidAmerica*, v. 11, 1984 for "'A Visioned End': Edgar Lee Masters and William Stafford" by Leland Krauth. Copyright © 1984 by the Society for the Study of Midwestern Literature. All rights reserved. Reproduced by permission of the publisher and the author.—*Midwest Quarterly*, v. 39, winter, 1998. Copyright © 1998 by the *Midwest Quarterly*, Pittsburgh State University. Reproduced by permission.—*Modern Poetry Studies*, v. 6, spring, 1975. Copyright © 1975 by Jerome Mazzaro. Reproduced by permission.—*Partisan Review*, v. 41, 1974 for "The Raw and the Cooked" by Paul Zweig. Copyright © 1974 by Paul Zweig. Reprinted by permission of Georges Borchardt, Inc. on behalf of the author.—*Rocky Mountain Review*, v. 54, fall, 2000. Reproduced by permission.—*Robert Frost Review*, fall, 1997; fall, 1999. Copyright © 1997, 1999 by the Robert Frost Society. All rights reserved. Reproduced by permission of the *Robert Frost Review*.—*South Carolina Review*, v. 7, April, 1975. Copyright © 1975 by Clemson University. Reproduced by permission.—*Studia Neophilologica*, v. 59, 1987 for "Willingly Local: A Conversation with William Stafford about Regionalism and Northwest Poetry" by Lars Nordstrom. Reproduced by permission of Taylor & Francis Group, www.taylorandfrancisgroup.com.—*Studies in English Literature 1500-1900*, v. 5, autumn, 1965. Copyright © 1965 the Johns Hopkins University Press. Reproduced by permission.—*Twentieth Century Literature*, v. 48, fall, 2002. Copyright © 2002 by Hofstra University Press. Reproduced by permission.—*Western American Literature*, v. 7, 1972. Copyright © 1972 by the Western Literature Association. Reproduced by permission.

COPYRIGHTED MATERIAL IN *PC*, VOLUME 71, WAS REPRODUCED FROM THE FOLLOWING BOOKS:

Allen, Gay Wilson. From *American Prosody*. Octagon Books, 1966. Copyright 1935 by American Book Company. Reproduced by permission.—Benediktsson, Thomas E. From "Montana Eclogue: The Pastoral Art of William Stafford," in *World, Self, Poem: Essays on Contemporary Poetry from the "Jubilation of Poets."* Edited by Leonard M. Trawick. The Kent State University Press, 1990. Copyright © 1990 by the Kent State University Press. Reproduced by permission.—Carter, Everett. From "The Typicality of Oliver Wendell Holmes," in *Themes and Directions in American Literature*. Edited by Ray B. Browne and Donald Pizer. Purdue University Studies, 1969. Copyright © 1969 by Purdue University Press. Reproduced by permission.—Faggen, Robert. From *Robert Frost and the Challenge of Darwin*. The University of Michigan Press, 1997. Copyright © 1997 by the University of Michigan Press. All rights reserved. Reproduced by permis-

Thomson Gale Literature Product Advisory Board

The members of the Thomson Gale Literature Product Advisory Board—reference librarians from public and academic library systems—represent a cross-section of our customer base and offer a variety of informed perspectives on both the presentation and content of our literature products. Advisory board members assess and define such quality issues as the relevance, currency, and usefulness of the author coverage, critical content, and literary topics included in our series; evaluate the layout, presentation, and general quality of our printed volumes; provide feedback on the criteria used for selecting authors and topics covered in our series; provide suggestions for potential enhancements to our series; identify any gaps in our coverage of authors or literary topics, recommending authors or topics for inclusion; analyze the appropriateness of our content and presentation for various user audiences, such as high school students, undergraduates, graduate students, librarians, and educators; and offer feedback on any proposed changes/enhancements to our series. We wish to thank the following advisors for their advice throughout the year.

"The Road Not Taken"

Robert Frost

The following entry represents criticism on Frost's 1915 poem "The Road Not Taken." For further information on Frost's life and career, see *Poetry Criticism,* Volumes 1 and 39.

INTRODUCTION

By Frost's own account, he wrote "The Road Not Taken" as ironic commentary on his friend Edward Thomas's Romantic nature. Biographical studies have held that Frost and the British poet often went walking in the English countryside and, on more than one occasion, Thomas expressed regret that they must choose one road over another.

It is believed that Frost began the poem in 1912, set it aside, then completed it in 1915, shortly after his return to New Hampshire. It was first published in the *Atlantic Monthly* in August, 1915, and later collected in his third book, *Mountain Interval* (1916). "The Road Not Taken" has always been one of Frost's most popular poems.

BIOGRAPHICAL INFORMATION

Frost was born March 26, 1874, in San Francisco, the son of William Prescott Frost, a newspaper reporter and editor, and Isabel Moodie Frost, a teacher. His family, originally from New England, moved to Massachusetts in 1884 after his father's death. Frost decided he wanted to be a poet early in life, graduating as class poet from Lawrence (Massachusetts) High School in 1892.

Frost married Elinor Miriam White on December 19, 1895; the couple had six children. He attended Dartmouth College in 1892 and Harvard University from 1897 to 1899. Although Frost was able to earn some money with sporadic publications and teaching jobs, he was frustrated over his unsuccessful career and moved his family to England in 1912. His first two books, *A Boy's Will* (1913) and *North of Boston* (1914) were published while he lived in England. Frost was a celebrated poet by the time he and his family returned to the United States in 1915.

In addition to his career as a prolific writer of poetry, Frost also held positions at many colleges and universities, including Tufts College, Amherst College, Harvard

University, Middlebury College, the University of Michigan, Columbia University, Yale University, and Dartmouth College. He was a cofounder of the Bread Loaf School and Conference of English held at Middlebury College in Vermont. Frost died in Boston on January 29, 1963.

PLOT AND MAJOR CHARACTERS

The only character featured in "The Road Not Taken" is the narrator, a traveler facing the choice between two roads. This figure is frequently identified as Frost's friend Thomas, about whom the poem is reported to have been written, although it is just as frequently identified as Frost himself.

In the first stanza, the traveler recalls standing at a junction of two roads. He expresses regret that he cannot travel on both roads "[a]nd be one traveler." He also describes one of the roads down the length that is visible from his vantage point.

In stanza two, the traveler suddenly relates how he took the other road and further describes that chosen way. The description compares the two roads, hinting at their similarity.

In the third stanza, the similarity of the two roads is reiterated. The traveler then describes how he had hoped to return to the other path another day but knew that he would probably not come back.

Stanza four projects into the traveler's future when he will still be wondering about that other path. He states here that the path he chose was indeed less traveled than the one he left behind, although the reader now understands that the difference between the two roads is subtle. While the narrator claims that his choice "has made all the difference," the precise nature of that difference is left unexplained.

MAJOR THEMES

The prevailing theme of Frost's "The Road Not Taken" is individualism. The traveler is alone and must face this difficult choice alone. Both roads seem very similar, and their differences may only be subjective. The traveler cannot go in both directions because he is but one person. The tension in the poem is provided by the individual's interaction with nature, which combines a sense of wonder at the beauty of the natural world with a sense of frustration as the individual tries to find a place for himself within nature's complexity.

Romanticism is another theme of "The Road Not Taken." Frost has made it clear in his essays and letters as to the origins of this poem and its inherent ironic nature as it pokes fun at the Romantic character of his close friend Thomas. Many critics still maintain that "The Road Not Taken" does not just describe another man's Romantic nature but also bears traces of Frost's own Romantic influences: William Wordsworth, John Keats, Emily Dickinson, and Henry David Thoreau. Frost's debt to Romanticism, which he tried to refute, is readily apparent in this poem, but is mitigated by his own ironic interpretation of the work.

CRITICAL RECEPTION

"The Road Not Taken" has always been extremely popular with readers and critics alike. On the surface, the poem's premise is simple, but critics have examined the poem in detail and have discovered depths of meaning not apparent in a casual reading. "The Road Not

Taken" is part of a larger literary and artistic tradition involving a choice between two paths, figurative and literal. George Monteiro and Jeffrey S. Cramer explore the literary history of this tradition and how it has come to a popular culmination with Frost's poem. Nicholas Cervo is concerned with Frost's choice of the word *road,* where wheeled vehicles travel, versus *path,* which would seemingly be more appropriate. While Cervo acknowledges that the choice was deliberate, he argues that it significantly alters the interpretation of the work.

David M. Wyatt views Frost as a poet who made surprise an important element in his writing. Wyatt explains that in "The Road Not Taken" the reader expects to be offered a choice, but that expectation is thwarted because the choice was made before the poem began. William George also addresses Frost's trickiness by examining the poem's point-of-view. George demonstrates how the poem is narrated by a middle-aged man mocking his younger self in the beginning of the poem and his future older self at the end.

Thomas Elwood Hart delves into the more technical aspects of "The Road Not Taken," dispelling the Romantic image of Frost composing this poem in one sitting. Instead Hart provides evidence that every word and phrase was carefully selected and placed so as to evoke layers of meaning for Frost, his readers, and for Thomas. Hart also examines Frost's revisions from the poem's initial publication in the *Atlantic Monthly* to its later appearance in *Mountain Interval.*

Many critics, such as Robert F. Fleissner and John H. Timmerman, have investigated Frost's Romantic influences at length in connection with "The Road Not Taken." Although Frost did not consider himself a Romantic poet, neither was he a Modernist. Fleissner and Timmerman point to Wordsworth and Keats as the most obvious influences on his work, but Dickinson and Thoreau, Romantics of the American Transcendentalist movement, appear also to have had a profound effect on Frost's technical and thematic approaches to poetry, as evidenced in "The Road Not Taken." Robert Faggen further explores Frost's connection to Thoreau by comparing "The Road Not Taken" to Thoreau's essay "Walking," published posthumously.

Manorama B. Trikha argues that "The Road Not Taken" is an example of how some important choices in life are guided by outward appearances. The critic views this poem as an "example of man's self-encounter and self-division." Investigating epistolary evidence, Larry Finger suggests that Frost's interpretation of "The Road Not Taken" changed later in his life from ironic commentary on his friend's Romantic nature to a more self-reflective representation of Frost's own choices. R. F. Fleissner disagrees, maintaining that Finger has not taken all evidence into account and, in some cases, has misinterpreted Frost's meaning in the letters. Fleissner maintains that Frost never changed his opinion about the meaning of "The Road Not Taken."

PRINCIPAL WORKS

Poetry

Twilight 1894
A Boy's Will 1913
North of Boston 1914
Mountain Interval 1916
New Hampshire 1923
Selected Poems 1923; revised, 1928 and 1934
Several Short Poems 1924
Selected Poems 1928
West-Running Brook 1928
The Lovely Shall Be Choosers 1929
Collected Poems of Robert Frost 1930
The Lone Striker 1933
Two Tramps in Mud Time 1934
The Gold Hesperidee 1935
Three Poems 1935
From Snow to Snow 1936
A Further Range 1936
Selected Poems 1936
A Witness Tree 1942
Come in and Other Poems 1943; revised as *The Road Not Taken,* 1951
Steeple Bush 1947
Greece 1948
Complete Poems of Robert Frost, 1949 1949
Hard Not to Be King 1951
Aforesaid 1954
Selected Poems 1955
The Gift Outright 1961
Poems 1961
In the Clearing 1962
Selected Poems of Robert Frost 1963
The Poetry of Robert Frost 1966
Complete Poems of Robert Frost 1968
The Poetry of Robert Frost: The Collected Poems, Complete and Unabridged 1969
Robert Frost: Poetry and Prose 1972
Selected Poems 1973
Stopping by Woods on a Snowy Evening 1978
Early Poems 1981
Spring Pools 1983
Collected Poems, Plays, and Prose 1995
Frost: Collected Poems, Prose, and Plays 1995
The Robert Frost Reader: Poetry and Prose 2002

Other Major Works

A Masque of Reason (verse drama) 1942
A Masque of Mercy (verse drama) 1947
Selected Letters [edited by Lawrence Thompson] (letters) 1964
Interviews with Robert Frost (interviews) 1966
Family Letters of Robert and Elinor Frost (letters) 1972
Robert Frost: A Living Voice (speeches) 1974

CRITICISM

David M. Wyatt (essay date 1976)

SOURCE: Wyatt, David M. "Choosing in Frost." In *Frost: Centennial Essays II,* edited by Jac Tharpe, pp. 129-40. Jackson: University Press of Mississippi, 1976.

[*In the following essay, Wyatt discusses the element of surprise in "The Road Not Taken."*]

Surprise: Robert Frost writes continually of it. As a disposition toward life it becomes a project for poetry, a way of moving through both. Even metaphor emerges as something come upon unawares. With a tenor firmly in mind, Frost can happen at any time upon a hidden vehicle. The pleasure is in falling for something one didn't expect to find, in a place one didn't know one was: "the pleasure of ulteriority."[1] So in the act of composition the poet remains absent from himself, waiting to surprise himself as he emerges onto the landing from which the climb into and out of the poem might be viewed. His "intention" is pleasantly ulterior, of "a particular mood that won't be satisfied with anything less than its own fulfillment. But it is not yet a thought concerned with what becomes it. One thing to know it by: it shrinks shyly from anticipatory expression. . . . A poem is the emotion of having a thought while the reader waits a little anxiously for the success of dawn." Unlike his forerunner Thoreau, Frost does not wish to prepare his own way, "To anticipate, not the sunrise and the dawn merely, but, if possible, Nature herself!" This is Frost's greatest fear: that he might anticipate himself and the unforeseen destiny of his poem.

Frost's anxiety that he might sacrifice wonder to order becomes his motive for metaphor. To preserve the "Order of Wonder" he follows a radically Emersonian impulse: "If you desire to arrest attention, to surprise, do not give me facts in the order of cause and effect, but drop one or two links in the chain, & give me with a cause, an effect two or three times removed."[2] Nowhere in Frost is the tension between surprise and anticipation, wayward experience and the form into which it is cast or forecast, more acute than in **"The Road Not Taken"**:

> Two roads diverged in a yellow wood,
> And sorry I could not travel both
> And be one traveler, long I stood
> And looked down one as far as I could
> To where it bent in the undergrowth;
>
> Then took the other, as just as fair,
> And having perhaps the better claim,
> Because it was grassy and wanted wear;
> Though as for that, the passing there
> Had worn them really about the same,
>
> And both that morning equally lay
> In leaves no step had trodden black.
> Oh, I kept the first for another day!
> Yet knowing how way leads on to way,
> I doubted if I should ever come back.
>
> I shall be telling this with a sigh
> Somewhere ages and ages hence:
> Two roads diverged in a wood, and I—
> I took the one less traveled by,
> And that has made all the difference.

Reuben Brower advances the traditional reading of this poem: "Although **'The Road Not Taken'** lends itself like some of Shakespeare's sonnets to over-easy identifications with the youthful self of the poet or the reader, it is still a powerful image of the choice of life."[3] I will argue that the much crankier response of Yvor Winters to the poem as written by "a man whom one might well call a spiritual drifter"[4] more accurately describes it. In surrendering to the "rightness of impulse," Frost is seen by Winters as conferring the active role in the poem upon the reader, who must assume the "burden of critical intelligence which ought to be borne by the poet." This is true, although it need not be lamented. Nor need we cringe when Winters pejoratively labels such impulses "Emersonian." The critic reveals his deep grasp of the Emersonian tradition even in the very act of trying to belittle it. For all of his unwillingness to honor it, Winters has correctly identified this tradition, and we should pause to outline its essential dimensions before going on to read Frost's central poetic extension of it.

The full force of Winters's objections to Frost has never been met. His attack begins to surface in *Maule's Curse* and adumbrates the later complaints—by Cowley, Pearce, Nitchie—that Frost fails of being a "serious" or a committed writer. While it took Winters twenty years to accuse Frost openly of being a spiritual drifter, any reader of *Maule's Curse* could have predicted that Frost would one day join Hawthorne, Emerson, Melville and James in the "History of American Obscurantism." Winters's argument is historical; his theme is the crisis of the will. By "obscurantism" he really means the

abandonment, by major American writers, of belief in a world of clear moral options. He sees this problem devolving inevitably from a conflict between Puritan theory and practice: "They may have denied the freedom of the will and the efficaciousness of good works by lip, but by habit, and without really grasping the fact, they believed in them and acted upon them."[5] While Perry Miller has given this conflict its most careful exposition, Winters can lay claim to having first lamented it as afflicting, through numerous transformations, our greatest literature. And he was also inspired in locating Emerson as the crucial vortex in which this conflicted experience of the will was concentrated and passed on: "In Emerson the exercise of the will is as active as ever, and his moral judgments are frequently made with force and with accuracy; but his central doctrine is that of submission to emotion, which for the pantheist is a kind of divine instigation: an inadmissible doctrine, for it eliminates at a stroke both choice and the values that serve as a basis for choice, it substitutes for a doctrine of values a doctrine of equivalence, thus rendering man an automaton and paralyzing all genuine action, so that Emerson's acceptable acts of expression are accidental poems or epigrams drawing their only nutriment from the fringe or from beyond the fringe of his doctrine." In the tradition flowing through Emerson attention shifts from the free exercise of choice to the difficulty of ever approaching it. "Maule's Curse" is to feel the will stimulated to no *end*.

Winters is more convincing as a literary critic than an historian of ideas. Yet however questionable his analysis of the origins of "Maule's Curse," he does prove that choosing rarely happens in the works he reads. Unfortunately the violence of Winters's judgments has obscured the accuracy of his descriptions. He complained of his book that it "was attacked . . . because it found obscurity where the reviewer found none." Yet the book very likely aroused more resistance because of its method and tone than its theme. On every page one encounters a sensibility unwilling to accept the demands this literature makes upon us. When Winters claims that "a work of art, like each detail comprising it, is by definition a judgment," he advances a definition none of these artists would recognize. They are by Winters's own persuasive description unwilling or unable to embody "judgment." Yet Winters's way of reading sheds just that negative light upon this literature which illuminates what it decidedly is not. Our debate with him should not be over whether such a tradition exists, but how to value it. These writers were not victims of a failure of nerve. They were intent upon creating a new way of being in the world. One thing they appear to have agreed upon: selves are not shaped through traditional acts of volition. So when Winters eventually includes Frost within this line and says of **"The Road Not Taken"** that it deals with "what in the hands of a more serious writer one could call the theme of moral choice,"[6] he proves himself of Frost's party without knowing it. This is just the response Frost's poem should encourage: the realization that the choice the poem appears to promise is not actually delivered. Winters writes as if he were Frost's **"Escapist—Never,"** that aggressive self-seeker for whom "All is an interminable chain of longing." The curse of his morality is to find identity the more receding as it is the more ambitiously sought. Frost inducts us into a contrary discipline: in his poetry identity is not pursued, but allowed spontaneously to emerge. He questions the narrow fiction that selves are formed only in the clash between the will and the world. People are, no more than poems, preconceived. Frost redeems "Maule's Curse" by initiating us into a world where the wonder of order has been superseded by the order of wonder.

The title of **"The Road Not Taken"** promises an anatomy of choice. We look forward to further dealings with a way not abandoned to. Most readers fail to relinquish this initial expectation, reading the poem as if it were of a fateful taking and a not-taking. The first stanza encourages this reaction by giving us the "facts in the order of cause and effect." We start by coming upon "two roads" diverging. As a literary situation, this could hardly be less original. As a moment bearing the burden of choice, the Western imagination knows few more compelling. The lines begin therefore to generate an anxiety so deep as to be obscure. Precisely because this possible divergence confounds so broad a range of fears, so many modes of loss, we are not sorry to linger "long" with the speaker at the fork. The necessary process of examination leading up to choice seems well underway as we complete the first stanza. At least "one" road has been "looked down" as far as we can look. Thus the semicolon after "undergrowth" prepares us for a turn of the head, a further gazing down the other road:

> Then took the other, as just as fair,
> And having perhaps the better claim,
> Because it was grassy and wanted wear;
> Though as for that, the passing there
> Had worn them really about the same,
>
> And both that morning equally lay
> In leaves no step had trodden black.

These seven lines complete the first sentence in the poem, though in ways wholly unexpected. Just as we begin to get lost in the undergrowth, the poem asks us to make a stylistic and experiential leap. That we expect merely a turn measures the surprising motion made between the two stanzas. For surely with "Then took the other" we are given an "effect two or three times removed" from a "cause." We seem to have jumped from stanza one to stanza three. The moment of choosing has been overshot—stanza two is missing—and we are already on the road. Why do so many readers fail to

experience this surprise? What devices work to mask it? The most profound answer evades literary analysis, since the device is deeply hidden within each reader. The poem triggers an anxiety we all feel in separating ourselves from our first source, in growing into division and maturity. Faced squarely with the crisis of separation, avoidance may be preferable to choice. In the moment of decision we leave as much behind as we find to carry with us. So the poem grants an impression of such a moment while actually shielding us from a true experience of it. By helping us to avoid the threat of self-division, Frost allows us to preserve an illusion of wholeness and eases us through a boundary situation in which it is barely possible to gather the reasons for moving:

> Wherever I am
> I am what is missing.
>
> . . . . .
>
> We all have reasons
> for moving.
> I move
> to keep things whole.[7]

Whatever our reasons for moving, we need not balk at a more practical analysis of how Frost makes us pass on. To describe this strategy an elaborate formula might be advanced: in lines six through twelve, the syntax of deliberation masks the rhetoric of equivocation. How different, really, are the two roads? Having missed our chance to examine them both, can we justify our course on the run?

We first find ourselves taking a rather undifferentiated road: "the other." Backing up, it seems as if "then took" carries a greater portentousness than "the other" can satisfy. This opening phrase certainly preserves our ignorance as to how or why we came here. The next equates both roads: this other is taken "as just as fair." But how are we to take the first "as"? Does it have the force of *since* or *though*? That is, does it signal a choice made, or a chance taken? The question passes as fleetingly through our minds as we do through the stanza, where we move on to a qualification in favor of the taken road. "Perhaps" scarcely works as self-congratulation, so the speaker goes on to shore it up with a "because." Hard evidence of "difference" seems to be at hand, if not underfoot. The frivolity of the claim—that being "grassy" and wanting "wear" are the necessary attractions of a road—may be overlooked in our relief at being granted some reasons for moving. But even this shaky rationale gets trodden down by a counter-qualification. "Though" in line nine initiates, for the attentive reader, the most disturbing revelation in the poem: as for "passing," it has "worn them really about the same." All the stanza's carefully measured phrases and counter-phrases finally contain no more capacity to differentiate the two roads than this.

The opening two lines of stanza three ask us to continue the process of equating the two roads through the agency of the poem's climactic, if often overlooked adverb—"equally." By the time we reach the first period in the poem, the two roads have registered themselves as the same and different, worn and untrodden. Frost has gone a good distance toward making "both" seem like "one" while preserving for the overeager reader the illusion of being on a unique course. The poem presents two roads through itself: one, the wide road toward easeful differentiation; the other, the straight and narrow way toward discovery of its choice as a hoax. Frost continues to play more upon our desire to master options than upon any reluctance to force our will onto our way. The exclamation in "Oh, I kept the first for another day!" sustains the illusion about some loss to regret. The resigned, forward-looking tone of the next two lines asks us to join in a manly acceptance of the consequence of choice. But the speaker undermines himself by being too knowing. He describes a choice becoming a fate. The "way" is to become what "leads" him. This fate might be the source of some concern had it not been his from the beginning of the poem. If "way leads on to way," doubts lead back to the self. The process of rationalization culminates in "I doubted if I should ever come back." Here we stumble over an extra half-foot; too many "I's" figure in this line. The speaker crams in an extra one at the beginning to throw off the rhythm of our stride through the poem. Nowhere do the anxieties of self-division, of being "one" and yet "both," surface more stubbornly than in this doubtful line, over-full of the reiterated singular self.

From a spurious resignation to the future in the third stanza we move in the fourth to a realization of that time. The burden of self-consciousness has become so great for the speaker that he projects the present into the future to think about it as the past. The main difficulty for the reader is in making out what "this" is. Does it refer to the choice (not made) or to the poem itself (still being said and read)? "This" usually testifies to the presence of a thing just as "that" does to its absence. Frost is fond of creating a sense of presentness by using *this*. But here the speaker is only present to his poem—not to the lived experience upon which it is based. He has already worked up this interval as a tale to tell, and one with a rhyme scheme so intricate as to challenge any notion that the end of each line remains unforeseen. "This" reduces and abstracts the poet's experience into portable content. As an abstraction, it distances us even further from the concrete immediacy of a moment of choice. It begs the question, as has the entire poem, of what did happen at the fork, while leaving the speaker (and willing auditors) free to point a moral and adorn a tale.

Thus the voice speaking the last stanza grows increasingly elegiac. It recapitulates the poem's first line—it

recommences to tell the tale—with a revealing distortion. "Two roads diverged in a wood, and I—" introduces a momentary stay into a process where none had been before. As we—now become a future audience—hover at the end of the line in wait for the choice to come, we get "I." Can we have expected anything else? Here "I" literally gets split from "I" to suggest the inevitable self-division consequent upon the failure to acknowledge the impossibility of choice. While the speaker misleads his listeners with "I took the one less traveled by," the attentive reader remembers that a moment of choosing between more and less never existed. This poem not only refuses to grant the time in which to choose; it presents a world void of difference which we might contemplate in such an interval. The crucial deception at the end turns upon "and." While we can understand that from a future vantage point any speaker might perceive "all the difference" between his past and his present self, we cannot agree that this particular difference flows from a fateful taking. The fictions of order a self projects back onto experience, even while that experience is still to be completed, here supplant the moment it actually lived. Overcome by what he has missed, the speaker tries to recreate the moment of choice and a world of alternatives "ages and ages" later. He has failed his trial by existence, but the watchful reader will not be unaware that the pure fate through which he has just gone "Admits no memory of choice" (**"The Trial by Existence,"** p. 21).

Frost spells out the poetic strategies appropriate to this view of experience in "The Figure a Poem Makes." This essay does not so much announce as embody Frost's aesthetic of surprise. Reading the essay is like reading the poem. Its initial question—"Why can't we have any one quality of poetry we choose by itself?"—is, at the end, still asking to be answered. Every time Frost seems to define in poetry a set of distinct qualities between which a poet must choose—"sound" and "soundness," "wildness" and "subject," "delight" and "wisdom"—he deftly whisks them away. To say of a poem that "It begins in delight and ends in wisdom" may satisfy our desire for formulaic symmetry. But it also breaks our experience of a poem into so discrete a series of steps as to advertise its inadequacy. Where does the transition between one mode of response and the other occur? This is a definition of an effect without a middle—no definition at all. And of poems, as of life, Frost says:

> Ends and beginnings—there are no such things.
> There are only middles.

> (p. 116)

Poems written by such formulas would have the reader meet himself coming from delight and going toward wisdom while remaining incapable of bridging their intervening confusion. No less aware of this compromise than his reader, Frost quickly takes refuge in a patent enigma: "The figure is the same as for love." Given this aesthetic, anything is a poem if you say it is. No one will object to this formulation—it is unarguable—just as no one will be able to agree as to its particular consequences. We must love a poem, as we love anything, of and for itself. And we take it, like this sentence, like a loved one's love, on faith.

As quickly as he broadens the range of belief in whatever poetic quality we will, Frost begins to narrow it: "No one can really hold that the ecstasy should be static and stand still in one place." And standing still is the last thing this prose permits us. Having affixed the poem through two figures, Frost now sets them moving. He substitutes "ecstasy" for the figure of love, motion for the object of emotion. To preserve the illusion of choice, of an argument discovered and agreed to by the reader rather than imposed by the poet, he inducts us through an "is" expressed as an "ought." For it is not possible, once we entertain the notion of poem as ecstasy, to "hold" that it should only stand and wait for us. So the next sentence unfolds the consequent stages of ecstasy: "It begins in delight, it inclines to the impulse, it assumes direction with the first line laid down, it runs a course of lucky events, and ends in a clarification of life—not necessarily a great clarification, such as sects and cults are founded on, but in a momentary stay against confusion." This is Frost's essential poetic. As each phrase advances our steps a little further, we remain in an ongoing present—it begins, inclines, assumes, runs, and ends—which can barely be glimpsed before it runs away. The sequence itself is stayed as its end proves not an end. Frost's most famous formula intrudes as an afterthought—a surprising stay against the sentence's gathering confusion. As we spiral through the sentence we are stayed by "momentary stay against confusion." During such moments it is ourselves we surprise in the act of figuring forth (not figuring out) a poem. The reader is the figure a Frost poem makes.

Such poetry asks us to focus on either the movement toward or the moment of staying. In his most authentic poems, Frost remains true to the discipline of surprise embodied in "The Figure a Poem Makes." Where "Form is for Frost identical with the act of creation and every poem is by virtue of its form a deed,"[8] the reading act becomes isomorphic with the ongoing creative one. Where form is imposed as an afterthought, the poem ceases to be a deed, and reading, instead of demanding existential readiness, dwindles into detached observation. Where wonder is not sacrificed to order Frost continues to fulfill an Emersonian bequest: "The one thing which we seek with insatiable desire is to forget ourselves, to be surprised out of our propriety, to lose our sempiternal memory and to do something without

knowing how or why; in short to draw a new circle. Nothing great was ever achieved without enthusiasm. The way of life is wonderful; it is by abandonment."[9]

For what Leslie Brisman has called the "Poetry of Choice,"[10] Frost substitutes the Poetry of Surprise. When his speaker stops to stand at the convergence of two roads, he does not, like Oedipus, or Milton's Adam or Wordsworth's Luke, experience "The moment of turning, when motion in one direction is about to begin" as "the still point at which the present is captured and alternatives are real." For no moment of presentness emerges in the poem during which the speaker and the reader might so choose. It is the entire process of conscious decision-making, the reality of a world of foreknown options, which Frost calls into question through his intentional strategies. Can poems get us to enact a life containing moments intersected by a conscious will? They may for some: "To those who fix today a point through which from earlier years they draw a line of life projected far into the future, this hour is of deep significance."[11] Frost's life in his poetry cannot be reduced to such a time-line. It is not the future that creates his present.

In **"The Road Not Taken,"** so fully in control of the experience he offers, Frost chooses to enact a mode of being he seems elsewhere merely to suffer. Through this very self-conscious performance he reveals the prevailing mode of his poetry: Frost does not choose form so much as find himself chosen by it. The surprise of the writer becomes the surprise of the reader. Reading Frost we acquire Coleridgian prejudices: "Remember there is a difference between form as proceeding, and shape as superinduced;—the latter is either the death or the imprisonment of the thing;—the former is its self-witnessing and self-effected sphere of agency."[12] Once inside a strong Frost poem, we find ourselves more chosen than choosing, doomed to anticipate only surprise. In this way we perhaps reenact the kind of life the poet himself seems to have lived, where devising surprise became his way of redeeming human time. The waywardness of poetry serves as consolation for a life otherwise impossible to bear, a release from the burden of the wholly fated. After the first choice, there is no other:

> 'Tis of the essence of life here,
> Though we choose greatly, still to lack
> The lasting memory at all clear,
> That life has for us on the wrack
> Nothing but what we somehow chose;
> Thus are we wholly stripped of pride
> In the pain that has but one close,
> Bearing it crushed and mystified.

(**"The Trial by Existence,"** p. 21)

Notes

1. *Robert Frost: Poetry and Prose,* ed. E. C. Lathem and Lawrance Thompson (New York: Holt, Rine-

hart and Winston, 1972), p. 401. The following quotation is from pp. 402-3.

2. *The Journals and Miscellaneous Notebooks of Ralph Waldo Emerson,* ed. A. W. Plumstead and Harrison Hayford (Cambridge, Mass: Harvard University Press, 1967), VII, 90.

3. Reuben E. Brower, *The Poetry of Robert Frost: Constellations of Intention* (New York: Oxford University Press, 1963), p. 231.

4. Yvor Winters, "Robert Frost; or, the Spiritual Drifter as Poet" in *Robert Frost: A Collection of Critical Essays,* ed. James M. Cox (Englewood Cliffs, N.J.: Prentice-Hall, 1962), p. 2.

5. Yvor Winters, *Maule's Curse,* in *In Defense of Reason* (New York: Swallow Press, 1947), p. 161. The following three quotations are from pp. 267, 153, and 227.

6. Winters, in Cox, p. 61.

7. Mark Strand, *Reasons For Moving* (New York: Atheneum, 1968), p. 40.

8. James M. Cox, "Introduction," in Cox, p. 2.

9. Emerson, "Circles."

10. See Leslie S. Brisman, *Milton's Poetry of Choice and Its Romantic Heirs* (Ithaca: Cornell University Press, 1973). The following quotation is from p. 61. Roy Harvey Pearce does not find in Frost's work a pattern of experience opposed to Brisman's poetry of choice: "Thus Frost has made his choice. He wills himself and his protagonists to choose, whereas Emerson willed himself to be chosen—unlike Frost, running the risk of losing control not only of his poems but his sense of himself. Frost has always known where he is going; or he says he has" (*The Continuity of American Poetry,* p. 281). This observation seems to invert the case. Emerson as writer chooses or is chosen by experience, depending upon the line or sentence one chooses to quote. Frost is manifestly denied the possibility of choice except as a retrospective imposition of form upon the flow of ongoing time. But Pearce comes close to admitting this, adding, as an afterthought, that when it comes to choosing, Frost only "says he has."

11. Lathem and Thompson, p. 206.

12. Coleridge, "On Poesy as Art."

Robert F. Fleissner (essay date 1979)

SOURCE: Fleissner, Robert F. "A Road Taken: The Romantically Different *Ruelle*." In *Robert Frost: Stud-*

ies of the Poetry, edited by Kathryn Gibbs Harris, pp. 117-31. Boston: G. K. Hall & Co., 1979.

[*In the following essay, Fleissner explores the influence of the Romantic poets on Frost's poetry, particularly William Wordsworth and John Keats, and contends that "The Road Not Taken" expresses Romantic individualism.*]

To J. Ryan Brownfield, author of "La Ruelle De Mon Choix"

Up! up! my Friend, and quit your books . . .
Let Nature be your Teacher.

Wordsworth, "The Tables Turned"

Scatter poems on the floor;
Turn the poet out of door.

Frost, **"The Thawing Wind"**

Clearly one of Frost's little ironies is the title of perhaps his most characteristic and controversial lyric, **"The Road Not Taken."** His main concern in the poem is evidently with the road he or the persona *did* take, and in this paper I shall identify it as the aesthetic route. The textual testimony indicates that the road is Wordsworth's. In particular, it is related to the path of the Lucy lyric that has become known to us rather by its first line than its title, "She Dwelt Among the Untrodden Ways." Wordsworth himself had a simpler lesser-known title for it: "Song." When the more common title is conflated with that by which Frost knew it, "The Lost Love," then we have a combination of two ideas subjoined in Frost's own title: an untaken path and an accompanying feeling of aloneness. "The Lost Love" is the title bestowed on the Lucy lyric by Palgrave in *The Golden Treasury,* Frost's favorite *vade mecum,* and hence I shall refer to the poem's title as such in this paper. When we raise the question of how Frost's sense of isolation in **"The Road Not Taken"** came into being, the answer is, again, Romantic. It is also, however, as we may find, ultimately more reminiscent of Keats in this respect than of Wordsworth, for although Frost has been related more to Wordsworth than to any other Romantic, he has deeper affinities with Keats, and the end of Keats's "Ode on a Grecian Urn" had a mythopoeic value for him that he was able to transform abstractly by way of a very concrete design in the two roads of his poem.

But is Frost truly a Romantic? In recent years various responsible scholars have from time to time called that designation into question, in effect qualifying his connection with Wordsworth. Indeed, Frost himself is on record for doubting whether the Romantic path was the one he should follow; he considered it perilously allied to escapism, which he found pusillanimous. Two well-known verses that serve as caveats against Romantic over-indulgence are **"Lucretius Versus the Lake Poets"** and **"Escapist (?)—Never."** Still, he could not fully abandon the legacy of Romanticism; in many a verse he adopts a Romantic framework almost in spite of himself. True, he insisted he was writing about man in nature, not merely about nature itself; he claimed to deplore a brand of Platonism which he found unscientific. Yet the Romantics have also put man back into nature; the image in Wordsworth's Lucy lyrics indicating that her hiddenness stems from nature refers to mankind. In any case, it is fortunate that the grounds we have for labeling one of Frost's best-known poems as Romantic have a solid objective or verbal basis.

Along with the critics who have qualified Frost's link to Romanticism are some who have recently observed that he was especially dependent on it. Any overall consideration of his sources cannot fail to cite his debt to the English, as well as American, Romantics.[1] Although Frost frequently made ambivalent remarks with regard to influences upon him or source study in general, a few key statements stand out, notably that a true poet "has to begin as a cloud of all the other poets he ever read."[2] Indeed, an excellent recent scholarly summing up of scholarship on Frost maintains that the name most often associated with him has been Wordsworth's.[3] Should we hesitate at this juncture and not travel on to his famous two roads because we recall only too well Wordsworth's admonition about the dangers of probing into a poet's raw material ("We murder to dissect")? Let us recollect Dryden's defense of Jonson's use of ancient writers: "What would be theft in other poets is only victory in him."[4] With his scientific concerns, Frost also would hardly have been apodictically opposed to dissection—whatever the specimen before us in the lab.

So let us examine with impunity his use of Wordsworth. Although, on one hand, he had claimed that Wordsworth's mind was "not . . . of the very first class,"[5] on the other, he eulogized him, especially during a Wordsworth Centenary address at Cornell during which he made the seeming casual confession:

> People ask me what I read. Why, I read Wordsworth . . .[6]

This admission, which went on to include other poets whose influence he conceded, was inspired at least as much, say, by the "nature" of the centennial occasion as it was by a Wordsworthian sense of "Nature." Yet, naturally enough, a poet like Frost who claimed to speak poems rather than recite them because he wanted his speech as much like that of ordinary people as possible, would find much kinship in the leading English Romantic who shifted from stilted eighteenth-century diction to a selection of the words used by everyday

man. Nevertheless, Frost was cagey in admitting any link with a poet whom he had dubbed a somewhat-less-than-first-class writer. "No," he once said apropos of his possible debt to Wordsworth, "you couldn't pin me there."[7] A strong statement, but then he straightaway allowed that he would "read all sorts of things," certainly including the arch-Romantic. We know also that his mother read Wordsworth to him when he was a child, that he often spoke of his delight in the Palgrave anthology and *The Oxford Book of English Verse* with their selections of Wordsworth and Keats which he so much admired.

Less known but nonetheless characteristic of Frost is that he indulged even in textual criticism of Wordsworth: he submitted an emendation for a line of the Lake Poet's, contending that "Bound each to each by natural piety" was in fact a misnomer and had better read "Bound each to each by nature piety."[8] Piety, to him, was not per se "natural." Bypassing the patristic commonplace that the natural builds on the supernatural, he evidently thought of piety as basically preternatural; or, if he did not think specifically of "nature piety" as piety toward nature rather than God, what he meant was simple or unsophisticated piety. With the hindsight of John Stuart Mill's essay "Nature," which allows for the complexity of meanings inherent in this abstraction, we can duly appreciate Frost's gloss—even if we do not count him here as a full-fledged textual emendator. But that is hardly irreverent, because he did not mean to be thought of as a scholar concerned with determining a substantive text based on authorial meaning. What is of more basic interest, ultimately, is that just as he realized that nature and piety are technically two very different universals, so he likewise found it difficult to combine two other Romantic abstractions: beauty and truth. The distinction between them is central to his thought, not only in **"The Road Not Taken,"** as we shall see, but in **"Two Tramps in Mud Time"** as well, regardless of whether or not he was specifically indebted to Keats's ode in each case. In so saying, I have no wish to contravene Louis Untermeyer's detection of a more comprehensive association of beauty and truth in Frost: "For him poetry was not only beauty but, in the Keatsian equivalent, truth."[9] I claim only that Frost himself would have been chary of it.

My purpose in this paper is not to start off on an ambitious road trip by showing Frost's major indebtedness to, say, parts of Wordsworth's epical vision in *The Prelude*; I leave that undertaking to such Frost scholars as Reuben Brower and Richard Poirier. My attempt is more modest. I propose that in **"The Road Not Taken"** we find that Romantic individualism is expressed in its very windings. Knowing some of the poet's background helps. Dissatisfied with academic life, Frost had chosen the bonafide American path of the rugged individualist, even as did his persona in the poem, but he also felt a hankering for the roadway he had failed to take. So the poet returned to academia to teach classes at Amherst, ones which inevitably turned out to be anything but "academic."[10] In his very rebelliousness, he was thus akin to the early Wordsworth. If we should ponder his more conservative interests, he would be like the older Wordsworth, though a better poet. He even predicts this comparison when, in **"Precaution,"** he slyly counters that he did not want to be radical when young for fear of becoming reactionary when old. Such a dichotomy already points to a kind of intellectual crossroads, as also depicted in **"The Road Not Taken,"** as we shall see. The concept of a "moral or mental cross-roads" intrigued him, and he wrote, as Elizabeth Shepley Sergeant tells us, that "some of the world's great geniuses (Goethe is one of them) have recorded similar meetings with their own images at a moral or mental cross-roads in life."[11] When we recall this summation—redolent as it is with the seeds of Goethean Romanticism in Germany—do we not find it helpful that two of his English predecessors also engaged in such troublesome roadwork, John Stuart Mill and William Hale White's Mark Rutherford, both of whom overcame their dilemmas expressly through their rediscovery of the heartfelt nature poetry of Wordsworth? What could then be more "natural" than to seek for similar Wordsworthian recollections in Frost's own poetic crossroads in **"The Road Not Taken"**—especially when we recollect that it was initially called "Two Roads"?

Frost's first published lyric, **"My Butterfly,"** is in the Wordsworthian mode, comparable to the Lake Poet's "To a Butterfly."[12] Both W. W. Robson and Reuben Brower have found traces of "Michael" in Frost.[13] But the most convincing interrelationship I have been able to detect in terms of verbal evidence is that between **"The Road Not Taken"** and "The Lost Love." This kinship, although extraordinary enough in its precise parallels and reversals, is most interesting thematically, but in that respect not as important philosophically, as what I should call the Keatsian subsurface, which represents the gravel base beneath the concrete. For Frost finally preferred the intensity of Keats to the plain style of Wordsworth. But let us start with the surface appearances and with Wordsworth—after the Edward Thomas matter is taken care of.

In any competent overview of source materials, previous "road crews" should be given their due. Sergeant and Thompson treat the genetic material in detail.[14] Among well-known views that have been proposed, the most common is that Frost remembered his poet friend Edward Thomas. As Reginald L. Cook tells us, "'What I had in mind that night,' Frost explains, 'was not myself but a friend of mine (Edward Thomas) who had gone to war. No matter what road he took, he would always have missed not having taken the other. I was thinking of him.'"[15] To some scholars, such a statement

would amount to a *donnée*. Why, they might ask, should we search about for other possible sources when the poet himself has assured us of what made him write what he did?

In answer, let us broach certain qualifications. First, I had my doubts that Frost told the whole story when he made this remark, so I put the matter to Cook, who knew the poet well, by asking if **"The Road Not Taken"** did not deal with something "more than Edward Thomas," and he readily agreed.[16] Second, Frost's statement could apply to certain other questions raised by the poem, specifically if it was about his problem of whether to stay in England (where he started writing it) or come to America (where he finished it). A further view has been that an experience on a "Plymouth wood road" led him to write what he did. Still another is Allen Tate's recent submission that Frost's road was his choice not to follow the learned style of Pound; thus since Pound was in the vanguard with his Chinese calligraphy and imagism, Frost's pastoral road was scarcely Pound's route.[17] On the other hand, the speaker's choice of the road less traveled by would point toward Pound's esoteric style, in a sense, not away from it.

In the light of Frost's specific statement, let us now discount these other views as not specifically bearing upon the occasion of the poem—that prompted by Thomas. Yet the occasion and the meaning are two very disparate matters. When we get to the significance of the road poem, we have to travel further than merely acknowledge that Frost, say, "parodied and quietly mocked" Thomas.[18] (The point was that Frost felt that whatever path Thomas would choose, he would always wish he had taken the other.) To say that the poem is "a joke at the romantic self-consciousness of making such a choice"[19] is better but not good enough, because it tends to disparage the very Romantic ingredients intrinsic to it. (Interestingly, however, Hartley Coleridge himself parodied "The Lost Love.")[20] Thompson helpfully posits eleven items relating to "the writing and reception of the poem," and two of them are relevant in that indirectly they also point to the Wordsworth poem.[21]

Thompson's item "g" claims attention first. He quotes from Frost as follows:

> That poem: there's a hint intended there. But you ought to know that yourself. One of the things I suffer from, you know, is being taken as intending a double meaning when I don't. Sometimes I do, and sometimes I don't. And I can't mark 'em—there's no way of marking them. I have to leave it to nice people to know the difference.[22]

Now the hint that I cull from that comment is in the last two words: "the difference." The last line of "The Lost Love" contains the key phrase "The difference," and the concluding line of **"The Road Not Taken"** echoes it—*au pied de la lettre*: "And that has / made all the difference." Whether or not Frost intended the last words in his comment as a hint would be curious but no great help because deep-seated indebtedness if often below the surface and not a matter of specific intent (though it should not contradict the latter). The Wordsworthian echo in Frost paradoxically represents a "difference" that conveys a similarity, one that is more than merely verbal. Aside from slyly informing the literary historian that what "made the difference" in Frost was Wordsworth's "the difference" transposed—in itself a rather simplistic gloss—the line is soulful. Wordsworth's speaker specifically sighs, and Frost present that exhalation in his own way. Whereas Wordsworth writes, "O!" Frost utters, "And I—/ I. . . ." The sigh becomes a dash, almost a stutter, a pause easily stimulated by the earlier dash in "The Lost Love." In a similar manner, there are exclamation points in both lyrics, one seemingly transferred from the other; thus whereas Wordsworth's point follows the "O," Frost's also does but at the end of the line instead. Whether these shifts are substantive effects rather than accidentals is hard to determine but at least they offer evidence for claiming influence. It might also be noticed that Frost's "ohs" are not always or merely sighs.

Next let us look at Frost's other comment (item "h") as cited by Thompson, who writes:

> On one occasion [Frost] told of receiving a letter from a grammarschool girl who asked a good question of him [on **"The Road Not Taken"**]: "Why the sigh?" That letter and that question, he said, had prompted an answer. End of the hint.[23]

Not much help? It is of some if we recall the Wordsworthian sigh. For Frost made much of sighs. During his unpublished lectures at the New School for Social Research, he said:

> Sometimes [some people] get a tone of grandeur . . . it starts with "oh," usually "oh world" "oh life" "oh time." You get to a prolonged "oh-ing" until you are dead . . . the same in speech . . . "oh thou that rollest about . . ." "oh king live forever" . . . one tone . . . probably a better one, I don't know whether it is or not. But there is a place where you show a difference.[24]

(Again that "difference.") Now "oh world, oh life, oh time" comes directly from Shelley.[25] But the phrase "rollest about" surely conjures up one of Wordsworth's other Lucy lyrics, "A Slumber Did My Spirit Seal," with its pantheistic ending, "Roll'd round in earth's diurnal course / With rocks, and stones, and trees." The poem appeared with "The Lost Love" in Palgrave. And once again Frost relates his exhalation to a "difference," recalling "The Lost Love."

In his lectures at the New School, Frost had more to say about "oh-ing," as he called it. His account of whether "ohs" should be pronounced long or short sug-

gests, at least on one level, the height of emotional Romanticism recollected, as Wordsworth had it, in tranquility. "One of my favorite places to have it out," he said, "was on the word 'oh.'" He contended that "those 'ohs' are subject matter of poetry . . . subject matter, not technique," and he claimed that he would like to exhibit his resources by the variety of "ohs" he could invent. With such emphasis upon this long vowel sound, is it any wonder that he took a hint from Wordsworth's "O!" in "The Lost Love" when he composed **"The Road Not Taken"**? Not only is the exhalation itself transformed, but also the long vowel sound at the end of a line becomes, for him, such a sound at the beginning of one. The "ways" of Wordsworth's lyric are echoed in Frost's "how way leads on to way," and "Fair as" at the start of line six becomes "as fair" at the conclusion of Frost's own line six.

With Frost's reference to "subject matter," we are back to meaning per se rather than merely occasion, so let us regard the intrinsic significance of Frost's Romantic *ruelle* (or metaphoric poetic alley). Lawrence Perrine is certainly on the right track when he analyzes the exhalation as not simply for "the road not taken," but instead a "sigh of regret that *both* choices were not possible" (italics Perrine's).[26] Such a positive interpretation removes the lyric from the realm of someone's "being different" (with modern negative connotations for twentieth-century Americans) and brings it into the arena of being "something different" (with more positive associations). These designations, after all, appealed to the conventions of the common man for whom Frost wrote. The speaker, in other words, is not sighing with regret because he finds himself "different" but observing that it would have also been a comfortable experience if he had been both layman and poet.

Ben W. Griffith notes that the two roads are described as "fair," an adjective which he takes to mean favorable (as in "a fair choice") because they diverged but did not separate at right angles.[27] One was therefore hardly bad and the other good. Consequently, it is probably being good—but too narrow—to claim, as Sister Catherine Theresa does in her otherwise expert analysis of Frost's religious imagery, that the source is the scriptural passage "It is a narrow gate and a hard road that leads to life, and only a few find it" (Matt. 7:13-14).[28] Yet the roads, although "about the same," are still different; that is the point of the poem. Ambivalence in the adjective "fair" implies that one road was fair in the ethical sense (thus "a fair choice") whereas the other was propitious in an aesthetic one. The effect is closely comparable to the meaning of "My right might be love but theirs was need," the key line in **"Two Tamps in Mud Time."** The road not taken becomes the way of prosaic truth; the pathway selected, the *ruelle* of beauty, "decadent" though it sometimes may seem to be. When the speaker sighs that he was incapable of accepting both roads, he is ruefully aware that, to him, truth and beauty are ir-reconcilable. Again compare a line in **"Two Tramps in Mud Time"**: "where the two exist in twain."

At this point, it is convenient to turn directly to Keats, since the Truth-Beauty calculus ushers in the ending of "Ode on a Grecian Urn." On one level, Frost's speaker finds himself a Romantic, seemingly escapist poet who would like to travel two routes but cannot because the creative artist is, *sui generis,* set apart from the multitude; on another, the persona expresses his inner doubts about the / mythopoeic Truth-Beauty identifica-tion at the end of Keats's poem, albeit indirectly. Since Frost is on record as having questioned the inherent meaning of the famous Keatsian equation, contending, for example, that truth is sometimes ugly—although he conceded that Keats got away with his Platonic formula poetically—[29] there is thus more to "the difference" in **"The Road Not Taken"** than initially would alert the eye. The sigh is not merely one of regret, but concomi-tantly one of gratitude. Herein lies the implicit paradox of the poem. The speaker inwardly is pleased that he is not run-of-the-mill. He is not harking back to the idea, now corrected by Perrine in his interpretation cited above, that there was no essential difference between the two roads.

It is time for a short, but required digression of Frost and his understanding of Keats's ode, because I wish to propose that he is the one who should be given credit for finally solving the famous problem at the end. His gloss on it elsewhere has a seemingly offhand quality but in point of fact it makes a good bit of sense. In a letter to Sidney Cox, he began, "You aren't influenced by that Beauty is Truth claptrap"; yet he hastened to add, "In poetry and under emotion every word is 'moved' a little or much—moved from its old place, heightened, made, made new."[30] Although his initial criticism very likely indicated his inability to resolve the life-versus-art dilemma as hinted at in the Keatsian equation, his qualification is of substantial value. Any scholarly consideration of the text of the lines has to take into account how the words "move"—that is, the "full set" of quotation marks, viz.:

> . . . to whom thou say'st,
> "'Beauty is truth, truth beauty.' That is all
> Ye know on earth, and all ye need to know."[31]

Although all these quotation marks are not formally found in the text, a modern emended edition could well put them in (or at least call attention to a grammatical need for them), because they reveal the critical consensus that the transcripts are, at least in part, superior to the printed versions. The purpose of the inverted commas around only the first five words found in the printed versions, however, far from indicating the specific words of a speaker or a quotation from someone

like Shaftesbury (the most recent conjecture),[32] was most certainly to show (and correctly so) that these words invoke a special meaning. Indeed, one accepted usage of quotation marks has always been to point to the special sense. Did not Frost himself intuit this sense when he said that "every word is 'moved' a little or much," even as his use of the participle is put within inverted commas to indicate *his* special sense? After noting that Keats's equation represents "a fine beautiful-sounding phrase as far as it goes,"[33] he remarked that ugliness is also truth; yet he was scarcely rejecting the Transcendentalist label of truth per se, if what he meant—and he surely did—was that beauty is simply not the whole of truth. Although Frost hardly admitted to being a Transcendentalist, at the same time his liking for Emerson showed that he was not apodictically op-posed to such a philosophical position; time and again I find he is exhibiting Transcendentalist qualities in spite of himself.

Metaphysically, the issue that arises is the following: Transcendentals may be accepted for what they are without their having to be equated; Aquinas, to cite a standard authority to whom Frost had explicit recourse, posited that there are three Transcendentals as aspects of God's Nature (that is, transcending His Being and found in His Creation): the *Unum* (Oneness), *Verum* (Truth), and *Bonum* (Goodness)—not, however, *Pul-chrum* (Beauty), which, though related, is not the same. Admittedly, Jacques Maritain interprets Aquinas somewhat differently, although associating beauty with goodness rather than truth,[34] but he is not in the mainstream, which has followed the age-old dictum that "beauty is in the eye of the beholder." Interestingly, Keats would have reversed the relationship imputed above to Frost (namely that ugliness is also truth or beauty is but a part of truth) by claiming that "truth is not all of beauty" in that a life of sensations, as he put it in his letters, or the aesthetic life, was superior to him than thought. What Frost's Puritanism reacted to was the patent affront to commonsense hazardously resonant in the Keatsian lines. It would be of interest if Frost was indebted in this respect to Ruskin's well-known es-say "The Greatness of Style," with its own famous critique of the Keatsian passage, but in any event other major writers of our time have criticized the equation as well.[35]

Although Frost intuitively grasped the special use of quotation marks—implying that Keats was not referring to beauty and truth as absolutes per se—did he also see that Keats evidently meant the speaker of the final two lines not to be the poet but the urn? Doubtfully so, because most readers have not, although that reading now has the endorsement of the Harvard Keatsians. As the leading expert on the crux informs us, "It seems better for the urn to tell us what we know and need to know than for the poet to do so."[36] Keats's idea was that the Truth-Beauty equation was merely an earthly solution to a mystery to be finally resolved in the afterlife. So the urn addresses the lovers on its surface, themselves things of beauty, and not primarily the speaker or reader at all. (If it is objected that common-sense is at stake with such a reading, we can respond that it makes as much sense for the urn to speak to the lovers as to speak in the first place.) How then would it "tease us out of thought"—like Keats's "life of sensa-tions"? How else but by inviting a teasing bit of pa-ronomasia on the words *on earth*? The wordplay implies that the lovers are depicted on an earthen vessel, one made of terra-cotta; their meaning is thereby based not on a worldly existence alone, or on an otherworldly one, but on an artistic one.[37]

If Frost did not catch on to Keats's meaning *in toto*—"How do I know," he once wrote, "whether a man has come close to Keats in reading Keats? It is hard for me to know"[38]—his limited formal understanding was prompted by his own difficulty in coming to terms with Platonism, a point frequently reiterated in the Thompson biography. In "Boeotian," he says, "I love to toy with the Platonic notion"; he thereby opposes what he designates "systematic" wisdom, presumably that, say, of Aristotle rather than Plato; yet at the same time he is more a disciple of Aristotle than Plato in his insistence on a formal or structured dimension to art, as in his poem "Pertinax." What might be called his unsystematic ordering of form, or his creative ability to make order out of chaos, pertinently, and pertinaciously, stands also behind the artistry of Keats.

But let us get back to **"The Road Not Taken."** Why did Frost shift poetic gears by changing the title from "Two Roads"? Since the reason is Wordsworthian, Keats must temporarily take a back seat. Did not the title derive from "The Lost Love"? As hinted at in the titles, both poems delineate a similar sense of deficiency. Frost's feeling of loss is a far cry, however, from what Yvor Winters unfortunately dubbed "spiritual drifting" in the seeming paradox of the two roads—that is, that one appears less worn, yet both are actually more or less alike.[39] The true deficiency described is also differ-ent from what a more recent critic terms the poet's rationalization in coming to a decision.[40] For these Fros-tian crossroads do not represent a vague turning off. Winters is quite wrong. The important point made is that their being described as "about" the same craftily indicates (as Perrine argues in his analysis cited earlier) that they are not really the same. To put it another way, roads that are "about" the same are *only* "about" the same, and therefore not equivalent. The word *about* should be stressed, not the word *really*.

Thus the intricate intersection of these roads is more evident than most critics have surmised: Frost intercon-nects with Wordsworth and, indirectly yet more basi-cally, with Keats. Aside from the strong verbal parallels with Wordsworth that I have already shown ("The dif-ference"—"the difference"; "O!"—"Oh . . . !" and "I—I," "ways"—"Way . . . way"; "Fair as"—"as fair"), Lucy's "untrodden ways" are *re*-presented as Frost's "leaves no step had trodden black"—both phrases signifying the immediacy and freshness of experience. Whereas Wordsworth tells of a landscape that is "mossy," Frost produces one which is, analogously, "grassy." From an elementary verbal perspective, however, the "-trodden" echo is the most remarkable.

But does Frost express regret at the symbolic death of *his* Lucy? Yes, inasmuch as Lucy is hardly a mere allu-sion to Dorothy Wordsworth, Marie-Anne Vallon, or Mary Hutchinson—recent "psychobiographical" criti-cism notwithstanding.[41] Derivable from the Latin *Lucia* (itself derivable from "light" in Latin), Lucy has a func-tion that is largely, if not entirely, symbolic. Now Frost too expresses regret at a symbolic passing away and imagines reciting the event in old age ("ages and ages hence"). Just as Lucy reflects Wordsworth's feeling of heavenly light or creative afflatus in terms of the diminution of his childhood vision as he gets older, Frost too finds his vision darkened. His lyric tells of a similar loss—not of untrodden ways by themselves but of the youthful dream encompassing both roads of life. Interestingly, Keats, like Frost, found the final words of "The Lost Love" exceptionally meaningful; he spoke them as "the best . . . that Wordsworth ever wrote."[42] This correlation enhances the overall Wordsworth-Keats-Frost relationship.

In sum, the road leading into the undergrowth in **"The Road Not Taken,"** the one which the speaker does not take, is that of the common man and his way of life, that of humdrum "truth" and thereby closer to "reality" in an ordinary sense. The other road may not seem to be beautiful at the outset, but it is the lonely road of the artist and it can lead to beauty. Frost does not of course make it that crystal clear, but we are at least on the road to the road. Frost's is certainly the road of the individualist, which the New Englander was, leading to isolation and longing, especially in old age. The reader can then draw out the more universal meaning.

Ultimately Frost's poem is more significant than Word-sworth's because, behind the façade of the com-monplace, our Puritan is able to imply that the basic philosophical dichotomy between ethics and aesthetics is by no means foreign to the nature of the artistic mind, that he is destined to come out on top even if, in the process, he has to forsake some of ordinary humdrum reality, or the "pedestrian" path. The aesthetic route, the speaker well realizes, is not identifiable with the whole truth of reality—except possibly on the anagogic level—but it is surely part of the reality of truth. The lyric informs us that when the road of "pedestrian" truth is passed by, the optional road of beauty may yet remain and that route is not essentially a detour at all. On the other hand, some modern critics who have compared the two poets aver that the Englishman is superior to the New Englander.[43] Louis Simpson has an apt reply for one of these castigators: "The reviewer compares Frost with Wordsworth, as though they were in some sort of competition."[44] Such competitive evaluation is indeed irrelevant. Frost did not personally accept the Lake Poet's special brand of pantheism. Yet in utilizing some of the aesthetic qualities of the English Romantics, Frost arrived at a new synthesis, which became a product all his own. In the process **"The Road Not Taken"** has ironically become, at least for numerous readers and scholars, a well-traveled thoroughfare.

THE WORDSWORTHIAN PARALLELS

	Wordsworth	Frost
Titles:	"The Lost Love" (the title of "She Dwelt..." in Palgrave)	"The Road Not Taken"
Lines:	"among the untrodden ways" (1.1)	"In leaves no step had trodden black" (1.12) "way leads on to way" (1.14)
	"mossy" (1.5)	"grassy" (1.8)
	"Fair as" (1.6)	"as fair" (1.6)
	", and O!" (1.11)	", and I – / I..." (11.18–19) "Oh" (1.13)
	"The difference" (1.12)	"The difference." (1.20)
Punctuation:	The use of the the single dash to indicate a sharp pause at the beginning of a line. (1.7)	The use of the single dash to indicate a sharp pause at the end of a line (1.18)
	The exclamation point (11.6, 11, 12)	The exclamation point (1.13)
Poetic devices:	Use of conjunction at the start of a line	Use of conjunction at the start of a line
	"And" (1.4) "But" (1.11)	"And" (11.2, 3, 4, 7, 11, 20) "Yet" (1.14)

Notes

1. The most comprehensive recent paper I have seen dealing with such literary indebtedness is by Sister Jeremy Finnegan, O.P., "Creative Borrowing: Auditory Memory in Robert Frost," presented at the annual convention of The Midwest Modern Language Association in 1976. (See her essay on this same topic in this volume.) See also Charles Carmichael, "Robert Frost as a Romantic," in *Frost: Centennial Essays* ed. Jac Tharpe (Jackson: Univ. Press of Mississippi, 1974), pp. 147-65. I have published separate studies on Frost's debt to individual Romantics; e.g., "Frost's Response to Keats's Risibility," *The Ball State University Forum* (Frost issue), 11 (1970), 40-43; on Coleridge: "Frost on Frost . . . at Midnight," *Studies in the Humanities,* 5 (1976), 32-38; on Tennyson as a Victorian Romantic "Like 'Pythagoras' Comparison of the Universe with Number': a Frost-Tennyson Correlation," in *Frost: Centennial Essays,* pp. 207-20; "'Frost . . . at . . . Play': a Frost-Dickinson Affinity Affirmed," *Research Studies,* 46 (1978), 28-39. Quotations from Frost are from *Complete Poems of Robert Frost* (New York: Holt, Rinehart and Winston, 1949) because Frost used that volume himself, but I have also consulted *The Poetry of Robert Frost,* ed. Edward Connery Lathem (New York: Holt, Rinehart and Winston, 1969). Lathem's more recent edition has an optional comma in the text of "The Road Not Taken." [Lathem's description of his textual scholarship on the Frost poems appears in Vol. I of the two-volume edition, *The Poetry of Robert Frost* (Barre, Mass: Imprint Society, 1971), pp. vii-xxvii.] Quotations from Wordsworth are taken not from the De Sélincourt edition, but from that to which Frost had access, Palgrave, *The Golden Treasury* (New York: Random House, 1944).

2. Lawrance Thompson, *Robert Frost: The Years of Triumph, 1915-1938* (New York: Holt, Rinehart and Winston, 1970), pp. 355, 650.

3. Reginald L. Cook, "Robert Frost," in *Fifteen Modern American Authors: A Survey of Research and Criticism,* ed. Jackson R. Bryer (Durham: Duke Univ. Press, 1969), p. 270.

4. "Of Dramatick Poesie," in *Essays of John Dryden,* ed. W. P. Kerr (New York: Russell and Russell, 1961), I, 43, 82. (As cited by Sister Jeremy Finnegan.)

5. Radcliffe Squires, *The Major Themes of Robert Frost* (Ann Arbor: Univ. of Michigan Press, 1963), p. 8.

6. This talk was published for the first time as "A Tribute to Wordsworth," *The Cornell Library Journal,* No. 11 (1970), 76-99. (Reference here is to p. 91).

7. Interview with Richard Poirier, *The Paris Review,* as cited in *Interviews with Robert Frost,* ed. Edward Connery Lathem (New York: Holt, Rinehart and Winston, 1960), p. 88.

8. Elizabeth Shepley Sergeant, *Robert Frost: The Trial by Existence* (New York: Holt, Rinehart and Winston, 1960), p. 88.

9. *Robert Frost: A Backward Look* (Washington: Library of Congress Ref. Dept., 1964), p. 23.

10. Thompson, *Years of Triumph,* p. 100.

11. Sergeant, p. 87.

12. In a recent study, however, George Monteiro traces "My Butterfly" to both Frost's stay at Dartmouth College in 1892 (as Thompson also did) and his reading of Dickinson: "Over the memory of the autobiographical moment which moved Frost to attempt this elegy hovered Dickinson's 'butterfly' poems." "Emily Dickinson and Robert Frost," *Prairie Schooner,* 51 (1977/78), 369-86. (This quotation from p. 374).

13. Robson, "The Achievement of Robert Frost," *The Southern Review,* NS 2 (1966), 735-61; Brower, *The Poetry of Robert Frost: Constellations of Intention* (New York: Oxford Univ. Press, 1968), pp. 174-79. Brower has a great deal to say on the Frost-Wordsworth-Keats relationship.

14. Sergeant, pp. 87-89; Thompson, *Years of Triumph,* pp. 88-89, 544-48.

15. "Frost on Frost: The Making of Poems," *American Literature,* 28 (1956-57), 65.

16. Quoted by permission from Reginald L. Cook.

17. Allen Tate, "'Inner Weather': Robert Frost as a Metaphysical Poet," in *Robert Frost: Lectures on the Centennial of His Birth* (Washington: Library of Congress, 1975), p. 65. Tate also relates Frost to Wordsworth (p. 66).

18. Thompson, *Years of Triumph,* pp. 88-89.

19. See Millicent Travis Lane, "Agnosticism as Technique: Robert Frost's Poetic Style," Diss. Cornell 1967, p. 128. The gravamen of this thesis should, however, be compared with the essay on Frost's religion by Dorothy Judd Hall, "An Old Testament Christian," in *Frost: Centennial Essays* III (Jackson: Univ. Press of Mississippi, 1978), pp. 316-49.

20. The poem is cited by G. E. (in "Wm. Wordsworth," *Notes and Queries,* 4th ser., 3 [1869], 580) in answer to a query. It is also cited by Herbert Hartman ("Wordsworth's 'Lucy' Poems: *Notes and Marginalia,*" *PMLA,* 49 [1934], 134-42) but only in part, which is misquoted, with an incorrect reference as to its source. The parody is interesting to compare with Frost's use of the same poem (but for more than parodic reasons); it is very amusing.

21. Thompson, *Years of Triumph,* pp. 545-48.

22. Thompson, *Years of Triumph,* p. 547.

23. Thompson, *Years of Triumph,* p. 547.

24. Lecture of 5 Feb. 1931, recorded by Genevieve Taggard in The Dartmouth College Library and cited with permission but with my pointing.

25. Frost quotes the line again, labeling it "Shelleyan," in his Cornell speech, p. 98. He discusses Wordsworth in close proximity.

26. "Robert Frost, 'The Road Not Taken,'" *The Explicator Cyclopedia,* ed. C. C. Walcutt and J. E. Whitesell, (Chicago: Quadrangle Books, 1966), I, 140. This explication counters David Wyatt's "Choosing in Frost," in *Frost: Centennial Essays* II, ed. Jac Tharpe (Jackson: Univ. of Mississippi Press, 1976).

27. Griffith, "Robert Frost, 'The Road Not Taken," in *Frost: Centennial Essays,* pp. 139-140.

28. Sr. Catherine Theresa, "New Testament Interpretations of Robert Frost's Poems," *The Ball State University Forum* (Frost issue), 50-54. Other religions have had similar maxims, notably Hinduism, which has a saying that the road to salvation is as straight as a razor's edge (thus influencing Maugham's *The Razor's Edge*). I do not see how Frost's poem is explicitly Christian, especially since he called himself an Old Testament Christian; in other words, that it is based at all on the New Testament has not been proved. But I like the idea.

29. *Selected Letters of Robert Frost,* ed. Lawrence Thompson (New York: Holt, Rinehart and Winston, 1964), pp. 140-42.

30. *Selected Letters,* pp. 140-42.

31. See Jack Stillinger's seminal article, "Keats's Grecian Urn and the Evidence of Transcripts," *PMLA,* 73 (1958), 447-48; and also the appendix "Who Says What to Whom at the End of Ode on a Grecian Urn?" in his book *The Hoodwinking of Madeline and Other Essays on Keats's Poems* (Urbana: Univ. of Illinois Press, 1971), pp. 167-73. I would add, however, one more category to his four: *(5) Urn to figures on the urn.*

32. Harry M. Solomon, "Shaftesbury's *Characteristics* and the Conclusion of 'Ode on a Grecian Urn,'" *Keats-Shelley Journal,* 24 (1975), 89-102.

33. See Daniel Smythe, *Robert Frost Speaks* (New York: Twayne, 1964), p. 62.

34. "So, although the beautiful is in close dependence upon what is metaphysically true, in the sense that every splendour of intelligibility in things presupposes some degree of conformity with that Intelligence which is the cause of things, the beautiful nevertheless is not a kind of truth, but a kind of good." *Art and Scholasticism with Other Essays,* tr. J. F. Scanlan (London: Sheed and Ward, 1949), p. 21.

35. E.g., T. S. Eliot, I. A. Richards, and William Carlos Williams. For a convenient reference work, see Harvey T. Lyon, ed., *Keats' Well-Read Urn: An Introduction to Literary Method* (New York: Holt, Rinehart and Winston, 1958), passim.

36. Stillinger, *Hoodwinking,* p. 173.

37. There has been disagreement in the scholarly ranks regarding the material out of which the Grecian Urn was composed. A typical reaction is the following one from a professor at St. Peter's College, Oxford during the summer of 1978: "Keats did not have in mind some great big marble thing." Such a reading ties in with my view that the last lines of the Ode suggest an earthen vessel ("That is all ye know on earth"). Yet the poem does refer to "marble," possibly because the poet had in the back of his mind the Elgin Marbles, about which he also wrote. Thus Keats biographer Amy Lowell asserted that "the inspiration . . . came from the Elgin Marbles" and that "no urn had anything to do with it," a view then accepted by Walter Jackson Bate. Miss Lowell's comment is of interest with regard to Frost because of his interest in her (he once memorably referred to a special dinner to which she had invited him as her "Keats eats"). Perhaps the best article on the subject of the Urn's composition is James Dickie's ("The Grecian Urn: An Archaeological Approach," *The Bulletin of the John Ryland Library,* 52 [1969], 1-19). Although Dickie apodictically contends that the urn is marble, as also in Keats's "Ode to Indolence," he remarks in regard to the latter reference that "Professor Corbett of University College, London, makes the interesting suggestion that Keats was here 'unconsciously thinking of a clay vessel, which you can turn easily by hand, unlike marble'" (p. 5). The same could apply to the Grecian Urn Ode, especially since Dickie believes that "the poet turns the urn round between stanzas 3 and 4" (p. 8). Moreover, "green altar" suggests a painted vessel.

38. *Selected Prose of Robert Frost,* ed. Hyde Cox and Edward Connery Lathem (New York: Holt, Rinehart and Winston, 1966), p. 43. Yet Frost later revised this essay and crossed these lines out. The article as initially revised appeared in *Amherst Graduates' Quarterly,* 4 (Feb. 1931), 5-15, and the crossed-out lines appear in the copy published in facsimile as a keepsake of a Robert Frost gathering held at Dartmouth, Baker Memorial Library, on July 3, 1966, and preserved now at Cornell. He cut the lines after the speech was published in the *Quarterly* as "An Uncompleted Revision of 'Education by Poetry,'" thus in effect revising his revision. To my knowledge, the final deletion is found only in the Cornell copy. Frost was this way denying any belief in what has now been paraded as "The Intentional Fallacy." He wanted instead to stress the need for seeking poetic intent, his own included, and he felt a close attachment to Keats's own meaning.

39. Winters, "Robert Frost; or, The Spiritual Drifter as Poet," *The Sewanee Review,* 56 (1948), 564-96. In spite of its negative verdict, Winters' article has become the most often cited critical article on Frost—thus underscoring *en passant* the popularity of "The Road Not Taken."

40. William B. Bache, "Rationalization in Two Frost Poems," *The Ball State University Forum* (Frost issue), 33-35.

41. Richard E. Matlak, "Wordsworth's Lucy Poems in Psychobiographical Context," *PMLA,* 93 (1978), 46-65. Matlak argues that Wordsworth was unconsciously basing Lucy on his sister Dorothy because he wanted to be free of her (and thus had Lucy die) to join Coleridge—a view with which I disagree.

42. See C. D. Narasimhaiah, "The Reputation of Robert Frost: A Point of View," *The Literary Criterion,* 9 (Winter 1969), 1-10. (This reference is to p. 5.) Narasimhaiah compares "The Road Not Taken" and "The Lost Love" critically, not historically.

43. Narasimhaiah, 1-10; see also the review of Thompson in The *Times Literary Supplement,* 16 April 1971, pp. 434-35; George W. Nitchie, *Human Values in the Poetry of Robert Frost* (Durham: Duke Univ. Press, 1960), pp. 27-28.

44. *TLS,* 30 April 1971, pp. 504-05.

Thomas Elwood Hart (essay date winter 1984)

SOURCE: Hart, Thomas Elwood. "Frost's 'The Road Not Taken': Text-Structure and Poetic Theory." *Language and Style* 17, no. 1 (winter 1984): 3-43.

[*In the following essay, Hart discusses in depth the technical mastery, word play, and compositional history of Frost's "The Road Not Taken."*]

If design govern in a thing so small[1]

Among the several poetic postures Robert Frost assumed in public, one is still widely cherished, even by some scholars: his claim that he composed his poems at one sitting (or walking), "like the stroke of a raquet [sic], club, or headman's ax" and "without fumbling a sentence."[2] This image of Frost remains popular because it is symbiotic with the even more widely cherished

Romantic myth of the inspired bard, writing as by orphic dictation, or in its secular form, the poem writing itself. Frost fueled this foolishness in "The Figure a Poem Makes":

> Like a piece of ice on a hot stove the poem must ride on its own melting. A poem may be worked over once it is in being, but may not be worried into being. Its most precious quality will remain its having run itself and carried away the poet with it.
>
> (*SP* [*Selected Prose of Robert Frost*], 20)[3]

A close reading of Frost often shows a first reading wrong. It is easy to take "not worried into being" to mean not designed, drafted, and revised, but this is not what Frost wrote. He himself once admitted when challenged: "I won't deny I have worried quite a number of my poems into existence."[4] In weighing Frost's assertions we must remember what he terms his "innate mischieveness" (*SL* [*Selected Letters of Robert Frost*], 344),[5] and heed his warning: "Don't trust me too far. I'm liable to tell you anything. . . . Check up on me some" (T1 [*Robert Frost: The Early Years, 1874-1915*], xiv).[6] When he makes claims like "I have never been good at revising" (*SL*, 237, 21 April 1919), we must attend closely to his counterassertions, even in the same letter: "I won't say I haven't learned with the years something of the tinker's art." Indeed, a few years earlier he had gone so far as to boast: "To be perfectly frank with you I am one of the most notable craftsmen of my time" (*SL*, 79, 4 July 1913).

This ambiguity persists also in his statements of later years. A conversation between Frost and Robert Francis offers a clear example:

> he [Frost] asked me what I had been doing and I said I had been trying to make my poems better. Disdainfully he asserted that poets don't improve, they only change. A poem must be written in one impulse, at one sitting, like a piece of ice on a hot stove that rides on its own melting. But a moment later he admitted that it had taken Gray eighteen years to complete his *Elegy*. I think Frost, if put in a corner, would concede that spontaneity sometimes has to be labored for.[7]

Perhaps the best known tale of Frost creating a poem is the one he told about **"Stopping by Woods."** One dewy dawn, having worked through the night, he was suddenly moved to hear the words, as though they were spoken to him, and he wrote them down so perfectly that they never needed revision. Lawrance Thompson checked up on the story's "mythical details" about revision. His conclusion: "The facts do not support these assertions" (T1, 595; cf. 594-97 and T2 [*The Years of Triumph, 1915-1938*], 236-37 and 596-98).

The present paper grew out of an attempt to "check up" on another of Frost's most beloved poems, **"The Road Not Taken"** (abbreviated **"RNT"**), which was first published in 1915.[8] In terms he rarely, if ever, applied to any of his other popular lyrics, Frost repeatedly warned his audiences about this poem. Typical is his statement on 26 August 1961 before a sophisticated audience at the Bread Loaf Writers' Conference: "You have to be careful of that; it's a tricky poem, very tricky" (T2, 546). Some of the reasons for this warning are biographical. The poem was written for Frost's very close friend, the English poet Edward Thomas, and much of its initial inspiration was playful parody of Thomas's romantic character. Yet, although the historical facts surrounding the parody have been clearly and repeatedly documented by Thompson, teachers and critics alike continue to make the surface text serve as a key witness on Frost's life-choices, philosophical affiliations, moral stature, and what have you, largely ignoring both the crucial significance of the parody element for such purposes and Frost's own repeated warnings.[9]

The poem's trickiness, however, goes beyond the parody and beyond even the levels of irony perceptively discerned by both Ted Hall and David M. Wyatt *without* reference to Frost's parodistic intent. It concerns subtleties of textual organization and formal craftsmanship that have not yet received the attention they deserve. Some of these subtleties fall in the realm of "performance," as Frost termed it. The meaning of "performance" as he used it still remains vague, though it is indisputably one of the two or three terms he relied on most frequently in later years to characterize his art. The word's etymological suggestiveness for Frost is most evident in the essay "The Constant Symbol" (1946) where it is contrasted with "conformance," ostensibly unoriginal art (*SP*, 26). Frost played on another note of the word's ambiguity in comparing poets and athletes as performers and proclaiming "Every poem . . . some sort of achievement in performance."[10] In both places he referred generally to aspects of poetic "performance"—like rhyme, meter, stanza, and the formal constraints of ode, sonnet, and sestine royal— dropping hints rather than defining or illustrating his use of the word specifically. Elaine Barry identified some of Frost's connotations when she glossed "performance" as "the self-definition achieved by technical mastery."[11] Yet without concrete illustrations, much of the word's vagueness carries over into the gloss. One purpose of the present study is to examine specific instances of Frost's technical mastery in one of his more successful poems and thus clarify what kinds of "performance" Frost actually performed.

Other structural subtleties exemplify a second principle of Frost's poetic theory, "association." Frost repeatedly emphasized how central verbal and conceptual associations were to his art: "All thought is a feat of association: having what's in front of you bring up something in your mind that you almost didn't know you knew. Putting this and that together. That click" (PR [*Writers at Work: The Paris Review Interviews*], 30). Returning to the topic moments later, Frost explicitly linked "performance" and "association" and even chided literary critics for neglecting such compositional features:

> The whole thing is performance and prowess and feats of association. Why don't critics talk about those things—what a feat it was to turn that that way, and what a feat it was to remember that, to be reminded of that by this? Why don't they talk about that?
>
> (PR, 32)

One type of association well documented in Frost's writings consists in foregrounding the etymological implications of words. Associations of this kind apparently had a strong formative influence during the composition of **"The Road Not Taken."** The text shows considerable evidence that Frost deliberately worked out patterns of association which, by exploiting etymological implications, interrelate various levels of textual structure: the literal meaning, the metaphors, the irony, the parodistic component, the stanzaic form, even intricacies of sound-play. This study will take up Frost's challenge and examine how these "feats of association" influenced the poem's shape and meaning.

These two closely related purposes are part of a larger concern with the *practice* of Frost's poetic theory, in particular what he meant by his repeated emphasis on "form," on imposing form on raw materials ("When in doubt there is always form for us to go on with. Anyone who has achieved the least form to be sure of it, is lost to the larger excruciations"; *SL*, 418), and whether he was referring to more than his theory of sentence-sounds when he claimed to be among the most notable "craftsmen" of his time and "one of the few artists writing" (*SL*, 88, 6 August 1913).[12] Since no worksheets of **"RNT"** appear to have survived, the only available access to the compositional process that produced the poem is by inference from the finished text. A third purpose of this study is to draw and substantiate textual inferences about Frost's compositional techniques and thereby to throw some light on the poetic theory these techniques imply.

This analysis falls into three interrelated parts: issues of "performance," "feats of association," and inferences about composition. Given the consistency of Frost's theoretical emphasis on form, the findings for **"RNT"** in all three areas will prove representative of at least some of his subsequent work. These findings are presented in detail in the hope that a better understanding of this poem's structure will facilitate "checking up" on Frost elsewhere. Following this analysis is an examination of some implications of these findings for Frost's general theory of poetic form and for the aesthetic impact of his achievements with form in this one "staggering" (Edward Thomas)[13] and "permanent" (Edwin Arlington Robinson)[14] poem.

I. PERFORMANCE

Much of what Frost had to say about poetic form is set against a backdrop of conflict between "chaos" and "order" (*SL*, 419), raw materials and shapeliness (*SL*, 418), "freedom" and "commitments" (*SP*, 25-26). Disdainful of those poets who avoid the rigors of form, like the "freeversters" and authors who "write huge shapeless novels, huge gobs of raw sincerity bellowing with pain" (*SL*, 418), Frost extolled formal constraints which, as in a sonnet, require both "the self-discipline" of theme and the "harsher discipline from without," that imposed by gradually entangling commitments to meter, length of line, rhyme, and stanza (*SP*, 27). Frost seems to relish it most when he must "acknowledge himself in a tighter and tighter place," when he must commend his spirit unto forms (*SP*, 26). This commitment he repeatedly portrayed in heroic terms: "Every poem is an epitome of the great predicament; a figure of the will braving alien entanglements" (*SP*, 25). In such heroic formulations of the poet's predicament Frost goes beyond mere acceptance to an active seeking out of new and more demanding challenges to achieve against, or, using his term, to show "prowess" in overcoming (PR, 30-33). The form created need not be heroic. It may even be "delicate or small": "To me any little form I assert . . . is velvet, as the saying is, and to be considered for how much more it is than nothing." Indeed, smaller may be better: "no forms are more engrossing, gratifying, comforting, staying, than those lesser ones we throw off like vortex rings of smoke. . . . For these we haven't to get a team together before we can play" (*SL*, 418-19). What is heroic is the challenge set and its achievement.

Among Frost's hints about which challenges to his prowess he valued most, two statements in a *Paris Review* interview stand out. One concerns rhyme:

> One of the ways of looking at a poem right away it's sent to me, right off, is to see if it's rhymed. Then I know just when to look at it. The rhymes come in pairs. . . . That is in the realm of performance, that's the deadly test with me. I want to be unable to tell which of those he thought of first.
>
> (PR, 33)

The other concerns stanza-structure:

> I'm always interested, you know, when I have three or four stanzas, in the way I *lay* the sentences in them. I'd

hate to have the sentences all lie the same in the stanzas. Every poem is like that: some sort of achievement in performance.

(PR, 30)

These categories of rhyme- and stanza-structure provided both starting-point and frame of reference for my analysis of form in **"RNT."** My chief assumptions, based on Frost's own theoretical statements, were that formal regularity would involve two fundamental dialectical principles of all life and art, repetition and variation, and that repetition, if structurally relevant, would reveal more or less perceptible patterns. As an expedient, therefore, the analysis focused on examples of repetition to determine which elements of the text Frost repeated, where they recur, and whether such recurrences do fall into regular patterns. The elements analyzed were rhyme-words and related sound-play, other words, concepts, and syntactic groups. What I found strongly suggests—if not in each individual item at least by cumulative testimony—that much of this text's present shape results from a conscious, even calculating method of composition.

The patterns that emerged are described below in summary style with a minimum of quotation. One danger of any structural analysis of poetry is that patterns tend to appear in isolation, separated from context, as if they had some autonomous existence and justification. The format of the description assumes that the reader will counter this difficulty by referring to the text throughout both to verify the patterns and to corroborate their role in shaping the poem (not merely themselves). To facilitate this, the text is printed in full in Figure 1 with supplementary numbering and structural rubrics keyed to some of the findings to be described.[15]

The text contains twenty lines divided formally into four equivalent stanzas. Frost's choice of these external limits and divisions represents a commitment to two formal moduli; in the abstract: fiveness of line within each stanza and fourness of stanza within the whole, or formulaicly, five times four equals twenty. The rhyme-structure a-b-a-a-b establishes a formal tension between three a-rhymes and two b-rhymes in each five-line stanza; in the abstract the proportionality may be expressed as $3/5 + 2/5 = 1$, both for each stanza and—since all four stanzas have the same rhyme-pattern—for the poem as a whole: 12/20 (or three-fifths a-rhymes) + 8/20 (two-fifths b-rhymes) = 20/20, or 1. The evidence is that Frost exploited this transferable, abstract property of his rhyme-pattern as one means of "performing" his text. Examples of the proportionality three-fifths (or its corollary, two-fifths) abound to such an extent and with such consistency in the text's physical organization that they may be viewed as components of a kind of

structural leitmotiv. This formal motif, which we may for convenience call the rhyme-system, consists of the following patterns (listed roughly in order of increasing conceptualization).

(a) Counterpointed against the end-rhyme in the first stanza are comparable anaphoric repetitions: thrice "And" (beginning lines 2, 3, and 4), twice "T(w)o" (beginning lines 1 and 5).[16]

FIGURE 1. *THE ROAD NOT TAKEN*

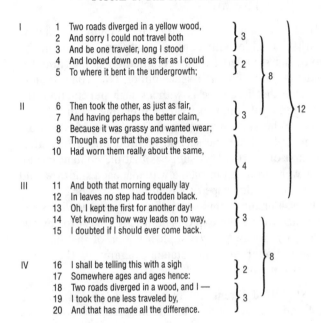

(b) The poem's syntactic units are grouped into four sentences (ending with lines 12, 13, 15, and 20). The way Frost managed to "*lay* the sentences" (PR, 30) in the four stanzas coincides with—and helps define—the poem's thematic organization. The first sentence is by far the longest, occupying more than half the poem, lines 1-12. It is primarily narrative in character. The remaining three sentences, occupying the last eight lines, are all primarily reflective. The twelve-line narrative sentence is formally marked, as is the poem as a whole (see below), by conceptual symmetry at start and finish: lines 1 and 12 both refer to the fall foliage and its color. The poem's major thematic division comes with the abrupt shift of mood in the immediately following sentence (the only line with anacrucis): "Oh, I kept the first for another day!" (line 13). The juncture between the first and second sentences, clearly marked by syntax, theme, conceptual symmetry, and change of mood, divides the twenty-line text into twelve lines (chiefly narrative) plus eight lines (chiefly reflective). That is, three-fifths (12/20) and two-fifths (8/20).

(c) The first sentence contains *three* subunits distinguished by semicolons (ending lines 5 and 8). These subunits contain *five, three,* and *four* lines (see A below) respectively. The chiefly reflective part contains *three* sentences of one, two, and *five* lines respectively. The two five-line syntactic units in each part fill the first and last stanzas. In the latter case the *five*-line sentence is further divided into *three* subunits by the colon ending line 17 and dash ending line 18. There are in all, then, eight (sub)units delimited by the eight major marks of punctuation. Eight marks in twenty lines—2/5. Part one (lines 1-12) has *three* syntactic (sub)units, part two (lines 13-20) has *five*[17]—3/5.

(d) The divisions marked off by these eight punctuation marks coincide with content groupings, although the divisions signaled by the exclamation point (line 13) and the dash (line 18) seem minor. Only one content juncture that I can see is without such punctuation, the turning of attention to road A after line 3. In all four stanzas the shifts from one content group to the next occur either after the second or third line, never after the first or fourth. This suggests that the content groupings were arranged in such a way that each stanza would have a thematic shape of either $3 + 2 = 5$ or $2 + 3 = 5$ lines. Pursuit of this possibility not only confirms the presence of the three/five pattern here, but also reveals a larger rationale governing distribution of the thematic material over all four stanzas, again by the same proportionality.

(e) Slightly different *sets* of content groupings may be distinguished according to which criteria are applied. The major criterion applied in (b) above, for example, is narrative versus reflective; this determines the fundamental division into twelve (part one) + eight (part two) = twenty lines. Another criterion is time. Part one is in the past. Part two proceeds in two stages of future time: in the *three* lines 13-15 the lyric "I" looks into the future ("another day"; "if I should ever come back"), though this act of reflection itself is described as a past event; in the *five* lines 16-20 the "I" projects recollection of the entire situation, including the anticipated future of lines 13-15, into a more distant future ("I shall"; "ages and ages hence"). There is subtle chiasmus in the way both past and future tenses and parallel time expressions ("should" and "shall," "day" and "ages") are interwoven here.

(f) Yet another criterion is the persona's relationship to the two roads. In the poem's first *three* lines the focus is on "both" of the "Two roads." This focus returns in the poem's central four lines, 9-12 ("both . . . equally") and near the end ("Two roads," line 18). Thus eight of the text's twenty lines concern *both* roads, again two-fifths (8/20).

(g) Otherwise, with the exception of lines 16 and 17, the focus is on either the one road or the other: on road A, the road not taken, in lines 4-5 and 13-15, and on

road B, the one taken, in lines 6-8 and 19-20. As suggested by the diagrammatic presentation in Figure 2, the design controlling the placement of these passages is extremely intricate. The following formal subtleties are worth stressing. The underlying proportionality is again $3/5 + 2/5 = 1$ (once for each road). In the two 2-line passages (lines 4-5 and 19-20, concluding stanzas I and IV respectively) the focus is exclusively on the one road or the other. In the two 3-line passages (lines 6-8 and 13-15, symmetrically balanced at the start and end of stanzas II and III respectively) each road is viewed in reference to the other ("took the other"; "kept the first"). Moreover, this pattern of content and proportion is formally highlighted by the marked repetition of the (singularly appropriate) words "one" or "(-)other" in the *initial lines of all four passages.* The chiasmic vectors in Figure 2 call attention to the correspondences is number, focus-type, and wording that interrelate the two sets of $2 + 3 = 5$ lines, one set for each road.[18]

FIGURE 2. FORMAL PATTERNS OF WORD, NUMBER, AND SENSE GOVERNING THE THREE- AND TWO-LINE PASSAGES DEVOTED TO THE ROAD NOT TAKEN AND THE ROAD TAKEN; THREE/FIVE PROPORTIONALITY

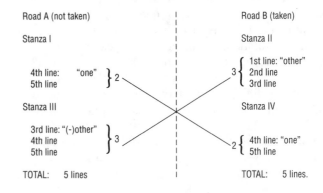

FIGURE 3. VERBAL ECHOES LINKING BEGINNING AND END

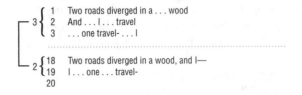

The rhyme-system is basically asymmetrical and dynamic, inhering in a tension of unequal parts, three and two in five, twelve and eight in twenty. If this were the only pattern-system in the text, one might question the relevance of its tension between *unequal* parts to a poem about choice between roads "really the same" which "equally lay." There is, however, another formal design against which the dynamic rhyme-system is counterpointed. It is the division of the text into four equal stanzas. In the abstract this division is basically symmetrical and static $(2 + 2 = 4)$, its formal, almost concentric balance calling attention to the middle and the two ends. But the "commitment" to four stanzas also offered the poet an opportunity for asymmetrical variation within the symmetry $(3 + 1 = 4)$. Examination of the text's verbal and thematic repetitions shows that Frost took advantage of both symmetrical and asymmetrical potential in his four stanzas, again in what appears to be a conscious, even systematic way of composing. The patterns based on fourness, both two/four and three/four proportionality, may be referred to collectively as the stanza-system. Patterns expressive of the more symmetrical two/four proportionality are summarized in (A) and (B) below, those reflecting three/four proportionality in (C).

(A) The most conspicuous repetitions occur at the beginning and near the end: "Two roads diverged in a [yellow] wood" (lines 1 and 18). These are accompanied, furthermore, by other symmetrical echoes linking lines 2 and 3 at the beginning with 18 and 19 (the third and second lines from the end). These are isolated in Figure 3. As noted in (f) above, the only other passage concerned with "both" of the "Two roads" is in the central four lines, 9-12. This passage, like the four stanzas, is divided by the central formal axis between stanzas II and III into $2 + 2$. The wording at this central axis, "same, / And both," is conceptually linked with the beginning and end—by synonymy with the beginning ("both" in line 11 repeating the initial b-rhyme in line 2) and by antonymy with the end ("same" in line 10 structurally contraposed with the final b-rhyme, "difference," in line 20). Unlike the other stanza junctures after lines 5 and 15, this central axis does not coincide with a major syntactic pause, the only punctuation here being the comma after line 10. Evidently, the centripetal focus of the stanza arrangement is aimed more at the central passage of four lines than at the formal axis itself, for the balanced syntactic and thematic enjambement that transcends the axis clearly connects stanzas II and III, emphasizing a coming together rather than separation in the middle. Thus, the overall formal symmetry apparently has to do less with the stanza junctures as such than with the thematic unity of the three passages near the junctures at beginning, middle, and end, those referring to the "two"-ness, "both"-ness, and "same"-ness of the roads—in a word, their twinness.[19]

(B) The thematic connection among initial, central, and final passages raises the question about possible symmetry in the passages intervening. In (g) and Figure 2 we observed the symmetrical balance of the two 3-line passages devoted to the road taken and the road not taken. The one passage immediately precedes, the other immediately follows the central four-line unit devoted to "both" roads. Stanzas II and III may thus be viewed

as a symmetrically disposed sequence of three (road B) + four (road A + B) + three (road A) = ten lines.[20]

Proceeding further outward we note that the next symmetrically aligned pair of content groups—the two lines ending stanza I and the two lines beginning stanza IV—also matches up passages of equal length.[21] A thematic correspondence between these parts of stanzas I and IV is not immediately evident by any of the criteria applied up to this point. On closer inspection, however, a more subtle parallel in wording and meaning begins to emerge. In lines 4 and 5 the persona portrays himself as looking down the one road (ultimately not taken) "as far as" he could; in the positionally corresponding lines 16 and 17 the persona looks into the future "ages and ages hence," in effect down the road to be taken. The shared motif of the persona trying to discern the future down the road, especially the deictic symbolism common to the two situations, is appropriately concentrated in the felicitous verbal correspondence that connects the two passages, aptly enough at the same focal point in both, the start of the second line: "To where" (5) and "Somewhere" (17). Thus, the symmetry unfolds yet another step: two (future down road A) + three + four + three + two (future down road B) = fourteen lines.

What remains, proceeding outward, are the three lines at the start and the three lines at the end, those containing the symmetrical focus on the "Two roads." These two 3-line passages both begin with the conspicuous repetitions in lines 1 and 18 and share the other notable verbal echoes summarized in Figure 3 above. Thematically, however, the second and third lines in each (2-3 and 19-20) are contrasted: indecision at the start versus both the decision and, as one critic appropriately termed it, "the romantic pose of finality" at the end.[22] The main lines of the organizational symmetry analyzed here are diagrammed in Figure 4.

FIGURE 4. SYMMETRY (RUBRICS FROM LEFT TO RIGHT: THEMES, VERBAL ECHOES, NUMBER OF LINES IN UNIT, MAJOR PUNCTUATION INVOLVED, LARGER GROUPINGS)

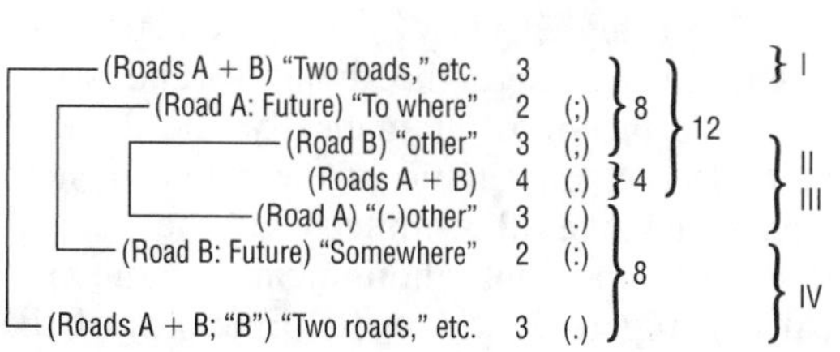

(C) A final content criterion implicit in the poem's thematic organization is the distinction between the past event at the crossroads and its future consequences. The first three stanzas present the past event, in both its narrative (lines 1-12) and reflective phases (lines 13-15). All the verbs are in the past tense. At the start of the fourth stanza the tense and setting shift to the future ("I shall be telling"), and in the projected future the persona recalls the past event and its consequences. From the perspective of this criterion of time, the relationship between stanzaic structure and thematic organization appears rather more asymmetrical, $3 + 1 = 4$. A striking set of verbal and conceptual correspondences gives reason to believe that Frost also consciously exploited this feature of his text's potential for formal patterning. The final three lines in effect summarize the first three stanzas: the "this" to be told (line 16) refers back to the first three stanzas and forward to the last three lines. As the italics in Figure 5 indicate, the wording that begins stanzas I, II, and III is echoed—in strictly sequential order but with gradually decreasing similarity in sound and sense—by the way the final three summary lines begin.

FIGURE 5. PARALLELS OF SOUND (AND SENSE) AT THE START OF THE FIRST THREE STANZAS AND THE LAST THREE SUMMARY LINES

Stanza I,   line 1: *Two roads diverged in a* yellow *wood,*
Stanza II,   line 1: Then *took the* other as just as fair,
Stanza III, line 1: *And both that* morning equally lay

Line 18: *Two roads diverged in a wood,* and I—
Line 19: I *took the* one less traveled by,
Line 20: *And that* has made all the difference.

From the foregoing (inter)relationships, it is evident that a fundamental principle of Frost's "performance" in **"RNT"** is what may be called structural counterpoint. A dynamic pattern comprising twelve + eight = twenty lines (the three/five rhyme-system; see the brackets at the right in Figure 1) is imposed on a static structure of four stanzas: five + five + five + five = twenty lines (the stanza-system). Within the stanza-system, moreover, two subpatterns, one symmetrical, the other asymmetrical ($3 + 1 = 4$), are superimposed in similar structural tension. All three designs share verbal and conceptual elements, but each is determined by different formal and thematic criteria. All three, however, also have formal properties in common that tend to integrate them in a higher unity. This is perhaps most evident in Figure 4, where the dynamic and static systems come together most dramatically: the three + two = five pattern characteristic of the rhyme-system coincides with the overall symmetry of the stanza-system. It is also apparent, though on a somewhat smaller scale, in Figure 2, where the principles of the two systems—basically fiveness and fourness—are similarly combined and resolved.

The two most important *formal* determinants of these patterns are verbal repetition[23] and number. The patterns described of course result from one person's "interpretation" of textual facts, since all description involves some interpretation. But this is not an interpretive read-

ing in the usual sense. Rather, the analysis is chiefly concerned with textual features that are readily accessible to objective verification, like repetitions and the numerical properties of rhyme and stanza, and therefore lays claim to some measure of objectivity. The patterns look to me, on the whole, too consistent to be reasonably explained as accidents or subconscious by-products. Moreover, patterns of "association" discussed in the following section give further grounds for seeing in these textual findings creatures of conscious design.

Although still not widely recognized, Frost's use of number in the service of form is no longer as surprising today as it might have appeared some years ago. In his analysis of **"The Wood-Pile,"** a poem published a year before **"RNT,"** J. Donald Crowley recently examined mathematical puns on the cord of wood, "measured, four by four by eight" (line 24), and cited statements by Frost to show that the poet "was himself fascinated by what he called 'carrying numbers into the realm of space and at the same time into the realm of time.'"[24] Frost's mother, who had a profound influence on his poetic education, was a teacher "in mathematics" (PR, 16), and Frost's own training in Greek exposed him early to interpenetrations of alphabet and number and the etymological kinship of much poetic and arithmetic terminology, for example in "rhythm," "meter," and "arithmetic," or "rhyme" (cf. OE rīm, 'number'), or even the earlier term for verse, "numbers."[25] In discussing the metaphorical origins of science one of Frost's essays, "Education by Poetry" (1931), traced the Greek connection explicitly: "The best and most fruitful [of the Greek metaphors] was Pythagoras's comparison of the universe with number" (SP, 37).[26] It may be stretching this statement too far to infer from it, as R. T. Fleissner recently did, that Frost was "perhaps . . . more of a conscious follower of Pythagoras than we might at first imagine."[27] But Fleissner seems justified in the more limited conclusion—one apparently corroborated by Reginald L. Cook's personal acquaintance with the poet—that for Frost "science and poetry have in common a mutual concern with numerical progression."[28]

The context of Fleissner's argument is an interpretation of **"The Gold Hesperidee,"** which attempts to show that the Golden Mean is both an aesthetic and an ethical determinant in the poem. Whether or not one accepts Fleissner's numerological conclusions, the similar use of the numbers five and three in Tennyson's "The Hesperides" and Frost's **"The Gold Hesperidee"** (perhaps also Coleridge's "Kubla Khan") is certainly striking.[29] Striking also in the present context is the intriguing fact that the numbers explicitly and repeatedly referred to in **"The Gold Hesperidee"** are five, three, and two (lines 2 and 13; 4, 5, 6, 25, and 27; 11, 12, and 25 there respectively), the same numbers Frost used in the rhyme-system (see Figure 2) and the symmetrical patterns (see Figure 4) described above.

Perhaps relevant too are the conceptual links Fleissner noted between **"The Gold Hesperidee"** (first published in 1921) and **"RNT."** Although Fleissner himself did not consider any numerical features of **"RNT"** in interpreting it as "motivated by a concern for temperance or the ideal of the Mean,"[30] it is possible that "Golden Rule" and "Golden Proportion" had something to do with the poem's formal structure. If the text's line total of twenty is repeatedly multiplied by the Golden Mean approximation (.618) to form a proportional series, the results (to nearest integer) are twenty, twelve, eight, five, three, and two, precisely the values operative in the rhyme-system (see Figure 1).[31] But here interpretation of a less objectively verifiable nature comes into play, one that will presumably have to take into consideration the findings discussed in the following sections.

II. "FEATS OF ASSOCIATION": EDWARDIAN TOMFOOLERY

In the foregoing analysis of Frost's "performance" in **"RNT,"** it seemed prudent procedure to be led gradually from the externals of printed format to patterns of increasing conceptualization. Analysis of Frost's "feats of association" in this poem could not proceed the same way because the associations involve rather private allusions and parody, which for most readers would remain inaccessible in the text without hints. Once the hints are given, however, it becomes possible for critics to rise to Frost's challenge and "talk about" patterns of association within the text. The present discussion therefore proceeds from extrinsic clues about parody to intrinsic patterns that develop the parody's textual implications, first in conceptual associations, then in formal subtleties of wording and sound-play that lead back into the "realm of performance."

Beyond what is available of Frost's correspondence with Edward Thomas about this poem during the early summer of 1915, the poet's earliest preserved hint about its hidden meanings are contained in his letter of September 9, 1915, to Louis Untermeyer: "Even here I am only fooling my way along as . . . particularly in **'The Road Not Taken.'** . . . I trust my meaning is not too hidden in any of these places. I can't help my way of coming at things" (LU [*The Letters of Robert Frost to Louis Untermeyer*], 14). This statement served to exemplify what Frost had written about friendship in the letter's opening paragraph, particularly his comment on playfulness between friends: "we shall be always fooling like a pair gay with love" (LU, 13). In commenting on this letter later, Untermeyer emphasized the importance of playfulness in their friendship:

> Apart from my admiration for Robert's poetry, which never failed to excite as much as move me, what endeared him to me was his irrepressible sense of play. It was a rich and surprising playfulness, unexpected and almost unknown to the readers of his monologues, a delight in fooling for its own sake, a drollery that ranged from literary badinage to absurdly bland double meanings and wildly nonsensical puns.
>
> (LU, 13)

In hindsight, Frost's choice of **"RNT"** as an example of such "fooling . . . along" seems particularly appropriate in this letter because of the profound meaning he experienced in the friendship established but a year earlier with the person for whom he had only recently written this poem, Edward Thomas.[32] But Untermeyer's intimation that Frost's playfulness could at times be overly subtle, even for the best of friends, was a danger Frost himself had had occasion to recognize only a few months earlier. Obviously expecting Thomas would see **"RNT"** for the parody it was, Frost had mailed him the poem without accompanying letter or explanation. It must have been a keen disappointment to Frost when he learned from Thomas's letters of June 13 and July 11, 1915, that Thomas had totally missed the poem's parodistic intent.[33] Moreover, even when the subtlety had been pointed out to him, Thomas cautioned Frost: "I doubt if you can get anyone to see the fun of the thing without showing them and advising them what kind of laugh they are to turn on" (11 July 1915, quoted in T2: 89). Frost could, with some justification, console himself about the parody's initial failure, since the poem caught Thomas at a time of what Frost later termed "exquisite . . . pain" in choosing between emigrating from England to be with Frost in New Hampshire or enlisting to fight for England in the war.[34] And he implies that he had come to terms with the initial disappointment and recognizing the limitations inherent in his kind of subtlety, for later in the same letter to Untermeyer he admitted:

> And as for your parodies . . . they are not my kind of fooling; but they are a constituted kind and of course much better than mine. The best of your parody of me was that it left me in no doubt as to where I was hit. I'll bet not half a dozen people can tell who was hit and where he was hit by my **Road Not Taken.**
>
> (LU, 14)

That was in 1915. The parody is now more accessible, at least to scholars, especially since Thompson pulled together so much of the pertinent biographical information (*SL,* xiv-xv, and T2, 87-89). Clearly, Edward Thomas was "hit" in his indecisiveness. It is also now evident how apt the road-traveler symbolism was for Frost's purpose. Not only was Thomas a noted walker and cyclist who loved roads,[35] but also the event that inspired this symbolism involved choosing between alternative roads during one of the walks the two men took together.[36] It may have been this symbolism Frost was referring to when he dropped hints about the poem's subtlety during public readings, or it may simply have been to caution audiences from identifying the sighing traveler with the poet.[37] Whatever his reasons, he repeatedly dropped hints about the poem like the one quoted earlier: "You have to be careful of that; it's a tricky poem, very tricky" (T2, 546).

But how "tricky"? Why did Frost single out this lyric as "very tricky," when so many of his poems are extremely subtle, some in fact considerably more difficult to understand? Is the parody of Edward Thomas, with its now evident road-traveler symbolism, the limit of the poem's trickiness? Is its teasing all the "fun of the thing" (Thomas) or all the playfulness to be expected from a craftsman who delighted "in fooling for its own sake, a drollery that ranged from literary badinage to . . . wildly nonsensical puns" (Untermeyer)? Or are there yet more subtle tricks tucked away in this text, even some which could seem "wildly nonsensical"?

There are signs that the poem's symbolism is more than an allusion to a romantic trait in Thomas's behavior. Close attention to the text's conceptual associations strongly suggests that the poem began as an elaborate metaphoric pun which Frost systematically developed to match the symbolic situation to the sound and sense of Thomas's *name*. The *Oxford English Dictionary* gives inter alia the following meanings for "Thomas": "Thomas . . . 1. A Greek, Latin, and common Christian name; well known as that of the 'doubting apostle' (see John xx. 25), and hence used allusively. . . . 2. Generic name for a footman . . ."; the etymological meaning of Thomas is *twin*.[38] It is not difficult to see how onomastic associations like these could have influenced the poem's symbolism; in short: the persona as vacillating doubting Thomas who must choose (as foot-man?) between equivalent or *twin* roads.

But it is difficult to know how far the playfulness in this goes and where seriousness begins. Before examining the textual evidence for this hypothesis, it may be worthwhile to consider several reasons why the underlying name metaphor, if indeed relevant, need not be read merely as the cute trick it may at first appear to be. Frost himself took his well-known (and occasionally criticized) sense of humor seriously: "The style is the man. . . . If it is with outer humor, it must be with inner seriousness. Neither one alone without the other under it will do" (*SP*, 65).[39] Louis Untermeyer, certainly one of those who knew Frost best, repeatedly cited this statement as "an almost perfect description of Frost himself."[40] He also cited, as representative, Frost's late description of his art—"It takes all sorts of in- and outdoor schooling / To get adapted to my kind of fooling" (originally entitled "The Poet" [1959])—and explained: "The 'fooling' was his [Frost's] particular mixture of levity and gravity, of outer humor and inner seriousness" (LU, 388).

Frost was also seriously concerned about names, their meaning, and the relation of name-meaning to character. The most probing example of this concern is his 170-line poem **"Maple"** (first published in 1921), the entire text of which is devoted to the effects of a name "having too much meaning": "Thus had a name with meaning, given in death, / Made a girl's marriage, and ruled in her life" (lines 45 and 163-64). Representative too are his numerous name puns in *A Masque of Mercy* (Jesse Bel, Keeper: "The name his mother gave him is to blame" [line 35]) and in *A Masque of Reason* (Job as job). One key to the puns in the latter is the suggestive allusion to Genesis 2: 19-20—perhaps as a symbolic source of science and poetry?—when Frost has God proclaim: "I'm a great stickler for the author's name. / By proper names I find I do my thinking" (lines 199-200).

Many other of Frost's name puns are more obviously spoofs, for example in **"The Wrights' Biplane"** ("Its makers' name . . . was writ in heaven doubly Wright.") and the limerick **"The Seven Arts"** (cf. T2, 113-14). The numerous name-games in his letters to Untermeyer appear to be in this category, for example: "Robt— perfect passive participle" (27 June 1918), "Robbered Frossed" (19-20 June 1920, 23 June 1920), "Robbed Frossed" (27 January 1921), and such as his reference to himself in Ann Arbor as "The Guessed of this University because I came as a riddle and was so soon solved" (23 November 1921). Many of these are, as Untermeyer called them, "nonsensical" and seem hardly comparable in significance with the way Maple's name "ruled in her life." But even the less significant of these puns give us a rounder picture of Frost's preoccupation with the sound and sense of names. Those that are more clearly significant should caution us from dismissing this preoccupation, especially when the person so preoccupied is a poet of Frost's stature. Did Frost's surname rule in his life? At least one critic found evidence that it did in his poetry. Noting the frequent occurrence of winter concepts like ice, snowy evenings, and frozen lakes in the early books, no less a critic than Theodore Maynard wrote in 1920: "If I had to sum up Frost with a word I would use the word 'frost.' Winter lies over all his landscape."[41] This is, of course, a hyperbole, but at the very least a provocative one. Would Frost have disagreed?

In the same spirit, but at some less risk of hyperbole, I would like to hazard an analogue: the name (Edward) Thomas lies over much of the verbal landscape in **"RNT."** Was it by proper names Frost was doing his thinking when developing the associations in this poem? The first clue, as we have seen, is the biographical connection with Thomas's behavior in Gloucestershire; in Thompson's summary formulation: "Frost pretended to 'carry himself' in the manner of Edward Thomas just long enough to write **'The Road Not Taken'**" (*SL*, xiv). We may expect from what we know of Frost's playfulness and ambition as a craftsman that a poem written for a person at once close friend and fellow poet might well be a technical tour de force. Encouraged by these circumstances to have a closer look at the poem's associations from this perspective, let us explore some of the ways Frost could have consciously exploited the poem's onomastic potential.

As noted, the name Thomas means "twin," "doubter," and "footman." The poem begins and ends with "Two roads" which, twinlike, are worn "really about the same."[42] Faced with choosing, the speaker wants to go two directions, to "travel both / And be one traveler," a kind of Siamese twin.[43] Perhaps as a "traveler" he could even be thought of as a "Thomas" ("footman").

The formal potential of twinness leads beyond purely conceptual association. On the syntactic and lexical levels too there are frequent doublings.[44] The setting involves "Two roads" (twice). The tale itself is twice told (lines 1-12 and 18-20) and "ages and ages" separate the two tellings. The minimal difference between the two roads is doubly described (one "was grassy and wanted wear") as is their essential similarity ("had worn them really about the same, / And both that morning equally lay"). Other important verbal repetitions are indicated in note 23 above, especially "travel(-)," "both," "took," "as . . . as" and, most conspicuously, "Two roads diverged in a . . . wood." Even the speaker's mental images appear in verbal pairs: he thinks not only of "ages and ages," but also "how way leads on to way." As David M. Wyatt has recently emphasized, the persona himself is literally divided in two by the hovering at the end of line 18: "and I—/ I took."[45]

These instances of syntactic and lexical doubling can of course be explained without recourse to name play. They also function as part of that repetition and variation of sound that gives poetry its musicality, what Frost called its "tune."[46] At first I took the repetitions to be little more than that. Then I noticed that Frost had been very selective about the sounds given formal emphasis by repetition and that his selection coincided more often than not with the sound and spelling of Edward Thomas's name. Moreover, these coincidences in sound proved, on inspection, to be rather more intricately patterned than could easily be credited to chance.

Four such sound groupings occupy structurally prominent places in the text. All four involve alphabetical play, but the methods by which the letters are patterned differ slightly in each. The first two, taken singly, could perhaps be considered fortuitous, were it not for the third and fourth. Taken together, however, the four seem to me too consistent with the poem's other subtleties in both sound and sense to be dismissed as mere accidents.

If intended as patterns—and their presence is particularly difficult to explain if they were not—they offer fresh insight into Frost's "kind of fooling," his mastery with formal constraints, and, more important, the process that shaped this poem.

The first is in the conspicuously repeated phrase, "*Two* roads diverged in a . . . *wood*," which may well have been the starting point for much of the poem's symbolic sound play. The phrase stands out prominently at the beginning and near the end of the poem and itself begins and ends with echoes of two of the four syllables in Ed*ward Tho*mas's name, the central two. The internal rigor of this pattern is brought out by the diagram in Figure 6. The distinguishing formal characteristics here are anaphora and, at least in line 1, rhyme; that is, the focus is on beginning and end. Particularly notable is the way this focus is carried through uniformly at each level: in the poem as a whole (lines 1 and 18), within these lines (at the start and near the end in each), and in the name syllables concerned (i.e., initial and final letters only are echoed).[47]

The second example, although not so conspicuously placed, comes at a point in the text that is conceptually and formally important, the syntactic and thematic juncture ending line 8 (two-fifths of the poem's twenty lines).

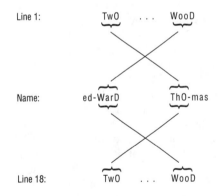

FIGURE 6. NAME PLAY AT THE BEGINNING AND END OF LINES 1 AND 18 (NEAR THE BEGINNING AND END OF THE TEXT)[48]

It is at this point, after both roads have been described and distinguished, that the tone shifts to one of qualification, and the central, four-line unit begins, showing that both roads are really about the same. The dominant sound at this juncture is the rhyme word "wear." Like the rhyme ending line 1, "wood," "wear" resembles the second syllable of the name Ed*ward*. Frost, it seems, exploited the resemblance this time by disposing the alphabetical play—here in strictly sequential order—around this important rhyme. As may be readily seen from the diagram in Figure 7, the two metrical feet at this juncture, "-ed wear; / Though as," closely parallel the spelling of the name in ten of its twelve letters. (The unusual phrase "though as" occurs only one other time in all of Frost's poetry, **"Some Science Fiction,"** line 9.)

FIGURE 7. NAME PLAY AT THE JUNCTURE BETWEEN LINES 8 AND 9 (TWO-FIFTHS OF THE POEM'S TEXT)

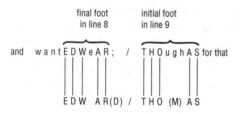

The third example is related to the first two, but more complicated in the textual demands it presumably made on the poet and therefore also a somewhat more reliable indicator of intent. As such, it also increases the likelihood of a larger purpose behind the first two examples. The challenge the pattern posed is perhaps most easily understood if approached from a hypothetical stance. Imagining ourselves in the poet's place, let us suppose Frost wished to echo Edward Thomas's name on the poem's formal highnotes, its rhymes. We know from the passage quoted near the start of the previous discussion on "performance" that Frost saw success in rhymes as "the deadly test" (PR, 33). It would seem to follow that encumbering the rhymes would be for him the most exacting challenge to technical skill. The extent of the challenge becomes apparent when we ask ourselves: Which rhymes will work for the four syllables ED, WARD, THO, MAS? They cannot be too obvious. But they should not be too difficult either, especially since the a-b-a-a-b scheme of masculine rhymes (perhaps already established in writing stanza IV; discussed below) is demanding enough as it is. We have almost decided to have the first line end in "wood," so we have the W-D for a start. The AR could be accommodated in some corresponding part of the pattern later, say in something easy like "air." THO is a bit trickier, but if we switch vowel and consonants (like other symmetrical features of structure we're contemplating), we'll have OTH, and that's manageable; "both," for example, would serve well. The problem with MAS is similar, but becomes even trickier if we invert the letters symmetrically to SAM. But how about imbedding the letters in something like "same"? Now all that's left is ED. It's difficult to work this in in a monosyllabic rhyme without being too obvious, and inversion to DE, as in "made," would be less appropriate in rhyme because of the silent *e*. To get just these two letter-sounds we're going to have to go with a close approximation like "day." Now let's see how we can arrange rhymes like these in a pattern to get the most onomastic sense from their sound. "Wood" in our first line would be an a-rhyme, so let's make all the a-rhymes go with "Edward." We have two letters in W-D, two in AR, and two in ED, so we can set them up in a kind of symmetry, the ends W-D and ED situated at the extremes and AR, appropriately, in the middle. That leaves the b-rhymes for "Thomas." Etc., etc.

This is doubtless a much abridged version of how Frost perhaps actually proceeded. But judging from what is now in the text, I suspect the fictional process just sketched is still closer to fact than fancy. The poem contains eight rhyme sets, two in each stanza, an a-rhyme with three members, a b-rhyme with two members (a-b-a-a-b). The sets are, for the four stanzas: -ood, -oth / -air, -aim / -ay, -ack / -igh, -ence. The initial five of these sets all employ words that meet the conditions for name play described above. The name-play design hidden in these five rhymes is summarized schematically in Figure 8.

FIGURE 8. THE POEM'S INITIAL FIVE RHYMES: NAME PLAY ON *EDWARD THOMAS*

Stanza:	Rhyme-word:	Rhyme-type:	Relevant letters:	Sum of letters:	Name syllables:	Names:
I	"wood"	a	W-D	2	-W(AR)D	
	"both"	b	OTH	3	THO-------	
II	"wear"	a	AR	2	-(W)AR(D)	EDWARD THOMAS
	"same"	b	SAM	3	-MAS---	
III	"day"	a	D(E)	(2)	ED-	

Does the pattern of sound-play in Figure 8 derive from a carefully wrought onomastic design? Or is it merely a chance cluster of lucky events? Having come to a conviction about the poem's artifice rather gradually myself, I can sympathize with initial skepticism. All five rhyme sets and all thirteen participating rhyme words sound so natural that it seems at first incredible they could have been erected upon so contrived a foundation of predetermined formal constraints. Indeed, unless the design features are explicitly "unconcealed" in diagrammatic isolation, the very success of the textual camouflage makes it hard to grasp the intricacy and regularity of how the details are organized. But if Frost was proud of his craft, and could claim to be one of the most notable craftsmen of his time, he was also proud of his ability to conceal that craft: "The great object of great art," he wrote to Thompson in 1942, "is to fool the average man in his first or second childhood into thinking it *isn't* art" (*SL*, 499).[49] By this measure **"RNT"** is artful indeed, and it is not surprising that Frost was especially proud of his accomplishment with rhyme in this poem. During a reading on June 30, 1958, he boasted: "you can go along over these rhymes [in **"RNT"**] just as if you didn't know that they were there—like this." And after reading the poem: "You see, that talks past the rhymes and almost hides them as it takes them."[50] Is Frost's justified pride here more justified than he's letting on?

To supplement the diagram in Figure 8, let us look briefly at a few of the more concealed intricacies of the pattern it summarizes. To begin with, the symmetry of the pattern is precise and consistent in all regards, even including rhyme-types and the number of letters. The two-letter forms apply to "Edward," the three-letter forms to "Thomas." The "Edward" rhymes read up, the "Thomas" rhymes read down. For the most part, the rhyme-sounds are fairly common in Frost's oeuvre. But the rhyme on "both" is notable, since this is the only time Frost used it in *all* of his published poetry. (I know of its further use only in one unpublished fragment, written in England in 1913 or 1914, now in the Amherst College collection.) The numerical properties of the design also harmonize well with the numerical aspects of the poem's syntactic and thematic structure discussed earlier, especially the tension between the numbers three and five. For example, the initial *five* rhymes generate (or are governed by) the name-pattern; the poem's final *three* rhymes do not participate. The pattern divides the name Edward Thomas (naturally?) into *five* components, (E)D, AR, WD, and THO, MAS, three two-letter forms and two three-letter syllables.[51]

In describing the name play to this point, I have treated the three patterns as if they were separate. They are discrete in some respects, but not in all. The first example (TwO . . . WooD) shares the word "wood" with the patterns of rhymes, which in turn shares the term "wear" with the alphabetical sequence ED WeAR; / THOugh AS in Figure 7. Not unlike the intersecting in a crossword puzzle, the echoes of Thomas's name appear to reach out *horizontally,* as it were, from the rhyme words "wood" and "wear" in the *vertical* array (Figure 8).

FIGURE 9. ALPHABETICAL PLAY ON "TWO ROADS"

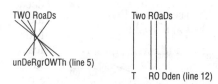

The same kind of horizontal development emanates from the rhyme word "same" at the poem's central axis. Before considering this fourth pattern, however, we should look briefly at a couple of the techniques by which Frost exploited the potential for alphabetical play in the top arm of the design, so to speak, line 1. The keynote words "Two roads," the poem's initial metrical foot, are echoed at two structurally important points in the text. The first is at the end of stanza I. As shown at the left in Figure 9, the rhyme word "undergrowth" not only contains the principal letters of its symmetrical counterpart at the start of the stanza, but has them in

exactly reversed sequence, creating a sort of mirror symmetry. The second comes near the end of the poem's long initial sentence (three-fifths of the text), the word "trodden" in line 12. The close resemblances in sound and spelling, here in sequential order, are also profiled in Figure 9. Since its musical value would be slight at such a distance, this "echo" may have been intended chiefly as a formal reflection of the crucial syntactic and structural division at the end of part one (lines 1-12), perhaps also as a phonetic parallel to the symmetrical references to foliage in these same two lines (see I, b above). It should be noted that the two sound-correspondences are similar in type to the first and second name-play patterns, one symmetrically chiasmic (like that in Figure 6), the other strictly sequential (like that in Figure 7).[52] "Undergrowth" completes the rhyme with "both." Is a closer connection with the name patterns intended? Did Frost perhaps see in the words "Two roads" yet another alphabetical echo of Thomas's name, one reinforcing the implication of "twinness" in them examined earlier? It is possible, since all the letters in "Two roads" also occur in "Edward Thomas." In fact, the words "Two roads" contain all but three of the letters which spell the name eDWARD ThOmAS. Perhaps this is another reason why Frost originally titled this poem "Two Roads."

In discussing the first three examples of name play we have focused on either meaning or sound. Now in the words "Two roads" we begin to see verbal and conceptual associations coinciding. The *convergence* of the meaning ("twinness") and the letters (eDWARD ThOmAS) is, in my judgment the best case for (what Frost called) "ulteriority" (*SP,* 24) in the phrase "Two roads"; the alphabetical element would be of negligible significant by itself. The last of the four name patterns exhibits a similar convergence of sense and sound, but one that is even more clear-cut because the independent cases for both sound and sense are strong. Just as the lesser name patterns reach out, so to speak, from the words "wood" and "wear" in the rhyme design, so too the rhyme word "same" has an important onomastic offshoot. The location of the word "same" is a significant factor here. It stands right before the central axis, the formal pause between stanzas II and III. This is also, it will be recalled, the midpoint of the central four-line unit (lines 9-12) in which we learn about the twinlike similarity of the two roads. The word with which "same" is paired at this formal axis, the first metrical stress in the next stanza, is a repetition of the form with which it is coupled by symmetrical alignment in the rhyme pattern (Figure 8), "both." Thus, it may be seen in the abstract in Figure 10, the pivotal components of the major name pattern are once again structurally juxtaposed, this time where one would perhaps ideally expect to find them, at the central point where the two halves of the text converge and diverge.

FIGURE 10. NAME PLAY AT THE POEM'S
CENTER

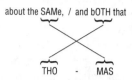

What probably delighted Frost most about this is the way sound and meaning come together in it. First off, the pattern splits up the two syllables of the name THO-MAS. Is this not much like Thomas himself at the middle of the crossroads, torn in both directions ("And sorry I could not travel both / And be one traveler"; "and I—/ I took")? Second, the letters in THO-MAS are spelt backwards. This too, it could be argued, harmonizes well with an important feature of the poem's allusive meaning: the parody of Thomas's way of looking back romantically to the road not taken ("Oh, I kept the first for another day!" Yet, "I doubted if I should ever come back").[53] Finally, the central *position* and central *significance* of SAMe bOTH for THO-MAS: what better choice of words could Frost have made for serious play on a name with meaning? "Both" and "same" not only sound "Thomas," they *mean* it: to be "twin" is to be *both* the *same*. To be "both" and the "same"—to travel two roads and be one traveler—was Thomas's romantic wish.

Remarkable as this may seem, there is more to this pattern at the axis. The two central lines share yet another set of features in which sound, sense, and name play are combined. Besides their pivotal meeting in "same, / And both," the two lines also echo one another phonetically in "worn" and "morn-," and (more in spelling than in sound) "really" and "equally." This phonetic parallelism reinforces parallel meaning, for it is these two lines that most explicitly denote the sameness of the two roads. Indeed, the two parallel verses may even have been designed to be prosodic analogues of the words they describe—two linguistic strings "about the same," as it were, diverging from their point of juncture. In any case, the parallelism calls attention to the fact that the name play is not restricted to the words at the juncture itself (SAMe and bOTH). In a manner corresponding to the focus on beginning and end in line 1, the name play in the parallel lines 10 and 11 involves the initial metrical foot as well as the rhyme. The "both" in line 11 is the verse's first metrical stress. It echoes the onomastic rhyme word "both" of line 2. The corresponding first metrical stress in the parallel line 10 is "worn." This echoes the key rhyme word "wear" of line 8. The terms "wear" and "worn" do not have the obvious semantic relevance to Edward Thomas's name that "both" does. But in sound and spelling the pun here is somewhat more pronounced: the phonetic contexts of "wear" and "worn" are the only two points in the poem

where a sequence of letters conforms to the alphabetical shape of "Edward" (see Figure 11).

FIGURE 11. RECURRENT SOUND PLAY ON
EDWARD

	Word(s):	Shape:
Name:	eDWaR(d)	vowel-D-W-vowel-R-(D)
Line 8 (end):	wanteDWeaR;/	vowel-D-W-vowel-R-(D)
Line 10 (start):	/haDWoRn	vowel-D-W-vowel-R-(D)

The pattern in the central lines (Figures 10 and 11) points up again what I consider the most compelling feature of the onomastic design: the overall *consistency* among its several constituent subpatterns. The intricate regularity of what may be termed the *vertical* subpattern among the first five rhymes, diagramed in Figure 8, is matched by a comparable uniformity of shape in the three *horizontal* subpatterns diagramed in Figures 6, 7, and 10-11. Common to all three is a twin focus on beginnings and ends, either initial and final sounds of words or, especially, initial and final metrical feet within the verse-lines. The latter type is particularly evident in the two subpatterns involving the repetitions of the verb "wear." As can be seen in Figure 12, both patterns have markedly similar profiles: the subtle differences are clearly subordinated to the overall parallel arrangement in each pair of lines (lines 8 and 9, 10 and 11); in both instances the parallel arrangement is reinforced by secondary sound correspondences like "worn" and "morn-" and "grass-" and "pass-" (the poem's only line pairs with such internal rhymes); and both patterns tie into the *vertical* subpattern of rhymes in very much the same way. It is almost as if the larger design embracing all four name patterns were a case of alphabetic *techno-paignia,* a giant capital letter E, in mirror image, comprised of lines 1, 8-9 (two-fifths of twenty), and 10-11 (half the twenty) and connected by the pun running down through the rhymes.

FIGURE 12. PARALLEL NAME PLAY IN LINES
8-9 AND 10-11

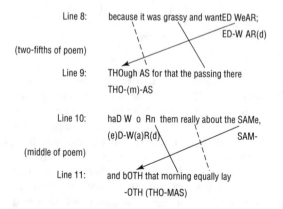

Clearly, then, for what became of sound and sense in this poem, both the character and the name of Edward

Thomas made a great difference. But not all the difference! The art of the poem is not only in its name play, for all Frost's subtlety at it. Nor do I mean to suggest that knowledge of these intricacies *must* play an important part in our enjoyment of the lyric (although surely for some it will). After all, the poem has been much enjoyed up to now without such knowledge (not, however, without the patterns themselves!). What I think can be fairly claimed is this: the structural and symbolic uses Frost made of Edward Thomas's name and character in this poem were fundamental factors in why and how the text was put together. Critics wishing to draw textual inferences about Frost's moral attitudes—and much of the recent scholarship on the poem has tended to drift this way—can hardly ignore the new evidence of the poem's "style," how the poet "carried himself" here.[54] Those interested in Frost's compositional practice as well as his theory can hardly ignore the kinds and degrees of formal constraint that his own ingenuity imposed on achievement in form. Whether or not one agrees with the apparent theoretical implication—art as a mastering of entanglements, alien or innate—it clearly must be weighed in alongside his inspirational qualities in a balanced assessment of Frost's stature as poet.

III. Composition

If the textual evidence examined above is any measure, **"RNT"** was composed with considerable forethought and revision, not in one stroke of racquet, club, walking stick, or orphic wand. Several of the questions this raises about Frost's compositional methods deserve at least preliminary attention in the present context: What do we know about the circumstances of the poem's composition? What did Frost himself say about these circumstances? What do the structural patterns reveal about the poem's genesis and therefore about which specific techniques lay behind notions like "performance and prowess and feats of association," "fooling around," and working over a poem "once it is in being"? The larger question, of course, is where Frost stood in the ancient debate between the claims of inspiration and craftsmanship. Because his theoretical statements are often coy, metaphorical, and even conflicting enough to leave his stance itself a matter of debate, the most promising source of insight into Frost's poetic theory may well be what can be reclaimed of his shaping process by analysis of textual shape. The importance of this larger issue seems sufficient reason to pursue the compositional questions, even though they lead into an inferential and increasingly speculative realm.

Lawrance Thompson assembled a number of comments by Frost and others relating to the composition and reception of **"RNT"** (T2, 545-48). The most important for insight into the poem's genesis is a remark Frost made almost forty years after the poem was composed: "One stanza of **'The Road Not Taken'** was written while I was sitting on a sofa in the middle of England; was found three or four years later, and I couldn't bear not to finish it" (23 August 1953). Thompson pointed out the slight inaccuracies and inconsistencies in this and related recollections by Frost and presented evidence to correct them. Taken together, Frost's comments and the other pertinent evidence indicate that different parts of the poem were written on at least two separate occasions falling within a period of less than a year, presumably between mid September 1914 and late April 1915.[55] Thompson's own conclusion was that Frost wrote "at least one stanza" in England, "near the end of his stay in Gloucestershire" (T2, 88), and the remaining stanzas some time after the Frosts returned to New Hampshire in early March 1915.[56] Thompson even indicated that the stanza written first in England was the one that now concludes the poem (T2, 88).

No worksheets for this poem are known to have survived, the earliest extant manuscript copy being the completed version Frost sent to Thomas "in April or very early May of 1915."[57] To judge from Thomas's letter of 13 June 1915 (T2, 545), line 10 originally read: "Had *gone to* them *both* about the same" (my emphasis). If line 11 was as we now have it, then the key name-word "both" originally appeared twice at the central axis in conjunction with "same" (THO-MAS in line 10 *and* lines 10-11). The deletion of the "periphrastic looseness" Thomas complained of in "gone to" gave occasion to echo the name play of line 8 by substituting "worn" (cf. Figure 11) and to establish the internal rhyme with "morn-" in line 11, a parallelism Frost apparently chose to develop further by replacing the "both" in line 10 with "really" (cf. Figure 12) to make the central two lines really about the same.

The first published version in the *Atlantic Monthly* (August 1915) differed from that in the first edition of **Mountain Interval** (1916) in three respects: line 8 ended in a comma rather than the semicolon; line 12 had "marked" for "kept"; and line 18 ended in a comma rather than the dash (also in the earliest MS; see quotation below). The wording change does not involve any of the patterns discussed, but the two punctuational changes (if the comma after line 8 in the magazine version is not simply an accident of printing) both call attention to important structural divisions in the first and last sentences—dividing each, incidentally, at the corresponding point, after the second of the three subdivisions in each.

The minute changes in the earliest published versions support the textual findings, but give little insight into the compositional process. It is to be hoped that the draft Frost said he "found . . . later," or some other early version, will still come to light.[58] But there seems no reason to doubt the essential accuracy of the chronology Thompson deduced from the known circumstances and from the later recollections Frost shared with him.

Two questions therefore arise: How does Thompson's chronology relate to what we have learned about the poem's formal structure? And what additional evidence does that structure provide concerning the poem's linear biography? At issue here in particular is Thompson's judgment that the last stanza was composed first. Although a response to such issues must of necessity be somewhat speculative, it is at least interesting to observe that the structural relationships between the last stanza and the other three involve nothing that conflicts with Thompson's judgment and several features that seem to support it. Obviously supportive is the fact that the last stanza states or implies, almost in summary form, the poem's major themes (cf. Figure 5). But perhaps more important, the very structure of the stanza seems to contain the seeds of many of the features we have seen in the organization of the poem, both in parts and in whole.

The earliest known version of this last stanza is quoted by Thompson from the manuscript copy Frost sent to Thomas (T2, 88):

> I shall be telling this with a sigh
> Somewhere ages and ages hence:
> Two roads diverged in a wood, and I,
> I took the one less traveled by,
> And that has made all the difference.

Let us accept, as a hypothesis, Thompson's view that Frost wrote this last stanza first and reexamine the poem from this perspective to see not only whether the hypothesis stands up, but also whether the exercise itself gives us a reasonable approximation of how the text-structure described above could have developed, almost organically, from the seeds in these five lines. Examination of possible structural "associations" will provide an additional check on the features of "performance" and "feats of association" discussed previously.

The tetrametric rhythm and a-b-a-a-b (3 + 2 = 5) rhyme scheme established here, or in a stanza closely resembling this, set the pattern for the other stanzas.[59] The text of the stanza consists of a single sentence. The syntactic juncture marked by the colon divides this sentence into two distinct units of meaning: the first unit, two lines in length, contains the speaker's reflection projected wistfully into the future and forming an *inquit* for what follows; the second unit, three lines long, describes the (anticipated) remembrance of a narrative situation and its consequences. This second part is further divided into three separate clauses joined by "and," two lines more and one line slightly less narrative in character. The fundamental division at the colon is clear both syntactically and thematically. In the distribution of its verbal material, the five-line stanza has the following numerical shape:

2/5 (:) more reflective

(lines 16-17)

3/5 (.) more narrative

(lines 18-20).

As the discussion in section I showed, the same proportions control the overall organization of the complete text. The first twelve lines, or three-fifths of the twenty-line whole, are devoted to the narrative situation proper, which is described in one long sentence. As in stanza IV, the "narrative" section here is further divided into three discrete subunits, joined this time by semicolons (after lines 5 and 8). The obvious change in tone beginning line 13 ("Oh, I kept . . .") shifts attention from the narrative situation to the speaker's inner response to the situation, and then, beginning with line 16 ("I shall be telling . . ."), to his (anticipated) response to that response. Again, therefore, we have a conspicuous syntactic and thematic break that is supported by the punctuation and exactly (though inversely) proportional to the model of the last stanza:

3/5 (.) (chiefly) narrative

(lines 1-12)

2/5 (.) (chiefly) reflective

(lines 13-20).

By corollary at least, and perhaps in part by design, stanzas III and IV thus have similar syntactic and thematic shapes:[60]

Stanza III:	Stanza IV:
2 lines (.) narrative	2 lines (:) reflection
+	+
3 lines (.) reflection	3 lines (.) narrative.

Perhaps the most obvious resemblance between the last stanza and the first three is in the series of verbal connections extending from the final three lines. As shown in Figure 5 earlier, stanzas I, II, and III all begin with verbal echoes from these three lines *in consecutive order*. The most developed of these echoes connects lines 1 and 18 ("Two roads . . ."), but it may be added that the pregnant pause concluding line 18 ("and I—") is drawn out into a threefold sound of "And . . . I" in lines 2, 3, and 4 of the first stanza. The relationships between line 19 and stanza II and between line 20 and stanza III also exhibit comparable amplification, but on a decreasing scale.

Viewed as the conclusion of the poem as we now have it, these last three lines appear to be something like a summary (albeit one that subtly and ironically reveals the person's romantic rationalization of his choice). We are not accustomed to viewing this finale as the emotional starting point of the poem, and of course need not in order to see these lines as the *compositional* starting point. But it requires only a small shift in perspective to understand rather easily how they could have been either or both for the poet. In fact, the principle of one-line-one-stanza, which emerges from at least the verbal echoes in Figure 5, may have been closely connected with the poet's choice of the four-stanza form. Interesting here too is the way the three/four principle of the poem's stanza-system governs the syntax of stanza IV: the sentence that fills the stanza has four clauses; Frost laid these in the stanza so that three of the four take up one line each in the three-fifths subunit after the colon. Certainly the last (first?) stanza is itself one of the clearest examples of how the principles of fiveness and fourness are adeptly harmonized in this poem.[61]

For all these reasons, then, it is not difficult to see how the poet could very well have developed the rest of the poem, both in shape and substance, out of the last stanza. But as a final test of how consistent all of this is with Frost's 1953 statement, two related issues need to be addressed. One concerns the possibility that some other stanza could have been the one Frost was referring to. Examination shows that none of the other three stanzas exhibits the degree of formal harmony with whole that is evident in stanza IV. Moreover, it is difficult to imagine how any other stanza could have been composed alone and left to stand alone even for a few months. Stanzas II and III are interlocked by enjambment of thought and syntax, and stanza I, though syntactically independent, is incomplete in thought, leaving the reader wondering what's down the other road.

The second issue is irony. Nowhere in the poem is its irony and ambiguity more evident than in the last stanza. But this subtlety reveals itself—to the careful reader—only through juxtaposition with what we know from the preceding three stanzas: "the one less traveled by" we know to have "equally" lain and to have been "worn . . . really about the same"; we know the choice to have been, in the words of one critic, "arbitrary, whimsical, undetermined"[62]; and we know "all the difference" to be richly ambiguous because of what we have learned about the speaker's tendency to retrospective rationalization.[63] To assume that stanza IV once stood prior and alone would of course seem to require that this irony was either in the poet's mind when he wrote the stanza or somehow sufficiently implicit for him in the text when he came back to it to write the rest. There is, however, no way to get at this with any finality. This Frost himself well knew:

> That poem ["RNT"]: there's a hint intended there. But you ought to know that yourself. One of the things I suffer from, you know, is being taken as intending a double meaning when I don't. Sometimes I do, and sometimes I don't. *And I can't mark 'em* [the hints]—*there's no way of marking them.* I have to leave it to nice people to know the difference.[64]

Nevertheless, both the finished poem and Frost's later comments about it give reason to conclude that the irony was likely under the surface of the stanza from the start. One reason is that the phrase "with a sigh" does in fact succeed in alerting the attentive reader to the irony.[65] Another stems from Frost's own repeated intimations that he intended this line to be a key to the irony; representative is the comment he made after reading the poem during a talk on July 2, 1956: "See, the tone of that is absolutely saving. You've got to look out for it, though. See. 'I shall be telling this with a sigh.'"[66] Such intimations are further corroborated by the anecdote Thompson related about Frost's response to a question from a schoolgirl about the "hint" in the word "sigh" (*SL,* xv and T2, 547). Thompson went so far as to state that when Frost sent the poem to Thomas with nothing else in the envelope he had "the expectation that his friend would notice how the poem pivots ironically on the un-Frostian phrase, 'I shall be telling this with a sigh'" (*SL,* xv). None of this of course proves conclusively that the irony was there from the start. But taken together these indications make this seem likely, especially when we recall that the poem was written, at least in part, to quietly mock an attitude toward choice that Edward Thomas had exhibited, and that Frost reportedly chided Thomas about this attitude *during* their walks together.[67]

What can be said for the irony seems no less applicable to the parody it supports. The very pervasiveness of name play in the poem's imagery strongly suggests that the web of onomastic "associations" was an original, formative factor in both parody and irony. Beyond that, the degree of subtlety in all this and the fact that Frost expected Thomas to discern the fun of the thing—without hints!—both seem grounds for suspicion that the two men had discussed such formal devices during their walks, perhaps even an analogue of such patterning in the ornate style of some Edwardian predecessor. In this connection two pieces of circumstantial evidence are particularly intriguing for the association they may imply with Gloucestershire and the topics of shop-talk among the poets there. The first is a comment in an essay entitled "Perfect Day—A Day of Prowess" (1956) where Frost explicitly linked his notion of "performance" with Edward Thomas himself: "another Welsh friend of mine, Edward Thomas, in England, [had] come to look on a poem as a performance one had to win" (*SP,* 88). Is this why Frost apparently felt he could expect Thomas to discern his "performance" of **"RNT"**? The other is in Frost's two-part letter to Lascelles Abercrombie dated 21 and 30 September 1915 (SL, 192-94). Although this letter deals largely with business difficulties between Frost and his publisher, Mrs. Nutt, it has a significant postscript asserting that the war had "made some sort of new man and a poet out of Edward Thomas" (*SL*, 193) and a suggestive, though apparently facetious request that Abercrombie recommend topics for the books Frost's contract with Mrs. Nutt obligated him to write. The letter concludes with a whimsical but perhaps characteristic strategy for revenge, one certainly eloquent of Frost's playful penchant for the cryptic (and cryptographic?)—and perhaps also, given all known circumstances, of private professionalisms familiar to the two poets: "For my own protection I intend to *sink a cryptogram in the text* that will say to the public when I furnish the key in the newspapers: Mrs. or Madam mistook her Man. Dont think too badly of me" (*SL*, 194; emphasis mine).

IV. Some Implications for Frost's Theory of Form and Aesthetics

At the outset I placed the study of form in **"RNT"** in the service of a larger concern with Frost's poetic theory and practice. The results of this study, particularly the evidence of highly calculative compositional techniques, provide one new touchstone by which we may "check up" on both Frost's theoretical pronouncements and the meaning of the poem itself. It will of course need to be looked into whether the formal complexity of this one poem is representative of Frost's practices elsewhere. But a number of inferences may be cautiously drawn from the findings as they now stand. Those of particular interest to me concern two areas of possible aesthetic justification for patterning of such precision and intricacy. The one has to do with cause, the other with purpose. That is: What do the patterns in **"RNT"** tell us about the concept of "form" that led to their being devised? And what is the relationship between such patterns and the poem's aesthetic impact?

Throughout I have cited from what Frost said about "performance" and "feats of association" as a means of access to the poem's formal and conceptual structure. To the extent the textual findings ring true, their most immediate implication for Frost's understanding of poetic form is in closing the hermeneutic circle and providing access back the other way to a richer understanding of what Frost meant by "performance" and "association." This implication need not be elaborated on, since the logic in sections I and II is easily reversed: performance defines "performance." The logic in the discussion of composition is somewhat less reversible because more speculative. Here the major implication concerns not only the composition of **"RNT,"** but the larger issue of "form" mentioned at the start of that discussion: the ancient debate between inspiration and craftsmanship.

In this debate I believe Frost has been widely misunderstood. Not that I question Frost's inspiration as poet. Quite the contrary. Indeed, formal analysis of **"RNT"**

would be meaningless if the poem were not, above all else, inspired poetry. But the popular image of Frost as inspired bard presents a lopsided view of his poetry. One unfortunate result of this has been that his achievements as craftsman have not received the attention they deserve. A recent assessment of Frost scholarship by one of Frost's former students applies to this context as well: "what is most needed now is a *balanced* view of Robert Frost, perhaps as much of the man as the poet since what we think of him as human being seems, now, out of all proportion, to be coloring and revising, upward or downward, what we think of him as a poet."[68]

"My object," Frost wrote in 1929, "is true form—is was and always will be—form true to any chance bit of true life" (*SL*, 361). What Frost meant by "form" is the subject of much that has been written on his scattered, largely offhand theoretical comments, and much of this scholarship has stressed the more Romantic, even rhapsodic formulations, the ones so frequently quoted because themselves so lyrical: "A poem . . . begins as a lump in the throat" (LU, 22); "Step by step the wonder of unexpected supply keeps growing"; "Its most precious quality will remain its having run itself and *carried away the poet with it*" (*SP*, 19-20, from "The Figure a Poem Makes"; emphasis added).[69] Little, however, has been written about the forms individual poems actually took, and that little has not always squared well with the usually quoted theoretical excerpts. As early as 1942, for example, in the first critical book on Frost, Lawrance Thompson showed that the poet's practice was more deliberate than suggested by the introduction to his collected poems ("The Figure a Poem Makes").[70] Most recently, Richard Poirier has called the tenor of this best known of Frost's theoretical essays into question by arguing that Frost's techniques involved "a good deal of premeditation and preplotting."[71]

The intricacies of form now found in **"RNT"** give reason to pursue this line of inquiry further. Rereading the essay(s) to see whether our former understanding holds up not only shows some statements in a different light, but also reveals passages that even seem to hint at a more calculative manner of composition.

Perhaps the clearest cases involve the paradoxes of wildness and regularness, crookedness and straightness discussed in "The Figure a Poem Makes" (1939) and "The Constant Symbol" (1946). The earlier and more often reprinted essay seems to stress crookedness and wildness, which is perhaps the chief reason why "the wild free ways of wit and art" (*SP*, 20) so strongly color the popular image of Frost as both bard and theorist. But not all critics have accepted this emphasis at face value. As Poirier, for example, put it: Frost's "claims . . . to the 'wildness of logic' are apt to strike some readers as disingenuous."[72] The later essay, on the other hand, seems to give the edge to straightness and regularness, and, in placing greater stress on what Frost called there the "straight crookedness" of a "poem written regular" (*SP*, 29, 24), almost appears designed to counterbalance the earlier overemphasis on wildness.

In reading both essays we should give due heed to what Frost stated in the later one about his penchant for the "ulteriority" of metaphor, for "saying one thing and meaning another, saying one thing in terms of another" (*SP*, 24). One of the only metaphors common to both essays is the paradoxical "straight crookedness" of a good "walking stick" (*SP*, 19 and 29). As the earlier essay stated it: "We enjoy the straight crookedness of a good walking stick. Modern instruments of precision are being used to make things crooked as if by eye and hand in the old days" (*SP*, 19). The wording here seems carefully chosen for subtlety. At first reading the emphasis appears to be on *crookedness,* but on scrutiny it reveals itself as doubly paradoxical. Not only is the crookedness straight; it is achieved with "Modern instruments of precision." Whether or not Frost's paradoxical metaphor is a deliberately veiled hint about his own compositional techniques—as I am inclined now to read it—the "straight crookedness of a good walking stick," wrought with "precision," is an apt image for the calculated artlessness of the surface text in **"The Road Not Taken."** Indeed, this poem illustrates concretely and specifically why I am convinced—with Poirier, but for partially differing reasons—that "what Frost says about 'modern instruments of precision' might sometimes apply to his own work on a poem."[73]

In "The Constant Symbol" there is no explicit reference to "precision," but here, in contrast with the generalities of the earlier essay, the emphasis on straightness and regularness extends to details of craftsmanship. One passage seems especially relevant to the issue of formal "precision." As we have seen, the structural evidence in **"RNT"** gives reason to infer that Frost's concept of form included even such details as the numerical properties of the textual materials and name play based on individual letters of the alphabet. It therefore seems particularly significant that one of Frost's most suggestive examples of the "constant symbol" for poetic form touches literally on both numerical and alphabetical features in one stroke:

> Jeremiah, it seems, has had his sincerity questioned because the anguish of his lamentations was *tamable to the form of twenty-two stanzas for the twenty-two letters of the alphabet.* The Hebrew alphabet has been kept to the twenty-two letters it came out of Egypt with, so the number twenty-two means as much form as ever.

> (*SP*, 28; emphasis added)[74]

I suppose Frost too will have his sincerity questioned by some because he used number as a formal tool or because so much of the poem's imagery and the parody

of Edward Thomas's character appears traceable to play on name-sounds, name-meanings, perhaps even name-numbers. True, the techniques are unfamiliar. But there are also some good reasons for taking them seriously. To start with, the fact that Frost structured this text the way he did—consciously, it seems, and for an accomplished fellow writer—suggests that he himself may have felt that deliberate design, including even precise attention to the kinds of formal details we have been examining, has something to do with the poem's aesthetic effectiveness. The main reason, however, is the recognized success of this poem as poetry. The fact that we have enjoyed this poem so much all along *despite* the patterns and our ignorance of them, at least on conscious levels, raises the question whether we have enjoyed the poem all along in part *because of* the patterns. In other words, do such submerged regularities of structure have a subliminal influence on our aesthetic response?

I for one strongly suspect that they do. My reasons are admittedly speculative, but the question seems important enough to run some risks in the hope of at least provoking discussion. My suspicions apply to both the numbers and the onomastic design, but in varying degrees, as will become clear.

Let us look first at the numbers. In addition to the considerations stated or implied in the analysis itself, it may be helpful to view the possible aesthetic effect of the numbers within a more widely drawn context. For some time now critics of music and especially art have been aware of the mathematical designs governing some great music (such as some works by J. S. Bach) and the geometric cartoons underlying many paintings of enduring appeal (for example, by Dürer and da Vinci). As regards at least the paintings, it is widely believed that these design features play a significant role in aesthetic experience even when they are not consciously perceived. Scholarly analysis of poetic uses of number began later, but has nevertheless matured to the point that some literary critics have started to ask whether and to what extent "the aesthetic emotion is affected . . . by unapprehended 'technical procedures.'"[75] This question touches one of the most intriguing humanistic issues raised by the discovery of number-based designs in works of poetry and art that we value: the possible capacity of man as an experience-structuring and structure-seeking being to respond intuitively to intricate regularities of structure he does not perceive. Perhaps the poets (composers, artists, architects) who used these techniques by design perceived something about their sense of beauty that most of us tend to overlook.

Accordingly, it seems at least possible, perhaps probable, that the underlying number-based design summarized in Figures 1 through 5 has had some subliminal effect on our enjoyment of this poem, since we are so evidently sensitive to rhythms of other kinds. By contrast, however, the aesthetic value of the onomastic design seems at first a solely cerebral affair, not subliminal. Certainly the alphabetical patterns in the design must be seen to be enjoyed. But the design also has at least one less cerebral effect: its influence on the poem's conceptual unity. Although the grounding of the poem's system of metaphors in the name "Thomas" is itself clearly private—since the text does not mention the name as such—and although the parody is now less private only because of Frost's hints, the way the imagery is unified, in both sense and sound, around Thomas's character, as the speaker portrays it, and around the concepts of twinness, indecision, and so forth, as Frost associated these with the character and the name, helped to shape the text and therefore also whatever appeal that text has had, even for readers unaware of the subtleties influencing their response.

Both the numerical and the onomastic patterns may, of course, elicit a conscious aesthetic response, be it the joy of recognition or sheer marvel at Frost's achievement over self-imposed hindrances. But beyond this the onomastic design has yet another aesthetic effect; it has expanded the poem's interpretive scope. **"RNT,"** it now appears, is a further example of Frost's long-term preoccupation with the relationship between name and character, a topic he addressed most directly in **"Maple"** (1921). Like **"Maple,"** but of course less fully and more obliquely, **"RNT"** touches what Elaine Barry in her reading of **"Maple"** termed "profound and complex ideas about the nature of knowledge, language, and personality," ideas that seem to place Frost "in the realm of I. A. Richards and Wittgenstein."[76] That these ideas had an important place in Frost's thinking is evident from the preoccupation with winter imagery in his poetry and from pregnant uses of the concept "name" in both poetry and theory. Perhaps the most suggestive of these is in "The Figure a Poem Makes": "It [a poem] *finds its own name as it goes* and discovers the best waiting for it in some final phrase at once wise and sad" (*SP*, 19; my emphasis).

Beyond these more or less conscious effects, I have observed that the poem's emotional appeal for me personally increased with awareness of the larger onomastic dimension. Perhaps the reasons for this increased appeal are not purely personal, as may be suggested by the following analogues. One of Frost's favorite and most striking metaphors for the compositional process is in the frequently cited passage from "The Figure a Poem Makes" quoted at the outset: "Like a piece of ice on a hot stove the poem must ride on its own melting." What role does the onomastic association of "ice" with "Frost" play in this metaphor's emotional appeal? What is lost by emendation: "Like a piece of lard on a hot stove the poem must ride on its own melting," or further removed: "Like a dollop of butter on a hot skillet the

poem must skate on its own melting"? Similarly, what is gained by the thinly veiled onomastic allusions so fundamental to the structure of **"Mending Wall,"** especially in lines 1-2 and 35-36: "Something there is that doesn't love a wall, / That sends the frozen-ground-swell under it"; and: "Something there is that doesn't love a wall, / That wants it down" (frost in nature, Frost the apple-grower as persona, Frost as poet—perhaps Frost as person)?

The playfulness in this "fooling" is firmly rooted in the post-Kantian aesthetic of play represented by Schiller, Nietzsche, William James, and Santayana.[77] But I suspect there is more to the play than playfulness. The same motif occurs too frequently and too seminally in Frost's work. It is "not just to no purpose," as Frost wrote of E. A. Robinson's "revel in the felicities of language" (*SP*, 67). Behind the motif I sense a deeper, almost epistemological concern with the interpretive process itself: how poems mean with aesthetic effect. If this judgment is accurate, the patterns of both name and number in **"RNT"** are probably an instance of the "literary criticism" Frost admitted to hiding in some poems. Once brought out into view, these at first seemingly arcane patterns of poetic play give unique insight into precisely the kinds of questions Richard Poirier saw raised by the other kinds of linguistic play that he examined in Frost's poetry—questions about the "limits of metaphor and the boundaries of form," or more fundamentally, "about what cannot quite be signified."[78]

What the numbers and name play in **"RNT"** tell us about both Frost's theory of poetic "form" and the poem's aesthetic achievement also reflects, by the hermeneutic process, back on the patterns themselves. The implications help us to see more clearly the context of theory in which the patterns appear organic, which in turn causes the patterns to appear less surprising. The poem and its subtle design grew out of the friendship between Frost and Thomas and perhaps needed no higher justification at the time than the wish—as Frost expressed it in the final line of **"To E. T."**—to "see you pleased once more with words of mine." But from all the linkages between text and theory, it seems to me unlikely that the patterning in **"RNT"** is unique in either kind or motivation.

In concluding his essay "The Constant Symbol," Frost stated: "I have written my verse regular all this time without knowing till yesterday that it was from fascination with this constant symbol I celebrate" (*SP*, 29). In **"The Road Not Taken"** we have one potentially instructive example not only of this fascination, but also of how one poem by Frost was "written . . . regular." If the symbol is in fact as constant in Frost's compositional practice as he claims in the essay, we should look to see if comparable structural techniques are also present in his other poems. If we were to find that similar patterning correlates with previously recognized success, perhaps it is not too much to hope that textual analysis of this kind will ultimately teach us something about the greater mystery: how design governing in parts so small makes poems please.

Notes

1. Except where otherwise indicated, all text citations are from *The Poetry of Robert Frost,* ed. Edward Connery Lathem (New York: Holt, Rinehart and Winston, 1969), here from the sonnet "Design," line 14. The present essay is dedicated to Kristina and Dawn, two poets in high school, for the part their interest played in prompting it.

2. Quoted from Frost's letter to Charles Madison, 26 February 1950, in: Cleanth Brooks and Robert Penn Warren, *Understanding Poetry,* rev. ed. (New York: Holt, 1950), p. 603.

3. Citations of Robert Frost's essays throughout are by page from *Selected Prose of Robert Frost,* ed. Hyde Cox and Edward Connery Lathem (New York: Collier, 1968), abbreviated *SP.*

4. In the letter cited in n. 2 above.

5. Quotations from Frost's letters are by page and, where relevant, by date from *Selected Letters of Robert Frost,* ed. Lawrance Thompson (New York: Holt, Rinehart and Winston, 1964), abbreviated *SL;* and *The Letters of Robert Frost to Louis Untermeyer,* ed. Louis Untermeyer (New York: Holt, Rinehart and Winston, 1963), abbreviated LU.

6. Quotations from the first two volumes of the three-volume official biography of Robert Frost by Lawrance Thompson is by volume and page: *Robert Frost: The Early Years, 1874-1915* (New York: Holt, Rinehart and Winston, 1966), abbreviated T1; *The Years of Triumph, 1915-1938* (1970), abbreviated T2.

7. Robert Francis, *Frost: A Time to Talk* (Amherst: Univ. of Massachusetts Press, 1972), p. 85.

8. Though the poem's popularity needs no documentation, Frost's own high regard for it is less well known. When asked to choose his "best" for the anthology, *105 Greatest Living Authors Present the World's Best,* ed. Whit Burnett (New York: Dial, 1950), he equivocated but nonetheless included "RNT" in the sixsome he looked "fondly back over as deserving more attention" (pp. 52-60).

9. Recent readings of "RNT" that ignore Thompson's documentation include: Ted Hall, "A Note on 'The Road Not Taken,'" in: *Gone into if not Explained: Essays on Poems by Robert Frost,* ed. Greg Kuzma (Crete, Nebraska: Best Cellar Press, 1976),

pp. 135-38 (my thanks to my colleague Thornton Parsons for alerting me to this article); Archibald MacLeish, "Robert Frost and New England," *National Geographic,* 149 (1976), 438-44; and David M. Wyatt, "Choosing in Frost," in: *Frost: Centennial Essays II,* ed. Jac Tharpe (Jackson: Univ. Press of Mississippi, 1976), pp. 129-40. Contrast with these the earlier perceptive interpretation by Elaine Barry, *Robert Frost* (New York: Ungar, 1973), pp. 12-13, and the repeated cautions and censures by Donald Greiner, *Robert Frost: The Poet and his Critics* (Chicago: American Library Assoc., 1974), pp. 41, 178, 222-23.

10. An interview with Richard Poirier reprinted in *Writers at Work: The* Paris Review *Interviews,* Second Series, ed. George Plimpton (New York: Viking, 1963), pp. 7-34, here p. 30; cited henceforth from this reprint as PR by page.

11. Elaine Barry, *Robert Frost on Writing* (New Brunswick, N. J.: Rutgers Univ. Press, 1973), p. 25.

12. On sentence-sounds (and this letter) see Tom Vander Ven, "Robert Frost's Dramatic Principle of 'Oversound,'" *American Literature,* 45 (1973), 238-51.

13. In his letter to Frost of 13 June 1915; see T2, 544-45.

14. In his letter to Frost of 2 February 1917, SL, 210.

15. The text follows the edition cited in n. 1 above, but does not incorporate the comma introduced by the editor, without justification, in line 9.

16. All three remaining stanzas have what may be considered alphabetical echoes of this anaphora, two lines beginning with the same sound, the other three different: stanza II "Th-" (1st and 4th lines), stanza III "I(-)" (2nd and 5th lines), and stanza IV "I" (1st and 4th lines). In stanzas II and IV the anaphora coincides with a-rhymes, in stanza III with b-rhymes.

17. Part one repeats the subject "I" *three* times (lines 2, 3, and 4); part two has the subject "I" *five* times, the last one doubled and emphasized by rhyme and the dash (lines 12, 15 twice, 16, and 18-19). Part one has line-initial "And" *five* times, part two line-initial "I" *three* times, perhaps a variation on the anaphora noted in (a) above.

18. A minor detail perhaps worth noting is the way the alphabetical anaphora described in n. 16 corresponds exactly with the limits of these passages in stanzas II (3 + 2), III (2 + 3), and IV (3 + 2).

19. Possible echoes of this centripetal focus are: the symmetrical anaphora in stanza I; the central comma (and quiet juncture) in stanza I (line 3);

the syntactic organization of stanzas III (2 + 1 + 2 = 5) and IV (2 + 1 + 2 = 5). Is a structural echo of the three/five patterns involved here? The four stanzas are defined by five junctures (beginning and end and three internal at lines 5, 10, and 15). The three connected passages are near three of these five junctures.

20. As already observed, both three-line passages have "(-)other" in their initial lines. In addition, the middle lines in each (lines 7 and 14), which are symmetrically opposite one another at the text's one-third and two-thirds points (6 + *1* + 6 + *1* + 6 = 20), are syntactically similar, containing the poem's only two participial phrases ("And having . . ."; "Yet knowing . . .").

21. Both numerically and positionally this 2 + 2 alignment linking stanzas I and IV exactly duplicates the 2 + 2 enjambment between stanzas II and III.

22. Barry (see n. 9), p. 13. Note too that the wording connections involve all three lines at the start, only two at the end: 3 + 2 = 5.

23. It may be helpful to summarize here in overview. Twelve words recur in metrical stress: roads, diverged, wood (1, 18), I (2, 13? 15, 16? 18, 19?), travel(-) (2, 3, 19), both (2, 11), one (4, 19), took (6, 19), (-)other (6, 13), that (9, 20), way (both in 14), ages (both in 17). All except "that" figure importantly in the patterns. Several other verbal echoes participate: two (1, 18), (-)where (5, 17), as . . . as (4, 6), And (. . .) that (11, 20). Cf. also wear/worn (8, 10).

24. J. Donald Crowley, "Hawthorne and Frost: The Making of a Poem," in: *Frost: Centennial Studies* (Jackson: Univ. Press of Mississippi, 1974), pp. 288-309, here p. 297; Frost's words here, excerpted from "Education by Poetry" (*SP*, 37), are quoted rather out of context, but Crowley's essential point seems valid.

25. The Georgian publication entitled *New Numbers,* edited at Abercrombie's thatched cottage in Gloucestershire, was presumably very familiar to Frost at the time of the walks with Edward Thomas there, which inspired this poem; see T2, 37.

26. Of science, but not mathematics. Frost excluded mathematics here ("The mathematical might be difficult for me to bring in, but the scientific is easy enough.") and set limits on the Pythagorean metaphor: "The metaphor has held and held, breaking down only when it came to the spiritual or psychological or the out of the way places of the physical" (*SP*, 37).

27. R. F. Fleissner, "Like 'Pythagoras's Comparison of the Universe with Number': A Frost-Tennyson

Correlation," in the collection cited in n. 24, pp. 207-20, here p. 209.

28. Fleissner, p. 210. The view Fleissner credited to Cook seems somewhat at odds with Cook's detailed analysis of Frost's poetic theory—Reginald L. Cook, *The Dimensions of Robert Frost* (New York: Rinehart, 1958), pp. 41-67—which stressed the more inspirational aspects: "The first dominant aspect in Frost's theory is a preference for the organic and the natural over the geometrical and the self-conscious" (p. 46). The book's many valuable insights need more balance in the direction of the view Fleissner cited and the present findings are pointing.

29. Fleissner's reading of Tennyson's line—"Five and three make an awful mystery"—could be applied almost verbatim to the rhyme-system of "RNT": "let us be satisfied with the meaning that three works together with five, as part of the larger number, and term this relationship the five/three cluster" (p. 208).

30. Fleissner, p. 215. In his reading Fleissner followed the lead of Tristram Coffin, *New Poetry of New England: Frost and Robinson* (Baltimore: Johns Hopkins Univ. Press, 1938), p. 133: "The wise man and the good, tries to keep to the middle of the road. . . . This is a New England farmer-poet's conception of the Golden Mean. . . . The Golden Mean is like the Golden Rule" (per Fleissner, p. 215).

31. For another possible reason for the choice of five and twenty, see the discussion in section II below, especially n. 51.

32. Louis Mertins—*Robert Frost: Life and Talks-Walking* (Norman: Univ. of Oklahoma Press, 1965), p. 135—quotes Frost as saying of Thomas: "He was my greatest friend since boyhood." The sentiments on friendship he wrote to Untermeyer can be compared with those expressed for Thomas in "To E. T.," especially: "I meant, you meant, that nothing should remain / Unsaid between us, brother . . ." (lines 9-10).

33. Both of Thomas's letters remain unpublished, except for excerpts in T2, 89, 545.

34. Quotation from Frost's letter to Thomas, 31 July 1915 (*SL*, 184). The tone of this letter in response to word of Thomas's decision to enlist suggests that Frost may have felt a bit guilty about the unfortunate timing of this particular parody. May he have also felt that the poem's gentle mocking about indecisiveness had had a part in Thomas's fateful decision? Compare the reasons Thompson gave (T2, 545-47) why Frost "could never bear to tell the truth about the failure of this lyric to perform as he intended it."

35. See his poem "Roads," which begins: "I love roads," first published in *An Annual of Poetry* (London: Constable, 1917), pp. 53-55, under the pseudonym Edward Eastaway; from his letters to Gordon Bottomley of 11 February and 18 February 1916—*Letters from Edward Thomas to Gordon Bottomley,* ed. R. George Thomas (London: Oxford Univ. Press, 1968), pp. 258ff.—it appears that the poem had just been composed and could thus have had no role in the allusions of Frost's parody completed at least a half year earlier. "Roads" is nonetheless indicative of Thomas's self-image.

36. Thompson reports it as follows, based on Frost's recollection on 16 August 1947: "Teasing gently, he accused Thomas of being such a romantic that he enjoyed crying over what might have been. After one of their best flower-gathering walks, he had said to Thomas, 'No matter which road you take, you'll always sigh, and wish you'd taken another'" (T2, 88). The flower-gathering suggests this walk took place in August rather than the fall of 1914.

37. A clear example of the latter is the comment he reportedly made on lines 16ff in March 1925: "This is the sigh I can imagine their wishing I would sigh, I guess." The comment is preserved in annotations by Elizabeth Shepley Sergeant in a copy of *Selected Poems,* 1923, a photocopy of which is in the Robert Frost Library, Amherst College; I wish to express my thanks to Will Bridegam, Director of the Library, and John Lancaster, Curator of Special Collections, for their generous assistance.

38. On Frost's predilection to use "common words in their etymological sense, playing with them," see Cook (cited in n. 28), p. 52.

39. This passage is from Frost's introduction to Robinson's *King Jasper* (1935). It is interesting to note that the specific example Frost cited to illustrate his point was an instance of apparent Robinsonian name play; the quote continues: "Robinson was thinking as much in his sonnet on Tom Hood."

40. Louis Untermeyer, *Play in Poetry,* the Henry Ward Beecher Lectures delivered at Amherst College, October 1937 (New York: Harcourt, 1938), p. 102. Frost had made arrangements for these lectures. That Frost heartily approved of Untermeyer's judgment is evident from his letters to Untermeyer of 17 October 1937 and 10 March 1938. Untermeyer reaffirmed it years later as an obituary notice; see LU, 387. Of his comments on Robinson, Frost once wrote: "That is so much me that you might suspect the application to him of being forced" (*SL,* 461; 24 February 1938).

41. Cited in an unsigned piece entitled "Poet of Frost," *Literary Digest,* 56 (17 July 1920), pp. 32-33.

42. "Twin" is of course a derivative of "two." The poem's original title, according to Thompson (T2, 88), was "Two Roads." The change to "The Road Not Taken" was apparently intended to help mark the irony. The wording of the original title still remains in the text, occurring prominently twice. The original elevation of the phrase to title status is perhaps further indication of Frost's onomastic intent. See the possible sound-play in these two words discussed below (at Figure 9).

43. Of at least parenthetical interest, Frost told Louis Mertins (book cited in n. 32, p. 136): "Thomas and I had become so inseparable that we came to be looked on as some sort of literary Siamese *twins* in a literary sense, with a spiritual bond holding us together" (emphasis added). Was the epithet "Siamese twins" the result of some etymological punning on Thomas's name by the Gloucestershire poets? Certainly Frost was drawing here on some historical "association" ("we came to be looked on as . . ."). It is intriguing to observe that Eleanor Farjeon—*Edward Thomas: The Last Four Years* (London: Oxford Univ. Press, 1958), pp. 94-95—referred to the poets *with the same term* in her account of a rural repast they and she shared at the home of a local family, the Farmers, in late August or early September 1914: "I rose, and Helen [Thomas] rose, and Elinor Frost. Mr. Farmer rose. The Poets attempted to rise, relapsed on to their seats, and regarded each other with comical consternation. They were perfectly sober, though exceedingly gay; but the gallons of strong cider, against which I had been inoculated, had gone to their legs, and not one of them could stand without support. I saw Edward [Thomas] and Robert [Frost] stagger to their feet, clutch each other, and go down; they rose again with great caution, clinging together. On the other side of the table Gibson and Abercrombie were behaving similarly. Two brace of poets staggered out into the moonlight and went hilariously homeward like *two sets of Siamese Twins.* I have boasted ever since of the night when I drank all the poets in Gloucestershire under the table" (emphasis mine).

44. Did Frost intertwine such devices even on the graphic level? The text appears to have more than its organic share of words with visually "geminated" consonants and vowels, at least one occurring in fifteen of the poem's twenty lines: yellow, wood, sorry, stood, looked, took, better, grassy, passing, really, equally, trodden, shall, telling, wood, took, all, difference.

45. Wyatt, "Choosing in Frost" (cited in n. 9), p. 136. Unfortunately, this is one of only a few points on

which I can agree with the conclusions Wyatt drew from his often perceptive textual analysis. The source of difficulty lay, as I see it, in his attempt to make the text yield information about Frost's attitudes toward choice without giving any attention to the various evidence for the ironical posture Frost was assuming here, not to mention the intended parody of Edward Thomas behind the irony.

46. See *SP,* 17-20. On the ambiguity of Frost's attitude toward musicality see Barry (cited in n. 9), pp. 20-21.

47. In the figures and subsequent discussion, uppercase letters are used to emphasize suspected pattern features; in quotations involving such emphasis all other capital letters are suppressed.

48. Within the name the *middle* syllables are involved (reflected by syllables at both ends of the first line). The name-letters excluded by this principle, particularly the name-syllables at both *ends* of the name, are: E-D-A-r-h-M-a-s. Is it an accident that all but one of these eight letters (r) form words that occur near the *middle* of the *last* line: "has" (in sequential order) and "made" (in reverse order, signified by the uppercase letters above)? Both words occur only here; the latter is one of only two words beginning with the letter *m.* See also the discussion at n. 52 below.

49. See also in a different context: "I should like to be so subtle at this game as to seem to the casual person altogether obvious" (LU, 47; 1 January 1917).

50. Quoted by Reginald Cook, *Robert Frost: A Living Voice* (Amherst: Univ. of Massachusetts Press, 1974), p. 123.

51. In view of Frost's statement about alphabetic number symbolism in "The Constant Symbol" (quoted at n. 74 below), it should at least be mentioned that the line total of each stanza (five) and of the entire text (twenty) coincides suspiciously well with the rest of the onomastic design: the fifth letter of the alphabet is E, the twentieth is T. Frost referred to Edward Thomas by the initials E. T., inter alia, in his commemorative poem "To E. T.," the text of which, interestingly enough, has a total again of twenty lines, this time arranged in five (four-line) stanzas in pentameter (rather than tetrameter). Both poems share the rhyme "day"/ "way," and these rhyme-words occupy corresponding positions in the two twenty-line texts, lines 13 and 14 in "RNT" and lines 14 and 16 in "To E. T." They also share one other line-final word, "both." In "To E. T." it does not rhyme, but it is located in the line symmetrically opposite the

"day" -rhyme (lines 7 and 14 respectively, the one-third and two-thirds points in the text; cf. n. 20 above: $6 + 1 + 6 + 1 + 6 = 20$). The positional symmetry here may have been intended to link these two shared words in a structural allusion to the earlier poem, especially since, as we have seen, "day" and "both" are the components of the rhyme-pattern (Figure 8) that yield the syllables ED(ward) and THO(mas) and therefore also the letters E and T, letters five and twenty. Moreover, the two comparable pairings of "bOTH" and "day" are echoed by an even more immediate coupling of these sounds; in both texts the "day"-rhymes are accompanied by the word "OTHer"; "anOTHer day"/"way" ("RNT") and "day"/"the OTHer way" ("To E. T."). (The presence of these onomastic constraints may explain, at least in part, the apparent stylistic awkwardness of line 16 in "To E. T.") The possibility that Frost consciously cultivated textual correspondences between discrete poems has intriguing critical implications for the study of his books. See also n. 61 below.

52. See also n. 48, where the same two principles reappear: chiasmic inversion in "made" and sequential order in "has."

53. Perhaps relevant here as a "feat of association" is Thompson's presumably informed suggestion that Frost's own viewpoint, the one against which the poem's ironic posture plays, was identified with a biblical proverb: "it often happened that . . . Thomas would regret the choice he had made and would sigh over what he might have shown Frost if they had taken a 'better' direction. More than once, on such occasions, the New Englander had teased his Welsh-English friend for those wasted regrets. Disciplined by the austere biblical notion that a man, having put his hand to the plow, *should not look back,* Frost found something quaintly romantic in sighing over what might have been" (*SL,* xiv; emphasis added). I suspect that it is this proverb (Luke 9.62) we see surfacing in the poem's least romantic lines, 14 and 15, heavily veiled though the allusion is by the ironic overlay.

54. LU, 165-66: a writer's "style is the way he carries himself toward his ideas and deed." It is "that which indicates how the writer takes himself and what he is saying." See also *SP,* 65, quoted in part at n. 39.

55. The walks with Edward Thomas, which Frost claimed occasioned the poem (T2, 88, 544), occurred in August 1914 and during two shorter visits in the following fall months. If Frost's comment of 23 August 1953 refers to the Gallows at Ryton Dymock, Gloucestershire—as Elizabeth Shepley Sergeant, *Robert Frost: The Trial by Existence* (New York: Holt, Rinehart and Winston,

1960), pp. 142-43, and Thompson (T2, 546) indicate-then composition would not likely have begun before the Frosts moved over there from Little Iddens in mid September 1914 (T1, 456). An early version of the completed poem was mailed to Thomas prior to the public reading Frost gave of it at Tufts on 5 May 1915 (T2, 546). It is, of course, possible that the poem owed a partial debt to latent insights or notes deriving from some earlier experiences. Compare, for example, the account—now superseded by Thompson's—given earlier by Sergeant, pp. 87-89, an interpretation echoed by Reuben A. Brower, *The Poetry of Robert Frost: Constellations of Intention* (New York: Oxford Univ. Press, 1963), p. 231.

56. "Not until he reached New Hampshire and began to find in the many letters from Thomas further reflections of the same wistful brooding over alternatives, did Frost complete this poem that he first called 'Two Roads'" (T2, 88).

57. According to Thompson (T2, 544), this "earliest known manuscript version" is preserved in the collection of Howard G. Schmitt. The manuscript in the Jones Library is Amherst is fair copy with no evidence of genesis or extensive revision; I wish to acknowledge the assistance of Dr. Philip N. Cronenwett, Curator of the Frost collection, during my visits there.

58. A perhaps vain hope—Frost claimed that he had not, in his words, "treasured my first drafts along with my baby shoes" (the letter cited in n. 2).

59. As Thompson pointed out—*Fire and Ice: The Art and Thought of Robert Frost* (New York: Holt, 1942), p. 86—Frost had already used this stanzaic form in three earlier poems ("In Neglect," "My November Guest," and "In a Vale"). Besides the 3 + 2 rhyme scheme the anaphoric repetition of "I" in two of the stanza's five lines could have suggested the fuller development of this device in stanza I: Two-And-And-And-To; perhaps also alphabetically is stanzas II and III: T-T, I-I.

60. In the later published version, the syntactic similarity is reinforced by the introductions of the dash after IV, 3, corresponding to the exclamation point concluding III, 3.

61. The congruence of syntax (3/4) and prosody (3/5) is found in all four stanzas, but is both most evident and most integral in stanza IV. Convenience in harmonizing the last stanza's three/four and three/five features may also have had something to do with the choice of a twenty-line (4 × 5) total. Regarding the other twenty-line poem devoted to Edward Thomas, "To E. T.," see n. 51 above. Is it coincidence that this poem has five

stanzas of four lines each and this time pentameter rather than tetrameter? That the first three of the five stanzas begin with "I"? Is it coincidental that "To E. T." is preceded by eighteen of the forty-four poems in the book *New Hampshire* and is thus three-fifths from the end of the collection? That the eighteenth from the end (or three-fifths from the start) is "To Earthward"? George W. Nitchie—*Human Values in the Poetry of Robert Frost* (Durham, N. C.: Duke Univ. Press, 1960), p. 198—has called attention to an analogous, but more conspicuous case of symmetry in *Mountain Interval,* the thematic correspondence between the "crucially placed" (and, incidentally, originally italicized) poems with which the collection began and ended, "RNT" and "The Sound of the Trees" (written in Gloucestershire). Taken individually, such uses of number and symmetry may not be significant. But the convergence of so many formal tricks with the same numbers in precisely the two poems most directly linked with Edward Thomas has a cumulative impact that should at least alert us to the possibility of similar design features in Frost's other poetry. Hesitant as some literary critics may be to vex the numerological issue, it is worth remembering that Frost would not be the first or foremost poet in the Western tradition to exploit the aesthetic potential of such subtleties. See recently R. G. Peterson, "Critical Calculations: Measure and Symmetry in Literature," *PMLA,* 91 (1976), 367-75, as well as my comments and Peterson's responses in *PMLA,* 92 (1977), 126-28.

62. Nitchie (cited in previous n.), p. 17.

63. What Wyatt (cited in n. 9), in referring to this line, aptly termed "the fictions of order a self projects back onto experience" (p. 136).

64. From a talk on 14 March 1950 as quoted by Thompson, T2, 547; italics mine.

65. Barry (cited in n. 9) took the word "sigh" as "the *first hint* that the poem is a gentle parody of the kind of person whose life in the present is distorted by nostalgic regrets for the possibilities of the past, who is less concerned for the road taken than the 'road not taken'" (p. 12, italics added). She did not discuss any other hints.

66. Transcribed by Cook (cited in n. 50), pp. 106ff, here p. 112.

67. See T2, 88 and n. 36.

68. Charles Edward Eaton, a review of Reginald Cook, *Robert Frost: A Living Voice,* in *Georgia Review,* 30 (1976), 447-60, here p. 448.

69. See the overview of this scholarship given by Greiner (cited in n. 9), especially chapter 6, and Barry (cited in n. 11), especially pp. 10-33.

70. Thompson, *Fire and Ice* (cited in n. 59).

71. Richard Poirier, *Robert Frost: The Work of Knowing* (New York: Oxford Univ. Press, 1977), p. 52.

72. Ibid.

73. Ibid.

74. See n. 51.

75. Peterson (cited in n. 61), p. 370. Compare in this context my analysis of formal patterns in one of the most anthologized German lyrics, and eight-line poem twenty years in the making, "Linguistic Patterns, Literary Structure, and the Genesis of C. F. Meyer's 'Der Römische Brunnen,'" *Language and Style,* 4 (1971), 83-115, especially pp. 114-15.

76. Barry (cited in n. 11), pp. 29-31.

77. See Frank Lentricchia, *Robert Frost: Modern Poetics and the Landscape of Self* (Durham, N. C.: Duke Univ. Press, 1975), especially pp. 165-70.

78. Poirier (cited in n. 71), pp. xi-xii.

George Monteiro (essay date 1988)

SOURCE: Monteiro, George. "Roads and Paths." In *Robert Frost and the New England Renaissance,* pp. 44-53. Lexington: The University Press of Kentucky, 1988.

[*In the following essay, Monteiro shows "The Road Not Taken" to be part of a long tradition involving the literary and pictorial trope known as "The Choice of the Two Paths." The critic also discusses the biographical background of Frost's poem.*]

> When a man thinks happily, he finds no foot-track in the field he traverses.
>
> —Ralph Waldo Emerson, "Quotation and Originality" (1859)

"The Road Not Taken" can be read against a literary and pictorial tradition that might be called "The Choice of the Two Paths," reaching not only back to the Gospels and beyond them to the Greeks but to ancient English verse as well.[1] In *Reson and Sensuallyte,* for example, John Lydgate explains how he dreamt that Dame Nature had offered him the choice between the Road of Reason and the Road of Sensuality. In art the same choice was often represented by the letter "Y," with the trunk of the letter representing the careless years of childhood and the two paths branching off at the age when the child is expected to exercise discretion. In one design the "Two Paths" are shown in great detail. "On one side a thin line of pious folk ascend a

hill past several churches and chapels, and so skyward to the Heavenly City where an angel stands proffering a crown. On the other side a crowd of men and women are engaged in feasting, music, love-making, and other carnal pleasures while close behind them yawns the flaming mouth of hell in which sinners are writhing. But hope is held out for the worldly, for some avoid hell and having passed through a dark forest come to the rude huts of Humility and Repentance."[2] Embedded in this quotation is a direct reference to the opening of Dante's *Inferno*:

> Midway upon the journey of our life
> I found myself within a forest dark,
> For the straightforward pathway had been lost.
> Ah me! how hard a thing it is to say
> What was the forest savage, rough, and stern,
> Which in the very thought renews the fear.
> So bitter is it, death is little more.[3]

From the beginning, when it appeared as the first poem in **Mountain Interval** (1916), many readers have overstated the importance of **"The Road Not Taken"** to Frost's work. Alexander Meiklejohn, president of Amherst College, did so when, announcing the appointment of the poet to the school's faculty, he recited it to a college assembly.

> Two roads diverged in a yellow wood,
> And sorry I could not travel both
> And be one traveler, long I stood
> And looked down one as far as I could
> To where it bent in the undergrowth;
>
> Then took the other, as just as fair,
> And having perhaps the better claim,
> Because it was grassy and wanted wear;
> Though as for that the passing there
> Had worn them really about the same,
>
> And both that morning equally lay
> In leaves no step had trodden black.
> Oh, I kept the first for another day!
> Yet knowing how way leads on to way,
> I doubted if I should ever come back.
>
> I shall be telling this with a sigh
> Somewhere ages and ages hence:
> Two roads diverged in a wood, and I—
> I took the one less traveled by,
> And that has made all the difference.[4]

"The Choice of Two Paths" is suggested in Frost's decision to make his two roads not very much different from one another, for passing over one of them had the effect of wearing them "really about the same." This is a far cry from, say, the description of the "two waies" offered in the seventeenth century by Henry Crosse:

> Two waies are proposed and laide open to all, the one inviting to virtue, the other alluring to vice; the first is combersome, intricate, untraded, overgrowne, and many

obstacles to dismay the passenger; the other plaine, even beaten, overshadowed with boughes, tapistried with flowers, and many objects to feed the eye; now a man that lookes but only to the outward shewe, will easily tread the broadest pathe, but if hee perceive that this smooth and even way leads to a neast of Scorpions: or a litter of Beares, he will rather take the other though it be rugged and unpleasant, than hazard himselfe in so great a daunger.[5]

Frost seems to have deliberately chosen the word "roads" rather than "waies" or "paths" or even "pathways." In fact, on one occasion when he was asked to recite his famous poem, "Two paths diverged in a yellow wood," Frost reacted with such feeling—"Two *roads*!"—that the transcription of his reply made it necessary both to italicize the word "roads" and to follow it with an exclamation point. Frost recited the poem all right, but, as his friend remembered, "he didn't let me get away with 'two paths!'"[6]

Convinced that the poem was deeply personal and directly self-revelatory, Frost's readers have insisted on tracing the poem to one or the other of two facts of Frost's life when he was in his late thirties. (At the beginning of the *Inferno* Dante is thirty-five, "midway on the road of life," notes Charles Eliot Norton.)[7] The first of these, an event, took place in the winter of 1911-1912 in the woods of Plymouth, New Hampshire, while the second, a general observation and a concomitant attitude, grew out of his long walks in England with Edward Thomas, his newfound Welsh-English poet-friend, in 1914.

In *Robert Frost: The Trial by Existence*, Elizabeth Shepley Sergeant locates in one of Frost's letters the source for **"The Road Not Taken."** To Susan Hayes Ward the poet wrote on February 10, 1912:

Two lonely cross-roads that themselves cross each other I have walked several times this winter without meeting or overtaking so much as a single person on foot or on runners. The practically unbroken condition of both for several days after a snow or a blow proves that neither is much travelled. Judge then how surprised I was the other evening as I came down one to see a man, who to my own unfamiliar eyes and in the dusk looked for all the world like myself, coming down the other, his approach to the point where our paths must intersect being so timed that unless one of us pulled up we must inevitably collide. I felt as if I was going to meet my own image in a slanting mirror. Or say I felt as we slowly converged on the same point with the same noiseless yet laborious stride as if we were two images about to float together with the uncrossing of someone's eyes. I verily expected to take up or absorb this other self and feel the stronger by the addition for the three-mile journey home. But I didn't go forward to the touch. I stood still in wonderment and let him pass by; and that, too, with the fatal omission of not trying to find out by a comparison of lives and immediate and remote interests what could have brought us by cross-

ing paths to the same point in a wilderness at the same moment of nightfall. Some purpose I doubt not, if we could but have made out. I like a coincidence almost as well as an incongruity.[8]

This portentous account of meeting "another" self (but not encountering that self directly and therefore not coming to terms with it) would eventually result in a poem quite different from **"The Road Not Taken"** and one that Frost would not publish for decades. Elizabeth Sergeant ties the moment with Frost's decision to go off at this time to some place where he could devote more time to poetry. He had also, she implies, filed away his dream for future poetic use.

That poetic use would occur three years later. In 1914 Frost arrived in England for what he then thought would be an extended sabbatical leave from farming in New Hampshire. By all the signs he was ready to settle down for a long stay. Settling in Gloucestershire, he soon became a close friend of Edward Thomas. Later, when readers persisted in misreading **"The Road Not Taken,"** Frost insisted that his poem had been intended as a sly jest at the expense of his friend and fellow poet. For Thomas had invariably fussed over irrevocable choices of the most minor sort made on daily walks with Frost in 1914, shortly before the writing of the poem. Later Frost insisted that in his case the line "And that has made all the difference"—taken straight—was all wrong. "Of course, it hasn't," he persisted, "it's just a poem, you know."[9] In 1915, moreover, his sole intention was to twit Thomas. Living in Gloucestershire, writes Lawrance Thompson, Frost had frequently taken long countryside walks with Thomas.

Repeatedly Thomas would choose a route which might enable him to show his American friend a rare plant or a special vista; but it often happened that before the end of such a walk Thomas would regret the choice he had made and would sigh over what he might have shown Frost if they had taken a "better" direction. More than once, on such occasions, the New Englander had teased his Welsh-English friend for those wasted regrets. . . . Frost found something quaintly romantic in sighing over what might have been. Such a course of action was a road never taken by Frost, a road he had been taught to avoid.[10]

If we are to believe Frost and his biographer, **"The Road Not Taken"** was intended to serve as Frost's gentle jest at Thomas's expense. But the poem might have had other targets. One such target was a text by another poet who in a different sense might also be considered a "friend": Henry Wadsworth Longfellow, whose poem, "My Lost Youth," had provided Frost with *A Boy's Will,* the title he chose for his first book.

"The Road Not Taken" can be placed against a passage in Longfellow's notebooks: "Round about what is, lies a whole mysterious world of might be,—a psychological romance of possibilities and things that do not happen. By going out a few minutes sooner or later, by stopping to speak with a friend at a corner, by meeting this man or that, or by turning down this street instead of the other, we may let slip some great occasion of good, or avoid some impending evil, by which the whole current of our lives would have been changed. There is no possible solution to the dark enigma but the one word, 'Providence.'"[11]

Longfellow's tone in this passage is sober, even somber, and anticipates the same qualities in Edward Thomas, as Frost so clearly perceived. Elizabeth Shepley Sergeant had insisted that Frost's dream encounter with his other self at a crossroads in the woods had a "subterranean connection" with the whole of **"The Road Not Taken,"** especially with the poem's last lines:

> I shall be telling this with a sigh
> Somewhere ages and ages hence:
> Two roads diverged in a wood, and I—
> I took the one less traveled by,
> And that has made all the difference.

Undoubtedly. But whereas Longfellow had invoked Providence to account for acts performed and actions not taken, Frost calls attention only to the role of human choice. A second target was the notion that "whatever choice we make, we make at our peril." The words just quoted are Fitz-James Stephen's, but it is more important that Frost encountered them in William James's essay "The Will to Believe." In fact, James concludes his final paragraph on the topic: "We stand on a mountain pass in the midst of whirling snow and blinding mist, through which we get glimpses now and then of paths which may be deceptive. If we take the wrong road we shall be dashed to pieces. We do not certainly know whether there is any right one. What must we do? 'Be strong and of a good courage.' Act for the best, hope for the best, and take what comes. . . . If death ends all, we cannot meet death better."[12] The danger inherent in decision, in this brave passage quoted with clear-cut approval by the teacher Frost "never had," does not play a part in **"The Road Not Taken."** Frost the "leaf-treader" will have none of it, though he will not refuse to make a choice. Nothing will happen to him through default. Nor, argues the poet, is it likely that anyone will melodramatically be dashed to pieces.

It is useful to see Frost's projected sigh as a nudging criticism of Thomas's characteristic regrets, to note that Frost's poem takes a sly poke at Longfellow's more generalized awe before the notion of what might have happened had it not been for the inexorable workings of Providence, and to see **"The Road Not Taken"** as a bravura tossing off of Fitz-James Stephen's mountainous and meteorological scenario. We can also project the poem against a poem by Emily Dickinson that Frost had encountered twenty years earlier in *Poems, Second Series* (1891).

> Our journey had advanced;
> Our feet were almost come
> To that odd fork in Being's road,
> Eternity by term.
>
> Our pace took sudden awe,
> Our feet reluctant led.
> Before were cities, but between,
> The forest of the dead.
>
> Retreat was out of hope,—
> Behind, a sealed route,
> Eternity's white flag before,
> And God at every gate.[13]

Dickinson's poem is straightforwardly and orthodoxically religious. But it can be seen that beyond the "journey" metaphor Dickinson's poem employs diction—"road" and "forest"—that recalls "The Choice of the Two Paths" trope, the opening lines of the *Inferno*, and Frost's secular poem **"The Road Not Taken."**

The "dark forest" in the tradition of "The Choice of the Two Paths" and the "forest dark" of Longfellow's translation of the *Inferno* also foreshadow the imagery of the famous Frost poem published in *New Hampshire* (1923), the last stanza of which begins: "The woods are lovely, dark and deep."[14] In spurning the word "forest" for "woods," a term that is perhaps more appropriate for New England, Frost was, whether he knew it or not, following Charles Eliot Norton, whose translation of the *Inferno* reads "dark wood" and who glosses the opening of Dante's poem: "The dark wood is the forest of the world of sense, 'the erroneous wood of this life' . . . , that is, the wood in which man loses his way."[15] In "the darkest evening of the year," the New England poet finds himself standing before a scene he finds attractive enough to make him linger. Frost's poem employs, significantly, the present tense. Dante's poem (through Longfellow) employs the past tense. It is as if Frost were casually remembering some familiar engraving that hung on a schoolroom wall in Lawrence as he was growing up in the 1880s, and the poet slides into the picture. He enters, so to speak, the mind of the figure who speaks the poem, a figure whose body is slowly turned into the scene, head fully away from the foreground, bulking small, holding the reins steadily and loosely. The horse and team are planted, though poised to move. And so begins the poet's dramatization of this rural and parochial tableau. "Whose woods these are I think I know. / His house is in the village though. / He will not see me stopping here / To watch his woods fill up with snow." And then, having entered the human being, he witnesses the natural drift of that human being's thoughts to the brain of his "little horse," who thinks it "queer" that the rider has decided to stop here. And then, in an equally easy transition, the teamster returns to himself, remembering that he has promises to keep and miles to go before he sleeps. Duties, responsibilities—many must have them, we think, as echolalia closes the poem, all other thoughts already turning away from the illustration on the schoolroom wall. And even as the "little horse" has been rid of the man's intrusion, so too must the rider's mind be freed of the poet's incursion. The poet's last line resonates, dismissing the reader from his, the poet's, dreamy mind and that mind's preoccupations, and returning to the poet's inside reading of the still-life drama that goes on forever within its frame hanging on the classroom wall.

The ways in which Frost's poem **"Stopping by Woods on a Snowy Evening"** converses with Longfellow's translation of Dante are evident from other shared echoes and images. The *Inferno* continues:

> I cannot well repeat how there I entered,
>   So full was I of slumber at the moment
>   In which I had abandoned the true way.
> But after I had reached a mountain's foot,
>   At that point where the valley terminated,
>   Which had with consternation pierced my heart,
> Upward I looked, and I beheld its shoulders,
>   Vested already with that planet's rays
>   Which leadeth others right by every road.
> Then was the fear a little quieted
>   That in my heart's lake had endured throughout
>   That night, which I had passed so piteously.[16]

What Frost "fetched" here (as in **"The Road Not Taken"**) were the motifs of risk and decision characterizing both "The Choice of the Two Paths" and Dante's *Inferno*.

"The Draft Horse," a poem published at the end of Frost's life in his final volume, *In the Clearing* (1962), reminds us curiously of Frost's anecdote in 1912 about recognizing "another" self and not encountering that self and also of the poem **"Stopping by Woods on a Snowy Evening."** In addition it is reminiscent of **"The Road Not Taken."** In each case—anecdote, autumnal poem, and winter poem—the poet must make a choice. Will he "go forward to the touch," or will he "stand still in wonderment and let him pass by" in the anecdote? He will choose the "road less traveled by" (but he will leave the other for a later passing, though he probably will not return to it). He will not succumb to the aesthetic (and perhaps psychological) attractions of the woods, which are "lovely, dark and deep," but will go forth to keep his promises—of both kinds (as Frost explained): "those that I myself make for myself and those that my ancestors made for me, known as the social contract."[17]

> With a lantern that wouldn't burn
> In too frail a buggy we drove
> Behind too heavy a horse
> Through a pitch-dark limitless grove.
>
> And a man came out of the trees
> And took our horse by the head

> And reaching back to his ribs
> Deliberately stabbed him dead.
>
> The ponderous beast went down
> With a crack of a broken shaft.
> And the night drew through the trees
> In one long invidious draft.
>
> The most unquestioning pair
> That ever accepted fate
> And the least disposed to ascribe
> Any more than we had to to hate,
>
> We assumed that the man himself
> Or someone he had to obey
> Wanted us to get down
> And walk the rest of the way.[18]

The "little horse" of the earlier poem is replaced by "the too-heavy horse" of the later one. The "woods" have now been replaced by "a pitch-dark limitless grove." The hint in "grove" is one of sacrificial rites and ordered violence. The "sweep of easy wind and downy flake" of **"Stopping by Woods"** is echoed more ominously in **"The Draft Horse"** in that after "the ponderous beast went down" "the night drew through the trees / In one long invidious draft." The man was alone; here he is part of an "unquestioning pair." **"Stopping by Woods"** was given in the first person. **"The Draft Horse,"** like the beginning of the *Inferno*, takes place in the past. There is resolution in the former— even if it evinces some fatigue; in the latter there is resignation. At the time of the poem and in an earlier day, the loss of a man's horse may be as great a loss as that of one's life—probably because its loss would often lead to the death of the horse's owner. And for the poet the assassination has no rhyme or reason that he will discern. He knows only that the man "came out of the trees" (compare the intruders in **"Two Tramps in Mud Time"** or the neighbor in **"Mending Wall"** who resembles "an old-stone savage armed"). Insofar as the poet knows, this act involves motiveless malevolence less than unmalevolent motive—if there is a motive. In the *Inferno*, the beast that threatens the poet's pathway gives way to the poet—"Not man; man once I was," he says—who will guide him. Frost's couple have the misfortune to encounter not a guide but an assassin. "A man feared that he might find an assassin; / Another that he might find a victim," wrote Stephen Crane. "One was more wise than the other."[19] It is not too far-fetched, I think, to see the equanimity of the poet at the end of **"The Draft Horse"** as a response to the anecdote, many years earlier, when the poet avoided meeting his "other" self, thereby committing the "fatal omission" of not trying to find out what "purpose . . . if we could but have made out" there was in the near-encounter. It is chilling to read the poem against its Frostian antecedents. Yet, as Keeper prefers in *A Masque of Mercy* (1947)—in words out of another context which might better fit the romantic poet of **"The Wood-Pile"**—"I say I'd rather be lost in the woods / Than found in church."[20]

Notes

1. See Samuel C. Chew, *The Pilgrimage of Life* (New Haven: Yale Univ. Press, 1962), pp. 175-81.

2. Ibid., p. 178.

3. *The Divine Comedy of Dante Alighieri,* trans. Henry Wadsworth Longfellow (Boston: Houghton Mifflin, 1895), p. 3.

4. "The Road Not Taken," in *Complete Poems, 1949,* p. 131.

5. Chew, *Pilgrimage of Life,* pp. 180-81.

6. Quoted in Philip L. Gerber, "Remembering Robert Frost: An Interview with William Jewell," *New England Quarterly* 59 (March 1986):21.

7. *The Divine Comedy of Dante Alighieri,* trans. Charles Eliot Norton, rev. ed., vol. 1: *Hell* (Boston: Houghton Mifflin, 1903), p. 1.

8. Sergeant, *Trial by Existence,* pp. 87-88.

9. Gerber, "Remembering Robert Frost," p. 21.

10. *Selected Letters of Robert Frost,* p. xiv.

11. Henry Wadsworth Longfellow, *Drift-Wood,* in *Outre-Mer and Drift-Wood* (Boston: Houghton Mifflin, 1886), pp. 405-6.

12. William James, "The Will to Believe," in *Pragmatism and Other Essays,* introduced by Joseph L. Blau (New York: Washington Square Press, 1963), p. 213.

13. *Poems (1890-1896) by Emily Dickinson,* p. 364.

14. "Stopping by Woods on a Snowy Evening," in *Complete Poems, 1949,* p. 275.

15. Norton, *Divine Comedy,* p. 1.

16. Longfellow, *Divine Comedy,* p. 3. In "conversation" Frost occasionally referred to the *Inferno*; see Cook, "Frost in Context," pp. 134, 138.

17. Quoted in Cook, *A Living Voice,* p. 81.

18. "The Draft Horse," in *In the Clearing,* p. 60.

19. Stephen Crane, *The Black Riders and Other Lines* (Boston: Copeland and Day, 1895), p. 62.

20. *A Masque of Mercy,* in *Complete Poems, 1949,* p. 632.

Nathan Cervo (essay date winter 1989)

SOURCE: Cervo, Nathan. "Frost's 'The Road Not Taken.'" *Explicator* 47, no. 2 (winter 1989): 42-3.

[*In the following essay, Cervo comments on Frost's choice of the word "road" over "path" in "The Road Not Taken" and the interpretative implications of this choice.*]

The tragic irony of Robert Frost's poem **"The Road Not Taken"** continues to go undetected, and this is not surprising because critics generally bring to the poem their own predisposition to read it as a statement of American individualism. Indeed, to my mind, the conscious side of Robert Frost, when he composed the poem, probably shared the same tendency. Poetry, however, comes into play when self-consciousness leaves off, and what speaks itself through the poem is an Abiding Mystery. In my opinion, this Abiding Mystery avails itself of that submerged racial memory that Jung, rather fatuously, it seems to me, sublimated into the Collective Unconscious. What I am saying is that one's genes have a hand in refracting and communicating the meaning of one's culture, even when consciousness is not alert to that meaning but only seems to savor it by way of vague intuition or intimation.

Thus, with reference to **"The Road Not Taken,"** a poem in which the word *not* functions as what I would call a *word of commanding deference*—that is, as a word that seems to defer to larger meanings but actually commands them, one can readily see that, on the level of conscious meaning, the word *road* is misused. The correct word would have been *path.* And here the Abiding Mystery makes its cultural presence and meaning felt; for road is, etymologically speaking, a synecdoche for the *way traveled by carts, cars, chariots, by anything advancing by means of wheels.* My point is that the Cultural Unconscious equates road with *rota* (Latin, wheel). The word path on the other hand, from Old English *paeth* (cognate to Latin *"pes,"* which means foot, step, pace), would oppose the idea of advancing by foot to that of advancing by wheel.

Fundamental to the poem's stated intimation of the truth about human existence, as sensed by Frost, is the idea of *rut* (the track carved out by wheels from the surface over which they travel) in its relationship to the ego (cf., "I," 2, 3, 4, implied in 6, 13, twice in 15, 16, 18, 19). In the poem's tragic intuition, egoism is figured as a wheel, an Ixionian torture (cf., Vergil, *"Ixionii rota orbis"*), which gouges out a road in the image of its own flange.

Because, in the poem, both paths are described as roads, it makes no difference, despite the pathetically muted last line ("And that has made all the difference"; 20), which road the "I" ironically takes, because "I" and road are conceived inextricably as the same entity. This is why the "I" of the poem prophesies, "I shall be telling this with a sigh / Somewhere ages and ages hence" (16-17). The "this" of line 16 is revealed to be the "that" of line 20. The identity of "this" and "that" is basically the same as the identity of the two ego-roads. In other words, morally and psychologically speaking, the "I" has made no choice at all. This is why "a sigh" (of regret? disappointment? anxiety?) will be the ego's guerdon. The diabolic aspect of the ego, the fact that it transcends the normal, and normative, apportionment of a human lifetime, is suggested in the phrase "ages and ages hence," which evokes the circular repetitiveness of Ixion's wheel in hell.

Frost's roads must ultimately, it seems to me, be read as being every bit as visionary as Rimbaud's "Ruts" (French, *Ornières*). Indeed, the setting and trajectory of both works are strikingly similar, each projecting at its outset "Two roads," a "right" and "left" bank of apperception. Rimbaud writes (*Illuminations*, translated by Louise Varèse. New York: New Directions, 1957, 58):

> A droite l'aube d'été éveille fes feuilles et les vapeurs et les bruits de ce coin du parc, et les talus de gauche tiennent dans leur ombre violette les milles rapides ornières de la route humide. Défilé de féeries.

> On the right the summer dawn awakens the leaves and exhalations and rumors of this park corner, and the slope on the left preserves in its violet shadow the thousand rapid ruts of the clammy horseway. Narrow descent into faery!

(My translation)

But whereas Rimbaud's descent appears to be into the Eleusinian Mysteries, Frost's roads both lead into a variant of Percy Miller's wilderness, that is, into "a yellow wood" (1) sere before its time and an extension of the New England (Puritan) psyche. For each poet, the world of consciousness (Rimbaud's *"A droite,"* Frost's "To where it bent in the undergrowth", 5) teeters within a frail, fantastic sphere that is encroached upon by the minatory domain of the Absolutely Eerie (Rimbaud's *"féeries,"* Frost's Puritanical "undergrowth").

In light of the above, Frost's roads, used instead of the correct paths, chime Rimbaud's *"les milles rapides ornieres de la route humide. Défilé de féeries."* But, at least to me, Rimbaud's *"parc"* (piece of enclosed ground) is more reassuring, that is, less illusory than Frost's wood (1, 18; *i.e.,* wilderness), which the Abiding Mystery (the Cultural Unconscious spoken of earlier) seems to be using to resonate the Old English word *wōd*, whose meaning is insane.

William George (essay date summer 1991)

SOURCE: George, William. "Frost's 'The Road Not Taken.'" *Explicator* 49, no. 4 (summer 1991): 230-32.

[*In the following essay, George claims "The Road Not Taken" involves the perspectives of a single poetic persona at three different stages of life—a middle-aged narrator who looks back on his younger self and ahead to his older self.*]

Robert Frost's **"The Road Not Taken"** has been included in several poetry texts with comments and notes that seem to me to imply mistaken interpretations. For example, Laurence Perrine, including the poem in his *Sound and Sense: An Introduction to Poetry*, states that "the general meaning of the poem is . . . an expression of regret that the possibilities of life-experience are so sharply limited. . . . The person with a craving for life, however satisfied with his own choice, will always long for the realms of experience that had to be passed by" (6th ed., New York: Harcourt, Brace and Jovanovich, 1982, 78). In another text, *The Norton Anthology of Modern Poetry,* the notes by Richard Ellmann and Robert O'Clair suggest that the poem is either a "slightly mocking parody" of Edward Thomas's indecisiveness or a poetic rendering of a doppelganger experience by Frost (New York: Norton, 1973, 196).

When I scrutinize the poem, however, I find details that such interpretations cannot explain. The complexity of the attack in **"The Road Not Taken"** depends upon our paying close heed to the three distinct ages of the persona in the poem and realizing that late in his life the speaker faces again a choice between a more- and a less-traveled road.

Readers of **"The Road Not Taken"** have been warned by Frost himself against casual readings; he stated that the poem is "very tricky"[1] and that its subtle mockery contains a "hit."[2] In addition, excellent explications, such as that by William H. Pritchard, help to counteract the tendency of some readers to ignore significant details of the poem in order to make of it "an inspiring credo stated by the farmer-poet of New Hampshire."[3] Yet, again and again readers seem to wish to see in the poem Frost "following his instinct, choos[ing] the road less traveled by."[4]

Like many literary voices, the speaker of **"The Road Not Taken"** holds up an earlier, less wise version of himself for gentle mockery. What distinguishes this poem from others, however, is that the speaker also holds up to us an older self, whom he also attacks. In many ways, this speaker's younger and older selves are alike. Compared with the middle-aged self, both are given to emotion, self-deception, and self-congratulation, and both face a decision which the middle-aged speaker sees with more objective eyes than do his younger and older selves.

The first three stanzas of the poem present the differences between the younger self and the poem's speaker, which I call the middle-aged self. It is this middle-aged self, not the younger self, who admits to and purposely stresses the similarity of the two roads. The younger self is perhaps too dismayed with or too "sorry" about the nature of choice to notice that "passing there / Had worn [the two roads] really about the same, / And both that morning equally lay / In leaves no step had trodden black." These observations about the roads' similarities come to us from the middle-aged self's corrective, more truth-seeking voice. While the younger self does admit to himself that the road he has chosen is "just as fair" as the other road, he ignores the two roads' sameness to congratulate himself because his choice—to him—had "perhaps the better claim." In contrast to the younger self, who does know life enough to doubt "if [he] should ever come back," the middle-aged self does not delude himself with exclamations such as "I kept the first for another day!" It is to the middle-aged self, therefore, that I think we should attribute the mocking "Oh" that begins line thirteen.

Like his younger self, the older self, whom the middle-aged self imagines, also faces a choice represented by a fork in the road:

> I shall be telling this with a sigh
> Somewhere ages and ages hence;
> Two roads diverged in a wood, and I—
> I took the one less traveled by

The older self's "sigh" is similar to the younger self's being "sorry I could not travel both / And be one traveler." Both emotional responses are strikingly different from the middle-aged self's objectivity in looking at his callow younger self and self-aggrandizing older self. Like the younger self, the older self comes to a point where "two roads diverge in a wood." Although William Pritchard suggests that "presumably Frost added [the dash] to make the whole thing more expressive and heartfelt" (127), I believe Frost's adding the dash clarifies that the older self is poised, like his younger self, before two roads, and like his younger self "long [he] stood" before making *his* choice. In this "age" of the persona, the choice will be either to tell the truth or to lie about the choice made "ages and ages" before. If the older self can no longer remember that the wood was "yellow," we certainly can forgive him this lapse. However, what is less forgivable to us is that the older self ignores what the middle-aged self had come to know about that first choice: that "both [roads] that morning equally lay." Only self-aggrandizing self-deception could cause the older self to ignore what the middle-aged self clearly knows. Therefore, the road not taken by the older self is the road of truth; the road the older self does take is that of deception, which is, I imagine Frost might say, actually the more traveled path, for it is the one traveled by both the speaker's younger and older selves.

The poem, therefore, presents to us three distinct "ages" of the persona. To attribute the sorrows, claims, and choices of the three-aged self to just one self leads, I think, to mistaken notions about the poem and to a failure to understand the complexity of a poem that presents a middle-aged self mocking less-objective versions of himself as a younger and an older man.

Notes

1. Lawrance Thompson, *Robert Frost: The Years of Triumph* (New York: Holt, Rinehart and Winston, 1970) 546.

2. Robert Frost. *Selected Letters of Robert Frost,* ed. Lawrance Thompson (New York: Holt, Rinehart and Winston, 1964) 190.

3. William H. Pritchard, *Frost: A Literary Life Reconsidered* (New York and Oxford: Oxford UP, 1984) 128.

4. Arthur M. Sampley, "The Myth and the Quest: The Stature of Robert Frost," *The South Atlantic Quarterly* (summer 1971), rpt. in *Critical Essays on Robert Frost,* ed. Philip L. Gerbert (Boston: G. K. Hall, 1982) 197.

Jeffrey S. Cramer (essay date 1996)

SOURCE: Cramer, Jeffrey S. "Mountain Interval: 'The Road Not Taken.'" In *Robert Frost among His Poems,* pp. 44-6. Jefferson, N.C.: McFarland & Company, Inc., 1996.

[*In the following essay, Cramer situates "The Road Not Taken" within the literary tradition of the two roads theme, citing examples from Virgil, Emily Dickinson, Henry David Thoreau, and others.*]

First published in *The Atlantic Monthly,* August 1915.

Frost began writing the poem in England in 1914 and completed it in Franconia before his first public use of it on May 5, 1915 [[Thompson]:546; [Angyal]:99, 117; [Cook, 1956]:65].

"I'll bet not half a dozen people can tell who was hit and where he was hit by my **'Road Not Taken,'**" Frost wrote to Louis Untermeyer [[Untermeyer]:14]. The poem had, in fact, been inspired by Frost's amusement regarding a familiar habit of Edward Thomas, his closest friend while living in England. In 1914, Frost and Thomas often took long walks through the Gloucestershire countryside. Thomas would try to choose a way which might allow him to show his botanizing friend a rare plant or a special scene. Often, before the walk ended, Thomas would regret his choice, sighing over what they could have seen if they had chosen a better route [[Frost]:xiv]. After one particular walk, Frost said to Thomas, "No matter which road you take, you'll always sigh, and wish you'd taken another" [[Thompson]:88]. Although it had been these walks with Thomas which inspired **"The Road Not Taken,"** the image of the two roads occupied Frost's mind earlier when he wrote to Susan Hayes Ward on February 10, 1912:

> Two lonely cross-roads that themselves cross each other I have walked several times this winter without meeting or overtaking so much as a single person on foot or on runners. The practically unbroken condition of both for several days after a snow or a blow proves that neither is much travelled.
>
>   [[Sergeant]:87]

That the above image was a catalyst for this poem is partially confirmed by his once dating the poem "1912? 1914" [[Angyal]:114].

The "two roads" theme has a long tradition in literature. Frost would have been aware of this archetypical pattern from a variety of sources. Following are a sampling of sources with which Frost would have been familiar.

In Virgil's *Aeneid* (book VI, *ll.* 540-543), the Sibyl tells Aeneas:

>   Here is the place
> Where the road forks: on the right hand it goes
> Past mighty Dis's walls, Elysium way,
> Our way; but the leftward road will punish
> Malefactors, taking them to Tartarus.
>
>   [[Virgil]:178]

In the section "Table-Talk" from *Drift-Wood*, Longfellow has this statement: "Round about what is, lies a whole mysterious world of might be [. . .] by turning down this street instead of the other, we may let slip some great occasion of good, or avoid some impending evil, by which the whole current of our lives would have been changed" [[Longfellow]:405-406].

Emily Dickinson wrote a poem beginning

> Our journey had advanced;
> Our feet were almost come
> To that odd fork in Being's road
>   . . .
>
>   [[*American Poetry*]:276]

In his essay "Circles," Emerson wrote, "The difference between talents and character is adroitness to keep the old and trodden road, and power and courage to make a new road to new and better goals" [[Emerson]:413].

Thoreau wrote in his journal on Sunday, August 31, 1851, that "our customs turn the hour of sunset to a trivial time as at the meeting of two roads—one coming from the noon and the other leading to the night [. . .]" [[Thoreau]:254].

William James, in the final paragraph to "The Will to Believe," wrote, "We stand on a mountain pass in the midst of whirling snow and blinding mist, through which we get glimpses now and then of paths which may be deceptive. [. . .] If we take the wrong road we shall be dashed to pieces" [[James]:479]. Even more to the point, James wrote in "The Dilemma of Determinism,"

> What is meant by saying that my choice of which way to walk home after the lecture is ambiguous and matter of chance as far as the present moment is concerned? It means that both Divinity Avenue and Oxford Street are called; but that only one, and that one *either* one, shall be chosen.
>
>   [[James]:573]

Frost was often dismayed at people reading more into his poems than he had intended. On interpreting the poem, Frost said during a reading at Wofford College in South Carolina:

> Should you take a hint when none is intended? Or should you, with more sensitive nature, only take hints when they *are* intended? And that's so in reading my poetry. That poem: there's a hint intended there. But you ought to know that yourself. One of the things I suffer from, you know, is being taken as intending a double meaning when I don't. Sometimes I do, and sometimes I don't. And I can't mark 'em [. . .]
>
>   [[Thompson]:547]

On the form of the poem, Frost said that when you read the poem you can just go past the rhymes as if they weren't noticed. Talking past the rhymes almost hides them. He said he was complimented whenever anyone said that when they read a poem of his they can hear him talking [[Cook, 1974]:123].

l. 16. *I shall be telling this with a sigh*: speaking of the sigh, Frost warned a Bread Loaf audience that "the tone of that is absolutely saving" [[Cook, 1974]:112].

Works Cited

American Poetry: The Nineteenth Century (New York: Library of America, 1994).

Angyal, Andrew J. "Robert Frost's Poetry Before 1913, A Checklist" (*Proof 5, The Year-book of American Bibliographical and Textual Studies,* 1977).

Cook, Reginald L. "Frost on Frost: The Making of Poems" (*American Literature,* March 1956).

———. *Robert Frost: A Living Voice* (Amherst: University of Massachusetts Press, 1974).

Emerson, Ralph Waldo. *Essays and Lectures* (New York: Literary Classics of the United States, 1983).

Frost, Robert. *Selected Letters of Robert Frost,* edited by Lawrance Thompson (New York: Holt, Rinehart and Winston, 1964).

James, William. *Writings, 1878-1899* (New York: Library of America, 1992).

Longfellow, Henry Wadsworth. *Outre-Mer and Drift-Wood* (Boston: Houghton Mifflin, 1886).

Sergeant, Elizabeth Shepley. *The Trial by Existence* (New York: Holt, Rinehart and Winston, 1960).

Thompson, Lawrance. *Robert Frost: The Years of Triumph, 1915-1938* (New York: Holt, Rinehart and Winston, 1970).

Thoreau, Henry David. *Journal* (New York: Dover Publications, 1962).

Untermeyer, Louis. *Letters of Robert Frost to Louis Untermeyer* (New York: Holt, Rinehart and Winston, 1963).

Virgil. *The Aeneid,* translated by Robert Fitzgerald (New York: Random House, 1983).

Larry Finger (essay date fall 1997)

SOURCE: Finger, Larry. "Frost's Reading of 'The Road Not Taken.'" *Robert Frost Review* (fall 1997): 73-6.

[*In the following essay, Finger asserts that Frost's own interpretation of "The Road Not Taken" changed over the years, from an ironic depiction of his friend Edward Thomas to a more sentimental description of Frost himself.*]

Who is the poet in **"The Road Not Taken"**? In his *Robert Frost Handbook*, James L. Potter contends that to read the poem as it should be read one must know that the poet in the poem is Edward Thomas, not Robert Frost. Potter says that if read as a statement about Frost the poem lacks irony and fades away into a "sentimental justification of following one's personal bent, of being an individual" (52). We fail to see, Potter continues, that Frost is "mocking Thomas's habit of fretting over choices, present and past" (52). Is the poem about Edward Thomas or Robert Frost? If read as a statement about Frost, is the poem merely a "sentimental justification"? What was Frost's response to the poem, in the beginning and through the years until his death in 1963?

Frost did write the poem in England in 1914 while spending a great deal of time with Thomas, his British friend. The poem does describe Thomas's rather lonely, isolated life, a way less traveled; and on numerous occasions, right after writing the poem especially, Frost said it was more about Thomas than himself (Sergeant 89). Thomas concurred. Not long after Frost returned to the States, he sent a copy of the poem without comment to Thomas, who saw in it a better description of himself than of Frost. In September of the following year, 1915,

in a letter to Lewis Untermeyer, Frost is apparently still holding out for the Edward Thomas reading of the poem. Frost says to Untermeyer: "I am only fooling my way along as I was in the poems in *The Atlantic* (particularly in **'The Road Not Taken'**) as I was in what I said about Spoon River. I trust my meaning is not too hidden in any of these places. I can't help my way of coming at things" (Thompson 189).

But in 1925, eleven years after writing the poem, Frost acknowledged in a letter to Crystine Yates, a young girl in Dickson, Tennessee, that the poem was about himself. Ms. Yates had written Frost to ask if the sigh in the last stanza were one of regret or one of satisfaction. Frost replied as follows:

> Amherst Mass April 1951
>
> Dear Miss Yates:
>
> No wonder you were a little puzzled over the end of my **"Road Not Taken."** It was my rather private jest at the expense of those who might *think* I would yet live to be sorry for the way I had taken in life. I supposed I was gently teasing them. I'm not really a very regretful person, but for your solicitousness on my behalf I'm
>
> Your friend always, Robert Frost[1]

This letter to Ms. Yates says nothing about Edward Thomas. Was Frost treating her as a special audience, content for her to read the poem autobiographically, *misread* the poem, that is? Would anyone think that Frost was still holding out for Edward Thomas as the poet in the poem?

I think it reasonable to assume that Frost's own interpretation of **"The Road Not Taken"** changed through the years. No doubt he wrote the poem with Thomas in mind; and for a number of years thereafter, insisting in correspondence with friends and in public meetings that the poem was "tricky," perhaps he was still thinking of Thomas. But by the time Frost responded to Ms. Yates in 1925, he had changed his mind. I don't believe he was treating her as a special audience. He was beginning to lose interest in any subtlety in the poem related to Edward Thomas. Perhaps his letter to Ms. Yates, the poet in the quiet of his study answering an honest question from a young student in a faraway state, expresses his most honest feelings about the poem.

It appears that in the public reading that turned out to be his last, Frost wanted **"The Road Not Taken"** to be the last poem his audience would hear that night. The occasion was his annual appearance at the Ford Forum at Jordan Hall in Boston, December, 1962, not long after his Russian tour. According to William Pritchard, Frost concluded his readings and remarks "rather abruptly" with **"The Road Not Taken"** (259). Why the abrupt ending? Could it be that Frost omitted poems he had intended to read so that the last poem of the evening would be **"The Road Not Taken"**? There is considerable evidence that at the time Frost strongly suspected that he was close to death. If he had decided that the poem described his own life, and if he thought this might be his last public reading, then it was not surprising that he would end the program with **"The Road Not Taken."** No one would argue that Frost wanted his audience to hear the poem as a statement about Edward Thomas, a final chance for them to catch the subtlety. Neither did he want his audience to universalize the poem, not at that moment anyway. He read the poem, I think, as a statement about himself. Perhaps as much as any other poem, this one had become his.

As it turned out that night, however, **"The Road Not Taken"** was not the last poem the audience heard. As was his custom, Frost allowed time after his reading for members of the audience to ask questions. During that time someone asked him to read **"Two Tramps in Mud Time"**; and Frost, perhaps still thinking of **"The Road Not Taken"** and his own choice to follow poetry, "said" only the last stanza of the poem:

> But yield who will to their separation
> My object in living is to unite
> My avocation and my vocation
> As my two eyes make one in sight.
> Only where love and need are one,
> And the work is play for mortal stakes,
> Is the deed ever really done
> For Heaven and the future's sakes.

After reading that stanza, Frost went on to talk about life's choices. Pritchard describes Frost's closing remarks that December night in Boston, just days before Frost's death: "It was all 'gamblin', and one had to bet nothing less than one's life; indeed, he said, one of the 'sweetest' of all expressions was 'You bet your sweet life'. There was 'nothing to life' unless one could say, 'I bet my sweet life on this'" (260). Many years earlier Frost had gambled. Choosing one road rather than another, he bet his sweet life on poetry.

So **"The Road Not Taken"** was for Frost a moving, a shifting thing. Clearly Frost liked the poem when he first wrote it: he read it publicly even before he published it, including it in his very first reading, held at Tufts College, May 5, 1915. His early attempts to get people to read it his way perhaps made him weary of the poem, not just the interpretive problems surrounding it. This weariness appears to manifest itself in letters Frost wrote to Louis Untermeyer during the early 30s. In preparing anthologies, Untermeyer made a practice of including Frost's poems, at times of course with Frost's encouragement. Frost even sent lists of poems he wanted Untermeyer to include. **"The Road Not Taken"** appears in none of the lists.

But through the years, it became clear to Frost that the poem described his own life; and the description is best seen in the last stanza, one that lifts the poem above sentimentality, one that gives the poem ambiguity if not irony, even when read autobiographically. The last stanza does not say whether Frost's decision to give his life to poetry turned out well or not. The stanza is ambiguous. And it is this very ambiguity that Frost, I believe, came to appreciate. His decision to write poetry at any cost brought him wonderful experiences, even world-wide fame; but it brought him great heartache, too. Frost's letters provide overwhelming evidence. For example, as early as 1937, he wrote to Untermeyer: "Water boy you are! Where are you hidin? Sometimes I feel as if I deserved a hidin myself for the selfish way I have behaved in life. I heard someone say to an audience in public that he was the opposite from me: whereas I had never done a thing except for the fun of it, he had never done a thing except from a sense of duty. Its [sic] an almost true picture of me" (Thompson 294). That is, while poetry brought him pleasure, it seduced him away from duty, at times familial duties, something he was never able to forgive himself for. Frost came to see in **"The Road Not Taken"** both the pleasure and the pain of his own life and, for that reason, especially during the later years, had a growing appreciation for it.

It seems clear that Frost wrote **"The Road Not Taken"** with Edward Thomas in mind. As Potter says, Frost was mocking Thomas's regretfulness. He played a game in writing the poem and continued the game for a number of years, holding out for a reading of the poem that was too much to ask of any reader. But by the time he wrote Ms. Yates in 1925, he was growing tired of the game and willing for her to read the poem as a statement about himself. When he read **"The Road Not Taken"** to Russian audiences a few months before his death, he read it as a statement about his own decision to give his life to poetry. The touch was even more personal when he read the poem to the Boston audience a few weeks before his death. With that reading, he was saying goodbye.

Note

1. Crystine Yates, whom I knew as Mrs. Aubrey F. Soyars, gave me the Frost letter while I was teaching in Nashville, Tennessee, in 1968.

   Permission to use the Frost letter here has been granted by the estate of Robert Frost, Alfred C. Edwards, Trustee. Any further use of the letter must be approved by the Estate.

Works Cited

Potter, James L. *Robert Frost Handbook*. University Park: Pennsylvania State UP, 1975.

Pritchard, William H. *Frost: A Literary Life Reconsidered*. New York: Oxford, 1984.

Sergeant, Elizabeth S. *Robert Frost: The Trial by Existence.* New York: Holt, 1960.

Thompson, Lawrance, ed. *Selected Letters of Robert Frost.* New York: Holt, 1964.

Robert Faggen (essay date 1997)

SOURCE: Faggen, Robert. "Descent into Matter: Natural History and the End of Theodicy." In *Robert Frost and the Challenge of Darwin,* pp. 245-302. Ann Arbor: The University of Michigan Press, 1997.

[*In the following excerpt, Faggen examines Thoreau's influence on Frost, comparing Thoreau's essay "Walking" to "The Road Not Taken."*]

"The Road Not Taken" is an ironic commentary on the autonomy of choice in a world governed by instincts, unpredictable contingencies, and limited possibilities. It parodies and demurs from the biblical idea that God is the "way" that can and should be followed and the American idea that nature provides the path to spiritual enlightenment. The title refers doubly to bravado for choosing a road less traveled but also to regret for a road of lost possibility and the eliminations and changes produced by choice. **"The Road Not Taken"** reminds us of the consequences of the principle of selection in all aspects of life, namely that all choices in knowledge or in action exclude many others and lead to an ironic recognition of the limitations of our achievements. At the heart of the poem is the romantic mythology of flight from a fixed world of limited possibility into a wilderness of many possibilities combined with trials and choices through which the pilgrim progresses to divine perfection. I agree with Frank Lentricchia's view that the poem draws on "the culturally ancient and pervasive idea of nature as allegorical book, out of which to draw explicit lessons for the conduct of life (nature as self-help text)."[1] I would argue that what it is subverting is something more profound than the sentimental expectations of genteel readers of fireside poetry.

In the context of American thought it is indebted, as is **"The Wood-Pile"** and **"Directive,"** to Thoreau's essay "Walking." That late essay, published a month after the author's death in 1862, represents his attempt to reconcile evolutionary theory with personal and American ideals. "Walking" describes the journey of the fettered, cultured European into a wilderness by which the past is continually transformed. I agree with Max Oelschlaeger's insight that in "Walking" Thoreau "brilliantly weds the implications of evolution with epistemology itself: *knowledge itself evolves, and intuition is fundamental to the process.*"[2] Oelschlaeger

adds that Thoreau's insight conveys the "essential notion that *cultural forms,* just as inorganic and organic ones, *must evolve in response to changing circumstance. . . .* the same evolutionary process that underpins life also nourishes the individual."[3] The walk westward represents both a quest for the Holy Land and a search for mythic origins in a primordial wilderness stripped of the layers of civilization:

> We go eastward to realize history and study the works of art and literature, retracing the steps of the race; we go westward as into the future, with a spirit of enterprise and adventure. The Atlantic is a Lethean stream, in our passage over which we have had the opportunity to forget the old world and its institutions.[4]

Thoreau naturalizes our "walking" escape and quest, making it analogous to great migrations of wildlife, something he views as ennobling rather than degrading in its effect on the idea of individual will and choice. Animal instinct and choice are praised as representing providence:

> I know not how significant it is, or how far it is an evidence of singularity, that an individual should then consent in his pettiest walk with the general movement of the race; but I know that something akin to the migratory instinct in birds and quadrupeds,—which, in some instances, is known to have affected the squirrel tribe, impelling them to a general and mysterious movement, in which they were seen, say some, crossing the broadest rivers, each on its particular chip, with its tail raised for a sail, and bridging narrower streams with their dead, that something like the *furor* which affects the domestic cattle in spring, and which is referred to as a worm in their tails,—affects both nations and individuals from time to time.[5]

The passage in Thoreau's essay to which Frost refers most pointedly in **"The Road Not Taken"** expresses a willingness to trust our choice to the magnetism of nature. It is only our "heedlessness" that makes for a wrong choice. The actual world, according to Thoreau, will mirror both an interior and an ideal world:

> What is it that makes it so hard sometimes to determine whither we will walk? I believe that there is a subtle magnetism in Nature, which, if we unconsciously yield to it, will direct us aright. It is not indifferent to us which way we walk. There is a right way, but we are very liable from heedlessness and stupidity to take the wrong one. We would fain take that walk, never yet taken by us through this actual world, which is perfectly symbolical of the path which we love to travel in the interior and ideal world, and sometimes, no doubt, we find it difficult to choose our direction, because it does not yet exist distinctly in our idea.[6]

"The Road Not Taken" appears on one level to support Thoreau's idealism and its ultimate alliance with the magnetism of nature. Dramatizing the way our ideals are often in discord with the contingencies of experience, Frost places us at the moment of decision in which our "choice" appears much more uncertain and nature's signals less magnetic or more ambiguous.

The drama of the poem is of the persona making a choice between two roads. As evolved creatures, we should be able to make choices, but the poem suggests that our choices are irrational and aesthetic. The sense of meaning and morality derived from choice is not reconciled but, rather obliterated and canceled by a nonmoral monism. Frost is trying to reconcile impulse with a conscience that needs goals and harbors deep regrets. The verb Frost uses is *taken,* which means something less conscious than *chosen.* The importance of this opposition to Frost is evident in the way he changed the title of **"Take Something Like a Star"** to **"Choose Something Like a Star,"** and he continued to alter titles in readings and publications.[7] *Take* suggests more of an unconscious grasp than a deliberate choice. (Of course, it also suggests action as opposed to deliberation.) In **"The Road Not Taken"** the persona's reasons wear thin, and choice is confined by circumstances and the irrational:

> Two roads diverged in a yellow wood,
> And sorry I could not travel both
> And be one traveler, long I stood
> And looked down one as far as I could
> To where it bent in the undergrowth;
>
> Then took the other, as just as fair,
> And having perhaps the better claim,
> Because it was grassy and wanted wear;
> Though as for that the passing there
> Had worn them really about the same,

Both roads had been worn "about the same," though his "taking" the second is based on its being less worn. The basis of selection is individuation, variation, and "difference": taking the one "less traveled by." That he "could not travel both / And be one traveler" means not only that he will never be able to return but also that experience alters the traveler; he would not be the same by the time he came back. Frost is presenting an antimyth in which origin, destination, and return are undermined by a nonprogressive development. And the hero has only illusory choice. This psychological representation of the developmental principle of divergence strikes to the core of Darwinian theory.[8] Species are made and survive when individuals diverge from others in a branching scheme, as the roads diverge for the speaker. The process of selection implies an unretracing process of change through which individual kinds are permanently altered by experience. Though the problem of making a choice at a crossroads is almost a commonplace, the drama of the poem conveys a larger mythology by including evolutionary metaphors and suggesting the passage of eons.

The change of tense in the penultimate line—to *took*—is part of the speaker's projection of what he "shall be telling," but only retrospectively and after "ages and ages." Though he cannot help feeling free in selection, the speaker's wisdom is proved only through survival of an unretraceable course of experience:

> And both that morning equally lay
> In leaves no step had trodden black.
> Oh, I kept the first for another day!
> Yet knowing how way leads on to way,
> I doubted if I should ever come back.
>
> I shall be telling this with a sigh
> Somewhere ages and ages hence:
> Two roads diverged in a wood, and I—
> I took the one less traveled by,
> And that has made all the difference.

The poem leaves one wondering how much "difference" is implied by *all,* given that the "roads" already exist, that possibilities are limited. Exhausted possibilities of human experience diminish great regret over "the road not taken" or bravado for "the road not taken" by everyone else. The poem does raise questions about whether there is any justice in the outcome of one's choices or anything other than aesthetics, being "fair," in our moral decisions. The speaker's impulse to individuation is mitigated by a moral dilemma of being unfair or cruel, in not stepping on leaves, "treading" enough to make them "black." It might also imply the speaker's recognition that individuation will mean treading on others.

Notes

1. Frank Lentricchia, "Lyric in the Culture of Capitalism," *American Literary History* (spring 1989): 85.

2. Max Oelschlaeger, *The Idea of Wilderness* (New Haven: Yale University Press, 1991), 167.

3. Ibid., 165.

4. Thoreau, "Walking," in *Great Short Works of Henry David Thoreau,* ed. Wendell Glick (New York: Harper and Row, 1982), 304.

5. Ibid., 305.

6. Ibid., 303.

7. See Edward Connery Lathem's editorial note on the history of this change in his edition of *The Poetry of Robert Frost* (New York: Henry Holt, 1969), 573.

8. Dov Ospovat, *The Development of Darwin's Theory* (Cambridge: Cambridge University Press, 1981), 191-209. Ospovat discusses the way Darwin's theory changed from one emphasizing diversity to one emphasizing divergence and difference through isolation.

R. F. Fleissner (essay date fall 1999)

SOURCE: Fleissner, R. F. "Whose 'Road Less Traveled by'? Frost's Intent Once Again." *Robert Frost Review* (fall 1999): 22-6.

[*In the following essay, Fleissner disagrees with critic Larry Finger's assertion that Frost changed his interpretation of "The Road Not Taken" later in life.*]

Once again Larry Finger has raised the issue of the true subject of Robert Frost's **"The Road Not Taken"** as being not Edward Thomas, after all,[1] though the author had regularly said that it was,[2] but rather the poet himself. Age-old as this dilemma truly seems to be, let us come to terms better now with some of the basic technicalities involved. For did this model, conservative lyricist really *change his mind* on such a noteworthy work, as has actually been twice claimed in print by Finger? In brief, the matter at stake is whether Thomas's own taking of the "road less traveled by" was basically on Frost's mind when he composed the poem and when he would discuss its genesis.

My proposal here is that the poetic intent was clearly enough to promote Thomas only, not himself (or also himself), and that that primary focus did not change; only incidental reference to himself there plausibly entered the genetic picture, not any related to his precise statements of intent. Granted Reginald L. Cook, who happened to discuss this very matter with him, did allow partly for Frost as subject. Here is an excerpt from correspondence that happened to be addressed even to me on the issue:

> Granted that consciously the poem does refer to Thomas's life style; however, when considered unconsciously, how self-revealing the poem really is. The human insight, which this poem expresses, is probably an awareness Frost had himself earned from his own life. I think it has this double-edge for two reasons: first, because Frost certainly had self-insight; and, secondly, he had the moral courage to face up to his own limitations. The road not taken was his as well as Edward Thomas's experience, and this is the irony of it.[3]

Although Cook does support a personal connection here he then specifically reveals that Frost himself unequivocally uttered that the subject was Thomas, not himself, as his article "A Walk with Robert Frost" shows.

According to the editorial introduction, Cook's essay is based on a walk through the woods with Frost during a "past summer" (in 1955). This is some twenty-six years after the letter cited by Finger in *American Literature.* In his account of his conversation with the poet, Cook states that he mentioned to him that readers would continually see the subject of the untaken-road poem as about Frost himself and that the latter agreed but then again reminded his companion that the subject was, in fact, Thomas. What counts here is poetic intent, after all. Here is the excerpt:

> When I said: "Well you know they'll always associate **'The Road Not Taken'** with you," he replied: "Yes, I suppose they will but it's about Edward Thomas."

> (26)[4]

Plausibly at least the indirect allusion in the poem to Frost himself, at any rate according to readers, is what Frost meant when he referred obliquely to "my rather private jest," in the letter from the poet cited by Finger.[5] What is then rather subtler than all this is that Frost could have been influenced of course by other things, notably for instance Wordsworth's familiar Lucy poems;[6] still, indebtedness in itself is never to be conflated or confused with explicit expression of intent. For that matter, as I happen to have suggested a number of times elsewhere, the very "Lucy" connection could at least obliquely have entered in by way of Thomas, who was himself admittedly strongly inspired by Wordsworthian lyrics and indeed is responsible for relating Frost to the Poet Laureate as well.[7]

After his original note on the subject appeared in *American Literature,* Finger suggested once more that such correspondence implies that Frost surely had some second thoughts, if only because he notified a young girl, Crystine Yates, to this effect.[8] She had written the poet originally to inquire if the sigh in the final stanza implied rather regret or satisfaction. Frost's response (April 1951) happens to refer to "the way I had taken in life."[9] Then Finger interprets this response again literally, as meaning the poet had actually changed his mind about his subject (from Thomas to himself).

But let us look at Frost's remark more in context. Evidently he then wrote the young lass the way he did because he wanted her to comprehend (or deduce) something rather general about the poem; if he had brought in Thomas, that biographical focus could have seemed too technical, would hardly have helped her overall understanding. For she presumably was unaware of there being any "occasion" for the verse. If he had been asked later, directly, whether he had had any change of mind, most probably Frost would have admitted that his remark to her was meant quite informally and so should not be taken out of context or too literally. True enough, even great poets can have their casual, light-hearted moments when the rudiments of the genetic thinking process have to be relaxed a bit.

In order to clarify the genetic issue more fully, permit me to relate, in passing, his friend T. S. Eliot's familiar comments in his celebrated work *The Three Voices of Poetry,* specifically the matter of the formal critical distinction between person and *persona.* In a word,

Eliot considered that the speaker in a lyric is not to be taken simply as some autobiographical reflection of himself as writer: that would be too innocent a view (though what the writer has previously experienced or read may indirectly also enter the picture). (Yet, admittedly, Eliot had to confess later that this distinction of his sometimes works out better in "theory" than in "practice.") So Frost evidently saw no need to inform his correspondent what the precise occasion was for his writing the poem (clearly Thomas's own habits); that would have complicated things unduly for her. Presumably when the girl would grow up, she would become acclimatized to the standard distinction between the poet and the mask he creatively assumes. This clearly relates to the commonplace that when one becomes adult, one sometimes has to put on a socialized, private act—if only not to have one's respondent become unnecessarily involved with one's own problems. It is worth remarking further that Eliot's distinction has come to the fore especially with regard to his passing comments about Jews (e.g., in "Gerontion"). But it is immature to term Eliot himself anti-Semitic simply because the speaker in a poem of his, having naturally to reflect the time and circumstances of his milieu, indulges somewhat liberally in expressions which can give the impression of such bias. Granted, Eliot, in a University of Virginia speech, cited "free-thinking Jews"; it was printed in his *After Strange Gods* (meaning Freud and Marx?) yet never reprinted; he confessed later that he did not mean to single out merely *Jewish* free-thinkers, that his paper, alas, was simply poorly composed. Then he allowed his poems with Jewish references to be reprinted because they simply did not reflect the poet's own stance, were not *intended* to do so in other words.

In turn, why else would *Frost* have asserted that he was not meant to be reflected in the speaker of **"The Road Not Taken"**? The answer appears to be that he felt a bit awkward in considering the poem as at all directly about himself, if only because he preferred to imagine his representative writing to be reflecting that of the average individual, not a person being at all "different." The point is that in America a certain acceptance of uniformity can have a major influence upon human behavior, as is evident from the common enough accusation of one's being different as suggesting abnormality (thus perhaps being politically incorrect). One standard response to the question then of *how* one is taken as "different," namely as being "different from everyone else," can represent a blunt put-down (except for bonafide nominalists). Frost was human enough to be sensitive to this framework, stereotypical though such a response may in fact now appear to be. He liked to think of his writing as reflecting well enough that of the ordinary (not the "different") individual, hence being more universal that way.

Finger's conclusion that Frost changed his mind about the focus of the poem is also subverted by the other factual concerns. For the poet had clearly stated in public forum after 1929 that the lyric was, in truth, not at all about himself, but dealing with Edward Thomas. He would not have really changed his mind about all this. I happen to have heard about this admission after he gave a recital, where I grew up, in Aurora and at Wells College (actually from one of my good friends, a neighbor and professor there, now deceased), and later it appeared again in a printed account of Reginald Cook's discussion of walks with him in Vermont, cited earlier. So let us take Frost at his word on this in terms of intention and not bring in the unconscious when it would oppose what he had in mind.

Notes

1. See his essay in the journal of the Robert Frost Society, which is a follow-up to his previous one in *American Literature* (though that is not acknowledged).

2. John Evangelist Walsh, for one, claims that Frost "repeatedly explained" that the lyric was "a mild satire on the chronic vacillating habits of Edward Thomas, his endless fine distinctions when faced with a choice" (211).

3. Letter of 16 August 1981. As a former student at The Bread Loaf School of English for several summers, I came to know "Doc" Cook (Director) fairly well. The quoted passage is followed by a statement giving me permission to quote: "Like Frost, I don't mind being quoted, if I'm quoted correctly." I can vouch that he is.

4. In this context, Frost also commented on his poem "The Soldier" as being also about Thomas, as is well recognized. One should likewise recall the lyric entitled "To E. T."

5. The letter is dated simply April 1951. Permission to quote has been granted by the estate of Robert Lee Frost.

6. See, in particular, my *Frost's Road Taken* 1-30. Originally my chapter was delivered as a paper at the Wordsworth bicentennial symposium at Wittenberg University (1970), then in revised form at a 1977 Modern Language Association Frost session, and finally entitled and published in my chapter "A Road Taken" in the Harris collection. But versions have since been augmented and have appeared in *The South Carolina Review* (special Frost issue) and delivered at various conferences. Most recently the conception was transformed into a paper read at the Wordsworth conference in Grasmere, England, during the summer of 1997 (entitled "Frost and Wordsworth: The British Allegiance," the subtitle being a borrowing from

Cook) and then, in new form, at the four-day Frost conference at Winthrop University (Autumn 1997), entitled "Onto the Road Not Taken—by Wordsworth, Frost, and Edward Thomas." The Frost-Wordsworth parallel with the untaken-road poem was, as I discovered necessarily belatedly (owing to the time factor), first commented on by C. D. Narasimhaiah, editor of the journal in which his article appeared.

7. Mainly see my essay in *The South Carolina Review.* For corroboration, cf. Walsh (190), who also cites Thomas's review of Frost in connection with Wordsworth, namely of *North of Boston.* In a letter to Frost of 11 Sept. 1916, as I have pointed out, Thomas referred specifically to Wordsworth's love poems under the cover of an "Old Cloak" metaphor.

8. See his follow-up in *The Robert Frost Review.*

9. Cited by Finger in his follow-up (73).

Works Cited

Cook, Reginald L. "A Walk with Robert Frost." *Yankee* Nov. 1955: 18-27.

Eliot, T. S. *The Three Voices of Poetry.* London: Cambridge UP, 1953. 16-24.

Finger, Larry L. "Frost's Reading of 'The Road Not Taken.'" *The Robert Frost Review* 7 (1997): 73-76.

———. "Frost's 'The Road Not Taken': A 1929 Letter Come to Light." *American Literature* 50 (1978): 478-79.

Fleissner, R. F. "A Road Taken: The Romantically Different *Ruelle.*" In Harris 117-31.

———. "Enveloped in that *Old Cloak*: Edward Thomas, Wordsworth, and Frost's Untaken Road." *The South Carolina Review* 19 (Summer 1987): 39-45.

———. *Frost's Road Taken,* New York: Lang, 1996. 1-30.

Harris, Kathryn Gibbs, ed. *Robert Frost: Studies of the Poetry.* Boston: G. K. Hall, 1979.

Narasimhaiah, C. D. "The Reputation of Robert Frost: A Point of View." *The Literary Criterion* 9 (1969): 1-10.

Thomas, Edward. Rev. of Frost's *North of Boston, The English Review* 18 (1914): 142-43.

Walsh, John Evangelist. *Into My Own: The English Years of Robert Frost.* New York: Grove P, 1988.

John H. Timmerman (essay date 2002)

SOURCE: Timmerman, John H. "Rationalist Ethics." In *Robert Frost: The Ethics of Ambiguity,* pp. 62-92. Lewisburg, Penn.: Bucknell University Press, 2002.

[*In the following excerpt, Timmerman explores the expression of Frost's Romantic side in "The Road Not*

Taken," concluding that the choice to be made in this poem "is not grounded in some rationalist scheme; rather, it is an existential product of the immediate moment."]

While he turned against the romantic excess in poetic form under the influence of Santayana, Frost nonetheless retained the unsettled, questing spirit of the romantic legacy. On a quest for personal value, or a validation of self, his poetic characters must choose and act to make that validation. The choices held open for the character, and the ambiguities of choices that prevent clear and decisive actions, are also those that confront the reader. One of Frost's best-known examples of this ambiguity appears in **"The Road Not Taken."**

> Two roads diverged in a yellow wood,
> And sorry I could not travel both
> And be one traveler, long I stood
> And looked down one as far as I could
> To where it bent in the undergrowth;
>
> Then took the other, as just as fair
> And having perhaps the better claim,
> Because it was grassy and wanted wear;
> Though as for that the passing there
> Had worn them really about the same,
>
> And both that morning equally lay
> In leaves no step had trodden black.
> Oh, I kept the first for another day!
> Yet knowing how way leads on to way,
> I doubted if I should ever come back.
>
> I shall be telling this with a sigh
> Somewhere ages and ages hence:
> Two roads diverged in a wood, and I—
> I took the one less traveled by,
> And that has made all the difference.

The poem may seem to many to be the great pastoral symphony of his works; upon closer probing, however, one uncovers discordant notes and tense ambiguities. To fully appreciate the achievement, the poem should be situated in several different contexts, each of which provides differing angles of vision on the work.

After selling his farm in Derry, New Hampshire, Frost moved in 1912 with Elinor and their children to England. There two of the most important events of his life occurred: the publication of his first volume of poetry, **A Boy's Will** (1913), and his deep friendship with the English poet, Edward Thomas. The friendship would be all too brief. Thomas died in 1917 in World War I, but the friendship left a profound and lasting impact upon Frost.

According to Lawrance Thompson's *Robert Frost* (vol. 2, 88-89, 544-48), **"The Road Not Taken"** was originally written in a piece of correspondence to Thomas, and, Thompson speculates, it was intended to satirize the indecisive Thomas. Indeed, it isn't difficult to detect a tone of jesting, but friendly, conversation in the poem. Regardless of the difficulty of Thompson's reading the author's intentions into the work, the poem itself nicely captures the frequent walks of Frost and Thomas across the English countryside.[1]

Substantial evidence, however, suggests that the idea of the poem antedates Frost's acquaintance with Thomas. In a 1912 letter to Susan Hayes Ward, Frost writes of "two lonely cross-roads" that he walked frequently during the winter. After a snowfall, he would observe the road lying trackless for days, showing that "neither is much traveled." Frost goes on to describe how one evening he was surprised to see a figure in the distance walking toward him. Oddly, he felt he was approaching his own image in "a slanted mirror," or as if two images were about to "float together." In the end, Frost writes, "I stood still in wonderment and let him pass by" (*Selected Letters* 45). That experience sheds substantial light upon the ambiguities that have perplexed readers of the poem, for certainly **"The Road Not Taken"** dramatizes the narrator's encounter with his own self.

The poem was first published in *The Atlantic Monthly* (August 1915), and was collected as the opening poem in Frost's third volume, **Mountain Interval** (1916). As he had done in his previous volume, **North of Boston,** Frost set the opening poem and the concluding poem, **"The Sound of Trees,"** in italic, rather than roman type. A comparison of the two poems brings forth many striking similarities beyond the function of introducing and concluding the volume. Both poems pose the narrator in a moment of ambiguity, where a choice may be made but no certain responses to that choice appear. While **"The Road Not Taken"** locates the narrator "in a yellow wood," **"The Sound of Trees"** locates the narrator in his lodging listening to the sound of trees. In fact, as the trees sway and bend, so too his whole body sways and bends to their pull. To what end, however? As in **"The Road Not Taken,"** the narrator of **"The Sound of Trees"** is not certain. He announces that "I shall set forth for somewhere / I shall make the reckless choice." But not now. Now he feels the tug of action, but leaves it in the tense ambiguity of "someday." Whereas in **"The Road Not Taken"** the narrator actually does step out on a "leap of faith," the action of the narrator of **"The Sound of Trees"** is indeterminate. Thus, the two poems frame conflicting actions when forced with ambiguous choices and ends.

As seen previously in his essay "The Constant Symbol," Frost declared that the "mind is a baby giant," hurling its toys ahead of itself. So too it is with the poet, flinging out words, prosody, and other playthings of the craft ahead of him. But they land in zigzag paths; thus, the "straight crookedness" of the poem. We should not

misunderstand so careful a poet as Frost as abdicating method and design, but rather as using them seductively to bring the reader into the poem and thereby to unveil shades of meaning to the reader. Such is one fundamental trait of his poetic ethics. Rather than shouting the truth, as his poem **"Mowing"** has it, the poet would prefer to whisper along the zigzag path that is the poem.

The point is important to **"The Road Not Taken"** for it is indeed one of his superb pastoral poems, perfectly capturing as if by camera one momentary scene in nature. The autumn setting, nearly always a nostalgic and sometimes melancholy season in Frost's poetry, evokes a tone of sweet wistfulness here. Nature's life is passing; if "Nature's first green is gold," its last green is yellow. But nature in this poem also acts upon the narrator, further than a mere evocation of wistfulness. As Johannes Kjorven has argued in *Robert Frost's Emergent Design,* the poem's focus centers primarily upon the choice/action of the narrator. In this case, nature, at one unexpected point, presents him with two leaf-fallen paths—divergent, branching off into the unseen distance. So it is in nature; one reaches such a point, one makes a decision, one travels on. But it is not that way for the narrator, and herein the poem itself branches off into complexities as we observe the narrator's reaction to the choice that nature presents him.

While the pastoral scene may seem simple, the form of the poem itself propels the zigzag paths. In fact, the form belies the pastoral quality for, unlike **"Mowing,"** it is far more intense, suggesting uncertainty and vacillation against the compelling need to make a decision. The stanzaic rhyme scheme appears in perfect regularity: ABAAB CDCCD EFEEF GHGGH. The rhymes are all masculine, with a curious twist in lines five and twenty where the penultimate syllable rhymes, pairing the "undergrowth" and the "difference." Within this tightly clad system, however, rhythm and word patterns shift and strain, reflecting the narrator's own mind. With his reliance upon sound-sense, as many scholars have pointed out, Frost should not—perhaps cannot—be placed tightly within a regular line prosody. Even his sweetly flowing **"Mowing"** is broken by irregular accents since he speaks as a laborer, not as a poet writing about a laborer. So too in **"The Road Not Taken"** accents shift spontaneously, trochees mixing freely with iambs. Frost captures the mind of the woods-walker in such a way, eliciting discovery, uncertainty, and sadness by the varied structures.

The linguistic deployment of the poem abets this fluctuation. The first thing one notices is a shift in the wood itself. Line 1 discovers two roads in a "yellow wood." The opening trochee manifests the surprise of the walker stumbling across those roads. His relationship with and decision according to those roads constitute the bulk of the "telling" of the poem until the last stanza where the decision is made. In line 18, however, the reader finds an echo of line 1. Something is missing. It reads simply, "Two roads diverged in a wood." The "yellow" wood, with its beauty and surprise, has been suspended, held in thrall by a decision between two roads that has to be made. It is possible, in fact, that if one follows this transition one could read the poem as expressing a wholly negative attitude toward decision making. The beauty of the world around us slips away under the weight of the need for pragmatic decisions. Whether read this way or not, the formal techniques of the poem nicely evidence the baby giant using its toys to set a zigzag course. In this case, it most powerfully lures the reader into that course for deeper probing. What further evidence in the poem's setting can be determined to guide that course?

After the objective description in stanza 1—what in fact lay before him—the narrator engages the why of his choice. The evidence in stanzas 2 and 3 is inconclusive. Yet, in the third stanza the imposition of the context of time on the poem again subtly shifts the meaning. At the present moment, the yellow leaves have not been "trodden black." Something of the narrator's passage will indelibly change that, but so too he will be changed. Although he claims to keep the first path for another day, he knows full well that with one step it disappears forever into the past. The "sigh" of the fourth stanza is anticipated in the third as the narrator makes his choice, "Oh, I kept the first for another day!" But there will be no other day, no other precise moment such as this.

Even as he stands in the present, then, at this seemingly harmless juncture in the woods, the poet feels the dramatic moment of the future. The fourth stanza shifts to the future, which, of course, he can't know. All he has is the present moment. The indecision of the narrator here contrasts sharply with the fierce energy of the narrator of **"A Leaf Treader,"** something of a parallel poem. There the narrator, by his own admission, has trod the leaves to stamp out fear. Not so with the narrator here. He steps out at last on the path that he chooses to call less traveled, but it is only his choosing to call it that that makes all the difference for his sense of the future. In his essay, "Whistling in the Dark: Robert Frost's Modernist Quest for Meaning," William Doxey emphasizes that the choice/act determines meaning since "each choice excludes its alternative." Doxey adds, "What is done cannot be undone, so the meaning here seems to be that one must live as though his judgment were correct, regardless."[2] In this context also, it is not difficult to see the implications for Frost's personal commitment to be a poet. His choice during the England years was fretted by unusually heavy financial concerns, a lack of a reading public, and a commitment to a poetic form unlike that practiced in the modernist trend. The risk of the future weighs like a sigh in the poem.

"The Road Not Taken" does indeed, then, follow several zigzag contours. It may be an ironic jest with his friend Thomas. It is indeed a pastoral scene. Its formal qualities expertly snare and lead the reader. It reveals nature working upon the narrator by offering the complexity of seemingly identical choices. Finally, it holds forth the tension—unresolved in spite of the last line—between the present moment and the unknown future, and the need to shape some ethical stance toward present and future through human action rather than received tradition. In these ways it also manifests what Langbaum calls "The Poetry of Experience." The choice to be made is not grounded in some rationalist scheme; rather, it is an existential product of the immediate moment.

Notes

1. For a substantially detailed biographical accounting of "The Road Not Taken," see Larry Finger, "Frost's Reading of 'The Road Not Taken'" in the 1997 issue of *Robert Frost Review.*

2. William S. Doxey, "Whistling in the Dark: Robert Frost's Modernist Quest for Meaning," *West Georgia College Review* 23 (May 1993), 31.

Works Cited

Thompson, Lawrance. *Robert Frost: The Years of Triumph, 1915-1938.* New York: Holt, Rinehart and Winston, 1970.

Frost, Robert. *Selected Letters of Robert Frost.* Edited by Lawrance Thompson. New York: Holt, Rinehart and Winston, 1964.

Doxey, William S. "Whistling in the Dark: Robert Frost's Modernist Quest for Meaning." *West Georgia College Review* 23 (May 1993): 29-33.

Kjorven, Johannes. *Robert Frost's Emergent Design: The Truth of the Self In-Between Belief and Unbelief.* New Jersey: Humanities Press International, 1987.

Langbaum, Robert. *The Poetry of Experience.* New York: W. W. Norton, 1963.

FURTHER READING

Biography

Parini, Jay. *Robert Frost: A Life.* New York: Henry Holt, 1999, 514 p.

Provides a sympathetic and balanced biography of Frost.

Criticism

Finger, Larry L. "Frost's 'The Road Not Taken': A 1925 Letter Come to Light." *American Literature* 50, no. 3 (November 1978): 478-79.

> Examines a letter in which Frost discusses the ending of "The Road Not Taken," describing it as a "private jest at the expense of those who might *think* I would yet live to be sorry for the way I had taken in life."

————. "That Frost Letter: Another Look." *CEA Critic* 43, no. 3 (March 1981): 36-9.

> Expands his comments about Frost's letter regarding "The Road Not Taken."

Fleissner, Robert F. "Frost's Use of Wordsworth and Keats Revamped." In *Frost's Road Taken,* pp. 1-30. New York: Peter Lang, 1996.

> Discusses "The Road Not Taken" and Frost's debts to Romantic poets William Wordsworth and John Keats.

Kearns, Katherine. "Irony II: This Is Not a Pipe." In *Robert Frost and a Poetics of Appetite,* pp. 56-85. Cambridge: Cambridge University Press, 1994.

> Includes an analysis of "The Road Not Taken" as a work of "conscious irony."

Kemp, John C. "The Poet in New England." In *Robert Frost and New England: The Poet as Regionalist,* pp. 185-236. Princeton, N.J.: Princeton University Press, 1979.

> Examines "The Road Not Taken," stating that "if we make too much of his being on the 'right' road, we will misjudge the depth and complexity of his verse."

Ketterer, David. "The Letter 'Y' in 'The Road Not Taken.'" *Robert Frost Review* (fall 1997): 77-8.

> Reads "The Road Not Taken" in terms of the letter 'Y,' observing that the letter graphically represents a forking road; that there is a proliferation of words in the poem with y-sounds; and that the letter is a homophone of "why," which remains a central unanswered question regarding the choice of roads.

Trikha, Manorama B. "Definitive Choices." In *Robert Frost: Poetry of Clarifications,* pp. 99-128. New Delhi, India: Arnold-Heinemann, 1983.

> Examines "The Road Not Taken" as an "example of man's self-encounter and self-division" and suggests that the poem demonstrates that many choices are guided by outward appearances.

Additional coverage of Frost's life and career is contained in the following sources published by Thomson Gale: *American Writers*; *American Writers Retrospective Supplement,* Vol. 1; *Authors and Artists for Young Adults,* Vol. 21; *Children's Literature Review,* Vol. 67; *Concise Dictionary of American Literary Biography, 1917-1929*; *Contemporary Authors,* Vols. 89-92; *Contemporary Authors New Revision Series,* Vol. 33; *Contemporary Literary Criticism,* Vols. 1, 3, 4, 9, 10, 13, 15, 26, 34, and 44; *Dictionary of Literary Biography,* Vols. 54 and 284; *Dictionary of Literary Biography Documentary Series,* Vol. 7; *DISCovering Authors*; *DISCovering Authors 3.0*; *DISCovering Authors: British Edition*; *DISCovering Authors: Canadian Edition*; *DISCovering Authors Modules: Most-studied Authors and Poets*; *Encyclopedia of World Literature in the 20th Century,* Ed. 3; *Exploring Poetry*; *Literature Resource Center*; *Major 20th-Century Writers,* Eds. 1 and 2; *Major 21st-Century Writers* (ebook), 2005; *Modern American Literature,* Ed. 5; *Poetry Criticism,* Vols. 1 and 39; *Poetry for Students,* Vols. 1, 2, 3, 4, 5, 6, 7, 10, and 13; *Poets: American and British*; *Reference Guide to American Literature,* Ed. 4; *Something About the Author,* Vol. 14; *Twayne's United States Authors*; *World Literature Criticism*; *World Poets*; **and** *Writers for Young Adults.*

Oliver Wendell Holmes
1809-1894

American poet, essayist, novelist, and biographer.

INTRODUCTION

Holmes was a popular nineteenth-century author celebrated for his wit and sense of humor. Many of his poems were composed in honor of an anniversary or other special occasion and most have been forgotten today. His best known individual poems are "Old Ironsides," "The Deacon's Masterpiece, or the Wonderful One-Hoss Shay," and "The Chambered Nautilus."

BIOGRAPHICAL INFORMATION

Born in 1809 in Cambridge, Massachusetts, Holmes was the eldest son of Sarah Wendell Holmes and the Reverend Abiel Holmes, a Calvinist minister. Holmes's early training in the Puritan-based religion of his father led to his lifelong animosity toward Calvinism—a sentiment that informed much of his writing. From 1824 to 1825 Holmes attended Phillips Academy in Andover after which he began studying law at Harvard. He soon became disenchanted with his studies, however, and switched to medicine. He graduated from Harvard in 1829, spent a year in Paris taking advanced courses, and returned to Harvard in 1833. He received his degree in medicine in 1836 and started a private practice. In 1839 he began teaching at Dartmouth College, and a year later married Amelia Lee Jackson, the daughter of Judge Charles Jackson. The couple had three children: Oliver Wendell Holmes, Jr., the future Supreme Court Justice, born in 1841; a daughter, Amelia, born in 1843; and another son, Edward, born in 1846. By this time Holmes was teaching at the Tremont Medical School, maintaining his medical practice, and establishing his reputation as a poet. In 1847 he became Parkman Professor of Anatomy and Physiology at the Massachusetts Medical College of Harvard University, where he taught for the next thirty-five years.

In addition to his multiple careers as writer, teacher, and physician, Holmes also became a much sought-after public speaker, lecturing on a variety of medical topics—some of them controversial—as well as on literature. He was a regular contributor to the *Atlantic Monthly* and wrote verses commemorating countless

anniversaries and celebrations. Holmes retired from Harvard in 1882, but he continued writing and speaking until his death in 1894 at the age of eighty-five.

MAJOR WORKS

In 1830, Holmes published "Old Ironsides" anonymously in a Boston newspaper, expressing his outrage at the government's reported plans to dismantle the *U.S.S. Constitution,* a frigate that had seen action against the Barbary Pirates early in the nineteenth century and against the British in the War of 1812. The resulting public outcry saved the ship and Holmes acknowledged authorship of the poem. From then on Holmes regularly supplied poetry to the local newspapers in Boston. *Poems,* his first published collection of verse, appeared in 1836 and was revised and expanded several times over the next thirteen years. Although he composed some serious poetry, his most popular pieces were humorous and occasional verses in the meter of the folk ballad or in heroic or octosyllabic couplets. Most of these occasional pieces were forgotten by the early years of the twentieth century, with the exception of "Old Ironsides"; "The Chambered Nautilus," speculating on the growth of the soul; "The Last Leaf," recounting the problems of old age; and "The Deacon's Masterpiece, or The Wonderful One-Hoss Shay," critiquing the inflexibility of Calvinism.

Holmes's poetry collections include *Songs in Many Keys* (1862), *Soundings from the Atlantic* (1864), and *Songs of Many Seasons* (1875). In addition, Holmes's most popular prose collections—*The Autocrat of the Breakfast-Table* (1858), *The Professor at the Breakfast-Table* (1860), and *The Poet at the Breakfast-Table* (1872)—all contain a number of poems.

CRITICAL RECEPTION

Holmes's poetry was very well received by his contemporaries. He was besieged with requests to provide poems in honor of a wide variety of occasions, and he was generally happy to oblige. James Ball, defining the genuine poet as "Singer, Revealer, Teacher, all combined in one harmonious whole," claims that Holmes was just such a true poet. Ball maintains that in Holmes's poetry "the thought is always so pure and true, the style always so graceful and worthy, and the rich and ripe genius of the author always so apparent." Most early observers, however, distinguished between Holmes's humorous verse and his serious poems, with the latter never so highly valued as the former. William Sloane Kennedy, among others, believed that Holmes's humorous poetry—particularly that written between 1830 and 1849—represented his best efforts. According to Kennedy, "not all of Dr. Holmes' memorial and anniversary productions, and verses kindly written by request, are of equal merit. Scores of them are nothing but rhymed rhetoric and sentiment." His humorous poetry, however, is deeper than it may first appear according to many of his early admirers, among them William Cranston Lawton, who asserts that "in the ability to bridge the narrow, but deep and dangerous, rift that parts humor from pathos, Holmes has, perhaps, no superior since [Thomas] Hood."

By the early twentieth century, however, most of Holmes's poetry was considered "very dusty," as C. Hartley Grattan described it in 1925. Grattan further complains that "the literary fame of Oliver Wendell Holmes has been erected into a chapter when it should be reduced to a footnote." Alfred Kreymborg also attests to the old-fashioned quality of the verse, suggesting that "his collected poems are reactionary. One needs historical spectacles to bring them back to reality." For Kreymborg, Holmes "never escaped the Eighteenth Century to

which his writings adhere." Gay Wilson Allen offers a similar assessment of Holmes as a poet, maintaining that "in many respects, he remained an eighteenth-century neo-classicist all of his life." His work was further limited by his training as a physician, according to Allen, who complains about "the scientific reserve that always held in check his poetic imagination." Everett Carter, however, considers Holmes's writing perfectly emblematic of the nineteenth century, at least in terms of its content. For Carter, "the historical force which flowed through most of the poems and essays of Holmes was the most important charge of symbolic energy of the American nineteenth century." Holmes's work, according to Carter, embodied the American Dream or, as James Russell Lowell and Ralph Waldo Emerson termed it, the American Idea, just coming into its own in Holmes's time.

PRINCIPAL WORKS

Poetry

Poems 1836
Urania: A Rhymed Lesson 1846
Astraea: The Balance of Illusions 1850
Songs in Many Keys 1862
Soundings from the Atlantic 1864
Humorous Poems 1865
Songs of Many Seasons 1875
Favorite Poems 1877
The Poetical Works of Oliver Wendell Holmes 1877
The School-Boy 1879
The Iron Gate, and Other Poems 1880
Grandmother's Story and Other Poems 1883
The One Hoss Shay with Its Companion Poems How the Old Horse Won the Bet and The Broomstick Train 1891
The Poetical Works of Oliver Wendell Holmes 1975

Other Major Works

Homeopathy and Its Kindred Delusions (essay) 1842
The Contagiousness of Puerperal Fever (essay) 1843
The Autocrat of the Breakfast-Table (essays) 1858
The Professor at the Breakfast-Table (essays) 1860
Currents and Counter-Currents in Medical Science (essays) 1861
Elsie Venner: A Romance of Destiny (novel) 1861
The Guardian Angel (novel) 1867
Mechanism in Thought and Morals (essays) 1871
The Poet at the Breakfast-Table (essays) 1872
Medical Essays, 1842-1882 (essays) 1883

Pages from an Old Volume of Life (essays) 1883
A Mortal Antipathy (novel) 1885
Ralph Waldo Emerson (biography) 1885
Our Hundred Days in Europe (essays) 1887
Over the Teacups (essays) 1891
The Writings of Oliver Wendell Holmes. 13 vols.
   (novels, essays, poetry, and biography) 1891

CRITICISM

James Ball (essay date 1878)

SOURCE: Ball, James. "Pertaining to Poetry." In *Dr. Oliver Wendell Holmes and His Works: Being a Brief Biography and Critical Review,* pp. 41-56. London: Elliot Stock, 1878.

[*In the following excerpt, Ball praises Holmes as a true poet whose rhymes reveal new truths.*]

> Fountain of Harmony! Thou Spirit blest,
>   By whom the troubled waves of earthly sound
> Are gathered into order, such as best
>   Some high-souled bard in his enchanted round
>
> May compass, Power divine! O spread thy wing,
>   Thy dove-like wing that makes confusion fly,
> Over my dark, void spirit, summoning
>   New worlds of music, strains that may not die.

In the verses above quoted from the dedication to Keble's Christian Year, is concealed one of the best definitions of poetry. It is a poet's "confession of faith," and it fits in with our own belief that poetry is something which is sung, and which should contain '*new* worlds of music.' We must first of all have the poet—the maker—who is gifted with a clearer vision than most of us, a vision which comprehends nature, and the good—or God—in nature, and the rule—which also is God—in nature, and the life and its purpose which make up nature. Then he must *make* for us new songs: all which songs must be either of new truths, with keen-edged, arrow-like motion and measure, to sink deep into our inmost consciousness and move our whole being; or of old truths which have failed to strike us before, dressed up anew and decked with all the grace he can command from his great poetic soul, in order that now they may reach us. Carlyle says, "All old poems, Homer's and the rest, are authentically songs. I would say, in strictness, that all right poems are:" and then he adds, in his candid, out-spoken manner, "that whatsoever is not *sung* is properly no poem, but a piece of prose cramped into jingling lines,—to the great injury of the grammar, to the great grief of the reader, for most part!"

The poet, then, is a Singer, Revealer, Teacher, all combined in one harmonious whole. Whoso rhymes without teaching is no poet; whoso gives us mere verses without a new truth or new beauty of an old truth to form the marrow of them is no poet; but he who sings to us in harmonious measure—now smooth, perchance; now rushing like a tumultuous flood with the mighty force of passion—words which teach us new truth and new beauties of truth, he is a poet, such work of his is poetry. It is subject to such conditions that we claim the title of poet for Oliver Wendell Holmes, and it will be found that his poetical work is able to bear the test of all that we have asserted poetry should be. Take here one example. Looking at the shell of a Nautilus, which to less gifted natures would be but a shell;—pretty, perhaps, nothing more—he with his poetic vision sees a song therein, which he has entitled, **"The Chambered Nautilus."** After describing how the occupant of the little shell—according to the wont of his species—built each year a new spiral of his coiling home, which was larger than the last year's spiral: and how he went on year by year building in a widening spiral, and each year living in the enlarged home, and giving up the smaller one of last year, he—the poet—hears a voice—the voice of his poetic nature—which sings:

> Build thee more stately mansions, O my soul,
>   As the swift seasons roll!
>   Leave thy low-vaulted past!
> Let each new temple, nobler than the last,
> Shut thee from heaven with a dome more vast,
>   Till thou at length art free,
> Leaving thine out-grown shell by life's unresting sea!

He, however, is more modest for himself than we are for him, and whilst he recognises the high ideal of poetry we have endeavoured to indicate, he thinks it beyond his reach. Thus in one of his early poems we find the following beautiful expression of a poetic truth that had flashed upon him, which shows at once his clear comprehension of what song should be:

> If to embody in a breathing word
> Tones that the spirit trembled when it heard;
> To fix the image all unveiled and warm,
> And carve in language its ethereal form,
> So pure, so perfect, that the lines express
> No meagre shrinking, no unlaced excess;
> To feel that art, in living truth, has taught
> Ourselves, reflected in the sculptured thought;—
> If this alone bestow the right to claim
> The deathless garland and the sacred name;
> Then none are poets, save the saints on high,
> Whose harps can murmur all that words deny.

Comment upon this is needless. The thought is simply sublime. In this example, and in many others which might be given, the poet is brimming over with sacred truth, for which he feels words cannot be found. It reveals to us a nature so deep, so extensive, that language is insufficient to utter all its longings: and in which there is much left to be expressed in that blissful time when the harp shall murmur what words now deny.

But, as we have already remarked, Dr. Holmes is practical as well as poetical: practical in his poetry, and he is not ashamed to own it. When asked, 'at the Breakfast-Table,' whether he would not confess at least to using a rhyming dictionary, he replied:

> I would as lief use that as any other dictionary, but I don't want it. When a word comes up fit to end a line with, I can *feel* all the rhymes in the language that are fit to go with it, without naming them. I know all the polygamous words, and all the monogamous ones, and all the unmarrying ones,—the whole lot that have no mates,—as soon as I hear their names called. Sometimes I run over a string of rhymes, but, generally speaking, it is strange what a short list it is of those that are good for anything. That is the pitiful side of all rhymed verse. Take two such words as *home* and *world*. What can you do with *chrome* or *loam* or *gnome* or *tome*? You have *dome, foam,* and *roam,* and not much more to use in your *pome,* ('Pome' is a name given in America to a baked cake of maize or Indian meal, about the size of an apple, but seems to be used here in another sense.) as some of our fellow-countrymen call it. As for *world,* you know that in all human probability somebody or something will be *hurled* into or out of it: its clouds may be *furled* or its grass *impearled*: possibly something may be *whirled* or *curled,* or even *swirled,*—one of Leigh Hunt's words, which with *lush,* one of Keats's, is an important part of the stock in trade of some dealers in rhyme.

In another place he says also:

> Poets, like painters, their machinery claim,
> And verse bestows the varnish and the frame.

Still, he is careful in maintaining, what the best definitions of poetry teach, that the poet is moved, or has a revelation made to him: and so we find in his treatise upon mechanism in thought and morals, the following truth laid down:

> The poet always recognises a dictation *ab extra*; and we hardly think it a figure of speech when we talk of his inspiration.

He illustrates this truth by observing that frequently the poet will sit down to pen some gay conceit; and then find his eyes suffused with tears, and his spirit moved, and write something quite different to his first purpose. This we think is a very correct way of putting the case.

Dr. Holmes frequently refers to ideas which strike him as to his literary work, as well as to those he has concerning general matters, and often he takes us behind the scenes, as it were, of the poet's manufactory: those comments suggested by the remark as to a rhyming dictionary, for example. He also gives us some really good hints as to literary work generally. Here is one. In the "Autocrat" he says:

> I want to make a literary confession now, which I believe nobody has made before me. You know very well that I write verses sometimes. Of course I write some lines or passages which are better than others: some which, compared with the others, might be called relatively excellent. It is in the nature of things that I should consider these relatively excellent lines or passages as absolutely good. So much may be pardoned to humanity. Now, I never wrote a 'good' line in my life, but the moment after it was written, it seemed a hundred years old. Very commonly I had a sudden conviction that I had seen it somewhere. Possibly I may have sometimes unconsciously stolen it, but I do not remember that I ever once detected any historical truth in these sudden convictions of the antiquity of my new thought or phrase. I have learned utterly to distrust them, and never allow them to bully me out of a thought or line.

> This is the philosophy of it. Any new formula which suddenly emerges in our consciousness has its roots in long trains of thought; it is virtually old when it first makes its appearance among the recognized growths of our intellect. Any crystalline group of musical words has had a long and still period to form in.

Again, in the "Autocrat" (which was written before he had published a novel) in reply to a question from one of the boarders "at the Breakfast-Table," why he did not write a story, or a novel, or something of that kind, he replies as follows:

> That every articulately-speaking human being has in him stuff for *one* novel in three volumes duodecimo has long been with me a cherished belief . . . Now, an author's first novel is naturally drawn, to a great extent, from his personal experiences—that is, it is a literal copy of nature under various slight disguises . . . I as an individual of the human family, could write one novel or story at any rate, if I would.

> Why don't I, then? Well, there are several reasons against it. In the first place, *I should tell all my secrets, and I maintain that verse is the proper medium for such revelations.* Rhythm and rhyme and the harmonies of musical language, the play of fancy, the fire of imagination, the flashes of passion, so hide the nakedness of a heart laid open, that hardly any confession, transfigured in the luminous halo of poetry, is reproached as self-exposure. A beauty shows herself under the chandeliers, protected by the glitter of her diamonds, with such a broad snow-drift of white arms and shoulders laid bare, that, were she unadorned and in plain calico, she would be unendurable—in the opinion of the ladies.

Notwithstanding the theory here playfully given forth, our author has written *two* novels, to which we shall refer later on. He has told a great many of his secrets in them, though not more perhaps than in his poems.

One of the best pieces of advice ever given to those poor, infatuated beings, who *imagine* they are poets is that extracted from the "Autocrat," to which we incidentally referred in the brief biography. After remarking that the habit of chewing on rhymes without sense and soul to match them is, like that of using any other narcotic, at once a proof of feebleness, and that a young man can get rid of the presumption against him that he is an inferior person by his writing verses, only by convincing us that they are verses worth writing, he says:

> I would always treat any given young person passing through the meteoric showers which rain down on the brief period of adolescence, with great tenderness. God forgive us if we ever speak harshly to young creatures on the strength of these ugly truths: and so, sooner or later, smite some tender-souled poet or poetess on the lips who might have sung the world into sweet trances, had we not silenced the matin song in its first low breathings! Just as my heart yearns over the unloved, just so it sorrows for the ungifted who are doomed to the pangs of an undeceived self-estimate . . . One doesn't like to be cruel—and yet one hates to lie. Therefore one softens down the ugly central truth of donkeyism—recommends study of good models, and that *writing verse should be an incidental occupation only, not interfering with the hoe, the needle, the lapstone, or the ledger.*

If it were possible to bring home this advice to many of our fancied poets—those with the *will* and *desire* to utter music, but without the *ability* to do so—how many importunities to take subscription-copies friends and acquaintances would be spared—how the "two-penny" boxes of the book-stalls would be emptied! It is pitiful this jingling together of bad prose into lines. It is wonderful so sensitive a nature as that of Dr. Holmes can be so patient with it. All honor to him for his great sympathy; for with most of us (to quote Carlyle again) "precisely as we love the true song, and are charmed by it as by something divine, so shall we hate the false song, and account it a mere wooden noise, a thing hollow, superfluous."

It will be a relief to turn from this to a little true poetry, a song by our author, which should bring comfort to those, who, having high aspirations and noble aims, cannot always reach them. The truth embodied in the song is suggested—as many truths are—by a simple matter: in this case it is a crooked footpath. After describing its devious turnings the poet sings thus:—

> Perhaps some lover trod the way
>   With shaking knees and leaping heart,—
> And so it often runs away
>   With sinuous sweep or sudden start.
>
> Or one, perchance, with clouded brain
>   From some unholy banquet reeled,—
> And since, our devious steps maintain
>   His track across the trodden field.
>
> Nay, deem not thus,—*no earth-born will*
>   *Could ever trace a faultless line;*
> Our truest steps are human still,—
>   To walk unswerving were divine!

> Truants from love, we dream of wrath;—
>   Or rather, let us trust the more!
> Through all the wanderings of the path,
>   We still can see our Father's door.

We do not pretend that all Dr. Holmes' verse is poetry: much is not so, and does not pretend to be so. There are many pretty ballads amongst his works, and other metrical scraps: but all bear the impress of the master hand which acts in conjunction with the poet's soul, and in all the serious poems, and in most of the humorous ones too, the language is well chosen as well as the metaphor.

As a hymn-writer, so far as can be judged from the few examples he has given us, he is only equalled by some of the choicest of those who in the last century made hymn-writing almost their sole poetical exercise. We give as examples of our author's great power in this direction the two hymns in the closing sections of the "Professor." One is supposed to be sung by Iris to the "little gentleman" (of whom you shall be told something in a future chapter) as the latter lay upon his death-bed. It is entitled—

"Hymn of Trust"

> O Love Divine, that stooped to share
>   Our sharpest pang, our bitterest tear,
> On Thee we cast each earth-born care,
>   We smile at pain while Thou art near!
>
> Though long the weary way we tread,
>   And sorrow crown each lingering year,
> No path we shun, no darkness dread,
>   Our hearts still whispering, Thou art near!
>
> When drooping pleasure turns to grief,
>   And trembling faith is changed to fear,
> The murmuring wind, the quivering leaf
>   Shall softly tell us, Thou art near!
>
> On Thee we fling our burdening woe,
>   O Love Divine, for ever dear,
> Content to suffer, while we know,
>   Living and dying, Thou art near!

There are few verses which so fitly express as these do that living, hopeful faith in a divine love, without which life would be an intolerable burden, and death the dread portal of an unknown, awful region beyond, towards which the shrinking soul would move with a terror no words can define.

The other hymn concludes the "Professor," and is introduced thus:—

> Thanks to all those friends who from time to time have sent their messages of kindly recognition and fellow-feeling! Peace to all such as may have been vexed in spirit by any utterance these pages have repeated! They

will, doubtless, forget for the moment the difference in the hues of truth we look at through our human prisms, and join in singing (inwardly) this hymn to the Source of the light we all need to lead us, and the warmth which alone can make us all brothers.

"A Sun-day Hymn."

Lord of all being! throned afar,
Thy glory flames from sun and star:
Centre and soul of every sphere,
Yet to each loving heart how near!

Sun of our life, Thy quickening ray
Sheds on our path the glow of day;
Star of our hope, Thy softened light
Cheers the long watches of the night.

Our midnight is Thy smile withdrawn;
Our noontide is Thy gracious dawn;
Our rainbow arch Thy mercy's sign;
All, save the clouds of sin, are Thine!

Lord of all life, below, above,
Whose light is truth, Whose warmth is love,
Before Thy ever-blazing throne
We ask no lustre of our own.

Grant us Thy truth to make us free,
And kindling hearts that burn for Thee,
Till all Thy living altars claim
One holy light, one heavenly flame.

Dr. Holmes' capacity for sacred poetry is equally well marked in **"The Living Temple,"** also called **"The Anatomist's Hymn"**; which is introduced thus:

Not in the world of light alone
Where God has built His blazing throne,
Nor yet alone in earth below,
With belted seas that come and go,
And endless isles of sunlit green,
Is all thy Maker's glory seen:
Look in upon thy wondrous frame—
Eternal Wisdom still the same!

Then follows a description of the human body, the breathing, the blood, the muscles and nerves, hearing, and the action of the brain; all lucid not only with poetical description: but with technical light also. Lastly there comes the closing thought—in which is embodied a foreshadowing of the time when no longer "the smooth, soft air, with pulse-like waves" shall pass through to give the blood its brightening purple and new vitality: and when that blood shall no longer leap forth "in unnumbered crossing tides," nor "creep back to find the throbbing heart:" when light, and sound, and will shall all have left the body:—this is the closing thought, which follows:

O Father! grant Thy love divine
To make these mystic temples Thine!
When wasting age and wearying strife
Have sapped the leaning walls of life,

When darkness gathers over all,
And the last tottering pillars fall,
Take the poor dust Thy mercy warms,
And mould it into heavenly forms!

Enough has been quoted and written probably to shew the reader that Oliver Wendell Holmes is really a poet—a poet of the first rank. His only fault—if it be a fault—is that he has written so much poetry that one is beset with difficulty as to what is best fitted for special mention and quotation. Again—in another point of view—the abundance of good things is perhaps a little apt to engender indifference as to their merit. However, this we may confidently say—whoever reads his poetry, whether the pieces interspersed throughout his prose works, or those collected into separate volumes, will be amply repaid. The thought is always so pure and true, the style always so graceful and worthy, and the rich and ripe genius of the author always so apparent, that their perusal must be attended not only with profit but with real pleasure. I know no specific more successful in chasing away depressing thoughts, than the perusal of some of these poems. They lift one above the accidents of time and space, reveal the glory and calm which lie beyond, and bring to the soul something of that divine peace which passes understanding. They touch the chords of immortality, and awaken sweet visions of another and higher sphere of being, in which the God-like in us shall have freer and fuller scope than now. They remind us of the grand fact that we are something more than animate dust. And to do so is the poet's privilege; for, as Longfellow says:—

God sent His singers upon earth
With songs of sadness and of mirth,
That they might touch the hearts of men,
And bring them back to heaven again.

William Sloane Kennedy (essay date 1883)

SOURCE: Kennedy, William Sloane. "Poetry." In *Oliver Wendell Holmes: Poet, Littérateur, Scientist*, pp. 267-91. Boston: S. E. Cassino and Company, 1883.

[*In the following excerpt, Kennedy assesses Holmes's poetry, maintaining that his humorous verse is far superior to his more serious work.*]

His the quaint trick to cram the pithy line
That cracks so crisply over bubbling wine.—

                                                                HOLMES

It is as a writer of humorous poetry that Holmes excels. His non-humorous poems are full of beautiful passages, as we shall see; but they are not, many of them, perfect works of art like the others; they have not the same unique flavor of individuality. A goodly proportion of his best comic and humorous pieces are *vers d'occasion,* written to be read at banquets or before select companies. From time immemorial wit has seasoned table-talk. A company at table assigns by instinct the chief *rôle* to the wit or humorist. The three meals of a day are its green oases, its sparkling poems. "The Poet at the Breakfast-Table,"—the title was well chosen. In the freshness and buoyancy of the morning hour the fancy plays most delicately and spontaneously, and the poet of Beacon Street has transferred to the pages of his prose and his poetry the vitality and intensity of spirits that the cup of coffee imparts. He also understands the soft illusory enchantment of the chandelier, what time its lustre mingles with the faint waxy aroma and flowery perfume of the banquet-room.

When the critic approaches the post-cœnatical and convivial poems of Holmes, he will throw aside his quill, if he is not a fool, and yield himself with others to the fun and riant humor of the moment.[1] If he does anything, he will long for an artist's brush to paint some such scene as this: (no Deipnosophistean Greek debauch, with wreaths and wine, but) an ample breakfast-table in a high and sunny room, the cheery crackle of blazing wood in a spacious fireplace, the delicate aroma of coffee gratefully inhaled (but you can't paint that), a cultured and merry company seated at the table, and at its head the genial face of one crowned

With white roses in place of the red,

whose tender-glancing eye is now moist with tears, and now gleaming with fun, and whose lips at one moment utter subtle and sententious truth, and at another bubble over with puns and rippling laughter, and jests which put the company into such a state of interior titillation and stomachic exhilaration of mood that the snowy table-cloth is momently in danger of amber stains from shaking cups. And upon the frieze of the room let there be a motley procession of figures,—weird Elsie, sweet Iris and the Little Gentleman hand in hand, the poor Tutor, roguish Benjamin Franklin, gaunt Silence Withers, wayward Myrtle, and honest Gridley,—with gargoyles and grotesques at intervals, a whizzing Comet, the immortal One-Hoss Shay at the moment of its dissolution, the Spectre Pig, and the pensive Oyster-man, and for scroll-work a chain of spiral, pearly shells with purpled wings outspread.

After reading a dozen or more pages of the neat Augustan couplets of Holmes' best *vers d'occasion*, packed and crammed with little *genre* images and neat concretes, you have the comfortable feeling of a man who has just despatched a dish of hickory-nuts cracked in halves, and intermingled with raisins,—the whole washed down with a *gläschen* of old sherry. Or you feel as if you had been at Mr. Aldrich's "Lunch":—

A melon cut in thin delicious slices,
A cake that seemed mosaic-work in pieces,
Two china cups with golden tulips sunny,
And rich inside with chocolate like honey.

But not all of Dr. Holmes' memorial and anniversary productions, and verses kindly written by request, are of equal merit. Scores of them are nothing but rhymed rhetoric and sentiment, and should never have been printed at all except in newspapers. Their author has said of late that he would like to go over his poetry and cull out the best for a final edition. It is to be hoped that he may find time for this task. He has told us of the origin of many of his verses:—

I'm a florist in verse, and what *would* people say,
If I came to a banquet without my bouquet?

And in another place:—

Here's the cousin of a king,—
Would I do the civil thing?
Here's the firstborn of a queen;
Here's a slant-eyed Mandarin.

Would I polish off Japan?
Would I greet this famous man,
Prince or Prelate, Sheik or Shah?
—Figaro çi and Figaro là!

What was a kind-hearted man to do? Of course he complied: the verses were ground out somehow,—and what poet could ever resist the temptation to publish? It is almost impossible to impart by quotations the spirit and hilarity of the best of these *vers d'occasion*: there is a whet and stimulant in every line: the humor of them is interior, below the midriff, and penetrates the thick integument of care and gravity with a slow, delicious feeling that finally breaks out into uncontrollable laughter. Read the **"Modest Request"** for an illustration; or the **"Chanson without Music,"**—a voluble polyglot medley that almost takes one's breath away, resembling nothing so much as the tipsy music of a bobolink, or the vocal pyrotechnics of the Southern mocking-bird:—

You bid me sing,—can I forget
    The classic ode of days gone by,—
How belle Fifine and Jeune Lisette
    Exclaimed, 'Anacreōn, gerōn ei'?
'Regardez donc,' those ladies said,—
    'You're getting bald and wrinkled too:
When summer's roses all are shed,
    Love's nullum ite, voyez-vous!'

In vain ce brave Anacreon's cry,
    'Of Love alone my banjo sings'
(Erōta mounon). 'Etiam si,—
    Eh b'en?' replied the saucy things,—
'Go find a maid whose hair is gray,
    And strike your lyre,—we sha'n't complain;

But parce nobis, s'il vous plaît,—
   Voilà Adolphe! Voilà Eugène!'
     . . . . .

Ginōsko. Scio. Yes, I'm told
   Some ancients like my rusty lay,
As Grandpa Noah loved the old
   Red-sandstone march of Jubal's day.

I used to carol like the birds,
   But time my wits has quite unfixed,
Et quoad verba,—for my words,—
   Ciel! Eheu! Whe-ew!—how they're mixed!

Some of Holmes' best anniversary poems have been those for the Phi Beta Kappa. **"Post-Prandial"** is one of these, and its rare fun will not be understood by those who are ignorant of the circumstance that Wendell Phillips, who is a distant "connection" of Holmes, and Charles G. Leland (Hans Breitmann) both had public parts to perform on the occasion that gave rise to the poem. **"Rip Van Winkle, M.D.—An after-dinner prescription taken by the Massachusetts Medical Society at their meeting, held May 25, 1870,"** is a capital piece of professional fun. It is full of sly thrusts at antiquated doctors. They are typified in the person of Rip Van Winkle (a grandson of Irving's hero), who goes to sleep with the request that he be awakened once a year for the doctors' meeting. Rip

     Had, in fact, an ancient, mildewed air,
  A long gray beard, a plenteous lack of hair,—
  The musty look that always recommends
  Your good old Doctor to his ailing friends.
  —Talk of your science! after all is said
  There's nothing like a bare and shiny head;
  Age lends the graces that are sure to please;
  Folks want their Doctors mouldy, like their cheese.

Holmes was class poet at college, and he has remained class poet all his life. Thirty-seven of his class anniversary poems appear in his complete poetical works. Some of them are in his finest vein and are of general interest. For example, **"The Boys,"** written in 1859:—

  Has there any old fellow got mixed with the boys?
  If there has, take him out without making a noise.
  Hang the Almanac's cheat, and the Catalogue's spite!
  Old Time is a liar! We're twenty to-night!

  We're twenty! We're twenty! Who says we are more?
  He's tipsy,—young jackanapes!—show him the door!
  'Gray temples at twenty?'—Yes! *white* if we please;
  Where the snowflakes fall thickest there's nothing can
    freeze!
     . . . . .

  Then here's to our boyhood, its gold and its gray!
  The stars of its winter, the dews of its May!
  And when we have done with our life-lasting toys,
  Dear Father, take care of thy children, THE BOYS!

"The Last Survivor" is one of those fine pieces of imagined retrospect, or forecasting of the future, which

is so excellently done in the **"Epilogue to the Breakfast-Table Series."** **"The Archbishop and Gil Blas"** may serve as the comic counterpart of **"The Iron Gate,"** and could, one thinks, scarcely have been written except by an old physician who had himself been a keen observer of old men:—

  Can you read as once you used to? Well, the
    printing is so bad,
  No young folks' eyes can read it like the books
    that once we had.
  Are you quite as quick of hearing? Please to
    say that once again.
  Don't I use plain words, your Reverence? Yes,
    I often use a cane,
  But it's not because I need it,—no, I always
    liked a stick;
  And as one might lean upon it, 'tis as well it
    should be thick.
  Oh, I'm smart, I'm spry, I'm lively,—I can
    walk, yes, that I can,
  On the days I feel like walking, just as well as
    you, young man!

The exquisite elegiac poem on his classmate, Prof. Benjamin Peirce—that grand old mathematician of lion aspect, whose very presence seemed a proof of immortality,—is pitched in a lofty key, as the subject, indeed, could not but inspire. Two of the stanzas may need a word of explanation:—

  To him the wandering stars revealed
  The secrets in their cradle sealed:
  The far-off, frozen sphere that swings
  Through ether, zoned with lucid rings;

  The orb that rolls in dim eclipse
  Wide wheeling round its long ellipse,—
  His name Urania writes with these
  And stamps it on her Pleiades.

The reference here is to Prof. Peirce's calculations of the perturbations of Uranus about the time of the discovery of Neptune by Leverrier and Adams, "Peirce" (says Dr. Thomas Hill of Portland, ex-President of Harvard University) "showed that the discovery of Neptune was a happy accident; not that Leverrier's calculations had not been exact and wonderfully laborious, and deserving of the highest honor, but because there were, in fact, two very different solutions of the perturbations of Uranus possible. Leverrier had correctly calculated one, but the actual planet solved the other, and the actual planet and Leverrier's ideal one lay in the same direction from the earth *only* in 1846." A writer in the New York *Nation,* October 14, 1880, says: "When, in 1846, he [Peirce] announced in the American Academy that Galle's discovery of Neptune in the place predicted by Leverrier was a happy accident, the President, Edward Everett, 'hoped the announcement would not be made public; nothing could be more improbable than such a coincidence.' 'Yes,' replied Peirce, 'but it would be still more strange if there were on error in my calculations'; a confident assertion which the lapse of time has vindicated."

The reader of Dr. Holmes' class poems may like to know the full names of certain classmates to whose memory poems are dedicated. The initials J. D. R. stand for Jacob D. Russell; F. W. C. for Frederick William Crocker; J. A. for Joseph Angier; and H. C. M., H. S., J. K. W., respectively for Horatius C. Merriam, Howard Sargent, and Josiah Kendall Waite.

There are no very strongly marked epochs in his poetical development; still his poetical activity may be roughly divided into four periods, each with characteristics of its own. During the first period—from 1830 to 1849—the greater portion of the best humorous poems were written. From 1849 to 1857—or from the fortieth to the forty-eighth year of the poet—he seems, as he himself has intimated, to have fallen into a sort of literary lethargy, and there was scarcely a poem produced which takes rank with the work of other periods in his life. There is scarcely a humorous poem in this group; and only three satirical ones which stick in one's memory,—namely, **"The Moral Bully," "The Old Man of the Sea,"** and **"The Sweet Little Man."** It is a curious coincidence that this barren period extends precisely over the period of his summerings at Pittsfield, and over his career as a lecturer. In 1857 came the *Atlantic Monthly*; and the first contributions of Holmes to its pages—prose and poetry—form the finest literary work of his life. The poems published in the "Autocrat" are of so uniformly high an order that one may consider them as forming a group by themselves (1857-1858). They include such famous pieces as **"The Chambered Nautilus," "Latter-Day Warnings," "Æstivation," "The One-Hoss Shay,"** and **"Ode for a Social Meeting."** The period from 1858 to the present time is distinguished by a very much larger proportion than before of anniversary and memorial verses, and other *vers d'occasion,* and for a decided preponderance of serious over humorous poems.

His early humorous poetry (and his later also) is idiomatic, pitched in a conversational key, full of bright fancies, rippling laughter, crisp and sparkling rhythm, and pleases most in virtue of the use of familiar and homely objects placed in the most incongruous relations. But we are not going to be betrayed into an analysis of Dr. Holmes' *vers de société.* Rash would be the man who should attempt it; and he would get no thanks for his pains either. Nor shall his early humorous poems be quoted. There is but one way: you must buy his poetical works and read them,—read them and laugh, and find your moral atmosphere cleared, your breath freer, your digestion better, and your whole nature sunnier than before.

A feature of all his versification is its neatness,—no slovenly rhymes, no slipshod metres. And Pope himself never crammed more meaning into single lines and stanzas, which gleam with the polish and delicate finish of fresh-minted coins of gold. Where will you find greater condensation (outside of the writings of Tacitus) than in such lines as these:—

> The sexton, stooping to the quivering floor
> *Till the great caldron spills its brassy roar,*
> Whirls the hot axle, etc.
>
> > **"The Bells"**

> These are the scenes: a boy appears;
>   Set life's round dial in the sun,
> Count the swift arc of seventy years,
>   His frame is dust; his work is done.
>
> > **"Birthday of Daniel Webster"**

> True to all truth the world denies,
>   Not tongue-tied for its gilded sin;
> Not always right in all men's eyes,
>   But faithful to the light within.
>
> > **"A Birthday Tribute to James Freeman Clarke"**

> Its irised ceiling rent, its sunless crypt unsealed.
>
> > **"The Chambered Nautilus"**

> For these the blossom-sprinkled turf
>   That floods the lonely graves
> *When Spring rolls in her sea-green surf*
>   *In flowery-foaming waves.*
>
> > **"The Two Armies"**

There is still another whole compartment in the mind of this many-sided man which we have not explored,—his tender passion and delicate feminine sensibility. Every person of mature years who passed through the fiery furnace of the American Civil War of 1861-65 came out chastened and purified and elevated in nature. Already in 1861 we seem to see the influence of the opening war upon Holmes, in the prelude to his **"Songs in Many Keys"** (1861). After this his mind seems sobered and elevated to more earnest and impassioned poetical thought. But perhaps it is only the sobering influence of years that we notice. The key-note of the change is struck in the prelude just mentioned:—

> Song is thin air; our hearts' exulting play
> Beats time but to the tread of marching deeds,
> Following the mighty van that Freedom leads,
> Her glorious standard flaming to the day!
> The crimsoned pavement where a hero bleeds
> Breathes nobler lessons than the poet's lay.
> Strong arms, broad breasts, brave hearts, are better
>   worth
> Than strains that sing the ravished echoes dumb.

The poem **"Musa"** is full of a youthful, rich, Oriental fire and passion that one had hardly suspected in Holmes,—reminds you of some of Bayard Taylor's poems of the East. So do the following two stanzas (**"Fantasia"**):—

> Kiss mine eyelids, beauteous Morn,
> Blushing into life new-born!
> Lend me violets for my hair,
> And thy russet robe to wear,
> And thy ring of rosiest hue
> Set in drops of diamond dew!
>
> Kiss my cheek, thou noontide ray,
> From my Love so far away!
> Let thy splendor streaming down
> Turn its pallid lilies brown,
> Till its darkening shade reveal
> Where his passion pressed its seal!

"Under the Violets" has the delicacy of **"Claribel,"** and all the artlessness of Herrick's pieces without their sensuality. **"Iris, her Book,"** is full of that subtle, tremulous feeling, and sensitive psychical affinity which unlocks for its author the inmost souls of such young girls as Iris and Myrtle Hazard. A poet never hung more breathlessly over an opening lily, or gazed more reverently into the innocent little face of the spring's first violet, than the creator of Iris and Elsie has watched the Psyche unfolding in a young girl's nature, or new-born Eros trying his wings in the rosy light of her fancy.

One topic still remains to be touched upon, and we would not treat it in an ungracious or complaining spirit,—namely, the Anglicism of his poetical vehicle or metrical style. That this is not original does not detract from the merit of his poetry in the eyes of those who were partially nourished by the poetry of the Queen Anne school. He is a man of the world, a university man, and we should hardly expect such a one to strike out a new style in poetry, like the great lovers of nature,—Wordsworth, Burns, Emerson, Whitman: still it remains to inquire how the style of the Boileau and Pope school acquired such a life-long hold upon him. The answer is doubtless to be found in the circumstance that in his father's house, and in the university town where he lived as a youth, that species of poesy was exclusively fashionable at the time when his poetical style was forming. If there is a great deal in Holmes that reminds one of William Spencer, of Crabbe, Pope, Hood, and the Prize Poets of the English universities,—it is because these were the popular poets when he was a boy and when he was in college. He tells us in the "Atlantic Almanac" that he and the other children of his father's house were educated on such English books as Miss Edgeworth's "Frank" and "Parent's Assistant," "Original Poems," "Evenings at Home," and "Cheap Repository Tracts," and says that he considers it to have been a great misfortune that they should have been fed on these English books instead of on American ones, for the former were full of words that had no meaning for them. They found themselves in a strange world where James was called "Jem," not Jim as they always heard it; where a young woman was called "a stout wench"; where the boys played, not at marbles, but at "taw"; where mischievous boys crawled through a gap in a hawthorn hedge to steal Farmer Giles' red-streaks, instead of shining over the fence to hook Daddy Jones' Baldwins; where Hodge used to go to the ale-house to get his mug of beer, whereas they used to see old Joe steering for the grocery to get his glass of rum; where toffy and lollypop were eaten in place of molasses-candy and gibraltars; where poachers were pulled up before the squire for knocking down hares with sticks, while to their knowledge boys hunted rabbits with guns, or set "figgery-fours" for them without fear of the constable; "where birds were taken with a wonderful substance they called bird-lime; where boys studied in *forms,* and where there were fags, and ushers, and barring-out; where there were shepherds, and gypsies, and tinkers, and orange-women, who sold *China* oranges out of barrows; where there were larks and nightingales instead of yellow-birds and bobolinks." Upon all this the Doctor remarks: "What a mess,—there is no better word for it,—what a mess was made of it in our young minds in the attempt to reconcile what we read about with what we saw. It was like putting a picture of Regent's Park on one side of a stereoscope, and a picture of Boston Common on the other, and trying to make one of them. The end was that we all grew up with a mental squint that we could never get rid of."

How closely the heroics of Dr. Holmes resemble those of Goldsmith and Pope no careful reader needs to be told. As for Hood, there is a striking resemblance between his features and those of Holmes, and there is a striking general resemblance between the style and literary methods of the two in some of their humorous poems. Holmes is unique and original in matter, only his style shows the influence of Hood. To show to what purpose Hood was read by Boston and Cambridge people about the time when Holmes was making his first poems, read the following stanza selected by the writer from many similar ones in the *Boston Daily Advertiser* for 1830. The verses are called **"Fashionable Eclogues"**:—

> Next year, papa! next year, mamma!
> You know I'm thirty-two,
> (I call myself but twenty-six,
> So this is *entre nous:*)
> *Next* year I shall be thirty-three,
> I've not a day to lose,
> Oh, let us go to town at once,
> I'm lost if you refuse.

Compare the metrical flow of this with Hood's "Sally Simpkins' Lament":—

Oh Jones, my dear! Oh dear! my Jones,
   What is become of you?

Oh! Sally dear, it is too true,—
   The half that you remark
Is come to say my other half
   Is bit off by a shark!'

Oh! Sally, sharks do things by halves,
   Yet most completely do!
A bite in one place seems enough,
   But I've been bit in two.

Hood's "Ode on a Distant Prospect of Clapham Academy" contains just the touch of Holmes in his **"Old Cambridge."** Hood says:—

Ay, that's the very house! I know
Its ugly windows, ten a-row!
   Its chimneys in the rear!
And there's the iron rod so high,
That drew the thunder from the sky
   And turned our table-beer!

And Mrs. S———? Doth she abet
(Like Pallas in the parlor) yet
   Some favor'd two or three,—
The little Crichtons of the hour,
Her muffin-medals that devour,
   And swill her prize—bohea?

And Holmes' metres run as follows:—

The yellow meetin' house,—can you tell
Just where it stood before it fell,
   Prey of the vandal foe,—
Our dear old temple, loved so well,
   By ruthless hands laid low?
Where, tell me, was the Deacon's pew?
Whose hair was braided in a queue?
(For there were pig-tails not a few),—
   That's what I'd like to know.

So much for the metrical vehicle of Holmes, and the models on which he formed his style. A poet must choose some style or other, and the Boston singer found that of the school of Pope and Hood best fitted for his use. By any other name the rose would smell as sweet. In the case of humorous or comic verse, we need not quarrel much with the style, if the matter be but good.

Inasmuch as Dr. Holmes has not yet edited a selection of his best poems, the following anthology may be an acceptable guide for hurried readers; and let it be premised that all the preludes of the poet are exquisite pieces of poetry and sentiment. The best poems, in the judgment of the writer, are these:—[2]

"Old Ironsides"; "The Last Leaf"; "The Cambridge Churchyard"; "My Aunt"; "Evening by a Tailor"; "The Dorchester Giant"; "The Comet"; "The Music Grinders"; "The September Gale"; "The Height of the Ridiculous"; "On Lending a Punch-Bowl"; "Nux Postcœnatica"; "A Modest Request"; "The Stethoscope Song"; "The Meeting of the Dryads"; "The Mysterious Visitor"; "The Toadstool"; "The Spectre Pig"; "The Ballad of the Oysterman"; "The Hot Season"; "The Moral Bully"; "The Old Man of the Sea"; "The Sweet Little Man"; "The Chambered Nautilus"; "The Two Armies"; "Musa"; "A Parting Health"; "Prologue"; "Latter-Day Warnings"; "A Good Time Going"; "The Last Blossom"; "Contentment"; "Æstivation"; "The Deacon's Masterpiece, or The Wonderful One-Hoss Shay"; "Ode for a Social Meeting"; "Under the Violets"; "Iris, her Book"; "Aunt Tabitha"; "Epilogue to the Breakfast-Table Series"; "The Old Man dreams"; "The Boys"; "The Last Survivor"; "The Archbishop and Gil Blas"; "Benjamin Peirce"; "Dorothy Q."; "The Organ-Blower"; "Rip Van Winkle, M. D."; "Chanson without Music"; "A Sea Dialogue"; "Grandmother's Story of Bunker-Hill Battle"; "Old Cambridge"; "How the Old Horse won the Bet"; "The Iron Gate"; "My Aviary"; "For Whittier's Seventieth Birthday"; "The Coming Era"; "Post-Prandial."

Notes

1. "I would go fifty miles on foot," says Yorick, "for I have not a horse worth riding on, to kiss the hand of that man whose generous heart will give up the reins of his imagination into his author's hands,—be pleased he knows not why, and cares not wherefore."

2. The poems are given in the order in which they occur in the latest edition (1882), and may therefore be read consecutively and chronologically by referring to the table of contents of the poems.

Walter Jerrold (essay date 1893)

SOURCE: Jerrold, Walter. "The Poet." In *Oliver Wendell Holmes*, pp. 29-61. London: Swan Sonnenschein and Co., 1893.

[*In the following excerpt, Jerrold discusses the critical reception of Holmes's work at the end of the nineteenth century.*]

The Chieftain, by William Winter.[1]

Read at the "Atlantic" Festival, in Commemoration of the Seventieth Birthday of Oliver Wendell Holmes, at Boston, December 3, 1879.

If that glad song had ebbed away,
   Which, rippling on through smiles and tears,
Has bathed with showers of diamond spray
   The rosy fields of seventy years,—

If that sweet voice were hushed to-day,
    What should we say?

At first we thought him but a jest
    A ray of laughter, quick to fade;
We did not dream how richly blest
    In his pure life our lives were made:
Till soon the aureole shone, confest,
    Upon his crest.

When violets fade the roses blow;
    When laughter dies the passions wake:
His royal song that slept below,
    Like Arthur's sword beneath the lake,
Long since has flashed its fiery glow
    O'er all we know.

That song has poured its sacred light
    On crimson flags in freedom's van,
And blessed their serried ranks, who fight
    Life's battle here for truth and man—
An oriflamme, to cheer the right,
    Through darkest night!

That song has flecked with rosy gold
    The sails that fade o'er fancy's sea;
Relumed the storied days of old;
    Presaged the glorious life to be;
And many a sorrowing heart consoled
    In grief untold.

When, shattered on the loftiest steep
    The statesman's glory ever found,
That heart, so like the boundless deep,
    Broke, in the deep no heart can bound,
How did his dirge of sorrow weep
    O'er Webster's sleep!

How sweetly did his spirit pour
    The strains that make the tear-drops start,
When, on this bleak New England shore,
    With Tara's harp and Erin's heart,
He thrilled us to the bosom's core
    With thoughts of Moore!

The shamrock, green on Liffey's side,
    The lichen 'neath New England snows,
White daisies of the fields of Clyde,
    Twined ardent round old Albion's rose,
Bloom in his verse, as blooms the bride
    With love and pride.

The silken tress, the mantling wine,
    Red roses, summer's whispering leaves,
The lips that kiss, the hands that twine,
    The heart that loves, the heart that grieves—
They all have found a deathless shrine
    In his rich line!

Ah well, that voice can charm us yet,
    And still that shining tide of song,
Beneath a sun not soon to set,
    In golden music flows along.
With dew of joy our eyes are wet—
    Not of regret.
For still, as comes the festal day,

In many a temple, far and near,
    The words that all have longed to say,
The words that all are proud to hear,
    Fall from his lips, with conquering sway,
        Or grave or gay.

No moment this for passion's heat,
    Nor mine the voice to give it scope,
When love and fame and beauty meet
    To crown their Memory and their Hope!
I cast white lilies, cool and sweet,
    Here at his feet.

True bard, true soul, true man, true friend!
    Ah, gently on that reverend head
Ye snows of wintry age descend,
    Ye shades of mortal night be shed!
Peace guide and guard him to the end,
    And God defend!

There is a rare pathetic touch about some of Holmes's unique *vers d'occasion* which, probably entirely overlooked at the time of the verses being spoken, is not too obvious even to those reading the poet in their study. It is found where the poet explains how well he is aware that all his listeners have come ready to smile at the anticipated "funny things," to pucker their lips at his first pun, and to roar with laughter at the coming *mot*—

I know my audience. All the gay and young
Love the light antics of a playful tongue;
And these, remembering some expansive line
My lips let loose among the nuts and wine,
Are all impatience till the opening pun
Proclaims the witty shamfight is begun.
Two-fifths at least, if not the total half,
Have come infuriate for an earthquake laugh.

. . . . .

I know a tailor, once a friend of mine,
Expects great doings in the button line,—
For mirth's concussions rip the outward case,
And plant the stitches in a tenderer place.
I know my audience,—these shall have their due;
A smile awaits them ere my song is through![2]

They have come, that is, to be amused and tickled by the humorist and wit rather than to be elevated and edified by the poet and philosopher. Yet though the poet recognises this, and in his quiet, half-playful, half-reproving way thus tells his audience that he does so, he manages to give them much wisdom and much beautiful poetry, along with the quaintness of expression and illustration—the verbal quips and cranks which had come to be looked upon as the most important of his literary merchandise, and the rightful due of those who listened to him. This character for pleasantry which he had so early acquired—**"Urania,"** from which the above passage is quoted, was written in 1846—has probably been largely responsible for the colouring of the whole, or at any rate a great part, of Holmes's poetic work. Even with some of the essentially pathetic pieces, there is yet an atmosphere of humour through which they are seen. Take, for example, from among the earlier poems, **"The Last Leaf,"** "suggested by the sight of old Major Melville in his cocked hat and breeches,"[3] which won the commendation of so fastidious a critic as Edgar Allan Poe, who indeed made a copy of it, which copy fell later into the hands of the gratified author. It was this same poem, too, which so fascinated Abraham Lincoln that he learned it by heart, and was fond of referring to the fourth verse as one of the most pathetic passages in literature:—

I saw him once before,
As he passed by the door,
   And again
The pavement stones resound,
As he totters o'er the ground
   With his cane.

They say that in his prime,
Ere the pruning-knife of Time
   Cut him down,
Not a better man was found
By the Crier on his round
   Through the town.

But now he walks the streets,
And he looks at all he meets
   Sad and wan,
And he shakes his feeble head,
That it seems as if he said,
   'They are gone.'

The mossy marbles rest
On the lips that he has prest
   In their bloom,
And the names he loved to hear
Have been carved for many a year
   On the tomb.

My grandmamma has said—
Poor old lady, she is dead
   Long ago—
That he had a Roman nose,
And his cheek was like a rose
   In the snow.

But now his nose is thin,
And it rests upon his chin
   Like a staff,
And a crook is in his back,
And a melancholy crack
   In his laugh.

I know it is a sin
For me to sit and grin
   At him here;
But the old three-cornered hat,
And the breeches and all that,
   Are so queer!

And if I should live to be
The last leaf upon the tree
   In the spring,

Let them smile, as I do now,
At the old forsaken bough
   Where I cling.[4]

The second and fifth verses show us the humourist rather over-colouring the work of the poet. "The pruning-knife of Time," for instance, seems to be out of keeping with the quiet pathetic feeling of the greater part of the poem, which is just sufficiently charged with humour to keep it truly pathetic without being sentimental; it is, indeed, a very good example of that close interconnection of humour and pathos which is so often remarked, and to which it is, perhaps, that such writers as Charles Lamb owe their peculiar place in our affections.

The too-pronounced presence of the humourist, although it may jar upon us in reading some of Holmes's pathetic poems, is yet only an occasional blemish; generally the humour is but like the glow of summer lightning, bringing what it illumines nearer to us, while at times the humourist is not present at all—no more than the Thomas Hood of *The Epping Hunt* and *The Tale of a Trumpet* is visible in the Thomas Hood of *The Bridge of Sighs* and *The Song of the Shirt*—witness the short, sharp, defiant yet exultant ring of **"Old Ironsides."** The fervour of the opening line—

Ay, tear her tattered ensign down—[5]

rings through the whole poem, making our pulses leap and our blood tingle as with a sudden blare of trumpet. Small wonder is it that this short impromptu[6] should have echoed and re-echoed throughout the States— serving effectually its object of saving the old frigate *Constitution,* popularly known as *Old Ironsides,* from proposed destruction. In another of these earlier poems also—**"The Cambridge Churchyard"**—we have a sustained flight of

The lonely spirit of the mournful lay,
Which lives immortal as the verse of Gray.[7]

How truly Gray-like in both form and spirit, for instance, is this single stanza—a stanza which embodies in itself the *motif* of the whole poem—

Hast thou a tear for buried love?
   A sigh for transient power?
All that a century left above
   Go, read it in an hour!"[8]

It is simple in expression, yet direct in meaning as Goldsmith himself might have written.

In 1851 Mary Russell Mitford devoted a section (xxxi.) of her pleasant *Recollections of a Literary Life* to Oliver Wendell Holmes, and this she did mainly on the strength of one poem, **"Astræa,"**—"a little book of less than forty pages"—that had been delivered before the

Phi Beta Kappa Society the previous year. This instant recognition by Miss Mitford of the poet from over sea is especially noteworthy as taking place before the publication of the first English edition of Holmes's poems. A year later that first English edition appeared, and probably owed its appearance at that time to the unqualified welcome extended to it by a critic of such true instinct as Mary Russell Mitford. A glance at these words of welcome, in the light of the poet's later great success, may well interest us. In introducing those passages from **"Astraea"** which had especially attracted her, the critic says: "In these days of curious novelty, nothing has taken me more pleasantly by surprise than the school of true and original poetry that has sprung up among our blood-relations (I had well-nigh called them our fellow-countrymen) across the Atlantic; they who speak the same tongue and inherit the same literature. And of all this flight of genuine poets, I hardly know any one so original as Dr. Holmes. For him we can find no living prototype; to track his footsteps, we must travel back as far as Pope or Dryden; and, to my mind, it would be well if some of our own bards would take the same journey—provided always it produced the same result. Lofty, poignant, graceful, grand, high of thought and clear of word, we could fancy ourselves reading some pungent page of *Absalom and Achitophel,* or of the *Moral Epistles,* if it were not for the pervading nationality, which, excepting Whittier, American poets have generally wanted,[9] and for that true reflection of the manners and the follies of the age, without which satire would fail alike of its purpose and its name."

Poetry has probably existed as long as human language, yet an adequate definition of what it really is that we mean by the word is yet to seek. It has been attempted numberless times by widely different persons; as often has it been sought, perhaps, as the true meaning of another word—wit. Yet, despite this, we are far from having a satisfactory definition of either of them. Indeed it is probable that when found it will be discovered that it embraces the two. I myself do not intend adding to the number of those who have sought to express in an axiom what poetry exactly is and what it is not, for, as quaint old Isaac Barrow expresses it with regard to wit, "often it consisteth in one knows not what, and springeth up one can hardly tell how." All that we can say is, I do not know what poetry is, but *this* is poetry, forthwith giving an example of much riches of thought in a little room of words. To show in Holmes's poetry the simple terseness of expression with which he conveys a deal of meaning, we may take such lines as these on the first approach of spring, where the second half of the first line—in its context—suggests so very much more than the words would ordinarily convey:—

> Doubtful at first, suspected more than seen,
> The southern slopes are fringed with tender green.[10]

Or, in another vein, we may take such an example as this—

> Alone, alone, the awful past I tread
> White with the marbles of the slumbering dead.

Or this couplet from **"Spring,"** the same poem from which is taken the first of the two preceding quotations,—a couplet which Miss Mitford instanced as being unmatched in flower painting—

> The spendthrift crocus, bursting through the mould
> Naked and shivering with his cup of gold.[11]

Holmes's occasional verse and his more particularly humorous writings we will consider later; here we are more especially concerned with his poetry, which has been—to use a much ill-treated expression—inspired, that is, written not so much in accordance with a request from without as in fulfilment of a command from within. To seek for such a poet's "models," to say he is of this or that "school," a follower of this or that "leader," a writer in this or the other "mould," were a difficult task and a thankless. An American critic,[12] who has exercised his ingenuity on this question, has found Holmes's chief master, the man by whom his style was most considerably influenced, in Thomas Hood! In support of his criticism, Mr. Kennedy quotes some verses which he implies, but does not state, are by Holmes, along with some stanzas from one of Hood's comic ballads. The examples given are both in common ballad metre, but there all similarity ends; the American verses do not at all "show to what purpose Hood was read by Boston and Cambridge people when Holmes was making his first poems."[13] Hood's poems might never have crossed the Atlantic for any influence of his style discernible in the **"Fashionable Eclogue"** quoted.

> Next year, papa! next year, mamma!
> You know I'm thirty-two,

is very much more in the style of Thomas Haynes Bayley, or even of Praed, than in that of Hood. Both Hood and Holmes are true humourists—both of them have "touched alike the springs of laughter and the source of tears;"[14] and examples might, it is true, be quoted, showing the apparent influence of Hood's punning style—

> Milton to Stilton would give in, and Solomon to Salmon,
> And Roger Bacon be a bore, and Francis Bacon gammon![15]

Or, again, one might take a single poem—**"Lexington,"** for instance—and declare that Holmes's poetry bore distinct evidence of having been influenced by the songs and melodies of Thomas Moore—

> Slowly the mist o'er the meadow was creeping,
> Bright on the dewy buds glistened the sun,

When from his couch, while his children were sleeping,
  Rose the bold rebel and shouldered his gun.[16]

Might we not imagine that Erin's laureate himself had
touched the harp-strings which responded thus? Or, yet
again, we might take that exquisite gem, **"The Chambered Nautilus,"** and say, Here is the work of a poet
who must have drunk deep and long at seventeenth-
century founts—who is closely and sympathetically
acquainted with Abraham Cowley, Andrew Marvell,
and kindred souls.

  This is the ship of pearl, which, poets feign,
    Sails the unshadowed main,—
    The venturous bark that flings
  On the sweet summer wind its purpled wings
  In gulfs enchanted, where the Siren sings,
    And coral reefs lie bare,
  Where the cold sea-maids rise to sun their streaming
  hair.[17]

The task of tracing each line of a poet's work to some
previous writer is, however, an ungracious one;
plagiarism and imitation are less common than some
would have us believe, and what often appear as such
would prove, if proof were possible, nothing but mere
coincidence. "Given certain factors," as the Autocrat
expresses it, "and a sound brain should always evolve
the same fixed product with the certainty of Babbage's
calculating machine."[18] The youthful poet, with but rar-
est, if there be any, exception, will, at first, express
himself in forms with which he is familiar, and the attainment of a form for himself will be a mere matter of
evolution, as he finds for himself the way in which it is
best for him to give out that which he has to impart. We
might take various isolated poems or passages from
Holmes's works, showing the apparent influence or
imitation of widely differing writers, as I have shown,
yet we should but little affect his title to originality;
indeed, early as her criticism was formulated, Miss Mitford was not far wrong in hailing Holmes as one of the
first of America's peculiarly *national* poets. He is not
national in the sense of having written for all time the
legends of the Indians in a *Hiawatha*; yet how much
more he represents the peculiar temper of his country-
men than Longfellow is very obvious on the slightest
comparison of their works. He is not national in the
sense of having treated of native places and legends—
with their names!—such as we have in *Mogg Megone*.
Yet there can, I think, be little doubt about his being
even more national than Whittier, with whom it is that
Miss Mitford brackets him. He is not national in the
sense of having caught and perpetuated in a poem the
dialect of a *Hosea Biglow*; yet I should place him before
Lowell in this regard. He is not national in the sense of
having struck a new vehicle for poetic expression such
as is given us in *The Leaves of Grass*; yet it is apparent
that even more than Walt Whitman is Holmes peculiarly

national. Longfellow and Lowell, Whittier and Whitman, each represents some particular phase of the
national life, character, traditions, or peculiarities; but
Holmes draws upon all these, and subtly, yet consistently, interweaves in his work any such real difference
as may exist between the American nation and the parent race from which it has mainly sprung. The result is
a curious interweaving of shrewd *Poor Richard*-like
common sense, with high and beautiful thoughts,—the
texture of poetry, which, as I take it, is the most
peculiarly national that America has yet produced. Pe-
gasus has not yet been thoroughly acclimatised, as yet
he is only allowed to fly with clipped wings, for fear he
should fly beyond the common bound of common sense,
or to feel when he tries a flight that

  The world's cart-collar hugs his throat.[19]

We have, scattered throughout Holmes's three volumes
of poems, delicate hints of stories and traditions of old
Colonial days, along with beautiful descriptive passages, and the constant recurrence of a mirth-provoking
humour often allied with high moral truths and touching pathos, in a way that is strikingly characteristic, and
which is very much wanting in what is called, or calls
itself, "the new humour." His many loving references to
the old days before the Declaration of Independence,
and also to "Mother" England, as Mistress Bradstreet
had called it, testify to a certain wholesome conservatism in the mind of the poet, and do not one whit lessen
his great love and admiration for the present Republic.
Among his themes, dealing with the old days in
America, not one is more delightful than **"Dorothy Q.,
a Family Portrait,"** a poem which, written in 1871,
has all the freshness and spirit of the author's earlier
works, and which is peculiarly representative of his
style both of thought and expression.

  O Damsel Dorothy! Dorothy Q.!
  Strange is the gift that I owe to you.
        · · · · ·

  What if a hundred years ago
  Those close-shut lips had answered No,
  When forth the tremulous question came
  That cost the maiden her Norman name,
  And under the folds that look so still
  The bodice swelled with the bosom's thrill?
  Should I be I, or would it be
  One-tenth another, to nine-tenths me?

  Soft is the breath of a maiden's YES:
  Not the light gossamer stirs with less;
  But never a cable that holds so fast
  Through all the battles of wave and blast,
  And never an echo of speech or song
  That lives in the babbling air so long!
  There were tones in the voice that whispered then
  You may hear to-day in a hundred men.

O lady and lover, how faint and far
Your images hover,—and here we are,
Solid and stirring in flesh and bone,—
Edward's and Dorothy's—all their own,—
A goodly record for Time to show
Of a syllable spoken so long ago!—
Shall I bless you, Dorothy, or forgive
For the tender whisper that bade me live?

It shall be a blessing, my little maid!
I will heal the stab of the Red-Coat's blade,
And freshen the gold of the tarnished frame,
And gild with a rhyme your household name.[20]

Dorothy Q. was Dorothy Quincy, Holmes's great-grandmother—

Grandmother's mother: her age, I guess,
Thirteen summers or something less.[21]

Another delightful story-poem of the old time is **"Grandmother's Story of Bunker-Hill Battle, as she saw it from the Belfry."** Curiously enough, in this poem we have at the conclusion a theme similar to that in the passage just quoted; after telling her grandchildren how, as a girl, she had watched the fight, and fainted, and been carried home—

When I woke from dreams affrighted the evening
lamps were lighted,—
On the floor a youth was lying; his bleeding breast
was bare.

. . . . .

For they all thought he was dying, as they gathered
round him crying,—
And they said, 'Oh, how they'll miss him!' and, 'What
will his mother do?'
Then, his eyelids just unclosing like a child's that has
been dozing,
He faintly murmured, 'Mother!'—and—I saw his eyes
were blue.

'Why, grandma, how you're winking!' Ah, my child,
it sets me thinking
Of a story not like this one. Well, he somehow lived
along;
So we came to know each other, and I nursed him like
a—mother,
Till at last he stood before me, tall, and rosy-cheeked,
and strong.

And we sometimes walked together in the pleasant
summer weather,—
'Please to tell us what his name was?' Just your own,
my little dear,—
There's his picture Copley painted: we became so
well acquainted,
That—in short, that's why I'm grandma, and you
children all are here![22]

Another old-world theme is touched upon in **"Agnes,"** which tells, in simple ballad metre and language, the pathetic story of a New England knight and his humble love; how he makes her his mistress and then, she having saved his life at Lisbon during the earthquake, marries her—

Thus Agnes won her noble name,
Her lawless lover's hand;
The lowly maiden so became
A lady in the land![23]

One of the most striking features of Holmes's writings—both prose and poetry—is the evidence of the remarkable power which he has of seizing upon happy similes; a page is often rich with a wealth of imagery that would serve a "minor" writer for a volume. That Holmes is a true poet is a matter about which there cannot be any doubt, despite the fact that many persons would add, "Yes, a true *humorous* poet,"—implying in their use of the word humorous a something derogatory to the man's genius as a poet. Yes, he is a humorous poet; and in the peculiar sense of being a true poet and a great humourist combined we can only find his equal in Thomas Hood. Although both as poets and as humourists they were quite unlike, still in the peculiar combination of the two functions they are the same. They are not poets, without the saving quality of humour; they are not versifying humorists like a Coleman, a Hook, or a W. S. Gilbert, who are humourists merely using the poetic vehicle stripped of all that makes it poetry. Holmes is a didactic poet, not

dealing counsel from a lofty height
That makes the lowly hate it,

but using his poetry as a means to teach men the truths that have come to him as one of themselves, and it is the *entente cordiale* consequently established between writer and readers that makes him so widely loved. It is not often in his pages that we light upon a purely imaginative poem, such as **"The Chambered Nautilus"** and **"Musa"** and a few more, but when we do we are sure to find that they bear instant evidence of their origin in the alembic of a pure poet's soul. Of the combination of humour and pathos referred to we have frequent examples in that most striking series of *vers d'occasion* entitled in the collected works, *Poems of the Class of '29*. This series, which extended from 1851 until 1889, while giving us examples of many different moods, has yet running like a silver thread through all a bright, unfailing, humour-loving optimism. After reading, one year, a half-regretful musing over their long past, their "class poet" would come before "The Boys," as he called them, with a rousing verse of humour:—

I like full well the deep resounding swell
Of mighty symphonies with chords inwoven;
But sometimes, too, a song of Burns—don't you?
After a solemn storm-blast of Beethoven.

Good to the heels the well-worn slipper feels
When the tired player shuffles off the buskin;

A page of Hood may do a fellow good
  After a scolding from Carlyle or Ruskin.[24]

The very next year we have a really pathetic picture called up before us of the last survivor of the class:—

Yes! the vacant chairs tell sadly we are going, going
  fast,
And the thought comes strangely o'er me, who will
  live to be the last?

. . . . .

His figure shows but dimly, his face I scarce can
  see,—
There's something that reminds me,—it looks like—is
  it he?
He? Who? No voice may whisper what wrinkled brow
  shall claim
The wreath of stars that circles our last survivor's
  name.[25]

Celebrated as they thus have been by the greatest of their number the members of the Harvard Class of '29 will enjoy a unique fame, for the poems written for their anniversary meeting are something far better in quality than we are accustomed to associate with poetical work produced in such circumstances.

Year by year, like milestones placed,
Mark the record Friendship traced.
Prisoned in the walls of time
Life has notched itself in rhyme.[26]

Holmes's occasional verse is really remarkable for its combination of the qualities which characterise the rest of his poetry—one becomes aware at once that the poems are no laboured task which the poet has badgered his brains to produce for the stated occasion, but are the fresh outpourings of a cheerful, healthy and remarkably ready poetic nature. Some beautiful pieces celebrate various Harvard anniversaries, other than those connected with the class of '29, meetings of alumni, etc. The "old boy" tells them, in verses always containing an undercurrent of deep thought, what they dreamed of when young, and what has come in the shape of experience with the gathering years—

We've seen the little tricks of life, its varnish and
  veneer,
Its stucco-fronts of character flake off and disappear,
We've learned that oft the brownest hands will heap
  the biggest pile,
And met with many a 'perfect brick' beneath a rimless
  'tile.'

What dreams we've had of deathless name, as
  scholars, statesmen, bards,
While Fame, the lady with the trump, held up her
  picture cards!
Till, having nearly played our game, she gaily
  whispered, 'Ah!
I said you should be something grand,—you'll soon
  be grandpapa.'[27]

In 1836 on the celebration of the two-hundredth anniversary of Harvard, Holmes—*felix audacia*—sang a song of his own. Fifty years later, at a similar celebration, he read a long poem, full of the fire, fervour, and character which we find in his earlier work. Whenever such occasions have arisen during his long life, Holmes has been called upon to celebrate the event in verse, and not alone on such occasions, but also on innumerable minor and more private ones, at times when people were gathered together to hail the coming, speed the parting guest. Preluding *Songs of Many Seasons* in 1874 the poet himself said,—

Not for glory, not for pelf,
Not, be sure, to please myself,
Not for any meaner ends,—
Always 'by request of friends.'

Here's the cousin of a King,—
Would I do the civil thing?
Here's the first-born of a Queen:
Here's a slant-eyed Mandarin.

Would I polish off Japan?
Would I greet this famous man,
Prince or Prelate, Sheik or Shah?—
Figaro çi and Figaro là!

Would I just this once comply?—
So they teased and teased till I
(Be the truth at once confessed)
Wavered—yielded—did my best.[28]

Even in his lighter poems, those dealing with essentially humorous subjects, or those with which he delighted after-dinner audiences, we have evidence that, as he expresses it, while his gay stanzas

pleased the banquet's lords,
The soul within was tuned to deeper chords![29]

Among the humorous poems which we find in Holmes's three volumes several have for many years been favourites of readers and reciters at popular entertainments—such, for instance, as the **"Deacon's Masterpiece; or, The Wonderful One-Hoss Shay,"**[30] a poem which may well stand as representative of the best expression of American humour. This is, however, but one of many poems which might be included in the same category. In these poems humour has been the *motif,* while in many others humour is used as a light the better to throw up the meaning which the author wishes to convey—as the jam of sweetness in which the doctor-poet often disguises a powder of teaching. Humour is certainly one of the essential factors in the constitution of Holmes's genius, although he can at times wax deadly serious when combating what appears to him as humbug or meanness, writing even with scathing satire at times, as when he addressed a poem, during the inter-States struggle, to **"The Sweet Little Man,"** and dedicated it to the "Stay-at-Home Rangers"—

> Bring him the buttonless garment of woman!
> 　Cover his face lest it freckle and tan;
> Muster the Apron-String Guards on the Common,
> 　That is the corps for the sweet little man![31]

This satiric turn to his humour is frequently given in snatches of his song, as though the philosopher were driving a truth home with a weapon lent him by the poet. Of the pen he says in **"The Schoolboy,"** a song which celebrated the centennial of Phillips's Academy,—[32]

> Too ready servant, whose deceitful ways
> Full many a slip-shod line, alas! betrays;
> Hence of the rhyming thousand not a few
> Have builded worse—a great deal—than they knew.[33]

Or we may take a passage such as this from a poem read at a Medical Society dinner—

> Strong is the moral blister that will draw
> Laid on the conscience of the Man of Law,
> Whom blindfold Justice lends her eyes to see
> Truth in the scale that holds his promised fee.[34]

Or this, from verses addressed to James Russell Lowell, where we have a very happy use made of one of the most famous lines from *Chevy Chase*—

> And if we lose him our lament will be
> We have 'five hundred'—*not* 'as good as he.'[35]

Of humour pure and simple, the humour of extravagance or of fun, we have many examples scattered up and down the pages.

> A health to stout Hans Breitmann! How long before
> 　we see
> Another Hans as handsome,—as bright a man as he![36]

Of the grand new gilded dome of Boston, "the hub of the solar system," he says—

> When first in his path a young asteroid found it,
> 　As he sailed through the skies with the stars in his
> 　　wake,
> He thought 'twas the sun, and kept circling around it
> 　Till Edison signalled, 'You've made a mistake.'[37]

In reading many of these purely humorous ebullitions of playful fancy, it seems difficult to realise that they are by the poet who could at times touch the lyre with such very different effect. It is interesting to notice that during the first years of his poethood Holmes wrote some of the most wildly humorous and at the same time some of the most obviously serious of his work.

The transition from the one to the other is probably but natural—youth knows no "happy mean," if the term be not inaccurate—it is wildly playful, or, when serious, it is so in deadly earnest. In middle and later life the poet has apparently realised that his work has received most attention, and therefore, it is to be presumed, has had most effect, when he has succeeded in subtly fusing the two qualities in such a way as he has made familiar to us in a great number of his poems. It has been said that we have to go back to the date of Dryden and Pope, or at least to that of Goldsmith, for poetry to which that of Holmes is most akin. In his didactic couplets we may perhaps frequently find passages suggestive of the earlier writers, and for forceful directness, combined with simplicity of expression, we might find many lines parallel with those of Oliver Goldsmith. The humour of Dryden and Pope was the grim humour of the satirist, and not of that harmless kind whose lambent light plays around so much of Holmes's writings. With Goldsmith, the kinship is perhaps somewhat closer, although the resources of the more modern poet-doctor—for did not Goldy, too, write himself M.D.?—are more plentiful, and his wide and various knowledge of men gives him an advantage over poor Nolly.

Holmes's faculty for seizing upon similes and allusions is extraordinary and perhaps unequalled. Thomas Moore plumed himself on a friend having totted up the similes in his *Life of Sheridan,* the abundance of which, said the self-satisfied singer, was strong evidence of his poetic nature; as though it was necessary that the writer of *Lalla Rookh* and the *Irish Melodies* should have compiled a *Life of Sheridan* to prove that he was a poet! The friend who should set about so thankless a task for Oliver Wendell Holmes would at any rate be able to produce a very large total on the completion of his misapplied labours. In this regard, Lowell, perhaps, may run Holmes rather close, for he also possesses in a remarkable degree the power of instantly calling up illustrations to point that which he may be saying; for instance, how very beautiful yet how unexpected is the simile in this verse describing Huldy in the later versions of *The Courtin'*!—

> For she was jest the quiet kind
> 　Whose naturs never vary,
> Like streams that keep a summer mind
> 　Snow-hid in Jenooary.

How happy, too, is the same writer's allusion in the *Biglow Papers*!—

> We begin to think it's nater
> 　To take sarse an' not be riled;—
> Who'd expect to see a tater
> 　All on eend at bein' biled?[38]

Every page that Holmes has written, of prose or poetry, reveals his possession of this power in a remarkable degree—a power which must have gone far to give his work the high place which it holds in the regard of present readers, and to which it will probably owe much of its fame in years to come. We may glance at one or two illustrative examples of what is here insisted upon. In describing the difference between the time of youth and of age he tells us that—

> The hearts that were thumping like ships on the rocks
> Beat as quiet and steady as meeting-house clocks.[39]

> Stick to your aim: the mongrel's hold will slip,
> But only crowbars loose the bulldog's grip.[40]

> On the blue flower a bluer flower you spy,
> You stretch to pluck it—'tis a butterfly;
> The flattened tree-toads so resemble bark,
> They're hard to find as Ethiops in the dark;
> The woodcock, stiffening to fictitious mud,
> Cheats the young sportsman thirsting for his blood;
> So by long living on a single lie,
> Nay, on one truth, will creatures get its dye.[41]

> Women, with tongues
> Like polar needles, ever on the jar;
> Men, plugless word-spouts, whose deep fountains are
> Within their lungs.[42]

> Time is the angel-thief which Nature sends us
> To break the cramping fetters of our past.[43]

> How the past spreads out in vision with its far-receding train,
> Like a long-embroidered arras in the chambers of the brain.[44]

It will be seen at once by these few examples how readily the poet lays hold of similes quite apposite, yet, entirely unhackneyed and unspoiled by endless repetition, they come upon us as we read with all the pleasure of that surprise which is said to lie at the root of our delight in wit.

It is very obvious that Holmes's work contrasts very sharply with that of those morbidly melancholy "albino-poets," as he terms them, "whose refrain is 'I shall die and be forgotten, and the world will go on just as if I had never been;—yet how I have loved! how I have longed! how I have aspired!'"[45]

There is, perhaps, no commoner—and at the same time there is no more dangerous form of criticism than that which attempts to forecast the view which the Future (capitalised) will take of a given piece of work, or the works of a given author. The criticism which consists in saying, "This will live when Homer is forgotten"—"and not *till* then," as a wit is reported to have added—is of course sweeping, but it is—if one may be permitted the apparent Hibernianism—sweepingly inconclusive; it is given with an air of assurance which is begotten of the fact that the critic knows that until the Future has

become the Present—in other words until "Homer is forgotten"—his judgment though it may be called in question cannot be refuted. It is true that the work so welcomed may be forgotten during the lifetime of both critic and author,—"'tis nothing," says the critic—the author, of course, saying "Ditto, to Mr. Burke"—while triumphantly pointing to great works which Fame, the jilt, has studiously neglected for long periods and then welcomed with a smile of recognition and taken into her favour. The work hailed with delight and ranked with the greatest is perchance soon forgotten, it becomes that nine-days' wonder, that thing for which the writer for cash must pray day and night, and for which the true literary artist must as earnestly pray may not be his—"the book of the season." Such as a topical song is to music, as a daily illustrated paper is to art, so is, most often, the book of the season to literature—it is for a season and *not* for all time. Another book, published it may be at the very same time, has fallen foul of the critics, or has fallen, apparently, stillborn from the press, and is yet destined to be one of the books of the world.

I will not say of Holmes that he will be remembered when Homer is forgotten; we may, however, consider the position which he occupies among his contemporaries—the leading men of letters of America. "Who"—asked Sydney Smith, in a famous review—"Who in all the four Continents reads an American book?" The century has seen great changes, and to-day we ask, "What English publisher does not profit by pirating American books for British readers?" Holmes's works alone are procurable from half a dozen publishers other than the firm which issues his authorised collected edition. As a poet, the position which rightfully belongs to Holmes is immediately after Longfellow in point of fame, while in point of popularity he is probably to-day the very first. It may yet be true, as has been suggested, that his work is less likely to live—through being scattered over so many short pieces—through there being no one great poem to remember him by—and through so much of it being written for certain stated occasions.

Notes

1. *The Poems of William Winter*: Boston, 1881, p. 151.

2. *Poems*, i., p. 108.

3. *Mortal Antipathy*, p. 8.

4. *Poems*, i., p. 3.

5. *Poems*, i., p. 2.

6. See *ante*, p. 8.

7. *Poems*, i., p. 41.

8. *Ibid.*, i., p. 6.

9. Whitman's first volume was not issued until four years later; while none of Lowell's "national" poetry had been issued.

10. *Poems*, i., p. 197.

11. *Ibid.*

12. Mr. W. S. Kennedy.

13. W. S. Kennedy, *O. W. Holmes*, p. 287.

14. Douglas Jerrold, dedication of *Cakes and Ale* to Hood.

15. *Poems*, i. p. 88.

16. *Ibid.*, i., p. 67.

17. *Poems*, ii., p. 107.

18. *Autocrat*, p. 8.

19. Coventry Patmore: *The Angel in the House.*

20. *Poems* ii., p. 206.

21. *Ibid.*, ii., p. 205.

22. *Poems*, iii., p. 10.

23. *Ibid.*, i., p. 190.

24. *Poems*, ii., p. 73.

25. *Poems*, ii., p. 78.

26. *Ibid.*, ii., p. 201.

27. *Poems*, i., p. 265.

28. *Poems*, ii., p. 201.

29. *Ibid.*, i., p. 109.

30. *Poems*, ii., p. 131.

31. *Ibid.*, ii., p. 236.

32. See *ante*, p. 6.

33. *Poems*, iii., p. 94.

34. *Poems*, iii., p. 112.

35. *Ibid.*, iii., p. 135.

36. *Ibid.*, iii., 157.

37. *Poems*, iii., p. 81.

38. J. R. Lowell: *Collected Works*, vol. viii., p. 45.

39. *Poems*, ii., p. 66.

40. *Poems*, i., p. 121.

41. *Ibid.*, i., p. 207.

42. *Poems*, i., p. 16.

43. *Ibid.*, ii., p. 103.

44. *Ibid.*, ii., p. 81.

45. *Autocrat*, p. 185.

J. E. A. Smith (essay date 1895)

SOURCE: Smith, J. E. A. "Berkshire Jubilee Speech and Poem." In *The Poet among the Hills: Oliver Wendell Holmes in Berkshire*, pp. 49-68. Pittsfield, Mass.: George Blatchford, 1895.

[*In the following excerpt, Smith describes the context in which Holmes delivered his "Poem of Welcome" at the Berkshire Jubilee of 1844.*]

Something of Oliver Wendell Holmes' relation to Pittsfield and Berkshire is intimated in the letter with which our prologue closes; but his affiliation with the town will appear more definitely as we proceed; still using his own words as a basis and guide. And we begin with those spoken at the Berkshire Jubilee of 1844. The Berkshire Jubilee:—Fifty years ago that name would have needed no interpretation in a connection like this. The unique character of the festival, the many famous participants in it, and the great number of the mountain country's sons and daughters who flocked to it from homes in all sections of the Union, secured liberal reports of, and comments upon, its proceedings in all considerable American journals. But all things are food for edacious Time; and even a little half-century is a ravenous devourer of newspaper fame. The story of the Jubilee is still locally extant; but even at home, although a little revived by the recurrence of its fiftieth anniversary, it begins to take on the phantom-like obscurity of tradition. Elsewhere, now and then, a minute biographer alludes to it in his memoir of some prominent actor in it; taking good care to provide an explanatory foot-note, or its equivalent. Yet it was a right memorable occasion; and one that deserves a permanent record. That its name and some hint of its character will be preserved is made sure by the inclusion of Dr. Holmes' poem of welcome to it in the permanent collection of his works; but even there it calls for the annotation we are to give it here.

THE JUBILEE

For some years previous to 1844, Rev. Russell S. Cook, of New York, a native of New Marlboro, a resident of Lenox in his youth, and a frequent loving visitor to it in his mature life, was secretary of the American Tract Society. His official duties called him to all sections of the country; and everywhere he found Berkshire men in respectable, and often in high, positions. Impressed by the spontaneous expressions of warm regard for their old mountain homes by those whom he earliest met, further inquiry wherever he went convinced him that this feeling was uniform and universal.

From these and cognate observations, Mr. Cook conceived the idea of bringing these emigrants together in a social reunion at some convenient central point in Berkshire, with a view to forming a band of union among them; awakening in the citizens of the county an interest in the fame and usefulness of those who had gone out from among them, and also of furnishing to the world an illustration of the influence New England was having in the formation of the character of the country. Mr. Cook suggested this idea from time to time in his official visits, and found it everywhere cordially approved; but its realization was postponed, awaiting the recovery of the country from the financial depression of 1837; and probably, also, the completion of the Western (now the Boston and Albany) Railroad to Pittsfield, which did not happen until the late fall of 1842. In the spring of 1843, Mr. Cook, incidentally meeting Judge Joshua A. Spencer, of Utica, a native of Great Barrington, broached the subject to him. The judge heartily concurred in his idea, and the two gentlemen agreed upon a plan which was afterward substantially carried out. Both were men of influence personally, as well as from their official positions. Leading New York newspapers gave their earnest assistance, the name "Berkshire Jubilee" being first printed in the *Journal of Commerce,* whose editor, Colonel Stone, was foremost in his helpfulness. There was no difficulty in organizing a "New York Committee" zealous for the proposed reunion, with names upon it fit to conjure with: such as William Cullen Bryant, Orville Dewey, Judge Samuel R. Betts, David Dudley Field, Theodore Sedgwick, Marshall S. Bidwell, and Drake Mills. This committee communicated with gentlemen in Pittsfield, where, and in the county, committees were formed for the local work.

Then all went swimmingly. It was determined to hold the Jubilee at Pittsfield, August 22 and 23, 1844. The program called for a sermon and historical poem on the first day, an oration in the forenoon and a dinner in the afternoon of the second: all preceded by formal and informal welcomes and greetings, which proved to be warm and heartfelt, and interspersed with poems, hymns, and other minor exercises, some of which were of very marked character; such as an essay upon the then recently deceased William Ellery Channing by his friend Miss Sedgwick, and an ode on Berkshire by Mrs. Frances Ann (Fanny) Kemble.

Near the Pittsfield Union Railroad passenger station— which indeed stands on the edge of its southern slope— there rises the most conspicuous natural elevation in the township, save its very narrow mountain borders. It is almost two hundred rods long and forty wide, and its summit is about sixty feet above the mean level of the city streets. It was originally the farm of Dr. Timothy Childs, one of the most honored of Pittsfield's Revolutionary patriots; and, although it is now covered with fine streets and avenues, in 1844 there was no house

upon it except the homestead which he built, and in his lifetime occupied. Thus it commanded an entirely unobstructed view of the noble valley, with ever-majestic Greylock looking down upon it from the north, and the graceful triune Lenox Range, with Yocun's Seat, its loftiest peak, not far away on the south. The Housatonic flowed along its western base, and the village lay smiling on the east.

All its memories and features marked this fair hill as the proper spot for most of the exercises of the Jubilee; and a platform was erected near the southern extremity of its summit upon which it was planned to conduct all, except the receptions and the dinner. But, when the people had assembled for the sermon, a violent rainstorm drove them, "in most admired disorder," from the hill to the time-honored, fairly handsome and spacious Congregational church. There the sermon was preached by that most eminent educator, metaphysician, and pulpit orator, President Mark Hopkins of Williams College. Dr. Hopkins has been happily characterized as "massive-minded;" and his Jubilee sermon was what was to be expected from such a preacher. But he was also a true son of one of the most Berkshire of all old Berkshire families. He dearly loved the scenery which had delighted him from childhood, and he was proud of the history in whose glories he had good right to share. He knew well how to prize all that went to make up the grand mountain-walled individuality which peculiarly characterizes the county. Naturally inspired by an occasion which kindled and concentrated thought of all this, many poetic passages glowed, like Alpine roses, among his massive sentences.

A poem by Rev. Dr. William Allen, of Northampton, ex-president of Bowdoin College, followed the sermon, and, if not such poetry as Bryant would have discoursed, it was excellent local history and topography, and well fitted to stimulate and gratify local pride. Dr. Allen was a scholar and biographical writer of decided merit; but his special claim to the position assigned him at the Jubilee was that he was a son of Rev. Thomas Allen, the first minister of Pittsfield and the "Fighting Parson of Bennington Field;" and that, succeeding his father in 1811, he had preached six years in the pulpit from which he read his poem; so that he might well have been regarded as a connecting link between the Berkshire men of the Revolution and those of the Jubilee time.

The oration on the second day, by Judge Joshua A. Spencer, was a terse *résumé* of Berkshire history, told with grace and spirit. Nature, grown more kindly, permitted it to be delivered, with other interesting exercises, from the platform on the hill. Up to this time this hill had been known simply as the "Childs Farm." But Rev. Dr. John Todd, the chairman of the Pittsfield committee, in his farewell address at the close of the Jubilee, in the dinner pavilion, said:

We have been thinking how we could erect some monument of this Jubilee. In our wisdom we have spoken of several; but, after all, God has been before us; and his mighty hand hath reared the monument. That hill from which we came to this pavilion will hereafter bear the name of JUBILEE HILL; and when our heads are laid in the grave, and we have passed away, and are forgotten, we hope that our children and our children's children will walk over that beautiful spot, and say, 'Here our fathers celebrated the Berkshire Jubilee.' This monument shall stand as long as the footstool of God shall remain.

The great assemblage gave a ringing response to these words; and the name was fixed forever.

THE JUBILEE DINNER

The successive parts of the Jubilee were remarkably well balanced; but the dinner was singularly memorable: the intellectual portion being an expansion of the thought and concentrated essence of the feeling which marked the preceding demonstration. Its story is certainly pertinent to our present essay, as Dr. Holmes was a conspicuous figure in it.

The main streets of Pittsfield that run north and south are, for some three-quarters of a mile, bordered by plains. Near the northern end of this distance there was in 1812 a large, perfectly level, open field. This attracted the attention of Maj.-Gen. H. A. S. Dearborn, who was organizing the Northern Military Department for the war that was just commencing; and he selected it as a site for a cantonment—a post of rendezvous, organization, and training for regiments raised in New England, and for the confinement of prisoners of war. Pittsfield had been chosen for the cantonment on account of its defensible position among the hills: a protection for which, at the Jubilee, years afterward, the assembled people returned thanks by singing with enthusiasm Mrs. Hemans' "Hymn of the Mountain Christians," of which we quote one verse:

> For the strength of the hills, we bless thee,
>   Our God, our fathers' God.
> Thou hast made thy children mighty
>   By the touch of the mountain sod.
> Thou hast fixed our ark of refuge
>   Where the spoiler's foot ne'er trod;
> For the strength of the hills we bless thee,
>   Our God, our fathers' God.

Barracks were erected for the cantonment and occupied by many of the soldiers who won honor in the northern campaigns, and by more than two thousand of the prisoners captured by them; the privates among the latter seeming to enjoy their captivity better than campaigning.

When the war was over the barracks gave place to three large buildings erected for the Berkshire Gymnasium, a high school for young men, founded on a peculiar German model by Professor Chester Dewey, one of the foremost American men of science of his time, and one who did a great work as a pioneer in the study of Western Massachusetts geology, mineralogy, and natural history generally. Professor Dewey having discontinued the gymnasium, to accept a professorship in the Rochester University, the buildings were occupied in 1844 by the Pittsfield Young Ladies' Institute, which, although recently founded, had already attained a national standing. Before these buildings, a pavilion for the Jubilee dinner was erected, in which tables were spread for a thousand guests.

The president of the day was George N. Briggs, who was then serving the first of seven terms as Governor of the Commonwealth after six in Congress: an admirable selection, not solely because Governor Briggs was the most eminent citizen of the town and county in official rank; but because he was unsurpassed in qualifications to preside at a festal table like this: never-failing tact, self-possession, and knowledge of men, ready and never misplaced wit and humor, wonderful familiarity with Berkshire character, history, tradition, and anecdote, together with the happiest faculty for making use of his local lore.

Some thirty sons of Berkshire responded to the president's call for short speeches or "sentiments;" all of them men of note in their several homes, and some of wider fame. Among them, besides several who have been named in other connections, were President Heman Humphrey of Amherst College—who before and after that presidency was an intense and ardent Pittsfield man—Rev. Drs. Orville and Chester Dewey, Theodore Sedgwick, of New York and Stockbridge; John Mills, of Springfield, and Julius Rockwell, the successor of Governor Briggs in Congress. An interesting speaker was Rev. Joshua Noble Danforth, of Alexandria, Virginia, a son of Pittsfield's Revolutionary hero, Col. Joshua Danforth; who said: "We stand here to-day, forty in relationship—twenty-five of us the direct descendants of David Noble of Williamstown—the upright judge, the exemplary Christian."

A peculiarly pleasant and striking incident of the day was the speech and the reading of Leigh Hunt's poem, "Abou Ben Adhem," by William Charles Macready, the distinguished English tragedian; which, with Mrs. Kemble's grand Berkshire ode, made a contribution to the occasion from the British stage that was little to be expected.

Another pleasant and notable feature was the presence of Rev. Dr. David Dudley Field, of Stockbridge, the first historian of Berkshire County, with two of his famous sons, David Dudley and Cyrus W. Naturally the great lawyer was the spokesman of the family: but it is not for that we now specially recall him. In President

Hopkins' sermon there occurred the following passage: "Probably most of us have read—for it was in an old New England school-book—of that 'Journey of a Day' that was a picture of human life. And, if it were given us to make the journey of a day that should be, not in its events, but in its scenery, the picture of our lives, where should we rather choose to make it than through the length of our Berkshire? What could be better than to watch the rising of the sun from the top of Greylock, and his setting from the Eagle's Nest?"

"This passage so fastened itself on Mr. Field's mind" that he followed its suggestions, the very next week; and his spirited account of the experience the excursion brought him was widely published in the journals of the time under the title of "A Journey of a Day," and is reproduced in the recent superb edition of his writings. "The entire length of the county"—he wrote—"from north to south is fifty miles; and if the ascent of Greylock is made the evening before, so that the journey may begin at sunrise, it is possible in thirteen hours to pass down the valley, ascend the Dome of the Taconics, and get a last view of the setting sun from the Eagle's Nest." This he accomplished: passing through Williamstown, New Ashford, Lanesboro, Pittsfield, Lenox, Stockbridge, Great Barrington; and, over the Dome of the Taconics in Egremont, into the wild, awe-inspiring gorge of the far-famed Bash-Bish Falls in the western side of Mount Washington, where, among the other almost Alpine features, a vast wall of rock rises two hundred feet, beetling twenty-five feet beyond its base at its top; the Eagle's Nest, from which Mr. Field and his companion had a glorious view of the setting sun; Greylock, Williamstown, Lanesboro, Pittsfield, Lenox, Stockbridge, Great Barrington, the Dome, and the Eagle's Nest: what a carcanet of golden landscapes jeweled with precious memories these names call to mind! And to each and all the great jurist dealt poetic justice, both as to scenery and to story. We can, however, only quote his words regarding the Jubilee, and so much of those concerning Pittsfield as relate to the town as its seat.

Arriving at Pontoosuc Lake, which he locates in Lanesboro, although half its surface is in Pittsfield, Mr. Field writes:

> One feature of uncommon beauty, the place [Lanesboro] has: its Pontoosuc Lake, or Shoonke Moonke, as it is sometimes called. It covers six hundred acres; and its bright waters, the road along its margin, and the tall trees that shade it make you sorry to leave it. We could not stay, but hurried on to Pittsfield. What shall we say of Pittsfield; the hospitable, the beautiful? Just fresh from the Jubilee—fresh from the open houses and the open hearts of her people—we drove into the village, with the scenes of those two days fresh in our vision. The intervening week had vanished. We stood again on Jubilee Hill; we went down to the field where the feast

was spread; we laughed under the Old Elm; we saw our friends—our fellows; as goodly a company as we shall see again for many a day. Truly it was a high festival: one worthy to be commemorated—to be repeated.

> The valley of the Housatonic here widens to its greatest breadth. Poontoosuck, the Indian name (pity it was not retained) signifies 'a field for the deer.' Pleasant place for hunting the Indians must have found it; and pleasant, too, for sojourn it is for the white man.

We must content us with one more contemporary description of the Jubilee; or a portion of one. It is from the pen of Catherine Sedgwick—there could be no better representatives of the people of southern Berkshire at the Jubilee, and of their feeling regarding it than Dudley Field and Catherine Sedgwick. An official report of the proceedings on the two days of the festival was published in an octavo volume, and Miss Sedgwick contributed to it a five-page *résumé* of the story, written in the Hebraic manner. We quote a few of the more detachable verses.

* * *

Hath not the Lord given us rest on every side! Now we will proclaim a Jubilee.—We will go up to our Jerusalem! We will worship in the temples of our fathers. We will kiss the sod that covers the graves of our kindred; and we will sit ourselves down in the old places where their shadows will pass before us!

We will rejoice and make merry with our brethren; and Memory and Hope shall be our pleasant ministers. And we will lay our hearts together, and stir up the smouldering embers of old friendships till the fire burns within us: and this, even this sacred fire, will we transmit to our children's children.

And even as they said, so did they; and in the summer solstice, with one heart and one mind, did they come together: the Pilgrims from afar and the Sojourners at home. Even from the valley of the Mississippi came they; and from the yet farther country of the Missouri, and from the Land of the Sun, even from the Southland; and from all the goodly lands about Massachusetts.

* * *

And they gathered together, a multitude of people, old men and elder women, young men and fair young maidens, and much children—a very great company were they.

And a great heart was in the people of Pittsfield; and they opened the doors of their pleasant dwellings and bade their brethren enter therein. And they spread fine linen on their beds, and they covered their tables with the fat of the land; for the Lord had greatly blessed the people of Pittsfield.

And they said to all their brethren: Come now and enter in and freely take of our abundance; for, lo, have we not spread our tables for you, and hath not the angel of sleep dressed our beds, that our brethren may sleep therein?

And the faces of their brethren shone, and they entered in; and they said: It was a true report we heard of thee; thy land doth excel, and thou hast greatly increased the riches and the beauty thereof.

Such was the occasion on which Oliver Wendell Holmes first addressed a Berkshire audience; and such were the men and women associated with him in it.

Dr. Holmes' Speech and Poem

Governor Briggs having made a cordial, interesting, and appropriate speech of welcome, to which Judge Betts responded in the same vein, the governor announced a poem by Dr. Holmes. The poet was already not unknown to fame, although very far from that which afterward celebrated his name; and its announcement was received with ringing cheers and cries of "Come forward!" The president suggested that he should rather follow the example of Judge Betts, and mount the table; remarking that this would be an advance on some old-fashioned feasts, where the tendency was rather to get under the table than upon it. Dr. Holmes followed this advice and took the table: and when the renewed cheers subsided read the following speech and poem.

He asked to be allowed, before he opened the paper in his hand, to assure his friends of the reason why he found himself there. He said:

Inasmuch as the company express willingness to hear historical incidents, any little incident which shall connect me with those to whom I cannot claim to be a brother, seems to be fairly brought forward. One of my earliest recollections is of an annual pilgrimage made by my parents to the west. The young horse was brought up, fatted by a week's rest and high feeding, prancing and caracoling to the door. It came to the corner and was soon over the western hills. He was gone a fortnight; and one afternoon—it always seems to me it was a sunny afternoon—we saw an equipage crawling from the west toward the old homestead; the young horse, who set out fat and prancing, worn thin and reduced by a long journey—the chaise covered with dust, and all speaking of a terrible crusade, a formidable pilgrimage. Winter-evening stories told me where—to Berkshire, to the borders of New York, to the old domain, owned so long that there seemed a kind of hereditary love for it. Many years passed away, and I traveled down the beautiful Rhine. I wished to see the equally beautiful Hudson. I found myself at Albany; a few hours' ride brought me to Pittsfield, and I went to the little spot, the scene of this pilgrimage—a mansion—and found it surrounded by a beautiful meadow, through which the winding river made its course in a thousand fantastic curves; the mountains reared their heads around it, the blue air which makes our city-pale cheeks again to deepen with the hue of health, coursing about it pure and free. I recognized it as the scene of the annual pilgrimage. Since then I have made an annual visit to it.

In 1735, Hon. Jacob Wendell, my grandfather in the maternal line, bought a township not then laid out—the township of Poontoosuck—and that little spot which

we still hold is the relic of twenty-four thousand acres of baronial territory. When I say this, no feeling which can be the subject of ridicule animates my bosom. I know too well that the hills and rocks outlast our families. I know we fall upon the places we claim, as the leaves of the forest fall, and as passed the soil from the hands of the original occupants into the hands of my immediate ancestors, I know it must pass from me and mine; and yet with pleasure and pride I feel I can take every inhabitant by the hand and say, If I am not a son or a grandson, or even a nephew of this fair county, I am at least allied to it by hereditary relation.

"Poem of Welcome."

Come back to your Mother, ye children, for shame,
Who have wandered like truants, for riches or fame!
With a smile on her face and a sprig on her cap,
She calls you to feast from her bountiful lap.

Come out from your alleys, your courts and your
  lanes,
And breathe, like young eagles, the air of our plains:
Take a whiff from our fields, and your excellent wives
Will declare it's all nonsense insuring your lives.

Come you of the law, who can talk if you please
Till the man in the moon will allow it's a cheese,
And leave "the old lady, that never tells lies,"
To sleep with her handkerchief over her eyes.

Ye healers of men, for a moment decline
Your feats in the rhubarb and ipecac line;
While you shut up your turnpike, your neighbors can
  go
The old roundabout road to the regions below.

You clerk, on whose ears are a couple of pens,
And whose head is an ant-hill of units and tens;
Though Plato denies you, we welcome you still
As a featherless biped, in spite of your quill.

Poor drudge of the city, how happy he feels
With the burs on his legs and the grass at his heels;
No dodger behind, his bandanas to share,
No constable grumbling "You mustn't walk there."

In yonder green meadow, to memory dear,
He slaps a mosquito and brushes a tear;
The dew-drops hang round him on blossoms and
  shoots,
He breathes but one sigh for his youth and his boots.

William Cranston Lawton (essay date 1898)

SOURCE: Lawton, William Cranston. "Holmes." In *The New England Poets: A Study of Emerson, Hawthorne, Longfellow, Whittier, Lowell, Holmes*, pp. 232-54. New York: The Macmillan Company, 1898.

[*In the following excerpt, Lawton offers an overview of Holmes's literary career, praising the poet's wit and sense of fun.*]

THE LAST LEAF

The recent departure of the Autocrat has brought freshly to the minds of us all the long peaceful career of this last survivor from the Round Table. It is a strange coincidence, at least, that from Bryant's birth to Holmes' death (1794-1894) was a hundred years to a month: a century which precisely includes the lives of our six most famous poets.

The gambrel-roofed house, close to Cambridge Common and the College yard, in which Dr. Holmes saw the light, most appropriately, on Commencement Day of 1809, was still standing until a dozen years ago. The new Gymnasium and Law School of the University displaced it at last. A few years later the Autocrat speaks of the well as alone remaining to mark the site. Perhaps that, too, has vanished. It is generally supposed the old house was pulled down about 1884. It is to be hoped the Autocrat died in that belief. As a matter of fact, however, the venerable abode of the race was cut into several sections, by a thrifty purchaser, hauled to the river side, and there doubtless it stands to-day, still unmistakable in its ignominy, tenanted by at least a half-dozen wretched families of various colors and races. *Books,* like men, "have a doom of their own," as Horace says, and Holmes has echoed it most effectively in his prelude:

> O sexton of the alcoved tomb,
>   Where souls in leathern cerements lie,
> Tell me each living poet's doom!
>   How long before his book shall die?

But even he would hardly have had the heart to sing, in gaiety or earnest, the real fate of the house of the Holmes family!

The author's earliest memories of the spot are gathered up in the first number of *The Poet at the Breakfast Table,* which should be read with Lowell's merrier "Cambridge Thirty Years Ago." Like Lowell and Emerson, Holmes was the son of a Congregationalist clergyman, a learned but not a witty man. It is said of the Autocrat, as of his younger townsman, that his poetic vein and his wit must have been inherited wholly from his mother.

At the dame's school of his childhood, Margaret Fuller and the second Richard H. Dana (who later spent *Two Years before the Mast*) were among his mates. His last school year was passed at the Phillips Academy in Andover; and in 1867 a visit to these early haunts produced the sheaf of reminiscences called "Cinders from the Ashes." "The ghost of a boy was at my side as I wandered among the places he knew so well." But when at the station the elderly man called for two tickets to Boston, "the little ghost whispered, 'When you leave

this place, you leave me behind you.'" Eleven years later, for the centennial of the famous Academy, these early memories were again recorded in verse:

> I, whose fresh voice yon red-faced temple knew,
> What tune is left me, fit to sing to you?
> . . . Much could I tell you, that you know too well.
> Much I remember, but I will not tell. . . .

(Mr. Aldrich is not the only self-confessed Bad Boy in the Atlantic circle.) This clashing heroic couplet, by the way, the favorite of Dryden, Pope, and Goldsmith, was almost a part of Dr. Holmes' poetic second nature his whole life through. He began, indeed, to use it as a boy at Andover, in a metrical version from Virgil which is still preserved.

He entered Harvard at sixteen, and graduated without mishap, as all the world knows, in the class of 1829. Even in college he published some verses now famous, especially, **"The Height of the Ridiculous"**:

> I wrote some lines once on a time
> In wondrous merry mood, . . .

and at graduation he was chosen Class Poet. This "merry mood" lasted, on the whole, through life, and in one of his most impressive farewells,—which were happily as numerous as Patti's,—I mean **"The Iron Gate,"** read for a breakfast given on his seventieth birthday, he says:

> I come not here your morning hour to sadden,
>   A limping pilgrim, leaning on my staff,
> I, who have never deemed it sin to gladden
>   This vale of sorrows with a wholesome laugh.

In these college verses indeed we see little purpose further than to raise an idle laugh. But the man and the poet awoke suddenly in full earnest when, in 1830, it was proposed to break up the frigate *Constitution,* popularly known as *Old Ironsides.* Every American schoolboy shouted the lines:

> Ay, tear her tattered ensign down!

written almost upon the instant by the youth of twenty-one, and published a day or two later in the *Boston Advertiser.* They were copied everywhere, and were not only successful in their immediate purpose, but gave their author national fame at a single bound. These verses have still the place of honor at the opening of the standard editions of his poems. A recent article in *St. Nicholas* gives interesting information upon the present whereabouts and condition of *Old Ironsides.*

We shall have more to say of Holmes' humor; but it is well to remember that this first great triumph was the clear, earnest cry of a patriotic heart. So the poet's own favorite, **"The Chambered Nautilus," "The Voice-**

less," and many another masterpiece, even the Prelude **"To My Readers,"** are wholly serious, almost sad. In the ability to bridge the narrow, but deep and dangerous, rift that parts humor from pathos, Holmes has, perhaps, no superior since Hood. He resents the suspicion that he is merely a jester more sharply than any other charge against himself. The singer is a true knight:

> Think not I come in manhood's fiery noon,
> To steal his laurels from the stage buffoon.
> His sword of lath the harlequin may wield;
> Behold the star upon my lifted shield!

For a year Holmes studied law, but this he abandoned more promptly than Lowell did later, and found his proper career in medicine. If we add the theological influences of his father's home, he thus combined an insight into all the three learned professions, which was happily utilized in the most successful of his three novels, *The Guardian Angel.* After two years' study of medicine at home, he spent three years abroad, chiefly in the schools and hospitals of Paris. Doubtless this French experience intensified the clear-cut crispness and directness of Holmes' style, especially in verse. Of direct reminiscence there is not so much. **"La Grisette,"** though Parisian in setting, has little of the Béranger flavor, save in its title. His welcome to Prince Napoleon, in 1861, with its **"Vive la France!"** has, perhaps, more warmth of feeling than most among his numerous songs of welcome and farewell. There are many recollections of these youthful years in the account of another pilgrimage, half a century later, "Our Hundred Days in Europe."

The year of his return, 1836, was an important one. He took his degree of M.D. at Harvard. He read his first long poem, **"Poetry, a Metrical Essay,"** before the Phi Beta Kappa in August; and he published a volume of poems, among which this **"Metrical Essay"** was the chief. The very title, like the metre and the style, recalled Dryden and Pope. His rapid couplets here ring all the changes of feeling

> From grave to gay, from lively to severe,

though indeed Holmes never can be really severe, very long, save when attacking rigid Calvinism in theology, or homœopathy in medicine; and even then the jest breaks through, just when his sternness begins to trouble us.

The connection of parts in this and in other sustained flights of Dr. Holmes' muse often baffles us. The clearness and completeness are always there—in the couplet or the stanza. His genius is distinctly lyrical. When he ventures beyond a hundred lines, on a single theme, his wings sag, or his course veers. As with his friend Emerson, the part is here sometimes more than the whole.

It might be supposed that poetry would have interfered with the young physician's success; but it was not so. Besides practising medicine in Boston, he wrote, during 1836-1837, medical essays which won three or four medals, offered as prizes in those years. Dr. Holmes has always had plenty of time!

After two years as Professor of Anatomy and Physiology at Dartmouth (the famous "small college" which Daniel Webster's plea had saved), Holmes returned to practise medicine in Boston, and to marry, in 1840. His position in the "best society" was never questioned. His liking for the good things of life is confessed delightfully in **"Contentment"**:

> Little I ask; my wants are few;
> I only wish a hut of stone
> (*A very plain* brown stone will do),
> . . . I care not much for gold or land;
>   Give me a mortgage here and there;
> Some good bank-stock, some note of hand,
>   Or trifling railroad share,—
> I only ask that Fortune send
> A *little* more than I shall spend.

He did not imperil his comfort by any premature devotion to abolition, or other unfashionable causes; indeed, there is a curious allusion to John Quincy Adams' gallant stand in his old age:

> Chiefs of New England! by your sires' renown,
> Dash the red torches of the rebel down!
> Flood his black hearthstone till its flames expire,
> Though your old Sachem fanned his council-fire!

Here the "rebel" is the Abolitionist! Not that Holmes was ever lacking in frankness or courage. Fortunately for the reformers themselves, conservatism will always be in the majority; and Dr. Holmes was a natural conservative in many things besides his love of the heroic couplet.

In 1847 he accepted a professorship in the Harvard Medical School, and for thirty-five years gave there his four weekly lectures, resigning in 1882. His lectures were as clear and interesting in themselves as the subject would permit, and illustrated with such wealth of anecdote and ludicrous allusion as no other demonstrator of anatomy ever had at his command.

In 1851 appeared the first of his many poems for the class of '29. The next year he began a successful career as "lyceum" orator, with a course on English poets of the nineteenth century. This was in the golden days of the lyceum, and this course in particular had much of that consecutiveness which we claim as a cardinal virtue in University Extension. His favorite subjects appear to have been Scott, Byron, Keats, Shelley, Moore, and in a less degree, Wordsworth. He had a delightful habit of closing each lecture with a poem upon the poet he had discussed. Of these, the most loftily inspired is, without question, the elegy describing the drowning of Shelley, the finding of the body, with a volume of his friend Keats' poems thrust, opened, into his bosom; the burning of the corpse on the Italian shore, and the depositing of his ashes beside Keats' grave in the famous little Protestant cemetery at Rome. The closing plea against hasty denial of the divine grace for the anti-Christian poet is especially beautiful. Each quatrain of this poem demands a picture to illustrate it, though I do not know that it has ever been so published.

And now we once again approach the year which drew all these gifted New Englanders more closely about the Round Table of the Atlantic. Lowell, it will be remembered, was made editor-in-chief, with enthusiastic unanimity, when the new magazine was started in the autumn of 1857. His first condition was, that Holmes should be a leading contributor. The two were then already the most famous wits of American letters; but Lowell, though not yet forty, had ten years before leaped into popularity with Hosea Biglow, and also won supremacy among the critics by his slashing Fable for the guild; while Holmes at fifty, a prosperous physician and popular professor, was in literature little more than a welcome writer of occasional verse.

The late and sudden flowering of his prose genius is as wonderful as anything in his career. In three successive years of the magazine appeared the first two delightful volumes of *Table Talk,* and the powerful novel, *Elsie Venner.* After half a dozen years' rest came in rapid succession his happiest novel, *The Guardian Angel,* and, in 1871, the third "Breakfast Table" book, *The Poet.* The plan of these three volumes of table talk is so flexible, that everything is "in order," except, indeed, a motion to adjourn; for it is not easy to lay the book down, though it is really much better read piecemeal and thoughtfully. There is not much dramatic characterization in the conversation. We rarely hear any voices but Holmes' own; yet this one voice, in prose as in song, has "many keys"; sweeps, indeed, almost the whole gamut of human feeling and experience. Those of us not blessed with a keen sense of the ludicrous will miss much of the best in these books; but not all by any means. It is breakfast *à la carte,* and he is hard indeed to please who cannot find much both toothsome and strengthening.

In still another field of letters Dr. Holmes was to win laurels, though not the loftiest. His biography of Motley, the historian, appeared in 1879, that of Emerson in 1884. If anything was still lacking to prove his versatility, we might mention an impressive oration delivered to Bostonians in the dark days of 1863, insisting that the war must now go on to the end, even though that end should be the utter destruction of our people and civilization.

My last remembrance, as indeed numberless Harvard men's, of Holmes and Lowell, is as poet and orator at the great Anniversary in 1886. Dr. Holmes' hair was already snow white, as Lowell reminded him with tender playfulness, later in the day. But for years longer the little Autocrat was as familiar a street figure to Bostonians as the stately form of Phillips Brooks or the gaunt shape of Edward Everett Hale. His summers were spent in his pretty cottage on the favorite "North Shore," at Beverly. The inevitable end of the cheerful life tale need not be recalled.

It has been attempted to follow, thus far, a chronological outline of biography. A pleasant final task remains: to recall the charm of Dr. Holmes' literary work. The traits unmistakable in it are swift versatility, a crisp simplicity and grace, depth of earnest thought, but above all a merry, ever-present wit and humor. Holmes' medical writings, of course, lie outside our field; so, indeed, strictly speaking, do his two essays in biography, though that of Emerson is indispensable to our knowledge of both author and subject. It is amusing to see that Holmes, who was as little of a mystic as any true poet can be, seems to share in some degree the popular estimate of "Brahma," which many, at least, if not all faithful Emersonians place near the head of his verses: "To the average Western mind it is the nearest approach to a Torricellian vacuum that language can pump out of itself."

To the three famous volumes of table talk, a fourth, greatly inferior in power, *Over the Teacups,* was added in his last years. The passage which will be remembered longest is the thrilling picture of the writer's sensations in advanced age: "At fifty, your vessel is staunch, and you are on deck with the rest in all weathers. At sixty, the vessel still floats, and you are in the cabin. At seventy, you with a few fellow-passengers are on a raft. At eighty, you are on a spar to which, possibly one, or two, or three friends of about your own age are still clinging." The yet more pathetic close of the paragraph need not be cited.

The opinion that Dr. Holmes' romances are chiefly breakfast-table chats still, is, I think, just, and, indeed, the general judgment of critics; but I am writing when fresh from a reperusal of them, and so am, happily, no critic. Their charm is so great and many-sided, that it is hard indeed to find any fault *while you read.* But there really are long stretches of monologue by the professor, while the story waits. The main plot is not skilfully woven, and does not show much originality. Indeed, in *The Guardian Angel,* the heroine's fortune is restored to her by so hackneyed a device as the long-lost will, which the villain finds by accident, conceals while he strives to win her hand, and thinks he destroys before her eyes when rejected. Of course, it is only a copy. The real document is safe in the honest partner's hands—and all ends happily! Dr. Holmes himself knew how to ridicule this sort of thing, at least upon the boards, deliciously, as we may see in the Prologue:

> 'The world's a stage,'—as Shakspeare said one day;
> The stage a world—was what he meant to say.
> The outside world's a blunder, that is clear;
> The real world that Nature meant is here.
> Here every foundling finds its lost mamma;
> Each rogue, repentant, melts his stern papa;
> Misers relent, the spendthrift's debts are paid,
> The cheats are taken in the traps they laid;
> One after one the troubles all are past,
> Till the fifth act comes right side up at last;
> When the young couple, old folks, rogues, and all
> Join hands, *so* happy, at the curtain's fall.

But in truth the chief value of these stories is to be sought elsewhere than in plot and construction. *Elsie Venner* is a rather grewsome account of a human being, changed in nature before her birth by the venom of a rattlesnake. Even this strange medical problem is of interest to the wise physician chiefly because behind it he sees a larger ethical question. As he says in a second preface: "Wherein lies the difference between her position at the bar of judgment, human or divine, and that of the unfortunate victim, who received a moral poison from a remote ancestor before he drew his first breath?" Not a promising beginning for an enjoyable romance, you say,—if you do not know your author. Yet it is as fascinating as anything of Rider Haggard's, and a thousand-fold more profitable to read. In passing, it may be said that one of the most delightful elements is the broad flavor of rustic Yankeeism, culminating in Major Sprowle's party. "Silas Peckham," the schoolmaster, is a merciless satire on the worst form of New England shrewdness and thrift. Students of the dialect will find here helpful additions to the vocabulary of Hosea Biglow.

The Guardian Angel treats the problem of heredity in a far more normal and pleasanter example. Myrtle Hazard, like every human being, is the complex result of many ancestral lives and natures. Through the eyes of the old doctor in the story, who in his ninety years has studied five generations of her race, we see a succession of her inherited traits rise to the surface and imperil her womanly life, until her own essentially healthy and noble nature comes safely to its own.

The last romance, *A Mortal Antipathy,* is a far less serious and less powerful illustration of a kindred problem: the enduring force of impressions made upon the mind in early infancy.

We must pass to the poetry of Holmes. He is doubtless most widely known as pure humorist. **"The September Gale," "The Deacon's One Hoss Shay," "How the Old Horse Won the Bet," "The Broomstick Train,"**

usually come first to our minds. Nor is this altogether unreasonable on our part. Holmes' most unique gift to literature is his pure fun and wit. But it is actually a gift *to literature*: that is, it appears, often, at least, as an inseparable element in the composition of enduring masterpieces, which, of course, possess other and higher qualities. Even the **"One Hoss Shay"** itself could only have been written by a master of sentiment and pathos. Where else do we hear so effectively indicated the terrible gliding, slipping, passing of the years, the ceaseless flight of time?

> Colts grew horses, beards turned gray,
> Deacon and deaconess dropped away,
> Children and grandchildren—where were they?
> But there stood the wonderful one hoss shay
> As fresh as on Lisbon-earthquake-day.
> . . . Little of all we value here
> Wakes on the morn of its hundredth year
> Without both feeling and looking queer.

Indeed, we may say of the entire poem, that full as it is of humor, and even of fun, yet there is method and art and deepest pathos in't no less.

There is much more pure fun in Holmes' poetic output than in Lowell's. "Hosea Biglow," especially, never allows us to forget his purpose, to drive home a moral lesson, or even to aid the political cause which he thought the cause of righteousness as well. Dr. Holmes himself truly describes his friend,

> Whose play is all earnest, whose wit is the edge
> (With a beetle behind) of a sham-splitting wedge.

"The Courtin'," again, is pure pathos, in a homely setting, and leaves us, at best, very like his heroine,

> Kind o' smily round the lips,
> And teary round the lashes.

Indeed, Lowell's really aimless fun, on the rare occasions when it appears, is the mirth of the scholar quite as often as of the Yankee. We may instance the piece written for a Harvard Commencement dinner, which is largely unintelligible save to college men, and even drops into Greek for a moment. The same remark is at least partly true of the delicious epitaph upon the brothers Snow, oystermen, in **"Cambridge Thirty Years Since,"** culminating in an exquisitely ludicrous citation from Horace, "Jam satis nivis!" (enough of snow!).

But Holmes' fun was a very large part of his nature, and quite able to stand alone, in prose or verse. Not to repeat names of poems already mentioned, **"The Ballad of the Young Oysterman," "Evening, by a Tailor,"** and plenty more are quite safe from any moral application. Single lines and stanzas from many of his poems have been made proverbial by their very grotesqueness, *e.g.:*

And silence, *like a poultice,* comes
To heal the wounds of sound.

Sometimes, in mock-dignified language, he alludes to a most familiar rhyme or bit of slang:

Like the filial John,
Whom sleep surprised with half his drapery on.

Fond as he is of the dignified heroic couplet, he will make it sing of things that would have shocked—not alone manly Dryden or precise Pope, but—even poor rollicking Noll Goldsmith. For instance, when he has received a **"Modest Request"** for a speech, a song, *and* a toast, all on the same occasion, he is reminded of the thirsty sailor:

'Jack,' said my lady, 'is it grog you'll try,
Or punch, or toddy, if perhaps you're dry?'
'Ah,' said the sailor, 'though I can't refuse,
You know, my lady, 'taint for me to choose—
I'll take the grog to finish off my lunch,
And drink the toddy—while you mix the punch.'

This element of drollery, I repeat, is essential to our appreciation of the real Holmes. No less essential, surely, is the pure pathos and lofty aspiration of his religious and imaginative verse:

Build thee more stately mansions, O my soul,
As the swift seasons roll!
Leave thy low-vaulted past!
Let each new temple, nobler than the last,
Shut thee from heaven with a dome more vast,
Till thou at length art free,
Leaving thine outgrown shell by life's unresting sea!

In a few poems, such as **"The Voiceless,"** we seem to hear the drip of the author's very life-blood in the verse:

O hearts that break and give no sign,
Save whitening lip and fading tresses,
Till Death pours out his cordial wine,
Slow-dropped from Misery's crushing presses!

But the complete charm of the poet is felt where these two elements, seemingly so diverse, are most completely fused. Perhaps the most perfect example of what is meant will be found in the poem, almost too familiar to be quoted here, which was the special favorite of Abraham Lincoln. Indeed, it is said that the great emancipator once gained his case, as counsel for a persecuted old man, by quoting the famous fourth stanza:

The mossy marbles rest
On the lips that he has pressed
In their bloom.

Strangest of all it seems, that Dr. Holmes himself should have lingered for *sixty years* to realize in full at last the prophetic closing stanza:

And if I should live to be
The last leaf upon the tree. . . .

C. Hartley Grattan (essay date January 1925)

SOURCE: Grattan, C. Hartley. "Oliver Wendell Holmes." *American Mercury* 4, no. 13 (January 1925): 37-41.

[*In the following essay, Grattan contends that Holmes's writing was provincial and unsophisticated, and that most of his poetry was already dated by the early twentieth century.*]

The literary fame of Oliver Wendell Holmes has been erected into a chapter when it should be reduced to a footnote. To have written one book of importance and a handful of occasional poems cannot make a man a figure of major significance. The impossibility appears the greater when it is recalled that the one book epitomizes the humor of a single region. It is *The Autocrat of the Breakfast Table,* and its importance today is not national, but sectional and local to Boston. Not all of his contemporaries were blind to the exaggerations in the old regard for Holmes, for Thomas Bailey Aldrich noted with unusual realism that "I can't imagine how he will stand by and by; at present his personality is a tower of strength."

If Boston society had been more integrated than it was, and the center of a firmly established leisure class, Holmes would have been simply a cultured gentleman with a literary talent. As it was, he had wit and ability enough to do occasional poems and light essays with a reasonable grace for a highly literate but by no means leisured circle. To him, and to his contemporaries, literature was never a primary consideration. He was a professor of anatomy for thirty-five years; his ability or lack of ability there need not deeply concern us, who are chiefly interested in his writings. It may be observed, however, in passing, that his biographer never once mentions Darwin, and that complaints were made before Holmes' resignation that he was failing to keep up to date in his professional information. He said of Pasteur, though, "I look upon him as one of the greatest experimenters that ever lived, one of the truest benefactors of his race," and he was much interested in the early experiments with artificial anesthetics. He wrote of *Homeopathy and Kindred Delusions,* and there is, too, his much quoted remark about dumping drugs into the sea.

It seems curious that he was regarded as a very dangerous enemy to religion in his day, and that his books were forbidden to the pious. Ostensibly he was a Unitarian. What he was most interested in was laying the ghost of his early training in old-fashioned Calvinism, and although he spoiled many books in his effort he never succeeded in doing so. His theological notions were rather amorphous, but it seems that he wanted to put abroad in the world the idea of a benevolent deity. The Calvinists made of God a cruel and arbitrary figure, quite apart from the world. The generation of Cotton Mather got God down to earth as an interfering old busybody. The deists proclaimed Him to be a gentleman, and the transcendentalists made man and nature and God all of one piece. Holmes never got as far as the last, but he did try to make God benevolent and gentlemanly. Such an enterprise does not seem daring to us today, but in Holmes' day it was tremendously so, especially to the "evangelical press." The constant return of his father's notions to his consciousness led him to recurring mental flagellations, stimulated of course by hostile criticism from without. Unfortunately, the issue was temporary and so his struggles are no longer interesting.

Outside of religion and medicine Holmes had no interests but Boston and Cambridge. The Statehouse at Boston was his "hub of the solar system." He made two trips to Europe; other than that his travelling was mainly on the lyceum circuit. "The story of my first visit to Europe is briefly this: my object was to study the medical profession, chiefly in Paris, and I was in Europe about two years and a half." The second he wrote about in *Our Hundred Days in Europe* (1886), and in that book he explains apologetically that it is only a record for his friends. One is certainly not moved by it now, save perhaps when he speaks of meeting "Oscar Wilde and his handsome wife." He makes no observation on Wilde's wit, however, but the situation is tantalizing. His most uncritical friends are forced to admit that he was most astonishingly provincial in his physical activity, but they contend that his writings are universal in appeal. But a man's letters need not move over so small an area as his body, and Holmes' letters do. Those to Motley, the most extensive series, are made up of Boston gossip, references to the Saturday Club, his personal religious notions, his family interests, and complaints on the drabness of his days, which he finds as regular as the pendulum of his clock. The Saturday Club meant a great deal to him and when it fell to pieces he lamented greatly. It was a really remarkable association of the major minds of New England, but in their conversation they simply flattered one another. The only figure that we are really interested in shunned its meetings; he was Thoreau, "the nullifier of civilization." The rest were all pleasant gentlemen and Holmes in horror wrote, "It must have been a terrible thing to have a friend like Chatterton or Burns." These pleasant gentlemen could not abide a cynic, for "his talk is to profitable conversation what the stone is to the pulp of a peach." Gay's couplet, "Life is jest and all things show it; I thought so once and now I know it," was

combated thus: "Life is a gest, an achievement, or always ought to be." Mr. Longfellow, of the club, wrote some verses called "The Psalm of Life," embodying the same thought, which "touched the heartstrings of the nation." Such was the Saturday Club. When other members went into the world Holmes stayed at home and wrote them the town gossip. He was of Boston, and he was for Boston. Even in religion his ideas did not spring from a universal curiosity, but are explicable only in terms of time and place.

When Holmes brought out his first novel, *Elsie Venner*, in 1861, he had already published several volumes of verse and two of his "Breakfast Table" series. He ventured into the form twice afterward in *The Guardian Angel* (1867) and in *A Mortal Antipathy* (1885). In these novels the modern reader will find almost nothing of interest; Holmes' score in this field, indeed, may be reduced to zero. They evidence his preoccupation with theology and medicine; the ideas behind two of them are "physiological conceptions fertilized by theological dogma," chiefly about heredity and free will. Elsie Venner suffered prenatal ophidian influences which gave her a snake-like character and enabled the author "to suggest the limitations of human responsibility in a simple and effective way." *The Guardian Angel* is also concerned with heredity, but there is not so horrific a manifestation of it. The third and last deals with a young man who has a mortal antipathy to young women because a beautiful one dropped him when he was young. He recovers only when another, also of great beauty, rescues him from fire. She wears bloomers, which eases off the shock.

The modern reader is staggered by all this nonsense, set forth in the utmost seriousness. Holmes documented his novels carefully. He stands, indeed, as one of the forerunners of the realism of Howells, but that need not give us pause, for so does Louisa Alcott with *Little Women*. Aside from their burden of impossible themes, his stories fail to interest as novels because the narrative is clogged by a too frequent intrusion of the manner of the essay. Some of the interpolated essays reflect pleasantly enough New England village life as it was before the alien deluge. When he prepared a final edition in 1891 he realized that his novels were fading and wrote in the new preface to *The Guardian Angel*: "If it fails to interest the reader who ventures upon it, it may find a place in an unfrequented book-shelf in common with other medicated novels."

II

Both as a doctor and as a novelist Holmes was singularly reticent about sex. When women began to clamor for admission to the Harvard Medical School he was rather indifferent, but inclined slightly toward opposition. As Dr. D. W. Cheever, one of his old pupils, observes, it is "interesting as an index of his delicacy and purity, that he affirmed that he was willing to teach women anatomy, but not with men in the same classes; and above all, that he should insist on two dissecting-rooms, which should strictly separate the sexes." In fact, it has been hinted that his modesty was one of the reasons for his lack of success as a practicing physician. When he wrote fiction he was similarly restrained. In *A Guardian Angel* the heroine is rescued from drowning while disguised as a boy and as the hero tears open her shirt in reviving her he discovers that "he" is a female—and then modestly replaces the shirt! When it is suggested that one of his beautiful heroines (and all of his women are beautiful) pose as a model for a statue, he observes that she is not so self-conscious a beauty as to dispute territory with the Venus de Milo "in defences as scanty and insufficient as those of the marble divinity." But on occasion he could be brave, and even bold: once he admitted in mixed Boston company that he had "heard of" Casanova.

"As a boy," Holmes once said, "I used to read the poetry of Pope, of Goldsmith and of Johnson." The influence of these men is discernible in all his verse. The most used foot is the iambus, and a good deal is rhymed couplet, of the *a-b-a-b* scheme. He was not technically ingenious, though he was facile in rhyming. All his work was done before 1880, when the newly discovered lyric forms from France provided the occasional versifier with novel and airy schemes for his fancies. The emotions played little part in what he wrote. His best effects are in occasional verse, of which, as literary handy man, he wrote a great deal. Every Boston birthday dedication, literary visit and so on demanded celebration, and to Holmes they always turned. He was even "offered pay for a poem in praise of a certain stove polish, but I declined." Verse "torn up by the roots," as he puts it, was naturally ephemeral, and though, collected, it fills three double-columned volumes, his friends now have regard only for what can be put into a slim volume of one hundred pages. Some of his poems have passed over into American folklore, among them, **"The Wonderful One Hoss Shay,"** and one has achieved the dubious immortality of being a favorite "speaking piece" for school children, **"Old Ironsides."** But most of it is now very dusty. Occasionally it survives as humor—**"The Height of the Ridiculous"** and **"The Broomstick Train,"** for example. The serious pieces do not seem to hold up. **"The Chambered Nautilus"** is an elaborate conceit with a trite moral, and in introducing it at the end of a breakfast-table conversation he calls particular attention to the moral. The best of Holmes seems to me to be in **"The Last Leaf,"** which appealed alike to the intellectual Poe and the emotional Lincoln. Mark Twain tells of

Holmes reciting it: "Then Doctor Holmes recited—as only Doctor Holmes could recite it—**'The Last Leaf,'** and the house rose as one individual and went mad with worshiping delight." Most of that was in tribute to his personality; nevertheless the poem does combine a good subject and felicity of expression.

When, in 1857, the Boston-Cambridge group established the *Atlantic Monthly* it was to Holmes that the first editor turned for popular material, and his reply was *The Autocrat of the Breakfast Table,* published as a book in 1858. It is incomparably the best volume of prose that he wrote; all his other books may be dismissed as relatively unimportant. They do contain flashes of wit, but they are also full of sandy stretches, and as a whole, barren. He quotes as applicable to *The Autocrat* a phrase out of the preface to "Gil Blas": "Here lies buried the soul of the licentiate." If that is true, then the soul of Holmes was dry and bookish; indeed, he always had an easy feeling among books, "as a stable-boy has among horses." There is no accent of talk in *The Autocrat,* but only careful writing. We do not hear a tone of voice. Holmes regarded conversation as a fine art, and was alleged to be the best talker in Boston, but his written discourse is didactic even when it is whimsical. One may reasonably suppose that *The Autocrat* epitomizes the literary humor of the Boston the author knew. When Mark Twain was in England the English made it plain to him that they could turn out polite humorists like Holmes by the dozen, but that Lincoln, Artemus Ward and Twain himself were beyond them. When the bookishness is taken away from Holmes nothing is left, or almost nothing; there is no body. One goes through his masterwork with amusement, but nothing memorable remains at the end. "Ah yes," one says, "This was humor in literary Boston."

The trouble probably lay in his inability to take a purely critical attitude toward anything but religion—and there he was fighting a dying dragon, and he did not give it its death blows. His kindliness assuaged the pain of those who still worshiped. He stuck in pins, but Emerson and William Ellery Channing did the heavy work. On social questions he was very conservative, and of morals I need not say more. He attacked the Knights of Labor in *Over the Teacups,* that record of his dotage, and told them that if they "did not like the country they could go elsewhere." By implication, he makes it appear that the Knights were chiefly Irish and Germans, anyway. "If all the cities of the world were reduced to ashes," he wrote elsewhere, "you'd have a new set of millionaires in a couple of years or so out of the trade in potash." Not even whimsicality can make that other than conservatively commonplace. The truth is that Holmes knew little and cared nothing about the social movements of his time. He was rebuked by Lowell for his indifference to Abolition, but when the Civil War came he said it was holy.

III

It could have been said in no other city than the Boston of 1857 that "society is a strong solution of books." To Holmes books meant those of Eighteenth Century England, and chiefly those of Goldsmith and the essay-ists. His prose is peppered with incidents out of Boswell, and was formed on the model of Addison and Steele. How he got through *Tom Jones* and *Roderick Random* and Sterne's novels, I don't know, for he could talk about books having "subjects which a fastidious conventionalism would approve." Not all the books of Swift, it appears, were on his list, for "one who has had the misfortune to soil his mind by reading certain poems of Swift will never cleanse it to its original whiteness." Of his contemporaries in England he preferred Words-worth, but he was also fond of Carlyle. Of the Bosto-nians he said little of much value, for he had a distaste for criticism, but he read them all and hailed them as immortal. His letters to Lowell are full of praises, and he wrote to Mrs. Stowe, "Your books, being immortal, must be purged from every earthly stain." But "I shrink from a lawless independence to which all the virile energy and trampling audacity of Mr. Whitman fail to reconcile me." Nor did he understand another independ-ent soul, Emerson, though he wrote a biography of him. It is anecdotal, and without insight. He thought *In-nocents Abroad* full of "frequently quaint and amusing conceits." He expected a great deal of Aldrich, and he was sure about William Dean Howells. He mentioned Ik Marvel as "one of the pleasantest of our American writers." The whole case may be summed up in his belief that "one of the best offices which women perform for men is that of tasting books for them." Thus it is not surprising that he disapproved of Zola as "one whose name must be looked for at the bottom of the alphabet, as if its natural place were as low down in the dregs of realism as it could find itself."

When he was a youth in Paris he saw many pictures, but in his own Boston he found little but Copley, Stuart and Washington Allston. This poverty is revealed in his remark, made in *Our Hundred Days in Europe,* about a visit to the Louvre: "I retained a vivid remembrance of many pictures, which had been kept bright by seeing great numbers of reproductions of them in photographs and engravings." No wonder he wrote that "the New World keeps the imagination on a plain and scanty diet." He knew little of the theatre, though he once said through one of his small boy characters: "D'd y'ever see Ed'in Forrest play Metamora? Bully, I tell you!" Fanny Elssler—to Emerson her dancing was a religion—was the woman who "danced the capstone onto Bunker

Hill Monument as Orpheus moved rocks to music." His most constant pleasures were horse-trotting—not rac-ing, for that stimulated betting—and measuring trees. He had endless data on the woodland giants of New England. He believed in temperance "for healthy people," and discouraged smoking.

Pleasantness and fastidious conventionalism thus make up all there is of Holmes. His religious radicalism no longer scares anyone, and it didn't scare many of any intelligence in his own day. In him is summed up the humor of literary Boston—in *The Autocrat* and a hand-ful of poems. His life and works are materials for a footnote to the history of an epoch. The charm of his personality made his contemporaries overrate him, and the adulators of New England continued the error. He took himself seriously, of course, though he once said slightingly that during his professorship at Harvard he had "paid some attention to literature." Such polite deprecation is a falsification of his real attitude. Better illustrative is an incident. When Lowell brought How-ells to meet Holmes, the latter said, "Well, James, this is something like the apostolic succession;—this is the laying on of hands!"

Gay Wilson Allen (essay date 1935)

SOURCE: Allen, Gay Wilson. "Oliver Wendell Holmes." In *American Prosody,* pp. 193-216. New York: Octagon Books, 1966.

[*In the following excerpt, originally published in 1935, Allen discusses the limitations of Holmes's poetic style, noting that it was informed by both eighteenth-century verse and the poet's scientific training.*]

I. INTRODUCTION

There is almost every reason for us not to expect a pro-sodic system from Holmes, or even much prosodic thinking at all. He was first of all a physician and professor of anatomy, and most of his poetry is colored to some extent by the scientist, directly in subject-matter and idiom and indirectly in the scientific reserve that always held in check his poetic imagination.

In the second place, he was a "throw back," as most critics have pointed out (though they often over-emphasize it). He says in his note to *Poetry,* **"A Metri-cal Essay"** written in 1836, that, "This Academic Poem presents the simple and partial views of a young person trained after the schools of classical English verse as represented by Pope, Goldsmith, and Campbell, with whose lines his memory was early stocked." And in many respects, he remained an eighteenth-century neo-classicist all of his life. But even in this confession we must remember Holmes's statement that the poem, which would of course include the versification, represents only his "partial views." It is plain, however, that this young poet was not headed toward any sort of prosodic revolution.

In the third place, Holmes was always primarily an "occasional" poet, despite the fact that he did write some fine poetry for more serious purposes; and the occasional poet, like the journalistic versifier, may be counted upon to follow the conventions. For new forms divert attention to technique, whereas the "occasional" poet wants all attention focused on what he has to say. So long, therefore, as Holmes remained the writer of after-dinner verse (and such he did remain until the end of his days), he was practically compelled to continue using the familiar octosyllabic couplet, the heroic couplet, ballad meter, and other simple and accepted forms.

Nevertheless, we do find Holmes now and then speculating on prosodic questions. The most widely known instance, of course, is "The Physiology of Versification," which is typical of Holmes the scientist, and which proclaims that there is a vital and necessary connection between the laws of versification and the respiration and the pulse, "the true time-keepers of the body." He takes as his starting point the fact that a normal person breathes about twenty times per minute, and then says:

> The 'fatal facility' of the octosyllabic measure has often been spoken of, without any reference to its real cause. The reason why eight syllable verse is so singularly easy to read aloud is that it follows more exactly than any other measure the natural rhythm of expiration. In reading aloud in the ordinary way from the 'Lay of the Last Minstrel,' from 'In Memoriam,' or from 'Hiawatha' . . . it will be found that not less than sixteen nor more than twenty-four lines will be spoken in a minute, probably about twenty. It is plain, therefore, that if one reads twenty lines in a minute, and naturally breathes the same number of times during that minute, he will pronounce one line to each expiration, taking advantage of the pause at its close for inspiration. The only effort required is that of vocalizing and articulating; the breathing takes care of itself, not even demanding a thought except where the sense may require a pause in the middle of a line. The very fault with these octosyllabic lines is that they slip away too fluently, and run easily into a monotonous sing-song.[1]

On the same grounds, Holmes argues that the "heroic line" is more difficult to read because only about fourteen verses are pronounced in a minute; so that, "If

a breath is allowed to each line the respiration will be longer and slower than natural, and a sense of effort and fatigue will soon be the consequence." Though the cæsura is a "breathing-place," it "entirely breaks up the natural rhythm of breathing." The twelve- and the fourteen-syllable lines are also found difficult for the same reasons.

Now this argument is ingenious and interesting, but it is so "scientific" that it fails to take into account all the facts. Holmes admits that different persons have different respiratory rhythms, and hence his argument may not hold for all people. Moreover, he does not consider the fact that in enjambed octosyllabics, two, three, or several lines are read at one breath-sweep. And in blank verse, which is undoubtedly the most "natural" speaking verse (as Shakespeare's dramas are sufficient to prove), the irregular variation of short and long breath-sweeps gives us the most pleasing effects. But still more important is the fact that this theory is an attempt to explain conventional, classical, accepted prosody, in which end-stopped lines predominate. It is more physiological than prosodic. The attempt to explain prosody on physiological principles is commendable, yet the chief value of the essay for the student of prosody lies in the fact that it is the best proof we could ask that Holmes took conventional prosody for granted.

As late as 1849, Holmes takes Lowell to task for his versification: "You laugh at the old square-toed heroic sometimes, and I must retort upon the rattlety-bang sort of verse in which you have indulged. I read a good deal of it as I used to go over the kittle-y-benders when a boy, horribly afraid of a slump every time I cross one of its up-and-down hump-backed lines. I don't mean that it cannot be done, or that you have not often done it so as to be readable and musical; but think of having to read a mouthful of such lines as this:—

For the frost's [?] swift shuttles its shroud had spun.[2]

In 1890, Holmes does admit that, "I find the burden and restrictions of rhyme more and more troublesome as I grow older."[3] But here he is probably referring more to his own infirmities than to any intrinsic restrictions of the system; certainly he never seems to have thought of trying to write poetry without the "burden" of rime (except, of course, in blank verse).

And yet, strangely enough, there is in his 1836 preface a doctrine which sounds curiously "modern," even "modernistic" or "cubistic." In defending the "extravagant" in poetry, he says: "A series of hyperbolical images is considered beneath criticism by the same judges who would write treatises upon the sculptured satyrs and painted arabesques of antiquity, which are only hyperbole in stone and colors. As material objects in different lights repeat themselves in shadows variously elongated, contracted, or exaggerated, so our solid and sober thoughts caricature themselves in fantastic shapes inseparable from their originals, and having a unity in their extravagance, which proves them to have retained their proportions in certain respects, however differing in outline from their prototypes."[4]

But this preface is apparently a defence of the poems in the 1836 volume, all of which obey the conventional rules of versification. Apparently Holmes never thought of trying to convey his "hyperbolical images" and "caricature" by a "fantastic" or "exaggerated" technique.

Holmes did make valuable contributions to the practice of American versification, and exerted a powerful influence toward reinstating the French polish and perfection of eighteenth-century English ideals; yet we must study him as a versifier and not as a conscious prosodist.

2. BALLADS AND BALLAD MEASURE

Though Holmes early began to use practically all the verse forms that he ever used, the ballad measure seems to be most characteristic of his earlier period. He never surpassed **"The Spectre Pig,"** for instance, in his imitations of the genuine folk ballad, despite the fact that he insisted on placing it in the last section of his collected poems under the heading of "Verses from the Oldest Portfolio." It is difficult to find anywhere a more subtle, ironical, and satirical parody of the thought, diction, and rhythm of the ballad.

> It was the stalwart butcher man,
>   That knit his swarthy brow,
> And said the gentle Pig must die,
>   And sealed it with a vow.
>
> And oh! it was the gentle Pig
>   Lay stretched upon the ground,
> And ah! it was the cruel knife
>   His little heart that found.

These inversions and parataxes are not awkward, as we might expect, but produce a rhythm which is an unmistakable folk ballad tune. We also find the same "tune" in **"The Mysterious Visitor."**

"Old Ironsides" (1830) is in the same ballad measure, yet is different in several details. The eight-line stanzas are fairly regular in meter and have a two-line thought-movement, as in **"The Spectre Pig"** and the genuine folk ballads; but only four of the twenty-four lines are enjambed, there are comparatively few metrical stresses, and the diction and syntactical constructions are more natural than in **"The Spectre Pig."** Occasionally the first foot is reversed:

> Nail to the mast her holy flag,
>   Set every threadbare sail,
> And give her to the god of storms,
>   The lightning and the gale!

"The Star and the Water-Lily" (1830) contains a generous sprinkling of anapestic feet, a variation which Holmes continued to use intermittently during his whole poetic career.

> The sun stepped down | from his gol | den throne,
>   And lay | in the sil | ent sea,
> And the Lil | y had fold | ed her sat | in leaves,
>   For a sleep | y thing was she;
> What is | the Lily dreaming of?
>   Why crisp the waters blue?
> See, see, | she is lif | ting her var | nished lid!
>   Her white leaves are glistening through!

"To an Insect" and **"My Aunt"** (1831), however, are more typical of Holmes's ballad measure, being straight iambic, 4 + 3. **"The Cambridge Churchyard"** is in precisely the same meter, but is less regular and inclined to singsong because of a skilful variation of stresses, including initial accented syllables, secondary accents, and spondees.

> Our ancient church! it's lowly tower,
>   Beneath the loftier spire,
> Is shadowed when the sunset hour
>   Clothes the | tall shaft | in fire;
> It sinks beyond the distant eye
>   Long ere | the glittering vane,
> High wheel | ing in the western sky,
>   Has faded o'er the plain.

Where alternate lines are enjambed, the ballad measure is really seven-stress, the 4 + 3 arrangement being entirely arbitrary. **"A Ballad of the Boston Tea-Party"** could be printed in seven-stress lines without in any way changing the rhythm, except possibly to tempt the reader to syncopate it.

> The waves that wrought a century's wreck
>   Have rolled o'er whig and tory;

"**The Ballad of the Oysterman**" is arranged in seven-stress lines, but is in the same rhythm as "**The Spectre Pig.**" These are early poems; later ones are "**Nux Postcœnatica**" (1848), "**Meeting of the Alumni of Harvard College**" (1857), and "**Post-Prandial**" (1881).

3. Four-Stress Iambics

Holmes used the four-stress iambic line extensively from his college days (*cf.* "**The Meeting of the Dryads**") until very near the end of his life. His four-stress verse includes simple stanza forms, such as the *abab* quatrain, octosyllabic couplets, and "clipped" four-stress iambic. No new, eccentric, or irregular versification is found in the handling of these forms, and since they are so common anyway, a full discussion of them should not be necessary.

His juvenile "**The Meeting of the Dryads**" is characteristic of much of Holmes's regular octosyllabic lines, with its inversions, smooth and regular beats, and couplet movement (even with alternate rime):

> In every julep that he drinks,
> 　May gout, and bile, and headache be;
> And when he strives to calm his pain,
> 　May colic mingle with his tea.

"**Under the Violets**" (1859) is different in its versification only in the greater enjambment of its third stanza, the first four lines being read at one sweep. Rarely are more than two lines enjambed in Holmes's four-stress verse.

"**The Parting Word**" is characteristic of the seven-syllable lines:

> I must leave thee, lady sweet!
> Months shall waste before we meet;
> Winds are fair and sails are spread,
> Anchors leave their ocean bed;

Only two lines of this poem depart from the regular pattern, and even this departure (primary-secondary-primary accents) is neither unusual nor especially important:

> When the first sad sun shall set, . . .

> While the first seven mornings last,

However, a few very pretty lines are produced in "**Fantasia**" partly by this device:

> Kiss mine eyelids, beauteous morn,

> Blushing into life new-born!

Some of the later seven- and eight-syllable couplets contain a good deal of parallelism accompanied by initial repetition and balancing of half-line against half-line, resulting in such a rocking-horse movement as that found in "**Programme**":

> Not for glory, not for pelf,
> Not, be sure, to please myself, . . .
> Turn my pages,—never mind
> If you like not all you find; . . .
> Every kernel has its shell,
> Every book its dullest leaf,

In "**The New Eden**" some of the parallelism is emphasized by alliteration:

> The rippling grass, the nodding grain, . . .
> To scanty sun and frequent rain. . . .
> The food was scant, the fruits were few: . . .
> Austere in taste, and tough at core,

Holmes's most famous four-stress couplets are those of "**The Deacon's Masterpiece, or The Wonderful One-Hoss Shay.**" Here anapestic substitution is used very freely:

> Have you heard | of the won | derful one | -hoss shay,
> That was built | in such a log | ical way?
> It ran a hundred years | to a day,
> And then, | of a sud | den, it — ah, | but stay,
> I'll tell | you what hap | pened without | delay,
> Scaring the parson into fits,
> Frightening people out | of their wits,—
> Have you ev | er heard of that, I say?

The monotonous rime and absurd rhythm are part of the humor of this piece, but the versification is little better than doggerel, especially in such passages as:

> Deacon and deaconess dropped away,
> Children and grandchildren—where were they?
> But there stood the stout old one-hoss shay
> As fresh as on Lisbon-earthquake-day! . . .
>
> End of the wonderful one-hoss shay.
> Logic is logic. That's all I say.

"**Parson Turell's Legacy,**" written in the same year as the "**One-Hoss Shay**" (1858), is, on the whole, more regular, though the rhythm in some passages is broken by short, elliptical sentences, resulting in a colloquialism very characteristic of Holmes's humorous verse:

> Facts respecting an old arm-chair.
> At Cambridge. Is kept in the College there.
> Seems but little the worse for wear.

Know old Cambridge? Hope you do.—
Born there? Don't say so! I was, too.

Another colloquial device is the use of abbreviations, with a consequent eccentricity of rhythm, as in **"How the Old Horse Won the Bet"**:

The swift g. m., old Hiram's nag,
The fleet s. h., Dan Pfeiffer's brag,
With these a third—and who is he
That stands beside his fast b. g.?

On the whole, **"Dorothy Q,"** with its very sparing enjambment and monotonous singsong rhythm, is characteristic of Holmes's four-stress couplets. Like Whittier's *Snow-Bound,* it is important for its description, not for its versification, though it is a much smoother and less awkward poem than Whittier's. **"At the Pantomime"** has greater enjambment, with more skilfully varied pauses, and contains some of Holmes's most pleasing octosyllabic couplets.

4. THE ANAPEST

We have already observed Holmes's use of anapestic feet in both his ballad and his four-stress couplets. **"The Stethoscope Song"** is not predominantly anapestic, but the use of some anapests is part of the pattern, a pattern which is itself somewhat uneven, individual lines often being as "rough and ready" as limerick verse, as in the first quatrain:

There was | a young man | in Boston town.

He bought | him a steth | oscope nice | and new,

All moun | ted and fin | ished and pol | ished down,

With an iv | ory cap | and a stop | per too.

But many of Holmes's poems are typically anapestic, such as **"The Old Man of the Sea."** Notice also the final repetitions in the first and third lines of each stanza:

Do you know | the Old Man | of the Sea, | of the Sea?

Have you met | with that dread | ful old man?

If you hav | en't been caught | you will be, | you will be;

For catch | you he must | and he can.

Or still more anapestic, with its feminine cæsuras, is **"Brother Jonathan's Lament for Sister Caroline,"** which begins:

She has gone |— she has left | us, [:] in pas | sion and pride,

Our storm | y-browed sis | ter, [:] so long | at our side!

Many of the later "class poems" are in this movement, as are several pieces in "Bunker-Hill Battle and Other Poems," 1874-1877. Note, for instance, **"Grandmother's Story of Bunker-Hill Battle,"** with its internal double rimes accompanying the triple rhythm:

'T is like stir | ring liv | ing embers | when, at eight | y, one
    remembers

All the achings | and the quakings | of "the times | that tried
    men's souls;"

When I talk | of *Whig* | and *Tory,* | when I tell | the *Reb* | el story,

To you the words are ashes, | but to me | they're burning coals.

The 1874 **"At the Atlantic Dinner"** contains three- and four-syllable rimes:

I suppose it's myself that you're making allusions to
And bringing the sense of dismay and confusion to.
Of course *some* must speak,—they are always selected
    to,
But pray what's the reason that I am expected to?
I'm not fond of wasting my breath as those fellows do
That want to be blowing forever as bellows do;
Their legs are uneasy, but why will you jog any
That long to stay quiet beneath the mahogany?

Though Holmes did use this meter fairly frequently, especially in his later period, he apparently adopted it merely as a variation to relieve the monotony of his octosyllabics and heroics. No one realized better than the poet himself that his style was limited, as he confesses in the anapestic **"For Whittier's Seventieth Birthday"** (1877):

Yes,—"the style is the man," and the nib of one's pen
Makes the same mark at twenty, and three-score and
    ten;

5. HEROIC COUPLET

We have already seen that Holmes admitted his eighteenth-century prosodic background, and that he seemed to resent Lowell's laughing "at the old square-toed heroic." In **"Poem Read at the Dinner Given to the Author by the Medical Profession,"** he proudly admits his allegiance to this measure:

And so the hand that takes the lyre for you
Plays the old tune on strings that once were new.
Nor let the rhymester of the hour deride
The straight-backed measure with its stately stride;
It gave the mighty voice of Dryden scope;
It sheathed the steel-bright epigrams of Pope;
In Goldsmith's verse it learned a sweeter strain;
Byron and Campbell wore its clanking chain;
I smile to listen while the critic's scorn
Flouts the proud purple kings have nobly worn;

This passage is also a good illustration of the metrical regularity of Holmes's heroics. Each line has exactly ten syllables, inverted feet are used sparingly, spondees rarely (but *cf.* "proud purple"), and each couplet is closed or "couplet moulded" in the eighteenth-century manner. Extra syllables can in nearly every case be accounted for by the usual rules of elision, as, for example, in the following lines from the 1836 *Poetry,* **"A Metrical Essay"**:

(1) Elision of "open vowels":

> Would wail its re*quiem* o'er a poet's grave! . . .
> And carve in language its ether*eal* form,

(2) "Pure *l*":

> The hot-cheeked rev*eller*, tossing down the wine

(3) "Pure *n*":

> The infant, list*ening* to the warbling bird;

(4) "Pure *r*":

> Scenes of my youth! awake its slumb*ering* fire!
> Ye winds of mem*ory,* sweep the silent lyre!

Holmes used this measure extensively, both for serious and "familiar" verse. Most of his long poems are in this form. His **"Five Stories and a Sequel,"** which he collected under the heading of "Readings Over the Teacups," are all in heroic couplets. They include **"To My Old Readers," "The Banker's Secret," "The Exile's Secret," "The Lover's Secret," "The Statesman's Secret," "The Mother's Secret,"** and **"The Secret of the Stars."** These poems are not so well known as Holmes's four-stress couplets of the **"One-Hoss Shay,"** yet they contain some good versification, such as **"The Secret of the Stars,"** which has some beautiful cadences, held in check only by the rime and a corresponding tendency toward the full stop after the completion of the rime. Many of the first lines of couplets, though, are enjambed:

> In vain the sweeping equatorial pries
> Through every world-sown corner of the skies,
> To the far orb that so remotely strays
> Our midnight darkness is its noonday blaze;
> In vain the climbing soul of creeping man
> Metes out the heavenly concave with a span,

These lines are less "couplet moulded" than the average eighteenth-century English heroics, but the neo-classical model is apparent. It is in this measure, however, that the eighteenth-century influence on Holmes's versification is strongest.

The pentameter in alternate rime is so nearly like the heroic couplets in versification that it need not be analyzed here. The most popular instance is **"The Iron Gate,"** in *abab* quatrains. **"Homesick in Heaven"** is sometimes highly praised. And some other examples are **"For the Commemoration Services"** and **"My Aviary."**

6. Blank Verse

Holmes wrote comparatively little blank verse, probably because it is not a very convenient form for "occasional" poems; and his few attempts are perhaps less known than any other poetic form that he used. But the little blank verse that he did write is, so far as versification goes, unusually good. The 1864 **"A Sea Dialogue"** contains some awkward lines, the worst being:

> Friend, you seem thoughtful. I not wonder much
> That he who sails the ocean should be sad.

Yet the 1872 **"Wind-Cloud and Star-Drifts"** shows complete mastery of the form. Especially commendable are the long breath-sweeps, permitting sustained cadences in the best blank verse tradition.

> With quickened heart-beats I shall hear the tongues
> That speak my praise; / but better far the sense
> That in the unshaped ages, / buried deep
> In the dark mines of unaccomplished time
> Yet to be stamped with morning's royal die
> And coined in golden days, /—in those dim years
> I shall be reckoned with the undying dead, /
> My name emblazoned on the fiery arch, /
> Unfading till the stars themselves shall fade. //

However much Holmes's heroic couplets may be in the eighteenth-century tradition, his blank verse is certainly not, for it shows scarcely a trace of the couplet influence. Yet it is more in the tradition of Freneau than of Bryant, since it echoes the good workmanship of Freneau (*cf. The Rising Glory of America*) and lacks the sonority of Bryant's *Thanatopsis*.

7. "The Chambered Nautilus"

The popularity of **"The Chambered Nautilus"** and the poet's own undisguised pride in this poem make a discussion of it almost imperative. In a letter to George Ticknor, Holmes declares, "I am as willing to submit this [poem] to criticism as any I have written, in form as well as substance, and I have not seen any English verse of just the same pattern."[5]

In none of his other poems do we find Holmes using such freely varied accents as in **"The Chambered Nautilus."** There are, in fact, so many reversed feet and interpolated spondees that no one stanza accurately indicates the underlying rhythmical pattern. Stated simply, the pattern is composed of iambic pentameter, trimeter, and a final alexandrine, in the following scheme: $a_5a_3b_3bb_5c_3c_6$. But to illustrate the basic pattern we must build up a composite stanza:

Its webs of living gauze no more unfurl; ...　　(a)

That spreads his lustrous coil; ...　　(a)

The venturous bark that flings ...　　(b)

Let each new temple, nobler than the last, ...　　(b)

In gulfs enchanted, where the Siren sings, ...　　(b)

Before thee lies revealed, —　　(c)

Its irised ceiling rent, its sunless crypt unsealed!　(c)

The following stanza is as typical as any:

Year af | ter year　beheld | the sil | ent toil

That spread | his lus | trous coil;

Still, as | the spir | al grew,

He left | the past | year's dwell | ing for | the new,

Stole with | soft step | its shin | ing arch | way through,

Built up | its id | le door,

Stretched in | his last | -found home, | and knew | the old | no

more.

While the first element of the compound, such as "last-found," is usually given primary stress, with secondary stress on the second element (as scanned above), this phrase and others, like "sea-maids," are nearly spondaic. "Sea-maids" is especially interesting. In the phrase "the sea-maids rise" the normal accentuation would be (× / \ /); but "the cold sea-maids rise" contains a conflict, the preceding monosyllable "cold" tending to reduce the accentuation of "sea" to secondary stress. Perhaps the whole line is normally pronounced as follows:

> Where the cold sea-maids rise to sun their streaming
> hair.

The poem contains an abundance of alliteration, much more, in fact, than we find in most of Holmes's poetry. Several examples are:

> On the sweet summer wind its purpled wings . . .
> Its irised ceiling rent, its sunless crypt unsealed! . . .
> Stole with soft step its shining archway through, . . .
> Build thee more stately mansions, O my soul, . . .
> Leaving thine outgrown shell by life's unresting sea!

It is probably unsafe to press very far a search for symbolism in the form of this poem, yet one wonders whether the rhythms (including the combinations of pentameter, trimeter, and alexandrine in the novel stanzaic arrangement) were not intended to symbolize the crenulated and scalloped shell of the chambered nautilus. At any rate, the form is, as Holmes himself believed, very unusual, and perhaps unique.

8. OTHER STANZA FORMS

Next to **"The Chambered Nautilus,"** Holmes perhaps took most pride in **"The Last Leaf,"** at least among his stanzaic poems. Certainly it is the only other poem which he believed he had written on an original model. His own explanation of why he happened to use the "somewhat singular measure" is amusing. "I had become a little known as a versifier, and I thought that one or two other young writers were following my efforts with imitations. . . . I determined to write in a measure which would at once betray any copyist." He mentions Campbell's *Battle of the Baltic* as having probably suggested the form, "But I do not remember any poem in the same measure, except such as have been written since its publication."[6]

It is a little puzzling why Holmes took so much pride in the form of this poem, but his handling of it is easy and dexterous.

I saw him once before,

As he passed by the door,

　And again

The pavement stones resound,

As he totters o'er the ground

　With his cane.

The rhythm does have a lilt which is more musical than anything else Holmes ever wrote. The only trouble is that it is almost too musical, the "tune" obtruding itself into the reading so much that the poem is mostly sound. Still, it is a competent lyric. And its music is reminiscent of the seventeenth-century English lyrics.

Holmes's most peculiar stanza is the unrimed trochaic quatrain of **"De Sauty,"** composed of three six-stress and one three-stress lines. This is unique in his poetry, for his only other unrimed verse is regular blank verse, and no other poem of his is so predominantly trochaic.

Many | things thou | askest, | jackknife | -bearing | stranger,

Much-conjecturing mortal, pork-and-treacle-waster!

Pretermit thy whittling, wheel thine earflap toward me,

　Thou shalt hear them answered.

When the charge galvanic tingled through the cable,

At the polar focus of the wire electric

Suddenly appeared a white-faced man among us:

　Called himself "DE SAUTY."

Though the great bulk of Holmes's poetry is in couplets and alternate rime (often paragraphed as stanzas), he did use several stanza arrangements. But since most of them are fairly conventional, and none of those not already discussed are of any special importance, it should be sufficient merely to list the main forms.

The quatrains have already been discussed, but we may add the form aab_5b_3, in **"But One Talent"** and **"To the Eleven Ladies."**

The tail-rime stanza appears to have been a favorite with Holmes. Examples of the main combinations are: $aa_3b_2ccc_3b_2$, **"International Ode"**; $ab_2bcc_4abdb_2$, **"Too Young for Love"**; $ABcc_4B_2$, **"Martha"**; $aa_4b_3ccc_4b_3$, **"The World's Homage,"** in *Two Poems to Harriet Beecher Stowe*; $abab_4cc_3d_4ee_3d_4$, **"Lexington"**; $a_5a_3bbccd_5a_3$ (var.), **"At the Summit,"** in *Two Poems to Harriet Beecher Stowe*; $abaa_5b_3$, **"The Rose and the Fern"**; and $abbcc_3a_2$, **"The Peau de Chagrin of State Street."**

The **"Two Sonnets: Harvard"** (1878) and the sonnet sequence to Longfellow, **"Our Dead Singer"** (1882), show that Holmes could handle the Italian form with ease and facility, and it is surprising and regrettable that he did not write more sonnets. These five adhere closely to the form, but the first obeys most strictly the quatrain divisions of the octave. Its opening quatrain is as follows:

> To God's Anointed and His Chosen Flock:
> So ran the phrase the black-robed conclave chose
> To guard the sacred cloisters that arose
> Like David's altar on Moriah's rock.

To judge by Holmes's random stanzas, his sonnets, his blank verse, and his few excellent lyrics, he could have achieved success in almost any conventional meter; yet as we have seen, he always remained essentially a poet of octosyllabics and the heroic couplet. In this connection, it is interesting to recall Lowell's qualified praise, whether or not we agree with it:

> He has perfect sway of what I call a sham metre,
> But many admire it, the English pentameter,
> And Campbell, I think, wrote most commonly worse,
> With less nerve, swing, and fire in the same kind of
> verse,

A Fable for Critics

While Holmes won considerable fame and distinction in his day, it is doubtful whether he has had much influence on American versification, (1) because he used the old measures without contributing anything new to their handling except an urbane unself-consciousness and an epigrammatic polish, and (2), and consequently, because his method called attention to content rather than technique.

9. THE FAMILIAR VERSE OF SAXE, FIELD, BUNNER

Since Holmes was preëminently a poet of *vers de société*—or, as Brander Matthews prefers to call the type,

"familiar verse,"—we may properly consider here some of the minor familiar versifiers of the period. In his anthology of *American Familiar Verse* Brander Matthews includes Benjamin Franklin's *Paper*, Freneau's *The Parting Glass* and *To a Caty-Did*, Paulding's *The Old Man's Carousal*, Bryant's *Robert of Lincoln*, Emerson's *The Humble-Bee*, Whittier's *The Barefoot Boy*, Longfellow's *Catawba Wine*, and selections from many other American poets, both major and minor. Indeed, most poets at one time or another write light lyrics which may be called familiar verse, but Holmes is the only major American poet with whom this verse was especially characteristic.

Likewise the number of significant minor poets who are distinguished chiefly for their familiar verse is small. In fact, we find only three of special importance. They are John Godfrey Saxe (1816-1887), Eugene Field (1850-1895), and Henry Cuyler Bunner (1855-1896). Matthews says that Saxe "is not only the earliest, he is also the most old-fashioned in his method and the least individual in his outlook. His verse is modelled upon Praed's, to whose dazzling brilliance he could not attain; and he borrowed also the pattern of Hood in his more broadly comic lyrics."[7]

Saxe himself made no secret of his imitation of Hood and Praed. He even labelled *The Beauty of Ballston*, for instance, as "After Praed." And it is also true, as Matthews says, that Saxe was conventional in his methods, as in his simple ballads, *The Briefless Barrister, Captain Jones's Misadventure*, and *The Cold Water-Man*; in his heroic couplets, as in *The Times*, with its balance and antithesis of half-line against half-line; in the rollicking but smoothly flowing anapestics of *A Benedict's Appeal to a Bachelor*; and the playful triplet and quadruplet feminine rimes of *The Devil of Names* can be paralleled in the humorous verse of many other poets. But *The Cold Water-Man* is a skilful burlesque of the folk ballad, though hardly so successful as Holmes's **"The Spectre Pig."**

One special characteristic of Saxe's versification is his fondness for "tail-rime." Some examples are: *A College Reminiscence*, $aa_4b_2cc_4b_2$; *The Proud Miss MacBride*, aaa_4—$b_3ccc_4b_3$; and many simple arrangements in the "Love Poems." We also find three-stress blank trochees in *Rhyme of the Rail*. Saxe's "Love Poems" is perhaps the most significant group for verse technique, being the most truly lyrical. His use of burdens, repetitions, and frequent iterations of the same rimes in these poems is analogous to the versification of the seventeenth-century English madrigals—and possibly to the late nineteenth-century adaptations of the fourteenth-century French forms, as practiced by both Swinburne and later Austin Dobson. One interesting example is *To My Love*, riming *abbBa abbBa abbBa*—apparently an original type of the rondel. *Roger Bontemps, The King of Nor-*

mandy, and *The Poet of this Garret* are translations and adaptations from Béranger.

The sentimentality of Eugene Field, is so out of fashion today with educated Americans that his smooth, facile, and melodious versification is generally unappreciated. But most of his poems have a truly musical lyricism hardly equalled by any other minor American poet of his time. His ballads, lullabys, and dialect poems are as singable as the original English ballads which he deliberately tried to imitate. He uses alternate rime, especially in trimeters and quatrameters, but his characteristic measure is the ballad. *Father's Way* is in seven-stress couplets, but the poem has an unmistakable ballad tune, as do likewise the long-line dialect poems, such as *Casey's Table D'hote,* which begins:

> Oh, the days on Red Hoss Mountain, when the skies
> wuz fair 'nd blue,
> When the money flowed like likker, 'nd the folks wuz
> brave 'nd true!
> When the nights wuz crisp 'nd balmy, 'nd the camp
> wuz all astir,
> When the joints all throwed wide open 'nd no sheriff
> to demur!

The singing quality of Field's poems is partly the result of his extensive use of couplet and alternate rime. But sometimes the excessive reiteration of similar rime sounds results in undesirable singsong—probably Field's greatest weakness. His best poems could all be set to folk ballad tunes. *Long Ago, Little Boy Blue, Dutch Lullaby,* and *Cornish Lullaby* are essentially songs anyway.

Practically all of Bunner's poems in conventional measures are distinguished for their grace, ease, and clever manipulation of meter to produce fresh and novel effects; but he is particularly important in the history of American versification for his adaptation and use of the fourteenth-century French forms which Austin Dobson had recently used so successfully in English. The American interest in these forms may be dated from the spring of 1878. In May of that year Brander Matthews reviewed one of Dobson's volumes for the *Nation,* and then in June he published "Varieties of Verse" (an essay on the history of these forms) in *Appleton's Journal.* Thereafter Matthews, Bunner, and many others began writing triolets, rondels, rondeaus, and ballades. Eugene Field wrote one ballade, called *Ballade of Women I Love,* but Bunner's experiments in the French forms are the most important ones of the period.

An example of the triolet is Bunner's *A Pitcher of Mignonette,* riming ABcAcbAB. *O Honey of Hymettus Hill* is a rondel on Dobson's variation, *viz.,* ABab baAB ababAB. *She was a Beauty* rimes ABab baAB babaAB. Some rondeaus are *An April Fool, Les Morts Vont Vite, Saint Valentine, That New Year's Call. Behold the Deeds* is a chant royal, one of the most complicated forms aside from the sestina.

Bunner was perhaps the cleverest of all the minor American poets of the late nineteenth century, but the *tour de force* apparently interested him more than the content of his poems. Some of his cleverest work is in *Home, Sweet Home, with Variations,* in which he cleverly burlesques the versification of Swinburne, Bret Harte, Dobson ("As Austin Dobson Might Have Translated it from Horace if it Had even Occurred to Horace to write it"), Oliver Goldsmith at 19 and Alexander Pope at 52, and Walt Whitman. These parodies also indicate that Bunner was a profound student of versification. Many of his lyrics are also reminiscent of Heine and Herrick.

Notes

1. "The Physiology of Versification" in *Pages from an Old Volume of Life* (Boston, 1892), p. 316.

2. John T. Morse, Jr. (ed.), *Life and Letters of Oliver Wendell Holmes* (Boston, 1896), II, 110.

3. Author's note to *Invitâ Minervâ.*

4. Printed as an introductory note to "Earlier Poems."

5. *Life and Letters, op. cit.,* p. 278.

6. Introductory note to the poem. (See Cambridge ed.)

7. Brander Matthews, "Writers of Familiar Verse," *Cambridge History of American Literature* (New York: G. P. Putnam's Sons, 1918), Vol. II, p. 242. By permission of The Macmillan Company, publishers.

Selected Bibliography

OLIVER WENDELL HOLMES

TEXT

Holmes, Oliver Wendell, *The Complete Poetical Works,* etc., ed. by H. E. Scudder. Boston: Houghton Mifflin Company, 1895.

———, *Life and Letters,* ed. by John T. Morse. Boston: Houghton Mifflin Company, 1896.

———, "The Physiology of Versification," in *Pages from an Old Volume of Life.* Boston: Houghton Mifflin Company, 1913. (Riverside edition.)

CRITICISM

Kreymborg, Alfred, "Dr. Holmes and the New England Decline," *Our Singing Strength.* New York: Coward-McCann, 1929. Chapter XI, pp. 134-150.

Matthews, Brander, "Writers of Familiar Verse," in *Cambridge History of American Literature.* New York: G. P. Putnam's Sons, 1918. Vol. II, Chapter XXIII, pp. 224-244.

Untermeyer, Louis, *American Poetry from the Beginning to Whitman.* New York: Harcourt, Brace and Company, 1931. Pp. 401-405.

MINOR POETS

Cohen, Helen Louise, *Lyric Forms from France.* New York: Harcourt, Brace and Company, 1922.

[A History and Anthology of the Ballads, Chants Royal, Rondels, Rondeaus, Triolets, Villanelles, and Sestinas in English and American verse.]

Matthews, Brander, *American Familiar Verse.* New York: Longmans, Green, and Company, 1904.

————, "Varieties of Verse," *Appleton's Journal* (June, 1878), 19, 565-567.

White, Gleeson, *Ballades and Rondeaus.* London: Walter Scott Publishing Company, Ltd., 1887.

[An anthology of English and American Ballades, Rondeaus, Chants Royal, Sestinas, Villanelles, etc., with a critical and historical Introduction.]

J. Chesley Mathews (essay date September 1957)

SOURCE: Mathews, J. Chesley. "Dr. Oliver Wendell Holmes and Dante." *Italica* 34, no. 3 (September 1957): 127-36.

[*In the following essay, Mathews explores the influence of Dante's poetry on Holmes's writing.*]

Oliver Wendell Holmes studied Italian under Dr. Pietro Bachi[1] during the third term of his sophomore year at Harvard College (1826-1827) and the first and second terms of his junior year (1827-1828),[2] and would have learned it at least well enough to be able to read it.[3] He also would have known Latin.[4] So he would have been able to read, though perhaps not easily, any of Dante's works in their original language. Furthermore, it is certain that he read at least the *Inferno* in his college course.[5] It is almost certain, too, that as a student he would have acquired a copy of the *Divina Commedia*;[6] and in 1931 Mr. Justice Holmes recalled that his father had the *Divina Commedia.*[7] Moreover, as will appear presently from Dr. Holmes' writings, he had available a copy of Cary's translation by 1863,[8] and acquired a copy of Longfellow's translation of the *Divine Comedy* and a copy of Parsons' translation of the *Inferno* in 1867, and a copy of Norton's translation of the *Inferno* in 1891. In addition, he had Parsons' *The First Ten Cantos of the Inferno*, Boston, 1843 (inscribed "for Oliver Wendell Holmes, with the respects of the translator"); Parsons' *Seventeen Cantos of the Inferno*, Boston, 1865 (inscribed "To Oliver Wendell Holmes, with the sincere esteem of T. W. P." A.l.s. from the translator, Boston, Apr. 20, [1865?] to Dr. Holmes, relative to the presentation of the book, tipped in); a three volume edition of Cary's translation, *The Vision . . .* , London, 1881; *La Divina Commedia . . .* , col comento di Pietro Fraticelli, 3v., Firenze, G. Barbera, 1884; Norton's translation of the *Purgatory* and *Paradise*, Boston and New York, 1891-92; and *The Divine Comedy*, translated by Parsons, Boston and New York, 1893. These books, as well as the Parsons and Norton volumes mentioned just above, are among the Dr. Holmes books in the Library of Congress.[9] It is a matter of record, also, that he attended meetings of the Dante Club at Longfellow's home on June 13, 1866, and February 27, 1867; and he probably attended such meetings a few more times, even though the fact is not recorded.[10]

If we turn to Holmes' writings, we find that he gave the first hint of having read Dante in *The Autocrat of the Breakfast Table* (written in 1857 and '58): there he wrote that "pride, in the sense of contemning others less gifted than herself, deserves the two lowest circles of a vulgar woman's Inferno."[11] The use of the word "Inferno," the conception of an Inferno with "circles," and the implied idea that the "lowest circles" are the worst—all these details suggest a knowledge of Dante's *Inferno.*[12] In *The Professor at the Breakfast Table* (published in 1860) his statement that "the old Latin tutor clove to 'Virgilius Maro,' . . . as closely as ever Dante did in his memorable journey"[13] implies that he had read the *Inferno*; for as Virgil and Dante journeyed through Hell, Dante always kept close to his leader, right beside him or behind him.[14] Then in "The Inevitable Trial" (written in 1863) he showed definitely that he had read at least part of it; he said,

> There is no neutrality for any single trueborn American. If any seek such a position, the stony finger of Dante's awful muse points them to their place in the antechamber of the Halls of Despair,—
>
>   —"With that ill band
> Of angels mixed, who nor rebellious proved,
> Nor yet were true to God, but for themselves
> Were only."
>
>   —"Fame of them the world hath none
> Nor suffers; mercy and justice scorn them both.
> Speak not of them, but look, and pass them by."[15]

The quotation is from the third canto, and is in Cary's translation.[16]

In the poem on **"Bryant's Seventieth Birthday"** (1864) he referred to Dante as "the wan-cheeked Florentine."[17] In *The Guardian Angel* (1867) he quoted the words "lasciate ogni speranza,"[18] from canto III of the *Inferno*; and gave clear evidence of having read canto V by alluding in a sentence,

> The book-dusting came to as abrupt a close as the reading
> of Lancelot,

to Francesca's statement that when Paolo kissed her, as they were reading together of Lancelot,

> Quel giorno più non vi leggemmo avante.[19]

Again in the same year, in "The Seasons," he alluded to canto III:

> . . . do you remember Richard Gunn and his wonderful toys, with the inscription over them, awe-inspiring as that we recollect so well in the mighty Tuscan's poem?
>
> "Look, but handle not!"[20]

He was thinking of the inscription over the gate of Hell, especially the final line of it; and may also have been thinking of Virgil's words to Dante, "guarda e passa."[21]

Having received a gift copy of volume I of Longfellow's translation of the *Divine Comedy*,[22] Holmes wrote to the author on May 10, 1867:[23] "I thank you, my dear Longfellow[,] for the copy of that noble work which your country and the English-speaking world will thank you for as long as genius and scholarship are honored. I will not praise it further." On September 12, 1867, having received a gift copy of T. W. Parsons' translation of the *Inferno*,[24] he wrote to his friend:[25]

> My Dear [Dr. Parsons]: I have received the beautiful volume, and though I have not yet had time to read it through I have read enough to appreciate the skill and the poetical beauty with which you have finished your translation. It is a great honor to our city and country and a proof of the rapid growth of our culture that two such versions as your own and Longfellow's should be given to the public in the course of the same year.
>
> I cannot help thinking that each will render the other more interesting. The difficulties of the text are so great that two or three independent renderings of it will be most acceptable to all the more interested and less profoundly instructed class of readers. But I do not wonder at these words "Tantus labor." To keep so close to the text and yet to turn it into harmonious and idiomatic English verse was a task which might well keep you busy for years. I feel sure that you will get honor and I hope profit for your faithful and admirable performance.
>
> . . . a day or two ago . . . the volume came.
>
> I thank you heartily for your beautiful gift. I thank you for this new and noble addition to our literature.

He spoke of Dante again in a letter to Harriet Beecher Stowe (dated November 17, 1867):

> I bow meekly to all your criticisms except the Dante paragraph. I believe I did not go to one of the "Inferno" séances, [to but] one or two of "Purgatorio," the others all "Paradiso." How often I have said, talking with Lowell, almost the same things you say about the hideousness, the savagery, of that mediaeval nightmare! . . . You cannot use too strong language.[26]

Here he indicates that he had been sufficiently interested in the *Divina Commedia* to talk often with Lowell about it and to attend some of the Dante Club meetings, at which the poem was discussed, although, as Howells remembered the meetings, Holmes' "voice was heard at the supper rather than at the criticism, for he was no Italianate."[27] Also, like not a few others, he was strongly impressed by what he called the savage, nightmare quality of it. Such an impression suggests that he knew the *Inferno* better than he did the other two parts, and that he appreciated even the *Inferno* not well enough. About a year later he expressed again the same feeling in his essay on "The Medical Profession in Massachusetts" (January, 1869):

> In the perpetual presence of this great Healing Agent, who stays the bleeding of wounds, who knits the fractured bone, . . . it is doubtless hard for the physician . . . to accept the God of Dante's "Inferno."[28]

On March 21, 1876, he wrote to James Russell Lowell that he had just a day or two before finished reading the latter's essay on Dante, and that he laid it down "with a sigh of regret that I could not earlier in my life have come under those influences (perhaps I ought to say could not have inherited those gifts) which would have fitted me to read such an Essay as a scholar and not as a school-boy."[29] In the essay on "Jonathan Edwards" (1880) he mentioned Dante five times.[30] Speaking of justice, according to Edwards' conception, he said, "Its work, as in the theology of Dante, is seen in the construction and perpetual maintenance of an *Inferno*, which Edwards mentions." Referring to Edwards' conception of Hell, as displayed in his sermons, he said, "We can endure much in the medieval verse of Dante which we cannot listen to in the comparatively raw and recent prose of Edwards." He also spoke of "Edwards' Dante-like descriptions of his 'Inferno.'" These statements show the same reaction to one quality of Dante's work as was revealed in the letter to Harriet Beecher Stowe and the medical essay: they also imply that Holmes knew the *Inferno* of Dante. Another statement in "Jonathan Edwards" shows definitely that he knew the story of Ugolino (told in canto XXXIII of the *Inferno*): he said, "The archbishop did not poison Ugolino and his boys,—he only withheld food from them."[31] And the other time he mentioned Dante in this essay, he referred to a statement

> to be found at the beginning of the fourth canto of Dante's "Paradiso." The passage is thus given in Mr. Longfellow's translation:—
>
> Between two viands equally removed
> And tempting, a free man would die of hunger,
> Ere either he could bring unto his teeth.[32]

So he had read at least some of the *Paradiso* too, in Longfellow's translation.

Holmes "Sent to 'The Philological Circle' of Florence for its meeting in commemoration of Dante, January 27, 1881, the anniversary of his first condemnation," a sonnet entitled **"Boston to Florence."** In it he spoke of the true homage Americans were paying to Dante, and of the fact that America's poets were making Dante ours (referring, presumably, to Longfellow's and Parsons' translating the *Divina Commedia,* and possibly also to Norton's translating the *Vita Nuova*), but did not show in it any definite knowledge of or indebtedness to any of Dante's work. Only the last ten lines deal with Dante:

> Thine exile's shrine thy sorrowing love embowers,
> Yet none with truer homage bends the knee,
> Or stronger pledge of fealty brings, than we,
> Whose poets make thy dead Immortal ours.
> Lonely the height, but ah, to heaven how near!
> Dante, whence flowed that solemn verse of thine
> Like the stern river from its Apennine
> Whose name the far-off Scythian thrilled with fear:
> Now to all lands thy deep-toned voice is dear,
> And every language knows the Song Divine![33]

In a letter to T. W. Parsons, dated November 12, 1881, and written to acknowledge the receipt of a poem, Holmes spoke of the former's translation of Dante:

> . . . your Dante, I judge from all that I have heard and read (for I feel a little diffident of my own judgment), will carry your name to posterity coupled with a noble and monumental achievement.[34]

In *A Mortal Antipathy* (1885)[35] he wrote a passage which contains clear echoes of the first canto of the *Inferno*:

> I was already at least
>
> *Nel mezzo del cammin di* mia *vita,*
>
> when I risked myself, with many misgivings, in little-tried paths of what looked at first like a wilderness, a *selva oscura,* where, if I did not meet the lion or the wolf, I should be sure to find the critic.[36]

The two quotations are from lines 1 and 2 of *Inferno* I; "the lion" and "the wolf" allude to the lion and wolf which Dante met in the "selva oscura" (lines 45, 49). Then in *Our Hundred Days in Europe* (1887) he parodied the ninth line of canto III, saying that "*Leave at home all your guineas, ye who enter here* would be a good motto to put over [the] door" of a certain book store;[37] and by the last four words of the line he suggested that he had Cary's translation in mind. In *Over the Teacups* (1890) he again showed definite knowledge of canto V. When he wrote,

> To say, as Dante says, that there is no greater grief than to remember past happiness in the hour of misery is not giving the whole truth,

he was giving in English the familiar "Nessun maggior dolore . . ." passage from that canto.[38] And when he wrote the following passage,

And Number Five and her young friend the Tutor,— have they kept on in their dangerous intimacy? Did they get through the *tutto tremante* passage, reading from the same old large edition of Dante which the Tutor recommended as the best, and in reading from which their heads were necessarily brought perilously near to each other?[39]

he was thinking of Francesca and Paolo's reading together of Lancelot, as the quotation "tutto tremante" (from line 136) shows. This passage also suggests that he might have been describing a copy of the *Commedia* owned by himself or which he had seen.[40] Twice more in *Over the Teacups* he referred to Dante, mentioning him as a classic along with Homer, Virgil, and Horace, and speaking of

> Dark, dim, Dante-like solitudes.[41]

The last three references to Dante in Holmes' writings were made in letters. One was in a letter to Charles Eliot Norton (dated October 17, 1891); there he wrote,

> During the delivery of [Lowell's] noble poem, read under the Washington elm, I could not keep my eyes from following the expression of your countenance. No Dante in the presence of Beatrice could have shown more truthfully in his features the delight with which he looked at her and listened to her.[42]

Now all through the *Paradiso* Dante was in Beatrice's company, and there are many passages in which he experienced great delight while looking at her or hearing her speak. One recalls especially that as they ascended to each higher circle he had to adjust his sight (physical and spiritual) to greater light, and did this, with joy, by gazing at her.[43] It seems, though, that Holmes was not alluding to any particular passage, but was speaking in general terms; and his statement suggests that he was familiar with the whole *Paradiso*.

Holmes spoke also in the same letter to Norton of the latter's translation of the *Inferno*:

> Perhaps I should not have written at this particular moment had I not found on my table your Translation of the first Part of the *Divine Comedy*. You must finish your work without his [i.e., Lowell's] eye to review its closing portions. But his presence will be with you still.[44]

The next was in a letter addressed to Maria S. Porter, April 3, 1893, or soon afterward:

> Parsons *is* appreciated by scholars; . . . To his lifelong devotion to Dante, by the absorbing study he has given him, I attribute the felicity of his style, the exquisite art that characterizes his work.[45]

And the final reference was in a letter to Mrs. George Lunt, December 19, 1893, written upon receiving a copy of the collected edition of Parsons' *Poems*:

Dr. Parsons was as true a poet as we had among us. His fondness for Dante and the admirable version he has given of the *Divina Commedia* showed the lofty range of his affinities.[46]

It appears, then, that Holmes read at least the *Inferno* in Italian as early as 1827 or 28; read, if not so early, then in later years, at least some and probably all of the *Purgatorio* and *Paradiso,* in translation if not in Italian; and during the last thirty-seven years of his life showed, by quotations and references in his writings, and by the interest expressed in the Dante translations done by his friends Longfellow, Parsons, and Norton, not only a moderate familiarity with Dante's major poem, but also not a little interest in it.

Notes

1. The Harvard College Catalogues and other records show that, beginning with the third term of 1825-26, Dr. Bachi was the teacher of Italian during Holmes' undergraduate years. (I am indebted to the officials of the Harvard College Library for the privilege of examining the College records referred to here and in the notes below, and I wish especially to acknowledge the assistance given me by Mr. Clifford K. Shipton, Custodian, and Mr. Kimball C. Elkins, Senior Assistant, of the Archives.)

2. The records of Holmes' course of study in his undergraduate years are not as detailed as the records given in the Term Books for later years; but they show that Holmes began Italian under Bachi on April 20, 1827, continued the study of it during the succeeding fall and winter terms, and did well in this subject. In his college course he had previously studied French, and later studied Spanish. (I am indebted to Mr. Shipton and Mr. Elkins for providing me with this information and having records microfilmed for me. See especially Bachi's Reports dated May 18 and Oct. 1, 1827, George Ticknor's Letter of March 21, 1828, and the "Rank Scales, 1827-58.") Holmes himself wrote in a letter dated at Cambridge, in December, 1828, that he had "studied French and Italian, and some Spanish" (J. T. Morse, *Life and Letters of Oliver Wendell Holmes,* 2 vols., Boston, 1896, I, 59f.). See also Eleanor M. Tilton, *Amiable Autocrat,* New York, 1947, pp. 38f.

3. A century later Mr. Justice Holmes believed that his father "did not really read Italian, but could make it out with a translation" (letter dated May 29, 1931, owned by J. C. Mathews). But one of the principles regulating the study of the modern languages at Harvard was that, once a student had chosen to study any one, he was not permitted to quit the study of it until he had learned the language (Fourth *Annual Report of the President* of *Harvard University to the Overseers,* for the year 1828-29, Cambridge, 1830, p. xxiv). Four students of Dr. Bachi's going up for the examination in Italian on March 30, 1829, even though they had been taught for only two terms, were reported by the head of the department as being "offered as able to read Italian into English easily and well" (Ticknor's Report of March 21, 1829, in *Reports of the Department of Modern Languages,* p. 10—in the Archives).

4. Mr. Ticknor recorded, on April 29, 1830, that "the students come to college with a considerable knowledge of Latin & Greek" (*Reports,* pp. [54-55]). And Harvard undergraduates studied Latin through the freshman and sophomore years and first two terms of the junior year (*Fourth Annual Report of the President,* pp. xv, xvi).

5. The records specifically show that the group of students with which Holmes was examined had read all of the *Inferno* (see letter of March 21, 1828, in *Ticknor's Letters,* p. 92; also the Second and Third *Annual Report of the President,* for the years 1826-27 and 1827-28, Cambridge, 1828 and 1829, pp. 33 and 35 respectively; and my "Thoreau's Reading in Dante," in *Italica,* XXVII, No. 2, June, 1950, p. 78).

6. "Dante Div. Commedia 3 vols., $1.88" was listed among the textbooks for Italian in the Second *Annual Report of the President,* for the year 1826-27, p. 51; and on June 26, 1832, Ticknor, in writing a request that twenty-five copies of the *Divina Commedia* be ordered for textbooks, suggested a three-volume edition (*Reports,* p. [105]).

7. However, the son doubted that his father "paid much attention to it, until perhaps the last years of his life" (letter mentioned in note 3, above).

8. One would guess that he had Cary's version many years earlier.

9. Mr. Frederick R. Goff, Chief of the Rare Books Division, the Library of Congress, kindly supplied me with an inventory of the Dante volumes in L.C. which once belonged to Dr. Holmes.

10. Samuel Longfellow, *Life of Henry Wadsworth Longfellow,* 3 vols., Boston and New York, 1891, III, 75, 85. (On the first date, *Paradiso* XXXIII was read.) Although Holmes apparently was not often present, he probably attended more than twice. Longfellow's MS Journals and known letters contain a record of only one-third of the Club meetings; and Holmes implied in a letter written to Harriet Beecher Stowe near the end of 1867, and in which he was speaking of the Dante readings which he had attended, that he had been present more than twice (see passage quoted on

page 129). Longfellow, in a letter to James T. Fields, March 4, 1867, wrote: "Do not forget to tell Holmes, that I expect him on Wednesday. Say to him how pleasant a thing it is to go to a house where he is not only welcome, but desired" (a.1.s. in the Longfellow House). W. D. Howells, too, in *Literary Friends and Acquaintances* (New York and London, 1901, pp. 152, 161), after remarking that he did not often see Dr. Holmes during the winter of 1866-67, said that in the spring and thereafter "I met him chiefly at Longfellow's, or . . . at the Fieldses'. . . . It was at certain meetings of the Dante Club . . . that one saw the doctor." "I met Dr. Holmes at the Fieldses', and at Longfellow's, when he came out to a Dante supper, which was not often." Holmes was present also at "a Dante Club supper" on "Wednesday 12" [Feb., 1868] (H. W. L.'s MS Journal, 1863-1869), after the translation had been published and the regular Dante Club meetings had ended.—In a letter to J. L. Motley (April 3, 1870) Holmes spoke of seeing Longfellow "last Saturday" at the Saturday Club, and remarked, "I think the work of translating Dante kept him easy, and that he is restless now" (Morse, *op. cit.,* II, 188f.).

11. *The Complete Works of Oliver Wendell Holmes,* Fireside Edition, 14 vols., Boston, 1909, hereinafter referred to as *Works,* I, 271.

12. In Dante, moreover, pride (though a different thing from what Holmes meant by pride) is punished in the lowest circle.

13. *Works,* II, 61. Dante's name is mentioned again on p. 85.

14. Only three times did they separate, and even then they were within sight of each other or within calling distance (*Inf.* VIII, 106ff.; XVII, 34ff.; XXI, 58ff.). Usually they were literally within reach of each other (*Inf.* III, 19; VIII, 43); and when frightened, Dante got as close as he could to his guide (*Inf.* XXI, 97f.).

15. *Works,* VIII, 117f.; *Inf.,* III, 37-39, 49-51.

16. "The Inevitable Trial" was a Fourth of July oration; so the speaker could not very appropriately have given the passage in Italian.

17. *Works,* XIII (*Poems,* II), 250.

18. *Works,* VI, 346.

19. *Works,* VI, 373; & *Inf.* V, 127-138.

20. *Works,* VIII, 160.

21. *Inf.* III, 9, 51. He had quoted line 51 before: see note 15, above.

22. Three volumes, with pages approximately seven by ten inches, ordinary edition, bound in green cloth (Boston, Ticknor and Fields, 1867). Holmes'

set is now in the Harvard College Library; and volume one is inscribed "Oliver Wendell Holmes with kindest regards of the Translator. May 1, 1867." I am indebted to Mr. William B. Todd, an Assistant to the Librarian, for supplying me with this information. Volumes II and III, published a little later, in May and June respectively, presumably were received soon afterward.

23. The letter is in the Longfellow House, in Cambridge. I am indebted to the late Dr. H. W. L. Dana and to Mr. Thomas H. DeValcourt for the privilege of examining materials there.

24. *The First Canticle (Inferno) of the Divine Comedy of Dante Alighieri,* translated by Thomas William Parsons, Boston, MDCCCLXVII.

25. Letter published by Maria S. Porter, in "Thomas William Parsons," in *The Century Magazine,* LXII, N.S. XL, 935 (Oct. 1901), though wrongly dated there. Corrections have been made by a photostat of the original, which is in the Huntington Library. In the letter Parsons' name has been erased. At the end of the translation, p. 216, T. W. P. had printed "Tantus labor non sit cassus!"

26. Morse, *op. cit.,* II, 225, and E. W. Emerson, *The Early Years of the Saturday Club,* Boston and New York, 1918, p. 439. Brackets are E. W. E.'s.

27. Howells, *op. cit.,* p. 152.

28. *Works,* IX, 365.

29. Morse, *op. cit.,* II, 115f.

30. *Works,* VIII, 368, 384, 386, 383, 374.

31. Dante names Ugolino and the Archbishop Ruggieri (lines 13f.), tells that Ugolino's sons were imprisoned with him in the tower (lines 38f.), and that they were starved to death by the Archbishop (16-21; 43ff.).

32. Lines 1-3. See above, p. 128, and note 22.

33. *Works,* XIV (*Poems,* III), 137f.

34. Porter, *op. cit.,* p. 935.

35. In the memoir of "R. W. Emerson" (1884) he mentioned Dante's name four times (*Works,* XI, 24, 156, 247, 295).

36. *Works,* VII, 11.

37. *Works,* X, 147.

38. *Works,* IV, 159, and 227 (cf. XIV, 192).

39. *Works,* IV, 302.

40. We know that Holmes' father "loved to buy rare old editions of classic works" (W. S. Kennedy, *Oliver Wendell Holmes,* Boston, 1883, p. 40) and

that he "had a library of between one and two thousand volumes," in which "the son browsed at will" (*C.H.A.L.,* New York, 1931, II, 225). And see above, p. 127, and note 6.

41. *Works,* IV, 159, and 227 (cf. XIV, 192).

42. Morse, *op. cit.,* II, 316f.

43. For example, when they entered into Mercury, he saw her "si lieta"

> Che più lucente se ne fè 'l pianeta.
> E se la stella si cambiò e rise.
> Qual mi fec' io!
>
> (*Par.* V, 96-99)

And when they entered into Mars, and his eyes were vanquished by the new lustre, Beatrice showed herself to him "sì bella e ridente" that he could not keep the sight in his memory, and therefrom his eyes regained power "A rilevarsi" (*Par.* XIV, 67-84. Cf. also X, 52-63; XVIII, 3-15; XXI, 1-3, 19-23; XXII, 124ff., 154; XXIII, 19-24, 34, 46ff.; XXVII, 88-96; XXX, 14-21, 26f. At other times, too, than at these ascents from circle to circle, he referred to his joy: he spoke of

> il piacer de li occhi belli,
> Ne' quai mirando, mio disio ha posa
>
> (*Par.* XIV, 131f.);

and at another time said,

> Poscia rivolsi a la mia donna il viso,
> E quinci e quindi stupefatto fui;
> Chè dentro a li occhi suoi ardea un riso
> Tal, ch'io pensai co' miei toccar lo fondo
> De la mia grazia e del mio paradiso.
>
> (XV, 32-36)

(Cf. also IV, 139-142; XXVIII, 11f.; XXXI, 79-93.) In section III of the *Vita Nuova,* too, Dante meets Beatrice and is greeted by her: he was in her presence, looked at her, heard her speak, and it seemed to him then that he saw "tutti li termini de la beatitudine," he took in "tanta dolcezza" that he became as it were "inebriato." (Cf. also *V. N.,* II, and XI.) But there is no evidence that Holmes knew the *Vita Nuova,* although one would expect him to have read Norton's translation of it, which was published in 1867.

44. *The Divine Comedy of Dante Alighieri,* translated by C. E. N., i.*Hell,* was published in Boston in 1891. Lowell died August 12, 1891.

45. Porter, *op. cit.,* pp. 934f. The date has been established by Professor Miriam R. Small, of Wells College.

46. Zoltán Haraszti, *Letters by T. W. Parsons,* Boston, [1939], p. 120.

Howard Webb (essay date October 1965)

SOURCE: Webb, Howard. "Holmes's 'The Deacon's Masterpiece.'" *Explicator* 24, no. 2 (November 1965): Item 17.

[*In the following essay, Webb considers a parallel between the theology implied in Holmes's poem "The Deacon's Masterpiece" and in his novel* Elsie Venner.]

> Now in building of chaises, I tell you what,
> There is always *somewhere* a weakest spot,—
> In hub, tire, felloe, in spring or thill,
> In panel, or crossbar, or floor, or sill,
> In screw, bolt, thoroughbrace,—lurking still,
> Find it somewhere you must and will,—
> Above or below, or within or without,—
> And that's the reason, beyond a doubt,
> That a chaise *breaks down,* but doesn't *wear out.*
>
> —OLIVER WENDELL HOLMES

"The Deacon's Masterpiece" is usually regarded as an attack on any logical system, but particularly on Calvinism (George Arms, *The Fields Were Green,* Stanford University Press, 1953, pp. 112-113; Miriam Small, *Oliver Wendell Holmes,* New York, 1963, pp. 99, 102). What has not been generally noted is that the poem contains more than this attack. In terms of its metaphor, it also states Holmes' alternative to such systems, and particularly to Calvinism. The proper kind of chaise, argues the third stanza, is one which may *"break down but doesn't wear out"*; a chaise, that is, which may have weak spots but which can be repaired and maintained in operating condition. Just so, a sound religious system is not one which wears out and must be discarded; rather, when it breaks down, when time and knowledge reveal weaknesses in it, the system should be capable of being repaired, healed, and thus continuously maintained in accord with fact.

The implied analogy of the poem, with its emphasis on healing, sets forth the same theological empiricism as that of the physician in *Elsie Venner*: doctors "always see [the Creator] trying to help his creatures out of their troubles. A man no sooner gets a cut, than the Great Physician, whose agency we often call *Nature,* goes to work, first to stop the blood, and then to heal the wound, and then to make the scar as small as possible" (*The Works of Oliver Wendell Holmes,* Boston, 1892, V, 320).

The good Doctor Holmes was a remarkably consistent man.

Everett Carter (essay date 1969)

SOURCE: Carter, Everett. "The Typicality of Oliver Wendell Holmes." In *Themes and Directions in Ameri-*

can Literature, edited by Ray B. Browne and Donald Pizer, pp. 38-55. Lafayette, Ind.: Purdue University Studies, 1969.

[*In the following essay, Carter discusses recurring themes in Holmes's writings, considering them perfectly representative of the spirit of his times.*]

In his description of the early career of James Russell Lowell, Leon Howard hinted at the approach which might be taken towards a writer whose virtues are typicality rather than originality, representativeness, rather than uniqueness. Observing how ". . . sterile and unrevealing purely aesthetic criticism"[1] of this kind of an author can be, we are forced into an awareness of the relationship between history and the art which comes out of history, between the large worlds of a culture's style of life and the little worlds created by the artist. In such representative writers, ". . . the subtler forces of history . . . flow from the past to the present . . ."[2] and to comprehend either the history or the author we must perceive the way in which the underlying commitments of a people in an age received their expression in that kind of imaginative literature which embodied, rather than rejected, the conventional acceptations of its times. I should like to examine the currently unfashionable prose and poetry of Lowell's friend and contemporary, Oliver Wendell Holmes, using with sympathy this technique of subtler historical analysis: that is, identifying the beliefs of his culture which Holmes typified, and then showing how these beliefs are involved in the forms of his most significant works.

The historical force which flowed through most of the poems and essays of Holmes was the most important charge of symbolic energy of the American nineteenth century. It has been variously termed the American Dream,[3] or the "official faith,"[4] or (by Lowell) the country's gospel;[5] or (by both Lowell and Emerson) the American Idea.[6] Like all deified concepts, this "Idea" has been often reverentially named, but never fully described. It would take much time and space to anatomize it fully, but it is possible to summarize a number of descriptions of its various components, and to say that the public style of the American nineteenth century is a triad of beliefs representing the culmination in America of the humanistic strains of the Western Renaissance: the optimistic belief in the significance of Nature and Man, the reliance upon experience as the test of value, and the belief in the possibilities of progress towards a morally as well as a physically improved world. One or another of this triad has been made the subject of many studies of the American imaginative experience,[7] studies which often, like Daniel Boorstin's, emphasize one of the ingredients without seeing that all three are interdependent and together form an unspoken ideology: faith in experience demands

an unspoken commitment to the underlying significance of the natural world in which that experience occurs, and a hope, at least, or an expectation, at most, that man can interact profitably with such an environment. Faith in nature and man, and faith in the possibility of progress as a basis for faith in experience, these together comprised the structure of feeling of most sentient Americans, to which Oliver Wendell Holmes gave significant imaginative form.

With the first element of the official faith, a belief in the universe as ordered and significant, Holmes was unreservedly in accord, never doubting that nature embodies a divine order according to which man must organize his moral and social life. "The great end of being is to harmonize man with the order of things,"[8] he said through the character of the Professor at the Breakfast Table. And in this order, man can involve himself with the material affairs of the world, strengthened by the conviction that truth will eventually prove its worth, and that error will eventually be corrected. The words he used were an echo of Bryant, whose statement he possibly found congenial because of its medical metaphor: ". . . Truth gets well if she is run over by a locomotive, while Error dies of lockjaw if she scratches her finger." (II, 109)

Health and sanity, for Holmes, were the norms of the universe, and a firm foundation for optimism. The doctrine of original sin, of evil at the heart of a fallen world, he declared, was an assertion that "all men's teeth are naturally in a state of total decay . . ." Nonsense, he told his listeners. "There are a good many bad teeth, we all know, but a great many more good ones." (II, 111) In just such a perspective appeared to him the brutality and the cruelty of men: these are symptoms of disease, of lack of health, or, to use the psychological term, of "insanity." "Anything that is brutal, cruel, heathenish, that makes life hopeless for the most of mankind and perhaps for entire races . . . ought to produce insanity in every well-regulated mind." (I, 42)

The principal "heathenishness" he saw in his own culture was the doctrine of original sin and its promulgation by the Puritan tradition. This was the "barbaric" notion to which he alluded when he talked of a theory which "makes life hopeless for most of mankind." The least violent of his attacks came during his speculation on the origins of the doctrine in Catholicism: "I have sometimes questioned," the Professor said, "whether the many libels on human nature had not been a natural consequence of the celibacy of the clergy." (II, 209) But often Augustinian pessimism, and its Protestant manifestations, was one of the few concepts that made him lose his tolerance and good humor. He called Puritanism that "miserable delusion," (II, 114) adding that "If a man hangs my ancient female relatives for sorcery, as they did in this neighborhood a little while ago, or burns my instructor for not believing as he does, I care no more for his religious edicts than I should for those of any other barbarian." (II, 106) The Puritans, he said, were "those wretched fools, reverend divines and others, who were strangling men and women for imaginary crimes a little more than a century ago . . ." (II, 114) Jonathan Edwards may have been a "remarkable man," but his brain was as well adjusted "for certain mechanical processes as Babbage's calculating machine," and his congregation treated him quite properly when they "turned him out by a vote of twenty to one, and passed a resolution that he should never preach for them again." (II, 114)

Edwards's rejection by his congregation was one of the pieces of evidence Holmes offered to prove the validity of his optimistic belief in the homely sense of common men as the best means of knowing reality. The mistake of Puritanism was to leave "common sense and common humanity" (II, 114) out of its premises. "The laymen," he declared, "have to keep setting the divines right constantly." (II, 113) As in theology, so it is in philosophy: the ultimate court of appeal is the common perceptions of most men. He described the philosopher as a man who unwraps a truth painfully, and, at the end of the process, "we recognize it as the diminutive and familiar whom we have known in the streets all our lives." (II, 38) From the point of view of literary criticism, the most significant aspect of Holmes' reliance upon common sense was his belief that value in art is a function of acceptance by an informed public. Not for him was the ideal of the solitary, alienated artist: "Produce anything really good, and an intelligent editor will jump at it." (I, 290)

Just as his view of the value of the world—its partial evil, but its substantial goodness and healthfulness—started with a revulsion from Puritan pessimism, so did his view of the way in which we know the world begin with an attack upon false modes of knowledge—the superstitions, the traditional errors, the false mythologies of the past. These outmoded beliefs were, for him, "lumps of nonsense" which *We the people,* Sir, some of us with nut-crackers, and some with trip-hammers, and some of us with pile-drivers, and some coming with a whish! like air-stones out of a lunar volcano, will crash down on . . . till we have made powder of them like Aaron's calf!" (II, 15) One of the proofs of human progress was, for him, the triumph of reason over superstition, and he therefore turned naturally to an identification of the past with darkness, and of the present with light. "Ancient error" was for him like the rock in whose dank shadows dwells the "old lying incubus" to which the empiricist puts "the staff of truth." (I, 108)

This belief in the superiority of scientific empiricism to all past forms of "knowing" was the major prop of his world view. The mythologies of the past, he insisted, must be carefully reconsidered, and the false mythologies distinguished from the true, by each generation: "Rough work, iconoclasm,—but the only way to get at the truth." Indeed, his scientific prejudice went even further, and suspected the value of the whole of the symbol-making and myth-making faculties of man. There is a sense of grudging in his admission that "Man is an idolator or symbol-worshipper by nature," for he added, "which, of course, is no fault of his." He tried to be fair, however, and said that his opposition was only to the "local and temporary symbols" which must be "ground to powder." (II, 110)

But Holmes was no traducer of the emotional life of man; far from it. His belief in science and the scientific method as the principal weapon in man's arsenal of cognition was not a belief that man should live a life of reason, but a belief that man should live in a way of which reason would approve. Instincts were given to us to be regulated, and any system which assumes the need for exterminating them is sheer insanity, he wrote. Like William James, whose views on science and religion would be much like his, he declared: "Science . . . in other words knowledge,—is not the enemy of religion; for, if so, then religion would mean ignorance. But it is often the antagonist of school-divinity." (II, 113) The emotional commitments of men, Holmes was aware, are their supreme commitments, and the most important aspects of their humanity; indeed, he recognized that they constituted the essence of their being. Illusions, he suggested, are necessary. All he asked was that illusions be subjected to the check of empirical reason, and, once they were shown to be at variance with the truths of experience, that they be renamed "delusions," and be discarded. But as illusions, they must be cherished: When one "has lost *all* his illusions, his feathers will soon soak through and he will fly no more." (I, 9) The many good men whom he saw around him, and, most important, the women whom he worshipped as the embodiment of the best tendencies of the species, carry in their hearts, he felt, the sentiment of love. Together with the sentiment of creation, and the sentiment of tenderness towards the weak and helpless, this sentiment, he declared, is the true religion for which America must make its new symbols. (II, 124-125)

The ways of knowing the world, then, are two-fold—a way of knowing natural things which may be measured quantitatively, and a way of knowing those things which cannot be measured nor analyzed. And the latter mode of "knowledge" is intuitive, immediate, and total. "What should you think of a lover," he asked, "who should describe the idol of his heart in the language of science, thus: Class, Mamallia; Order, Primate; Genus, Homo;

Species, Europeus; Variety, Brown; Individual, Ann Eliza; Dental Formula,

i $\frac{2\text{-}2}{2\text{-}2}$ c $\frac{1\text{-}1}{1\text{-}1}$ p $\frac{2\text{-}2}{2\text{-}2}$ m $\frac{3\text{-}3}{3\text{-}3}$ . . . ?" (I, 231)

For love, for the perception of beauty, the sentiments are the proper faculty and "poetry" the only proper language. In talking of trees, for example, the Autocrat of the Breakfast Table urged his companions to speak of them "as we see them, love them, adore them in the fields, where they are alive. . . ." (I, 231) Not a philosopher, Holmes made no attempt to reconcile these two areas of knowledge—knowledge of physical facts which could be described in the language of science, and knowledge of universal ideals. But this duality is everywhere apparent in his essays and poems, and foretells the same duality in William James and the American pragmatists.

One of the outmoded beliefs to which Holmes put the staff of scientific analysis, one of the false myths he tried to exorcise, was that of the superiority of the savage to the civilized, of the ignorant to the cultivated. While he believed in the common sense of common man, he meant by "common" the consensus of mature men, and by "sense" the achievements of civilized minds that had learned their lessons from experience. In him, therefore, we find an early example of the reassessment and rejection of one of the myths that had been used to foster a part of the American official faith: the idea of natural goodness had received its mythological expression in the parables of the noble savage and the superior child; translated into the second half of the nineteenth century, these parables became an anti-intellectual defense of the primitive and an attack upon the civilized. Instead of bolstering the idea of progress with the affirmation of the capabilities of man, they became a weapon for the attack upon progress; in other words, to use Holmes' terms, "natural goodness" became not an illusion but a delusion.⁹ And as such it was the object of his attack. Children, he said, with the cheerfulness which took away the sting, are "little wretches . . . as superstitious as naked savages. . . ." (I, 204) All other things being equal, he admitted, he preferred the man of family to the man with none, for "the man who inherits family traditions and the cumulative humanities for at least four or five generations" (I, 23) is more likely to possess the qualities of reason, tolerance, and decency which, to him, meant civilization.

Part of the reason for his rejection of the myth of the noble savage and the divine child was his awareness of the importance of heredity in determining behavior. And here Holmes made an interesting defense of progress on the basis of an awareness of the natural inevitability of certain moral and physical evils. The disposition to these evils, Holmes knew, is as inevitable,

as "determined" as are the other processes of nature. But they *are* processes of nature, and hence are open to man's understanding and his social control. They are not the products of a super-nature about which man has no knowledge and over which he has no domain. Moral evils, therefore, like disease, have their causes; these causes can be understood; they can also be the object of sympathy rather than of fear, and of a sober hopefulness rather than despair. Don't tell me about children coming into the world trailing clouds of glory, said the doctor to the minister in *Elsie Venner.* And then he went on to say that he often, though not normally, saw them coming into the world trailing hereditary diseases. The motive behind Holmes' two "medicated novels" was to demonstrate the operation of natural causality in the formation of aberrations of character and behavior. On another, less serious occasion, Holmes declared: "It is such a sad thing to be born a sneaking fellow;" if one happens to be born with "such congenital incapacity that nothing can make a gentleman of him" he is entitled "not to our wrath, but to our profoundest sympathy." (I, 219) The transfer of evil from the realm of mystery and the supernatural absolute to the realm of the definable, the knowable, and hence, the controllable, was a source of chastened hope, rather than of despair. It was chastened, because it included the acceptance of the reality of evil; there was no feeling that evil, as Emerson put it, was "merely privative;" but for Holmes, evil was subject to the sovereignty of man's reason; it had natural causes; it could be confronted; it could be understood, and perhaps, meliorated.

The myth of the noble savage, then, was no longer needed, and, indeed, could be a temptation to a false and blind view of reality. Instead, the moderate, reasonable assumption that man and nature were mixtures of good and evil, with the evidence pointing to a supremacy of the good—this belief was a sufficient prop for his acquiescence in the idea of progress. His attitude towards the relation between English and American civilization is instructive in this connection. Holmes felt himself and his society a normal development from English eighteenth century culture; he argued that ". . . the American is the Englishman reinforced." (I, 238) The feeling here is of progression, advancement, improvement over the past, at the same time that there is a due acknowledgment of the values of the past upon which the present can build. This attitude is even more apparent in *The Professor at the Breakfast Table,* where he contrasts the old world with the new, and declares, in a startling reversal of the usual attitude towards the comparative youth and maturity of the two civilizations: "They are children to us in certain points of view. They are playing with toys we have done with for whole generations." The superiority was based upon the widening of the democratic spirit: "We do think more of a man, as such . . . than any people that ever lived did think of him. Our reverence is a great deal wider, if it is less intense." (II, 33-34) This increase in the range of humanism, he felt, was the basis for the new literature and the new religion of America: "Democratic America has a different humanity from feudal Europe, and so must have a new divinity." (II, 115)

Such was the identity of Holmes' view of man, nature, and history with the structure of feeling of his culture. And the literary forms in which this world view was presented were variations upon the forms that eighteenth century England had used for its literature of cultural affirmation. The Spectator Papers of Steele and Addison were the precedents for the series of charming, informal essays on society, science, literature, history, religion, philosophy which Holmes wrote as the series entitled *The Autocrat, The Professor,* and *The Poet at the Breakfast Table.* The setting of the essays was significant: to use a boarding house as the place for the conversations, to describe the interplay between a group of thoroughly common-place and middle-class participants and their social "autocrat,"—surely this tells us much about the commitments of the author. The Autocrat and the Professor and the Poet were the author's various disguises, and, like the Autocrat, Holmes could say to this undistinguished group of listeners: "I hope you all love me none the less for anything I have told you." (I, 314) The "Professor" described himself early in the volume given to his lucubrations, and the description is of Holmes himself: essentially optimistic, believing in the significance of the world of common experience, proud of his breadth of interest, skeptical of narrowness, and intolerant only of fanaticism: "Here am I . . . a man who has lived long enough to have plucked the flowers of life and come to the berries,—which are not always sad-coloured, but sometimes golden-hued as the crocus of April . . . contented enough with daily realities, but twirling on his finger the key of a private Bedlam of ideals . . . loving better the breadth of a fertilizing inundation than the depth of a narrow artesian well . . ." (II, 21-22) The Autocrat-Professor-Poet reigned over an oval table about which were collected the other boarders; with one exception they are fairly dull people; but, "what a comfort a dull but kindly person is, to be sure, at times." They comprised the Landlady, her son named Benjamin Franklin (!), her daughter, the "Koh-inoor" (a business man who sports a diamond), the Venerable Gentleman, the Divinity Student, A Young Fellow, the Landlady's Poor Relation, and then, the most completely defined of the characters: the "Little Gentleman," so ugly he is called "The Sculpin," but gallant, generous, high-minded, a perfect embodiment of the poor homely commonplace of moderate American life in which Holmes believed so deeply.

But The Sculpin was a trifle ridiculous, too. Holmes put in his mouth statements of many of the extreme positions to which Holmes himself was often attracted—the superiority of America to Europe, the heady sense of a new revelation for a new world, the infinite superiority of Boston to any other place in the universe. ". . . Boston sunsets . . ." cried the ugly and endearing little enthusiast, "perhaps they're as good in some other places, but I know 'em best here . . . American skies are different from anything they see in the Old World. . . . A new nursery, Sir, with Lake Superior and Huron and all the rest of 'em for wash-basins! A new race, and a whole new world for the new-born human soul to work in!" (II, 83) This device of projecting his opinions through a comic character, looking at him objectively, and laughing at him satirically and fondly—this was but an overstatement of the self-satire which was a tone of all his essays. For the Autocrat, the Professor, and the Poet, too, are fictional characters; and while Holmes, in the preface to *The Autocrat* indirectly assumed responsibility for their views (an earlier "Autocrat," he said, was his immature "son"), still the assumption of the mask, no matter how transparent, afforded him an opportunity to detach himself, to step back, to achieve a distance, and gently to mock his own pretensions as well as those of his fellow man.

The style and structure of the Autocrat series, then, are precisely suitable to their vision. Holmes chose as his setting a commonplace environment; he peopled it with a group who represented many of the ordinary aspects of that environment; business, housekeeping, clerkdom. The homely gathering about the board of a rooming house, the sympathetic cast of middle-class characters, the clear rendering of their language, the avoidance of symbolisms that would shift the focus from the ordinary to the extraordinary, the avoidance of plot (or mythos imposed upon the material),—all these comprised the elements of a fundamentally affirmative work of art. Above all, the tone of satire and self-satire was an aesthetic counterpart of his ideas. In holding up to ridicule the distance between his society's ideals and its practices, he gave an unspoken assent to those shared ideals; he must have started with an agreement with his reader about the nature of the vision they both possess. But were he to adopt the satiric mode alone, he would be risking the danger of setting himself up, as an artist, as superior to his fellow man, capable of standing apart from them and creating visions radically different from theirs. Through the constant control of self-satire, through such devices as the little Sculpin, he ridicules himself and demonstrates how the author is like the audience he is satirizing, not apart from or superior to them.

The same gentle self-depreciation that provides the major tone of his prose pervades most of his poetry as well. Indeed, it determines his stance as a semi-professional, rather than a professional maker of verse. He disliked the excessiveness, the immoderation of the claim that the fine art of poetry (as distinguished from "poetic sentiment," common to all men) is a supreme and unconditioned human activity. "There are times," the Autocrat told his listeners, "in which every active mind feels itself above any and all human books." Even more, there are physiological sensations which are "entirely beyond the reach of symbols . . . Think of human passions as compared with all phrases," he told the divinity student. "Did you ever hear of a man's growing lean by the reading of 'Romeo and Juliet,' or blowing his brains out because Desdemona was maligned?" (I, 132-133) This hierarchy of values which gave a contingent and subordinate place to art was summarized by his assertion: "I have always believed in life rather than in books. I suppose every day of earth with its hundred thousand deaths and something more of births,—with its love and hates, its triumphs and defeats, its pangs and its blisses, has more of humanity in it than all the books that were ever written, put together." (I, 134)

The very willingness to write occasional verse, celebrating many minor, and some major, social events is a testimonial to his commitment to the superiority of life over art. Sometimes these "events" or experiences were centered upon individuals, and Holmes treated them generally with an affectionate satire, so gentle that it borders on reverence:

> My aunt! My dear unmarried aunt
> Long years have o'er her flown;
> Yet still she strains the aching clasp
> That binds her virgin zone;

> (XII, 12)

And the rest of the poem told of the mistaken caution of her father, whose excessive care resulted in the pathos of "one sad, ungathered rose / On my ancestral tree." His poem written on the occasion of the *Atlantic* dinner for its contributors, combined the same sense of poetry as an occasion, with an optimism about the possibilities of progress; there was the tone of sustained gentle mockery, a mockery directed at himself and his hopes, identical with the hopes of all those gathered about him. He proclaimed the illusion of progress, but then stepped away from it and objectively observed the self-contradictions built into the illusion. To their great experiment in spreading culture through the medium of the *Atlantic Monthly,* he addressed his toast: that it shall grow "till all we are groping for / Has reached the fulfilment we're all of us hoping for. . . ." When it came to describing the consummation devoutly to be wished, Holmes gently pointed out the inadequacy of all Utopian ideals based upon imposing the dreamer's standards of goodness upon the world: we will hope for the growth of the *Atlantic,* and all it represents, he said,

> Till the roughs, as we call them, grown loving dutiful
> Shall worship the true and the pure and the beautiful,

> And, preying no longer as tiger and vulture do,
> All read the 'Atlantic' as persons of culture do!

> (XIII, 162-169)

The self-depreciation of the occasional poems is one aspect of the affirmative satirical vision—the satire directed against one's own pretensions. The satire he directed at others was usually tempered by this self-mockery, but there was no moderation in several of his poems which dealt with Puritanism and religious bigotry. The portrait of the "whey-faced" preacher in **"The Moral Bully"** was a devastating one, and had none of the usual softening touch of sympathy with a common human failing. The whole history of Puritan intolerance, and of the Enlightenment's rage against it, was summarized in Holmes' description of the pastor as one "whom small disturbance whitens round the lip." There was a picture of life-denying fanaticism in the "lean phantom, whose extended glove, / Points to the text of universal love;" the portrait was filled out with a summary of his sermons which "with grim logic" proved "That all we love is worthiest of our hate." The poem reached a real anger at the conclusion, and asked bitterly if "every scarecrow, whose cachetic soul / Seems fresh from Bedlam . . ." has "The right to stick us with his cutthroat terms, / And bait his homilies with his brother worms?" (XII, 204-205)

But this tone is as unusual in his religious poems as it is in his secular verse; and the most famous of his verses, **"The Deacon's Masterpiece; or, The Wonderful One-Horse Shay,"** is in exactly the mode of his normal posture of good-humor. **"The Deacon's Masterpiece"** is one of the poems which tests most severely the critical faculty, and, indeed, the whole nature of literary criticism. Its simplicity, its ease, its accessibility, its unpretentiousness appears to make comment unnecessary, and explication an affectation. It seems to lie there, cheerful, impudent, open to the inspection of any and the enjoyment of all. Its very qualities, in other words, seem to deny its seriousness; and yet, they should not deny its value, for its worth is bound up with its lack of pretence, and its expression of the dominant beliefs of its culture. Not a major work of art, it is none the less pleasing, significant, and satisfying, and a criticism which cannot include works like these is an incomplete criticism.

Its subject is the opposition between absolute systems that enslave the minds of theologians and philosophers, and the hero of Holmes' world view: the common sense of the common man. Holmes gave the prose argument for the poem a year or so later in *The Professor at the Breakfast Table,* when, during a running attack on Jonathan Edwards, the Professor, declared: "A man's logical and analytical adjustments are of little consequence, compared to his primary relations with Nature and truth; and people have sense enough to find it out in the long run; they know what 'logic' is worth."[10] So the important thing about the poem is its folk perspective: the world is seen through this "sense of the people" which reduces pretentiousness, no matter how sanctioned by intellectual tradition, to dust.

The voice of this people's sense is in an imitation of the doggerel rhythms of the poem—so close to the ballad voice of the folk. The voice of the people is in the concern of the poem, too; for the concern are the folk concerns: the attention to details of building, making good use of proper materials, traditions of craftsmanship for utilitarian purposes. It is what has been termed the "vernacular perspective." The stanza which deals with the construction of the shay is the longest one of the poem, and it dwells with loving attention on the details of its construction, and on the utility, and, therefore, the beauty of the materials with which its parts were made:

> The crossbars were ash, from the straightest trees,
> The panels of white-wood, that cuts like cheese,
> But lasts like iron for things like these;

The folk perspective, the vernacular, is maintained through to the end; the conclusion is the perennial joke of the people—the "pratfall"—the surest way to humble pride: the actual descent of the proud to the hard earth, the ending of pretentiousness on the painful fact of the buttocks black and blue.

The "pratfall" of comedy is the counterpart of the fall of man in tragedy—the counterpart and the radical opposite. It reduces a cosmic and final descent to a terrestrial, and temporary mishap, and uses the mishap as a warning, a chastening lesson which will improve the future. In a way, **"The Deacon's Masterpiece"** is a general "pratfall" for western man. It is not a tragedy that man's systems are imperfect; it is not a tragedy that nature's systems are involved with decay and with radical, even cataclysmic change; it is rather an affirmation of the truth that the Universe is an open universe, in which the only absolute is change. Anything man constructs, whether it be carriages or systems of belief, must be part of this truth; and any absolute system, whether it be of theology, government, or technology, will fall afoul of the common sense knowledge of an open-ended universe. This was the attitude which received its expression in **"The Wonderful One-Hoss Shay."**

Seen in this light, certain elements of the poem assume an added resonance. For example, Holmes placed the year of the shay's construction in three historical contexts. One was the American triumph over English despotism; and the transitoriness of this aspect of the world's historical evils was made apparent by the casual dismissal implied in the lines describing George the Second of England: "Snuffy old drone from a German hive." A second identification of the shay is with the royal system of warfare: Americans had been skeptical of the rigid battle formations of Braddock's army, and both Franklin and Washington warned the English that they were ill-suited to the New World's conditions. When Braddock's army, then, was "left without a scalp to its crown," there was a large admixture of the comic sense of satisfaction at the spectacle of humbled pride in the reaction of the American colonists. The third, the most significant event of the year, was the Lisbon Earthquake—a cataclysm which religious zealots had used to postulate the essential evil of the world, and had insisted upon viewing as a retribution for man's wickedness. But the galloping cadences of the rhymed couplets made the horror one event, like many others, in the mutability of the world, and removed it from any sense of tragic significance:

> That was the year when Lisbon town
> Saw the earth open and gulp her down . . .

At the end, a hundred years later, precisely, the instantaneous dissolution of the chaise provided a minor, a very minor echo of the instant destruction of a far-off European city. The systems of men, and the constructions of men, this juxtaposition tells us, are ridiculously small when compared to the "earthquake shock," yet at the same time, these same shocks are domesticated to the scale of man; they in turn have little more effect on the world's history than the thrill that the earth felt when it received the parson's rump; thus are both natural events and human institutions absorbed in a comic perspective; for both have a comic objective: the humbling of pride and the implication of a happy ending, either cosmic or historical, both for nature and for suitably chastened man.

The occasional poems, and **"The Deacon's Masterpiece,"** are meant as light verse, but Holmes also addressed himself with high seriousness to the major question of his century: the relation between knowledge and belief, religion and science, and he wrote two impressive poems on this subject. The less successful of the two was the more pretentious: **"Wind-Clouds and Star-Drifts"**; yet it is not without its beauty; it is a dignified statement of the man-centered optimistic creed of the nineteenth-century scientist. It was a poem in twelve parts which began with the musings of "a young astronomer" as he waits for the sky to clear. While he waits, he thinks of the history of human aspirations and inevitably compares them to the vastness of the universe. Such comparisons make him feel the gloom of those for whom space has become the new monster, elbowing man out of the cosmos, and he does not

> . . . marvel at him who scorns his kind
> And thinks not sadly of the time foretold
> When the old hulk we tread shall be a wreck,

A slag, a cinder drifting through the sky
Without its crew of fools!

Leaping ahead in his imagination to the end of the earth, and speculating whether it will perish in ice or in fire, he chooses fire as his preference, for it may be that then the earth will become "a new sun for earths that shall be born." Such visions make him feel the oneness of men who have always searched for knowledge: "I am as old as Egypt to myself. . . ." But they bring him back to the neo-classical longing to limit himself to "one poor patch / Of this dull spheroid and a little breath / To shape in word or deed to serve my kind."

His heart, he knows, "is simply human; / All my care for them whose dust is fashioned like mine own." He will express himself in verse, as one of the "veils of language" beneath which he dares to be himself; he knows that his will be no great talent: only "A slender-margined, unillumined page;" but he will trust his fellows to read it "in the gracious light of love." So concludes the first three sections; they have posed the problems; the next sections discussed his growth as a scientist—as one who has learned from a master as the neophyte learns from the priest; and there is the strong sense of science as the new religion in these lines: he was trained to

. . . find the glimmering specks of light
Beyond the unaided sense, and on my chart
To string them one by one, in order due,
As on a rosary a saint his beads.

And in this religion of scientific quest, he "learned to search" that he might "know / The whence and why of all beneath the stars. . . ." His life, therefore, will be "a challenge, not a truce." And he could not believe that the Father who had given him the urge to quest would deny his right to ask his questions.

The following sections dealt with the kind of God in whom the scientist is able to believe. It was not the God of the barbarians, nor of Greece and Rome, nor the vengeful God of Israel. It must be a God worthy of the dignity of enlightened and emancipated man.

This is the new world's gospel: Be ye men!
Try well the legends of the children's time . . .
Ye are as gods! Nay, makers of your gods,—
Each day ye break an image in your shrine
And plant a fairer image where it stood. . . .

The images that men would make in a new world and a new age comprised the subject of the last sections of the poem. The image must be made: it is part of "our subtle selves" to long to have images and idols. But these new images, worthy of the dignity of scientific man, would be in the image of the best of men, and, more especially, would present the face of woman's unselfish love. Holmes, a decade earlier had said, with the self-mockery of his guise as the Autocrat of the Breakfast Table: ". . . I have been ready to believe that we have even now a new revelation, and the name of its Messiah is WOMAN!" (II, 125) But he was deadly serious when, in **"Wind-Clouds and Star-Drifts,"** he wrote that

Love must be still our master; till we learn
What he can teach us of a woman's heart
We know not Him whose love embraces all.

This was Holmes' unabashedly sentimental belief, and demonstrated the way in which his scientific awareness, his knowledge that "God has made / This world a strife of atoms and of spheres . . ." was made part of a general faith in the essential beneficence of Nature and of Man.

A less pretentious, and more successful fusing of science and religion was his little poem **"The Chambered Nautilus."** It bears informative comparison with Poe's sonnet *Science*. Poe insisted that the vulturous eye of scientific analysis necessarily destroyed beauty. Holmes' vision was exactly opposite. The kind of scientific dissection which Poe found intolerable, the section of a beautiful organic object, prepared by an empirical scientist, was precisely the stimulus for **"The Chambered Nautilus."** But instead of drawing from the spectacle a moral of despair, Holmes drew from it a counsel of cosmic hope and affirmation.

The sketch of the Nautilus in a scientific encyclopedia had taken the shell out of mythology and romance, with the kind of "peering eye" that Poe deplored. And this wrench from the world of myth to the world of empirical reality was the subject of the first two stanzas of Holmes' poem; the first dealt with the shell as it was surrounded by the romantic imagination, sailing

In gulfs enchanted, where the Siren sings
And coral reefs lie bare,
Where the cold sea-maids rise to sun their streaming
  hair.

The second stanza introduced a world in which realities have replaced the dream: the myth of the shell as a ship is "wrecked," the innermost secrets of its actual construction no longer can excite the mythical imagination, for the secret lies stripped and bared: "Its irised ceiling rent, its sunless crypt unsealed!" At this point Holmes apparently reached the usual romantic agony—the pain at the sight of beauty violated by the prurient prying of the scientist. But Holmes had prepared us for something quite different when he described the inner reality of the shell as a "crypt"—with the word's sense of primitive concealment and gloomy decay, and when he called it "sunless." In contrast, the following stanza, which gives in detail the actuality of the shell's physical construction seen by the empirical investigator, is filled with light: "lustrous" and "shining" are the two adjectives which dominate the atmosphere of the lines. We trace the progress of the organism, from its small center, outward around the spiral of growth, each of the cells becoming larger and more beautiful. At each cycle of growth the body of the creature, "Stretched in its last-found home, and knew the old no more."

The next stanza pointed out the direction we can expect the poem to take. From an object that lies dead comes a new life; from the dead mysteries are born truths clearer than any proposed by mythology or romance. These truths contain both the possibilities and the significance of moral and spiritual progress. The possibilities are that man can build his larger mansions, and that each temple can be nobler than the last. The significance of these successive enlargements of rational concepts is that each of them is a growth which apparently cuts off man from heaven at the same moment that it shelters him (each temple shuts him from heaven with a "dome more vast"); yet, by a logical continuation of the process, each successive expansion of the rational is the means by which the ineffable is finally accomplished. The scientist's empirical curiosity has been no bar to this achievement; on the contrary, it has been the means by which the ceilings of man's aspirations are lifted from the low vault of the past to the horizons of knowledge that stretch out to the infinite.

This good and lasting poem, the gracious Breakfast Table series, and the best of Holmes' occasional poetry are in no danger of overevaluation. In the current critical temper, his virtues are at a discount. As Leo Marx has said about the evaluation of another writer whose qualities are a response to the "desires of his country-men," the "holistic standards" of contemporary analysis are incapable of a proper assessment. Holmes, like Howells, Mark Twain, and Robert Frost, demands to be read and valued for his typicality, for the way in which he responded to the deepest commitments of his culture; to these commitments he gave effective forms which must be identified and judged in their ideational context.

Notes

1. Leon Howard, *Victorian Knight-Errant* (Berkeley and Los Angeles, 1952), p. viii.

2. Howard, *loc. cit.*

3. The bibliography of the term would be immense; the most recent acknowledgement of the ubiquity of the concept is Frank M. Collins, "Cooper and the American Dream," *PMLA* 81 (March 1966), 79-94. "Chroniclers of the American Dream have made progressively clear . . . 'dialogue' . . . it produced was the distinguishing feature of the nineteenth century American literature."

4. "Official faith;" I'm sure many have used the term before him, but Perry Miller's acceptance of the concept as well as his employing this phrase appears in "The Romantic Dilemma in American Nationalism and the Concept of Nature," *The Harvard Theological Review* (October, 1955), 158, p. 241.

5.   "Our country hath a gospel of her own
       To preach and practice before all the world."

      The Poetical Works of James Russell Lowell
      (Boston, 1904), I, 78

   Holmes also wrote of the "new world's gospel: Be ye men!" *The Poet at the Breakfast Table*, in *The Works of Oliver Wendell Holmes* (Boston, 1891), p. 232.

6. James Russell Lowell, Letter to C. F. Briggs, December 1848, *Letters of James Russell Lowell*, ed. C. E. Norton (New York, 1894), I, 148, and Ralph Waldo Emerson, *English Traits* (Philadelphia, n.d.), p. 276.

7. There have been a large variety of explorations of the official "faith" or "style;" Daniel Boorstin, in his works *The Americans* (New York, 1958), and in *The Genius of American Politics* (Chicago, 1953), identifies the style with an absence of ideology combined with a presence of faith in experience. This analysis is not dissimilar from H. B. Parkes' in *The American Experience* (New York, 1955). A. N. Kaul in *The American Vision* (New Haven, 1963), indicates that the rejection of the past and the vision toward the future is the common denominator. A. A. Ekirch has seen the Idea of Progress as the single most significant part of the faith in *The Idea of Progress in America, 1815-1860* (New York, 1951). In a wonderfully insightful introduction to his *American Literature and the Dream* (New York, 1955), Frederick Ives Carpenter has declared that the Dream escapes definition but is involved with optimism and a faith in man. Almost every foreign observer from de Tocqueville to Brogan has observed that sanguinity was a salient feature of the American attitude towards destiny.

8. Oliver Wendell Holmes, *The Works of Oliver Wendell Holmes* (Boston, 1891), II, 4. Subsequent volume and page numbers appear in the text.

9. The "official philosophy" of his times, Scottish Common Sense, had answered the problem of the apparent contradiction between a belief in the "natural goodness" of natural man, and a belief in the value of civilization which would necessarily destroy the "naturalness" of man. Its answer was that it is man's nature to strive to create better societies, and that the progress of mankind

towards more complex social organizations was a fulfillment of its natural potentialities. See Adam Ferguson, *An Essay on the History of Civil Society* (London, 1793), p. 113.

10. Holmes, *Works,* II, 114. There has been an interesting little battle going on about the specific reference of this poem to Puritanism. Barrett Wendell had made the suggestion at the turn of the century, and DeWolfe Howe had discovered the supporting quotations in *The Professor at the Breakfast Table.* Elizabeth Tilton rejected the allusion as unfounded, but Marian Rossiter Small, having the last word, finds Wendell's insight a good one. Elizabeth Tilton, *Amiable Autocrat* (New York, 1947), pp. 419-420; M. A. DeWolfe Howe, *Holmes of the Breakfast Table* (London, and New York, 1939), pp. 117-118; Marian Rossiter Small, *Oliver Wendell Holmes* (New York, 1962), p. 99.

Eleanor M. Tilton (essay date 1975)

SOURCE: Tilton, Eleanor M. Introduction to *The Poetical Works of Oliver Wendell Holmes,* pp. xvii-xxxv. Boston: Houghton Mifflin, 1975.

[In the following essay, Tilton surveys Holmes's life and career as a poet.]

Like fireworks the day after or like the "banquet's dead bouquet"—with such similes Oliver Wendell Holmes describes the verses he provided his classmates, his colleagues, his club, his university, and his city. From the day he was elected poet of the Class of '29 to the last year of his life, Holmes was in demand to celebrate an anniversary, welcome a celebrity, eulogize the dead, bid the traveler farewell, supply a hymn, reply to a toast, or "play Orpheus to the stones" of a monument. He had reason to complain that 'the mere touch of a warm adjective blisters my palm." His readiness of rhyme made him all too open to "men with argument and women with entreaty" when what was wanted was a poem.

With the popularity of *The Autocrat of the Breakfast-Table,* the requests increased until he became weary of his "corn-stalk fiddle" and spent his ingenuity devising ways to say "No." "You must call upon some other street musician," he crossly told a colleague. Among fellow-physicians he was "celebrated for ready wit, a good song, and a candid investigation," and the doctors claimed their share of songs. He begged for privacy, described the debilitating effects of composition upon the nervous system, and deployed his humor, rhetoric, and even rhyme to frame refusals, unless "struck full in the centre of volition." Out of the practice of refusal came "A Familiar Letter to Several Correspondents" of

1876, a confession disguised as admonition; the man bitten by "the rhyming tarantula" is beyond cure. In the same year, he gave the undergraduate editors of the *Harvard Advocate* **"How the Old Horse Won the Bet"** with its closing line: "A horse *can* trot, for all he's old." He was rather less confident than the line suggests.

He had long been exploring the puzzle of his own personality in essay and novel, playing off one alter ego against another, discovering how many there were, only one of them The Poet. Aware that his mind was "discursive, erratic, subject to electric attractions and repulsions," that to him life was "so vivid" that he was always "too eager to seize and exhaust its multitudinous impressions," he could in the persona of The Poet speak as if he supposed himself to be one. In another guise, that of The Master, he corrected himself: "I *have* some of the qualities that make a man a poet, and yet, I am not one."

In 1872, when he wrote these lines, he was inclined to retrospection. The younger Wendell Holmes was displaying an uncomfortably fierce concentration, even bringing his work to the dinner table, a spectacle that made the elder Holmes uneasy. At the same time the gambrel-roofed house in which he had been born was sold to the University. He had begun raking "cinders from the ashes" in 1869, and a succession of anniversaries in the 1870's would keep him at it. What he found was a life vivid to memory, but not laid out along any line of single-minded achievement.

On August 29, 1809, the Reverend Abiel Holmes, minister of the First Church of Cambridge, noted in his almanac the birth of the first boy in a household of daughters. The minister was a modified Calvinist, "liberal—for a Connecticut man," said a parishioner. Abiel Holmes had written a little poetry, published a history modestly called *Annals of America,* and contributed astronomical observations to the *Memoirs* of the American Academy of Arts and Sciences. He remained for a time undisturbed by the battle in the New England churches. In the struggle between the orthodox forces from his own college, Yale, and those of liberalism from Harvard, Abiel Holmes "maintained a . . . middle station" until a few months before his son's eighteenth birthday.

As a boy Wendell Holmes knew no unsettling crisis in a household slightly darkened by Calvinist teaching but brightened by a genial mother, a pair of lively sisters with Harvard beaux in attendance, a whimsical brother, ample space for play, and not very arduous schooling. There were disadvantages to being undersized, but he discovered that words and wit might be as effective in defense as fists. He had a rival with words, the overeducated daughter of Congressman Fuller. Margaret probably read more modern books than he, for the library in the gambrel-roofed house was deficient in light reading. It had a good supply of poetry, a little old-fashioned to be sure, but still poetry. He was entranced by the "sonorous resonance" of Pope's translation of Homer, and his ear caught the cadences of the heroic line of Dryden and Pope. He took to making up couplets in his head.

Abiel Holmes extracted admonitions from pear trees and bookworms for a son whose quickness of wit was not matched by industry, but he apparently did not consider a passion for fast horses and a precocious taste for cigars as signs of original sin. Holmes was taught that he was "conceived in sin, & born in iniquity" but could say of his parents that in them "nature never allowed 'Grace' to lead them to inhuman conclusions." The strict observance of the sabbath was sometimes made more dreary by visiting ministers with the Yankee whine and dark allusions to damnation.

Holmes's first exposure to intense orthodoxy came during his year at Andover. In this "Dove's nest of Puritan faith," he encountered too many representatives of "rectilinear theology," a headmaster "bigoted, narrow-minded, and uncivilized," and a smiling teacher who turned out to be unjust and brutal. On his sixteenth birthday he appeared before the examiners of Harvard College, happy to exchange a "doctrinal boiler" for "a rational ice-chest."

When Holmes joined the Class of '29, he joined for life; only three classmates survived him, and of these the two that were able-bodied attended his funeral. Holmes had never agreed with the one, the abolitionist Samuel May, and had tried hard to convert the other, the Baptist Samuel Francis Smith, to a liberal religion. Such were loyalty and affection, however, that when politics or religion threatened to splinter the class, they chose a ground on which they could stand together, even to drink a toast during the Civil War to a southern classmate and "*his* constitution." Among the factions that divided the class as undergraduates, Holmes moved easily.

As a student, he maintained a respectable place on the rank lists, struck his teachers as "gifted" in languages, discovered the pleasure of chemistry, and acquired a reputation as a poet. In November 1828, the Reverend Andrews Norton solicited poems for a gift book *The Offering.* Here Holmes first appears in a book, bound in green silk as he boasted to his Andover friend Phineas Barnes. He supplied his clubs with verses and at least one song.

In his senior year, the college commanded his muse for the Exhibition on April 28 and Commencement on August 26, 1829. The class elected him its poet. These commissions he executed to the satisfaction of the

newspapers and the audiences. The class-day poem of his "hapless amour with too tall a maid" does not survive; the other two are here first collected. The Commencement program shows that Holmes had no enviable spot on the long program of orations and colloquia. The exercises were held in the First Church which was filled by nine o'clock in the morning; it was eight minutes of one before Holmes took the stage. Very small in stature and youthful in looks, he followed the tallest man in the class. He must have been even then an accomplished public performer, for annotated programs grade him as very good and "excellent," neither annotator otherwise lavish of praise. Emerson would later say of one of Holmes's occasional poems that he could not be sure how good it was, so skillfully had the poet delivered it. At not yet twenty Holmes could hold a hungry audience to attention; he was doing so still at seventy-four. During all the years he taught at the Harvard Medical School, he was assigned the one o'clock lecture hour because he could keep the hungry and the weary alert.

Equipped with a "fatal facility for rhyme," with "literary bantlings" in print, he had also a catholic curiosity. No subject of study was altogether repellent to him, although he was uncomfortable with mathematics and irritated by metaphysics. His classmate James Freeman Clarke reports Holmes as saying: "I'll tell you, James, what I think metaphysics is like. It is like a man splitting a log. When it is done, he has two more to split." Holmes was not among the young men excited by Coleridge's *Aids to Reflection.* For his future, he looked to law or medicine.

He had reason not to consider the ministry. In July 1827, the liberal parishioners of the First Church at Cambridge had addressed a memorial to their minister. After two years of moves and countermoves, the struggle ended with Abiel Holmes ousted from his pulpit two months before his son entered the same church for his commencement day. In the opinion of the press and even of the *ex parte* council that determined his removal, the minister was sacrificed to both his liberal opponents and his orthodox supporters. Of what his son thought at the time, there is no record. On his father's death in 1837, he had occasion to speak. He saw the two parties as "pressing upon" his father "with much care and policy for their own interests, and too little anxiety with regard to him." Recollected indignation breaks into scorn of the "machinery of modern Jesuitism" and "the Machiavellian contrivances" of deacons. In *Elsie Venner* and *The Guardian Angel,* Holmes tells the story as he wished it had turned out. Rankling more than the liberal party's behavior is that of the orthodox deacons and the assistant these deacons hired for their minister after the split in the church. The minister's son takes his revenge in the characters of Deacon Shearer and the Reverend Bellamy Stoker.

Holmes tried first the law. How little the law attracted him is attested to by the number of verses he contrived to write the moment he had encouragement. A group of undergraduates founded a paper and invited Holmes to contribute. By May of 1830 he was "writing poetry like a madman." He saw his poems in print, not only in *The Collegian,* but in *The New-England Galaxy* and in *The Amateur.* Anonymity did not conceal authorship, and he was asked to contribute to two gift-books. To see his verses handsomely bound and accompanied by an engraving was gratifying. He signed these poems with the distinctive initials: O. W. H. Perhaps the editor of *The Token* knew that the "H." appended to three stanzas in the *Boston Daily Advertiser* of September 16, 1830 stood for Holmes. The poem was **"Old Ironsides."**

The poetic frenzy carried him through 1831 and inspired one of his best poems, **"The Last Leaf."** Holmes said later that he invented the stanza pattern of the poem to entrap an imitator. Whatever his motive, the melancholy cadence effected by the short lines of the tail-rhyme suffuses the comic details of the poem with a rueful tone. Pathos and comedy are held in delicate equilibrium.

The young writer had some reason for self-satisfaction but no illusions about the "poet's lot," as he informed readers of *The New-England Magazine.* To it he contributed two papers called "The Autocrat of the Breakfast-Table," trying his hand at prose. One realization is sharp: "How much easier it is to be witty on some old, hackneyed subjects, than to find out the ridiculous for one's self." By 1832, Holmes was writing noticeably less. He had abandoned the law for medicine and declared himself "in love with his starving delusion."

Fortunate in his teachers, Jacob Bigelow, John Collins Warren, and James Jackson, Holmes gave the study of medicine concentration and devotion. He became a skilled dissector. In the pharmacy of the Massachusetts General Hospital, he used his love of chemistry. With Jackson, he went through the wards, learning more of the cases than any of the other students. Other young men including Jackson's son had already gone to Paris to extend their study; Holmes resolved to follow them. Dr. Jackson wrote to his son: "Do not mind his apparent frivolity and you will soon find that he is intelligent and well-informed. *He has the true zeal.*"

Holmes sailed for Europe on March 29, 1833 and returned on December 15, 1835. In that interval he wrote no poetry, refused to write though asked, and referred rather grandly to "my own science." Philosophers, poets, and revolutionaries still frequented the Café Procope, but for the "medicals" from America the iniquities of Louis Phillipe mattered far less than the numerical method of Pierre Louis. Holmes sampled the theater and the Louvre, cultivated a passionate liking for painting, bought violets, books, and engravings, flirted with a grisette, but he went every morning to the wards of La Pitié. Before the regular sessions began, he would hear the admired Pierre Louis say to him: "Vous travaillez, monsieur, c'est bien ça." Affected by the "concentrated scientific atmosphere" of Paris, he wrote home earnestly of his new "passion for truth." From Louis he learned "not to take authority when I can have facts, not to guess when I can know." Elected to membership in the Société Médicale d'Observation and given access to Louis' wards, he learned to be "exact, methodical, and rigorous." Founded for work not for vanity, the society led by Louis made severe demands upon its members for attendance, papers, and self-criticism. Louis urged that young men engage in research before entering into practice, and he so advised the elder Jackson. In his memoir of his son, Dr. Jackson wrote sadly, regretting that he had not heeded Louis' advice, but in America "such a course would have been so singular, as in a measure to have separated him from other men."

The training itself made for separation, especially from admirers of Coleridge and Carlyle. On a Sunday evening in 1836 Holmes met an old acquaintance—Margaret Fuller. According to her, the conversation turned upon the question: "What view should the man of science take of his relation to eternal interests and his temporal pursuits?" The topic was surely hers; one cannot imagine a lapsed Calvinist fresh from a rigorous French medical training posing such a question. The diarist reports: "W. H. took the ground that there was no settling any-thing about God and the world, that if you went on zealously with any study, seeking truth alone, you would be led unconsciously to the proper ground." Complacently Miss Fuller concludes that she is Holmes's superior "in precision of thought and clearness of utterance." She is the more gratified because Holmes is her own age and one of those "who have really good minds." Behind Holmes's later satire of *The Dial* and its arrogant contributors lay the model of Pierre Louis' "modesty in the presence of nature." The principle "not to guess when you can know" underlay his lectures on the delusions of homeopathy, phrenology, hydropathy, and quack applications of mesmerism, all of which were resorted to by his fellow poets. He had come home with a mind sharpened to the difference between the aesthetic and the scientific modes of perceiving relationships; the difference was always present to him.

He came home to demands for poetry. In his absence his friends had kept his name alive by extravagant allusions to him in periodicals they edited. Park Benjamin asked for a poem for his *American Monthly Magazine,* was given among others **"The Last Reader,"** and earned Holmes's wrath by amending a word. Although shaken by the editor's presumption and by a candid friend who thought the new poems not so good as the old, Holmes set himself to provide a song for the Harvard bicentennial dinner and a poem for Phi Beta Kappa. The song he had the audacity (the "brass," his brother said) to sing himself. The long poem for Phi Beta Kappa he learned by heart and delivered "with charming ease and propriety," according to the secretary of the Board of Overseers.

Welcomed by poets, editors, and his alma mater, Holmes claimed in the same year the attention of the doctors. He entered and won the competition for the Boylston Prize for Medicine. Not attempting an ambitious treatment of the set topic, he focused his essay, "Direct Exploration," upon a new instrument, the stethoscope, and its use. Mentioning his "zealous devotion" and "amiable disposition," his teachers got him the job of visiting physician at the Boston Dispensary.

Holmes wanted "a regular occupation," by which he could support himself and secure "a hold on the community." Being a poet would not satisfy this modest ambition; writing the preface to the volume of poems to appear in November, he renounced the rôle. He was rebuked for "literary suicide" and told by *The North American Review* that there was "no profession so engrossing as to leave no time for poetry." Ignoring this encouragement, he labored doggedly on the research for his essay on Intermittent Fever. The paper was historical rather than scientific, but the principles he had learned in Paris held. He was again competing for a prize; two were offered in 1837 and he won both. "It is almost useless to contend with him in an enterprise of this kind," said the local medical journal. *Poems* of November 1836 was followed by *Boylston Prize Dissertations* of January 1838 dedicated to P. Cha. A. Louis . . . "in the Recollection of His Invaluable Instructions and Unvarying Kindness."

In the twenty years between 1833 and 1853, Holmes wrote only as many poems as he had produced in the four years between 1829 and 1833. The poems were those his place in the community might require: occasional poems written to please his fellow physicians or his summer neighbors in Pittsfield, verses for Harvard and poems for Phi Beta Kappa at Dartmouth (1838) and Yale (1850). He resolved not to keep his reputation as a poet alive by "periodical gaspings." To this resolution, he made a few exceptions. He provided his classmate Clarke with verses for the *Western Messenger* and found himself in the unlikely company of Emerson and Margaret Fuller. He liked **"An After-Dinner Poem"** of 1843 well enough to offer it to *Graham's*. Originally called **"Terpsichore,"** the poem dances over a wide field of contemporary follies; he probably knew that, clever as it was, its topicality required that it be published at once.

Earlier in 1843, he had written his most important medical essay, *The Contagiousness of Puerperal Fever,* a "candid investigation" in which he did not spare his colleagues grief. Written "in a great heat and with passionate indignation," the essay was the product of twenty-one days' intensive research in the literature of the disease and in the experiences of physicians he could cross-examine. That puerperal fever might be contagious had been suggested in 1842 by Dr. Francis Condie of Philadelphia, but the guess had been scouted by Dr. Charles D. Meigs, author of the standard American textbooks on obstetrics. In Boston Dr. Walter Channing had three times reported to the Boston Society for Medical Improvement on successive cases in his own practice; he too rejected the notion of contagion. The society had heard also of two deaths from dissection wounds incurred during autopsies on puerperal fever victims. On January 23, the pathologist John B. S. Jackson raised the question of the possibility of contagion. Within twenty-four hours, Holmes, done with "trivial discussion," was at work. On February 13 he presented his paper.

Asserting at the start that any doubter was ignorant of the evidence, he marshalled the facts to make good his thesis that doctors and nurses were culpable agents of infection. What had been suggested as early as 1773 and as recently as 1842 was made incontrovertible by Holmes's essay. It was printed in *The New England Journal of Medicine*; Holmes circulated an offprint, and an abstract was printed in *The American Journal of Medical Science*. It was the abstract that attracted attention in this country and in England, but with the evidence trimmed and without Holmes's eloquence, the argument did not convince all readers. Noticeably, obstetricians were least persuaded, including Channing, who had seen the full essay yet considered his "experience" sufficient rebuttal. Dr. Meigs attacked the concept of contagion, labelled Holmes's essay as among the "jejeune and fizzenless dreamings of sophomore writers," and loftily attributed deaths from puerperal fever to "Providence." To take arms against fatuity requires a compelling motive. Holmes reprinted his essay in 1855. Addressing his new introduction to medical students, he wrote: "I had rather rescue one mother from being poisoned by her attendant, than claim to have saved forty or fifty patients to whom I had carried the disease." He closed with his most splendid rhetoric:

> . . . Indifference will not do here; our Journals and Committees have no right to take up their pages with minute anatomy and tediously detailed cases, while it is a question whether the 'black death' of child-bed is to be scattered broadcast by the agency of the mother's friend and adviser. Let the men who mould opinions look to it: if there is any voluntary blindness, any culpable negligence, even in such a matter, and the facts shall reach the public ear; the pestilence-carrier of the lying-in chamber must look to God for pardon, for man will never forgive him.

The motive behind the *Boylston Prize Dissertations* was ambition; that behind the puerperal fever essay of 1843 and 1855 was altruistic. But always the impetus to put his talents to work had to be immediate. Separated from colleagues who boasted of "cures," assumed that "experience" constituted evidence, and offered "Providence" as an explanation of what they were unwilling to face, he was separated also from his fellow poets who trusted to "intuition." With his eye on the immediate, Holmes struck his German-indoctrinated contemporaries as a man of "mere understanding," not a man of "imagination."

While Holmes taught the use of the microscope, the transcendentalists listened to papers on such modest subjects as "Man in the Ages." When they began to show themselves in their periodical *The Dial,* Holmes took notice of them. In **"Terpsichore"** he mocks their presumption. Addressing them as "Deluded infants," the doctor asks: "Will they ever know / Some doubts must darken here below." A sane man might expect to answer the question: Is puerperal fever contagious? Only a "Bedlamite" would put conundrums to "Earth the tongueless" and "the deaf-mute Time!"

By 1843, Holmes had found his place in the community. In 1840 he married Amelia Lee Jackson, daughter of Judge Charles Jackson and niece of his loved teacher Dr. James Jackson. Holmes's first son and namesake, future Justice of the Supreme Court, was born March 9, 1841; his daughter Amelia on October 20, 1843; and his son Edward on October 17, 1846. The family lived at 8 Montgomery Place, not far from the Tremont Medical School where he now taught. By 1846, he had developed a respectable practice, had joined the staff of the Massachusetts General Hospital, had maintained his reputation as a poet, and had earned what he shrewdly called the "flattery of abuse." In April 1847, he received notice of his appointment as Parkman Professor of Anatomy and Physiology at the Massachusetts Medical College (i.e., Harvard). In May he attended the first meeting of the American Medical Association. He was made chairman of the Committee on Medical Literature; the devastating report presented the following year was entirely his work. He charged his colleagues with servility to England, the "habit of indolence," and poverty of mind, and documented the charges in a "scathing review" that took two hours to deliver.

Meanwhile his appointment as Parkman Professor entailed his making the Introductory Lecture. Such was his reputation that a number of gentlemen, transcendentalists among them, attended the lecture and even considered enrolling in his course. Holding the office of Dean, he supported the application of a woman; thereafter he consistently voted for the admission of women, more often than not their only advocate. Withdrawing from private practice in 1849, he began to appear with more regularity on the public lecture platform where he may be said to have been rehearsing for *The Autocrat.* Invited to give a series of lectures for the Lowell Institute of 1853, he chose the subject of "The English Poets of the Nineteenth Century." Romantic idealists, willing to hear him on anatomy or the "Races of Man," were astonished at his temerity in choosing to speak on Wordsworth and Coleridge.

Two letters written before he gave these lectures suggest his expectations as a reader. Writing Emerson to acknowledge the gift of *Poems* (1846), he admired the "genuineness" of Emerson's "descriptions of common scene and feelings" but admitted that much was to him "vague and mystical." What to Emerson was "a clear and simple image" seemed to him "to refract and distort" the idea. He wondered that Emerson could "undervalue" rhythm as a "means of expression." He is the more surprised because passages that have moved him most by the "beauty and strength of thought" have been "melodious" in spite of Emerson's "carelessness." Acknowledging that his mind is "different in tendencies and habits" from the minds of Emerson's intimates, he had found much to delight him.

To Hawthorne in 1851 he wrote without reservations:

> The imagination of our lean country men has always seemed to me as emaciated as their faces. I had been so morbidly set in this belief that but for your last two stories I should have . . . believed that all we were to look for in the way of such spontaneous growth were such languid, lifeless, sexless creations as in the view of certain people constitute the chief triumphs of a sister art as manifested among us.
>
> . . . The Yankee mind has for the most part . . . flowered in pots of English earth—but you have . . . raised yours . . . in the natural soil . . . the moment a fresh mind takes in the elements of common life about us and transfigures them I am contented to enjoy and admire . . .

The criteria he brought to his lectures on the English poets are revealed in these letters. He asked for melody and in the "prolix" Wordsworth found prose, or rhythms so elusive as to be undetectable to ears attuned to Pope; he found the "elements of common life," and the "homely truthfulness of the actual," but not yet for him their "transfiguration." In Byron and Moore he heard strong melodies, but both had too often found their matter elsewhere than in their "natural soil." The lectures were so well subscribed that the press wildly overestimated his profit from the size of the crowds. Even an unsympathetic reviewer observed: "His peculiar magnetism makes itself felt before his voice is heard." The "chime and emphasis of his voice" were as pleasing as his wit. The newspaper reports are less than coherent. Holmes's speech was distinct but rapid; the reporters had trouble keeping up with him. The chief victim of his wit was Carlyle whose judgment of Scott he satirically diagnosed. He is reported to have treated "tenderly" weaknesses he had been expected to mock. Some of his hearers regretted that he was not more reverential in his handling of Wordsworth, more censorious in his judgment of Byron, and more melodramatic in his account of the opium-eating Coleridge.

Originally the lecture room had been a place where serious listeners hoped to be instructed, but by the fifties it had become, as Holmes knew, a lion-trap, a place of amusement. The traveling was arduous for Holmes, liable to homesickness and asthma. Immaculate in his person, he suffered in ill-kept rural taverns. From the business of lecturing he was rescued by the founding of *The Atlantic Monthly*. The first editor, James Russell Lowell, made Holmes's promise to contribute a condition of his acceptance of the job; and thereafter each successive editor made sure of his contributions.

Holmes did not escape from the lecture room unscathed. In 1855, in his Address for the New England Society of New York, he had satirized the prohibitionists and abolitionists; reformers in the audience hissed. To the hisses he referred forgivingly in his poem the following evening, but the false reports of his lecture in the newspapers brought him letters. He did not answer the journalists, but the letters from Theodore Parker and Emerson, he had to answer. He told Parker: "I don't want to be bullied into Heaven by the pulpit—neither do I wish to be called hard names to make me better or more humane. But surely my attacks on this spirit, as shown in moral warfare, do not prove that I am a glutton, or a drunkard, or a defender of slavery." To Emerson he wrote: "If the law of conscience *carried out fully only by the ultra-abolitionists,* had been proclaimed in strict accordance with the law of love, I believe the question would be far more nearly solved than it is at present." He assures Emerson that he is not "undergoing any process of moral disintegration." Transcendentalists could be as dogmatic as Calvinists; between irresistible grace and the infallible conscience there was not much to choose.

The human race might require criticism, but Holmes thought it required charity even more, and the papers shortly to appear in the new magazine would try to show why. Lowell had wanted variety, and his first number guaranteed it. On page 48 appeared Emerson's "Brahma" followed by *The Autocrat of the Breakfast-Table*. All contributions were unsigned, but no reader was deceived. Holmes's provocative talk and Emerson's provoking poem drew attention to the first number. As successive numbers came out, the press repeatedly praised the Autocrat's talk. With the founding of *The Atlantic* and his admission to the Saturday Club in 1857, Holmes joined a second "community."

The format of the Breakfast-Table papers owes to the two papers written twenty-five years earlier only the title. The notion that every man might be his own Boswell had not then occurred to him, nor had he attempted to fill out the boarding-house table with refracting characters. The new format allowed his "discursive" mind free play. There was nothing in his life that could not evoke suggestive ideas. Cant, quackery, and fatuity were the objects of stringent comment in the breakfast-table books and in the novels. The religious press charged him with being a semi-infidel who poisoned the minds of his readers. The socially conscious, then as now, misapplied his definition of the "Brahmin." Chosen by Holmes for its association with learning and the priesthood, the word identified a physical and psychological type of which Edwards, Channing, and Emerson were representative as he makes plain in *Elsie Venner* of 1861 and in the poem **"At the Saturday Club"** of 1884.

Holmes delighted as many as he offended. Yet few of his contemporaries responded to that subject he thought "the noblest and most interesting"; namely, psychology. He asked for the study of "man, the individual, not the abstraction, the metaphysical or theological lay-figure." In *The Autocrat* he offers his image of the limited will as a drop of water imprisoned in a crystal. With the theme of human limitation, he made ready for **"The Coming Era."** In this poem of 1880 he foresees a day when the muse will yield to science, and "Physics will grasp imagination's wings," or so, in the fiction of the poem, he is being told by a new generation of "youthful sages."

He was prepared to psychologize even his addiction to verse. Whatever a poem cost him in nervous energy and however often he was moved to warn the tyro to beware of the rhymer's disease, he had still to write poetry. Late in life, asked to choose between *The Contagiousness of Puerperal Fever* and **"The Chambered Nautilus,"** Holmes refused to answer. To have saved lives was reason for satisfaction, but he could not recall with any self-congratulation his savage frame of mind at the time of writing. The poem, on the other hand, had been written in a state of exhilaration he recalled with pleasure. In his lecture on Keats, the poet who had chosen poetry over medicine, Holmes had unequivocally expressed his approval of the choice. In the best account of the lecture (in Bryant's *New York Evening Post*), he is reported as saying: "it is a good thing to save a few lives, but it is better to have infused a new life into our language."

In *The Poet*, he suggests that he had not found a voice. He might more accurately have said that among many voices, he had not chosen one to be unmistakably his. The poems in *The Autocrat* alone illustrate his range from the romantic sublime of **"The Chambered Nauti-**

lus" through the clever play of Latin and English in "Æstivation," to the colloquial **"Deacon's Master-piece"**; rhythm, diction, tone are all radically different. **"Contentment"** and **"Latter-Day Warnings"** are less far apart, but the stance of the speaker in each is not the same. The gathering includes occasional poems in which good humor and appropriate sentiment are held together by the poet's sense of the occasion. Complementing them is the mock occasional poem **"Ode for a Social Meeting"** carefully revised to satisfy a teetotaler's taste. The voice of the professor in love with his subject is heard in the anatomist's hymn **"The Living Temple."** Only two poems are at all alike; **"Parson Turrell's Legacy"** matches **"The Deacon's Master-piece,"** to show that he could "do it twice."

So sure is Holmes's control of his tunes and his lyrics in whatever mode he chooses that he appears to speak in rhyme as easily as in prose. He can make the heroic couplet expressive of the harshest sarcasm, of genial humor, of solemn praise, of common talk. In some occasional poems he skates close to the cliché, but his diction is usually crisp; he tries to avoid the blurring word and the limp epithet. With a more sensitive ear than his contemporaries, he can make his cadences remarkably expressive.

Choosing the Professor to succeed the Autocrat, he carried on a running debate with the religious press. For the book he invented the alter ego of the crippled "Little Boston," provincial patriot and fierce defender of religious liberty. With this invention, he anticipated the admissions he would make seven years later in letters to Harriet Beecher Stowe. His necessary resistance to Calvinist training had, he thought, injured the "balance" of his intelligence: "I suppose all I write may show something of this, as the lame child limps at every step, as the crooked back shows through every garment."

The persistent misinterpretation of **"The Deacon's Masterpiece"** as an attack upon Calvinism is understandable in the light of Holmes's obsession. For this interpretation, first offered by Barrett Wendell, there is no evidence; Holmes's son testified to his father's never so describing it. In its context in *The Autocrat,* there is nothing to warrant such a reading. In a note of 1885, Holmes presents the poem in terms of its subtitle "A Logical Story" and its final line: "Logic is logic. That's all I say." In the first number of *The Autocrat,* the question is asked: "If a logical mind ever found out anything with its logic?" The answer promptly returned is: "I should say that its most frequent work was to build a *pons asinorum* over chasms which shrewd people can bestride without such a structure." The critic who reads the poem as a parable should apply it to all logical systems which, whatever their perfection of artificial structure, must collapse under pressure from nature.

Holmes's first novel, *Elsie Venner: A Romance of Destiny,* carried a warning in its subtitle. Not altogether fusing science and poetry, the novel is in part a "medicated" fantasy designed "to test the doctrine of 'original sin,'" and in part a documentary of New England village life. Fresh from exercising a license to be discursive, Holmes does not bring the varied matter of his novel into harmony. His psychological speculations are not suited to his heroine, for his image of the will as a moving drop of water enclosed in a crystal is not applicable to a child poisoned before birth. Minor figures in the novel are more suggestive than the ophidian heroine and her Gothic cousin Dick. The schoolteacher Helen Darley is a mild hysteric puzzled by her own aberrations and those of some of the children she teaches. She is moved to question the creed she had been taught. For this indictment of orthodox training Holmes was charged with "moral parricide" and accused of dissecting "before the world the character and memory of his father." A second figure in the novel, the vacillating preacher Fairweather, is represented as lost in his own spiritual needs and incapacitated for the care of other souls; he seeks refuge in the Catholic Church.

While the novel was running in *The Atlantic,* Holmes addressed his colleagues. "Currents and Counter-Currents in Medical Science" has as one topic the discoveries of the geologists who have "remodelled the beliefs of half the civilized world." The unsettling of traditional ideas has sent some men scurrying to the oldest dogma or the newest mystical fancy. Holmes recognizes here the comforts of Catholicism, which had drawn a number of recent converts from among the young, and the increasing attraction of spiritualism. Able to welcome the discoveries of the geologists, Holmes was able to welcome Darwinism and became at Boston dinner-tables the explicator of the new texts derived from nature not scripture.

In the following year, all questions went down before the one fact of the Civil War. The war, foreseen and feared by Unionists, evoked in Holmes the ardent patriot. In spirit he was deeply engaged, and that not solely because he had a son at the front. He had argued consistently for Union and the compromises undertaken to ensure it; now he threw his talent into the Union cause. With lecture, hymn, and exhortatory verse, he earned attack from the Copperheads.

Confident in public, in private he was anxious. Three times the alarming messages came to the house on Charles Street; it was the second that sent him on his "Hunt after the Captain." The psychologist found it curious that anxiety and weariness instead of blinding him to what he saw should have made him more alert and observant. He wrote out his worries to John Lothrop Motley. To this loved friend, he could write with freedom, shocked by the Jeremiahs he met in the street, by those prepared to abandon the Union, those prepared to submit to the South, and those whose chief concern was their pocketbooks. He met them all in the streets of Boston. He found more meanness than he supposed possible: "I believe our people are worked up to the *paying* point, which, I take it, is to the fighting point as boiling heat (212°) is to blood heat (98°)." He encountered young men whose temperatures were well below normal and old men who supposed that a little prudence might have prevented the "unlucky accident."

The correspondence with Motley prepared him for the Fourth of July oration of 1863. He had made fun of Fourth of July oratory in the past; now the motive for inventing his own was irresistible. Arguing for the inevitability of the conflict, he eloquently establishes what he calls (out of Spencer) the "law of simultaneous intellectual movement." He draws his illustrations from art, literature, science, and history, deploying the device of the wide-ranging catalogue to persuasive effect. To rebuke those who count the cost in dollars, he catalogues with manifest contempt the luxuries the northerner still enjoys: "If our property is taxed, it is only to teach us that liberty is worth paying for as well as fighting for." The rhetoric now shows tarnish but then comforted the speaker as well as the audience.

Holmes needed comfort; the letters from the battlefield were increasingly pessimistic. The view from Fredricksburg in 1862 was not the same as the view from Boston and Vienna; young Holmes charged his father and Motley with "ignorance." Not doubting the "right of our cause," he despaired of "success by arms." He concluded this "blowoff" by asking for six photographs of himself and had the envelope addressed by someone else "so that you may think it a bill." In the still harrowing days of 1864, Captain Holmes felt acutely the prolonged physical and emotional pressures of the war. He wrote ambiguously: "I have made up my mind to stay on the staff till the end of the campaign & then if I am alive, I shall resign—I have felt for some time that I didn't any longer believe in this being a duty . . ." By "this" he meant returning to service as a line officer after his three-year term ended, but only later letters explain the vague pronoun. Misunderstanding, the father replied at once; his letter, arriving the day after the young man had heroically carried a message through a nest of rebel raiders, provoked resentment. Conscious of virtue and exhausted by days of battle and nights of marching, the son wrote angrily of misunderstanding that impugned his honor. Five days later, with "a thousand loving thoughts," he acknowledged "delightful letters" from both parents and a box of cigars from his father.

When young Holmes supposed that he might die of the wounds received at Bull's Bluff, he recalled agreeing with his father, whose religious scepticism he shared,

that there could be no deathbed recantation. Toward his father, he freely expressed respect, "sass," anger, and love. Between two vain, quick-witted, argumentative men, there was likely to be friction as well as love. The father admitted to being vain; the son, to being "disagreeable." Twenty years later in retrospective speeches about the war, the veteran echoes the sentiments of his father's address of July 4, 1863, and in "The Soldier's Faith" (1895) he remembers the "cynic force with which thoughts of common sense will assail the soldier in times of stress." The details of the speech suggest that he was rereading his own letters.

In 1865 with his hero at home, Dr. Holmes was meditating on heredity; he had a "case" before him—sceptic, poet (of the class of '61), patriot, and, the father hoped, potential judge. With heredity in mind, Holmes was glad to say: "Luckily my wife is one of the smartest and most capable women going." Heredity would be a theme in *The Guardian Angel* of 1867. James T. Fields had asked for "An American story," and Holmes took a hint from a medical friend for "a book on education with a physiological base." The novel fulfils these specifications, too explicitly the hostile reviewer in *The Nation* thought, lamenting the "atmosphere of carnality" he detected in the book. In his heroine Myrtle Hazard, Holmes created a more plausible case than Elsie Venner. Myrtle's difficulties in weathering the storms of adolescence, which so offended the sensibilities of *The Nation,* are worked out in terms of her conflicting inherited traits. To describe his sense that human beings have an unconscious knowledge of themselves that has only to be brought into consciousness for recognition to follow, Holmes uses the image of the undeveloped photographic plate from which the picture emerges as the photographer applies his wash. Shortly after he published the novel, Holmes had the satisfaction of finding similar conceptions in the writings of the Englishman Henry Maudsley (sometimes labeled the first psychiatrist).

With his usual sense of occasion, Holmes prepared his Phi Beta Kappa Address of 1870, *Mechanism in Thought and Morals.* In a sparkling performance, the professor and poet speak in one voice. Holmes uses his talent for selecting the bright image to show all that is known about the brain and the process of thinking in so far as thinking can be the subject of testing and measurement. With manifest delight he suggests the questions that can be asked and describes his own experiments, some devised to check the findings of others and some anticipatory of future experiments. He had traced the idea of unconscious thought to Leibnitz and then considered its variations in later theorists. His continuing attack on supposedly moribund theologies is prompted by his recognition of the subterranean life of old beliefs. He turns his address in this direction; it is not the scientist who can be charged with materialism, but the moralist:

> We hang men for our convenience and safety; sometimes shoot them for revenge. Thus we come to associate the infliction of punishment for offences as their satisfactory settlement,—a kind of neutralization of them, as of an acid with an alkali: so that we feel as if a jarring moral universe would be all right if only suffering enough were added to it.

The address was neatly timed. *The American Journal of Medical Psychology* was founded in 1870; in 1871, John E. Tyler, who had been a special lecturer in "Psychology and Medicine," became a full professor at the Medical School with his own department of neurology.

Among the visitors to the old house on Charles Street and the new house on Beacon Street, were the younger Holmes's brilliant friends: William James and his brother Henry; Charles Saunders Peirce, Henry Adams. In *The Poet at the Breakfast-Table* Holmes acknowledges that sons "do not walk in our ruts of thought or begin exactly where we left off, but they have a standpoint of their own." No scientist as his son's generation conceived of the scientist, Holmes took refuge in the fact that he was a poet and turned the breakfast table over to that alter ego. He might regret not having made himself a specialist, but as he confessed to S. Weir Mitchell, his "nature was to snatch at all the fruits of knowledge." The new book with his candid letters to Mitchell of the same year reveals that the fruits of psychological knowledge might be bitter, but nothing could put him to flight from the immediate world in which he was as interested as he was in his own "vicious and kicking brain." He could use the book to explain the new science to the old and to defend sentiment from the young. Through the Poet and the Master, the well-informed doctor speaks of Darwinism, the nebular hypothesis, the theories of Alexander Bain and Francis Galton, and the latest in bacteriology.

Moving easily into the post-Darwinian world, Holmes yet felt his years and the demands made upon him not only by a longer University term but by the responsibility of being a celebrity not shy in public. So much in love with "his native planet" that he hoped leaves of absence were permitted from heaven, even Holmes could find the "gilded age" too rich for absorption. He took in all he could and bore as well as he could a melancholy succession of losses: Agassiz, his sister Ann, his son-in-law, first Mary Motley and then Motley himself. His biography of Motley he wrote with love. He had never loved Sumner, but the senator's death and the disgraceful spectacle of drunken politicians at the funeral underscored "the ignoble aspect of the great republic." Was there any other way to treat the disorderly Tilden-Hayes campaign save by mocking it as he does in the poem **"How Not to Settle It"**?

With the loss of loved friends and relatives, he approached his seventieth birthday with "cheerful despair." Three years later on November 28, 1882 he entered his lecture room at the medical school for the last time and discovered more affection than he had bargained for. For once in his life he was speechless. Even the New York medical profession was prepared to subject the Boston celebrity to dinners and receptions. Expected to sing for his supper, Holmes resorted to the familiar "straight-backed measure with its stately stride." He is not sure that praise from the doctors is merited "For nature's servant far too often seen / A loiterer by the wave of Hippocrene."

He was not done with his profession, for he had to perform at the dedication of the new Medical School Building. At that moment, Governor Ben Butler was investigating the Tewksbury Almshouse, exploiting the disposal of bodies to the medical school and the presumed horrors of the dissecting room—Holmes's domain. Butler made much of Holmes's having shown a piece of human skin to his classes. The dedication had been scheduled for May, but before evening on May 11, the building was gutted by fire. When the postponed day of dedication came in October, the building was to be opened for inspection, but someone locked the dissecting-room. At the end of his speech Holmes introduced the shocking topic of "the Anthropotomic Laboratory, known to plainer speech as the Dissecting-Room."

He let forth all his love for his subject and all his contempt for politicians whose "inflammatory representations" might provoke "midday mobs or midnight incendiarism." It is in the interest of intelligent citizens to "defend the anatomist and his place of labor." He went on to give examples of the relation between anatomical studies and surgery and concluded: "I cannot stop to moan over a scrap of human integument . . . for every lifeless body which served for these experiments a hundred or a thousand fellow-creatures have been saved from unutterable anguish, and many of them from premature death." Some member of the chastened medical faculty unlocked the doors of the dissecting room before the audience was released to make its tour of inspection.

Ostensibly retired, Holmes summoned in his final decade the spirit to write a second biography, a third novel, an account of one hundred days abroad, the tea-table coda to the breakfast-table series, and, of course, poems. Yet at Parker's of a Saturday he found "the company . . . more of ghosts than of flesh and blood." He put the feeling into a poem. **"At the Saturday Club"** is in the loved measure of the heroic couplet. Holmes steps lightly over the pavement of rhyme. He brings us naturally to the Parker House and into the empty dining room, the more empty for the detail of "the waiters lounging round the marble stairs." He gives his ghosts "robes of flesh," bringing Longfellow, Agassiz, Hawthorne, and Emerson before the eye and to the ear. He gives too the qualities of mind and work, and suggests his judgment so obliquely that it takes a moment to see that the effect of the epithets attached to Longfellow is that of unvarying softness; those attached to Agassiz give us the robust and vigorous. His admiration of Hawthorne's work is implicit in every line; the man is a mystery the poet is willing to leave unsolved. Still no lover of transcendentalism, Holmes exempts Emerson from censure. His simile descriptive of Emerson's slow searching for the right word is somewhat labored, but he finds the right images for this "wingéd Franklin."

When he wrote the poem, he was already at work on the biography of Emerson for the American Men of Letters series. The book brought him letters of praise. Lowell, a professor of literature inclined to snub the professor of anatomy, was grateful to be shown that Emerson, without "sensuous passion," had "spiritual passion enough and to spare." Perhaps more gratifying was a letter from Henry Adams, a contemporary of his son. Adams wished that the chapter on poetry had been longer, at the expense of the judgments of Emerson's admirers, for he preferred Holmes to "Mr. Emerson's echoes . . ." Holmes at close to seventy-five was surely pleased by Adams's comment on "the lightness of touch and the breadth of sympathy that makes your work so much superior to anything we other men, who call ourselves younger, succeed in doing." The work had tired Holmes; his brother John urged him to read novels "and have a blow-out at tea if you won't go anything stronger."

Instead of reading novels, he wrote one, beginning at once on *A Mortal Antipathy*. A novel by courtesy, the book does not control the author's discursive mind; on the contrary, the device of a literary society, which publishes its members' contributions, allows Holmes to disport himself on such subjects as interviewers, intellectual humility, and psychological relations to bodies of water. The book has two topics: the woman question and a case of childhood trauma. Satirizing the feminist and her opponent, he creates two bizarre maidens to expose the weakness of the intellectual arguments of the one and physiological arguments of the other. The "case" of the hero with his trauma-induced phobia was credible to Dr. S. Weir Mitchell but not to the ordinary reader. However casual a novel, the book shows that its author is still alert to his world.

Besieged by interviewers and flooded with letters, Holmes issued "A Cry From the Study" only to invite more letters, among them invitations to visit England.

Leaving with his daughter in April, he arrived in time for the London "season." The round of breakfasts, luncheons, teas, and dinners persuaded Holmes that the "season" was suited to ruminants with several stomachs but not to an old man with only one. He went to the parties and took his three honorary degrees graciously, but he had his own desires. He was determined to see the Derby again. Traveling in state in the special train of the Prince of Wales, he was amused to compare his grandeur of 1886 with his lowly status of 1834. The poor student had seen Plenipotentiary in 1834; now the celebrity was to see Ormonde—two great horses, which the greater experts could not tell.

A compelling desire was to see his coevals. In intense excitement on June 7, Holmes heard Gladstone urge the passage of the Irish Home Rule bill, saw him go down to defeat, and heard him cheered even so. He walked home alone at two in the morning not displeased at the performance of this other gentleman of seventy-seven. Three days later he went to the Isle of Wight and wandered under the trees with Tennyson whose seclusion he respected too much to write of him. A sentimental traveler, Holmes looked for associations with his own past and with poets. He could not see the lark rising from Salisbury Plain, but at Windsor he heard the cuckoo's "wandering voice." In the same spirit he went to Paris, revisited remembered places, took coffee at the Café Procope, and made one visit to the modern world. In the rue Vauquelin, he presented his compliments to Louis Pasteur.

The return home was darkened by his wife's illness, but he wrote his book while his journey was fresh in his mind. Of his infirmities he made light; but griefs crowded one upon the other. His younger son had died in 1884, and now he would lose his wife. One number of *Over the Teacups* had appeared in *The Atlantic*; he abandoned the book. For a while his daughter's coming to live with him rejuvenated his bleak household and revived his waning spirits, but in 1889, his daughter too died. He met his griefs with fortitude, and in 1890, he picked up the abandoned book.

Candidly Holmes told his readers that he expected to repeat himself: "The area of consciousness is covered by layers of habitual thought . . . When we think we are thinking, we are . . . only listening to the sound of attrition between those inert elements of our intelligence." The Dictator presides over the tea-table along with a new alter ego "The Crank," on to whom Holmes shoves the responsibility for his firmest prejudices. He has new topics; though he has not the terms, he explores semantics and extrasensory perception. In 1858 he had delighted his readers with **"The Deacon's Masterpiece"**; in 1890 he matches his record with **"The Broomstick Train."** His readers rejoiced in this revivification of wit turned upon the new invention of the electric trolley car, but he himself called his last book the "wintry product of my freezing wits."

He was not idle in the last four years of his life and could meet demanding occasions with speech and rhyme. The work of preparing the Riverside Edition of his *Writings* [*The Writings of Oliver Wendell Holmes*] could scarcely have been easy. He felt like Hamlet, "fat and short of breath," he told one of the editors at 2 Park Street. What appears to be his last poem, his translation from Sappho, is written in a very shaky hand. The poem is a love poem, but the stricken lover and the translator know too well the signs of impending death. On October 7, 1894, talking with his son, Holmes "simply ceased to breathe."

In 1872 in *The Poet at the Breakfast-Table,* Holmes had written: "Life is a fatal complaint and an eminently contagious one." Because life was an infection he was never tempted to avoid, Holmes had grown younger as he grew older, able to meet his son's generation more than halfway. Admiring his father's "fertile and suggestive intellect," Justice Holmes concluded that his father had "the most penetrating mind of all that lot."

Not bound to any literary fashion, Holmes's poetry cannot be confidently "placed." Poetry was for him "the science of the heart," and through every change of tune and topic, he consistently suggests that the human race is the better for candor and kindness, truth and laughter. Suffering and grief he acknowledges as realities, but not sin and evil. Against the moral earnestness that would rub the sheen from the many bright facets "in the crystalline order of things," he would all his life protest. It cannot be said that Holmes was no poet; it has to be said that he was so many other things as well.

Acknowledgments

For permission to use Holmes's manuscripts, I am indebted to the Houghton Library, Harvard University; the Countway Library, Harvard Medical School; Harvard Law Library, Harvard University; the Harvard University Archives, The Henry E. Huntington Library, the Manuscript Division of the Library of Congress, Miss Miriam R. Small, and Mrs. Ward I. Gregg. The fragment from Margaret Fuller's diary is quoted with the permission of Houghton Library. For permission to use texts first printed in Currier's *Bibliography of Oliver Wendell Holmes,* I wish to thank New York University Press. The firm of Abelard-Schuman has allowed me to use poems first printed in my *Amiable Autocrat.* Harvard University Press has permitted the use of passages from *Touched With Fire.*

Of incalculable value were Thomas Franklin Currier's manuscript notes of variant readings. These notes (in my possession) were particularly useful in checking the

1895 texts. I have a special debt to Miss Carolyn Jakeman and Mr. Rodney G. Dennis of Houghton Library and Mr. Morris Cohen and Mrs. Erika S. Chadburn of the Harvard Law Library, all of whom were very helpful in the crisis of the "lost" manuscripts. I wish to thank also Mr. Richard J. Wolfe of the Countway Medical Library and his staff. The notes added to this edition are the fuller because of the labor of Margaret Notley Yackulic who also patiently typed and retyped revised manuscript.

The principal secondary works consulted are listed below with note of the abbreviations used in the notes. Titles marked with an asterisk are the sources of matter quoted in the Introduction.

Currier, Thomas Franklin. *Bibliography of Oliver Wendell Holmes,* ed. Eleanor M. Tilton. New York: 1953. (C. & T.)

————. "Oliver Wendell Holmes, Poet Laureate of Harvard," *Proceedings of the Massachusetts Historical Society,* LXVII (1945), 436-451.

*Holmes, Oliver Wendell, Jr. *Speeches.* Boston: 1934.

*————. *Touched With Fire,* ed. Mark De Wolfe Howe. Cambridge, Massachusetts: 1946.

Ives, George B. *A Bibliography of Oliver Wendell Holmes.* Boston: 1907.

Lokensgard, Hjalmar. "Holmes Quizzes the Professors," *American Literature,* XIII (May 1941), 157-162.

*Morse, John T. *Life and Letters of Oliver Wendell Holmes.* Boston: 1897.

Small, Miriam R. "First and Last Surviving Poems of Dr. Oliver Wendell Holmes," *American Literature,* XV (January 1944), 416-420.

*Tilton, Eleanor M. *Amiable Autocrat.* New York: 1947. (A. A.)

————. "'Literary Bantlings': Addenda to the Holmes Bibliography," *Papers of the Bibliographical Society of America,* LI (1957), 1-18.

————. "Dr. Holmes Answers the Question," *North Carolina Medical Journal,* VIII (1947), 12-14.

————. "Science and Sentiment," *Transactions of the Studies of the College of Physicians of Philadelphia,* 4th ser. XXVI (August, 1958), 89-98.

Edwin P. Hoyt (essay date 1979)

SOURCE: Hoyt, Edwin P. "The Sad End of A Budding Poet" and "The Old Branch Begins to Wither." In *The Improper Bostonian: Dr. Oliver Wendell Holmes,* pp.

38-45 and 272-80. New York: William Morrow and Company, Inc., 1979.

[In the following excerpt, Hoyt discusses two periods in Holmes's life as a writer: the first, when his literary output became subordinate to his medical career, and the second, after his retirement from Harvard when he could again devote time to writing poetry.]

Graduation from Harvard College had far less impact on the life of Oliver Wendell Holmes than on most of his classmates. It meant only moving out of Stoughton Hall back across the common to the big yellow house, where he could live until he completed his education. That fall, for reasons that were never entirely clear to succeeding generations, Wendell chose to make law his profession, and enrolled in the Dane Law School to study under Judge Joseph Story and John Hooker Ashmun. He had considered going away, perhaps to Yale, to study law, but was persuaded by the coming of Judge Story and Professor Ashmun that Harvard was the place to be. Perhaps because the law school was located just next to the big yellow house, Holmes felt altogether sequestered there. In a matter of weeks it became apparent that the law did not suit him, and by winter he was thoroughly disgruntled, admitting as much to Phineas Barnes, although he did not mention the reason.

By way of amusement he produced poems for a literary magazine called the *Collegian,* published by Harvard friends. The poems gave him more pleasure than Blackstone, by far. By spring he had published fifteen poems in the four issues of the *Collegian,* and they had been copied by various other newspapers and literary journals around New England; but since they were unsigned, they brought him little more than self-satisfaction.

The *Collegian*'s "admirable comic poetry" became known to Frederick Hill, editor of the *New England Galaxy.* Hill made it a point to learn the name of the poet. He was particularly taken by **"The Height of the Ridiculous,"** Holmes's simplest and most professional work to date. It brought him new commissions from editor Hill.

So in the summer of 1830 the poet labored and the advocate slumbered. From this period came **"The Ballad of the Oysterman"**:

> It was a tall young oysterman lived by the riverside,
> His shop was just upon the bank, his boat was on the tide;
> The daughter of a fisherman, that was so straight and slim,
> Lived over on the other bank, right opposite to him.
>
> It was the pensive oysterman that saw a lovely maid,
> Upon a moonlight evening, a-sitting in the shade,
> He saw her wave her handkerchief, as much as if to say,

> "I'm wide awake, young oysterman, and all the folks away."
>
> Then up arose the oysterman, and to himself, said he,
> "I guess I'll leave the skiff at home, for fear that folks should see:
> I read it in the story book, that for to kiss his dear,
> Leander swam the Hellespont,—and I will swim this here."
>
> And he has leaped into the waves, and crossed the shining stream,
> And he has clambered up the bank, all in the moonlight gleam;
> Oh, there were kisses sweet as dew, and words as soft as rain,
> But they have heard her father's step, and in he leaps again.
>
> Out spoke the ancient fisherman,—"Oh what was that, my daughter?"
> "Twas nothing but a pebble, sir, I threw into the water."
> "And what was that, pray tell me, love, that paddles off so fast?"
> "It's nothing but a porpoise, sir, that's been a-swimming past."
>
> Out spoke the ancient fisherman,—"Now bring me my harpoon!
> I'll get into my fishing boat, and fix that fellow soon."
> Down fell that pretty innocent, as falls a snowwhite lamb,
> Her hair drooped round her pallid cheeks, like seaweed on a clam.
>
> Alas for those two loving ones! She waked not from her swound,
> And he was taken with the cramp, and in the waves was drowned;
> But Fate has metamorphosed them, in pity of their woe,
> And now they keep an oyster shop for mermaids down below.

This poem achieved instant fame at Harvard. It was put to music and sung in taverns and restaurants where men made merry. But only a handful knew the name of its author, for again these verses were unsigned. Holmes, then, by his twenty-first birthday, was an accomplished creator of humor, although still unknown outside a select circle.

Then came a change.

The morning of September 14, which should have found Oliver Wendell Holmes deep in his case studies, instead found him deep in the pages of the Boston *Daily Advertiser.* There he read a short news item reprinted from a New York newspaper:

> *Old Ironsides*—It has been affirmed upon good authority that the Secretary of the Navy has recommended to the Board of Navy Commissioners to dispose of the frigate *Constitution.* . . .
>
> —*New York Journal of Commerce*

When the young poet Oliver Wendell Holmes saw those lines, his Massachusetts man's soul flamed up. If a New York editor lamented the fact that the Secretary of the Navy was considering scrapping the famous frigate, the matter was of far more interest in Boston and its suburbs. The *Constitution* was Boston's own ship, built in Boston harbor by Massachusetts men and sailed by Massachusetts men, by and large, in wars against the French, the Barbary pirates, and the British.

She was an old ship now, her timbers were rotting and her refurbishment would cost the navy a pretty penny at a time when Congress was complaining about expenditures. The pressure was on in Washington to break up the ship and stop the rot. But as the editor of the *Journal of Commerce* suggested, public pressure should stop the attempt.

Holmes took pen in hand and dashed off three rousing stanzas of sardonic poesy, and hastened by horsecar to Boston to offer them to the editor of the *Advertiser.*

"Old Ironsides"

Ay, tear her tattered ensign down!
Long has it waved on high,
And many an eye has danced to see
That banner in the sky;
Beneath it rung the battle shout,
And burst the cannon's roar;—
The meteor of the ocean air
Shall sweep the clouds no more.

Her deck, once red with heroes' blood,
Where knelt the vanquished foe,
When winds were hurrying o'er the flood,
And waves were white below,
No more shall feel the victor's tread,
Or know the conquered knee;—
The harpies of the shore shall pluck
The eagle of the sea!

Oh, better that her shattered hulk
Should sink beneath the wave;
Her thunders shook the mighty deep,
And there should be her grave;
Nail to the mast her holy flag,
Set every threadbare sail,
And give her to the god of storms,
The lightning and the gale!

The editor read, and knew a sensation when he saw one. It was indignant, damning, patriotic, and loving all at once. Next day the *Advertiser* ran the three-stanza poem. A few days later it was picked up in New York, and then in Philadelphia, and in Washington; and soon it had traversed the nation, north and south, east and west. Everyone knew something of the saga of **"Old Ironsides,"** and she represented the finest tradition of America. So the protests began to arrive at the navy yard, and if there had been any serious thought of actu-

ally junking the old frigate (which is debatable), minds were changed and a warning was issued for the future: nineteenth-century Americans did not like government meddling with their traditions.

"Old Ironsides" was signed only with a timid *H.* So while the poem became a national institution, its author continued to be unknown outside the literary circles of Boston and Cambridge.

In his work for the *Collegian* Holmes was joined by a number of young men whose paths would cross his constantly in future years. C. C. Felton would become professor and then president of Harvard. Chauncy Emerson would die, but his brother Ralph Waldo would carry the family name to literary greatness. James Freeman Clarke, often Holmes's rival as class poet, would become his steadfast friend.

In a few months Holmes had written a number of poems for "gift books." A gift book was precisely what the name indicated: a volume of lighthearted miscellany, printed with care on fine paper, handsomely illustrated, and bound in morocco. Its purpose was the same as that of the "coffee-table books" of a later generation; almost all the sales were for gifts, usually from a man to a woman. The gift book *Token,* published in 1831, contained Holmes's **"The Lost Boy,"** and two prose pieces by an unknown writer from Salem, Nathaniel Hawthorne.

Already the Boston area was attracting figures who would make it the literary center of the United States.

Holmes wrote only a few more poems that year. They were notable for their excellence and originality, a major step above his sophomoric collegiate work. Those poems of 1830 and 1831 rank among his best, and among the best work produced anywhere in America at the time.

That might not be saying much. In the 1830s American literature had not yet found itself. Cambridge's Richard Henry Dana had written his *Two Years Before the Mast*; New York's Washington Irving was busy with his stories; and James Fenimore Cooper was weaving his tales of the northeast frontier. But Cambridge's Henry Wadsworth Longfellow was as yet no more known than Hawthorne; John Greenleaf Whittier was just beginning his writing. James Russell Lowell was a schoolboy. Ralph Waldo Emerson was still a Boston preacher.

When Americans talked about "literature," their minds turned to England. As far as America was concerned, it was the age of the orator, and books were more likely to contain extracts from a speech of Daniel Webster or Edward Everett than a story by an American writer.

New York's William Cullen Bryant was the most famous poet of the period, yet he was primarily a newspaper editor.

So while Holmes dearly loved writing—"the intoxicating pleasure of authorship," he termed it in a serious moment, and "lead-poisoning" when in a jovial mood—he felt he needed a profession. And tiring of the law, he considered only one alternative, medicine. Others who would become famous in the world of letters put their hands to occupations close to the pen, but not Holmes.

Perhaps it was the family background that kept him from considering journalism, perhaps it was the influence of Harvard College. But he might have given thought, as did Longfellow, to teaching in the literary field. He did not. He turned from law to the harsh mistress of medicine, a field even more difficult in America in the 1830s than now, principally because there was so little knowledge of scientific medicine.

For years most of Holmes's intellectual efforts would be devoted to his new profession. And when he resumed poetry it would be on a different basis than before. The promise of this short early period would never be fully realized; the genius that had produced **"Old Ironsides"** would be concentrated elsewhere, not even concentrated, some said, but scattered so widely that the full effect would never be felt in any field.

Holmes wrote one more major poem in the next year, **"The Last Leaf."**

> I saw him once before,
> As he passed by the door,
> And again
> The pavement stones resound
> As he totters o'er the ground
> With his cane.
>
> They say that in his prime,
> Ere the pruning-knife of time
> Cut him down,
> Not a better man was found
> By the Crier on his round
> Through the town.
>
> But now he walks the streets,
> And he looks at all he meets,
> Sad and wan,
> And he shakes his feeble head,
> That it seems as if he said,
> "They are gone."
>
> The mossy marbles rest
> On the lips that he has prest
> In their bloom,
> And the names he loved to hear
> Have been carved for many a year
> On the tomb.

> My grandmamma has said—
> Por old lady, she is dead
> Long ago—
> That he had a Roman nose
> And his cheek was like a rose
> In the snow.
>
> But now his nose is thin,
> And it rests upon his chin,
> Like a staff,
> And a crook is in his back,
> And a melancholy crack
> In his laugh.
>
> I know it is a sin
> For me to sit and grin
> At him here;
> But the old three-cornered hat,
> And the breeches, and all that,
> Are so queer.
>
> And if I should live to be
> The last leaf upon the tree
> In the spring,
> Let them smile, as I do now,
> At the old forsaken bough,
> Where I cling.

When Edgar Allan Poe saw this poem, in his capacity as literary critic he acclaimed it as one of the finest works in the English language. Holmes would scribble other verses, and many of them would be printed. But for all practical purposes, when Oliver Wendell Holmes left his childhood Cambridge home in the autumn of 1830 to move into a boardinghouse in Boston and study medicine, he cut not only his close family ties, but his literary ties as well.

Neither the man nor his writings would ever be quite the same.

*   *   *

The Atlantic was after Holmes again. Editor Aldrich wanted another series, another *Autocrat,* if that were possible.

What is possible when you are seventy-eight years old? The question had interested the scientist in Holmes for many years. He rather thought something *was* possible, if Aldrich did. He had given this new editor the same instructions he had given to Howells: if he found Holmes slipping into the ways of senility, warn the author before he made a fool of himself.

It had not happened. No evidence of weakness had appeared, Aldrich said; so Holmes undertook the new series.

The new group of articles to grace the pages of *The Atlantic* would be called "Over the Teacups." Holmes delivered the first of these essays at the end of 1887.

Holmes was not at all sure a new generation of *Atlantic* readers would be in the slightest bit interested in what he had to say. ". . . Nobody can blame the young people for preferring the thoughts and language of their own generation, with all its future before it, to those of their grandfathers' contemporaries."

Holmes then launched into one of his favorite areas of discussion: psychology and psychological oddities.

Holmes was already working on his next installment of "Over the Teacups," in February 1888, when Amelia died. That shock was intensified the same month by the death of James Freeman Clarke, his Harvard classmate and friendly poetic competitor of years past, but more recently his pastor and close friend. Two more important lights in Holmes's life had been snuffed out.

Holmes felt he could not continue the *Atlantic* series. There was the estate to be settled. Then, hardly had Little Amelia become established in the house, when she took sick. She seemed to recover, but the improvement was illusory; she died the next year. Holmes had just been getting ready to write again. Once more the process was stopped in midstream.

What was he to do?

This time the transition was more painful for all concerned. Wendell—the judge—and Fanny had no option under the moral code of nineteenth-century New England: they moved back into 296 Beacon Street, and Fanny took over the household. Judge Holmes was not so affected by it; he lived in a world of his own, largely untouched by the lesser emotions of family life, and he traveled a good deal to make speeches and to attend meetings. The burden of coping with the demands and problems of her father-in-law fell on Fanny. She never complained about the obligation, but performed in a manner that truly endeared her to Holmes.

Those deaths, emphasized by the constant trickling away of the lives of his acquaintances, gave Holmes a sense of living on borrowed time. People were forever asking him for "a few lines" in the volumes and papers he inscribed for them. He took to writing the last verse of **"The Last Leaf"**:

> And if I should live to be
> The last leaf upon the tree
> In the spring,
> Let them smile, as I do now,
> At the old forsaken bough,
> Where I cling.

New friends swept into his life to replace, in a measure, those he had lost. Little Amelia had taken him up to visit Mrs. Julia Dorr at Bar Harbor. Mrs. Dorr lived in Vermont during most of the year and wrote poetry. She had begun summering at the new resort of the wealthy merchants and businessmen who found Saratoga old-fashioned and Newport too glossy for their taste. She and Holmes corresponded regularly after Amelia's death, and Mrs. Dorr became very dear to Holmes. She tried to persuade Holmes to come up to Bar Harbor again in the summer of 1889, but he would not.

"I have no Amelia to talk it over and live it over with me," he protested. But the real reason was his growing weakness and his unwillingness to move from familiar surroundings. He was troubled by asthmatic attacks. And he felt very old, very tired, very much alone. "My son and his wife are doing all they can to make and keep me comfortable and cheerful, and I do my best—but the world cannot be what it has been for me."

Too many shocks had come too suddenly. The class of '29 assembled that year, and Holmes had a poem for them. But there were only six leaves left on the bough, and they all felt a little self-conscious. Who would go next? The question hung heavy in the air.

That summer Holmes was eighty years old. From Beverly Farms he was writing cheerful little notes to announce the fact, as though a new baby had come to the house. Fanny and Wendell had accompanied him to the Beverly Farms cottage for the summer. The area was growing and becoming a little pretentious. Next door to Beverly was the town of Manchester, and some of his acquaintances who lived there began giving names to their houses and calling their community Manchester-by-the-Sea. Holmes laughed and began heading his notes, "Beverly-by-the-Depot."

Whittier wrote him a poetic birthday tribute, and he was touched. He had hundreds of letters of congratulation.

By the beginning of the next year, although Holmes felt able to continue the Teacups series, he was tidying up his affairs. He gave his extensive medical library (one thousand volumes) to the Boston Medical Library Association. He spent many hours trying to persuade President Eliot to confer an honorary degree on classmate Samuel Francis Smith for "My Country, 'Tis of Thee." Eliot found that an insufficient reason for the granting of a Harvard LL.D., no matter how much he liked and respected Dr. Holmes.

Holmes had given up the boats, but the familiar figure in black broadcloth suit and coat and black beaver hat marched out every day for a stroll. Dr. Holmes was as much a part of the scenery as the trees that graced the grassy common. Nannies pointed him out to their charges, "See, there's Doctor Holmes." Schoolgirls who were studying his poems passed him open-mouthed; an artist came to sketch him and caught the figure, slightly bent, moving briskly along, in front of 296 Beacon Street.

Holmes admitted in the Teacups papers that he was preoccupied with old age. "The octogenarian loves to read about people ninety and over. He peers among the asterisks of the triennial catalogue of the University for the names of graduates who have been seventy years out of college and remain still unstarred . . ."

He seemed to make a game of it. He'd said to Longfellow years before at the Saturday Club that poets weren't long-lived. Longfellow had looked at him calmly and said he didn't believe a word of it. Next meeting, Longfellow handed Holmes a list of poets who had lived to ripe old age. Now Holmes drew up his own. "Bryant lived to be eighty-three years old, . . . Longfellow seventy-five . . . Halleck seventy-seven . . . Whittier, still living . . . eighty-two. Tennyson is still writing at eighty and Browning reached the age of seventy-seven . . ."

And Dr. Oliver Wendell Holmes was eighty-one and going like a house afire; well, still smoldering, anyhow.

Holmes raised the question of poetry: could an old man write poetry, with his "ossified" arteries? He answered with a poem:

> To the Eleven Ladies
> Who Presented Me with a Silver Loving Cup on the
> Twenty-ninth of August, M DCCC LXXXIX

It ended:

> Better love's perfume in the empty bowl
> Than wine's nepenthe for the aching soul,
> Sweeter than song that ever poet sung,
> It makes an old heart young!

The answer seemed to be *no*.

The Teacups papers were more personal than any of the other series had been. When Helen Keller, the deaf-blind woman who had conquered all those odds to learn to read braille and write, wrote him a letter, he included it in one of the Teacups papers. He put a poem at the end of one paper: **"La Maison D'Or (Bar Harbor)."** Julia Dorr knew what he meant.

He did not seem to care about the general reader.

He meandered along the road of his own life as he wrote, and many readers found that road duller than his past; his older readers found more to interest them by far than the younger ones. His continued popularity with the editors seems a little odd today. It must have been due to his position as "the living monument" of literary Boston.

The one real spark from Holmes was a poem that had much of the old-fashioned New England charm of **"The Deacon's Masterpiece"**:

"The Broomstick Train, or, the Return of the Witches"[1]

Look out! Look out, boys! Clear the track!
The witches are here! They've all come back!
They hanged them high,—No use! No use!
What cares a witch for a hangman's noose?
They buried them deep, but they wouldn't lie still,
For cats and witches are hard to kill;
They swore they shouldn't and wouldn't die,—
Books said they did, but they lie! they lie!

—A couple of hundred years, or so,
They had knocked about in the world below,
When an Essex Deacon dropped in to call,
And a homesick feeling seized them all;
For he came from a place they knew full well,
And many a tale he had to tell.
They long to visit the haunts of men,
To see the old dwellings they knew again,
And ride on their broomsticks all around
Their wide domain of unhallowed ground.

Well did they know, those gray old wives,
The sights we see in our daily drives:
Shimmer of lake and shine of sea,
Brown's bare hill with its lonely tree,
(It wasn't then as we see it now,
With one scant scalp-lock to shade its brow;)
Dusky nooks in the Essex woods,
Dark, dim, Dante-like solitudes,
Where the tree-toad watches the sinuous snake
Glide through his forests of fern and brake;
Ipswich River; its old stone bridge;
Far off Andover's Indian Ridge,
And many a scene where history tells
Some shadow of bygone terror dwells,—
Of "Norman's Woe" with its tale of dread,
Of the Screeching Woman of Marblehead,
(The fearful story that turns men pale:
Don't bid me tell it,—my speech would fail.)

Who would not, will not, if he can,
Bathe in the breezes of fair Cape Ann,—
Rest in the bowers her bays enfold.
Loved by the sachems and squaws of old?
Home where the white magnolias bloom,
Sweet with the bayberry's chaste perfume,
Hugged by the woods and kissed by the sea!
Where is the Eden like to thee?

For that "couple of hundred years or so,"
There had been no peace in the world below;
The witches still grumbling, "It isn't fair;
Come, give us a taste of the upper air!
We've had enough of your sulphur springs,
And the evil odor that round them clings;
We long for a drink that is cool and nice,—
Great buckets of water with Wenham ice;
We've served you well upstairs, you know;
You're a good old—fellow—come, let us go!"

I don't feel sure of his being good,
But he happened to be in a pleasant mood,—
As fiends with their skins full sometimes are,—
(He'd been drinking with "roughs" at a Boston bar.)

So what does he do but up and shout
To a graybeard turnkey, "Let 'em out!"

To mind his orders was all he knew;
The gates swung open, and out they flew.
"Where are our broomsticks?" the beldams cried.
"Here are your broomsticks," an imp replied.
"They've been in—the place you know—so long
They smell of brimstone uncommon strong;
But they've gained by being left alone,—
Just look, and you'll see how tall they've grown."
—"And where is my cat?" a vixen squalled.
"Yes, where are our cats?" the witches bawled,
And began to call them all by name:
As fast as they called the cats, they came:
There was bob-tailed Tommy and long-tailed Tim,
And wall-eyed Jacky and green-eyed Jim,
And splay-foot Benny and slim-legged Bean,
And Skinny and Squally, and Jerry and Joe,
The driver may just unhitch his team,
We don't want horses, we don't want steam;
You may keep your old black cats to hug,
But the loaded train you've got to lug.

Since then on many a car you'll see
A broomstick plain as plain can be;
On every stick there's a witch astride,—
The string you see to her leg is tied.
She will do a mischief if she can,
But the string is held by a careful man,
And whenever the evil-minded witch
Would cut some caper, he gives a twitch.
As for the hag, you can't see her,
But hark! you can hear her black cat's purr
And now and then, as a car goes by,
You may catch a gleam from her wicked eye.
Often you've looked on a rushing train,
But just what moved it was not so plain.
It couldn't be those wires above,
For they could neither pull nor shove;
Where was the motor that made it go
You couldn't guess, *but now you know.*

Remember my rhymes when you ride again
On the rattling rail by the broomstick train!

Lowell wrote him in congratulation, almost Lowell's last letter.

In a way, Lowell's praise of the poem confirmed what Holmes suspected, that the rest of "Teacups" was not scintillating. He had grown too old, and was too far out of touch with the ideas of the 1890s.

"Over the Teacups" was concluded just before Lowell's death, at the end of 1890. In the last number Holmes announced that he would not write another series.

His Afterword was brighter than almost any of it. Holmes mentioned again his difficulties in keeping up with his fan mail. He made a joke of it in "my unwritten answers to correspondents," by an author driven to the wall by too much mail:

Answer 1. To the autograph hunter:

Want my autograph do you? And don't know how to spell my name. An *A* for an *E* in my middle name. Leave out the *L* in my last name. Do you know how people hate to have their names misspelled? What do you suppose are the sentiments entertained by the Thompsons with a *P* toward those who address them in writing as Thomson?

Answer 2. To the flatterer:

Think the lines you mention are by far the best I ever wrote, hey? Well, I didn't write those lines. What is more I think they are as detestable a string of rhymes as I could wish my worst enemy had written. A very pleasant frame of mind I am in for writing a letter, after reading yours!

Answer 3. To a pest who has named a child for the author:

I am glad to hear that my namesake, whom I never saw and never expect to see, has cut another tooth; but why write four pages on the strength of that . . .

Answer 4. To the eclectic critic:

You wish to correct an error in my Broomstick poem do you? You give me to understand that Wilmington is not in Essex County, but in Middlesex. Very well, but are they separated by *running water*? Because if they are not, what could hinder a witch from crossing the line that separates Wilmington from Andover, I should like to know?

He was tired, the reader need expect but little more from him in the future.

It was not quite a good-bye, but he was warning them; the last leaf was trembling on the bough.

Notes

Very little is known about the philosophical decision that led Holmes to try the law before he entered medicine. He never explained why he chose the law, and only briefly and usually indirectly did he indicate that he found it too boring to continue. From that some have deduced that Holmes had no use for lawyers, and Catherine Drinker Bowen, in *Yankee from Olympus* (Boston: Atlantic Monthly Press, 1944), invented conversation in which Dr. Holmes indicated his contempt for lawyers. But Mark DeWolfe Howe, in his later biography, *Justice Oliver Wendell Holmes, The Shaping Years, 1841-1870* (Cambridge: Belknap Press, 1957), said flatly that the younger Holmes was pushed into the legal profession by his father, and that seems much more in character. As a Brahmin, Holmes had utmost respect for the profession; he was married to the daughter of a distinguished judge, and his brother John and many of his friends were lawyers and judges.

I have included several of the poems Holmes wrote in the early 1830s, because these are among his most successful, and certainly "Old Ironsides" is the most famous. Holmes's energy and growing ability to deal with poetic theme seems apparent here, culminating in "The Last Leaf," which he wrote shortly before embarking on the medical studies that would demand his total concentration for the next five years. Had Holmes continued as he was going in "The Last Leaf," he might have become the important poet that Edgar Allan Poe, for one, already then thought him to be.

Holmes's perennial popularity is given credence by editor T. B. Aldrich's request of him, when he was nearly eighty years old, to write another series for *The Atlantic.* That series, *Over the Teacups,* could have a renewed meaning in the last quarter of the twentieth century, as American eyes turn to the aging processes, and the aging are so many among us. For Holmes never lost his scientific eye for the phenomena of nature, just as he never lost his sensuousness. Up to the last he went to concerts, and then to rehearsals when the formality of concert-going grew too much for him. He loved the pleasures of the table, although he had long since quit smoking because of his asthma, and drank virtually nothing in these last years. His poem, "The Broomstick Train," was a recognition of the collision between the old (Holmes's world) and the new (the world of his son). But much of what he wrote was timeless, as his colloquy on the irritation of the writer and public figure who is bedeviled by a loving public.

1. This poem was suggested to Holmes by the coming of the electric railway, with its high wires and apparently magic method of propulsion (in the eyes of one born in 1809). The "broomsticks" of stanza nine were tall protrusions on each car, peculiar to the early electrified railroads—now long-since vanished. Although a modern reader has missed that era entirely, the poem had another charm: it was Holmes's celebration of the vast changes that had come to Massachusetts in his lifetime.

FURTHER READING

Bibliography

Currier, Thomas Franklin. *A Bibliography of Oliver Wendell Holmes,* edited by Eleanor M. Tilton. New York: New York University Press, 1953, 707 p.

Listing of biographical and critical texts on Holmes through the mid-twentieth century.

Biography

Holmes, Oliver Wendell. *The Poetical Works of Oliver Wendell Holmes: Household Edition.* Boston: Houghton Mifflin, 1884, 357 p.

Collection of poems accompanied by brief biographical sketch.

Criticism

Brenner, Rica. "Oliver Wendell Holmes." In *Twelve American Poets before 1900,* pp. 169-98. New York: Harcourt, Brace and Co., 1933.

Examination of Holmes's career and the connections between his life and his works.

Old South Leaflets. "Certain Writings of Oliver Wendell Holmes," no. 201 (August 1909): 1-20.

Selected poems with a brief biographical sketch and critical annotations.

Kreymborg, Alfred. "Dr. Holmes and the New England Decline." In *Our Singing Strength: An Outline of American Poetry (1620-1930),* pp. 134-50. New York: Coward-McCann, Inc., 1929.

Discusses the New England poets, maintaining that Holmes's work had more in common with the poetry of the eighteenth century than with that of his nineteenth-century contemporaries.

Additional coverage of Holmes's life and career is contained in the following sources published by Thomson Gale: *American Writers Supplement,* **Vol. 1;** *Concise Dictionary of American Literary Biography, 1640-1865;* *Dictionary of Literary Biography,* **Vols. 1, 189, and 235;** *Exploring Poetry;* *Literature Resource Center;* *Nineteenth-Century Literature Criticism,* **Vols. 14 and 81;** *Reference Guide to American Literature,* **Ed. 4; and** *Something About the Author,* **Vol. 34.**

Stephen Spender
1909-1995

English poet, critic, autobiographer, essayist, playwright, short story writer, novelist, translator, editor, and nonfiction writer.

INTRODUCTION

A member of the so-called Auden Circle, Spender is best known for poetry that combines direct commentary on social and political issues with the lyricism typically associated with Romanticism.

BIOGRAPHICAL INFORMATION

Spender was born on February 28, 1909, in London, to Violet Schuster Spender, an invalid of German and Jewish descent, and Harold Spender, a liberal English author and political journalist. Spender's parents were puritanical and overprotective and "kept him from children who were rough," as Spender later complained in one of his poems. At the onset of World War I, the family, which included Spender's older brother Michael, older sister Christine, and younger brother Humphrey, moved to Sheringham, Norfolk. Spender and his sister were initially enrolled at Miss Harcourt's School in East Runton, but in 1919 he joined Michael at boarding school. That same year the family returned to London and in 1921 Spender's mother died following an operation. Five years later Spender's father died under similar circumstances following surgery. The children's maternal grandmother, Hilda Schuster, took over the care of the children. In 1928 Spender enrolled in University College, Oxford, where he fell in love with a fellow student to whom he gave the name Marston and who provided the inspiration for a number of Spender's early poems. W. H. Auden and Christopher Isherwood were also at Oxford at the time and in 1930, just before his senior year, Spender left school without earning a degree in order to join Isherwood in Berlin. Their adventures in the hedonistic, homosexual community of the German capital were chronicled by Spender in his 1951 autobiography *World within World* and by Isherwood's stories that formed the basis for the musical *Cabaret*. Auden and Spender, along with Louis MacNeice and Cecil Day Lewis, became known as the Oxford Generation or, later, the Auden Circle, after its most famous member.

During the 1930s Spender, like many young men of his class, became disillusioned with democracy and capitalism and saw communism as the answer to the growing threat of fascism. He embraced the Republican cause in the Spanish Civil War, but as a pacifist he refused to join the fighting. He traveled to Spain twice to write about the war, the first time for the communist paper *The Daily Worker* and the second time representing Great Britain, but after witnessing abuses on both sides of the conflict, quickly became disenchanted both with the communist cause in Spain and with communism in general.

During World War II Spender served as a fireman in the National Fire Service in London until 1944 when he was transferred to the Foreign Office. A year later he served with the British Control Commission in occupied Germany and in 1946 with UNESCO in Paris. He traveled to the United States several times over the next several years and held a variety of academic posts including Elliston Professor of Poetry at the University of Cincinnati and Beckman Professor at the University of California at Berkeley. He also taught at Cornell, Vanderbilt, Connecticut, Loyola, and Northwestern and served as poetry consultant to the Library of Congress. From 1970 to 1977 he served as professor of English at University College, London University, and in 1979 he was made an honorary fellow of University College, Oxford. He was knighted in 1983.

Spender was married twice. In 1936, he married Agnes Marie (Inez) Pearn, a student of Spanish literature at Oxford; the union ended in divorce three years later. In 1941, he wed Natasha Litvin, a pianist, to whom he was married for more than fifty years. They had two children, Elizabeth, known as Lizzie, and Matthew. Spender continued to write poetry, criticism, and essays, publishing his last book of poetry in 1994. He died on July 16, 1995, in London.

MAJOR WORKS

Spender published his first book of poetry, *Nine Experiments,* in 1928, when he was only nineteen years old. This was followed by *Twenty Poems* two years later, and by *Poems* in 1933. The latter volume contains some of the most frequently anthologized of his individual poems, including "The Express," "My Parents," and "I Think Continually," all of which had originally appeared in Michael Roberts's 1932 anthology, *New Signatures.* *Poems* also included the first of his political poems revealing his early enthusiasm for communism, a stance which was ultimately to harm Spender's reputation as a poet, according to some scholars. A second edition of *Poems* was published in 1934, and Spender's only long poem, the four-part *Vienna,* appeared that same year. The work deals with the insurgency of the socialists in Austria and their complete defeat in early 1934; viewed in light of subsequent events in Germany culminating in the Holocaust, it is in some ways considered a prophetic work.

In 1939 Spender produced his most famous and most critically acclaimed volume of poetry, *The Still Centre,* which includes such notable individual poems as "The Uncreating Chaos," "Exiles from Their Land, History Their Domicile," and "An Elementary School Class Room in a Slum." Although two of the four sections of the book deal with the Spanish Civil War, many poems in the volume represent less political, more personal writing. This was the direction Spender's poetry would take from that point on in such collections as *Ruins and Visions* (1942), *Poems of Dedication* (1947), and *The Edge of Being* (1949). Two expanded collections of Spender's poetry were published: *Collected Poems, 1928-1953* (1955) and *Collected Poems, 1928-1985* (1985). Spender produced his final volume of poetry, *Dolphins* in 1994, the year before he died.

In addition to his poetry, Spender also produced numerous works in other genres including *The Burning Cactus* (1936), a volume of short stories; *Trial of a Judge* (1938), a verse drama; as well as two novels, an autobiography, and several works of criticism and other nonfiction. He also served as editor or coeditor of a number of books and periodicals. He coedited, with Louis MacNeice, the 1929 issue of *Oxford Poetry;* he served as coeditor of *Horizon* magazine from 1935 to 1941; and he was coeditor of *Encounter* magazine from 1953 to 1967. He also edited the works of Percy Bysshe Shelley, D. H. Lawrence, and his old Oxford classmate W. H. Auden.

CRITICAL RECEPTION

Although Spender's poetry was popular in his own time, his literary reputation dimmed somewhat in the later years of the twentieth century. Several critics have suggested that Spender's poetry falls short and that Spender himself failed to live up to his early promise. One such critic is Willis D. Jacobs, who has written that Spender, "once hailed as the Shelley of our times," went on to produce poems that lack energy and that, with few exceptions, miss the mark of true greatness. "Spender's political poems are strident; his personal lyrics are weary," according to Jacobs, but he acknowledges that Spender reached some measure of success as "the wistful elegist of man's loneliness and death." Derek Stanford maintains that Spender's work is uneven and that "many of his interesting poems, which hold us by reason of their sensitiveness or evident sincerity, fail to achieve full harmony of style or total unity of effect." A. K. Weatherhead suggests that Spender's reputation has waned because of the "quality of uncertainty" that pervades his poetry. Although the critic considers Spender "one of the purest lyrical talents of the century in English," he complains that his talent "has never been entirely liberated from the conscience, the call of duty, the structural needs of the poem, and the world itself to issue its own spontaneous utterances."

According to some critics, Spender's poetry harkens back to the Romantic era and evokes comparisons to such nineteenth-century poets as William Wordsworth and Walt Whitman. W. H. Sellers compares Spender's use of rhyme to Wordsworth's, maintaining that "perhaps even more than Wordsworth he is aware of the subtle possibilities of this device." H. B. Kulkarni has studied Spender's treatment of nature, claiming that "Spender was not affected by the popular view of nature in the post-Darwinian era as 'red in tooth and claw' and forever engaged in a deadly struggle for existence. Spender's picture of nature comes closer to the vision of the romantic poets." Weatherhead, however, contends that Spender's work often overturns Romantic conventions, citing a poem in which "the traditional beauty of the country is pitted to its disadvantage against the iron railway lines." Spender's tendency to comment directly in his poetry on social and political problems was also in conflict with his Romantic tendencies, according to several scholars. Sanford Sternlicht asserts that "the major characteristic of Spender's poetry is a constant tension between an engagement with the objective world outside—the salient mark of the thirties poets—and the need for his soaring spirit to rise above the mundane considerations of the workaday world."

The published details of Spender's personal life have also affected his critical reputation and many critics now question the strength of his commitment to a variety of liberal political causes. Surya Nath Pandey, for example, contends that "his exhortations to his comrades for building up a just society were all genuine but they went little beyond their rhetoric and propaganda." Nonetheless, Pandey rebuts those commentators who criticize Spender for refusing to fight in the Spanish Civil War despite his avowed support for the cause: "True, Spender was neither a Spaniard nor a soldier but he was emotionally involved in the Spanish conflict and to condemn his poems as those of a 'tourist' or an 'observer' would be a travesty of truth." Other critics have been less kind. Richard Danson Brown, among others, recalls Roy Campbell's satirical conflation of MacNeice, Spender, Auden, and Day-Lewis into "MacSpaunday" to suggest that together the poets "formed a homogenous clique of interchangeable, mutually aggrandizing talents." Christopher Hitchens sums up the view of several recent scholars: "Spender never quite succeeded in overcoming the widespread impression . . . that there was something vaguely preposterous about him."

PRINCIPAL WORKS

Poetry

Nine Experiments: Being Poems Written at the Age of Eighteen 1928
Twenty Poems 1930
Poems 1933; revised and enlarged edition, 1934
Vienna 1934
The Still Centre 1939
Selected Poems 1940
Ruins and Visions: Poems, 1934-1942 1942
Poems of Dedication 1947
The Edge of Being 1949
Collected Poems, 1928-1953 1955

Selected Poems 1964
The Generous Days: Ten Poems 1969; enlarged edition, 1971
Recent Poems 1978
Collected Poems, 1928-1985 1985
Dolphins 1994

Other Major Works

W. H. Auden, Poems [editor] (poetry) 1928
The Destructive Element: A Study of Modern Writers and Beliefs (criticism) 1935
The Burning Cactus (short stories) 1936
Forward from Liberalism (nonfiction) 1937
Trial of a Judge: A Tragedy in Five Acts (play) 1938
The Backward Son (novel) 1940
Life and the Poet (criticism) 1942
Selected Poems of Federico Garcia Lorca [translator, with J. L. Gili] (poetry) 1943
European Witness (nonfiction) 1946
World within World: The Autobiography of Stephen Spender (autobiography) 1951
Learning Laughter (essay) 1952
The Creative Element: A Study of Vision, Despair, and Orthodoxy among Some Modern Writers (criticism) 1953
The Making of a Poem (criticism) 1955
Engaged in Writing and The Fool and the Princess (short stories) 1958
The Imagination in the Modern World: Three Lectures (lectures) 1962
The Struggle of the Modern (essay) 1963
Chaos and Control in Poetry (criticism) 1966
The Year of the Young Rebels (essay) 1969
The Poems of Percy Bysshe Shelley [editor] (poetry) 1971
D. H. Lawrence: Novelist, Poet, Prophet [editor] (criticism) 1973
Love-Hate Relations: A Study of Anglo-American Sensibilities (essay) 1974
Eliot (criticism) 1975
The Thirties and After: Poetry, Politics, People, 1933-1970 (nonfiction) 1978
Henry Moore: Sculptures in Landscape (essay) 1979
Letters to Christopher: Stephen Spender's Letters to Christopher Isherwood, 1929-1939, with "The Line of the Branch"—Two Thirties Journals (letters and journals) 1980
In Irina's Garden with Henry Moore's Sculpture (essay) 1986
The Temple (novel) 1988

CRITICISM

Willis D. Jacobs (essay date April 1956)

SOURCE: Jacobs, Willis D. "The Moderate Poetical Success of Stephen Spender." *College English* 17, no. 7 (April 1956): 374-78.

[*In the following essay, Jacobs discusses Spender's failure to achieve greatness as a poet despite his sensitivity, intelligence, and early promise.*]

Has ever distinguished poet attempted so much and accomplished so little? Of course if one counts the sheer bulk of Stephen Spender's work—poems, essays, criticism, travelogue, autobiography, humorous squibs, lectures, and what not (he is tireless)—one is overwhelmed by the quantity done; yet the thought persists that we have from such an enormous mountain precious little mouse.

This is all the more puzzling because Spender is clearly gifted with sensitivity, intelligence, knowledge, courage, and industry. Is his comparative failure as poet due to insufficiency of poetic talent or to certain personal and literary flaws which cripple his gifts in the act? These are embarrassing questions, and only a real affection for the poet *manqué* and sympathetic human being that is Stephen Spender could encourage one to decipher this mystery.

Here is a man once hailed as the Shelley of our times. That was twenty and more years ago, and Spender is called our Shelley no more. Here is a man once the pride and enthusiasm of young political rebels and aspiring young poets. The first have abandoned him as he abandoned them; the second have turned, long since, to Dylan Thomas for what once they hungered to find in Spender. It is indeed too many years since Spender was welcomed as a brilliant new light in the world of poetry; he is now seen as both a much older man—as we all are—and a much lesser poet. This last is sad and perhaps not fully charitable, but Spender once appeared to possess such ability and still possesses such admirable qualities as artist and man that he deserves a tentative examination to discover, if may be, why his success as poet has been moderate, or, perhaps, even tepid.

Reading affectionately through the poetry of this likeable and noble man, one does encounter here and there lines, even brief poems, of some charm and warmth. The pathos comes as one notes the brevity and scarcity. Frequently in longer works one winces over poem after poem spoiled as an entity by bathos, eruptions of false notes, and dismaying errors in taste—both in language and in the very structure of the poems.

His success, when he succeeds, generally arrives in stanzas of no more than twelve or fifteen lines, and yet there it is a success that leaves one touched, even haunted, but convinced that this is a pretty little talent, not a warm, rich, enduring gift. Such a successful poem, on its level of the not quite immemorial, is his **"Discovered in Mid-Ocean."** In this poem reminiscent of the Daedalus legend are a number of ramifications: Spender himself as an Icarus, political or poetical, aspiring to the stars, but failing and falling and wrecked; implications of man as artificer, whose mechanical inventions (like the aircraft here) serve both to raise him and destroy him; insinuations of man as creator of weapons (perhaps a war-plane here), destroying others with them, and himself destroyed in them. In short there is richness here, and one notes that, appreciates it, remembers the poem—and feels that it misses any true greatness. It is too mild and too timid. Spender's political poems are strident; his personal lyrics are weary.

Shelley too has some lines about a man lost at sea. His words seem almost commonplace:

> Many a green isle needs must be
> In the deep wide sea of Misery,
> Or the mariner, worn and wan,
> Never thus could voyage on—
> Day and night, and night and day,
> Drifting on his weary way. . . .

But as one reads these simple words he feels a force of emotion—a surge of soul—flooding the lines. It is the great heart beat of Shelley. With Spender, however, there is generally a tiredness. The heart beats, but sadly, sluggishly. His is the lyrical poetry of the defeated. Not that defeat creates only weak verse; Thomas Hardy proves otherwise. Defeat is a powerful motive and noble quality too. Spender's defeat is the sapless defeat of mere and unstruggling surrender; from it comes poetry of wistfulness, not poetry of grief—poetry of charm, not poetry of passion and strength. Stephen Spender is the wistful poet.

He has written an excellent poem called **"What I Expected."** If society is changed, he tells us, it is not by a dramatic moment, but by the daily straining of suffering men, and meanwhile from them drop away courage, hope, and faith:

> What I expected was
> Thunder, fighting,
> Long struggles with men
> And climbing. . . .
>
> What I had not foreseen
> Was the gradual day
> Weakening the will
> Leaking the brightness away. . . .

This is moving, but once more the theme is of the hurt man, wincing at his hurt. I lost and it hurts; the world has changed and it hurts. Can superb poetry be written from this velleity? "Within my head, aches the perpetual winter Of this violent time," Spender sighs; and since we too have been frozen and betrayed by the ignoble days of this world we understand and feel affection for this spokesman of our dismay. Yet his simple wistfulness and regret have not led to poetry of the first rank.

In Spender's political verse—his call to reform or revolution—he found a real force and inspiration. For a period he discerned in Communism the means to a democratic and peaceful world. His political verse, however, was generally flawed by either crass tendentiousness or venal technique. That political verse can be effective and poetically true is apparent; one has only to recall Shelley again, or William Morris even in his blunter moments:

> For that which the worker winneth shall
>   then be his indeed,
> Nor shall half be reaped for nothing by him
>   that sowed no seed.

The political verse of Spender is eloquent and imperfect. "The writer who grasps anything of the Marxist theory," he once wrote, "feels that he is moving in a world of reality and in a purposive world." This conviction lent him force but not poetic sureness. The wistfulness and hurt in the poetry that follows his Communist period probably have a dual cause—his disenchantment with that political doctrine, and his shamed awareness that he had often betrayed the integrity of poetry in his effort to preach. He had, thus, not really a poet's firm hand or great faith; he was poetaster instead. He had failed politically and poetically; he failed politically because, he had became convinced, he had mistaken the nature of Communism; he failed poetically because he was not a *natural* poet, one who knows spontaneously and strongly what poetry must be and what perjuries it must never allow itself. Spender became aware, that is, that he was a man with great yearning to be a poet, sensitivity to ideas and words, and insufficient poetic talent.

Once the political afflatus is past, the writer himself can see and flush at the poetic falseness at the end of **"The Landscape Near an Aerodrome."** A landing aircraft is described with eye, ear, and love:

> More beautiful and soft than any moth
> With burring furred antennæ feeling its huge path . . .
>   Gently, broadly, she falls,
> Scarcely disturbing charted currents of air.

The plane passes over the bleak suburbs of the city, reaches the aerodrome, and frees its passengers. Up to the final stanza this is a poetically notable work. When Spender describes the wind-sleeve of the airport he does so with "l's" that picture its reaching height: "sleeves set trailing tall"—with the hissing of the wind

in the "s's" as well. Describing the passengers peering down at the land he refers to their "eyes trained by watching"—creating an effective ambiguity: "eyes-strained by watching." Describing the frayed factory area, where amid ugliness men labor at producing objects of luxury like aircraft for others to enjoy, he puts his rage and hurt into monosyllables, the way men speak in pain: "Here they may see what is being done." Near the airport, chimneys poke into the sky, and Spender provides the words and letters that create the sight: "Chimneys like lank black fingers." The industrial area itself is called the "outposts of work," with the military term "outposts" indicating that the workers there suffer a life of military subservience, command, and regimentation. All this is poetically right. From the words we receive not only idea but picture, and not only idea and picture but an emotional response to both. Up to the last stanza the work is a beautiful and thoughtful poem contrasting the comfort of the few to the squalor of the many, the luxurious indolence of some to the drab cheerlessness of others. The poem has made its statement. But then comes—as so often with Spender's political verse—the jarring note, the poetical flaw. The final lines are:

> Then, as they land, they hear the tolling bell
> Reaching across the landscape of hysteria
> To where, larger than all the charcoaled batteries
> And imaged towers against that dying sky,
> Religion stands, the church blocking the sun.

Religion, we are suddenly told, blocks out the light; as an institution, the church abets industry to bring darkness to man. This may be so; but to say it here, at this time, in this poem, is poetically false. This is not a poem about the church; to thrust it in as an afterthought is a structural flaw that bespeaks an earnest and dedicated young man but also an imperfect artist.

So too with the bathetic poem called **"The Funeral."** In this appears an image of striking beauty—but in the wrong place and contrary to the sense of the poem as Spender conceived it. Spender is saying (as he has every right to say) that our times have new heroes, better heroes than those of our traditional past. These new heroes are the men whose labor produces the physical wealth of the world. Such men are more valuable, he says, than a classical culture "Mourned by scholars who dream of the ghosts of Greek boys." But in the same poem we are asked to mourn the death of a contemporary hero—a Stakhanovite: "This one excelled all others in making driving-belts." This disparity in language and imagery makes the Stakhanovite absurd. The beauty of the Greek image—its long vowels, the sweetness and solemnity of its sounds—engenders nobility and loveliness in the past, in the very era Spender is terming inferior through the rest of the poem. Spender's language contradicts his intention, and he is not artist enough to recognize and excise the fatal anomaly. He too, despite himself, mourns the ghosts of Greek boys more than he does the nameless fabricator of driving-belts, and so his language bears witness. Enamored with a lovely statement, he employs it, though its gravity and melody dwarf the other lines and turn to absurdity the expression Spender sought to make before it.

Similarly the poem called **"Not Palaces"** ultimately disappoints because of false tone. It is a call to youth to change the world, to strive for economic betterment and human brotherhood. It is a cry for justice, equality, and love. Yet it ends:

> Our program like this, yet opposite:
> Death to the killers, bringing light to life.

The paradox of stimulating brotherhood and love by wide-scale murder ("Death to the killers") is not resolved. Worse, it is not seen. What matters here is not so much the logical confusion; rather it is the artistic failing, the structural flaw whereby the final lines strike a note of murderous vindictiveness in a poem purportedly expressing high idealism and love of humankind. The contradiction is redoubled within the poem. In the new society, Spender writes at the beginning, there will be no people "ordered like a single mind." Some few lines later, nonetheless, he states: "Our goal which we compel: Man shall be man." If there is a difference between *order* and *compel*, surely it is the latter which is the more stern and inflexible. Spender, in short, asserts within a few lines that in his new world man will be *freed* for individual life and then *compelled* to accept goals set by others. Once more we have a contradiction which makes one feel that both as thinker and poet Spender is too frivolous.

What Spender often lacks, it appears, is the "fundamental brainwork" which D. G. Rossetti declared indispensable for a poet. Emotion he has; intelligent control over the structure and language of his poem he too frequently has not. Randall Jarrell had something like this idea in mind when he remarked of Spender:

> Stephen Spender is, I think, an open, awkward, emotional, conscientiously well-intentioned, and simple-minded poet. To like his poems as much as we shouldn't, we need to respond to what they are meant to be, not to what they are—and it is surprisingly easy to do this. Most of his virtues and vices cluster around the word *sincere*. One likes his **Collected Poems** neither for their development (most of his experience and intelligence are excluded from the poems, so any great development is impossible) nor for their general excellence, but for a few touching, truthful poems that seem the products of observation, moral insight, and inspiration.
>
> (*Harper's,* Oct. 1955, p. 100)

Once we approach Spender on his true level, we can enjoy him, even though we will occasionally wince. He is no Shelley; he has neither the power nor the instant swoop of that falcon. He is not even Auden; he has not the easiness and breadth of that bright-eyed sparrow. He lacks the gorgeous plumage of a Wallace Stevens. At his best, Spender is the poet who knows that our world, our sex, and our sorrows are ever with us and ever too much for us. He is essentially an elegist. Even his poems of celebration incline toward sadness. **"I Think Continually of Those"** appears an exhortation to action and the apotheosis of those

> who in their lives fought for life,
> Who wore at their hearts the fire's center.

It is a poem glowing with imagery from Freud and D. H. Lawrence—imagery not only of birth but equally of short life and of swift oncoming destruction. The blaze of the sun and the heat of fire burn throughout the poem. Those who were truly great are dead (perhaps Marx and Lenin, perhaps Shelley and Lawrence). They traveled but "a short while towards the sun"—consumed by the fire of their passage and by the blazing goal they approached. They "left the vivid air signed with their honor," but their life was brief as they flared into death.

In another place, Spender reminds us:

> You were born; must die . . .
>   The miles and hours upon you feed.
> They eat your eyes out with their distance
> They eat your heart out with devouring need
> They eat your death out with lost significance.

And says finally that the song of life is "Of love, of loneliness, of life being death."

To be at one's best the wistful elegist of man's loneliness and death is no dismal fate for a poet, even if it is not the highest either. Essentially that is Spender's achievement. He feels "The furious volleys of charioteering power Behind the sun, racing to destroy." He hears "the groaning of the wasted lives." He knows the horror of "incommunicable grief." He reflects

> That the kingdom of heaven on earth must always
> Reiterate the garden of Eden,
> And each day's revolution be betrayed.

Behind each man's mask Spender discerns the timorous, uncertain child. He recognizes that child, for he of course is the child. Like the child he seeks some warmth, some haven: "Come home at last; come, end of loneliness."

It is not a mean thing to be a minor poet. Stephen Spender belongs not with Shelley and Keats, but he can interest and please those who fondly remember poets as disparate as Fulke Greville, Sir John Davies, and Wilfred Owen.

W. H. Sellers (essay date autumn 1965)

SOURCE: Sellers, W. H. "Wordsworth and Spender: Some Speculations on the Use of Rhyme." *Studies in English Literature 1500-1900* 5, no. 4 (autumn 1965): 641-50.

[*In the following essay, Sellers compares Spender's use of rhyme with that of William Wordsworth, noting how their handling of this poetic device is representative of their respective historical periods.*]

The material out of which poems are made is words, and words are amenable to a patterning that yields special devices. Being peculiar to poetry these devices assist the poet in establishing the necessary psychical distance between his constructed illusion and actuality. But poetry is more than words: what many poets ultimately create is the illusion of the feeling of thinking a thought, the illusion of the logic of feeling. Consequently, the feeling as well as the sense organizes a poem, giving it form and using words as its material. And the feeling is intimately related to the specific devices in a poem, for the effect of any device must be in harmony with the nature of the feeling.[1] An examination of the use of one device, rhyme, in the works of two poets of different historical periods, William Wordsworth and Stephen Spender, confirms this view and at the same time refutes an assertion made by Louis MacNeice that "changes in poetic technique are on a level with the changes each season of woman's fashion in dress. In the latter it is admitted that there is a certain deference to utility (appropriateness to the occasion) but the majority of innovations are due to the love of novelty."[2]

II

Herbert Read has said that Wordsworth is the poet who reintroduced into English poetry devices that had been neglected during the preceding century.[3] Much of the freedom exercised in contemporary verse is the result of his experiments, not the least important of which involved rhyme. Although he wrote first in rhyme and did not abandon it until 1795 in the short poem "Lines (left under a seat in a yew-tree)," Wordsworth apparently found that certain of the thoughts he wished to create suffered when presented in rhyme. In general these thoughts were for him what might be called "great" thoughts: that is, deeply significant and highly complex thoughts that had to be expressed, and expressed in a form that would do their significance and complexity absolute justice. There are four such great poems in the Wordsworth canon, and three of them, "Lines Composed a Few Miles Above Tintern Abbey" (1798), *The Prelude* (1805), and *The Excursion* (1814), are written in blank verse, while the fourth, "Ode: Intimations of Immortality" (1807), for reasons that I shall offer later, is written in rhyme.

"Tintern Abbey" is an intensely lyrical creation. The feeling it renders is highly impassioned: the poem is so constructed that the reader is swept along by the rapidly moving lines, removed from actuality by the rich imagery and the recurring alliteration and assonance. What Wordsworth sought to create is precisely the illusion of ecstatic feeling, and in attempting to do so he found rhyme inappropriate because it impeded the urgent movement of the whole by inviting the reader to pause at the end of lines. A representative passage from the poem illustrates the effects that he achieved:

> And so I dare to hope,
> Though changed, no doubt, from what I was when first
> I came among these hills; when like a roe
> I bounded o'er the mountains by the sides
> Of the deep rivers, and the lonely streams,
> Wherever nature led: more like a man
> Flying from something that he dreads than one
> Who sought the thing he loved. For nature then
> (The coarser pleasures of my boyish days,
> And their glad animal movements all gone by)
> To me was all in all.—I cannot paint
> What then I was. The sounding cataract
> Haunted me like a passion: the tall rock,
> The mountain, and the deep and gloomy wood,
> Their colours and their forms, were then to me
> An appetite; a feeling and a love,
> That had no need of a remoter charm,
> By thought supplied, nor any interest
> Unborrowed from the eye.

> (65-83)

Here, because there is little end-stopping, the lines flow freely; and this freedom, along with the absence of rhyme, allows Wordsworth to fit the lines to the image, as in lines 67-69. There is a suggestion of off-rhyme endings in the run of *n*'s in "man/one/then," but, because these words are all passing rhyme with no assigned pause, their effect as rhyme is negligible. More striking, however, is the way in which assonantal and consonantal off-rhyme is used internally: "led/loved, all/was," and "appetite/eye." Each of these occurs before a marked pause, thereby receiving an emphasis that must have been intentional. Instances of this practice can be found elsewhere in the poem. So, while abandoning end rhyme, Wordsworth retained a vestigial form of rhyme inside the lines. By using rhyme in this way he was able to control his lines, contribute to the making of his illusion, and at the same time gain intensity of feeling through freedom of movement.

In the next significant non-rhyme poem, *The Prelude*, Wordsworth moves even farther away from the use of rhyme. There are again some suggestions of assonantal and consonantal end rhymes, but far fewer than in "Tintern Abbey," and internal off-rhyme is used much less emphatically. It is probably the most perfect of his non-rhyme poems. And it had to be written without rhyme because, as Read says, it is "the epic of the man of feeling."[4] It is the creation of feelings of extraordinary intensity, feelings that could be expressed only in sweeping lines charged with imagery:

> Oh! many a time have I, a five years' Child,
> A naked Boy, in one delightful Rill,
> A little Mill-race sever'd from his stream,
> Made one long bathing of a summer's day,
> Bask'd in the sun, and plunged, and bask'd again
> Alternate all a summer's day, or cours'd
> Over the sandy fields, leaping through groves
> Of yellow grunsel, or when crag and hill,
> The woods, and distant Skiddaw's lofty height,
> Were bronz'd with a deep radiance, stood alone
> Beneath the sky, as if I had been born
> On Indian Plains, and from my Mother's hut
> Had run abroad in wantonness, to sport,
> A naked Savage, in the thunder shower.
>
> (I.291-304)[5]

Seldom can a poet sustain such lyricism for any great length, and this achievement, if nothing else, makes the nearly 8500 lines of *The Prelude* remarkable. Rarely, in fact, have feeling and intensity come so strongly together, even in far shorter poems. To be sure, there are moments, particularly towards the end of the poem, when the intensity tends to let up; but in general the inspired lyricism transmutes successfully the philosophical subject matter.

Of course, the vast majority of Wordsworth's poems employ rhyme. In these poems, it is clear, he was dealing with thoughts that to him were not extraordinarily great and therefore not suited to intense expression. The "Lucy" poems and the sonnets are of this nature: though highly lyrical, they do not embody sufficiently significant or complex thoughts to warrant either unusual length or technical license. Some poems suggest a profound feeling without elaborating it, as in "Green Linnet"; others are primarily narratives in which the poet aims not so much at creating an illusion of feeling as an illusion of a train of events, so that subject matter is of prime importance. In this type of poem the lyricism must be controlled, and one of the easiest ways to gain such control is through rhyme. On the other hand, there are some narrative poems in which Wordsworth is more concerned with creating an illusion of the most intense kind of feeling, and in these he turned to non-rhyme. In "Michael," for instance, the feeling is more significant than the chain of events; in fact, the narrative merely provides a frame for the lyricism.

At first sight "Ode: Intimations of Immortality" is an exception to Wordsworth's use of rhyme, for it has all of the characteristics of a lyrical poem, but is written in rhyme. And perhaps it is an exception; there is no law binding a poet to one creative method. But at least part of the poem's singularity can be explained by the

realization that its intensely lyrical element is paradoxically freed and controlled by the rhyme. Ordinarily rhyme gives a poem a feeling of control, but the run-on lines, the rich imagery, and pervading intensity seem to overpower this control in such a way that the lyricism is actually heightened. And perhaps in order to further this effect Wordsworth used the ode's fluid rhyme scheme.

In *The Excursion* Wordsworth works with rhyme in still another way. Heretofore he had dispensed with rhyme only when the thoughts he sought to create were sufficiently great and the subject matter sufficiently rich to merit sustained lyricism. In *The Excursion,* however, neither of these requirements is immediately apparent, with the result that the poem seems often to lack vitality. Yet, viewed as a whole, the poem does reveal a pattern, a muted lyrical pattern: for Wordsworth, it becomes clear, is gradually building up the illusion of feeling, gradually moving towards a climax. As a result, of course, *The Excursion* falls far below the sustained intensity of *The Prelude*; in spite of the presence of internal assonance, relatively flat passages occur throughout:

> Turn wheresoe'er we would, he was a light
> Unfailing; not a hamlet could we pass,
> Rarely a house, that did not yield to him
> Remembrances; or from his tongue call forth
> Some way-beguiling tale. Nor less regard
> Accompanied those strains of apt discourse,
> Which nature's various objects might inspire;
> And in the silence of his face I read
> His overflowing spirit. Birds and beasts,
> And the mute fish that glances in the stream,
> And harmless reptile coiling in the sun,
> And gorgeous insect hovering in the air,
> The fowl domestic, and the household dog—
> In his capacious mind, he loved them all:
> Their rights acknowledging he felt for all.
>
> (II.32-47)

The familiar epithets, the generally unvarying meter, and the ponderous catalogue do not make for moving lyricism. Nor do the frequent pauses permit the lines to attain any rhythmic momentum. There are, of course, passages in the poem which do achieve considerable power:

> —We followed, taking as he led, a path
> Along a hedge of hollies dark and tall,
> Whose flexile boughs low bending with a weight
> Of leafy spray, concealed the stems and roots
> That gave them nourishment. When frosty winds
> Howl from the north, what kindly warmth, methought
> Is here—how grateful this impervious screen!
>
> (VIII.441-447)

Here Wordsworth, avoiding end-stops and exploiting assonance more fully, produces a compelling rhythm well suited to the thought being expressed. In brief, *The*

Excursion often does have feelings that parallel its thinking, and, as the thinking moves towards its climax, so does the feeling. Where the poem suffers, however, is where the subject matter, in itself heavily philosophical, proves too much for the feeling; far too frequently, unaided by rhyme, the lines lose psychical distance and become little more than prose.

All that can be safely said of Wordsworth's practices is that, in general, he does not use rhyme when the thought he wants to express is not only great but at the same time intense. The absence of rhyme is made up for by the use of various other devices that, unlike rhyme, will not interfere with the necessary free movement of the lines. When the thought is neither great nor intense, however, Wordsworth uses rhyme.

III

Stephen Spender is certainly one of the most lyrical of modern poets, and his use of rhyme is of particular interest because of the numerous variations that he effects. Perhaps even more than Wordsworth he is aware of the subtle possibilities of this device. Among the chief causes of these variations has been Spender's shift in thematic emphasis from the outer to the inner world: he has tried to create in his poetry feelings of vastly different kinds, and in doing so he has found it expedient to bring into play diverse devices.

An examination of Spender's poems published before 1939 indicates that, wherever his subject matter is of a sufficient richness, he has done away with regular rhyme. This is conducive to the feelings he is often trying to create, such feelings as sympathy for the unemployed or disgust with prevailing social conditions. Rhyme in poems concerned with such feelings would give a sense of order artistically inimical to the intended effect. The thirtieth poem in *Poems* (1933) illustrates Spender's early method:

> In railway halls, on pavements near the traffic,
> They beg, their eyes made big by empty staring
> And only measuring Time, like the blank clock.
>
> No, I shall weave no tracery of pen-ornament
> To make them birds upon my singing-tree:
> Time merely drives these lives which do not live
> As tides push rotten stuff along the shore.
>
> —There is no consolation, no, none
> In the curving beauty of that line
> Traced on our graphs through history, where the oppressor
> Starves and deprives the poor.
>
> Paint here no draped despairs, no saddening clouds
> Where the soul rests, proclaims eternity.
> But let the wrong cry out as raw as wounds
> This Time forgets and never heals, far less transcends.

Not only is the subject matter here extremely rich, but the absence of rhyme gives to the poem a feeling similar to that which Wilfred Owen, to whom Spender is much indebted, had obtained in part through the use of half-rhyme: a feeling of disorder deserving of deep pity.[6] In Owen this feeling is enhanced not only by half-rhyme but by falling vowel sound, as in the opening lines of "Strange Meeting":

> It seemed that out of battle I escaped
> Down some profound dull tunnel, long since scooped
> Through granites which titanic wars had groined.
> Yet also there encumbered sleepers groaned
> Too fast in thought or death to be bestirred.

Spender, however, relies completely on off-rhyme only when, as in the third stanza, the richness of his material falls off. Elsewhere in the poem he avoids the restricting regularity of rhyme and instead creates feeling by an intense lyrical quality conveyed by such words as "empty," "blank," "rotten," and "raw," and by such emotive phrases as "draped despairs" and "saddening clouds."

Spender does use rhyme in some of the early poems, usually those dealing with subjective themes; but even in these poems it is usually off-rhyme or half-rhyme, seldom regular rhyme. And when he deals with the external world, as in **"Two Armies,"** one of his Spanish War poems in *The Still Centre* (1939), he tends to use non-rhyme as Owen used half-rhyme to aid in creating the feeling appropriate to chaos, a feeling conveyed primarily by an intense lyricism. Similarly, in **"The Coward,"** he contributes to the illusion of flatness, of dull monotony, by using off-rhyme.

Vienna (1934) holds great interest for the student of rhyme, for this long four-part poem, which marks the closest Spender has come to writing a "great" poem in the Wordsworthian sense, attempts to create the complex illusion of the varied and often contrasting feelings experienced during and after a futile uprising against an unjust social order. It is a remarkable mixture of intense lyricism and flat statement. The lyrical passages are brilliantly wrought:

> There were some suffered from the destruction of
>   houses
> More than from the death of men: they weep for their
>   houses
> That endured enormous wounds, a man's abyss.
> So the once sun-flaked walls, our elaborated pride,
> Were more our life than any man's one life, though
>   proud.
> Heroes are instantly replaced: civilization
> Wears concrete sides: destroy these walls
> With shell-holes, and our children wear their weals.

With particular effectiveness, the half-rhyme here suggests disintegration. The non-rhyme and off-rhyme in the following passage, however, do little to transmute its prosaic flatness:

The square windows of the prison square surround
　him dumbly
Where a ditch was dug by criminals and a gallows set
And sand sprinkled. Then 56 soldiers
Armed to the teeth looked rather ridiculous
To guard one man. But we were watching
From our cells, prison cells, cells of labour,
Our leader. They brought him out in a hurry
For Dollfuss had phoned through to complain of the
　delay;
Dollfuss, Dollfuss said "Hang him low."
Wallisch stood on the platform and before he died
"Live Socialism," and "Hail Freedom," he said.

Given enough length perhaps, such lines may achieve a
low degree of lyricism; but, because Spender juxtaposes
them to passages of considerably more intensity, their
essential flatness is exposed and an overall unevenness
prevails throughout the poem.

In the foreword to *The Still Centre* Spender declared
". . . in my most recent poems I have deliberately
turned back to a kind of writing which is more personal,
and I have included within my subjects weakness and
fantasy and illusion." And this preoccupation with the
feeling of subjective experience has continued up to the
present. With it there has been an increasingly more
flexible and more subtle use of rhyme and off-rhyme. In
Ruins and Visions (1942) he freely mixes the two in
order to augment the feelings he seeks to create, as in
these lines from **"The Journey"**:

> Oh, but then suddenly the line
> 　Swung on to another view
> Barren with myself, and the blank pain
> 　Of the crammed world without you.

The off-rhyme, "line/pain," gives added intensity to the
feeling of regret that the lines create. His confident
control of the effects of rhyme is clearly seen in the
opening stanzas of **"The Air Raid Across the Bay"**:

> Above the dead flat sea
> And watching rocks of black coast
> Across the bay, the high
> Searchlights probe the centre of the sky
> Their ends fusing in cones of light.
> For a brilliant instant held up
> Then shattered like a cup.
>
> They rub white rules through leaden dark,
> Projecting tall phantom
> Masts of swaying derricks
> Above the sea's broad level decks.

Here Spender combines subtly the freedom of non-
rhyme and the control of rhyme. This mastery is seen
more and more clearly in his later poems. **"Seascape,"**
in *Poems of Dedication* (1947), for instance, uses a
relatively strict rhyme without end-stops even though
its subject matter is extremely rich:

> The azure vibrancy of the air tires
> And a sigh, like a woman's, from inland

Brushes the golden wires with shadowing hand
Drawing across their chords some gull's sharp cries
Or bell, or gasp from distant hedged-in shires:
These, deep as anchors, the silent wave buries.

Even when the subject matter is not instrinsically rich,
the same rather strict combination of rhyme and off-
rhyme proves highly effective, as can be seen in one of
Spender's most simple yet most moving poems, **"Empty
House"** in *The Edge of Being* (1949):

> Then, when the child was gone,
> I was alone
> In the house, suddenly grown huge. Each noise
> Explained its cause away,
> Animal, vegetable, mineral,
> Nail, creaking board, or mouse.
> But mostly there was quiet of after battle
> Where round the room still lay
> The soldiers and the paintbox, all the toys.
> 　　Then, when I went to tidy these away,
> My hands refused to serve:
> My body was the house,
> And everything he'd touched, an exposed nerve.

These later poems contrast with such early works as **"I
Think Continually of Those Who Were Truly Great"**
in *Poems* (1933) in which rich material and urgent
rhythm, untrammeled by rhyme, sustain the lyricism. It
would seem that Spender came only gradually to realize
the possibilities of rhyme, to recognize the subtle effects that he could gain by using off-rhyme sparingly
for special emphasis like that achieved in **"Seascape"**
by the words "cries/buries" and in **"Empty House"** by
the words "gone/alone," effects that contribute much to
the illusion he seeks to create in each poem. In his later
poetry, with a few exceptions, the feeling involved
determines the function of rhyme: if the feeling is one
of disorder, he tends to use occasional off-rhyme; if the
feeling suggests some kind of order, then he introduces
an appropriate measure of rhyme.

IV

This cursory examination of the work of only two poets
scarcely permits the drawing of any broad conclusions
about the use of rhyme in poetry. It does suggest,
however, that this poetic device is functional, that when
the illusion to be created is one of intense feelings, the
poet moves away from strict rhyme. And it proves that
the use of rhyme has nothing to do with anything so
whimsical as fashion and everything to do with the
poet's pursuit of aesthetic harmony.

Notes

1. The theoretical basis of this paper derives in large
part from the work of Suzanne K. Langer, especially from chapters 13, 14, and 15 of *Feeling and
Form* (New York, 1953).

2. "Poetry," *The Arts To-day,* ed. G. Grigson
(London, 1935), p. 46.

3. *Phases of English Poetry* (London, 1928), pp. 144-146.

4. *Phases of English Poetry,* p. 135.

5. From the 1805 text of *The Prelude,* ed. Ernest de Selincourt and Helen Darbishire (O.U.P., 1959). All other quotations are from *Wordsworth's Poetical Works,* ed. Ernest de Selincourt and Helen Darbishire, First Edition, 5 Vols. (O.U.P., 1940-1949).

6. See D. S. Welland's "Half-Rhyme in Wilfred Owen," *RES* [*Research in English Studies*], I (1950), 226-241.

James L. Potter (essay date February 1966)

SOURCE: Potter, James L. "The 'Destined Pattern' of Spender's 'Express.'" *College English* 27, no. 5 (February 1966): 426-28.

[*In the following essay, Potter examines six successive drafts of Spender's "The Express" as a means of studying the development of the poem's form.*]

> After the first powerful plain manifesto
> The black statement of pistons, without more fuss
> But gliding like a queen, she leaves the station.
> Without bowing and with restrained unconcern
> She passes the houses which humbly crowd outside,
> The gasworks and at last the heavy page
> Of death, printed by gravestones in the cemetery.
> Beyond the town there lies the open country
> Where, gathering speed, she acquires mystery,
> The luminous self-possession of ships on ocean.
> It is now she begins to sing—at first quite low
> Then loud, and at last with a jazzy madness—
> The song of her whistle screaming at curves,
> Of deafening tunnels, brakes, innumerable bolts.
> And always light, aerial, underneath
> Goes the elate metre of her wheels.
> Steaming through metal landscape on her lines
> She plunges new eras of wild happiness
> Where speed throws up strange shapes, broad curves
> And parallels clean like the steel of guns.
> At last, further than Edinburgh or Rome,
> Beyond the crest of the world, she reaches night
> Where only a low streamline brightness
> Of phosphorus on the tossing hills is white.
> Ah, like a comet through flame she moves entranced
> Wrapt in her music no bird song, no, nor bough
> Breaking with honey buds, shall ever equal.[1]

When Robert Frost hit upon the line, "And miles to go before I sleep," he evidently found the chord that enabled him to resolve "Stopping by Woods on a Snowy Evening"; he had tried a different line first, but this one finally made it possible for him to achieve the poem "as it meant itself to be written," to release its "destined pattern," as John Holmes put it (in Paul Engle and W.

Carrier, *Reading Modern Poetry* [Chicago, 1955]). If this seems too romantic a conception of literary composition, suggestive of "Kubla Khan" or the direction of a Muse, it is nevertheless evident in the work of many different poets. Often there seems to be no special reason why a certain line or figure should "unlock" the poem, but occasionally we can see from manuscript recensions just what it is that the others failed to do.

In successive drafts of **"The Express"**[2] we can see how Stephen Spender finally achieved the poem's "destined pattern," and further, just in what sense that pattern was "destined." Spender's manuscript has been examined a number of times, of course, for one reason or another. Karl Shapiro has used it as a means of penetrating the writer's psyche,[3] and to Spender himself it has afforded insights into the general process of artistic creation as manifested in the poet's way of thinking.[4] And in many classrooms it has been used to illuminate the effects of various literary techniques and devices (such as imagery, as in line 2, where Spender replaced his original "clear statement of pistons" with "black statement . . ."). Our concern, however, will be with the developing manifestation of an aesthetic phenomenon, with the emergence of the poem's form—what Northrop Frye calls "the true father or shaping spirit of the poem."[5]

There are six drafts of **"The Express"** in Spender's workbook, and these differ in more than details; the resolution of the poem—its final form—was obviously not arrived at easily or automatically. Indeed, as we shall see, it emerged only when a radical change was made in the focus of the basic imagery, the poem seemingly refusing to "jell" in the first four drafts, at least. The development of the poem's form went, briefly, as follows:

Drafts A and B are almost identical. First, in draft A, Spender produced the first twelve or thirteen lines of the poem almost as they appear in the final version: he describes the train leaving the station and picking up speed until "she" begins to "sing." In these lines he concurrently determined that the poem was to be in blank verse, which implied that it would have an "organic" structure rather than one imposed by conventions of rime and meter, as in a sonnet. The form of **"The Express,"** thus, had to emerge from within itself, through its own working-out. Draft A ends in a few lines that point toward a conclusion to the poem by suggesting the "meaning" of the train:

> We travel further than Edinburgh or Rome
>   wild
> ~~For we~~ r [R]eaching new eras of ~~insane~~
>   happiness
> When night falls   (l. 20)
>   Explore new areas of happiness
>   "   "   eras of wild happiness

Finally, draft B is practically the same as A except that at the end the "We" (representing the passengers, clearly, in 1. 18) is replaced first by "Travellers," and then that is deleted in favor of "Her passengers."

The next two drafts, C and D, are another stage in the formation of the poem, though not really a new tack. The line of development is epitomized in the increased emphasis Spender put on describing the effect of the train ride on the passengers. The basic pattern for the poem represented in C and D had been established rudimentarily in A and B, in the description of the train's movement followed by the suggestion of its significance in terms of the passengers' impressions. In C and D Spender tried even harder to indicate this significance explicitly; he had little success, however, in describing the reactions of the passengers in order to bring out that significance, as the end of draft D will illustrate:

> ~~They are r~~[R]uled round with
>   iron lines   (l. 25)
> ~~And stamped with—?—imagery which makes~~
>   ~~new worlds:~~
> ~~This strange new world~~
> And strange new forms of rods and jets of
>   steam
> Stamp on their brains an image of new
>   worlds
> ~~Their brains are stamped pressed on by~~
>   ~~forms poured on by steam~~
> The images of power stamp their brain (l. 31)
> They watch
> ~~And of works whose fires~~
> ~~And of metals moulten to create new works~~
>   ~~worlds~~
> And hear
>
>   (ll. 25-34)

The many deletions seem to indicate that Spender hit a dead end in trying to make the symbolic significance of the train explicit.

The next draft, E, is so neat that it is almost a shock. It is so close to the finished work that the last draft, F, is no more than a copy of E with a few touchings-up.

The essential difference between these two drafts and the others is two-fold. First, the references to the passengers have been dropped completely, in favor of references to the train itself. Second, the attempts to describe the passengers' perceptions have also been dropped, and instead, the significance is evoked for the reader directly, symbolically, by the train itself. We can understand now the difficulties encountered in drafts A through D: it was as if Spender had been trying to write the poem in the same terms as a cautionary tale like "Peter Rabbit," where the adventures of the hero are described and then a moral is stated. The consequence of applying this method in the earlier drafts of **"The Express"** was first that the tone and style began to

sound tendentious, while the work as a whole became less of a symbolic poem than a piece of propaganda. Second, and more important, the introduction of the passengers produced a shift in focus that distorted the essential pattern of the poem.

This, one might say of draft E, is the way the poem "meant itself to be written." Or, to be rather less romantic, we can say that the final version is artistically coherent because of persistent focus on a central symbol, whereas the earlier versions were not thus unified, and that at the same time the final poem is unified modally because the theme is consistently embodied in the central symbol rather than being stated explicitly, "discursively," at some point. There are, of course, good literary works in which we do not find these kinds of unity or consistency, but **"The Express"** is the better for having them. They are responsible for the continuity and the unity of the poem's effect, for bringing the imagery to bear concertedly in order to "condition" our minds for the response implicitly expected. This formal continuity was evidently the poem's "destined pattern."

Notes

1. Stephen Spender's poem "The Express," which appears in *Poems* (London, 1934), is reoriented here by the kind permission of Random House, Inc.

2. In Spender's workbook, now in the Lockwood Memorial Library of the University of Buffalo. The manuscript versions of the poem are also reproduced in Wright Thomas and S. G. Brown, *Reading Poems* (New York, 1941), pp. 624-629.

3. "The Meaning of the Discarded Poem," in *Poets at Work,* ed. Charles D. Abbott, New York, 1948.

4. In *The Making of a Poem,* New York, 1962.

5. *Anatomy of Criticism* (Princeton, 1957), p. 98.

Derek Stanford (essay date 1969)

SOURCE: Stanford, Derek. "Introduction" and "Stephen Spender." In *Stephen Spender, Louis MacNeice, Cecil Day Lewis,* pp. 3-23. Grand Rapids. Mich.: William B. Eerdmans, 1969.

[*In the following excerpt, Stanford offers an overview of Spender's position within the group of his contemporaries known as the "Pylon Poets," which included W. H. Auden, Louis MacNeice, and Cecil Day Lewis.*]

"A PARTICULAR LABEL"

> The secret of these hills was stone, and cottages
> Of that stone made,
> And crumbling roads
> That turned on sudden hidden villages.

> Now over these small hills, they have built the
>   concrete
> That trails black wire;
> Pylons, those pillars
> Bare like nude giant girls that have no secret.

So wrote Stephen Spender in 1933, his poem **"The Pylons"** providing—as he remarked twenty-one-years later—"a particular label for some of the poetry of the 'Thirties: an embarrassment to my friends' luggage more even than to my own." At the time these verses were written, however, there may have been naivete, as of a child with a new train set, but embarrassment was out of the question. Rimbaud, in the last century, had said that it was "necessary to be absolutely modern"; and Auden, Spender, Day Lewis and MacNeice were all busily bent on taking poetry and making it new. The contemporary look required by the Muse seemed to these young poets partly a matter of reflecting in their poetry the industrial society of their day. Images from the world of machines were particularly favored by them. Thus Spender writes of the noise of the express,

> The song of her whistle screaming at curves,
> Of deafening tunnels, brakes, innumerable bolts,

and, though he has to employ romantic imagery to make his point, insists upon the triumph of the mechanical over the pastoral:

> Ah, like a comet through the flame, she moves
>   entranced,
> Wrapped in her music no bird song, no, nor bough
> Breaking with honey buds shall ever equal.

In a more subtle fashion, Day Lewis uses railway images to express the end of a love-relationship:

> Suppose that we, tomorrow or the next day,
> Came to an end—in storm the shafting broken,
> Or a mistaken signal, the flange lifting—
> Would that be premature, a test for sorrow?

while MacNeice selects urban images to express disintegration and threat in the years between the wars:

> The street is up again, gas, electricity or drains,
> Ever-changing conveniences, nothing comfortable
>   remains
> Un-improved, as flagging Rome improved villa and
>   sewer
> (A sound-proof library and a stable temperature).
>
> Our street is up, red lights sullenly mark
> The long trench of pipes, iron guts in the dark,
> And not till the Goths again come swarming down the
>   hill
> Will cease the clangour of the pneumatic drill.

Such mechanical ornaments as trains, drains, and pylons—though they provided a group name for these poets—were, however, only a small part of their

program. The Italian futurists and the Russian Mayakovsky had earlier made much of these devices, while Eliot's first volumes of verse resort to a background use of such means, as adroit and atmospheric as they are unobtrusive: "The memory throws up high and dry / A crowd of twisted things / . . . A broken spring in a factory yard," "While I was fishing in the dull canal / On a winter evening round behind the gashouse."

Turning back to Spender's poem **"The Pylons,"** we see what lay behind this employment of engineering adornments:

> The valley with its gilt and evening look
> And the green chestnut of customary root,
> Are mocked dry like the parched bed of a brook.
>
> But far above and far as sight endures
> Like whips of anger
> With lightning's danger
> There runs the quick perspective of the future.

The sinister potency attributed to the pylons is indicative of the way in which these poets looked at modern existence. The poem brings into sharp collision two ways of life—the past and the future—and suggests how the settled tenor of the first is disturbed and disrupted by the second. The Pylon poets saw how industrial living constituted a challenge to the traditional image of man established within an agrarian ethos. Nor was that challenge a pretty one. A contemporary critic has indicted the period in which these poets wrote as one of "mass unemployment through the world, workers' poverty and homes, humbug from famous people, the importance of money in worldly estimates of worth, the lack of meaning in accepted creeds."

This was certainly how these poets interpreted industrial living in our Western democracies. For Auden, capitalist economy in the slump is represented by those "silted harbours, derelict works" which figure so often in his lines; images to be set against Spender's starry-eyed song of Stakhanovite heroics in what then seemed to the Left a land of promise:

> Death is another milestone on their way.
> With laughter on their lips and with winds blowing
>   round them
>
> They record simply
> How this one excelled all others in making driving
>   belts.

To this perhaps fanciful saga of labor ("This is festivity, it is the time of statistics") Spender opposed his elegy for the unemployed:

> In railway halls, on pavements near the traffic,
> They beg, their eyes made big by empty staring
> And only measuring time, like the blank clock.

Nor was the debate between capitalism and communism the only theme of these poets. Outside, in Germany, there was fascism. As Spender noted:

> Meagre men shoot up. Rockets, rockets,
> A corporal's flaming tongue wags above flaming
>   parliament
>
> The tide of killers now, behold the whip-masters!
> Breeches and gaiters camouflage mud.

while for Auden the war in Spain became an image of the human conscience ("I am your choice, your decision: yes, I am Spain").

Employed superficially, the industrial-mechanical imagery of these poets appeared often as a mere fad or fashion; but when it was used with a deeper sense of the social context it gained significance. Thus, for Auden, the city becomes the locality that best expresses the discrepancy between our way of living and man's fundamental nature:

> In unlighted streets you hide away the appalling
> Factories where lives are made for a temporary use
> Like collars or chairs, rooms where the lonely are bat-
>   tered
> Slowly like pebbles into fortuitous shapes.

Looking at a bust of Apollo, Rilke tells us in his *Sonnets to Orpheus* that the stone head with its accumulated beauty seemed to say to him, "You must change your life." Regarding the Medusan landscape of industrial England in the thirties, with its depressed areas, unemployment and malnutrition, the Pylon poets heard the same admonition. They, too, must change their way of living, and learn to show others, also, how to change.

It is at this point that these poets become of more than historical interest, though our concern with them is related to the history of their times. It has been customary to think of them as revolutionary poets—poets dedicated to a cult of violent political change. It is true that such an hypothesis of action did exist as one element in their work; but anything like a planned program of change appears never to have gained their assent and must certainly be looked for in vain in their verse.

What they *did* insist upon was an internal change—a revolution within the self. "Harrow the house of the dead," wrote Auden, "look shining at / New styles of architecture, a change of heart." Spender realized even more clearly that the individual person is the pivot of change. If revolution is to be transformation, then revolution begins at home. Spiritual implications are obvious here.

> Different living is not living in different places
> But creating in the mind a map

> And willing on the map a desert.
> Pinnacled mountain, or saving resort.

At the same time, the change that these poets stipulated was not envisaged in quietist terms. Their desire was not to create little lonely cells of harmonious living withdrawn from society as a whole and content not to influence its decisions. Instead, they imagined their salvationist words carried like a revivalist's gospel. Essentially they were unconcerned with the isolated perfectionist, paring his spirit's finger nails. Beginning with the "I," they nonetheless contended that "the proper study of mankind is man"; and Michael Roberts, a contemporary critic, noted how their attitude was nearer to "the Greek conception of good citizenship than to the stoical austerity of recent verse" (1932). "Our goal which we compel: Man shall be man," declared Spender emphatically, in a line more charged with conviction than precision.

It is this vision of change, and the transvaluation of values it implies, that particularly demands the attention of Christian sensibilities. Out of the four poets thought of as a group—Auden, Spender, Day Lewis, MacNeice—only one, Auden, gave his later assent to the basic tenets of the Christian faith. In all of them however, to some extent, we witness the manifestation of Christian values and beatitudes dissociated from orthodox terminology. What we discover is a striving for grace in terms that fit neither a traditionally supernatural nor a conventionally rationalistic usage. And since in the most powerful poetry there is always a suggestion of revelation, what we find in the best work of these four is the sense of charisma in secular context. As MacNeice wrote in *An Eclogue for Christmas*:

> Goodbye to you, this day remember is Christmas, this
>   morn
> They say, interpret it your own way, Christ is born.

A STRANGE ANALOGY

If we seek to date the birth of this movement, then Spender's hand-printing of an edition ("about thirty copies") of Auden's first volume entitled *Poems* in 1928 makes a convenient start. It also serves to spotlight Auden, who was the seminal mind of the group as well as being its impresario. On account of his larger status, Auden merits separate treatment in this series; but no summary of the Pylon poets can explain the nature or direction of their work without some preliminary reference to him. We have only to read Spender's autobiography *World within World,* or note the many references and dedications to him in the volumes of the Pylon poets, to see the influence he exerted.

From the Introduction that he wrote to *Oxford Poetry,* 1927, it is clear that Auden possessed a mind sharper and more subtle than most undergraduates. He disclaimed, straight away, any appeal to the teen-age cult which was rife in the post-War years. "Those," he wrote, "who believe that there is anything valuable in our youth as such, we have neither the patience to consider nor the power to condone: our youth should be a period of spiritual discipline." (Here one is reminded of the statement Eliot was to make a few years later in "Thoughts after Lambeth," namely that what the young need to be taught is "chastity, humility, austerity, and discipline." Auden and Eliot hold different ends in view, but both stress the necessity of self-ascesis as a means.)

Auden evidently exercised the ringmaster's function to the manner-born. "He had," Spender tells us, "the strangest sense of looking for colleagues and disciples . . . He looked at a still life on the wall and said: 'He will be the Painter . . .' His friend Isherwood was to be the Novelist. Chalmers was another of the Gang. Cecil Day Lewis was a colleague. A group of emergent artists existed in his mind, like a cabinet in the mind of a party leader."

The spell of Auden—the shaman-like effect of his personality—is apparent from all that Spender recounts. "I took to showing Auden my poems," he confesses. "I would arrive with my pockets stuffed with manuscripts and watch him reading them. Occasionally he would grunt. Beyond this his comment was restrained to selecting one line for praise. I showed him a long poem, after reading which he said,

'In a new land shooting is necessary

is a beautiful line,' and immediately the line entered as it were his own poetic landscape of deserted mines, spies, shootings—terse syllables enclosed within a music like the wind in a deserted shaft."

Auden at Oxford made the deep impression he did because he appeared to know all the answers and because the answers he gave appeared new. "At this early age," Spender relates, "Auden had already an extensive knowledge of the theories of modern psychology, which he used as a means of understanding himself and dominating his friends." Largely speaking, these theories were of a Freudian nature, but the key one, or pet one, concerned the psychosomatic origins of illness. "In 1929," as Isherwood narrates, "during a visit to Berlin, he came into contact with the doctrines of the American psychologist Homer Lane . . . Auden was particularly interested in Lane's theories of the psychological causes of disease—if you refuse to make use of your creative powers, you grow a cancer, etc."—which is exactly what that poor spinster did in Auden's ballad of Miss Gee. Isherwood remarks how "references to these theories can be found in many of the early poems," and indeed in the early poems of his friends. Without knowledge of these theories—namely,

"If you are sick, this merely means that your desires are urging you, through sickness, to do what you really want, not what you think you ought to"—it is well-nigh impossible to understand the import of such a phrase as "the liar's quinsy" in Auden's key poem "Sir, No Man's Enemy."

In this poem, the person of the Healer (suggested presumably by Lane) is identified with the God-figure and addressed as such:

> Sir, no man's enemy, forgiving all
> But will his negative inversion, be prodigal:
> Send us power and light, a sovereign touch
> Curing the intolerable neural itch . . .

The poem follows the petitionary structure of a prayer. (Note how the supplication "Harrow the house of the dead" suggests here Christ's harrowing of hell.)

The status that Freud and Lane occupy in the Pylon poets is analogous to that which Christ's ministry of healing occupies in the Gospel records. With the analysts as guides, these poets hoped to exercise, extend, and explore the therapeutic miracle.

It is important to stress the psychological aspect of their vision. For them, the revolution was first to be a personal and internal affair. Writing of the year 1928 at Oxford, MacNeice states that "neither Auden nor Spender had yet shown the slightest interest in politics and, with a few exceptions such as Clare Parsons [an undergraduate poet who died young], the cult of Soviet Russia was something almost unknown."

Isherwood endorses this by telling us that the creative revolt of these poets was not primarily political.

> The Angry Young Man of my generation was angry with the Family and its official representatives; he called them hypocrites, he challenged the truth of what they taught. He declared that a Freudian revolution had taken place of which they were trying to remain unaware. He accused them of reactionary dullness, snobbery, complacency, apathy. While they mouthed their platitudes, he exclaimed, we were all drifting towards mental disease, sex crime, alcoholism, suicide.

The activity of the young Pylon poets in their early years suggests a parallel with the first Christian communities: supporting and encouraging one another in a hostile world, and seeking, all the time, to carry over their conviction into that larger arena. There is the same cooperative effort: Auden and Isherwood combined to write their three verse-plays together (*The Dog Beneath the Skin*, 1935; *The Ascent of F6*, 1936; and *On the Frontier*, 1938), followed by their prose-verse account of a trip to China entitled *Journey to a War*, in 1939; Auden and MacNeice collaborated in *Letters from Iceland*, in 1936.

Then, too, there is the equivalent of the first Christians' certitude, their sense of uniquely possessing the Word, in what Peter Porter has called—while speaking of the last work—a sort of "'in-group' knowingness." Another parallel presents itself in what might metaphorically be termed the chiliasm of the Pylon poets; for whereas the early Christians believed in a second coming of Christ as king of this world, so these poets believed in a passing away of the present order of things and the establishment of a more equitable community, a society in which "No one / Shall hunger: Man shall spend equally," a kingdom, in short, wherein "Man shall be man."

"No one shall hunger" ("Feed my flock") . . . "The palpable and obvious love of man for man" ("Love thy neighbor as thyself"). It was, then, ultimately the attempt of the Pylon poets to fulfill *both* of Christ's commands, external and internal, in purely secular terms, that sustains the parallel between them and the early adherents of the Faith. Finally, by an act of fancy, we see Auden cast in the role of St. Paul, exhorting, approving, condemning, casting out, and generally stage-managing the poetic revolution. "You came away from his presence always encouraged," MacNeice declared, recalling him at Oxford. It was certainly not without reason that Auden, in his *New Year Letter*, 1941, accused himself of having employed "the preacher's loose immodest tone"; nor should Isherwood's recollection of Auden's various hats, among which was included "a panama with a black ribbon—representing, I think, Auden's conception of himself as a lunatic clergyman," be entirely discounted as evidence.

Perhaps there is something indicative too in the fact that Auden's parents were devoutly practicing Anglo-Catholics; that Day Lewis's father was a Church of Ireland vicar, and MacNeice's father a Church of Ireland bishop. In their late adolescent rebellion against the family and its values, could they have been driven to seek a father-figure, a savior-figure, a healer-figure elsewhere? "O descend," wrote Auden in his poem "Spain," ironically invoking the life-force, "O descend as a dove or / A furious papa or a mild engineer, but descend." The facetious tone and the irony need not imply the absence of emotional identification here.

In endeavoring to find a twin solution to man's economic and emotional needs, the poets were thinking along advanced contemporary lines. The two sage-figures in terms of which the writers of the thirties understood man's existence were Marx and Freud, two prophets not always reconcilable. Nothing possibly was more significant of the avant-garde's attempt to unify the culture of the times than the convenient synthesis effected by Osborne in his book *Freud and Marx*; and the work of the Pylon poets can be seen as an imaginative attempt to produce an equivalent synthesis. Indeed,

their view of life might lead us to speak of their work in terms of Eros among the economists. As Spender wrote in **"After they have tired"**:

> And our strength is now the strength of our bones
> Clean and equal like the shine from snow
> And the strength of famine and enforced idleness,
> And it is the strength of our love for each other.

* * *

"Son of the Puritan Decadent"

Some slight knowledge of Spender's family background helps to make clear to the reader the direction in which his poetry moved.

Stephen Spender was born in London on February 28, 1909, the son of an ambitious but ineffectual political journalist. He was of partly German descent on his mother's side, and felt always a greater affinity with German than French literature, as, indeed, did Auden and Isherwood.

His high-minded parents brought him up in a too guarded way, trying to screen him from reality. There is a reflection of this in his poem **"The Fates,"** which summarizes the price one pays for an upbringing that excludes the facts and removes the pain from reality. Here, it is the mother-figure who is censured:

> You were that painted mask of motherhood
> For twenty years, while you denied the real
> Was anything but the exceptional.

"Poverty, adultery, disease"—all these unfortunate undeniables were, for this good lady, monstrosities to be blinked away, conditions it was best to close one's eyes to:

> This is the stage where nothing happens that can matter
> Except that we look well-produced and bright.

One of the realities from which the young Spender was protected was the horseplay of poorer children. As a result of this, Spender with his compassionate, masochistic, and complex nature grew up to find a strange appealing glamor in the poor and unemployed.

There was certainly a strong sacrificial strain in his makeup; and he tells us how when young, "lying in bed, there were times when I regretted not having my arms extended on a cross with rusty nails driven through my hands."

In the first poem, about poor children, it is the sacrificial-masochistic urge that is obvious:

> They threw mud
> While I looked the other way, pretending to smile,
> I longed to forgive them, but they never smiled.

while in the second poem, about the unemployed, it is compassion that the poet mainly feels:

> I'm jealous of the weeping hours
> They stare through with such hungry eyes.
> I'm haunted by these images,
> I'm haunted by their emptiness.

The other factors in Spender's life that have a strong bearing on his poetry can be shortly related. After an early love affair in Vienna, he formed an attachment to a young man called Jimmy Younger who later joined the International Brigade, was wounded, deserted, and finally shot. Spender has described this friendship with great honesty in his autobiography. He was twice married: first in 1936 to Inez Holden, an Oxford student and eager Communist; then, in 1941, to the pianist Natasha Litvin (to whom his **Collected Poems,** 1945, were dedicated).

Another relationship important to the poet was that with his sister-in-law Margaret Spender, who died of cancer, after great suffering, on Christmas day 1945. Margaret was his confidante during those months when his first marriage was breaking up, and showed him, as he said, "a courage and hope which seemed the final development of a line through her fearless and happy life which even illness could not break." Spender commemorates her in a series of eight poems, **"Elegy for Margaret,"** written in 1945.

Little else in Spender's life is relative to his poetry. In World War II he served in the Auxiliary Fire Service, about which he has written amusingly in *World within World.* His experience of enforced communal life does not appear to have triggered the lyrical impulse associated with the idea of fraternity in his earlier poems. The London blitz, however, was responsible for one vivid apocalyptic poem, **"Epilogue to a Human Drama"** ("When pavements were blown up, exposing nerves, / And the gas mains burned blue and gold").

For the rest, the chief landmarks of his existence have a professional rather than a poetic importance. For a while he helped Cyril Connolly edit the magazine *Horizon,* an important wartime meeting-ground for writers of all generations. After the war era he became editor of the more intellectualist journal *Encounter*; in 1965 he was appointed Consultant in Poetry to the Library of Congress at Washington.

"The Most Personal Poet"

Of the four Pylon poets Spender's output in verse is the smallest. His **Collected Poems** (1954) contains fewer pages than those of the other members of the movement, and since that date he has also published little work in verse. What is important about his poetry is its sensibility, the quality of which we shall examine. A further distinction must also be made, in that the perception and feeling-tone of the poems is often in advance of their artistic success. Spender is an uneven poet, and many of his interesting poems, which hold us by reason of their sensitiveness or evident sincerity, fail to achieve full harmony of style or total unity of effect. One may, in fact, say that whereas Auden is the "idea man" of the group, Day Lewis its most instinctive artist, and MacNeice its brilliant verbal *tour-de-force* writer, Spender is the most *personal* poet. Auden's poems are fables and parables, Day Lewis's songs and *objets d'art,* MacNeice's are subtle analyses, and Spender's largely private confessions. Philip O'Connor has put this very well when he remarks that "critics, who now make a mystique of impersonality, have given up hope of the other, have sometimes affected amusement at his 'emotionality' (which requires actually a grinding impersonality to achieve in poetry). But this is precisely his courage and integrity." He also explains what lies behind the poet's unevenness and the curious "unprofessional" live interest of his verse—its "human document" hold upon the reader—when he suggests for Spender's obituary: "He never rested in peace." "His anxiety," writes O'Connor, "was original, and he has never overcome it."

Of Spender's chief work in verse and prose, in addition to those already spoken of, mention must be made of **Nine Entertainments** (1928) published when he was only nineteen; **Twenty Poems** (1930); **Poems** (1933), which marked his first clear statement of political commitment; and **The Still Centre** (1939), published when he was still "preoccupied with various kinds of political activity" and "written directly and fairly quickly from the experiences which suggested them." Cyril Connolly has remarked how the poems in this volume on the Spanish Civil War are "far removed from his Communist enthusiasm of 1933"; and Spender himself has commented that the book contains a section of poems where "I have deliberately turned back to a kind of writing which is more personal, and . . . have included within my subjects weakness and fantasy and illusion." For many critics and readers **The Still Centre** is Spender's key volume. **Ruins and Visions** (1942) ended, remarks O'Connor, the poet's "flirtation with social reality, and reflected the 'blues' theme of our day, now also cracking up. Personal relations are asked to do the impossible: to stand in for a society that has failed the poet." Other books of verse include **Poems of Dedication** (1947) and **The Edge of Being** (1949).

His best criticism, as Kenneth Allott remarks, is contained in *The Destructive Element* (1935). The thesis of this book, rather over-simplified in MacNeice's words, is that Henry James, "like Proust [and other writers] was a herald of the Revolution; not being born at the right moment, all such writers could do was to immerse in the destructive element [James's phrase for the soul-destroying existence of a corrupt society]. But now the right moment had come." *The Destructive Element* was a subtle prolegomena to the pro-communistic *Forward from Liberalism* (1937). This acceptance of "Marxism as a working creed" was formally repudiated by Spender in *Life and the Poet* (1942), in which he declares that

> the ultimate aim of politics is not politics, but the activities which can be practised within the political framework of the state. Therefore an effective statement of these activities—such as science, art, religion—is in itself a declaration of ultimate aims around which political means will crystallize . . . A society with no values outside politics is a machine carrying its human cargo, with no purpose in its institutions reflecting their cares, eternal aspirations, loneliness, need for love.

This is Spender's fundamental declaration of a personalist position from which he has not substantially diverged. Other works of criticism are his monographs *Shelly* (1960) and *Poetry since 1939* (1946), *The Creative Element* (1953), and *The Making of a Poem* (1955).

"ONLY CONNECT . . ."

All that is most positive in Spender's poetry would seem to spring from gestures of imaginative and emotional charity; and it is, of course, this aspect of his work that most engages the Christian critical mind. Against Spender's disposition of mind and his poems, which may be viewed as his "good works" (both being interpretable in a pan-Christian fashion), must be placed his rejection of belief and his repudiation of the church as an enemy of light and the forces of the new. Thus, in his poem **"Landscape near an Aerodrome,"** the passengers in the arriving plane hear "the tolling bell" and see where, below them, "Religion stands, the church blocking the sun." Spender, intellectually, has proclaimed himself a sceptic, but defined his scepticism in an open and flexible way: "By scepticism," he told O'Connor, "I . . . mean scepticism about all dogmatic views. Atheism seems to me just as dogmatic as belief, and much narrower. Scepticism is quite consistent with respecting beliefs." Spender's scepticism, indeed, is of the sort that registers the emotional and imaginative impact of faith without that of its intellectual content. It is this which causes him to confess that he is "frightened by visions of belief, because with my kind of scepticism, any lot of believers may be right; I do not know anything to prove they are not right. For all I know, Hell is exactly as Dante described it . . . and Hell is something I certainly give a lot of thought to." Spender's position with regard to faith is therefore not an anti- but a non-relational one.

St. Paul, speaking of faith, hope, and charity, would seem to equate the workings of the first two with prophecy, preaching, and doctrine: "but whether *there*

be prophecies, they shall fail; whether *there be* tongues, they shall cease; whether *there be* knowledge, it shall vanish away." Against the inadequacy of these two gifts ("now we see through a glass darkly"), St. Paul posits the perennial nature of the third: "Charity never faileth," being the greatest of these three. It is along some such line of thought that Spender may be reckoned a pan-Christian poet.

The critic Middleton Murry once described the First World War as a "defeat of the imagination"—a failure, namely, to identify ourselves with the conditions of others, since this would have made war unthinkable. E. M. Forster, likewise, has emphasized the same need for identification in his epigraph to *Howard's End*: "Only connect." It is the distinction of Spender as a poet that he almost invariably makes this connection of identification, particularly with those who, remote, alien, or even hostile, stand most in need of it. One sees this power of his to "connect" with others in poem after poem, in present terms, with the pupils in an elementary school classroom in a slum (where the future for these children is "painted with a fog / A narrow street sealed in with a lead sky, / For far from rivers, capes, and stars of words"); or in historical terms, with the exploited children of the nineteenth century, engaged in chimney-sweeping, factory labor, and work in mines ("You are the birds of a songless age / . . . You whisper among wheels / Calling to your stripped and sacred mothers / With straps tied round their waists / For dragging trucks along a line"). One finds it in certain poems on the English Civil War when he imagines how a mist, like "common suffering"

> Whitens the air with breath and makes both one
> As though these enemies slept in each other's arms.

It is easy to see how Spender could never have been a successful Communist Party poet. A Party man must *hate* the other side; whereas Spender's tendency is, always, to seek to understand and forgive. And when he does speak of hatred, it is seldom of a collective kind geared to a standard ideology, but something at once both personal and universal. Thus, in the same poem, when he describes two armies confronting each other, dug deep in the winter plain, he observes how

> All have become so nervous and so cold
> That each man hates the cause and distant words
> That brought him here, more terrible than bullets.
> Once a boy hummed a popular marching song;
> The voice was choked, the lifted hand fell
> Shot through the wrist by those of his own side.

One can imagine how such truths must have endeared the poet to the literary commissars of the Left. Other poems of his expressing pity are **"The Prisoners," "The Drowned," "The Coward"**—all dealing with those types whom fate has cast as underdogs.

And when the subject of the poem is nearer to the poet himself, the charity increases. Such a poem is **"Song,"** which treats of the break-up of his marriage and speaks of himself, his wife, and her lover. In it the charity is magnificently sustained because each party in the situation is granted a measure of justice. This is one of the great love poems of all time. Beside it, the wit and irony of Catullus and Donne are those of conceited playboys with the clever understanding of cock-sparrow. The charity in this poem is complex in the extreme. It cannot be equated with Christian forgiveness; it is rather a vision of justice, at an elemental psychological level—a justification of those facts and forces that give to each his identity.

One of the great exercises in charity found in Spender's verse is discoverable in his poem-sequence **"Elegy for Margaret,"** the composition that combines a description of his sister-in-law's inch-by-inch dying with a sensitive commemoration of her spirit. Here Spender seems to demonstrate that an act of the imagination, in such a context as this, is almost synonymous with an act of charity. Here, to observe is to self-identify:

> You are so quiet: your hand on the sheet seems a
>   mouse
> Yet when we turn away, the flails
> That pound and beat you down with ceaseless pulse
> Shake like steam hammers through the house.

G. S. Fraser has noted Spender's sympathy with those who manifest "self-pity rather than stoicism, weakness rather than strength, failure rather than success." It should be remarked, however, that Spender's own self-pity is balanced always by a powerful self-knowledge which permits him no deception. In the splendid poem that speaks of the aftermath of his broken marriage, he ends with a statement of self-analysis tantamount to self-condemnation:

> At first you did not love enough
> And afterwards you loved too much
> And you lacked the confidence to choose
> And you have only yourself to blame.
>
> ("The Double Shame")

Spender's attitude of "humility about one's own weakness and charity for the weakness of others" sets him apart from his colleagues. When he writes that "An 'I' can never be a great man / . . . / The great 'I' is an unfortunate intruder / Quarrelling with 'I tiring' and 'I sleeping' / And all those other I's who long for 'We dying'," he is, by implication, criticizing the sin of pride and presenting the human image scaled down to a sense of mortal limitation. Spender appears to see man in terms of Original Sin—Original Sin operating without God.

In the poet's scheme of things, love takes the place of deity, though he is careful to allot it no omnipotent power. As has been said, part of Spender's originality lay in his thinking of *eros* as *agape*. He envisaged libidinal self-fulfilment in terms of the love-feast of brothers, camaraderie and intimacy between all men, and a personal care and concern for their condition.

It was during his early years in Germany that he developed these notions. This personal liberation of his repressions took place within a landscape of political revolution.

> Christopher [Isherwood] and I, leading our life in which we used Germany as a kind of cure for our personal problems, became even more aware that the care-free personal lives of our friends were facades in the front of the immense social chaos. There was more and more a feeling that this life would be swept away. When we were on holiday at Insel Ruegen, where the naked bathers in their hundreds lay stretched on the beach under the drugging sun, sometimes we heard orders rapped out, and even shots, from the forest whose edges skirted the shore, where the Storm Troopers were training like executioners waiting to martyr the naked and self-disarmed.

The political timing of these activities synchronized, then, with the timing of Spender's own private emancipation; and just as he reacted against the extreme erotic license of the German libertarians to work out his own idea of love, so he reacted against the antihumanitarian Nazism to develop his own notion of a personalist socialism.

Sometimes Spender writes, in a personal poem, of the therapeutic value of *eros*:

> My healing fills the night
> And hangs its flags in worlds I cannot near.
> Our movements range through miles, and when we
>   kiss
> The moment widens to enclose the years.

At other times, it is not love received but love projected that offers the solution. Thus, in his poem on a deserted spot in the Spanish War, he concludes with these sentiments:

> Nothing can count but love, to pour
> Out its useless comfort here.
> To populate his loneliness
> And to bring his ghost release
> Love and pity dare not cease
> For a lifetime, at the least.

Speaking of Whitman, in one of his excellent Introductions to *Poets of the English Language*, Auden characterizes three distinctive attitudes to the body: the pagan, the puritan, and the liberal-idealistic. This third point of view regards the body as a nuisance, an irrelevance, something that impedes the "real" activities of life which take place in the mind or the spirit. Spender's experience in Germany, and the poetry he made out of it, rectify this transcendental imbalance. Both in his poetry of love and in his socialist poetry, he stresses the *relevance* of the body—something that gives the "real" activities of mind and spirit a proper context. Spender, of course, had himself been brought up in a family atmosphere where the body was regarded, at the best, as troublesome; at the worst, as unclean. The figure of the son in his poem **"The Fates"** conveys this censorship of the *superego*:

> And yet he had his moments of uneasiness
> When, in the dazzling garden of his family,
> With green sunlight reflected on your dress,
> His body suddenly seemed an obscenity,
> A changeling smuggled to the wrong address.

It is, of course, the mother—with her rejection of the physical—who makes the son uneasy (note, too, how the mother's personality is presented in terms of "sunlight" and "dress," i.e. unearthly and inanimate elements, while the son's is presented in terms of "His body" as if, seen through her eyes, he was nothing but the carnal part of his make-up).

The distance between the imprisonment of the body in the first poem and its liberation, both personally and collectively, in the composition "O young men oh young comrades" is enormous. A whole internal revolution in the poet's nature has taken place, something that required as catalytic agents German nudism, hitchhiking, and free love. Against the inheritance of money and property, the poet tells the young men to

> Count rather those fabulous possessions
> which begin with your body and your fiery soul:
> the hairs on your head the muscles extending
> in ranges with lakes across your limbs.
> Count your eyes as jewels and your valued sex
> then count the sun and the innumerable coined light
> sparkling in waves and spangling under trees.

In the last three lines of the above passage, we see Spender reintegrating man with nature (viewed as his proper habitation) as distinct from the urban landscape of an acquisitive society:

> it is too late now to stay in those houses
> your fathers built where they built you to breed
> money on money.

Instead, the young men are exhorted to "step beautifully from the solid wall / advance to rebuild and sleep with friend on hill / advance to rebel." Here, in what might be called a radical democracy of touch, the erotic and the political are closely associated.

In this poem, as elsewhere, Spender envisages socialism in clearly physical terms. There is much of Whitman's fraternalism in it; but in Spender's case the brotherly feelings imply a "brotherly politic" while Whitman's moments of brotherly nearness are isolated within a politic of cutthroat competitive individualism. The American poet's social optimism seems to us now a lapse of intelligence.

Everywhere, in speaking of love and socialism, Spender seeks to present an organic image—a physical objective correlative, which shall express the actual or potential concrete living of the situation. Thus, we have metaphors from botany or animal biology to represent the nascent life of revolutionary sensibility. The "comrades" who have "tired of the brilliance of cities," "the failure of banks," and "the failure of cathedrals" (urban inanimate imagery) are exhorted not to lack "the springlike resources of the tiger / Or of plants which strike out new roots to urgent waters."

Spender's large avoidance of the abstract, with which Marxist thought is overloaded, gave to his poetry an immediate appeal all too rare in Communist poets. He leaves a clear visual impression when he speaks about one particular moment in history—the interbellum peace in 1929 before Hitler's coming to power—

> A whim of time, the general arbiter,
> Proclaims the love, instead of death, of friends.
> Under the doomed sky and athletic sun
> Three stand naked: the new bronzed German,
> The communist clerk, and myself, being English.

This stands in interesting contrast to the Marxist poet John Cornford's "Full Moon at Tierz: Before the Storming of Huesca":

> The past, a glacier, gripped the mountain wall,
> And time was inches, dark was all.
> But here it scales the end of the range,
> The dialectic's point of change,
> Crashes in light and minutes to its fall.

Without the title to inform us, we should not know what Cornford referred to. There is no setting of the scene; and whereas, with Spender's passage, the abstract noun "time" is soon given "local habitation and a name," here it is integrated in a web of other abstract terms: time, inches, dialectic, minutes. It is, of course, the word "dialectic" that obfuscates the whole passage. In the same poem, Cornford tells us that "with my Party, I stand quite alone"; and his statement explains the failure of his language. He has used Party-speech, the connotations of which have no common usage. Unless we are read in historical materialism, the term "dialectic" here is all but meaningless. It is Spender's distinction that, surrendering for a while, in part, to a philosophy alien to his nature, he preserved his own speech. Unless a poet's tongue is his own, he is little better than a hack.

The final remark remains to be made about Spender's revolutionary verse, namely, the sense of limitation that the poet speaks about at work in the Utopias and their millennial program:

What I had not foreseen
Was the gradual day
Weakening the will
Leaking the brightness away,
The lack of good to touch,
The fading of body and soul
—Smoke before wind.
Corrupt, unsubstantial.

One could have no finer summing up of man's natural bias to defection, as implied by Original Sin, than this.

"A SENSITIVE AGNOSTIC"

If Spender's poetry lacks wit, it is certainly, like Falstaff, the cause of wit in others. Sometimes, as in the description of him as "the Rupert Brooke of the depression," it is little more than a malicious half-truth (though Cyril Connolly's statement that "Spender's early poetry was characterized by an inspired innocence" should not be forgotten here). Francis Scarfe's phrase for him—"the Wilfred Owen of the Peace"—certainly comes much nearer the mark, though Scarfe himself felt it was not adequate to represent Spender's attitude, finding in the poet "far more than a negation" and "the clamorous pitiful protest of Owen." (Again, however, one should remember that for Spender, as for the War poet, clearly "the poetry is in the pity.")

Little has been written on the nature and quality of his language, though Francis Scarfe in *Auden and After* and G. S. Fraser in *Vision and Rhetoric* both have excellent essays on him. MacNeice once described him as a poet patiently pressing clichés into poetic shape with steady and powerful hands. This is not the destructive epigram it seems. Spender is too prone to poeticisms, to frilly and tinselly speech, or to its converse, flat, awkward diction. Sometimes this is evidently due to the boring necessity of the subject (a matter of the poet's expending his powers "on the flat ephemeral pamphlet" or some such political homily). Scarfe, indeed, notices how "the lyrical passages in Spender's propagandist poems occur largely as reactions against what he is preaching," while Fraser remarks that "The typical quality of his style, arising from [a] paradoxical combination of a desire 'to let himself go' and a fear 'of letting himself go' is a stumbling eloquence or a sweeping gesture suddenly arrested."

Verbally and temperamentally, poets may obviously be divided into soft-and hard-center types. Spender is distinctly a soft-center poet just as Auden is a hard. These epithets do not imply value-judgments: they merely suggest the operation of two distinct modes of sensibility. In this context it seems appropriate to comment on Thom Gunn's notorious attack on Spender in his *Lines to a Book,* since it assumes soft-center sensibility to be intrinsically valueless and also distorts Spender's text. "I think," writes Gunn,

of all the toughs through history
And thank heaven they lived continually.
I praise the overdogs from Alexander
To those who would not play with Stephen Spender.

The reference, of course, is to Spender's poem which begins **"My parents kept me from children who were rough,"** implying that it was the poet who was *not allowed* to play with rough children and not the children who *would not* play with the poet. Gunn's poem, by the way, is as nice a compendium of nasty virtues as one could easily come by—a version of Nietzsche as a leather-jacket boy.

Only one critic, so far as I know, considers Spender the superior of Auden. The latter's (sometimes showy) brilliance with words and ideas is so disarming that we forget that poetry is something besides an intellectual conjuring act plus a verbal *tour de force*. That something is, of course, the property on which Spender's backers must stake their claim.

Scarfe describes the poet's basic theme when he writes that "Spender has his own drama: a struggle to adapt his individualism to his social views, and a struggle to understand and perfect his individuality." O'Connor sees Spender as suffering from the personification of a social ailment, "more so than Auden making him, in my opinion, a more important poet—more representative, more articulately sensitive."

This last opinion brings once more into focus the sacrificial scapegoat element in Spender, so that when G. S. Fraser describes the poet as "as sensitive agnostic, whose soul indeed might be described as naturally religious or even *naturaliter Christiana*," we readily assent.

Selected Bibliography

GENERAL

WORKS

Oxford Poetry, with Introduction by W. H. Auden, Oxford, Blackwell 1927.

Poems by W. H. Auden, London, Faber 1930.

The Dog Beneath the Skin by W. H. Auden and Christopher Isherwood, London, Faber 1935 (verse drama).

The Ascent of F6 by W. H. Auden and Christopher Isherwood, London, Faber 1936 (verse drama).

On the Frontier by W. H. Auden and Christopher Isherwood, London, Faber 1938 (verse drama).

Journey to a War by W. H. Auden and Christopher Isherwood, London, Faber 1939 (a prose and verse travelogue).

Letters from Iceland by W. H. Auden and L. MacNeice, London, Faber 1936 (a prose and verse travelogue).

New Year Letter by W. H. Auden, London, Faber 1941.

CRITICISM

Auden and After by Francis Scarfe, London, Routledge 1942.

The Modern Writer and His Work by G. S. Fraser, London, Penguin 1964.

Vision and Rhetoric by G. S. Fraser, London, Faber 1959.

A Vision of Reality by Frederick Grubb, London, Chatto & Windus 1965.

Auden by Richard Hogart, London, Chatto & Windus 1951.

STEPHEN SPENDER

WORKS

Collected Poems, London, Faber 1954.

Twenty Poems, privately printed 1930.

Poems, London, Faber 1933.

Vienna, London, Faber 1934 (verse drama).

Forward from Liberalism, London, Gollancz 1935 (prose).

Trial of a Judge, London, Faber 1938 (verse drama).

The Still Centre, London, Faber 1939.

Ruins and Visions, London, Faber 1942.

Poems of Dedication, London, Faber 1942.

The Edge of Being, London, Faber 1949.

World within a World, London, Hamilton 1951 (autobiography).

The Creative Element, London, Hamilton 1953 (criticism).

The Making of a Poem, London, Hamilton 1955 (criticism).

CRITICISM

The first three critical titles listed in the "General" section all have essays or passages on Spender.

H. B. Kulkarni (essay date 1970)

SOURCE: Kulkarni, H. B. "Centre and Circumference: Spender's Poetic Themes and Techniques." In *Stephen Spender: Poet in Crisis,* pp. 73-110. Bombay, India: Blackie & Son Ltd, 1970.

[*In the following excerpt, Kulkarni explores Spender's treatment of nature and of love—both homosexual and heterosexual—in his poetry.*]

> The iron arc of the avoiding journey
> Curves back upon my weakness at the end;
> Whether the faint light spark against my face
> Or in the dark my sight hide from my sight,
> Centre and circumference are both my weakness.
>
> Stephen Spender

1. NATURE

In spite of his urban upbringing, nature was one of Spender's earliest passions. During his childhood he was taken away on occasions from the city on visits to the countryside where he lived in close contact with nature. This intimate companionship with nature was for Spender a memorable experience:

> My childhood was the nature I remember: the thickness of the grass in the pasture fields, amongst whose roots were to be found heartsease . . . , speedwell of a blue as intense as a bead of sky. There were scabious and cornflower and waving grasses and bracken which came as high as my shoulders.[1]

The family had moved to Sherringham in Norfolk, and close to where they lived, there were fields, beyond them the woods, and far on the horizon was range upon range of mountains "sculptured on the sky out of clouds." For young Spender familiar with the sights and sounds of the city, nature provided a thrilling experience. He played with the flowers, sang with the winds, and dreamt with the distant hills and clouds. But when he was forced to remain indoors during school hours, he felt "as though a wall had been raised between me and nature to which I belonged."[2] All the while he would be thinking of nature from which he had been temporarily segregated. He says: "I had a sensation of the garden, which I could just see through a window, twisted through with bird song as with forking flame, and of the limbs of trees running like veins through the sky, which poured down on earth in an enormous cataract a blue light."[3] After his class he used to run into the garden "where there was a pond, and lying on the ground beside it, stare down into that strange life" in the water:

> The life of the pond was like a theatre whose surface was the front of the stage; and peering down upon this stage I saw naked dramas, glutinous loves, voracious murders, incredibly fertile births, taking place in the utter stillness of unnatural light.[4]

It is no wonder that Spender had nursed an ambition to be "a naturalist, an old man with a long white beard, like a photograph I had seen of Charles Darwin."[5]

With this childhood passion for nature is associated Spender's first experience of poetry. He tells us how he experienced the pleasures of poetry when he was spending one summer vacation with his parents at Skelgill Farm, near Derwentwater:

This countryside is fused in my mind with my first sustained experience of poetry. For here my father used to read to me the simple ballad poems of Wordsworth. . . . the words of these poems dropped into my mind like cool pebbles, so shining and so pure, and they brought with them the atmosphere of rain and sunsets, and a sense of the sacred cloaked vocation of the poet.[6]

When Spender's mind awoke to the beauty of nature and the joy of poetry, a war was going on in Europe. The child's world of fancy and dream was rudely disturbed by the knowledge of the war which reached him in bits from various quarters. Sometimes as if out of nowhere, a zeppelin, "an enormous, cleanly-shaped monster," would suddenly burst in a clear blue sky before his startled eyes. Sometimes he would hear his mother cry out in anguish: "This is the most terrible war that has ever been." Members of the family as well as the servants would be constantly talking of pre-war days, "as poets sing of a Golden Age." To this ceaseless impact of war was added the interminable illness of his mother. It was, indeed, against "a background of calamity" that Spender grew up. The crisis of the times seems to have been an unchanging background of his life, and its awareness, to have split up his entire consciousness. To knit it up into a unity has been a major problem in Spender's life. His whole life appears to have been a struggle to balance opposing forces like nature and war, town and country, beauty and ugliness, ideals and reality, hope and despair, and so on. But the struggle makes his poetry a startling and intense experience.

One of his early poems, **"The Cries of Evening,"**[7] reveals the tension between opposites. The cries of evening—"sheep bleating, swaying gull's cry, the rook's 'caw,' the hammering surf"—remind the poet that he is "town-bred" and therefore a stranger—restless in a world which possesses "the constancy of natural rest." He loves nature, but nature does not seem to care for him:

> Sheep's love, gull's peace—I feel my chattering
> Uncared by these.

Nature's indifference stands contrasted with the poet's intense feeling. His passion seems to break through in every stanza of the poem in a succession of strong images suggesting the poet's restless state of mind. Worlds like 'pull,' 'grip,' 'tear,' and 'pluck' are used to describe the effect of the evening cries upon the poet. The animal imagery in which the night is described impresses the reader with its strength: "The paw of dark creeps up the turf;" "the dog Night bites sharp." The total impression of imagery in this poem is that of power and passion. Yet the restful images seem to be equally striking. References are made to the easy movements of the beasts, the peace of the gull and love of the sheep. As one reads the poem one gets a sensation of peace in the midst of restlessness and violence.

In another poem[8] Spender presents the luxuriance of midsummer drowning the houses "in fever of dust and roses" and the longings it produces:

> Would I might be that bough to night
> Will dip in dews! And, wrung
> From my impregnated phosphorescence,
> Honeyed song of my tongue.

But this is almost an impossible dream for one who is a prisoner "within our distraught gale of time":

> I am tied on strips of time,
>   Caged in minutes, made
> By men, exiled from the day's brilliance
>   In a deliberate shade.

Sometimes a moment may slip "between the bars of the raging machines" and "gleam with eternal rumours." But man cannot get hold of such moments, for

> Man is that prison where his will
>   Has shut without pity
> In a clock eternity,
> In his fist, rose of infinity.

Spender frequently uses contrast as a medium of his symbolic vision. In a bombed city stands an almond tree in bloom. The poet imagines it to be an angel bringing new life in the midst of death and destruction:

> This flesh-petalled tree
> Angel of Fra Angelico
> With folded hands, bended knee
> And arc of eloquent wing . . .
> To our world of ash will bring
> Annunciation of Spring.[9]

The poem is short and simple, yet vivid and powerful. Its beauty does not lie merely in the contrast between the world of ash and the blooming almond tree but in the power of description with which he combines the solidity of sculpture and the delicacy of painting. James Southworth, in his essay on Spender, says that

> The strength of a poet lies in his imagination, in his ability to fix indelibly in the mind of the reader by the apt choice of epithet the picture not only of the exterior of the person being described, but also of the inmost recesses of his character and soul. He not only reveals the object, but everything around it. Mr. Spender, with a freshness and vividness of characterization not unlike those of Lawrence, is able to combine the seemingly incongruous to form unforgettable images.[10]

The description of the angel of Fra Angelico is not only vivid and vigorous but communicates effectively the delicate emotion of hope and prayer and the angelic quality of life to arise out of the world of ash.

"Easter Monday"[11] deals with the same theme but works out the symbolism in greater detail. Yet it relies mainly on description without recourse to myth or fable other than the one suggested in the title. The poem begins by describing the splendour of summer bursting through a burnt-out city:

> *The corroded charred*
> *Stems of iron town trees shoot jets*
> *Of burning leaf.*

In this virtually deserted city, the poet comes upon green meadows where girls are playing in their first summer dresses. Children are seen gathering "pap-smelling cowslips." But there are workers too in every place:

> *But look, rough hands*
> *From trams, 'buses, bicycles, and of tramps*
> *Like one hand red with labour, grasp*
> *The furred and future bloom*
> *Of their falling, falling world.*

Contrast is the principal method of construction in this poem. The charred places, the broken columns stand contrasted with the summer green, the girls in summer clothes and the children gathering flowers; the red colour of flame that burns is also the burning colour of leaves, and red also are the hands of workers that labour and create; is it not also the banner of Communist Revolution? Thus by means of a combination of destructive and creative imagery the poet produces an impression of resurrection through revolution. This is Spender's usual technique of symbolism.

His method, however, is better illustrated in his poem **"Seascape."**[12] Spender himself explains the symbolism in this poem while commenting upon the making of his own poetry:[13] "The idea of this poem," he says, "is a vision of the sea. The faith of the poet is that if this vision is clearly stated, it will be significant." It is a bright summer day, and the ocean lies "like an unfingered harp." "The shore, heaped up with roses, horses, spires" is reflected in the sea. "The land, reflected in the sea, appears to enter into the sea, as though it lies under it, like Atlantis. The wires of the harp are like a seen music fusing seascape and landscape."[14]

This brief indication of what the poem contains should enable the reader to grasp its underlying symbolism. The following passage quoted at some length is an important part of what may be described as a manifesto of method. It throws light not only on the meaning of the poem we have been considering but also on Spender's creative process in general:

> Looking at the vision in another way, it obviously has symbolic value. The sea represents death and eternity, the land represents the brief life of the summer and of one human generation which passes into the sea of eternity. But let me here say at once that although the poet may be conscious of this aspect of his vision, it is exactly what he wants to avoid stating, or even being too concerned with. His job is to recreate his vision,

and let it speak its moral for itself. The poet must distinguish clearly in his own mind between that which most definitely must be said and that which must not be said. The unsaid inner meaning is revealed in the music and the tonality of the poem, and the poet is conscious of it in his knowledge that a certain tone of voice, a certain rhythm, are necessary.[15]

Explicit statement of meaning in poetry may not be a great virtue, but mere tone and rhythm would be found to be inadequate to convey symbolic significance in a poem. The metaphor of the angel and the reference to annunciation are necessary to make the symbol of the almond tree in a bombed city definite and clear. Without a reference to Easter in the title of the poem and the description of workers as carrying the furred and future bloom of their falling, falling world and a reference to their *red* hands of labour, the symbolic meaning of the poem is likely to be lost. Similarly the reference to ships, treasures, cities and legendary heroes engulfed by the sea takes the poem beyond visual experience, and lines like "these, deep as anchors, the silent wave *buries*" (italics mine) make the poem something more than mere description—an effective symbol. But a poem cannot offer more than general hints and yet remain a good poem. While discussing Spender's **"Seascape"** and his comments upon it, Cecil Day Lewis points to what he describes as a "law of imagery": "The images of a good poem are oriented to its general truth."[16]

> Mr. Spender's *Seascape* is an example of this. Its images, when you examine them, are seen to be all pointing one way: the shore, reflected, 'wanders in water'; a sigh of air draws inland noises out over the sea, where 'the gilded wave buries' them; . . . All these word pictures—and here perhaps we have hit upon a law of imagery—are only something more than word-pictures, *only become* images in relation to a general truth.[17]

In spite of this pointed direction of imagery, the reader may, as Day Lewis says, miss the meaning which Spender assigns to it. But it is enough that the poet creates a feeling in the reader that the poem means something more than its surface significance. The reader may not find exactly what the poet had intended. But a poem which is ambiguous may have rich possibilities of multiple interpretation. If for Spender **"Seascape"** stands for death or eternity, for another reader it might symbolize unity of the universe, unity of space and time, suggested by the reflection of the land in the sea and the burial of the dead past mirrored along with the visible present. But whatever the method by which Spender creates his symbols, it is evident even from the poems we have so far discussed that his descriptions are concrete and his symbols rooted in closely observed phenomena of life and nature. Moreover, the exploitation of nature for symbolic purpose introduces an element of freshness and colour which in the drab world of ours strikes the reader as romantic.

But nature in Spender is not merely a poetic device; it is an entity in itself. Nature makes life significant and love, rich and meaningful:

> We climbed together. Any feeling was
> Formed with the hills. It was like trees' unheard
> And monumental sign of country peace.

But when the lover returns alone to his room, he realizes the emptiness of life:

> Oh empty walls, book-carcases, blank chairs
> All splintered in my head and cried for you.[18]

It is because of nature that every awaking is forever new, though it is ever the same:

> So I remember each new morning
> From childhood, when pebbles amaze
>
> . . . . .
>
> The whole sky opens to an O,
> The cobweb dries, the petals spread . . .[19]

The sight of hills is peaceful to the mind, and "soft on the flesh the green scene reposes."[20] The poet's pen and paper would carry the weight of all the beauty of nature, but he finds that experience of nature is inexpressible in words:

> Had I pen and ink and paper
> I think that they could carry
> The weight of all these roses,
> These rocks and massive trees.
>
> . . . . .
>
> But that the singing of those birds
>
> . . . . .
>
> Tears through the listening writing of the eye.[21]

In this warring world of ours man seems to have lost even the knowledge of what nature can do to him. Spender thinks that nature has the power to heal, but we are caught up in the cruelties of the world to such an extent that we have refused to avail ourselves of the beneficial powers of nature: A soldier is going in a train to the war; he watches the green fields vanish swiftly from view, and the disappearing vision strikes him as unreal as a painted picture:

> Like the quick spool of a film
> I watched hasten away the simple green
>   which can heal
> All sadness . . .
> Real were iron lines, and smashing the grass
> The cars in which we ride, and real our compelled
>   time.
> Painted on enamel beneath the moving glass
> Unreal were cows, the wave-winged storks, the
>   lime; . . .[22]

Thus we are forced away from the companionship of nature to be cast into the realities of human cruelty and war. Perhaps the greatest evil of slums in cities is that the children in slums are shut away from the open air and freshness of nature. Spender protests against the misery of slum-children in his poem **"An Elementary School Classroom in a Slum"**:[23]

> All of their time and space are foggy slum.
> So blot their maps with slums as big as doom.
> Unless . . .
> This map becomes their window and these windows
> That shut upon their lives like catacombs,
> Break O break open till they break the town
> And show the children to green fields, and
>   make their world
> Run azure on gold sands . . .

But it is not only the children of the slums who have been deprived of the healing contact with nature. It is indeed a universal calamity. In **"June 1940,"**[24] watching the early summer preparing its green feasts in the garden, Spender remembers the war across the channel:

> In the German caterpillar-wheeled dreams,
> Imagined into steel, volley
> Through the spring songs and the green hedges,
> Crushing the lark's nest, with a roar of smoke
> Through the weak barriers of France.

Man has destroyed nature and thereby has turned this world into a veritable hell:

> Man's world is not nature, but Hell
> Where he struggles to make nightmare whole.

Therefore it appears that

> False is this feast which the summer, all one garden
> Spreads before the senses. Our minds must harden.

The idea that the beauty of nature is oftentimes a false appearance covering a horrible reality is recurrent in Spender:

> Poor child, you wear your summer dress
> And your scarf striped with gold
> As the earth wears a variegated cover
> Of coloured flowers
> Covering chaos and destruction over
> Where deaths are told.[25]

In **"Winter and Summer"**[26] Spender develops a similar idea:

> Within my head, aches the perpetual winter
> Of this violent time, where pleasures freeze.

And so when there is summer in the fields he thinks that

> . . . the luxurious lazy meadows
> Are a deceiving canvass covering
> . . . the furious volleys of charioteering power
> Behind the sun, racing to destroy.

But when he looks back on his childhood he finds that this contrast of appearance and reality was exactly in reverse, and winter with its "falsified snow" was only an accident and summer was real and eternal:

> . . . if my shadowed mind affirmed the light
> It would return to those green, foolish years
> When to live seemed to stand knee-deep in flowers
> There, winter was an indoor accident . . .

It is thus obvious that the difference between appearance and reality in nature is only a reflection of the poet's moods and the conditions in the world of man.

In quantity nature does not seem to be a dominant theme of Spender's poetry. But nature is never far from Spender's consciousness, and whatever the subject-matter, it seems to peep through as simile, metaphor or symbol with a pleasing suddenness and surprise. Whatever the quantitative measure of its importance, there seems to be no doubt that Spender's concept of nature provides an important clue to our understanding of his view of man and the world. Spender was not affected by the popular view of nature in the post-Darwinian era as "red in tooth and claw" and forever engaged in a deadly struggle for existence. Spender's picture of nature comes closer to the vision of the romantic poets. Spender does not exhibit any mystic longing of a Wordsworth for the "visionary gleam," but he was driven to the worship of nature, like Wordsworth, by the "inhumanity of man to man." "The still, sad music of humanity" is never out of Spender's mind; it does not even seem to be ever out of his sight. The landscape, as Spender paints it, is almost always a picture with the ravages of man's inhumanity presented in close proximity to nature's beauty and charm: A blooming almond tree stands in the centre of a bombed city; jets of burning summer leaves shoot up and resurrect a charred and broken city; dawn "cracks through mud-flats of despair"; the moon looks down upon a battlefield, and

> Upon this plain she makes a shining bone
> Cut by the shadows of many thousand bones.[27]

A soldier falls to the ground

> From his living comrade split
> By dividers of the bullet
> Opening wide the distances
> Of his final loneliness.
> All under the olive trees.

In this poem entitled **"A Stopwatch and an Ordnance Map"**[28] describing the death of a soldier, Spender repeats the last line "All under the olive trees" in every stanza and underlines it. Even the image of the moon and moon's timelessness is fixed in the centre of this story of the soldier's death. When Spender thinks of German-caterpillars, he does not think of them as destroying human lives but as crushing larks' nests, which perhaps creates a sense of extreme tenderness. When soldiers are put under the earth, grass and flowers grow above their graves:

> The grass will grow its summer beard and beams
> Of sunlight melt the iron slumber
> Where soldiers lie locked in their final dreams.[29]

As in the Ariel song, the dead really suffer a change and send flowers above the ground to reach the very stars. Flying above the landscape in an airplane the poet sees "feminine land indulging its easy limbs in miles of softness" but soon comes upon what he describes as "outposts of work":

> . . . chimneys like lank black fingers
> Or figures, frightening and mad: and squat buildings
> . . . like women's faces
> Shattered by grief. Here where few houses
> Moan . . . like a dog
> Shut out, and shivering at the foreign moon.[30]

Thus it is clear that nature is an important element which supplies Spender with a measure of beauty, humanity and eternity with which he evaluates the world about him and which sharpens our awareness of the ugliness and misery in the world of man. Spender does not use nature as a means of escape into the comfort and quietness of isolation, and therefore we do not find him singing of nature in lyrical rapture. Whenever he sees or thinks of nature, he invariably remembers what man has made of man and his world. Therefore, the impression made by his poems of nature is one of tension sometimes relieved by symbols of spring and summer signifying the poet's hope for mankind:

> We built
> Upon their earth the wave of a new world
> From flowers: each morning . . .
> . . . the police, afraid of daisies
> Trampled the flowers.[31]

When Spender started writing, poetry had for the most part left the country paths and had been wandering, perhaps in the company of Prufrock, the city-streets that

> . . . follow like a tedious argument
> Of insidious intent.

Spender did not take poetry back to nature but brought to the cities charred with war and violence a nostalgia for "natural piety." Here, in Spender, we do not have the romantic indulgence in soft sentimentalities of the Georgian poets for moonlight and flowers, nor do we have the feeling of exhaustion and sterility of *The Waste Land*. Spender's observation is sharp and clear, his imagery fresh and forceful. There is an air of youthful hope and strength which blends urban cruelties with the irrepressible charm of nature.

2. LOVE

(1) URNINGISM

If we understand love in its widest sense as an "emotional element in social relations," it appears in a variety of forms in the poems of Spender. Critics have discovered urningism in some of them. But one has to be extremely cautious in using psychological labels, for sometimes they tend to obliterate distinctions between normalcy and perversion in human behaviour. Urningism within bounds of normalcy is respectable friendship. Spender has described in his autobiography at some length his intimacies with Marston and Jimmy, but it would be difficult to describe them in terms like "urningism" or "homosexuality," carrying connotations of perversion and morbidity. Spender himself did not approve of these labels to signify his relation with his friends:

> I leave it to the reader to apply the psychiatric labels to the various relationships which I have to describe. Yet I have come to wonder whether many contemporaries in labelling themselves do not also condemn themselves to a kind of doom of being that which they consider themselves in the psychological text-book.[32]

Spender believes that "a relationship of the highest understanding can be between two people of the same sex," and it need not always be condemned as homosexuality. Spender's friendship with Marston was motivated by a desire to enrich his personality by going beyond the scope of his personal self. He asked Jimmy to come and live with him; for, as he says, he was feeling lonely and was not ready for marriage. They set up house together, but in the meantime Spender fell in love with Elizabeth. Indeed, he found it difficult to discard Jimmy for Elizabeth. But the conflict of choice between Jimmy and Elizabeth was really a moral conflict, for Spender was not able to overcome his feeling of responsibility for Jimmy not only because Jimmy had come to depend upon him for everything but also because Jimmy had become for Spender the symbol of the poor and unemployed through whom he was indeed expiating the bourgeois sin of exploitation. Spender found in Jimmy a valuable link between the crisis within and the crisis in the world. To label this relationship as homosexual is not merely to misunderstand Spender's personality but also to miss important aspects in human relations.

The poems which deal with Spender's emotional involvements with persons of his own sex are few, and were chiefly written in the early part of his career. They have variety as well as an intensity which we usually associate with the romantic passion of love, but they do not exhibit any trace of morbidity or perversion. James Southworth, while commenting on Spender's interest in urningism, says: "Mr. Spender makes no apologia for

that state. He accepts it; one might almost say he accepts it as the norm. Certainly there is no trace of morbidity in his presentation."[33]

One aspect of the so-called "homosexual" poems is the great admiration the poet feels for his lover. The admiration includes even the physical features:

> *Your light hair, your smile*
> *I watch burn in a land*
> *Bright in the cave of night.*
>   . . . . .
> *Like the summer dew*
> *Glaze me from head to toe.*[34]

In another poem, he compares his friend to constant April:

> *. . . when you laughed, your laughter*
> *Was like the bright cascade.*
> *The sun sheds on a cloud,*
>   . . . . .
> *And if you frowned, your frowning*
> *Was knit as these*
> *Slight showers.*[35]

The poet's admiration sometimes verges on adoration:

> *I vow he was born of light*
>   . . . . .
> *So, born of nature, amongst humans divine,*
> *He copied, and was, our sun.*
> *His mood was thunder*
> *For anger . . .*[36]

Here is another poem in a similar vein:

> *Your body is stars whose million glitter here:*
> *I am lost amongst the branches of the sky.*[37]

But, like love, even friendship has its ups and downs, joys and sorrows, unions and separations. Some of the better poems deal with the theme of separation and loss:

> *His figure passes, and I confess*
> *No suddenness of pain.*
> *. . . All happiness rolled away—again revealed*
> *That sore and flaming wheel I must live by.*[38]

Friendship filled Spender's life with meaning. When his friend is gone, life seems to dwindle into emptiness:

> *Oh empty walls, book-carcases, blank chairs*
> *All splintered in my head and cried for you.*[39]

But the poet cherishes the memory of this rich, though brief, experience of warm friendship:

> *For me this memory which now I behold,*
> *When, from the pasturage, azure rounds me in rings,*
> *And the lark ascends, and his voice still rings,*
>   *still rings.*[40]

These poems associated by critics with homosexuality have their origin in the attempts of the poet at friendship with Marston, his college mate. The relation had a lasting influence on Spender's personality and poetry. He realized for the first time in his life his heart's potentiality for love:

> . . . if these were tricklings through a dam,
> I must have love enough to run a factory on,
> Or give a city power, or drive a train.[41]

Spender came to think of his friendship with Marston as "one phase of a search for the identification of my own aims with those of another man. For different as we were, there was a kind of innocence and integrity in him which was also in my poetry."[42]

Spender's friendship with Marston affected his poetry as deeply as it did his personality. He found a subject to which he could relate his feelings and give them a sense of depth and reality which is difficult to achieve in a purely fictitious situation. Moreover, Spender felt that it was wrong to invent situations which did not reflect his true feelings merely to serve the purpose of poetry:

> My poems were all attempts to record, as truthfully as I could, experiences which, within reality, seemed to be poetry. Whenever the poetry, for the purpose of ending satisfactorily a poem, seemed to require something which was not true to my own experience, I abandoned it.[43]

Spender tells us that after his experience of friendship with Marston, he began to write poems which were "different from any others I had done." He explains that "a concrete situation had suddenly crystallized feelings which until then had been diffused and focussed no object."[44]

Spender was right in thinking so, for the "Marston" poems do strike the reader by their quality of firmness and vigour. The reality of his friendship seemed to have provided something like a bony structure which has given these poems a kind of muscular shape and strength. "He will watch the hawk with an indifferent eye" is an example of this comely compactness:

> This aristocrat, superb of all instinct,
>   With death close linked
> Had paced the enormous cloud, almost had won
>   War on the sun;
> Till now, like Icarus mid-ocean-drowned,
>   Hands, wings, are found.[45]

This poem is brief yet achieves concreteness by its appropriate imagery. Most of these so-called homosexual poems may be read simply for the pleasure of their fresh and precise imagery. **"To T. A. R. H."** is a fine example in this kind.[46] "The quick laugh of the wasp-gold eyes," "the glint of the quick lids," "the wiry cop-per hair," "the notched mothlike lips" and such other phrases give an etched sharpness to the portrait of his lover. Vivid and surprisingly pleasing are similes like:

> . . . the small vivid longings
> Gnaw the flesh, like minnows.

But the final impression of these poems is the sense of failure which the poet felt about his striving to achieve union with another person: "Never being, but always at the edge of Being" reads like a philosophic conclusion to this experiment:

> I move lips for tasting, I move hands for touching,
> But never come nearer than touching
> Though spirit lean outward for seeing.
> Observing rose, gold, eyes, an admired landscape,
> My senses record the act of wishing,
> Wishing to be
> Rose, gold, landscape or another.
> I claim fulfilment in the fact of loving.[47]

These poems which are associated with the theme of homosexuality should really be considered as a part of Spender's spiritual quest for "Being," an attempt at "wholeness" of personality. They are his first poetic expressions of his striving to move outward from the centre of his self toward the circumference of objective reality. Spender's experiment in friendship is like a concentric circle he has drawn about himself. If his experiment failed, it gave him a depth and width of personality which in turn enriched his poetry. Louis Untermeyer says of the "Marston" verses that they "sound a depth untouched by any of the younger generation."[48]

(II) ORPHEUS TO EURYDICE

But Spender's poems of love strike a deeper note and provide a richer variety than the ones we considered under the heading, "urningism." In several of these poems the influence of D. H. Lawrence is evident. As James Southworth puts it,

> I think it is true that no young poet of today, whether he admits it or not, is wholly free from the influence of D. H. Lawrence. Certainly he has been an important factor in Mr. Spender's poetry. From the point of view of subject matter he has encouraged him through example to a courageous frankness of statement and an incisive clarity of observation.[49]

In his poem, **"Oh young men, oh young comrades,"**[50] Spender "admonishes the younger generation properly to evaluate their physical attributes." "Passing, men are sorry for birds in cages"[51] speaks of another kind of bird—"the pleasant bird, physical dalliance." Spender advocates the necessity of releasing this bird from its long confinement:

> Yes! And if you still bar your pretty bird, remember
> Revenge and despair make their home in your bowels.

Physical dalliance, the poet feels, is the way to happiness. The error of centuries has forbidden pleasures of the senses and

> . . . quite banned like grass,
> Where the fields are covered with suburban houses.

It is, perhaps, this "suburban" culture which is responsible for the false sense of morality contemptuous of sense-pleasures as evil. **"I think continually of those who were truly great"**[52] states with emphasis that physical desire is a precious thing:

> What is precious, is never to forget
> The essential delight of the blood drawn from ageless
> springs
> Breaking through rocks in worlds before our earth
> Never to deny its pleasure in the morning simple light
> Nor its grave evening demand for love.
> Never to allow gradually the traffic to smother
> With noise and fog, the flowering of the spirit.

Spender implies that the pleasures of the senses are the flowers of the spirit. There is almost always an unmistakable suggestion of the metaphysical in most of his descriptions of physical experiences. In this connection we may examine **"O Night O Trembling Night,"**[53] a poem which is starkly physical and highly passionate in its description of the sexual union:

> O night when my body was a rod o night
> When my mouth was a vague animal cry
> Pasturing on her flesh o night
> When the close darkness was a nest
> Made of her hair and filled with my eyes . . .

The animal imagery suggests intensity of the sex passion as boldly as it describes the sensuality of the act, while the figure of the nest in the last two lines above is made to convey the sense of union—the nest is feathered by "her" hair and is filled by "his" eyes. But with the break of day comes the knowledge of love like the sensational headlines of a newspaper. Day covers her body but uncovers her love: "Her naked love, my great good news."

"Day Break"[54] suggests the union of the physical and the spiritual in still clearer terms: The poet is watching his beloved at dawn lying "with her profile at that angle," and suddenly

> From her dew of lips, the drop of one word
> Fell . . . when she murmured
> "Darling",—upon my heart the song of the first bird.
> "My dream glides in my dream," she said, "come
> true.
> I waken from you to my dream of you."
> O, then my waking dream dared to assume
> The audacity of her sleep. Our dreams
> Flowed into each other's arms, like streams.

Thus love fulfils itself in the physical union, but the union does not remain physical.

> Our bodies, stripped of clothes that seem,
> And our souls, stripped of beauty's mesh,
> Meet our true selves, their charms outwitted.[55]

It is also a meeting of the angel and the devil in the lovers:

> Our angel with our devil meets
> In the atrocious night, nor do they part
> But each forgives and greets,
> And their mutual terrors heal
> Within our love's deep miracle.[56]

When opposites clash in the miracle of lovers' meeting evil is cancelled and good is enhanced. The lovers by sharing fully each other's life become united. Physical union is of minor consideration in the achievement of true union; in fact, physical union is no union at all. However close the lovers may get physically, they may still remain divided:

> And when we meet—the ribs will still
> Divide the flesh-enfolding dream.[57]

The lovers have to strip themselves of time and space like clothes from their bodies:

> When tomorrow divides us, we shall fill
> That space with this peace as now the space
> Which, when we are closest, divides us still.[58]

The poet believes that he can eliminate the barriers of space and time and achieve complete union with his beloved:

> 'Distances between us will be crystal
> Traversed with illuminating rays
> Where our eyes fuse the rainbow of their gaze.
> 'Gazing into that crystal, behold the possible
> Nakedness nakeder than nakedness
> Where stripped of time and place as of dress,
> We meet again, being invisible.'[59]

In spite of a world that may separate them they can become united:

> Your mind and mine became one vase
> Where gaze flowed into gaze
> Under the surfaces
> Of our curved embraces.
> Our eyes see with each other's eyes
> Though half a world between us lies.[60]

Although the union has been described in physical imagery

> —Our lips melt into our lips
> . . . . .
> On my tongue your tongue
> Rustles with your song my song—

it obviously transcends the physical:

> *These distances which separate*
> *Drove our lives through that gate*
> *Beyond which our impossible*
> *Presences became invisible*
> *Our meeting indivisible.*[61]

There are numerous poems that deal with the complex nature of lover's union. In a poem addressed to his wife, Natasha, Spender describes her love for him:[62]

> *Your fingers of music*
> *Pressing down a rebellion of mistakes*
> *Raise here our devout tower of mutual prayer.*

He realizes that their love has removed the boulders of the past and brought peace and serenity into their present. In another poem,[63] Spender describes how love brings into birth a future of hope and joy:

> *Locked*
> *Within the lens of their embrace*
> *They watched the life their lives had wrought*
> *The folded future active street*
> *With walls of flesh complete,*
> *Between their clinging bodies rocked.*

In fact, the light and joy of the whole world seems to flow through their love:

> *World of summer which lies*
> *Buried in loved and lover*
>   . . . . .
> *Through their four eyes, light*
> *Of world and world streams.*[64]

It is not merely the ecstasy of union that the poet sings about, but he realizes that love is a great power in the universal scheme of things. It is a divine blessing:

> *. . . to love means to bless*
> *Everything and everyone.*[65]

The power of love is so great that it goes beyond the sphere of human life and affects even moons and tides:

> *Through man's love and woman's love*
> *Moons and tides move.*[66]

Its influence on human beings is so complete that they experience a rebirth of their life and personality:

> *Mixing in naked passion*
> *Those who naked new life fashion*[67]
> *Are themselves reborn in naked grace.*

Compared to love, books and the knowledge they contain seem to be dusty and futile. That is the reason why the great scholar Faust chose the living warmth of a woman's love in preference to a whole library of books filled with cobwebs:

> *Freed from these cobwebs, dust and phials of knowl-*
> *edge*

> *Would I might in her hell of heaven flit.*
> *To wake on peaks at dawn among the inhuman*
> *Rose-towering dreams—*
> *Reborn in the blonde landscape of a woman*
> *And dying in the river of her eyes.*[68]

Spender feels the same way; his greatest wish is to have love, to accept it, to accept it entirely including the undesirable things that may go with it:

> *Oh to be taken by it, and to hold*
> *My ear against its ever-female heart,*
> *And to accept its fleas and all its sins,*
> *To explore all its gifts*
> *And nothing, nothing to refuse.*[69]

Other interests and considerations are driven out, and the poet's mind is filled with the light of love:

> *. . . I shut the other*
> *Stars out from my sky.*
> *All but one star, my sun,*
> *My womanly companion,*
> *Revolving round me with light.*[70]

Of course, the woman he loves is not perfect; but as he begins to think of the defects his beloved may have, they seem to vanish altogether, and "I see only the pure you in your eyes."

> *Arrows of light pierce through the mist,*
> *Lapis Lazuli has pressed*
> *Its burning way through smothering cloud*
> *To show upon the world your face which seems*
> *A miracle among macabre dreams,*
> *Like a madonna painted on a shroud.*[71]

Love stands as the image of the good, the beautiful and the holy. It is a creative principle functioning in a world filled with hatred and evil. Spender places a quotation from Apollinaire at the head of one of his finest love poems:[72]

> *Que mon amour a la semblance*
> *Du beau Phénix, s'il meurt un soir*
> *Le Matin voit sa Renaissance.*

Later he develops this very theme of love as a phoenix emerging brightly out of the flames of a war-scorched city as a reborn city:

> *Then the sun scrawled*
> *Across the white sheet of the day*
> *Twisted iron black realities*
> *Broken boulevards through which humanity's*
> *Sprawling river Styx*
> *Of corroding shadows crawled.*
>
> *O but our love was the Phoenix*
>
> *Above the destroyed city reborn city*
> *conjoining spires of flame*
> *Tower of wings climbing spear-shaken skies*

Within the ensphered luminous air of eyes
Image by our faith sustained the same.

This faith in the power of love burns like a flame at the centre of Spender's poetry. It has the idealism of youth, but not the softness of a dreamer seeking his escape from the sphere of reality. Love for him is not a dreamy sentiment but a strong faith struggling in a hostile world of stern realities:

The final act of love
Is not of dear and dear
Blue-bird-shell eye pink-sea-shell ear
Dove twining voice with dove.

O no, it is the world-storm fruit,
Sperm of tangling distress,
Mouth roaring in the wilderness,
Fingernail tearing at dry root[73]

Spender's faith in love was built not only on the pleasures he enjoyed but also on the loss he suffered through separation, betrayal, and death. Loss of the loved one strengthened his belief in the power of love, for it had come to him not merely as the consummation of physical longing, but mainly as a state of holy blessedness. In his **"Epithalamion,"**[74] Spender reveals how tenderly he feels for lovers and how anxious he is for the perpetuation of their love:

Within this dragon-haunted era,
Let these two their faith perfect
To dome within their meeting mind
One clear sky of the intellect
Which no ill fate can make unkind.

O flesh and spirit of charity,
Hammer that ring from their fused minute
Moulten where they are, part to part,
Whose circle appears absolute
And of the pure gold of their heart.

He looks for love everywhere in the world and pays his deepest homage to it whenever and wherever he finds it. Travelling in a train where the eyes of other passengers would be

. . . searching for hope on the horizon,
The beam of a lost dawn,
Or browsing on the furnace fires of doom,

Spender would be longing to enter the life behind the drawn blinds of houses at the edge of railway lines,

A sun behind the clouds
Of slums, suburbs and farms
Where love fills rooms, as gold
Pours into a valid mould.[75]

With love Spender feels secure; without it he feels life empty and meaningless. In **"The Room on the Square,"**[76] the poet describes how his security of love was destroyed by war as peace in Europe was destroyed by it:

The light in the window seemed perpetual,

but now the light is fallen, the room is dark, for

. . . you are hidden
In sunbright peninsulas of the sword:
Torn like leaves through Europe is the peace
Which through me flowed.

"Lost"[77] is also a sad story of how his life filled with the most precious and gracious love has ended.

That is the room where the world was most precious
. . . . .
Here lamp and wooden furniture are gracious.
All other times and places seem atrocious.

The loss of love has been ascribed by Spender to many causes; one of them is the faithlessness of woman:

Lightly, lightly from my sleep
She stole, our vows of dew to break,
Upon a day of melting rain
Another love to take.

The poet thinks that she was justified in doing so, for she had to satisfy "the compulsive needs of sense" by pursuing "the plausible happiness of a new experience." Thoughts of murder and suicide justifiably cross his mind. But he sensibly decides on the harmless alternative of escaping into the loneliness of himself and writing

. . . round my high paper walls
Anything and everything
Which I know and do not know[78]

But it does not seem to help. Separation was an act of will, but the heart was out of it, for

How can the heart decide
To banish this loved face forever?

There is no consolation for a heart that cannot forget, nor cease to love,

When under sleep, under the day,
Under the world, under the bones,
The unturning changeless heart,
Burning in suns and snows of protestations
And breaks, with vows and declarations?[79]

Painful, indeed, is the memory of his beloved who has gone. Every place and object in the house has associations that remind him acutely of her tenderness and love:

Solid and usual objects are ghosts
The furniture carries cargoes of memory,
The staircase has corners which remember.

The poet pulls down the blind, lies on the bed and takes up a book to read, thinking that he might forget the pain. But the printed letters in the book turn into eyes and accuse him of "the double way of shame":

> *At first you did not love enough*
> *And afterwards you loved too much*
> *And you lacked the confidence to choose*
> *And you have yourself to blame.*[80]

Perhaps the loss is as painful to her as it is to him:

> *For how can he believe*
> *Her loss less than his?*
> *"True it is that she did leave*
> *Me for another's kiss;*
> *Yet our lives did so entwine*
> *That the blank space of my heart*
> *Torn from hers apart,*
> *Tore hers too from mine."*[81]

He dreams of his darling as standing "in a piteous attitude"

> *. . . waiting in sweet grace*
> *For him to follow . . .*

and considers himself to be Orpheus and her, Eurydice. He feels he should rise and undertake a journey to the underworld and bring her beloved back. But he soon realizes that such a journey would be futile:

> *If, with nerves strung to a harp,*
> *He searched among the spirits there,*
> *Looking and singing for his wife*
> *To follow him back into life*
> *Out of this dull leaden place,*
> *He would never find there*
> *Her cold, starry, wondering face.*
> *For he is no Orpheus,*
> *She no Eurydice.*
> *She has truly packed and gone*
> *To live with someone*
> *Else, in pleasures of the sun,*
> *Far from his kingdoms of despair.*[82]

Perhaps the beloved does not deserve to be called Eurydice, but the lover seems to possess qualities worthy of comparison with Orpheus. He possesses not merely the despair of Orpheus but the strength of his faith in love which prompts him to journey to the underworld and snatch his beloved from the clutches of death. In this case the lover seems to believe in the conquest of death by love, but his partner has betrayed him and has left for the pleasures of the sun, reluctant to return to her Orpheus.

But Spender does not cry merely over the spilt happiness in his personal life. He is aware that

> *Each is involved in the tears and blood of all.*

Spender's personal experiences of love and loss, union and separation, betrayal and death must have tremendously enlarged his sympathies. **"The Vase of Tears"**[83] explains how the poet's heart has become a vase in which the bitter tears of the world for its daughter's grief are collected:

> *Let me dry your eyes with these kisses.*
> *I pour what comfort of ordinariness*
> *I can; faint light upon your night alone.*
> . . . . .
> *Something in me gentle and delicate*
> *Sees through those eyes an ocean of green water*
> *And one by one the bitter drops collects*
> *Into my heart, a glass vase which reflects*
> *The world's grief weeping in its daughter.*

The wreck of love which Spender experienced in his personal life was witnessed by him on a larger scale in the world around him. This helped him to outgrow his mood of self-pity which dominates some of his love poems and to direct his feelings towards outside tragedies. When he does so, he brings to an impersonal situation the intensity of personal emotion and loads it with implications of universal significance. In his poem, **"Weep, Girl, Weep,"**[84] Spender addresses a girl who has lost her lover in war:

> *Weep, girl, weep, for you have cause to weep.*
> *His face is uprooted from your sleep,*
> *His eyes torn from your eyes, dream from your dream.*

But the sorrow of the girl is the tragedy of the world demanding tears from all:

> *The wet tears on your face gleam*
> *Down spires of the cathedral,*
> *And in the crowded squares your lament*
> *Makes a great angel whose instrument*
> *Is strung on the heart behind the face of all.*

By means of images like the cathedral and the angel, Spender achieves enlargement and sublimation of his theme. The method of contrast is often used for the same purpose. **"Two Kisses"**[85] creates a setting of sharp contrasts; the quay where the river suggests

> *The dirt off all the streets*
> *And the rotting feet of factories*

is set against the beauty of swans and boats, the far shore and day-green spaces. The kiss is related to this contrasting background and is compared to the proud launching of a boat among swans and lights:

> *And then the heart in its white sailing pride*
> *Launches among the swans and the stretched lights*
> *Laid on the water, as on your cheek*
> *The other kiss . . .*

The contrasts worked out in this poem carry the theme beyond the limits of subjective experience and give it a wider implication—the purity and beauty of love in a dirty world. Such a contrast is apparent in the imagery of most of Spender's love-poems. Some of the notable images that stick to our memory may here be repeated: "a miracle among macabre dreams," "Madonna painted on a shroud," "the Phoenix above the destroyed city," and so on. These images enlarge love's scope and significance and help us to understand its value in relation to the world in which the poet is destined to love and lose.

Perhaps the strongest influence that shaped Spender's concept of love was the disease and death of Margaret, his sister-in-law. The group of poems called **"Elegy for Margaret"**[86] was composed at various intervals during a period of six years. The sorrow that lingered for such a long time must have been a terribly shattering experience for Spender. At least the poems which were prompted by it are marked by a great concentration of imagery and emotion and a maturity and strength in suffering:

Margaret is bedridden. A deadly disease has been pasturing on her flesh, twisting her

> . . . on that rack of pain
> Where the skeleton cuts through you like a knife.[87]

Spender has been watching her, looking into her sunken eyes. Outwardly both pretend to be gay, but

> Under our lips, our minds
> Become one with the weeping
> Of the mortality
> Which through sleep is unsleeping.[88]

Death seems to be certain; this is the "granite fact" around her bed,

> Poverty-stricken hopeless ugliness
> Of the fact that you will soon be dead.[89]

Death stares through her gaze, and with her beautiful summer dress and shoes striped with gold she looks like the earth which

> . . . wears a variegated cover
> Of grass and flowers
> Covering caverns of destruction over
> Where hollow deaths are told.[90]

In the corner of her bed, Margaret looks like a ghost.

> A whispering scratching existing almost lost
> To our blatant life. . . .[91]

Her "hand on the sheet seems a mouse." Spender tries to reconcile himself to this fact with a philosophic observation that weeping would be futile and vain:

> Of what use is my weeping?
> It does not carry a surgeon's knife
> To cut the wrongly multiplying cells
> At the root of your life.[92]

Spender thinks it would be difficult to cut off the memory of her death from his life, for he would dream of her every day not as dead and gone but as restored to her prime of youth:

> Since, darling, there is never a night
> But the restored prime of your youth
> With all its flags does not float
> Upon my sleep like a boat,
> With the glance which will live
> Inescapably as truth.[93]

Even while she is dying, she brings together "all the love we knew" and reveals it in the smile of her "living, dying eyes." She looks like

> . . . a tree choked by ivy, rotted
> By kidney-shaped fungus on the bark,[94]

with a spray of leaves on a topmost branch

> As though the dying tree could launch
> The drained life of the sap
> Into the shoot of one last glance
> Above the lapping shining discs of evergreen.[95]

Thus Margaret's dying brings forth the best and the brightest elements in her life so that her death would be a restoration of her youth and beauty. She will wear her death "not like destruction, but like a white dress."

To accept death may be to accept the worst, but it is also to accept truth. So he wears her death next his heart, where others wear their love. For it is indeed his love, his link with life. He tells his brother that by losing we learn "with singleness to love."

> Better in death to know
> The happiness we lose
> Than die in life in meaningless
> Misery of those
> Who lie beside chosen
> Companions they never chose.[96]

Orpheus learned the value of love in the loss of love, and it became the inspiration of his creativity:

> Then of his poems, the uttermost
> Laurel sprang from his side.[97]

So the death of Margaret was a terrible lesson of nature that life's gains are often acquired through its losses. Moreover, the poet did not think that the dying woman he loved was a unique example. In the violence of our time each dying sailor holds in his fading darkening irises "the vision of some lost still living girl." In the eyes of Spender the picture of dying Margaret and other girls lost to their lovers becomes the image of

> The possible attainable happy peace
> Of Europe, with its pastures fertile,
> Dying, like a girl, of a doomed, hidden disease.[98]

Thus the personal tragedy in the life of Spender becomes the symbol of a tragedy that was being enacted in European civilization.

It is now clear that the love poems of Spender are personal and passionate, but they do not remain locked up in a world of private sensation. The most important quality of these poems is the poet's effort of imagination to enlarge the centre of personal love with its joys and sorrows to a circle which is coextensive with civilization itself. The extension of sympathy in Spender is achieved not by means of drama or fable but by a lyrical exposition of the theme. It consists of direct emotional statement, as we observed in poems like **"Weep, Girl, Weep"** and **"Elegy for Margaret."** A particular disposition of imagery connects the subjective experience with an objective situation and extends its meaning without losing the intensity and intimacy of personal emotion. The methods of similarity and contrast are both utilized for this purpose. As we have already noted, love may be described as "Madonna painted on a shroud" or a dying girl may bring up a vision of the peace of Europe destroyed by a deadly disease.

So we may conclude that Spender's love poems, like the poems on nature and friendship, stretch the centre of self to a wide circle of sympathy with the objective world, in an attempt to achieve identity with it. . . .

Notes

1. Spender, *World Within World* (London, 1951), p. 323.

2. *Ibid.*, p. 324.

3. *Ibid.*, pp. 324-325.

4. *Ibid.*, p. 325.

5. *Ibid.*

6. *Ibid.*, p. 87.

7. Spender, *Collected Poems* (New York, 1955), p. 197.

8. Spender, "Midsummer," *Poems of Dedication* (London, 1947), pp. 51-52.

9. Spender, "Almond Tree in a Bombed City," *The Edge of Being* (London, 1949), p. 35.

10. James Southworth, "Stephen Spender," *Sewanee Review*, XLV (July, 1937), p. 280.

11. Spender, *The Still Centre* (London, 1939), pp. 19-20.

12. *Poems of Dedication*, pp. 53-54.

13. Spender, *The Making of a Poem* (London, 1955), pp. 50-51.

14. *Ibid.*

15. *Ibid.*

16. Cecil Day Lewis, *The Poetic Image* (London, 1947), p. 139.

17. *Ibid.*

18. Spender, *Poems* (London, 1933), p. 14.

19. Spender, *The Edge of Being*, p. 15.

20. Spender, "In a Garden," *Ruins and Visions* (London, 1942), p. 126.

21. *Ibid.*

22. Spender, *Poems*, p. 16.

23. Spender, *Collected Poems*, p. 65.

24. Spender, *Ruins and Visions*, p. 107.

25. *Ibid.*, p. 115.

26. *Ibid.*, p. 104.

27. "Two Armies," *Collected Poems*, p. 84.

28. "A Stopwatch and an Ordnance Map," *ibid.*, p. 87.

29. "In No Man's Land," *ibid.*, p. 88.

30. "The Landscape Near an Aerodrome," *ibid.*, p. 41.

31. Spender, *Vienna* (New York, 1935), p. 29.

32. *World Within World*, p. 67.

33. James Southworth, *op. cit.*, p. 273.

34. "XXXV," *Poems*, p. 59.

35. "Constant April," *Twenty Poems* (Oxford, 1930), p. 12.

36. *Collected Poems*, p. 200.

37. *Ibid.*, p. 33.

38. "His Figure Passes," *Twenty Poems*.

39. *Collected Poems*, p. 4.

40. *Ibid.*, p. 24.

41. *Ibid.*, p. 7.

42. *World Within World*, p. 67.

43. *Ibid.*, p. 59.

44. *Ibid.*, p. 67.

45. *Collected Poems*, p. 3.

46. *Ibid.*, p. 25.

47. *Ibid.*, p. 13.

48. Louis Untermeyer, "Poetry of Power," *Saturday Review of Literature*, XI (November 10, 1934), pp. 274-75.

49. James Southworth, *op. cit.*, p. 277.

50. *Collected Poems*, p. 31.

51. *Ibid.*, pp. 29-30.

52. *Ibid.*, p. 32.

53. *The Edge of Being*, p. 12.

54. *Ruins and Visions*, p. 82.

55. "The Trance," *Poems of Dedication*, p. 31.

56. *Ibid.*, p. 32.

57. *The Still Centre*, p. 84.

58. *Poems of Dedication*, p. 55.

59. *Ibid.*, pp. 55-56.

60. *Ibid.*, p. 56.

61. *Ibid.*, p. 57.

62. "To Natasha," *Ruins and Visions*, pp. 83-84.

63. *Poems of Dedication*, p. 29.

64. *Ibid.*, p. 28.

65. *Ibid.*, p. 23.

66. "Man and Woman," *ibid.*, p. 30.

67. *Ibid.*

68. "Faust's Song," *The Edge of Being*, p. 16.

69. "Variations on My Life," *Ruins and Visions*, p. 91.

70. "The Human Situation," *The Still Centre*, p. 80.

71. "Absence," *Poems of Dedication*, p. 34.

72. "Meeting," *ibid.*, pp. 55-57.

73. *Poems of Dedication*, p. 22.

74. *The Edge of Being*, p. 48.

75. *The Still Centre*, p. 103.

76. *Ibid.*, p. 40.

77. *Poems of Dedication*, p. 35.

78. "Song," *Ruins and Visions*, pp. 11-12.

79. "A Separation," *ibid.*, p. 13.

80. "The Double Shame," *ibid.*, pp. 15-16.

81. "No Orpheus, No Eurydice," *ibid.*, p. 21.

82. *Ibid.*, p. 22.

83. *Ibid.*, p. 14.

84. *The Edge of Being*, p. 27.

85. *The Still Centre*, p. 86.

86. *Poems of Dedication*, pp. 11-22.

87. *Ibid.*, p. 11.

88. *Ibid.*, p. 18.

89. *Ibid.*, p. 19.

90. *Ibid.*, p. 18.

91. *Ibid.*, p. 20.

92. *Ibid.*, p. 18.

93. *Ibid.*, p. 17.

94. *Ibid.*, p. 16.

95. *Ibid.*

96. *Ibid.*, p. 13.

97. *Ibid.*

98. *Ibid.*, p. 12.

A. K. Weatherhead (essay date autumn 1971)

SOURCE: Weatherhead, A. K. "Stephen Spender: Lyric Impulse and Will." *Contemporary Literature* 12, no. 4 (autumn 1971): 451-65.

[*In the following essay, Weatherhead contends that nearly all of Spender's poetry is informed by the conflict between the will and the senses, or between the call of duty and the desire for spontaneity.*]

Since the 1930s, the poetry of Stephen Spender has been in relative obscurity,[1] partly, no doubt, on account of other poetry which has successfully competed for general attention and partly for certain of its intrinsic qualities. Many of the poems are pure: they do not come to us immediately; they are detached from the everyday things of the world and cannot be approached in the workaday frame of mind in which one comes in from the street to read the headlines and throw away the bulk mail. Their neglect is due also, perhaps, to the quality of uncertainty, which results in embarrassment to the reader when his expectations in a poem are suddenly defeated by a word or phrase which injures the tone that had been established. For often there seem to be two impulses at work, which do not blend but remain awkwardly at odds. It is these conflicting impulses that I wish to consider in this essay.

In the well-known poem **"Not palaces, an era's crown,"** number XXXIII of *Poems* (1933), Spender reveals more clearly than anywhere else a conflict that determines the features of many of his poems. This particular poem has a political message, and the conflict here has a political coloration incidental to one's immediate interests; but it presents in more or less fundamental terms the two poles between the influences of which the poetry is largely composed. The poet instructs the senses—his reader's or his own—to leave their "gardens" and their "singing feasts" and submit themselves to the purposes of the will. The lines have been anthologized often enough, but I quote them here again because they speak so immediately to principles sometimes underlying and sometimes more evident in much of Spender's poetry:

> Drink from here energy and only energy,
> As from the electric charge of a battery,
> To will this Time's change.
> Eye, gazelle, delicate wanderer,
> Drinker of horizon's fluid line;
> Ear that suspends on a chord
> The spirit drinking timelessness;
> Touch, love, all senses;
> Leave your gardens, your singing feasts,
> Your dreams of suns circling before our sun,
> Of heaven after our world.
> Instead, watch images of flashing brass
> That strike the outward sense, the polished will
> Flag of our purpose which the wind engraves.[2]

The conflict is between the will, on the one hand, which is to work in the outside world, and the senses, on the other, that work in their own leisure to spell out the lyrical poetry. If, as I suggest, these lines reveal a principle that works throughout the poetry of Stephen Spender, they remind one also to remark that this talent, one of the purest lyrical talents of the century in English, has never been entirely liberated from the conscience, the call of duty, the structural needs of the poem, and the world itself to issue its own spontaneous utterances.

These then are the poles exerting the influences of which the conflict can be felt in the large parts of a long poem or even the small elements of a line. With the will is associated the outer world and the poet as a person in that world and in its light; also associated with the will is the descriptive poem (or the descriptive elements in a poem), of which there are only a few in Spender, and the structure, the form of the poem. Associated with the other pole is the spontaneous lyric impulse, the nondescriptive or "literal" poem or images that do not primarily reflect the world, the poet's withdrawn self—his self at the "still centre," to use his own term, or what in a political discussion, in defiance of the Marxist theory of the economic control of the intellect, he calls that margin of freedom which no system can deny where there is room always for "pure states of being";[3] and, finally, associated with this pole is what seems to be a species of negative capability that in one important poem the poet designates his weakness. If in Milton or Dante the colossal informing will is the chief agent of the poetry, it is not so in the lyrical poetry of Spender, for whom the will opposes the poetry.

Nowhere are the poet's north and south so clearly manifested as in **"Not palaces."** In a later poem, however, they are in explicit conflict, although the terms of that conflict are abstracted from the sensible outside world. Whereas in **"Not palaces"** the imagery has a tenuous relation to the world of the senses, in **"Dark and Light"** it points to things conceived of rather than seen. The poem as a whole tends to be literal—literal in the sense that the elements do not designate things outside the poem but refer to other elements within. In Spender's own phrase, such a poem will "resist the mere flow of things."[4] It is faithful to its own form, a loose sestina; and one must forbear from making a paraphrase that merely substitutes another meaningless formula for its own. It may be said, however, that it records the poet's incompatible wishes: to live in the still center of his being, the dark, and to preserve this center but also at the same time to live at the circumference, in the world, the light, where will is effective. The first two stanzas play variations upon a limited number of images and references: dark and light, center and circumference, eye, violence, curve, and stone. In the first stanza, the inward self is straining outward toward the light of the external world:

> To break out of the chaos of my darkness
> Into a lucid day is all my will.
> My words like eyes in night, stare to reach
> A centre for their light: and my acts thrown
> To distant places by impatient violence
> Yet lock together to mould a path of stone
> Out of my darkness into a lucid day.

The second stanza negates the first:

> Yet, equally, to avoid that lucid day
> And to preserve my darkness, is all my will.[5]

His words avoid the light; his acts shatter the path. Following thesis and antithesis is a synthesis, discovered in the poet's weakness, more particularly in his fears. But his weakness is now identified, somehow, with will—that which nourishes the center with that which promotes the willed external personality:

> To break out of my darkness towards the centre
> Illumines my own weakness, when I fail;
> The iron arc of the avoiding journey
> Curves back upon my weakness at the end . . .
>
>   . . . . .
>
> Centre and circumference are both my weakness.
>
> O strange identity of my will and weakness!

The poem formally resolves its paradoxes. The resolution resists paraphrase: the poet is perhaps reporting arrival at a condition like that enjoyed by Rilke's angels in which the normal human contradictions are reconciled. But the words, repetitions, rhymes, and dialectic do their duty mainly to the form of the poem as an autonomous entity. In life the conflict is not to be resolved. "Throughout these years," says Spender, referring to the early thirties, "I had always the sense of living on the circumference of a circle at whose centre I could never be."[6] The union of the will and the self in the world with the self of the center is an individuation process fulfilled in the form of the poem only. The poem is not reporting; it is merely fulfilling art's function to assimilate our profound waywardnesses into a unity whose speciousness the reader or the artist himself is momentarily pleased to overlook.

The individuation process suggested here is not the same as the repeated efforts of Spender to relate the self to the outer world, efforts which are recorded throughout his work. He follows Rilke in his belief that it is the poet's job to transform external phenomena so that they symbolize inner experience: "Ideally," he says, "the artist should transform the environment into his own world."[7] And we repeatedly find him using the outside world for inward symbolic purposes, covertly or overtly. Looking, for instance, from a train, a frequent vantage point, he explicitly searches for a reflection of the self: "I look and look to read a sign," he says (*SC* [*The Still Centre*], p. 46). Or, in **"The Human Situation,"** he contracts the world into the glasses of his eyes making it entirely subjective: his

> . . . single pair of eyes
> Contain the universe they see;
> Their mirrored multiplicity
> Is packed into a hollow body
> Where I reflect the many, in my one.

> (*SC,* p. 79)

In this connection it may be observed that the poet is profoundly uncertain about the reality of the outside world. His poetry and his prose repeatedly show that no fact about it is bare and obvious to him, no idea about it is unmuddied by complexity, no sensation is clear, and permanence is an illusion. He longs for the pure static certainty that the world cannot provide: he had expected, he says,

> Some brightness to hold in trust,
> Some final innocence
> To save from dust;
> That, hanging solid,
> Would dangle through all
> Like the created poem
> Or the dazzling crystal.

> (*P* [*Poems*], p. 25)

In *The Still Centre,* the volume in which **"Dark and Light"** appears, there is much more emphasis upon the incompatibility of the will and the inward self than upon such artificial unification as that poem proposes. Spender is concerned in this volume with unity of being, which he calls one of his "obsessive themes."[8] The condition of unity may be achieved by some men after their death; of his poem **"Exiles from Their Land,**

History Their Domicile," he remarks that it is about "those who have, after their deaths, obtained for their lives a symbolic significance which certainly passed unnoticed when they were living." Death in this poem is the divinity that shapes ends and selects purposes and acts that will endow lives with symbolic significance; and again in another poem the poet looks forward to entering "The cloudless posthumous door / Where the slack guts are drawn into taut music" (*SC,* p. 89). But this significance, this unity of being, need not be the product only of death; there is also will. Death has enshrined the exiles as great because it has made them "one with what they willed" (*SC,* p. 24) or "cast / Their wills into those signatory moulds." In **"The Human Situation"** (*SC,* p. 81), the poet describes with resentful admiration figures whose wills are firm: the father, the captain of the school, a certain woman, and heroes of legend or history. When he reveals envy of those with firm wills, Spender reminds us of the young Matthew Arnold, whom he quotes, in a slightly different connection, in *Forward from Liberalism*:

> I too have long'd for trenchant force,
> And will like a dividing spear;
> Have praised the keen, unscrupulous course,
> Which knows no doubt, which feels no fear.[9]

Will is also admired in Spender's poems in nonhuman forms: the Midlands Express, for example, which "with unerring power" drives straight to its goal, ravishing England that lies beneath it like a woman (*SC,* p. 47).

He is thoroughly ambivalent, however; if he is drawn toward the will and the world in which it is operative, he is also attracted away from them. In **"The Uncreating Chaos,"** he thinks of his own will as faltering (*SC,* p. 33); but he recognizes what would be lost if the will took over, or what had been lost in such circumstances. He knows, in **"The Human Situation,"** that it would be impossible for him to enter the symbolic beings of those people whom he envies for their firm wills: it would be "Death to me and my way of perceiving / As much as if I became a stone" (*SC,* p. 82)—the stone being the image he had used in *Trial of a Judge* to express single-minded absorption in public passion, which he may have derived from Yeats' "Easter, 1916" where it has the same symbolic value ("Yeats," says Spender in his autobiography, "was perhaps the writer who best understood that public passion can 'make a stone of the heart'"). It is this that he risks doing in **"Not palaces,"** the poem already looked at, when he exhorts the senses to leave their singing feasts and turn to images of flashing brass, "the polished will / Flag of our purpose. . . ." In the short poem, **"Houses at Edge of Railway Lines,"** on the other hand, Spender contemplates with favor a life whose richness lies in the absence of effective will, which is symbolized by the train which rushes by outside (*SC,* pp. 103-104). And then there is Napoleon, the subject of a long poem (*SC*, pp. 96-100), who is "ruled / By a dead will," burdened by the fixed image of self—that which in other poems of Spender's seems desirable. It is clear that the cultivation of the still center of being calls for the abnegation of will. In **"The Uncreating Chaos,"** the center of being is a lucid condition

> where nothing's pious
> And life no longer willed,
> Nor the human will conscious. . . .
>
>   (*SC*, p. 34)

It is a

> field guarded by stones
> Precious in the stone mountains,
> Where the scytheless wind
> Flushes the warm grasses. . . .

In the same poem, on the other hand, will goes wrong and is characterized by images of the Nazis: ". . . the whip masters, / Breeches and gaiters camouflage blood" (*SC*, p. 33). Though he may be ambivalent, the poet is more strongly attracted to the center and tends to look back from images and examples of will, hankering toward the pure state, the still center, to live in which one would need to discard the fallible exertion of will and its influence:

> Shuttered by dark at the still centre
> Of the world's circular terror,
> O tender birth of life and mirror
> Of lips, where love at last finds peace
> Released from the will's error.
>
>   (*SC*, p. 85)

But the will and the world constantly make their claims, and the poetry manifests the resulting conflict.

The conflict in **"Not palaces"** has a political color: the play of the senses is to be replaced by acts of will in order to effect change. The conflict is overt, as it is again in **"The Pylons,"** where there is a similar theme of social progress. Spender has chosen a subject where the traditional poetic items of the English countryside are contrasted with the symbols of progress, the pylons, the monstrous appearance of which is augmented if that were possible by comparing them and their stance to "nude, giant girls that have no secret" (*P*, p. 47). The poetic things and the inward self associated with them go down once more before the things from the world of the will. So they do again in another early poem, **"At the end of two months' Holiday,"** in which the traditional beauty of the country is pitted to its disadvantage against the iron railway lines. The poet is dreaming that he is looking from a train:

> Like the quick spool of a film
> I watched hasten away the simple green which can heal

> All sadness. Abruptly the sign *Ferry to Wilm*
> And the cottage by the lake, were vivid, but unreal.

The countryside, the scene of the weekend escape of the bourgeoisie (and the scene of the Georgian picnic), is declared unreal; the train, symbolizing progress and the "iron time," is real enough:

> Real were iron lines, and, smashing the grass
> The cars in which we ride, and real our compelled
>   time:
> Painted on enamel beneath the moving glass
> Unreal were cows, the wave-winged storks, the
>   lime. . . .[10]

In **"The Funeral,"** on the other hand, where the old and traditional is opposed to the new communist regime, while the rhetoric gives a victory to the new world and the action in it, the poetic inward self is spontaneously asserted in the imagery; as has been pointed out, the lyrical sound of the last line, "Mourned by scholars who dream of the ghosts of Greek boys," implicitly approving traditional customs, betrays the rhetorical intentions of the poem.[11] The poet's weakness momentarily overwhelms the will.

Many of Spender's poems seem to speak from the center of the self almost in their entirety: in these poems the images derived from the outside world appear to have been refined of their mundane origins and turned into the elements of pure song. As to whether a poem ought to aim at such purity Spender is again ambivalent: he speaks sometimes on behalf of and sometimes against its independence from the world. In one of his contributions to the long debate over the role of poetry in the proletarian revolution, opposing the idea of propaganda in poetry, he says: "the writing of a poem in itself solves the poem's problem. Separate poems are separate and complete and ideal worlds. If a poem is not complete in itself and if its content spills over into our world of confused emotions, then it is a bad poem. . . ."[12] But in his autobiography he recalls an early difference with W. H. Auden, as follows:

> When Auden said at one of our earliest meetings, "The subject of a poem is a peg to hang the poetry on," he had indicated what I gradually realized to be another basic difference between our attitudes. For I could not accept the idea that the poetic experience in reality, which led into a poem, was then, as it were, left behind, while the poem developed according to verbal needs of its own which had no relation to the experience.[13]

Auden, for his part, says much later in a complaint about Shelley's poetry that he "cannot believe . . . that any artist can be good who is not more than a bit of a reporting journalist," and he wants, he says, "plenty of news" in literature. With many a poem of Spender's, on the other hand, one strongly suspects that the shape it has taken has been determined by internal rather than external needs—which is not to say that such needs have no longer any relation to the original experience.

An example of a pure poem is **"I think continually of those who were truly great"** (*P,* pp. 37-38). Geoffrey Grigson reports that Spender did, in fact, while at Oxford think continually of those who were frequently photographed and longed for their acquaintance. But the poem itself has refined away its expression of this sentiment and contains, in fact, very little news at all. The first and third of its three stanzas celebrate the "truly great" in imagery which associates them with fire and, more particularly, with the sun; and they have very little descriptive meaning. The middle stanza consists of three prescriptions; whether they are prescriptions *for* greatness or whether they are simply offered in the light of contemplated greatness is not clear: ". . . never to forget / The essential delight of the blood," never to deny its pleasure, and never to allow the traffic to smother the flowering of the spirit. Stanzas 1 and 3 consist of lyrical passages with literal meanings, relating only to other elements within the poem. It would thus be hard to substantiate the claims for the poem of C. Day Lewis, who attempts to make too much of its flimsy linkages to the outside world and sees it as "a successful attempt to re-establish communication with the past, a minor miracle of healing." It takes, he says, "the form of ancestor worship." But it is not, in fact, nearly as palpable as this suggests.

> . . . those who were truly great
> . . . remembered the soul's history
> Through corridors of light where the hours are suns
> Endless and singing.

They "hoarded from the Spring branches / The desires falling across their bodies like blossoms"; in the "highest fields" their names were "fêted by the waving grass"; finally, "Born of the sun they travelled a short while towards the sun, / And left the vivid air signed with their honour." In its exquisite phrasing, the poem sings mainly to itself, reflecting upon itself in its own structure and delivering only the vaguest kind of intelligence. Surely it is not merely the product of will reacting upon the world outside and describing conditions there as Lewis suggests; it is rather the lyric meditation of the inward self. And the use of the image of the "waving grass" in the high fields, which, as we have seen, is later associated with the still center, is perhaps no coincidence.

There are other poems of this kind, in which the song is unimpeded by the intrusion of the outside world and the sensibility is uncorrupted by the will. One need not, in fact, assume that the poem is an artifact refined from its source in the world, for it may originate not as description but purely in the realm of art. The following passage from one of Spender's essays suggests that, on certain occasions at least, the poem arises as an autonomous thing and certainly not as a medium for communicating description or any news:

Sometimes, when I lie in a state of half-waking and half-sleeping, I am conscious of a stream of words which seem to pass through my mind, without their having a meaning, but they have a sound, a sound of passion, or a sound recalling poetry that I know. Again sometimes when I am writing, the music of the words I am trying to shape takes me far beyond the words, I am aware of a rhythm, a dance, a fury, which is as yet empty of words.[14]

In the same essay we are shown an instance of how a poem arises from experience, where Spender is demonstrating the play of memory. But what emerges most remarkably from the example is how remote the fragment of poetry is from the experience, the reproduction of which has apparently undergone repeated refinement. Here is the fragment:

> . . . Knowledge of a full sun
> That runs up his big sky, above
> The hill, then in those trees and throws
> His smiling on the turf.

Spender says: "That is an incomplete idea of fifteen years ago, and I remember exactly a balcony of a house facing a road, and, on the other side of the road, pine trees, beyond which lay the sea. Every morning the sun sprang up, first of all above the horizon of the sea, then it climbed to the tops of the trees and shone on my window."[15] The poem has come some way from the sharp, sensuous particularity of the perception. All in all Spender manifests a much stronger fidelity to art than to the world of which art is normally representative and from which it takes its raw materials. And perhaps such an emphasis was not untoward at a time when the comrades were enjoining poets to be the trained canaries of the proletarian revolution.

These are some aspects of Spender's generally overwhelming predilection for the kind of purity which lifts the poem from its source in the world as experienced, precluding it from bringing news, shaping it as an artifact in its own world with its own internal needs and satisfactions. Very frequently, however, the exercise of the lyrical part of the self in spontaneous song is sharply halted by one device or another, at the prompting of the opposite part. There is first the injury or destruction of the lyrical pitch by calculated crudity, of which the prosaic "guts" and "skewers" in the following two passages are examples:

> To the hanging despair of eyes in the street, offer
> Your making hands and your guts on skewers of pity.

(*SC,* p. 30)

> All their perceptions in one instant,
> And his true gaze, the sum of present,
> Saw his guts lie beneath the trees.

(*SC,* pp. 59-60)

The crudity lies not in the anatomical location of the thing but in the sharp concrete designation among the insubstantial substantives; the same ridiculous effect that is gained in **"The Funeral"** when "laughter on their lips and winds blowing round them" gives way without warning to "this one excelled all others in making driving belts."

In other poems the lyrical pitch is destroyed by the crude assertion of structure. Structure belongs to the will; and it is imposed upon some poems, distressing the lyrical imagery and producing bathos. In **"Responsibility: The Pilots Who Destroyed Germany, Spring, 1945,"** a later poem, we observe the forced recapitulation of imagery as a means of imposing a curious kind of wooden unity. First, the poet sees the bombers as weaving a cage—a favorite image in Spender, found ubiquitously in his work along with the threads, the strings, and the wires. The whole first stanza is a remarkable example of his characteristic refinement of the news; whatever these scintillating objects are engaged in has been decently removed from any recognizable act of war:

> I stood on a roof-top and they wove their cage,
> Their murmuring, throbbing cage, in the air of blue
>   crystal,
> I saw them gleam above the town like diamond bolts
> Conjoining invisible struts of wire,
> Carrying through the sky their squadrons' cage
> Woven by instincts delicate as a shoal of flashing fish.[16]

Then the planes go, leaving silence and a network, now material and visible, of vapor trails, which melt into "satin ribbons / Falling over heaven's terraces near the sun." The planes, says the poet, had "carried [his] will" and bombed the German city. The imagery is linked up in the last stanza as follows:

> Now I tie the ribbons torn down from those terraces
> Around the most hidden image in my lines,
> And my life, which never paid the price of their
>   wounds,
> Turns thoughts over and over like a propeller,
> Assumes their guilt, honours, repents, prays for them.

One uses ribbons to make a presentation, a gift, perhaps, made to assuage a sense of guilt, or a wreath; and the image is related to the "satin ribbons," the vapor trails, earlier in the poem. And the thoughts turn like the propellers of the planes which went over in the first stanza. But thoughts simply do not turn over like propellers, and the effort to imagine them doing so injures the pitch. At the same time the repetition provides a kind of forced unity, such as Spender imposes upon an appreciable number of his poems, early and late. In controlling the lyrical feeling, however, and keeping down the singing pitch, the simile no doubt performs the function that the will requires of it. And in providing structured unity for the poem the will operates as it

does in Spender's notions of psychology, purveying unity of being while impairing the poetry-making faculty.

Perhaps more remarkable than the sudden onset of crudity and the imposition of a wooden unity is the destructive device of elaborating a metaphor or a simile to the point where it becomes ludicrous. It is a ubiquitous practice: the simile of thoughts turning over like a propeller is one example. Others are:

> . . . threw words like stones . . .
>
> (*P,* p. 23)

> . . . your heart fretted by winds like rocks at Land's
> End . . .
>
> (*SC,* p. 3)

> Vivid longings / Gnaw the flesh, like minnows
> (*CP* [*Collected Poems*], p. 40)

> Hearts wound up with love, like little watch springs.
> (*CP,* p. 71)

> . . . whose cries, like wild birds,
> Settle upon the nearest roofs . . .
>
> (*P,* p. 46)

> . . . fills her linen night-gown
> As the air fills a balloon.
>
> (*SC,* p. 104)

> With songs buried beneath the ground like rotted
>   leaves
> To spring as cucumbers . . .[17]

> Then your happiness bound cords
> Around his treasured glance, like a blue bow.[18]

In all these passages a lyrical pitch is destroyed by an elaboration of the vehicle of the simile. In that elaboration, the figure becomes subject to too close a scrutiny. One might accept that vivid longings gnaw the flesh, but with the addition of "like minnows" the poem suddenly becomes an animated cartoon; nor, similarly, with the addition of "like little watch springs" can one live with the fiction that the heart is wound up; "cries, like wild birds" is a lovely conceit, quite spoiled with the addition; and so forth. The practice does not enrich the poem by adding a complexity to be fused into the poem; what is added is, as it were, a voice from another dimension, striking the poem at an angle, making it absurd. The establishment of lyrical pitch, and then its destruction, results from two impulses, the lyrical and the prosaic. And, maintaining the terms Spender uses in the poem, we may say that these are derived from his dark inner and the light outer selves respectively. Keats, we are told, was forever contriving to maneuver himself out of sensuous enjoyment into misery, and, in many poems, Spender shows an analogous kind of shift. It is as if a stern voice from the pragmatic world called the poet back from his lyrical journey.

At the same time there are other devices by means of which the poetry moves in the opposite direction, evading the structure and organization of the pragmatic world, registering the poet's distrust of its reality, or quite simply embodying his escape from it—a process he registers in the early lines, "The city builds its horror in my brain, / This writing is my only wings away." Imagery, for example, that is descriptive of the world may become insubstantial, a movement in the opposite direction from that which ended with "guts" and "skewers": "voices / Murmured at night from the garden, as if flowering from water" (*P,* p. 55):

> Belsen Theresenstadt Buchenwald where
> Faces were clenched fists of prayer
> Knocking at the bird-song-fretted air.
>
> **(*EB* [*The Edge of Being*], p. 48)**

As well as by imagery that loses contact with the senses, the poet may detach himself from the world of will by means of conceptions so intricate as to be inconceivable. Of a debauchee poet of the last century, for instance, he says

> . . . that sigh, which hovers
> Through spaces between letters, white and far,
> Is on his page the print of what we are.
>
> **(*EB,* p. 50)**

There is much of this kind of thing in Spender, as any cursory glance at his work will reveal. These devices and others move the poem, momentarily at least, away from the outside world and restore it to the center.

An early poem of Spender's begins, "Never being, but always at the edge of Being." The poet proceeds to say that he moves lips for tasting and hands for touching but never comes nearer than touching,

> Though the Spirit lean outward for seeing.
> Observing rose, gold, eyes, an admired landscape,
> My senses record the act of wishing
> Wishing to be
> Rose, gold, landscape or another—
> Claiming fulfilment in the act of loving.[19]

The poem is an early expression of the sense of the split self, which consists of what later comes to be called the still center and the self in the world of the will. The spirit from the center leans outward to contact the other half of the self which it can do no more than touch. It observes the self in the world, the poet's body, as a landscape with which it desires to identify itself and, so the poem implies, is frustrated. But the act of loving (in later versions of the poem, the "fact of loving") establishes some kind of integration and hence "fulfilment." It is significant that Spender made an exception to the chronological order of the poems in his first book so that he might set this poem at the forefront of his published work[20] and that the phrase "edge of Being"[21] should have remained with him to be used twenty years later as the title for a volume of poems. For if being is the personality unified by will, then it is at the edge that the poet wishes to be, where his poetic abilities will not be injured or destroyed. And at the same time he wants to be no nearer than the edge to a world whose reality he thoroughly doubts. Between the two, spirit and world, deriving from the one its lyricism and from the other the ballast of will, the poetry seeks its difficult equilibrium.

Notes

1. Existing criticism includes: G. S. Fraser, "A Poetry of Search (Stephen Spender)," in his *Vision and Rhetoric: Studies in Modern Poetry* (London: Faber, 1959), pp. 202-210; Willis D. Jacobs, "The Moderate Poetical Success of Stephen Spender," *College English,* 17 (1956), 374-378; Howard Nemerov, "A Wild Civility," in his *Poetry and Fiction: Essays* (New Brunswick, N. J.: Rutgers Univ. Press, 1963), pp. 125-128; Morton Seif, "The Impact of T. S. Eliot on Auden and Spender," *South Atlantic Quarterly,* 13 (1954), 61-69; James G. Southworth, "Stephen Spender," *Sewanee Review,* 45 (1937), 272-283.

2. *Poems* (London: Faber, 1933), p. 56; referred to hereafter as *P.*

3. *Life and the Poet* (London: Secker and Warburg, 1942), p. 35.

4. "Inside the Cage," *The Making of a Poem* (London: Hamish Hamilton, 1955), p. 16.

5. *The Still Centre* (London: Faber, 1939), pp. 77-78; referred to hereafter as *SC.*

6. *World within World* (London: Hamish Hamilton, 1951), p. 192.

7. "Inside the Cage," *The Making of a Poem,* p. 15.

8. Introduction, *Collected Poems 1928-1953* (London: Faber, 1955), p. 15; referred to as *CP.*

9. From Arnold's "A Farewell," quoted in *Forward from Liberalism* (New York: Random, 1937), p. 86.

10. *Poems,* 2nd ed. (London: Faber, 1934), p. 16.

11. *Poems* (1933), p. 42. See Jacobs, "The Moderate Poetical Success of Stephen Spender."

12. "Poetry and Revolution," *New Country,* ed. Michael Roberts (London: Hogarth, 1933), p. 62.

13. *World within World,* p. 59.

14. "The Making of a Poem," *The Making of a Poem,* p. 60.

15. *Ibid.,* p. 56.

16. *The Edge of Being* (New York: Random, 1949), p. 36; referred to as *EB.*

17. *Vienna* (New York: Random, 1935), p. 11.

18. *Ruins and Visions* (London: Faber, 1942), p. 57.

19. *Twenty Poems* (Oxford: Basil Blackwell, n.d.), p. 2.

20. Not counting *Nine Experiments,* printed on Spender's own press in 1928. The poem "At the Edge of Being" is number 1 in *Twenty Poems.* The volume is introduced by a note which declares that with the exception of the first, the poems are arranged "almost" chronologically.

21. In all the versions of the poem, the noun is capitalized, the participle not.

Rose Kamel (essay date June 1975)

SOURCE: Kamel, Rose. "The Impending Holocaust: Spender's *Vienna* and *Trial of a Judge." Durham University Journal* 36 (June 1975): 189-99.

[*In the following essay, Kamel discusses the prophetic nature of Spender's poem* Vienna *and his verse drama* Trial of a Judge, *both of which anticipate the approaching Holocaust.*]

In *Poems* 1934 we occasionally discover a poem that's awry, jarred, one that anticipates the loss of illusion that the poet experienced after Hitler came to power. For example, a melancholy tone pervades the final stanza of **'What I Expected.'**

> For I had expected always
> Some brightness to hold in trust
> Some final innocence
> To save from dust;
> That, hanging solid,
> Would dangle through all
> Like the created poem
> Or the dazzling crystal.[1]

Spender's characteristically normal syntax is sometimes fragmented,

> The explosion of a bomb
> the submarine—a burst bubble filled with water—
> the chancellor clutching his shot arm. . . .

> (*Poems,* 49)

Spender was always ambivalent about committing himself to Marxist ideology. Justin Replogle's comment that 'of all the members of the [Auden] group,[2] Spender was least temperamentally fitted for Marxism. . . . From the beginning of his writing demonstrates such an unbroken record of concern for his own experience and the inner nature of all humans that it seems almost superfluous to state that the individual was always at the centre of his social thought . . .' is indeed apt. Seldom can Spender overcome his preoccupation with his own experience as a way of identifying with the others.[3] Nevertheless, the final section of this volume manages to integrate poetry and politics. We discover here a basically Marxist interpretation of history, undoubtedly impelled by the world-wide depression, the spread of Fascism in Italy and Germany, and the belief in the growing strength of the Soviet Union as a defence against both evils.

But these Marxist poems differ sharply from their ideological counterpart, **Vienna,** published the same year. That the tone of both volumes should differ so markedly indicates more than the poet's exacerbated sensibility or his confessional stance typical of the 1930's: 'As for me, I was an autobiographer searching for forms in which I could express the stages of my development.'[4] For one thing, his vantage point as a traveller through a central Europe besieged by portentious upheavals put him in the unusual position of being part of, yet outside the events: he could, therefore, both participate in and judge history.[5] But Spender also expanded his perception of these events by his almost visceral sympathy with the *force* of Fascism, with the sheer energy with which it could obliterate the conventions of ordinary political struggle by tapping the most destructive impulses of the human personality. In this respect his prescience was prophetic: it adumbrated the holocaust, the full effects of which Europe would not realize for another ten years.

More concretely, in *Poems* 1934 we see Spender's acceptance of Marxism through his presentation of time. Marxists thought historically and chronologically. They denied the permanence of any social order, for they believe that social contradictions form, become sharply defined and impel change:

> A Whim of Time, the general arbiter,
> Proclaims the love instead of death of friends.
> Under the domed sky and athletic sun
> The three stand naked: the new, bronzed German,
> The communist clerk, and myself, being English.

* * *

Our fathers killed. And yet there lives no feud
Like prompting Hamlet on the castle stair;
There falls no shade across our blank of peace,
We being together, struck across our path,
Or taper finger threatening solitude.

(*Poems,* 27)

This change would be essentially ameliorative, forward moving, embodying higher forms of social production and interaction. Above all, writers in the thirties felt the need for a rebirth out of chaotic change. In his succinct analysis of the period Julian Symons writes: 'This idea, with sometimes the chaos and catastrophe stressed, sometimes the rebirth, was the basis of the art of the Thirties.'[6]

Oh young men oh young comrades
it is too late now to stay in those houses
your fathers built where they built you to breed
money on money it is too late
to make or even to count what has been made
Count rather those fabulous possessions
Which begin with your body and your fiery soul:—

(*Poems,* 44)

In spite of the lyric, incantatory quality of this passage, Spender presents time chronologically with a clear separation between past, present and future: 'your fathers *built*', 'it *is* too late', 'what *has been* made'. Syntactical inversions are practically non-existent. Images of light flourish.

Spender capitalizes and personifies time: 'A Whim of Time', 'The wearing of Time', 'This Time forgets and never heals', (*Poems,* 27, 25, 60). He supports the concept of personified time with a constant flow of contemporary industrial images—pylons, trains, dams, pistons, aeroplanes, factories. But it is his image of the sun in this volume that stands for a dazzling socialist future. For the energy that derives from the sun not only flows into the humans who man the machines, enveloping the workers with purposeful proletarian fervour; energy informs the very machinery the workers use:

Not palaces, an era's crown
Where the man swells, intrigues, rests;
The architectural gold-leaved flower
From people ordered like a single mind,
I build. This only what I tell:
It is too late for rare accumulation
For family pride, for beauty's filtered dusts;
I say, stamping the words with emphasis
Drink from here energy and only energy
As from the electric charge of a battery,
To will this Time's change.
Eye, gazelle, delicate wanderer,
Drinker of horizon's fluid line;
Ear that suspends on a chord

The spirit drinking timelessness;
Touch, love all senses;
Leave your gardens, your singing feasts,
Your dreams of suns circling before our sun,
Of heaven after our world . . .

(*Poems,* 67)

Sun and battery images combine with the verb 'build' to render the forceful nature of modern technology affirmative, progressive.

In Spender's most famous lyric, a panegyric to the heroes of history, light and energy come from the sun:

I think continually of those who were truly great.
Who, from the womb, remembered the soul's history
Through the corridors of light where the hours are
    suns
Endless and singing. Whose lovely ambition
Was that their lips, still touched with fire,
Should tell of the spirit clothed from head to foot in
    song . . .

(*Poems,* 45)

Dazzling light images infuse these opening lines and the entire poem. They elaborate the key image 'spirit', defined by its position as the object of an elaborate relative clause. Many laterals / 1 / subtly underscore the force of the light image as a catalyst that links body to spirit. The light images are organic, linking the heroes with history, expressing the vision of a radiantly hopeful future.

In **'The Express'** mechanical energy as a catalyst integrates the machine metaphor with the lyric vision of an industrial paradise:

And always light, aerial, underneath
Goes the elate metre of her wheels.
Steaming through metal landscape on her lines
She plunges new eras of wild happiness
Where speed throws up strange shapes, broad curves
And parallels clean like the steel of guns.
At last, further than Edinburgh or Rome,
Beyond the crest of the world, she reaches night
Where only a low streamline brightness
Of phosphorus on the tossing hills is white.
Ah, like a comet through flame she moves entranced
Wrapt in her music no bird song, no, nor bough
Breaking with honey buds, shall ever equal.

(*Poems,* 53-54)

The light images affirm forceful energy, shift emphasis from fact to feeling, from the descriptive to the evaluative. The white light glowing in the darkness gives the night magic and song—'flame' and 'comet' light up the future. Technology transcends nature.

These poems express the concept of energy that Christopher Caudwell summarizes so incisively:

Men cannot live without acting. Even to cease to act, to let things go their own way, is a form of acting, as when I drop a stone that perhaps starts an avalanche. And since man is always acting, he is always exerting force, always altering or maintaining the position of things, always revolutionary or conservative. Existence is the exercise of force on the physical environment and on other men.[7]

Yet, as we have discovered, Spender occasionally demonstrates a fear of action antithetical to the dominant Marxist impulse in *Poems* 1934.

> Who live under the shadow of a war,
> What can I do that matters?
> My pen stops, and my laughter, dancing, stop
> Or ride to a gap.
>
> How often, on the powerful crest of pride,
> I am shot with the thought
> That halts the untamed horses of the blood,
> The grip on good.
>
> That moving whimpering and mating bear
> Tunes to deaf ears:
> Stuffed with the realer passions of the earth
> Beneath this hearth.

> *(Poems, 31)*

What about these 'realer passions of the earth beneath this hearth'?

Years later Spender analysed them in *World Within World* in which he described his travels through central Europe during the period that Hitler came to power.

> The cultured Europeans recognized in this political movement [Fascism] some of their most hidden fantasies. Hatred of it was deeply involved with a sense of their own guilt.

Disturbingly, Spender found himself responding to a violence he outwardly abhorred:

> External things over which I had no control had usurped my deepest personal life, so that my inner world became dependent on an outer one, and if that outer one failed to provide me with its daily stimulus of crime and indignation, I felt often a kind of emptiness. At the very worst there were moments when I felt that there was a conspirational relationship between the evil passions of the Fascists—which I so profoundly understood—and my own anti-Fascist virulence. . . . In poetry I was confronted with the dilemma of stating a public emotion which had become a private one, and which yet never became my own inner experience because, as I have explained, it evaded my personality rather than sprang out of it.[8]

This is the mood that pervades *Vienna,* the first and only long poem Spender ever wrote. Admittedly uneven[9] with its lyrical parallels, bleak narrative, fragments of dialogue and strident rhetoric, what unifies it is an extreme tension of tone, a feeling of encroaching personal and social chaos.

Vienna deals with the resistance of the Austrian workers to the Dollfuss conspiracy to destroy the Socialist party.[10] Spender's empathy for the poor, his identification with their plight as victims gives us passages of lyrical beauty: 'Dispersed like idle points of a vague star / Huddled on benches, nude at bathing places / And made invisible by crucifying suns / Day after day, again with grief afire at night, / They do not watch what we show.'[11] But we cannot believe in the workers' potential strength and affirmation of purpose because the narrator's voice undercuts this potential by projecting a nightmarish sense of futility and oncoming disaster. In this context Marxist affirmation seems to be meaningless.

> Supposing a stranger
>
> One totally disinterested, not a sucker
> Of his mother's milk from nipple of a shell
> Soon to destroy him—his arterial circulation
> Not a modern currency corrupted by inflation
> Should stand within northern range of us
>
> A stranger, a witness free from danger, observing
> The lying snakes, the favourites of the sun
> Those twisting ministers, infest a land
> Where all the twigs seem snakes, and where all pops
> The backfire of a car, a tactless cough
> The traitor Fey, seem bombs; watching
> The squall of fear an instant catch
> A thousand faces, like the death sphinx paw
> Murmuring on million deserts: a stranger answering
> *What is wrong?*

> *(Vienna, 19-20)*

The stranger ostensibly functions as the narrator's alter-ego, possibly to offset the intensely subjective tone, and to express a more dispassionate point of view. But the syntactic order of the narration is undercut by the savage diction, the eerie sense of disorder in the adjectives 'lying' and 'death sphinx', and the cumulative voiced and voiceless sibilants: 'stranger', 'witness', 'snakes', 'favourites', 'sun', 'twisting', 'ministers', 'infest', 'twigs', 'tactless', 'seem', 'bombs', which express a hissing, menacing quality. The stranger, then, does not report facts objectively, but describes reversals of conventional order; he becomes, therefore, an articulator of strangeness.

In other passages Spender's customarily normal syntax order becomes logically disconnected. Justin Replogle has commented on Spender's unusual use of ellipses that give these passages 'the quality of disconnected floating voices. This is the most common technique in the poem, one not significantly different from Eliot's similar device'.[12] Sometimes Eliot-like fragments of dialogue give a pastiche effect to the lines:

> 'Why, in Chicago. . . . Yes, more of a *sports-man. . . .*

'How much, how much did that tie cost?
'How much, how much do you think I lost
'What with the war and the inflation and what with
   our old picturesque estate gone? . . .[13]

Indeed, a comparison of Spender to Eliot is no idle one. *Vienna* reminds us of a wasteland in which events appear to be virtually apocalyptic. Clearly logical, coherent constructions reinforced by Marxist affirmations were alien to Spender's experience at this time and it is not surprising that he borrowed from a poet of the twenties who could best articulate disintegration.

> Whether the man living or the man dying
> Whether this man's dead life, or that man's life dying
> His real life a fading light his real death a light grow-
>   ing
>
> (***Vienna***, 9)

In this and many other passages 'dying' and 'death' are the most frequent verbs and adjectives, augmenting the ambiguity of these clauses, their lack of a concrete objective in time and space. Images of physical sickness and decay enlarge the death concept. Sometimes these images are grossly overstrained, but occasionally, as in the following lines, they enrich and enhance the poem's texture:

> The part true to this town is a square quarter:
> Unhomely windows, floors scrubbed clean of love
> A waste canvas sky, uniformed nuns,
> Streets tinkling with the silver ambulance.
> We breathe the bandaged air and watch through
>   windows
> Metal limbs, glass eyes, ourselves frozen on fires.
>
> (***Vienna***, 12)

Here the adjectives and adverbs change the therapeutic connotation of a hospital into something strange and menacing: 'unhomely', 'uniformed nuns'. Nouns denoting human features are distorted by the adjectives 'metal' and 'glass', so that human traits assume the mien of crippled automatons. 'Waste canvas sky' and 'bandaged air' transform nature into universal pathology. The effect of this passage is to render all of society helpless or wounded.

Spender also seems to have abandoned Time and the sun as images of hope:

> The Time is
> Dawn in the city with light dripping
> On speechless pavement, on mirroring parallels
> Of a surviving and dead wish, the defeated
> Staring, white canal.
>   The Place meets
> The Time: with difficult light creaking
> To fill the streets up to the level roofs
> To fill the morning which is a dulled cistern.
>
> (***Vienna***, 12-13)

Note the eeriness of 'a speechless pavement', 'staring white canal', and 'dulled cistern', which do not convey the city's actuality, but give it instead a surreal dimension. Furthermore, the light, previously associated with energy, ardour, human love and reason now becomes threatening: 'light dripping' suggests blood and 'light creaking', an arresting example of synesthesia, expresses danger. Throughout *Vienna* the sun image recedes and the diction that once conveyed light, warmth, hope, now gives way to recurring images of an ice age:

> At the North Pole where this world is all white flesh
> North Ocean reflecting vast speechless
> Aims of ice stabbed in its depths.
>
> (***Vienna***, 9 19)

Spender's fear reveal an attraction for violence not uncommon in writers of the 1930's. Julian Symons points out that 'in their adherence to collective security there was a masochistic feeling for violence, a longing for immersion in the virtuous strength of the Soviet Union, a desire to identify goodness with success'.[14] But in *Vienna* this need to act (which Caudwell pinpointed so well) in response to the threat of Fascism not only doesn't channel human energy into affirmative patterns of Marxist ideology—it unleashes amorphous energy as well; amorphous because the energy lacks direction and control. Destructive, rather than affirmative, it is the energy of nihilism. Years later Spender was to write of *Vienna*'s turbulence: 'To believe in political action and economic forces which will release new energies in the world is a release of energy in oneself.'[15] His implication is that this release is cathartic. But purposeless energy, proliferating tension, play a much more disturbing role in *Vienna* than in anything Spender had written before. The need to act as a means to an end, e.g. socialism, now underscores action existing in and for itself. In this context we lose the distinction between human beings and animals.

> Faces (so-called) utter a positive weakness
> The sulky heifer, the furnished goat, the
> Famished blonde, the conscious good.
> *What is wrong?*
>
> (***Vienna***, 19)

Recurring parallels, sadistic verbs combined with passive-voice constructions give a sado-masochistic quality to the savage energy:

> Lucky: those who were shot dead
> Outright not being and being those
> Thrown down cellar and trampled with nailed boots;
> Made to swallow the badge with three arrows
> That excellently deflect harmless into
> A ground pegged out for making decent houses;
> Beaten to death; left frozen
> In the so gentle snow breeding all iron
> Solid with their clenched rifles; or hanged
> By an ignoring justice, fit only for colonies.
>
> (***Vienna***, Part III, 21)

Adjectives and adverbs delineate a society where mass murder assumes an efficiency formerly associated with mass production.

Portions of the poem have an unusual number of syntactic copulas. These copular constructions result in a rigid juxtaposition of subject and predicate that makes the language reductive. In the following passage, for example, the accumulation of copulas undercuts the lyrical expansive impulse of the verse:

> We can read their bodies like advertisements
> On hoardings, shouting with common answers.
> Not saying, life is unhappy, unhappy is ill,
> Death is reward, law just, but only
> Life is life, body is body, a day
> Is the sun: there is left only beauty
> Of merest being . . .
>
> (*Vienna*, 15-16)

Not that copulas dominate **Vienna**. Obviously, in this long and uneven poem, no one style *can dominate*. But Spender begins to use copulas more frequently—partly, perhaps to impose an order on the basic disorder of the disintegrating scene he describes. But this schematic method expresses both an automatic response to life with regard for cause and effect, and an 'either-or-ness' that expresses polarity. Thus, the subject of a sentence becomes defined in terms of what we immediately perceive it is or isn't. Ambiguity, dialectical complexity, subtlety have little or no place in this kind of structure. Instead, Spender can only impose order by declaring that 'a' equals 'b'. Paradoxically this insistent need to repeat copulas only underscores the chaos upon which they have been superimposed. In a remarkable scene that depicts the systematic hunting and destroying of political fugitives, we see how copulas combine with sentence fragments and similes to render a nightmare:

> Fading, fading. On Wednesday, snow muffling
> Our resistance. There were those escaping
> Over the mountain bone-white desert and falling
> Dust, our land. Like stains of ink on satin
> Is blood spreading in snow—the joy of huntin'
> Their best since years. Life seems black against the
>   snow.
> To pick men with a gun is delicate
> As pointing cleanest crochet. The vivid runner falls
> From his hare-breathed anxiety: his undisputing
> Hold on terror. O gently, whitely buried.
>
> (*Vienna*, 25)

Gerundives—'fading', 'muffling', 'falling', 'spreading'—augment the feeling of helplessness. The simile linking inkstains to blood contrives to make murder mundane, as does the frighteningly domestic imagery of 'delicate . . . as cleanest crochet'. The craftsmanship of daily life now becomes a means of mass murder. And the effect of fading light, of a triumphant ice-age renders the rhetoric of the left futile,

unconvincing, unable to offer a viable alternative to the clear-cut menace of Fascism. In a schematic black and white age, the man of good will has no place to go. Seldom was this more true than in 1938, two years after the Austro-German Anschluss and two years after the onset of the Spanish Civil War. In *Trial of a Judge*, 1938, Spender puts the man of good will in an untenable situation.

This verse drama examines the fate of a liberal Judge who must act upon the premeditated murder of a young Communist intellectual by Fascists. When the Judge adheres to the law and condemns the murderers to death, the Fascists start a counterrevolution. He must now reverse the death sentence and impose it instead on some hapless communists who have been caught with illegal weapons. But it is too late even to capitulate to terror. Having staged a successful coup, the Fascists try the Judge and impose the death sentence upon him.

The sheer redundancy of sadistic images and aggressive verbs give this play a grotesquely over-strained quality. Some of this excess, of course, reflects the expressionistic dramaturgy popular in the 1930's. For instance, Spender tells us that the first act may be a dream in the Judge's mind, and the flunkey, Hümmeldorf, apparently dreams the fourth act. Likewise, the actors who play the 'audience' often shift their role from accuser to accused. Expressionist and surrealist techniques turn the Judge and all the other characters into types with little or no personal dimension.[16] We expect that this is what the style will reflect; what we are not prepared for is the uniformly strident incantatory aspect of the language, so that even the liberal Judge, ostensibly the last voice of reason in a world where 'judgement' has 'fled to brutish beasts' declaims in as extreme a manner as the others:

> The carotid artery was severed
> Petra's body mangled out of recognition
> What could I say except assert
> That my famous gentleness, changed to outrage,
> Would stamp their lives out with a kind of pleasure?[17]

As compared with **Vienna**, *Trial of a Judge* exhibits a greater frequency of past participles and passive verbs, a greater preponderance of copulas and antonyms:

> Dear friend, your world is the antipodes
> Of the world of those
> Who seal us in this living tomb:
> And travelling there, where all seems opposite,
> Yet all will be the same; only
> Those who are now oppressed will be the oppressors,
> The oppressors the oppressed.
>
> (*TOAJ* [*Trial of a Judge*], 83)

All of these stylistic devices express a rigidity and the apparent division of a society into Communists and Fascists:

Then, from the impregnable centre
Of what we are, we answer
Their *injustice* with *justice,* their running
Terroristic *lie* with fixed *truth.*
Our single and simple being
Will be the terrible angel
And *white* witness which though they deny
Dazzles even their convoluted *darkness*

(*TOAJ,* 85) (Italics mine)

As in **Vienna** black and white images contribute to this sense of dichotomy, but balanced though these images may be, even more than in **Vienna** the play moves toward a total eclipse of light:

How strange it seems
That to me justice was once delineated by an inner
  eye
As sensibly as what is solid
In this room, tables chairs and walls,
Is made indubitable by the sun.
But now crumbles away
In coals of darkness, and the existence
Of what was black, white, evil, right
Becomes invisible, founders against us
Like lumber in a lightless garret.

(*TOAJ,* 37)

To whatever place I turn my sight
I stare at my own weakness
Which brings down a Polar night
Groaning with more than winter-long distress.
These nightmare-calving fields of ice
Through black air challenge my eyes

(*TOAJ,* 49-50)

The overwhelming effect of both passages is one of an approaching darkness. Both darkness and coldness express totalitarianism that belies the ostensible presentation of a true dichotomy. Let us explore this point further. The Fascists are presented as mechanical men. Their strident, metallic, automaton-like sloganizing robs them of any human quality:

BLACK TROOP LEADER:

Learn there
The inner peace of killing; touch bugle colours
Like golden ridges in the conscript's mind

(*TOAJ,* 45)

SIXTH BLACK, SEVENTH BLACK, AND BLACK TROOP LEADER:

Our light floods the machinery of State power
Now. The lever craves the hand of the Leader.

But strident, mechanical speech comes from the left as well:

BLACK CHORUS:

Blasphemers against the Word;

RED CHORUS:

Kneelers before dictators and the
sword!

BLACK CHORUS:

You, who, after this life, will
suffer eternal death!

RED CHORUS:

This life, which you would turn to
death!

BLACK CHORUS:

We gain life after death.

RED CHORUS:

You make death in life.

BLACK CHORUS:

DEATH!

RED CHORUS:

DEATH!

(*TOAJ,* 50)

The images of death, the repetitive focus on death make the Judge's ultimate fate predictable. Justin Replogle argues that the Judge fails because 'his position is untenable. The liberal pacifism of the Judge is unrealistic; harsh realities demand opposing power with power, physical violence with physical violence'.[18] Clearly his liberalism can no longer be a source of power. But the physical violence that the left embraces *also* cannot offer hope and cannot, therefore, present a genuinely life-affirming antithesis to the encroaching void. An uniformly Fascistic shadow has eclipsed even the glimmer of a vision that somehow these historically necessary blood baths will result in an end to human oppression.

Again, we must remember that Spender wrote *Trial of a Judge* before 1939, the year that marked the end of the Spanish Civil War and the signing of the Nazi-Soviet pact. Writers of the 1930's believed that the time of the apocalypse was surely at hand and that the Soviet Union would proclaim the day of redemption. Despite Spender's fundamental ambivalence about following the party line, he apparently was willing to concede the Marxist millennium and the means necessary to procure it. It was only later in retrospect that he could analyse the dehumanizing implications of this stance.

Thus, when men have decided to pursue a course of action, everything which serves to support this seems vivid and real; everything which stands against it becomes abstraction. Your friends are allies and therefore real human beings with flesh and blood sympathies like yourself. Your opponents are just tiresome, unreasonable, unnecessary theses, whose lives are so many false statements which you would like to strike out with a lead bullet as you would put the stroke of a lead pencil through a bungled paragraph.[19]

Unfortunately, most of *Trial of a Judge* and much of **Vienna** is one-dimensional. To see life in terms of simple polarity was to schematize and distort art; to deny life's complexity was to deny art breadth of vision. But Spender also recognized that the problem was more than a matter of aesthetics. To abstract and deny individuals their human variability and possibility is a reductive process. Ultimately, the political opponent is reduced to the dangling corpse on the gallows—the Jew to an ash heap in a death camp. In this respect Spender's poetic response to political excess was appallingly prophetic. It was prophetic in another respect as well. The bronzed young Germans with whom he sunbathed before Hitler's ascent to power elicited from him a response to the destructive psychic energy of Fascism, its sheer demonology. This is what the Judge implies in the final lines of his last soliloquy:

> I have become
> The centre of that clamorous drum
> To which I listened all my life
> Whose letters spell time's meaning
> In this prison and my death.
>
> (*TOAJ*, 90)

These final lines foreshadow a statement Spender was to make later:

> Perhaps the world in which I was living was too terrible for this fusion [public and private] to take place: the only people who attained it were the murderers and the murdered. Throughout these years I had always the sense of living on the circumference of a circle at whose centre I could never be. . . . Somewhere I felt that there was a place which was at the very centre of this world, some terrible place like the core of a raging fire. . . . If I could ever approach it I felt it would be the centre where the greatest evil of our time was understood and endured. But at this thought I was appalled, for it made me realize that the centre of our time was perhaps the violent, incommunicable death of an innocent victim.[20]

It is this final vision, rather than the repetitive chant of the Red Chorus, 'We shall be free / We shall find peace,' that we are left with at the close of the play.

Notes

1. Stephen Spender, *Poems* 1934 (London: Faber, 1934), p. 26. Hereafter cited as *Poems* and included in the text.

2. Justin Replogle, 'The Auden Group,' *WSCL*, [*Wisconsin Studies in Contemporary Literature*] 5 (Summer, 1964), 143.

3. D. E. S. Maxwell comments rather caustically on Spender's concern with his own sense of selfhood. He notes that the poet turns to Marxism as he later would to psychoanalysis in an attempt to cope with the problems of selfhood. See D. E. S. Maxwell, *Poets of the Thirties* (London: Routledge & Kegan Paul, 1969), pp. 200-201.

4. Stephen Spender, *World Within World* (Berkeley: Univ. of Calif. Press, 1966), p. 138. Hereafter cited as *WWW*.

5. *World Within World* frequently makes this point. See pp. 134, 191-204.

6. Julian Symons, *The Thirties. A Dream Revisited* (London: Cresset Press, 1960), p. 8.

7. Christopher Caudwell, *Studies in a Dying Culture* (New York: Dodd Mead & Co., 1938), p. 125.

8. *WWW*, pp. 190-191.

9. Spender comments: 'The poem fails because it does not fuse the two halves of a split situation, and attain a unity where the inner passion becomes inseparable from the outer one.' See *WWW*, p. 192.

10. Dollfuss, chancellor of Austria, had connived with Major Fey and Prince Von Starhemberg, in charge of the Austrian Heimwehr, to fight the Nazis on condition that the Socialist party be destroyed. They voted in a Fascist constitution. The Nazis then resorted to terrorism, assassinated Dollfuss, and became powerful, albeit briefly, for the Heimwehr finally ejected them temporarily from Austria.

11. Stephen Spender, *Vienna* (London: Random House, 1934), p. 14. Hereafter cited as *Vienna* and included in the text.

12. Justin Replogle, *The Auden Group. The 1930's Poetry of W. H. Auden, C. Day Lewis and Stephen Spender.* Dissertation (Wisconsin: Univ. of Wisconsin Press, 1956), p. 503.

13. Cf. 'In the mountains, there you feel free. / I read, much of the night, and go south in the winter.' See T. S. Eliot, 'The Waste Land,' in *The Complete Poems and Plays 1909-1950* (New York: Harcourt, Brace & Co., 1952), p. 37. Spender writes that even in the Marxist mid-1930's, Eliot influenced the Auden group more profoundly than did any other poet. See Stephen Spender, 'Writers and Revolutionaries. The Spanish War,' *NYRB* [*New York Review of Books*], September, 1969, p. 3.

14. Julian Symons, pp. 49-50.

15. Stephen Spender in *The God That Failed*, ed. Richard Crossman (New York: Harper, 1949), p. 237.

16. It is interesting to compare *Trial of a Judge* produced for the Group Theatre under the direction of Rupert Doone and Auden with Auden and Isherwood's *The Dog Beneath the Skin* (1935), *The Ascent of F6* (1936) and *On the Frontier* (1938). These plays were also expressionistic, but are also intellectually playful: they lack the singular intensity of mood of Spender's drama.

17. Stephen Spender, *Trial of a Judge* (London: Faber, 1938), p. 9. Hereafter cited as *TOAJ* and included in the text.

18. Replogle, *The Auden Group,* p. 462.

19. Spender in *The God That Failed,* p. 253.

20. *WWW,* pp. 192-193.

List of Books Consulted

CAUDWELL, CHRISTOPHER. *Studies in a Dying Culture.* New York: Dodd Mead & Co., 1938.

The God That Failed, ed. Richard Crossman. New York: Harper, 1949.

ELIOT, THOMAS STEARNS. *The Complete Poems and Plays 1909-1950.* New York: Harcourt Brace & Co., 1952.

MAXWELL, D. E. S. *Poets of the Thirties.* London: Routledge & Kegan Paul, 1969.

REPLOGLE, JUSTIN. *The Auden Group. The 1930's Poetry of W. H. Auden, C. Day Lewis and Stephen Spender.* Dissertation. Wisconsin: Univ. of Wisconsin Press, 1956.

REPLOGLE, JUSTIN. 'The Auden Group,' *WSCL,* 5 (Summer, 1964), 143.

SPENDER, STEPHEN. *Poems* 1934. London: Faber, 1934.

SPENDER, STEPHEN. *Vienna.* London: Random House, 1934.

SPENDER, STEPHEN. *Trial of a Judge.* London: Faber, 1938.

SPENDER, STEPHEN. *World Within World.* Berkeley: Univ. of Calif. Press. 1966.

SPENDER, STEPHEN. 'Writers and Revolutionaries. The Spanish War,' *NYRB* [*New York Review of Books*], September, 1969, p. 3.

SYMONS, JULIAN. *The Thirties. A Dream Revisited.* London: Cresset Press, 1960.

A. Kingsley Weatherhead (essay date 1975)

SOURCE: Weatherhead, A. Kingsley. "Spender's Volumes of Verse." In *Stephen Spender and the Thirties,* pp. 155-200. Lewisburg, Penn.: Bucknell University Press, 1975.

[In the following excerpt, Weatherhead provides an overview of the publication history of Spender's poetry and the critical reception of his work.]

Spender's first poems appeared in 1928, printed on his own small hand press at No. 10 Frognal, Hampstead, London, N. W. 3, in an edition of 500 copies. The press was also used for printing chemists' labels and the earliest edition of Auden's poems (1928). In the middle of producing these, however, it collapsed.[1] The volume of his own work is entitled *Nine Experiments: Being Poems Written at the Age of Eighteen.* Spender says he subsequently rounded up and destroyed as many copies as he could. None of the poems is later reprinted.

The volume opens with **"Invocation,"** which sounds as if it were inspired by Shelley's "Ode to the West Wind":

> Blow forever in my head!
> And ever let the violins, tempest-sworn
> Lash out their hurricane. . . .

The prevalence of imagery related to light in this volume, such as "sun" and "eye," is also reminiscent of Shelley; and since it is a regular feature of all Spender's subsequent poetry, his early susceptibility to light is worth remarking. He makes more use here than later of the repetition of individual words, though it is always among his stock techniques; much of it here is a matter of trifling. There is also a certain playfulness in rhyming, which may be what he refers to when he says, "When I wrote **NINE EXPERIMENTS,** I was still in the stage of putting my money on an appearance of madness in my poems" (p. x). Thus in **"Gilles"** he writes,

> Gilles de Rais'
>   FACE,
> How blue the fringes shone!
> The tassels were
>   Torn from the air,
> (The sky is made of silk there). . . .

And **"Ovation for Spring"** goes

> The nineteenth time, from bough to bough
> I see the mocking fires of spring;
> And twice I've rhymed the name with 'king',
> But I am grown more *blasé* now.

He is very blasé and very self-conscious throughout. One doesn't want to pin too much solemn deduction on a few instances of self-consciousness and play. But it would be interesting if this technique, to be superseded later by others, were a means, conscious or otherwise, of protecting a rather raw-nerved, naked engagement with the poetic object. Other poems testify in part to an impulse to shield the sensibilities. Thus, for instance, the "whorl/whirl" play in the following passage from **"Evening on the Lake—(dolce),"** acts as some sort of stiffener in an otherwise passive Shelleyan response to beauty:

> Beauty cometh: See how gently
> Graven in the   Water, play

> The lazy whorls, which   Whirl absently
> Round the prow, and   Glide away. . . .

Later on we shall see techniques that are apparently calculated to break in and destroy romantic excitement or lyrical pitch, controlling emotion by deliberately introducing bathos. So, similarly, on certain occasions in his career, Spender dealt with his overpowering feeling: when seeing the fascist stage effects in Rome or upon receiving a brief glimpse of General Goering as he entered Dubrovnik, he burst into a high-pitched giggle.[2]

A poem called **"Appeal"** should be noted for it anticipates sympathies that are to be developed further: it opens, "The voices of the poor, like birds / that thud against a sullen pane, / Have worn my heart. . . ." The simile too is characteristic of Spender's later verse.

There is not a great deal of merit in these poems; Spender remarked thirty-six years after they were composed that he did not publish anything "worth preserving" until Blackwell's came out with his *Twenty Poems* in 1930.[3] This volume is made of more durable stuff: fourteen of the twenty poems are reproduced in the *Collected Poems* of 1955,[4] having appeared again before that in both editions of *Poems,* 1933 and 1934.[5] The poems appear in the order of composition except for the first one, **"At the Edge of Being,"** which was composed later than its position indicates. Poem II, **"Discovered in Mid-Ocean"** (first line: "He will watch the hawk with an indifferent eye"), is surmounted by a rubric, "The 'Marston' Poems," which, though the title is not repeated at the top of each following page, is presumably a series that includes numbers II to XII, for above No. XIII is the heading "Other Poems." Only six of the Marston series were reprinted in the *Collected Poems,* and then not as a group. "Other Poems" consists of eight unrelated pieces, including **"'I' Can Never Be Great Man"** and **"Beethoven's Death Mask,"** familiar to anthologies. All but one of these eight, **"Always Between Hope and Fear,"** are reprinted in *Collected Poems.*

The "Marston" poems are related to an experience Spender describes in his autobiography.[6] Marston is the name he gives to a fellow undergraduate at Oxford, who was a boxer, skier, and pilot but who was withdrawn, Spender felt, from the other college athletes, the "hearties," as they were generally known. Spender developed an emotional attachment to him which was unilateral and frustrating:

> Rushing in room and door flung wide, I knew.
> Oh empty walls, book-carcases, blank chairs
> All splintered in my head and cried for you.[7]

His enthusiasm was met with "quiet politeness" and the indifference that seems, paradoxically, to have been Marston's most attractive quality. After the relationship was over, Spender began, he says, to write poems different from any previous ones. "A concrete situation had suddenly crystallized feelings which until then had been diffused and found no object." The Marston series begins with the superman poem, **"Discovered in Mid-Ocean,"** in which Spender as poet has resolved the oppression of his real personal predicament by a species of amputation—making an image of the unattainable beloved as dead:

> This aristocrat, superb of all instinct,
>   With death close linked
> Had paced the enormous cloud, almost had won
>   War on the sun;
> Till now like Icarus mid-ocean-drowned,
>   Hands, wings, are found. . . .
>
>   (p. 3)

In another of the series, "Marston, dropping it in the grate, broke his pipe," Spender celebrates the pipe Marston had bought on a continental holiday, appreciating it for its associations. He is using the poetry here as a means of taking possession of a part of Marston's coveted activities; as in another poem, **"Saying 'good morning,'"** he recognizes that conversation is "a form of possession / Like taking your wrists. . . ." In the second poem of the series, **"The Dust Made Flesh,"** which has not been reprinted, the poet describes how he has created four figures. It is a creation somewhat in the manner in which Yeats created his characters, and Spender's lines recall the rhythms of Yeats. Marston, although we know him to have been real, is here designated one of the poets' creations:

> First made I Marston the superb boxer
> More than with men who dealt with death,
> Marston who ski-ed through snow,
> Curved through the whiteness, ran,
> Helmeted drove through air. . . .

After Marston came Helen, "Dark-eyed, words piercing night like stars"; then Catherine, who "sprang in sky" and "Along the ice-fleeced rocks shot chamois down." Finally there is Ainger, the poet

> . . . severe, voiced raucous-reed,
> With fascinating facets of crude mind,
> An enormous percipient mass on the plain.

Spender did not in fact *make* Marston as the poem claims; and the others are perhaps no more fictitious than he—Ainger, indeed, might for some features be Auden, briefly sketched.[8] But they may all be allowed to be the poet's imaginative creations; while each is very unlike him, each perhaps embodies desirable characteristics and is a coveted projection of himself; Spender is like Yeats again, who summoned the image of the "most unlike" who was his anti-self.

The characters are more likely to be coveted because each of them seems all of a piece: each can be briefly epitomized in one or more swift studies of imagery. In this respect the poem anticipates a later expression of Spender's qualified admiration for people whose personalities were so unified that they could be summed up in a single image or phrase: the "truly great," for example, of the poem that begins, **"I think continually of those who were truly great,"**[9] who leave the air "signed with their honour." There are others who appear in the later poetry, especially in *The Still Centre,* who are of this kind of distinction. They are unlike the complex, disjointed "I" who can never be a great man, in the poem on that subject, on account of all the disparate parts, "'I eating' / 'I loving,' 'I angry,' 'I excreting'"; and Spender repeatedly recognizes their appeal to him.

In the poems of the Marston series that follow **"The Dust Made Flesh,"** only Marston appears again by name, and he in only one of them; Helen, Catherine, and Ainger are not again identifiable. The remaining poems either celebrate a man or address a person, who may be man or woman, to whom the speaker is apparently emotionally attached; in each case it is presumably Marston. The last poem in the series, **"The Port,"** is incongruous in that it neither mentions nor addresses any single person, being only a well-packed description of a port; but perhaps the sinister imagery of graves, caves, skewed faces, lightning, and so on are an objective equivalent for the poet's feelings of frustration and grief.

One poem of this volume not in the Marston series is related to an incident in life: **"Written Whilst Walking Down the Rhine,"** in *Collected Poems* titled **"In 1929,"** refers to a meeting of three young men—the poet and two Germans, Joachim and Heinrich, a communist clerk. The story of Heinrich, Spender says, was a "fragment of the saga of all this German youth which had been born into war, starved in the blockade, stripped in the inflation—and which now . . . sprang like a breed of dragon's teeth . . ."[10] The poem looks back ten years and finds two of the three young men at war; it looks forward ten and finds Heinrich, the communist, building his world out of "our bones." There is now no prompting by the dead fathers for revenge:

> Now I suppose that the once-envious dead
> Have learned a strict philosophy of clay
> After these centuries, to haunt us no longer
> In the churchyard, or at the end of the lane
> Or howling at the edge of the city
> Beyond the last bean-rows, near the new factory.[11]

When the poem reappeared in Spender's next volume, Allen Tate pronounced it one of the finest in the century, remarking in it a clarity and a mastery of words that had been absent from English verse since Landor.

The poems in *Twenty Poems* are rich in concrete imagery. One or two of them are even descriptive as wholes: **"The Port,"** for instance, or **"I hear the cries**

of evening,"** the Georgian type of poem that describes evening in the country; and such poetry is unusual among Spender's shorter pieces. In one of the Marston poems there is also humor, which is also somewhat rare: shocked at the magnitude of his affection upon a small occasion, he thought,

> . . . if these were tricklings through a dam,
> I must have love enough to run a factory on,
> Or give a city power, or drive a train.

(p. 9)

In his autobiography, Spender mentions that Harold Nicolson offered to notice *Twenty Poems* in his column in the *Daily Express* but that he, Spender, declined the offer, saying that the volume was not for public sale, "but really out of pride and for no other reason."[12]

Spender's next volume, *Poems,* was published in 1933, by Faber and Faber. He had arrived in Russell Square. In this volume are gathered those poems for which, judging by the anthologies, he has been chiefly known throughout his poetic career. There are thirty-three poems in all, ten of which had already appeared in *Twenty Poems*: these include five of the Marston poems, **"At the Edge of Being,"** deprived now of its title and relegated to a position later in the volume (No. X), **"'I' Can Never Be Great Man,"** **"Different Living,"** **"Beethoven's Death Mask,"** and **"I hear the cries of evening."** Of the other twenty-three in the new volume, seven had already appeared in 1932 in Michael Roberts's *New Signatures.*[13] These seven were the poems that first brought Spender to the attention of the public and first linked him in its mind with Auden and C. Day Lewis. The poems are **"Oh Young Men,"** **"The Prisoners,"** **"I Think Continually,"** **"Who Live Under the Shadow,"** **"The Express,"** **"My Parents"** (**"My parents kept me from children who were rough"**), and **"The Funeral."** *Poems* contains in addition such familiar anthologized pieces as **"What I expected,"** **"After they have tired,"** **"The Landscape Near an Aerodrome,"** **"The Pylons,"** and **"Not palaces, an era's crown."** Among these are expressions of leftist sentiment which, while they were received by the doctrinaire Marxists without enthusiasm, as we have seen, have somewhat colored Spender's poetical reputation. In the introduction to *Collected Poems,* Spender says that he has included in that volume certain poems like **"The Pylons"** and **"The Funeral"** because "there seemed an obligation to 'own up'" to them, "when they were written [they] provided a particular label for some of the poetry of the 'Thirties: an embarrassment to my friends' luggage more even than to my own."[14] There are, as a matter of fact, relatively few poems that are unequivocally leftist.

Poems, 1933, was noticed in a bland paragraph in the *Times Literary Supplement* of July 6, 1933. The use both of the idiom of the day and also of an older vocabulary is remarked. The poet's main defect is said to be a lyrical exaggeration not always germane to the starker material, a comment that is surely an expression of the uneasiness incurred on account of the ill-assortment of the lyricism and the bathos in such poems as **"Not palaces"** and **"The Funeral."** But the main impression received by the *TLS* reviewer is of gentleness and a peculiar sweetness of temperament—so far from the so-called modern world. The rhythms are found to be personal and persuasive. F. R. Leavis also noticed this volume, but in a manner a little more strenuous. He found immaturity and instability in the technique, he observed unrealized imagery, and he said Spender was given to the "glamorous-ineffable-vague." Illustrating these defects he quotes from four poems: **"My parents quarrel in the neighbour room," "The Port," "I hear the cries of evening,"** and **"Your body is stars whose million glitter here."** Of the first of these, Leavis says, "Mr. Spender is unformed enough to be able to reproduce (quite unwittingly, it seems) the Meredith of *Modern Love*." The echo of Meredith is admittedly clear enough:

> My parents quarrel in the neighbour room.
> "How did you sleep last night?" "I woke at four
> To hear the wind that sulks along the floor
> Blowing up dust like ashes from the tomb."[15]

It is audible also incidentally in one of the Marston poems, **"Acts passed beyond the boundary of mere wishing"**:

> Then once you said "Waiting was very kind"
> And looked surprised: surprising for me too
> Whose every movement had been missionary,
> A pleading tongue unheard. I had not thought
> That you, who nothing else saw, would see this.
>
> (p. 15)

Spender is not by any means alone in speaking in a voice like Meredith's: the echo of *Modern Love* is heard repeatedly throughout the decade in lyrics that poetize an emotionally charged relationship.

Leavis uses **"I hear the cries of evening"** to illustrate his contention that "slightly disguised in the technical modernizing, there is a good deal of the Georgian" in the volume, saying the poem might have come from one of the Georgian anthologies. The poem about parents did not reappear in Spender's later volumes; **"I hear the cries of evening,"** dropped from the second edition of *Poems,* turned up again in the *Collected Poems.* **"The Port"** and **"Your body is stars"** have remained.

For the second edition, nine poems were added to the first, which, with the withdrawal of the two just mentioned, made a total of forty. Three of those added had appeared in Michael Robert's *New Country*;[16] about half of them were to appear again in *Collected Poems.* Among those added is **"Van der Lubbe,"** which is the name of the young Dutch communist who in the year previous had been blamed for the burning of the *Reichstag.* In the defendant's laughter Spender sees reflected the madness and twisted justice of contemporary Germany. The poem was not reprinted. Another poem added, **"For T. A. R. H.,"** is based on the poet's relationship with the young man Hyndman, which he discusses at some length in the autobiography. The poem is reprinted in *Poems* (1934), with revisions, from the *New Oxford Outlook* and appears again, with more revision, in *Collected Poems.*

> Even whilst I watch him I am remembering
> The quick laugh of the wasp gold eyes. . . .
>   . . . for love
> Is soaked in memory and says
> I have seen what I see, and I wear
> All pasts and futures like a doomed, domed sky. . . .[17]

There is much of Spender in this short poem; some of its features are characteristics that have already been mentioned; others are those that remain to be discussed. Biographically, there is the affection for another man, a kind of love of which the incidence in society is no doubt greater than the frequency with which it is discussed. It is fairly typical also inasmuch as the poem is not immediately concerned with Hyndman (its title after all is **"For T. A. R. H."**) but with Spender's own inner world in its response to Hyndman. And accordingly, in consonance with this fact, the substance of the poem has been largely withdrawn from the facts in the external world that gave it impetus; the imagery is relatively insubstantial, and it has been refined into a structure where the laws of art prevail, and sounds determine word selection:

>   . . . a doomed, domed sky.
> Thus I wear always the glint of quick lids
> And the blue axel turning. . . .

In 1934, the same year as the second edition of *Poems,* Spender's long poem, *Vienna,* appeared.[18] It celebrates certain of the details of the defeat of the socialist insurrectionists in February 1934, in Austria, where Spender had traveled shortly after it occurred. This was socialism's first battle and its first defeat. But although there is an image in a poem of Charles Madge's and a reference or two in John Lehmann's poems, *Vienna* is the only major literary work in English devoted to the tragedy. It uses a passage from Wilfred Owen's "Strange Meeting" for epigraph: "They will be swift with swiftness of the tigress, / None will break ranks, though nations trek from progress."

The poem is in four parts; it presents images of the political life of Austria and details of the fighting, particularly the heroic episodes of the capture, trial, and killing of Kaloman Wallisch, the socialist mayor of Bruck-an-der-Mur. Then, along with this public material and awkwardly associated with it, the poem presents certain purely personal feelings of the poet's that are attached to an entirely different and separate matter, a love affair he had pursued in Austria, in the spring of the same year as the insurrection, with an American woman, whom he calls Elizabeth in the autobiography.[19] In the poem, no concrete details of the affair are given; only feelings, presented expressionistically or in abstraction. In the autobiography Spender dwells on the reason that he had imposed the private matter upon the public: "public events had swamped our personal lives," he writes, "and usurped our personal experiences." But characteristically he had hung on to his private life, and thus "a poetry which rejected private experience would have been untrue to me." He says of *Vienna* that it was intended to express his indignation at the suppression of the socialists;

> but in part also it was concerned with a love relationship. I meant to show that the two experiences were different, yet related. For both were intense, emotional and personal, although the one was public, the other private. The validity of the one was dependent on that of the other: for in a world where humanity was trampled on publicly, private affection was also undermined.
>
> (p. 192)

These things are not quite so. The validities of socialism and human love are not necessarily dependent upon one another; private affection is not undermined by the presence of inhumanity in the world at large; and things that are intense and emotional are not necessarily thereby related. The effects named are not consequent upon the causes given, unless, by fiat of his imagination, the poet, drawing all things into his personal center, effectively make them so. This was no doubt his intention, and the product was to have been one variety of this poet's pervading expressionism.

But Spender recognizes that *Vienna* was a failure; certainly the relationship he claims and the interdependence of validities quite fail to manifest themselves, and they do not assist the flimsy structure in its unequal burden of containing both the objective and the subjective elements. We may observe here, however, that Spender's poetry most characteristically strains beyond its ability to make unity where diversity is overwhelming and to make resolutions out of unresolvable conflicts. More than for most poets, for Stephen Spender throughout his work, not to have failed would be not to have assayed a sufficiently tough project, to have shortchanged the complexity of things, to have taken the simplicity of appearances too much on trust, simplicity that has not won its way through complexity not being worth having.

The first part of the poem, "Arrival at the City," describes the unwholesome *patron* of the Pension Beaurepas, who brings to the poet's mind that "many men so beautiful" lay dead while this vulgarian lived on, and he compares him implicitly with Wallisch, whom he makes the hero of the rising. The contrast between them informs the first part of the poem; but in this part also, undisciplined by the structural scheme, there is the expression of feelings, which as mentioned, are not strictly germane to the objective parts of the poem. The poetry fluctuates between description of the outside objective world and description of inward sentiments; both efforts may employ concrete imagery; and thus, the movements from one thing to another not being marked, it is obscure.

After some fragments of self-revealing dialogue from the female residents of the Pension, the poem proceeds to force the paradox that the life of the patron is a decaying wound while the wounds and the death of the hero are an "Opening to life like a flower him overarching." Of the two examples, the poet says he chooses "the wholly dead." He adds, "their courtesy / Like lamps through the orange fog, with a glazed eye / Can preach still"; and the image is a small embodiment of the idea Spender develops later in **"Exiles from their Land, History their Domicile,"** a poem in *The Still Centre,* that the dead, in his own words, have "obtained for their lives a symbolic significance which certainly passed unnoticed when they were living" and have imposed on the imagination of posterity a "legend of their unity of being."[20]

It is not death we fear, the poem goes on, but disloyalty to an ideal memory of peace in the past and disloyalty toward the dead. The poet wants to keep the past firm; just as the dead are to appear in the unity of being with which death has endowed them, so the past should be kept inviolate, though already the "settled mountain . . . Slides its burnt slopes." So later, in Spender's play, *Trial of a Judge,* the Judge wishes to act for the sake of peace and "for the survival of a vision / Within the human memory / Of absolute justice. . . ."

A sense of the drabness of reality presides over the last thirty lines or so of this part of the poem, drabness that is momentarily escaped in the possibility of forgiveness. The poet presents first the real situation in images that point to the ordinariness of a part of the town—"Unhomely windows, floors scrubbed clean of love, / A waste canvas sky," and the like. These images are presumably correlative to the poet's feelings about the revolution, from which the idea of forgiveness provides temporary relief. It provides also a link with the second theme of the poem, the love affair. A sense of guilt and the need for forgiveness simply for being a member of the renter class and being thus immune to the sorrows of the workers was regularly manifested in Spender and in some of his colleagues. But for Spender guilt arose also out of his love affair with Elizabeth, because it conflicted with his feelings and his duties toward his secretary, T. A. R. Hyndman. We learn from the autobiography that Elizabeth and Spender discussed his guilt; and he wondered whether their explanations, "which made [his] 'psychology' responsible for everything, did not actually increase [his] sense of guilt."[21]

The idea of forgiveness comes to his mind glowing, paradoxically, like the first sin of loving in Eden:

> Instantly released, in joy and sorrow they fall,
> Escaping the whole world, two separate worlds of one,
> Writing a new world with their figure 2.

But reality returns in images of murky or "difficult" light, light "dripping / On speechless pavement," "The defeated / Staring, white canal." Part I closes with the same lines as those it opened with:

> Whether the man living or the man dying,
> Whether this man's dead life, or that man's life dying.

Part II, "Parade of the Executive," is itself divided into four parts marked by marginal subtitles in italics. The first part, *The Executive,* presents the rulers, Dolfuss, Fey, and Staremberg, as waxwork models in a parade, "Looking like bad sculptures of their photographs." They are parading in their fancy dress in order to "illustrate the truth" that they are our ancestors. We are exhorted at the very end of the poem, however, that not these representatives of order but the revolutionaries whom they crushed are in fact our ancestors. Next, presented as counterpoint, there are the unemployed, who, reduced to an attitude of basic realism, "politely" stay away from the parade. One noticeable feature in a number of Spender's poems is the manner in which he swings from one theme to its polar opposite or to another contrasting theme, then swings back: and then sometimes, but not here, he comes finally to a resolution at a midway point. In the third section of this part of *Vienna* we come back to *The Executive* with images that show the determination and the strength of this group. Then at the end of this part, the poet introduces a figure called *The Stranger,* the observer of the political scene who, unlike the poet himself, is objective and impartial. "Would he forgive us?" the poem asks, returning at the end to the obsessive guilt, of which the poet is determined to cut himself a large share:

> Would he
> Glance at a minister who smiles and smiles
> "How now! A rat? Dead for a ducat." Shoot!

In Part II, "The Death of Heroes," the poet identifies himself with the revolution, analyzes the causes of its failure, and presents vignettes of the action, some of which are quotations in prose to which he adds verse summaries. The poem describes the retreat of Wallisch to the mountains and how he was hunted down and caught by ski-patrols, then his defense in court, then his death, and finally how sympathizers brought flowers for his grave and for the graves of the other dead revolutionaries. The villain of the piece is Vice-Chancellor Fey.

Part IV is titled "Analysis and Final Statement." First, five voices whose speeches are labeled with the letters A to E make a composite commentary; the poem here totally withdraws into the world within, where the poet wants to deal with his feelings. Voices representing the participants of the conflict brought on by the love relationship all speak here. Voices A and B recognize the value in the relationship. C admits the harm it does to "a friend / Who is external," presumably Hyndman. Then D, thus introduced, who has the longest speech of the five, speaks as that friend:

> It is not what they stole nor what they spoiled . . .
> It is that my devotion they have spilled
> And bled my veins of trust across their sport.[22]

He forgives them, but he sometimes wishes, he says, that he were

> loud and angry
> Without this human mind like a doomed sky
> That loves, as it must enclose, all.

The image of the doomed sky is associated with Hyndman in the poem **"For T. A. R. H.,"** published in the second edition of *Poems* in 1934 (p. 36). In the passage in *Vienna,* D is no doubt expressing Spender's own hankering after the strength of will as he sees it in powerful men, as Arnold had hankered after it in the poem Spender quotes in *Forward From Liberalism.* The Judge in *Trial of a Judge* also regrets an inability to respond to situations with animal fierceness—an inability he considers characteristic of the liberal: "I envy, I envy / Those who had faith in the past to work the good / Or evil which they willed."[23] The comment of E (to return to *Vienna*) is obscure: he or she seems to be bringing the problem into alignment with the political matter by declaring that we rely upon corruption in men inasmuch as we rely upon their own self-esteem to motivate their heroism. Such an attitude spreads the guilt wide, bringing it to inhere in our very virtues.

Following the comments of the five voices, the poet begins to draw phrases and images from the earlier part of the poem, using these presumably to knit the parts together. But between such phrases, there are still the inward explorations of the poet's own "unknown, mental country." At last, the personal data and the political are fused—"yoked by violence together," rather—in a disintegrated profusion of imagery.

The failure of the poem to bring together its components was not one of the main charges brought by reviewers, who concentrated their objections on the images. D. M. T. in *New Verse*[24] finds in certain passages and image clusters a "falsity and affected ugliness," which he attributes to the current affiliation of Spender with political poets to whom he was, temporarily it seems, lending his moral weight. Tom Wintringham would have considered such moral weight to be negligible: as we have seen, he found Spender "unable to associate himself with the living stuff of the revolution," which inability produced in *Vienna* "a remoteness a coldness of image. . . ."[25] There is, certainly, a self-conscious contrivance about Spender's images all the way through *Vienna* and elsewhere that often makes them seem remote and cold; but there is no reason to attribute this to a lack of engagement in politics. It is conceivable that if he had abandoned himself to a burning political passion he would have fused all his materials into a unity; but, for better for worse, Spender never abandoned himself to anything. He never wrote out of excitement generated in the lower levels of the soul, whence come, for example, the terrifying or ecstatic outcries of Yeats or Roethke or Robert Graves; he brought forth no poetry that was not mediated through an analytic cerebration.

All this is not to say, obviously, that he had no feelings; probably these were in fact so strong that he was at pains to suppress them. Edwin Muir, one of Spender's most sensitive critics, notes that in *Vienna* there is no natural voice and nothing seems to be felt with definiteness, such feeling as there is being muffled in the "latest kind of poetic diction." And we need not suppose that this muffling was unintentional.

Trial of a Judge, 1938, produced by Rupert Doone for the Group Theatre, presents again the conflict between left and right, and with it that between public and private life, conflicts which, although very much Spender's own, have from the beginning of this century become familiar by their monstrous prodigies to every household in Europe and have not ceased since then to trouble the sleep of all sensible men. The conflict in the major key in this play is engaged between blacks (fascists) and reds (communists); between these two factions stands the liberal Judge. The fascists have murdered Petra, on the mistaken assumption that he was a Jew, and the Judge has condemned them to death. The communists, molested while handing out leaflets, have shot and wounded a policeman in the arm; and because the carrying of firearms is so punishable, the Judge has condemned them to death also. Hummeldorf, a minister of the government, asks the Judge to reprieve the fascists; the Judge desires the President to reprieve the communists. Power in the state moves to the right, however; and the Judge, the reds, and also Hummeldorf, now converted to the liberal position, are imprisoned.

The conflict in the minor key is that between the private life and the public, which in one particular form the poet had attempted to resolve earlier in his poem *Vienna.* The Judge champions the private against the total claims of the state, asserted by both the blackshirts and the reds. In the following passage, which has already been referred to, the city is the *res publica*; and the natural world, the "greenness," symbolizes the private life. The Judge is speaking:

> Petra's murder
> Printed in a million newspapers
> Torn and carried by the wind,
> Tugs like entrails on the blackthorn
> And fouls the edges of the city
> Where greenness first begins[26]

Part of the private life is the vision of absolute justice—a memory from the past to be kept and kept sacred like the same kind of memory in *Vienna*; again the Judge speaks:

> Then, for the sake of such a peace
> As still does mantle sunset villages
> Where the heart may love and rest,
> Which still to Europe I may restore;
> And, for the survival of a vision
> Within the human memory
> Of absolute justice accepted by consent. . . .

(p. 30)

For the fascists, of course, the nation is indivisible and "Embossed beneath one iron will"—everyone bearing the same stamp. One reviewer points out that the private life receives little enough dramatization in the play;[27] but, as will appear, Spender's distribution of dramatic life in the play is altogether gratuitous.

Like a number of Spender's shorter poems, the play has a dialectical structure: blacks versus reds, as thesis and antithesis, with the Judge not so much forming a synthesis as abjuring both their houses. The Judge's quarrel with the blackshirts has its obvious causes; and theirs with him is for his liberalism and his idealism: "this Judge," says the Black Troop Leader,

> believed
> That an argument would govern the state which drew
>   its form
> From the same sources as the symmetry of music
> Or the most sensitive arrangement of poetic words
> Or the ultimate purification of a Day of Judgment.[28]

The Judge's quarrel with the reds is that he will not condone their policy of answering violence with violence and using lies and hate in their struggle, as if the ends justified all. For using their methods

> we betray
> The achievement in ourselves; our truth
> Becomes the prisoner of necessity

Equally with their untruth, ourselves
Their stone and stupid opposite.

(pp. 103-4)

"Yeats," says Spender elsewhere, "was perhaps the writer who best understood that public passion can 'make a stone of the heart.'"[29] Between the Judge and the reds also falls the idea of abstract justice,[30] which the pragmatic reds reject, as indeed they reject the very idea of abstraction: the fiancée of Petra says to the Judge

Let your self-pitying eyes sink
Deep into their bone wells and stare
At the world's tragedy played out in that one skull.[31]

Louis MacNeice says that the "intended moral of the play was that liberalism today was weak and wrong, communism was strong and right. But this moral was sabotaged by [Spender's] unconscious integrity; the Liberal Judge, his example of what-not-to-be, walked away with one's sympathy."[32] One reviewer of the play calls it a morality play, and this is reasonable since we find the villains declaring their villainy as they used to do in the old drama.

A verbal victory is awarded to the Communists with their party line of tit-for-tat against the Fascists and the notion that finally power (the power of the proletariat) is right. But all the best arguments and all the feeling speeches go into the mouth of the judge with his defence of abstract justice. . . . Spender may have intended one moral for his play and diffidently suggested another. The only moral I could find was that Stephen Spender ought not to be a Communist. As a result of this contradiction in the play the judge walks out of the mosaic and becomes a character.[33]

This review demonstrates another instance in which Spender's "real" nature reveals itself through the ill-adjusted robes of the propagandist. The Judge seemed to Edwin Muir the most impressive figure in contemporary drama. "He is an embodiment of the spirit of man at a particular stage of history; he is a representative figure. . . . Every one needs such a figure, as an embodiment of itself and of what it wants to be."[34]

The play is not entirely dramatic, not exactly conceived as an artifact to be visible and audible on the stage: "Producers are not expected to follow too closely the details of sound (drums), lighting, scene shifting—" says the prefatory note. One stage direction runs, "raising her with a gesture which is really his own self-pity"; another, "Lighting suggesting illusion." The action of Act I, we are directed, is to suggest "that this act is a dream in the Judge's mind." Act IV involves another willing suspension of belief, being the dream of Hummeldorf. "Realism and symbolism were never quite reconciled," Gavin Ewart remarks, recording that the play opened with the Judge lying on the bier of the murdered Petra, indicating his sympathy but wrongly

suggesting that he was dying.[35] Edwin Muir commented that "the actual struggle is neither between the Fascists and the Communists, nor between the Judge and the world he lives in: it takes place within himself."[36] This condition is like that which contemporaries found in Spender himself, for whom the large conflicts in the world were said to reflect a conflict within.[37] Muir goes on: "This is perhaps a defect, dramatically; and it is paralleled by a corresponding defect: that the dramatic speech, with its involution, is more suited to monologue than to dialogue. The verse has some times great beauty, but it has rarely the direct speaking quality of dramatic utterance." In addition to these factors, which tend to sap the play of its dramatic strength, the imagery, as was pointed out in *Scrutiny*,[38] does not regularly lead into the subject; it is often vague. There are places where it is clear and objective and reveals the poet's intended meaning of its own accord, without his curious manipulation; but these places, effective as they are, are unusual. One reviewer found nothing more convincing in the play than the objective passage of prose in which the Black Troop Leader sells himself to us as a harmless bourgeois.[39] Here the imagery is clear and offers its own message. The "harmless bourgeois" sounds like one of the knights out of *Murder in the Cathedral* who has read Auden:

. . . most of us are happily married and myself, I may add, the proud father of six. Most of us own a little scrap of harmless property, a small shop with a bell that tinkles happily to summon mother when you open the door, or an acre or so of land, perhaps even a vineyard with the soft tendrils of the grapes and the fine globular fruit clustering around the ripe cheeks of our laughing children and young wives.[40]

More often we get verse, and verse with tortured and complex imagery, more suited to monologue, as Edwin Muir pointed out, than to dialogue: Of Petra:

They shot only his face
That's still the face of what he is:
Their leaden bullets against a knife edge
Of steel, have tried to turn the blade:
But instantly when he died, the entire knife
Of what he thought and strove, glued to my hand.

(p. 22)

These metaphoric equivalences would not be easily grasped in the theater. Spender even as dramatist is not content to be the mere choreographer, disposing his counters for objective vision and audition, revealing his meanings in their movements. Throughout all his work, images tend to be strained or twisted in the poet's restless, sophisticated effort to express the refinements and nuances of a truth that is not to be expressed by the normal blunt means of articulation. But there is a place in drama for bluntness; and in life itself there is a point at which something of the endless complexity of the truth inherent in things must be sacrificed for the sake of simplicity of expression and communication itself.

The Still Centre, published in May 1939, contains nearly all the poems written since the publication of the second edition of *Poems.* Many of these are about the civil war in Spain, grounded in experiences the poet had had there during 1937. The volume also contains longer poems: in the 1933 and 1934 volumes, no poem had gone much beyond thirty lines; some in *The Still Centre,* on the other hand, run to around a hundred and thirty. Among the longer ones, **"The Uncreating Chaos"** and **"Exiles from Their Land, History Their Domicile"** have been extensively revised, the poet tells us, since their first appearance, as had the shorter poem, **"An Elementary School Class Room in a Slum."** In his foreword Spender also says that external pressures had tended to make poets write of what was outside their own individual experiences, which had been dwarfed by the violence of the times. Therefore, he says, he has himself "deliberately turned back to a kind of writing which is more personal."

If, as he implies, Spender has now resigned his commitment to action in the "violence of the times" and presumably then also to poems bearing political burdens, he is still diversely drawn to the outer and the inner worlds respectively, and the tension is felt in many poems. The foreword includes a reference once again to the poet's need to relate the private world within to the public outer one; "Even while he is writing about the little portion of reality which is part of his experience, the poet may be conscious of a different reality outside. His problem is to relate the small truth to the sense of a wider, perhaps theoretically known, truth outside his experience."[41]

The theme that recurs most frequently in this volume is that of the achievement of unity of being or of an image of the integrated self. This has been attained to, apparently, by those who are dead, those who were (or are) "truly great," and those who exert will. Spender has suggested that the achievement is one of the "obsessive themes" that are always with him.[42] In a recent poem he recalls that as a child he thought that being grown up was "when / How they look from the outside / Is what they have become all through."[43] In the first poem of the Marston series, in *Twenty Poems,* he shows his predilection for personalities that can be condensed each into a single image which is as clear, vivid, and uncomplex as a mere sign—in Yeats's words, "Character isolated by a deed / To engross the present and dominate memory." We learned also in Spender's early volume, in **"'I' Can Never Be Great Man,"** that because the "I" is various, disintegrated, and not single, it can never be great.

In *The Still Centre* we find these ideas taken up again: there is the poem **"Exiles from Their Land"** of which Spender remarked that it was about "those who have, after their deaths, obtained for their lives a symbolic

significance. . . ."[44] In this poem death is the divinity that shapes ends and selects purposes and acts that will endow us with symbolic significance; in another poem, the poet looks forward to entering "The cloudless posthumous door / Where the slack guts are drawn into taut music."[45] But this significance, this unity of being, as Spender calls it (and Yeats before him), is not necessarily the product of death: there is also the will. Death has enshrined those exiles as great because it has made them "one with what they willed" (p. 24) or "cast / Their wills into signatory moulds. . . ."

The poet of *The Still Centre* thinks of his own will as "faltering" (p. 33); Spender wrote in his diary in Hamburg, "I have no character or will-power outside my work"[46]; in **"The Human Situation"** he envies figures whose wills are firm:[47] the father, the captain of the school, heroes of legend or history, a certain woman. Will is admired also in nonhuman forms: the Midlands Express, for example, which "with unerring power" drives straight to its goal, ravishing England that lies beneath it like a woman (p. 47).

Along with the admiration and the envy, however, there is firm recognition in this volume of what would be lost if the will took over, or what has been lost in circumstances where it had taken over. In **"The Human Situation"** the poet again observes that it would be impossible for him to enter, or imagine or wish to enter the symbolic beings of those he envies; it would be "Death to me and my way of perceiving / As much as if I became a stone," the Yeatsian image used in *Trial of a Judge* to express the result of singleminded absorption in public passion. His multivalence with all its liabilities is necessary to him. And he recognizes in others the importance of weakness as we have seen; declaring it valuable in George Barker, while the will is an obstacle to Rex Warner. In the short poem, **"Houses at Edge of Railway Lines,"** he contemplates with favor a life of which the richness lies in the absence of effective will—a train, once more, that rushes by outside (pp. 103-4) and in a later volume, under the same metaphor, he distrusts the will and the "confident iron rails."[48] Then in *The Still Centre* again, there is Napoleon, the subject of a long poem,[49] who is "ruled / By a dead will," burdened by the fixed image of self—the kind of image that in some other poems of Spender's is devoutly to be wished.

The poet, then, calls for the strength of will to become a being of integrity and at the same time knows he needs his own essential lack of will, what he designates weakness, for his very way of life. Weakness as the opposite of will is what he refers to when he says in the foreword that he has included in his subjects "weakness and fantasy and illusion." But a recurring process in this volume is the courtship of incompatible opposites, seen in such poems as **"The Human Situation," "The**

Separation," "The Mask," and especially **"Darkness and Light."** According to a reviewer in the *Times Literary Supplement,* the still center is the point from which all opposites can be reconciled.[50] Another reviewer of the book finds the still center to be a symbol for "that position from which the poet can stabilize his values and thus come to terms with his world."[51] But, no, it is a pole and not a point of equilibrium, and it cannot be the point of reconcilement: the peace at the still center, in the last stanza of **"The Separation,"** is obtained by release from the will's error; and that is no reconcilement or compromise with the will but the removal of its influence:

> Shuttered by dark at the still centre
> Of the world's circular terror,
> O tender birth of life and mirror
> Of lips, where love at last find peace
> Released from the will's error.[52]

The still center is, surely, that residue of the self, as Spender was later to designate it, which, washed over by all tides of public occurrences, is finally untouched and lives independent of any conditioning whatsoever.

The *TLS* noticed also that "a cry for release into reality through a profound acceptance of it sounds repeatedly through these poems, a cry to be recalled 'from life's exile. . . .'"[53] The final lines of **"To a Spanish Poet"** are quoted, including the following passage, which reproduces once again the Keatsian sentiment that was discovered to have much relevance in the decade:

> . . . only when the terrible river
> Of grief and indignation
> Has poured through all my brain
> Can I make from lamentation
> A world of happiness. . . .

But if the acceptance of reality sounds repeatedly throughout this volume, so too does the instinct to withdraw from it—"out of rapid day" into "the tunnel of my dream," or into "symbolic being" or to be at the still center where there is peace.

We have observed above in connection with the Marston poems a simple instance of how Spender uses the poem to resolve his own real-life quandary, the poetic death of Marston satisfying the grievous frustration Spender had incurred on being repudiated by him. **"Darkness and Light"** performs, no doubt, a similar act: behind the poem there presumably lies the personal problem of individuation, or at least the integration of various parts of the personality, say, the inner and outer worlds. The poem resolves that problem poetically, and, the effort at integration having grown the very habit of Spender's soul, it is not surprising that the poet uses the poem, with modifications, as epigraph for *World Within World.* It will be considered below in some detail.

Meanwhile, as a poetic welding of incompatibles, it is of interest to observe it in passing as an example of the use of the poem toward the solution of an insoluble problem.

In *Ruins and Visions* and in *Poems of Dedication,* which follows it, Spender puts his art to service in assuaging the grief of two personal afflictions, the departure of his wife and the mortal illness of a beloved sister-in-law, Margaret. At the same time, however, he questions the efficacy of art in resolving problems in reality. *Ruins and Visions* (1942) consists of four parts: the first three, "A Separation," "Ironies of War," and "Deaths" constitute the ruins; Part IV is "Visions." The poems of Part I express grief at the loss of a loved woman, who is presumably a reflection of Inez, who had left Spender in 1939. The substance of most of the poems is defined and decently removed from the literal source of the grief; but there are some occasional, telling, realistic details: "She was never one to miss / The plausible happiness / Of a new experience," for example, or, addressing himself, recognizing the deficiency he shared with Matthew Arnold:

> At first you did not love enough
> And afterwards you loved too much
> And you lacked the confidence to choose
> And you have only yourself to blame.[54]

There are only a limited number of realistic touches such as these in **"A Separation,"** but Spender seems to be concerned throughout this and the two following parts with the essential falsity of dreams, of certain thoughts, and of the artistic resolution of real problems—the kind of resolution, for example, that he created in **"Darkness and Light."** In **"No Orpheus No Eurydice"** the poet imagines his lost wife, his "pale darling," as dead, "waiting in sweet grace / For him to follow when she calls." But really she is not beautifully dead or able to "follow him back into life":

> For he is no Orpheus
> She no Eurydice
> She has truly packed and gone
> To live with someone
> Else. . . .

The poet's despair at the frailty of the poetic art in the face of an intransigent reality is seen in other poems in these earlier parts of *Ruins and Visions.* The force of an immutable reality is nowhere so powerfully felt in Spender as in this volume. One of the poems, **"Wings of the Dove,"** which is concerned with Margaret and her incurable disease and which becomes a part of the **"Elegy for Margaret"** in the next volume, recognizes the frivolousness, even, of grief. "Oh but my grief is thought, a dream. . . . It does not wake every day" to the "granite facts around your bed, / Poverty-stricken hopeless ugliness / Of the fact that you will soon be dead" (p. 116). In one or two poems in the early parts, the poet is scornful of people who do not acknowledge the real, like the mother in **"The Fates"** who brought up her son in a climate insulated even from the news of poverty, adultery, or disease (pp. 117-22), or like the old men of the last war whose voices he mocks in **"June 1940."**

The poet does not give all to objective truth, however. In Part IV, "Visions," the real and manifest are subordinated to the visionary and the numinous. The section opens with a poem **"At Night,"** which describes the release from pressures of the real which is effected by darkness. Then elsewhere there are references to liberation from the space defined by words: birdsong takes the poet to a "space beyond words"; sleep brings men to where they see "more / Than a landscape of words." In **"Dusk,"** as men drift into sleep, "the great lost river," which must have some atavistic meaning, "crepitates / Through creeks of their brains." Spender wrote subsequently of this part of the book that it reflected a tendency in poetry of that period, shared by the works of other poets, to turn inward to personal subjects (although this act he had already performed in **The Still Centre,** and he had so indicated in the preface). The poems of the last part of **Ruins and Visions,** he said, were "in search of universal experience through subjective contemplation."[55] This, as we have seen, tends to reverse the procedures of the rest of the book.

The last poem in **Ruins and Visions** is **"To Natasha,"** which is the name of the woman Spender married in 1941; and this poem of union balances those of separation at the beginning of the volume. Now, once again, art, whose resolutions had been suspected in some of the other poems, is allowed to bring harmony out of chaos. "Your fingers of music," says the poet, "Pressing down a rebellion of mistakes / Raise here our devout tower of mutual prayer." But even more is to be attributed to artistic vision: "Daily through vigorous imagining / I summon my being again / Out of a chaos of nothing."[56]

Part I of **Poems of Dedication**[57] is **"Elegy for Margaret,"** which contains six poems, versions of two of which had appeared already in **Ruins and Visions.** Part II, "Love, Birth, and Absence," consists of seven poems, ecstatic lyrical meditations on the poet's marriage, refined and insubstantial. Part III is a series, mostly sonnets, called "Spiritual Explorations," and Part IV consists of three poems, **"Midsummer," "Seascape,"** and **"Meeting."**

In view of the questions raised in **Ruins and Visions** as to the ability of art to solve problems, it is interesting to observe in **Poems of Dedication** how the poet faces the dying by cancer of his sister-in-law. For one thing, he resorts to a notion from Plato, coming to it, perhaps, by way of Shelley's "Lift Not the Painted Veil":[58] "the well," those who are healthy, that is, "are those who hide / In dreams of life painted by dying desire / From violence of our time outside. . . ." Addressing his brother, Margaret's husband, he appeals also to the idea that death bestows the legend of unity of being, which he had developed in **The Still Centre**: ". . . those we lose, we learn / With singleness to love." He brings no consolation, he says, but ". . . to accept the worst / Is finally to revive. . . ." And, last, in an illogical, poetic resolution,

> . . . she will live who, candle-lit,
> Floats upon her final breath,
> The ceiling of the frosty night
> And her high room beneath,
> Wearing not like destruction, but
> Like a white dress, her death.[59]

In the last poem of the elegy, by means of wild and distressed imagery, the act of love is relegated from flesh to bone, and the conception of love from eros to agape: ". . . to love means to bless / Everything and everyone." The reduction from flesh to bone is a part of a pervading motif in this volume, which appears especially as a stripping down to nakedness, or in one poem as a passing beyond nakedness. The main theme of the sequence "Spiritual Explorations," eight poems, mostly sonnets, that constitute Part III of **Poems of Dedication,** if indeed it may be spoken of as having a theme, is this descent into some pure, basic condition that underlies most of the phenomena of existence, where "Each circular life gnaws round its little leaf / Of here and now." Beneath all these is the immortal spirit. Spender says the sequence is an attempt to penetrate "the very nature of human existence";[60] the means of the attempt seems to be that of exploring the words, their potential ambiguities and paradoxes, that describe our condition: "All that I am I am not," for instance, or "I who say I call that eye I."[61]

There is some word play too in the opening poem of **The Edge of Being,**[62] **"O Omega, Invocation."** It dwells on the familiar motif of getting beyond present sensations now; indeed, the poet would proceed "beyond silence," in one place. The motif appears throughout the volume:

> . . . O, whose black
> Hoop, circling on white
> Paper, vanishes where the eye
> Springs through thee, O,
> Beyond space silence image,
> O thou, word of beginning
> Oh with what wordless end.[63]

Other poems in this volume dwell on the idea of withdrawing beyond the worlds of sense: in **"Judas Iscariot,"** a slightly dramatic monologue, Judas posits himself and Christ as eternal opposites beyond the world of "hypocrite eyes"; or in **"The Angel,"** there is a hankering for the "inviolate instants where we are / Solid happiness hewn from day, set apart / From others far"; ". . . the real is the terrible," declares the angel. This poem begins with the assertion that "each is involved in the tears and blood of all," the sentiment Spender had adopted in the thirties along with all the other poets who abided by the Keatsian exhortation in *Hyperion.* But now in this late volume the poet hardly conceals his wishes that it were otherwise. In *Vienna, 1934,* he had tried to fuse the story of the workers with the story of his own love affair, and this effort had failed. Now in a long poem in *The Edge of Being,* **"Returning to Vienna, 1947,"** he recognizes that his mind will not, in Eliot's famous phrase, digest such "disparate experiences": the crystal bowl of the love affair is flawed by the reality, the unemployed:

> There was reality, the flaw
> Within the golden crystal bowl, where life
> Was not entirely love nor even
> Baroque frozen in dolphin attitudes
> But was the unemployed who starved. . . .
>
> (p. 21)

The antitheses notified here introduce us to new terms for the conflict that Spender's foregoing volumes have variously revealed. It is, in general, the same conflict; it finds new terms and new images: in the early poems there are the traditionally good and lovely things, nature and culture, on the one hand, and progress and communism on the other; there is the world of will and that of sensibility, say, in *The Still Centre;* there is the ruined world and the visionary in *Ruins and Visions;* and now, at least related, is a conflict between the gilt statuary and the destructive dust. It will be recalled that in *Vienna* he had wanted to keep the past inviolate; but it is not to be so. **"Returning to Vienna"** proceeds to link the love affair with the architecture and sculpture of the old city; but the "seeming permanence was an illusion," and

> . . . what was real was transitory dust
> True to our time dust blowing into dust
> The dust a vital inward spring with power
> To shatter history-frozen visions
> And burst through cities and break down their
>   walls. . . .

In other poems of this volume dust appears again as the destroyer. (One recalls the showers of acrid dust that followed the explosion of bombs in air raids that Spender witnessed as a fireman at the time of the writing of some of these poems.) In **"We Cannot Hold onto the World"** the poet describes two deaths, that of an athlete who has been shot and that of Virginia Woolf; then he says in conclusion: "Who shall regain / The concentrated mind / From blowing dust outside, and

seas, and driving rain?" (p. 54). In the last stanza of the last poem of the volume, **"Time in Our Time,"** the poet writes, "Oh save me in this day, when Now / Is a towering pillar of dust which sucks / The ruin of a world into its column" (p. 56).

The title of this volume, derived from the poem that Spender had set at the forefront of his first published work, is apt enough for a group of poems in which his wishes to be suspended between the concrete being and the abstract nonbeing are once again made manifest. "I was cast naked out of non-existence," he says. And in another poem, **"Speaking to the Dead in the Language of the Dead,"** he contrasts the dead who have arrived at being—"the perfecting dead. Their night / Is words and statues"—with us, we, who under Yeatsian "blood and mire," are suffering on "the harsh edge of existence" (p. 52). Throughout, anticipated by the opening poem in which the eye springs through the word on paper, there is homage paid to the unreified. In **"Rejoice in the Abyss,"** with echoes of Owen's "Strange Meeting" and stronger echoes of Eliot's "compound ghost" in *Little Gidding,* the poet is instructed after an air raid to rejoice in the abyss and to accept emptiness:

> Unless your minds accept that emptiness
> As the centre of your building and your love,
>
>   . . . .
>
> All human aims are stupefied denial. . . .
>
> (p. 31)

In his lines on Virginia Woolf the poet dwells on the "un": "Her mind unstrung—mirror unspoken / Thoughts (white now as her bones) / Pages of an unwritten book."

In the last poem of the volume, from which quotation has been made above, Spender seems to want some kind of fusion between being and nonbeing of the order he conceived in the fusion between darkness and light in *The Still Centre.* The poem sets up men's past and future as fixities "pivoted / On the irreducible secret diamond / His Now." He concludes

> . . . may all that was
> Once idea integrated into stone
> Enter my secret mind at the whirling centre
> Of the external storm: and combine with
> A love which penetrates through falling flesh
> To paint the image in my heart
> Of that past greatness and that once-willed Future,
> Beyond the storm, which still can make a world.

Collected Poems[64] adds a handful of poems that had not previously appeared in the volumes. What is of more interest than the poems added is the fact that, of the one hundred and eleven poems printed, a large proportion are poems that Spender wrote in the thirties. Of the first edition of *Poems* (1933), only two poems are not reproduced, **"Those fireballs, those ashes"** and **"My**

parents quarrel in the neighbour room," the poem in which F. R. Leavis had heard the strong echoes of *Modern Love.* The space devoted to this one part of his poetic output up to that date is interesting. In addition, the poems about the Spanish Civil War, which had appeared in *The Still Centre,* are very fully represented. So that, even discounting his compulsion to "own up," as he says in the introduction, to certain poems of the period, it seems that Spender saw himself in 1955 predominantly as a poet of the thirties, or at least supposed that that is how his public saw him and was not displeased with the image.

Second, the changes the poet has made or has not made are interesting, though they do not demonstrate a single principle at work. Many of the earlier poems reappear with only minor changes; "A temptation I have guarded against," he says, "is that of making more than a discreet and almost unnoticeable minimum of technical tidyings up. . . . [T]he technical flaw in an early poem may reflect a true inadequacy to impose a finished form upon an incomplete experience. It may even . . . have a certain beauty in realizing the rightness of such an incompleteness."[65] There is, of course, no attempt made in the *Collected Poems* to change the image of the poet from that of a communist to that of a humanist by deft manipulation here and there of the diction in the earlier poems.

Apart from the changes made in those poems in which the poet has, in his own phrase, reinvented the ideas— **"Exiles from their Land, History their Domicile,"** for example,—changes tend sometimes simply to make for clarity in rhetorical statement. For instance, lines from **"Perhaps"** in the second edition of *Poems* are altered to release a metaphor and substitute abstract terms with more precise meaning and a simile: "is it leviathan, that revolution / hugely nosing at edge of antarctic?" (p. 50) becomes "Is it The Shape of Things to Come, that revolution / nosing whale-like at Antarctic edge?"[66] Or ". . . rays / Where our eyes fuse the rainbow of their gaze," in *Poems of Dedication* (p. 55), becomes ". . . rays / In which our eyes meet when, near or far, they gaze."[67] A number of such changes purchase clarity at the slight cost, sometimes, of richness.

His poetry often being so little dependent upon the descriptive function of its words, Spender is occasionally not loth to substitute words that change the literal meaning of a sentence, slightly or entirely. Thus, in **"Perhaps"** again, from the second edition of *Poems.*

> Out there
> perhaps growth of humanity above the plain
> hangs: not the timed explosion, oh but Time
> monstrous with stillness like himalayan range
>
> (p. 5)

becomes

> Out there
> Perhaps it is the dead above the plain
> who grow; not our time bombs but Time
> monstrous with stillness like that Alpine range.[68]

Other examples of such changes abound in poems that have been "reinvented."

Sometimes changes augment rather than reduce the richness of a poem. The greatest number of this kind are accounted for by the aim to increase the concretion of an image, to give a line particularity, or to make what was literal metaphorical. The last change quoted above shows Spender calling upon his wartime experiences and introducing the time bomb, with which as a fireman he had no doubt become acquainted. Another war experience feeds a poem that Spender changes in the direction of enrichment of image and increasing power of metaphor: the version in *The Edge of Being* of **"Epilogue to a Human Drama"** reads

> The City burned with unsentimental dignity
> Of resigned wisdom: those stores and churches
> Which had glittered emptily in gold and silk,
> Stood near the crowning dome of the cathedral
> Like courtiers round the Royal Martyr.
>
> (p. 28)

The *Collected Poems* version reads,

> London burned with unsentimental dignity
> Of resigned kingship: those stores and Churches
> Which had glittered century-long in dusty gold
> Stood near the throne of domed St. Paul's
> Like courtiers round the Royal sainted martyr.
>
> (p. 145)

The earlier and later renderings of two passages from **"Elegy for Margaret"** may be compared:

> . . . a villain
> Seizes on the pastures of your life
> Then gives you back some pounds of flesh, only again
> To twist you on that rack of pain. . . .[69]

in *Collected Poems*:

> . . . a villain,
> Seizes on the pastures of your flesh,
> Then gives you back some acres, soon again
> To set you on that rack of pain. . . .
>
> (p. 155)

> Since, darling, there is never a night
> But the restored prime of your youth
> With all its flags does not float
> Upon my sleep like a boat. . . .[70]

becomes in *Collected Poems*:

Since, Margaret, there is never a night,
But the beflagged pride of your youth
In all its joy, does not float
Upon my sleep, as on a boat.

(p. 157)

Finally, a change increasing the vividness of a poem suggests that an unconscious borrowing (or perhaps a borrowing back of what was once loaned) has influenced the modification: The *Still Centre* version of **"An Elementary School Class Room in a Slum"** closes as follows:

. . . show the children to the fields and all their world
Azure on their sands, to let their tongues
Run naked into books, the white and green leaves
　open
The history theirs whose language is the sun.

(p. 29)

The *Collected Poems* version has enriched the imagery:

. . . show the children to green fields, and make their
　world
Run azure on gold sands, and let their tongues
Run naked into books, the white and green leaves
　open
History theirs whose language is the sun.

(p. 81)

The "green" and "gold" additions to the description of the children running into grace remind us of Dylan Thomas's children, "green and golden" themselves who depart from grace in "Fern Hill," which had appeared in *Horizon* after the first but before the second version of Spender's poem.

Much of Spender's familiar imagery is repeated in his latest poems: eyes, winds, suns, waves, nets, and light, whole or broken, in all forms. Poems dwell upon children—the poet's son and his grandchild; and they also recall people from the past, some of whom are now dead and others, living, are changed. Some of the poems are still concerned with the old question of being: the poet is absorbed with the concept of the separate being of the child, for instance: "His glance is grave / Already with some secret hidden from me / . . . My one my own endlessly far from me."[71] Or again, in **"One More New Botched Beginning,"** the boy doesn't see his father but, absorbed in a study of some hens, he becomes a "bird boy" (p. 32).

More often than the separate beings of children, however, Spender is concerned in these recent poems with the identities of those dead or of those who have changed through the years. **"On a Photograph of a Friend, Dead"** explores the matter of the subject's unity and whether the subject can be represented by a single image like the figures in **"The Dust Made**

Flesh,"** in the Marston poems in Spender's earliest work. "Your gaze oblique under sun-sculptured lids / Endlessly asks me: 'Is this all we have?'" Other poems also show concern about the past and about the identities of figures therefrom, living or dead: in **"One More New Botched Beginning,"** the poet remembers walking with Merleau-Ponty, who though dead is no more irrevocable, says the poet, "than the I that day who was / Beside him"—and the poet himself is still living. Then again in the same poem, he recalls Louis MacNeice, Bernard Spencer, and himself exchanging poems. The other two are dead. "Their lives are now those poems that were / Pointers to the poems to be their lives." The meaning isn't clear, but the lines are apparently concerned with the identity of men's works and their lives. **"Auden Aetat XX, LX"** rehearses the well-known memories of Auden at Oxford (including the war-games) and then sets against these the present image of the poet with sixty winters on his head:

Forty years later now, benevolent
In carpet slippers, you still make devices,
Sitting at table like one playing patience
Grumpily fitting our lives to your game,
Whose rules are dogma of objective Love.[72]

The longest poem that Spender has attempted since *Vienna* is **"Pronouns of This Time,"** from which I have quoted earlier; and, judging by the first section,[73] it also is to be concerned with identity. It opens with a memory of childhood, the boy lying awake in his attic room at night watching the stars and ruminating on his selfhood. He reduces himself beneath the stars to nothingness, which renders him identical with everyone:

. . . I lay under that pane of glass
Covered with stars,
　　　. . . . .
And knew then: "I am nothing
But also everyone
Outside me, knows he's nothing
But knowing he is 'I'.
And knowing this I know
The being everyone
Within his dark heart knows
Awake at night alone."

He thinks of others—the cook and the maids and his father; but he can only imagine their daytime selves, the persons, supposedly, of will and world, their inner realities masked.

I could not think my father even
Except at breakfast with *The Times*
Spread out behind an egg. . . .

Earlier poems concerned with identity dwelt upon fragmentation and/or unification within the single person. The identity of all is a new concept, but it seems to be governed to some extent by familiar rules. Spender exercises the concept in this developing poem by considering the identity of himself as an unathletic boy with that of another boy of a very different type, the captain of cricket, each reduced by night time to nothing. Tomorrow

> he must go
> Out on to the field, assume
> Fresh muscle and new eye:
> Attired in pads and flannels
> Be Templar, win our praise.
> In bed now, he is I. . . . .

The poet works on the idea: there must have been a time when the communal selfhood was recognized by all, a time divided from us by a fault: "Something had gone wrong." But he will declare to people that they are one. The prelapsarian community, however, is an inward thing, both creating and depending upon "the world within":

> "In thee, in each of these,
> Differently the same,
> Light separates from dark
> And thou art Adam seeing
> Eden each day the first
> Created in his sight—
>
> "And not by thy sole seeing
> But by addition of those others
> Thy world within is made. . . ."

And once again, the will is the anathema:

> "Therefore whoever casts
> His will, a shadow over
> Another's life, his own,
> Plucks out the hidden nerve
> That is his own eye's seeing. . . ."

Along with the poems, we may glance at some things in the five stories that comprise the volume, *The Burning Cactus* (1936): "The Dead Island," which is a novelette, "The Cousins," the title story, "Two Deaths," and "By the Lake." These stories are of a kind of narrative different from that of *The Backward Son,* Spender's conventional boarding-school novel, full of happening and people, or that of the later novelettes: the stories are closer in style to the poems, using some of the same techniques and showing similar features. Very occasionally the prose gives way to verse with no appreciable jolt. They reveal more of Spender than do the poems: everything he writes, he says, is a fragment of autobiography; but the stories bring us closer, even if not very close at that, to the man himself behind the artifacts. And a brief study of them, noticing certain repeated techniques, will begin to reveal something of the main features of the cast of mind of their author, anticipating and introducing the matter of the final chapter of this essay.

There is, for example, in each story a manifestation of the need of one human for another. There are different kinds of need, but they are not social. In "By the Lake"

two boys at a pensionnat "for the backward and nervous sons of rich people," such, perhaps, as Spender attended himself as a boy, develop a friendship that satisfies familiar adolescent needs. In other stories there is a more covert need on the part of one character for another by means of whom he can define himself, and this feature is not merely a technique of the telling. In "Two Deaths," for example, the character of the narrator is in part revealed to him and displayed to the reader by the description of another man, a Dr. Mur, a phoney. "But if I could think of Dr. Mur as a ghost, what was I, leading this life divided between the sanatorium, my endless exploration of the streets, and my meals at a boarding house full of old ladies?"[74] This is a fairly clear case of what takes place in other stories a little less overtly—in "The Cousins," for instance, where Werner, the hero, as well as the reader, sees more certainly what Werner is by seeing in his cousins what he is not.

The hero in most of these stories is apt to be sick in body or mind or both, and he is gravely misunderstood. He is often a double personality. The adolescent hero in "By the Lake" is broad minded and progressive, and he argues quite hotly in favor of contraception; but he is embarrassed at overhearing the bawdy reminiscence of a fellow passenger on a steamer: "Richard flushed. Yet even whilst he despised this talk, he felt it was illogical that he was shocked" (p. 226). Others have more profound divisions in themselves: the "dear boy," so designated, in "The Dead Island," is a Dr. Jekyll who conceals within himself a Mr. Hyde who robs a bank and scatters the banknotes among the prostitutes in a brothel; the protagonist of "The Burning Cactus" is told that when he is unhappy he is a "different person . . . like a primitive savage, or a hunted animal" (p. 171).

The sick and misunderstood heroes are related to rooms, those they actually inhabit and, for contrast, those they do not but sometimes aspire to. Similarly, a room, often a lighted room, features quite frequently in the poems. In "The Cousins," Werner lives in a bed-sitting room in Victoria (London), to which he has recently escaped from the "dark" house of his earlier years; and these are in contrast to the house where the story is set, especially the "airy white room whose tall windows with window seats on either side of the bow window opened directly on to the cropped lawn" a room which, along with its inhabitants, tells him he is unhappy. Till, of "The Burning Cactus," lives in a "small clean room with metal walls," once light but now darkened by a new building that has been put up in front of it; and the diminished light symbolizes the decline in Till's sense of well-being from the time that he had come to the house; contrasted to this room is that of his friends, Pearl and Roger, who follow a relatively unhaunted and sensual existence in a room with arsenic green wallpaper. In "The Dead Island" the male youth seeking identity with the woman symbolically takes possession of her by daily sweeping her room.

One feature of these stories that has its equivalent in the poems and is felt throughout is the author's unconcern about the sheer objective action in the external world; things happen, often for symbolic effect, which the reader cannot visualize as happening. The clearest example is in "The Cousins," when a rook is shot by one of the cousins because, he says, rooks are vermin. The action is symbolic: Werner, the progressive liberal who "felt he represented international socialism and the arts," who writes poetry and is emancipated from conventional behavior with women, is to be disposed of as obnoxious by the wealthy philistine family with its large aim of self-preservation and its traditional code. Beyond its symbolic significance, the incident doesn't interest the author and he doesn't expect it to interest us: thus, although when shot it "came flapping and planing down," half a dozen lines below we are instructed that the bird "had fallen like a black rotten weighted fruit." Other incidents confirm that the dramatic facts themselves are insignificant to Spender. He is awkward in the way he moves people across rooms, has them introduced, and gets glasses of sherry into their hands; characters always have special looks on their faces, and it is what lies behind these that he is anxious to engage us with. He likes to pin significance upon insignificant details: in "The Cousins," again, Werner fumbles the catch of the card table and the incident is made to bear much symbolic weight. Throughout the stories, people are always liable to do things that people don't do, like Till in the title story, who puts a match to a cactus.

Physical description, whether of persons or things, is sometimes flawed for the same reason—that the author is far more interested in what is not purely objective fact. We learn, for instance, that one hero "noticed under the warm skin the movement of tender bones at the base of [another's] neck: there was a nervous, spilt eagerness about them." Of another we read, "One hand was now pressed to his head, whilst the other clutched at his thigh with coarse exhibitionism, giving his whole body an expression of excluding mountain, port, sea and sky, while pointing singly to the speaker's own personality" (pp. 154-55); of yet another, "it was so easy to read on the rounded flesh of her smiling face framed by the raven hair, that she had made her power and happiness all of one unshatterable shining coloured piece, apprehended from the sea . . ." (p. 48). These things are not to be perceived by our muddy human senses: who has ever discerned spilt eagerness in cervical vertebrae? Sometimes description is lost in a simile that is only dimly apprehensible: "his dark brown eyes, shot with the red blood smeared across their whites, were threatening like the light of street lamp discs struggling redly through yellow fog." There are places,

however, where description is objective and clear and not emasculated by the ideas that have invaded it; but it is most often bestowed upon scenes that have no essential parts in the stories and persons who don't matter. Such description is often vivid. We are shown Dolfuss, for example, who is not one of the principal figures in the story he enters: "A very short man with round boyish peasant eyes, full lips, snub nose, a small moustache and a very high forehead rather pathetically and prematurely lined, with the hair brushed back above it . . ." (p. 200) and Fey, "with a face white and creased like a dirty handkerchief, shot through with bloodless lips and eyes like bullets"; though the latter picture is not without the marks of the author's attitude. A woman walking through a Mediterranean port sees "a bearded nomad from a Turkish village who had spread some coloured carpets on the pavement in front of the hotel, and hung others on a lattice fence: she could see holes of blue sky through those that were hung up" (p. 63); she sees the "lithe hotel porter . . . with a springing step and a smile on his broad mongol face," "a sailing ship . . . being unloaded by five peasants whose dungarees, hands and faces were whitened by the cargo of meal," and so on.

The symbolism in the stories is sometimes presented as such: "'The life I lead here is like that cactus,'" says Till as he sets it alight. "'It's dry and bitter and cutting'" (p. 157). When the boys buy chocolate in "By the Lake," we learn that "This was one of those symbolic actions . . . which made them both return to their childhood" (p. 243). The symbolism is not always explicit; more often it is covert, and sometimes its presence is revealed by dramatic awkwardness, as in the instance of the shot bird. It is perhaps already apparent that the characters in these stories, whether they are the sensitive protagonists or their philistine opposites, all tend to respond to the symbolic values of actions, sometimes accepting things exclusively for their inward meanings. So the cousins, in their story, respond to Werner's fumbling of the catch on the card table.

It is partly with the aid of symbolism that the dialectic comes to be felt in certain stories. In "By the Lake" the adolescent boys are conscious on the one hand of their own youth, its innocence and ignorance and swift passage, and on the other of maturity, experience, knowledge, and evil. The incidents and discussions in the story constitute overt confrontations, but the structure is enriched by situations such as the following:

> . . . they watched the near shore go past fast and the shore of the other side of the lake with its huge mountains seem not to move. Richard noticed such things closely and he noticed himself noticing them. On the far shore were the mountains, but on the near shore towards Lausanne and Vevey there were only

slopes, terraced for vineyards. Occasionally rising from the verge of the lake were old villages with roofs recalling Dürer engravings.

(pp. 226-27)

The symbolic values of islands and mountain suggest a dialectic. Others are more overtly displayed: the ruling class and the noncommitted in "The Cousins," the two sides of Till's character in "The Burning Cactus."

The pervasive sensibility and the use of symbols and imagery with less-than-precise symbolic equivalence give these stories a pitch that reminds us of the poems. We are reminded of them too by such an occasional overwrought figure as we see in the poetry: "The conversation, like a wave striking a sunny rock, exploded into a million atoms of spray, some of which formed rainbows" (p. 115). The reader's mind, an instinctive cerebrator, crossword solver, code-breaker, and de-allegorizer, looks up for the meaning of the rainbow and is not fed. But what above all stamps these stories with the same imprint as the poems is the height of the stage on which both are enacted. In a word, it is elevated above the ground where objects, deeds, speeches, and feelings actually belong, to where thoughts and ideas interact, where high and subtle dramas flicker in the penumbra, and what Spender calls "moral interests" are compared. This is no doubt the nature of a good deal of fiction; but normally today the elevated drama grows by hint and insinuation or by the subtle interplay of symbol out of the muscular, physical things that are happening where we watch; and the writer behaves only as an impresario between objective facts on the one hand and the reader's active intelligence on the other. Spender's way is not this: the physical drama is a bare sequence, the author having observed in the rich ground level of reality only those details that will thrust the mental drama upon us, passive spectators. Occasionally reality makes itself felt, especially in "Two Deaths," where there are details that smack strongly of reality, of objective truth. But Spender's more usual practice, in these stories as in the poems, is to refine the blunt sensory experience and to render it again in terms of the categories of his own mind. Thus it comes about that, in these stories as in the poems, whatever the setting, images of light, whiteness, and eyes abound.

Notes

1. Stephen Spender, Foreword to Facsimile of *Nine Experiments: Being Poems Written at the Age of Eighteen* (Cincinatti: University of Cincinatti, 1944).

2. Geoffrey Grigson, *The Crest on the Silver* (London: Cresset Press, 1950), pp. 169-70.

3. (Oxford: Blackwell).

4. (London: Faber and Faber).

5. Both published in London by Faber and Faber. One poem from *Twenty Poems,* "I hear the cries of evening," was dropped from the 1934 edition of *Poems.*

6. *World Within World: The Autobiography of Stephen Spender* (London: Hamish Hamilton, 1951), pp. 64-67.

7. *Twenty Poems,* p. 7.

8. C. Day Lewis has a similar piece, but more clearly Yeatsian, in *Transitional Poem,* in which those who have his allegiance are mustered, like the friends of Yeats "that cannot sup with us" ("In Memory of Major Robert Gregory"): Lewis's last-named figure is "the tow-haired poet," who breeds "a piebald strain of truth and nonsense"—a more accurate rendering of Auden.

9. *Poems,* 1933, p. 37.

10. *World Within World,* p. 116.

11. *Twenty Poems,* p. 15.

12. *World Within World,* pp. 144-45.

13. *New Signatures: Poems by Several Hands,* ed. Michael Roberts (London: Leonard and Virginia Woolf, 1932).

14. *Collected Poems: 1928-1953* (London: Faber and Faber, 1955), p. 13.

15. *Poems,* p. 22.

16. *New Country: Prose and Poetry by the Authors of "New Signatures,"* ed. Michael Roberts (London: Leonard and Virginia Woolf, 1933).

17. *Poems.* 2nd ed. (London: Faber and Faber, 1934), p. 36.

18. (London: Faber and Faber, 1934). Spender is mistaken in saying, in *World Within World,* that he wrote it in 1935.

19. *World Within World,* pp. 193-201.

20. *Collected Poems,* p. 14.

21. *World Within World,* p. 197.

22. A different interpretation of this passage was made by W. H. Sellers in "Spender and Vienna," *Humanities Association Bulletin* 18 (Spring 1967): 59-68.

23. (London: Faber and Faber, 1938), p. 73.

24. No. 12 (Dec. 1934), p. 20.

25. "Artists in Uniform," *Left Review* 1 (Feb. 1935): 158 n.

26. *Trial of a Judge* (London: Faber and Faber, 1938), p. 29.

27. Janet Adam Smith, in *Criterion* 17 (July 1938): 730-34.

28. *Trial of a Judge,* p. 109.

29. *World Within World,* p. 191. He elaborates the idea in his discussion of Yeats's "Easter 1916" in *The Creative Element* (London: Hamish Hamilton, 1953), pp. 118-19. The "doctrine of necessity" of the communists, says Spender, "taught them not only that necessity justified bad means and individual suffering, but also that it was necessary to deny that it did" (*The Creative Element,* p. 154).

30. Louis MacNeice describes how, at the meeting arranged by the Group Theater to discuss the play, which was attended by a "squad" of comrades, an old man announced he was worried about one thing: "of course he knew S. could not have meant it, there must have been a mistake, but the writing seemed to imply an acceptance of Abstract Justice, a thing which we know is non-existent. [Spender] deliberately towered into blasphemy. Abstract Justice, he said, of course he meant it; and what was more it existed." (*The Strings are False: An Unfinished Autobiography* [London: Faber and Faber, 1965] p. 168).

31. *Trial of a Judge,* p. 73.

32. *Strings are False,* p. 167.

33. K. A., "Play for Puritans," *New Verse,* no. 30 (Summer 1938), p. 20.

34. *The Present Age from 1914* (London: Cresset Press, 1939), pp. 179-80.

35. "Two Views of a Play," *Twentieth Century Verse,* no. 10 (May 1938), p. 52.

36. *The Present Age,* p. 180.

37. As the reviewers of *Forward From Liberalism,* for instance, were not slow to instruct him.

38. H. A. Mason, "Mr. Spender's Play," *Scrutiny* 7 (September 1938): 222.

39. X., Review of *Trial of a Judge, Twentieth Century Verse,* no. 10 (May 1938).

40. *Trial of a Judge,* pp. 86-87.

41. *The Still Centre* (London: Faber and Faber, 1939), p. 10.

42. "Introduction," *Collected Poems,* p. 15.

43. "Draft of the First Five Selections of Part One," *Pronouns of this Time, Shenandoah* 16 (Autumn 1964): 9.

44. *Collected Poems,* p. 14.

45. *Still Centre,* p. 89.

46. *World Within World,* p. 205.

47. *Still Centre,* p. 81.

48. "The Journey," *Ruins and Visions: Poems 1934-1942* (New York: Random House, 1942), p. 91.

49. *Still Centre,* pp. 96-100. (Francis Scarfe finds the figure of Napoleon untrue to the facts of history; he is, rather, an immense Spender with all the complexities and defeatisms magnified ["Stephen Spender: A Sensitive," *Auden and After,* p. 47]. Charles Madge finds the poet's own reflections about greatness and defeat projected onto Napoleon ["Spender," *Poetry* (London) 1 (Nov. 15, 1940): 85].

50. Anon., "The Poet's Dilemma: the Impact of Events," May 6, 1939, p. 266.

51. Robert D. Harper, "Back to the Personal," *Poetry* 57 (October 1940): 49.

52. *Still Centre,* p. 85.

53. Anon., "The Poet's Dilemma: the Impact of Events," *TLS* [*Times Literary Supplement*], May 6, 1939, p. 266.

54. *Ruins and Visions,* p. 90.

55. *Poetry Since 1939* (London: Longmans Green, 1946), p. 34.

56. *Ruins and Visions,* p. 137.

57. (London: Faber and Faber, 1947).

58.   Lift not the painted veil which those who live
        Call Life: though unreal shapes be pictured there,
        And it but mimic all we would believe
        With colours idly spread,—behind, lurk Fear
        And Hope, twin Destinies. . . .

59. *Poems of Dedication,* p. 15.

60. *Poetry Since 1939* (London: Longmans Green, 1946), p. 37.

61. *Poems of Dedication,* p. 44.

62. (New York: Random House, 1949).

63. *Edge of Being,* pp. 9-10.

64. (London: Faber and Faber, 1955).

65. "Introduction," p. 15.

66. *Collected Poems,* p. 52.

67. *Ibid.,* p. 177.

68. *Ibid.,* p. 52.

69. *Poems of Dedication,* p. 11.

70. *Ibid.,* p. 17.

71. "Mein Kind Kam Heim," *The Generous Days* (New York: Random House, 1971), p. 20.

72. *Shenandoah* 18 (Winter 1967): 5.

73. *Shenandoah* 16 (Autumn 1964): 5-20. A note reads: "The poem is planned to be in three parts. Part one: *Thou and I.* Part two: *We.* Part three: *They.* These sections form approximately half of Part one."

74. *The Burning Cactus* (London: Faber and Faber, 1936), p. 193.

Surya Nath Pandey (essay date 1982)

SOURCE: Pandey, Surya Nath. "Spender's Poetic Pilgrimage II—Redemption through Action." In *Stephen Spender: A Study in Poetic Growth,* pp. 81-134. Salzburg, Austria: Institut für Anglistik und Amerikanistik, 1982.

[*In the following excerpt, Pandey traces Spender's development as a poet from* Vienna *(1934) through* The Still Centre *(1939).*]

[Spender's] involvement in human misery led him to explore the causes of exploitation, disparity and injustice in society. It also prompted him to give a passionate call for rebellion to other equally enthusiastic young men, who shared his sense of disgust at the existing state of affairs. But in the first phase of his poetic career, Spender's activities were confined simply to chalking out programmes and issuing manifestos. His exhortations to his comrades for building up a just society were all genuine but they went little beyond their rhetoric and propaganda. However, it was this concern with the contemporary problems that plunged him into hectic political activity when he visited the riot-torn city of Vienna in 1934. Spender was, now, horrified to see the vast spectacle of destruction and chaos brought about by Dollfuss and his army. Here he gathered the first-hand knowledge of human brutality with which the socialist uprising was suppressed. It was the deep feeling of identification with the cause of the Viennese workers that urged Spender to commemorate this event in *Vienna,* which has been hailed as "one of the most widely read of single poems in this century."[1] This poem marks a definite note of change in the poetic development of Spender as, henceforward, politics becomes a thing of primary concern for him.

Vienna deals with "the most heroic episode of modern times,"[2] namely, the fall of the Viennese socialists in 1934 and the victory of the Fascists under Dollfuss.

The poem consists of four sections. It opens with Spender's arrival in Vienna, shortly after the brutal suppression of the rebellion. The Austrian capital wears an anomalous look of confusion and upheaval as the aftermath of the event. The first section entitled 'Arrival at the City' is the interior monologue of a young man in a Viennese pension. The poet is stunned to see (imaginatively, of course, as *Vienna* is "an attempt to cope imaginatively with political events")[3] that the society around him is full of death. In utter confusion, he broods over the significance of the harrowing spectacle:

> Whether the man living or the man dying
> Whether this man's dead life, or that man's life dying
> His real life a fading light his real death a light
>   growing.
> Whether the live dead I live with.[4]

The poet is putting up in the Pension Beaurepas with old people for its inmates. He is surrounded by old ladies who prattle ceaselessly about their old loves and diseases. The boarders of the pension look like figures "printed in papers and cut out with scissors." The proprietor, immersed in sensual pleasures, is almost unaffected by the happenings outside. He chatters about girls and proudly introduces the poet to the festivities of *penis in circensem.* There is an effective caricature of this proprietor in the following lines:

> Winged tie. Winged nose. A bleared, active eye.
> The stick and strut of a sprucer day.[5]

This vivid picture of the proprietor exemplifies Spender's ability to combine the seemingly incongruous elements to form unforgettable images, which is believed to be the strength of a poet. The poet doubts whether this man, symbolising the decaying bourgeoisie, is really alive. Then he saunters through the city and looks at "statues of desirable angels" and is impressed by the sight of their "stone hair shitted by birds" and soothed with a cooing prayer. To the poet they seem to be more alive than the living creatures he has encountered in the city so far, and this makes him "choose the wholly dead." The 'dead' had lived up to their ideals and sacrificed their lives for them. He regrets the vanishing of the human touch, when bombs dismember senseless corpses:

> . . . for harmless bombs
> Ticking in bushes, shock us with their bangs,
> Tearing anonymous limbs from senseless corpses.[6]

The poet moves to another part of the city, perhaps, in search of a congenial atmosphere free from filth and pollution. But contrary to his expectations he arrives at a busy square smelling of disease and death:

> Unhomely windows, floors scrubbed clean of love,
> A waste canvas sky, uninformed nuns,

> Streets tinkling with the silver ambulance.
> We breathe the bandaged air and watch through
>   windows
> Metal limbs, glass eyes. . . .[7]

However, among these living dead, the workers are alive with an iron will to change the existing conditions. When these dead sleep, the workers get up early in the morning and go to work:

> The bins are emptied, the streets washed of their dung,
> The first trucks shunted;

But they too

> . . . behold the world's
> Utter margin where all is stone and iron,
> And wrong.[8]

Out of their work and vision will emerge "the will on alteration"—"the will to alleviate 'certain material evils'."

But this death-life confusion persists and the entire section almost resounds with what Martin Gilkes calls "the leitmotif of the preliminary section of the poem":[9]

> Whether the man living or the man dying,
> Whether this man's dead life, or that man's life dying.

Moved by such a scene of confusion and horror, the poet is disposed to inquire at length into the nature of the crisis. His task is made easy as a result of a public meeting on the 27th of May, at which the leaders of the Austrian government make their policy statements. The second section, 'Parade of the executive', highlights, though ironically, the ceremonies of the bourgeois rulers. There are "flags like whippets tugging" and "4 loudspeakers over the baroque porch, blowing our gilt trumpets." On the beach are seated Major Fey with "his 'strong' white face, a wet handkerchief shot through with two lead bullets" and Dr. Dollfuss with his daughter, smiling. They are flanked by the ministers on the dais. These are the people we trust, but behind their trustful and smiling faces are hidden the minds that deceive and destroy:

> Ministerial lips smile, but what's transparent
> As thin glass is their transparent smile
> Over thin lips: the glass is dashed down suddenly
> And murder glares. Their right hands hold
> Their right hands, but the dangerous left
> Fingers an invisible revolver.[10]

The sight of the unemployed young men is too striking to be overlooked. They are full of anger and Spender fails to understand why they stare even at the strangers like him with indifference. With "their eyes fixed upon an economic margin", they are "Dispersed like idle points of a vague star / Huddled on benches, nude at bathing places". Their indifference towards the bour-

geoisie (onlookers or the government itself) is understandable. Being unemployed and reduced to living on the primitive level, which is mostly making love in an irresponsible and even venal way, these proletarian crowds are perfectly indifferent to the pomp and grandeur of a government that promises no improvement in their condition.

Spender refers to the unfeeling propaganda and the lying of the Viennese authorities in regard to the tenements of the workers. Suddenly he turns for comfort to the thought of the crocus, as a symbol of something in nature that would resist the treacheries and inhumanities of politics:

> If only one can silence every voice,
> Assertion of the primitive crocus,
> Flooded with snow, but melting not to water,
> Melting into summer.[11]

The section ends with the imagined arrival of a stranger, who answers the question—"What is wrong?" The identity of the man is not clear. However, he is Hamlet-like in the rotten state of Vienna and the point of his answer is clear enough—"Shoot!".

The third section, "The Death of Heroes", is the most touching part of the poem, which describes the execution of Wallisch and the death of other worker-heroes. An old man, a survivor of the tragedy, narrates the story of the uprising and points to the 'fatal unconfidence' of the social Democrats as the sole cause of the failure. He also condemns the essentially liberal attitude of the rebels because moderation is incapable of coping successfully with ruthless rightist forces. The unfortunate man painfully alludes to the murder of his son by Fey's men, which was followed by "four more whose dying choked the stairs." He also narrates how a worker, who had betrayed the cause of the proletariat, melted to pity at such a scene of man-slaughter, realized his mistake and returned to the fold wishing to be killed for his treachery:

> "I forsook the workers to kill the workers because
> I was fed by these traitors. Now kill me."[12]

But it is the death of Wallisch, the socialist leader, which is the central story of this section. While comforting his affectionate wife in the court-room, Wallisch exposes the ruthless measures adopted by the Dollfuss government. We are also acquainted with the history of this hero, whose life has been a ceaseless struggle against victimization and oppression. His message to his followers to dedicate their lives to the cause of the proletariat is quite forceful:

> I have devoted my whole life to the workers
> To serve their cause. I have enemies only
> Because I fought for the workers so faithfully,

One must be ready to do all,
Ready to sacrifice oneself, even to lay down one's
life.[13]

And he does lay down his life in the workers' cause. Trapped and betrayed, he is taken prisoner. Spender's description of the arrest and execution of Wallisch is concentrated in its effect:

They brought him out in a hurry
For Dollfuss had phoned through to complain of the
day;
Dollfuss, Dollfuss said 'Hang him low'.
Wallisch stood on the platform and before he died
'Live Socialism', and 'Hail Freedom', he said.
The word 'Freedom' was choked by the rope.[14]

The prisoners learn of his death and as a token of their grief offer flowers on his unmarked grave. "Frequently Mr. Spender", writes Southworth, "uses single epithets with telling force."[15] The use of the word 'easy' in the following description of flowers stirs the imagination of the reader:

We brought easy flowers in crude wreaths
Daisies, nasturtium, corn flower, sorrel, dandelion.[16]

The death of heroes forces the survivors to think that "those who were killed outright" were lucky, and unlucky are those "burrowing survivors" who have no "tasks fit for heroes."

This brings us to the final section, "Analysis and Statement", which is the most introspective part in the whole poem. After his account of the attempted socialist uprising, the poet wishes to register a judgement on the historical event. The section begins with five voices, labelled A to E, which are apparently aspects of one person and which categorize his weaknesses. These different voices, which annoyingly repeat the personal pronoun, the "I, I, I", surprisingly merge into the 'I':

Beneath the lower ribs and the navel
I hold the desert, dividing my health
With five voices.[17]

The poet makes an appeal to an imaginary stranger to cure the "desert" he feels in his heart. First, he enumerates the types of persons he would not like his ideal stranger to be. In that context, Spender's use of the 'islands' image is meaningful. He does not want him (the ideal stranger) to be one of

Those who go to islands,
Whose salvaged happiness can greet their friends,
A few worthy of jokes.[18]

The poet is convinced that the right word on the Vienna affair might not be spoken by those who seek private satisfactions to make up for inner emptiness and discontent. 'Islands' symbolize the selfish and personal as opposed to the collective interest. The poet expects the stranger to integrate the creative and revolutionary forces into a new life. The poem ends with references to Wallisch and Weissel, the great heroes of the revolt. It is remarkable that the objectivity, which was maintained throughout the poem breaks down in the final section, with a sudden spurt of subjective feeling:

I think often of a woman
With dark eyes neglected, a demanding turn of the
head
And hair of black silky beasts.[19]

A reference to this woman in identical words was made earlier in the passage describing the unemployed in the first section.[20] In fact, the whole poem is loaded with references to sex in all its variety. It is, perhaps, this interweaving of sex with the main theme of political struggle and despair which led some critics to believe that sexual crisis is a crucial part of the Vienna experience.[21]

We can trace multiple references to sex in the poem. The old ladies of the Pension speak about their old loves. The proprietor chatters about girls: "I know she's a bitch, but quite my type." In the picture of the festivities of *penis in circensem,* the electric lights hanging on doorways have gestures with "glance like rape." Ivy smothers phallic chimneys. The unemployed young men strip naked, bathe and betray girls. There are even scatological aspects of sex. For example, mention is made of "oil-tarred pissoirs" and lavatories. There are descriptions of sexual perverts who

. . . hang about
At jaws of lavatories, advertising their want of love
Pilloried by their open failure.[22]

In the final section, we go back to the memory of the poet's experience of love:

Our sexes are the valid flowers
Sprinkled across the total world and wet
With night.[23]

"Flowers sprinkled across the world" seems to be the right description of the way sex figures in the poem. But the poet's love has been an experience of failure, due mainly to the fear he has inherited from his father:

It surely was my father
His dry love his dry falling
Through dust and death to stamp my feature
That made me ever fear that fortunate posture.[24]

This failure is not just a personal failure of a private desire.

The image of scattered flowers brings to the mind the picture of prisoners offering flowers on the grave of heroes like Wallisch:

We built
Upon their earth the wave of a new world
From flowers. . . .[25]

And this dream of a new world is trampled into dust by the police, symbolizing the Austrian dictators. It is this parallelism between love and politics which Hynes underlines in his comment:

> . . . there is an uncertain mixture in the poem of politics and self, public and private working in opposite directions and obscuring each other.[26]

It was a tug of war between the public and the private that was dividing the conscience of Spender when he wrote this poem. He himself felt that *Vienna* failed to "fuse the two halves of a split situation [public catastrophe and private affection], and attain a unity where the inner passion becomes inseparable from the outer one."[27] This points to a significant trait in Spender's poetic development. It has been observed earlier that the bias of the poet's personality was essentially subjective, though, he was mindful of the outer reality. This peculiar 'dilemma' is best described in his own words:

> In poetry I was confronted with the dilemma of stating a public emotion [hatred against fascism] which had become a private one, and which yet never became completely my own inner experience because, as I have explained, it invaded my personality rather than sprang out of it.[28]

Edwin Muir felt that the poem did not leave a powerful impression. The defeat of the uprising was disastrous and he wanted a grand treatment of it like a tragedy.[29] It may be recalled here that this was Spender's communist phase. In Marxist terms, the historical reversals are not tragic but simply inevitable parts of the dialectical process. The poet accepts defeat with a glimpse of revolutionary hope towards the end of the poem. The Vienna uprising failed but out of it emerged a heroic story of workers' resistance to the Fascist forces.

Vienna is a bold attempt to treat an important event of contemporary life in aesthetic terms. The social and political perception which was implicit in *Poems* is here vastly expanded but not at the cost of poetic excellence. In fact, it is a long lyric poem in which the events of the uprising are filtered through a private sensibility. The impassioned lyricism which is a hallmark of Spender's first poetic phase can be discerned here too as in the following lines:

'I love a friend
'Who is external: to him the sky is brass
'Solid the grass where his behaving runs
'At night he sleeps well with limpid hands silent,
'His character rings like the single stroke of a bell,
'Loving, I've struck and struck upon this bell
'Until at last I have become

'A singular phantom
'That haunts his constant dream.'[30]

It is these lyrical touches of exceptional intensity which prompted Henry Warren to comment:

> But would so sensitive [as marked in *Poems*] a lyricism survive, in this harsh age, beyond a first volume? *Vienna* is Mr. Spender's answer.[31]

Louis Untermeyer, perhaps, misses the point when he searches for the element of propaganda in the poem.[32] Spender, nowhere, indulges in preaching the philosophy of dialectical materialism, or shows the tendency of stepping down to a direct appeal to the masses. His emotional involvement in the struggle should not be viewed in terms of pure rhetorical didacticism. To do so would be to misunderstand the poetic concept of the 'thirties. Moreover, the private self of the poet is so significantly pronounced in the poem that it hardly leaves any room for such misconceptions and unsympathetic comments.

Vienna has been very often regarded as *The Waste Land* of Spender,[33] not because it is as great as Eliot's poem but because it can be definitely counted as one of the major poems of the 'thirties. Though deeply concerned with the crisis of the time, Spender has not taken recourse to myths or legends either borrowed from the past as in the case of Eliot, or created by himself, like Auden's 'Airman' and 'The dog beneath the skin'. To Spender, the situations of extreme crisis are their own symbols. The theme of *Vienna* is larger than its particular incident, for it was part of a larger conflict in which the Dollfuss government succeeded in suppressing the socialist movement in their state. Even this is part of a still larger theme of history in which Vienna would look like any other city—"Berlin, Paris, London, this Vienna"[34]—where the same conflict was taking toll of human lives and on the sacrifice of these people, who are described as a light to the living, we build our walls as on a foundation. Even then the gaze of Spender is concentrated upon the surface of society, upon political conflict and struggle, victory and defeat, violence and oppression, unlike Eliot whose attention is focussed upon the spiritual degeneration of modern society. Eliot again in *The Waste Land* has taken recourse to a definite technique for effecting a union of the temporal and the timeless elements so that the post-war London melts into any capital of Europe, and the cultural crisis of today becomes a recurring event in the history of mankind through the ages. Because of this profundity of thought and the complexity of technique, Eliot's *The Waste Land* has been rightly adjudged a superior work of art. This comparison, however, should not be construed as something derogatory to the excellence of Spender's poem, because comparison with a superior artist is not intended to belittle the achievement of the younger poet.

Trial of a Judge is the next milestone in Spender's poetic development. It is a poetic drama, a literary *genre* which Spender regards as an effective medium for presenting the problems of contemporary crisis. In his essay on "Poetry and Expressionism", he holds that all poetry is dramatic and all serious drama, whether written in verse or not, is essentially poetic. Both the forms cut through the surface realism of facts and details and reach the core of universal significance. Both achieve "a fusion of forces", "producing a crisis followed by a new synthesis". The overwhelming nature of the chaotic situation could be best expressed in dramatic form:

> Owing to war, political tyrannies, rival ideologies, uncertainty about the future, the attention even of the complacent middle class theatre-going public is more and more directed outwards from themselves and their families to a picture of an extensive conflict which had the world as its scene, and in which their lives are less significant than pawns.[35]

This conviction regarding the essentially poetic nature of drama makes Spender give every Act of *Trial of a Judge* a title, as if the Acts were different sections of a long poem. It was published and first performed in March 1938, the month in which the Anschluss added Austria to the Third Reich, and six months before the Czechoslovakian crisis. But Spender wrote it presumably with the collapse of democracy and the rise of the Nazi State in Germany in 1932 at the back of his mind.[36]

As the title suggests, the play centres in the problems of the liberal Judge. The failure of liberalism and the law under the pressure of Fascism are the principal themes of the play. The play opens with the soliloquy of the Judge, who is pondering over the trial of five Fascist murderers of Petra, the Jewish Communist. He interrogates the criminals later and it is in the course of his cross examination that we learn of the brutality of their crime. In the grip of poverty, Petra was leading a very miserable life but the light of his mission gave him hope and sustenance for existence. The atrocity of the act is highlighted in the speech of the Fifth Black Prisoner:

> We dragged him screaming
> Out of the straw bed by the heels.
> I shot him, stripped. Then we stamped on him
> And kicked his face in.[37]

We also have a detailed account of the murder as given by Petra's Brother and Mother. The Judge is moved at the heinous crime and sentences the murderers to death. The Act comes to an end with the threatening Chorus of Black Prisoners that they will get this order retracted by the force of their influence.

In the beginning of the Second Act, we find the Wife of the Judge talking with Hummeldorf, the Home Secretary in the government and an old friend of the Judge. He has come to the Judge's residence to request him on behalf of the government to revoke the sentence of death. We are also acquainted with the fact that three Communists have also been given equally harsh punishment for injuring a policeman in the process of defending themselves. The following remark of the Home Secretary while persuading the Judge well highlights the distortions of law and justice to suit the convenience of the Fascists:

> You seem to forget that the law is intended to protect the State from enemies and not to fulfil an abstract ideal of justice.[38]

Hummeldorf is assisted by the Judge's Wife in his mission and finally they succeed in getting the order retracted, though at the cost of anguish and pain in the mind of the Judge who wants the Communists also to be condoned. This announcement of acquittal is welcomed with cheers and loud slogans by the Fascists and their sympathisers.

In the Third Act there is an interesting dialogue between Black Chorus and Red Chorus, each justifying his mode of action. In the meantime the Judge comes on the stage and declares his resignation in utter frustration, as he fails to reconcile himself to the reprieve granted to Petra's murderers while under pressure from Fascists he is restrained from doing the same in the case of the Communists:

> Do not put away your revolvers.
> If you wish, shoot, I may not protest,
> For I come to announce not my own resignation
> But the resignation of the law.[39]

On being asked by Petra's Brother to mete out justice to Communists also, the Judge regrets his inability because the law is helpless under the growing menace of Fascism. The speech of the Sixth Black Prisoner is relevant in this context:

> Your Judge has no power! His law is founded on weakness.
> His rulings are not backed by armies.[40]

However, the Judge has experienced a tragic sacrifice of his conscience. All the time he is haunted by the sense of guilt and when Petra's Brother is also killed by the Fascists, he ultimately declares

> . . . now I retract
> The reprieve of Petra's murderers,
> And I order the arrest of those who shot
> Petra's brother here; and those
> Three communists who were unjustly sentenced
> My Court will try again.[41]

All of a sudden Hummeldorf appears and communicates to him that his resignation has been accepted by the government and he has been divested of all authority.

This Act closes with the determination of Black Prisoners to pass judgement on the Judge himself by whom they were condemned to death. The Judge is flanked by the Fascists and taken prisoner with the Communists.

This brings us to the next Act, viz., the trial scene, where the Judge is prosecuted on the charges of "dishonouring the cause of our heroic dead", by his old friend Hummeldorf himself, now occupying the position of the patron of justice. The Judge pleads guilty, "for by your law, the jungle is established," and proclaims:

> O let them witness
> That my fate is the angel of their fate,
> The angel of Europe,
> And the spirit of Europe destroyed with my defeat.[42]

But the trial does not proceed smoothly and the Judge is frequently interrupted and humiliated, so that the trial turns out to be a huge farce. Hummeldorf realizes the enormity of his error, steps down in repentance from his seat of judgement and asks his old friend to pardon him. Hummeldorf is also seized and carried to a cell.

The last Act reveals the Nazi cells where we see persons frenzied by Fascist torture and also listen to a significant dialogue between the Judge and the Red Prisoners. The Communists wish to build their new world on the bones of the oppressors. The Judge is worried by the thought that the means used by the Fascists and the Communists are the same, and today's oppressed would be tomorrow's oppressors and thus hatred and violence will be perpetuated:

> . . . for they transmit
> The violence and hatred which we used
> Into the children's faces which we breed
> Until their faces become that single face
> We gave our lives to kill.[43]

The Judge, therefore, resolves that we must "reject the violence they use" and

> . . . from the impregnable centre
> Of what we are, we answer
> Their injustice with justice, their running
> Terroristic lie with fixed truth.[44]

Strangely enough the Liberals are attacked both by the Fascists and the Communists. The First Black Prisoner is vehemently against the Liberals:

> Kill the liberals, who make us ridiculous in the eyes
> Of the world. Kill. Kill these shadows quickly,
> before they overwhelm us in their universal night of
> chaos.[45]

The Communists also have a similar attitude towards them:

> Yet see with their hypocrite mind; you disclaim
> The necessary killing hatred,

> And ignore that you or they must die.
> You accept gentility, plead for their approval,
> Even in death you sign the martyrs' truce
> Of Christians who have let themselves be killed,
> Clasping the lovely flowering crown and white
> Innocence of a saint's winding sheet; . . .[46]

The dilemma of the Liberal Judge is acute. He is torn between his faith in absolute truth and justice and the hard realities of life which are opposed to them. The crisis of conscience revealed in the Judge corresponds to the poet's own inner struggles. As Desmond MacCarthy puts it:

> The Judge himself strikes me as a sensitive projection of an imaginative creator who is in that kind of predicament I have conjectured. The life-blood of an inner conflict has gone to the inspiration of the Judge's words.[47]

Spender and the Judge had grown up in similar Liberal environments. The soliloquy[48] of the Judge just before his execution sounds almost autobiographical. It is pertinent to recall that, like the Judge, one of Spender's most passionate dreams of childhood was to be a Christ on the cross:

> If, lying in bed awake, there were times when I regretted not having my arms extended on a cross with rusty nails driven through my hands, there were others when I craved for a savagery, a daemonism which seemed to have gone out of the world.[49]

The sacrifice of the "poor dear lamb" appears to be an unconscious fulfilment of Spender's thwarted childhood-wish. One can easily see in the dilemma of the Judge the poet's ambivalent bent of personality.

Intermingled with this political theme is the theme of the destruction of love by the forces of hatred. Petra, the Jew, is a lover as well as a radical. After his murder by Fascists, his brother assumes Petra's role of the protector of Petra's fiancee (who is pregnant), and he too is killed. The Judge's barren and unhappy wife hates both Petra and his girl and revels in the expansion of hate:

> In the larger hate which destroys the world
> The time is redeemed and I am content.
> Let the unconsidering compact bomb cut through
> Tenements and the horizontal thoughts
> Of civilization. It was all false, false,
> Only my hatred and abrupt death were real.[50]

Fascism is the denial of love and life, and life-deniers get easily drawn to it. But personal feelings are also denied to those on the other side, i.e., the Communist camp. In the conflict of Right and Left, it seems that there can be no place for private emotions: love, like Liberalism and law, must wait for a time of peace. Spender, indeed, gives the Chorus of Red Prisoners the ringing last line, "We shall be free, We shall find peace", but it is only a whispered slogan. The words sound farcical and the rage impotent.

Trial of a Judge is really the story of a civilization on trial.[51] The martyrdom of the Judge and his associates is the martyrdom of Truth and Justice. And like the story of crucifixion, the sacrifice of innocent human lives holds the promise of resurrection. The theme is fused with the poetic qualities of Spender and his lyricism is evident in the following lines:

> Civilization which was sweet
> With love and words, after great wars
> Terrifies; architraves
> Or flowering leaf of the Corinthian capital
> Momently threaten; then fall
> In marble waves on life.[52]

By giving a dramatic mould to this lyricism Spender reaches the highest level of objectivity in his treatment of the most urgent political problems of the age. An engaging political allegory is enriched and deepened by a soul-searching introspection.

Spender's involvement in politics ultimately culminated in *The Still Centre* (1939) rightly hailed as "the best work of one of the most competent and sincere of living poets."[53] The turmoil of the times haunted the poet and he plunged himself into hectic political activities. Though the book is divided into four sections dealing with different problems, we would begin the analysis with his political activities in the Spanish Civil War which is the major theme and which occupies the second and third sections of the book. Spender had gone to the fighting fronts in the momentous War which apart from its political significance for him, "seemed a struggle for the conditions without which the writing and reading of poetry are almost impossible in modern society."[54] During his visits to Spain, the actual experience of human suffering wrought by war moved Spender deeply and he realized the deceptiveness of war rhetoric. The 'foreword' to *The Still Centre* is implicative:

> As I have decidedly supported one side—the Republican—in that conflict, perhaps I should explain why I do not strike a more heroic note. My reason is that a poet can only write about what is true to his own experience, not about what he would like to be true to his experience.

> Poetry does not state truth, it states the conditions within which something felt is true. Even while he is writing about the little portion of reality which is part of his experience, the poet may be conscious of a different reality outside.[55]

This statement reveals the poet's distrust of the propagandist heroics. His intention was to highlight the inhuman aspects of war and hence one finds *The Still*

Centre treating the Civil War in a personal and non-political manner. Instead of glorifying the old lie of 'arms and the man', Spender's poems touch upon death, suffering, fear and concern over the fate of the innocent and the cowardly. His war poems fall into two groups: those that depict the impact of war upon his sensibility and are defeatist, as for example, **'Ultima Ratio Regum'**, **'The Coward'**, **'Two Armies'**, **'Thoughts During an Air Raid'** and **'War Photograph'**; and those that render wartime events objectively, with a few oblique references to the tragic implications of the struggle, like **'At Castellon'**, **'Fall of a City'** and **'To a Spanish Poet'**.

The first group of Civil War poems in their solemnity of tone and ironic mood reminds one of Wilfred Owen's poems. Like Owen, Spender in these poems conceives of war as the great destroyer, a kind of impersonal phenomenon indiscriminately brutalizing and maiming humanity. The poem **'Ultima Ratio Regum'** dwells on the disparity between the powerful war-making world of money and arms and the death of one boy. The Latin title comes from the motto that was embossed on the cannons of Louis XIV: 'Force is the final argument of kings'. The first line, "The guns spell money's ultimate reason", is an energetic and sarcastic image of the inevitable belligerence of big money. An anonymous soldier, a victim of the economic system, was killed while guns focussed lethally on "the spring hillside." The poet ironically points to the extremely inhuman nature of the war-mongers who killed this boy "too young and too silly", "a better target for a kiss" than for bullets. The background information about the boy sharpens our sense of sympathy for him. He had been too young to be employed, never had been inside a fine restaurant, nor been written up in the newspapers. While business magnates were protected, this boy, being outside the mainstream, was vulnerable. The simile "intangible as a Stock Exchange rumour" suggests the vagueness and the unimportance of the boy in the materialistic world. The havoc wrought by war on man and nature is perceptively described in the following lines:

> Machine-gun anger quickly scythed the grasses;
> Flags and leaves fell from hands and branches;
> The tweed cap rotted in the nettles.[56]

The concluding stanza ironically asks the reader to regard the boy's life as "valueless" in ordinary economic terms and obscure by accepted social standards. The bitterness and the irony gain a sharper edge when Spender compares the insignificant life of the boy with the huge expense involved in the process of killing him. The poem ends with a rhetorical question:

. . . Was so much expenditure justified
On the death of one so young and so silly
Lying under the olive trees, O world, O death?[57]

The repetition of "so young and so silly" makes a final appeal to an outraged sense of justice.

The comparative directness of metaphors used in the poem is worth noting. 'Money' and 'gold' symbolize the business interests supporting the cost of the war. 'Factory', 'restaurant' and 'hotel' represent the social system. The aspects of war are shown by 'guns' and 'lead', the fallen 'tweed cap' and the mowing down of grass, flags and leaves. Ironically the poet has used investment terminology of gain and loss to express the absurdity of the entire enterprise: "money's ultimate reason", "gold sunk deep as well", "valueless", "was so much expenditure justified".

The anonymous soldier was "lying under the olive trees"; coincidentally enough, a flower has sprouted on the grave of a coward buried "under the olive trees". This coward was tricked into fighting by the false slogans of chivalry and heroism. However, in the final moments of life, he realized the "hidden truth" about war. Spender has feelingly described the death of this soldier and has built up a powerful effect in the logic of images:

> The mother's care, the lover's kiss,
> The following handkerchiefs of spray,
> All led to the bullet and to this.
> Flesh, bone, muscle and eyes
> Assembled in a tower of lies
> Were scattered on an icy breeze. . . .[58]

The psychology of **'The Coward'** might have stemmed from Spender's knowledge of the situation of Jimmy Younger, an intimate friend of the poet who joined the Brigade under the compulsion of personal circumstances. The villains are the propagandists, not the dead coward who experienced "rings of terror" more dreadful than any hero has ever known. The sense of pity and sympathy for such helpless victims of war is movingly stirred.

This concern with the weak and the timid shirkers extends in **'Two Armies'**, to all the men who happen to be involved in a struggle without realising all the implications of it and who would gladly get out of it if they possibly could. It is a poem about two opposing armies during wartime. It is winter and the two armies are equipping themselves with arms and ammunition to destroy each other. The hardships of war are stressed; "men freeze and hunger". It is really unfortunate that the very unemployed young men standing with vacant eyes at street corners whom we confronted in the early 'thirties are now conscripted for a bloody war. Then they were starving on account of joblessness and now

they are famished and frozen. Ironically Spender notes: "No one is given leave / . . . except the dead, and wounded." He adds bitterly that new battalions would replace them, providing "violent peace" for the recently-removed souls.

The second stanza also deals with the nervousness and tension that have gripped the soldiers of both the armies. They have developed hatred and disgust for the people who entangled them unnecessarily in the war. It is really strange that those who caused and planned the war do not have to go through the same predicament as those who fight it. Those distant manipulators with their political propaganda have become anathema much more detestable "than bullets" themselves. The victims of war are in fact innocent and harmless people: one who "hummed a marching song" and the other who "flapped the salute." It is all the more tragic that the saluting boy was "shot through the wrist by those of his own side." It may mean that the politicians of "his own side" heaped death on him by creating war. Another likely explanation is Spender's objection to the ruthless methods employed by the Communists to force men to stay in the line and to kill those who do not do so. The poem might be referring to the deliberate shooting of a fellow-soldier, who wished to desert.

The metaphor "numb harvest" is loaded with double meaning: numb psychologically, because war is an ordeal; and physically, because the weather is cold. The so-called harvest produces not crops, except in the minds of the perverted, but discomfort, suffering and death. Perhaps the soldiers wish to run away but they are watched by severe taskmasters and forced to stay "at the point of a revolver." Their secret desire to desert the army finds vent during sleep, when the sweet memory of homely love and affections is irresistible, which in their waking moments remains "a mass unspoken poem."

Spender penetrates further into the psychology of exhaustion when he observes that both the armies are rendered insensitive to hatred for each other as well as to the cause for which they are supposed to fight. They become "tormented animals" and their numbness and servility reveal themselves in a "dumb patience," while waiting for the fighting to end. At night nothing less ethereal than silence and sleep separates the enemy armies. The picture of the two armies resting at night only a few yards apart has emotional authenticity:

> When the machines are stilled, a common suffering
> Whitens the air with breath and makes both one
> As though these enemies slept in each other's arms.[59]

Wartime enemies are practically indistinguishable in their "common suffering". The inherent humanity of the soldiers sharply set against the brutality they are forced to share and contribute to reminds the reader of Hardy's 'The Man He Killed' or Wilfred Owen's 'Insensibility'. The lyrical effect of "Clean silence falls at night" is both soothing and sad.

The final stanza uses the cosmic and romantic elements associated with the moon entirely to a different end. The moon is a "brilliant pilot" who "stares down / Upon the plain she makes a shining bone / Cut by the shadow of many thousand bones". The unexpected ghastliness of the image converges in angry comment when the moon is presented as regarding "death and time throw up / The furious words and minerals which kill life." The poet's sense of the irretrievable loss during war is universal, rather than limited to a specific war. The poem also shows Spender's effort to adapt his romantic inclination to a grimly modern situation.

The idea of common suffering is personalised in **'Thoughts During an Air Raid.'** Instead of the sacrifice of the coward or the dispirited volunteer, the poet contemplates his own chances of dying. The whole effort, Spender contends, "is to put myself / Outside the ordinary range / Of what are called statistics"[60] and to maintain an "impersonal" attitude which can ignore the hundred killed "in the outer suburbs." Above all, everyone "should remain separate . . . and no one suffer / For his neighbour." That among people subjected to war the thought of personal survival may predominate over any humane concern with others is entirely possible, and perhaps normal. "But Spender's repulsion," writes H. D. Ford, "forces him to draw too weighty and ironic a moral."[61] The unfeeling

> . . . horror is postponed
> For everyone until it settles on him.
> And drags him to that incommunicable grief
> Which is all mystery or nothing.[62]

The same theme recurs in **'War Photograph'**. The title itself is ironic. A photograph is a valuable memorial of one of the happiest moments of life. Visualizing this corpse "a photograph taken by fate", the poet imagines it withstanding the passage of time:

> Only the world changes, and time its tense,
> Against the creeping inches of whose moon
> I launch my wooden continual present.[63]

The terrible sacrifice may be forgotten by the "years and fields" but the "whitened bones" will serve as lasting reminders of the cruelty of war.

The second group of the Spanish war poems attempts to express the feelings of a people struggling for their existence. Though hardly heroic, these poems, nevertheless, hint at the generous emotion, courage and devotion of the Spanish people. In **'At Castellon'**, the realistic images successfully evoke the tense atmosphere of a city about to be bombed. But here Spender's depiction of the "working man" is warmly sympathetic. Ordered to drive a comrade (presumably the poet) away from the city to a safe place, the working man lifts the ravaged lines of his face into a smile:

> . . . the eyes gleam
> And then relapse into their dream.
> Head bent, he shuffles forward
> And in without a word.[64]

The man embodies the will of a people "who dared to move / From the furrow, their life's groove." Examples of partisanship seldom occur in Spender's verse. And what he celebrates here is not a political ideal but the admirable courage of a people who dared to disturb "life's groove."

The idealism and devotion of people can be short-lived, however, as **'Fall of a City'** illustrates. The poem presents a pathetic trial of defeat which yokes a whole population to the alien ideology of the victors. It vividly communicates the upheaval and turmoil wrought by the conquering forces. The destruction of art-treasures is really touching:

> All the names of heroes in the hall
> Where the feet thundered and the bronze throats roared,
> FOX and LORCA claimed as history on the walls,
> Are now angrily deleted
> Or to dust surrender their dust,
> From golden praise excluded.[65]

It is ironic that not only the physical bodies of the great politicians have returned unto dust after their death but their pictures, which were believed to be exempt from death and decay, have also been dashed to the ground. The poem, however, is redeemed from defeatist sentiments in the final stanza. Some great old man remembers the days of liberty before the city was conquered. This message of liberty is preserved by the child and thus the spark of a once vital idealism passes to the succeeding generation. The present deception is mere expediency and beneath the disguise a vivid memory exists:

> But somewhere some word presses
> On the high door of a skull, and in some corner
> Of an irrefrangible eye
> Some old man's memory jumps to a child
> —Spark from the days of energy.
> And the child hoards it like a bitter toy.[66]

From the old man who had enjoyed the peace and serenity of liberty and then saw it being trampled upon by the victorious army, we come to Spender's elegy **'To a Spanish Poet'**. Though this poem is included in the fourth section, it may justifiably be studied with war poems because of its background relevance. The poem is localized in its dedication to the Spanish poet Manuel Altolaguirre, to whom the "you" refers. It opens with the poet looking out of his window during wartime. The metaphor which compares his sensitivity to that of a child "who sees for the first time things happen" is apt. War is supremely dreadful and as remote to the experience of the uninitiated as evil is to the innocent.

In the second stanza, there is a reference to the stucco pigeon falling from the roof and uttering a coo that augured the disintegration to come. The disorder and confusion brought about by war dazed the poet "in frozen wonder." However, he himself managed to survive that holocaust. Here, it may be remembered that prior to the massive bombings of the Second World War, the attacks on Spanish cities were the widest and the deadliest the world had yet seen. Spender's description of the poet stunned at such an upheaval is very powerful in its suggested contrast:

> With astonishment whitening in your gaze
> Which still retains in the black central irises
> Laughing images. . . .[67]

The laughter originates from the several interesting anecdotes spread during wartime. One concerns "a man lost in the hills near Malaga" during an unlikely mission in pursuit of a partridge. The other mocks at a general, saddened by his failure to breed a green-eyed bull. Both of these absurd quests appear grotesque amid the real trials and contingencies of war.

Spender now reverts to the present. He has been reading newspapers containing dramatic descriptions of war events. Their sensationalism reminds the poet of the likelihood of his Spanish friend's death. It is at this point that he grows philosophical and broods over the life-death paradox. The imagery in this stanza is extended and complex. The resurrection motif ascribes greater reality to the corpse buried. Those who bury the dead, on the contrary, live in an unreal and dead world that "revolves . . . explodes." Beneath the earth the "flowering eyes grow upwards through the grave," and gaze through "a rectangular window" to see the stars. The "rectangular window" suggests the shape of a coffin and the poet ironically describes the casualties in the war as comedies.

The stanza that follows is rather anatomical. The heart of the Spanish poet "looks through the breaking body." Spender envisions it as "axle through the turning wheel" and the Spanish poet stares through his "revolving bones":

> Where all my side is opened
> With ribs drawn back like springs to let you enter
> And replace my heart that is more living and more
> cold.[68]

The bone imagery is strongly reminiscent of Eliot through Webster.

The final stanza appeals to the sense of sight. It well testifies to Spender's excellent employment of romantic imagery. The following lines almost burst into lyrical rapture:

> Oh let the violent time
> Cut eyes into my limbs
> As the sky is pierced with stars that look upon
> . . . . .
> With your voice that still rejoices
> In the centre of its night,
> As, buried in this night,
> The stars burn with their brilliant light.[69]

The poem ends with the poet's wishing to identify himself with the misery of the world and sensitively involving himself in the grief and indignation that have overwhelmed humanity.

This concern with the imaginative death of the Spanish friend leads Spender to **'Port Bou'**—a beautiful poem that deals with the pathos of the firing practice overtaking the peaceful inhabitants of a town. In his autobiography, the poet refers to this poem:

> Crossing the Spanish frontier from France, I spent a day in Port-Bou, alone. This was a charming little port, with two headlands like green arms stretched into the sea and almost embracing, but leaving a little gap between, which was the harbour mouth. Port-Bou was bombed, though the quay was intact.[70]

The description of the port in the poem is very lively and appealing. The image of the child holding a pet corresponds very well to the lay out of the harbour. The fanciful introduction of dolphins might represent a romantic landlubber's conception of the sea; at the same time it aptly conveys the bobbing motion of the ship—a motion also suggested convincingly in the rhyme of the line:

> As a child holds a pet
> Arms clutching but with hands that do not join
> And the coiled animal watches the gap
> To outer freedom in animal air,
> So the earth-and-rock flesh arms of this harbour
> Embrace but do not enclose the sea
> Which, though a gap, vibrates to the open sea.
> Where ships and dolphins swim and above is the sun.[71]

Entranced by the beauty of the port, the poet sits "at a table in front of the quayside cafe, reading the newspapers," while waiting for his "connection to Barcelona." As the poet is busy recollecting some childhood image of the headlands of the port, a lorry full of Republican soldiers in their dirty uniforms stops before him. They look down at the poet's newspaper and ask: "How do they speak of our struggle, over the frontier?" The poet offers the newspaper but they refuse to accept "anything so precious" but only "friendly words." In a short while, the lorry roars away bearing its cargo of uplifted clenched fists. The firing practice begins from headland to headland across the harbour and the bullets fleck the sea to white foam. The whole town becomes agitated. An old man, running along the road, calls out "pom-pom-pom," perhaps in blissful imitation of the firing:

> An old man passes, his running mouth,
> With three teeth like bullets, spits out 'pom-pom-pom.'
> The children run after; and, more slowly, the women
> Clutching their clothes, ...[72]

The image of the sewing-machine describing the burden of pain on the poet is an indication of Spender's penchant for machine terminology.

Besides these major poems, the destructive connotations of some of his poetic images, viz., "torn like leaves through Europe is the peace,"[73] "the bursting tide of an unharnessed power / Drowning the contours of the present,"[74] are expressive of the poet's sense of anxiety and shock. The pathos of war can be discerned in the death of two comrades in **"A Stopwatch and an Ordnance Map."** The worst aspect of the war is that together with revolutionaries and soldiers, it kills and maims the innocent children and destroys the sleeping babies:

> This timed, exploding heart that breaks
> The loved and little hearts, is also one
> Splintered through the lungs and wombs
> And fragments of squares in the sun,
> And crushing the floating, sleeping babe
> Into a deeper sleep.[75]

It is in this extension of sympathy even to the ordinary civilian that Spender steals an edge over his great predecessor Wilfred Owen. The vision of the First World War poets was confined to the physical hardships of the soldier. "It is difficult," writes Davidson, "to say whether Owen and Sassoon were against the war itself (apart from the suffering of the soldiers) because they do not take the reasons for it into account."[76] The limited nature of their views of war is borne out by the subsequent writings of the soldier-poets who survived it. And it becomes amply clear that they were not interested in the forces that produced suffering. The value of Spender lies in his coming to grips with the idea of war, with its consequences and its meaning for the human race. He rises above the party and side affiliations in his war poems. His achievement is not just evocation of humanitarian feelings. What is more, it is a fruitful appeal to the good sense of people to save the human race from dehumanization.

Very often unsympathetic critics have found fault with Spender's Civil War poems. Mildred Davidson has pointed to "the lack of emotional impetus behind his [Spender's] peculiar sensitivity," and questioned their genuineness as they were written in his "position of observer."[77] Samuel Hynes is harsher still:

> There is something missing from Spender's war poems, some authority for the right to pity; without that authority, which perhaps a poet must earn by sharing in suffering, pity becomes a patronising, distant attitude . . . but these feelings [compassion for fighters and anger for propagandists] had been distanced by the fact that Spender was neither a soldier nor a Spaniard. . . . They [the war poems] are, even the best of them, the war poems of a tourist.[78]

True, Spender was neither a Spaniard nor a soldier but he was emotionally involved in the Spanish conflict and to condemn his poems as those of a "tourist" or an "observer" would be a travesty of truth. A "tourist" is a detached observer interested simply in reporting and recording the events. It is the passion of involvement and the imaginative participation in human suffering that bridges the gulf between the actual soldier and Spender. The poet could hardly be expected to have been either the murderer or the murdered. Genuine objectivity shakes off the accidents and crudity of the actual and personal experiences and achieves emotional identity with the impersonal world outside. Moreover, the perpetual suffering makes the soldier immune to the onslaughts of war and custom blunts the edge of its tortures. Besides, the sufferer may develop false notions of heroism about himself and find warmth and glow of joy in his suffering. Imaginative participation, on the other hand, sharpens the sensibility of the poet and enables him to probe deeper and deeper into its implications, unhampered by 'the film of familiarity'. To regard active participation in the war to be the only touchstone of authority about it, is far from convincing. Byron fought and died in the Greek War of Independence but he cannot be regarded as a greater revolutionary than Shelley, who never took any active part in violent activities. Imaginative visualization affords a broader vision to the poet and it is no less heroic. G. S. Fraser's remark is very pertinent in this context:

> . . . suffering is an inescapable feature of our time and that in a persistent active sympathy with suffering, a refusal to withdraw from imaginative participation in it, there *is* something heroic.[79]

This controversy, however, pinpoints the contention of the present study that Spender's poetic development has been along ambivalent lines. His approach to Civil War was more poetical than political. He joined the movement not simply because ideological issues were at stake but also because of the beauty of its background—the enchanting landscape of Spain and the poetry and the passion of its colourful people:

> The European Fascist versus anti-Fascist struggle was dramatized in Spain as in a theatre. The peculiar Spanish passion, idealism and violence of temperament, and even the Spanish landscape, colored the struggle and gave it intensity and a kind of poetic purity which it scarcely had before or afterward. Above all, this was a

war in which the individual, with his passion and comparative independence of mechanical methods, still counted. It was in part an anarchist's war, a poet's war. At least five of the best young English writers gave their lives as did the poets of the other countries. This drew the intellectuals still deeper into the struggle.[80]

Therefore, what seemed to fascinate Spender in this anti-Fascist struggle was more the poetry it evoked than the politics it involved. Even when he was convinced of the need of sacrifice in this struggle, he did not plunge into it as a fighting soldier. It is strange but true that his intimate associate, Jimmy Younger, with whom he had almost identified himself at one time, joined the International Brigade to fight on behalf of the Republicans but Spender chose to remain on the fringes of the war as its "observer." Here, it may be remembered that his friend, the Spanish poet Altolaguirre, about whose safety he was so deeply concerned, "stared out of the window on the emptiness / Of a world exploding," instead of coming on to the streets and sharing the suffering it involved. This sense of anxiety from a distance is meaningful. The forces of poetic aloofness and actual political involvement which pulled Spender in different directions turned him into a sympathetic humanitarian watching the war with an unbiased and detached attitude. What moved the poet was the utter destruction heaped by them on each other and he was led almost to ignore the justness of the cause he had intellectually espoused, to brood over the futility of it all. He did involve himself in politics in his own way but refused to be a partisan like the politician. His unbounded sympathies helped him overcome political partisanship and broke down the barrier between the friend and the foe. The following excerpt brings out his transcendental outlook on war:

> Suddenly the front seemed to me like a love relationship between the two sides, locked in their opposite trenches, committed to one another unto death, unable to separate, and for a visitor to intervene in their deathly orgasm seemed a terrible frivolity.[81]

Thus the emotion contained in Spender's War poems cannot be dubbed indifferent or dishonest. It was genuine emotion reaching out from personal to poetic, with the aesthetic distance necessary for successful communication. The foregoing analyses of poems are sufficient proof. But had Spender remained contented with this attitude, he would, perhaps, have developed his poetic personality along the right lines. He regretted that he was not able to participate fully in the struggle:

> Throughout these years I had always the sense of living on the circumference of a circle at whose centre I could never be.[82]

There was something in the very nature of the poet which held him back and deprived him of the identity he was craving to achieve through total surrender and sacrifice. He defines his position in the poem **'Port Bou,'** in which he pictures himself standing alone "at the exact centre" of a bridge, some distance from and yet within earshot of the firing practice going on nearby. The location almost perfectly represents his disengagement:

> And I am left alone on the bridge at the exact centre
> Where the cleaving river trickles like saliva.
> At the exact centre, solitary as a target.[83]

This duality of outlook has been the main tension behind Spender's creativity. His poetic sensibility, which was "naturally lyrical and emotional", experienced a conflict when he attempted to "deal in history and abstractions."[84]

Here, we may glance back at the first section, comprising the poems written on subjects that captured the attention of the poet by their extraordinariness. In fact, the poems included in this part were written between 1934 and 1939 and glow with Spender's topical awareness. Most of them are in continuation of the themes taken up by him in his first volume entitled *Poems*. These poems reveal the poet's lively interest in art. There are remarkable moments of imaginative flight and heightened lyricism. At times, he also gives evidence of high sensuousness. The picture of summer in **'Polar Exploration'** is replete with sensuousness:

> . . . Summer struck
> Water over rocks, and half the world
> Became a ship with a deep keel, the booming floes
> And icebergs with their little birds:
> Twittering Snow Bunting, Greenland Wheatear,
> Red-throated Divers; imagine butterflies
> Sulphurous cloudy yellow; glory of bees
> That suck from saxifrage; crowberry,
> Bilberry, cranberry, *Pyrola Uniflora*.[85]

'Easter Monday' celebrates the hope Spender cherished in his passionate enthusiasm to wipe out poverty from the face of the earth. Easter is an occasion of joy marking the anniversary of the Resurrection of Christ. This poem relies mainly on description without recourse to myth or fable other than the one suggested in the title. It opens with the description of the splendour of summer bursting through a burnt-out city:

> The corroded charred
> Stems of iron town trees shoot pure jets
> Of burning leaf.[86]

In this virtually deserted city, the poet comes upon green meadows where girls are playing in their first summer dresses. Children are seen gathering "pap-smelling cowslips." But there are workers too in every place and the poet exults at the thought of the victory of the worker over the disintegrating bourgeoisie:

> . . . But look, rough hands
> From trams, 'buses, bicycles, and of tramps,

Like one hand red with labour, grasp
The furred and future bloom
Of their falling, falling world.[87]

Contrast is the principal method of construction in this poem. The charred places and the broken columns stand contrasted with the summer green, the girls in summer clothes and the children gathering flowers; the red colour of the flame that burns is also the burning colour of leaves, and red also are the hands of workers that labour and create. And this reminds us of the banner of the Communist Revolution. Thus by means of a combination of destructive and creative imagery the poet produces an impression of resurrection through revolution. This is Spender's usual technique of symbolism.

C. Day Lewis regarded the following lines of the poem **'Experience'** as an excellent example of what he meant by "pure poetry" and asserted that "it would be impossible, not merely to give an adequate transcription in prose of the first two lines, but to give any hint of their sense in any other form whatsoever:[88]

Good-bye now, good-bye: to the early and sad hills,
Dazed with their houses, like a faint migraine.
Orchards bear memory in cloudy branches.
The entire world roared in a child's brain.[89]

This poem traces the evolution of the poet from innocence to maturity. The first two lines quoted above are supremely evocative and recreate the nostalgic mood of the poet and the shadowing-off of images into the remote vista of childhood. We can point to the 'good-bye now' as the clue, and trace it through the word 'early' with its suggestion both of childhood and of dawn (in the 'early' morning, the eye is still 'dazed' with sleep, an impression transferred to physical objects). Interfused with this can be traced the sensation of nostalgia and its dulled-painful and visually blurred quality, through the words 'goodbye', 'sad', 'dazed' and 'faint migraine'. It is this aesthetic sense that checked Spender from indulging in barren propaganda and boring rhetoric.

Spender's sense of nostalgia for childhood is supplementary to his interest in the past and its heroes as discernible in **'Exiles from their land, history their domicile.'** The people with extraordinary will-power, who, unable to find a congenial environment at home, proceeded to foreign garrets on their noble enterprises and sacrificed their lives for those ideals, were looked down upon by their contemporaries as exiles. Ironically enough, these exiles and outcasts have gone down in history while the mocking contemporaries of theirs, with meaningless existence are sinking into oblivion. Those "freedom's friends" are now "laurelled" and resurrected as harbingers of spring. The poet arrives at the bitter realization:

. . . We, who are living, seem
Exiles from them more living; for we endure

Perpetual winter, waiting
Spring that will break our hardness into flowers
To set against their just and summer skies.[90]

The sense of utter worthlessness of living bursts into a craving for noble ideals and the poet invokes these heroes of history to enthuse him:

O utter with your tongues
Of angels, fire your guns—O save and praise—
Recall me from life's exile. . . .[91]

This celebration of courage looks like something anachronistic in a valueless age, and Spender grapples with this theme in **'The Past Values'**. It is a metaphysical comparison of young men killed in battle to the pictures of old masters, the lives of both being rendered static and fixed at a point by their remoteness from us. The parallel is strengthened by a conceit. The glazed eyes of the dead have been compared to the glass and the glaze of varnish which come between us and the pictures. This thought is given added potency as Spender emphasizes the transparent wall which separates us from the dead as a means of effecting an unexpected awareness:

Through glass their eyes meet ours
Like standards of the masters
That shock us with their peace.[92]

This sense of shock gets intensified when Spender visits a classroom in a slum. The boys whose "future's painted with a fog" recite their "father's gnarled disease" in the school. Their poverty-stricken faces powerfully communicate the anguish in their heart. To these slum children with their stunted bodies, Shakespeare and the maps of other lands are meaningless. The poem appeals to the good sense of the people to adopt immediate measures to ameliorate their condition before they themselves are stirred up to remove social disparities by revolutionary activities. The lyrical touch saves the following lines from degenerating into pure propaganda:

Break, O break open, till they break the town
And show the children to the fields and all their world
Azure on their sands, to let their tongues
Run naked into books, the white and green leaves
   open
The history theirs whose language is the sun.[93]

The scene of social anomaly reflected in "the hanging despair of eyes in the street" compels Spender to call for offering hands and guts "on skewers of pity" in **'The Uncreating Chaos.'** The poem quivers with the apprehension of a coming disaster:

I stand so close to you,
I will confess to you.
At night I'm flooded by a sense of future,
The bursting tide of an unharnessed power
Drowning the contours of the present.[94]

It shows the poet's genuine concern about the disintegration of a civilization torn by war, political intrigues and confusion of moral values. He is deeply distressed by the violence of the time, which has become the order of the day. The confusion has expanded into uncreating chaos and the poem ends with a question, a favourite ending in Spender:

> Shall I never reach
> The field guarded by stones
> Precious in the stone mountains,
> Where the scytheless wind
> Flushes the warm grasses:
> Where clouds without rain
> Add to the sun
> Their lucid sailing shine?[95]

It must be noted that whatever the subject of Spender, the mode of expression is lyrical and the imagery rooted in the romantic impulse.

From this picture of a fragmented situation with little hope of redemption, we pass to the last section of the book that "contains the most highly personal and lyrical poems, which are perhaps the best things Spender has written."[96] These poems mark a definite change in Spender's poetic development. In justification of this group of poems, Spender devoted part of his 'Foreword' to *The Still Centre*:

> I think that there is a certain pressure of external events on poets today, making them tend to write about what is outside their own limited experience. The violence of the times we are living in, the necessity of sweeping and general and immediate action, tend to dwarf the experience of the individual, and to make his immediate environment and occupations perhaps something that he is even ashamed of. For this reason, in my most recent poems, I have deliberately turned back to a kind of writing which is more personal, and I have included within my subjects weakness and fantasy and illusion.[97]

Spender's reference to "the violence of the times" reminds us of the actual happenings of the year 1939. The Spanish Civil War ended in March 1939, when Madrid surrendered. German troops occupied Czechoslovakia in the same month. Chamberlain's policy of appeasement ended when Britain and France pledged their support to Poland (also in March 1939). Persons with leftist leanings were disillusioned with the Soviet Union, when the Russo-German Pact was signed in August the same year. It was a year of endings, but of no beginnings. In such a time one might expect that the thoughts of writers would turn away from the external remedies to the personal values for the redemption of society. Up till now, Spender's poetry shows a general movement from the centre of the poet's personal life towards increasingly wider circles of political and social phenomena. But the fateful year shattered the illusion that the world could be saved from Fascism and War. In the life of Spender, it was, perhaps an equally significant moment of soul-searching and self-analysis. In his autobiography, he frankly states:

> After my return from Spain I reacted from the attempt to achieve Communist self-righteousness towards an extreme preoccupation with the problems of self. I wrote poems in which I took as my theme the sense of being isolated within my personal existence: but I tried to state the condition of the isolated self as the universal condition of all existence.[98]

Spender's 'Foreword' quoted earlier has no tinge of despair and retreat in it. Rather, it can be interpreted as a reassertion of hope in a crumbling world. As a conscious alternative to the earlier, more public and committed poetry, Spender turns towards introspective verse highlighting the efficacy of human values. He rejects the ready-made remedies and theoretical formulae prescribed by political quacks. **'The Still Centre'** is not a peaceful centre of a walled-in personality but a disturbed sensibility invaded on all sides by the "world's circular terror." Harper's remark is worth reproducing in this context:

> . . . 'the still centre' is a symbol for that position from which the poet can stabilize his values and thus come to terms with his world. It is the nebulous goal toward which Spender is consciously striving.[99]

The title, **'The Still Centre'**, has been culled from the **'Darkness and Light'**, which is the most significant poem of this volume. It reflects the conflict between the subjective self and the objective reality which had overtaken Spender and which he found difficult to resolve. The poem begins:

> To break out of the chaos of my darkness
> Into a lucid day is all my will.

but continues in the second stanza:

> Yet, equally, to avoid that lucid day
> And to preserve my darkness, is all my will.[100]

Day and darkness, the objective world and the self are imaged as the centre and the circumference of a circle—the antithetical impulses towards and away from subjectivism, which are equally part of human identity. The resolution of the poem is an acceptance of both in the whole circle of the self:

> I grow towards the acceptance of that sun
> Which hews the day from night. . . .
> . . . . .
> The world, my body, binds the dark and light
> Together, reconciles and separates
> In lucid day the chaos of my darkness.[101]

This "acceptance of that sun which hews the day from night" is part of the process of growth. Growing up, maturing, developing—whatever one may call it—has two aspects. There is the realization that comes with added years that life, "instead of being something swiftly and romantically experienced, is something slowly and painstakingly lived."[102] That is a far from joyous discovery. Whatever sense of loss follows, the disillusionment is to some extent offset by the other aspect of growth, the enriching realization of the self, not as a completely isolated and self-contained identity, but as the product of innumerable forces—"My history is my ancestry / Written in veins upon my body."[103]— and as the small part of a vast and multitudinous whole:

> My single pair of eyes
> Contain the universe they see;
> Their mirrored multiplicity
> Is packed into a hollow body
> Where I reflect the many, in my one.[104]

Thus **'Darkness and Light'** is very close to Spender's expressed intention in the 'Foreword.' It is a programmatic poem, a demonstration of his turn-back to the personal. All the poems of this section are significant for what they exclude: there are no suffering poor, no exiles, no heroes and no politics here. Spender takes his body as the world, and the self as the whole subject. The poet has subjected himself to strict self-examination and the theme of lost love has been dealt with in most of the poems. It is only in his elegy on the Spanish poet (which we have analysed with war poems) that the poet returns to the public world, but even that world becomes an inner landscape, a parable of the sense of personal loss. Napoleon, the Great, as presented in **'Napoleon in 1814'** is not at all true to the facts, but an immense Spender, with all the complexes and defeatisms a thousand times magnified.

'The Separation' is a love-lyric, in which the lover laments his separation from the beloved because of some fault of his will or twist of the ego. The sense of isolation has been conveyed by the island symbol. The lover at a great distance stares, beyond his "dark and climbing fears," to where

> Your answering warm island lies
> In the gilt wave of desire.[105]

He images the far journey back to the other, but without hope of a satisfactory union. The sense of separation outweighs all considerations of joy:

> And when we meet—the ribs will still
> Divide the flesh—enfolding dream
> And the winds and seas of time
> Ruin the islands with their stream
> However compassed be the will.[106]

Yet he longs for the union with the beloved, which is the sole means of salvation in tragic times:

> Shuttered by dark at the still centre
> Of the world's circular terror,

> O tender birth of life and mirror
> Of lips, where love at last finds peace
> Released from the will's error.[107]

'Variations on my Life' is another melancholy love poem that describes the yearning of a lover for his beloved. Though largely nostalgic, it demonstrates Spender's power of grappling with a personal problem in a purely objective way. For the poet love is the most valuable possession. He wishes to get it and enjoy it completely, including the undesirable things that may go with it:

> Oh to be taken by it, and to hold
> My ear against its ever-female heart,
> And to accept its fleas and all its sins,
> To explore all its gifts
> And nothing, nothing to refuse.[108]

The poet longs to return

> To the first loved friend, you
> Whose life seemed most unlike my own
> As though you existed on an island
> In seas of an archaic time,
> Hidden under bird song and olive trees. . . .[109]

He goes on to give an attractive picture of the summer evening in the lover's island. Then he outlines the psychological conditions (happiness and acceptance of self) on his part that would enable him to return and to be received. For he has this at least to offer:

> I was the sea, I was the island
> Where the casqued heroic head
> Lay and was remembered;
> My innocent crystal mirrored your heart,
> My mind was your legendary sky of love.[110]

Further follow the conditions of improvement in his way of regarding himself and finally;

> O then my body would enter
> Its island and its summer
> The questions find their answer
> And my head its resting-place
> Where the other heart lies. . . .[111]

In **'The Human Situation'**, the poet scrutinizes his individuality and finds it to be a bundle of contradictions. This poem is, in some respects, a catalogue of fears and enemies, reinforced by a certain pride of self:

> And if this I were destroyed,
> The image shattered
> My perceived, rent world would fly
> In an explosion of final judgement
> To the ends of the sky,
> The colour in the iris of the eye.[112]

But he ends with the logical acceptance of self, the very solution which was forced upon such writers as Nietzsche and Gide, the realisation that their weakness is their strength:

Here I am forced on to my knees,
On to my real and own and only being
As into the fortress of my final weakness.[113]

The light of love, however, gets the upper hand over other interests and considerations:

. . . I shut the other
Stars out from my sky.
All but one star, my sun,
My womanly companion,
Revolving round me with light. . . .[114]

The poet looks for love everywhere and pays his deepest homage to it whenever and wherever he finds it. Travelling in a train where the eyes of the other passengers would be "searching for hope on the horizon," Spender would be longing to enter the life behind the drawn blinds of houses situated at the edge of railway lines:

A sun behind the clouds
Of slums, suburbs and farms
Where love fills rooms, as gold
Pours into a valid mould.[115]

The poet achieves enlargement and sublimation of his love themes by employing the method of contrast. **'Two Kisses'** creates a setting of sharp contrast; the quay where the river suggests

The dirt off all the streets
And the rotting feet of factories,

is set against the beauty of swans and boats, "the far shore and day-green spaces." The kiss is related to this contrasting background and is compared to the proud launching of a boat among swans and lights:

And then the heart is its white sailing pride
Launches among the swans and the stretched lights
Laid on the water, as on your cheek
The other kiss. . . .[116]

The contrasts worked out in this poem carry the theme beyond the limits of subjective experience and give it a wide implication—the purity and beauty of love in an otherwise dirty world. Such a contrast is apparent in the imagery of most of Spender's love poems. These images enlarge love's scope and significance and help us to understand its value in relation to the world in which the poet is destined to love and lose. For Spender it was natural to visualize the pangs of separation while earnestly craving for the pleasure of union. The following lines from **'The Little Coat'** are relevant:

—O hold me in that solemn kiss
Where our lips are changed to eyes
And in the deep lens of their gaze
Smiles and tears grow side by side
From the loving stillness.[117]

Robert Harper, though otherwise happy with Spender's achievement in *The Still Centre,* feels disappointed with what he calls "the obvious inability of the poet to come to any sort of terms with his world" and observes:

. . . he is still engaged in the same search for positive values that has sent him on so many fruitless literary ventures in the past seven years. There is no evidence in *The Still Centre* that he is approaching the end of this quest.[118]

Harper's argument is far from convincing. Spender does try to come to terms with the world in *The Still Centre.* In his foreword to this volume, he clarifies that his poems "do not strike a more heroic note", thereby implying that the current causes are not only inadequate, but even hostile to the deepest human needs. He confirmed the fact that the material of poetry is not to be picked up by hearsay; it should be true to the poet's experience. Such a voluntarily subjective orientation relates these poems to their milieu. They evince poetry's essential virtue in this that by quietly mysterious lyricism, echoing a profound and scrupulous inner life, they bespeak the most representative and indispensable principles of man's existence.

Utilitarian heroics and ideological victories would have been easier than Spender's quest for an understanding and social correlation of personal experience. He grapples with a protean problem, the subjective-objective dichotomy as a perennial dilemma intensified at the time. Many of his poems, some speculatively psychological, some descriptive of the war, in both Spanish and English settings, and some concerning love revolve about the fate of man in the nature of things, and also under socio-political exigencies. The poet ponders over the identity of man, the matrix of his inheritance and the isolation of his consciousness. Faces are as masks beholding other masks, appearance is a mirror, a surface reflecting a surface, the two-dimensional unreality of a portrait. As mind is bounded by flickering glimpses of an indeterminable externality, so the very bodies and breath of man are subject nowadays to world-ranging forces mechanically systematic and wasteful of human values. It is an overwhelming sense of pathos that prompted Spender to resist the "pressure of external events" and to deliberately turn back "to a kind of writing which is more personal." His 'still centre' is large enough to be a circle embracing the grief of the world stricken by violence and war. Pity here has broken the dams of dialectical materialism and has become free, personal and spontaneous. The value of love has been assessed as the only cherishable ideal in tragic times.

Thus, in the second phase of his poetic career, Spender took a deep plunge into the political life of the times. During the Vienna uprising, he felt stunned at the brutal suppression of the socialist revolution. His awareness was so sharpened that he obtained the membership of the Communist party, in whose programme of social millennium, he visualized a future for humanity. But the instinctive liberal bias remained his obsession and the poet experienced a conflict when confronted with the grim reality. His emotional upsurge in the Civil War was in tune with his concern about the rising trends of Fascism. However, the Marxist betrayal of the Republican cause warned him of its hypocrisy and *Trial of a Judge* expresses the dilemma of the poet's conscience. The liberal Judge, who like his creator, possesses a proportion of Jewish blood in his veins, and is condemned to death for his liberal views, reveals the tormented soul of the poet himself and hence is so remarkably able to elicit our sympathy. Spender's fascination for Communism almost ceased after the Spanish debacle and he did not renew his membership of the Communist party. He refrained from delving into political abstractions and turned inwards with **The Still Centre,** which "announced the end of Spender's uneasy alliance with Communism."[119] The personal note became more pronounced which he had unsuccessfully tried to suppress during all these years. He ultimately came to the conclusion:

> Within even a good social cause, there is a duty to fight for the pre-eminence of individual conscience. The public is necessary, but the private must not be abolished by it; and the individual must not be swallowed up by the concept of social man.[120]

However, this preoccupation with the freedom of the individual was not narrow and egocentric. He universalized his sense of the human situation and viewed it with the utmost objectivity. But his essentially subjective temperament was a great hurdle here as Southworth perceptively notes:

> Although autobiographical, it [Spender's poetry] is not narrowly egocentric. Objective though he attempts to be, subjectivity is the result.[121]

Notes

1. J. W. Beach, *Obsessive Images* (Minneapolis: University of Minnesota Press, 1962), p. 29.

2. Edwin Muir, "Society and the Poet", *London Mercury,* Vol. 31 (February 1935), p. 382.

3. *Times Literary Supplement,* "Vienna", Vol. 33 (13 December, 1934) p. 890.

4. *Vienna,* p. 13.

5. *Vienna,* p. 14.

6. *Vienna,* p. 15.

7. *Ibid.,* p. 16.

8. *Ibid.,* p. 17.

9. Martin Gilkes, *A Key to Modern English Poetry* (London: Blackie & Son, 1938), p. 101.

10. *Vienna,* pp. 21-22.

11. *Ibid.,* p. 23.

12. *Ibid.,* p. 31.

13. *Ibid.,* p. 34.

14. *Ibid.*

15. *Sowing the Spring,* p. 162.

16. *Vienna,* p. 35.

17. *Ibid.,* p. 39.

18. *Ibid.,* p. 41.

19. *Ibid.,* p. 39.

20. *Ibid.,* p. 20.

21. Hynes, *The Auden Generation,* p. 147.

22. *Vienna,* p. 41.

23. *Ibid.,* pp. 39-40.

24. *Ibid.,* p. 40.

25. *Ibid.,* p. 35.

26. Hynes, *The Auden Generation,* p. 148.

27. *World Within World,* p. 192.

28. *Ibid.,* p. 191.

29. Edwin Muir, "Society and the Poet," *London Mercury,* Vol. 31 (February 1935), p. 382.

30. *Vienna,* p. 37.

31. Henry Warren, "Vienna", *The Fortnightly,* Vol. 137 (February 1935), p. 250.

32. Untermeyer, ed., *Modern British Poetry,* p. 486.

33. W. Y. Tindall, *Forces in Modern British Literature* (New York: Alfred A. Knopf, 1947), p. 58.

34. *Vienna,* p. 42.

35. Stephen Spender, "Poetry and Expressionism", *The New Statesman and Nation,* Vol. 15 (12 March 1938), p. 408.

36. S. F. Morse, "Prophecy and Fact", *Poetry,* Vol. 52 (August 1938), p. 293.

37. Stephen Spender, *Trial of a Judge* (London: Faber, May 1938), p. 17.

38. *Ibid.,* p. 42.

39. *Ibid.,* p. 57.

40. *Ibid.,* p. 64.

41. *Ibid.*, p. 71.

42. *Ibid.*, p. 91.

43. *Ibid.*, p. 104.

44. *Ibid.*, p. 103.

45. *Ibid.*, p. 80.

46. *Ibid.*, p. 103.

47. Desmond MacCarthy, "The Trial of a Judge", *The New Statesman and Nation,* Vol. 15 (12 March 1938), p. 524.

48. *Trial of a Judge,* p. 108.

49. *World Within World,* p. 2.

50. *Trial of a Judge,* pp. 49-50.

51. Cf. "The Judge is the spirit of European liberalism. His refusal to condone the crimes committed in the name of nationalism, his trial and condemnation are a symbol of tragedies which were being enacted all over Europe in 1938 and 1939 . . ." V. de Sola Pinto, *Crisis in English Poetry 1880-1940,* p. 226.

52. *Trial of a Judge,* p. 56.

53. R. D. Harper, "Back to the Personal", *Poetry,* Vol. 57 (October 1940), p. 49.

54. Stephen Spender & John Lehmann, eds., "Introduction", *Poems for Spain* (London: Hogarth Press, 1939), p. 7.

55. *The Still Centre,* p. 10.

56. *Ibid.*, p. 57.

57. *Ibid.*, p. 58.

58. *Ibid.*, p. 59.

59. *Ibid.*, p. 56.

60. *Ibid.*, p. 45.

61. H. D. Ford, *A Poet's War: British Poets and the Spanish Civil War,* p. 229.

62. *The Still Centre,* p. 45.

63. *Ibid.*, p. 62.

64. *Ibid.*, p. 67.

65. *Ibid.*, p. 65.

66. *Ibid.*, p. 66.

67. *Ibid.*, pp. 105-6.

68. *Ibid.*, p. 107.

69. *Ibid.*

70. *World Within World,* p. 218.

71. *The Still Centre,* p. 71.

72. *Ibid.*, p. 72.

73. *Ibid.*, p. 40.

74. *Ibid.*, p. 31.

75. *Ibid.*, p. 69.

76. Davidson, *The Poetry is in the Pity,* p. 91.

77. *Ibid.*, p. 50.

78. Hynes, *The Auden Generation,* p. 251.

79. G. S. Fraser, *Vision and Rhetoric,* p. 207.

80. Richard Crossman, ed., *The God that Failed,* p. 222.

81. *World Within World,* p. 223.

82. *Ibid.*, p. 192.

83. *The Still Centre,* p. 72.

84. Hynes, *The Auden Generation,* p. 249.

85. *The Still Centre,* p. 17.

86. *Ibid.*, p. 19.

87. *Ibid.*, pp. 19-20.

88. C. Day Lewis, *A Hope for Poetry,* p. 95.

89. *The Still Centre,* pp. 21-22.

90. *Ibid.*, p. 24.

91. *Ibid.*, p. 25.

92. *Ibid.*, p. 27.

93. *Ibid.*, p. 29.

94. *Ibid.*, p. 31.

95. *Ibid.*, p. 33.

96. R. D. Harper, "Back to the Personal," *Poetry,* Vol. 57 (October 1940), p. 47.

97. *The Still Centre,* pp. 10-11.

98. *World Within World,* pp. 254-55.

99. R. D. Harper, "Back to the Personal," *Poetry,* Vol. 57 (October 1940), p. 49.

100. *The Still Centre,* p. 77.

101. *Ibid.*, p. 78.

102. Rica Brenner, *Poets of Our Time* (New York: Harcourt, Brace & World, 1941), p. 290.

103. *The Still Centre,* p. 80.

104. *Ibid.*, p. 79.

105. *Ibid.*, p. 83.

106. *Ibid.,* p. 84.

107. *Ibid.,* p. 91.

108. *Ibid.,* p. 91.

109. *Ibid.,* p. 93.

110. *Ibid.,* p. 94.

111. *Ibid.,* p. 95.

112. *Ibid.,* p. 79.

113. *Ibid.,* p. 82.

114. *Ibid.,* p. 80.

115. *Ibid.,* p. 103.

116. *Ibid.,* p. 86.

117. *Ibid.,* p. 88.

118. R. D. Harper, "Back to the Personal," *Poetry,* Vol. 57 (October 1940), p. 46.

119. Samuel Hynes, *The Auden Generation,* p. 366.

120. *World Within World,* p. 312.

121. Southworth, *Sowing the Spring,* p. 149.

Select Bibliography

I. STEPHEN SPENDER

(A) ORIGINAL WORKS:

The Still Centre. London: Faber and Faber, December 1944.

Trial of a Judge. London: Faber and Faber, May 1938.

Vienna. London: Faber and Faber, 1934.

World Within World. London: Faber and Faber, 1951.

(B) ARTICLES:

"Poetry and Expressionism", *The New Statesman and Nation,* Vol. 15 (12 March 1938).

II. CRITICAL LITERATURE ON SPENDER AND HIS AGE

(A) BOOKS:

Beach, Joseph Warren. *Obsessive Images.* Minneapolis: University of Minnesota Press, 1962.

Davidson, Mildred. *The Poetry Is in the Pity.* London: Chatto and Windus, 1972.

Ford, H. D. *A Poet's War: British Poets and the Spanish Civil War.* Philadelphia: University of Pennsylvania Press, 1965.

Fraser, G. S. *Vision and Rhetoric.* London: Faber and Faber, 1959.

Gilkes, Martin. *A Key to Modern English Poetry.* London: Blackie & Son, 1938.

Hynes, Samuel. *The Auden Generation.* London: The Bodley Head, 1976.

Lewis, C. Day. *A Hope for Poetry.* Oxford: Basil Blackwell, 1936.

Pinto, V. de Sola. *Crisis in English Poetry, 1880-1940.* London: Arrow Books, 1963.

Southworth, J. G. *Sowing the Spring.* Oxford: Basil Blackwell, 1940.

(B) JOURNALS:

Harper, R. D. "Back to the Personal", *Poetry,* Vol. 57 (October 1940).

MacCarthy, Desmond. "The Trial of a Judge", *The New Statesman and Nation,* Vol. 15 (12 March 1938).

Morse, S. F. "Prophecy and Fact", *Poetry,* Vol. 52 (August 1938).

Muir, Edwin. "Society and the Poet", *London Mercury,* Vol. 31 (February 1935).

Times Literary Supplement. "Vienna", Vol. 33 (13 December 1934).

Warren, Henry. "Vienna", *The Fortnightly,* Vol. 137 (February 1935).

Sanford Sternlicht (essay date 1992)

SOURCE: Sternlicht, Sanford. "A Thirties Poet: Early Verse." In *Stephen Spender,* pp. 18-52. New York: Twayne, 1992.

[*In the following excerpt, Sternlicht examines the poetry from Spender's first five volumes of poetry, from 1928 through 1939.*]

Tagged "the Auden Group," "the Oxford Poets," "the Pylon Poets," and other sobriquets, W. H. Auden, Stephen Spender, and C. Day Lewis were the leaders—and in critical opinion the only notable members—of a group of politically radical poets concerned with humanity and society and the dilemma of the seemingly unavoidable choice between necessity and freedom. They sought a truer vision of human existence. "They held that man was a product of his environment, that to change him the environment had to be transformed."[1] Michael Roberts, in his preface to *New Signatures* (1932), describes the rebellion of the new poets against the long tradition of introspective and esoteric poetry.[2] The group disintegrated with the advent of World War II, when the Marxist beliefs that bound them to each other were found wanting. Spender became the first to fall away.

The major characteristic of Spender's poetry is a constant tension between an engagement with the objective world outside—the salient mark of the thirties poets—and the need for his soaring spirit to rise above the mundane considerations of the workaday world. The result was "the fragmentation of self."[3] Forever in Spender's favor is his perpetual belief that poetry is a human gesture. As a poet emerging between the two great wars of this sad century, he naturally took as his subjects fear and death, love and war, inhibition and weakness, but always Spender had his own private drama to play out before his readers—"a struggle to adapt his individualism to his social views, and a struggle to understand and perfect his individuality."[4]

Auden was Spender's leader, mentor, and benign Svengali. Day Lewis and MacNeice were coequals with Spender in a "gang of four." In retrospect, the members of the group appear more different than alike, and at least one critic now believes that "Spender was . . . Auden's superior as a poet."[5]

NINE EXPERIMENTS

Spender's juvenilia is relatively impressive. During the summer vacation of 1928, Spender obtained a small hand-operated printing press and published his *Nine Experiments: Being Poems Written at the Age of Eighteen.* Exactly eighteen hand-numbered copies were issued. Spender soon became dissatisfied with his venture, tore up the loose sheets, and tried to retrieve and destroy the copies he had distributed. However, in 1964 he allowed a facsimile edition to be published by the Elliston Poetry Foundation at the University of Cincinnati.

The nine poems encompass a variety of subjects, but the major theme of *Nine Experiments* is the redeeming power of love in relation to the social problems of humankind. From the precocious beginning, Spender was intent on using and transforming much of the seemingly nonpoetic material of life in an industrial society. The noisy, malodorous, machine-run world of technology must be reconciled with the inherent beauty and majesty of the natural world.

In **"Come, Let Us Praise the Gasworks!"** Spender challenges the commonplace and shows his desire to explore new realms of experience, even (hypothetically of course) hard manual labor, surely a romantic trait:

> And man, the grimmest, starkest
> Of all those intimate machines; the harshest
> Grate grate [sic]. I'd love
> In an archaically perfect mechanic to move
> With clock-work limbs.[6]

The gasworks, providers of energy, are vital to an industrial society with a huge population. Louis Untermeyer very quickly perceived that "while the belated

Georgians were still invoking literary laverocks, lonely lambs, and traditionally deathless nightingales, Spender was hailing the advent of another order and writing such poems as **'Come, Let Us Praise the Gasworks.'"**[7]

> Walking beside a stenchy black canal,
> Regarding skies obtusely animal,
> Contemplating rubbish heaps, and smoke,
> And tumid furnaces, obediently at work.

> (*NE* [*Nine Experiments*], 14)

In trying to circumscribe the effects of poverty, **"Appeal"** anticipates Spender's later sympathies. It opens thus: "The voices of the poor, like birds / That thud against a sullen pane, / Have worn my heart" (*NE*, 8). However, the persona finds himself growing indifferent to the victims of society because their suffering is not as great as his grief for an unrequited love: *"It is upon your heart, your heart / That knows not charity"* (*NE*, 8).

The opening poem of *Nine Experiments*, **"Invocation,"** self-consciously echoes Shelley's "Ode to the West Wind": "Blow for ever in my head! / And ever let the violins, tempest-sworn, / Lash out their hurricane" (*NE*, 7). Fortunately, Spender never again would mix a metaphorical stew of violins and a hurricane.

Exploring the world of nature, **"Evening on the Lake—(dolce)"** pulsates with romantic vocabulary and imagery:

> Beauty cometh: See how gently
> Graven in the Water, play
> The lazy whorls, which, Whirl absently
> Round the prow, and Glide away.

> (*NE*, 17)

The almost 19-year-old poet sees himself, as teenagers are wont to do, as sophisticated and world-weary in **"Ovation for Spring"**:

> The nineteenth time, from bough to bough
> I see the mocking fires of spring;
> And twice I've rhymed the name with "king,"
> But I am grown more *blasé* now.

> (*NE*, 19)

The beauty of spring has lost its romantic hold on the persona. "The world is too much with him." Spring

> cannot stir me with her sound,
> Her light no longer makes me burn:
> I only see earth wake, and turn
> Again in penitential round.

> (*NE*, 19)

In *Nine Experiments,* Spender initiates his iterative light imagery with the related sun and eye references. Also, he begins to allude to glass and windowpanes as dividers of realities. As a group, these first poems show the promise of a young, intelligent, sensitive, impassioned poet striving to go beyond seeing to find a perspective into a personal realm of feeling, a poet at his best when working with the common idiom. **"Invocation," "Epistle," "I must repress," "Boiling the desperate coffee," "From 'The Enshrinement of the Ideal,' Part iv," "Made Sober,"** and **"The Farewell"** were all deemed forgettable by Spender and critics and never anthologized or collected.

Twenty Poems

The first critical attention to Spender's poetry was provoked by *Twenty Poems* of 1930 (*WW*, [*World within World*] 131). The collection proved much more durable than *Nine Experiments.* Fourteen of the pieces appear in *Poems* (1933), 13 in the slightly revised 1934 edition, and the 14 of the 1933 volume in *Collected Poems* (1955).

In these poems the Spenderian conflict between his basic romanticism and his growing understanding of the harsh realities of society grows more evident. The true poet must be affected by the climate of his age. G. S. Fraser notes, "There is a deep inherited wish in Mr Spender to yield to the romantic afflatus; there is also a strong contemporary impulse to question it and check it."[8] It is this duality, this tense entwining of thesis and antithesis, that provides the foundation for the earlier and greater part of the Spender canon.

In *Twenty Poems,* Spender begins to evince an individual style and work out the concept of the poem not only as statement but as act. Thus, there is a prescient openness in the verse. A distinct voice begins to emerge from the center of self.

The initial poem in *Twenty Poems* is so significant a statement for Spender that he used a phrase from it 20 years later as the title for the volume of poems *The Edge of Being* (1949). The poem **"At the Edge of Being"** begins, "Never being, but always at the edge of Being." The persona has decided to separate himself from full participation in life. He moves his lips for tasting and his hands for touching but can never get nearer to life than allowed by sensory limitations:

> Though the Spirit lean outward for seeing.
> Observing rose, gold, eyes, an admired landscape.
> My senses record the act of wishing
> Wishing to be
> Rose, gold, landscape or another—
> Claiming fulfilment in the act of loving.[9]

As happens often in the Spender canon, the self is split: part is in the world of the will and part remains in what Spender would later call "the still centre." The spirit in the center can only lean out and touch the world. Yet

"the act of loving" ("the fact of loving" in later versions), desirable as it is, tempts the persona toward oneness, the convergence of world and self. The poet, however, prefers the safety of the edge, where his fragile art is inviolable.

One series of personal verses in *Twenty Poems* is called the "Marston Poems," four of which were published in *Oxford Poetry* (1929) and six of which were reprinted in *Poems* (1933). They relate to Spender's infatuation with a fellow undergraduate at Oxford, an athletic but sensitive young man. The one-sided relationship was heartbreakingly frustrating (*WW*, 64-67): "Rushing in room and door flung wide, I knew. / On empty walls, book-carcases, blank chairs / All splintered in my head and cried for you" (*TP* [*Twenty Poems*], 7). "Marston" did not reciprocate Spender's passion, but nevertheless treated his young admirer politely, a quality that further endeared him to the poet. The "Marston Poems" commence with **"Discovered in Mid-Ocean,"** in which the persona alleviates his suffering by envisioning his lover as dead, while employing heroic classical sun imagery as an architectonic element:

> This aristocrat, superb of all instinct,
>   With death close linked
> Has paced the enormous cloud, almost had won
>   War on the sun;
> Till now like Icarus mid-ocean-drowned
>   Hands, wings, are found.

> (*TP*, 3)

Still the overwhelming need is to possess his beloved. In **"Saying 'good morning' becomes painful,"** conversation is "a form of possession like taking your wrists" (*TP*, 13). To know what Marston is doing, to dwell on his activities is yet another way to possess. In **"Marston, dropping it in the grate, broke his pipe"** (*TP*, 8), the persona, in an obvious Freudian gesture, builds possession on his knowledge of a pipe that his friend had bought during a continental holiday and that had given him much pleasure.

The young poet anoints himself God in **"The Dust made Flesh"** as he describes creating four figures: Marston, Helen, Catherine, and Ainger, a poet, Marston, close friend to the persona, thereby becomes a fabrication, perhaps because Spender wishes to back away from overt biographical exposure:

> First made I Marston the superb boxer
> More than with most men who dealt with death
> Marston who ski-ed through snow,
> Curved through the whiteness, ran,
> Helmeted drove through air.

> (*TP*, 4)

Marston's athleticism and purity are well established as the persona moves on to create "dark-eyed," cerebral Helen, with "words piercing night like stars," and the athletic Catherine, "who sprang in sky" and, like the goddess Diana, "along the ice-fleeced rocks shot chamois down." Spender certainly did not "make" Ainger, the poet, who is Auden cast as Byron—"severe, voiced raucous-reed, / With fascinating facets of crude mind, / An enormous percipient mass on the plain" (*TP*, 5). Spender was insecure and often ill at ease at Oxford, and thus liked to summarize his qualified admiration of friends with strong personalities, as if, by inference, he were deploring his own perceived lack of single-mindedness and ambition.

In **"Acts passed beyond the boundary of mere wishing,"** the persona has tried to ingratiate himself with his lover, but the simple, ingenuous courtesy of "waiting for the tram" carrying his lover provokes gratitude and an explosion of ecstasy in the persona: "Thinking, if these were tricklings through a dam, / I must have love enough to run a factory on, / Or give a city power, or drive a train" (*TP*, 9).

In **"I can never be a great man,"** one of the finest of the *Twenty Poems,* Spender comes out strongly against egotism as the proper motivating force behind great people. He proposes that those who rise above the rest of humanity do so through a complete selflessness that is far removed from the day-to-day working of body and mind. It is in the interior:

> Central "I" is surrounded by "I eating,"
> "I loving," "I angry," "I excreting,"
> And the "great I" planted in him
> Has nothing to do with all these.
>
> It can never claim its true place
> Resting in the forehead, and secure in his gaze.
> The "great I" is an unfortunate intruder
> Quarrelling with "I tiring" and "I sleeping"
> And all those other "I's" who long for "We dying."
>
> (*TP*, 17)

Although not immortal, the "great I," like a personified superego, has an energy and a love for life that serves in lieu of immortality. It tolerates all the weak, indolent, death-directed attitudes of body and mind, while making uncomfortable all the little "I's," the people who recognize that their drifting lives are wasted. Ultimately, "the first person singular can no longer be central; now the one who would seek fame must sink his personal identity in the first person plural."[10]

The "Marston Poems" after **"The Dust made Flesh"** either celebrate a man or address a man or a woman to whom the persona has an emotional attachment, but presumably it is Marston himself. Spender's early homoerotic poems, personal though they may be, are also a part of a tradition of such verse, a poetry that flowered in the trenches of World War I and was nearly as formalized and ritualized as the Renaissance sonnet sequence. Indeed, the great antecedent to these poems is Shakespeare's *Sonnets.*[11]

"Constant April" finds the persona lingering over the sensuous charms of his lover, relating him to the pleasant month:

> When you laughed, your laughter
> Was like the bright cascade.
> The sun sheds on a cloud,
>
> . . . . .
>
> And if you frowned, your frowning
> Was knit as these
> Slight showers.
>
> (*TP*, 12)

Of course, platonic friendship and aesthetic appreciation are also expressed in **"Constant April,"** as they are in **"His Figure Passes"** (*TP*, 6). The search for deep, sincere friendship is always a corollary to Spender's youthful passion for physical love and his need to find self-identity and worth in the reflections from a relationship.

The finest and most typically Spenderian poem in *Twenty Poems* is **"The Port."** Presumably a part of the "Marston Poems," it is really independent, describing the industrialized hub of commerce where sea, seashore, factory, and people meet. The port is where "the sea exerts his huge mandate" and where men work in "furnace" and "shipyards." As a collective image, the port is an objective correlative for the poet's frustration and unhappiness, manifest in the imagery of graves, caves, hard faces, lightning, confusion, and turmoil. The persona is of the industrial north. In the south, merchants dwell happily in "fat gardens" with "bronze-faced sons." In the port "the pale lily boys flaunt their bright lips, / Such pretty cups for money, and older whores / Scuttle rat-toothed into the dark outdoors" (*TP*, 14). For homosexuals and men who are disgusted with women and wavering on the sexual verge, the port is a titillating place full of sailors and boys.

"Written whilst walking down the Rhine"—which appears in subsequent collections as **"In 1929"**—shows Spender at his ceremonial best. The poem depicts the persona's friendship with two Germans, a bourgeois and a communist clerk. They are able to transcend the hatred their fathers felt in World War I:

> Our fathers killed. And yet there lives no feud
> Like Hamlet prompted on the castle stair;
> There falls no shade across our blank of peace
> We being together, struck across our path,
> Nor taper finger threatening solitude.
>
> (*TP*, 15)

However, if the past does not hinder, it nevertheless does not help, and separation is always the outcome:

> Lives risen a moment, joined or separate,
> Fall heavily, then are always separate,

Stratum unreckoned by geologists,
Sod lifted, turned, slapped back again with spade.

(*TP,* 16)

This noble, haunting poem, notes D. E. S. Maxwell, "stands with the best work of Spender's contemporaries."[12]

In **"Beethoven's Death Mask,"** also long recognized as superior Spender, the author again distances himself from a great person. He paints the composer as Rodin would have sculpted him, establishing depth, genius, mystery, and profundity:

I imagine him still with heavy brow.
Huge, black, with bent head and falling hair
He ploughs the landscape. His face
Is this hanging mask transfigured,
This mask of the death which white lights make stare.
I see the thick hands clasped; the scare-crow coat;
The light strike upward at the holes for eyes.

(*TP,* 23)

The persona remains fascinated by genius and the creative process that transforms experience and sound with negative capability. Spender explores the possibilities of spiritual aspiration through the achievement of Beethoven. He tries to imitate a master of music with the music and meaning of poetry:

Then the drums move away, the Distance shows;
Now cloud-hid peaks are bared; the mystic One
Horizons haze, as the blue incense heaven.
Peace, peace. . . . Then splitting skull and dream,
    there comes
Blotting our lights, the trumpeter, the sun.

(*TP,* 23)

The horror, ugliness, and death behind the mask, with light (Spender's image source for creative energy) striking at "the hole for eyes," is mitigated by the poem's lyrical values, and thus the poem transforms itself and becomes its own subject.

Twenty Poems, although a youthful work, has humor, passionate intensity, deep feeling, clarity, and rich, concrete imagery. It is a quantum leap from ***Nine Experiments*** and would have been no small achievement for any poet, let alone a youth of 21.

MICHAEL ROBERTS'S *NEW SIGNATURES*

In 1932 a young enthusiast of modern poetry, Michael Roberts, working with Leonard and Virginia Woolf at their Hogarth Press, put together an anthology of poems by young, recently discovered writers. The key poets were Spender, Auden, Day Lewis, William Empson, John Lehmann, and the American Richard Eberhart. Roberts's intention was to survey the imagery of modern life and to develop a new intellectual and

imaginative synthesis that would deal positively with the problems of life in the twentieth century. The anthology was a great success, selling out quickly, and had to be reprinted in a few weeks. The book was hailed as a "manifesto of new poetry, and the poets within its pages found themselves lumped together in the imagination of readers as 'New Signatures poets.'"[13] *New Signatures* spawned *New Country* in 1933 and John Lehmann's magazine *New Writing,* which unlike the *Left Review* was more interested in literature than in politics.

Spender contributed more poetry to *New Signatures* than any of the other eight poets represented therein. Most of his seven contributions are part of the permanent canon of twentieth-century British poetry. Spender included all of them in **Poems** of 1933.

"The Express" is considered one of Spender's signature poems, embodying as it does the very essence of the aesthetics of the Pylon Poets: the transmutation of the antipoetic material of modern life into poetry. **"The Express"** is an art moderne painting in words. As in some Edward Hopper paintings, there are no people in this poem, wherein a train, a machine as terrible as death, is personified as a lovely woman:

And always light, aeriel underneath
Goes the elate metre of her wheels.
Steaming through metal landscape on her lines
She plunges new eras of wild happiness
Where speed throws up strange shapes, broad curves
And parallels clean like the steel of guns.

(*NS* [*New Signatures*], 92)

For the train and the plane and the gasworks are more significant in modern life than the fields and forms of ancient song: "Ah, like a comet through flame, she moves entranced / Wrapped in her music no bird song, no, nor bough / Breaking with honey bud, shall ever equal" (*NS,* 93). The train "acquires mystery" and "she begins to sing." Then she screams and is heard "further than Edinburgh or Rome / Beyond the crest of the world." Here is orgasm. Here, too, is political élan, for the express symbolizes the force of "the first, powerful, plain manifesto" driving the revolution to its appointment with destiny.

"The Funeral" is one of Spender's great short poems in which lyric sensibility wars manifestly with political statement. It is vintage Spender, as is **"The Landscape near an Aerodrome"** written a short while later. Spender is fascinated with the processes and products of industry, and he both admires and envies the workers in factory and mill. The virile pride in the description of the funeral of the worker who "excelled all others in making drivingbelts" and the future that his labor has made possible sound like an anthem and recalls huge Soviet posters of the 1930s and 1940s:

They walk home remembering the straining red flags;
And with pennons of song fluttering through their
    blood
They dream of the World State
With its towns like brain-centres and its pulsing
    arteries.

(NS, 95)

Later on Spender would find the overtness of poems like **"The Funeral"** somewhat embarrassing and would include them in anthologies and collections only because the public expected to see them there, but the fact is that youthful panache and the lyric fusion of romantic and modern images continue to thrill new readers, especially the young and idealistic.

"I Think Continually" is an elegiac poem reminiscent of Laurence Binyon's "For the Fallen." With exquisite phrasing, Spender admires those strong personalities who are so unified that a single expression may be their apt signature. The great are imagistically with fire and sun in their struggle to aid and to save their fellow humans:

The names of those who in their lives fought for life,
—Who wore at their hearts the flame's centre:
Born of the sun, they travelled a short while towards
    the sun
And left the vivid air signed with their honour.

(NS, 90)

These are the people with a destiny, who bring with them from the spiritual realm of perfection a memory of glory:

I think continually of those who were truly great.
Who, from the womb, remembered the soul's history
Through corridors of light where the hours are suns
Endless and singing. Whose lovely ambition
Was that their lips, still touched with fire,
Should tell of the Spirit clothed from head to foot in
    song.

(NS, 89)

Spender may not be one of the truly great, and the poem may express a degree of envy and resignation, but the awareness of the spiritual dimension of greatness is of significance. "Who lives under the shadow of war" reminds the reader that Spender's generation is an interwar group of survivors. The young poet knows that no writer's words can stop the next war.

"On Young Men" is a poem of political commitment exhorting his fellow youth to leave "those ladies like flies perfect in amber" and "those financiers like fossils of bones in coal" to "advance to rebuild" their society, not forgetting to "sleep with friend on hill" (*NS*, 86). The images are intense and precise, but also somewhat labored, and one recalls MacNeice's mean description of Spender as a poet patiently pressing clichés into

poetic shape with steady and powerful hands.[14] Spender did "press" in much of his earliest poetry, but he pressed metaphysical imagery, not clichés.

"My Parents" deplores an upbringing that separated him from boys of the working class and made him their perceived enemy: "My parents kept me from children who were rough." The persona came to fear them when they "sprang out behind hedges / Like dogs to bark at our world." He "longed to forgive them, but they never smiled" (*NS*, 94).

"The Prisoners" is a weaker poem, flabbily self-referential and unable to evoke much of a credible sense of life in prison. The employment of the pathetic fallacy does not help. It is hard to imagine a "liquid door / Melted with anger" (*NS*, 87). Perhaps the persona or the prisoners are melting it with their anger.

It is easy to see how Spender's committed, exuberant poems excited a poetry-reading public in the early 1930s seeking a poetry of social hope, a public prepared to sort out and grace the machine-dominated environment it seemed somehow to have wandered into.

Michael Robert's next anthology, *New Country* (1933), contains four personal Spender poems, but they are not as distinguished as his contributions to *New Signatures*. One, **"The morning road with the electric trains,"** Spender dropped from the canon immediately. **"At the end of two month's holiday there came a night,"** **"Alas, when he laughs it is not he,"** and **"After success, your little afternoon, success"** were included in the second edition of the 1933 *Poems,* as were all of the *New Signatures* pieces.

POEMS

Poems (1933) contains 33 poems of which 16 had appeared in previous volumes, including *New Signatures* and *New Country*. Changes are minor. The second edition of *Poems,* published in September 1934, contains 40 poems, Spender having dropped 2 (**"I hear the cries of evening"** and **"My parents quarrel in the neighbour room"**) and added 9 (**"At the end of two months' holiday," "After success, your little afternoon success," "Alas, when he laughs it is not he," "The Shapes of Death," "For T. A. H. R.," "Van der Lubbe," "Passing, men are sorry for the birds in cages," "Perhaps,"** and **"New Year"**). The 1934 American edition, Spender's first book published in the United States, restored the 2 omitted poems. The American edition is considered definitive.

Within two years of the publication of ***Poems,*** Morton Zabel, in *Poetry,* called Spender "one of the most important young poets in England," one who would prove to be "a writer not only of immediate values but of permanent and convincing truth."[15] *Poems* is an estimable achievement, projecting an exuberant quality to be long remembered and happily recalled, like Shelley's, that of a young bard of wide-eyed affirmation. "The naïveté *is* Spender . . . it goes along with a genuine innocence of eye, and a capacity not only for being easily moved, but for honouring that emotion in strong and direct expression."[16]

Variations of subject and style abound in *Poems*; rhetorical declamations, conversations, commentaries on current issues and public events, and psychological portraits intermingle. **"The Express," "The Pylons"** and **"The Landscape near an Aerodrome"** employ imagery from modern technology instead of from traditional, outdated sources. The eponymous pylons, carrying electrical power above a valley, introduce the landscape of the future: "Like whips of anger / With lightning's danger / There runs the quick perspective of the future."[17] Nature is diminished by the power of human ingenuity, and the anthropomorphized pylons take on an aura of sexuality:

> Now over these small hills they have built the concrete
> That trails black wire:
> Pylons, those pillars
> Bare like nude, giant girls that have no secret.

(P [Poems], 57)

"The Landscape near an Aerodrome" depicts the changing concept of what is beautiful and fascinating, turning away from traditional landscape, ruined towns, and the displays of religion, to the sleek, streamlined machines of speed and mechanical power. A descending airliner is like a great eagle alighting:

> More beautiful and soft than any moth
> With burring furred antennae feeling its huge path
> Through dusk, the air-liner with shut-off engines
> Glides over suburbs and the sleeves set trailing tall
> To point the wind. Gently, broadly, she falls
> Scarcely disturbing charted currents of air.

(P, 55)

The passengers now can see the ruins that rampant, uncaring, capitalistic industrialization has wrought:

> now let their eyes trained by watching
> Penetrate through dusk the outskirts of this town
> Here where industry shows a fraying edge.
> Here they may see what is being done.

(P, 55)

Finally, as the earth images grow larger and larger,

> Beyond the winking masthead light
> And the landing-ground, they observe the outposts
> Of work: chimneys like lank black fingers
> Or figures frightening and mad: and squat buildings
> With their strange air behind trees, like women's faces
> Shattered by grief.

(P, 55)

And they find a "landscape of hysteria" where a church is blocking that imagistic source of creativity and love, the sun:

> Then, as they land, they hear the tolling bell
> Reaching across the landscape of hysteria
> To where, larger than all the charcoaled batteries
> And imaged towers against that dying sky,
> Religion stands, the church blocking the sun.

(P, 56)

The message is to have faith in the new forces symbolized by train, plane, and pylon and to abandon the old institutions like the church because they block the guiding light to the future.

In **"In railway halls"** and **"Moving through the silent crowd"** Spender paints a drama of despair in which institutions created for the welfare of humans have failed and the pitiful poor have nothing but time: "In railway halls, on pavements near the traffic, / They beg, their eyes made big by empty staring / And only measuring Time, like the blank clock" (*P*, 60).

The unemployed teem on the streets in **"Moving through the silent crowd"**:

> They lounge at corners of the street
> And greet friends with a shrug of shoulder
> And turn their empty pockets out,
> The cynical gestures of the poor.

(P, 30)

The predominant emotion in these early poems is pity. This recurring theme, the keystone of Spender's poetry, is partly a result of the influence of Wilfred Owen, who took as his subject pity for the suffering soldiers in war. Spender pitied the suffering of the victims of economic crisis.[18]

Another iterative Spender theme consolidated in *Poems* is the primary significance of personal relations in life. In poems like **"Those fireballs, those ashes"** and the earlier **"Oh young men"** and **"I think continually,"** Spender emphasizes the centrality of the physical aspect of human greatness. The sensuous being comes first. Relationships must have their physical dimensions, and this is true for great and small. Friends and lovers are more vital to physical and mental health, artistic achievement, and political action than are family, country, ideals, or ideology. MacNeice recalls Spender's "building what castles he could out of personal relations."[19] The power of the intimate exalted all.

"For T. A. R. H.," somewhat revised later, is based on Spender's relationship with his sometime secretary, Tony Hyndman, but primarily deals with the poet's inner-world reaction to the creative and destructive powers of love and to love's capacity to induce forgiveness:

At night my life lies with no past nor future
But only space. It watches
Hope and despair and the small vivid longings
Like minnows gnaw the body. Where it drank love
It lives in sameness. Here are
Gestures indelible.

(*P*, 36)

"How strangely this sun reminds me of my love"
finds the persona staring longingly at the other male's
face, taking his photograph, so to speak, with the retinas
of his eyes in order to remember the glorious day. The
young lover is like the god Apollo.

In **"Your body is stars whose million glitter here,"** a
lover is anatomized metaphorically as Spender uses
parataxis to paint a surrealistic canvas:

Your body is stars whose million glitter here:
I am lost amongst the branches of this sky
Here near my breast, here in my nostrils, here
Where our vast arms like streams of fire lie.

(*P*, 35)

Unfortunately, the plethora of images seems to melt and
drip, and when in the end "there comes the shutting of
a door," the reader does not know on what it shuts.

"What I expected" debunks the youthful fancy of the
poet's heroic self-image:

What I expected was
Thunder, fighting,
Long struggles with men
And climbing.
After continual straining
I should grow strong;
Then the rocks would shake
And I should rest long.

(*P*, 25)

Alas, he could not foresee the common fate of love and
life: "The pulverous grief / Melting the bones with pity,
/ The sick falling from earth" (*P*, 25-26).

"Without that once clear aim, the path of flight"
despairs that the twentieth century is like the Dark Ages,
in that social and psychological truth lie both "in
dungeons" of the mind and the real dungeons of political repression. Another type of repression is dealt with
in **"Passing, men are sorry for the birds in cages."**
Here the persona is able to announce the release of "the
bird of delight" from its cage and denounce the false
ideas that have kept it in prison. Those who lock up the
joys of life destroy themselves.

"Van der Lubbe," named for the innocent defendant
tried by the Nazis on a trumped-up charge of causing
the Reichstag fire, is a political poem emphasizing the
correlation between public and private Thanatos, which
together shape the destructive element in humankind.
Other very political poems are **"Perhaps,"** in which
several violent acts take place, their settings, time, and
purpose remaining vague. **"After they have tired"**
expects the revolution to bring a dazzling dawn without
banks, cathedrals, and insane rulers. In **"New Year"** the
persona urges the oppressed to rise up and create that
new dawn but "effect . . . beauty without robbery" (*P*,
64). Spender is always a little chary of revolution; he
cannot accommodate himself to the bloodshed.

"My parents quarrel in the neighbour room," which
complements **"My parents kept me from children
who were rough,"** from *New Signatures,* is a miniature
version of George Meredith's *Modern Love.* The
persona, here a horrified son, listens to his parents wage
war in their bedroom.

The last poem in the collection, **"Not palaces, an era's
crown,"** is an awkward Marxist piece with some foolish metaphors, such as a "battleship towering from hilly
waves." Yet the poem is also a call to duty. The poet
instructs his senses and his readers' to abandon their
"gardens" and their "singing feasts" and submit to the
design of the will to serve the "flag of our purpose" (*P*,
67).

Despite the seemingly political nature of much of *Poems,* a large percentage of the pieces are about self. In
one sense, the collection is a course in personal analysis,
the self being reconciled with internal needs and social
concerns. The id and the superego struggle but accommodate. After all, if Marx saw change as predicated on
material forces in society, Freud believed that change
was motivated by forces within the individual. In *Civilization and Its Discontents* (1930) Freud is concerned
with a person's relation to his guilt and to his society.
In respect to the latter, Spender's early poems are as
much Freudian as they are Marxist. The widespread
fascination with Freud in the 1930s could no more have
escaped Spender's attention than it did Auden's.

Poems is a remarkable achievement for a very young
poet in a great hurry to get things said. Samuel Hynes,
in *The Auden Generation,* poses a key question that
imaginative writers faced throughout the 1930s: "Is the
role of a poet a defensible one in such a time? And if it
is, what sort of poem should he write? Is the traditional
private context of lyric poetry appropriate . . . to a
time of public distress?"[20] Spender's answer in *Poems*
is a resounding yes. A lyric could be both private and
public, both a song and a manifesto. This was the accomplishment of *Poems*: capturing the interest of a
British public still exhausted by World War I, still grieving over the decimation of the brightest of a generation,
and continually disappointed with its leadership. That
public wanted to understand the inherent nature, the
psychological makeup, and the source of energy of the

inspiring figures of the human race, "those who were truly great." **Poems** addressed the need.

VIENNA

Vienna (1934) is Spender's grand attempt to project into public view "the conflict between personal life and public causes" (*WW*, 174). The experiences of a love relationship and the poet's indignation at the suppression of the Viennese Socialists by Prime Minister Engelbert Dollfuss were different but related, for although one was public and one private, both were intensely emotional and personal. Spender felt "the poem fails because it does not fuse the two halves of a split situation, and attain a unity where the inner passion becomes inseparable from the outer one" (*WW*, 174).

In **Poems** the cure for human ills lies in making the individual more happy and more aware of instincts, freeing sexuality, and developing emotional potential. In **Vienna** Spender explicitly considers the notion of "individual love as a cultural panacea" and then rejects it "in favor of a Marxist program."[21]

The four-part, 37-page **Vienna** is Spender's longest and most ambitious poem. It, more than any other work of his, shows Eliot's influence. The fact that Spender not only spent so much time in Austria and Germany but also chose to set his "epic" in a Central European capital at what he immediately recognized as a pivotal place and point in twentieth-century European history underscores Eliot's position that English "writers cannot afford to throw over the European tradition."[22] In Eliot's view, the English artist needs to turn his or her mind east to the Continent and away from the west (America) and the world (the British Empire). For Spender's generation of poets *The Waste Land* was the great "epic" of the century. In Spender's construct and interpretation of events, Vienna, embattled, gutted, and raped of its hope, becomes a "wasteland" in which the dream of a socialist civilization perishes. Vienna is, then, symbolic of the European cities in which the lights of political and individual freedom were going out in the 1930s. **Vienna** is a prophecy. The very imagery of the poem is Eliotic, with strings of images sequencing in emotional rather than logical iterations while fulfilling the precept of the objective correlative.

The first section of the poem, "Arrival at the City," describes the persona's coming to Vienna, where he takes up residence in the Pension Beaurepas, in which most of the inhabitants are old ladies who prattle on about their medical problems and elderly lovers. The proprietor, an ex-actor who likes to pass as an Englishman and who wishes to introduce the persona to his obscene version of *panen et circenses* (bread and circuses)—*"penis in circensem."*[23] The proprietor, a faded dandy, sports "wing tie. Winged nose. A bleared,

active eye. / The stick and strut of a sprucer day" (*V* [*Vienna*], 10). But "this man's dead life stinking" is like an open wound decaying. He is so obscene that the persona prefers "the wholly dead" to the living corpse and bag of corruption.

The persona wanders to another part of the city, a square quarter that is "the part true to this town" (*V*, 12). It is like a hospital for a sick city:

> Unhomely windows, floors scrubbed clean of love,
> A waste canvas sky, uniformed nuns,
> Streets tinkling with the silver ambulance.
> We breathe the bandaged air and watch through
>   windows
> Metal limbs, glass eyes, ourselves frozen on
>   fires.
>
> (*V*, 12)

"Arrival at the City" thus provides the backdrop for the tragedy of the oppression and murder of a decayed city, whose sacrifice may provide understanding and inspiration for those trying to prevent the death of Western civilization.

The second section, "Parade of the Executive," is even more abstract than the first. The suggestion of a foreign journalist surveying and recording the degeneration of an exotic city, like Isherwood in Berlin, disappears as the poem metamorphoses into a position paper by "the Executive," who advocates obedience to the dictator and his henchmen and the maintenance of appearances:

> Let no one disagree let Dollfuss
> Fey, Stahremberg, the whole bloody lot
> Appear frequently, shaking hands at street corners
> Looking like bad sculptures of their photographs.
> Let there be bands and stands and preparations
> And grateful peasants in costumed deputations
> Create the ghost of an emperor's coronation
> Stalking the streets and holding up the trams.
>
> (*V*, 14)

Meanwhile, there are the unemployed who are

> Dispersed like idle points of a vague star:
> Huddled on benches, nude at bathing places,
> And made invisible by crucifying suns
> Day after day, again with grief afire at night,
> They do not watch what we show.
> Their eyes are fixed upon an economic margin.
>
> (*V*, 14)

And there is a stranger, an observer, "a witness free from danger," like Spender, who sees a government minister, after a deceitful public event "who smiles and smiles." The stranger cries out like Hamlet, "How now! a rat? Dead for a ducat" (*V*, 20). The city of Vienna is as rotten as the state of Denmark.

The third part, "The Death of Heroes," describes the brave attempt and tragic failure of the workers and students who fought the fascists at Karl-Marx-Hof. This section of the poem is most powerful and stirring as it describes the suffering of the besieged. The slaughter is appalling: "Life seems black against the snow." A sniper fires and "the vivid runner falls / From his hare-breathed anxiety: his undisputing / Hold on terror. O gently, whitely buried" (*V*, 25). In the end the beaten and burrowing survivors without "tasks fit for heroes" must find new roles and "change death's signal honour for a life of moles" (*V*, 30). The dead are lucky; they are not dehumanized by the loss of freedom.

In the fourth part, "Analysis and Final Statement," the persona, the stranger, like a Prufrock, listens to coffeehouse voices, trying to understand, excuse, exculpate, and somehow assimilate what has happened around him. The persona, however, loses his frayed journalistic objectivity, his voyeuristic perspective, and turns inward to "I, I, I" and the love of a woman in order to heal his psyche:

> I think often of a woman
> With dark eyes neglected, a demanding turn of the
>   head
> And hair of black silky beasts.
> How admirable it is
> They offer a surface bright as fruit in rain
> That feeds on kissing. Loving is their conqueror
> That turns all sunshine, fructifying lemons.
>
>   (*V*, 33)

The heterosexuality that has been repressed in the persona, but leaks out in the description by the elderly ladies in the pension of their gray loves, in the proprietor's lust, and in other sexual references, blossoms into the conscious understanding that "our sexes are the valid flowers / Sprinkled across the total world and wet / With night" (*V*, 34).

Unlike Eliot's *The Waste Land,* published 12 years earlier, Spender's *Vienna* does not present a coherent, overall vision. Its obscurity seems imposed. However, as Samuel Hynes points out, "*Vienna* is a poem not so much about the history of the uprising as about the mythology. It is not a narrative, though it includes narrative passages: it does not tell the whole story, it ignores chronology, and it does not explain. What Spender seems to have aimed at was the expression of his own personal sense of Vienna."[24]

THE STILL CENTRE

The Still Centre (1939) contains 39 poems written between 1934 and 1939. They are grouped into four parts and preceded by a forward in which Spender explains that the poems in Part One were the first written and are subject-oriented. Parts Two and Three contain political poems, the last of which are concerned with Spain. Part Four is not directly referred to, but Spender states that the violence of the times he was liv-

ing in and the need for action could make a writer feel that writing was "perhaps something that he is ashamed of. For this reason, in my most recent poems [the bulk of Part Four], I have deliberately turned back to a kind of writing which is more personal, and I have included within my subjects weakness and fantasy and illusion."[25] No more *Vienna*s for him. Intrepid Spender flew in the face of expectations: he would write a song of himself when all thought he would continue to engage in political battle with fascism. Disillusionment with communism may have partly caused this turn, but the change was primarily the result of an unleashing of the pent-up romantic in the poet. Spender had come to feel that he was his own manifesto. As Eliot fled from the wasteland to religion and as Auden ran away to America to escape the coming chaos, Spender retreated to the still center on the isle of self.

Speaking of *The Still Centre,* David Daiches says, "The vein of lyrical speculation in this volume sometimes produces poetry which can hold its own with anything produced in the century."[26] The collection's value was immediately recognized, receiving such critical accolades as "the best work of one of the most competent and sincere of living poets."[27]

The title of the collection derives from Spender's sense of living on "the edge of being," on the periphery of events in the 1930s. "I had always the sense of living on the circumference of a circle at whose centre I could never be" (*WW*, 174-75). In *The Still Centre,* Spender is here less concerned with relating the self to the outside world. Instead, like Rainer Maria Rilke, he strives to convert external phenomena into symbols of the inner experience: "Ideally, the artist should transform the environment into his own world."[28] Looking out the window of a train he sees his image against the traveling landscape. That outside world is fleeting and unreal.

In the introduction to *The Still Centre,* Spender says that "poetry does not state truth, it states the conditions within which something felt is true. Even while he is writing about the little portion of reality which is part of his experience, the poet may be conscious of a different reality outside. His problem is to relate the small truth to the sense of a wider, perhaps theoretically known truth outside his experience" (*SC* [*The Still Centre*], 10). Spender had struggled throughout the decade from pre-Oxford isolation through fervent desire for social action, to political disappointment, and finally to a renewal of hope for human survival, humanistic values, and personal love.

Part One's rather didactic poetry begins with **"Polar Exploration,"** an early-1930s poem in which arctic explorers march through a world of white to winter quarters, exploring the realm of male relationships as much as external nature. Their intense lives contrast with the dull, bourgeois existence at home. The persona has come to realize that he is symbolically living in a new Ice Age: "Was / Ice our anger transformed?" But the more evil place "Is the North / Over there," presumably Germany, with "a tangible, real madness" and led by "A glittering simpleton" (*SC* [*The Still Centre*], 18), an underestimation of Hitler.

"Easter Monday," another early poem in the collection, is a political piece. On the day after the Resurrection

> The bourgeois in tweeds
> Holds in his golden spectacles'
> Twin lenses, the velvet and far
> Mountains. But look, rough hands
> From trams, 'buses, bicycles, and of tramps,
> Like one hand red with labour, grasp
> The furred and future bloom
> Of their falling, falling world.
>
> (*SC*, 19-20)

The Resurrection is like a revolution, but the "one hand red with labour," not with blood, will shape the future. The political position is more Fabian than Marxian.

The important love motive in *The Still Centre* begins with **"Experience."** Indeed, love is the ultimate "centre" the poet seeks. In obtaining experience, the persona bids farewell to childhood, to the "headaching" world before heterosexual experience, and enters the new world of Eros in which exists "two people . . . and both double, yet different. I entered with myself, I left with a woman" (*SC*, 21).

For C. Day Lewis the following lines were "pure poetry," impossible to transcribe into prose without impairing meaning:[29]

> Good-bye now, good-bye: to the early and sad hills
> Dazed with their houses, like a faint migraine.
> Orchards bear memory in cloudy branches.
> The entire world roars in a child's brain.
>
> (*SC*, 21-22)

One of Spender's "obsessive themes" is the unity of being. Humans struggle toward that state. Some may achieve the condition of unity after death. **"Exiles from Their Land, History Their Domicile"** is "about those who have, after their deaths, obtained for their lives a symbolic significance which certainly passed unnoticed when they were living."[30] Death chooses purposes and actions that give lives symbolic significance: "What miracle divides / Our purpose from our weakness?" (*SC*, 25). Great historical exiles bring their values to bear on the present. They are "freedom's friends." Although they "were jokes to children," their will, their courage, "their deeds and deaths are birds" (*SC*, 24). The persona prays to them:

> Recall me from life's exile, let me join
> Those who now kneel to kiss their sands,
> And let my words restore
> Their printed, laurelled, victoried message.
>
> (*SC*, 25)

Spender yet thinks "continually of those who were truly great."

In **"The Past Values,"** retitled **"The Living Values"** in *Collected Poems, 1928-1953,* the past is challenged as being destructive. The glazed look in the portraits of old masters appears like "the eyes of the freshly young dead / sprawled in the mud of battle" (*SC*, 26). A metaphysical conceit locks together the sad eyes of the inspirers, the dusty glass over portraits, the fog, and those poor soldiers "struck . . . with lead so swift / Their falling sight stared through its glass" (*SC*, 27). At the same time, **"The Past Values"** laments that modern war perverts and destroys the greatness of our legacy. Eros and Thanatos ever entwine. The old masters inspire creation and destruction, for they have also left us the patriotism and lust that have brought young soldiers to their deaths and ended their "dream of girls."

Although close to propaganda, **"An Elementary School Class Room in a Slum"** presents the poet's sincere concern for the social anomaly of children with their future "painted with a fog." Shakespeare and geography are meaningless to hungry children who "wear skins peeped through by bones and spectacles of steel / with mended glass." Their maps are blotted "with slums as big as doom" (*SC*, 29). The poem succeeds because of its sheer lyrical quality, its deep pity, its justifiable anger, and its prescription for the salvation of all parties to the social contract: create a Laurentian world for children where sensation and intellect unite to "break the town" and find a history "whose language is the sun," while the children joyously "let their tongues / Run naked into books" (*SC*, 29).

Because it is also about children and rebirth, **"A Footnote (from Marx's Chapter on the Working Day)"** in Part Two is discussed here. At the opening, children in school mouth foolishness and errors until, as in the speeches of Lear's Fool, the images have deeper meaning than the denotation:

> "So perhaps all the people are dead, and we're birds
> "Shut in steel cages by the devil who's good,
> "Like the miners in their pit cages
> "And us in our chimneys to climb, as we should."
>
> (*SC*, 43)

Children in their "angel infancy" are indeed birds, and the adults are dead, their souls imprisoned in error. Yet the children, with instinctive cognition, understand their tragic fate.

The last poem in Part One, **"The Uncreated Chaos,"** in four parts and 84 lines, is the second longest and one of the most significant in the collection. In it Spender expresses what for him was the great modern dilemma: being drawn toward the will and the world in which it is operative while simultaneously desiring to escape both will and world to the still center.

The world requires our obeisance: "To the hanging despair of eyes in the street, offer / Your making hands and your guts on skewers of pity" (*SC*, 30). At the same time, we poor spirits feed a fantasy:

> When the pyramid sky is piled with clouds of sand
>> which the yellow
> Sun blasts above, respond to that day's doom
> With a headache. Let your ghost follow
> The young men to the Pole, up Everest, to war: by
>> love, be shot.
>
>> (*SC*, 30)

But always "the uncreating chaos" of modern life descends upon us and destroys integrity while promoting selfishness, vanity, and hedonism:

> For the uncreating chaos descends
> And claims you in marriage: though a man, you were
>> ever a bride:
> Ever beneath the supple surface of summer muscle,
> The fountain evening talk cupping the summer stars,
> The student who chucks back the lock from his hair in
>> front of a silver glass,
> You were only anxious that all these passions should
>> last.
>
>> (*SC*, 30)

Part of the uncreating chaos, developing like a cosmic storm, is the rise of the Nazis, a truly destructive element:

> Meagre men shoot up. Rockets, rockets,
> A corporal's [Hitler] fiery tongue wags about burning
>> parliament.
> There flows in the tide of killers, the whip-masters,
> Breeches and gaiters camouflage blood.
>
>> (*SC*, 32-33)

What is to be done when a terrible world is too much with us? One does one's work. That is the only answer. One changes what one can and returns to "the simple mechanism. . . . Clear day, thoughts of the work-room, the desk, / The hand, symbols of power" (*SC*, 33). The progress of **"The Uncreating Chaos"** is in the desperate struggle between the archetypal forces of creation and destruction, with human love on the I-Thou scale the saving grace and the hope of rebirth. Thus, **"The Uncreating Chaos"** is the turning point in Spender's poetry. The poet has defined his work: it is poetry. The cost in isolation must be borne.

Part Two of *The Still Centre* is a miscellany of Marxist poems, sketches, love poems, and typical Spender machinery pieces, such as **"View from a Train"** and **"The Midlands Express."** These, along with **"Houses at Edge of Railway Lines"** in Part Four, show that Spender had not quite finished with what Auden called the "strict beauty of locomotive."

"View from a Train" again finds the persona seeing himself reflected in a train's window superimposed upon the landscape and remembering that the "man behind his mask still wears a child." **"The Midlands Express"** is another **"The Express."** This train is a "Muscular Virtuoso!" and very sexy, for "all England lies beneath you like a woman / With limbs ravished" (*SC*, 47). The train is compared, not quite convincingly, to "great art. . . . Whose giant travelling ease / Is the vessel of its effort and fatigue" (*SC*, 47).

In **"Houses at Edge of Railway Lines"** the persona looks for love while journeying on a train. It is "an age of bombs" and the passengers search for "hope on the horizon," but the persona, looking elsewhere, wishes "without knocking to enter / The life that lies behind / the edges of drawn blinds" (*SC*, 103), as if he were a lover calling. In the tranquil home we all long for "love fills rooms, as gold / Pours into a valid mould" (*SC*, 103).

"Hoelderlin's Old Age," like **"Beethoven's Death Mask,"** is an elegy and a celebration of old age and evening. In the German romantic tradition, the old poet Johann Hölderlin defies death's power as his "soul sings / Burning vividly in the centre of a cold sky" (*SC*, 37). Hölderlin has found his still center.

Three poems in Part Two are quite personal. **"Hampstead Autumn"** is a childhood reminiscence of a mature man who sorts out what he can and what he cannot regain from the past. In the end, the sun sets on "images, / Continuous and fragile as China" (*SC*, 38). The four-line **"In the Street"** is unusually aphoristic for Spender. The persona comes out in favor of isolation, "a blank wall with my self face to face," having grown weary of "the lies and lights of the complex street" (*SC*, 39). **"In the Street"** counters the sentimentality of **"Hampstead Autumn"** with existential self-reliance. **"The Room on the Square"** finds a rejected lover accepting his isolation as he climbs to "the dark room / Which hangs above the square." Again, as in **"Houses at the Edge of Railway Lines,"** the persona sees love happening elsewhere and to others, and he misses it sorely. The dark room once had a "light in the window [that] seemed perpetual" (*SC*, 40) because love was there for him. Yet love and loss are natural to the human experience, begetting growth.

"The Indifferent One" and **"Three Days"** are also love poems about loss. Although personal and obscure in their reference, they remain accessible in emotion, description, and sensuality. The former asks the loved one for "the smile's indifference which forgives" (*SC*, 49), and the latter finds the persona reminiscing on "sensual memories" and "your image and those days of glass" (*SC*, 51).

"The Marginal Field" is a socialist poem that deplores the exploitation of the farmer, but strained language militates against the message, although the opening stanza is lyrically fine, presenting yet again a view through a glass:

> On the chalk cliff edge struggles the final field
> Of barley smutted with tares and marbled
> With veins of rusted poppy as though the plough had
>   bled.
> The sun is drowned in bird-wailing mist,
> The sea and sky meet outside distinction,
> The landscape glares and stares—white poverty
> Of gaslight diffused through frosted glass.

> (*SC*, 41)

"Thoughts during an Air Raid" really belongs among Spender's poems of the Spanish Civil War in Part Three, the strongest, most significant, and most famous section of *The Still Centre.* These war poems show the strong influence of the soldier poet of pity, Wifred Owen. Unlike Owen, Spender was an observer of war, not a participant, and thus in his war poems he balances emotional reactions with his lifelong antiwar commitment. The sheer honesty of these war poems is compelling. "Some of them are among the most celebrated poems of the war."[31] **"Thoughts during an Air Raid"** finds the persona, "the great 'I,'" in a hotel bed in Madrid wondering if "a bomb should dive / Its nose right through this bed" (*SC*, 45). The persona, truly and reasonably frightened, tries to be flippant when confronted by the thought of imminent death. He generalizes his experiences into the terror most humans have at the thought of their own ending, but "horror is postponed / For everyone until it settles on him" (*SC*, 45). Solipsism is, after all, a defense against the anonymity of death. Even a Stalingrad is for one participant an individual experience. One wonders how many thousands of Londoners recalled this poem during the Blitz?

Part Three, mislocated in the Contents, really begins with **"Two Armies,"** a recollection of the bitterness of war in winter wherein "two armies / Dig their machinery" and "men freeze and hunger" (*SC*, 55). Yet, in war there is also much serenity between battles. The imagery borders on the erotic in a scene reminiscent of Shakespeare's *Henry V*:

> Clean silence drops at night when a little walk
> Divides the sleeping armies, each
> Huddled in linen woven by remote hands.
> When the machines are stilled, a common suffering
> Whitens the air with breath and makes both one
> As though these enemies slept in each other's arms.

> (*SC*, 56)

Clarity bursts over Spender's war poetry like a flare in the night. **"Two Armies"** dominates the panorama of war. More intimate scenes, comparable to cinematic close-ups, come later.

The sardonic **"Ultima Ratio Regum"** (The final argument of kings) describes the death of an insignificant, unknown soldier killed in a cause he did not comprehend: "The boy lying dead under the olive trees / Was too young and too silly / To have been notable to their important eye." The next line, so shocking, emphasizes the odd eroticism of war: "He was a better target for a kiss" (*SC*, 57). Yet war is foolish and wasteful:

> Consider. One bullet in ten thousand kills a man.
> Ask. Was so much expenditure justified
> On the death of one so young and so silly
> Lying under the olive trees, O world, O death?

> (*SC*, 58)

There are no heroes or heroics in Spender's view of war. In that sense, he is an "antiwar poet" rather than a "war poet," and in World War II he would pointedly refuse the proffered role of war poet. In the introduction to *The Still Centre* Spender makes it clear that he cannot write about heroism because it was not his experience (*SC*, 10). He could write about pity. That he knew. So did Wilfred Owen, who said, "My subject is war and the pity of war. The poetry is in the pity."[32]

For a noncombatant—perhaps because he could keep some distance, physically and emotionally—Spender's war imagery is unusually evocative: "The unflowering wall sprouted with guns, / Machine-gun anger quickly scythed the grasses" (*SC*, 57). His only American equal in this kind of imagery is Randall Jarrell in such poems as "The Death of the Ball Turret Gunner."

"The Coward" shows the persona's pity for a soldier who has destroyed his whole life in a moment of cowardice: "I gather all my life and pour / Out its love and comfort here" (*SC*, 60). The referential image is of a soldier emptying his canteen. But there is a drop of human kindness left for him. The persona states, "My love and pity shall not cease / for a lifetime at least" (*SC*, 60). Spender was accused of being a tourist at war.[33] Unfair! He was committed to the Spanish Republic, and his anguish was as real as anyone's. By his own admission, he would not have been much of a soldier.

In the fine poem **"A Stopwatch and an Ordnance Map,"** Spender again depicts the death of a soldier, one who will no longer need to know the time and place. A moment of violence and pain "and the bones are fixed at five / Under the moon's timelessness" (*SC*, 61).

"War Photograph" is surely a commentary on the most famous photo of the Spanish Civil War, Robert Capa's picture of a Republican soldier at the moment he was shot: "the instant lurks / With its metal fang planned for my heart" (*SC*, 62). The dying soldier knows that the ultimate photo is taken by fate: "My corpse be covered with the snows' December / And roots push through skin's silent drum / When the years and fields forget, but the whitened bones remember" (*SC*, 63). Perhaps to avoid the Capa connection, Spender changed the poem's title to **"In No Man's Land"** and shortened the piece in *Collected Poems, 1928-1953*.

In the Petrarchan **"Sonnet"** the persona criticizes the world for looking at his lover as a surface image "moving upon the social glass of silver" (*SC*, 64), but he plunges through those mirrored rays to his lover's "hidden inner self." The persona cannot solve the troubles of the world, but he can drown in the life of his love.

"Fall of a City" depicts the despair of a city that falls to the fascists. Although probably about Madrid, the poem prophesies the fall of Prague, Warsaw, and Paris in World War II. Perhaps the greatest loss is to culture:

> All the names of heroes in the hall
> Where the feet thundered and the bronze throats
>   roared,
> Fox and Lorca claimed as history on the walls,
> Are now angrily deleted
> Or to dust surrender their dust,
> From golden praise excluded.
>
> (*SC*, 65)

While for the poor children "all the lessons learned, [are] unlearnt" (*SC*, 66). Finally, though, the next generation must find the "spark from the days of energy." It did. Spain is now free. It may be because the Spanish child of the late 1930s hoarded liberty's energy "like a bitter toy" (*SC*, 66).

"At Castellon" (referring to a large Mediterranean port 50 miles north of Valencia) evokes the desperately tense atmosphere of a city about to be bombed. A worker is asked to drive the poet to the next village. They leave behind them what "the winged black roaring gates unload. / Cargoes of iron and of fire" (*SC*, 68). **"The Bombed Happiness"** presents an extended metaphor of the result of a bomb burst on children, who are turned into dancing harlequins by the force of the blast. Their flesh is stripped and "their blood twisted in rivers of song" (*SC*, 69). The state has played cruelly with these children. Its "toy was human happiness" (*SC*, 70). **"At Castellon"** and **"The Bombed Happiness"** are both rhymed pieces, unusual for Spender, who recognized that rhyme was not his forte. The delicacy of rhyme seems inappropriate for these violent poems.

"Port Bou," which takes its title from the small Spanish port that was Spender's entry point from France (*WW*, 199) and that had been bombed before he arrived, skillfully sums up the themes and attitudes of the Span-

ish Civil War poems. The extended metaphor of the poem is a broken circle representing the open bay, the incompleteness of the social revolution, the imperfection of war, and the unfulfilled hope of children:

> As a child holds a pet
> Arms clutching but with hands that do not join
>   . . . . .
> So the earth-and-rock flesh arms of this harbour
> Embrace but do not enclose the sea.
>
> (*SC*, 71)

The persona symbolically tries to bring the diverse parts of incompleteness together and find the truth: "My circling arms rest on a newspaper / Empty in my mind as the glittering stone / Because I search for an image" (*SC*, 71). But then nothing is complete in the waste and chaos of war, and the poet, after the port is evacuated, "is left alone on the bridge / Where the cleaving river trickles like saliva / At the exact centre, solitary as a target" (*SC*, 72). **"Port Bou"** is one of Spender's most accessible and powerful poems. The poet stands there, almost asking to be wounded. He cannot actively participate in the cause, but through his poetic sensibility he can express the suffering, the folly, and the pity. That is some service after all. That is the purpose of the Spanish Civil War poems.

Hugh D. Ford notes that instead of descanting on "fundamental ideas about freedom and liberty," Spender's "poems expound upon death, suffering, fear and concern over the fate of the innocent and the cowardly."[34] In the Spanish Civil War poems, Spender ceased to try to fuse poetry and public policy. The poems are without villains. The subjects are the dead, the defeated, and the frightened. Spender's good friend and coeditor of *Horizon*, Cyril Connolly, authored a colossal understatement when he referred to "Mr Spender's not very martial muse."[35] As Katherine Bail Hoskins says, "No absolute pacifist wrote more convincing antiwar poems during the thirties than this fervent apologist for collective security."[36]

Part Four of *The Still Centre* disappoints somewhat after the intensity of Part Three, but its contents logically follow Spender's retreat from political commitment. These poems seek primarily, but not exclusively, to deal with the inanition and breakdown of Spender's first marriage and the resulting loss, isolation, and disappointment with love. Significantly and sadly, Spender dedicated *The Still Centre* to the wife he was losing.

The poems of loss of love begin with **"The Human Situation,"** wherein the persona's troubled past is exorcised by Eros and "my Womanly companion, / Revolving around me with light" (*SC*, 80). **"The Separation"** is a poem in which lovers are parted because the persona has been busy traveling, but unlike **"The

Human Situation," it falls back on clichés such as "my map / With meaningless names of places" (*SC,* 84). The lament is prosy:

> To bring me back to you, the earth
> Must turn, the aeroplane
> Must fly across the glittering spaces,
> The clocks must run, the scenery change
> From mountains into town.
>
> (*SC,* 84)

But then comes the last stanza of the poem, which is strong Spender. The lovers will find peace together when the will to serve the outside world is curbed:

> Shuttered by dark at the still centre
> Of the world's circular terror,
> O tender birth of life and mirror
> Of lips, where love at last finds peace
> Released from the will's error.
>
> (*SC,* 85)

"Two Kisses" and **"The Little Coat"** are two more love poems. The former has the longing persona remembering the kiss he wears "like a feather / Laid upon my cheek" (*SC,* 86), and the latter presents an extended metaphor in which a torn coat presages loss "like dolls in attics / When the children have grown and ceased to play" (*SC,* 87). The persona desires to be held in a "solemn kiss" that will provide "the loving stillness" (*SC,* 88).

"Variations on My Life: The First" and **"Variations on My Life: The Second,"** the last love poems in the collection, are enigmatic pieces in which the tormented persona, with never enough air, space, or light, laments love past and lost, but realizes he will never abandon loving, "which nothing does refuse / and only death denies" (*SC,* 92).

In **"The Mask,"** Spender again employs glass and reflection imagery as the persona sees "the world with lenses." The eyes are the windows on reality: "My life confronts my life with eyes" (*SC,* 101). Other people revolve around the circles of his sight, but their passions are invisible. "They are the mirrors of the foreign masks / Stamped into shapes" (*SC,* 102). We can only know people one at a time, and then, because of masks, only imperfectly, for reality is merely our own consciousness. Thus, the solipsism of **"The Mask"** is the perfect paradigm of modernity.

"Napoleon in 1814" is the longest (114 lines) poem in *The Still Centre* and clearly the product of prolonged and troubled political thought. Napoleon represents Stalin, who in the 1930s was "the Man of Destiny": "Men spoke of you as Nature, and they made / a science of your moods" (*SC,* 97). Was ever the idea of dictator encapsulated in so few words? Napoleon is presented in

what Valentine Cunningham calls "heroic '30s images," such as "In you the Caesars," "sun," and "a superhuman shadow."[37] Spender was seeking to express the essence of a Napoleon. He had changed his mind about power politics and the morality of "good" tyranny fighting evil tyranny (i.e., Stalin versus Hitler). As in **"The Mask,"** individual consciousness shapes Napoleon's self-image as "the genius whom all envied," but with a difference:

> You were the last to see what they all saw
> That you, the blinding one, were now the blind
> The Man of Destiny, ill destined.
>
> For, as your face grew older, there hung a lag
> Like a double chin in your mind. The jaw
> Had in its always forward thrust
> Grown heavy.
>
> (*SC,* 96)

Napoleon should have truly studied and understood himself. Instead, he was left with the "wreck of deeds, the empty words." And after all, what is history but words? Great rhetoric, now like Hitler's and Stalin's, is "hidden in the hollow bones." **"Napoleon in 1814"** is a fine example of how Spender could bring his knowledge of history, his admiration for greatness and strength, his distrust of military force, and his puissant imagery of war and death to bear on an issue of the gravest importance: the attraction and the peril of the cult of personality.

"To a Spanish Poet (for Manuel Altolaguirre)" is the last poem in *The Still Centre.* It is an *ave atque vale* to all that the "idea" of Spain connoted in the 1930s, to the decade itself, and to the poet's youth. An English poet eulogizes a Spanish poet who was driven from Spain by the fascists at the very end (*WW,* 238-39). Spender employs the key image of *The Still Centre* in **"To a Spanish Poet"**—the glass mirror—as he has the Spaniard stand absurdly in the ruins of his bombed home:

> Everything in the room was shattered;
> Only you remained whole
> In frozen wonder, as though you stared
> At your image in the broken mirror
> Where it had always been silverly carried.
>
> (*SC,* 105)

Both Spender and Altolaguirre have "stared out the window on the emptiness of a world exploding." Spender reminds us of the individual's powerlessness in the face of the egotism of states that create "these comedies of falling stone" (*SC,* 106). Spender is so moved by the suffering of Altolaguirre and his compatriots that he reaches back into his cultural heritage to employ Jacobean imagery by way of Eliot:

> Unbroken heart,
> You stare through my revolving bones

On the transparent rim of the dissolving world
Where all my side is opened
With ribs drawn back like springs to let you enter
And replace my heart that is more living and more
  cold.

(SC, 107)

Yet the poem ends on a note of hope. The song goes on. It may be night but the stars still shine:

With your voice that still rejoices
In the centre of its night,
As, buried in this night,
The stars burn with their brilliant light.

(SC, 107)

I have left the first poem in Part Four, **"Darkness And Light,"** until last because, like **"The Uncreating Chaos,"** it is a crucial piece in the poet's struggle "to break out of the chaos of my darkness / Into a lucid day" (*SC*, 77). His words have become "eyes in night" trying "to reach a centre for their light" (*SC*, 77). He must find a place in the center of his will, but also, somehow, in the center of life and society. Paradoxically, the poet's conflicting postulates meet an artistic requirement: to have distant vision, to seek perspective, to stand aside and witness. He must stand "on a circumference to avoid the centre." Thus the dilemma that "centre and circumference are both my weakness" (*SC*, 77). Spender has located the source of modern artistic and intellectual paresis.

Finally, the persona in **The Still Centre** reveals the ambivalence and anxiety that foment modernism. The poet seeks strength of will to become a person of truth and integrity, and yet he knows, and reminds us, that human weakness is ever present, creating an inertia that leads to dangerous illusions. The "still centre" symbolizes that quiet, eternal place "from which the poet can stabilize his values and then come to terms with his world."[38] He has returned to the "edge of being." It is not surprising that Spender chose **"Darkness and Light"** as the epigram for *World within World*. How better could he summarize and preface the Manichaean conflict between freedom and determinism that structured the first half of his life?

SELECTED POEMS

At just past the age of 30 Stephen Spender was internationally recognized as a major English poet. Faber and Faber, in an effort to bring to mass popular attention the works of the most significant contemporary poets, launched a series, rather ingenuously named Sesame Books, and Spender's **Selected Poems** (1940) appeared therein, as did books of Eliot, Auden, MacNeice, and others. **Selected Poems** contains 12 poems from **Poems,** 19 from **The Still Centre,** and selections from each of the five acts of the verse play *Trial of a Judge.*

During World War II, British poetry quite understandably went into a tailspin. All the poets, even those who had emigrated, were traumatized by the desperate struggle. Many magazines were suspended. Book publishing was curtailed. Most writers did various kinds of war service. Thus, Spender and his contemporaries held their relative positions during the conflict. With Auden in America and in disgrace with the general public, if not with his friends, the publication of **Selected Poems** authenticated Spender in Britain as the premier poet of the younger generation growing just a little long in the tooth. He was considered a spokesperson and a visionary striving to integrate self and society. Slowly but inexorably, Spender would slip from his justly held position of eminence through several collections of successively diminishing promise, until the public perceived him not as a fine poet but as that valuable but lesser contributor to culture, the essaying critic.

Notes and References

1. Justin Replogle, "The Auden Group," *Wisconsin Studies in Contemporary Literature* 5 (1964), 136.

2. Michael Roberts, ed., *New Signatures* (London: Hogarth Press, 1932), 12; hereafter cited in the text as *NS*.

3. A. Kingsley Weatherhead, *Stephen Spender and the Thirties* (Lewisburg, Pa.: Bucknell University Press, 1975), 221.

4. Francis Scarfe, "Stephen Spender: A Sensitive," *Auden and After: The Liberation of Poetry, 1930-1941* (London: Routledge, 1942), 35.

5. [Geoffrey] Thurley, "A Kind of Scapegoat [: A Retrospective on Stephen Spender" *The Ironic Harvest: English Poetry in the Twentieth Century* (London: Edward Arnold, 1974)], 79.

6. *Nine Experiments* (Hampstead: privately printed, 1928; facsimile repr., Elliston Poetry Foundation, University of Cincinnati, 1964), 13; hereafter cited in the text as *NE*.

7. Louis Untermeyer, "Poetry of Power," *Saturday Review of Literature,* 10 November 1934, 274.

8. G. S. Fraser, *Vision and Rhetoric* (London: Faber and Faber, 1959), 205.

9. *Twenty Poems* (London: Blackwell, 1930), 2; hereafter cited in the text as *TP*.

10. Elton Edward Smith, "Stephen Spender, the Proletarian Poet," *The Angry Young Men of the Thirties* (Carbondale: Southern Illinois University Press, 1975), 65.

11. See Paul Fussell, *The Great War and Modern Memory* (London: Oxford University Press, 1975), 279-86.

12. D. E. S. Maxwell, *Poets of the Thirties* (London: Routledge and Kegan Paul, 1969), 196.

13. [Charles] Osborne, *W. H. Auden* [: *The Life of a Poet* (New York: Harcourt Brace Jovanovich, 1979)], 96.

14. Fraser, *Vision and Rhetoric*, 207-8.

15. Morton Zabel, "The Purpose of Stephen Spender," *Poetry* 45, no. 4 (January 1935), 209.

16. Thurley, "A Kind of Scapegoat," 81.

17. *Poems,* 2nd ed. (New York: Random House, 1934), 57; hereafter cited in the text as *P.*

18. James Southworth, "Stephen Spender," *Sewanee Review* 45 (July 1937), 275.

19. [Louis] MacNeice, *The Strings Are False* [(London: Faber and Faber, 1965)], 128.

20. Samuel Hynes, *The Auden Generation* (New York: Viking, 1972), 67.

21. Replogle, "The Auden Group," 139.

22. Morton Seif, "The Impact of T. S. Eliot on Auden and Spender," *South Atlantic Quarterly* 53 (January 1954), 62.

23. *Vienna* (New York: Random House, 1935), 10; hereafter cited in the text as *V.*

24. Hynes, *The Auden Generation,* 145.

25. *The Still Centre* (London: Faber and Faber, 1939), 11; hereafter cited in the text as *SC.*

26. David Daiches, *Poetry and the Modern World* (Chicago: University of Chicago Press, 1940), 237.

27. Robert D. Harper, "Back to the Personal," *Poetry* 57 (October 1940), 49.

28. "Inside the Cage," *The Making of a Poet* (London: Hamish Hamilton, 1955), 15.

29. C. Day Lewis, *A Hope for Poetry* (Oxford: Basil Blackwell, 1934), 95.

30. Introduction, *Collected Poems, 1928-1953* (New York: Random House, 1955), xvi.

31. A. T. Tolley, *The Poetry of the Thirties* (London: Victor Gollancz, 1975), 352.

32. Preface to *The Collected Poems of Wilfred Owen,* ed. C. Day Lewis (London: Chatto and Windus, 1963), 31.

33. Hynes, *The Auden Generation,* 251.

34. Hugh D. Ford, *A Poet's War: British Poets and the Spanish Civil War* (Philadelphia: University of Pennsylvania Press, 1965), 232.

35. Cyril Connolly, "Today the Struggle," *New Statesman and Nation,* 5 June 1937, 926.

36. Katherine Bail Hoskins, *Today the Struggle: Literature and Politics in England during the Spanish Civil War* (Austin: University of Texas Press, 1969), 227.

37. [Valentine] Cunningham, *British Writers of the Thirties* [(New York: Oxford, 1988)], 199.

38. Harper, "Back to the Personal," 49.

Dave Cummings (essay date 2002)

SOURCE: Cummings, Dave. "'Now With My Hand I Cover Africa': A Love-Poem Sent by Stephen Spender to William Plomer." *Journal of European Studies* 32, nos. 2 and 3 (2002): 223-33.

[*In the following essay, Cummings analyzes Spender's treatment of the colonized "other" in his love poem to the South African poet William Plomer.*]

> The bodies of those I love engirth me and I engirth them
>
> Walt Whitman, 'I Sing the Body Electric'[1]

William Plomer (1903-1973), addressee and recipient of the love poem discussed in this paper ["**Now with My Hand I Cover Africa**"], was born in Pietersburg, South Africa, shortly after the British-South African war of 1899-1902. He had travelled between England and South Africa for much of his early life, his mother loathing South Africa after the death in Johannesburg of her second son, John, in 1908. She felt that the family should return to England but two factors worked against this: Plomer's father loved South Africa and its people, and there was never enough money to provide a secure life-style if they actually returned.

When Plomer finally left school in Johannesburg, his wish to study at Oxford was denied on financial grounds, so he worked first in Molteno and then with his father in a general store in Entumeni, experiences which were to inspire his first novel *Turbott Wolfe,*[2] a biting attack on racism in South Africa. *Turbott Wolfe* was well received in both Britain and the United States but, not unsurprisingly, was condemned in most quarters of South Africa where its open handling of the taboo subjects of racism, brutality and miscegenation horrified the white inhabitants. The public response to the book was partly responsible for Roy Campbell and Laurens van der Post inviting Plomer on to the editorial board of *Voorslag* (Whiplash), a new South African journal dedicated to art and literature. This collaboration was short-lived, however, because the editors' criticism of

South African people and South Africa's political establishment was too much for the financial backers to accept. After the effective sacking of the trio, Plomer made his way in 1926 to Japan where he stayed for three years. This departure was accompanied by another burst of creative energy: Japan with its landscape and its growing militaristic power was perfect for Plomer's style of pastoral poetry and satirical prose narrative. The result was the collection of short stories *I Speak of Africa* (1927), the 'Japanese' novel *Sado* (1932) and two collections of poetry, *Notes for Poems* and *Five-Fold Screen*.[3]

In 1929 Plomer travelled to England, where he was to spend the rest of his life. He became 'reader' for the publishers Jonathan Cape, and perhaps the single issue he is now remembered for is his promotion of the writer Ian Fleming, creator of James Bond. He developed a friendship with Benjamin Britten and wrote libretti for the operas *Gloriana,*[4] and *Curlew River,*[5] the latter inspired by Britten's and Pears' visit to Japan in 1956, a trip organized by Plomer. After *Sado* his novels descended into weak Edwardian satires; it seems that without a powerful political edge his prose lost direction and importance. *Museum Pieces,* his last novel, was written in 1952, twenty years before his death. However, he continued to write poems until his death, the best of which retained a political edge, dealing with, for example, apartheid.

Perhaps Plomer's greatest (and certainly his bulkiest) legacy is his correspondence with literary figures of the twentieth century. The boxes of correspondence held by Durham University Library hold 24 metres of letters to Plomer. We are fortunate that he apparently refused to throw away any of this richly-ranging correspondence, including letters from E. M. Forster, Virginia Woolf, through to Spender, Isherwood and Auden, up to Derek Walcott and Nadine Gordimer towards the end of Plomer's life. With a few writers he maintained a life-time correspondence, notably E. M. Forster and Stephen Spender. Many of the 'queer' letters show how the homosexual middle-class writers of the 1930s had a particular attraction to working-class men, and to labourers and soldiers in particular. The links between homosexuality, upper-middle-class identity and left-wing politics and Thirties writers, such as Spender, Auden and Isherwood, appear to have been pivotal: as Spender would say later in life 'Sex with the working class of course had political connotations [. . .] It was a way in which people with left wing sympathies could feel that they were really getting in contact with the working class'.[6] In one early letter, part of the large volume of correspondence between Spender and Plomer from 1930 until Plomer's death in 1973, Spender sent a poem to Plomer that somehow displaces this working-class fetish to one that focuses on the cultural, African,

Other. It is this epistolary enclosure, which dates from the very beginning of their friendship, that is the subject of this essay.

In early 1930 William Plomer met Stephen Spender at the Oxford English Club,[7] Plomer having been invited to speak there on the topic of Japanese literature. He became a close friend of Spender, and they developed a friendship that was to last Plomer's lifetime. On 4 May 1930 Stephen Spender sent William Plomer a letter, in itself rather pedestrian, but intriguingly containing a rather tortured, half-competent 'love' poem, written between February and May of that year. It is the only fragment of their correspondence in which Spender views Plomer as 'exotic' and worthy of erotic attention. The poem is clearly sexual in nature, and gives fascinating insight into Spender's portrayal of the addressee's Otherness, which can be seen to be fetishized. This paper offers a reading of the poem, an understanding of which is based on the perception of a double fear of both homosexuality and the colonial subject.

In this early poem by Spender, the erotic appeal of the working-class male is translated into the allure of the colonial, so that this poem illustrates how those issues of class and the colonial subject can interact and function as a similar sexual fetish. Of course, there is nothing new in middle-class queer men objectifying either working-class or black men. This problematic of sexual desire and the objective fetishism of the working class and/or the colonial subject appear in the most unexpected of places.

When dealing with the relationship between the fetish, the homosexual and class difference, we need to consider their connections within the context of psychoanalysis and materialism. Yet the former—at least classical Freudian psychoanalysis—has been problematic with regards to the fetish and homosexuality. For Freud it seems that the homosexual and the fetish are two mutually exclusive matters:

> Probably no male human being is spared the fright of castration at the sight of a female genital. Why some people become homosexual as a consequence of that impression, while others fend it off by creating a fetish, and in the great majority surmount it, we are frankly not able to explain.[8]

The 1930s writers' sexual attachment to the working class or, as here, the colonial subject, cannot be framed within the mechanism of the Freudian fetish, as the homosexual's horror at the female's *lack* is actualized not through an object fetish (fur, boots, luggage) but through a sexual relationship with the *self-same,* or a manifestation through narcissism. A more fluid, and inclusive, definition of the fetish has been offered by Laura Mulvey:

A fetish is something in which someone invests a meaning and a value beyond or beside its actual meaning and value [. . .] Like a red-flag at the point of danger, the fetish object calls attention to a nodal point of vulnerability, whether within the psychic structure of an individual or the structure of a social group.[9]

Spender's poem can be framed within Mulvey's definition of the fetish, concerning itself with feelings of vulnerability, fear and desire; and I will be arguing that the fetish (or the value and meaning) of working-class men is transposed on to the colonial subject.

It is obviously impossible to tell whether this poem alludes to an actual sexual experience, but, even if it does not, it is clearly a love-poem. We get an indication that there may have been some erotic encounter between the European 'I' with his 'gusty, Northern passion' and an African 'you' of 'imprisoned skies'. Yet if intimacy did happen, we see that this is an unsatisfactory union, 'we were strangers lying side by side'. The yearning and feelings of guilt in the poem are somehow uncontrollable.

Given Plomer's 'action-packed' and fruitful literary life, it is understandable that the young Spender would see him as a figure of hero-worship. His poem presents a strange mixture of admiration and sexual desire, suggesting both a naïf attitude to politics and an almost uncomfortable attitude to colonial subjectification. The opening stanza contains a worldliness that seems too precocious for the 19-year-old Spender:

> This world grows tracks in my heart, maps the brow
> . . .
> Yes, with brow bent troubled like Europe
> I feel Africa push roots already,
> The ports you rest at grow like cancers in me.

These opening lines seem to refer to the state of a Europe 'troubled' by post-war poverty, the repercussions of the Wall Street crash of 1929 and the rise of politics polarized between extreme left and right. However, political allegory gives way to an image of sexuality and colonialism, disease and disgust. Africa is presented as a subterranean conqueror, its tentacles 'pushing' the ground beneath Europe, quaking a decaying civilization. The line, 'I feel Africa push roots' already overtly sexualizes the stanza by suggesting the image of sexual penetration. As this poem was written for and to Plomer, may we assume that we are dealing with reference to anal penetration? The African roots take on a phallic function, evoking a fantasy of Plomer the African penetrating the European Spender. These lines seem to be connected to two ideas, or fears, of colonialism. The first is within the discourse of the black man (in this case, read African) as phallus, as put forward by Fanon, 'He [the Negro] *is* a penis';[10] the second, a colonial reverse or fear of the colonized pushing back into the European 'origin'.

Yet this penetration is not accompanied by any form of *jouissance* on the part of the speaker. The ports the addressee rests in (for much of 1929-30 Plomer travelled Europe) are both literal ports and metaphorical orifices. A port is a site of entry, and of course exit, from the national body; moreover, ports are traditionally sites of promiscuous sex where sexually-transmitted diseases are rife. Leo Bersani points out in 'Is the rectum a grave?' that in the context of the HIV pandemic, contagion and infection are defined in terms of sexuality: children and heterosexuals with HIV are seen as innocent, but men who have sex with men are seen as guilty, 'It is as if gay men's "guilt" were the real agent of infection'.[11] Although, of course, Spender was writing decades before the advent of Aids, the analogy with Bersani is useful because Spender himself seems to be connecting sexual guilt and anxiety with sodomy and disease. The bodily guilt which Bersani has analysed in terms of heterosexist anxiety is heavily implied through Spender's metaphor of a cancerous growth, connected to the port—that is, the rectum. The poem thus puts into play the image of the diseased, cancerous rectum contaminated by the Other, the colonized.

Whether the anxiety controlling these tropes is a fear of the unknown (Africa), or guilt about same-sex desire, is never clarified in the poem, whose emotional tangle grows more complex as it proceeds. The second stanza embodies the personal and the political, not in a unified fashion but by creating a fissure between the sexual self and the political representation of Africa:

> Now with my hand I cover Africa
> If it were I struck here, you there
> The hands could reach across darkness.
> Surely the heart would not fear.

The first of these lines suggests both the European lover with his hand over the body of the African (an act of tenderness after sex?) and the active colonial desire of occupying Africa. This is a disturbing image, in that the European feels that he has enough power to eclipse the whole continent of Africa with just one hand, and this colonial arrogance can be seen to continue in the rest of the stanza. We may also see a connection with the idea of a map. Given the close friendship between Spender and W. H. Auden, and Auden's fondness for the map as a trope of psychosexual life,[12] it seems plausible to read this image in geographical terms, as if the poem envisages the Mercator map of the world, with Europe looking 'troubled' on top of Africa down below it.

More tricky are the lines 'The hands could reach across darkness / Surely the heart would not fear'. Spender's apparent reference to Conrad's *Heart of Darkness* (1899) reveals further complexities within his own poem. What is the purpose of the invocation of this text by the young poet? As an epistemological offering on the nature and substance of colonialism? After his death in 1924 Conrad's reputation was riding high, and importantly one could read his work as a critique of the colonial process. The *Heart of Darkness* allusion in this poem offers to Plomer Spender's anti-colonial sympathies, even though they seem to be framed in a confused colonial mind-set. One other explanation for this reference to Conrad is based on a homosocial/homosexual reading, along the lines suggested by Gregory Woods,[13] from which it may be suggested that Spender's apparently crude allusion may be pointing to darker, deeper possibilities. Woods has pointed out the strong homosociality, bordering on homosexual desire, between Marlow and Kurtz. It may be that Spender positions himself in the role of Marlow in search of a Kurtz who is perceived to have 'gone native'. The lines evoke the images of separation and journeying from *Heart of Darkness*; and ultimately, if the simile is extended to Conrad's narrative conclusion, the thought of a separation made final through death can be read back into the poem as the impossibility, undesirability and fear of a relationship. Kurtz (Plomer) was too hot for this Marlow to handle. This poem points to a conclusion that denies the possibility of two lives shared.

We must address ourselves to the question of why this relationship is doomed, at least sexually, before it begins. What is Spender's own 'Horror!' in this poem? Is it the fear of sex with men? Clearly not, for other correspondence sent from Spender to Plomer after this poem, indicates that he seemed to have no problems with one-night stands and affairs with men. Was it Plomer's connection with the Other, his African roots—the fetish, as Mulvey says, that flags up a point of danger? This is surely the answer, for how else could we read the admission in the third stanza that 'we are divided before parting; / Not miles not seas could so divide.' Spender attempts to reconcile the metaphorical and literal Africa and Europe, yet even during the sexual act there is a distance that cannot be bridged. It is not the geographical distance that divides these two individuals, it is the psychological and material burdens.

So far this poem reads as a tortured lament, a poem that sets out the impossibility of love, of only transitory sexual desire, ridden with guilt and rejection. The impediment is identified in the next line of the poem which sees the African Other as the abject: 'the unknown that cut between us / We were two strangers lying side by side.' The textual unknown in *Heart of Darkness* is translated to the explicitly unknown of this poem, cutting right into its heart. This cut, painful as any surely must be, is phonetically repeated in the final stanza's 'ruts blossoming in my heart'—where 'rut' means a hollow or mark in a road in the geographical landscape, and also an animalistic urge or sexual excitement. This poem is both avowing and disavowing sexual desire, yet its fetishist connection to the

'unknownness' of the addressee never lets go. The sexual desire at first emanates from the ontological nature of the addressee, and yet it must be disavowed because of the same. Does this confusion arise from Plomer's double-life? He is clearly African for Spender, yet he is the product of a white, middle-class, émigré family. 'We were strangers' implies we do not know each other and, also, we are the strange, the foreign, the unfamiliar.

At this point the poem seems to lose momentum, becoming overly metaphorical in style. It is unable to resolve the subject matter in hand, and resorts to the clichéd rhetoric of the love poem:

> And the great gulf swept up between us in the dark
> Yours were the sun and the imprisoned skies
> My gusty, Northern passion must destroy.

The unknown that cuts has now become 'a great gulf'. The quake that begins in the first stanza, leads to a bridgeable cut in stanzas two and three, and becomes a gulf in stanza four, making the process of rejection and abjection complete. The 'troubled' Europe of the opening simile is sexually destructive, it is a 'Northern passion that must destroy' the 'sun and the imprisoned skies'. Read in terms of colonialism, Spender's love is both destructive, destroying or at least eclipsing the sun, and redemptive in that it has the power to destroy 'the imprisoned skies', presumably representing the racial abuse and forced occupation of South Africa. It is a raw passion that cannot be harnessed for good or bad, it is directionless and arbitrary. Or is it? The final verse of the fourth stanza asks 'How could I quench that candle in your eyes?' The line rests on the modality of the verb 'could'; how could I possibly do that, to you? Again we turn from the political to the personal. This again points to a poem about the rejection of an individual, yet is undermined and subverted by a love that cannot let go—a love not merely sexual desire, but a redemptive longing.

The final stanza interestingly connects the 'cut' of stanza three with the themes of separation and animalistic desire:

> Thus from my heart the ruts collected and scatter
> Times painful blossoming shoots forth these words
> From a town's smoke and the black telegraph,
> Not like my thoughts under the feet of birds.

These 'ruts' are also emotional scars, once again desire and love are played off against one another. In these lines Spender is also setting up a contrast between smoky towns and black communications technology of industrialized Europe and pastoral Africa. Yet Plomer himself did not often enter into such a pastoral in his own writing on South Africa. The veldt described by Plomer in *Turbott Wolfe* is a violent landscape contaminated by the brutalities and inaction of the white set-tlers. One of his earliest poems, 'A Fall of Rock', which prefigures one of his best short stories *Ula Masondo,* is an attack on the inhumane conduct of mine owners and white workers towards the black workers which reads as a humane, politically charged manifesto against the capitalist system that creates such inequalities:

> [. . .] 'Oh!' Cry two or three, while red and blue
> Sparks fly from diamond earrings; several men
> Are glad for the excuse to squeeze white hands
> And murmur reassurance in small ears
> They say perhaps it was a fall of rock
> In the deep mines below.
>
> . . . . .
>
> [. . .] Two kaffirs trapped
> Up to the waist in dirty water. All the care
> That went to keep them fit - !
> Concrete bathrooms, carbolic soap,
> A balanced diet and free hospitals
> Made them efficient, but they die alone [. . .][14]

(It is ironic that, as we shall see, Spender was shortly to criticize Plomer's work as politically lightweight.) Conversely, Spender's own image of industrial 'smoky towns' may remind those familiar with Plomer's work of the Blakean landscape seen by the eponymous hero of *Ula Masondo* entering Johannesburg for the first time, '[. . .] distant ships between dark sky and dark sea, and from round them, as from ships, stood out faint fumes of smoke, faint fumes in space'[15]—a long way from the romanticized idyll of birds pecking in the kraal. It seems that Spender's poem is reflecting a certain naïf perception of a South Africa which was heavily industrial in parts, and equally brutal throughout. The last line is, to this reader, the strangest of the poem; we may see the poet's 'thoughts under the feet of birds' as a rather bizarre intertextual allusion to Yeats' 'Tread softly for you tread on my dreams',[16] asking his ad-dressee to think kindly of the words that he has transcribed. After all Spender is presenting this poem to a poet and novelist who, at that time, was better known than himself.

In the surviving letters from Spender to Plomer, this is the only item that resembles a love statement. Plomer obviously very quickly became demoted from erotic/exotic object to friend status, not so much somebody to be respected as somebody to see as an equal—an at-titude which at times clearly irritated Plomer. When *Sado* was published in 1931, Spender wrote to Plomer that

> Your book interests me in a way it is very unsympa-thetic to me. There is a didactic note in it which is no doubt deliberate and creates its effect [. . .] Some of the statements you make are true, but I am curious to know what standpoint you make them? [. . .] It seems to me that the only thing a writer can do is draw atten-tion to the real issues [. . .] of fucking, money, religion, food, and all the primitive needs in life [. . .][17]

Plomer's response must have expressed annoyance at Spender's letter, for in the following letter Spender states

> I'm awfully sorry if my remarks seemed inappropriate, I was not so much criticizing your book as trying to explain my point of view by putting myself on the op-position side as it were . . .
>
> . . . I think that your novel would have been so much more terrific if instead of walking between two civiliza-tions, the East and West—and the other two civiliza-tions—the past and present—and making statements about the people in your novel, who really represent nothing more that they are going to disappear (so how can one be didactic about them?) that you had *accepted* the fact stated in p. 156. [of *Sado*] that the masses are going to dominate.[18]

Spender's own inconsistencies with regard to aesthetics are obvious. Firstly he criticizes Plomer for being didactic instead of talking of 'fucking and money', and in the later letter he attacks his novel for not being didactic enough because it (or Plomer) does not accept that the 'masses are going to dominate'. Perhaps we can forgive the young Spender this incoherence on the grounds of youth and political incertitude. Certainly his reply to Plomer's letter alerts us to the fact that Plomer was still a figure not to be crossed aesthetically. A sharper division came when Christopher Isherwood read *Sado,* after which Spender had the back-up he needed in terms of Isherwood's critique of the text. He sent Plomer a rather long letter, naïvely criticizing the text for its lack of political content:

> Christopher told me that he liked your book very much although he criticized it on rather the same political or social grounds as I had done. He seemed to feel that when your characters were talking although they talked about the East and West, etc, etc, they were only really interested in their own individualities. Of course the people in your book may have been like that in actual life, but somehow I feel that nowadays unless an artist shows great awareness of the much more important social problems behind the lives of his characters, his work tends to be disappointing.[19]

In fact nothing could be further from the truth. In a similar vein to Plomer's first novel, *Turbott Wolfe, Sado* is an excellent account of Japan in the 1920s and the rise of militarism.

These letters of 1932 suggest that Plomer very quickly ceased to be an object of sexual fascination for Spender. The excitement of the African very quickly began to wear off; when Plomer began to play his part in the English literary circle his exotic nature dissolved, leav-ing just another middle-class homosexual. For Spender fun was to be found elsewhere. He wrote to Plomer in 1931 that he was

> looking for a Friend. [. . .] I still hope that the Anarchists or Syndicalists Union of Neu Köhn may yield something. Or failing that the Winter Swimming

Baths, the Ping Pong [. . .] the Turkish Baths, the Six Day Bicycling Race, the International Football Matches, Skating, Ice-Hockey, hockey, Gymnastics, rowing, Literature [. . .] the Flicks, the New Cinema, the New Art, the New Photography. There are many roads to Rome . . .[20]

After the brief token of love or affection offered by the poem, Spender's relationship with Plomer becomes one of friendship. Their correspondence illustrates the development of that relationship and the change in Spender's own politics and sexuality. After the radicalism of the thirties, we see Spender becoming the 'family-man' to whose son Plomer stands godfather, and the promotion of both men to figures within the artistic and cultural establishment of Britain. The poem in itself may represent nothing more than a young man's infatuation with a rising light in the arts who had a certain erotic and exotic allure. Yet it remains culturally important for the way in which the African Other was given form and was made into a fetish.

Notes

1. Walt Whitman, 'I Sing the Body Electric', in *The Complete Poems* (London: Penguin, 1996), 127.

2. William Plomer, *Turbott Wolfe* (London: Hogarth Press, 1925).

3. William Plomer, *I Speak of Africa* (London: Hogarth Press, 1927); *Sado* (London: Hogarth Press, 1931); *Notes for Poems* (London: Hogarth Press, 1927); *The Five-Fold Screen* (London: Hogarth Press, 1932).

4. William Plomer, *Gloriana: An Opera in Three Acts* (London: Boosey & Hawkes, 1953); set to music by Benjamin Britten.

5. William Plomer, *Curlew River: A Parable for Church Performance* (London: Boosey & Hawkes, 1964); set to music by Benjamin Britten.

6. Peter Alexander, *William Plomer: A Biography* (Oxford: Oxford, 1989), 166.

7. *Ibid.*, 164.

8. Sigmund Freud, 'Fetishism', in *On Sexuality,* Vol. 7 of *The Penguin Freud Library,* eds. Angela Richards and Albert Dickson, trans. James Strachey (London: Penguin, 1977), 354.

9. Laura Mulvey, 'Xala, *Ousmane Sembene 1976: The Carapace That Failed*', in Patrick Williams and Laura Chrisman (eds.), *Colonial Discourse and Post-Colonial Theory* (Hemel Hempstead: Harvester-Wheatsheaf, 1993), 520.

10. Cited by Caroline Rooney, *African Literature, Animism and Politics* (London: Routledge, 2000), 172.

11. Leo Bersani, 'Is the rectum a grave?', *October,* 43 (1987), 197-222 (p. 210).

12. W. H. Auden 'We have brought you, they said, a map of the country', in *The Orators: An English Study* (London: Faber, 1932), 46-7. My thanks to Jan Montefiore for this suggestion.

13. Gregory Woods, *A History of Gay Literature: The Male Tradition* (New Haven: Yale University Press, 1998), 192.

14. William Plomer, 'A Fall of Rock', in *Collected Poems* (London: Jonathan Cape, 1973), 19-20.

15. William Plomer, *Selected Stories,* ed. Stephen Gray (Johannesburg: Africasouth Paperbacks, 1984), 55.

16. W. B. Yeats 'He Wishes for the Cloths of Heaven', in *Collected Poems* (London: Macmillan, 1968), 81.

17. Letter from Spender to Plomer, Plomer 213/11, Durham University Library, [probably October], 1931, unpublished.

18. Letter from Spender to Plomer, Plomer 213/8, Durham University Library, Wednesday [1931], unpublished.

19. Letter from Spender to Plomer, Plomer 213/12, Durham University Library, Bei Weiss, Kleiststr. 15, Berlin, Armistice Day and Nov. 12 [1931], unpublished.

20. *Ibid.*

Richard Danson Brown (essay date fall 2002)

SOURCE: Brown, Richard Danson. "'Your Thoughts Make Shape Like Snow': Louis MacNeice on Stephen Spender." *Twentieth Century Literature* 48, no. 3 (fall 2002): 292-323.

[*In the following essay, Brown discusses Louis MacNeice's criticism of Spender's poetry and Spender's influence on MacNeice's own work.*]

The notion that the left-wing writers of the 1930s formed a homogenous clique of interchangeable, mutually aggrandizing talents has become one of the clichés of twentieth-century literary history. Roy Campbell's satirical figure "MacSpaunday" typifies such accounts (Alexander 199). Campbell's amalgamation of MacNeice, Spender, Auden, and Day-Lewis into a single careerist, cowardly poetaster has often been recycled as a convenient shorthand for "the Auden group." Yet as influential studies of the period and the writers have shown, such accounts misrepresent the complex affiliations that existed between men like Louis MacNeice and Stephen Spender.[1] This essay focuses on MacNeice and Spender during the early 1930s to explore two related issues: first, how MacNeice's reading of Spender's **Poems** (1933) shaped his own break-through volume, *Poems* (1935); and second, how the observation of this relationship can help to refine understanding of MacNeice's poetics at this pivotal stage in his career.

* * *

MacNeice and Spender were never altogether at ease with one another. Contemporaries at Oxford, fellow aspiring poets who jointly edited the 1929 *Oxford Poetry,* their accounts of each other are indicative of a rivalry sporadically tempered by mutual affection. According to Spender, MacNeice was ironic and supercilious, always ready to put the innocent Spender down with a wry witticism (*Journals* 263-64); according to MacNeice, Spender was an archetype of the romantic poet, always self-consciously advertising his poethood to an indifferent world (*Strings* 113). Such rivalry is hardly surprising: MacNeice was two years older than Spender, yet Spender achieved literary celebrity ahead of MacNeice. Though MacNeice's *Blind Fireworks* was published in 1929 while he was still an undergraduate, the volume was not a significant success. In contrast, Spender had seven poems in Michael Roberts's influential *New Signatures* anthology of 1932, while his **Poems** (1933) received wildly enthusiastic notices.[2] During the early 1930s, he was lionized by literary London while MacNeice worked in relative obscurity as a lecturer in classics at the University of Birmingham.[3]

The main evidence of tetchy collegiality is MacNeice's portrait of Spender in *The Strings Are False,* and Spender's response after its posthumous publication in 1965. MacNeice applauds Spender's integrity to his artistic vision in his account of the furor that surrounded the performance of Spender's play *Trial of a Judge* by the Group Theatre in 1938—which communist spectators felt endorsed the moral qualms of its liberal protagonist—but also enjoys himself at Spender's expense in the clash between interior décor and political commitment:

> Stephen Spender . . . was now living in a chic apartment with a colour scheme out of *Vogue*, a huge vulcanite writing-desk and over the fireplace an abstract picture by Wyndham Lewis. Very comfortable and elegant but not quite big enough for Stephen; his enormous craggy apostolic flaring face seemed liable to burst the walls . . . [in *Forward from Liberalism*] S. argued (accepting the dialectic) liberalism had played its part; once the vanguard, was now reaction; the man of good will today must acknowledge the Third International. His book, however, offended many in all parties. The Right did not like it, the Liberals did not like it, and the Comrades . . . could not help noticing

that S., who wanted to be at home with Stalin, was much more at ease with J. S. Mill.

(*Strings* 166-67)

Though broadly sympathetic to Spender's dilemma, MacNeice's account retains a critical detachment, a sense that Stephen really should have known better. This is highlighted in the image of Spender as being too big for his designer flat: just as Spender's face threatens "to burst the walls" of his physical milieu, he threatens to break the constraints of his ideological milieu, though crucially without being fully conscious of his position. The irony of this portrait is in the implied gap between Spender's commitment and his self-awareness. As MacNeice comments with an apparently effortless detachment, Spender "had not been born for dogma" (*Strings* 168), though again it takes Spender much longer to realize this than it takes MacNeice. Spender's *Journals* from November 1965 make clear that it was MacNeice's "almost cold-blooded air of supercilious disdain" that he found most irritating in *The Strings Are False*:

> To judge from his recollections he always seems to have been fully conscious at the time of any one relationship he had of his own attitude towards it, e.g., in the account of his first marriage, it seems that he had from the moment of falling in love with Mary Beasley[4] the same detached awareness of her character. He certainly did seem to "cast a cold eye" on the world around him. One thought of him leaning back, regarding one with amused detachment through half-closed eyes. In fact his memoir shows that he did regard me in this way. But I can't believe—from remembering them together at Oxford—that he judged Mary quite as objectively, at the time of their engagement even, as here appears.

(*Journals* 263-64)

Yet the MacNeice-Spender relationship is more important for its implications about their poetry than for its intimations of gossipy indiscretion. My interest is in how MacNeice uses Spender's **Poems** in the articulation of his poetic in the essay "Poetry To-day" and in the development of his own work in *Poems*. In this context, Spender's response to MacNeice's memoirs has a critical as well as a biographical relevance: MacNeice's later recapitulations of the past tend to suggest a lucidity and poise in his observation both of events and himself as an observer. Even a poem as devastating as "Autobiography" casts the past coolly;[5] it articulates not so much the trauma of an unhappy childhood as the self-cauterized and ultimately illusory objectivity of its subject. The poem keeps the processes of repression more vivid than what is being repressed; even the pain in "When my silent terror cried / Nobody, nobody replied" is felt as something "silent" and unobserved by the adult world.[6] Similarly, the final couplet, "I got up; the chilly sun / Saw me walk away alone" expresses less the pain of emotional isolation than the absence of such pain (*Collected Poems* 183-84). The haunting refrain *"Come back early or never come"* depends for its effect on the strategic repression of the expected internal rhyme "home": we half anticipate "Come back early or never come home," but the text shrewdly denies such an emphatic sentimental gesture. The poem's popularity is unsurprising: through its focus on repression, MacNeice's poetic "Autobiography" can easily be generalized.

On the other hand, though MacNeice was to present himself as an ironic observer of the literary and political zeitgeist in texts like *Autumn Journal* and *The Strings Are False, Poems* displays a young poet struggling between conflicting priorities and potential voices. The volume represents MacNeice's not always successful attempts to clarify his poetic and his poetry. Such self-conscious endeavor is also evident in "Poetry Today," which cites Spender as an influence while remaining cautious about the more intimidating precedents set by Yeats, Eliot, and Auden. Studying MacNeice's critical assessment and poetic reaction to Spender's work in the mid-1930s thus illuminates the processes through which MacNeice came to his habitual self-presentation as a detached observer.

* * *

Differences of political emphasis seem to have been at the root of MacNeice's suspicion of Spender. His review of *The Destructive Element: A Study of Modern Writers and Beliefs* (May 1935) is simultaneously sympathetic to Spender's theory—that James, Yeats, Eliot, and Lawrence "are all concerned with the same 'political subject'"—and skeptical of Marxist theories of literature and Spender's acceptance of these:

> At the moment, even the most intelligent communist tends to relapse into crude generalizations. Thus Mr. Spender quotes, apparently with approval, Lenin's statement "Art belongs to the people." . . . Lenin is here repeating the fallacies of Tolstoy.
>
> (*Criticism* 5, 7)

Though MacNeice was intrigued by the intellectual possibilities of communism, he remained dubious about the translation of such theories into practice. Accordingly, Lenin's socialist puritanism is connected with Tolstoy's Christian puritanism. In each case, ideological systems inappropriately constrict creativity. Because Spender identifies himself with the Communist Party and the Soviet experience,[7] for MacNeice his work has a bogus flavor—note the condescension implicit in what is essentially a positive review: "having read this book with a *moderately* open mind, I do not find that the thread or plot of it is arbitrary" (my emphasis, *Criticism* 5).[8]

This impression that MacNeice's resisted communist doctrine is supported by his earlier reply to the questionnaire inquiry carried out by Geoffrey Grigson for the October 1934 edition of *New Verse*. Responding to the question "Do you take your stand with any political or politico-economic party or creed?," MacNeice answered, "No. In weaker moments I wish I could" (*Criticism* 4). Literary historians have taken this as a general statement of MacNeice's attitude towards political commitment.[9] It is worth observing that MacNeice's ideological detachment has worn rather better than his contemporaries' conviction. His resistance to communism is unusual because it neither resolves into a right-wing critique of socialism (in the manner of Wyndham Lewis) nor a reassertion of liberalism (in the manner of Day-Lewis). As late as 1942, MacNeice would write that he "distrust[s] all parties but consider[s] capitalism must go" (*Prose* 72). MacNeice's politics were characteristically independent; as Margot Heinemann observes, "He was never a Communist . . . but he did come, however unwillingly, to a strongly felt antifascist and socialist commitment which—unlike Auden and Spender—he never seems to have felt much need to modify" (345). Moreover, the wit of his reply to the *New Verse* questionnaire can distract attention from the fact that he was troubled by the same concerns as those writers who were Communist Party members. In this sense, Spender and MacNeice's *Poems* explore analogous problems: the tensions between individualism and commitment alongside pervasive feelings of cultural and emotional estrangement.

As an illustration of this, consider two texts that in MacNeice's *Poems* are printed on adjacent pages, "Turf-stacks" and "The Individualist Speaks" (30-31).[10] A critical consensus has emerged about these poems: they embody MacNeice's suspicion of communism and his desire to deflate the controlling patterns set up by such theories.[11] In this view, "Turf-stacks" juxtaposes a positive pastoral landscape with a negative image of an industrial city. Yet when it was first published in *New Verse,* it had the unadorned title "Poem."[12] By renaming it for volume publication, MacNeice implies that it is a pastoral. The earlier title, however, betokens a deeper uncertainty about the poem's orientation that is truer to its representations of town and country:

> Among these turf-stacks graze no iron horses
> Such as stalk, such as champ in towns and the soul of
>   crowds,
> Here is no mass-production of neat thoughts
> No canvas shrouds for the mind nor any black hearses:
> The peasant shambles on his boots like hooves
> Without thinking at all or wanting to run in grooves.
>
> (*Collected Poems* 18)

Though the pastoral landscape might seem preferable to the "iron" city, the peasant is reduced in the couplet to a human horse who "shambles . . . Without thinking at all." While he escapes the "mass-production of neat thoughts," such freedom does not endow him with autonomy or even consciousness. The dichotomy between an authentic countryside and a mechanized city thus hardly implies a traditional preference of the one over the other.

Uncertainty continues in the second stanza, which presents what is usually seen as MacNeice's attack on communist intellectuals: "those who lack the peasant's conspirators . . . Will feel the need of a fortress against ideas and against the / Shuddering insidious shock of the theory vendors." While the review of *The Destructive Element* does attack "the theory vendors" of Marxist criticism, it is misleading to read this stanza as an uncomplicated amplification of that view. The speaker of "Turf-stacks" is indiscriminately hostile to "theory" and "ideas" alike. Where in the first stanza the peasant is thoughtless, so here the speaker wants "a fortress" not only against Marxist "theory" but also "against ideas" of any kind. In the final stanza, the attack on ideas precipitates a retreat to a "tunnel where the world recedes":

> For we are obsolete who like the lesser things
> Who play in corners with looking-glasses or beads;
> It is better we should go quickly; go into Asia
> Or any other tunnel where the world recedes,
> Or turn blind wantons like the gulls who scream
> And rip the edge off any ideal or dream.
>
> (19)

The focus has shifted from satire of "theory vendors" to the expression of a self-consciously aesthetic sensibility. The speaker concedes the obsolescence of his class, languidly imagines a retreat into Asia, and a final transformation of such aesthetes into "blind wantons" who "rip the edge off any ideal or dream." Even if MacNeice sympathizes with the desire to retreat and "play in corners with looking-glasses or beads," this is hardly a ringing endorsement of such a strategy. As "Aubade"—another poem concerned with the interplay of subjectivity and the external world—puts it, we have "to look forward to . . . a precise dawn / Of sallow grey bricks, and newsboys crying war" (*Collected Poems* 30). Retreat in such conditions is not an option: "Aubade" reluctantly admits that whether "we" like it or not, the outside world increasingly impinges on the interior. Hence "Turf-stacks" envisages such detachment resolving into the screaming, destructive cynicism of "the gulls." It anticipates the bitterness of the wartime poem "The Satirist," where the perception of the failure of "large ideals" creates "a heartless type / Whose hobby is giving everyone else the lie" (*Collected Poems* 210). MacNeice's consistent suspicion of anti-intellectualism suggests that the speaker of "Turf-stacks" is a Bloomsbury-ite, an aesthete resistant to the alleged contamination of art with ideas. Two years later he

would attack this rarefied constituency more directly in his "Letter to W. H. Auden": "it is a blessing to our generation, though one in the eye for Bloomsbury, that you discharged into poetry the subject-matters of psycho-analysis, politics and economics" (MacNeice, *Criticism* 83).[13]

Similarly, the individualist of "The Individualist Speaks" celebrates drunken violence, travestying any ethic of social solidarity: "we / Knock our brains together extravagantly / Instead of planting them to make more trees" (*Collected Poems* 22). This image is reminiscent of MacNeice's positive definition of communism in *The Destructive Element* review: "Communism in the truer sense is an effort to think, and think into action, human society as an organism (*not* a machine, which is too static a metaphor)" (MacNeice, *Criticism* 6). The individualist scorns the sort of "organic" activity MacNeice himself advocates. As Peter McDonald observes of the review, "the bite of this passage . . . comes from its radical questioning of any privileged and secure perspectives. . . . [MacNeice is] rejecting the fixed, panoptic gaze of Marxist analysis along with the entrenched positions of bourgeois liberalism" (17). Similarly, in the poem, despite the glamour of his nonconformity, the individualist is, like the sensibility explored in "Turf-stacks," a destructive opponent of any such attempts to "think into action, human society as an organism." As a poetic diptych in *Poems,* "Turf-stacks" and "The Individualist Speaks" point to the limitations of both communism and individualism.

So while MacNeice may seem to have achieved his political sang-froid without effort, the evidence of *Poems* suggests otherwise. His suspicion of communism is not at this stage a fully formulated skepticism but rather a reluctant resistance to an apparently oversimplified creed, all the while conscious that in the contemporary political landscape there were few realistic alternatives to that creed. It is worth remembering that the collapse of the Labour government in 1931, and its replacement by Ramsay MacDonald's National Government, signaled for MacNeice's contemporaries the death of constitutional socialism.[14] MacNeice's response to these events some 10 years later, though predictably worldweary, retains a tinge of satiric bitterness: "the deplorable trinity of MacDonald, Jimmy Thomas and Snowden—suddenly called themselves 'National', sold their birthright" (*Strings* 135).

"Poetry To-day" offers a revealing insight into MacNeice's thinking, since it was written at the same time as the later texts in *Poems*: both were first published in September 1935.[15] MacNeice contextualizes the current poetic scene through a condensed history of recent developments alongside case studies of selected poets, notably Auden and Spender. As in "Modern Writers and

Beliefs," MacNeice discusses how communism might aid the writing of poetry. And like "Turf-stacks" and "The Individualist Speaks," MacNeice's account veers between an individualist critique of communism's totalizing claims alongside the recognition that some aspects of communist thought could be useful to contemporary poets. Recapitulating the analogy between the views of Lenin and Tolstoy, he writes:

> I have no patience with those who think poetry will become merely a handmaid of communism. Christianity, in the time of the Fathers, made the same threats; all poetry but hymns was bogus, no one was to write anything but hymns.

This warning, however, is followed by the caveat that "intoxication with a creed is . . . a good antidote to defeatist individualism" (*Criticism* 25).

MacNeice's ambiguity about the politics of literature is particularly evident in his readings of Spender. Valentine Cunningham has written of the "vogue" for "Critical toughness" during the 1930s, citing among others MacNeice's review of Auden and Isherwood's *On the Frontier*: "The mystical love scenes of Eric and Anna made one long for a sack to put one's head in" (34-35).[16] The presentation of Spender in "Poetry To-day" would seem to support this reading: he "is a naïf who uses communism as a frame for his personal thrills"; he "has swallowed D. H. Lawrence whole and mixed him up with Shelley, Nakt-Kultur and Communist Evangelism" (26, 38). However, MacNeice's account of Spender's *Poems* is significantly more complex than such bitchy sound bites might suggest. MacNeice repeatedly draws attention to the fragmentary quality of Spender's work:

> He will . . . be the man for posterity, if our poetry is ever dug up in fragments; here is someone who really *felt* posterity will say; and will conclude that he died young. His poems have a fragmentary appearance as it is . . . [they] have not got that crystal self-contained perfection which is so glibly attributed to the ideal lyric.
>
> (38)

MacNeice is uncharacteristically hesitant. The fragmentary, excavated Spender sounds like a type of Chatterton—a romantic, self-destructive figure, awkwardly baring his soul through a patchy lyricism. Yet if posterity's imagined verdict suggests an attack, the charge that Spender's work lacks "crystal self-contained perfection" is identified as a virtue. But even here MacNeice is unsure; the fragmentariness of Spender's poems points in opposing directions: "I sometimes think that this is vicious but prefer to think that is their virtue" (38).

MacNeice's ambivalence is partly indicative of his broader suspicion of the collage technique characteristic of the first generation of modernists. Earlier in the es-

say, he praises Eliot as an innovator and technician, but then attacks Pound's *Cantos* for their indiscriminate use of what Grigson had called "the cultural reference rock-climbing style" (qtd. in *Criticism* 17). Indeed, Spender's 1933 essay "Poetry and Revolution" (first published in the *New Country* anthology) begins with a traditional assertion of the need for poems to be "separate and complete and ideal worlds" (*Thirties* 48). In this essay, Spender is concerned to face up to the tensions between revolutionary demands for a propagandist poetry and "the bourgeois tradition" to which he belonged (51). In such a context, his espousal of a traditional poetic is unsurprising: Spender needs the authority of the tradition—and its notions of the necessary autonomy and coherence of poetic texts—to resist a propagandist model of the function poetry. Fragmentation, in other words, was a rather dubious virtue in the early 1930s. A fragmentary poem was either the ultimate recherché highbrowism of Pound's *Cantos,* with attendant right-wing sympathies, or an aesthetically feeble work of left-wing propaganda.

MacNeice continues: "if you read Spender's one volume of **Poems** through several times, you will *probably* decide that he is an interesting and valuable poet" (my emphasis; 38). That *probably* is characteristic: MacNeice thinks that he thinks that Spender is "interesting and valuable," but he is not altogether sure. Hence he cites Robert Penn Warren's damning critique of Spender's "thoroughly conventional 'poetical' idiom, his relaxed rhythms, and his thin, almost feminine, subject matter" before mounting his case for the defense:

> This is a point of view which it is only too easy to take up. . . . [Spender] is patently very limited. But . . . he has made the most of his limitations. The poet's "hands" are in this case not deft and virtuoso but they have a patient tact . . . which presses his confused world of emotional clichés into a harmony which is, fittingly, incomplete. His "relaxed rhythms" are entirely suited to his subject matter; slickness is alien to him. I find myself that when I want to make sure not to be fulsome, I tend to write in this way. Thus two lines of mine which I consider good—
>
> These moments let him retain like limbs,
> His time not crippled by flaws of faith or memory
>
> —are, if I am not mistaken, typical of Spender's manner.
>
> (38-39)

MacNeice's uncertainty is partly a product of Spender's failure to accord with the stylistic directives given elsewhere in "Poetry To-day." While Auden and Day-Lewis are praised for having pruned "exclamatory sentimentality," Spender is noted as an exception to this tendency (35). This passage underlines the clichéd aspect of Spender's verse and its debts to Shelley—a debt that was to MacNeice symptomatic of an unpurged adolescence.[17] Yet what is absorbing about this critique is the sense that MacNeice seems to change his mind in the process of writing: Spender's weaknesses are itemized but are subsequently recuperated as virtues. The value of Spender's poetry is that its fragmentary form exactly complements its emotionally contorted subject matter.

That MacNeice acknowledges borrowing "Spender's manner" is significant. While "Poetry To-day" is variously admiring of Eliot and Yeats, MacNeice cautions against using them as models. They are

> not to be too closely copied. If we must copy we must either copy people of our own age and society . . . or else people so far removed from us by time or language that our copying will not impose on anyone. Thus I avoided reading Eliot for three years or so that I might not write fake Eliot. But when I wrote the Spenderesque lines quoted above, I did not regard them as fake Spender because I knew they were proper to me; whereas Eliotesque lines would not have been proper to me but merely composed *ab extra*.
>
> (41)

Despite MacNeice's best intentions, "fake Eliot" is apparent within *Poems*. "Trapeze" strikes a series of would-be Prufrockian poses: "Blood slavers over the evening sky . . . On the skyline shaggy spears of grass / Itch ominously and the moon / Limps on a crutch whose ferrule taps to us / Doom (if rightly we decodify)" (57). Unsurprisingly, such poems were later dropped.[18] "Poetry To-day" suggests MacNeice's acute awareness of the difficulties inherent in such imitation. Copying Eliot is riskier than copying Spender because of the dangers of "impos[ing] on anyone." In other words, the imitator imposes on the model by the borrowing; implicitly, the imitator risks having the model's vision imposed on his own text. This is certainly what happens with poems like "Trapeze": MacNeice's emergent voice is swamped by the noisy echoes of Eliot's stronger originals. But borrowing from Spender is permissible, MacNeice argues, because his "Spenderesque lines . . . were proper to me."

We can get a clearer sense of the issues implicit here by examining the passage in "Poetry To-day" that MacNeice cites in detail. It comes from the long poem that concludes *Poems,* the "Ode" written for MacNeice's son Daniel. The text that lies behind "Ode" is Yeats's "A Prayer for my Daughter." As Stallworthy notes, both Yeats's and MacNeice's prayers for their children are connected to prayers for Ireland in times of uncertainty (168). Yeats warns his daughter off the "intellectual hatred" that has made Maud Gonne "Barter . . . every good . . . For old bellows full of angry wind" (189). Similarly, in times of "mob mania," MacNeice "pray[s] off from my son the love of that infinite / Which is too greedy and too obvious; let his Absolute / Like any

four-walled house be put up decently" (MacNeice, *Poems* 60-61). Yet as we have seen, MacNeice was sensitive to the pitfalls of imitating writers of the authority of Eliot or Yeats. In December 1935, he warned would-be imitators of Yeats's plays that he "is a very single-minded or whole-minded artist. Take hints if you like but for God's sake don't imitate him. You would have to be him first, which you're not" ("Some Notes" 8). Hence though prompted by "A Prayer for my Daughter," "Ode" is not a direct imitation; rather, MacNeice follows the occasion of Yeats's poem but eschews much of its form, rhetoric, and attitudes. He does not adopt the tenor of Yeats's advice, his diction, or his "ceremonious" (190) eight-line stanzas. Indeed, "Ode" is unusual for MacNeice in adopting a kind of free verse. Its stanzas come in a range of different sizes; its rhyming is unpredictable and unstable. This is why I think that in "Poetry To-day" MacNeice connects "Ode" with Spender: Spender's less intimidating style gave him a means of assimilating the stronger influence of Yeats to his own poetic vocabulary.

The image of Daniel MacNeice's "time not crippled by flaws of faith and memory" echoes the third stanza of Spender's **"What I expected"**:

> The wearing of Time,
> And the watching of cripples pass
> With limbs shaped like questions
> In their odd twist,
> The pulverous grief
> Melting the bones with pity,
> The sick falling from earth—
> These, I could not foresee.
>
> (*Poems* 25-26)[19]

Spender juxtaposes anticipation with actuality: his persona had not expected "the watching of cripples pass / With limbs shaped like questions," or his inability to remedy their plight. "Ode" by contrast is couched as a didactic poem; MacNeice issues a string of metaphysical and aesthetic nostrums. Spender's cripples are transposed into a metaphor that conveys the wholeness of experience MacNeice wishes for his son:

> Therefore let not my son, halving the truth
> Be caught between jagged edges;
> And let him not falsify the world
> By taking it to pieces;
> The marriage of Cause and Effect, Form and Content
> Let him not part asunder.
> Wisdom for him in the time of tulips
> Monastic repose, martial élan,
> Then the opening mouth a dragon or a voluptuary—
> These moments let him retain like limbs
> His time not crippled by flaws of faith or memory.
>
> (*Poems* 64-65)[20]

While this stanza recalls the manner of "A Prayer for my Daughter" (for example "May she become a flourishing hidden tree / That all her thoughts may like the linnet be" [189]), its poetic effect is substantially different. Line length is dictated more by syntax than by verse pattern, as in the prosy sprawl of the trimeter lines "By taking it to pieces" and "Let him not part asunder"; half- and para-rhymes proliferate ("edges" / "pieces"; "voluptuary" / "memory"); in short, there is none of the traditional couplet music of Yeats's stanzas. To be sure, MacNeice was not writing the modernist free verse of poets like Williams or cummings: this stanza retains relatively traditional rhythms and juxtapositions—it displays what "Poetry To-day" calls "the reappearing beat of the old verse" (30). But the point is that it avoids the elaborate formalism of "A Prayer for my Daughter" and recalls the very different formal effects of Spender's best work. These have been well described by O'Neill and Reeves:

> Spender's stanzaic shapes and overall structures are held open to the often ragged mass of feeling; tentative and exploratory, they are concerned to mirror the emergence into words of consciousness.
>
> (126)

This captures the loose and open structures of such key texts in Spender's *Poems* as **"In 1929,"** "oh young men oh young comrades," and "After they have tired of the brilliance of cities" and mirrors MacNeice's description of the fragmentary appearance of Spender's lyrics.

"What I expected" is slightly more formal in that it is made up of four eight-line stanzas with a largely regular rhyme scheme. Nevertheless, as in "Ode," line length and rhyme are shaped more by the exigencies of syntax than by adherence to a formal pattern. Hence in the first half of the third stanza, Spender sacrifices the expected rhyme at the end of the fourth line to emphasize the impact of "The sick falling from earth" on the speaker:

> The wearing of Time,
> And the watching of cripples pass
> With limbs shaped like questions
> In their odd twist,

"What I expected" is an adroit compromise between the impulses to form and to freedom: "twist" fails to rhyme convincingly with "pass," but in that failure assonates and alliterates with "questions." Spender dexterously manages the shape of his verse so that it mirrors the "odd twist" of the cripples it describes and underlines the "questions" the passing cripples make the speaker ask himself. Such a subtle marriage of "Form and Content" is in keeping with the poem's broader agenda, in which Spender appears to deflate the speaker's naiveté with a lesson in sober reality: "I had not foreseen . . . The lack of good to touch / The fading of body and soul" (25). The expected trajectory, however, is weakened by the poem's restatement of the speaker's original vision in the final stanza: "I had expected always . . . Some final innocence / To save

from dust . . . Like the created poem / Or the dazzling crystal" (26). Spender laconically refuses to interiorize the lesson he teaches himself, and in so doing frustrates the reader's expectation that the poem will endorse the potentially platitudinous wisdom of experience.

I suggest therefore that the stanzaic form of "Ode" is reminiscent of Spender's practice in *Poems*. It could be further argued that the shifting perspectives of **"What I expected"** inform "Ode" and are mobilized against the ultimately authoritarian shadow of Yeats. As MacNeice was to observe in 1941, "A Prayer for my Daughter" articulates Yeats's nostalgia for a more ceremonious and structured past (*Poetry of Yeats* 120). "Ode" catches MacNeice at his most anti-Yeatsian in his characteristic reluctance to dogmatize: "I cannot draw up any code / There are too many qualifications / Too many asterisk asides / Too many crosses in the margin" (65). Immediately before this, MacNeice offers a direct rebuke to the style of parenting implied by "A Prayer for My Daughter":

> I remember all the houses where parents
> Have reared their children to be parents
> (Cut box and privet and parrot's voice)
> To be clerks to total the flow of alien money
> To be florists to design these wreaths and wedding
>   bouquets
>
> (65)

Though MacNeice's ostensible target is the bourgeoisie of "Cut box and privet," this passage registers a resistance to the assumptions that underlie Yeats's poem. Where Yeats envisages his daughter "Rooted in one dear perpetual place," brought by "her bridegroom" to an aristocratic and "ceremonious" house (189-90), MacNeice asserts the folly of rearing "children to be parents" and in the final line equates "wedding bouquets" with funereal "wreaths." As John Engle puts it, "'Ode' is MacNeice's 'no thanks'" to Yeats (73). Hence at the close of a text ostensibly composed of paternal wisdom, MacNeice becomes radically skeptical of the tradition he is working in. What is the point, he asks, of rearing children to become facsimiles of their parents who will unquestioningly "parrot" the same values? Such resistance to the hortatory mode in what is a designedly didactic poem recalls the paradoxical structure of **"What I expected."** In both texts, the poets seem to be offering an exemplary moral pattern that they ultimately deny.

Thus "Poetry To-day" indicates MacNeice's tempered admiration for the technique of Spender's *Poems*, and in particular the complementary relationship between his "relaxed rhythms" and his subject matter. "Ode" demonstrates this in practice as MacNeice adopts Spender's manner as a means of avoiding the "slickness"—or rather the rhetorical amplitude and grandeur—of Yeats's "A Prayer for my Daughter." Yet as we have seen, "Poetry To-day" is far from a ringing endorsement of Spender. If MacNeice admired the formal accomplishment of his lyrics, he remained skeptical about Spender's progressive politicization of his work in **Poems** and beyond.[21] The critical relation between the two poets' work can be felt most clearly when MacNeice's "To a Communist" is read alongside the poem to which it probably replies, Spender's **"After they have tired of the brilliance of cities."**

* * *

MacNeice's admiration for Spender's poem is shown by the fact that he cited it twice in important contexts. First in "Poetry To-day," the last four lines of the poem's first stanza illustrate the new poets' technical economy, resulting in an innovative poetry of "simple statement" as opposed to the overenumerative verse of writers like Pound and Sacheverell Sitwell (MacNeice, *Criticism* 30-31). But the more revealing comment is in *Modern Poetry* (1938):

> Spender's most effective use of imagery is when one image pervades and controls a whole poem, as in the poem beginning **"After they have tired of the brilliance of cities. . . ."** This poem is dominated by the word "snow" with its associations of hunger, universality and clarity:
>
>   It is death stalks through life
> Grinning white through all faces
> Clean and equal like the shine from snow . . .
>
> And our strength is now the strength of our bones
> Clean and equal like the shine from snow . . .
>
> We have come at last to a country
> Where light equal, like the shine from snow, strikes
>   all faces . . .
>
> But through torn-down portions of old fabric let their
>   eyes
> Watch the admiring dawn explode like a shell
> Around us, dazing us with its light like snow.
>
> (109-10)[22]

Once again, MacNeice's criticism is almost as interesting for its omissions as for its assertions. **"After they have tired . . ."** is a lyrical anticipation of a communist revolution. Although Spender was not to become a member of the Communist Party until later in the decade, poems like this were to mark him as an enthusiastic sympathizer with the cause.[23] As early as 1932, Roberts's *New Signatures* included such communistic poems as **"The Funeral"** (a utopian vision of "the World State" replacing "individual grief"), and "oh young men oh comrades" (a lyric incitement to revolutionary consciousness).[24] **"After they have tired . . ."** looks forward with a wide-eyed gasp of delight to the

end of capitalism: after "they"—presumably the bourgeoisie—"have tired of the brilliance of cities . . . Then those streets the rich built with their easy love / Fade like old cloths" (*Poems* 47). Spender keeps the process of revolution unspecific; it is evoked as a seamless development in human consciousness as the "We" of the second stanza become aware of social injustice. Hence the third stanza presents the communist millennium in terms that are almost reminiscent of the discovery of a new and more beautiful planet:

> Readers of this strange language,
> We have come at last to a country
> Where light equal, like the shine from snow, strikes
>   all faces,
> Here you may wonder
> How it was that works, money, interest, building,
>   could ever hide
> The palpable and obvious love of man for man.
>
> (48)

As MacNeice's comments suggest, the poem is breathtakingly assured in its use of traditional lyric resources to fit new social and political contexts: this stanza catches Spender's exhilaration in the new "country" with an unlikely precision. Through its focus on the strangeness of the "language" he employs, and the "wonder" experienced by the "Readers" and participants in this cataclysmic change, the poem cannily licenses and embodies the reader's astonishment. Spender attempts to redirect the skepticism of his bourgeois readers into the more politically tractable response of "wonder." However, the lyric beauty of the poem leaves it open to less sympathetic constructions. In the context of his positive discussion of Spender's imagery, it is unsurprising that MacNeice did not quote the beginning of the final stanza:

> Oh comrades, let not those who follow after
> —The beautiful generation that shall spring from our
>   sides—
> Let not them wonder how after the failure of banks
> The failure of cathedrals and the declared insanity of
>   our rulers,
> We lacked the Spring-like resources of the tiger
> Or of plants who strike out new roots to gushing
>   waters.
>
> (48)

These lines recall MacNeice's description of Spender in "Poetry To-day" as having "swallowed D. H. Lawrence whole and mixed him up with Shelley . . . and Communist Evangelism." The communist idioms of comrades, banks, and insane rulers nestle uneasily beside the vaguer imagery of "The beautiful generation that shall spring from our sides" and "plants who strike out new roots to gushing waters." In other words, neoromantic images and diction are assimilated to the poetic task of anticipating the new revolutionary dawn. As Julian Symons has written of his reading of Auden's "A

Communist to Others" in the early 1930s, "Rupert Brookeian gush" was detectable in Spender's poem (Bucknell and Jenkins 178). Whether this is a fair reading or not, **"After they have tired . . ."** can seem to be a poem of unalloyed utopianism that naively deploys romantic idioms in support of revolutionary doctrine. While MacNeice admired the technical accomplishment of the poem—its organization around the image of snow—he was resistant to what he took to be its overly optimistic vision. I suggest that this resistance is clarified in "To a Communist."

There has been little detailed commentary on this poem, perhaps because it seems to be a self-explanatory satire of a generic communist, just as "The Individualist Speaks" portrays a generalized individualist.[25] But Mac-Neicean personae are a slippery bunch; as he was to comment later in the prefatory note to *Springboard* (1944), poems like "The Satirist" and "The Conscript" were intended as particular portraits with the potential for universalization: "'The Conscript' does not stand for all conscripts but for an imagined individual; any such individual seems to me to have an absolute quality which the definite article recognizes" (7). "The Casualty" is exemplary of this aesthetic: it memorializes MacNeice's school friend Graham Shepard (killed at sea in 1943) and, through its generalizing title, other casualties of the war.[26] Though "To a Communist" lacks the kind of subheading that connects "The Casualty" to Shepard—*"in memoriam G. H. S."* (*Collected Poems* 245)—its echoes of **"After they have tired . . ."** strongly imply that the communist was Spender.

The only other substantial candidate to have been proposed is Auden. According to Jon Stallworthy, addressing the communist as "my dear" targets the homosexual Auden (154).[27] This is plausible inasmuch as during the early 1930s, Auden seemed to be the model left-leaning intellectual; as Symons recalls, "We never doubted that [Auden] was himself a Party member" (Bucknell and Jenkins 178). Indeed, it could be argued that MacNeice's title satirically recalls Auden's "A Communist to Others."[28] Equally, the straight MacNeice was not averse to mocking the sexual proclivities of his homosexual contemporaries. His account of Oxford in the late 1920s shows that he saw "my dear" as a general marker of homosexuality rather than as the private property of Auden:

> the air was full of the pansy phrase "my dear". I discovered that in Oxford homosexuality and "intelligence", heterosexuality and brawn were almost inexorably paired. This left me out in the cold and I took to drink.
>
> (*Strings* 103)

The suggestion that Auden was MacNeice's communist, however, rests on arguments that would work equally well for Spender. During the early 1930s, Spender was

as openly homosexual as Auden. Part of the charge of *Poems* was that Spender's love objects were tantalizingly male. In **"For T. A. R. H.,"** addressed to his lover Tony Hyndman, the gender of the subject and the emotional involvement of the speaker are unambiguous: "Even whilst I watch him I am remembering / The quick laugh of the wasp gold eyes . . . love / Is soaked in memory" (36).[29] Published alongside such poems, even a text as ostensibly political as **"After they have tired . . ."** is inflected with homoerotic resonance, especially in its rhapsodic evocation of the postrevolutionary world. Phrases like "The palpable and obvious love of man for man" (where the physicality of "palpable" is underlined by its being linked with the synonymic "obvious") and "The beautiful generation that shall spring from our sides" (with its suggestion of parthenogenetic reproduction) give the postrevolutionary world a homoerotic flavor. Moreover, E. R. Dodds observes that "Of the so-called 'Thirties poets' [MacNeice] seems to have known only Stephen Spender at all well [during the early 1930s]; his acquaintance with Auden did not ripen into intimacy until later" (115). But the case for Spender can be made most persuasively by the close reading of MacNeice's poem.

Rather than being a general satire of communism, "To a Communist" is cast as a dialogic poem. It responds to **"After they have tired . . ."** through a discussion of revolutionary metaphorics:

> Your thoughts make shape like snow; in one night only
>   The gawky earth grows breasts,
> Snow's unity engrosses
> Particular pettiness of stones and grasses.
> But before you proclaim the millennium, my dear,
> Consult the barometer—
> The poise is perfect but maintained
> For one day only.
>
> (*Collected Poems* 22)

Where "Ode" recasts Spender's physical image as a metaphor, "To a Communist" reverses the process. As the commentary in *Modern Poetry* indicates, **"After they have tired . . ."** uses snow as a broad symbol of social and psychological upheaval. Through the repetition of variants of the key phrase "Clean and equal like the shine from snow," Spender focuses on the sensuous impression made by newly fallen snow. Thus in the first stanza, the "death" of the capitalist conception of the city grins "white through all faces" like snow; similarly in the final stanza, the orgasmic explosion of the new dawn dazes us "with its light like snow." MacNeice ironically paraphrases Spender's "thoughts": the unity of snow absorbs and resolves differences in the perceptual world "of stones and grasses" with the suddenness of revolutionary change: "in one night only / The gawky earth grows breasts." "Gawky" encapsulates MacNeice's perspective: to the communist, the earth's geophysical particularities are awkward impediments to the more unified (or just, or equal) world which revolutionary change will bring. The feminization of the earth, moreover, mockingly glances at Spender's homoerotic utopia. Each phrase is freighted with a crisp resistance to this alleged unity; note how the half rhyme of "engrosses" with "grasses" undermines the process of absorption it describes. Indeed, the form of "To a Communist" is another illustration of MacNeice's attentiveness to Spender's poetry. As **"After they have tired . . ."** eschews traditional rhyme and stanzaic patterns while retaining "the reappearing beat of the old verse," so "To a Communist" deftly interweaves short and long lines with sporadic half rhymes. And whereas in "Ode" Spenderesque technique was used to avoid sounding too much like Yeats, here it is adopted for the purpose of mocking Spenderesque politics.

In the second half of the poem, the satiric edge becomes sharper: the snow "millennium" is ridiculed through the reminder that the "poise" of snow is "maintained / For one day only." MacNeice amplifies his point through the patronizing chumminess of calling the communist "my dear." Set against the third stanza of **"After they have tired,"** with its evocation of a new country where equality has suddenly become "palpable," "To a Communist" brings the reader to the "gawky earth" with a bump. Indeed, MacNeice registers his amused disdain for his target's lyrical communism by connecting him to an English middle-class milieu (in the choice of the barometer[30]) and English weather conditions (where snow is unlikely to remain untarnished for more than "one day"). As we shall see, Spender's Englishness as against MacNeice's Irishness was an important component of their rivalry.

As a rebuke to a colleague, "To a Communist" partly confirms Spender's allegations of MacNeice's aloofness. The poem adopts a donnish hauteur for the comic purpose of exposing the silliness of the analogy between snowfall and revolution. It also indicates MacNeice's fascination with snow as a metaphor. This is evident in "Snow," the most celebrated poem in the 1935 volume, in which the incongruous juxtaposition of "snow and pink roses" prompts metaphysical reflection on "The drunkenness of things being various" (*Collected Poems* 30). In this case, snow has ceased to be a political metaphor and is restored to the "collateral and incompatible" world that poem evokes. But "To a Communist" is more than just a satirical squib; its satire depends on MacNeice's literary-critical reading of Spender's text.[31] In this sense, it is a miniature version of debates implicit throughout *Poems*: what subjects should poetry be concerned with, and what are the best treatments of those subjects? This poem addresses the first question by its resistance to a politically engaged poetry, just as "Turf-stacks" and "The Individualist Speaks" point to the limitations of individualism. Indeed, these poems

collectively suggest an impasse in MacNeice's aesthetics, alongside his awareness of the limitations of the political alternatives available to him.

* * *

Spender's review of MacNeice's *Poems* (to which we will return shortly) notes that "MacNeice always knows what he is doing" ("Mr MacNeice's Poems" 17). Indeed, the texts that make up *Poems* are self-conscious in their preoccupation with questions of poetics. As Peter McDonald has argued in relation to the eclogues that begin the volume, "it is possible to see in them the crux of an aesthetic and ideological debate which MacNeice was conducting . . . both with himself and contemporary writing" (20-21). In "An Eclogue for Christmas," the city-dwelling speaker A, reacting against the aestheticism of earlier modernists, complains that he has not "been allowed to be / Myself in flesh or face . . . They have made of me pure form, a symbol or pastiche" (*Collected Poems* 33). In "Eclogue by a Five-barred Gate," Death mocks the aestheticized verse of the shepherds by travestying Yeats's "Easter 1916": "All you do is burke the other and terrible beauty . . . Poetry you think is only the surface vanity . . . The hooks and eyes of words; but it is not that only" (*Collected Poems* 37-38).[32]

As I have suggested, much of the intellectual endeavor of *Poems* is preoccupied with addressing the question of what else poetry might be. Texts like "To a Communist" and "Turf-stacks" frustrate any expectation of an easy resolution to such questions. Joining the Communist Party or turning one's back on abstract thinking are represented as equally bogus alternatives: MacNeice will not allow his subjects or his readers such simplified options. But what is most remarkable about *Poems* is the extent to which MacNeice is capable of turning his critical disdain onto his own formulations. I will conclude by looking at "Wolves" as a poem that not only rejects the by now familiar targets of individualism and communism but also MacNeice's own poetic identity, either as a fallen aesthete or the neo-Heraclitan of "Snow."

The opening stanza of "Wolves" impatiently recapitulates the aesthetic of MacNeice's first volume, *Blind Fireworks* (1929):[33]

> I do not want to be reflective any more
> Envying and despising unreflective things
> Finding pathos in dogs and undeveloped handwriting
> And young girls doing their hair and all the castles of sand
> Flushed by the children's bedtime, level with the shore.

> (*Collected Poems* 29)

"Finding pathos in dogs . . . . / And young girls" summarizes an earlier poem, "The Lugubrious, Salubrious Seaside," in which "dogs' tails tick like metronomes" and "bathing girls / Deign to illuminate the sea," while the speaker reflects with an uncertain mixture of aggression and nostalgia on childhood: "Those wooden spades that dig the mind, / Unearthing memories of spades / When we were the protagonists / Flaunting down juvenile parades" (*Collected Poems* 8). "Wolves" rejects such aestheticized retrospection: MacNeice is unwilling to play this poetic game "any more." But this move away from the styles of his undergraduate poems is undercut by the second stanza's rejection of the perspective outlined in poems like "Snow" and "An Eclogue for Christmas":

> The tide comes in and goes out again, I do not want
> To be always stressing either its flux or permanence,
> I do not want to be a tragic or philosophic chorus
> But to keep my eye only on the nearer future
> And after that let the sea flow over us.
>
> (29)

Most critics have downplayed this passage as a temporary derogation of habitual modes of thinking (see Marsack 16 and Longley, *Louis MacNeice* 143-44). Though "Wolves" is by no means MacNeice's last word on "the thesis that everything is flux" (*Strings* 96), it is also more than empty attitudinizing. Rather, it suggests that the poetics of flux trailed in *Poems* is as inherently problematic as the nostalgist reflections of *Blind Fireworks*. The stanza asserts that all poetic categories are vulnerable in the face of the incoming sea. Adopting a Heraclitan pose, or that of "a tragic or philosophic chorus," will ultimately be just that: a construction that may not be adequate to the challenges of "the nearer future." It is in this spirit that the final stanza queries the collective ethos:

> Come then all of you, come closer, form a circle,
> Join hands and make believe that joined
> Hands will keep away the wolves of water
> Who howl along our coast. And be it assumed
> That no one hears them among the talk and laughter.
>
> (29)

"Wolves" is congruent with poems like "To a Communist" inasmuch as it draws attention to the wishful thinking implicit in communistic aspirations. But it is more complex than the shorter poem: though this passage questions collective solidarity, its focus is not so much the shortcomings of communism as the inevitability of the coming crisis. Indeed, the pathos of the image is that the "make believe" of the close-knit circle is so potentially attractive: note the urgent, would-be seductive imperatives that organize the first line of this stanza. As Terence Brown has observed in relation to "Wolves," though apocalyptic rhetoric is common among writers of the 1930s, "MacNeice is unique . . . in conveying a sense of total doom" (51). This stanza exemplifies that sense: the closed circle of friends will not hear the tidal approach of the "wolves of water." What is so impres-

sive is that the poem's apocalyptic eschews the merely rhetorical by its critique of MacNeice's own poetic poses. The reader is more likely to feel that the crisis is genuine because the writer has not spared his own formulations in his anticipation of the future.

Like other texts in *Poems*, "Wolves" closes with impasse, not resolution: the sea's advance on the shore is imminent; no resolves can stop it. It might then seem to confirm Samuel Hynes's portrait of MacNeice as a chronic melancholic whose lack of conviction is indicative of a pessimistic and ultimately passive response to the upheavals of the 1930s (367-73). As others have observed, Hynes's account depends on the valorization of Auden at the expense of MacNeice.[34] But the articulation of an impasse is not the same thing as the surrender to passivity. Though the advance of the "wolves of water" is inevitable, the poem counsels neither quiescence nor the nostalgia it rejects in the first stanza. Rather, like "To a Communist" and "Turf-stacks," "Wolves" presents a situation that cannot easily be resolved: MacNeice is not giving up, he is attempting to outline the problem—what I have called the impasse—as clearly as possible.

If this suggests that MacNeice consciously played with, and undermined, the role of the disengaged poseur, Spender's reading of MacNeice's *Poems* was rather different. For Spender, MacNeice was to remain something of a poseur both as a man and a poet. His review in the October-November 1935 issue of *New Verse* is generally enthusiastic in urging readers to buy *Poems*, yet praise for MacNeice's technical skill is leavened with criticism of his overall approach. Spender claims to refuse to criticize MacNeice's work on the pretext that it "is difficult to 'place'"; his insistence that the review "does not pretend to criticism" ("Mr MacNeice's Poems" 17, 19) may be a prickly response to the claim made in "Poetry To-day" that it "is unconvincing to analyse" Spender (MacNeice, *Criticism* 39). But the review does criticize MacNeice on the grounds that he sacrifices too much for aesthetic effect:

> The impression left by this book is of a series of pictures painted with precision in a very limited range of colours. . . . To say that these pictures are unexceptionally done, is also to question the poet's whole approach to his medium. The fact that Mr MacNeice so abundantly insists on his double (his poet's and his painter's) eye results in the sacrifice of a single image. He often achieves a brilliant, a dazzling line . . . yet he never achieves a crystalline phrase, nor a hard statement.
>
> (17-18)

As we have seen, in his critical account of Spender, MacNeice rejected the traditional aspiration to a "crystalline" lyricism. Yet the real force of Spender's critique is that MacNeice offers little more than beautifully painted poetic pictures. Spender implies that Mac-Neice willfully avoids making the "hard statement[s]" demanded of a politically engaged poetry. Hence his account of the musicality of MacNeice's verse develops into an image of its glamorous, even commercial, slipperiness: "It is too infectious . . . it infects and turns in on itself, like a snake in a Walt Disney film, involved in its own coils" (18). The cartoon snake anticipates a pervasive trend in the reception of MacNeice as an aesthete out of place in a political generation. Yet Spender emphasizes the painterly quality of *Poems* at the expense of any sense of the volume's real intellectual complexity. In short, it is a review that powerfully enacts the ways in which critical judgment can be influenced by personal animosity.

Spender's poem **"Louis MacNeice,"** written long after MacNeice's death, is a franker and more convincing account of the tensions in the relationship between the two poets.[35] He describes MacNeice as "aloof," as "Looking down at you, smiling to himself":

> The superior head slanted back
> With dancing eyes summing you up
> And laughter only just arrested
> At some joke about you, known only to himself
> (Perhaps the cutting phrase sharpening in his forehead)
> He half-beckoned you up into his high mind
> For a shared view of your clumsiness.

> *(Collected Poems 1928-1985*, 177)

The poem focuses on the dynamics of embarrassment: Spender catches the squirming feeling of his own "clumsiness" as set against MacNeice's poised superiority. Two-thirds of the poem makes no reference to MacNeice's poetry, and when Spender finally turns to the poem's ostensible occasion—a reading at which he was to perform "Bagpipe Music"—the vocabulary of MacNeice's text mercilessly exposes Spender's parochialism:

> Now, reading his poem "Bagpipe Music", I don't
>   know how to pronounce
> C-e-i-l-i-d-h—nor what it means—
> He looks down from high heaven
> The mocking eyes search-lighting
> My ignorance again.

> (177-78)

There is something very uneasy about Spender's poem. While it appears to be a memorial to a dead colleague (especially as published in *The Thirties and After,* which explains the circumstances in which it was written), its real focus is Spender's emotional reaction to MacNeice, his unpurged sense that MacNeice retains the high ground—that even dead his "mocking eyes" are able to "search-light" Spender's ignorance and clumsiness. Indeed, it is this unease that makes **"Louis MacNeice"** an effective poem. Unlike the previous poem in *Col-*

lected Poems 1928-1985, **"One More New Botched Beginning,"** it does not simply reassert the value of MacNeice's life and works.[36] Rather, Spender gives awkward testimony to the problems he found with MacNeice as a man, and ultimately as a poet. The poem's sense of inferiority is precisely located in the Gaelic word "Ceilidh." "Bagpipe Music" evokes the Hebridean communities MacNeice encountered during 1937 while collecting material for his travel book *I Crossed the Minch* (1938); the relevant passage reads "It's no go the gossip column, it's no go the Ceilidh, / All we want is a mother's help and a sugar-stick for the baby" (*Collected Poems* 97). By singling out "Ceilidh," Spender points to the cultural differences between himself and MacNeice: the English writer fails to appreciate the Irish writer's Celtic background and affiliations. Indeed, the comic irony of Spender's passage is intensified by the fact that the half-rhyme with "baby" partly guides the reader's pronunciation of "Ceilidh" in "Bagpipe Music." In **"Louis MacNeice,"** by contrast, the word becomes a dismembered verbal symbol of Spender's failure to understand a fundamental component of MacNeice as the text painfully spells out the letters: "C-e-i-l-i-d-h."

That nationality was an issue between the writers is underlined by a passage in Spender's *Journals.* Immediately after his comment on *The Strings Are False,* Spender recounts a wartime anecdote about MacNeice and a British diplomat. MacNeice is decisively worsted in this encounter: the diplomat identifies MacNeice's northern Irish origins and implies that his detachment confirms "'the story that I have heard that a school of seals went on shore and interbred with the people living on that part of the coast of Ireland'" (*Journals* 264). Spender uses this story to amplify his sense of "Louis's almost cold-blooded air of superiority," but it also indicates the power of the rivalry that **"Louis MacNeice"** mutes through its focus on Spender's sense of his inferiority (*Journals* 264). Cumulatively, the passage from *Journals* suggests the tensions between Spender and MacNeice, and the extent to which the stereotypical binaries of the "cold-blooded" Ulsterman and the "clumsy" Englishman divided writers of ostensibly similar affiliations.

MacNeice saw Spender as a contemporary with a defined yet limited style, who could be safely used as a model, unlike the more compelling and dangerous Yeats and Eliot. MacNeice's study of Spender's *Poems* furnished him at a pivotal moment in his own development with an example he could successfully emulate. Yet Spender represented more than a stylistic influence. For MacNeice, he also embodied the intellectual and poetic pitfalls of communism. But it is misleading to characterize MacNeice as a knee-jerk political skeptic. He largely shared his communist contemporaries' suspicion of capitalism and was critical throughout *Poems* of bourgeois taste and politics. Collegial rivalry allowed MacNeice to see in Spender's work an example both of what could be done poetically and what should not be trusted politically. In turn, MacNeice's reflection on Spender's more politically engaged work enabled him to articulate both his resistance to such optimism and his foreboding for the future.

Notes

1. See Hynes for the major "Auden-centred" reading of the 1930s. Cunningham 13-35 and McDonald 4-9 provide important riders to Hynes's model.

2. The dust jacket of the 1934 second edition begins with the comment from the *Fortnightly Review* that *Poems* is "An unmistakable declaration of genius."

3. For details of MacNeice's and Spender's careers in the early 1930s, see Stallworthy 131-58 and Leeming 55-71.

4. Mary's stepfather's name was in fact Beazley; see Stallworthy 121-24.

5. "Autobiography" was written in September 1940, roughly the same period at which he was at work on *The Strings Are False*. See *Strings* 11-12 for E. R. Dodds's account of the genesis of the prose text.

6. In this sense, "Autobiography" accords with Freud's classic account of the workings of obsessional repression in the "Rat Man" case study (*Notes upon a Case of Obsessional Neurosis* [1909]). Contrasting the behavior of obsessives with that of hysterics, who forget what they repress, Freud writes: "The trauma, instead of being forgotten, is deprived of its affective cathexis; so that what remains in consciousness is nothing but its ideational content, which is perfectly colorless and is judged to be unimportant" (76). The point here is not that MacNeice was an obsessive like "Rat Man" but rather that "Autobiography" poetically enacts a similar kind of repression.

7. See in particular *The Destructive Element* ch. 13.

8. In fact, *The Destructive Element* is less doctrinaire than MacNeice allows for. In discussing *The Orators,* Spender observes "It seems likely . . . that the communist explanation of our society is not adequate to produce considerable art: it is only adequate to produce art to serve its purposes" (254).

9. See for example Cunningham 32. More generally, see Brown, where MacNeice's habitual lack of and suspicion of conviction is generalized into a thoroughgoing philosophical skepticism.

10. In *Collected Poems,* these texts are separated by four pages (18-22), following MacNeice's own resequencing of his earlier volumes for *Collected*

Poems 1925-1948; see Dodds's editorial preface for a rationale of these decisions (*Collected Poems* xv-xvi). While Dodds's strategy was sensible in the late 1960s (when an updated *Collected Poems* was urgently needed), general readers and specialists would now be best served by a collected edition that would reprint the poems in the sequence they originally appeared in individual volumes. This would have the advantage of reprinting the many poems rejected by MacNeice in 1949 (see *Collected Poems* 560-61 for details), as well as presenting the oeuvre in a more historically nuanced form. As it stands, Dodds's edition conflates the editorial decisions MacNeice took for *Collected Poems 1925-1948* with the straight reprinting of the five volumes MacNeice published between 1951 and 1963.

11. This approach has a long history: see Powell 603. For more recent commentary, see Marsack 7-8; Longley, *Louis MacNeice* 43; and McDonald 32.

12. See MacNeice's "Poem." Apart from the addition of a few commas, the title is the only change MacNeice made to the poem for volume publication.

13. See also MacNeice's review of Auden's *Look, Stranger!* (MacNeice, *Criticism* 76).

14. See Hynes (65-67) for the impact of the collapse of the Labour government on the "Auden Generation."

15. See Stallworthy 167 and MacNeice, *Criticism* 10n1. The texts in *Poems* were written over a longer period of time, between 1929 and 1935; see *Collected Poems* v-vi.

16. For the full review, see *Criticism* 101-03. I have corrected Cunningham's misquotation (reading "make" for "made").

17. "For about a year and a half I thought of Shelley as *the* great poet. While I was 17 I wrote, as I think many people do when they are 17, a number of Shelleyan poems defying or renouncing everyday life and its codes" (*Modern Poetry* 50).

18. Both "Trapeze" and "Insidiae" were dropped from *Collected Poems 1925-1948*; another Eliotic poem, "Everyman his own Pygmalion," was—wisely—not reprinted after its initial appearance in *New Verse* no. 1 (Jan. 1933), 10-11. For Eliot's influence, see "Eliot and the Adolescent" (1948) (MacNeice, *Criticism* 148-53) and Marsack 3-4.

19. The textual history of Spender's *Poems* is yet more complicated than MacNeice's. The texts of *Poems* (1933) as they appear in *Collected Poems 1928-1985* are often substantially revised; key poems (for example "After they have tired of the brilliance of cities") are omitted altogether. The

difficulties are concisely stated by O'Neill and Reeves: until the earlier—and often stronger—versions of *Poems* are reprinted, interested readers will have to search out original editions (35-36). I therefore quote from the second, expanded, edition of *Poems* published in 1934.

20. For "Ode," I quote directly from *Poems* because Dodds's *Collected Poems* prints a stanza break between "By taking it to pieces" and "The marriage of Cause and Effect," though he retains the semicolon after "pieces" (*Collected Poems* 58). Dodds was probably misled by *Collected Poems 1925-1948*, where these lines straddle separate pages (45-46). The stanza is also spread over two pages in *Poems*, but there is no indication of a break between "Let him not part asunder" and "Wisdom for him." Given its subject matter, wisdom would indicate that the stanza should not be parted asunder.

21. See MacNeice's comment on Spender's political miniepic *Vienna* (1934): "Unsuccessful, I think (still too *voulu*)" (*Criticism* 42). *"Voulu"* implies that Spender was trying too hard; certainly, *Vienna*'s amalgam of modernist collage and revolutionary idealism was unlikely to have appealed to MacNeice.

22. For the full text of the poem, see Spender, *Poems* 47-48. It can also be found in *Collected Poems 1928-1953* (49-50), though this version is marred by rewriting.

23. For Spender's protracted flirtation with communism, see Leeming 52-54, 63-64, and 93-103. Spender did not become a party member until 1937 and the publication by the Left Book Club of *Forward from Liberalism,* though he had been advocating revolutionary arguments for a long time before this.

24. See Roberts 86, 95-96. Both were collected in *Poems.*

25. See McKinnon 96-97; Longley, *Louis MacNeice* 43; and McDonald 30.

26. For Shepard's death, and a reading of "The Casualty," see Stallworthy 319-22.

27. Stallworthy also suggests Anthony Blunt as a "less likely addressee" (154n).

28. Though not collected until *Look! Stranger* (1936), Auden's poem was written in August 1932 and published a month later in *Twentieth Century*; it achieved wider circulation still when republished in *New Country* (1933); see Fuller 163. "To a Communist" is dated to 1933 by Dodds; it first appeared in *The Criterion* 13.51, published in January 1934. By this time, MacNeice would have

been familiar with both Auden's poem and Spender's: "After they have tired . . ." appeared in the first edition of Spender's *Poems* (1933), published in January 1933.

29. This poem was added to the second edition of *Poems.* For Spender and Hyndman, see Leeming 74-88. Also relevant in this context is Spender's early novel *The Temple,* whose primary focus is homosexual relationships in Weimar Germany.

30. The communist's barometer is worth comparing with that of "Mayfly," a love poem, which begins "Barometer of my moods today, mayfly, / Up and down one among a million" (*Collected Poems* 13-14). Though "To a Communist" and "Mayfly" represent different poles within *Poems,* like "To a Communist," "Mayfly" evokes a pastoral idea of England, and in this case Oxford; see also *Strings* 122.

31. See Longley, ""Something Wrong Somewhere?" for an account of MacNeice's criticism, which argues that "literary criticism is rarely a wholly separable category for MacNeice" (56).

32. See McDonald 22 for the view that this passage attacks Auden's therapeutic model of poetry and the *New Country* notion that art is about communication.

33. See MacNeice's foreword: "I have called this collection *Blind Fireworks* because they go quickly through their antics against an important background, and fall and go out quickly" (qtd. in Stallworthy 131).

34. See Cunningham 16-17 for a critique of Hynes's view of the 1930s as "an affair of a group of chums clustered about their mutual friend"; see McDonald 4-9 for consideration of how ideas of nationality contribute to Hynes's caricature of MacNeice as a "professional lacrymose Irishman" (334).

35. In *The Thirties and After,* the poem appears under the different title "Seeing MacNeice Stand Before Me" (265).

36. This poem elegizes MacNeice alongside Merleau-Ponty and Bernard Spencer: "Louis caught cold in the rain, Bernard fell from a train door. / / Their lives are now those poems that were / Pointers to the poems they made their lives." (*Collected Poems 1928-1985,* 176).

Works Cited

Alexander, Peter. *Roy Campbell: A Critical Biography.* Oxford: Oxford UP, 1982.

Brown, Terence. *Louis MacNeice: Sceptical Vision.* Dublin: Gill and Macmillan, 1975.

Bucknell, Katherine, and Nicholas Jenkins, eds. *W. H. Auden: "The Map of All My Youth."* Oxford: Clarendon, 1990.

Cunningham, Valentine. *British Writers of the Thirties.* Oxford: Oxford UP, 1988.

Dodds, E. R. *Missing Persons: An Autobiography.* Oxford: Clarendon, 1977.

Engle, John. "A Modest Refusal: Yeats, MacNeice, and Irish Poetry." *Learning the Trade: Essays on W. B. Yeats and Contemporary Poetry.* Ed. Deborah Fleming. West Cornwall: Locust Hill, 1993. 71-88.

Freud, Sigmund. *Case Histories 2.* Ed. A. Richards. Harmondsworth: Penguin, 1979.

Fuller, John. *W. H. Auden: A Commentary.* London: Faber, 1998.

Heinemann, Margot. "Three Left-Wing Poets: Louis MacNeice, John Cornford, Clive Branson." *Marxism Today* 20:11 (Nov. 1976): 343-54.

Hynes, Samuel. *The Auden Generation: Literature and Politics in England in the 1930s.* 1976. London: Pimlico, 1992.

Leeming, David. *Stephen Spender: A Life in Modernism.* London: Duckworth, 1999.

Longley, Edna. *Louis MacNeice: A Critical Study.* London: Faber, 1988.

———. "'Something Wrong Somewhere?': MacNeice as Critic." *Louis MacNeice and His Influence.* Ed. K. Devine and A. J. Peacock. Gerrards Cross: Colin Smythe, 1998. 53-67.

MacNeice, Louis. *Collected Poems.* Ed. E. R. Dodds. London: Faber, 1966.

———. *Collected Poems 1925-1948.* London: Faber, 1949.

———. "Everyman His Own Pygmalion." *New Verse* 1 (Jan. 1933): 10-11.

———. "Four Poems" ["To a Communist," "Museums," "A Contact," "Sunday Morning"]. *The Criterion* 13:51 (Jan. 1934): 230-31.

———. *Modern Poetry: A Personal Essay.* 1938. New York: Haskell House, 1969.

———. "Poem" ["Turf-stacks"]. *New Verse* 2 (Mar. 1933): 14-15.

———. *Poems.* London: Faber, 1935.

———. *The Poetry of W. B. Yeats.* 1941. London: Faber, 1967.

———. *Selected Literary Criticism of Louis MacNeice.* Ed. Alan Heuser. Oxford: Clarendon, 1987.

———. *Selected Prose of Louis MacNeice.* Ed. Alan Heuser. Oxford: Clarendon, 1990.

———. "Some Notes on Mr Yeats' Plays." *New Verse* 18 (Dec. 1935): 7-9.

———. *Springboard: Poems 1941-1944.* London: Faber, 1944.

———. *The Strings Are False: An Unfinished Autobiography by Louis MacNeice.* Ed. E. R. Dodds. London: Faber, 1965.

Marsack, Robyn. *The Cave of Making: The Poetry of Louis MacNeice.* Oxford: Clarendon, 1982.

McDonald, Peter. *Louis MacNeice: The Poet in His Contexts.* Oxford: Clarendon, 1991.

McKinnon, William T. *Apollo's Blended Dream: A Study of the Poetry of Louis MacNeice.* London: Oxford UP, 1971.

O'Neill, Michael, and Gareth Reeves. *Auden, MacNeice, Spender: The Thirties Poetry.* Basingstoke: Macmillan, 1992.

Powell, Dillys. "Disillusion Again." *London Mercury* 32.192 (Oct. 1935): 603-04.

Roberts, Michael, ed. *New Signatures: Poems by Several Hands.* London: Hogarth, 1932.

Spender, Stephen. *Collected Poems 1928-1953.* London: Faber, 1955.

———. *Collected Poems 1928-1985.* London: Faber, 1985.

———. *The Destructive Element: A Study of Modern Writers and Beliefs.* London: Cape, 1935.

———. *Journals 1939-1983.* Ed. John Goldsmith. London: Faber, 1985.

———. "Mr MacNeice's Poems." *New Verse* 17 (Oct.-Nov. 1935): 17-19.

———. *Poems.* London: Faber, 1933.

———. *Poems.* 2nd ed. London: Faber, 1934.

———. *The Temple.* London: Faber, 1988.

———. *The Thirties and After: Poetry, Politics, and People (1933-75).* London: Macmillan, 1978.

Stallworthy, John. *Louis MacNeice.* London: Faber, 1995.

Yeats, W. B. *The Poems.* Ed. Richard J. Finneran. London: Macmillan, 1984.

Christopher Hitchens (essay date January-February 2005)

SOURCE: Hitchens, Christopher. "A Nice Bloody Fool." *Atlantic Monthly* 295, no. 1 (January-February 2005): 174-78.

[*In the following essay, Hitchens recounts some of the less flattering aspects of Spender's personal and literary reputation.*]

One of the early poems with which Stephen Spender made his name opens like this: **"My parents kept me from children who were rough."**

In 1957, in *The Sense of Movement*, Thom Gunn proclaimed: "I praise the overdogs from Alexander / To those who would not play with Stephen Spender."

Not long afterward two distinguished Englishmen of letters decided that "Stephen" had earned his very own limerick, and wrote,

> Then up spake the bold Stephen Spender
> "You may think my conscience is tender.
> You might think my heart
> Was my sensitive part—
> But you should see my poor old pudenda."

In a long life Spender never quite succeeded in overcoming the widespread impression (which he may have privately shared) that there was something vaguely preposterous about him. His official biographer, John Sutherland, perhaps unwittingly and certainly unwillingly, provides armfuls of ammunition for this view. He does not cite either of the cracks I have just mentioned, but he does give the passage below, taken from Spender's memoir *World Within World*. In 1930 T. S. Eliot had decided to publish four of the young man's poems in the *Criterion*, and furthermore invited him to lunch.

> At our first luncheon he asked me what I wanted to do. I said: "Be a poet" "I can understand you wanting to write poems, but I don't quite know what you mean by 'being a poet,'" he objected.

I think this is quite funny on its own, but additionally so because it inverts what ought to be the proper Jamesian scenario—the stuffy English don admonishing the brash young American student. Be that as it may, Stephen Spender was to pass a great deal more of his life "being a poet" than he ever did writing poetry.

The thought lay about him in his infancy (which was marked by an awful father, a frightful elder brother, and a hideous torment of a boarding school education—so far, "on track" for English writing). At the age of nine he went to the Lake District on a family holiday and was exposed to "the simple ballad poems of Wordsworth," which, as he further phrased it, "dropped into my mind like cool pebbles, so shining and so pure, and they brought with them the atmosphere of rain and sunsets, and a sense of the sacred cloaked vocation of the poet." He was already, in other words, what Byron witheringly called "a Laker." An early school poem sustains the same note of moist wonderment about the weather, yearning for the spring in Devonshire but opening, "The rain drops from the mist endless and slow / The trees are bare and black . . ."

This culminates in the line "O God! . . . would I were there." Sutherland misses a trick, I think, in failing to point out the obvious debt to Rupert Brooke and his Grantchester, inspiration of drooping and sensitive versifiers at that time and since. (Ten years later Geoffrey Grigson was dryly to say, in reviewing Spender's book *The Destructive Element*, "Stephen Spender is the Rupert Brooke of the Depression.")

Indeed, it was above all the sense of an epoch, and of a decade, that allowed Spender to get away with "being a poet." Crucial to this image were his friendships from Oxford days with W. H. Auden, Louis MacNeice, Christopher Isherwood, and Cecil Day-Lewis. This cabal provoked Roy Campbell's joke about the "MacSpaunday" school: a joke that was a source of embarrassment (and rage, given Campbell's open sympathy for fascism) while simultaneously furnishing a near guarantee of immortality.

Among this book's assembly of sometimes very striking unpublished photographs is a shot of Spender, Auden, and Isherwood on the beach at Fire Island in 1947. Spender stands commandingly erect in the center, with his arms around the shoulders of his two much shorter comrades. There would be no doubt in the mind of the untutored as to which of them was the senior (the photo is presumably from Spender's private trove). And yet, as Sutherland shows very skillfully, it was Auden who was the literary boss from the beginning, and Isherwood (sometimes with Auden, and sometimes without) who was the sexually tougher and more resourceful one. Auden demonstrated his mastery from the very first, demanding to know of Spender how often he wrote poetry.

> Without reflecting, I replied that I wrote about four poems a day. He was astonished and exclaimed: "What energy!" I asked him how often he wrote a poem. He replied: "I write about one in three weeks." After this I started writing only one poem in three weeks.

So silly. Up until then, of course, Spender had been so impressed at attending the same Oxford college as Shelley that he had felt compelled to adopt yet another poetic pose: that of the agonized and alienated young dreamer.

Anyone who has seen *Cabaret* can read several of the succeeding chapters at speed. The three men pursued boys of various sorts and conditions (usually proletarian) all over Berlin and over much of Germany and Austria as well. (Auden ended up with a painful rectal fissure, which led him to write his wince-makingly titled *Letter to a Wound*.) They seem to have done most of it on borrowed money or on tiny publishing advances. Orwell's vicious remark, about the "nancy poets" who spent on sodomy what they had gained by sponging, was barely a match for the amazing narcissism revealed in these pages. However (and as Orwell was later to ruefully admit), there was a core of principle involved. Spender could feel fascism coming on, and was appalled by the premonitory symptoms of it. He may have made a complete fool of himself by going briefly to Spain. (The leader of the British Communist Party, the cynical Harry Pollitt, probably did say that he thought Spender's only usefulness would be to die the death of a Byronic martyr: another potential poetic "character" for him to have adopted, had he been less prudent than he was.) Spender may have written a fatuous book titled *Forward From Liberalism,* which among other things defended Stalin's show trials. But beneath all this playacting and conceit and gullibility was a pith of seriousness.

We can reconstruct this, not from *Goodbye to Berlin* but from the words of Isaiah. Dr. Berlin, whatever his many drawbacks, was an excellent judge of character. What he saw in Spender was an open-faced, vulnerable, rather captivating readiness to take chances. Most bullied English public school boys with oppressive fathers would soon have learned how to wear a protective carapace of some sort; Spender remained a naif in the best sense of that term, even as he remained something of an adolescent in matters of the pudendum. (The reason I don't name the authors of the above limerick, written by contemporaries of his, is that even now they regard it as accurate but unkind.)

The hinge moment, if I read Sutherland correctly, came with the outbreak of the Second World War. Spender had become an admirer of America, but it would not have occurred to him to take ship and leave England at that moment, as Auden and Isherwood both famously did. In the course of an earlier quarrel Spender had exclaimed to Isherwood, "If we're going to part, at least let's part like men." Isherwood had won that round, replying bitchily, "But Stephen, we aren't men." In some fashion or manner brittleness of that sort was to become de trop after Dunkirk. Spender "stayed on," tried to enlist and was rejected on health grounds (which ranged from tapeworm to varicose veins), joined the London Fire Brigade (not a soft option at that time), and also became a husband and father. Sutherland rightly doesn't speculate about this, but there appears to me to have been a latent connection between the advent of war and the triumph of Spender's heterosexual side. His disastrous earlier, "open" marriage, to the bohemian hell-minx Inez Pearn, had been a failure partly because of his reluctance to break things off with his lover Tony Hyndman, here depicted as sponger and sodomite on a majestic scale. By falling for Natasha Litvin, a gifted musician and a considerable beauty, Spender found himself not only able to hold on to a serious woman for the first time but also—and perhaps not without its own significance that year—to confirm and affirm the slightly suppressed Jewish element in his family background.

(His mother, Violet Schuster, was from a long line of converted and assimilated English Jews originating in Frankfurt.)

The war also improved his poetry. In the thirties Spender had had to contend with the criticism—obviously wounding to an aspiring writer and poet—that he didn't write very well at all. Eliot noticed it. Auden noticed it. Cyril Connolly noticed it. To Connolly, Spender wrote in that disarming manner that Isaiah Berlin so adored, "You are quite right about the bad writing. I am very sorry. It disturbs me very much." Hilarious. Even his most famous poem, **"I Think Continually of Those Who Were Truly Great,"** with its closing line, "And left the vivid air signed with their honor," had to be retouched by Isherwood before it "sang." Spender's readers often had to put up with things like **"Hampstead Autumn"** (1932), yet another rumination on the seasons: "In the fat autumn evening street / Hands from my childhood stretch out / And ring muffin bells."

Possibly . . . But in 1943 he published **"Exercises/ Explorations,"** the third "exercise" of which read,

> Since we are what we are, what shall we be
> But what we are? We are, we have
> Six feet and seventy years, to see
> The light, and then release it for the grave.
> We are not worlds, no, nor infinity,
> We have no claims on stone, except to prove
> In the invention of the city
> Our hearts, our intellect, our love.

This is very fine, and Sutherland is not stretching too far in comparing it, with its "mortuary sonorousness," to Donne's "Holy Sonnets."

Spender was more than six feet tall and lived on to be well over seventy. He easily outlived all his more famous contemporaries, and became in a sense their living witness as well as their official obituarist. I heard him give a rather beautiful address at Auden's memorial in Oxford in the fall of 1973. His long, spare frame and his nimbus of white hair had by then become familiar at dozens of international conferences and seminars. Sutherland speaks of him as a pioneer version of what we now call "the public intellectual." But Noel Annan went a bit further in terming him a "cultural statesman": a concept with a trapdoor of absurdity built right into it. This trapdoor was soon to fall open with a dismaying bang.

Having stayed in wartime England while keeping lines open to America, Spender was ideally positioned after 1945 to become a figure in the Anglo-U.S. "special relationship" and in one of its aspects, the cultural Cold War. The flagship symbol of both was the magazine *Encounter,* published in London but financed from across the Atlantic. Spender was a distinguished member of the team of anti-communist liberals (Isaiah Berlin, Richard Wollheim) and not-so-liberals (Irving Kristol, Melvin Lasky) who characterized the magazine. His wife, Natasha, came up with the name.

Square miles of print have now been devoted to the scandal that occurred in the late 1960s when Conor Cruise O'Brien flatly accused *Encounter* of being a self- or at least semi-conscious organ of the Central Intelligence Agency. That it had long been receiving a thick-envelope CIA subvention was quickly established. But who among the editors had known all along? Lasky certainly had, and Berlin (in my opinion) equally certainly. Spender staked, and nearly lost, his reputation on the stubborn assertion that he had had absolutely no idea. It will be quickly seen that he was making it certain that he would look a fool. The English subdivide this title into categories, starting with plain fool, moving through damn fool to bloody fool, and ending with fucking fool—for which one has to be sinister as well as silly. By throwing wine over William Empson for even suggesting anything covert about *Encounter*'s finances, Spender qualified as at least a bloody fool. But a nice kind of fool for all that: the sort who could write, as he had in Germany many years before, "On the whole though I've decided that the best thing is to stick through thick and thin to the best one can find in one's fellow creatures, even though one is humiliated by having one's weakness and lack of pride exposed by one's dependence on them."

In the end, after dodging much collapsing scenery at *Encounter*, Spender announced that one was frightfully hurt to find that one's colleagues had been deceiving one. I don't doubt that this was largely genuine. But Sutherland provides a detail that was hitherto unknown to me. It seems that Spender had been unable to recruit the support of T. S. Eliot for the enterprise. The conservative sage of Faber had from the first been "chronically suspicious of the 'American auspices' of the magazine." Well then, how could Spender really maintain that the thought had never even occurred to him?

He managed, with that providence that sometimes protects the terminally innocent, to escape into a third act of his life. This period might be described as "Backward to Liberalism." There was always a threat of the farcical or the undignified in the interest Spender took in the young, but Sutherland makes a convincing case that he was kept young, in a sense, by the growth of his gifted children, Matthew and Lizzie. Thus his book about the events of 1968, with the potentially embarrassing title *Year of the Young Rebels,* did not go over the abyss into a glassy admiration of student revolt. And he became one of the first to see the moral importance of the dissident movement in the Soviet

Union, with its synthesis of literary and ideological opposition. Having been an early defender of Boris Pasternak, he became an equally early patron of the exiled Joseph Brodsky and a vigorous organizer of petitions and support groups. This sympathy took institutional shape in the 1970s, with the imaginative inauguration of the magazine *Index on Censorship.* Devoted to the battle against repressive governments on all continents, this journal was and remains highly worthwhile. So over the long term Spender had had a part in launching *Horizon,* which for all Cyril Connolly's idiosyncrasies was indispensable to keeping alive a literary pulse in England during the war. Despite being despised by the true editor of *Encounter* and being kept on only as a "useful idiot" by the surreptitious moneymen, he ran a more than respectable "back half" of books pages for the magazine. This is a not altogether shabby record.

Attempts were made to smirch it all the same. Spender rather trustingly indulged a young opportunist named Hugh David, who then produced a scabrous "biography" titled *Spender: A Portrait With Background.* This gave infinite pain, both in its numerous falsifications and in its pitiless exposure of the old boy's days as a gay boy. The same trope was exploited without scruple by the forgettable American "gay writer" David Leavitt, who in 1993 extruded a novel called *While England Sleeps* and simply annexed some passages of *World Within World* in order to do so. Yet none of this seems to have prevented Spender from continuing to form friendships with writers younger than himself, of the generation of Peter Ackroyd and James Fenton (two rather acute choices). If his lifelong vice was that he could not stop himself from RSVPing to any old card of invitation, it can still be said of Spender that he continued to take the cheery chance of new encounters.

It may be that Sutherland felt a need to compensate for previous injustices in the writing of this biography, but one sometimes has the sense that his dutiful-ness became a chore to him. The word "idyllic" is employed so many times, even for scenes of relatively ordinary satisfaction at the seaside or in the countryside, that after a while I stopped circling it. Nothing excuses the use of "prevaricate" for "procrastinate," or "refute" for "repudiate." And Spender may well have been discharged from the Fire Brigade on June 13, 1944, but it is an abuse of a crucial word to say "Ironically, it was the same day that the first of the V-1 buzz bombs fell on London." That barely rises to the level of coincidence. An author has furthermore become far too close to his subject if he can write—this time unironically, and of a domestic row in the ski resort of Gstaad—that "the upheaval dwarfed the Suez crisis."

Still, by the time of his much mourned death, in 1995 (which occurred just after his unprecedented last-minute decision to decline a social invitation from the Holroyd/

Drabble household), Spender had managed to outlive the sorts of taunt and nickname ("Stainless Splendor," "Stephen Savage") that his parents had feared when they first forbade him—pointlessly, as it was to turn out—the company of "rough" boys. He had never stopped working. He had never ceased to take an interest. And he had perhaps earned himself the most sentimental line of the much less sentimental poet Philip Larkin: "What will survive of us is love."

FURTHER READING

Bibliography

Kulkarni, H. B. *Stephen Spender Works and Criticism: An Annotated Bibliography.* New York: Garland, 1976, 264 p.

Comprehensive bibliography of Spender's published books, with a complete listing of the prose and poetry included in anthologies, as well as of sound recordings, manuscripts, and criticism.

Biography

David, Hugh. *Stephen Spender: A Portrait with Background.* London: Heinemann, 1992, 308 p.

Unauthorized biography of Spender repudiated by the poet and his wife.

Criticism

Brett, Michael. Introduction to *New Collected Poems: Stephen Spender,* edited by Michael Brett, pp. xvi-xxi. London: Faber and Faber, 2004.

Brief introduction to Spender's poetry and the historical and personal events that informed it.

Harper, George Mills. "'Necessary Murder': The Auden Circle and the Spanish Civil War." In *On Modern Poetry: Essays Presented to Donald Davie,* edited by Vereen Bell and Laurence Lerner, pp. 67-80. Nashville, Tenn.: Vanderbilt University Press, 1988.

Account of the activities of Spender, Auden, and other poets during the 1936 Spanish Civil War, and of the poetry inspired by the war.

Jacobs, Willis D. "Spender's 'I Think Continually of Those.'" *Modern Language Notes* 65, no. 7 (November 1950): 491-92.

Brief exploration of the ambiguity of the last line of Spender's celebrated poem.

Spender, Stephen, Peter Marchant, and Stan Sanvel Rubin. "An Interview with Stephen Spender." *Partisan Review* 55, no. 1 (winter 1988): 45-54.

Interview in which Spender discusses the role of the poet in society and his own ability to continue producing poetry into old age. This text is an edited transcription of a videotape produced on February 14, 1978.

——, and James Naiden. "A Conversation with Stephen Spender." *North Stone Review* 10 (fall 1991-winter 1992): 203-23.

Interview conducted on March 31, 1982, in which Spender discusses the relationship between poetry and politics and offers an evaluation of some contemporary poets.

Sutherland, John. "The 1990's: 'Five Years He Shouldn't Have Had.'" In *Stephen Spender: The Authorized Biography,* pp. 539-61. London: Viking, 2004.

Discusses Spender's reputation at the end of his life and the publication of his final book of poetry, *Dolphins,* in 1994.

Tasker, John. "Sir Stephen Spender: The Alroy Kear of Our Time." *Literary Criterion* 28, no. 3 (1993): 1-15.

Compares Spender to the self-promoting character Alroy Kear from Somerset Maugham's novel *Cakes and Ale.*

Additional coverage of Spender's life and career is contained in the following sources published by Thomson Gale: *British Writers Supplement,* Vol. 2; *Concise Dictionary of British Literary Biography, 1945-1960; Contemporary Authors,* Vols. 9-12R; *Contemporary Authors New Revision Series,* Vols. 31 and 54; *Contemporary Authors—Obituary,* Vol. 149; *Contemporary Literary Criticism,* Vols. 1, 2, 5, 10, 41, and 91; *Contemporary Poets,* Ed. 1, 2, 3, and 4; *Dictionary of Literary Biography,* Vol. 20; *DISCovering Authors 3.0; DISCovering Authors Modules: Poets; Encyclopedia of World Literature in the 20th Century,* Ed. 3; *Literature Resource Center; Major 20th-Century Writers,* Eds. 1 and 2; *Major 21st-Century Writers* (ebook), 2005; *Poetry for Students,* Vol. 23; *Poets: American and British; Reference Guide to English Literature,* Ed. 2; and *Twayne's English Authors.*

William Stafford
1914-1993

American poet, essayist, translator, and editor.

INTRODUCTION

Stafford was a prize-winning poet whose themes include the conflict between nature and culture, the power of myth, and the horrors of war. Many of his more than 3,000 published poems deal with the landscapes of Kansas, his birthplace, and the Pacific Northwest, where he lived most of his adult life.

BIOGRAPHICAL INFORMATION

The eldest of three children, Stafford was born January 17, 1914, in Hutchinson, Kansas, to Earl Ingersoll and Ruby Mayher Stafford. His father, seeking work wherever he could find it during the Great Depression, moved the family from town to town, and young Stafford contributed to the family's income by delivering newspapers and selling vegetables he had grown himself. The family's devotion to justice, tolerance, and hard work were instilled in Stafford at a young age. After graduating from high school, Stafford attended a junior college in El Dorado, Kansas, and then transferred to the University of Kansas, working his way through school as a waiter. He earned a B.A. in 1937.

During World War II, Stafford, a registered conscientious objector, put in long hours doing manual labor in a variety of Civilian Public Service camps in Illinois, Arkansas, and California. In 1944, while stationed in California, he married Dorothy Frantz, a local schoolteacher whose father was a pacifist minister. After the war the couple returned to Kansas, where Stafford resumed his university studies and earned an M.A. in 1946. The Staffords had four children—two sons and two daughters. In 1948 Stafford accepted a teaching position at Lewis and Clark College in Portland, Oregon. He took a leave of absence from 1950 through 1956 to earn a doctorate in creative writing from the University of Iowa and to teach for a year at Manchester College and for another year at San Jose State College. He returned to Lewis and Clark in 1957 and remained there until he retired from teaching in 1980. Stafford's numerous awards include the National Book Award for Poetry in 1963, the Shelley Memorial Award from the Poetry Society of America in 1964, and a

Guggenheim fellowship in 1966. In 1970 he was named Poetry Consultant to the Library of Congress. Stafford died on August 28, 1993, in Lake Oswego, Oregon.

MAJOR WORKS

Although Stafford started writing at a young age, he didn't begin to take it seriously until he was in college and he did not publish a volume of poetry until he was almost forty-six years old. He went on to become one of the most prolific poets of twentieth-century America, publishing more than 3,000 poems as well as numerous essays on the art of poetry writing. His first volume of poetry, *West of Your City,* appeared in a limited edition in 1960 and was soon out of print. It was followed two years later by *Traveling through the Dark,* which won the National Book Award and established Stafford's reputation as an important poet. The volume's title poem, his most popular and most frequently anthologized single work, articulates the conflict between civilization and the wilderness that informs much of Stafford's work as a whole. In 1966 Stafford published *The Rescued Year,* which reprinted fourteen of the poems from *West of Your City* along with a number of new poems. In 1970 *Allegiances* was published and in 1973, the highly acclaimed *Someday, Maybe.* Both volumes contain poems that refer to the original inhabitants of the land, before the arrival of European Americans. Previously uncollected poems, along with a number of new ones, appeared in *Stories That Could Be True: New and Collected Poems* (1977). Stafford's later volumes include *A Glass Face in the Rain* (1982) and *An Oregon Message* (1987). These collections represent only a portion of his published poetry since he also produced more than twenty smaller books, or chapbooks, printed by small, independent presses.

In addition to his poetry, Stafford produced numerous works of nonfiction. His first book, *Down in My Heart* (1947), is a collection of essays based on his experiences as a conscientious objector in the Civilian Public Service camps during World War II. He also published a number of essay collections on the writing process, most notably *Writing the Australian Crawl* (1978) and *You Must Revise Your Life* (1986).

CRITICAL RECEPTION

Stafford is considered a regional poet—sometimes in the pejorative sense of the term—and a landscape poet. The poet and critic Richard Hugo differentiates between Stafford's poems that describe the Great Plains of his native Kansas and those that feature the Pacific Northwest, where he spent more than forty years of his life. Hugo claims that many of Stafford's Northwest poems fail because the poet is "not at home" within the landscape. "The Northwest is rich and Stafford has always been Kansas dirt poor," according to Hugo, referring to what he calls Stafford's "early poetic failures to conquer the Northwest." In contrast, William Young praises Stafford for "his continuing faith in the open road and his sense of being 'at home' no matter where he is." Similarly, John Lauber contends that "Stafford country" encompasses both of the geographical areas primarily associated with the poet: "His region, in fact, is simply the American West with its plains and deserts and mountains and rivers, its farms and its towns (but rarely its cities)."

Stafford's use of the plain style has generated a fair amount of critical controversy. Lauber has noted the "leisurely and colloquial" syntax and "the simplest possible" diction often employed by Stafford. "The effect is of primer-style, of the Dick and Sally of a first-grade reader," reports Lauber in his analysis of the poem "In California." Paul Zweig, although he praises Stafford's use of conversational style in his early poetry, finds that by 1973 "the simple language has become a mannerism." According to Zweig, although Stafford is aiming for a sense of childlike innocence in the poems of *Sometimes, Maybe,* what he achieves is more often "commonplace statements and coy sentimentality." George S. Lensing suggests that a certain amount of critical neglect of Stafford's work can be attributed to the fact that most of Stafford's poems "shun grandiose and portentous statements in favor of forms that are brief, calm, and even-tempered." Nonetheless, notes Lensing, "[t]o speak of a poetry of unostentation, however, is not to deny the remarkable power of many of the poems, even though it has led critics to dismiss him."

Roger Dickinson-Brown suggests that Stafford's reputation is becoming "to some extent a cult reputation," with people outside the circle finding his poetry dull. "The first and major cause of Stafford's dullness is a muting overexposure. The quantity of what he publishes is out of proportion to the really few things he has to say," claims Dickinson-Brown. Judith Kitchen acknowledges that the quality vs. quantity problem has hurt Stafford's reputation: "Stafford's refusal to edit his own work and to limit the amount he publishes has caused critics to take him less seriously than they should." To many scholars, however, Stafford's poetry appears remarkably consistent over the years. Lensing and Ronald Moran have remarked on this aspect of Stafford's work. Moran notes that "[t]he juxtaposition of almost any poem from *West of Your City* with one from the 1973 volume *Someday, Maybe* would not evince startling differences in style or themes." Kitchen agrees, maintaining that "it is difficult to tell poems that were first printed in *West of Your City* from poems that appeared over twenty-five years later in *An Oregon Message.* Both the themes and the methods have remained consistent."

Several critics have also commented on Stafford's use of point of view in his poetry; he often writes from the perspective of the Other—of an animal, of the landscape, or, in the case of the poem "1080," of a chemical pesticide that enters the food chain, destroying everything it touches. Carol Kyle has studied Stafford's adoption of a Native American persona as a representative of the lost wilderness, although she maintains that he sometimes personifies even the wilderness itself, "alternately active and passive." She cites one poem in which "the tiger at the zoo and the man watching him outside his cage change position and point of view as the bars of the cage melt into a pattern of stripes on the tiger's back." Henry Taylor points out that often the speakers of Stafford's poems "are not the observer, but the thing observed—wind, seeds, trees, ducks—and they speak of how things are with them." Lars Nordström discusses the poem "Whispered into the Ground," which features a speaking seed, and "Beaver Talk," which presents two animals exchanging information on "the nature of lakes, and how to deal with the discovery of a new one."

The autobiographical nature of much of Stafford's work has drawn critical attention, too, particularly with reference to his idealized portrayal of childhood and the opposing representations of his two parents. Stafford's habit of presenting his father in heroic, romantic terms in his poetry has been discussed by several critics. Lensing, for example, claims that Earl Ingersoll Stafford "is exalted by the heroic virtues of the wilderness" and notes the many poems that "celebrate the elder Stafford's taciturn strength and life-giving sustenance." Lensing and Moran maintain that in glorifying childhood "Stafford goes beyond even [Theodore] Roethke . . . in defining the father as the central occupant of that near-perfect world." In recent years, feminist critics have begun commenting on the far more negative representation of the mother in Stafford's poetry. Kitchen reports that Stafford, writing extensively about the influence of both his mother and father, "sees two sides of himself" based on their respective contributions to his character, which he described as "the judgmental, fearful side and the receptive, open side." Sally Bishop Shigley has studied numerous representations of parenthood in Stafford's poetry and contends that Stafford consistently portrays mothers as weak, fearful, and sullen, whereas fathers are almost universally "wise and strong." "Stafford is not anti-female or anti-feminist by any means," Shigley acknowledges, "yet his general yearning to close the gaps between men and wilderness, men and their fathers, men and their history, and men and technology does not seem to extend specifically to the gap between men and women."

PRINCIPAL WORKS

Poetry

Winterward (unpublished doctoral dissertation) 1954
West of Your City 1960
Traveling through the Dark 1962
The Rescued Year 1966
Eleven Untitled Poems 1968
Weather: Poems 1969
Allegiances 1970
Someday, Maybe 1973
Going Places: Poems 1974
The Design on the Oriole 1977

Stories That Could Be True: New and Collected Poems 1977
Tuft by Puff 1978
Things That Happen Where There Aren't Any People 1980
Sometimes Like a Legend: Puget Sound Poetry 1981
A Glass Face in the Rain 1982
Roving across Fields: A Conversation and Uncollected Poems, 1942-1982 1983
Listening Deep 1984
An Oregon Message 1987
Kansas Poems 1990
Passwords 1991
My Name Is William Tell 1992
The Darkness around Us Is Deep: Selected Poems 1993
Learning to Live in the World: Earth Poems 1994
The Methow River Poems 1995
Even in Quiet Places 1996
The Way It Is: New & Selected Poems 1998
Every War Has Two Losers: William Stafford on Peace and War (poetry and prose) 2003

Other Major Works

Down in My Heart (essays) 1947
Modern Poetry of Western America [editor, with Clinton Larsen] (poetry) 1975
Writing the Australian Crawl: Views on the Writer's Vocation (essays) 1978
You Must Revise Your Life (essays) 1986
Window on the Black Sea: Bulgarian Poetry in Translation [translator; edited by Richard Harteis] (poetry) 1992
Crossing Unmarked Snow: Further Views on the Writer's Vocation (essays) 1997

CRITICISM

Richard Hugo (essay date spring 1970)

SOURCE: Hugo, Richard. "Problems with Landscapes in Early Stafford Poems." *Kansas Quarterly* 2, no. 2 (spring 1970): 33-8.

[*In the following essay, Hugo maintains that Stafford's landscape poems of the Northwest are not always successful because the poet never feels entirely at home in that region.*]

William Stafford is more than just a landscape poet, but as a landscape poet he is one of the very best. By landscape poet I mean a poet who uses places and experiences in those places as starting points for poems.

For such a poet, as several critics have noted, there are two landscapes, one external and one internal. The external one is simply "used"—indeed, usually sacrificed—to get to the internal landscape where the poem is. The difference in the two scapes is probably arbitrary and in reality nonexistent. However, some immediate problems are evident. What to leave out of the real picture? What to add? How to lie about the world in *your* way in order to get at truths about yourself?

Then there is the major problem of possession, of being "at home" in the external scape used, of putting yourself in the scene. This is difficult. Willing a persona is usually too feeble for the purpose. The poem cannot merely happen because the poet saw the nice farm in the sunset and would "like to write a poem about it." First he must steal the farm. He must emotionally own the external landscape because selfishness precedes sharing. Most bad landscape poems are bad not because, as we usually presume, they were written by a sentimental old lady or are filled with the clichés of youth, but because before the poem was started, the poet had generously presumed that the external landscape belonged to others as well as himself and that attitudes toward the external were shared or communal. Such generosity and warmth may be commendable in life but seldom find their way into good poems. (All this assumes is that to be good a poem should have some depth of personal commitment. Actually, I suppose all a good poem need do is to be interesting.)

I'll limit myself here to two external landscapes in William Stafford's poems, the Midwest and the Far West, specially the Pacific Northwest, and of Stafford's relative success in each area. His first book, *West of Your City,* brought much critical acclaim, and called enough attention to Stafford to help his second book win the National Book Award. As astute a critic as Louis Simpson praised the true originality at work in the early poems. The first poem, after an introductory piece, is called **"One Home,"** and the poem opens "Mine was a midwest home—you can keep your world." This could mean: what was mine is mine and you can have yours. That would indicate that Stafford selfishly owns his material, his external scape. It could also imply: you can keep your world because there's no danger of my stealing it as long I'm obsessed with mine. Either way, the rest of the poem works out. Stafford's world was limited by forces long dead: "Indians pulled the West over the edge of the sky." Throughout the poem, Stafford's landscape, his external one, is working poetically for him, helping him and us to his internal scape where the poem is. The sun is "like a blade" that is always over man, threatening. And to escape the drabness of a world where "plain black hats rode the thoughts that made our code," where "we sang hymns in the house; the roof was near God," the oppression of a God and a sun always too close, the loneliness where

"To anyone who looked at us we said 'My Friend,'" "we ran toward storms." In other words, anything to get away, even running toward danger to find the escape of excitement. This theme is developed in a later, profoundly touching poem called **"Thinking for Berky."** But there is no getting away: "Wherever we looked the land would hold us up." Of course, the land also held them up the way a child is held up to see a parade. The world is psychologically restricted but the vision is vast.

In such a world one dreams, gropes, tries to make his way like a catfish with "feelers noncommital and black" (**"In the Deep Channel"**), and one's deepest feelings, "the deep current," fights the desire to grow or perhaps to break away: "tugged at the tree roots below the river." Nor is any amount of questioning helpful. In **"At the Salt Marsh,"** Stafford's questioning of the world in which he finds himself becomes as morally inconsequential as the firing of a shotgun. Nothing will tell him what's right or wrong and only reality, here the head of a dead duck, remains. In **"Hail Mary"** the shadows of cedars in graveyards become obsequious in the face of a threat of detection and yet are lonely enough to bow "to the wind that noticed them." What we can do is listen, and whatever can touch us will seldom come from the drab and barren world of Stafford's childhood (except of course that we are touched constantly in the poems) but from "that other place."

On page 19 of Stafford's first book is this poem:

"The Farm on the Great Plains"

A telephone line goes cold;
birds tread it wherever it goes.
A farm back of a great plain
tugs an end of the line.

I call that farm every year,
ringing it, listening, still;
no one is home at the farm,
the line gives only a hum.

Some year I will ring the line
on a night at last the right one,
and with an eye tapered for braille
from the phone on the wall

I will see the tenant who waits—
the last one left at the place;
through the dark my braille eye
will lovingly touch his face.

"Hello, is Mother at home?"
No one is home today.
"But Father—he should be there."
No one—no one is here.

"But you—are you the one . . . ?"
Then the line will be gone
because both ends will be home:
no space, no birds, no farm.

My self will be the plain,
wise as winter is gray,
pure as cold posts go
pacing toward what I know.

People have frequently remarked that Stafford, like many good poets, has little personal taste about his own work. It is said he doesn't know his good poems from his bad ones. It's not for me to discuss his bad poems (**"The Gun of Billy the Kid"** and **"B.C."** are hopelessly awful), but I have noticed that his best poems seem to appear in the best (often highest paying) magazines, and the above poem is placed at the end of the first section of the first book, a conspicuous position. It also appears next to last in the first section of his third book, *The Rescued Year,* and is followed by **"Listening,"** another fine poem from his first volume; together they make a strong ending for the first section of his third volume. Of course, editing could account for all this, but I suspect Stafford is a shrewder judge of his work than some people, including myself, used to give him credit for. At any rate, he'd have to be really dense not to know that the above poem is the one we are all looking for.

If a poet can find out how he feels and then have the courage to state it, he has done almost all he can. This sounds simple, and maybe it is. It is anything but easy. This poem is so simple and direct, so emotionally honest that it goes beyond its affecting impact and begins to haunt the reader. At least it haunts me, and has for years. By naming things this way Stafford resolves many of the problems he has been trying to solve in the first section (called "Midwest") of his first book. Much of the poetic energy has gone into illuminating, demonstrating and, in the weaker moments, talking about problems imposed by environment, problems of outer and inner landscapes affecting each other, being at odds with each other, complementing and supplementing each other. He has been finding ways to cope, discovering escapes, developing strategies (Stafford's word).

"The Farm on the Great Plains," on one level, is the poet's battle against and victory over regression. The poem is central to an understanding of Stafford as landscape poet. Home tries to reclaim him first, the telephone line is cold yet the farm (the past) tugs it. He calls every year but no one is home until on the right night he finds someone, who is of course himself and who is obliged to tell him what he already knows—no one is home. It is Stafford's peculiar kind of courage that he can admit to playing the childish games we all play, asking himself over and over the question to which he already knows the answer, taking strange comfort in his desperation. Finally, the cycle of regressive dependence on the past is broken when his final question, weakened perhaps by repetition and certainly by

his preceding firmness with self, trails off to nothing. He hangs up on himself. The phone line (umbilical cord if you want to be smartass) is severed for good. The last self left at home dissolves, and the poet is left with only those selves of the past he took with him. Everything, including death, can be faced. He is home anywhere with his plain, gray sensibility, once he has accepted what he is.

Once a poem as excellent as **"The Farm on the Great Plains"** has given license for freedom, the poet might be presumed free to write in any landscape. But poets always have troubles. If not, they create them. And we find in the second section (entitled "Far West") that the poet is not as at home as he might have hoped. It is one thing to say both ends of the line will be home and another to know it's true. Some of the reasons for Stafford's poetic difficulties in the second section become apparent. Stafford's original external landscape, and (since he is an honest poet) his internal one as well, is Kansas. Flat vistas, a harsh cruel weather but one that comes from far off, can be predicted, even spotted early, and consequently prepared for (strategy?): drab customs, at least in Stafford's day, drab towns, repressive social codes. This is the Kansas represented in the poems.

The west, especially the Pacific Northwest, is another matter. In western Washington and Oregon, vistas are usually limited. Trees are tall and thick, and in your way. Hills and mountains are in your way. The deep, long, uninterrupted gaze is rarely possible. Air is often hazy. Clouds are heavy and frequently low—something is oppressive no matter where you are. The scenery is dramatic and sudden, the weather mild, and the moral and social codes, what there are of them, are at best diffuse, free of a single rigid influence. Most of all, it is an area of surprise. You need not run toward storms to get your kicks. Just innocently drive around the next curve and a grand snow-covered mountain you never expected will bang your eyes.

In the first poem in the section, **"Walking West,"** Stafford is forced to more regular rhythms than we've come to expect in his best work. He goes to externally half-rhymed quatrains, and while **"The Farm on the Great Plains"** is in quatrains, there one feels the poem found the form. Here, the form seems superimposed. Standard form is one resort of a poet in trouble. **"Walking West"** is not a bad poem but anyone might have written it. Certainly this is not Stafford at his best. At his best he is subtly rhythmic in an exciting way, or can grope morally about, planning his strategies.

In other pieces you can sense he is not at home. In his town "To anyone who looked at us we said 'My Friend.'" But in **"The Research Team in the Moun-**

tains," which appears in his second volume, *Traveling through the Dark,*

> If your policy is to be friends in the mountains
> a rock falls on you: the only real friends—
> you can't help it.

I suppose that's true, if one can generalize that people in the Far West are not as friendly as people in the Midwest, though who in hell knows? The point here is that although nature in the Midwest is far less hospitable to man than in the Far West, Stafford finds it more so, at least in the poems. But the real danger in the Far West, I suspect, is neither the threat of falling rocks nor of unfriendly people but rather the danger of not writing his own poems. (He would write poems—and good ones—anywhere). Here, external and internal landscapes are at unpoetic odds.

Going back to the first volume, in **"A Survey"** Stafford is once again reduced to being "poetic" to bring off the poem. And nowhere does Stafford seem more uncreatively foreign than in **"In the Oregon Country."** Here he can do little more than pile up names of places and tribes and in an effort to mold the poem, he fails to escape the "tyranny of narration." He seems dazzled by the relatively rich history, topography, and myths. The Northwest is rich and Stafford has always been Kansas dirt poor. The external Northwest landscape bears no relation to his internal one, at least none strong enough to get to the poem. They do not supplement or complement each other and there is no *mutual* alienation.

Stafford's early poetic failures to conquer the Northwest are the result of his abandoning his capacity for ruthlessness. He does not own the places he tries to use for poems, and so he can only *try* to use them. The obsessive quality of emotional ownership is missing. It is essential; the external must be possessed, not just observed. Anyone can snap a camera. (I should qualify what I'm saying by emphasizing that all early poems growing out of the Far West are not bad poems. Far from it. Some are very good. What I'm saying is that the real poem, the one growing out of the inner landscape and revealing previously unknown personal relationships with the world, is often missed. Good or bad, it was seldom missed back home.) This failure to reach out and make the "new world" his, to treat the pines, gulls, mountains, and streams as if he were the first man to see them, leads Stafford to resolve early Far West poems with overly-public "poetic" statements: "So many Chinook souls, so many Silverside." But of course he succeeds. He was always too much the poet not to:

"Traveling through the Dark"

> Traveling through the dark I found a deer
> dead on the edge of the Wilson River road.
> It is usually best to roll them into the canyon:
> that road is narrow; to swerve might make more dead.

> By glow of the tail-light I stumbled back of the car
> and stood by the heap, a doe, a recent killing;
> she had stiffened already, almost cold.
> I dragged her off; she was large in the belly.

> My fingers touching her side brought me the reason—
> her side was warm; her fawn lay there waiting,
> alive, still, never to be born.
> Beside that mountain road I hesitated.

> The car aimed ahead its lowered parking lights;
> under the hood purred the steady engine.
> I stood in the glare of the warm exhaust turning red;
> around our group I could hear the wilderness listen.

> I thought hard for us all—my only swerving—,
> then pushed her over the edge into the river.

This poem seems a great favorite of Stafford readers; it appears everywhere. I happen not to care for it much, but for irresponsible reasons which I'll state later. Let's say the world is right, I'm wrong, and the poem is a success. If so, one reason is that it transcends the difficulties he had with the earlier Far West poems. The elements of the Pacific Northwest are there: the night-dark limit on vision contrasted to the unlimited views of bright, open Kansas plains (sometimes the Midwest is brighter at night than the Northwest during day), the surprise you can't plan for because you can't see it coming from far off (what road ever curved in Kansas or ran straight in western Oregon?), the dead deer suddenly there, the canyon, the narrow road, and Stafford honestly awkward in the scene: "I stumbled back of the car." His magic is gone.

> In scenery I like flat country.
> In life I don't like much to happen.

he says in **"Passing Remark,"** and so the situation on the Wilson River road is definitely not his kind. What strategy will handle this? He takes some strength from the car, the indifferently relentless headlights and from the steady purr of the engine, etc., before he finds a way out.

Now for my sour digression, my irrelevant reasons for not liking the poem—this may be my only chance. Simply put, it jars my Northwest soul. I could argue aesthetically that a poem cannot afford time to wait for a decision, only time for the decision to be rendered or better, named. But I can't defend this. Besides, it's probably wrong. Being from the Northwest, however, I have no doubt what the decision should be, and at least I can understand my impatient urge to say: stop thinking hard for us all, Bill, and get that damned deer off the road before somebody kills himself.

Why he uses this as the first and title poem of his second book is probably the more important question. I think he realized that he had "used" that foreign external landscape and managed to write a sound poem (I'm sure one he likes much) out of himself. Stafford's world may not be large but his poems are big enough. Here, I think he knew he had literally traveled through the dark and now both ends of the Kansas line are home. He carries his world within him for good, and no matter how foreign the external landscape, he will travel through its darks and find his poem. Of course, he had already demonstrated this in other poems before writing this one, but this time he has convinced himself he can do it. The real sacrifice is not the deer but the external world, and the real salvation is not the life of the next motorist but the poem itself. If this was a moment he told himself as poet he would go on writing his poems anywhere, it must have been one of the best moments in a career that has had more good ones than most.

Carol Kyle (essay date 1972)

SOURCE: Kyle, Carol. "Point of View in 'Returned to Say' and the Wilderness of William Stafford." *Western American Literature* 7, no. 3 (1972): 191-201.

[*In the following essay, Kyle discusses Stafford's use of place and perspective in his wilderness poems.*]

The perspective in William Stafford's **"Returned to Say"** is probably the most interesting of the approaches to an understanding of the poem. From the title of the book of poetry, ***Traveling through the Dark,*** the perspective is clearly that of the *traveler*; in this poem, the traveler seems to have emerged from the other world, to have come back from the other side of the grave, as the title again **"Returned to Say"** suggests. The returned figure is a "lost Cree / on some new shore"; from all accounts an Indian could only be lost in a world totally alien, on the shore of a kingdom not his own.

The exact identification of the persona of the Indian is not so important as an identification of co-existent possibilities. A spirit returned from the other world like a ghost haunting a cove does not rule out the interpretation of the spirit as a sort of guide, or a kind of guardian angel. Information on the Cree Indian identifies the tribe to which he belongs as the North American Cristineaux Indian living in the forests and plains of Montana through Ontario and Saskatchewan, thus the allusion to facing north, and also to *traveling* north. But more than this, the Cree tribes believed that the basis for success in life was the acquisition of a guardian spirit acquired at adolescence. The return of a spirit to guard another person just starting his adult life is not at all inconsistent with the general view of the returned spirit, but it is difficult to reconcile with the fact given in the poem that the supposed guide is "lost." This is

hardly explained in the name of irony since the tone of the poem suggests an ideal world of romance or dream vision, or trance, not a world of absurd contradictions. The reconciliation *might* be made however on the grounds that the Cree, having just returned, must begin anew to reacquaint himself with the topography of the North American wilderness. Like a true American, descended from Christopher Columbus who lost his way to find America, the Indian must temporarily lose himself to find himself. Like Frost's "Directive" in a pre-historic, geologically-strange wilderness, the directions lead only to one's getting lost; the road to the children's playhouse back into time, the closed-off road to the center of one's childhood, the map for the finding of the treasure buried with the Holy Grail, lie in one's self. The "directive" is St. Mark's from the Bible, losing one's self as a part of the process of growing up, of moving through childhood and adolescence to a kind of self-knowledge.

Perhaps this is the reason for the strength of the identification of the spiritual guide as one's alter-ego. The clearest support for this theory comes from the point of view registered in the poem of the gradual merging of the first and third persons after the initial split. That is, originally, the speaker is the "I" of the poem and the two figures are definitely traveling separately: "he in a hurry and I beside him" closes the first stanza. The person shifts back and forth from first to third person in the second stanza:

> It will be a long trip; he will be a new chief;
> we have drunk new water from an unnamed stream;
> under little dark trees he is to find a path
> we both must travel because we have met.
>
> (ll. 5-8)

The two symbolically drink water as "we," but then "he" finds the path and both the pathfinder and his pupils follow. This pattern continues throughout the poem: in stanza three "we" gesture, but the Indian performs the ritual alone of blowing the grain of sand off his knifeblade. Again this Indian history shows a special devotion to certain symbolic objects, sometimes recommended in a dream or vision. As the breathing of this by now very physically present Indian "darkens the steel," "his eyes become set / And start a new vision" (ll. 11-13). At this point, the most ambiguous of the uses of the peronal pronoun occurs: "the rest of his life. / We will mean what he does" (ll. 13-14). The syntax can be taken two ways: either the new vision will exist for the rest of his life, or for the rest of his life, ignoring the period punctuating the end of the line, "We will mean what he does." Again, there is no reason why *both* could not work: the vision established for the rest of his life will serve as guide for them both as they are parts of the same person. In this way, the developed part of the original "I," the Indian part, suggests a concentration on one's own ancestral pathfinder, on a return, perhaps, to Indian lore as a guide.

The present Black Mountain poets, of course, are the chief exponents of the return to lost cultures as a kind of restoration of the imagination. The term offered by Robert Duncan is, in fact, the description of such a place as a "made place"; I prefer the term "found place" as in "found poetry" or "found art" of any kind. The temptation here is to immediately identify this territory as found culture; as Olson's *The Kingfishers* refinds and embraces the lost Mayan culture as his own, the lost and refound Cree culture shifts the Indian locale from Central America to North America. The difference between Olson's found culture and Stafford's located place, however, is enormous: the difference exists chiefly in the distinction between that which is imaginative as projective verse projects the mind into the past, into a once actual place, and that which is actual as the place is identifiable in the present and marked for travel in the future. Stafford's place is more locatable on a map; Olson's is down there somewhere in a rain swamp as he himself suggested, and occupies more a theory of space than an actual place. Stafford's Indian steps out of, perhaps, *The Pathfinder* or out of the pages of Indian history and folklore: "Back of this page / the path turns north" (11. 14-15), but this, of course, is part of the poetry. The difference lies in the perception of the degree of the emergence of reality from a dream, or perhaps the difference lies in the power of the imagination to conjure up the real world from the imagined world. In this latter case, if Olson's theoretical found place is more imagined, Stafford's poetic imagination is certainly stronger, for the Indian actually emerges from the past, is recalled to life, is resurrected and in *person* proceeds to restore the spirits of the main speaker of the poem. The emphasis on actuality and on *action* as part of actuality cannot be ignored. To 'mean' and to 'do' are different; Olson only *means,* but only Stafford's Indian *does.* He is silent; he travels quietly north. The moccasins of both swift runners, travelers, by the last line of the poem, "do not mark the ground," and the integration of the two companions is complete.

The word "mark" is a kind of pun here as the line above read "We are looking for a sign" (1. 15). The imagery of sight in the poem reinforces the multileveled interpretation of the speaker as seer searching for a direction. The sign of the compass for north is just one example of the possible puns on language as first sign and then symbol; the South American Spanish have an expression: *tener un norte en la vida* and the implications are clear that the poet holds the north as a desirable direction in more than one way. The habit of "looking for a sign, is, of course, more developed than inherited although a certain set of mind is required. This set of mind is, again, reflected in the setting: the new shore shows "rock in the light and noon for see-

ing" as if every possible detail of the environment is visibly intensified by the sun at midday reflected off the blanched rock.

II

The general question of the spirit of Stafford's wilderness is raised by the inferences in the specific example. A set of descriptions of his state of nature emerges from which certain conclusions may be drawn. One clear element discernible in **"Returned to Say"** is the very palpable imagination of the forest; this wilderness of Stafford's truly has a life apart capable of producing an echo of its own mysterious personality in the actual figure of the Indian. The Indian here represents the nature that he seeks to know; the energy required for the resurrection of the spirit of nature must be enormous; it is the wilderness itself who has "returned to say" that what is mandatory in this city-plagued time is a return to nature. Nature then becomes the new chief as the Indian, at first lost and unsure, retrieves his confidence and merges with the spirit around him. Again, in this twentieth-century Renaissance, the harmony between body and spirit has been re-established and a direction toward integrity achieved. The beginning of the journey is blessed by the ritual of baptism: "we have drunk new water from an unnamed stream" and nourished by the peace of soul that characterizes the quiet of the line "Henceforth we gesture even by waiting."

As usual in Stafford and in most romantic poetry, nature is also somewhat dependent upon the state of mind and the state of activity of the men in the poem. Here, the noon brightness reflects the open vision of clarity that distinguishes the lucidity of this direction. The effect is dramatically anthropomorphic. In this poem also the drama depends upon the confrontation, the *meeting* of two people: "because we have met" is characteristically grand, majestic, definitive. The same reaction in nature to a meeting of two people appears in **"Glances"**:

> Two people meet. The sky turns winter,
> quells whatever they would say.
> Then, a periphery glance into danger—
> and an avalanche already on its way.

(11. 1-4)

The second stanza proceeds to explain how careful, how calculating these two people have always been; however, "they didn't know what it is to *meet*" and the italics are Stafford's. The romantic notion that a whole world can crumble at a glance supports the suspicion that the poet's world, though large and grand, is not so strong as the psychic bond behind two people, or that the spiritual bond created between men is supported by the physical and instinctively responsive force of nature. Such consequences to a single act of man are dangerous, like an avalanche, but man rides its force like the sea, looking firmly at the present, concentrating on the balance needed for the motion of the ride "calm and still on a speeding stone" (1. 14).

The form of the poem supports the theme behind this phenomenon of "meeting." The rhyme scheme is consistently either whole or slanted in the alternate lines. For instance, in the first stanza, the whole rhymes are *say* and *way*, the slanted *winter* and *danger*. In the third stanza, the rhymes are eye and slant: *gone, stone*, and *avalanche, stand*. But right in the center, the eye of the hurricane, *haste* and *waste* rhyme, but the two outstanding words of the poem, the words *lives* and *meet* do not conform, do not rhyme at all. Since *meet* is the only word in the poem that appears in italics and since it is the other word in the poem that does not rhyme, it is certain that the attention drawn to the word significantly intensifies the poetic description of the theme of encounter.

The wilderness in Stafford's poem is alternately active and passive; the degree of activity changes from poem to poem, and also sometimes within the same poem as the latent power of the wilderness emerges after a long wait. For instance, in **"Representing Far Places,"** the realization of the life of the universe occurs in the first stanza; it is necessary to quote the entire stanza in order to see the transformation take place:

> In the canoe wilderness branches wait for winter;
> every leaf concentrates; a drop from the paddle falls.
> Up through water at the dip of a falling leaf
> to the sky's drop of light or the smell of another star
> fish in the lake leap arcs of realization,
> hard fins prying out from the dark below.
>
> (11. 1-6)

The arc appears through the transformation of the extraordinary energy required to convert a passive mass into an active, moving force. The laws of physics govern both atoms of water and light, as well as the astronomical world of "the smell of another star" which turns out to be a star / fish emerging from the under-world of the sea, traveling through the dark. The ocean represents the "far place" of space just as the place of the poem represents the "far place" conjured up by the mind "in society when the talk turns witty" (1. 7). Then, "you think of that place, and can't polarize at all" (1. 8), can't, that is, locate the pole exactly, but the "land fans in your head / canyon by canyon" (11. 9-10) and the mind itself becomes a representation of not only far places but of the concept of place itself. Like a seventeenth-century cosmographical description of the human body, this twentieth-century cosmographical description of the human mind sees in "one little room an everywhere" as: "Representing far places you stand in the room . . . among contradictory ridges in some crescendo of knowing" (11. 11, 14).

The opposite also occurs frequently in Stafford, that is when the wilderness, the place, assumes human characteristics. In **"Traveling through the Dark,"** it is not only nature who responds instinctively to life, the fawn ready to be born inside a deer dead on the edge of the road, but also the mechanical world of the car that responds organically:

> The car aimed ahead its lowered parking lights;
> under the hood purred the steady engine.
> I stood in the glare of the warm exhaust turning red;
> around our group I could hear the wilderness listen.
>
> (11. 13-16)

The point of view very often, then, becomes what the words literally signify—the point of view from a particular place. You travel through the dark to reach the place and that intersection of the traveler and space becomes the X spot. In **"Elegy,"** the spots are marked as signs:

> At sight of angels or anything unusual
> you are to mark the spot with a cross,
> for I have set out to follow you
> and these marked places are expected,
> but in between I can hear no sound.
>
> (11. 36-42)

In **"Time's Exile"** the place is marked by sunflowers; they mark the meeting place, the original encounter between two people and as well the path of the traveler "who finds his way by sunflowers through the dark," in the last line of the poem. A "groove in the grass" marks one's **"Vocation"** so that the place again becomes the point of view and the vocation or task of the poet is to find the place and thus "to find what the world is trying to be," as that last line suggests. Sometimes the search is very subtle and strong, when, for instance, the magnetism of the spot repels the deer but draws the poet: "a fear peace, / where you always had to go to listen" (11. 16-17 **"The Thought Machine"**), and an exchange takes place between man and nature: after-wards, "the forehead / has the noble look that hill had" (1. 21). Again, although the title of **"Things We Did That Meant Something"** is very directive, the process of locating the place through color is very imaginative, delicate, and suggestive. In a very fine, precise way, the act is reminiscent of the geometrical process of finding the "locus"; the direction is haphazard but sure. The poet, for instance, tells us "I often glance at a winter color—/ husk or stalk, a sunlight touch" (11. 3-4) or maybe the color of a wasp nest in the bush "near the winter river with silt like silver" (1. 6). He tells us that he may get "lost" walking toward this color, and disap-pear on "the edge of a new knowing" (1. 2), but that is the risk of beauty as Charles Olson would say.

Other times, the parallel is much too obvious. Nature is alive and shouting in **"Requiem"** where: "A tree in the forest fell; the air remembered. / Two rocks clinked in the night to signal some meaning" (11. 3-4). Or, the point of view from the position of nature's animals is appalling: the view for example of the **"Chickens the Weasel Killed"** appealing to the ground with their wings, or **"The View from Here"** of the cold Antarctic penguins who, supposedly like Milton and like us, stand and wait. In **"Captive,"** the tiger at the zoo and the man watching him outside his cage change position and point of view as the bars of the cage melt into a pattern of stripes on the tiger's back.

Also somewhat weak but interesting from the point of view of originality and technique are the museum poems. The problem of writing poems about objects in a museum is that the objects themselves as works of art are already once removed from the concrete level of image, already abstracted from the senses to begin with. The phenomenon is like writing a poem about a painting or about a piece of music: the instinct is to *see* the object rather than write about it. But aside from that initial artistic problem, the point of view as technique is extraordinary: the objects are more capable of staring than Emily Dickinson's frozen nature: "Still faces on the wall: that look / the early camera gave—hold still for time" are opening lines for the perspective of **"The Museum at Tillamook."** The faces on the wall watch the traveler in the museum "looking history / back and forth." Then the perspective shifts back to the traveler describing the men who belong to the faces: Joe Champion first white settler, with his carved cradles, one for the baby and the other for the grain. "Where's his grave," Stafford asks, and you see the figure, the wax ghost of the settler for the first time perhaps as an unburied corpse, a purgatorial soul wandering through the museums of the world. A grave in the form of a canoe—"canoe or coffin"—*does* appear then to demonstrate the flood of '49 and the eyes of one of the old men stare at something "above the camera: the eyes go back" (1. 23).

The very macabre tableau of the historical cycle of life and death is paralleled by a tableau of natural history on the next floor:

> Upstairs other creatures from the wild
> have gathered—cold, natural scenes: an owl of snow,
> a wolf with clear eyes looking down over the blown
> birds' eggs, through the floor
>
> . . . . .
>
> into Joe's hollow tree
>
> (11.24-29)

The reproduction of the natural scene suggests what probably originally took place as the natural scene watches the settlers, and the settlers in turn attempt to protect themselves against the natural forces: animals, winter, hunger, flood, death.

Somewhat less effective—lacking the two dimensional vision of the tunneled watching hole through the floor

to the tree—is the poem **"In the Museum."** The speaker puts a talisman, a shard, a relic, a fragment, into the hand of his companion and the effect is supposedly like that of radium—the waves of energy and association circle out in ripples from the center. The idea is fine, but the chosen metaphor and closing lines are weak: "Let one by one things come alive like fish / and swim away into their future waves."

The shard in **"In the Night Desert"** is much more of a talisman although Stafford does not say so. Instead, its power appears in its effects, in the ordering of the night desert behind its back and in the analogy with language which gives the energy to the relic: the "Apache word for love" is a "talk-flake / chipped like obsidian," so strong that, once said, it is never said again, the tongue so twisted and numb, the desert so placed out of the way that it can never interfere again. The magic talisman, the ancient Indian word for love, controls person and place through time; lesser words succumb to time and the desert like dead Indians: "one / more word that spins / In the dust." (11. 5-7). Although the colon after this dust introduces the "talk-flake," it is the word for love Stafford is talking about and the colon represents antithesis rather than similarity. Here the talisman is strange and alive, twisting like a tornado, powerful as the empty space of silence when missing. Its setting is out-of-doors, and since that is Stafford's special place, it could be the contributing reason for the poem's success.

Again, **"The Old Hamer Place"** is effective because the natural scene claims the abandoned house. The old place is haunted by the animals rushing the house, crashing into the hills, by the "moaning / seasons" wandering through the room, by the shadows of living nature that grow in the dark. The place is vulnerable to nature because it is so hollow, so deserted, so like a "night desert." So even the poet can cause the place to fall:

> I touch that wall, collapsing it there where
> no one knows, by the quavering owl sound
> in a forest no one knows.
>
> (11. 16-18)

But at the same time the place is fragile for collapse, it is also open for restoration and can "come shuddering back" at a magic touch. "A place that / changed is a different place" says the poet but the process of change allows the object to become its former self—sliding back or forward along the same nerve. In the same way, the poet can touch these places in his mind and find them: Stafford is no projectionist; the places that he conjures up in his mind as a look-out from which to view the world are real, have names like **"The Old Hamer Place."**

Stafford's strongest places, however, are those which are not so visible, not so well named although in fact they are very palpable to and locatable by the imagination. Like **"Returned to Say," "A Look Returned"** represents a borderline between one world and another. Between two states "where Montana meets Alberta" lies the "border of October," or the beginning of change from one season to another. Between the grass and the sky the border is drawn, but the line is imperceptible: "a hill twisted the line / of the seamless land" and "clouds correct the fence's stance" (11. 8-9-10). This is the day relating "winter's province to the state" (1. 7) so that each territory is clear but none is defined. The same "wild" country appears in **"Late Thinker"** where the "pale fields meet winter" (1. 33); two unequal states meet, and the meeting is dynamically uneven. All that the two states ever share is the condition of neighborhood: two countries share the common quality of being next to each other as two seasons and two people. But as Stafford suggests, good fences do *not* make good neighbors, and in this attempt to "find a place" in "unlikely places" as he says in **"In Dear Detail, by Ideal Light,"** sometimes it is necessary to stand right on the border, right at the edge, right at the intersection where two things meet and nothing exists really by itself. This is the **"Late Thinker"** again hiding in the woods with the fern or hiding behind the map like the northern state afraid of cold and curled behind the paper of the map to avoid the wind and snow. The speaker too, like a tree that acts out what is happening to it in **"At Cove on the Crooked River,"** holds the map before his face and looks and hides at the same time, stalking place like the sun in Lake Chelan, dodging peaks of mountains like an intruder trespassing on forbidden ground. This traveler moves like an instinctive natural force but reads the map like the map reads him. The **"Look Returned"** then is continual as the relationship between man and nature knows no end, as the hands of nature—the swirling snow—touch the face of man in a prototypal Stafford interchange of attributes, as the poem closes:

> But that state so north it curled behind
> the map in hands of snow and wind,
> clutching the end of no place—
> I hold that state before my face,
> and learn my life.
>
> (11.16-20)

The one dimension of place left so far only slightly touched is time; Stafford's poetry, like obedient twentieth-century poetry, sees time as an extension of space so that a certain time in fact becomes a place. In **"The Only Card I Got on My Birthday Was from an Insurance Man,"** the point of view is from the fixed position of a star: "on a line meridian high / state by state my birthday star comes on / and peers" (11. 2-4). Just as "peers" puns on the point of view from the peering star and the contemporary view of his "peers," "Past its light" also suggests that past is a time as well as a space and the dark well of time is a double representation of time and space like the spoked wheel that turns both the clock and the weather. A candle "marks" the instant of birth like a star marks space. By the end of the poem the deep well of space has merged with the well of time until the space traveler can say: "Who travel these lonely wells can drink that star"; the line is separate from the rest of the poem and closes it. The speaker has found a birthday place and any strong enough to do the same can follow and watch. The whole world could fall away but like the speakers in **"Before the Big Storm,"** the actors are quiet at the moment of expectation, at the edge of the town.

John Lauber (essay date spring 1974)

SOURCE: Lauber, John. "World's Guest—William Stafford." *Iowa Review* 5, no. 2 (spring 1974): 88-100.

[*In the following essay, Lauber explores Stafford's sense of awe and reverence toward nature, an attitude toward the earth that Lauber maintains has not been seen in American literature since Henry David Thoreau.*]

The poetry of William Stafford is rooted in a series of natural pieties rare in contemporary life or literature: piety toward the earth itself, toward the region, the home, the parents, toward one's total past.[1] First, the essential, piety toward the earth. Has it been *fully* felt by anyone in America (except Thoreau!) since the Indian? White American man has cut himself off from his past, racial as well as personal, and from the earth—maybe you cannot possess one without the other. To discover that past, to find man at one with the earth in America, Stafford must turn to the Indian:

> Under the killdeer cry
> our people hunted all day
> graying toward winter, their lodges
> thin to the north wind's edge.
>
> Watching miles of marsh grass
> take the supreme caress,
> they looked out over the earth,
> and the north wind felt like the truth.
>
> Fluttering in that wind
> they stood there on the world,
> clenched in their own lived story
> under the killdeer cry.
>
> **("Our People,"** *RY* [*The Rescued Year*], 50)

Aided by the aptness of the bird's name, the opening lines imply much: hunters signalling with bird calls (a thin and piping sound, always on the verge of fading out), and an occupation that not only supported life but was life for them. They see the land as animate, receiving the caress which may be that of the wind, or of

God. It is a supreme caress because it is the last, presaging winter, which is also the winter of their culture. "Fluttering in that wind" implies their exposure and vulnerability to wind and cold, and a kind of insubstantiality in themselves, about to fade from history. "Clenched in their own lived story," they have lived their time and sense it; "clenched" expresses tautness and completion. And the poem completes itself by returning to its opening, in keeping with the cycle of the seasons and of their lives which it implies. Half-rhyme and regular stanza form contribute to a sense of the ceremonial and elegiac, providing a formal dignity which combines with clear images to avoid the easy sentimentality.

Stafford's fullest image of a completely natural man, whose identity is inseparable from the earth on which he lives, is found in **"The Concealment: Ishi, the Last Wild Indian."** The last survivor of his tribe, living his primitive life in early twentieth-century California, Ishi succeeded for years in hiding all traces of his existence:

> A rock, a leaf, mud, even the grass
> Ishi the shadow man had to put back where it was.
> In order to live, he had to hide that he did.
>
> (*RY*, 56-57)

in which he is the exact opposite of modern man, especially modern California man.

With beautiful economy the poem presents the physical elements of Ishi's life and his relationship to them:

> Erased
> footprints, berries that purify the breath, rituals
> before dawn with water.

Here is an attitude that transcends the utilitarian—berries purify, water is sacramental as well as thirst-quenching. While Stafford is no primitivist, he sees the life of natural man as significantly more than "nasty, brutish, and short." Discovered and uprooted from his world (though humanely treated), Ishi soon died. The poem is suffused with pathos, both for this archaic and doomed survivor and by implication for ourselves, who have lost what he had.

To be rooted means also to be rooted in one's own past, and in poem after poem Stafford discovers, recreates, and accepts his parents, his relatives, his high school classmates, his town, the farms around it. **"The Rescued Year"** (a phrase that sums up the intent of much of Stafford's work) is the title both of a book and of a poem that explores a year from the poet's boyhood. In a pair of images it creates the Depression on the prairie:

> That Christmas Mother made paper
> presents; we colored them with crayons
> and hung up a tumbleweed for a tree

and culminates in a remembrance of the father: "In all his ways I hold that rescued year."

The memory of the father, a man close to the earth ("He lived by trapping and hunting / wherever the old slough ran"—**"Some Shadows,"** *A* [*Allegiances*], 4), in but not quite of the prairie towns in which the family lives, dominates many of these poems. Adolescent rebellion is absent; the father appears not as rival or oppressor, but as teacher, initiator, gift-bearer, and the gift he brings is a way of perceiving or of being in the world:

> My father could hear a little animal step,
> or a moth in the dark against the screen,
> and every far sound called the listening out
> into places where the rest of us had never been.
>
> (**"Listening,"** *RY*, 27)

It is a poem about perception, not as a passive receiving but as a search (the listening goes out), and the father seems a kind of primordial poet, whose own perceptions remain unverbalized. "Inviting the quiet by turning the face," he scents and he hears the easily overlooked, the small and the distant.

The prairie town itself, the town of an adolescent boy, appears typically in **"Garden City."** Given that title, we expect irony or sentimentality; Stafford provides neither:

> That town, those days, composed grand
> arching pictures down by the river.
> A cloud or a girl strayed by. Any storm
> was temporary. Those hills to the south
> rush into the lens, emboss the world;
> and I can see so well that the hawks grow
> pin feathers. Our class picnic
> blossoms in ribbons and watermelons.
>
> (*A*, 38)

This is an active rather than a passive vision. Verbs animate the landscape, give life to the stanza; the hills "rush" and "emboss the world." That unexpected "emboss" provides a roughness of texture that the poem requires to save itself from its own charm. But the world of class picnics, ribbons and watermelons, seen without mockery or condescension, is part of Stafford's rescued past.

The prairie culture receives definitive statement, and full comprehension, in **"One Home,"** a key poem in the Stafford canon:

> Mine was a Midwest home—you can keep your world.
> Plain black hats rode the thoughts that made our code.
> We sang hymns in the house; the roof was near God.
>
> The light bulb that hung in the pantry made a wan
>   light,

but we could read by it the names of preserves—
outside, the buffalo grass, and the wind in the night.

A wildcat sprang at Grandpa on the Fourth of July
when he was cutting plum bushes for fuel,
before Indians pulled the West over the edge of the
sky.

To anyone who looked at us we said, "My friend":
liking the cut of a thought, we could say, "Hello."
(But plain black hats rode the thoughts that made our
code.)

The sun was over our town; it was like a blade.
Kicking cottonwood leaves we ran toward storms.
Wherever we looked the land would hold us up.

                                        (*RY,* 18-19)

There's not only a statement of theme but a gesture of defiance in the opening line, no doubt in recognition of the long-continuing Revolt Against the Prairie in American literature. The poem deliberately avoids fashionable literary clichés, at the risk of falling into old-fashioned, sentimental ones: "We sang hymns in the house," or "To anyone who looked at us we said, 'My friend.'" It's saved by the directness and simplicity of its language (which is yet witty and unexpected in "before Indians pulled the West over the edge of the sky"), by that grotesquely appropriate detail of the wildcat's spring—on the Fourth of July!—and above all by one line, "Plain black hats rode the thoughts that made our code." For all its absolute simplicity of diction, the line is richly suggestive, both of stereotypes and of realities. The monosyllables are appropriate to the culture as a whole and to the tradition of Western taciturnity. The cowboy is implied, but without glamour; the plain black hats connote starkness of life and of thought.

In the repetition at the end of the fourth stanza, "but" makes all the difference, instantly suggesting the limitations of thought, belief and action implied by the image, and showing that the poet is quite as well aware of them as we are. With that reassurance, and with the harshness of "blade" and "storm," we can accept the sense of oneness with the land, and resulting security, given by the final line. This poem offers something better than a drearily predictable rebellion—it offers understanding.

"Stafford country" includes the farms and little towns of the plains during the Depression (the period is important; his attitude differs radically when dealing with contemporary America) and also the Northwest where he has lived since 1948, teaching at a small college in Portland, Oregon. His region, in fact, is simply the American West with its plains and deserts and mountains and rivers, its farms and its towns (but rarely its cities), its highways and railroads, its animals and its plants, and its people from the Indian to contemporary man.

"At Cove on the Crooked River" states the relationship between modern man and the Western scene:

At Cove at our camp in the open canyon
it was the kind of place where you might look out
some evening and see trouble walking away.

And the river there meant something
always coming from snow and flashing around
    boulders
after shadow-fish lurking below the mesa.

We stood with wet towels over our heads for shade,
looking past the Indian picture rock and the kind of
    trees
that act out whatever has happened to them.

Oh civilization, I want to carve you like this,
decisively outward the way evening comes
over that kind of twist in the scenery

When people cramp into their station wagons
and roll up the windows, and drive away.

                (*TD* [*Traveling through the Dark*], 81)

A cove is a harbor, a place of rest and refuge, and these connotations are important. "Crooked" is unexpected, and the alliteration of "Cove" and "Crooked" adds a harshness of sound that's apt for the desert setting. Syntax is leisurely and colloquial ("At Cove . . . it was the kind of place"). Diction too is colloquial, appropriate to the homely personification of "and see trouble walking away." The first stanza is raised above the prosaic by only a few details: the hard c's and emphatic rhythm of the opening line, the faint image of the third. In stanza 2, simultaneously the images become more particularized and the scope of the poem expands to show the course of the river from its beginning. The "Indian picture rock" and the "trees that act out whatever has happened to them" are (like this poem) records of and responses to the setting; they introduce a human continuity between past and present as well as a continuity between the human and natural response to the environment. They also provide models for the poet to follow, as shown by "carve" in the next stanza.

With the invocative "Oh civilization," the poem heightens in emotion and generalizes in significance. "Carve" simultaneously implies the hardness of the landscape and refers back to the incised pictures on the rock. It means both to carve an image of the poet's civilization and to carve the civilization itself into the desired shape. Evening ends the day and the poem as stanza 4, not self-contained like the earlier ones, flows into the final couplet with its ironic image of visitors "cramping into their station wagons and rolling up their windows," shutting out everything the poem has presented before they escape it completely by driving away. "Cramping" is immensely suggestive.

"The Move to California," a sequence of five poems in *The Rescued Year,* presents a modern version of the archetypal American experience—the journey West, including visions of heaven and hell. The tone is neither illusioned nor disillusioned; the poet is equally aware of promise and reality. The move begins with **"The Summons in Indiana"** (a casual, modern summons by "an angel of blown newspaper") and reaches an unclimactic climax, the Great Divide, in **"At the Summit."** Instead of the sweeping vista of cliché, the reader is offered the unexpected image of "a little tree just three feet high" that "shared our space between the clouds." The true climax occurs in the fourth poem, **"Springs Near Hagerman"**:

> Water leaps from lava near Hagerman,
> piles down riverward over rock
> reverberating tons of exploding shock
>   out of that stilled world.

The startlingly active opening ("water *leaps* from lava"), the strongly rhythmical five-beat lines, the careful alliteration of r's and hard consonants (d's and t's), and the fusion of mass, energy and sound in "reverberating tons of exploding shock" communicate enormous power. In the final stanza the springs offer a vision and a promise: "At work when I vision that sacred land . . . I go blind with hope." The word "sacred" is rare in Stafford, and gains force accordingly.

But the paradisal vision is instantly balanced by an infernal one, in **"Along Highway 40"**:

> Those who wear green glasses through Nevada
> travel a ghastly road in unbelievable cars
> and lose pale dollars
> under violet hoods when they park at gambling houses.

There is a movement from water to drought, from hope to satire, although the final stanza offers escape: "I crossed the Sierras in my old Dodge . . . and slept in the wilderness on the hard ground." That rough contact with physical reality is necessary, after the tourists who insulate themselves completely from it.

The title of the last poem, **"Written on the Stub of the First Paycheck,"** ironically indicates arrival, the goal achieved.

> Gasoline makes game scarce.
> In Elko, Nevada, I remember a stuffed wildcat
> someone had shot on Bing Crosby's ranch.
> I stood in the filling station
> breathing fumes and reading the snarl of a map.

Anticlimax? Undoubtedly. Betrayal of the American dream? Hardly anything so melodramatic. "Gasoline makes game scarce" sums up the development of the modern West, while the vanished Old West is commemorated by the stuffed wildcat, shot on a movie star's ranch. The conclusion is deliberately ambiguous, passing no judgment. "We moved into a housing tract"—the

ultimate flatness and boredom of modern America. But "every dodging animal carries my hope in Nevada," so at least dodging animals and hope survive.

"In California," published in *The Southern Review* (Spring, 1971) provides a sequel and an allegory of modern America.

> Someone is running.
> Someone has to get somewhere.
> He is running to stay the same.
> The rest of the world runs with him.
> Women are taking turns to be with him,
>   to try to be real.
>
> Each of them runs and then finds
> It is another man she is with.
> They all run faster and faster.
> It is America, and everyone
> is finding Today somewhere in the sound
>   or breath or touch of Tomorrow.
>
> They all tell each other their dreams,
> then draw slowly apart. All their
> dance adds to a solemn sway in their cities.
> Away out in the evening the orchards
> and fields hold still and grow. Their steady
>   green follows the sunset down.

That anonymous "someone" instantly establishes tone and theme. In his anonymity, he is the representative modern man; his running, seeming to exist purely for its own sake, gives the effect of a looking-glass race. The stanza moves by jerks, with almost every line a complete sentence; diction is the simplest possible. The effect is of primer-style, of the Dick and Sally of a first-grade reader (individualized only in their names) nominally grown up. The search is for Reality, or Identity, doomed from the start because the goal is placed outside the self, in the nonexistent: "finding Today . . . in the sound / or breath or touch of Tomorrow." The answer would be to find Today in today, and this is a function of poetry—to restore us to the present, which is all that can exist. Those who "live in the future" are of course living in the present (they cannot live anywhere else) but are living in fantasies and abstractions. If the human movement, seen from a distance, appears to gain solemnity from its sheer mass, it's promptly placed by the reference to orchards and fields (which both hold still and grow, unlike the humans who do neither) and to their "steady green"— the only steadiness present. The poem ends with the colors of life—green and the red of the sunset—and the natural cycle of the sun replacing the futile running of the earlier stanzas.

"Our car was fierce enough; / no one could tell we were only ourselves" (**"The Trip,"** *TD,* 72). The modern American seeks his own reality in possessions and in the image of himself that possessions create. Even the prairie town has changed, and its present condition requires almost surrealistic metaphors:

Here in our cloud we talk
baking powder. Our yeast feet
make tracks that fill up with fog.
Tongue like a sponge, we describe
the air that we eat—how it has its own
lungs, inhales many a stranger.

The images have a nearly metaphysical consistency, but lack the metaphysical rationality. It is suggestion that counts—suggestions of unreality, ineffectuality, softness, blurredness, loss of clarity, all somehow devouring. Beneath the softness, violence proceeding from fear. The poem concludes with a double explosion:

Overhead planes mutter our fear
and are dangerous, are bombs exploding
a long time, carrying bombs elsewhere to explode.

That explosion, at least, is real.

Modern poets habitually deal in apocalypse and Stafford is no exception, though his are characteristically quiet— "soft apocalypses," one might call them, yet they can be sweeping, too. **"The Epitaph Ending in And"** suggests a total, not merely a human, destruction:

In the last storm, when hawks
blast upward and a dove is
driven into the grass, its broken wings
a delicate design, the air between
wracked thin where it stretched before,
a clear spring bent close too often
(that Earth should ever have such wings
burnt on in blind color!), this will be
good as an epitaph:

Doves did not know where to fly, and

The soft and the hard, the weak and the strong, the gentle and the cruel—all these contrasts are implied in the contrast of hawks and doves, and are reinforced by their fates. Verbs beginning lines ("blast," "driven," "wracked," "burnt") suggest an irresistible destructive force, with a resulting delicate pathos: "The earth should ever have such wings / burnt on in blind color" (in which line division works interestingly, as the wings seem momentarily to belong to the earth). The poem leaves one with questions. "Doves did not know where to fly": to escape destruction? Does the statement apply to all past time? The ending is tantalizing, frustrating— but there is no more to say, as one realizes after trying to say it.

But the pure apocalyptic stance is rare in Stafford, perhaps because it seems to require a self-dramatization that's alien to him, perhaps because in its purity it tends to be completely destructive; **"From the Gradual Grass"** (which might have been called "The Two Voices," if Wordsworth hadn't pre-empted the title) contrasts the apocalyptic in this sense with the affirmative. The first voice seems to exist only to announce

itself ("Imagine a voice calling, / 'There is a voice now calling'") and to create the conditions it prophesies ("'Walls are falling!' / as it makes walls be falling"). The theme is suggested by form as well; circularity is created by repetition as the voice does what it announces. The poem continues, to proclaim a second voice "from the gradual grass . . . making words, a voice: / Destruction is ending . . . *That voice is calling.*" Indeed it is, it is the voice of Stafford's poetry.

"Apocalypse" need not be always or only destructive, a fact which those who use the word freely often forget. It implies also a making new or a seeing of all things as new, and Stafford's **"Summer Will Rise"** presents this regenerative process with a dionysiac abandon unique in his work:

Summer will rise till the houses fear;
streets will hear underground streams;
purple, the banished color, will flare.
This is the town where the vine will come.

People will listen but will not hear.
Eyes will wizen to find a friend.
When no one is watching the candleflame
this is the town where the wind will come.

The trees will hear, farther than winter,
over the town a coming of birds.
What great wild hands will reach for them?
*—and for all who are here when those wanderers
come?*

It's a poem that gains from being read in context; only then can one appreciate, for example, the startling contrast of "purple, the banished color" to Stafford's favorite grays and browns.

There's a potentially frightening movement as the unknown and the repressed invade the town—the area of the human—and take possession. But perhaps what comes is akin to the human, or a part of the human which the town has banished. The invasion therefore is joyful, a joy communicated by the lilting anapests of the refrain. After the initial, shriveled response implied by "wizen," the poem reaches its emotional climax in the last stanza as the rising current is embodied in the "coming of birds." What hands?—or whose?—one might ask—but should not. It's enough that they reach for trees, for birds, for townspeople, for "all who are here" to shelter and protect.

Again and again the poems approach a moment of intense realization, hinting at a possible Reality that we could reach—or that could reach us—if only we would open ourselves to it. In **"Remember"** the goal is nearly attained in the unlikely setting of a "sheep town, say, in Nevada":

That was almost, through quiet, the time:
the world stilled for dawn.

As the poem admits, "Nothing was new," yet "the horizon gained something / more than color." What was gained, if not a true epiphany, was a realization of its possibility that is in itself transforming. The poet achieves escape from the ego, from the daily routine, into a sense of something beyond the self, or perhaps in the self—a different way of perceiving.

And what would the world be like, if we could once realize it fully? **"Earth Dweller"** gives an answer:

> It was all the clods at once become
> precious; it was the barn, and the shed,
> and the windmill, my hands, the crack
> Arlie made in the axe handle . . .
>
>   . . . . .
>
> . . . somewhere inside, the clods are
> vaulted mansions, lines through the barn sing
> for the saints forever, the shed and windmill
> rear so glorious the sun shudders like a gong.

The experience is of ecstasy, the ecstasy that results when, as Blake writes in *The Marriage of Heaven and Hell,* "My senses discovered the infinite in everything." Gaining power from the unexpected "shudders," the last two lines reach an intensity of affirmation unequalled anywhere else in Stafford's poetry. In its imagery the stanza may suggest Thomas, or Traherne in his *Centuries of Meditation* ("The corn was orient and immortal wheat . . . The dust and stones of the street were as precious as gold . . . Eternity was manifest in the light of the day"). But the conclusion is pure Stafford in its sober naturalism:

>   the world speaks.
> The world speaks everything to us.
> It is our only friend.

As Stafford has written in prose, "We hear each other but we do not hear the earth." The poet opens his senses to the influences of the earth, he speaks for it, he comes as one **"Representing Far Places"** (to borrow the title of a poem from *Traveling Through the Dark*) to remind us of winter and cold and storm and dark, and of something more too. He faces those storms for us, strengthens us to face them ourselves. Stafford is a traditional poet, in the basic Romantic tradition of the last century and three quarters. Poetry not only shares its perceptions with us, but teaches us to perceive, or to induce perception: "inviting the quiet by turning the face." The image of the father in that poem (**"Listening"**) must also be an image of the poet:

> More spoke to him from the soft wild night
> than came to our porch for us on the wind;
> we would watch him look up and his face go keen
> till the walls of the world flared, widened.

That incredibly compressed final line simultaneously presents a perceiving in all its elements and identifies perception with the world itself—a world actively cre-

ated for each of us by his own senses. Which is not to say that reality is arbitrary or capricious. "The world speaks everything to us," and it can only speak through the senses.

But if Stafford writes in a Romantic tradition, he lives in an unromantic age, as he's very well aware. In **"Near"** he characteristically deals with the predicament of the modern poet by exemplifying it:

> Walking along in this not quite prose way
> we both know it is not quite prose we speak
> and it is time to notice this intolerable snow
> innumerably touching, before we sink.
>
> It is time to notice, I say, the freezing snow
> hesitating toward us from its gray heaven:
> listen—it is falling not quite silently
> and under it still you and I are walking.
>
> Maybe there are trumpets in the houses we pass
> and a redbird watching from an evergreen—
> but nothing will happen until we pause
> to flame what we know, before any signal's given.

Sound reinforces meaning in the heavy clumping of accents on the last four words of the opening line. The first and second lines pair off, one concerned with the rhythm of poetry, the other with its content. That content is a world of blurred imprecision, an effect reinforced by the snow that follows. The abstract modifiers "intolerable" and "innumerably" heighten emotional intensity, raising the stanza above the prosaic, and imply the symbolic nature of the poem. The first two stanzas offer a world of gray (the only color named), of cold, of "not quite." Even the snow doesn't do anything as forceful as falling; it is only "hesitating toward us." The trumpets enter as abruptly as in Eliot's "A Cooking Egg" ("Where are the eagles and the trumpets? / Buried beneath some snow-deep Alps"). But the poem is no pastiche; the image of the redbird in the evergreen (colors of life again) belongs to a poetic world very different from Eliot's. Only in the last line is there a really active verb, "flame"—both destructive and life-giving. "To flame what we know"—that is, in unsatisfying abstract terms, to affirm our individuality, our desires, our tie to the earth, our *life,* and to do so spontaneously ("before any signal's given"). Nothing could be more remote from Eliot, or indicate more clearly Stafford's essential romanticism.

Understatement no doubt reflects the poet's personality. It is also strategic; Stafford seems to hold a Wordsworthian distrust of "rhetoric." He would surely accept Wordsworth's opinion (so much more true of our age!) that "a multitude of causes, unknown to former times, are now acting with a combined force to blunt the discriminating powers of the mind, and . . . to reduce it to a state of almost savage torpor," and the conclusion that to rouse the mind from its savage torpor is a major function of poetry. This arousal is to be achieved by encouraging the mind to exert its powers of subtle discrimination and of response to delicate stimuli through a poetry of calculated understatement.

The result is a style that might be called "minimum writing," corresponding exactly to the "minimum living" recommended by the poetry:

> The earth says every summer have a ranch
> that's minimum: one tree, one well, a landscape
> that proclaims a universe.

("**In Response to a Question,**" *TD,* 33)

Verse forms approach the traditional (Stafford has even written a few unrhymed sonnets), rhyme appears occasionally, rhythms tend to be clearly patterned. Images draw attention to themselves by their rightness to the occasion and their precision of detail rather than by the shock of surprise. The diction itself is remarkably "pure"; that is, nontechnical and unspecialized, neither highbrow nor lowbrow, neither aggressively contemporary nor "literary" and conventional. In other words, *central.* Not the language that educated people speak, but the language one wishes they spoke. It's likely to sound surprisingly modern to readers of the twenty-first century. Syntax too has an air of disarming simplicity but may conceal a good deal of artfulness, as with the suspended structure and meaning of the opening participial phrase in **"Near,"** or the careful progression of "walking," "touching," "freezing," "falling."

Asked by an interviewer whether he saw any "recurring patterns of ideas" in his own work, Stafford answered that "one of the elements is not a pattern of ideas, but a feeling of coziness or a feeling of being at home. It's like the delight of having shelter in a storm or it's like the feeling of becoming oriented where you've been temporarily disoriented." That final clause brings to mind Frost's famous definition of a poem as "a momentary stay against confusion," but here confusion, rather than clarity, is seen as the temporary state. The unknown, the nonhuman, are constantly present, and their power is admitted, but the poetry does not assume that they are finally inimical. As Stafford has put it, in his closest approach to a prose poetic (the essay "At Home," *Hudson Review,* Autumn, 1970): "In the world where what is outside man extends into mystery, awe, worship, respect, reverence—poetry, *the stance that accepts,* may be salvational. The psyche may depend on limitation, recurrence, stability, as do organic processes." But acceptance is no good if it's not believable. To be more than a platitude, it must include and give full weight to both sides: winter-spring, darkness-light, cold-warmth, transience-permanence, separation-unity. Stafford's poetry does, and doing so constructs an image of man at one with himself and with the earth (and everything that word implies), feeling toward it an awe

and a reverence, and extending that piety toward his own nature—refusing to mutilate himself by uprooting himself from his past or by cutting his ties to the earth and living in machines and abstractions. It's not surprising to hear Stafford say that poetry comes easily, that there is never a morning when he can't write. Making poetry, for him, is a matter of opening the self to the self and to the world (denying any final separation between them) and of trusting the impulse that follows. The result is a poetry at once completely personal and uniquely free from egotism, a poetry that places man firmly within the world and finds its hope in that.

> World, I am your slow guest,
> one of the common things
>   that move in the sun and have
>   close, reliable friends
>   in the earth, in the air, in the rock.

Notes

1. Stafford has published five volumes of poetry to date: *West of Your City* (1960); *Traveling Through the Dark* (1962); *The Rescued Year* (1966); *Allegiances* (1970). The last three are abbreviated in my citations as *TD, RY* and *A.* (The best poems of *West of Your City* are reprinted in *The Rescued Year.*) His most recent volume is *Someday, Maybe* (1973).

Paul Zweig (essay date 1974)

SOURCE: Zweig, Paul. "The Raw and the Cooked." *Partisan Review* 41, no. 4 (1974): 604-12.

[*In the following essay, Zweig examines Stafford's* Someday, Maybe *and maintains that it represents a trend toward plain style and a refusal of rhetorical authority that contrasts with the poetry of his contemporary A. R. Ammons.*]

I

It has seemed at times as if the poetry of the 1960s spoke one language: simple, sensitive to conversational rhythms, and deliberately "unliterary." In order to be believed, it was felt, a poem had to create a feeling of honest talk. Indeed, a rhetoric of "honesty" developed, the main features of which were a slight clumsiness, the avoidance of culturally charged words in favor of common speech, and a rhythm of understatement, as if the poem's "honesty" required that it avoid a sense of authority. The poem was supposed to have "happened." It was not an artifact of words, but an outgrowth of the poet's integrity. The reader was meant to be surprised by leaps of insight emerging simply and vulnerably, as if a man were saying more than he thought he knew. This rhetoric of honesty exerted an enormous attraction on poets of the most varied gifts. The feeling seemed to be that language had to be held in check if it were not to lie; that language, the poet's only tool, was fundamentally untrustworthy. He had, therefore, to use it minimally. He had to write as if it were not language at all, but a pure transmission of intimacy, like Rousseau's language of hearts.

Along with this attitude toward language went a distrust of the sort of conceptual ambition which characterized the poetry of a preceding generation. Poets of the 1960s did not trust the reflective power of a Stevens or an Eliot. They chose humbler models, for example, Chinese poetry, with its mood of domestic mystery and unsophisticated emotions. This surely is an irony of cultural influence, since Chinese poetry is in fact highly conventional. The casual "honesty" of Tu Fu or Li Po is the result of a codified rhetoric, and not at all a "language of the heart." But, as Harold Bloom has argued, such misreadings are of the very nature of cultural influence.

A sustaining irony of this plain style, perhaps a source of the energy it released for so many poets, is political, though covertly and probably unconsciously so. The refusal of rhetorical authority, the humble rhythms of intimacy, the focus on fleeting moments and small perceptions, represents, perhaps, a distrust of power itself which was expressed in many other ways in the culture of the 1960s. As the nation had come to value control over the material world and coercive authority, enforced by the machines of war, its poets relinquished the material world and the language of power; they relinquished the public and historical realms, and retreated into the freedom of "inwardness." This relinquishment became a political act, issuing eventually into the political poetry of the late 1960s.

As with any language which settles into a code and a set of conventions, the conversational style of the 1960s has gradually discovered its limits. All too often "honesty" has become a formula, slack rhythms a vehicle for unfocused energy, smallness of perception a form of avoidance. The enormous release which many poets experienced in the early 1960s has been replaced by mannerisms of release.

This weakening of the language is apparent in William Stafford's new book, *Someday, Maybe.*[1] Stafford is one of the finest poets of the conversational style. His poems are limpid and controlled, with a sort of narrative plainness that recalls Robert Frost. Like Frost too, he writes out of an experience of America, in particular of the American Northwest, though rarely with the insistent localism which characterized other poets of the 1960s, who loaded their poems with folk history and picturesque place-names. For Stafford the American landscape is the embodiment of a way of seeing. It supplies a

solitary vastness crossed by languages which reach from one blind place to another; not only human languages, confined to the long loops of telephone wire which appear so often in Stafford's poems, but natural languages spoken by snowflakes, by echoes, by tumbleweed. Stafford's "language of hearts" speaks across the distance which separates man from his own created objects, and from nature, as in this poem from *The Rescued Year*:

> Some catastrophes are better than others.
> Wheat under the snow lived by blizzards
> that massacred stock on Uncle George's farm.
> Only telephone poles remember the place, and the
>   wire
> thrills a mile at a time into that intent blast
> where the wind going by fascinated whole
> millions of flakes and thousands of acres of tum-
>   bleweeds.

These connections come easily to Stafford. He perceives them with a child's immediacy, but a child who has grown older and learned to understand the irremediable quality of distance. When he is at his best, Stafford's plain style has some of the feeling of folk stories and myth: it does not need complexities of language in order to create its vision, because the vision belongs to the world the poet sees, and not to the poet himself.

These marvelous qualities are only sparsely present in *Someday, Maybe.* Instead, the simple language has become a mannerism. The transparent sense of myth or folktale has become a deliberate naïveté. There are too many lines in the book like these:

> A person mixing colors bends low
> when we walk there. "Why are you
> so intent on that bottle you are stirring?"
> And then I know: in that little bottle
> he has the sky.

and

> But many things in the world
> haven't yet happened. You help
> them by thinking and writing and acting.
> Where they begin, you greet them
> or stop them. You come along
> and sustain the new things.

This sounds like the sort of idea an adult would mistakenly invent to amuse a child. But the child would miss the point, because the images do not have the innocence of something "seen" for the first time. Although they try for that quality, they come up instead with commonplace statements and coy sentimentality. Much of *Someday, Maybe* fails in the same way. Here is another example of what I mean:

> One day Sun found a new canyon.
> It hid for miles and ran far away,

then it went under a mountain. Now Sun
goes over but knows it is there. And that
is why Sun shines—it is always looking.
Be like the sun.

The attempted myth creates no echoes here. The strained simplicity of the poem chokes it off before it can gather resonance. One need only recall Stafford's extraordinary myth poem in *The Rescued Year,* **"The Animal That Drank Up Sound,"** to see how powerfully this mode has worked for him in the past. But in *Someday, Maybe* the ideas fall limply on the page. One has the sense of a formula being offered, instead of a perception still damp with its birth-water.

But Stafford is too good a poet to be defined by his failures, even in a book as disappointing as *Someday, Maybe.* Here and there one comes upon poems which are as quietly startling as any Stafford has written. In the end, one feels that *Someday, Maybe* represents not so much a flagging of Stafford's powers as an editorial mistake, made all too easily because the convention of simple talk lay at hand, ready to speak on when the poet himself had fallen silent. Here is one of the wholly lovely poems in the book which must be added to the number of Stafford's finest; it is entitled, **"The Widow Who Taught at an Army School"**:

> *She planted bullets in a window box,*
> *lead tips up like a row of buds,*
> *and she told the children: "Every charge*
> *the Indians made was a dance for their horses,*
> *but serious men made the Gatling gun;*
> *its bullets come true forever—you go*
> *mad from shooting the gun.*
>
> *"From east of the mountains, from Daylight Lake,*
> *morning begins," she said,*
> *"and it loves us all; its edge opens the field.*
> *Children, let's sing 'Rescue Me, Day,'*
> *for we are all prisoners here."*
>
> *There are widows like that in many schools,*
> *and officers with eyes like badges*
> *that follow a look past the window box,*
> *ready for a dance but mad from the gun,*
> *and stare out over the field.*

II

In recent years, there has been a casting about for heroes in American life. Perhaps the anxious confusion of the period has caused among us a particularly great longing to relax into admiration. We want to bask in the stability of a great talent. We want to experience the steady, warming influence of genius. Because it is exhausting to have to make up one's mind every day, we are thankful that certain results endure. Shakespeare and his companions in the heaven of literature offer us secure ecstasies.

But this is an unstable time in America. Great men are tossed high, and brought low too quickly. The empyrean of heroes no longer hovers at a lovely distance. Instead of Fred Astaire, Clark Gable, and Greta Garbo, we have Dustin Hoffman and Jane Fonda, who are good, who are very good, but who are vulnerable, close enough to our grey level of confusion to cause a hint of envy; a suspicion that the difference between us and them is not genius, but luck. So our heroes don't last. Nixon soars to the heights and is shot down in months. Norman Mailer is scarcely anointed, when he skids into ridicule. The heaven of heroes refuses our burnt offerings.

In this respect the little world of poetry has reflected the larger world. Almost yearly another banquet is set, another talent is seated at the place of honor, another offering of praise is elaborately prepared, with overtones of reverence and grim respect. But there are no sustained hosannas, no beatitude of settled values. The subtle acids of doubt topple the celebration, and a year or two later the hero has subsided into the unfinishable labor of becoming a poet—a labor which he himself has never discontinued. But now we leave him to it, buying his books perhaps, but exhausted once again by the need to make up our minds. Alan Dugan, Robert Bly, James Wright, John Ashbery, W. S. Merwin, Allen Ginsberg, all have received the pomp of celebration only to be returned to the world of unfinished men. Robert Lowell lasted longer. The praise still billows around his knotty countenance, but there is less of it, and, apparently, less of him. John Berryman had his hour, and a second effort may be gathering now that he is not here to undermine it with the elaborate cunning of his drunkenness and despair. Sylvia Plath has lasted remarkably long, despite her sentimental partisans.

Meanwhile the table has been set again, and the guests are swarming. Another good poet has been declared hopefully, tentatively, major. The poet is A. R. Ammons, the occasion the publication last year of his *Collected Poems.*[2] Ammons has written a great deal. Although his *Collected Poems* are not complete—it leaves out a long poem, "Tape For the Turn of the Year," published several years ago as a separate volume—it represents almost four hundred pages, and Ammons's career is young.

Collection is the opposite of selection and, in the case of poetry, it is rarely to the poet's advantage. Few of us are Yeats or Baudelaire. In the past, most collections were done after the poet's death by scholars seeking to establish a historical document. But poets these days have taken to "collecting" themselves, and the result often blurs more than it clarifies the achievement of the work. In his collection, Ammons includes every moment and modulation of his talent: the luminous leafed in with the trivial, the carefully achieved with the self-indulgent, the too long with the too short. One has to wade through a great deal of tentative language before coming upon the fine sparse poems which represent

Ammons's best. But the labor is by no means all loss. The very shagginess and roughness of the collection forces the reader to become intimate with Ammons's elusive rhythms. One has the experience not so much of reading a work, as of entering into a process, in the course of which finished poems emerge, like pure crystals, their stony husk refined away. There is power in all of this. The roughness and profusion of Ammons's work becomes, somehow, a figure for his obsession; the sense of a process rushing brilliantly, though inconclusively forward is, finally, true to the idea of his poetry. As a result of sifting and panning all of this ore—a labor not without tedium—one understands, finally, why Ammons's turn at the banquet table has come.

At a time when the limits of the conversational style have come to be felt more and more strongly, Ammons offers, in great abundance, precisely those qualities neglected during the 1960s: intricate language and conceptual ambition. Reading through many of his longer poems, one is impressed by Ammons's attempt to connect a density of style reminiscent of Gerard Manley Hopkins, with an elaborate reflective framework which recalls Wallace Stevens. The echo of Stevens is inevitable, since Ammons's main concern is to articulate a philosophy of perception which must be simultaneously argued and demonstrated in the poetry. The main point of Ammons's conception seems to be his view that the mind and the world are joined together in a seamless intricacy. It is not simply that the mind and the world mirror each other, for mirrors contain settled forms, they connect but they also interpose limits. Like Alice, the poet has solved the surface of the mirror. He perceives, and renders in language, the interpenetrating gusts of movement by which the mind and the world make each other whole. As Ammons writes in "Corsons Inlet":

> I have reached no conclusions, have erected no bound-
> aries,
> shutting out and shutting in, separating inside
>   from outside: I have
>   drawn no lines:
>   as
>
> manifold events of sand
> change the dune's shape that will not be the same
>   shape
> tomorrow,
>
> so I am willing to go along, to accept
> the becoming
> thought, to stake off no beginnings or ends, establish
>   no walls:

This is Ammons at his clearest, yet somehow not at his best. The statement he makes is accurate enough: the aim of his poetry is not finishing, but unfinishing; it is to cut the world loose from the illusion of settled forms, and set it flowing in the ever new flood of perception.

His words cascade irregularly on the page in a mimetism of released energy. The "idea" is there all right. But the poetry is cold, the experience, for all its intricacy, is thin. And here is Ammons's gravest fault. All too often he fails to connect the conceptual framework of the poem with the local effects of his language. This is especially true in the early work, but it remains true of his longer, more ambitious poems throughout. His images turn moments of experience into sensuous complexities; Hopkins-like compressions of syntax offer the reader "a hundred sensations a second," as Ammons remarks. But a gap yawns between this brilliant seething of impressions and the overarching discourse which Ammons intends as his "idea of order." Between sensuous mimetism and cold philosophy there is a space, which Ammons does not fill often enough. But the space between is where we live. It is where the "idea" thickens into passion, where passions clarify into thought and perception. "Corsons Inlet" and "Saliences" are often cited as examples of Ammons's conceptual power. We are invited by critics to think of Wordsworth in "Tintern Abbey," of Emerson, of Eliot's discursive passages in "Four Quartets." But "Corsons Inlet" is governed by windy and abstract rhetoric, as in the passage quoted above. The poem begins crisply enough, with a description of the poet walking along a beachfront, exploring the uncertain margin between land and sea, reflecting on the perpetual movement which dissolves shapes through an alchemy of slow transitions, as the sand dune simultaneously stands and blows away, as the tide is a tireless alternation of land and water. But the landscape is quickly dimmed by the fog of meaning which Ammons projects upon it. Ammons's power of perception, his most brilliant quality, lapses into a compromise which is neither sensuous, nor especially thoughtful either:

> in nature there are few sharp lines: there are areas of
> primrose
>   more or less dispersed;
> disorderly orders of bayberry; between the rows
> of dunes,
> irregular swamps of reeds,
> though not reeds alone, but grass, bayberry, yarrow,
> all . . .
> predominantly reeds:

Academic critics like Harold Bloom and Geoffrey Hartman have been partly responsible for the enlarged interest in Ammons's work. *Diacritics*, a university magazine devoted to literary theory, recently published an entire issue on Ammons. One is happy for this renewed interest on the part of the academy for poets and for poetry. Bloom's and Hartman's enthusiasm for Ammons probably reflects their sense of a failure in the antirhetorical poetry of the past decade. After years of a poetic style which militated against ideas and repudiated conceptual ambition, they found in Ammons a poet both thoughtful and complex, whose work invites the sort of critical scrutiny which the great works of modernism also invited. Like Stevens, Pound, and Eliot, Ammons in his poetry demands explication. And let us be reminded, explication is not simply a form of detached analysis. It is a mode of reading required by, and appropriate to, complex poems. As practiced by the great critics of modernism—Blackmur, Empson—it becomes a form of intellectual ascesis, mobilizing the passions of thought in an activity akin to the methods of meditation about which Louis Martz has written.

But these critics have done Ammons a curious disservice, for they have focused their praise on his weakest quality—his attempt to formulate complicated ideas in poetry—and overlooked what seems to me to be his real achievement: the lyrical articulation of small moments of experience; his ability to organize shapes of language into an epiphany of movement, a frozen flood of perceptions which is visionary not because of any passionate metaphysics, but because of the sheer clarity of the poet's ability to recreate what he "sees." I don't mean to say that Ammons doesn't think well, or that his ideas are not interesting. They are; more important, they provide a framework which releases the intensity of his best short poems. But they do not make good poetry. Unlike Eliot or Stevens, Ammons does not write well about ideas. His conceptual reach does not intensify his language. When he writes "philosophical" poems, or inserts reflective passages into poems, he becomes boring and abstract. Only when his poem plunges into the moment itself does it gain the exhilarating clarity which is Ammons's best quality, as in this short poem, "Winter Scene":

> There is now not a single
> leaf on the cherry tree:
>
> except when the jay
> plummets in, lights, and,
>
> in pure clarity, squalls:
> then every branch
>
> quivers and
> breaks out in blue leaves.

The shock of hard, swift vision here is powerful and lovely. It recalls the sort of naked language which William Carlos Williams made possible in American poetry. There are many poems like this in the *Collected Poems*. One comes upon them as upon wells of clear drink in a complicated landscape. The seamless intricacy of world and mind is not a subject matter of the poem, but a medium into which the poet has been launched. In poems like these, the scaffolding has been forgotten; the poet is naked in the world, and the world has become naked to him. He is thinking with his "eyes" not his mind, or rather, his mind has let itself loose into the fusing brilliance of perception.

In another mode more special to his vision, Ammons has written poems which are intricate mimetisms of change, expressing his sense of the unceasing movement which is all we can know of experience, and of the world. Such poems succeed when they grasp the form of movement in a kind of visual onomatopoeia, instead of offering conclusions about a metaphysics of change. Given Ammons's obsession with instability and process, it is no surprise that he should have trouble with conclusions, both in the philosophical and in the formal sense. It is only in mid-movement, like a sudden vision of all the drops in a column of falling water, that his poetry attains a sort of cold ecstasy. There is fascinating strength in a passage like this

> From silence to silence:
> as a woods stream
> over a
> rock holding on
>
> breaks into clusters of sound
> multiple and declaring as
> leaves, each one,
>
> filling
> the continuum between leaves,

but a typical letdown in the poem's concluding lines:

> I stand up,
> fracturing the equilibrium,
> hold on,
> my disturbing, skinny speech
> declaring
> the cosmos.

Elsewhere the processes of thought and feeling themselves are made into cataracts of imagery. The inner world becomes not a space, as in much poetry of the 1960s, but a sinuous energy, as in "Landscape With Figures":

> When I go back of my head
>   down the cervical well, roots
>   branch
> thinning, figuring
>   into flesh
> and flesh
> glimmers with man-old fires
> and ghosts
> hollowing up into mind
>   cry from ancient narrowing
>   needle-like caves:

A. R. Ammons is an excellent poet. His *Collected Poems* resembles a flood of scraps and pieces mingled with finely wrought objects. The power of the flood is blurred but it is governed by a vision which imposes itself and, gradually convinces, not as an argument, which Ammons manages with only moderate skill, but as a lived clarity; and that, finally, is much more rare and precious.

Clearly, a poet refuses the dominant language of his time at his peril. Often those poets who succeed create a new language, as Allen Ginsberg did when he wrote *Howl* amid the overpolished tones of the 1950s. At first glance Ammons too seems to be a maverick, working vigorously against the limitations of the plain style, making a case in his work for a new intricacy of conception. Yet his best poems are closer to the plain style than one might think. It is when one hears William Carlos Williams in the background of his voice that the poems work clearly and solidly, not when one hears Hopkins or Stevens. Like so many other poets of the 1960s, Ammons's strengths and limitations derive from his flight into immediacy, his unwillingness to work with or against the limiting framework of culture and tradition. In this sense, of course, Ammons is extraordinarily American. But the impulse to reinvent all language, and all thought, falls short in his work. What survives is Ammons's version of the dream which is at the heart of so much recent poetry: the anticultural, Rousseauean dream of a purer, more articulate nature.

Notes

1. *Someday, Maybe.* By William Stafford. Harper & Row.

2. *Collected Poems 1951-1971.* By A. R. Ammons. Norton.

George S. Lensing (essay date spring 1975)

SOURCE: Lensing, George S. "William Stafford, Mythmaker." *Modern Poetry Studies* 6, no. 1 (spring 1975): 1-17.

[*In the following essay, Lensing examines the relationship of Stafford's poetry to myth.*]

William Stafford's poems have been appearing widely and regularly in America since the late 1940's. His five volumes, *West of Your City* (1960), *Traveling through the Dark* (1962), *The Rescued Year* (1966), *Allegiances* (1970), and *Someday, Maybe* (1973), have been received with general critical acclaim, and *Traveling through the Dark* earned a National Book Award for Poetry. Stafford chose not to include a large number of his poems in these volumes. They appear separately in scores of magazines, newspapers, and journals. In spite of this, the poetry is not well known; critical attention to his work, beyond the reviews of his various volumes, is almost nonexistent. There are, for example, no poems by him in Richard Ellmann and Robert O'Clair's *Norton Anthology of Modern Poetry* (1973). Earlier he had been left out of A. Poulin's *Contemporary American Poetry* (1971). While the neglect of the work is shortsighted and costly, there are, I think, reasons for it.

In one sense, Stafford's is a poetry of unostentation. His poems, almost without exception, shun grandiose and portentous statements in favor of forms that are brief, calm, and even-tempered. There is nothing of the bardic in his poetry, but rather a meanness, a terseness of remark, that is totally free of the meretricious: "Mine was a Midwest home—you can keep your world. / Plain black hats rode the thoughts that made our code."[1] Neither has the poet made an effort to aggrandize the work through noisy promotion or personal notoriety. Born in Hutchinson, Kansas in 1914 and reared there and in other southern Kansas towns (Wichita, Liberal, Garden City, El Dorado), he exhibits a rural and Western identity. A conscientious objector during World War II, he worked in Civilian Public Service camps from 1942 to 1946.[2] He has been teaching at Lewis and Clark College in Portland, Oregon since 1948, with time out for a Ph.D. in creative writing from the State University of Iowa in 1954.

Living in Lake Oswego, Oregon, near Portland, Stafford and his wife, Dorothy Frantz Stafford, are the parents of four children. Unlike Robert Lowell, Stafford has not written poems of indignation in the context of his role during World War II and, unlike many other contemporary poets who share with him the experience of university teaching, he avoids "academic" verse. In a statement about one of his poems in *Poet's Choice,* he acknowledges in his work a "moral commitment mixed with a deliberate—even a flaunted—nonsophistication."[3] In another place, he describes the greater influence of his mother's voice over that of T. S. Eliot: "Not to assert very much, but on the other hand, to assert what she felt" ("An Interview With William Stafford," 93). It is clear that both the poet and his poetry eschew poses that are in any way contrived or self-inflating. "The authentic . . . ," says Stafford in the first poem of *Someday, Maybe,* "holds / together something more than the world, / this line" (*SM* [*Someday, Maybe*], 2).

To speak of a poetry of unostentation, however, is not to deny the remarkable power of many of the poems, even though it has led critics to dismiss him. Poems like **"Traveling through the Dark," "At Liberty School," "Returned to Say," "Connections,"** and **"Shadows"** seem to me to be highly successful, and the list is far from exhaustive. But the preponderant impact of the work is not based on single poems; it is cumulative and derives from a familiarity with the larger canon. For this reason, I hope that the "collected" (or "selected") poems will soon be available in a single volume. Stafford's finest poems are scattered almost indiscriminately over his career. One has little sense of major evolution and change in his work; both method and matter are relatively consistent from volume to volume. Like Wallace Stevens, he was in his mid-forties when his first collection, **West of Your City,** was published. Earlier, when he completed in 1954 his doctoral dissertation, a grouping of 35 short poems, some of which had previously been published in magazines like *Poetry: A Magazine of Verse* and the *Nation,* he had already found his mature voice. This first unpublished collection, **Winterward,** is not notably different from the poems of his most recent volume, and, in fact, with some minor revisions, seven poems from **West of Your City,** one from **Traveling through the Dark,** and four from **The Rescued Year** originally appeared in it.

In appraising the totality of Stafford's achievement to date, the critic might choose any of several approaches. Poems of family and particularly those which describe the poet's father make up a continuing theme: the same may be said about the poems treating the American Indian. Stafford as a poet of the Emotive Imagination[4] or deep image can also be explored. The celebration of the American wilderness, both past and present, is a central theme, and the theme could be examined from any number of perspectives. Countermanding the riches of the wilderness is the insidiously enveloping technological society, and Stafford's commemoration of it is marked by fear and repudiation. Another approach, the one adopted here, is to speak of the mythic quality of the poetry. This approach embraces many of the characteristics listed above and is one which Stafford has adumbrated in several interviews and essays. The quest for myth, comprising both a technique and a theme, takes the reader to the heart of the poetry.

I

Stafford's interest in myth is not based upon ancient literatures and classical narratives, though there are occasional allusions to some of these sources in poems like **"In Medias Res"** and **"At Liberty School."** The mythmaking of the poet does not consist in the recasting of those characters and episodes which have become permanent endowments of the Western psyche. Instead, the poet sets out to discover new "patterns" and "reverberations" which speak with the same universal urgency. In a 1970 interview, he describes this ambitious undertaking:

> The key word might be myth. Every now and then we find ourselves encountering some story or pattern that wields more power over us than we would expect. I suppose that if I refer to the Oedipus story, we'll immediately have a reference point here. Someone, Sophocles or whoever, blundered into this pattern, and it has a lot of power. My assumption is that these patterns lie all around us. But as a writer it's too abrupt and cheap of me to think my job is take a pattern that Sophocles found and drape what I write around it. Instead of that, I would like to stumble on something new as Sophocles did. Of course, such patterns are rare, I realize.

("Keeping the Lines Wet," 124-25)

It is significant that Stafford's search for myth is conducted within the frame of "some story." His poems, though occasionally surrealistic in part, are founded on narrative, the imparting to the reader a human event in time. Though most of his work is relatively short, few poems are without a narrative structure. As he says in "An Introduction to Some Poems," "we have to live that dream into stories" (*SM,* 2). In the writing of one of his best known poems, **"Traveling through the Dark,"** the poet began with a story: the "actual experience of coming around a bend on Wilson River Road near Jordan Creek in Oregon, and finding this deer, dead." The poem did not emerge, however, until the poet later converted it into an account of the event to his children: "As I was recounting the story to my kids the next day, I discovered by the expressions on their faces that I was arriving at some area of enhancement in the narrative. It wasn't until I saw their expressions that I felt my narrative itself helping to produce a kind of redoubling of experience" ("Keeping the Lines Wet," 132). Stafford also refers here to the "patterns" in which mythic identities are enfolded. The word is used frequently when the poet is describing these identities.

In another 1970 statement, Stafford outlines his own practice of writing poetry by making himself receptive to impulse: "indulgences of my impulses will bring recurrent patterns and meanings again" ("A Way of Writing," 11). If Stafford's mythic embarkation thus begins in "story" by his pursuing "patterns" of elusive but peculiar psychic power, the resources of that pursuit locate finally in images. The images are fitted into patterns, and in the arrangement and timing of them, mythic revelation becomes a possibility. These images in the work of Stafford invariably belong to the wilderness, to the unspoiled world of natural life set in the poet's own familiar West. Even the titles of many of his poems imply this orientation: **"West of Your City," "Walking West," "Across Kansas," "The Farm on the Great Plains," "Sunset: Southwest," "Stories from Kansas," "From Eastern Oregon," "What I Heard Whispered at the Edge of Liberal, Kansas."** In a private letter, he has described the discovery of myth through the Western outdoors: "For me, myth comes at you in the way it did before it was formulated by anyone else. It comes from the influences on us all the time—gravity, wind, time, the immediacy of near things and the farness of far things—everything that touches you."[5]

Stafford does not assume that the poet rationally invents myth or that, through the use of narrative and image, myth inevitably emerges. When he asserts in the quotation above that "I would like to stumble on something new as Sophocles did," he implies that its discovery may be accidental and unexpected. This acknowledgement of accident and surprise, as Stafford repeatedly insists, governs the process of his method. In "Writing the Australian Crawl," he declares, "When I write, grammar is my enemy; the materials of my craft come at me in a succession of emergencies in which my feelings are ambivalent; I do not have any commitments, just opportunities" (p. 12). In the *Iowa Review* interview he affirms the method of random association: "I just start to write whatever occurs to me, no matter how trivial, in order to get into motion, and the process of writing calls up other things, and a kind of train sets in, the sequence that comes about because I'm in motion" ("An Interview with William Stafford," 101). Again, in another essay: "I must be willing to fail. If I am to keep writing, I cannot bother to insist on high standards. I must get into action and not let anything stop me, or even slow me much. . . . I am thinking about what many people would consider 'important' standards, such matters as social significance, positive values, consistency, etc. I resolutely disregard these" ("A Way of Writing," 10-11). Finally, responding to a description of his writing by Donald Hall, the poet claims, "My way of writing, however, is much more groping and less programmed than he—or anyone else so far as I know—has ever glimpsed' (Letter to author, 15 July 1972).

I emphasize these scattered remarks because they underlie the fact that Stafford's poetry does not begin with a preconceived "message" or even a formal method. To "stumble" on myth necessitates a complete openness to the resources of the imagination. It also invites the risk of artistic failure. In either case, the writing begins simply. **"The Woman at Banff"** had its origin, the poet discloses, with a simple and isolated clause: "While she was talking" ("Writing the Australian Crawl," 13). Or, the sounds of language and stress may spur the poem forward: "But meanwhile there exist always those sleeping resources in language—connotations, sound reinforcements, allusions, myth-residues, and so on" ("A Poet's Voice: An Approach through Prose," 190). Stanley Edgar Hyman has rightly warned that the literary artist can confuse his personal and private imagination with the universality of myth: "Literature is analogous to myth, we have to insist, but it is not itself myth. . . . What such modern writers as Melville or Kafka create is not myth but an individual fantasy expressing a symbolic action, equivalent to and related to the myth's expression of a public rite."[6] I think it is Stafford's acute awareness of this distinction that enables him to remain on guard against poems that are too self-consciously "literary," too indebted to exterior criteria. In a restricted sense, a poem *can* be the "expression of a public rite" if the poet's individual fantasy links up with the public archetype. Stafford cites Sophocles as such an artist. Again, story and image serve as his "ritual" and, as Ernst Cassirer has put it, the poet's own "emotion" becomes "myth" through "image": "Myth cannot be described as bare emotion

because it is the *expression* of emotion. The expression of a feeling is not the feeling itself—it is emotion turned into image."[7]

II

Two poems, **"Connections"** and **"Shadows,"** demonstrate in particular the resourcefulness of Stafford's quest for myth. The first is an early poem, appearing in his initial volume *West of Your City*; it was later reprinted in *The Rescued Year.* **"Shadows"** has not yet been included in any of the volumes. It appeared in the Spring, 1970 number of *Field,* along with two earlier manuscript versions. Both poems have received little if any critical analysis, and they seem to me to belong among the poet's finest achievements. They also demonstrate more general qualities typical of the verse, especially the attributes of myth as he defines them. **"Connections,"** as its title tells us, seeks to chart the ties between the human perceiver and the mysteries of the wilderness:

> Ours is a low curst, under-swamp land
> the raccoon puts his hand in,
> gazing through his mask for tendrils
> that will hold it all together.
>
> No touch can find that thread, it is too small.
> Sometimes we think we learn its course—
> through evidence no court allows
> a sneeze may glimpse us Paradise.
>
> But ways without a surface we can find
> flash through the mask only by surprise—
> a touch of mud, a raccoon smile.
> And if we purify the pond, the lilies die.

> (*RY* [*The Rescued Year*], 43)

The poem's elements are threefold: the onlookers ("we"), the raccoon, and a pond covered with water-lilies. In the alignment of human, animal, and vegetative life, Stafford shows how, in its separateness, each element seeks to discover insight into and unity with the others. One notes at once a series of contraries on which he begins: the surface of the pond vs. its hidden under-surface; the mask of the raccoon vs. his smile; the "low, curst" and muddy swamp vs. the threat of purification. The first agent in the poem's drama is the raccoon, who seeks to penetrate the pond's mystery by inserting his hand under the water to find "tendrils / that will hold it all together." He fails. "No touch can find that thread, it is too small." The search, however, is not forsaken. The human onlookers, themselves in quest of the same hidden vitality of the wilderness as the raccoon, turn to the animal. Like the pond, the raccoon is also described in terms of surface and under-surface. The poem twice informs us that his face is a "mask," suggesting not only a metaphor for the spotted face of a raccoon, but implying again a life that is concealed by an exterior "surface." Now, however, a revelation occurs, and the barriers between the human and the wild prove not totally impenetrable.

If the "tendrils / that will hold it all together" remain undisclosed, the raccoon, himself an extension of the same wilderness as the pond, is less elusive. Paws covered with mud from the pond, he bestows a smile beneath his mask: "But ways without a surface we can find / flash through the mask only by surprise—/ a touch of mud, a raccoon smile." The earlier "gazing" and "glimpse" suddenly and miraculously "flash" with vision. The poem forcefully declares that the essence of the wilderness is hidden behind surfaces; it can, however, be briefly undisguised as spontaneously and irrationally as a sneeze ("a sneeze may glimpse us Paradise"). Also like a sneeze, the glimpse is fleeting. The masks and surfaces are reimposed; "connections" are temporary. Ultimately, the separateness of the three elements of life is absolute, and the ominous concluding line warns that this separation must remain. To appropriate the pond to human ends by purifying it will come at the price of the lilies' life.

"Connections" illustrates clearly what David Bidney means when he says that the ritual acts of myth "presuppose an intuition of cosmic unity of life and a feeling of identity of man with nature."[8] Myth seeks through ritual performances to peel away the impediments that separate the divine, the human, and the sub-human. Stafford's poem suggests a partial disclosure of that unity, but it also demonstrates the evasion and distance separating man from nature. In other poems as well, the key to the meaning of the wilderness is frequently hidden under surfaces. An underground badger, for example, hovers under the feet of the explorer in **"Walking West"** (*WYC* [*West of Your City*], 22). Here, "in deep flint another time is / Caught." Corn planted by Indians many centuries ago can still be harvested ("that corn still lies") in **"West of Your City"** (*WYC,* 10). A catfish teems with its secret life in **"In the Deep Channel"** (*WYC,* 13). **"Bi-Focal,"** the final poem of the dissertation collection and reproduced in *West of Your City* and *The Rescued Year,* explicitly distinguishes exterior surfaces from the deeper "legend":

> Love is of the earth only,
> the surface, a map of roads
> leading wherever go miles
> or little bushes nod.
>
> Not so the legend under,
> fixed, inexorable,
> deep as the darkest mine
> the thick rocks won't tell.

(*RY,* 63)

Stafford is preeminently the poet of earth and its topography. In and under the earth—and it is usually the plains of the West—lies the enduring "legend" of

human value. In the poem **"The Earth,"** the earth is hailed as "this great friend," the locus of our identities and lives: "When the earth doesn't shake, when the sky / is still, we feel something under the earth: / a shock of steadiness" (*SM,* 52). And in **"Earth Dweller,"** its contents are again celebrated: "Somewhere inside, the clods are / vaulted mansions." The poem concludes with the exclamation: "The world speaks everything to us. / It is our only friend," (*A* [*Allegiances*], 79). **"Shadows,"** too, is a poem of the earth and, with its reference to the mole tunnels, it also hints at the earth's secret and subterranean life. It is, however, a poem more ostensibly symbolic than **"Connections"** and one that relies to a lesser degree upon a single narrative frame. It is, in fact, a series of brief narratives united by the common symbol of the shadow:

> Out in places like Wyoming some of the shadows
> are cut out and pasted on fossils.
> There are mountains that erode when
> clouds drag across them. You hear the tick
> of sunlight breaking edge off white stones.
>
> At a fountain on Main Street I saw
> our shadow. It did not drink but
> waited on cement and water while I drank.
> There were two people and but one shadow.
> I looked up so hard outward that a bird
> flying past made a shadow on the sky.
>
> There is a place in the air where
> our old house used to be.
>
> Once I crawled through grassblades to hear
> the sounds of their shadows. One shadow
> moved, and it was the earth where a mole
> was passing. I could hear little
> paws in the dirt, and fur brush along
> the tunnel, and even, somehow, the mole shadow.
>
> In my prayers I let yesterday begin
> and then go behind this hour now,
> in churches where hearts pump sermons
> from wells full of shadows.

(**"*Field,*"** [Spring, 1970], 15)

The poem at first may appear to be disjunctive and discursive. It lacks the clear narrative continuity of works like **"Connections"** or **"Traveling through the Dark."** Each stanza, nonetheless, tells a separate story, just as each story is united by the image of the shadow. Furthermore, the contiguous shadows work to establish associations (not unlike the "connections" of the poem of that title) between sounds and silence, between present and past, and between the exterior world and the speaker's interior self. The first stanza locates the reader in the open and impersonal setting of "places like Wyoming." Clouds create shadows which act upon fossils, mountains, and stones. The erosion and breaking of these objects by sun and shadow create the impression of the slow passage of great periods of time:

clouds "drag across" mountains which are themselves inhabited by "fossils." (The use of long vowels, dipthongs and monosyllabic words determines the stately tone and pace of the stanza.)

Already in stanza one, the poet suggests the auditory power of the sunlight as it breaks off the stones with a clock-like "tick." The primal activity of shadows acting upon earth is central to the development of the poem, and it is noteworthy that in its revision Stafford has moved this stanza from its location as fifth in the holograph version to first. Here, in almost godlike power, shadows inform the earth and themselves transcend its slow mutations. The second stanza introduces the personal perceiver and shifts the poem from the wilderness to "Main Street." Stooping to drink from a fountain, the speaker perceives the shadow "on cement and water." He then remarks, "There were two people and but one shadow." The line is perplexing since the second person is unidentified in the poem. (In the reproduced holograph there is the added line, "Two people in love have but one shadow." It is obvious that in his revisions of the poem throughout, the poet has taken pains to render his own presence more impersonally and universally.) In any case, so amazed is the poet by the conjoining activity of the shadow that his attention is directed upward and he becomes the source for a ray of light blotting a shadow on the sky: "I looked up so hard outward that a bird / flying past made a shadow on the sky." The power of the shadows already demonstrated in stanza one is now shared by the poet through the force of his own intense gaze; the poem symbolically translates the strength of the shadow from the outer to the inner.

Accordingly, in the next stanza, the briefest of the poem and occurring at its midway point, the "old house" of the poet's youth is evoked. The energy of the shadow in merging "two people" into "one shadow" enables the poet, himself participating in the shadow's efficacy, to "cut out" and "erode" time. In stanza four, a scene from the poet's past is reenacted. The significance of Stafford's preoccupation with his youth and parentage will be returned to later. Here, however, the poet remembers directing his attention downward rather than "outward," as in the second stanza, and he returns to his familiar earth. Among the blades of grass a mole moves, projecting a shadow. The auditory quality of the shadow is reiterated as the speaker hears its purely visible motion, along with that of the paws and brushing fur of the creature. An earlier poem, **"Fieldpath,"** parallels closely the activity of this stanza. In this six line lyric from **Winterward,** the dissertation collection, the poet rather than an animal forms shadows as "monuments" of the earth:

> I helped make this groove,
> and other helpless monuments I have carved—

turning them over, this evening,
I see no way to escape immortality:
my shadow with its Christian name
has worn out through this grass so long.

(**W** [**Winterward**], 30)

The symbolic dimension of the shadow image expands at the poem's end. The "prayers," "churches," and "sermons" suggest a religious power, not so much from a Christian source as from "wells of shadows" that are profoundly human and personal: "hearts" pump the sermons. The poet's capacity to transcend time in and through the force of the shadows has been demonstrated in each preceding stanza. Now "yesterday" can "begin," and he, like shadows, is concealed "behind this hour." The meaning of the symbol in the poem is not simple, but, inclusively, it represents the intense union of the poet with the earth and sky, ancient and contemporary life, fossils, moles and the unidentified companion of stanza two. In this union, the poet merges past and present; each stanza in the poem had represented a temporal shift. The present is enhanced and enlarged by the accessibility of yesterday's beginnings, and the activities of the shadows of stanza one intimate the immortal. In their very auditory power, the shadows suggest a force greater than the natural. A capaciousness in the poem's use of the image and in the pattern which emerges from it hints at the kind of mythic pursuit that Stafford describes in his prose remarks.

I do not believe that in his use of the shadow Stafford intends to suggest the well-known Jungian archetype; for him it is another manifestation of qualities like "gravity, wind, time, the immediacy of near things and the farness of far things," as he refers to them in the letter cited earlier. This poem suggests symbolically, nonetheless, that the shadows posses a direct psychological significance. They are projected not only from the sun, but from the human self as the poet gazes outward forcing a shadow of the bird upon the sky, or as "hearts pump sermons / from wells full of shadows" in the poem's concluding lines. In these instances, the shadows may share something of the hidden and unconscious shadow-power that Jung describes in *Aion: Researches into the Phenomenology of the Self* (1959). As the Swiss psychologist states in "On the Psychology of the Unconscious," "The conscious mind is on top, the shadow underneath, and just as high always longs for low and hot for cold, so all consciousness, perhaps without being aware of it, seeks its unconscious opposite, lacking which it is doomed to stagnation, congestion, and ossification. Life is born only of the spark of opposites."[9] In the poet's image of the inner self, particularly that of the pumping wells, there is such an integration between perceptions of the present and memories of the past.

Another poem, **"Some Shadows,"** plays upon the image, again associated with the past and the prominent figures of the poet's youth, his parents. Especially the father, Earl Ingersoll Stafford, who died in 1942, is exalted by the heroic virtues of the wilderness. **"Listening," "Elegy," "Parentage," "Fall Journey," "My Father: October 1942," "Father's Voice," "Father and Son," "The Swerve,"** and many other poems celebrate the elder Stafford's taciturn strength and lifegiving sustenance. In many of these poems, the father also evokes a nostalgia for the poet's own youth attached to an edenic wilderness and his joyous participation in it. In **"Some Shadows,"** both father and mother are cherished for their simplicity: "Forgive me these shadows I cling to, good people" (*TRY,* 4). In other poems, North American Indians share the heroic qualities of his father. The lost Cree, the Shawnees, Geronimo and Crazy Horse are all subjects of poems, and Ishi, another "shadow man," lives like the parents in self-effacing concealment in **"The Concealment: Ishi, the Last Wild Indian"** (*TRY,* 56). Throughout his work, shadow imagery is attached to inner sources of strength, self-possession and courage.

III

The various projections of shadows in **"Shadows"** and the various surfaces and under-surfaces of **"Connections"** create "patterns" of images. These alignments permit Stafford to pursue the myth "that wields more power over us than we expect." His work consequently belongs to the experimental in contemporary American poetry. One recalls, for example, the mythology of Theodore Roethke's greenhouse world and his psychic identity with the nudging and reptilian creatures of a pre-human life: "I believe that to go forward as a spiritual man it is necessary first to go back."[10] James Dickey, too, more surrealistically than Stafford or Roethke, seeks to possess the exterior world through the agency of the imagination: "I also discovered that I worked most fruitfully in cases in which there was no clear-cut distinction between what was actually happening and what was happening in the mind of a character in the poem."[11] Stafford's participation in the outer world is far less preoccupied with the pre-human evolutionary concerns of Roethke or with the phantasmagoric fusions of Dickey. His perception of the earth and the objects thereof are colored by metaphor, but their solid reality remains whole and intact. Asked in an interview about how the poet mythologizes his world, Stafford responded precisely: "If I could think of an image for myself, instead of domesticating the world to me, I'm domesticating myself to the world. I enter that world like water or air . . . everywhere. Mythologizing, yes. I'm writing the myth of the world, not the myth of me" ("An Interview with William Stafford," 36). Unlike Roethke or Dickey, his first loyalty is to the integrity of the undistorted world.

Stafford in several places acknowledges his admiration for Thomas Hardy's poetry; Stafford's work, in turn, has been compared to Robert Frost's. In his use of the Emotive Imagination, Stafford recalls Robert Bly, James Wright, Louis Simpson, and some of the Latin American, German and Scandinavian poets who have influenced them. His mode of mythmaking, however, is his own, just as his Western setting containing the themes of family, wilderness and protestation against the artificialities of modern life is formulated in an idiom peculiarly his. In the unostentation of his verse, he does not embrace the flamboyant or the eccentric. "In scenery I like flat country. / In life I don't like much to happen," he admits in **"Passing Remark"** (*TRY,* 45). What does happen, of course, is the endless act of awe in finding himself part of the earth's largess. In this, his artistry is pastoral and romantic, even though the boundaries of his verse remain simple and tightly marked.

No one would claim that Stafford's poetry is everywhere successful. Eluding the pretentious, some of his poems succumb to a false folksiness. He often fails when he quotes dialogue in his verse, and his attempts to coin a pithy aphorism at the end of a poem sometimes emerge flat and clichéish: "Some days, I think about it." (*SM,* 27); "I like their / clean little coveralls." (*SM,* 80); "But that was good tea, Friend," (*A,* 41). Some of the poems are so undramatic they hardly seem to begin. What the poet has achieved in his finest work, however, is an extraordinary tone of self-possession, a firmness of identity coupled with a sense of personal humility as he fills his own place in the world. These are traits that we do not often identify with the romantic. Robert Bly has said that "in another fifty to sixty years we will have a much clearer idea of what a poet is, and I think it is going to have something to do with men like Stafford, who are able to live in this country with a certain gentleness."[12] For over a quarter century William Stafford has quietly but steadily constructed a body of poetry, the dimensions of which we have tardily begun to perceive. Our critical appreciation, however, will have to reckon with his craft of making myth, an ingredient basic to his art.

Notes

1. *The Rescued Year* (New York, 1966), p. 18. For this essay I have used the following abbreviations or summaries: *W: Winterward* (University Microfilms, Ann Arbor, 1954); *WYC: West of Your City* (Los Gatos, Calif., 1960); *TTD: Traveling through the Dark* (New York, 1962); *TRY: The Rescued Year* (New York, 1966); *A: Allegiances* (New York, 1970); *SM: Someday, Maybe* (New York, 1973); "Keeping the Lines Wet": "Keeping the Lines Wet: A Conversation with William Stafford," ed. Philip L. Gerber and Robert J. Gemmett, *Prairie Schooner,* 44 (Summer 1970); 123-36; "A Way of Writing": William Stafford, "A Way of Writing," *Field,*

2 (Spring 1970), 10-12; "Writing the Australian Crawl": William Stafford "Writing the Australian Crawl," *College Composition and Communication,* 15 (February 1964), 12-15; "An Interview with William Stafford": "An Interview with William Stafford," ed. Cynthia Lofsness, *The Iowa Review,* 3 (Summer 1972), 92-106; "A Poet's Voice: an Approach through Prose": William Stafford, "A Poet's Voice: an Approach through Prose," in *The Distinctive Voice,* ed. William J. Martz (Glenville, Ill., 1966), p. 190; "An Interview with William Stafford," *Crazy Horse,* 7 (June 1971), 36-41.

2. *Down In My Heart,* a collection of essays by Stafford describing his affiliation with the Civilian Public Service program during the War, was first published in 1947 by the Brethren Publishing House and reissued in 1971.

3. [*Poet's Choice*], ed. Paul Engle and Joseph Langland (New York, 1962), p. 143.

4. See Ronald Moran and George Lensing, "The Emotive Imagination: A New Departure in American Poetry," *Southern Review,* 3 (Winter 1967), 51-67.

5. William Stafford, letter to the author, 15 July 1972.

6. Stanley Edgar Hyman, "The Ritual View of Myth and the Mythic," in *Myth and Literature,* ed. John B. Vickery (Lincoln, Neb., 1966), p. 57.

7. Ernst Cassirer, *The Myth of the State* (New Haven, 1946), p. 43.

8. David Bidney, "Myth, Symbolism, and Truth," in *Myth and Literature,* ed. John B. Vickery (Lincoln, Neb., 1966), p. 11.

9. In [Carl G. Jung], *Two Essays on Analytical Psychology,* trans. R. F. C. Hull (New York, 1953), p. 64.

10. Theodore Roethke, "Open Letter," in *On the Poet and His Craft, Selected Prose of Theodore Roethke,* ed. Ralph J. Mills Jr. (Seattle, 1965), p. 39.

11. James Dickey, "The Poet Turns on Himself," in *Babel to Byzantium, Poets and Poetry Now* (New York, 1968), p. 287.

12. "An Interview with Robert Bly," ed. Kathy Otto and Cynthia Lofsness, *Tennessee Poetry Journal,* 2 (Winter 1969), 42.

Roger Dickinson-Brown (essay date spring 1975)

SOURCE: Dickinson-Brown, Roger. "The Wise, The Dull, The Bewildered: What Happens in William Stafford." *Modern Poetry Studies* 6, no. 1 (spring 1975): 30-8.

[*In the following essay, Dickinson-Brown suggests that the reason many readers find Stafford's poetry dull is that the poet has written too many poems that reiterate the same sentiments.*]

A friend once said to me that William Stafford's poems are "nice, but dull." My friend is a good artist, and she wasn't trying to be smug or clever. She knew the poems and had heard him read, and I am afraid she was partly right. Stafford's reputation is now growing beyond that even of most important, "established" contemporary poets; but his is to some extent a cult reputation. Outside the cult many people still find his writing dull. To make things worse, the poems seem to have become duller as they have improved. Yet this dullness has not seemed to mar the poet's best work. Some of his early as well as his late poems are not only very good, but interesting and exciting as well. To show this I shall have to consider the dullness first: I don't want to speak only to advocates and friends.

There are some interesting early poems. The title poem from *Traveling through the Dark* (1962) is an example:

Traveling through the dark I found a deer
dead on the edge of the Wilson River road.
It is usually best to roll them into the canyon:
that road is narrow, to swerve might make more dead.

. . . . .

I dragged her off; she was large in the belly.
My fingers touching her side brought me the reason—
her side was warm; her fawn lay there waiting,
alive, still, never to be born.
Beside that mountain road I hesitated.

The car aimed ahead its lowered parking lights;
under the hood purred the steady engine.
I stood in the glare of the warm exhaust turning red;
around our group I could hear the wilderness listen.

I thought hard for us all—my only swerving—,
then pushed her over the edge into the river.

This poem is typical of Stafford's tact. In it are the little details, the wild subject, the ghosts of traditional poetic forms, and the implicit distrust of humanity that generally characterize his old and his new work; and the subject is interesting. It might be objected that whatever interest the poem offers exists in the simple subject or reported experience itself, and not in the artistic treatment or understanding of that experience. In spite of the efforts of the penultimate line, it would appear that this objection is valid. Nonetheless, one cannot fault a poem for having an interesting subject: that part of the poem which is the subject is memorable, even if the language—the understanding—isn't. But Stafford can go further and write better and still be interesting.

This is **"At the Bomb Testing Site"** from the even earlier *West of Your City* (1960):

At noon in the desert a panting lizard
waited for history, its elbows tense,

watching the curve of a particular road
as if something might happen.

It was looking at something farther off
than people could see, an important scene
acted in stone for little selves
at the flute end of consequences.

There was just a continent without much on it
under a sky that never cared less.
Ready for a change, the elbows waited.
The hands gripped hard on the desert.

The poem is in every way better than **"Traveling through the Dark."** Its subject is better than the accidental occasion of the deer; it is perfectly clean of trivial or irrelevant details; and it is so far from being an inartistic description of experience—that is, experience without understanding—that almost the only experience in it is the experience of understanding. The few necessary supportive and illustrative details are sharp and perceptive—the lizard is real—and the prosodical form is swift, artful in the best sense, and effective. I will return to some of these points shortly. The point now is that this poem is in many ways both interesting and exciting. Because he can write this well, it is especially regrettable that he is often thought to be, and really is, a dull writer also.

The first and major cause of Stafford's dullness is a muting overexposure. The quantity of what he publishes is out of proportion to the really few things he has to say. Even allowing for the process of his development, the "complete" statement of what he has had to say could be contained in the space of any one of the approximately eighty-page volumes we get every four years or so. A restrained selection now, instead of restraint before, would be difficult, since what we have in the corpus of Stafford's writing is not eighty pages of good poems and a few hundred of dross, but rather hundreds of redundant poems, spread thin. Much of what is tiresome in Stafford is simply a matter of reading the same attitude and perception poem after poem. At its best, it is a good attitude, worth reading, but it is a simple one, profound but with few aspects. The release of the poems for publication should have been gauged accordingly. Further, in Stafford's poems detail does not figure very importantly either as subject or as ornament, nor even as illustration (not even, really, in the deer poem). Perhaps this means that he is a very serious poet, but the relatively minor importance of detail should have resulted in a small rather than a large number of poems. Stafford likes to write, and this is his prerogative; but the overabundant output has also become our problem. Already the excess has created a need for severe editing. Someone other than the poet will have to produce a "definitive" Selected Poems, or he will be buried in the clutter and culture he so eloquently observes. It would not be an unprecedented fate for a writer; we are all at the mercy of editors and anthologists. Yet even with this paring down, the problem of Stafford's "thinness" remains.

Another problem in the writing has already been named: the dominating wisdom of his poems tends to deprive all human, and even wild, physical details—the grace of gesture, the motion of leaves—of any kind of significance—even of that hollow beauty embodied in Wallace Stevens' work. This is especially true in the later work, where details appear more rarely and where, by their own context, little can be made of them, even as items of pleasure. This deprives Stafford of one minor but prolific source of poetry. In the most successful poems, these details are replaced by a profound understanding of the limits of human nature. This understanding of man's limits is the subject of the conclusion of this essay. Nonetheless, in most of the late poems, a second source of interest is gone. Compare the remarkable lizard of the early **"At the Bomb Testing Site"** to these lines from **"Witness,"** in the most recent *Someday, Maybe* (1973):

> On top of Fort Rock in the sun I spread
> these fingers to hold the world in the wind;
> along that cliff, in that old cave
> where men used to live, I grubbed in the dirt
> for those cool springs again.

The problem here is not abstraction; abstraction can cut deepest of all, and sometimes does in these late poems. The problem is that the style has become, through a peculiar philosophical process, concrete and vague.

A further cause of Stafford's dullness is prosodic. Along with an increasing number of contemporary writers, he uses what, alas, strikes me as a kind of genteel quasi-formalism: random rhyme and off-rhyme; lines that nearly scan to one system or another; groups of lines that look but don't act like stanzas. All of these are potential sources of extremely subtle and effective modulation, and sometimes that happens, as in these lines from one of the best poems in *Someday, Maybe*, **"The Whole Story"**:

> When we shuddered and took into ourselves
> the cost of the way we had lived,
> I was a victim, touched by the blast.
> Death! I have death in me!
> No one will take me in from the cold.

This is a traditional accentual meter, the ancient beat of limericks and children's poems, folk poems, and art songs of the Middle Ages. Stafford almost never writes entirely in it, but he is often near it. Here a momentary traditional four-beat, three-beat line alternation is more or less sustained ("Christ that my love were in my arms / and I in my bed again"), but abandoned elsewhere in the poem. Line-lengths vary, the rhythm shifts in and out of meter, there is no rhyme. Except for this last characteristic, the poem is representative. Here, everything works very well, but the procedures more often yield different results: a certain smooth, uninteresting movement, as in these lines from **"Hero"** in the same volume:

> What if he came back, astounded
> to find his name so honored, schools
> named after him, a flame at his tomb,
> his careless words cherished? How could
> he ever face the people again, knowing
> all he would know in that great clarity
> of the other side? (His eyes flare into
> the eyes of his wife. He searches his brothers'
> drawn faces turned toward him suddenly still.)

This is not even graceful, much less perceptive: it is uneventful and banal.

The last source of dullness in Stafford's poetry is especially difficult to define. Perhaps no one not already convinced will be persuaded that there is a complacency of tone throughout his poems that kills perception and what might be called perfectly true feeling. I suspect that this is "heresy," that Stafford is regarded, by those who like him, as an apostle of alert humility and radical wisdom. Sometimes I too see this, but more often I see a man seduced by his own habit of being very simple and very wise. Consider **"Deerslayer's Campfire Talk"** from *Allegiances*:

> Wherever I go they quote people
> who talk too much, the ones who
> do not care, just so they take the center
> and call the plans.

Or **"Any Time"** from the same volume:

> (Waves will quiet, wind lull; and in that
> instant I will have all the time in the world;
> something deeper than birthdays will tell me all I
>   need.)

The complacency is often ghostly, but I believe it is almost always there. Only a thorough reading can really bring it out. It takes his edge away.

II.

The best of William Stafford's poetry goes far beyond these limitations. The writing is abstract, distant, inhuman, almost inarticulate. Stafford's achievement is that he *is* here articulate. He has reached a profundity by pursuing a double path, and I must say that I have no sympathy for part of the pursuit. Everywhere he distrusts—in fact, he demeans—what is specifically human ("political" in Hannah Arendt's definition of the word), individually identified, mortal, not wild (therefore victimized in time, and transitory). This prejudice against social identities is most often neatly presup-

posed. For me, it is tiresome and annoying for being the cant of the last century or two. Take the views of **"Composed, Composed"** in *Someday, Maybe,* for example:

> The flat people in magazines hear
> the flat god of their tabletop say,
> "Let there be flat people," and
> there are ads and editorials.

Or there are Stafford's rather silly leaves in **"The Little Lost Orphans"** from the same volume:

>   . . . every vein guides
> fate. I agree with all that happens
> at the end; right, right, right.
> No other guide but is
> leads onward. . . .

Hackneyed, comfortable, sentimental. And, again, in **"The Eskimo National Anthem"**:

> Now while the boss talks or while an official
> tells me what to do, the bears at Talkeetna
> begin to dance, and the escaping files of
> birch trees make it away over the pass. . . .

The bears and the trees aren't bad, but the presentation in these poems of bosses and officials is slick and unexamined. God knows, officials, magazines, ads and editorials are imperfect, but all they get here is a place in a zealot's naive catalogue of evil: bosses and magazines are evil because they are bosses and magazines (This includes, presumably, the editors who choose Stafford's poems for publication in magazines). It is all very exasperating and silly.

It is important not to confuse this easy naiveté with something close to it, but deep and not familiar enough, though we have heard it in the poetry of Emily Dickinson and Robert Frost and some others. There is a subtle but real difference in what emerges as wisdom; human and social actions are not rendered foolish simply for being human or social, but they are depicted as terribly small and insignificant. Humanity is not demeaned, it is belittled, in a special modern way. **"Now"** from *Someday, Maybe* offers an example:

>   . . . Fern arrives to
> batter the window. Every day gets lost
> in a stray sunset and little touches of air.
> Someone opens a door. It is this year.

This is something close to great art, not because it is new but because it is realized: the perception is important, difficult, and perfectly rendered. Detail illustrates and advances idea, is nowhere ornamental or superfluous. Exactly the right degree of particularity is achieved in every part, especially in the brilliant vagueness of "Someone opens a door. It is this year." The difference between this and the flat gods is huge.

If there are not as many aspects of this and other Stafford perceptions as there are poems, there are, nonetheless, different facets. Perhaps the most important of the facets in the most recent poems is what Stafford calls "now." Part of "now," as **"The Earth"** suggests, is simply *carpe diem* celebration, always worth a few lines:

> we come, we
> celebrate with our breath, we join on the curve
> of our street, never lost, the surge of the land
> all around us that always is ours,
> the beginning of the world and the end.

But "now" in poems like **"The Moment"** from the same volume becomes the best of Stafford: it becomes the poverty of all we have, tragic, the great distress. It becomes loss:

> Is it just you, Wind?
> Maybe. But it is Now;
> it is what happens, the moment,
> the stare of the moon, an
> opening birds call out of,
> anything true. We have it.
> That's what the rich old
> shepherd meant, pointing
> through the storm at
> the blowing past wind
> passing nothing:
> "Those who have gone
> and those who never existed,
> they don't have it."

Parts of this poem are perfectly focused, alive, and lonely. They realize what champions of Stafford's poetry wish readers to see in all the poems. Partly conventional, the perception and expression are not very new, but alertly realized and far away from the trite and the dull: clear, alive, alone—spoken, whatever Stafford's theories may be, not for people who have no names, but as **"The Whole Story"** affirms, out of a grown sense of what happens:

> . . . through the light on the hills
> I let children approach. In a pale straw slant
> the sun angles down. Maybe the children will not see
> the victims, will somehow survive. The sun touches
> along and goes away, and while the stars
> come out the sky waits and wherever they look
> it is now and there is still time.

Alberta T. Turner (essay date April 1975)

SOURCE: Turner, Alberta T. "William Stafford and the Surprise Cliché." *South Carolina Review* 7, no. 2 (April 1975): 28-33.

[*In the following essay, Turner discusses Stafford's use of cliché for ironic effect, which the poet achieves by substituting a single word in a clichéd phrase or by placing the cliché in an unexpected context.*]

To say that a poet uses cliché is enough to warn off editors of little magazines, prevent readings on prestigious campuses, and turn foundation awards in the direction of more bold and risk-taking writers. William Stafford has suffered none of these reversals, yet a close reading of his poems shows that one of the most frequent devices which creates his special originality, or voice, is a skillful handling of cliché.

Stafford's method is to draw attention to the cliché *as* cliché—to make the reader recognize the familiar phrase by using exactly the expected words or enough of them so that the reader knows what specific substitution has been made. The surprise is created by using the familiar phrase (1) in an unusual context, (2) in an expected context but in such a way that the meaning becomes ironic, or (3) by changing the phrase just enough so that the expected words become even more applicable than they would have been before the change.

All three methods can be illustrated from the poem **"Glimpse Between Buildings"**:

"Glimpse Between Buildings"

> Now that the moon is out of a job
> it has an easy climb, these nights,
> finds an empty farm where a family could live,
> slides wide over the forest—all those
> million still violins before they are
> carved—and follows those paths only air
> ever uses. I feel my breath follow
> those aisles and stumble on the moon
> deep in forest pools. . . .
>
> Moon, you old unsinkable submarine,
> leaf admirer, be partly mine,
> guide me tonight along city streets.
> Help me do right.[1]

At least eight phrases in the poem are familiar enough to appear in a cliché dictionary:

1. out of a job

2. an easy climb

3. follow those paths

4. stumble on

5. you old [so and so]

6. be mine

7. guide me tonight

8. help me do right

All but two (nos. 5 and 6) are used in their expected forms. The first exception, *be mine*, contains the insertion *partly*, which alters but does not disguise the poetic lover's usual proposal to his lady. The second altered cliché, *you old so and so,* substitutes *unsinkable submarine* for *so and so,* a change which, again, does not disguise the fact that Stafford is using the familiar phrase in its familiar affectionate, slightly amused tone. Of the remainder, phrases nos. 3, 7, and 8 are clichés of the hymnal, and nos. 1, 2, and 4 are colloquial, everyday expressions. Their occurrence in a poem whose last four lines are an address to the moon and whose last line is a familiar address to God suggests that Stafford is being either tritely sentimental or ironic. The way that he mixes these clichés of the love and religious traditions with the colloquial and mundane ones leaves sentiment intact, but gives an ironic twist which prevents sentimentality. The moon is not Diana; it is an old man out of a job (the moon's job as inciter of love and poetic madness has been abolished, the moon-man thrown out, and his moonscape taken over by a research laboratory). The old man is not only unemployed but a vagrant and a dreamer: he uses his older mythic occupations just for fun. Instead of haunting empty houses, he examines them as possible family homes; instead of inspiring moonlight sonatas, he admires the forests as still, uncarved violins; instead of laying moon paths that bewitch and lead lovers astray, he follows paths that are nameless and to no mortal or lunar purpose; where once he lit pools for lovers and dryads, he now takes his own midnight dip and submerges for his own pleasure. But the speaker still prays to him in the clichés of the lover and the religious believer. "Be mine," "guide me tonight," "help me do right." By changing "be mine" to "be partly mine" and adding "along city streets" to "guide me tonight" Stafford alerts his reader to the fact that the clichés must not be taken in their usual senses. In this context the unchanged phrase from a hundred Christian prayers, "Help me do right," becomes "Help me realize that the so-called easy climb may be the hard one, that the traditional job may be easier than a discriminating and truly fulfilling vagrancy, and that the glimpse of the moon as vagrant, from between buildings, may be just the perspective on regimentation which makes human civilization bearable." Without the clichés, phrased as they are, there would be no tension between the expected and the unexpected. There would be only a flat prose statement.

Cliché as Stafford has used it in this poem acquires the strength of historical or literary allusion. We follow its expectedness just short of complacence, then by addition of a word, or by placing it in an unexpected context, he makes the old phrase tilt us in a new direction.

A second poem in which Stafford uses cliché in the same way is **"Sophocles Says"**:

"Sophocles Says"

History is a story God is telling,
by means of hidden meanings written closely
inside the skins of things. Far over the sun
lonesome curves are meeting, and in the clouds
birds bend the wind. Hunting a rendezvous,
soft as snowflakes ride through a storm their pattern
  down,
men hesitate a step, touched by home.

A man passes among strangers; he never smiles;
the way a flame goes begging among the trees
he goes, and he suffers, himself, the kind of dark
that anything sent from God experiences,
until he finds through trees the lights of a town—
a street, the houses blinded in the rain—
and he hesitates a step, shocked—at home.

For God will take a man, no matter where,
and make some scene a part of what goes on:
there will be a flame; there will be a snowflake form;
and riding with the birds, wherever they are,
bending the wind, finding a rendezvous
beyond the sun or under the earth—that man
will hesitate a step—and meet his home.[2]

In this poem few of the clichés are used in their usual forms, though modifications clearly imply those forms:

CLICHÉS	IN STAFFORD'S FORMS
Simon says	Sopocles says
The heavens are telling the glory of God	History is a story God is telling
lonesome people are meeting	lonesome curves are meeting
birds are blown by the wind	birds bend the wind
keeping a rendezvous	hunting a rendezvous
at home	touched by home
	meet his home
a man goes begging	a flame goes begging
suffers indignity, shame, injustice	suffers the kind of dark that anything sent from God experiences
eyes blinded by rain	houses blinded in the rain
hesitates a moment	hesitates a step.

The especially heavy concentration of clichés in this poem can be attributed to the poem's central point—a modification of the popular understanding of what Sophocles said about fate: that it comes to men as a surprise, that they cannot forestall it, that it is grim and tragic, but that its very tragedy can leave a heroic man wiser and resigned. Stafford says the same thing, but changes the tone of Sophocles' statement. *Fate* becomes *home.* To the denotation of justice and inevitability and surprise, he adds the connotation of comfort, of personal completeness. A cliché situation is twisted just enough to make it a new situation. Each cliché strengthens this effect: "Simon says" is a child's game, and Stafford is about to take the threat out of Sophocles: Astronomical curves are humanized by being called lonesome; the wind becomes less threatening because birds bend it; a rendezvous with destiny is not imposed, but sought; flame does not scar or blind or beckon, it begs; man does not suffer a unique and impersonal cosmic punishment, but the kind of warm darkness that anything sent from God knows. Conversely, the clichés of absolute comfort have been made less comforting: the houses that offer welcome and security to travelers lost in the woods in the stock fairytale situation are blinded by rain. Most important, the word *home* goes through a gradual change which makes the reader aware that it both *is* and *is more than* the cliché concept of stove, wife and security blanket: the seeker is *touched by home* (surprised); shocked to find he is already *at home,* and finally made (as Sophocles' heroes were) aware enough of the nature of home to meet it. Home is security only in the sense that it is fate. Sophocles says that fate will surprise, fit, determine, enlighten, and Stafford says he should have added that fate will also comfort us.

The two poems I have selected work the device of surprise cliché harder than many of Stafford's poems do. But the device occurs often enough in other poems to show that it is one of Stafford's most powerful tools for suggesting mystery in a mundane situation. For example, in **"At the Fair"** (*The Rescued Year,* p. 44) the lines "What more could anyone ask / We had our money's worth" come just after the list of usual sideshow attractions and just before an incident which is both less than and much more than any of these: "And then besides, outside the gate, / for nothing, we met one of those lithe women—/ The whirling girl, laughing with a crooked old man." In **"The Well Rising"** (*West of Your City,* p. 50) the substitution of *brimming* for *cutting* in the expression "plowshare brimming through deep ground" occurs while Stafford is taking the usually unnoticed commonplaces of the field and interpreting them as actions of "thunderous" intent; he ends with the lines, ". . . I place my feet / with care in such a world." In **"At the Bomb Testing Site"** (*West of Your City,* p. 31.) he substitutes "at the flute end of consequences" for the usual "at the tail end," in order to say that a lizard waiting for an important change, its hands gripping the desert, is waiting for a beginning rather than merely for the final explosion which the rest of us have been taught to expect. In **"Aunt Mable"** (*The Rescued Year,* p. 17) he writes, "shaken by intermittent trust, / stricken with friendliness" where custom would lead us to expect "shaken by intermittent pain, stricken by fear." Again the modification is organically necessary to the thrust of the poem, which is saying that we are so accustomed to being shaken by mistrust and fear that we are numb to it, that the only thing which can really shake us is trust and friendliness. And I could cite dozens more.

To use this device entails great risk, for the poetic "decorum" of the 1970's forbids the too-familiar phrase in the expected context, whether that phrase be allusion, pathetic fallacy, or everyday colloquialism. Yet Stafford has found it a risk worth taking because it insures that the reader will go at least part way with the poet on the strength of his old awareness before he is jerked into or flooded with new awareness, that he will come close for a look and so give the poet a chance to surprise him. If everything in a poem is entirely original, the reader may not get a firm enough grasp on it to permit it to take him anywhere. Stafford does invite a quick or cursory reader to see the familiar signs, think he's been there already, and turn back too soon. But more often than not he succeeds in surprising his reader into going farther than he thought he could go. When his method succeeds, the reader can agree with him that

> Walking along in this not quite prose way
> we both know it is not quite prose we speak.

(**"Near,"** *The Rescued Year,* p. 77)

Notes

1. "Glimpse Between Buildings" from *Someday, Maybe* by William Stafford. Copyright © 1973 by William Stafford.

2. "Sophocles Says" from *The Rescued Year* by William Stafford. Copyright © 1966 by William E. Stafford.

George S. Lensing and Ronald Moran (essay date 1976)

SOURCE: Lensing, George S., and Ronald Moran. "William Stafford." In *Four Poets and the Emotive Imagination: Robert Bly, James Wright, Louis Simpson, and William Stafford,* pp. 177-216. Baton Rouge, La.: Louisiana State University Press, 1976.

[*In the following excerpt, Lensing and Moran examine elements of surrealism and independence in Stafford's poetry, praising his experimental handling of what they term the "emotive imagination."*]

William Stafford's poetic alliance with the makers of the Emotive Imagination is a unique and largely fortuitous one. He has never embraced unequivocally the method of the imagination as we have defined it here, though major versions of it appear in all his volumes. Nor has he totally abandoned traditional prosodic structures—even though experimentation in meter and rhyme has been constant. A significant number of Stafford's poems are written in free verse. He has never been strongly identified with the poetics of Robert Bly, though his work has received the commendation of Bly, Louis Simpson, Donald Hall, James Dickey, and others. Furthermore, short poems by Stafford demonstrating a poetry of surreal images which appeal to certain alogical associations appeared as early as the collection which made up his doctoral dissertation in 1954. Poems by Stafford employing qualities of the Emotive Imagination are therefore important, not only because they demonstrate an independence and individuality in the emergence of the new poetry, but also because they rank among the finest lyrics written in America in the past two decades.

Stafford has published more poems than any of the other three poets considered here; he is also the oldest (born in 1914), though he came to the serious writing of poetry relatively late. One would not speak of the emergence of Stafford's poetry so much from the Imagist-Projectivist tradition as from that of the Transcendentalists and Robert Frost.

Both in metrics and in theme, the poems of William Stafford are relatively consistent. The poet was forty years old when he submitted a collection of thirty-five short poems as his doctoral dissertation at the State University of Iowa under the title *Winterward*. This group, largely unknown, was drawn upon for succeeding volumes. With the publication of *West of Your City* in 1960 Stafford reprinted four poems from *Winterward* identically and three others with only minor modifications. **"Elegy"** was reprinted with slight alterations in *Traveling through the Dark* in 1962. His 1966 volume *The Rescued Year* printed one poem identically from the dissertation and three others slightly revised. The juxtaposition of almost any poem from *West of Your City* with one from the 1973 volume *Someday, Maybe,* for example, would not evince startling differences in style or themes.

Stafford's poems reveal thematically a singular and unified preoccupation. The voice of his work speaks from a sheltered vista of calm and steady deliberation. The speaker looks backward to a western childhood world that is joyous and at times edenic, even as he gazes with suspicion and some sense of peril upon the state of modern American society. The crux of each volume by Stafford involves the search for that earlier age identifiable by certain spiritual values associated with the wilderness, values which can sustain him and his family as well as the whole of the technological and urban society which surrounds him. The means to this search come through a poetry of images, images frequently and profoundly mythic. The investigation of these themes in the work of Stafford will constitute the discussion which follows. Before tracing them, however, one should be aware of the mode of the Emotive Imagination at work in Stafford's poetry and how it, specifically, contributes to the moral concerns of his work.

The setting of Stafford's poetry is western, ranging from Kansas, the state of his birth and boyhood, to Oregon, where he has taught for more than two decades.

As a result, Stafford's outdoor world is a landscape of nature writ large: there is the wind of poems like **"Tornado"** and **"Before the Big Storm"** and the sky of **"Holding the Sky."** His preferred world is **"The Farm on the Great Plains,"** as one poem has it, or **"At Cove on the Crooked River."** In almost every case, the descriptive imagery accompanying these poems discloses a deeply human value symbolically inherent in the landscape. It is, in short, a setting ideally suitable to the poetry of the Emotive Imagination and one markedly distinct from the more midwestern settings of Bly and Wright. If a lyric by Robert Bly is likely to be set in a snowy Minnesota corn field, for example, one by Stafford will be located on the side of a mountain or along a riverbank. The setting is partially accountable for a distinction in the tone of the given lyric. There is less of the soft effusiveness one is likely to find, for example, in a poem by James Wright. As Stafford says in **"The Preacher at the Corner,"** "Unavoidable / hills have made me stern, determined not to be wavery." Another quality that forestalls the "waveryness" of Stafford's poetry is his relative adherence to regular and formal metrical and stanzaic patterns.

The qualities which Stafford shares with the other poets of the Emotive Imagination, however, are basic. Although the poem itself more often speaks through the first person plural in a Stafford poem than the first person singular, the poet's activity is often solitary. Stafford's use of the collective "we" universalizes his own experiences. While the drama underlying the poem may originate in the external world, it can dart inward with sharp abruptness. The inward propulsion of the poem also follows upon the juxtaposition of images. The state of silence in a given poem, essential to the poetics of Robert Bly, is prominent in two of Stafford's finest poems: **"From the Gradual Grass"** and **"The Animal That Drank Up Sound."** In the former, a poem Paul Ramsey calls "one of the few great lyrics of this century,"[1] it is a silence itself which emerges from the "gradual grass," portending a hopeful prospect in a world where "Walls are falling!" In the latter, an unidentified animal simply subsumes the sounds of nature:

> In all the wilderness around he
> drained the rustle from the leaves into the mountain-
>   side
>
>   . . . . .
>
> he buried—
> thousands of autumns deep—the noise that used to
>   come there.

The poems of *West of Your City* (1960) are almost all written in colloquial diction but, even so, in fixed meters. They also depend heavily on images. A poem like **"Vacation,"** discussed in Part I, Chapter 1, shows Stafford's mastery of the essential process of the Emotive Imagination. One could also point to **"Hail Mary,"** **"Lore," "Weather Report," "The Well Rising,"** and especially **"Two Evenings"** as examples of Stafford's serious experimentation with the juxtaposition of images in semisurrealist constructions. The narrative background is minimal in these examples; images gather and meaning inheres in their accumulation.

Traveling through the Dark (1962) reveals a greater commitment to a poetry that makes its pitch not so much to logical continuity in narration as to unconscious association through images. The volume also discloses Stafford's first elaborate use of free verse. **"Universe Is One Place,"** a minor poem, displays openly the new looseness. The poem begins:

> Crisis they call it?—when
> when the gentle wheat leans at the combine and
> and the farm girl brings cool jugs wrapped in burlap
> slapping at her legs?

The question of line 1 is answered through the images of the question in lines 2-4. The poem's principal punctuation is that of the question mark and dash, opening up the structure. Repetition of words from the end of one line to the beginning of the next undercuts more conventional, logical connectives. Personification of certain images ("the gentle wheat leans") is strongly reminiscent of Bly and Wright. The final response to the "crisis" of line 1 is contained in the poem's concluding line, a line which defies syntactical, though not imagistic, clarity: "City folks make / Make such a stir. / Farm girl away through the wheat."

Stafford has alluded briefly to this method which relies more upon syllabic content than full rhymes or regular meter: "Instead of assuming that the language has syllables with many sounds, only certain ones matched for rhyme or equivalent duration or emphasis, I assume that all syllables rhyme, sort of. That is, any syllable sounds more like any other syllable than it sounds like silence. . . . Once the writer accepts this total relation to the language, most discussions about meter and form (in regard to sound) become inadequate."[2] In the first stanza of **"Universe Is One Place"** quoted above, there are no full rhymes among the terminal syllables of any lines. There are, of course, the total rhymes involved in the repetition of "when / when" as well as "and / and." Equally important, however, Stafford's open and loose syntax invites more subtle syllabic echoes: the vocalic rhyme of "wheat leans," the proximate rhyme of "wrapped" and "slapping," the consonant rhyme of "jugs" and "legs." This mode of "syllabic rhyme," as Stafford calls it, eschews the obvious and inevitable rhyme, one which would distract from the quiet flow of the images. Conversely, the more hidden rhymes actually enhance the psychic play of the same images.

Since *Traveling through the Dark,* each of Stafford's succeeding volumes has contained poems similar in

method to **"Universe Is One Place."** *The Rescued Year* in 1966 reprinted early poems from *West of Your City* like **"Vacation"** and **"The Well Rising"** and included new poems such as **"Across Kansas"** and **"Right Now"**—all of which draw upon a procession of images which culminate in disclosing a state of the unconscious. *Weather,* a private 1969 collection, continues the practice, especially in a poem like **"When We Got to Chitina."** Again in *Allegiances,* 1970, poems of the Emotive Imagination are present. **"In Fog,"** one of the more memorable, is quoted here in entirety:

> In fog a tree steps back.
>
> Once gone, it joins those hordes
> blizzards rage for over tundra.
>
> With new respect I tell
> my dreams to grant all claims;
>
> Lavishly, my eyes close between
> what they saw and that far flood
>
> Inside: the universe that happens
> deep and steadily.

The title of the poem, coupled with the dream of the poem's speaker, introduces the reader to a surreal world where boundaries of ordinary perception are blurred. The poem also illustrates the particular metaphoric quality of the Emotive Imagination. The tree's envelopment in fog identifies with the speaker's dream and its recession into "that far flood / Inside." The two phenomena, the trees and the dream, otherwise seem to have little in common. They are, however, related by their absorption in uncontrollable weather. The fog-bound tree joins "those hordes / blizzards rage for over tundra." Similarly, the dream is divided by the "far flood / Inside." The two elements of the metaphor coalesce fully when the "blizzards" without and the "flood" within are brought to tranquillity by the poem's concluding statement: "The universe that happens / deep and steadily." That which was distinctly personal becomes general and accessible to the reader's own experience. Even the tree, perhaps the most objective element of the poem, is personified into the subjective: "In fog a tree steps back." The poem's first line consequently encapsulates the movement of the Emotive Imagination. As the real is rendered surreal, the fog merges with the dream. At the end, both images unite in the general. It is the images, in any case, which propel the reader inward; the poem stops at the instant of recognition. Stafford employs similar processes in other poems from *Allegiances,* especially **"Stories from Kansas"** and **"What I Heard Whispered at the Edge of Liberal, Kansas."**

"Owl," from *Someday, Maybe,* (1973) presents a winter setting, within which are juxtaposed an owl, a snowflake, the stars, and extinct tribes of men. In the third stanza, each image links up with the others, and ultimately with the fate of all men, in the proclamation of evanescence and mortality:

> No witness but the eyes,
>   no flake at large but wings,
>   no sound but the flow of stars,
>   and a claw of moon
>   in the wood.

Another poem from the same volume, **"Dreams To Have,"** situates images as frames on a strip of film or painting in a gallery, images which arrest the flux of time, but also epitomize it: "I remember that place / the rest of my life."

"Universe Is One Place," "In Fog," and **"Owl"** are poems which recall the achievements of Bly and Wright; they are not, however, representative in the larger sense of Stafford's own work. Many of his poems are not markedly surrealistic; most are not as prosodically loose as these poems. Furthermore, while these are essentially without narrative plot, most of Stafford's poems adhere rather closely to some narrative substructure; as he asserts in "An Introduction to Some Poems," "we have to live that dream into stories."

Stafford's affinities with and contribution to the poetry of the Emotive Imagination are perhaps more general, involving both theme and technique. In its larger context, his poetry is essentially Janus-faced: it looks back with nostalgia upon an idealized childhood, but never at a removal from a far more foreboding perspective of modern society. His poetry seeks to chart the connectives between these two worlds. What, then, is the relation between such a thematic preoccupation and the Emotive Imagination? It is precisely in the way by which the poetic imagination seeks to link up the two perspectives. The childhood world is extolled through images of the wilderness; the validity of that world and the accessibility of its values are revealed through a poetry of distinctly archetypal images. If "the rescued year" is indeed recoverable, it will inevitably be found "west of your city." In **"Watching the Jet Planes Dive,"** Stafford exclaims, "We must find something forgotten by everyone alive, / and make some fabulous gesture."

Perhaps William Stafford is equaled only by Theodore Roethke among American poets who cherish the memory of childhood. Stafford goes beyond even Roethke, however, in defining the father as the central occupant of that near-perfect world. If for Dylan Thomas the childhood eden of "Fern Hill" finds him "honoured among foxes and pheasants" and "prince of the apple towns," Stafford's eden is appreciably simpler: "Plain black hats rode the thoughts that made our code." The Kansas boyhood of Stafford, marking an epoch of American life between the two wars, is rural, austere, inhabited by companionable neighbors and dominated by family. Its value for Stafford, though, is more than sentimental. It ultimately represents a way of life that forcibly contradicts the urban world of the 1960s and '70s. Its moral precepts derive directly from an intimate familiarity with the land and the wilderness: ". . . we ran toward storms. / Wherever we looked the land would hold us up."

The nature of that plain childhood world provides a key to Stafford's own attitude, one that shuns the fanciful in favor of the ordinary. In a brief comment on his poem **"The Farm on the Great Plains,"** Stafford has acknowledged the presence of a "moral commitment mixed with a deliberate—even a flaunted—nonsophistication."[3] The occasional weakness of some of these poems occurs precisely when nonsophistication succumbs to the trite ("There was popcorn on the stove, / and her mother recalled the old days, inviting me back.") Stafford's nonsophistication is "flaunted," one suspects, to avoid the slightest trace of the meretricious or the mannered; in this attempt he has been successful. There is a kind of *Winesburg, Ohio* quality to these poems, an attempt to capture a whole family, a whole town. Even the titles suggest it: **"The Preacher at the Corner," "The Girl Engaged to the Boy Who Died."** However, if George Willard seeks to escape the small town at the end, William Stafford desperately tries to recover it.

In some poems Stafford casts the vision of his youth through mythic characters and settings. **"In Medias Res,"** for example, is a poem whose title points to the epic conventions which underlie its statement. Possibly as a dream, the first stanza situates the poet on the streets of a town at night surrounded by his father and his son. The unity of the generations through the love of the poet sends out the mythic spell: "There was a one-stride god on Main that night, / all walkers in a cloud." The power of the familial bond ignites the setting of the poem so that the town becomes the conflagration of Troy. It concludes in an outcry: "'Aeneas!' I cried, 'just man, defender!' / And our town burned and burned." In other poems similar mythic contexts, all with overtones of the golden age, are invoked. **"At Liberty School,"** for example, reproduces the schoolboy world and the emotional power of the "Girl in the front row who had no mother." (Stafford lived one year in Liberal, Kansas, and graduated from Liberal High School.) The mounting force of the poet's memory of the girl transforms the poem in the fourth stanza into the heroic utopia of Atlantis. The images are characteristic of the Emotive Imagination:

> Our town now is Atlantis, crystal-water bound;
>   at the door of the schoolhouse fish are swimming
>   round;
>   thinking in and out of the church tower go deep waves.

Another poem, **"Twelve Years Old,"** reenacts an episode from the poet's childhood; the principal allusion is indirect, but it draws upon the promise of the land of milk and honey given to Moses and the exiled Jews. The twelve-year-old boy and his companions "found / honey in an old tree." The loss of that childhood is accompanied by the dissipation of the promised land:

> Far to a land all curved and green,
> a place the wind blew from,
> a poured-out land all honey smooth—
> a land that never did come.

In **"That Weather,"** Stafford recasts the untroubled world of childhood in the life of his own son Bret, "a millionaire / of days he would never lose." It is, as Stafford says in the poem's last lines, a veritable golden age:

> These few lines record that time,
> for the annals of the world. There are such
> golden things, and all the rest is about them.
> Rome rose, and fell, for these.

From Virgil to Exodus, from Atlantis to Rome, Stafford's nostalgia for his youth on the plains of the American midwest is mythically shaped. There is a certain irony in these allusions, however; the appeal of that childhood world is deliberately unheroic in its outward activity. Its memory is precious for the very fact that it is undramatic.

Occasionally, the mythic transformation of Stafford's childhood is less literary and more atavistic: "We were a people together / alive in the bush again," in **"Folk Song." "In the Old Days"** revolves around the memory of the mother's stories of "the wide field" which surrounds the home, a field occupied by "strange animals" who approach the house and call out to its inhabitants: "Then Mother sang. But we listened, beyond: / we knew that the night she had put into a story was real." In both instances, the focus is not so much on family as on the land itself. If Stafford's poetry is religious or mystical in its response to the wilderness, that impulse emerges not only from the Bible but from the natural world: "Around our home were such tall legends, / everything carved by winds and rivers."

The mythic quality of the childhood world is dominated by the figure of the father who appears in dozens of Stafford's poems. Earl Ingersoll Stafford worked for Bell Telephone and K-T Oil Company before his death in 1942. These positions caused the Stafford family to move about throughout Kansas—though Stafford himself lived in Hutchinson, Kansas, the town of his birth, for all but three or four years before his graduation from high school in Liberty, Kansas. In these poems the father is always regarded from the point of view of the son who has survived him, but who continues to look to him as preceptor and guide. In a private letter Stafford acknowledges, "My father did in fact represent a fervent and sustaining influence. When I read of others who find themselves rebelling against their fathers and so on, I have to use my imagination."[4] The father who appears in the poems is heroic: he is provider and protector; his moral strength is steady and independent of worldly expectations; most important of all, he is the high priest of the wilderness. Like Sam Fathers to Isaac McCaslin or Natty Bumppo to the neophytes of the frontier, Stafford's father is initiator and instructor to the son, not only in relation to the wilderness itself, but in the moral values which inhere within it. Again like Fathers and Leatherstocking, he is imbued with certain mystical, almost superhuman, powers. An early poem, **"Listening,"** exalts the father's prowess in perceiving the steps of animals or the moths against the screen: "we would watch him look up and his face go keen / till the walls of the world flared, widened." A visionary power is attributed to him in **"The Swerve"** where his ability to drive across a bridge at night after the car "went blind" derives from "a light he kept in mind." In **"The Rescued Year"** the father is described in religious terms and is given a vision of prophetic magnitude. The poem recounts the church-going of Stafford's youth, the response to which, on the father's part, is "mean." He then recalls the rides home from church:

> —and going home his wonderfully level gaze
> would hold the state I liked, where little happened
> and much was understood. I watched my father's finger
> mark off huge eye-scans of what happened in the creed.

The figure of the father in these poems occasionally assumes the archetypal dimensions of the universal father. One of the titles, **"Parentage,"** suggests this enlargement from the individual to the universal. Under the general title "Following the *Markings* of Dag Hammarskjöld: A Gathering of Poems in the Spirit of His Life and Writings" appears another of these poems, again implying the extension of the father beyond the individual. The psychological ramifications of this relationship between son and father consequently take on a general application, one which lends itself, perhaps not consciously on Stafford's part, to specific Freudian and Jungian illustrations. The correspondences between the father as he appears in the poetry and certain analytical psychologies remain partial and tentative; but to the degree that the figure transcends the individual in the universal, such systems can be insightful.

The Oedipal pattern in the father-son relation is clearest in **"Some Shadows,"** a poem which celebrates the gentle reserve and fragility of Stafford's mother: "A lean man, a cruel, took her. / I am his son." But if the father of this poem is in any sense a tyrant in the Freudian scheme, he is quickly recast in the ideal.[5]

The heroic pattern of the father's life serves as a model for the aspirant son, but ultimately it is unattainable. The function of the father according to this scheme unfolds in **"Parentage."** Here he is remembered as alienated from society, so strong in himself as to be self-sufficient, though to the world "he was overwhelmed." The son cannot model himself upon such a measure, preferring "to be saved and not, like him, heroic." The conclusion, one which is contradicted in other poems, is the relief of dissociation: "I want to be as afraid as the teeth are big, / I want to be as dumb as the wise are wrong: / I'd just as soon be pushed by events to where I belong."

The ambivalence of the son is revealed in another poem from the same volume, *Traveling through the Dark.* In "Elegy" the opposite of dissociation is desired—even though again the activity of the father is heroic, here cosmic:

> At sight of angels or anything unusual
> you are to mark the spot with a cross,
> for I have set out to follow you
> and these marked places are expected,
> but in between I can hear no sound.

The presence of the father is manifest in Stafford's poetry according to a variety of psychological tensions: association/disassociation; cruelty/love; success/failure—and underlying is a sense of continuing awe.

In one poem, **"Some Shadows,"** Stafford honors the memory of both his parents in terms of the forces they continue to hold over him. The shadow itself is an image commonly enough associated with the dead. Carl Jung, however, defines the shadow as a major archetype latent in the unconscious: "The conscious mind is on top, the shadow underneath, and just as high always longs for low and hot for cold, so all consciousness, perhaps without being aware of it, seeks its unconscious opposite."[6] From this perspective one might also regard the pressing memory of parents, partially conscious, partially unconscious, as Jungian: "Forgive me these shadows I cling to, good people." Another poem, **"Shadows,"** which appeared in the Spring, 1970, issue of *Field,* is archetypal. It includes the setting of boyhood: "There is a place in the air where / our old house used to be." The poem goes on to define Jung's "shadow life":

> At a fountain on Main Street I saw
> our shadow. It did not drink but
> waited on cement and water while I drank.
> There were two people and but one shadow.
> I looked up so hard outward that a bird
> flying past made a shadow on the sky.

Jung's discussion of the father insists that the son's "imago" of the father is conditioned by the image of the son's own unconscious. The father is never imaged as he objectively exists, but as a "compound" containing the specific reactions of the child. The "imago" is therefore both subjective and objective. In "The Relation between the Ego and the Unconscious," Jung describes the effect of the "imago" upon the son after the father's death: "The image is unconsciously projected, and when the parents die, the projected image goes on working as though it were a spirit existing on its own. The primitive then speaks of parental spirits who return by night (revenants), while the modern man calls it a father or mother complex."[7] The father as revenant, a projection of the son's own unconscious memory, is not uncommon in these poems. One can see the manner in which the Jungian spiritvision corresponds to the process of the Emotive Imagination. Images fix upon the external world; they evoke, however, an appearance or revelation which is interior. Objective phenomena summon the psychic vision. **"Fall Journey"** operates as a poem according to this pattern:

> Evening came, a paw, to the gray hut by the river.
> Pushing the door with a stick, I opened it.
> Only a long walk had brought me there,
> steps into the continents they had placed before me.
>
> I read weathered log, stone fireplace, broken chair,
> the dead grass outside under the cottonwood tree—
> and it all stared back. We've met before, my memory
> started to say, somewhere. . . .
>
> And then I stopped: my father's eyes were gray.

The final line, in gathering the other images of gray in the poem, dramatically reveals the "imago" of the spiritfather. In another context Stafford has spoken of the role which memory of the father plays in the actual writing of poems: "I sometimes find myself thinking of a phrasing and then ascribing it to him in a poem—but there is a certain kind of justice in that, as I come close to thinking that he continues to say things!"[8]

The specific moral influence of Stafford's father is of course less universal and more personal. Through all these poems he emerges as the man at peace with himself and the world. In **"Father's Voice,"** this is his bequest to his son: "He wanted me to be rich / the only way we could, / easy with what we had." In a highly personal way, Stafford's own pacifism seems to have found a precedent in his father.[9] But the poet is sparing in specific details, a fact which reinforces the universality of the figure.

Another character-type who corresponds to the father in the poetry of Stafford is the American Indian. Like the father, the Indians and their chiefs are dead; and their wisdom also derives from intimacy with the wilderness.

They too impart their wisdom, heroically purchased, to their survivors through the agency of the poem. **"Boone Children,"** from *Weather,* presents the Indians, here Shawnees, as aged figures who speak to the "children." The chief acquiesces paternally in the request of the children for passage through the territory. He then "went back into the leaves." The poem concludes,

> Today we might find that chief, and the right thing
> might get said, till the calendar moaned away through
> the trees, as the Boone children said yes.

The rediscovery of the lost chief whose prophetic counsel might yet prevail is the subject of many of the Indian poems. The barriers of time are dissolved ("the calendar moaned away").

The qualities by which the Indian is most consistently defined are not ferocity and warfare, but reticence and concealment, an insight common to the Indian poems of both Wright and Simpson. His life is enacted according to rituals and symbolic patterns which bring him into harmony with the wilderness. He is marked by his withdrawal, both imposed and preferred, from the predator-settlers. In **"The Concealment: Ishi, the Last Wild Indian,"** Ishi is defined as "the shadow man" whose survival depends upon hiding. He fails and with his death the mythic ritual of Indian life also dissolves: "Erased / footprints, berries that purify the breath, rituals / before dawn with water." In **"The Last Day,"** Ishi is replaced by Geronimo, another doomed figure whose final refuge is concealment. His extinction corresponds in the poem to Heraclitus' ascent from rocks to water to air: "To Geronimo rocks were the truth, / water less, air not at all; / but the opposite he had to learn."

Perhaps the two most successful Indian poems are from *Traveling through the Dark*: **"A Stared Story"** and **"Returned to Say."** The former is a sonnet where, in the octave, the Indians, upon returning to camp "feasted till dark in the lodge of their chief." They then rode away over the "earth their mother." The sestet suggests a contemporary reenactment of the earlier cyclical life of the Indians now gone: "Often at cutbacks where roots hold dirt together / survivors pause in the sunlight, quiet, pretending / that stared story. . . ." The "wild world" is momentarily recaptured, as the poem's last words prescribe, "by imagination."

"Returned to Say" is Stafford's most purely mythopoeic Indian poem. It describes a meeting between the speaker and "a lost Cree." Together, they embark upon an ancient journey which leads to the discovery of a "new vision." There are overtones of the medieval grail romance where the knight is met by a father-helper figure who leads the knight through a series of initiatory and purifying acts. The quest is defined by hardship: "It will be a long trip"; "he is to find a path." A series of sacramental acts must be performed before the disclosure of the looked-for "sign." In part, the activity is baptismal: "we have drunk new water from an unnamed stream." Even the breathing of the Cree is an act of consecration: "there is a grain of sand on his knife-blade / so small he blows it and while his breathing / darkens the steel his eyes become set." The "sign" turns out to be, not the holy grail, but the very activity of the journey itself: "We will mean what he does." And the poem's final irony is contained in the idea that, while the journey involves the physical world of the wilderness, its reality is spiritual: "Our moccasins do not mark the ground." The poem illustrates a tenet which underlies all of Stafford's Indian poems: most of the Indians have been violently removed;[10] their pattern of life, adherent to the values of the wilderness, remains a richly attractive alternative to contemporary society. In this sense, the lost Cree, the Shawnees, Ishi, Geronimo, Crazy Horse, and the rest have "returned to say."

The childhood world, for all its mythic import, is past, and "the rescued year" is saved from oblivion only through the language of poetry. Family and friends of youth have departed; the Indian civilizations of the past are reduced to captive feebleness. The values by which that lost world existed, however, remain possible; they are indeed a desperately prescribed remedy in the face of perils which Stafford sees on every side. The nature of those perils occupies a major portion of Stafford's canon as a poet. The precarious world in which the poet finds himself is described through three principal categories. The first is composed of the dangers of the wilderness and nature itself, dangers that existed as much in the past as in the present, though they seem more acute now. The second category is made up of specific descriptions of modern, technological society. The poems here are concerned with the threats of nuclear war, of a ravaging industrial society, and of a mechanical existence that divorces the individual from authentic human values. Finally, some poems form a category which exposes the sham and vapidity of modern social behavior.

It is important to note that in the last two instances Stafford is presenting the reader with an impression of modern society that is diametrically opposed to the idealized world of childhood. The two worlds, in fact, stand almost irreconcilably apart. Finally, it is the vocation of the poet to discover the means by which the two poles can be brought together so that modern society can be redeemed. That will only occur, however, by the unequivocal embrace of the ethos which informed the life of the western boyhood of Stafford.

Although many of his poems suggest that Stafford's view of the childhood world is innocently utopian, this vision does not hold universally. The same resources of the wilderness which nourish the happiest human existence also disclose a kind of Darwinian struggle wherein predation and decay lurk. **"With One Launched Look,"** **"Chickens the Weasel Killed," "Love the Butcher Bird Lurks Everywhere"** are poems which, as their titles suggest, betray the inhospitable in nature. A fundamental lesson of the nature world is that all life is defined by insecurity and transitoriness. **"Winterward,"** for example, hints at the seasonal thrust of the year toward winter and death. The movement itself is beset with "threatenings":

> a foxfire of fear, the distrust
> of sighting under a willow tree
> a little eggshell, burst.

"Small Items" and **"Things We Did that Mean Something"** elaborate the same theme: nature falling over in winter and prefiguring the inevitable fall of the human observer. In such instances, "a fateful diagram" is the only acceptable reading of the world.

Persons who populate such a world are themselves marked victims. Their existence is so precarious that even the inhalation of the next breath of air is uncertain. **"In the Cold"** allegorically defines the abandoned astronaut locked outside his rocket on a hostile planet:

> And listen: the wind has come.
> Finally, it always does.
> It will touch everything.

As its title allegorizes, **"A Human Condition"** disabuses one of the security of home, farm, and forest; all "will indict." Even the wilderness and the land offer no permanent refuge: "These places could have been home, / are lost to you now. They are foreign but good."

Being alert and cautious affords some protection against the natural disasters of the world. In any case, human volition is relatively helpless in correcting the aberrances themselves. The same cannot be said for the more ominous threats that emerge in Stafford's verse. These are humanly invented and humanly imposed.

Of special concern to Stafford are those means of technology that endanger the wilderness. It is a theme to which he returns in every volume. "They have killed the river and built a dam," he asserts in **"The Fish Counter at Bonneville."** Oil well engines have outlasted the vigilance of the snakes in **"Boom Town."** Especially in **"Quiet Town"** the ironic silence and reserve of the community only thinly cover various acts of delinquency: "Technicians in suicide plan courses / in high school for as long as it takes." The automobile graveyard is taken as a symbol of contemporary standards for succeeding generations in **"Time"**: "The river was choked with old Chevies and Fords. / And that was the day the world ended."

In poems such as these Stafford shares with Bly, Wright, and Simpson a distrust and disavowal of much of what he finds in modern society. Unlike these poets, however, Stafford's appraisal of that scene is not so much founded upon the disparity between the wealthy and the poor, or between unscrupulous capitalists and ostracized misfits. Rather, it is the rapacious destruction of the natural world, the environment of all men, that most perplexes him.

Perhaps most heinous of all is the threat of imminent nuclear annihilation. The presence of bomb testing sites and missile silos upon the plains of the wilderness elicits a particular horror. **"Our City Is Guarded by Automatic Rockets"** speaks of the "cornered cat," the rocket itself, which is "now ready to spend / all there is left of the wilderness, embracing / its blood." A similar imagistic setting occurs in **"At the Bomb Testing Site,"** a poem which Bly includes in his *Forty Poems Touching on Recent American History*. Here, a lizard braces itself for existence in a world which has become a desert, "a continent without much on it." Less apocalyptically, **"Evening News"** fixes on the nighly ritual of hearing war reports, presumably those from Vietnam, as they are broadcast over television (". . . a war happens, / only an eighth of an inch thick."). The poet's recourse is to immerse himself, somewhat desperately, in the surroundings of his own life, to which he addresses a prayer:

> In the yard I pray birds,
> wind, unscheduled grass,
> that they please help to make
> everything go deep again.

As victim of the holocaust in **"The Whole Story,"** the poet is subsumed by leaves, sky, and winter through which he reaches out toward the children-survivors.

Stafford's dismay at the war in Indo-China is neither faddish nor a pose. During the years of World War II (Stafford was twenty-seven in 1941), he was a conscientious objector who served in several Civilian Public Service camps for religious objectors in Arkansas and California. A collection of essays describing various work details, friends he made in the alternate service, and the hostility he encountered during these years was published in 1947 under the title *Down in My Heart*.[11] Stafford has indicated that his deferment was technically granted on religious grounds, though his objection was not purely sectarian: "I was more a social objector, with benevolence but no firm doctrinal bent."[12] Stafford's introductory essay to *The Achievement of Brother Antoninus* takes note of the San Francisco poet's refusal to serve in the armed forces in World War II; the description of that poet's response to war and "political turmoil" might apply to much of Stafford's own work: "Pressures in the long development spring from the distinguishing issues of our time—World War II, the moral crises incident to war and the uprootings that go with it, the political turmoil felt by a whole alienated group, and the emotional revulsions of a conscientious and sensitive human being subjected to such pressures."[13]

"Traveling through the Dark" is probably Stafford's most popular and frequently anthologized single poem. In its broadest outline it reiterates the theme of confrontation between technology and wilderness, one which leads to the jeopardy of the latter. The poem is a narrative description of the poet's sojourn along a road at night leading to his discovery of a doe, victim of an earlier collision with another automobile. In a different context, Stafford has recalled the origin of the poem in a personal episode: "The poem concerns my finding a dead deer on the highway. This grew out of an actual experience of coming around a bend on the Wilson River Road near Jordan Creek in Oregon, and finding this deer, dead. As I was recounting the story to my kids the next day, I discovered by the expressions on their faces that I was arriving at some area of enhancement in the narrative."[14] The poet's crisis of discovery is rendered even more acute by his sudden recognition of the unborn fawn: "her fawn lay there waiting, / alive, still, never to be born." As a result, he is thrust, both literally and symbolically, between the vulnerable world of the wilderness represented by the doe and the predatory world of technocracy represented by his own automobile. The moral dilemma consequently is transferred to him: "I thought hard for us all." In its outward sense, the decision is an obvious and easy one. The dead doe and the unborn fawn must be removed from the path of traffic: "It is usually best to roll them into the canyon: / that road is narrow; to swerve might make more dead." This he finally elects to do. The poet's removal of the obstacle, however, is attended with irony and, through the images of the poem, a sense of self-incrimination. As he hesitates in making the decision about what to do with the doe, "my only swerving," he becomes aware of his personal relation to the animal and the larger life of which she is a part: "I could hear the wilderness listen."

The poem's imagery alone, without further obtrusive commentary, defines his personal moral stance. The doe is "almost cold," while "her side was warm" with the life of the unborn fawn. The imagery of coldness-warmth is ironically inverted through the description of the automobile in which the poet himself, innocent of the actual killing, has been driving. He sees the victim "By glow of the tail-light." The car "aimed ahead its lowered parking lights." Even the poet stands "in the glare of the warm exhaust turning red." The life of the wilderness is ironically replaced in this manner by the life of the car. The poet's self-indictment emerges through his obvious identity with both worlds. He is

able to abdicate neither. Furthermore, both worlds are presented in terms of life that suggest the human. The wilderness "listens," even as the car sinisterly has "aimed ahead its lowered parking lights," during which time the "steady engine" has "purred." Personifications bring home the fact that, while neither phenomenon is itself human, both are influences on human values.

"Traveling through the Dark" recalls the Emotive Imagination through its use of personifications and images. The images, however, are not surreal, and the poem itself remains consistently an objective narration. Stafford structures the poem upon four four-line stanzas and a concluding couplet. Irregular in meter, the poem employs no regular rhyme scheme—only occasional half-rhymes: "road / dead," "canyon / reason," "engine / listen." In its formal aspects, the poem is characterized by its economy of statement. Its easy colloquialism camouflages to a degree this organization. As Charles F. Greiner has pointed out, the use of a single word can be significant. The unborn fawn is described as "alive, still, never to be born." The word "still" sustains meanings on at least three levels: (1) still as *yet* alive; (2) still as *quiet*, indeed, so silent he hears "the wilderness listen"; (3) still as "stillborn," an inevitable association with the appearance of both "still" and "born" within the same phrase.[15]

"Traveling through the Dark" defines in trenchant terms the invasion of the wilderness by a new civilization. At times, as other poems express, the poet is forced, more directly than through the use of an automobile, to intercept that world. Stafford himself has not lived in isolation outside modern social environments. Like Wright and Simpson, he holds a Ph.D., having studied at the State University of Iowa. He has been affiliated with the teaching of literature at various universities for more than twenty-five years. As poetry consultant to the Library of Congress, he lived in Washington, D.C., in 1970/71, and has traveled extensively around the United States giving poetry readings. While he is no stranger to modern society, Stafford's poems leave little doubt that his allegiances belong to the untamed, natural world of the West. One poem, "The Trip," describes a visit by the poet to a drive-in restaurant, the whole of that episode enveloped in the artificial and dehumanizing: "A waitress with eyes made up to be Eyes / brought food spiced by the neon light." This impersonal world is characterized as "hollow on the outside, some kind of solid veneer." In "Have You Heard This One?" a stewardess on an airplane has "forged her face" cosmetically. She meets a passenger who asks, "'Haven't I seen / you everyplace before?'" They marry "that very night in a motel." The poem ends, "This is a true story. / It happened in New York / and Los Angeles / and Chicago / and. . . ." Other poems evince further the attempt by Stafford to shun the artificial world. "At the Chairman's House-

warming," for example, speaks of the banal conversation at a party where the talk is "like a jellyfish" in its course of idle banter. The poet does not absolve himself from this world and its conversation, but he implores at the end of the poem: "let me live definite, shock by shock." As a credo of his own poetics, Stafford proclaims in **"An Introduction to Some Poems"** that the individual and the poem pursue the same end: "The authentic . . . holds / together something more than the world, / this line."

Stafford's best poem on the artificiality of modern life is **"A Documentary from America."** It recounts a visit to a political rally where a presidential candidate is speaking. The rally is followed by the viewing of that event on a television report later in the day. The entire experience suggests manipulation and contrivance. The candidate's speech is "written by a committee"; the participants at the rally find that the television coverage makes them into unwitting supporters. As the poet witnesses the rally later on television, he is interrupted by yet another reporter:

> "Oh God," we said, "we were watching us, watching us." And in a terrible voice he roared, "Quick, be smiling; you are on the air again!" and—a terrible thing—we said just as he said, "How do you do."

The poetry of Stafford has been thematically examined up to this point in terms of two poles. The first is the idealized world of childhood upon the western plains of America in the earlier part of the twentieth century. It is dominated by the figure of the father and, by extension, the earlier Indian chieftains. This world is evanescent and exists principally through nostalgia, or, as Stafford says in **"A Stared Story,"** "by imagination." The second pole fixes firmly upon the present world which surrounds Stafford's adult life. It is seen almost exclusively in terms of fretful risk. The mechanized state of modern society which has forced the removal of man from his intimate identity with the land and nature is not only a threat to the continuation of the wilderness itself but insidiously reduces the terms of human existence to debilitating distortions and artificialities.

There is finally, however, a third state in the poetry of Stafford which is posited upon the kind of life the poet has attempted to stake for himself and his family. It is to some degree a romantic world which entails, necessarily, a partial retreat from the other and larger society which encloses him. But as a world of retreat it is not one of illusion. In the final analysis, the entire thrust of Stafford's work taken as a whole is toward the disclosure of a life that seeks to recapture the values of that other elusive and boyhood world. Consequently, these poems refuse to submit to the inflictions against the wilderness—both physical and spiritual. Rather, they are poems of desperate retrenchment.

The image in which Stafford casts himself in these poems is, to some extent, that of an isolated, sometimes lonely, advocate. Robert Creeley has spoken with some disapproval of Stafford's "wry wit, often, which can make peace with the complexities of times and places. . . . The danger is simply that things will become cozy ('The earth says have a place . . .'), and that each thing will be humanized to an impression of it merely."[16] It should be remembered, though, that Stafford's thematic conservatism in these poems does not emerge out of ignorance or insensitivity to the compelling issues of the larger world. To the contrary, he suggests that some form of retreat is finally the only remedy with which he can address those issues. The poems of what one might call the "modern wilderness" are calculated on Stafford's part to this end.

A major premise of these poems is that one's moral choices that lead to personal happiness depend integrally on the location of *where* one lives. Geography is the primary ingredient of personal gratification. In this sense, Stafford's poetry is as regionalist as that of southern poets like James Dickey. Many of the titles of poems suggest this regionalism: **"West of Your City," "Walking West," "Across Kansas," "The Farm on the Great Plains," "Sunset: Southwest," "Stories from Kansas."** All of these poems offer an alternative to an America where lives are marked by mobility, rootlessness, and insulation from the soil. Stafford is most overtly didactic on precisely this point: "One's duty: to find a place / that grows from his part of the world," or "The earth says have a place, be what that place / requires." A second criterion is a kind of burrowing in once the individual has found that location, a stubborn resolution to hold fast to one's chosen land. In **"A Story,"** the poem's speaker observes mysterious climbers whose objectives are unknown: "they crawl far before they die." His own response is the opposite: "I make my hole the deepest one / this high on the mountainside." Another requirement is isolation. The secrets of the wilderness are divulged only to the one who removes himself from civilization. The "apparition river" of **"By the Snake River"** is lost when the poet "went / among the people to be one of them." Especially the spiritual life of nature is discernible only when "The railroad dies by a yellow depot, / town falls away toward a muddy creek." Finally, the fruits of the wilderness can never be discovered by rational chartings. "You thinkers, prisoners of what will work," are disavowed by Stafford in **"An Epiphany"** as he describes a brief and almost mystical encounter with a dog "in quick unthought." Such revelations are spontaneous, fleeting, and granted at moments when least expected.

The method of the Emotive Imagination is most apparent in the poems of the modern wilderness when Stafford seeks to define its concealed meanings. The deepest life of nature is revealed only rarely and under conditions outlined above. Even so, Stafford suggests an ambivalence in presenting the accessibility of those meanings. Glimpses (a favorite Stafford word) are possible; and, at times, a profound linking between the human and the nonhuman natural world occurs. On the other hand, Stafford occasionally suggests that the boundaries between the two worlds are impenetrable, and the imposition of the human is a tainting activity.

Stafford's depiction of the essential wilderness is set up through images—almost always in terms of a vertical hierarchy. The outer world is one of surfaces and shadows; it is available to everyone and yields many precious moments. The other world, concealed and far less accessible, is underground; its perception becomes the abiding vocation of the poet. **"Bi-Focal"** is one of the clearest definitions of the two separate dimensions of the wilderness:

> Love is of the earth only,
> the surface, a map of roads
> leading wherever go miles
> or little bushes nod.
>
> Not so the legend under,
> fixed, inexorable,
> deep as the darkest mine
> the thick rocks won't tell.

The "legend under" occupies the mythical gropings in this division of Stafford's verse. The imagistic arrangement of the concealed wilderness takes many forms, but almost always conforming to the vertical hierarchy. In **"On the Glass Ice"** it is the frozen fish under the surface over which the poet skates. In **"Walking West"** it is an underground badger: "Anyone with quiet pace who / walks a gray road in the West / may hear a badger underground." Here, "in deep flint another time is / caught." Corn planted by "starving Indians" of ancient generations can still be brought to harvest—*"that corn still lies"*—in **"West of Your City." "In the Deep Channel,"** as the title suggests, is another account of revelation from under—here "a secret-headed channel cat." In moments of calm, the steadiness of life under the earth is sensed, as Stafford sets forth in **"The Earth"**: "When the earth doesn't shake, when the sky / is still, we feel something under the earth: / a shock of steadiness." Although the truest reality of the wilderness is concealed below, its presence is manifest above. The opening stanza of **"Weeds"** attests to the irrepressible will of nature to "witness forth":

> What's down in the earth
> comes forth in cold water,
> in mist at night, in muttering
> volcanoes that ring oceans
> moving strangely at times.

One of Stafford's finest lyrics, **"Connections,"** demonstrates again the vertical hierarchy of the wilderness life; it also summarizes the prerequisites for human perception of that life. The poem appeared originally in *West of Your City* and was selected by Stafford for republication in *The Rescued Year*:

> Ours is a low, curst, under-swamp land
> the raccoon puts his hand in,
> gazing through his mask for tendrils
> that will hold it all together.
>
> No touch can find that thread, it is too small.
> Sometimes we think we learn its course—
> through evidence no court allows
> a sneeze may glimpse us Paradise.
>
> But ways without a surface we can find
> flash through the mask only by surprise—
> a touch of mud, a raccoon smile.
>
> And if we purify the pond, the lilies die.

The several conditions for revelation of the concealed wilderness are all at work in this short lyric: its geographical setting is that of the poet's personal allotment in the wilderness ("Ours is a low, curst, under-swamp land"); it occurs in a remote and isolated location as the poet clandestinely witnesses the activity of the raccoon; the sought-after "glimpse" occurs "only by surprise" and not by a rational process ("evidence no court allows").

"Connections" treats of two kinds of "surfaces" and two kinds of under-surfaces in the wilderness life. As its title suggests, it is an exploration of the linkings between the two levels. In the first five lines of the poem, direct human activity is removed. The raccoon itself stands over the surface of a pond and "puts his hand in." The animal seeks a manifestation of the vital undersurface life of the wilderness: "tendrils / that will hold it all together." He fails, as line five explains. In the remainder of the poem, the human pursuit of the same manifestation ensues. Again, "ways without a surface" must be tried; the true vitality of the wilderness is concealed below. Here, the attempt is more successful and occurs through deliberate irony. Like the raccoon, the human cannot put his hand in to discover the "thread." In absolute terms the boundaries between the two worlds are unbreachable. A "glimpse," however, is possible, and this occurs through the intercession of the raccoon itself. While the animal could not itself "find that thread," it can become for the human perceiver a mediator in the revelation of the wilderness. Accordingly, the raccoon itself, an animal of the same untamed world, becomes an extension of the same surface/undersurface division of the wilderness. The face of the animal is twice described as a "mask"—another surface that conceals the authentic life behind it. The "touch of mud" and the "raccoon smile" become for the human perceiver the instruments of revelation. The images of the poem gather here to a climax of the Emotive Imagination. The "under-swamp land" does reveal itself briefly but dramatically through the smile of the raccoon, the removal of the mask. Irony is crucial here: the swamp and the raccoon are finally one in that the wilderness emanates from both. The human perceiver is granted a miraculous insight into the world of nature, both swamp and animal, through the raccoon's smile.

The poem concludes with an admonition: "And if we purify the pond, the lilies die." Human control can only be an ironic pollutant. The separation between human and wilderness life is absolute, and the latter claims its final autonomy.

The role of the raccoon in **"Connections"** is not unique. Animals are frequently invested with elevated positions in the life of the wilderness. The "comfortable earth" has excluded animal life, Stafford exclaims, in **"Outside."** Meanwhile, constantly encircling the periphery of human life is the coyote, ancient symbol of wisdom. The poem concludes with the suggestion that such wisdom can be reclaimed:

> For all we have taken into our keeping
> and polished with our hands belongs to a truth
> greater than ours, in the animals' keeping."

Similarly, the song of the sparrow in **"In Response to a Question"** or the singing of fish in **"On the Glass Ice,"** become moral directives, as do deer tracks in **"Deer Stolen."** The idealized existence of animals is perhaps most comprehensively imparted in the poem **"In Fur"**: "Owning the wilderness, they're not lost."

If **"Connections"** suggests that the unity between the wilderness and twentieth-century man is relative and fleeting, other poems pursue more positively that linking. *"Wild things wait,"* he insists in **"West of Your City,"** and there are overlappings between the two worlds which suggest, at times, an almost mystical relationship. Asked about mysticism in his verse, Stafford does not deny it, although he insists that "I would like to be as clear and unambiguous as possible in my work."[17] Elsewhere, he has acknowledged "unanalyzed impressions of holiness" as a major theme in his work.[18] Occasionally, such as in a poem like **"A Walk in the Country,"** the description of the communion between poet and world seems spiritual in such a manner that the experience approaches the purely religious:

> I felt a burden of silver come:
> my back had caught moonlight
> pouring through the trees like money.
>
> That walk was late, though.
> Late, I gently came into town,
> and a terrible thing had happened:
> the world, wide, unbearably bright,
> had leaped on me. I carried mountains.

Less prodigiously, other poems recognize instants of tangential mergings with nature that also appear sacramental. **"Ceremony,"** for example, describes an episode where a muskrat bites the finger of the poet while his hand is in the waters of the Ninnescah River. His blood trails the current in the direction of the ocean, effecting a momentary transformation of the wilderness "by a kind of marriage." A similar though more recent poem, **"Witness,"** acknowledges "the hand I dipped in the Missouri / above Council Bluffs and found the springs." The hand, successful in its touch with the undersurface secret of the wilderness, becomes permanently blessed by the experience. These poems of semi-mystical encounters with the natural world recall those poems of James Dickey that center on fishing and hunting outings. Stafford's, however, are less surrealistic and accompanied by calmer, deliberately less dazzling psychological effects on the part of the speaker: "we study how to deserve / what has already been given us."

In most of his work, Stafford's quest for the wilderness does not seem aimed at portentous or mystical encounters. The western wilds, in fact, are niggardly in revealing their secrets to human explorers. **"A Survey"** recounts the attempt to map the area of the "Frantic Mountains," a mythological wilderness. The "field boot crew" cannot even approach the area because of its flooded rivers. Recalling the raccoon of **"Connections,"** wildcats are then commissioned for a survey of their own kind, the only possible one, Stafford suggests. As we have seen, the wilderness does not altogether elude, though, and if the imposing conditions set forth by nature are met and if the perceiver will wait the "glimpses" and "surprises," he will not be totally impeded.

In most cases, the value in the actual pursuit of the unclaimed territories of nature is self-discovery—"to find / what I am," as he says in **"By the Snake River."** In the title poem of *Allegiances,* the making of oneself "sturdy for common things" as opposed to "strange mountains and creatures" is the most appealing human ambition. Finally, the wilderness remains the surest antidote for a world which, as we have seen in other poems, has run amuck in its misdirected course:

> "Some day, tame (therefore lost) men, the wild
> will come over the highest wall, waving
> its banner voice, beating its gifted fist:
> *Begin again, you tame ones; listen—the roads*
> *are your home again."*

In the poems of the modern wilderness, Stafford again employs a form of myth,[19] but one which does not conform directly to patterns of earlier history or literature. He has, in fact, described these poems as a search for new myths:

I don't have any sense of larger purposes, just little immediate encounters. Beyond this, of course, aside from language there is a kind of resonance among our experiences. The key word might be *myth*. Every now and then we find ourselves encountering some story or pattern that wields more power over us than we would expect. I suppose that if I refer to the Oedipus story, we'll immediately have a reference point here. Someone, Sophocles or whoever, blundered into this pattern, and it has a lot of power. My assumption is that these patterns lie all around us. But as a writer it's too abrupt and cheap of me to think that my job is to take a pattern that Sophocles found and drape what I write around it. Instead of that, I would like to stumble on something new as Sophocles did. Of course, such patterns are rare, I realize.[20]

This "resonance among our experiences" almost always is rooted for Stafford in the location of the wilderness. In a private letter he has elaborated upon this setting of mythic investigation: "For me, myth comes at you in the way it did before it was formulated by anyone else. It comes from the influences on us all the time—gravity, wind, time, the immediacy of near things and the farness of far things—anything that touches you."[21]

Stafford's poetry does not give evidence of the attainment of a radically original and self-contained mythology. Indeed, many of the mythic patterns in his poems of the modern wilderness conform to fairly traditional romantic polarities: the superiority of the pastoral over the urban, the spontaneous over the rational, the isolated over the social. Even in more particularized versions of the wilderness certain traditional constructs are repeated. Stafford's play with mythic invention or modification occurs most noticeably when he seeks to establish some means of linking the human questor and the hidden wilderness. Some examples have already been witnessed, such as the raccoon's smile in **"Connections"** or the blood from the poet's finger in **"Ceremony."**

In a more traditional mythic framework some of the poems incorporate devices which seem almost inevitable in a poetry of this nature. As with the other poets of the Emotive Imagination, Stafford's exploration of the unconscious through the arrangement of images takes on certain primitive and archetypal impulses in some of the poems. **"Reporting Back"** from *Traveling through the Dark,* a short lyric of three couplets, hints at earlier forms of life which have been misplaced in the course of time. The image of the lost path is central: "Is there a way to walk that living has obscured? / (Our feet are trying to remember some path we are walking toward.)" The quest of feet is replaced by the groping of hands in a notably similar poem, **"Origins."** More extensively, **"From Eastern Oregon"** depicts the typical removal from "the world's problem." In this case, the speaker enters a symbolic cave of ancient civilization where he reads "the carved story." The cave functions analogously to the path of **"Reporting Back."** The speaker himself

goes on to assume an atavistic personality that leads him to "the swell of knowing":

> Your eyes an owl, your skin a new part of the earth,
> you let obsidian flakes in the dust discover your feet
> while somewhere drops of water tell a rock.

The cave of prehistoric life may be accessible symbolically, but its actuality is remote. For this reason, Stafford comes up short in comparison with a poet like Roethke, for example, in his recourse to primordial environments. The treasures of the wilderness can be poetically approached through real and contemporary measures. **"In the Museum"** presents objects from ancient and distant points, "a broken urn volcano-finished." Having viewed the various artifacts, the museum goer senses the impulse to identify with their origins—an impossible task, the poem implies. Instead, one fixes upon the present: "You never can get back, but there'll be other / talismans." Most of Stafford's modern wilderness poems investigate the nature of these "other talismans."

One would not wish to impose too stringently diagrammatic outlines upon Stafford's verse. The poems do not themselves conform to mechanical formulas. Yet, if the concealed wilderness and its essential vitality are presented beneath a variety of surfaces—below a river or underground, for example—the symbolic linkings between that part of the wilderness and its human perceiver are almost always presented as linear and horizontal. A vertical hierarchy functions in the various levels of the wilderness itself; a horizontal network describes the avenues between those levels and the poet's own person. This network consists of a variety of symbolic formulations, which also constitute a primary element in Stafford's mythological schema. Some, indeed, conform to traditional and archetypal associations. The journey is one example of this; the corridor is another.

We have already seen one illustration of the horizontal network in **"Reporting Back,"** and that, of course, is the path. **"Watching the Jet Planes Dive"** is one of the poems where Stafford is most explicit in his discussion of the mythological overtones which emanate from the pursuit of the wilderness. Here, he advocates not the return to aboriginal sources, but to a forgotten past more intimately connected with the land. It is an activity that is "ritual" and one which entails the discovery of a "trail on the ground." Only such "wild beginnings" will counter the frenetic and eccentric patterns of modern life represented by the plunging of the jets overhead: "If roads are unconnected we must make a path, / no matter how far it is, or how lowly we arrive."

Closely related to the path is the more generalized notion of the journey itself. An inevitable motif in the search for the concealed wilderness, it is frequently incorporated in Stafford's verse. **"Returned to Say"** has already been considered as a kind of grail quest on the part of the poem's speaker and the lost Cree. The journey also informs, though less mythologically, the automobile passage of the poet in **"Traveling through the Dark."** In the lyric entitled **"Journey"** from *Someday, Maybe* human and animal life become a shared identity through the horizontal visual glance. The human perceiver ("You") encounters "a bear or / a wolf": "Eyes / give each other their flame and go out / when you meet."

The attractiveness of the journey motif to Stafford is partially attributable to its correspondence to earliest frontier life. The frontier journey by America's first explorers and settlers yielded the original and most fructifying manifestations of the unspoiled wilderness. **"Boone Children"** and **"For the Grave of Daniel Boone"** are two illustrations of this idealized journey. The latter recounts Boone's westward trek in terms of the construction of an ever-enlarging "home." Those of modern society who are Boone's "heirs" seek to repeat the same journey:

> Children, we live in a barbwire time
> but like to follow the old hands back—
> the ring in the light, the knuckle, the palm,
> all the way to Daniel Boone,
> hunting our own kind of deepening home.

The same journey is transferred to the poet himself in **"Glimpses in the Woods."** In this poem he describes a succession of yew trees deep within the woods, "giver of bows, drinker of shade." The poet allegorically defines "incidents of my journey" through this passageway and invites the reader to accompany him. The trees then provide a "corridor like a question, / a tunnel with one end, a mine meant / to escape from the dark." The column of trees symbolically serves both as an extension of the wilderness itself and a channel into its meaning, "the sacred blur." Another "twinned corridor" appears in **"A Farewell Picture,"** one which extends from the poet's own eyes back to the war years of his youth and his father's steadfast resolution to shoot "only game with his rifle. / People, no."

Beyond the corridor, the trail, and the path—all of which contain the idea of journey—Stafford's other representations of the horizontal network are more surreal. Telephone wires, for example, have been a less conventional addition to this pattern. In **"Long Distance,"** the sound of "ghostly voices" over the telephone elicits for the poet the prospect of overcoming time and returning to his youth and "the town back home." The same symbol informs **"The Farm on the Great Plains"** where the poet describes again his attempt to recover the idyllic life of his boyhood. Eventually, he speculates, "the line will be gone" and the meaning of his youth on the plains will be self-possessed:

> My self will be the plain,
> wise as winter is gray,
> pure as cold posts go
> pacing toward what I know.

The wire is further reduced to a ray of light in **"Level Light,"** a poem that recalls Emily Dickinson's "There is a certain slant of light." In both poems a ray of afternoon sunlight signals the arrival of winter as a reminder of human mortality. Stafford's poem leads to the conclusion that failure in the eyes of the world, like the succumbing of afternoon and season, is the only manner of human progression.

Finally, a brief lyric of only eight lines, **"Recoil,"** introduces the arrow dispatched from the bow. That burst of motion becomes metaphorically the poet's recollection as he seeks to "be myself again" by remembering home. The bow is appropriate to this act of moral release and recovery because it is a product of the wilderness, one that also remembers home:

> The bow bent remembers home long,
> the years of its tree, the whine
> of wind all night conditioning
> it, and its answer—Twang!

The images of the horizontal network have in common the fact that they are all representative of a psychological state: the reaching out of the human toward the wilderness—whether it be the modern wilderness, the wilderness of the poet's youth, or the wilderness of the American frontier. Each of these images—path, corridor, trail, tunnel, a visual glimpse, wire, ray of light, arrow—becomes a means of moral trajectory toward what is most authentic in human values; each represents what in **"Found in a Storm"** Stafford calls "meanings in search of a world."

The upshot of Stafford's poetry of the modern wilderness is a reaffirmation of American life in the twentieth century. It is true that poems like **"At the Bomb Testing Site,"** **"A Documentary from America,"** **"Traveling through the Dark,"** and others remind us of the tenuous and imperiled state of that life. At times a meager stoicism seems the best resort: "Today we have to stand in absolute rain / and face whatever comes from God." Stafford's poetry epitomizes the quality of the Emotive Imagination—that for all its romanticism, this poetry will not take refuge in illusions or pretensions about the state of modern society. Part of his confidence in the future is founded upon the miraculous ability of the wilderness, independent of any human agency, to renew itself. It is this of which he speaks in **"As Pippa Lilted"**: "It will be soon; / good things will happen." Or, the acceptance of the unheroic and unexalted in human nature, an honest perspective, allows "a pretty good world" in **"Adults Only."** Most important of all, however, and that which underlies Stafford's continued didacticism, is the faith that the life he once enjoyed upon the Kansas wilderness and the one he seeks to reclaim upon the modern wilderness is still dynamic and accessible.

Stafford seems to have been the first American poet to incorporate successfully the Emotive Imagination during the 1950s. Each succeeding volume by him has reconfirmed its viability and vitality to him as a poet. Yet, it is worth a final note to acknowledge again that he has never embraced this mode of poetry to the exclusion of other and more traditional kinds of verse.

The importance of the Emotive Imagination to [Bly, Wright, Simpson, and Stafford] and to others may rest on the premise that its use not be exclusive of other forms of poetry; it may be true that the method does not offer a sustaining idiom for a poet whose intent is experimentation over a continuing career. The achievements of Bly, Wright, Simpson, and Stafford nonetheless establish that its practice offers a major lyric experimentation in American poetry, one which lends itself abundantly to a variety of sensibilities and subjects, and one which has yielded individual poems of permanent importance to American letters.

Notes

1. Paul Ramsey, "What the Light Struck," *Tennessee Poetry Journal,* II (Spring, 1969), 19.

2. William E. Stafford, "Finding the Language," in Stephen Berg and Robert Mezey (eds.), *Naked Poetry* (New York: The Bobbs-Merrill Co., 1969), 82.

3. William E. Stafford in Paul Engle and Joseph Langland (eds.), *Poet's Choice* (New York: Dell Publishing Co., 1962), 143.

4. Stafford to George Lensing, July 15, 1972.

5. *Totem and Taboo,* one of Freud's most anthropological studies, speaks of the pattern by which the despised father, following his desired death, is exalted: "The ambivalent attitude towards the father has found a plastic expression in it, and so, too, has the victory of the son's affectionate emotions over his hostile ones. The scene of the father's vanquishment, of his greatest defeat, has become the stuff for the representation of his supreme triumph. The importance which is everywhere, without exception, ascribed to sacrifice lies in the fact that it offers satisfaction to the father for the outrage inflicted on him in the same act in which that deed is commemorated." *Totem and Taboo,* trans. James Strachey (New York: W. W. Norton and Co., 1950), 149-50. It should be pointed out, however, that at no point do Stafford's poems explicitly entertain a death

wish for the father. He has said elsewhere, "My father was far from oppressive." Letter to George Lensing, July 15, 1972.

6. C. G. Jung, "On the Psychology of the Unconscious," in *Two Essays on Analytical Psychology* (New York: 1953), 64.

7. C. G. Jung, "The Relations Between the Ego and the Unconscious," *ibid.,* 196.

8. Stafford to George Lensing, July 15, 1972.

9. See "A Farewell Picture" from *Weather* (Mt. Horeb, Wis.: The Perishable Press, 1969).

10. See "In the Oregon Country" from *West of Your City* (Los Gatos, Calif.: The Talisman Press, 1960).

11. A third printing of *Down in My Heart* in a paperback edition was issued in 1971 from The Brethren Press, Elgin, Illinois.

12. Stafford to George Lensing, July 31, 1972.

13. William E. Stafford, "Brother Antoninus—The World as a Metaphor" in *The Achievement of Brother Antoninus* (Glenview, Ill.: Scott, Foresman and Company, 1967), 3.

14. Philip L. Gerber and Robert J. Gemmett, "Keeping the Lines Wet: A Conversation with William Stafford," *Prairie Schooner,* XLIV (Summer, 1970), 132.

15. Charles F. Grenier, "Stafford's 'Traveling through the Dark': A Discussion of Style," *English Journal,* LV (November, 1966), 1018.

16. Robert Creeley, "'Think What's Got Away,'" *Poetry,* CII (April, 1963), 44.

17. Gerber and Gemmett, "Keeping the Lines Wet: A Conversation with William Stafford," 128.

18. "Reciprocity vs. Suicide, Interview with William Stafford," *Trace,* XLVI (Summer, 1962), 223.

19. See George S. Lensing, "William Stafford, Mythmaker," *Modern Poetry Studies,* VI (Spring, 1975), 1-17.

20. Gerber and Gemmett, "Keeping the Lines Wet: A Conversation with William Stafford," 124-25.

21. Stafford to George Lensing, July 15, 1972.

Leland Krauth (essay date 1984)

SOURCE: Krauth, Leland. "'A Visioned End': Edgar Lee Masters and William Stafford." *MidAmerica* 11 (1984): 90-107.

[*In the following essay, Krauth explores affinities between Stafford's poetry and the work of Edgar Lee Masters.*]

Comet-like, Edgar Lee Masters emerged with the publication of *Spoon River Anthology* in 1915 from dark obscurity to shimmering prominence, only to disappear again into ethereal night. Pound's expatriate enthusiasm—"AT LAST," he announced, "At last America has discovered a poet"—quickly gave way to reiterated complaints against Masters's dejected vision.[1] Amy Lowell struck the reverberating note when she pronounced the book as depressing as the Newgate Calendar.[2] For more recent critics, however, the criminals are not the citizens of Spoon River, Masters's grim self-elegists, but his critical judges. In *Beyond Spoon River,* one of his most sympathetic readers, Ronald Primeau, has noted that even Masters's "admirers" don't know the whole of his work.[3] This neglect, together with the insistently negative view of the tenor of his poems, has isolated Masters, stranded him on an all but forgotten shoal far upstream from the rapids of contemporary poetry.

But Masters is closer to us than we realize. Consider these three recent descriptions of contemporary American poetry—the first, a definition of subject matter; the second, a description of postmodern poetic form; the third, an assessment of current practice in prosody:

1) a poetry of immersion . . . an embrace not only of the raw and chaotic energies of contemporary life, but also of the interior life of individual subjects.

2) Postmodern American poetic form . . . is *analogical* . . . [employing] non-literary analogues such as conversation, confession, dream and other kinds of discourse . . .

3) Free verse is clearly the *Lingua Franca* of our time. . . . What we hear in it is the music of the land, and the words we say it with.[4]

What is striking here is how well these summaries fit the Masters of *Spoon River.* Like our contemporary poets, he embraces the raw and chaotic energies of life by driving into the interiors of individual lives; like our contemporary poets, he employs an analogical form by writing verse epigraphs; and like our contemporary poets, he exploits free verse to voice the music of the land. Such unexpected congruencies suggest anew the lasting power of Masters's finest poetry. They also suggest, I think, that we might usefully reexamine Masters's work by comparing his *Spoon River* poems to those of an eminent contemporary poet, William Stafford. For the distance from Masters to Stafford is not as far as it appears on most maps of postmodern poetry.

Stafford himself feels a kinship with Masters. Although he has never discussed Masters publicly in his essays or interviews, Stafford knows his poetry well and considers it one of the seminal influences on his own career. Explaining not only his knowledge of Masters but also his debt to him, he writes:

Specifically, about Masters—yes, oh yes. My parents early introduced us to the Spoon River world, and I know those poems as old friends. My mother could quote some, and I can too . . .

You make me realize that encountering Masters' direct, sceptical and ironic, but caring, bits of insight printed in an arching collection of poems—this kind of reading was a steady encouragement to me:—something called poems could be right out of the lives around me.[5]

Stafford's silence in public about Masters is, he explains, like not "saying much about my brother or anything else so near that I forgot it was an influence."[6] Beyond encouragement and even direct influence, there is between the two poets, I believe, a fundamental congruence of feeling and vision.

Four things specially mark the connections between Masters and Stafford: a common reliance on memory as the generative source of poetry; a common feel for the remembered world of their Midwestern pasts; a common concern over the creative life of the artist in a materialistic society; and a common belief that the darkness of life can be transcended by acts of spirit—by visionary seeing. In more encompassing terms, both poets have a bifocal vision, looking at experience through what Masters called "realistic" and "mystical" eyes.[7] In Masters the realistic view seems to predominate, while in Stafford one is more aware of mystical glimmerings. But whatever the emphasis, both see beyond the empirical world into a sphere of haunting otherness; both write toward "a visioned end."[8]

For Masters and Stafford alike importance lies, in F. Scott Fitzgerald's memorable phrasing, "somewhere back in that vast obscurity beyond the city, where the dark fields of the republic" roll on "under the night." Both poets are "borne back," if not "ceaselessly," at least recurrently, "into the past." Memory opens the space for many of their finest poems. Stafford insists that his writing is "a reckless encounter with whatever comes along," a process of "accepting sequential signals and adjustments toward an always-arriving present," but paradoxically the content of that "always-arriving present" is often the past made available through memory.[9] He is inspired by recollections "stretching back through daily life, into early experiences."[10] Masters was similarly enthralled by his past. He acknowledged, in a sentimental way not often associated with the infamous poet of ascerbic bitterness, that "his heart" lay always in the river valleys of his youth, clenched by "a thousand memories."[11] He insisted that "the story" of his "ancestors" was "woven into . . . [the] fabric" of *Spoon River,* and he was, by his own account at least, devoted not only to his relatives but to all the villagers of his past.[12] "I loved the people there then," he averred, "and I love their memory."[13]

Memory for Stafford arises within the "cave of yourself where you know / and are lifted by important events";

it is "what holds the days together."[14] Knitting his present to his past, memory often functions as both well-spring and matrix of his poems. It leads him back to indelible events—to the class picnic at Garden City, for instance, or to catching catfish in the deep channel—and back to unforgettable people—to his father and mother, of course, to his Aunt Mabel, his Uncle George, to Ella, Bess, Ruth, Althea, Ellen, and the preacher at the corner who "talked like an old gun killing buffalo."[15] Two of his earlier books, *The Rescued Year* (1966) and *Allegiances* (1970), in particular, exploit memory. To a notable degree, both are, like Master's *Spoon River Anthology*, gatherings of remembered people. But once memory has opened for Stafford the world of his poem, imagination holds sway. Some of his seemingly real people are, as he has admitted, invented figures.[16] For Stafford, memory is less literal recall than a vista revealing the unexpected, multiplying possibilities. Commenting in effect on how his poems come into being, Stafford says in **"The Rescued Year,"** "I rubbed / the wonderful old lamp of our dull town" (*N&CP* [*Stories That Could Be True: New and Collected Poems*], 117)—and then, of course, anything can happen: genies or genius can appear.

Masters has a similar sense of the power of memory. "Memory," he insists, "is a kind of reading glass under which spots of earth long beloved take on the aspect of something magical."[17] *Spoon River Anthology* itself came into being when Masters, spending time with his mother "recalling . . . old days," found that he remembered "the whole past" of his village years.[18] In the book memory is in fact doubled, for Masters brings his characters into existence by remembering—and like Stafford, freely inventing—the people of his past, and the characters in turn define themselves by recalling their lives in elegy. Memory for Masters is thus not only an engendering power, as it is for Stafford, but also a primary technique. For both poets, however, memory is more than a recollection of things past; it is the very ontology of the individual present.

What both poets most often remember is place—and the ways of living that take shape from it. Both have an abiding feel for the particularities of their regional past; both know what Stafford says he learned from Masters: that poems can come right out of the world around them. Each poet has testified to the power of the first homeplace. In *The Sangamon* Masters muses in passionate wonder over the hold everyday things exert on the poet:

I'd like to know what it is that catches the imagination like a strange touch on the very heart, the very spiritual being of prenatal memories, that persist with reference to earthplaces, like little streams bordered by willows, like fields of yellow wheat, like hills with the summoning sky above them against which may stand an old corncrib? Why should such common things stir down where there is no explanation in the heart?[19]

And Stafford, having selected a poem out of his Midwestern past, **"The Farm on the Great Plains,"** as his favorite for Paul Engle and Joseph Langland's anthology, *Poet's Choice*, glosses it with an amaze equal to Masters's by remarking that "the *things*" in the poem—"plains, farm, home, winter"—command his "allegiance" in a way that is, he insists, beyond his "power to analyze" for they "possess" him.[20] Both poets are spell-bound by the magic of place.

Most often Masters recreates place in the *Spoon River Anthology* by describing lives played out within the confines of regional life. The details of so simple a declaration as Indignation Jones's, for instance, reverberate with the felt import of lived space:

No more you hear my footsteps in the morning,
Resounding on the hollow sidewalk,
Going to the grocery store for a little corn meal
And a nickel's worth of bacon.[21]

Such lines evoke a past, a place, a whole ethos and its special ways of living. So strong is the grip of locale on Masters that his most natural affirmations are little more than itemizations of remembered regional pastimes:

Do the boys and girls still go to Siever's?
For cider, after school, in late September?
Or gather hazel nuts among the thickets
On Aaron Hatfield's farm when the frosts begin?
For many times with the laughing girls and boys
Played I along the road and over the hills
When the sun was low and the air was cool,
Stopping to club the walnut tree
Standing leafless against a flaming west.
Now, the smell of the autumn smoke,
And the dropping acorns,
And the echoes about the vales
Bring dreams of life. They hover over me.

(*SR* [*Spoon River Anthology*], 52)

Dreams of his past life on the Midwestern plains also hover over Stafford. Throughout his career he has repeatedly made poems out of his familial past. **"A Family Turn"** is a representative portrait, one that "links" for Stafford himself "to a quality in Masters:"[22]

All her Kamikaze friends admired my aunt,
their leader, charmed in vinegar,
a woman who could blaze with such white blasts
as Lawrence's that lit Arabia.
Her mean opinions bent her hatpins.

. . . . .

We swept headlines from under rugs, names
all over town, which I learned her way, by heart,
and blazed with love that burns because it's real.
With a turn that's our family's own,
she'd say, "Our town is not the same"—

Pause—"And it's never been."

(*N&CP*, 114)

While the affectionate humor is distinctly Stafford's, the honest acknowledgement of his aunt's meanness, the slight shock that comes with the revelation that she busybodies and gossips all over town, and, more complexly, the sense that her critical prying breeds genuine love, all these recall Masters's visioning of experience. Stafford's feel for his regional past takes in the landscape, as well as the people who inhabit it, and he often allows place to bespeak its own meanings, to voice the music of the land:

> The well rising without sound,
> the spring on a hillside,
> the plowshare brimming through deep ground
> everywhere in the field—
>
> (*N&CP*, 51)

Sometimes, however, Stafford attaches general reflections to the specifics that prompt them:

> Mine was a Midwest home—you can keep your world.
> Plain black hats rode the thoughts that made our code.
> We sang hymns in the house; the roof was near God.
>
> The light bulb that hung in the pantry made a wan
>   light,
> but we could read by it the names of preserves—
> outside, the buffalo grass, and the wind in the night.
>
> . . . . .
>
> The sun was over our town; it was like a blade.
> Kicking cottonwood leaves we ran toward storms.
> Wherever we looked the land would hold us up.
>
> (*N&CP*, 29-30)

Here, as in Masters, place becomes compelling presence, real in itself, redolent of past delight, and emblematic of something larger still, of something that might be called existential sufficiency. In both poets this sense of adequacy—"the land would hold us up," Stafford tells us—is associated with the deeply felt particularities of the Midwestern world.

While finding stability as well as beauty in the world of their past, Masters and Stafford alike look askance at much of the present. They have in common a strong didactic impulse, an urge to instruct their age, one which is in fact out of sync with the two eras they bridge, being at odds not only with the tenets of modernism but also with the tenor of postmodern poetry. Yet Masters and Stafford are poet-critics of their society. Both view with alarm the increasing commercialism of America; both fear the stifling of liberal ideology; and both object to the madness of war.

Much of their discontent with America is in the familiar vein of Midwestern protest. From Howells and Twain on though Garland to Anderson, Dreiser, and Lewis, Midwestern writers have inveighed against the drift of American life. More specifically the Midwestern writer has characteristically complained of a cultural impoverishment. Garland strikes this recurrent note with poignant humor in his diaries:

> I've been rereading Hawthorne's *Mosses [from] an Old Manse* and contrasting his life with mine. How little I have to work with as compared to his Concord. . . . The only moss I have is on the woodshed.[23]

The Midwestern writer has typically attributed the vacancy in his field of vision, to borrow James's famous phrase, not only to the crude newness of his region but also to the steady drive toward materialism in American life in general. Anderson made the contrast between artistic endeavor and practical business the very center of his personally liberating self-mythologizing. "My own nature," he exclaimed, again and again, "was in revolt against moneymaking as an end in life."[24] The classic formulation of the case, however, is Dreiser's polemic, "Life, Art and America":

> Here in America, by reason of an idealistic Constitution which is largely a work of art and not a workable system, you see a nation dedicated to so-called intellectual and spiritual freedom, but actually devoted with an almost bee-like industry to the gathering and storing and articulation and organization and use of purely material things. In spite of all our base-drum announcement of our servitude to the intellectual ideals of the world (copied mostly, by the way, from England) no nation has ever contributed less, philosophically or artistically or spiritually, to the actual development of the intellect and the spirit.[25]

The same strain can be heard in the pronouncements, as well as the poems, of Masters and Stafford. Masters centers his autobiography, *Across Spoon River,* on his struggle to free himself from a business environment inimical to art. "And here was I," he writes at one summarizing moment, "in this apartment badly deviled to make a living, and doing that in a business which destroyed every imaginative impulse."[26] Having freed himself from such entanglement sooner in his career than Masters, Stafford still feels his estrangement, even from those who profess respect for his art:

> Oh, the people around me voice regard for art, writing, and so on. But I confess: they like poetry and poets in terms which seem to me not valid. I do not have the qualities, motives, purposes, hopes that they seem to think poets have. In short, I do—as a poet, that is—feel alien.[27]

From their "alien's" point of view, both Masters and Stafford assail the misdirection of American life.

For Masters in *Spoon River* the chief destroyer of humanity is money—the love of it, the striving for it, the power it entails. Masters sees in someone like Anthony Findley, an archetypal figure of success in the Horatio Alger mold, a basic perversion of values: "I say of man," Findley says, "'tis worse to lose / Money than friends"; and, "'Tis better to be feared than loved." (*SR*, 152) Masters's principal embodiment of the corruption of American life and character, however, is of course Thomas Rhodes—the financial, political, and ecclesiastical kingpin of Spoon River. Masters makes Rhodes not only grasping, self-serving, and morally depraved, but also actively hostile toward the creative artists of Spoon River. Pointedly he has Rhodes dismiss Petit, the Poet, Margaret Fuller Slack, the would-be novelist, and Percival Sharp, the ironic reader of icons often taken to be one of Masters's self-portraits. He thus dramatizes what he feels as the antagonism of money-men toward all imaginative endeavor, thereby endorsing the Midwestern notion that there is an irreconcilable antithesis between materialism and the creative life itself. The fall of Rhodes, incomplete as it is, is Masters's rebuke to the human arrogance born of wealth and power. It is also, perhaps, a sign of his hope, fragile though it is, for the life of the mind.

Like Masters, although in softer tones, Stafford often objects in general to much of American life:

> Counting the secretaries coming out of a building
> there were more people than purposes.
>
>   (*N&CP*, 51)

> And the great national events danced
> their grotesque, fake importance.
>
>   (*N&CP*, 152)

Stafford is far less the social critic than Masters, but there is no mistaking his feeling that a money-mad culture is perverting the human. In the fifth section of the long poem, **"The Move to California,"** he is for once almost savagely ironic in condemning America's debilitating obsessions:

> Those who wear green glasses through Nevada
> travel a ghastly road in unbelievable cars
> and lose pale dollars
> under violet hoods when they park at gambling houses.

> I saw those martyrs—all sure of their cars in the open
> and always believers in any handle they pulled—
> wracked on an invisible cross
> and staring at a green table.
>
>   (*N&CP*, 47)

Stafford marks the loss of the human in these representative Americans by making them exotic. His ironic evocation of the traditionally religious—"martyrs," "wracked on an invisible cross"—anticipates the antidote to their illness which he dramatizes in the next stanza:

> While the stars were watching
> I crossed the Sierras in my old Dodge

> letting the speedometer measure God's kindness,
> and slept in the wilderness on the hard ground.
>
>   (*N&CP*, 47)

For Stafford, nature often seems to offer a norm for human action. More explicitly than Masters, Stafford calls for a return to the elemental: "We must go back and find a trail on the ground," yet like Masters, he challenges all present-day hubris: "we must travel on our knees." (*N&CP*, 44) Nature in Stafford's poetry is never static (even his rocks move and intend) but always becoming. He dismisses those "Deaf to process, alive only to ends," "the logical ones." (*N&CP*, 55) The epiphanies in his poetry are sudden illuminations of mystery that defy rationality as well as materiality. They occur by chance or by an imaginative knowing at one with nature's beckoning essences. For as Jonathan Holden has observed, a major theme of Stafford's work is "the imagination—its resilience, its stubborn and playful instinct for deriving meaning and awe from the world."[28] Apprehending the natural world aright is for Stafford a necessary act of imagination, the crucial exercise of the very creativity Masters feels is jeopardized by the likes of Thomas Rhodes. With an urgency equal to Masters's, Stafford envisions as disaster any loss of imaginative power (see in particular **"The Animal That Drank Up Sound"**). While Masters characteristically condemns those who thwart the creative life, Stafford typically exhorts his readers to release their imperiled potentialities. Here, for instance, he enjoins humanity to remain human through imaginative responsiveness to the portents of earth:

> The earth says have a place, be what that place
> requires; hear the sound the birds imply
> and see as deep as ridges go behind
> each other.
>
>   (*N&CP*, 75)

Of course for both Masters and Stafford one must not only imagine what the world suggests but also face what it presents. Perhaps the most notorious aspect of Masters's poetry is its bleakness, its insistent sense of catastrophe, befallen or impending. This mood, too, has its counterpart in Stafford's poems. Both poets envision humankind in large perspective, as, in Masters's terms, "a part of the scheme of things," "a part of the question / Of what the drama means." (*SR*, 262) Both see human life played out against a dark cosmic backdrop; both are haunted by a sense of apocalyptic peril, a fear of ominous endings near at hand. Here, from one of Masters's poems, is their common atmosphere:

> Then the sun went down between great drifts
> Of distant storms. For a rising wind
> Swept clean the sky and blew the flames
> of the unprotected stars . . .
>
>   (*SR*, 211)

Or again, even more terribly and explicitly from Stafford:

> Now we hear the stars torn upward
> out of the sky; the alarm
> shadows us as we run away
> from this fact of a life, our home.

(*N&CP*, 127)

The similarity of mood is arresting. This dark vision is by no means exclusive to Masters and Stafford (one could in fact argue that it is common to most twentieth-century poets). But it is one they share, and it is one of the things Stafford has singled out as central to his own appreciation of Masters. "I had an appetite," he writes, "for that bitter but sustaining way of seeing."[29]

In neither poet, finally, is the bitter way of seeing life at large confirmed. Despite the prevailing critical view to the contrary, Masters's poetry resists its own darkness. And Stafford's not only counters its darkness but transfigures it, not into light but into a signifying obscurity worthy of human embrace. In both, to use Stafford's phrase, the "bitter . . . way of seeing" is also "sustaining."

The other side of the bleakness of *Spoon River* is, as careful readers know, a celebration of human nature, an affirmation of lived life, and an assertion of at least the possibility of metaphysical meaning. The point is worth emphasizing because the negative view of Masters persists. As recently as 1982 one critic, sensitively rediscovering the regional literature of Illinois, rediscovered only the misanthropic Masters.[30] Yet Masters invested the world of Spoon River with glimmerings of hope, joy, and faith. We need to re-see his poems, both one by one (for they are often technically more interesting than criticism has acknowledged) and as an anthology. His gathering, it seems to me, might best be reviewed as a dialectic. Positions—social, political, moral, psychological, intellectual, sexual, philosophical, and accidental—are balanced by their opposites. The striking, discontinuous utterance of Dippold the Optician, who shifts the lens of vision from color to families to knights of old to women to fields of grain to goblets to space to nothing to trees to lakes to sky to depths of air, should teach us how to see Masters's book. (see *SR*, 201-202) The energy of *Spoon River* arises from the constant interplay of conflicting perspectives. It is an exchange without final resolution but with a clear inclination.

The inclination is a desire to uphold, to affirm and believe. Masters himself suggested as much when he spoke of the joy in the book, of its celebrations, and especially of its design. He understood his structure as one that would move his reader from confusion, failure, and limitation to heroism and truth, or as he defined the final sequence, to "heroes and the enlightened spirits."[31]

His celebration of human nature careens between love and self-sacrifice, on the one side, and courage and endurance, on the other. His pioneers loom as heroes of accomplishment:

> We went by oxen to Tennessee,
> Thence after years to Illinois,
> At last to Spoon River.
> We cut the buffalo grass,
> We felled the forests,
> We built the school houses, built the bridges,
> Leveled the roads and tilled the fields
> Where the leaves fall,

and as mystical spirits whose essence is as unfathomable as it is riveting

> What was it in their eyes?—
> . . . . .
>
> It was like a pool of water,
> Amid oak trees at the edge of a forest,
> Where the leaves fall,
> As you hear the crow of a cock
> From a far-off house . . .

(*SR*, 237)

His affirmation of life lived fully, whatever the result, pervades the volume, providing the sounding board against which all the elegiac cries—of joy or pain or triumph or despair or frustration or fullment—are to be heard. This note, enjoining all to embrace life, is struck most fully by that fictive version of Masters's grandmother, Lucinda Matlock, who voices it through a denunciation of succeeding generations (thereby allowing later critics to hear only its bitter strain):

> Degenerate sons and daughters,
> Life is too strong for you—
> It takes life to love Life.

(*SR*, 239)

She only proclaims, however, her version of the drive and joy that many Spoon Riverites testify to in their varying tones: "In the morning of life I knew aspiration and saw glory," (*SR*, 37) and again, "I lived in wonder, worshipping earth and heaven"; (*SR*, 252) and again, "We were ready then to walk together / And sing in chorus and chant the dawn / Of life that is wholly life." (*SR*, 270)

Spoon River as a whole "confronts the problem of the meaning of existence,"[32] and despite the numerous examples of those who fail to find any meaning in their lives, despite those who vociferously insist that there is no meaning to be found, Masters entertains the possibility that there is purpose and design to human living. He does so most emphatically by giving the final part of *Spoon River* over to the "enlightened spirits." Throughout the book we hear from a number of visionaries, but their number increases as the book unfolds (it is far less static and repetitive than most readers allow) until they actually dominate the close. Even a partial list of them would include Jacob Goodpasture, Benjamin Fraser, Aaron Hatfield, Jennie McGrew, Faith Matheny, Willie Metcalf, Willie Pennington, Zilpha Marsh, Gustav Richter, Isaiah Beethoven, Arlo Will, Elijah Browning, and the Village Atheist, who ends up, of course, as a believer. Their visions range from the conventional to the crackpot (for a sampling of extremes, see Aaron Hatfield, modeled on Masters's grandfather, and Benjamin Fraser), and from the earth-immersive, Roethesque—"On spring days I tramped through the country / To get the feeling . . . / That I was not a separate thing from the earth" but one that had "flowers growing in me" (*SR*, 257)—to the absolute ethereal *other*: "And there you sit thrilling lest the Mystery / Stand before you and strike you dead / With a splendor like the sun's." (*SR*, 255) But the point, I believe, is not *what* any one visionary beholds, but just the fact that she or he *sees*. Vision alone is elevating; vision alone provides a meaning beyond the moil of ordinary living. To go a bit beyond *Spoon River* in Masters's own writing is to discover quite clearly the pattern of importance latent within the work. In a later poem, a reminiscent response to the prairies of his youth, Masters asserts the uplifting union of the seer and the seen that defines his *Spoon River* visionaries:

> To contemplate the prairie is
> To fathom time, to guess at infinite space,
> To find the Earth-spirit in a dreaming mood.
> In Illinois the prairies are a soul . . .
>   . . . . .
>
>   above all
> Is the spirit of the scene, the mystical
> Presence, not wholly nature, and not man,
> But made of these . . .[33]

Like Masters's, the world of Stafford's poetry is shrouded in darkness (it is perhaps fitting that his best known poem, the title piece for his National Book Award, is **"Traveling Through the Dark"**). He creates moments of human loss, intensified by a piercing awareness of mortality:

> But I stood on the skull of the world the night he
>   died, and
> knew that I leased a place to live with my white
>   breath.
>
>   (*N&CP*, 32)

He acknowledges existential confusions and anxieties:

> lost in hydrogen—we live by seems things
>   . . . . .
>
> And, whatever is happening, we are here;
> a lurch or a god has brought us together.
> We do our jobs—listening in fear . . .
>
>   (*N&CP*, 75)

He insists, Masters-like, upon the bleakness of life:

> Today we have to stand in absolute rain
> and face whatever comes from God,
> or stoop to smooth the earth over little things
> that went into dirt, out of the world.
>
>   (*N&CP*, 89)

And he finds portents of possible meaninglessness all around him—in the sky, for instance, when geese lose their direction:

> faltering back through their circle they came.
>
> Were they lost up there in the night?
> They always knew the way, we thought.
> You looked at me across the room:—
>
> We live in a terrible season.
>
>   (*N&CP*, 86)

But Stafford's attitude toward the painful, bleak, uncertain aspect of life is accepting. Although he is sharply aware of "how cold, / unmanageable the real world" is (*N&CP*, 119), he welcomes it. His acquiescence is so pronounced that Robert Creeley has declared it a clear and present "danger" that "things will become cozy" in Stafford's poems.[34] Whether dangerous or not, Stafford embraces life in all its darkness. His affirmations equal, even exceed, Masters's. Matching Masters's "It takes life to love Life," Stafford proclaims,

> we ordinary beings can cling to the earth and love
> where we are, sturdy for common things.
>
>   (*N&CP*, 193)

And echoing both Masters's cries of life's tangled darkness *and* his insistence upon stoic engagement, Stafford grimly announces:

> Better to stand in the dark of things and crash,
> hark yourself, blink in the day, eat bitter bush
> and look out over the world.
>
>   (*N&CP*, 126)

Stafford's stance of acceptance is anchored, I believe, by his abiding sense of what he has variously termed "a certain directional feeling we have," "reverberating patterns," or "impressions of holiness."[35]

As in Masters's poetry, this underlying or overarching significance is apprehended by heroic questers, ordinary wanderers, and visionary seers. Like Masters, Stafford celebrates "the star-striding men / who crossed the continent." (*N&CP*, 104) He creates a series of legendary figures—some historical, like Daniel Boone, most imaginary, like Deerslayer, Logue, Sublette, and the Wanderer—who confront, as Logue does, the "world of the farthest." (*N&CP*, 167) They are Stafford's counterparts to Master's pioneers and visionaries. And again like Masters, who endows his grandparents with heroic vision, Stafford makes his own father into one of these far-seeing guides. He mythologizes his father as someone who teaches him to listen out "into places" where "the walls of the world flared, widened" (*N&CP,* 33), as someone who teaches him to believe in the "sight of angels or anything unusual" (*N&CP,* 63), as someone who teaches him to know that he is the world's "slow guest, / one of the common things / that move in the sun and have / close, reliable friends / in the earth, in the air, in the rock." (*N&CP,* 157) Above all, his mythic father gives him his life's occupation: "'Your job is to find what the world is trying to be.'" (*N&CP,* 107)

Heeding this father's advice, Stafford is the chief visionary in his own poetry. It is Stafford himself who propounds the visions of metaphysical meaning which correspond to those set forth by Masters beyond the mundane world of Spoon River. These seeings are some of Stafford's most famous poems. **"Bi-Focal"** encapsulates his visionary faith:

Sometimes up out of this land
a legend begins to move.
Is it a coming near
of something under love?

Love is of the earth only,
the surface, a map of roads
leading wherever go miles
or little bushes nod.

Not so the legend under,
fixed, inexorable,
deep as the darkest mine
the thick rocks won't tell.

As fire burns the leaf
and out of the green appears
the vein in the center line
and the legend veins under there,

So, the world happens twice—
once what we see it as;
second it legends itself
deep, the way it is.

(*N&CP,* 48)

To any skeptical reader, the certitude of the last stanza is in question, and the way the world "legends itself" may be indistinguishable from, only an instance of, "what we see it as." But as with Masters's seers, so with the visionary Stafford himself, what matters most is just the capacity to discover meanings—meanings which may or may not actually inhere in the universe. To the extent that Stafford and Masters believe in the legends that write life into the universe they participate in what has been defined as the central postmodern poetic concern: "to uncover the ways man and nature are unified, so that value can be seen as the result of

immanent processes in which man is as much object as he is agent of creativity."[36] To see Stafford in this light is to see him as a poet of his age, our moment; to see Masters's similarity is to see, in yet another way, that he too is our contemporary. Placing the two together reveals a basic continuity in Midwestern writing. Both poets present "a visioned end," and find in such discovering, as Stafford suggests, the essential human activity:

And all, slung here in our cynical constellation,
whistle the wild world, live by imagination.

(*N&CP,* 64)

Notes

1. Ezra Pound, "Webster Ford," *Egoist,* 2 (June 1, 1915), pp. 11-12.

2. See Amy Lowell, *Tendencies in Modern American Poetry* (Boston and New York: Houghton Mifflin Co., 1917), pp. 174-75.

3. Ronald Primeau, *Beyond "Spoon River": The Legacy of Edgar Lee Masters* (Austin: Univ. of Texas Press, 1981), p. x.

4. Charles Molesworth, *The Fierce Embrace: A Study of Contemporary American Poetry* (Columbia: Univ. of Missouri Press, 1979), p. ix; Jonathan Holden, "Postmodern Poetic Form: A Theory," *New England Review,* 6, No. 1 (Autumn 1983), 3; Wayne Dodd, "And The Look Of The Bay Mare Shames Silliness Out Of Me," *The Ohio Review,* No. 28 (1982), p. 36.

5. William Stafford to Leland Krauth, 26 March 1984.

6. *Ibid.*

7. Edgar Lee Masters, *Across Spoon River: An Autobiography* (New York: Farrar & Rinehart, 1936), p. 318.

8. *Ibid.,* p. 402.

9. William Stafford, *Writing the Australian Crawl: Views on the Writer's Vocation* (Ann Arbor: Univ. of Michigan Press, 1978), pp. 66-67.

10. *Ibid.,* p. 38.

11. Edgar Lee Masters, "The Genesis of Spoon River," *American Mercury,* 27 (Jan. 1933), p. 40.

12. *Ibid.*

13. Edgar Lee Masters, *The Sangamon* (New York: Farrar & Rinehart, 1942), p. 116. The enthusiasm for his townsmen expressed here by Masters should be compared to his contempt for them registered in his autobiography (see *Across Spoon River,* p. 410).

14. William Stafford, *Roving Across Fields* (Daleville, Ind.: The Barwood Press Cooperative, 1983), p. 49.

15. William Stafford, *Stories That Could Be True: New and Collected Poems* (New York: Harper & Row, 1977), p. 163; hereafter cited parenthetically in my text as *N&CP*.

16. See Jonathan Holden, *The Mark to Turn: A Reading of William Stafford's Poetry* (Lawrence: The Univ. Press of Kansas, 1976), pp. 3-6. This is the best extended critical study of Stafford.

17. Masters, *The Sangamon*, p. 23.

18. Masters, *Across Spoon River*, pp. 338-39.

19. Masters, *The Sangamon*, pp. 87-88.

20. William Stafford, in *Poet's Choice*, ed. Paul Engle and Joseph Langland (New York: The Dial Press, 1962), p. 143.

21. Edgar Lee Masters, *Spoon River Anthology* (1915; rpt. New York: Macmillan Pub. Co., 1962), p. 45; hereafter cited parenthetically in my text as *SR*. Whenever I use one of Masters's Spoon River speakers as the voice of his own attitudes, I do so believing that the normally suspect identification between author and created character can be established in the specific instance by Masters's other personal writings. I imagine that for Masters generally what Stafford once said of himself was also true: "Successive poems are . . . like multiplying self." (Stafford, *Roving Across Fields*, p. 20)

22. Stafford to Krauth, 26 March 1984.

23. *Hamlin Garland's Diaries*, ed. Donald Pizer (San Marino, California: The Huntington Library, 1968), p. 53.

24. *Letters of Sherwood Anderson*, ed. Howard Mumford Jones and Walter B. Rideout (Boston: Little Brown and Co., 1953), p. 82.

25. Theodore Dreiser, "Life, Art and America," *Hey Rub-A-Dub-Dub: A Book Of The Mystery And Wonder And Terror Of Life* (New York: Boni and Liveright, 1920), p. 258.

26. Masters, *Across Spoon River*, p. 209.

27. "Reciprocity vs. Suicide: Interview with William Stafford," *Trace*, 46 (Summer 1962), 224.

28. Holden, *The Mark to Turn*, p. 6.

29. Stafford to Krauth, 26 March 1984.

30. See Robert C. Bray, *Rediscoveries: Literature and Place in Illinois* (Urbana: Univ. of Illinois Press, 1982), pp. 152-56. An extensive review of critical response to Masters is provided in John T. Flanagan, *Edgar Lee Masters: The Spoon River Poet and His Critics* (Metuchen, New Jersey: The Scarecrow Press, 1974). For somewhat more recent commentaries and bibliography, see *The Vision of This Land: Studies of Vachel Lindsay, Edgar Lee Masters, and Carl Sandburg*, ed. John E. Hallwas and Dennis J. Reader (Macomb: Western Illinois Univ. Press, 1976).

31. Masters, "Genesis of Spoon River," p. 50.

32. Cesare Pavese, "The Spoon River Anthology," *American Literature, Essays and Opinions*, trans. Edwin Fussell (Berkeley: Univ. of Cal. Press, 1970), p. 43.

33. Masters, *The Sangamon*, p. 25. For an excellent discussion of Masters's mysticism, see Primeau, *Beyond Spoon River*, pp. 168-205.

34. Robert Creeley, "'Think What's Got Away . . .'," *Poetry*, 102 (April 1963), p. 44.

35. Stafford, in "Discussions During the Spring Poetry Festival, Martin, April 16-17, 1971," *Tennessee Poetry Journal*, 4, No. 3 (Spring 1971), p. 18; "Keeping the Lines Wet: A Conversation With William Stafford," ed. Philip L. Gerber and Robert J. Gemmett, *Prairie Schooner*, 44 (Summer 1970), p. 126; "Reciprocity vs. Suicide," p. 223.

36. Charles Altieri, "From Symbolist Thought To Immanence: The Ground of Postmodern Poetics," *Boundary 2*, 1, No. 3 (Spring 1973), p. 608.

William Stafford and Lars Nordström (interview date 20 December 1985)

SOURCE: Stafford, William, and Lars Nordström. "Willingly Local: A Conversation with William Stafford about Regionalism and Northwest Poetry." *Studia Neophilologica* 59 (1987): 41-57.

[*In the following interview, conducted in December 1985, Stafford discusses changing critical perceptions of American regionalism.*]

[*Lars Nordström*]: *You tend to use material both from the Midwest and the Pacific Northwest.*

[William Stafford]: Or any place.

Or any place—right! And by regional material people who talk about this, critics, seem to mean both that which is readily identifiable and that which demands knowledge of the region to identify, but which is unique to the place. Like a particular place or person . . . anything in time and space. I realize that you write a great deal that has no obvious regional ties, but when you do, and when you notice that a poem starts to include material from a place, say the Northwest, do you recognize any recurring patterns, thoughts, or themes in your treatment of this material?

Yes, I have several reactions to that. One is that writers and critics like to talk about region and sense of place. It's very popular. I've been on panels about it in this country. And I can understand why this attracts people, but I have another angle about it. I think that any artist is sustained by the things of this world, and the things that are near loom larger, impinge, and they are important because they are near. But they are not important because they are any certain part of the world. Or so it seems to me. But to relate easily and quickly, I suppose, to what is near you is a gracious thing. It's a positive thing. So, wherever you are you are regional if you are an artist. Or so it seems to me, because you use the things that are there. That's what you rebound to, reverberate with, but I wouldn't like to make the jump to say that therefore it's important that Theodore Roethke was in the Northwest, for instance. I think if he'd stayed in Michigan, or gone to New York, or wherever he'd gone, he'd been a poet if the other conditions had been right.

Now, there's another thing, that is, if I find myself beginning to write a poem that feels regional—and I'm intrigued by the way you said that because I certainly do understand it—because anything you begin to write that begins to be whatever it is, if you encourage it to go on being just exactly what it is, you do so. So if it sounds regional when I'm writing it, or feels regional, I'm very likely to make it even more regional. And, I guess maybe this will be my finale too—you urged me on—that is, you use the terminology, the local names, the things that will feel exotic to someone from somewhere else for several reasons. For one reason, you use whatever names, nouns, locutions come natural to you, and you don't change them unless there is a reason. And the reason of trying to talk like everybody else is not a good reason, because those peculiarities are sometimes the flavorful part of what you are doing.

Yes, that seems to make sense. There are problems with the words "region" and "regionalism" too, depending on how you define them.

Yeah, that's right.

The associations vary a great deal. There was a survey of regionalism made by The South Dakota Review *about ten years ago, and I believe you were in it and so were several other Northwest poets.*

I remember that.

It was interesting to read the reactions, because, first of all, most of the people from the Northwest were in favor of the word regionalism. It seemed to me that the way they reacted to the word regionalism depended on how they defined it. Because it has been, especially in this country I think, associated with provincialism, things that cannot be appreciated outside the region; you know local in a negative sense; parochialism.

Yes, that jumpiness I think comes from a historical thing that happened in the literature of the United States. There was the regionalism group, Hamlin Garland and so on. And there was the feeling that these people are quaint, they are limited, uninteresting. So some writers get jumpy about it. I don't feel jumpy about it, partly because everyone is regional, place is everywhere. So I have a kind of joking way of identifying this: A national writer in America is a regional writer who lives in New York.

(Laughter.)

That's a good way of putting it. I see your point, even though I know there are others, like Richard Hugo, who in a conversation with you in the Northwest Review *said that he thought there was more landscape coming into Northwest poetry than elsewhere. As an example he compared it to the work of W. S. Merwin, who, even though having lived all over the world, has no strong, continuous sense of place in his work. In your poetry one has that sense. I think Hugo has a point there, and it has to do with your poetics, with what kind of material you use for your poems.*

Well, maybe so. Northwest writers—it's interesting that they are the ones who impinged on your attention as the ones who embraced regionalism—they like their region. But there are other regions where the writers like it too, the South for example. *I'll Take My Stand* is the title of one book from the South. And Northwesterners take their stand. Hugo worked at it pretty hard to embrace regionalism. He had Duwamish and so on in his poems, all sorts of regional words.

Does using regional material mean, as you see it, that the user becomes part of a kind of regionalism? How would you define the difference between being involved in a sense of place or in regionalism?

Yes, I think in the parlance used in America, regionalism would imply that the writer is deliberately exaggerating the localness of material. That part of what the writer is counting on, and that the readers are savoring, is a flavor that is from elsewhere, or that is quaint. A sense of place would be different, I think, because you would not be deliberately exploiting or making hay out of the exoticness of the material; you would just be in the material, just be using what is natural to you in your kind of life. So there is a kind of a literary posturing that goes with regionalism, and sometimes they even use the odd spellings, you know, and they use words like "tarnation" and so on.

Well, that was the charge levelled against many of the regionalists of the 30s, and the critics then used the term "local color." But the regionalists separated regionalism, which they saw as the realistic investigation of the place, from local color, which stood for the quaint exaggeration, distortion, or exploitation.

I can accept any of that terminology, it would not bother me.

It's interesting that you say that today, giving "sense of place" a positive meaning and calling regionalism the exaggeration, because it suggests a similar situation. Meanings change.

I'm afraid language is like that.

I read something in an essay by you called "The End of a Golden String," where you say: "Retreating into the snug little weaving shed of the writer, I would advance, timidly, an idea contrary to the scholarly, the masterful, the eloquent. Sometimes it seems to me that a writer habitually touches the earth, touches home, clings to all that passes. Even to start a poem is to unreel stingily from the starting place, and to make each successive move out of minimum psychic expenditure . . .

Let me say that a poem comes from a life, not a study."

First, is this an understated retort to the theoreticians of "High Modernism," supporting objectivity, universality, timelessness? And secondly, is it unreserved support of the openness to the subjective and particular impulses from one's sense of place or region?

Well, if I'd use your terminology I would embrace the last thing you said. I think it is openness to what comes to the person. In fact, I would base my aesthetic, such as it is, on this concept: That art comes from total experience, not just experience of other art. So it often seems to me that many people who are in the arts, and who are critics of art, assume that an artist is a person who learns from other artists. That art is like a relay race passed from Picasso to somebody else to me, you know. Well, Picasso is a little kid in some town and all those experiences have a bearing on his life and on his art. So to narrow it down to say that his art derives from other art is a drastic exclusion of the influences on a human being. So I would try to make art, and conceptualize art, and let my own art be an embracing of the whole experience. So I've tried, I even have some terminology, but it hasn't taken a hold: It's the tradition of total experience, rather than the tradition of art.

Yes, I realize that there is an ironic line in one of your poems about Yeats, Eliot and Pound and how they studied art.

That's right, I remember how it goes. It's from the poem **"Things I Learned Last Week"**: "Yeats, Pound and Eliot saw art as / growing from other art. They studied that."

In the Northwest, has the local poetry community been of importance? By "local poetry community" I simply mean other poets living in the area, local poetry magazines, local poetry readings, local presses, the various grants which have enabled writers to stay at home and dedicate themselves to writing, and so on. In short, does this reinforce a sense of place?

Yes, I think those things are all important. To the community of artists here I'd also add bookstores, libraries. These things that are a part of your life are either convenient or inconvenient, and it helps—it helps me at least—to feel a part of a community. I feel sociable, and the existence of these other writers, say, just to restrict it to one element that is local, would be gratifying and stimulating. Partly because, maybe mostly because we just happen to be interested in the same things, and when we get together we have a lot to interchange about. Contrary to what many people say that writers are a close mouthed group, and hide what they are doing from others, I found they are just as eager to sprawl all over the place and tell what they're doing and try out things that they have done. Trying out things that one has done is not my style in the sociability of a group, I think it inhibits sociability. But I do enjoy the company of others who are doing writing.

You have published seven major collections of poetry, but you have also published over two dozen small editions of poetry, mostly in the Midwest, but in the Northwest too. Can one interpret this as support for a decentralization of the literary publishing business, and support for local publishing?

Yes, I'm a participant in small press publishing in the sense that it includes many small collections that I've published, still, I'm an outsider in the sense that it happened. I did not engineer it to happen, it just happened to me.

Is that right?

That is, people would say: "Don't you have some poems we could make a chapbook out of?" This happened very recently, maybe things you have not seen which I have around here. I'll show you. So whenever that's part of sociability they say: "Well, I have this press, and I'm thinking of doing this and that;" or "I've already done a few and I would like to do something of yours.

Do you have anything?" Well, if they're really interested, sure I have things. I'm writing all the time. So these things have just trickled out by invitation, and they have been in the Northwest partly because I am here, and would meet people here, but they have been in other parts of the country, even in the central parts of the country, and so on. Wherever there is a small press. Just recently someone from New York had a press, and they published something of mine called **The Quiet of the Land.** They did a good job with the printing, and it happened just the way all the others happened. Someone said: "Don't you have some poems we could put together?"

Why do you think there is this great interest in publishing small editions? Is it the result of the National Endowment for the Arts, or is it partly because of the dissatisfaction with the New York publishers?

Yes, well I guess it would seem that you would have to account for it since it grew up out of nothing. And you immediately alerted me when you said the National Endowment for the Arts; it's true that they have nourished these things with money.

They did in the past.

Yeah, that's right. Well, these things come and go, but there are always sources around here and there. The way I'd see it is this: You live somewhere in the country; you are interested in reading and writing and printing, and making things. And you don't move to New York just in order to make a chapbook. You happen to be here, why go anywhere else? You have got a press here, the mail costs the same all over the country, and you can get as many poems in Hawaii as you could anywhere else. That is, if people are alert enough to realize that you don't have to go and hand it to someone; you mail it. So, you know, you can live, you can put out *Milkweed Chronicle* in Minneapolis, or put out "Poetry Southwest" or something, wherever you are.

It's a fascinating situation, but it makes it very difficult too for the scholar to track things down because there is so much that is not available.

Yeah, that's right. The channels of distribution are centralized, but the printing is decentralized, so how do you get into the channels? That's where the National Endowment tried to help, that's where all sorts of things like Poets & Writers tried to help.

Do you feel that establishing a major publishing house in the Northwest is of great importance? Do you think such a thing would alter Northwest poetry?

Well, you know it's happened, again and again. So establishing it and seeing it nourish and grow, those are two different things. Of course, there are publishers

here who have been here for years, but in order to survive they have to turn to something other than pushing little chapbooks around in bookstores. They just can't live like that. Now there are some that are doing fairly well now, I suppose Copper Canyon, Graywolf, Breitenbush, and so on. But the ones that have been here a long time and have sort of got solid like Binford-Mort; they do everything, rock climbing books, everything.

The university presses seem to have cut down on their poetry publishing. In the 70s they published a great deal of poetry it seemed—the University of Washington would publish poetry, but now that does not seem to be the case.

I have not really been aware of that myself, because what one university decides not to do, another university decides to do. It's sort of like things bumping up all over the country, Ohio, Georgia, Southern Methodist, University of Utah, I don't know, all sorts of places. It's true, I do remember Washington put out quite a few, but for all I know they'd do another one if they get a hold of a good manuscript.

Perhaps I am projecting a non-existent pattern onto some of your poems, but it seems to me that in those rare instances when other poets find their way into your poems, they seem to be Northwest or Western poets, like Roethke, Hugo, and Jeffers. And you have edited a book of Western poetry. I also know that you have written on other writers from other parts of the country, I can think of Thoreau and Willa Cather right off the top of my head. But does this mean that you feel a sort of kinship with Westerners, that these poets are somehow more intimately connected to you? Is that why they come up in poetry, or is this not really true?

Well, I think it's not my volition that has made this happen. It's circumstances. For instance, one book that I wrote was called *The Achievement of Brother Antoninus.* Scott, Foresman wrote to me and asked me to write in their series "The Achievement of . . ." They have several ones, and they said: "There are two people we are especially interested in at the moment, Richard Wilbur, up in New England, and William Everson, on the West Coast." Well, I wrote back and I said: "I've always been fascinated by Richard Wilbur, and I have a lot of his books here. I'd like to write a book on Richard Wilbur." Well, they ran into trouble because they could not get permission to use a lot of poems we needed for that book from Richard Wilbur's publishers. So I wrote the book about William Everson, then you come along and say "How come you always write about Western writers?" And I say, well, you know, they thought of me in relation to Everson because we were both conscientious objectors, that's one thing. And I did know him, not much, but I knew him a little. I knew him a lot better than I knew Richard Wilbur. But those things are partly in the minds of publishers.

I'll give you a story that will maybe help you on your whole outlook. When I was in Alaska, the writers complained: "When we write something we send it out; if we get a pleasant response from a New York publisher they usually say something like: 'Don't you have some Alaska material?' Because they think we live in Alaska, we must represent Alaska." So you see that's forced upon them.

That's been a complaint often, that things are imposed from the East as to what you are supposed to do as a Western writer too.

Yes, I don't feel imposed upon, I just feel it's a quirk of the human mind. So it's going to happen wherever you are. You know, if you are running a magazine you think: "Well, I want to know what the scene is like in New York." So you get in touch with New York writers because they would already be steeped in it.

I was thinking also when I said this about Western writers that you have written poems about Roethke and Hugo and Jeffers.

That's true. What you meet you react to. I have met them. I have also written poems about Eberhardt and . . . (Stafford's pause) Keats (laughs), and so on.

But it seems to me though, that you do have an interest in Western poetry?

Yes, I'm not denying an interest, but I'm just saying that it's not a deliberate thing; it's a spontaneous reaction to things that come to my attention.

Yes, being in the West, they would come to your attention.

Not long ago I had a letter from someone down in Kentucky. He sent me a newspaper clipping that was listing Southern writers, and it listed me. He said: "How come you're in it?" Well, I have been sending things to Southern magazines.

That's interesting. Earlier I mentioned that dialog with Richard Hugo called "The Third Time the World Happens," because in it you ask Richard Hugo: "Dick, some people are asking if there are characteristics peculiar to NW poetry." And he replied: "I think maybe in Northwest poets there is a tendency to use more landscape . . . There's just less of the outside world gets into Eastern poetry, at least less than I see in the Northwest. I think that we go outside more than people do in the East." So now, more than ten years later, I would like to ask you the same question.

Well, I rejoiced in Hugo's opinions, and his voicing of them, good and emphatic, and he sort of welcomed the world when he talked. But I don't really feel this. I immediately think of someone like Robert Frost, "I'm going out to clean the pasture spring," and so on. I don't know whether you are outside in Montana in the winter (laughs) or outside in Florida in the winter, or something like that. So I just don't quite know what to say about it. I think Hugo himself was a fisherman, and he liked those placenames, so he was outside. Once he bought himself a car without a top you know. He took us for a tour in it, and we went to an Indian reservation and so on. He liked the outdoors, so he'd see that way.

So you think that would be more his point of view?

I think so.

I don't know if I mentioned it to you, but when I first read A Geography of Poets *it really struck me that Northwest poetry had a lot of responses to the natural world to a much higher degree, it seemed to me, than poetry from other parts of the country.*

Well, editors choose. That is a geography of poets, you know.

You know the book, right?

Yeah, I do know it. I have a copy. And they choose the things that link to the area they have chosen to make the focus. So it's the Northwest, the California scene, the East, and so on. And I guess, if you are from somewhere else you think: what makes a Northwest poem? How are they going to tell it is a Northwest poem? Well, if it says Dungeness Spit, or it says Puget Sound or something like this, then it is the Northwest. So they do it that way. That would be one influence.

I realize too that there is the bias of the editor, still I was just wondering.

Participating in a panel on regionalism in 1981, called "The Realities of Regionalism," during a discussion on the importance of research, you wanted to put less emphasis on research and instead "maximize the sensitivity." You said: "I think there's another way to think about literature and regionalism. And that is that it's not something you decide to do; it's the recognition of a place you're already in. And you just accept this, and you can't help representing your region, because, to the degree that you belong there, you exactly do." My question here is, if not this approach implies an established poetics with commitment and attention to the specifics and details of a place? A different kind of poetics would, under the same circumstances, produce an entirely different poem, perhaps entirely separated from this "place," and still be a valid and good poem. We talked about this a little bit earlier, and perhaps I'm repeating the same question.

Well, it's always a little different; you come at it from a different angle. I can give you an example, and I can narrate my plight on this kind of issue. When I was travelling in Pakistan someone said to me: "Are you writing poems about Pakistan while you're here?" And I was able to say, yes. But I did not want this person to go on and ask me more, because actually what I had been writing that morning, was a poem about the pattern of cracks on the ceiling in the hotel room. Now, is it in Pakistan? Yes. Is it a Pakistan poem? No. In fact, I think later that I modified that poem and sold it as "Cracks On the Ceiling in a Hotel in Pullman, Washington," (laughs) or something like that. But that's the way it started, and that illustrates what I am up against. You can say, yes, but it might signify more than you really mean.

I see your point. But I really do think that you have a strong commitment in your poetry to the language you use, to details. And there is a concreteness, certain specifics in your poetry, which someone like Merwin does not have. In this respect he is not as specific; on the whole there is a certain vagueness as to the physical locality, even in a poem which might have been triggered by the same place. So what I'm saying is that two different kinds of poetics could react to the same place in totally different ways.

Yes, I feel alive by touching the earth where I am, and this is said in various ways by various people. But I do feel local, willingly local, in fact gloriously local. And it's just a matter of liking to eat the diet where you happen to live, and that's both a fact and an ideal.

Responding to the place you live in, is, as you have said, important to your work. This seems to me also to be related to the concept of home as well—something which comes up again and again in your work. In a relatively early essay called "Problems with Landscapes in Early Stafford Poems," by Richard Hugo, he basically argues that you lack "emotional possession" of the Northwest landscape, something which, he also argues, is not true of course for your Midwestern poems. In 1970, how did you respond to this? And how do you feel today—has the Northwest become a home emotionally possessed?

(Laughs) It's easy to respond how I responded in 1970. I did not do anything. It did not have any effect. I like to hear Hugo, I like to read Hugo, but I did not take it seriously. And there are two reasons not to take it seriously: I did not feel that his harpoon got me. And the other thing is, that even if it should be true, or make a difference—and those are two different things—I would

not want to respond to it because I wouldn't want, artificially, to become a Northwesterner. I mean, if it happens naturally, that's the way you do it: You are an artist. If you try to put it on, because grants are given to people who do that, then you're neglecting those essential parts of your art that have to do with where it comes from in the most sensitive parts of your being. So there would be several reasons to shy away from paying much attention to that.

Now about now, oh . . . yes, I'm at home. I'm still at home in the Midwest, I'm at home in the Northwest, I'm at home in the South. Anywhere—is the feeling, because for me the crucial parts of writing have to do with what is shared by all human beings. And what is shared by all human beings is so much more important than those superficial differences. Inhale, exhale. We share these important things with all living beings.

Do you feel that living on the far edge of Western civilization, the "end" of European thought and culture—At the End of the Open Road, as Louis Simpson has called one of his books—gives you a perspective which enables you to evaluate it more easily?

Yes, I'm familiar with Simpson's *At the End of the Open Road*, ending in a used car lot in California and so on. Part of me says yes, I value perspective wherever it comes from, but there's a part of me that isn't quite ready to be sure that the geographical location of a writer in this age of communication is more than just kind of a metaphorical thing. I mean, I don't think it's an essential perspective giver. Of course, anything that helps is welcome, and you do want the perspective tied into events that are happening far away. Maybe the most crucial events are happening in China, in which case people in New York are as far from it as I am. Maybe they are happening in the Soviet Union, or Sweden, or wherever, and my suspicion is that they are happening somewhere none of us has figured out yet. So how can I tell how far away I am from it?

I should perhaps have been more specific in my question—to some extent I was asking about the end of the frontier. Perhaps there still is a frontier left in Alaska, definitely more so than here. But I see it as a clash, when the frontier myth which is so widely embraced by popular culture in this country, suddenly finds itself out of space here at the edge. There is no way left to go. You all of a sudden have to look back and you have this continent that has already been settled. And you have this myth which embodies so many things: That there is still open space, so go ahead and grab what's there, use it and move on. And it seems to me that at that point when you have reached the end, there must be a reevaluation of this myth, or perhaps an emphasis on a different myth.

Yes, well in my own life I feel a kind of yearning for the frontier, and I feel reluctance to rely on other people, for instance. And when Daniel Boone needs elbow room somewhat within a hundred miles, I understand that. So John Haines is a spectacular example of someone who sought all those miles, and I understand that too. It's partly the impulse to do it yourself; if a tree is in the way my impulse is still to use an axe, and not a chain-saw. If I take a picture, I want to develop it, print it myself; if I could, I'd make the film and the camera. It's sort of wanting to start at zero. Zero based technology. That is not a way to get ahead today, I mean nobody can do it, of course. It's a real fantasy. If you're into computers, that does not mean that you're into the theories of computers and doing the parts, it means that you are using what other people have done. I'm still reluctant to do that.

That's interesting. It strikes me as a European too, because we don't have that desire to the same extent, because we, for so long, by necessity, have been forced to rely upon each other, and also, the government has had such power over people's actions for centuries that people know that they cannot do what they want to do because the government will restrict them.

Yeah, there is that different feeling. I am very much part then, of that Western feeling. But our son Kim has a story for you. He was with a group of writers, and when they were talking about someone who had a word processor, somebody spoke up and said: "What, you use a word processor? I couldn't do that, I have my electric typewriter." Another person said: "Electric typewriter! I have my manual typewriter." Someone else spoke up and said: "I use a pencil!" Right on down.

I really sense this, especially in Western poetry, a Western myth or something related to the frontier feel-ing.

Well, I'd like to put in this, that maybe all artists have that feeling of frontier, and maybe this is too closely tied to the chances of history when we think of it as a human impulse. It may be the impulse to do it yourself, you know, do the painting yourself, do a piece of music, compose the music, write the book, and in that sense we all always live on the frontier. It's just a question of recognizing it. And maybe people who create things, or people who feel that edge, that others don't feel, want to go beyond that edge. That kind of Daniel Boone impulse to get into Kentucky or to get into "How would it feel if I put in more violins?" sort of thing.

It seems to me that the complex of values and attitudes commonly referred to as the "Frontier Mentality," stressing the lack of restrictions on personal behavior; that progress always is seen in terms of expansion of human enterprise; the vision of waiting resources or potential for the ambitious individual, and so on, even though firmly rooted in the popular culture, has very

little support among poets. And I'm thinking now about its ecological implications. Because as we have seen, the consequences of technology have been disastrous. Do you feel that Northwest poets especially take a stand, and do you yourself take a strong stand on this?

I do take a stand myself, and I do think Northwest writers take a stand on this. For several reasons. For one thing, it's possible from out here to view Cleveland, Pittsburgh, and say no, no, let's not have it happen. So it's a perspective that we are talking about. Also, the Northwest happens to exist in a more pristine—it's not pristine, but it's more so—than places that have suffered the disasters that have alerted us to this danger. So in my own life I feel living at the edge, that's always interested me, but I also feel the vaingloriousness of assuming that you can bend the world any way you want to. You can't do that. And I'm quite ready to knuckle under, and to say uncle to the forces of nature. So it's sort of a complex situation for me: I like the Daniel Boone impulse, but I do not trust the universal and everlasting availability of that kind of frontier.

In a fairly recent issue of the Northwest Review, *called* The Nuclear Peril, *you contributed a poem which clearly had, I think, what most people would call political implications. Just as a great many medical doctors have organized "Physicians for Social Responsibility," do you feel that poets, or perhaps more generally poetry, has a responsibility to stress humanistic and life preserving values, and provide a sense of ecological awareness? Or is it simply a responsibility we must have as human beings?*

Well, I think it would be desirable if all human beings had this feeling of responsibility, but it is true that the activities of some human beings promote in them vision, perspective. They are sort of outriders for civilization, and the poets live by that commitment, I guess, to being available to the implications of things. Northwest poets, and poets in general of course, have been gung ho participants in these reforms, or in the perception of the need for reform. So that's very much part of my life and it would be nice if we all agreed about that, but I can understand that someone who is working in a coal mine wants to know where the job is going to be before he wants to quit mining coal. So it behooves us not only to see the danger from black lung, and, you know, smoke, but also to stay and be sympathetic with, and cooperative with people who are going to do something that will enable all human beings to have that kind of perspective.

In poetry though, you have said in an essay too that "intent endangers creation."

Yes.

And to adopt a stance where you say that poets have that responsibility, does not poetry move into that dangerous zone again here, where intent, where trying to provide a perspective could be dangerous for the creative act?

Well, maybe you noticed that I sidled into that last issue by saying it seems to me that it would be a nice thing if everybody were alert, but the circumstances of some people make them alert. And if that alertness comes naturally to you out of your whole life, that's what you use when you write poetry. But if you have been persuaded by someone who comes to your door and tells you about the ecological peril, and won't you quickly write us a poem about it, then your intent to be helpful will make that sensibility that you use suffer, because you will be turning away from some of the signals you get from your whole self in order to devote a part of yourself to what someone else has told you you ought to be. It just seems to me as a writer, that you lose something when you do that. Of course, you gain something too, but what you gain in social effectiveness you lose in that outrider feeling, that uniqueness that you have.

In 1970, in an essay-review called "At Home on Earth," you wrote: "There is a stillness about the ecological threat. We are surrounded, but the danger hardly appears—but it is there. Was there yesterday, but not so demanding." How do you feel about those words today, 15 years later?

Of course, the threat is getting louder and louder, more things are getting through to us. I remember—I had forgotten the title of that review—the editor of *The Hudson Review* sent me this big box of ecological books and asked me to do that review. I thought it was a burden, they were so big!

Yes, you mentioned in the review that some of those books were about 900 pages long, and there were a dozen books.

Yes, I went through those, and was properly horrified in various ways. I feel essentially the same way, I mean, the ecological threat is still relatively quiet. It's possible to go live in polluted air for quite a while, it may not get you for years. But it's getting you all the time. So our intellect can be alerted, we can supplement our senses with our intellect, and that's what we ought to do.

That review, "At Home on Earth," reveals that you gave twelve books on various aspects of ecology a great deal of sustained critical attention. Have your concern and interest in ecological matters continued with the same intensity over the years?

Yes, you know the magazines we get here, such things as *National Wildlife,* the Sierra Club things and so on. Like many people in our circumstances, in the arts, or in academic life, we are aware of these things. Now, I did feel that as a burden when I got that boxful of big, heavy books, and it was a distraction from my usual life and kind of writing—it was not poetry. I felt harnessed to the plow. Still, I felt it was something I ought to do, and I would probably feel the same again, but I would be sorry: Why not somebody else?

Many of your poems evoke an ominous and pessimistic view of man's fate, which you seem to relate to the application of modern technology to nature. Just to quote one little thing here called "Scientists" in **Tuft by Puff***:*

> These intellectuals banging their heads
> till they flare—
> they are burning the world down.

I had forgotten about that.

There are several other poems like "Stadium High, Tacoma" from **Sometimes Like a Legend,** *or "Ferns" from the same book which opens: "After the firestorms that end history," or the one "With a Gift of a Flower, for the First / Birthday of the Computer of Humble / Oil on the North Slope of Alaska" from* **Going Places,** *and so on. There are several other poems, but I'm not going to list them all here. Is the position of poetry in today's society like giving a flower to a computer?*

(Laughs) No, I don't think so. It seems to be natural to compare art to something fragile like a flower, but I never have felt that way about art. I have felt that—well, Wordsworth said something like this: "When the scientist goes as far as he can, poetry will be right beside him." I have this feeling too, that it is not something that is a frill, or an expendable thing, but it's going to be with everyone forever. I mean, that kind of impulse. I mean the distinctions you make between natural impulses and inhibited ones. The joy you feel on some occasions and not on others, so long as you are alive you feel these differences, and those differences are what make poetry.

Are you pessimistic though about man's fate?

Yes, yes I am, intellectually. There were a couple of people here yesterday, or the day before from up at Tacoma, or near there, who are doing a kind of oral history. I want to mention them to you. One of them is named Steve Jaech, he teaches at Steilacoom Community College, and he and a historian from Seattle were here and they had told me they had also interviewed a historian who is an unusual, unusually good professor up there. And they said: "He is very pessimistic, but he seems happy!" (Laughs) Yeah, I understand it. Animal spirits is one thing, but cool assessment is another. But there is another way to look at it, and that is—and I tried this on those two who came too—we don't know enough to be pessimistic.

It's a good thing to keep in mind.

I would also like to quote a passage from the essay "Writing the Australian Crawl": "We must forgive ourselves and each other much, in our writing and in our talking. We must abjure the 'I wrote this last night and it looked good, but today I see it is terrible' stance. When you write, simply tell me something. Maybe you can tell me how we should live." This last line interests me a lot. There seems to be an implication here that even if the individual poem is started without direct, wilful intent as far as writing a particular poem, there seems to be an underlying assumption behind the creative act that would like to discover a guide of some sort. That is, that the poem to some extent is defined in terms of its moral function. And this, then, relates to man's relationship to other men, to nature, and to God. Would you agree to this?

Yes, I would agree to that. And just to expand on it a little, or try to justify this quick embrace of that idea: It seems to me that moral positions are really derived from aesthetic considerations. That is, "the Good Book," is a good book. If it weren't a good book, it wouldn't be "the Good Book." That back of, unbeknownst to individuals, their positive response to life giving things is the source of their moral values. So, it might seem as if you were heroically harnessing art to something that is different, but I think that you are just recognizing that the trouble with the bad life is that it does not feel good, ultimately. And all decisions that you make have to do with the quality of living.

There is a revealing anecdote in the opening section of the essay "Making a Poem / Starting a Car on Ice," which says something about the function of poetry on the most elemental and pragmatic level. Do you remember, the poem about no smoking while you were at the University of Washington?

Oh yeah, yeah.

The moral of the story, with that explicitly created poem representing poetry that "should function as a part of the information system for society," as that student put it, is that poetry does not work on this level, that poetry is not read as instruction. The poem is understood as a message which has no relation to the actions of one's daily life.

(Laughs)

Is it correct to assume, then, that in view of your hope for poetry—"Maybe you can tell me how we should live"—that the problem resides in the general reader, and not in the ambition of the artist?

Yes, I, you know . . . I'll have to think this one over. But to respond as directly as I can, it seems to me that even instruction is literature. I mean, this person who

sees the sign which in effect says "No Smoking," when I say it's a poem, he says: "Oh, well," and then smokes. It's an attitude toward what is creative, and what is creative is a trying out of things. You read it not as gospel, and not as instruction, but as an excursion of the intellect and the feelings.

I guess I can't go do it as bluntly as I started out when I said even instruction is a poem. But I would say, ideally for me, no matter what anyone said to me, I would view it, or take it, as something aesthetic. I mean, not— What does that person say? but What does that mean?— when a person says that. Enlarge the frame. Political speeches think they are delivering information. No, no. I say, what does it mean when so and so says that. And of course analysts, that's exactly what they do. They say: "Well, the reason this happens is that this is a certain kind of posturing getting ready for the summit, you know, something like that." Sure. So we understand that. It still has meaning, but it's not true. (Both laughing.)

Well, I think you've got to take in art, and in reading, and in thinking that there is no local determination. That is, there is no holding place; there are just a whole bunch of influences. So you could have this little poem that induces people not to smoke—it does not instruct them not to smoke—it induces them not to smoke. So it could still have an inducing value, without being prohibition. I don't know, it's complex.

Yes, it is a complex thing. The effects of art, as you say, are inducive . . .

A poem is something that enlarges your life. Even when it seems to be instructing you to do something destructive, in the context, it might be something positive. I mean, there are ironies; even I, in my mild way, have those in my poems. And if someone would isolate a part of it, they'd say "Why do you say that?" Well, the total effect of the poem might be the opposite. Well, I'm just stirring around in the complexity of all this.

Yes, it seems to me too that the poems that are written, say, about nuclear peril in that Northwest Review *issue, are basically saying: "Don't drop the Bomb!" That's the bottom line of all those poems.*

But apparently that's not enough. You know, the poem's got to do something else. It's got to give the reader an experience of a life that's so good they don't want to drop the bomb. Something like that. So it's not enough to give instruction, even when you are giving instruction. Human beings have some bounce in them, that will react. They won't be just an inert receiver of a message.

In "The SAR Interview" in 1972 you were asked "What new writers on the current scene impress you the most?" You answered Robert Lowell. But then you went on to say the following: "The next, sustained, influential poet will come with few sounds of bells and cymbals, I suspect; he may come looming at us from a regional or somehow a continuous sense of aim—maybe someone like Wendell Berry." No poet, except for possibly Gary Snyder, has been more intimately associated with a combination of sense of place and ecological concerns. How do you see your statement today about Berry or the next poet coming from that direction?

I think I was maneuvered into identifying someone of influence rather than someone of transcendent poetic value. They are two different things, and it is just as hard now as it was then to know who that is. You know, I could give you some different names. Lowell's gone; Gary Snyder is a guru, rather than a poet in a certain sense, and maybe the same is true about Wendell Berry. So, I'd give you different names, but I'm subject to the same fallibility as everybody else, of course, so that my criticism of those who are now recognized would also be, implicitly, criticism of the unrecognized. But of course I have my opinions. And that's the way we gradually come to realize: Who is this, who has begun to loom?

Well, I was thinking about what you said here during our talk, that poetry should come from one's whole way of life, and so on, and I understand that ecological concerns and these other things that we have talked about are of great importance to you. Do you also see that they would be important, or be an important part of another new, major American poet?

No, I don't. I think, insofar as I am adequate to conceptualize all this, that poetry is always a surprise. I couldn't predict that a person would have ecological concerns who would be a transcendent poet. For all I know, there are more insidious dangers than the ecological one. Insidious may not be the word, but, you know, less seen or less understood, less perceived. On the other hand there may be more positive glories, incipiently, in the surrounding human beings than I perceived. That's what I hope to find out from the speaker. So I couldn't predict what kind of concern they would have. For instance, Lowell, I don't remember any ecological concerns in his poems. They are all something else— they were social, that is, within the psyche. And there may be wondrous, new developments in the psyche, or, on the other hand, terrible ones that no poet has happened on at the moment.

I think one can safely say that a poet like Theodore Roethke was a kind of neotranscendentalist, believing that the divine is manifested in nature, and that man's goal is a mystical union with nature, and so on. In several of your poems, for example **"By the Deschutes Shores"** *and* **"Crossing the Desert,"** *you also explicitly see nature as a religious domain. Apart from Roethke's mystical desire, do you share his views in this respect?*

Well, one short answer is no. But that human beings should find themselves writing poems in which the things and processes, the sort of flavors and emanations of nature, should be significant, and mysteriously significant, is not to make those poets very close; it just indicates that they are both human beings. I mean, nature has this all but universal effect, and if you find yourself oriented toward that kind of metaphor it is not surprising that you would come up with what seems to be similar religious attitudes. But my own religious attitudes would be not necessarily connected with any of my poems.

So you don't have a fascination for the transcendental movement then?

Oh, I'm interested, but not committed.

There is a poem of yours called **"Atavism,"** *in* **Roving Across Fields,** *and it struck me that it is very close to a passage in Roethke's "North American Sequence," in the poem "The Far Field," where the protagonist of the poem—a young boy—sits on a log in a river and slides into the sand, and sort of experiences having been a part of evolution. Which is also something that comes into your poems, a feeling of close kinship with animals and plants. You know, accepting the fact that we have been different natural forms.*

Yeah, I remember a Roethke poem like that, you know, a worm or something. "I may be a worm someday."

Is there a connection here?

Well, I can't help smiling when I think about this because for me, writing a poem is trying on a coat in a store. That's a coat I tried on, and it felt good. But there are other coats, is the sort of feeling I have. It's not an identification of me or my views or commitments, it is an excursion into an area that I have heard about and want to try. Something like that. No one poem feels like the coat I wear all my life. You know, I've got sweaters, sweater coats, hooded jackets, all sorts of things.

I wish I had brought the quote from the critic who said something like: "Mr. Stafford never uses persona."

Is that right?

Yes, somebody said that. I can't remember exactly where I saw that, I have gone through so much stuff.

That's fantastic!

Yes, because it really threw me off.

Well, maybe he is saying that you don't reach for a voice, find a voice. I don't like that idea myself. However, I immediately think of a poem in which I'm an old guitar up in Alaska. Is that persona or not? (Laughs.)

Yes, Jonathan Holden points out that somebody had interpreted "Some Shadows," the line about Hawk, "I am his son" as straight biography and drawn some interesting, but obviously false conclusions from it.

Yes, I just tried on that coat.

Yes, that was another coat. But I had another little question that I thought of when we talked about being part of evolution. What are the consequences in your life and poetry of acknowledging this heritage?

Well, that's different. I do feel a part of evolution, as a short way of saying a complex thing. A consequence of accepting that is that you are suspicious of individual human beings who speak to you as if they have corralled some total wisdom in the world, or something like that. I feel a part of it. We're all worms together there (Laughs.).

I was wondering about the poems where you assume the perspective of nature, adopting the view of a plant or animal. Roethke said: "I can project myself easier into a flower than a person." There are several poems of yours which speak from an animal persona. For example, the untitled poem which begins: "After they passed I climbed / out of my hole and sat / in the sun again" in **Eleven Untitled Poems.**

(Laughs) Yes, persona again.

And in "Terms of Surrender" in **Going Places, "Beaver Talk" in Tuft by Puff,** *and so on. For Roethke, many of these animistic impulses had a religious-mystical purpose, from where do these impulses come in your work?*

Just variety, just to be somebody else like a beaver or something for a while. What he said about speaking for a flower more easily than for a human being is a creative thing to say. Not necessarily true, but it's a challenge, it's an exercise, it's exciting, it's an exploration to be somebody else or something else for a while. I like to try that.

There is another dimension too. Somebody like Gary Snyder takes it up on the level of responsibility from the ecological point of view, that poets have a responsibility to speak for the wilderness, to be their representatives since they have no way of speaking out for themselves against the destruction from us.

It's scary out there when you get to thinking about such things as that. It might be that the animals have a responsibility to die for the wilderness that we are creating, which is a different wilderness but a wilderness nevertheless. I mean, human beings have a feeling that

what they create will be ordered, somehow superior. Alas, I don't think that. It's a wilderness all over again with different animals called human beings.

I would like to ask you a little bit about your use of American Indian material in your poetry. One thing that interests me is, again, the function of poetry. The function of the stories, myths and legends within the culture of the North American Indians was—and now I'm loosely paraphrasing Jarold Ramsey's introduction to Coyote Was Going There—*to transmit practical knowledge, history, morality, religion, myths, and to entertain. All this was through story telling. By adopting the American Indian story form in many of your poems, or using that type of material, do you hope to see poetry established on similar terms in our culture today? Is it even possible to talk about the function of poetry in today's society, or is poetry, as some critics have it, simply a fairly exclusive club?*

I do think it's possible to talk about function of poetry in today's society; it's a problem, but talking about anything is as far as I am concerned. That's a function.

But so far as the material in my poems is concerned, it's just something that happened to come along to me when I was writing and thinking. I suddenly realized that just this morning, again, when I was writing, there are some Indians in that thing! It's about some people who come down from timberline to the Yukon Highway, and they watch the cars go by. And they think: "This is civilization? Does this go on for ever?" And things like that. And the last line says something like: "They do not feel the need to tell their story." Now, I don't know whether that would be true of Indians, but it occurred to me, when I was writing, that they do not feel the need to tell their story. It was just the line that appealed to me. So I put it in my poem.

So I've just used that as a kind of emblem of how it comes to me. They are a salient group, they are in evidence around us, some of my best friends are Indians. That sort of feeling. By the way, there are some in Portland that might interest you. Do you know a person named Ed Edmo?

I've seen the name in several periodicals.

He's an Indian, and he frequently calls up to let me know of his latest triumphs. Sort of a war dance, Ed Edmo. And there are others around, Klamath Jackson, he was in a Conscientious Objectors' camp and he lives in Portland. So it's just part of the world, it just gets into some of the poems.

I recently also saw that a part of your heritage was American Indian.

Well, Dorothy laughs about this. My father had this story, he said: "Uncle Charlie, he said that he were part Indian and were from the Crowfoot group in upstate New York," and so on. Actually I have heard that anyone who has been in America very long, I mean some generations, have got Indian blood because the Indians were here. But I couldn't get any allotment on the reservation or anything like that. But every now and then Ed Edmo sort of treats me as an Indian, and other Indians do partly because I show up in those antholo-gies of Indian writers. I like that.

So it's an identification with their values or their at-titudes that in many ways appeals to you too?

It does appeal to me. But if I could claim to be black, I would, because that's also part of the scene that I would like to share.

What do you think the most important contribution of the culture of the Indians would be to modern American civilization?

I think for most Americans they are a metaphor.

You mean as place is a metaphor?

Yeah, they are a reference point in thinking. The people who were here before, the old days, something differ-ent, from outside looking in. They stand for difference, they stand for when the continent was unspoiled. They certainly are not that now—they are in the continent as much as we are. Someone said when I was up in Alaska: "If you want to see pollution, you ought to visit an Indian village." So they said. So, you know, the mystique of it is on a shaky foundation I think, but the metaphorical significance of it is very important. So you can have literary articles on palefaces and redskins and so on.

So it's primarily as metaphor rather than as anthropo-logical source.

I'm afraid so.

Today several American Indian writers have established themselves. This is a fairly recent development in American literature, and in terms of your own work, has this been an important source of stimulation?

Yes. But it's not just recently. Well, when I was a kid, I would be reading people like Lew Sarrett. Have you ever heard of him?

No.

Canadian poet. Or I would be reading James Willard Shultz. He was white, but he lived with the Blackfoot Indians. He wrote *My Life as an Indian.* I just devoured

these books. Come to think about it, I just reread James Fenimore Cooper's *Deerslayer,* about Chingachgook, the Mohican (laughs) and all that. Well, these books are part literary, they came to me through literature. But they came through to me through literature by way of some Indian writers. Eastman was one. Very few Indians went to Harvard in those days and became writers, but they were imaginatively important in what I read. And I would read books by someone named Altsheler, old series of frontier books. Or many, many Stewart Edward White, James Oliver Curwood, Jack London, people like that.

It's perhaps more that the Indian writers are receiving a great deal of attention now.

Yes, it's like saying that the women's movement started in the seventies or sixties. No, no, it started in day one. (Laughs.)

In an interview with Kip Stratton in The Greenfield Review, *you talked about your interest in native American culture a little bit. You said: "And then when you begin to write, one of the many effects of entering an art is, I think, that you are ready for the salient and extreme elements in your life. And one of the salient elements is the Indian element. It sort of stands for when the continent was cleaner and purer and better, more interesting." This last sentence sounds like something Gary Snyder would say . . .*

Yes!

. . . when he argues that the life of pre-historic man, or before man was organized into cities, was actually superior to that of modern civilization.

Yes, unspoiled countryside. Yeah, I share that. You know we go hiking into the wilderness looking for it. People will walk a long way and scramble over mountains to get that feeling. People go to Alaska for that reason, and stay there. And they go off to Hawaii or the South Seas or the Alps, and go skiing and so on, and all those impulses I share. Or to Sweden. (Laughs.)

Yes, lots of wilderness there. I also have that instinctive desire to get lost in the woods; it's easy if it's right outside your door.

I like the idea of getting lost, but in one of my poems I have someone accuse me of not being able to get lost. It's called **"The Preacher at the Corner."** He suddenly turns to me and says something like: "You can't get lost!"

Henry Taylor (essay date 1989)

SOURCE: Taylor, Henry. "'Thinking for Berky': Mil-lions of Intricate Moves." In *On William Stafford: The*

Worth of Local Things, edited by Tom Andrews, pp. 221-32. Ann Arbor: The University of Michigan Press, 1993.

[*In the following essay, originally published in 1989, Taylor analyzes "Thinking for Berky" and contends that it is one of Stafford's best and most representative poems.*]

I

In **"Thinking for Berky,"** many of the qualities that make Stafford's poetry what it is are at their best. The meter, strictly speaking, is unstable; some of the lines are iambic pentameter, and others stray from that toward fourteen syllables, yet the rhythmical rightness of each line is firmly there, not to be quarreled with. Similarly, the rhyme is the very opposite of insistent; though the rhymes between the first and fourth lines of each stanza are solid and true, there is enough between the rhymes to keep them from being more than a gentle and mysterious reminder that this is utterance weighed and wrought. Within this delicate scheme, the sentences move easily from immediate description to generalization and back again, the tone never modulating beyond the conversational. And yet there is something close to bravura in the calm statements of large truths: "there are things time passing can never make come true," "justice will take us millions of intricate moves."

Certain qualities of calmness and unpretentious gravity may create the impression that this voice is not easily modulated, or inclusive of various tones. But many of the qualities evident in **"Thinking for Berky"**—discursiveness, directness, delicacy of meter, specificity of description, definitiveness of general statement—are to be found in **"Adults Only,"** a recollection of an evening at the state fair, in the tent reserved for the striptease act. The poem begins with a general statement: "Animals own a fur world; / people own worlds that are variously, pleasingly, bare." The rest of the stanza recalls how those worlds came clear to "us kids" the night they found themselves in that tent. The poem ends:

> Better women exist, no doubt, than that one,
> and occasions more edifying, too, I suppose.
> But we have to witness for ourselves what comes for
>   us,
> nor be distracted by barkers of irrelevant ware;
> and a pretty good world, I say, arrived that night
> when that woman came farming right out of her
>   clothes, by God,
>
> At the state fair.[1]

Certain lines in this stanza—the first two, the last four—are quite clearly different from anything in **"Thinking for Berky"**; they are looser, more conversational. But only a few of the words—*pretty good,* for example—are foreign to the diction of the other poem. The use of the word *farming* in each poem is indicative of Stafford's unusual sensitivity to context: in **"Thinking for Berky"** the word has a hard and desperate sound, as if the parents farmed mostly with sickles and whips. In **"Adults Only"** the word is quirky but exact: the woman comes rolling out of her clothes like a combine out of a wheat field.

Along the spectrum from pure conversation to elaborate oratory, Stafford's poems occupy a relatively narrow range. But his acquaintance with that zone, and his sense of what context can yield, seem to have been, from the beginning, more than sufficient to the creation of explosions which many other poets would expend far more energy to bring about.

Stafford's first collection, *West of Your City* (1960), was published in an elegant limited edition by a small press; except for a few poems which have been widely anthologized, and fourteen which were reprinted in *The Rescued Year,* the work in it was unavailable for several years, until the appearance of *Stories That Could Be True: New and Collected Poems* (1977), which reprints Stafford's first two books, and three others: *The Rescued Year* (1966), *Allegiances* (1970), and *Someday, Maybe* (1973). *West of Your City* turns out to be a first book of great maturity, distinctiveness, and understated power; Stafford, it seems, is among those rare poets who do not publish a book before they have hit their stride. We are in danger now of taking Stafford's particular stride for granted, but it must have been earned courageously; most of the noisier proponents of this or that way of writing poems in the 1950s would have been reluctant to embrace these quiet, durable poems. In meters that are never too insistent, yet never out of control, the poems in *West of Your City* record the observations of a questing spirit—evoking the past, revealing in the present many small but significant signs of where we are, and heading westward, into the future. The tone is discursive, the diction conversational, but everywhere in these poems shines Stafford's amazing gift for arranging ordinary words into resonant truth and mystery: "Wherever we looked the land would hold us up."

Though *West of Your City* was out of print before it came to wide attention, *Traveling Through the Dark* (1962) immediately established Stafford as a poet of rare gifts and unusual productivity. As the citation of the poetry judges for the National Book Award put it: "William Stafford's poems are clean, direct and whole. They are both tough and gentle; their music knows the value of silence." True enough; and one is then awestruck to realize that these splendid poems—seventy-six of them, enough for two collections—were published only two years after *West of Your City*. As James Dickey once said, poetry appears not only to be the best way for Stafford to say what he wants to say but also to be the easiest. This may be an exaggeration, but it is true that even in the most casual of circumstances, Stafford's utterances can have the distinctive and memorable flavor of his poetry, as when he closes a letter, "So long—I look toward seeing you everywhere."

In *Traveling Through the Dark,* the major advance over the first book is in breadth of tone. Looking at the ways in which his poems can break into humor, I begin to think that Stafford has a talent, never quite indulged, for self-parody. He is attuned to the effects he can create, and so sensitive to various modes of surprise, that even within a restricted range of word choices, he can be haunting, wistful, or slyly humorous.

In *The Rescued Year,* there are many poems which surprise only because they did not exist before; they are otherwise very much like Stafford's earlier work. As he says at the end of **"Believer,"**

> You don't hear me yell to test the quiet or try to shake
> the wall, for I understand that the wrong sound weakens
> what no sound could ever save, and I am the one
> to live by the hum that shivers till the world can sing:—
> May my voice hover and wait for fate,
>   when the right note shakes everything.

> (*Stories* [*Stories That Could Be True*], 123)

But if the poems continue to sound exactly like the poems his earlier work led us to expect, there are among the subjects of these poems a few matters which Stafford had not previously staked out as his kind of territory. The title poem, longer and more leisurely than most of Stafford's earlier poems, is a fine evocation of a year of happiness lived in his youth, when his father had a job in another town and moved the family there. In **"Following the *Markings* of Dag Hammarskjöld: A Gathering of Poems in the Spirit of His Life and Writings,"** Stafford fashions a moving long sequence of related poems, the more valuable because they do not depend too heavily on the inspiration acknowledged in the title. And in **"The Animal That Drank Up Sound,"** he creates a myth of remarkable freshness, which has yet the flavor of folklore that makes it sound ancient. The first part of the poem tells how the animal came down and swallowed the sounds of the earth, until at last all sound was gone, and he starved. In the second section, a cricket, who had been hiding when the animal came by, awoke to a heavy stillness, and with one tentative sound, brought everything back:

> It all returned, our precious world with its life and
>   sound,
> where sometimes loud over the hill the moon,
> wild again, looks for its animal to roam, still,

down out of the hills, any time.
But somewhere a cricket waits.

It listens now, and practices at night.

> (*Stories,* 147)

The boldness of this poem and others in *The Rescued Year* is carried forward into *Allegiances* and *Someday, Maybe.* The strain of odd metaphor against discursive diction is rewardingly increased: "He talked like an old gun killing buffalo, / and in what he said a giant was trying to get out."

As always, any observation might start a poem, but in *Allegiances* Stafford seems freer to let the observation go either as far as necessary or to let it stop when it should. Several of these poems are tiny, fragmentary, but complete, like **"Note"**:

> straw, feathers, dust—
> little things
>
> but if they all go one way,
> that's the way the wind goes.

> (*Stories,* 181)

Sometimes these small observations are gathered in bunches under one title, like **"Brevities"** or **"Religion Back Home."** In these clusters of short poems, the tension between their disparateness and their being gathered under one title reminds us of Stafford's sense of his vocation: "The world speaks everything to us. / It is our only friend."

More and more often in *Allegiances* and *Someday, Maybe,* Stafford evokes the spirits of those whose ancestors lived here before white people came. **"People of the South Wind,"** for example, is a mythic explanation of where a person's breath goes after he dies; the tone is radically conversational, even for Stafford, but the effect is, magically, dignified. And the title poem of *Someday, Maybe,* **"The Eskimo National Anthem,"** recalls a song, "Aleena, Al-wona," that echoes often through the speaker's daily life. The phrase is translated as **"Someday, Maybe."** (A small misfortune has befallen the version of the poem in *Stories*: "Someday" is misprinted as "Somebody.") The poem ends with the observation that the song might be to blame if the speaker's life never amounts to anything, though it is a comforting keepsake. The paradox is gracefully concealed; it is hardly possible, in the poetic world of William Stafford, to notice so much, and still live a life that amounts to nothing.

The gathering of previously uncollected poems, *Stories That Could Be True,* extends the range of Stafford's apparently boundless empathy. Many of the speakers in these poems are not the observer, but the thing observed—wind, seeds, trees, ducks—and they speak of how things are with them, in a voice that is of course truly Stafford's, but which is profoundly convincing; it is a lively extension of the myth-making tendency that began to be displayed in *The Rescued Year.* It is also noteworthy that in these more recent poems, Stafford often permits himself a strictness of meter and rhyme that is rare in his earlier work. He has usually preferred to suggest a form rather than commit himself fully to it; but there are poems here whose simplicity, memorability, and charm are like the verses people who speak English have had in their heads from childhood. It takes a lifetime of thoughtful and wide-ranging work to arrive at the stage where one can write a miniature masterpiece like **"At the Playground,"** which in its way can speak for what Stafford has been up to all along, and for what he has been looking for in the books he has published since:

> Away down deep and away up high,
> a swing drops you into the sky.
> Back, it draws you away down deep,
> forth, it flings you in a sweep
> all the way to the stars and back
> —Goodby, Jill; Goodby, Jack:
> shuddering climb wild and steep,
> away up high, away down deep.

(Stories, 11)

II

In the past few years, Stafford has published a number of prose pieces about how his poems come to be. Many of these have been collected in *Writing the Australian Crawl* (1978) and *You Must Revise Your Life* (1986), both published in the University of Michigan's Poets on Poetry series. It is widely recognized by now that Stafford presents himself as a poet for whom the process is in many ways more important than the product. He wants an openness to any possibility during the initial stages of—I almost said *composition.* He is therefore suspicious of technique, especially if it is used for its own sake, or used to force a poem in a preconceived direction. His rhetorical stance toward these matters is exemplified in "Some Notes on Writing," a prose statement at the beginning of his most recent collection of poems, *An Oregon Message* (1987):

> My poems are organically grown, and it is my habit to allow language its own freedom and confidence. The results will sometimes bewilder conservative readers and hearers, especially those who try to control all emergent elements in discourse for the service of predetermined ends.
>
> Each poem is a miracle that has been invited to happen. But these words, after they come, you look at what's there. Why these? Why not some calculated careful contenders? Because these chosen ones must survive as they were made, by the reckless impulse of a fallible but susceptible person. I must be willingly fallible in order to deserve a place in the realm where miracles happen.

> Writing poems is living in that realm. Each poem is a gift, a surprise that emerges as itself and is only later subjected to order and evaluation.

(10)

As direct as these paragraphs seem, there are certain questions which they do not quite answer. Is Stafford describing a process like automatic writing? Language must have "its own freedom and confidence," and "after they come," by "reckless impulse," the words "must survive as they were made." This is certainly suggestive of a method which involves little in the way of revision. On the other hand, the poems are "later subjected to order and evaluation," whatever "order" might mean here.

In "A Way of Writing," one of the essays collected in *Writing the Australian Crawl,* Stafford notes that others "talk about 'skills' in writing." He goes on to explain his difficulty with the concept:

> Without denying that I do have experience, wide reading, automatic orthodoxies and maneuvers of various kinds, I still must insist that I am often baffled about what "skill" has to do with the precious little area of confusion when I do not know what I am going to say and then I find out what I am going to say. That precious interval I am unable to bridge by skill. . . . Skill? If so, it is a skill we all have, something we learned before the age of three or four.

(19)

It is statements like that last one, taken out of context—sometimes, admittedly, by Stafford himself—which have recently given rise to the notions that Stafford wants all poems to be equally valued, that writing teachers should not evaluate student work, and that a kind of open basking in possibility is more important than any talk of how to make a poem better than it is. "Well," we hear the teacher saying, "this might show us something important. Next?" I ponder the Zen of workshopping, the guru as wise ignoramus.

Again. In an interview with Cynthia Lofsness (in *Writing the Australian Crawl*) Stafford speaks suspiciously of technique:

> It's not a technique, it's a kind of stance to take toward experience, or an attitude to take toward immediate feelings and thoughts while you're writing. That seems important to me, but technique is something I believe I would like to avoid.

(98)

In conversation on various occasions since that interview, which was first published in 1972, Stafford has said similar things; but in those contexts, the interviewer's definition of technique, included in her question, has not always been present as a background: "I would define technique as a belief on the part of the poet that there are certain rules or forms into which his ideas must be channeled for proper expression. A belief that there is a proper 'framework,' into which he must fit his specific feelings. . . ."

It is instructive to note the extremism of the positions Stafford opposes when he talks about these things. In one case, we have the desire to control absolutely every impulse, to work everything toward a predetermined effect or end; in another, we have a belief in rules, in a proper framework. The first method is obsessive, the second oversimplified and ignorant. Of course these ways of trying to write poems are doomed; and of course it is better to be ready for surprises. More conservative voices than Stafford's have been heard to say, for example, that a poem glides on its own melting, like a piece of ice on a hot stove, or that poetry should come as naturally as leaves to a tree.

Perhaps Stafford is increasingly concerned to address the notion that all one needs to be a poet is to learn the things that are taught in writing classes. It may be that his own extraordinarily prolific output has often brought him questioners who want to know exactly how he does it. It is certain that he falls rather easily into moods that inspire him to easily misunderstood pronouncements; he says what he means, most of the time, but the most audible part of what he says is the more radical part. In the passage about "skill" above, for example, he is careful to establish that he has "experience, wide reading, automatic orthodoxies and maneuvers of various kinds."

In a couple of passages from *You Must Revise Your Life* there are useful examples, first of the haste with which Stafford can sometimes say things which his poems contradict, and second, of the ease and friendliness with which he can discuss matters of great technical importance. In a short piece about a short poem, "Where **'Yellow Cars'** Comes From," there are these sentences about sound:

> As for sound, I live in one great bell of sound when doing a poem; and I like how the syllables do-si-do along. I am not after rhyme—so limited, so mechanical. No, I want all the syllables to be in there like a school of fish, flashing, relating to other syllables in other words (even words not in this poem, of course), fluently carrying the reader by subliminal felicities all the way to the limber last line.

(44)

The paragraph begins with the general and modulates toward the specific poem, but the dismissal of rhyme sounds general.

A few pages later, in another essay about the same poem, he writes:

> And line breaks, too, happen along. By now, in my writing, many considerations occur to me in jotting down even first hints of a poem. I like to feel pat-

terns—number of stresses, multi-unstressed or few-unstressed sound units, lines that carry over and make a reader reach a bit, pauses in the line that come at varying, helpful places: early in the line, middle of the line, later in the line. But I make the lines be the way they are by welcoming opportunities that come to me, not by having a pattern in mind.

(47)

If we think of technique, not as some rigid belief in proper frameworks and rules, but as a partial and growing understanding of an enormous array of verbal effects and opportunities, some of them traditional and some of them more nearly unprecedented, then it becomes harder to entertain the idea that Stafford cares much less about it than Richard Wilbur does.

III

In the light of these remarks, it is useful to look more closely at **"Thinking for Berky,"** and at one or two poems from Stafford's most recent collections. A sense of Stafford's skill, or technique, or outrageous good fortune, is barely suggested in the brief metrical description at the beginning of this essay.

For some readers, the metrical question will be difficult; for even more doctrinaire readers, it will be easy, or nonexistent. There are respectable people, in the school of J. V. Cunningham, who believe that lines either exemplify a strict meter, or that they do not, and that a mixture of both kinds of line in one poem is some sort of default on the contract. But Stafford has arrived at the contract, if any, with nearly evasive tact: the meter of the first three lines is so far from firmly established that it is purely a matter of opinion where to place stresses among the syllables "must have some" in the fourth. Yet, even veering as they do between nine and twelve syllables, and between four and six stresses, the first four lines arrive satisfyingly at their ends, and at the rhyme. Much of the satisfaction emerges almost unnoticed from rhymes and echoes elsewhere than at the ends of lines: *joined-kind-end, screaming-drama,* the march of four *l* sounds proceeding from beginning to end of words in the first two lines.

This kind of local sonic richness continues throughout the poem, even as a larger net is also being cast, to make connections among stanzas by means of end-words not included in the "official" rhyme scheme (*patrol-soul,* both connecting with the second stanza's rhymes; *come-came*; *wood-misunderstood*), and over the whole poem by the echo between *bed* and *beds,* and the repetition of *listening* and *night* in the first and final lines.[2] Meanwhile, another aspect of the poem's rhythmical balance is maintained by the tension between lengthening lines and shortening sentences.

Stafford's prose remarks seem intended to forestall the conclusion that these kinds of things are always calculated. Very inexperienced readers often want to know how many of a poem's effects could have been planned, and most practitioners know that many are not. But most practitioners also know that thinking about such matters, in one's own poems and in others', is a useful way to deepen acquaintance with them, and to grow toward recognizing them when an unpressurized knowledge, disguised as good luck, brings them into the lines we are writing.

The convergence of impulses—from the tradition and from the individual train of thought—can even result in a sonnet. The discovery that a sonnet is under way is usually made before all the rhymes are in place, so some searching and rephrasing must usually be done. During that process, I imagine, Stafford might constantly weigh the effects of either staying with tradition, or noticeably departing from it, perhaps to the point that strict readers might decide that the result is not a sonnet. Here, for example, is **"Seeing and Perceiving,"** from *A Glass Face in the Rain* (1982):

> You learn to like the scene that everything
> in passing loans to you—a crooked tree
> syncopated upward branch by pre-
> established branch, its pattern suddening
> as you study it; or a piece of string
> forwarding itself, that straight knot so free
> you puzzle slowly at its form (you see
> intricate but fail at simple); or a wing,
> the lost birds trailing home.
> These random pieces begin to dance at night
> or when you look away. You cling to them
> for form, the only way that it will come
> to the fallible: little bits of light
> reflected by the sympathy of sight.
>
> (46)

I believe it is possible to be drawn into this poem, to follow its sentences with enough absorption not to notice rhyme until the final couplet. It is unusual to find a sonnet, or near-sonnet, in which the form itself does not seem to constitute much in the way of a statement; these days, to elect the sonnet form is usually to make a gesture with something behind it. Here, the form seems gradually to evolve, as it might "come / to the fallible," so that the short ninth line has a rightness that outweighs its failure to meet rigid expectation.

Rhyme is infrequent in Stafford's most recent collection, *An Oregon Message* (1987). One of its more obtrusive manifestations is in **"Brother,"** a mysterious poem which defies literal paraphrase:

> Somebody came to the door that night.
> "Where is your son, the one with the scar?"
> No moon has ever shone so bright.
>
> A bridge, a dark figure, and then the train—
> "My son went away. I can't help you."
> Many a clear night since then. And rain.

> I was the younger, the one with the blood.
> "You better tell Lefty what his brother done."
> They went off cursing down the road.
>
> A boy in the loft watching a star.
> "Son, your big brother has saved your life."
> He never came back, the one with the scar.
>
> (98)

The difficulty of assembling the details into coherence is emphasized by the self-contained lines, each of which is resonant with possibility. There is reference to what sounds like a threatening encounter, and possibly some catastrophe; but the details hang in the memory as they might in the mind of a traumatized victim of imperfect recall. Because it borders on the incomprehensible, in most prose senses of the term, the poem benefits immeasurably from the added mystery of regular rhyme. A line such as the fourth, with its assortment of three images which could add up in several ways concluding in departure, death, or rescue, becomes one of twelve beads on a string, attractive in itself; the same is true of the seventh, in which the phrase "the one with the blood" could suggest several paraphrases. The poem is reminiscent of certain ballads, like "Sir Patrick Spens," from which such usual narrative elements as motivation are absent, so that the events take on a stark necessity.

Some readers have called Stafford's poetry "simple," as if it had failed to comprehend our civilization's great variety and complexity. But the simplicity exemplified in **"Brother"** is exactly the kind that makes for complexity in contemporary life. None of us knows enough, it seems. William Stafford's many ways of reminding us of that, and of offering consolation, constitute one of the most secure and solid of recent poetic achievements.

Notes

1. William Stafford, *Stories That Could Be True: New and Collected Poems* (New York: Harper and Row, 1977), 93. Subsequent citations of this book will be made in the text, to *Stories* and a page number; quotations from other collections, all published by Harper and Row, will be identified in the text and followed by a page number.

2. For a while in the early 1970s, Stafford read this poem aloud, and authorized reprinting it, with a slightly different last line: "While in the night you lie, so far and good." It has admirable qualities, but Stafford had reverted to the original ending by the time he assembled *Stories That Could Be True*.

Lars Nordström (essay date 1989)

SOURCE: Nordström, Lars. "William Stafford's Ecological Metaphor." In *Theodore Roethke, William Staff-*

ord, and Gary Snyder: The Ecological Metaphor as Transformed Regionalism, pp. 57-100. Stockholm: Uppsala, 1989.

[In the following excerpt, Nordström discusses Stafford's pessimistic attitude toward technology and modern life.]

1. INTRODUCTION[1]

When we turn to William Stafford's use of the ecological metaphor, we find a somewhat different expression of it from that found in Theodore Roethke. Whereas Roethke emphasizes the cyclical nature of all being, the continuous transformation of different life forms, the desire to merge with the subhuman world, and, through those poetic strategies, implies an environmental ethic, Stafford's poems attempt to articulate how we are to live correctly and responsibly within the natural order. In this respect Stafford's poetry is much more explicitly ethical. There are, however, direct links between the two poets. Stafford's ecological metaphor reflects a similar sense of opposition between technology and wilderness, with an ultimate affirmation of the latter. The car, for example, is often perceived as responsible for the death of wild animals. The poem **"The Move to California,"** ends by lamenting the destruction of wildlife by the great number of cars, "Gasoline makes game scarce" (*WYC* [*West of Your City*], *SCBT* [*Stories That Could Be True*], p. 47), and in **"Traveling through the Dark"** (*TTD* [*Traveling through the Dark*], *SCBT*, p. 61), the car is certainly described as a death bringer.

But in Stafford's poems there is also a deeper pessimism about the direction of our modern, technological society, especially expressed through images of the military "machine." These poems include not only his famous anti-war poems, such as **"At the Bomb Testing Site"** (*WYC, SCBT,* p. 41), and many others, but those envisioning the end of human life on planet Earth.[2] Yet Stafford is convinced that pessimism is not the only valid attitude one can have either as a person or a poet; a sense of possibility and happiness is still essential. The consequence of his stance is not, in other words, an overpowering sense of doom or an implied fatalism free from personal responsibility.[3] The nature of his pessimism must therefore be taken into consideration when we look at his pessimistic poems within the context of the ecological metaphor. In a sense one could say that his pessimistic poems assume the function of backdrop against which our responsibilities as human beings in the natural order must become clear. Here we find that against the threat of disaster due to technological arrogance at one end of the scale, wilderness is affirmed at the other, and the two act as poles against which we understand contemporary human hubris and humility. The Kentucky poet, novelist, essayist and farmer Wendell Berry, with whom Stafford shares many affinities,

elegantly sums up this polarity in his book of essays on culture and agriculture, *The Unsettling of America*:

> And the most dangerous tendency in modern society, now rapidly emerging as a scientific-industrial ambition, is the tendency toward encapsulation of human order—the severance, once and for all, of the umbilical cord fastening us to the wilderness or the Creation. The threat is not only in the totalitarian desire for absolute control. It lies in the willingness to ignore an essential paradox: the natural forces that so threaten us are the same forces that preserve and renew us.[4]

The importance of listening to the wilderness for an awareness of its regenerative values, and to affirm them (to live without losing one's "umbilical cord"), is as crucial to Stafford as it is to Berry.

Since the ecological metaphor expresses an ethical position which involves the natural world, it inevitably points towards a relationship to the place where such values are (or could be) realized through action. The place referred to as home consequently assumes special significance.[5] Home, in this sense, is the Northwest region Stafford has made his own, where he has lived most of his daily adult life since 1948, and the home he uses metaphorically as a point of reference connected to his environmental ethic. In other words, the expression of place goes far beyond the impulse of mere description of the geographical landscape, but must be understood as serving a more symbolic role. In the early 1970s Stafford affirmed this more abstract and moral sense during a poetry festival: "Actually, a poet's place is just a metaphor for something that is harder to identify. It's not the place that is important. It's a more fundamental kind of orientation . . . It's toward some kind of little something in our minds that says yes and no all the time."[6] The central aspect of the ecological metaphor is, in other words, its ethical position, which assumes precedence over geographical referentiality when the two are coupled.

The early 1970s must also be considered a crucial time in Stafford's ecological awareness, because in 1970 he published a review of twelve books on ecology for *The Hudson Review* called "At Home on Earth."[7] The review is important for several reasons. First of all, the title of the review gives an additional meaning to the word "home" by signifying more than just the place where one lives; to be "at home" also carries with it the implication of responsibilities defined in terms of environmental ethics, and this new, articulated relationship to place is certainly reflected in his poetry. In a few prefatory statements to the actual review he also acknowledges the significance of the natural world as a source of moral and spiritual guidance for poetry, and implies an ethical function of poetry itself: "In the world where what is outside man extends into mystery, awe, worship, respect, reverence—poetry, the stance that accepts, may be salvational."[8] Further into the review he takes a clear, active stand based on the conclusions he is able to draw from the material: "Once the reader picks up connections, a sense of responsibility comes alive; and the more you learn the more immediate becomes involvement."[9] This review demonstrates, in other words, a commitment to involvement in environmental issues which is related to his view of the function of poetry. Sixteen years later, when asked whether his concern and interest in ecological matters had continued with the same intensity after that book review, Stafford answered affirmatively:

> Yes, you know the magazines we get here, such things as *National Wildlife,* the Sierra Club things and so on. Like many people in our circumstances, in the arts, or in academic life, we are aware of these things. Now, I did feel that as a burden when I got that boxful of big, heavy books, and it was a distraction from my usual life and kind of writing—it was not poetry. I felt harnessed to the plow. Still, I felt it was something I ought to do, and I would probably feel the same again, but I would be sorry: Why not somebody else?[10]

The importance of the wilderness in Stafford's vision has already been noticed by several critics and will only be discussed insofar as it adds to earlier studies. Jonathan Holden, for example, in his fine, pioneering study *The Mark To Turn,* observes that the "imaginative use of Nature as an emblem of propriety, as a model for 'salvation,' is a major theme in Stafford's poetry."[11] By looking at several early poems Holden approaches the ecological metaphor when he defines this theme as one where "there is an ideal human 'place' in the world, that this 'place' is a humble one, that this 'place' is defined through process, that the way to find this 'place' is to live economically and, through faith in 'the wings / within,' be 'guided.'"[12] I certainly agree with Holden about this, but due to the fact that his study is limited to Stafford's first five, major collections, and that Stafford's ecological metaphor is more complex and different in focus, his study is not complete. There are several aspects of the ecological metaphor which are not included in Holden's study, which will be explored here: the backdrop of pessimism concerning man's fate, the importance of Native American material for this vision, the religious overtones echoed in some wilderness material, the symbolic polarity of technology/city on the one hand, and the wilderness on the other (with criticism of the former), the use of animal personae, and how the ecological metaphor often is defined in some kind of "regional" way. Another excellent early study which also gropes towards the ecological metaphor along Holden's approach, is John Lauber's "World's Guest—William Stafford," in which he explores "a series of natural pieties" including "piety toward the earth itself, toward the region, the home, the parents, towards one's total past."[13]

The sense of home evoked in the context of the ecological metaphor has also another important dimension, and that is in its broader sense of an American uniqueness. This expression of home is that conveyed through Stafford's sense of identity with the Native Americans, which is based on a lifelong interest in literature about, or by, Native Americans. In an interview, Stafford recalls:

> Well, when I was a kid, I would be reading people like Lew Sarrett. . . . Or I would be reading James Willard Shultz. He was white, but he lived with the Blackfoot Indians. He wrote *My Life as an Indian.* I just devoured these books. Come to think about it, I just reread James Fenimore Cooper's *Deerslayer,* about Chingachgook, the Mohican (laughs) and all that. Well, these books are part literary, they came to me through literature. But they came through to me through literature by way of some Indian writers. Eastman was one. Very few Indians went to Harvard in those days and became writers, but they were imaginatively important in what I read.[14]

Consequently it is not surprising that one discovers a relatively high frequency of Native American material in Stafford's poetry, appearing long before it became in vogue to write about the Native Americans. In the use of this material one can observe how his initial, more factual treatment in some of his early poems disappears and is replaced by a more symbolic way of handling the same material. For example, the early poem "In the Oregon Country,"[15] which could even be termed a traditional regional poem in that it explores concrete details of Northwest history, or the poem "At the Custer Monument" dated 1953,[16] belong to a type of poem which later disappears from Stafford's work. Still, there are important early poems, for example "Our People,"[17] which initiate Stafford's crucial sense of identification with the Native Americans, and the poem "The Fish Counter at Bonneville" (*WYC, SCBT,* p. 43), with its early signals of ecological awareness in the opening line: "Downstream they have killed the river and built a dam;" a statement which also parallels the Native American point of view, since the Columbia River tribes lost their ancient village sites and fishing rocks and had to be relocated due to the dam's construction. In other words, what is significant about these two early Native American poems, is the perspective they establish; it is clear where the poet's sympathies are. Later poems which continue the exploration of this material usually demonstrate, as we will see, the centrality of the ecological metaphor. For example, the poem "The Concealment: Ishi, the Last Wild Indian" (*TRY* [*The Rescued Year*], *SCBT,* p. 136), even though factual in a certain sense and based on a well-known book,[18] becomes a more symbolic expression desiring an open realization of Ishi's life, because his way of life demonstrated the possibility of an existence leaving "a land unspoiled."

Not many critics have discussed, or even touched on Stafford's use of Native American material. For example, Carol Kyle discusses the poem **"Returned to Say"** (*TTD, SCBT,* pp. 102-3), in her essay "Point of View in **'Returned to Say'** and the Wilderness of William Stafford."[19] She reads the poem in a manner which approaches the ecological metaphor, but still remains crucially different: "The Indian here represents the nature that he seeks to know; the energy required for the resurrection of the spirit of nature must be enormous; it is the wilderness itself who has 'returned to say' that what is mandatory in this city-plagued time is a return to nature."[20] Equating the "lost Cree" with the wilderness is not, according to the context provided by the ecological metaphor, a complete reading of the poem. The "lost Cree" is simply just not the wilderness incarnated, but the emblem of an attitude *toward* the wilderness. His new vision evokes the new ethic guiding human behavior in the realm of nature, which is evoked in the final line of the poem with its dream of living without damaging the earth: "Our moccasins do not mark the ground."

Another poet and scholar, Jarold Ramsey, has suggested a parallel in imaginative approach between Native American stories and Stafford's work in the "Introduction" to *Coyote Was Going There*. Ramsey claims that the Native American oral tradition demonstrates "an imagination that celebrates a profound sense of harmony with the natural order. . . . The distinguished Oregon poet William Stafford, a keen student of western Indian culture, often summons in his poems the positive aspect of this mentality and the imagination that sustains it."[21] In the same "Introduction," Ramsey also points to the fact that he was struck by the profound sense of place these Oregon country stories demonstrated. Actually, it was so pervasive that Ramsey used the ecological awareness of place as the organizing principle of his collection:

> Bearing in mind, then, the diverse terrains and climates that constituted "Oregon" to its first peoples as they still do to us, I have tried to select and arrange the myths by ecological regions, so as to suggest how deeply and variously the literature of the state's native inhabitants reflects their responses to the special natural environments they knew as home, and of which we are the unlikely inheritors.[22]

A general parallel exists here to many of the Stafford poems which deal with the ecological metaphor: they too often exhibit a sense of place which is associated with the Northwest, or at least with the western landscape. And as was mentioned earlier in the introduction, this might very well be associated to Stafford's sense of home.

Stafford himself has also articulated his awareness of the symbolic value of Native American material in poetry. When asked what he thought the most important contribution of the culture of the American Indians would be to modern American civilization, he replied:

> I think for most Americans they are a metaphor . . . they are a reference point in thinking. The people who were here before, the old days, something different, from outside looking in. They stand for difference, they stand for when the continent was unspoiled. They certainly are not that now—they are in the continent as much as we are. Someone said when I was up in Alaska: "If you want to see pollution, you ought to visit an Indian village." So they said. So, you know, the mystique of it is on a shaky foundation I think, but the metaphorical significance of it is very important. So you can have literary articles on palefaces and redskins and so on.[23]

In other words, Stafford's interest in the Native American is not primarily focused on the reality of their wars, slaves, social habits and so on, but on positive aspects which suggests a kind of modern transformation of the Rousseauan concept of the Noble Savage. In the context of the ecological metaphor the Native American has been transformed into the emblem of a positive innocence dwelling without conflict within the natural world. The use of Native American material should therefore be interpreted as a kind of submetaphor within the larger ecological metaphor.[24]

There is also a dimension of the oral Native American storytelling tradition echoed in Stafford's poetry within the ecological metaphor. The function of the original oral Native American story tradition seems to have been basically threefold: to transmit the fundamental values of the culture, to explain nature (both exterior and interior), and to entertain.[25] It is interesting to note that Stafford primarily leans toward the didactic aspects of the tradition, and that his poems often transmit a particular point of view in the form of a parabolical teaching of some kind. That is, they are moral in that they convey a vision of the world offered as right, or as a vision from which one understands what is right. The system of values these poems transmit is not that of the traditional cultures of the Native Americans, of course, but within the context of the ecological metaphor we find a pattern of environmental ethics which is affirmed.

A few words about the ecological metaphor as a transformed regional impulse are necessary as well. Many of the poems gravitating toward the ecological metaphor often seem grounded in identifiable places in the Pacific Northwest. But, one might argue, so do many of Stafford's "un-ecological" poems, just as there often is a regional impulse in poems from his childhood and youth in the Midwest, or even from places of his frequent travels. What does this signify? We have to recognize that the general presence of a specific regional reference of some sort in a poem is the result of Stafford's poetics, which pays attention to particulars and to ordinary things.

Stafford himself answered like this when asked about the use of material from one's region:

> I think that any artist is sustained by the things of this world, and the things that are near loom larger, impinge, and they are important because they are near. But they are not important because they are any certain part of the world. . . .
>
> So if it sounds regional when I'm writing it, or feels regional, I'm very likely to make it even more regional. And, I guess maybe this will be my finale too—you urged me on—that is, you use the terminology, the local names, the things that will feel exotic to someone from somewhere else for several reasons. For one reason, you use whatever names, nouns, locutions come natural to you, and you don't change them unless there is a reason. And the reason of trying to talk like everybody else is not a good reason, because those peculiarities are sometimes the flavorful part of what you are doing.[26]

Stafford's comment reveals an aesthetic position which affirms the importance of the details and particulars of a specific place, but does so without any exclusive intent. He opens the poem **"Lake Chelan"** (*TTD, SCBT,* pp. 84-85) with a demonstration of this aesthetic: "They call it regional, this relevance—/ the deepest place we have." The poems are created with a sense of place because, as the poet puts it elsewhere, what is near and close, "local nudges from day-to-day life" have much more significance than "large influences, national tendencies, or tendencies of a period in literature."[27] Consequently many of the poems will look regional, or seem to pay a great deal of attention to place. But it is not a deliberate act of seeking out these references. As he also says: "I certainly don't have a program about defending the West. But it's part of my life, and also those things usually identified with the West are part of my commitments, I guess."[28] His aesthetic acknowledges a sense of place as a point of reference to the reader by locating the poem in an often clearly defined time and space; on the other hand, the poems are not regional to the extent that the reader must know the significance of the reference in order to comprehend the poem. For example, J. Russell Roberts, Sr. argues this point when he says that in the third stanza from the poem **"Things That Happen"** (*A* [*Allegiances*], *SCBT,* pp. 177-78),

> We were back of three mountains called
> "Sisters" along the Green Lakes trail
> and had crossed a ridge when that
> one little puff of air touched us,
> hardly felt at all.

"the place names are incidental and might be changed without altering the meaning of the experience which could happen to mountaineers anywhere in the world."[29] Looking at an individual poem, this argument is correct. Yet there is another dimension to the inclusion of regional references which has to do with the ac-

cumulated effect of regional material in the totality of a poet's work. It is when we look at all the poems with references to the Pacific Northwest that certain patterns begin to emerge, and a reverberation between place and theme becomes noticeable, especially since this place is synonymous with a concept of home. While talking with Sanford Pinsker about the poem **"With Kit, Age 7, At the Beach"** (*A, SCBT,* pp. 151-52), Stafford adds this:

> You suggested something about using the landscape there as a model for a deeper meaning. *All* particulars reflect something, if looked at alertly enough. The job in writing is the repeated encounter with particulars. It may be that you hit on a succession of particulars that reinforce each other—and in that case you have a poem.[30]

It is clear here, that the inclusion of the particulars of a specific place is not executed primarily for the sake of a regional investigation (due to the specialness of a particular place), but for the symbolic significance, the associations of certain words or images, and so on. Whether a certain particular is included or excluded, depends on its ability "to reflect something" larger than itself, rather than whether it is regional or not. With this in mind it becomes impossible to say that any place is equally suited for inclusion into a poem; that is not the correct criterion. The criterion is that of its power of suggestion. In short, there is no "regionalist" ambition behind Stafford's poems in the sense that they attempt to document or explore a particular place in a consistent and persistent manner.[31] This does not mean that there are no Northwest poems with regionalist flavors in Stafford's canon; one could argue that poems like the already mentioned **"In the Oregon Country"** (*WYC, SCBT,* p. 37), **"The Museum at Tillamook"** (*TTD, SCBT,* pp. 86-7), **"Out West"** (*TRY, SCBT,* pp. 129-30), and many others, belong to this category.

Stafford's statement, that particulars drawn from the sense of place are selected because they "reflect something," indicates that these references must be understood symbolically. It has now become a critical commonplace to state that there is a correspondence between the outer and inner landscape in Stafford's work. Raymond Benoit seems to have been among the first to state that "geography is often close to psychology in Stafford."[32] A year later Richard Hugo goes into more detail in the opening paragraph of his study "Problems with Landscapes in Early Stafford Poems," where he establishes the following definition: "By landscape poet I mean a poet who uses places and experiences in those places as starting points for poems. For such a poet, as several critics have noted, there are two landscapes, one external and one internal. The external one is simply 'used'—indeed, usually sacrificed—to get to the internal landscape where the poem is."[33]

The fact that the poem, in Stafford's point of view, should be willing to embrace not only regional impulses, but all sorts of particulars that "are near," puts his poetic approach in contrast to some of the tenets of Modernism. In Stafford's essay "The End of a Golden String," he says: "Sometimes it seems to me that a writer habitually touches the earth, touches home, clings to all that passes. Even to start a poem is to unreel stingily from the starting place, and to make each successive move out of minimum psychic expenditure. . . . Let me say that a poem comes from a life, not a study" (*WAC* [*Writing the Australian Crawl*], pp. 43-44).[34] For example, the importance of what exists outside literary tradition, and especially the importance of the natural world/wilderness, is humorously expressed in a somewhat unusual, regional poem from the collection with his son, called ***Braided Apart*** (1976):[35]

"The PMLA Biblio. is Limited to Certain Printed Works"

There are others, and mss.
And then talk.
And the animals.
And all the leaves.
And the taciturn sand.

So here is an unlisted item:
Beach Grass and
Co., Agate Cove,
Oregon. A windy day, 1964.
The title and all the content:

"Shhh!"

The poem cautions the reader that what we find in this poem is not something we will be able to track to any literary source. This kind of text does not rely on art growing out of, or referring to art; it tells us to listen to the place at hand.[36] Stafford's position is important to understand, because it suggests that the poems accumulate deeper meaning more through the context they establish with the world, and to some extent with other Stafford poems, than through any extensive dialogue with literary tradition.[37] This is not to say that these poems stand free and dissociated from literary tradition. As Holden points out, Stafford's poetry "exhibits a steady consciousness of Romantic tradition, particularly Wordsworth and Thoreau."[38]

Finally a note on the scope of this study. In order to perceive the totality of Stafford's ecological metaphor, it is also necessary to include the poetry from his many small editions, most of which have been published during the 1970s.[39] The reasons for this are simple: first of all, it is roughly during this period that the ecological metaphor receives its most articulated expression. The poet's "early period," containing the poetry published in book form during the early 1960s, represents the commencing coalescence of the metaphor, but certainly not its complete realization.[40] It is also interesting to

observe that the ecological metaphor has received less sustained expression in Stafford's latest collections of poetry, *A Glass Face in the Rain* (1982) and *An Oregon Message* (1987), which, for the sake of this argument, we could call his "later poetry." This suggests that the process of articulating an environmental ethic in his earlier poetry was a response to one of the new concerns of the 1960s and 1970s, and that this process seems to have reached a sense of completion. So while ecological and environmental issues have remained important in the public discourse of the 1980s, perhaps the attempt to keep arguing an ethical position in the poetry seems less urgent once such a stance has been articulated. Furthermore, selecting poems outside his major collections reveal a more pronounced articulation of the ecological metaphor (which might be the result of other editorial criteria than those at Harper and Row), and thus constitute an important, emphasized thematic addition to the poems in the major collections. A final reason for looking at these poems is that they belong to a body of the poet's work fairly inaccessible and unknown to the general reader, and that these poems have remained completely ignored by earlier critics. Apart from a few scattered and local book reviews, there is very little mention of the poetry of his small press publications.

2. PESSIMISM AS A BACKDROP TO THE ECOLOGICAL METAPHOR

By looking at some of William Stafford's pessimistic poems concerning man's fate on earth, it is possible to perceive how the ecological metaphor to a certain extent is defined against that pessimism, and how that gives it such a central position. All of the poems discussed here have been published in small edition books, but interestingly enough, not yet collected in any major volume. By bringing these lesser known poems to light, I hope to demonstrate that this is an aspect of Stafford's work which has been largely ignored (perhaps simply because the small editions have been ignored), but which is crucial when we look at some of the contexts of his poems. A pessimistic mood is not completely missing from Stafford's major books. For example, the poem **"The Epitaph Ending in And"** (*TRY, SCBT*, p. 127), expresses the same sense of finality with its opening words "In the last storm," and similarly, one could argue that a poem like **"Our City Is Guarded by Automatic Rockets"** (*TRY, SCBT*, pp. 121-22), suggests this pessimism as well with its ending: "because I think our story should not end—/ or go on in the dark with nobody listening." Or that the more recent **"Ground Zero"** (*AOM* [*An Oregon Message*], p. 36), with its post-bomb evocation, expresses it too. Still, the focus here is less on pessimism than it is on protest, which, after all, might be construed as a kind of optimism.

As we have seen in the introduction to this chapter, William Stafford is fundamentally pessimistic about man's fate on earth. His pessimism is not an obsession, not a subject he continually returns to, but a conviction at the very foundation of his outlook. One could say that this point of view shapes our understanding of some of his other poems, even explicates certain attitudes expressed in the general body of poems related to the ecological metaphor. These poems represent explorations into the emotions of pessimism, while at the same time implying the ways of hope. They are steps in the process of trying to come to an understanding of the complexity of this feeling. Stafford seems to suggest several reasons for this pessimism: 1) that we should distrust the rational intellect because of its tendency to suppress the quiet voice of the heart that is only heard by careful and sustained listening;[41] 2) that our sense of being exiled from participation in the world of nature might be due to our emphasis on technology; 3) that we fail to assume personal responsibility for the consequences of our actions as human beings; 4) that the very nature of Western civilization is inherently destructive; 5) that we are not perceptive enough to be guided by the "faint presence" of nature; 6) or that there simply is no explicit reason for man's end on earth—that this destruction is ultimately incomprehensible to us.

In short then, one could say that Stafford explores these different possible causes without adopting a single one as solely responsible. Furthermore, in line with Stafford's poetic strategy of not to "simply assert something" (*YMR* [*You Must Revise Your Life*], p. 68), these poems do not directly present alternatives to the pessimism they exhibit. The reader must draw his own conclusions. The poem **"Scientists,"** which is part of a sequence called "Some Short Poems" in *Tuft by Puff* (1978, unpaginated), suggests one cause for pessimism: an unbalanced reliance on the rational intellect:

"Scientists"

These intellectuals banging their heads
till they flare—
they are burning the world down.

The poem clearly points to a central consequence of this reliance on the "head" without acknowledging the traditional opposite, the "heart," the seat of feeling. In its general sense this short poem is a comment on the emphasis of our present culture, dominated by science and technology. Stafford's mistrust of the rational intellect can be found scattered throughout his poetry. Take, for example, the ending of **"Traveling through the Dark"** (*TTD, SCBT,* p. 61), where the narrator characterizes his own thinking as identical to that act which killed the deer: "I thought hard for us all—my only swerving—, / then pushed her over the edge into the river." What this poem affirms is, of course, a reliance on feeling or intuition as the right source for action.

The affirmation of the heart as the right source for action (implicitly rejecting the head) is also found throughout his poetry. At the ending of the poem **"The Well Rising"** (*WYC, SCBT,* pp. 51-2), the bird is seen as an ideal model: "The swallow heart from wing beat to wing beat / counseling decision, decision: / thunderous examples. I place my feet / with care in such a world."

In the poem **"End of the Man Experiment,"** published in *Things That Happen Where There Aren't Any People* (1980, p. 15), the end of human existence is associated with the North.

"End of the Man Experiment"

In The North a great wind lived.
Its mighty hand
scoured a kingdom out
and formed the last snowman.

What a strange carol he sang!—
himself blowing away,
lips, head, hands,
whimpering low, forlorn,

Till only the level wind
lived in that land,
the whole bowed world
one storm.

Contrary to Stafford's other pessimistic poems, this poem does not try to point to any specific cause for the final "storm." Instead, the "great wind" of "The North" seems to be an extended metaphor of the mysterious force that rules all life. According to Holden, "The North" is part of Stafford's set of symbols representing "Nature in its uncontrollable aspect," which certainly elucidates the nature of this force.[42] In the description in the first stanza of how the "mighty hand" of this wind "scoured a kingdom out / and formed the last snowman," the "last snowman" seems to suggest modern man himself, brought to total humiliation by this great power before he is destroyed. The second stanza depicts his "strange carol" of disintegration, and the third stanza gives us a final vision of a "whole bowed world / one storm." Perhaps the poem suggests that man's end is inherent in the nature of the world, that the death of a species is an inevitable consequence of its birth. Perhaps the poem wants to suggest a point where coexistence between man and nature is no longer possible.

Ultimately the poem must be read as a kind of bleak reminder of the true relationship in the world between man and Creation: that man is not in control of natural forces in spite of all the other things he believes that he is in control of. But there are no final reasons given here why this is happening: no lack of humility, no hubris, no lack of responsibility, no disregard for nature. This vision seems more related to the uncaring, powerful universe found in the poetry of Stephen Crane or Robinson Jeffers, than any of the other poems discussed here. It is a universe ruled by a force which is not only incomprehensible, but also apparently completely unconcerned with the fate of human beings. At the end the poem leaves all possibilities open: we cannot really know why things happen, the world of nature is a mystery, and all this poem claims is to present a vision of such a world. In this respect it echoes the sentiment of the last stanza of one of Stafford's most famous poems, **"At the Bomb Testing Site"**: "There was just a continent without much on it / under a sky that never cared less" (**WYC, SCBT** p. 41).

The poem **"A Story for a Winter Night,"** published in *Stories and Storms and Strangers* (1984, pp. 6-7), describes a rather pessimistic view of the situation man is creating for himself:

"A Story for a Winter Night"

Late one winter night in The North
sleepers awoke in a frozen town:
the whole earth shuddered around their beds
as a chomping monster came over a hill, and down.

And suddenly they remembered—the military post:
a band of men had been told
to build forts up there with a giant machine
that could traverse the cold.

"Ravager," they called it, and they left it running,
its deep engine tame, but the gears tight,
mumbling savagely, its white plume
smoke-ringing deliberately in the moonlight.

Ravager's clang tracks mowed that town.
Its big blade sliced right over a sleeping child.
Then stamping and charging Ravager howled
furiously away into the wild,

Where it still tramps—its great sound
whispering distantly in the northern sky
where now and then a whole mountain avalanches
as it goes inexorably by.

Too big to stop, too strong to wear out, Ravager haunts
those men who let it rear and escape.
They go listening with their children to stand
on the porch or the back step,

As my father took me, the saved child: away off
its blared light flickering its own road, we heard
Ravager feeding on some distant mistake and grunting
hungrily through the night at the adversary world.

The poem suggests a kind of modern Frankenstein story possessing the ingredients of often feared disaster, involving clandestine military activities, nuclear power and/or arms, as well as ecological disaster.[43] "Ravager," the destructive aspect or consequence of human behavior, has gone out of control and become threatening, even though it has not yet destroyed all life. It is

alive and free to ravage up under the "northern sky," echoing the same symbolic geographical source as the previous poem.[44] Ravager destroys a town, kills innocence, "a sleeping child." It also ruins nature, "a whole mountain avalanches / as it goes inexorably by." It is "too big to stop, too strong to wear out," and its enemy is the "world." In short, it is a force directed against all life, created by man.

What does Ravager really stand for? We know that it is built at "the military post" by "a band of men" who "had been told" to do so, suggesting that Ravager is the result of men who obey orders from others instead of their own conscience—that is, by men avoiding responsibility for their actions. Consequently, "Ravager haunts / those men who let it rear and escape." The fact that this breaking free surprises its builders reveals the degree of hubris in their exaggerated belief in the power to control technology. (The association to a technological construction is beyond doubt, as it is referred to as "a giant machine" with an "engine," and that it evokes a tank with its "clang tracks" and so on.) The final irony of this human creation is that Ravager is built for the opposite purpose: for protection, for "forts."

So instead of simply being a description of the destructive forces threatening man, this poem takes on the quality of a parable. The narrator of the poem is "the saved child," apparently saved by the instruction of his father, and the moral of the poem seems to be that there certainly is a way to avoid becoming one "of the band of men." The way to prevent the world from being "ravaged," the poem seems to imply, is to establish an individual, responsible moral code. By being guided by an ideal opposite that of taking orders, we will also be responsible for the world in a small but significant way. If "the band of men" had been guided by this principle, "Ravager" would not be in existence.

The point of view assumed in this poem, is very close to the conclusion of one of the stories in *Down In My Heart*, Stafford's largely autobiographical accounts from four years as a conscientious objector during WW II. In a story called "Mountain Conscription" a man named George expresses a similar feeling of disillusioned pessimism about the existence of the war:

> "It's as if the war is a game," George said. "People retain the same qualities throughout big historical changes; a fad comes along, something like peewee golf, but with a slightly murderous effect, and people go along—with their same friendly feelings—murdering each other."[45]

So in spite of the possibility of being guided by responsibility, the poem leaves us with a pessimistic point of view. Ravager is still at large, "feeding on some distant mistake and grunting / hungrily through the night at the adversary world."

The poem **"Stadium High, Tacoma,"** from *Sometimes Like a Legend* (1981, p. 24), uses a different technique to convey a similar kind of pessimism:

"Stadium High, Tacoma"

This building in front is Greek, copper
on top. It looks over Indian space.
I feel, when I walk its hall, some other space.

Below by the water lies many a wrecked old place,
walls broken and soaked, but floors
of a marvelous strength,
where beams and the years have hid.

To the east, whole cities of smoke fall toward
a final sky, where Boeing hovers, and fate,
and Europe, and Africa, and Asia.

The poem juxtaposes two entirely different cultures, that of Western origin and that of American Indian origin, and evokes the destructiveness of the former. Even the title contains that juxtaposition. Stadium High, of course, refers to a particular high school, but the Greek etymology ("stadion" means racetrack), adds a sense of football aggressiveness. Tacoma, on the other hand, is known to have received its name from a novel by Theodore Winthrop, *The Canoe and the Saddle* (1863), in which it is said that Tacoma is the word the Indians used for Mount Rainer, by which they meant "near to heaven," "nourishing breast," and "mother of waters."[46]

The opening line informs us that the building "in front is Greek," suggesting that whatever it tries to be, it is inevitably a façade. This structure confronts "Indian space." Walking inside the building the narrator does not "feel" its presence, but experiences "some other space." That is, he does not feel part of this Greek heritage alone. The second stanza tells us that close by, but now hidden from us because it lies "below" the ground, are "wrecked" remnants of the Indian dwellings. We also learn that even though their walls are "broken and soaked," their floors have "a marvelous strength." Metaphorically speaking, this image suggests that what they were is still strong and good to build on. The first and second stanza thus use these two buildings symbolically to evoke two opposite relationships to the world. It is clear which one the narrator favors. Standing almost on the very edge of the North American continent, the narrator in the third and last stanza looks back over the settled continent:

To the east, whole cities of smoke fall toward
a final sky, where Boeing hovers, and fate,
and Europe, and Africa, and Asia.

What he sees looking east (and in a sense back in time), is the result of the industrial expansion of Western civilization: polluting, alienated from its Native American culture (and by implication, nature), to such a degree that it suggests complete destruction, "the final sky." The word "fall," of course, also carries overtones of a moral fall. Part of this vision of doom includes the airplane manufacturers, not simply because Boeing is located just north of Tacoma, but because the airplane is such a succinct metaphor of twentieth century technological development. Here, by the connective "and" it is inseparably bound with a "fate" that will involve the entire planet. Technology seems to be, in other words, intimately connected to this "final sky."

A poem which does not explicitly articulate a sense of doom, but nevertheless implies a profound pessimism about civilization, would be **"At Cove on the Crooked River"** (*TTD, SCBT,* pp. 99-100). It is interesting to note that this poem uses the same images of contrast as the preceding poem: the Native American point of view from the wilderness versus modern civilization as represented by the car. The poem opens with the narrator in the wilderness by an "Indian picture rock," taking in the view of the camp and the scenery. This place should be, the narrator says, where you "see trouble walking away." What kind of trouble this is, we do not yet know. Then two stanzas follow which affirm the significance of nature: "the river meant something," and the trees are seen as possessing a kind of true responsiveness by acting "out whatever has happened to them." In the third stanza we suddenly find out what the trouble is: "civilization." The narrator's language becomes metaphorically charged at this point, when he says that he wants to "carve" civilization "decisively outward the way evening comes," which is then compared to the way "people cramp into their station wagons / . . . and drive away." The three images here of carving and removing, of night and darkness approaching, and of cars disappearing, makes it clear that Stafford views the wilderness as the antithesis to a civilization he wants to go away.

The poem **"Ferns,"** also from *Sometimes Like a Legend* (1981, p. 54), begins with a rather matter-of-fact statement of the end of man's existence:

"Ferns"

After the firestorms that end history,
a fern may print on the rock
some pattern about chance, and
the reaching for it, and the odds.

Already they are prints for us:
lace in dusk, thin
stem, wide hand, faint presence; and
I know something fainter, fern:

The map under this country
that shows where we are while
we wander lost and the sun pulls
and our thought swims into the air.

The poem gains immediate momentum by switching from an initial statement of the end of man (calmly posited as fact), and by reversing our expectations of a continued focus on man, to what *may* happen to a single frond of a fern. It is as if the imagined image of the fern printed on rock by an atomic blaze, must become the mysterious emblem preventing it from happening. The following two stanzas explore reasons why this would not have to happen. First of all, already these ferns "are prints for us," which implies that their message can be received right now. We already know the "chance" and the "odds." Then the fern is depicted as a "wide hand, faint presence," a personification suggesting a greeting or signal indicating that it really is here and possible to get in touch with. The last stanza points even further by stating the existence of a "map under this country / that shows where we are." A map suggests a description that tells us where things are in proportion to each other, and which could guide us if we only find it. This map should not simply be construed as geological formations, but is probably more akin to the "legend" under the land in the poem **"Bi-focal"** (*WYC, SCBT* p. 48). The earth holds both mystery and guidance if observed carefully, but it is a dark and deep truth. Instead "we," as the poem ends, "wander lost and the sun pulls / and our thought swims into the air." The last line is especially revealing: "thought" and "air" seem to be the opposites of the ideal "feeling" and "earth." Again, the recurring distrust of intellect and theory comes through in this poem, and possibly it is even construed as the tragic flaw which will lead us to doom.

We also catch a glimpse of the poet's vision of doom in the third stanza of the second part of **"Montana Eclogue"** (*A, SCBT,* p. 167), where "We glimpse that last storm when the wolves / get the mountains back." The association of doom and wolves reappears in a much later poem too, but with a very different perspective. **"Later"** (*GF* [*A Glass Face in the Rain*], p. 50) evokes a sense of pessimism not through the end of man in a nuclear war, but through modern man's lack of concern for the wilderness. In this poem the wolf is at the center of attention as the emblem of the wilderness itself. "Now they are almost extinguished," the second stanza tells us in the opening line. And the significance of that, the poem concludes, "means we are on the trail the wolves have gone." A clearer link between an ecological awareness and a profound sense of pessimism concerning man's fate is hard to find in Stafford's poetry.

3. THE ECOLOGICAL METAPHOR AND THE WILDERNESS

In his book, *The Unsettling of America,* Wendell Berry voices a commonly held agreement (at least among ecologically-oriented poets), about the need for a revision of the current, anti-ecological direction of society. Even though this book argues from a primarily agricultural point of view and focuses its criticism on the consequences of modern agribusiness, it contains some fundamental comments on the man-wilderness relationship which are representative for Stafford's fundamental point of view as well. Berry discusses, in a chapter called "The Body and the Earth," the importance of an attitude which respects the wilderness for what it is and puts man in a proper relationship with it.

> That humans are small within the Creation is an ancient perception, represented often enough in art that it must be supposed to have an elemental importance. On one of the painted walls of the Lascaux cave (20,000—15,000 B.C.), surrounded by the exquisitely shaped, shaded, and colored bodies of animals, there is the childish stick figure of a man, a huntsman who, having cast his spear into the guts of a bison, is now weaponless and vulnerable, poignantly frail, exposed, and incomplete. The message seems essentially that of the voice out of the whirlwind in the Book of Job: the Creation is bounteous and mysterious, and humanity is only a part of it—not its equal, much less its master.

> Old Chinese landscape paintings reveal, among towering mountains, the frail outline of a roof or a tiny human figure passing along a road on foot or horseback. These landscapes are almost always populated. There is no implication of a dehumanized interest in nature "for its own sake." What is represented is a world in which humans belong, but which does not belong to humans in any tidy economic sense; the Creation provides a place for humans, but it is greater than humanity and within it even great men are small. Such humility is the consequence of an accurate insight, ecological in its bearing, not a pious deference to "spiritual" value.[47]

The perspective Wendell Berry describes here, of man acknowledging his proper size in the totality of the natural world, is central in Stafford's poetry as well. The image of a cave drawing, for example, recurs in Stafford's poems not only to show the frailty of man within Creation, but to suggest a more intense and intimate relationship with it. To live in a cave becomes the ultimate symbol of living with the earth, and to be one with it. The poem **"Querencia"** (*AOM,* p. 31), describes a cave in which paintings were made a long time ago. "Rockslides now have hidden that room," the poem continues, and "nobody believes in that room anymore." Still, the poem ends with the assertion: "It is there." The idea that the earth contains meanings that are now hidden from, and forgotten by an industrial-technological age, is clearly linked to the pervasive articulation of environmental ethics. In the poem **"Touches"** (*SM,* [*Someday, Maybe*] *SCBT,* p. 223), for example, the non-human universe is given a voice in the opening line: "Late, you can hear the stars." Tuned in to this voice, standing in a deep canyon, the speaker of the poem recognizes the significance of the setting: "you are in the earth and / it guides you;" and later in the poem he is indeed inside a cave too. The idea that the earth is our guide to a proper way of living, certainly becomes a central symbol, "ecological in its bearing" as Berry puts it. The ecological dimension of living in a cave is also implied in **"A Sound from the Earth"** (*A, SCBT*, p. 172) where the grandfather of Crazy Horse is said to be living inside a cave, emphasizing the Native American intimacy with the earth.[48]

To adopt a proper attitude toward the earth, Stafford's poetry suggests a reconnection with the wilderness. It becomes a place where we can establish a more profound, often mysterious, link with ourselves. But the possibility of connecting with the wilderness rests on the assumption that there still is a wilderness to connect to, something which no longer can be taken for granted since the modern industrial-technological civilization is able to expand only at the expense of the wilderness. The image of the wilderness taken hostage by civilization is succinctly expressed in a short poem from ***The Design on the Oriole*** (1977, unpaginated):

"The Coyote in the Zoo"

A yellow eye meets mine:
I suddenly know, too late,
the land outside belongs
to the one that looks away.

In one sense the poem is a sad comment on the absurdity of trying to preserve a manifestation of the wilderness in a cage. The instant there is eye contact, the poem raises the question of what we, as human beings, have done not only to this animal, but to the wilderness, and with what right.[49] But there is yet another implication of this poem, and that is on the level of metaphor. In the Native American oral tradition in the Pacific Northwest, (except for the tradition of the coastal tribes) Coyote the Trickster was the central character. The roles he played in these stories varied from that of Transformer/Creator hero to "Delightful Rogue and Horrible Example."[50] In short, one could say that Coyote in this sense is a symbolic incarnation of the imagination: humorous, incredibly creative, often terrible, always unpredictable, and even uncontrollably wild since he is part of the wilderness.

When Coyote is locked up in a cage longing to get out, it is a clear indication that things are not as they should be. The speaker of the poem understands that the creative principle is a free principle, like the wilderness, and must remain wild and uncontrolled. Advocating the necessity of preserving the wilderness thus becomes part of the ecological metaphor because it illustrates an important connection to the human mind. To accept the wildness of the wilderness is to accept the creative principle, without which man is not whole. To connect with the wilderness thus becomes a process of creating wholeness.

The symbolic role played by Coyote as a guide to our understanding of the creative impulse comes out in the poem **"Outside"** (*WYC, SCBT*, pp. 48-49) as well. This poem argues that "We need to let animals loose in our houses," which could be interpreted as another way of saying that we must once again make our home among the wild animals. And this is, of course, exactly how the Native American lived. The reason we have to do this, is due to the fact that "all we have taken into our keeping / . . . belongs to a truth / greater than ours, in the animals' keeping." Just as the earth itself contains a truth we need to find again, we need to rediscover the animals by opening ourselves up to them. As the poem concludes: "Coyotes are circling around our truth."

In **"Hearing the Song"** (*AOM*, p. 101), overcoming the initial fear in the Coyote's sound and being able to hear its beauty, its song, is the focus of this poem. The ability to do that is, of course, parallel to the ability to affirm the wilderness. It is interesting to note that the attitude toward the wilderness in this poem is identical to the Gary Snyder poem "The Call of the Wild,"[51] where he laments his neighbors' inability to stand listening to this song: "And the Coyote singing / is shut away / for they fear / the call / of the wild" (*TI* [*Turtle Island*], p. 22). A similar theme, of killing coyotes, also appears as the triggering point in the poem **"1080,"** *Listening Deep* (1984, p. 26), even though the ecological consequences of using a poison entering the food chain assumes centrality in this poem.

"1080"

"Ten-Eighty," they say it, when they call
for me, and I kill so well they'd
give me a medal, stockmen
would. They love me. Right down
the food chain I go: after
the coyote dies, the vulture that
eats it does, then the ant and
anteater and on. I sift
for death, and find it again
and again. I carry many ghosts
multiplying with me as I go.
Even the swallows flittering for
tainted flies hear me in the grass.
"My name is Ten-Eighty," I whisper—
"you come too." And they come.

Again there is the articulation of conflict between nature and culture. In the context of other Stafford poems dealing with coyotes, this coyote must also be understood as a symbol of the wilderness, and the thoughtless use of toxins reverberating through the food chain as a criticism of a shallow and shortsighted view of the true complexity of natural systems.

In the poem **"How to Regain Your Soul,"** from the same collection, *Listening Deep* (1984, p. 14), the way of regaining perspective is described in terms of mental balancing through a journey into the wilderness:

"How to Regain Your Soul"

Come down Canyon Creek trail on a summer
   afternoon
that one place where the valley floor opens out.
   You will see
the white butterflies. Because of the way
   shadows
come off those vertical rocks in the west,
   shafts of sunlight hitting the river and
   a deep
long purple gorge straight ahead. Put down
   your pack.

Above, air sighs the pines. It was
   this way
when Rome was clanging, when Troy was
   being built,
when campfires lighted caves. The white
   butterflies dance
by the thousands in the still sunshine.
   Suddenly anything
could happen to you. Your soul pulls toward
   the canyon
and then shines back through the white wings
   to be you again.

Several things alert the reader in this poem: the western landscape evoked without the use of any specific geographical references, the wilderness setting defined against the beginnings of modern Western civilization, and the interaction between "soul" and wilderness. As the title of the poem indicates, something is needed in order to regain one's soul. Becoming one with "the canyon" returns the soul to the speaker and suggests the necessity of establishing contact with the constant, timeless reality present in the wilderness. The assumption behind this poem is, in other words, that the "soul" has been lost. If the soul can be regained in the wilderness, the implication is that the cause behind this loss must be attributable to the lack of wilderness. Since the absence of wilderness is the direct result of an expanding civilization, evoked through the references to "Rome" and "Troy," the poem establishes a clear polarity between the values associated with them. The two cities are, incidentally, the same as those evoked in the poem discussed earlier, **"Stadium High, Tacoma."**

In many ways this poem is an exact correspondence to the old Chinese landscape paintings Wendell Berry spoke about. There is a specific, western American setting, an overwhelming wilderness, and the image of a lone traveler. But the wilderness is not unchartered. There is a path, the "Canyon Creek trail" passing through it. So just as in the Chinese paintings, there is a place for man in Stafford's wilderness, but it is a place which portrays him in a different perspective from that of the control-oriented modern society.

The idea of letting go of control is also stressed in this poem. The advice of the speaker (speaking with a clear sense of experience) to the reader, is one of passive at-

tentiveness: "Suddenly anything / could happen to you." There is no volition on the part of the hiker. You don't make it happen; this is something which happens to you once you invite the possibility by hiking into the wilderness. The idea of mental centering is also reinforced by the symbolic "white butterflies." The symbol of the butterfly larva shedding its cocoon to become a winged butterfly has, in religious literature, often suggested events of transformation from bodily to spiritual, or from one level of insight to another, and so on. Here, the "thousands" of dancing "white butterflies" suggest the beauty and the transcendent quality of the wilderness itself. And in the very last image of the poem, the soul is clearly associated with that quality of the butterflies when it "shines back through the white wings / to be you again." As in so many of Stafford's poems, one could possibly interpret the journey into the wilderness as a metaphor of creative activity since it generally resembles Stafford's ideas about creative writing as an excursion into something unknown that produces a text.[52] Even so, it points to the parallel between the imagination and the wilderness, and the importance of the possibility of interaction.

"By the Deschutes Shore," from *The Design on the Oriole* (1977, unpaginated) as well, also suggests several recurring themes in Stafford's work. There is the focus on the small event, a certain spiritual atmosphere saturating it, and a kind of passive acceptance of what is and what has happened. Light, or more specifically the sun, takes on the significance of being the conveyor of wisdom:

"By the Deschutes Shore"

Millions of miles away at evening the sun
touches the little folded hands of the dead
mouse in the grass church by the river.
No tuft but gains a halo in the service, no
rock unwarmed. Having no hands, the world
learns everything by shouldering down in the
dusk and waiting like this while the sun
repeats its lesson color by color toward
the brown mouse, brown paws, brown, brown grass.

Simply describing a dead mouse by a river during sunset, the poem also takes on the additional dimensions of being both an affirmation of a transcendental natural world and an illustration of humility. The event is directly compared to a church funeral, in which the surrounding congregation of tufts of grass and rocks becomes saturated with a religious dimension. The natural environment and the light are thus established as synonymous with body and spirit. The meaning of the poem is then gently conveyed. The grass and the rocks, "the world," are passive and accepting to the presence of the light, which "repeats its lesson color by color." The "lesson" is simply the color of the earth itself, the color "brown," and the implication is that this simplicity must be accepted. The suggestion of the last line is that "brown" is the greatest denominator, the color in the landscape which stands out the least. Brown means being inconspicuous, an inseparable part of the landscape. The sense of nature transformed into a place of religious communion between man and nature is also suggested in very similar terms in a poem like **"Crossing the Desert"** (*SM, SCBT,* p. 234), where "Little animals call / us" and "a ditch at night is a church," and so on.

"By the Deschutes Shore" can, in other words, be read as a parable where a small event in nature parallels our own true human situation. Humans are, just like the mouse, very small and mortal in the greater order of nature. The poem also urges a stance of "shouldering down in the / dusk and waiting" until the light will teach its lesson of letting go. Related to the light metaphor is the suggestion in the first stanza of **"People of the South Wind,"** which urges "Be like the sun" (*SM, SCBT,* p. 222), because the sun stands for perception and insight.

Stafford's perception of nature as a spiritual realm seems to be based not primarily on a direct commitment to the literary tradition in, say, the Transcendental sense. Instead, it seems grounded in what Stafford has referred to as his most profound religious experience:

> The most impressive such experience I recall was on the banks of the Cimarron River in western Kansas one mild summer evening, when sky, air, birdcalls, and the setting sun combined to expand the universe for me and to give me the feeling of being sustained, cherished, *included* somehow in a great, reverent story.[53]

Since the direction of contemporary technological/ industrial society indicates that a general perception of this kind of inclusion has not been allowed to advise our behavior toward the earth, how do we find a way which allows us to perceive a new perspective? In the poem **"Atavism"** from *Roving Across Fields* (1983, p. 47), the speaker acknowledges not only the unity of man and nature, but suggests nature as the mask of the world's ultimate mystery. The poem also hints that since we are part of evolution we still possess a kind of memory of our earlier animal forms, and that attention to these feelings becomes a process of rediscovering the wilderness as our home:

"Atavism"

1.

Sometimes in the open you look up
where birds go by, or just nothing,
and wait. A dim feeling comes—
you were like this once: there was air,
and quiet; it was by a lake, or
maybe a river—you were alert

as an otter and were suddenly born
like the evening star into wide
still worlds like this one you have found
again, for a moment, in the open.

2.

Something is being told in the woods: aisles of
shadow lead away; a branch waves;
a pencil of sunlight slowly travels its
path. A withheld presence almost
speaks, but then retreats, rustles
a patch of brush. You can feel
the centuries ripple—generations
of wandering, discovering, being lost
and found, eating, dying, being born.
A walk through the forest strokes your fur,
the fur you no longer have. And your gaze
down a forest aisle is a strange, long
plunge, dark eyes looking for home.
For delicious minutes you can feel your whiskers
wider than your mind, away out over everything.

Again, as in so many other poems, the stance toward the wilderness is one of passive alertness; one must be still and "wait" in order to become perceptive. The waiting then invites "a dim feeling" of identity with an animal spirit in a "quiet" landscape. The opening of the poem suggests a rediscovery of the wilderness as one's original source of being. That "Something is being told in the woods," is enhanced by the image of the "pencil of sunlight slowly" writing a message to the observer. This long wait, measured not in minutes or hours, but in a spot of sunlight wandering across the ground, brings the listener to the edge of mystery, to the perception of a presence: "A withheld presence almost / speaks, but then retreats." The mystery is keenly associated with the wheel of life and death of all living beings, suggesting a sense of equality between all forms of life and a recognition of identity rather than alienation. The attempt to grasp this presence, the "gaze / down a forest aisle," is finally recognized as a search "looking for home." That this "home" is found is also manifested in the two following lines which end the poem, where a total identification with a whiskered animal is reached and described as in terms of a transcendental experience: "For delicious minutes you can feel your whiskers / wider than your mind, away out over everything."

Experiences of a related nature can also be found in the poem **"Journey"** (*SM, SCBT,* p. 235), which by employing an animal persona, affirms the experience of having had animal shape. The poem **"Origins"** (*SM, SCBT,* p. 221) which opens "So long ago that we weren't people then," also points to this idea of having belonged to the animal world.

The poem **"Terms of Surrender"** from the chapbook *Going Places* (1974, p. 42) demonstrates an interesting division in attitudes towards men on one hand, and nature on the other, which reinforces the importance of the ecological metaphor. The speaker assuming the voice of "we" in the poem, belongs to a group of people doing everything possible in order to survive. Their surrender does not apply to the world of men, which they deal with acknowledging its evil, but to the world of nature, which they revere. Perhaps this is an indication that "we" suggests a Native American persona:

"Terms of Surrender"

We hide in the dead grass.
Heat makes the rocks tremble.
Before night rescues us we have
accepted the terms: crawled,
lied, cheated—lived.

We take what the world gives.
We bow our heads like flowers
and think of the ways we came.
Before sleep each night we put
our mouths against a clod
and breathe our share of common air—

The truest way there is to say God's name.

Whoever "we" are hiding from and trying to escape in the first stanza, they do not surrender to them; "night rescues" them. What they do surrender to is an unsentimental acceptance of not always being able to be morally good since survival is paramount. But in spite of this, "we" demonstrate a great deal of humility towards the earth through the complete acceptance of "what the world gives." They also "bow" their heads and respect their place in the natural order, acknowledging "the ways we came." There is a sense of proportion preserved in this. Living humbly in this manner, literally giving one's spirit to the ground itself, is a celebration of the interconnectedness between man and nature, the "truest way there is to say God's name." The act of breathing spirit into mud or clay also echoes, of course, many of the creation myths of the Native Americans in the Northwest, and hints at a creative interaction with the earth.[54]

Many of Stafford's poems celebrate a sense of existence in the world characterized by living without doing any damage to it, and urge a vision of man in balance with nature. **"On an Un-named Mountain"** from *Listening Deep* (1984, p. 16) is such a poem:

"On an Un-named Mountain"

You try to be sure while you stand
quiet: quiet will reach you—
no voice, not even a whisper
miles away where you are. It is
while your closed eyes and silence
protect you that you hold the day
arched over nothing: nobody cares,
and without hurting the world you have

taken a breath again and given it away.
You open your eyes. It is an afternoon
on earth, and you are there.

The poem's search for quiet involves a balancing of internal and external wilderness, and affirms that as one establishes a silence within, "quiet" will come from without. As in so many other poems, this attitude becomes the embodiment of a proper relationship with the world. The ecological dimension is indicated by the fact that this is a way of being "without hurting the world." The implication is that an active, aggressive attitude which excludes listening, and which puts the emphasis on imposing rational order, is a destructive attitude. As the poem **"It Is the Time You Think"** (*WYC, SCBT,* p. 55) opens: "Deaf to process, alive only to ends, / such are the thinkers around me, the logical ones—" which are later identified as the "sudden men in jets who hunt the world."

A poem set on the Oregon coast in the collection *Sometimes Like A Legend* (1981, p. 30), also points towards an implied rejection of civilization in favor of the wilderness. The poem argues, through a rather basic contrast, but with great delight in the sounds and associations of local places, that human trust must be directed toward nature and not civilization:

"Places and Punctuation: The Coast"

Seaside-Rockaway, Tillamook-Astoria.
Port Orford-Coos. Down below Yachats.
Salmon Mouth Dunes. Pirate Cove.
From Siletz to Waldport. Where the
Nestucca goes into the hills. Haystack—
a windy day, late, no one on all
that miles of sand south of Neahkhanie.
A couple in gray, anywhere, looking
west. Shelter in the rocks.

At first sight, the poem sums up a common image anywhere on the Oregon coast: a single couple on a huge, empty beach while the sun sets over the ocean. But the last line adds another dimension to the poem. In spite of all these places along the Oregon coast, filled as they are with tourist accommodations and taking up most of the space of the poem, the end turns around and briefly but intensely focuses on the shelter nature provides. It is like a scale on which the first eight lines are balanced against the last one, and the last is found most substantial.[55]

The affirmation of nature does not mean the exclusion of human civilization, only that the two must be in proper balance: neither city nor wilderness, but the country in between. The speaker's preferences are clearly expressed in the poem **"Sub-Urban"** from *Sometimes Like A Legend* (1981, p. 9), which is just such a middle ground:

"Sub-Urban"

In any town I must live near the rind,
where the animals come around nibbling.
Everything else inside may be designed,
but near is an edge, not confined.

They must be animals that, though mild,
come straying in only by night-time.
They don't belong, but come anyway, beguiled
by light, but ready to bolt for the wild.

That's how the wilds and I belong
around any kind of a city:
in front of us lights and all the glory and stir,
but back of us—country, as friendly as fur.

Accepting a more metaphorical meaning of the speaker's place of residence as an imaginative and intellectual place, we again see a connection to the vital source of the wilderness. What the speaker affirms is the necessity of having the wilderness present on at least one "edge" of his house, a common symbol of the mind and the intellect. This suggests that human life must be able to acknowledge a wild and uncontrolled aspect, containing the unknown side of the "night-time" and the free animals of that dark. These visitors are connections to the mysterious other, to the unknown.

The city, on the other hand, does not carry these positive associations with its "lights and all the glory and stir"; there seems to be something vain or ironic about its exaggerated appearance. With lights (much energy and activity), glory (conspicuous heroic achievements and events), and motion (restlessness and little time for listening), it stands at the opposite pole from the quiet dark with its careful, alert and shy animals. This division is further emphasized by the city "in front of us" and the "country" "back of us," which could be read both in spatial and temporal terms. In either case, the poem implies a reservation about the on-going process of urbanization of society.[56]

Another of Stafford's recurring strategies to evoke the necessity of humility toward nature is to adopt the perspective of a small animal or plant in a poem. The implication is, of course, that just as the small accentuate a different relationship between the part and the whole, we should acknowledge our true size within the whole of creation. The poem **"Whispered into the Ground"** (*SCBT,* p. 25), for example, has a seed speaking about moving with "the wind" and waiting "quietly" on the ground. Stafford's use of persona is not limited to that of animals or plants in poems which directly suggest or imply an ecological awareness, but there are several poems of this kind.[57]

The poem **"Beaver Talk"** from *Tuft by Puff* (1978, unpaginated) humorously uses this strategy:

"Beaver Talk"

Not all the lakes have names;
they trade shapes with the air
and because they help the clouds,
the clouds protect them.

If you find one, christen it
"Splash." But don't tell where—say
"Far on a trail where nothing
made any tracks," or "It was

Out there where the wind blows."

The poem presents, as the title indicates, one beaver talking to another about the nature of lakes, and how to deal with the discovery of a new one. He understands the fluidity of water, how it evaporates and comes back, and how it is part of the clouds. The advice he gives, to keep any discovery of a new lake to himself, makes sense if we think in terms of the expansion pattern of beaver behavior in the wild. But there is another level in the poem as well. First of all, the beaver is the Oregon state animal; on the flag it is displayed in gold against a blue background. Also, as one book on beavers puts it: "Beavers are peaceful, sociable creatures and not given to a great deal of fighting."[58] That is, they exhibit some of the qualities which Stafford considers so essential. Furthermore, talking beavers also suggest stories from the Native American tradition, where animals are considered people possessing most human attributes. With this in mind, the persona in the poem becomes more clearly Oregonian. From this point of view, the poem evokes the constant flux of nature in a system of mutual interdependence, of the changing "shapes" of water "with the air," where lakes "help the clouds" and they in turn "protect them." Read in this way, the second stanza must be understood as an urging to preserve the wilderness. It has to remain unmapped or undefined in order to remain wild, so one should not "tell where" it is. The advice to refer to it as "a trail where nothing / made any tracks," or "out there where the wind blows," of course evokes the water in which the beaver moves, but it also suggests the quality of the wilderness as the untracked, wild space which must be left as it always has been.

Another poem which also uses the beaver persona, but is more explicitly parabolical, is **"Beaver People"** from *Sometimes Like A Legend* (1981, p. 35). The problem the poem raises and tries to respond to, is how do we live in the best possible way in the world? The answer, such as it is, certainly seems related to the ecological point of view:

"Beaver People"

Beaver people are trying to figure out the good water.
All winter they feel a dark deep touch
around their house. "Somewhere," one says, "there is

the good water." But another one, drowsing with a
  paw
over the edge of the bunk, just says,
"But how could it be different, very much?"

Around them sweep currents from up-country—
whatever happened there: leaves, dirt, a spring
that flowed a slow promise every day last summer.
To live—real—in their house is to belong to all that,
yielding to it a face of many-muscled confession:
  where
you have been—a face that never avoided anything.

Beaver people swirl that scenario for us; trail
before our faces too a world streaming
ready for our kind of knowing, a river in thought-
  color.
They declare the Renaissance in any patch of alders.
While we drowse, a paw flips to all of us drowned
  here
in our own pageant, under this ice, dreaming.

This three-partite poem basically sets up a structure of establishing a focus on the theme, illustrating a situation, and pointing to its human relevance. In the first stanza, there is a disagreement as to where the ideal situation or place, "the good water," exists. Is it somewhere else or right here? The implication is, of course, that it is right here, in the present, because "how could it be different, very much?" (The emphasis on now is also pointed out in the third stanza, where the beavers "declare the Renaissance in any patch of alders.") In the second stanza the beaver life in the river is portrayed as a way of being in harmony with the world of motion surrounding it. The current is both an indication of seasons, "leaves, dirt" after fall rains, as well as a "promise" of the never ending motion of life suggested by the river. To live a beaver life is to "belong to all that," to be an inseparable part of the cycles of nature confronting it uncompromisingly with faces "that never avoided anything."

In the third stanza the parabolical leap is taken: "Beaver people swirl that scenario for us." Our life's river is one "in thought-color," but the beaver attitude toward it is applicable and "ready for our kind of knowing." We too must declare "the Renaissance" in the now of our lives. The last two lines portray us as "drowned here / in our own pageant, under the ice, dreaming." Our attention is, in other words, not turned toward the now of life in nature; we are lost in a kind of spectacle, isolated and living in the world of dreams.

4. WILLIAM STAFFORD'S USE OF NATIVE AMERICAN MATERIAL

Expressing an identification with the Native Americans is, as Stafford put it in the introduction to this chapter, "a metaphor." So even though part of his family claims to have had Indian ancestry, this is not what Stafford considers important for his Native American point of view.[59] Stafford argues that any American after having lived in North America for some generations, will have acquired some genetic trace of the Native Americans. So the claim to "Indian blood" thus mainly becomes yet another way of identifying American uniqueness. This "democratic" assumption is also important in the sense that an identification applies not to a minority, but to a majority of Americans. It is a common heritage with which a great many could feel comfortable, and a way of stating a deeper bond to the land defined in terms of home. But it is not the main reason for identifying with the Native Americans. The crucial aspect is the perspective this metaphor gives him as a poet, and the cluster of values and attitudes which are associated with it.[60]

As was also mentioned in the introduction, one must think of some of Stafford's later poems dealing with the Native American material as attempts, at least on one level, to graft onto a storytelling tradition. It is important to point out, however, that they are not simply retellings of old, already documented Indian material, or even primary outgrowths of such material. In that respect they are quite different in both content and spirit from the "story-poems" collected and retold by another Northwest poet, David Wagoner, in *Who Shall Be the Sun?*[61] The debt in Stafford's poems is less obvious, because his attempt is not to render anew what has already been documented, or make garbled story fragments comprehensible by supplying a context. Instead one should see this group of Stafford's poems as new creative efforts to continue the spirit of these stories and to reactivate some Native American views of the world.

What we find in many of Stafford's poems are, in other words, narrative structures or patterns which are more or less evocative of the original Native American stories themselves, and which explicitly or implicitly identify the narrator as a Native American. By doing that, they read like traditional Native American stories even though their concerns and subject matters are contemporary. For example, the poem **"The Animal That Drank Up Sound"** (*TRY, SCBT,* pp. 145-47), is reminiscent in tone of such a traditional story. The Native American qualities that this poem evokes are triggered by several pointers in the text. First there is the opening line: "One day across the lake where echoes come now / an animal that needed sound came down." This fits the pattern of using a particular geographical locus as the triggering point for a story, emphasizing the participation of place in the creation of the mythos of a tribe. Furthermore, we have the central character in the shape of an animal with supernatural qualities, which is a common feature in the Native American storytelling tradition. Finally, there is the timelessness of the language employed by the poem: the vocabulary belongs to pre-civilized man (no modern objects are to be found), which frees it from contemporary times and instead associates it with a time found in Native American stories set before the arrival of the white man.

Then, if we briefly look at the poem not so much in terms of what it refers back to but what it refers forward to in the eyes of a contemporary reader, the ecological metaphor provides a helpful matrix for interpretation. Read in this manner, the animal becomes the embodiment of the threat to the environment, and the poem articulates a warning of the possibility of the extinction of life on earth. In this context we can even understand the title as echoing the main thrust of Rachel Carson's *Silent Spring.*[62]

Another of Stafford's poems, **"Heard Under a Tin Sign at the Beach"** (*SCBT,* p. 8), demonstrates the same poetic strategy. The opening line of the poem establishes: 1) a wind persona speaking to the narrator of the poem, "I am the wind"; 2) the wind then tells the narrator that he "had a home"; 3) that he has "three brothers" who liked to quarrel, and that this is related to having had to leave home; 4) that he is "looking . . . for someone, / examining everything"; 5) that he and his brothers "wrestle" when they meet; and 6) finally, that he remembers his earlier encounters with the narrator and that they will meet again. If we briefly compare this poem to a short story from *Coyote Was Going There* called "The Battle of the Winds," we immediately see some direct correspondences to a Native American point of view:

> The brothers of the Southwest Wind were always fighting with the brothers of the Northeast Wind and their sister, whose name was Tekstye.

> Finally Tekstye's brothers were killed, and she ran away. But just as she reached the Columbia River, one of the Southwest Wind brothers caught up with her, and knocked her into the water.

> Then he said to Tekstye, "From now on you will no longer be a person and go around freezing people. You can blow once in awhile, then I will come and overpower you. Rain will be your enemy too. You will blow and freeze everything, but then he and I will come; we will thaw out the ground, warm everything up, and make the earth green and beautiful again."[63]

In this story the winds are personified as brothers and sisters; the different winds battle (wrestle and quarrel) with each other to the extent that some are killed; and the result of the battle is that one wind loses its home. It would be farfetched indeed, to argue a direct relationship between these two specific texts and claim that the poem has its roots in the story. It might, but it does not seem very likely, because comparisons with other Native American wind stories could yield similar correspondences as well. The important point here is not direct influence, but the story's illustration of Stafford's poetic technique of transforming traditional Native American storytelling elements, with which he is obviously familiar, into his own poems.

Read within the context of the ecological metaphor, the wind persona of **"Heard Under a Tin Sign at the Beach"** assumes the representational position of the force of the world of nature. The final stanza, where the wind embraces the narrator, thus points to a clear awareness of the intimate relationship between nature and man, and the wind's final words, "There will be / these times again, no matter how far," must be understood as a serious reminder to man that he will never be totally free or disengaged from the world of nature.

It is also interesting to note that this poem, **"Heard Under a Tin Sign at the Beach,"** has a kind of companion poem, **"Wind World"** (*SM, SCBT,* pp. 229-30), which echoes the former poem both in content and structure. A brief look at the poem shows that again the wind is personified: Wind World is the name of a wind person. Furthermore, there is a narrator (only here he is explicitly defined as a Native American) telling us about the wind: "Wind World always made friends with / us Indians, who wore feathers for him." Finally, the narrator is "told" these things about Wind World from a tree-like plant (a "Joshua tree near Mojave"), suggesting the important ability to perceive and understand the voice of nature. So here we have a poem which stresses how the Native American is at peace with Wind World (in spite of the fact that Wind World does have the menacing child Thirst, whose "ragged little dolls" suggests those dead from lack of water), and how the narrator's final observation nevertheless focuses on Wind World's beauty singing "a song."[64]

The same fundamental reverence the Native Americans showed for the Earth occurs again and again in Stafford's poetry evoking Native American material. The poem **"Dawn on the Warm Springs Reservation"** from the collection *Things That Happen Where There Aren't Any People* (1980, p. 30) is a good illustration of the adoption of that reverence:

"Dawn on the Warm Springs Reservation"

Into its frost-white branches
a juniper draws the light,
a bowl of it, softly glowing, quiet.

Off through the fog all day
miles of these file away,
faint pearls of white.

And all spirits in the world so bide,
one for every thing:
a place, a tree, a rock. . . .

You can't give away, or buy,
or sell, or assign these hills—
they hold what they always held.

And it's the same all over the world—
any tree, any rock, any hill.

This poem seems to focus on two aspects of the Native American point of view clearly related to certain aspects of environmental ethics. The views the poem illustrates are that the world possesses not only a sense of beauty and mystery available to our human perception, but an intrinsic value as well, by emphasizing that nature is saturated with "spirits"; that is, that the earth is alive independently of human beings, and that this presence is found in entities everywhere, in "a place, a tree, a rock. . . ." If nature is acknowledged as the abode of these spirits, respect and reverence seem to be the only proper attitudes towards it, and living in such a world must become a process of responsible interaction with it.

The opening line of the fourth stanza: "You can't give away, or buy / or sell, or assign these hills—" is a statement absolutely contrary to the world we know and live in, where every single piece of land is claimed by nations, divided into public or private property, measured, sold and taxed and so on. Why then, does the poem claim the opposite, that land cannot be bought or sold? First of all, this stance reflects the traditional Native American point of view toward the ownership of land, which, together with the title of the poem, identifies the speaker as a Native American. Furthermore, apart from raising the inevitable question with what right anyone claims ownership to any land, the poem also implies that there is something in an attitude treating the world as real estate which destroys an awareness of what the land has "always held." As soon as the land is divided into private property the ability to perceive its spiritual presence, and with that, our respect is lost. The image of an undivided world, free from boundaries and divisions, evokes a dream of completeness and unity with non-human nature.

There is another realization implicit in this image as well. Land that is possessed in our modern sense of property can permit and even justify exploitation or abuse, since ownership allows the right to decide over land reduced to the concept of natural resources. With the loss of the perception of spiritual presence in nature, land is reduced to various forms of objects of income and thus open to environmental destruction. The last lines of the poem are, in other words, an affirmation of the universal applicability of an environmental ethic demonstrating responsibility towards the land: "And it's the same all over the world—/ any tree, any rock, any hill."

What many poems utilizing Native American material also point to is a state of being both passive and intensely alert at the same time, which pays attention to and heeds the voice of nature. The voice of nature is often a quiet voice, and in a number of poems it can be heard from the nature within as well as without. This attitude seems to be a complex feeling including a sense of humility, attention, respect, and carefulness. In the poem **"At the Klamath Berry Festival"** (*TRY, SCBT,* pp. 131-32), we learn the difference between what can and what cannot be known.

In this poem with the dancing chief, the narrator of the poem, and the sociologist, we have a statement that what the narrator conceives of as central in the attitude of the dancer is not measurable in sociological terms. On one level, this could be seen as a qualification of the use of local or regional material in poetry: even though the poem is clearly placed in a particular, Northwest setting and includes the unique facts of an event in that place, that is not the main concern of the poem. What lies at the center of the poem is a distinction of what three different ways of perception (the chief's, the narrator's, and the sociologist's) reveal to the reader.

The attempt of the observing narrator and sociologist consists of trying to catch glimpses of "the old way" of being. But already in the last line of the first stanza the narrator becomes ironic toward the task of the sociologist: "I envied him the places where he had not been." The implication is, of course, that the "places" the speaker of the poem so strongly desires to visit are the ones where the sociologist has not been, that is, the places which cannot be mapped and described in sociological terms. The sociologist can observe the events at the festival, but ultimately, as the last line indicates, the meaning of the dance is concealed to him: the dancer moves "past the sociologist."

The narrator thus recognizes that the sociologist does not really know, but that the dancer does. The chief becomes the central character of the poem. He represents the ideal, a kind of modest hero who makes the speaker see another significance beyond the merely factual. He dances "the old way," which is the unobtrusive way. His feet are "still-moccasined," suggesting both that they are quiet, and that they are still following a tradition, still in moccasins. The eagle wing held in front of his mouth indicates silence as well as identification with the bird itself. That this is important is conveyed by the fact that it is stated twice in the poem. We also find out that the chief is "bashful," and that his attention is directed toward "listening and listening," and not to the audience. Again, an importance emphasized by the repetition. The fact that "he danced after others stopped" implies that his dance is not simply a scheduled performance at a festival, but that he is dancing as a result of his listening. The opening three lines of the last stanza, "He took two steps, the boom caught up, / the mountains rose, the still deep river / slid but never broke its quiet," relate the act of listening to the processes of nature. Nature is quiet to the narrator, but the dancer is nevertheless able to hear something.[65]

The poem can, consequently, be read as a description of a chief who possesses the power to hear a realm of nature silent to the narrator, and therefore also as an indication of where to look for spiritual and/or moral guidance. Perhaps one could even interpret it as an extended metaphor describing the act, and true source, of poetic creativity. In either case, the poem relies on an image drawn from the ecological metaphor: to follow ("dance") "the old way" of the Native Americans by being adopted by a manifestation of its "spirit." In other words, a mysterious bond exists between any listening dancer and the world of nature.[66]

Part of the task of the poet, then, is to re-establish a connection with the Native American point of view. Because of the pessimism Stafford expresses about the future of modern civilization, this attempt is often articulated as a rediscovery of something that has been, which might be again. The short poem **"Indian Caves in the Dry Country"** (*SM, SCBT,* p. 222) expresses this idea very succinctly: "These are some canyons / we might use again / sometime." The assumption behind the poem is, of course, that the civilization modern technology has created might not be there to support us. As in all short poems, what is left out, unsaid, assumes crucial importance. Here, the unsaid points towards our complete dependency on the natural world—something which is too often forgotten in our urban, industrial age—and works as a *memento mori* for the reader. Again, it is a warning against the hubris created by this missing acknowledgment. The poem could therefore be said to argue a way of life re-establishing a direct and explicit intimacy with the earth itself, as well as an implied respect for it.

Another poem, **"The Indian Cave Jerry Ramsey Found"** from the chapbook *Going Places* (1974, p. 22), demonstrates both Stafford's deep interest in Native American material and his imaginative reconnection with another way of being.

"The Indian Cave Jerry Ramsey Found"

Brown, brittle, wait-a-bit weeds
block the entrance. I untangle their
whole summer embrace. Inside—soot from
a cold fire, powder of bones,
a piece of ceremonial horn: cool
history comes off on my hands.
Outside, I stand in a canyon so
quiet its pool almost remembers its
old reflections. And then I breathe.

There are several links in this poem between the old ways and the poet. The title itself points not only to a factual discovery made by a person recognized for his thorough knowledge of Native American material, but also, because of the direction of the poem, suggests a sense of quest, a way of finding the past and bringing it back into the present. The speaker of the poem also "finds" this "cave" which takes on symbolical dimensions as a depository for the Indian way of life. Entering the cave also suggests entering this whole tradition. Importantly, it is not only a tradition visited by the speaker, looked at as in a glass counter in a museum, but actually and physically transmitted to him: "cool / history comes off on my hands." The fact that the transmission takes place through his hands is an evocative image of taking something up literally, of carrying it on, of holding a certain set of values.

The last three lines of the poem establishes the balance between the need for interior centering in old way of life, a visit to the cave, and living in the "outside" world. The way of living in that outside world, which, by the way, also is a canyon, is a way which reduces the significance of the human presence. The speaker is there, but unobtrusive, deemphasizing himself. Instead he lets the landscape of the canyon manifest itself, and because he has adopted the old ways he "almost" enables the pool to remember "its / old reflections." "Almost" is a crucial modification. The speaker knows that even though he has visited the cave, the rest of the world out there in eastern Oregon has not. The old way cannot be brought back that simply. He breathes; he belongs to the present world but is in touch with the old one. The reader has followed the speaker through his process of centering, and a new transmission of "cool history" takes place through the poem.

At a first glance, this poem might not seem to be an explicit facet of the ecological metaphor, but taken as a part of the matrix established in the canon of Stafford's poems dealing with Native American material, it gathers additional meaning. The central point of view advocated by the speaker is one of humility, of unobtrusive human presence in the natural environment. The lack of any references to the existence of modern civilization is also significant; it is only implied because we know it represents a diametrically opposite view from that represented by the Indians.

The poem **"The Early Ones"** from the collection *Things That Happen Where There Aren't Any People* (1980, p. 14), also suggests the primitive way of life as an ideal which can be rediscovered:

"The Early Ones"

They kept it all level. And low. Even
little stones they swept away. They went on
for miles, a bend at a hill, then a bend
back. Around them birch forest mostly
or openings for lakes, and a few hidden lakes.

They carved on the rocks—these are what stay,
hardly worn at all if sheltered, some
broken and all of them gray, that distant

gray that clouds have, or storms that moan
at the coast. They carved and went away.

Level and low. And the carved things. And one
more thing: when you look around and listen,
the last thing is there. You hear it wait.
Because they were early and quiet, and because
of that last bend, and because of the gray—

There is something left. We'll find it some day.

This poem also points toward the importance of reconnecting with "the early ones," because they stand for an ideal way of existing harmoniously within the environment "around them." The opening line, "They kept it all level. And low," suggests a life in balance with a minimum impact. The sense of an inherent system of environmental ethics is conveyed through the way the early ones keep things neat, keep their home "swept." Furthermore, there is an interesting link between creativity and environmental ethics implied here: "They carved on the rocks" but "went away." With their disappearance their attitudes seem to have disappeared as well, which might suggest that the discovery lies in the reversal of the process; that is, that it is through the creative act, the writing of poetry in Stafford's case, that this missing element is rediscovered.

The third stanza affirms that a mysterious "last thing" is also left. We are told that if we adopt the attitude of the early ones, "look around and listen," (the early ones were "quiet," that is, listening,) we can "hear it wait." This "last thing" is not specified, it cannot be, because it represents an undeveloped potential. The poem only affirms that we can know that it is there, not exactly what it is. In other words, what the early ones had still exists, but since we have not found it we cannot define it. The poem ends on an optimistic note with the belief that this will be found: "There is something left. We'll find it some day." Because of the emphasis in the poem on a basic humility, this "last thing" seems to point to a kind of reverence and respect towards one's environment.

The poem **"Wovoka's Witness"** (*SCBT*, pp. 5-6), is an interesting example of the way Stafford transforms existing historical material of the Native Americans to articulate an environmental ethic. Wovoka was a Paiute, who lived in Mason Valley in Nevada. His visions in the late 1880s and early 1890s transformed him into a messiah, and his teachings became the direct source of the widespread ghost-dance movement among most of the western tribes. Wovoka's important contribution to all the western tribes that adopted his prophecy was, according to James Mooney, a revolution of their moral code.[67] Briefly summarized, the moral aspects of Wovoka's vision were: "Do no harm to any one"; "Do right always"; "Do not tell lies"; "When your friends die, you must not cry"; and finally, "You must not fight."

Especially the last commandment, Mooney argues, radically transformed the warrior-oriented Plains tribes. It was, in other words, a radically new, basically pacifist movement. If these tenets were obeyed, Wovoka said, and the ghost-dance ritual he taught was obeyed, soon the white people and their world would be wiped out through some magical action by the Great Spirit, the wild game would reappear, and all the Native Americans would be reunited with their ancestors in a state of perpetual bliss.

At a first glance, little of this appears in the poem. The title also hints that it is not Wovoka himself who is speaking, but his witness, suggesting someone who has understood his teaching. (Since Wovoka was reverentially referred to as "Our Father" by most of the ghost-dancers, the title certainly echoes the familiar Christian "Jehovah's Witness.") Instead, what Stafford's poem initially focuses on is the general importance of alertness, of being alive in the most keen sense of the word. A kind of religious awakening is implied here. Then, in the last two stanzas, the poem takes a new turn. The opening of the third stanza tells us: "My people, now it is time / for us all to shake hands with the rain." What this suggests is a new interpretation of Wovoka's "You must not fight," adding a dimension applying to environmental ethics: make peace with rain as the emblem of natural process and the element of all life. That this kind of peace must be understood in ecological terms is made explicit in the opening of the last stanza: "My own people, now listen—if we fail / all the trees in the forest will cease / to exist, or only their ghosts will stand / there fooling everyone." Pollution, acid rain, whatever destroys the trees, will be the result of an attitude which has not made peace with nature.

Another Wovoka poem, **"Wovoka in Nevada"** (*GF*, p. 131), opens by including a more explicit fragment from the prophet's vision, "buffalo all over / the plains again," to evoke the dream of a reestablished pristine North American continent, by contrasting it to a series of negative images from contemporary America: "bottle caps kicked in the ditch," or "fast cars" whose "blind windshields dismiss you," or the ironic "worship in a casino." Still, in spite of the focus of so much of contemporary American life, the poem ends with a reminder of the presence of Wovoka by having "Wheels on the tracks going 'Wovoka, Wovoka, Wovoka.'" So again, as in the poem **"Stadium High, Tacoma,"** there seems to be an implicit juxtaposition between Western and Native American culture, where the latter is affirmed.

These Stafford poems all seem to advocate a stance which affirms a Native American way of life expressing an inherent gentleness toward the earth—the place where one lives. This attitude, the various speakers of these poems argue, has been lost by our society. Quite clearly the speakers feel positive towards reestablishing these values, and seem hopeful, if not convinced, that we today will find them again. In this context the ecological metaphor works by pointing out what has been an inherently good environmental ethic, and not by pointing out what modern society or technology has done or can do wrong. What the speaker conceives of as wrong is in these poems only implied as an absent opposite.

Notes

1. The following abbreviations of Stafford's books are used throughout the text and notes:

WYC. West of Your City (Los Gatos, Calif.: Talisman Press, 1960).

TTD. Traveling Through the Dark (New York: Harper and Row, 1962).

TRY. The Rescued Year (New York: Harper and Row, 1966).

A. Allegiances (New York: Harper and Row, 1970).

SM. Someday, Maybe (New York: Harper and Row, 1973).

SCBT. Stories That Could Be True (New York: Harper and Row, 1977).

WAC. Writing the Australian Crawl (Ann Arbor: The University of Michigan Press, 1978).

GF. A Glass Face in the Rain (New York: Harper and Row, 1982).

YMR. You Must Revise Your Life (Ann Arbor: The University of Michigan Press, 1986).

AOM. An Oregon Message (New York: Harper and Row, 1987).

References to poems from the first five volumes will, for the sake of simplicity, be followed by the page location in Stories That Could Be True since that collection contains all the poems of the earlier books. Small editions will be identified in the text by title and year of publication only (for full bibliographical information, please consult the William Stafford bibliography), and since the poems contained there are so difficult to find, these poems will be fully included in the text. Finally, due to the large number of limited editions, the titles of these books will be given in full in order to avoid a confusion of abbreviations.

2. One perceives the legacy of Robinson Jeffers' philosophy of inhumanism in Stafford's poems expressing this sense of pessimism, even though Stafford balances his pessimism with a refusal to be ruled by it. As two examples of Stafford's awareness and appreciation of Jeffers' work, see Stafford's prose piece entitled "Robinson Jeffers' Groceryman," Northwest Review 13, No. 3 (1973), 64-68, and the poem "Jeffers," North By West (Seattle: Spring Rain Press, 1975), pp. 38-39. Since Jeffers' sense of ecology already has been discussed at some length by earlier critics, I will simply refer the reader to them. See for example, James D. Cleghorn, "Chapter II: Predecessors," in "Preservation of the Wilderness: A Contemporary View of Nature Poetry" (unpublished Ph.D. dissertation, University of Massachusetts, 1974), pp. 46-51, and Nabil Mahmoud El-Sharif, "Chapter Two: Views of Nature in Twentieth-Century American Poetry," in "Ecological Themes in the Poetry of A. R. Ammons, Allen Ginsberg, and Gary Snyder" (unpublished Ph.D. dissertation, Indiana University, 1983), pp. 39-49.

3. When asked whether he was pessimistic about man's fate, Stafford replied:

Yes, yes I am, intellectually. There were a couple of people here yesterday . . . from up at Tacoma . . . who are doing a kind of oral history . . . they had also interviewed a historian who is an unusual, unusually good professor up there. And they said: "He is very pessimistic, but he seems happy!" (Laughs) Yeah, I understand it. Animal spirits is one thing, but cool assessment is another. But there is another way to look at it, and that is—and I tried this on those two who came too—we don't know enough to be pessimistic.

Lars Nordström, "Willingly Local: A Conversation with William Stafford about Regionalism and Northwest Poetry," Studia Neophilologica, 59 (1987), 51. Hereafter referred to as "Willingly Local."

4. Wendell Berry, The Unsettling of America (New York: Avon Books, 1978), p. 130.

5. A qualification of the term "home" is perhaps in order here; it is not to be confused with another, equally important sense of home which Stafford has explored at great length, namely his childhood home in the Midwest. This is a theme which has remained important to him, and which has drawn the attention of several critics. For discussions on the various aspects of Stafford's Midwest home, see for example: Jonathan Holden, Ch. 4 "My Self Will Be the Plain," The Mark to Turn (Lawrence: The University Press of Kansas, 1976), pp. 51-66 (hereafter referred to as The Mark to Turn); Richard Hugo, "Problems with Landscapes in Early Stafford Poems," Kansas Quarterly, 2 (Spring 1970), 33-38; or Nathan D. Sumner, "The Poetry of William Stafford: Nature, Time, and Father," Research Studies at Washington State University, 36 (September 1968), 187-195.

6. "Discussions During the Spring Poetry Festival, Martin, Tennessee, April 16-17, 1971," Tennessee Poetry Journal, 4 (Spring 1971), 17-18.

7. William Stafford, "At Home on Earth," The Hudson Review, 23 (Autumn 1970), 481-98.

8. "At Home on Earth," 481.

9. "At Home on Earth," 485.

10. "Willingly Local," 50.

11. Ch. 3, "The Earth Says—," *The Mark to Turn*, p. 34.

12. *The Mark to Turn*, p. 39.

13. John Lauber, "World's Guest—William Stafford," *Iowa Review*, 5 (Spring 1974), 88.

14. "Willingly Local," 56-57.

15. First collected in *Poems*, Portland, OR: Portland Art Museum, 1959, later included in *WYC* (1960) and *SCBT* (1977), p. 37.

16. *Roving Across Fields: A Conversation and Uncollected Poems 1942-82* (Daleville, Indiana: The Barnwood Press Cooperative, 1983), p. 35.

17. Also from *Poems*, and later collected in *WYC* (1960), and *SCBT*, p. 36.

18. Theodora Kroeber, *Ishi: Last of His Tribe* (Berkeley: Parnassus Press, 1964).

19. Carol Kyle, "Point of View in 'Returned to Say' and the Wilderness of William Stafford," *Western American Literature*, 7 (Fall 1972), 191-201. Hereafter referred to as Kyle.

20. Kyle, 194. Her reading of this poem might also be influenced by the fact that she does not look at any other poem dealing with Native American material at any length.

21. Jarold Ramsey, ed., "Introduction" to *Coyote Was Going There* (Seattle: University of Washington Press, 1977), p. xxi. Hereafter referred to as *Coyote Was Going There*.

22. *Coyote Was Going There*, pp. xx-xxi.

23. "Willingly Local," 56. That the main concern of the Indian metaphor is ecological, is acknowledged by Stafford elsewhere too. A brief comment in Kip Stratton's "An Interview with William Stafford" in *The Greenfield Review*, 7 (Spring/Summer 1979), 91, confirms this. In a response to a question on his early interest in Native American culture Stafford replies that it was "a feeling of interest and sympathy for the country and for natural things—birds, animals—and we always, partly because of the kind of literature we read, relate that to Indians in our country. . . . It sort of stands for when the continent was cleaner and purer and better, more interesting."

24. There are exceptions, of course, of poems which do not fit this kind of categorization. For example, we catch a glimpse of the bleak reality of contemporary Native American life contrasted to the pleasant comfort of some train travelers in a poem like "Vacation." (*WYC, SCBT,* p. 39) There is certainly empathy here, and social indignation, but no ecological dimension. It is, however, interesting to note that it is the train, the traditional machine symbol representing an advancing technology intruding in the American garden, which is involved here carrying the vacationers. Another exception would be the poem "Slave on the Headland," (*SCBT*, pp. 15—16) which uses the persona of the captured slave to tell a story evoking the less positive aspects of a reality of the Native American past in the Pacific Northwest.

25. See Ella E. Clark, "Why And When the Tales Were Told," in *Indian Legends of the Pacific Northwest* (Berkeley: University of California Press, 1953), pp. 129-132. (Hereafter referred to as *Indian Legends of the Pacific Northwest*.) Jarold Ramsey points to the same general functions of the Native American storytelling in *Coyote Was Going There*, p. xxix.

26. "Willingly Local," p. 41.

27. William Stafford, "The Practice of Composing in Language," *Agenda*, 11 (Spring-Summer 1973), 63.

28. Ralph Hammond, "Little Gadgets to be Realized: An Interview with William Stafford," *Negative Capability*, 5 (Fall 1985), 40-41. And one of the "things usually identified with the West," especially in the context of "commitments," is certainly ecological concerns. See for example Thomas J. Lyon, "Western Poetry," *Journal of the West*, 19 (January 1980), 45-53.

29. J. Russell Roberts, Sr., "Listening to the Wilderness With William Stafford," *Western American Literature*, 3 (Fall 1968), 224.

30. From Sanford Pinsker's interview, *WAC*, p. 120.

31. For an eloquent statement on his position, see Stafford's "The Realities of Regionalism," *South Dakota Review*, 18 (Winter 1981), 54-63.

32. Raymond Benoit, in "The New American Poetry," *Thought*, 44 (Summer 1969), 207.

33. Richard Hugo, "Problems with Landscapes in Early Stafford Poems," *Kansas Quarterly*, 2 (Spring 1970), 33.

34. This attitude towards Modernism is also concisely summed up in the poem "Things I Learned Last Week" (*GF*, p. 66), "Yeats, Pound, and Eliot saw art as / growing from other art. They studied that." That is, Stafford's aesthetics does not put an emphasis on a direct dialogue with literary tradition or erudite learning so common within Modernism. In spite of having spent most of his adult life teaching college students how to read and write literature, his poems are not primarily "literary" in this sense.

35. William Stafford and Kim Robert Stafford, *Braided Apart* (Lewiston, Idaho: Confluence Press, 1976), p. 27.

36. Stafford certainly has his share of poems dealing more or less explicitly with writers or ideas from the domain of literature too, since that has been part of his encounters with the world. See for example "Meeting Roethke," in *Sometimes Like A Legend* (Port Townsend, WA.: Copper Canyon Press, 1981), p. 22; "Roethke," in *The Southern Review,* 3 (October 1967), 946-947; "Jeffers," in *North By West,* pp. 38-39; a number of poems in *SCBT*: "Willa Cather" (p. 40), "'The Lyf So Short . . .'" (p. 89), "Jack London" (pp. 135-36), "Sophocles Says" (p. 144), "Holcomb, Kansas" (pp. 153-54), "On Don Quixote's Horse" (pp. 179-80), "New Letters from Thomas Jefferson" (pp. 202-203), "A Song in the Manner of Flannery O'Connor" (pp. 244-245), "Ozymandia's Brother" (pp. 245-246); and from *GF,* "An Old Pickerel in Walden Pond" (p. 34) and "If I Could Be Like Wallace Stevens" (p. 102), and so on.

37. Stafford takes this stand from the very beginning of his writing career: "Literature holds a high place as a generator of values and insights. Human engagement with the materials of consciousness, the enhancement of simple experience by imaginative adjustment, looms as the central distinction of intellectual life; and literature is a great realm for that kind of activity. Subjected to modern analysis, our values, religions, laws, and truths of all kinds cannot any longer merely be ascribed to earlier sources." *Friends to this Ground: A Statement for Readers, Teachers, and Writers of Literature* (Champaign, Illinois: National Council of Teachers of English, 1967), p. 2.

38. *The Mark To Turn,* p. 6.

39. Not counting Stafford's creative Ph.D. dissertation at the University of Iowa, there is also the work collected in twenty-seven small editions, twenty-four of which have been published since 1970. (For a complete list of titles, publishers, and dates, see the bibliography.) A few of these editions contain only one poem or a handful of poems, and some of them have been included in the major collections, but there is still a great deal of relatively unknown poetry collected here.

40. The first published Stafford poems I have been able to locate ("Easy," and "Face") are from *The Illiterati,* No. 3 (Summer 1944), published in the Conscientious Objector's camp in Waldport, Oregon during World War II. Considering the fact that Stafford's first book was not published until 1960 (when the poet was 46 years old), after 16 years of magazine publications and a collection of poems for his creative Ph.D. dissertation at the University of Iowa in 1954 called *Winterward,* and that several books rapidly followed, a substantial part of the poetry published in the 1960s was probably written earlier than that.

41. For an excellent discussion of the importance of listening inward and its relationship to Stafford's Quaker childhood, see Chapter II, "Talk to Prayer to Truth," in "Herald and Oracle: The Poetics of William Stafford," unpublished Ph.D. dissertation by Norman Dennis Leavens, University of Notre Dame, Indiana, 1983.

42. *The Mark To Turn,* p. 17. For an extended discussion of Holden's interpretation, see pp. 16-23.

43. Stafford's views on nuclear power are quite clearly established at the very end of the poem "Incident" (*GF,* p. 67): "Let's get out of here," which, of course, fits the pattern of an environmental ethic established through the ecological metaphor.

44. The same pessimism associated with the symbolic "The North" and ecological disaster, is present in a most unusual Stafford poem, "A Piece of Newspaper," *Northwest Review,* 13, No. 3 (1973), 71, where "Tomorrow's News" is summed up as "Nobody."

45. William Stafford, *Down In My Heart* (Swarthmore, Pennsylvania: The Bench Press, 1985), p. 72.

46. According to Edmond S. Meany in *Origin of Washington Geographic Names* (Seattle: University of Washington Press, 1923), pp. 299-301, Winthrop had probably transcribed a word from the Chinook Jargon, "t'kope," of Algonkin origin, as "tacoma." This word was defined as "white (snowcapped) mountain." The Algonkin meaning of the word seems to have been manifold: "near to heaven," "nourishing breast," "mother of waters," or "frozen waters." George R. Stewart, in *American Place Names* (New York: Oxford University Press, 1970), p. 470, writes that "tacoma" "has been translated as 'the mountain,' and 'the gods,' and by various other terms. Since some Indians associated mountains and spirits, a combination of the two ideas may be considered possible."

47. *The Unsettling of America,* pp. 97-98.

48. There is quite a collection of poems that deal with caves in various ways, and with different emphases, which indicates the importance of its symbolic value. Apart from the ones that I discuss, see for example the following poems: "Solstice" (*Going Places,* 1974, p. 9), "Fort Rock" (*Going Places,* p. 20), "They Carved an Animal" (*Stories and*

Storms and Strangers, 1984, p. 13), "Kinship" (*Sometimes Like A Legend*, 1981, p. 43), "Cave Painting" (*All About Light*, 1978, unpaginated), "Things in the Wild Need Salt" (*SCBT*, pp. 6-7), "From Eastern Oregon" (*TRY, SCBT*, pp. 139-140), "Behind the Falls" (*A, SCBT*, p. 166), "Existences" (*SM, SCBT*, p. 220), "Our Cave" (*GF*, p. 24), and "Much Have I Traveled" (*GF*, p. 110).

49. See for example Mary Anne Warren, "The Rights of the Nonhuman World," in *Environmental Philosophy: A Collection of Readings,* ed. by Robert Elliot and Arran Gare (University Park: The Pennsylvania State University Press, 1983), pp. 109-134.

50. See Ramsey, *Coyote Was Going There*, pp. xxx-xxxi. But see also Gary Snyder, "The Incredible Survival of Coyote," *The Old Ways* (San Francisco: City Lights Books, 1977), pp. 67-93.

51. Gary Snyder, *Turtle Island* (New York: New Directions, 1974), pp. 21-23. Hereafter referred to as *TI*.

52. See for example "A Way of Writing," (*WAC*, pp. 17-20).

53. From Clinton F. Larson's "The Poet as Religious Moralist: An Interview with William Stafford," *Literature and Belief*, 2 (1982), 8. Reprinted in *YMR*.

54. See for example "Creation of the Animal People," *Indian Legends of the Pacific Northwest*, pp. 83-84.

55. There might also be something of William Everson's "Archetype West" evoked here, "the sun-down associated with death."

56. The image also echoes the title of a book by Gary Snyder, *The Back Country* (New York: New Directions, 1968), which works with a similar division of city and wilderness and the metaphorical significance of these two. According to the back cover Snyder intends the title to have at least three levels of association: "wilderness, the 'backward' countries, and the 'back country' of the mind with its levels of being in the unconscious."

57. See for example the following poems with plant and animal personae: "Blackbirds" (*SCBT*, p. 7), "Weeds" (*SM, SCBT*, pp. 217-18), "Existences" (*SM, SCBT*, p. 220), or "A Day Last Summer" (*AOM*, p. 85). Additionally, there are poems which are not strict animal or plant persona poems, but which uses animals or plants in third person to express a similar stance. See for example "B.C." (*TTD, SCBT*, p. 76), "From the Gradual Grass" (*TTD, SCBT*, p. 98), or "In Fur" (*A, SCBT*, p. 185).

58. Leonard Lee Rue III, *The World of the Beaver* (Philadelphia: J. B. Lippincott Co., 1964), p. 68.

59. When I asked Stafford about a reference in an earlier interview, Kip Stratton's "An Interview with William Stafford," *Greenfield Review,* 7 (Spring/Summer 1979), 91, which suggested that he considered part of his heritage American Indian, he replied:

> Well, Dorothy laughs about this. My father had this story, he said: "Uncle Charlie, he said that he were part Indian and were from the Crowfoot group in upstate New York," and so on. Actually I have heard that anyone who has been in America very long, I mean some generations, have got Indian blood because the Indians were here. But I couldn't get any allotment on the reservation or anything like that. But every now and then Ed Edmo sort of treats me as an Indian. And other Indians do partly because I show up in those anthologies of Indian writers. I like that.

"Willingly Local," 56

60. Even though this study focuses on the way in which Native American material articulates the ecological metaphor, there are other important values expressed through this material as well. The most consistently important theme besides the ecological metaphor, would be the empathy the speaker of the poems demonstrates toward the fate of the Native Americans. Feelings of respect and sadness are, for example, evoked in poems like "The Last Day" (*A, SCBT*, p. 156), or "A Sound from the Earth" (*A, SCBT*, p. 172).

61. David Wagoner, *Who Shall Be the Sun?* (Bloomington: Indiana University Press, 1978). The reliance of these poems on previous anthropological, linguistic, and literary documentation is acknowledged in the long subtitle of the book: *Poems Based on the Lore, Legends, and Myths of Northwest Coast and Plateau Indians.* For an excellent discussion of Wagoner's process of transformation of Native American material into contemporary "story-poems," see Jarold Ramsey's "Essay Review" of Wagoner's book, *Western American Literature* 15 (May 1980), 37-40.

62. A poem like this one is certainly open to many different readings. Stafford himself, at a poetry reading in Hillsboro, Oregon in 1985, told the audience an anecdote about how this poem was interpreted in Iran, while he was there on a reading tour during the regime of the Shah. He was warned that such a dangerously political poem, evoking the Iranian secret police (notorious for its elimination of oppositional voices) as an animal drinking up sound, could get him into trouble, and that he should be very careful with such poems.

63. "The Battle of the Winds," *Coyote Was Going There*, p. 71. A similar, more elaborated version of

the same basic story with almost identical traits is Ella E. Clark's retelling of "The Chinook Wind," *Indian Legends of the Pacific Northwest,* pp. 169-171.

64. Other poems that have a distinct Native American flavor would be, for example, several under the heading "Wind World": "Origins" (*SM, SCBT,* p. 221), "People of the South Wind" (*SM, SCBT,* p. 222), "Report to Crazy Horse" (*SM, SCBT,* pp. 225-27), or "Stories to Live in the World with" (*SM, SCBT,* pp. 228-29). A list of this kind could easily be made a great deal longer.

65. Some additional understanding in our reading of this poem can also be gained from a few brief glimpses from a text on the nature of Native American dancing in the Pacific Northwest. Reginald and Gladys Laubin states that: "Generally it can be said for the entire area that obtaining *spirit power* was a primary drive among these people"; and that: "The greatest power one could receive was said to be Eagle, recognized here and elsewhere as greatest of all the dwellers in the heavens, most powerful in the spirit realm." [Reginald and Gladys Laubin, *Indian Dances of North America* (Norman, Oklahoma: University of Oklahoma Press, 1977), pp. 397-398.] And the expression of these central concerns were, as the poem describes, often the subject of these usually individualistic dances; they were non-verbal communications of that found vision (Laubin, pp. 398-399).

66. It is interesting to note that Gary Snyder uses the same image in the "Hunting" section of *Myths & Texts*: "Brush back smoke from the eyes, / dust from the mind, / With the wing-feather fan of an eagle," to suggest the process of gaining insight through the Native American dance. Gary Snyder, "Hunting," *Myths & Texts* (New York: New Directions, 1978), p. 21.

67. For a discussion of Mooney's analysis of the ghost-dance doctrine, see Ch. 2, "The Doctrine of the Ghost Dance," *The Ghost-Dance Religion and the Sioux Outbreak of 1890,* edited by Anthony F. C. Wallace (Chicago: The University of Chicago Press, 1965), pp. 19-45, but especially pp. 24-25.

Judith Kitchen (essay date 1989)

SOURCE: Kitchen, Judith. "Understanding William Stafford." In *Understanding William Stafford,* pp. 3-38. Columbia, S.C.: University of South Carolina Press, 1989.

[*In the following excerpt, Kitchen examines Stafford's unusual use of perspective and the sense of moral responsibility that pervades his work.*]

CAREER

William Stafford spans poetic generations. Born in 1914, chronologically belonging to the generation of Robert Lowell, Randall Jarrell, and John Berryman, older than Sylvia Plath, Stafford seems to be the odd man out. Unlike the others, who can be termed "confessional" poets, Stafford chose to write a "personal" poetry; this includes a unique perspective coupled with a sense of moral and spiritual responsibility. He has been what he himself terms a "witness for poetry."

William Edgar Stafford, first son of Earl Ingersoll and Ruby Mayher Stafford, was born in Hutchinson, Kansas. Raised in a stubbornly nonconformist household, Stafford learned early the value of hard moral decisions and the security of firmly held convictions. Though neither parent formally belonged to a church, church was a central part of the social life of small Kansas towns, and the family often attended services. His parents instilled in him a sense of justice, individuality, and tolerance. The oldest of three children, Stafford was close to each of his parents in different ways, looking to his father for gentle but firm guidance in ethical matters, to his mother for the more personal responses to everything from gossip to literature.

During the 1930s, while Stafford was an adolescent, his father moved the family from town to town within Kansas, following whatever jobs were available during the depth of the Depression. Within a small span of time the Stafford family moved from Hutchinson to Wichita to Hutchinson to Liberal to Garden City to El Dorado. William carried his share of the load in each of these places, delivering papers (at one point the family's only source of income), raising vegetables, working in the sugar beet fields and as an electrician's mate. During this time, he graduated from high school, went to Garden City and El Dorado Junior Colleges, and then enrolled at the University of Kansas, where he worked his way through school waiting on tables. While at the university Stafford began to take his writing seriously (mostly stories from the experiences he'd had moving from place to place). He also took seriously his social and political responsibilities, demonstrating against the policy of segregation in the Student Union cafe.

With the advent of World War II Stafford's convictions were tested. He registered as a pacifist (the commander of the American Legion of El Dorado spoke to the draft board in his behalf) and spent the duration of the war in camps for conscientious objectors in Arkansas, California, and Illinois, working on soil conservation projects, forestry, and fighting fires. His choice was a courageous one. World War II was a popular war; to be a conscientious objector was to remove oneself from the mainstream of society. Stafford writes, "My four years of 'alternative service under civilian direction' turned my life sharply into that independent channel of the second river—a course hereafter distinguished from any unexamined life, from the way it might have been in any of my hometowns."[1] It was during these years (1942-46) that Stafford developed the habit of spending the early part of the morning writing. Because his work was physically exhausting, it was impossible to write when he was through for the day. But he found he could always find an hour before work began. He carried this habit into marriage, fatherhood (he has four children), and a life of teaching.

The years spent in the Civilian Public Service were formative years; what had previously been belief hardened into practice. His emphasis on listening, his patience, his long-range goal of internal change—all stem from this period of his life. In addition, he developed a tool for survival—flexibility. Stafford learned to look hard at both sides of any question. In the end he emerged with a social vision that served him in his many other endeavors.

While still in CO camps in southern California Stafford met Dorothy Frantz, the daughter of a minister of the Church of the Brethren. They married, and Dorothy lived nearby, teaching in the public schools. When he was discharged from the camp in 1946 they could at last establish a home. Stafford finished a master's degree at the University of Kansas, with the basic text of *Down in My Heart,* memoirs of the CO camps, forming his thesis; tried high school teaching in southern California; then moved to the San Francisco area to work for Church World Service, a relief agency. During this time *Down in My Heart* was published (1947), and Stafford continued to write each morning, publishing several poems in small magazines and such distinguished literary journals as *Poetry.* In 1948 he was offered a teaching position at Lewis and Clark College in Portland, Oregon. He remained there until retirement, using Oregon as the base from which he could make occasional forays into the country at large.

One brief period away turned out to be of importance to his career as a writer. In 1950-52 Stafford worked on a writing degree at the University of Iowa, receiving his PhD in 1954. He was able to hear, or study under, various writers such as Robert Penn Warren, Randall Jarrell, Reed Whittemore, and Karl Shapiro. He refers to these years as the "principal reference point I have for the literary life as lived by others."[2] Even then he was putting some distance between his experience and that of his colleagues. For one thing, his experience of the war was wholly different from theirs; he was older, married, and had at that time two small children. His writing habits were established. But the courses and workshops at Iowa did have some effect; they served almost as a foil for the development of his own idiosyncratic attitudes toward the teaching of writing.

In 1960, eight years after he left Iowa, Robert Greenwood and Newton Baird asked to print some of Stafford's work at their newly formed Talisman Press, a small press in southern California—not, as he had hoped for, a major publishing company. *West of Your City,* Stafford's first book of poems, was published that year in a beautiful edition of a few hundred copies. At that time Stafford was forty-six years old.

Traveling Through the Dark, Stafford's second book, was published by Harper and Row in 1962, and to some it must have seemed like a first book from a promising writer. It won the National Book Award for Poetry in 1963 and became fairly quickly a touchstone for a new generation of readers and poets who were looking for something different from the dominant mode of the "confessionals." Seven books from Harper and Row followed: *The Rescued Year* in 1966, *Allegiances* in 1970, *Someday, Maybe* in 1973, *Stories That Could Be True: New and Collected Poems* in 1977, *A Glass Face in the Rain* in 1982, and *An Oregon Message* in 1987. Seven books in twenty-five years would seem a prodigious amount from any poet, but this list represents only the titles from one publisher. Over twenty other books or chapbooks of poetry, published by small presses; several books of prose, including essays on writing or writers, translations, talks; a poetic "dialogue" with Marvin Bell; and a reprint of *Down in My Heart* were also published in the quarter century following *Traveling Through the Dark.* In 1964 Stafford was awarded the Shelley Memorial Award from the Poetry Society of America and in 1966 he received a Guggenheim fellowship. His prominence was confirmed in 1970 when he was named Consultant in Poetry to the Library of Congress. He traveled widely with the United States Information Service, reading in such countries as India, Pakistan, Iran, Egypt, and Thailand.

In the late 1960s and early 1970s, when unrest over the Vietnam war was at its height, students on campuses all over the country discovered the work of William Stafford. It seemed—in its pacifist leanings, its careful wisdom—to speak to and *for* them. Stafford was invited to read on campus after campus. This he did—Kent State, Berkeley, Madison, Hawaii, Alaska—but the visits were not always what either he or the students had expected. He was truly a nonviolent man, and the antiwar demonstrators were at times disposed to a violent method of making their views known. Stafford was uncomfortable with the role of spokesman, but he was still willing to be a witness. He says, of this time, "Both sides spread out leaving pacifists where they usually were, alone."[3] His easy-going, conversational reading style became one more statement about the place of poetry in a difficult and despairing world.

In 1980 Stafford retired from teaching, but not from the world of poetry. He published two major new collections, *A Glass Face in the Rain* and *An Oregon Mes-*

sage, and was given the Award in Literature by the American Academy and Institute of Arts and Letters. Even though Stafford has not had the critical attention he deserves, **"Traveling through the Dark"** has become one of the most widely anthologized contemporary poems. His influence, not only on the teaching of writing, but on what to expect from poetry itself, has quietly grown. It is only now that other poets are beginning to realize just how much effect William Stafford and his poetry had on their way of looking at the world.

OVERVIEW

William Stafford's complete work constitutes a testament for living. At first reading it might appear to recall an almost idyllic childhood, to reflect a lifetime of longing for the past—a harking back to a time that was simpler, when man could make peace with nature, when Indians lived in harmony with the world. But his poems are aimed, deliberately, at modern man with the bomb hanging over his head. How to live in a world like ours? Stafford consistently notes the ways in which technology threatens to sever us from our humanity. His answer is not the stereotypical "nature as salvation"; his poems exhibit complex and complicated relationships— between people, between people and the land, between the public and the private person. In **"Representing Far Places"** he concludes, "It is all right to be simply the way you have to be, / among contradictory ridges in some crescendo of knowing."[4] This "permission" that he gives himself feels hard won, as though wrested from deep doubt.

What underlies all Stafford's poetry is a fixed vision. Stafford himself would balk at the use of a word like *fixed,* careful as he is to test all sides of a question, to entertain all possible meanings. But *fixed* may be broad enough to encompass the idea of flexibility and to make room for change. In that context, it is firmly held convictions, as well as a clarity of vision, that give Stafford the strength to roam freely in his imagination and to test every aspect of his vision.

This vision seems to have solidified during the four years spent in CO camps during World War II. William Stafford spent formative years of his youth tucked away in the backwoods of the country, digging ditches, building bridges, learning to find his way in uneasy situations, learning to speak softly but firmly for what he believed to be the truth. He emerged with a mature sensibility that characterizes both his writing and his teaching; he is patient, receptive, ready to learn. In the 1985 foreword to *Down in My Heart,* which he entitled "A Side Glance at History," Stafford looks back at that time: "Back then—and now—one group stays apart from the usual ways of facing war. They exist now— and they did then—in all countries. Those who refuse the steps along that way are a small group, and their

small role is a footnote in the big histories."[5] But Stafford considers, in hindsight, that theirs was a significant role. He continued to play the role in the writing of his poetry—not that he wrote polemical or cautionary poetry, but that he allowed himself to "stay apart" and make small noises for the good of mankind, the good *in* mankind. Stafford himself chronicles the connection between that period of his life and his writing: "We were surrounded by challenges that had to do with that tension between open, ordinary daily life and the interior life that distinguishes individuals from each other. The two parts of my life that blended or clashed in making my writing were in constant alertness. I felt my morning writings as maintenance work or repair work on my integrity.[6]

If Stafford's vision is considered as having coalesced around his conscientious objector's experience, then it is possible to look at the subsequent poetry to see just what the angle of that vision is. This is subtle work, since Stafford's glance will always be sideways, and his work will slant toward meaning rather than embody it directly. The natural world serves as a source of imagery; but often it is an imagery that is general, even abstract—stone, bird, tree, as opposed to granite, chickadee, elm. The imagery, especially as it recurs, becomes symbolic. The "ideas" do reside in the "things,"[7] but the things are often blurred by their generality or by qualifying adjectives and skewed uses of verbs. To enter Stafford's world it is necessary to step lightly, to follow his footsteps over unmarked snow, to be receptive to the small sounds and the fleeting moments that hold a mystery, and a delight.

It is possible to view William Stafford's work, more than the work of most other poets, as if it had been written all at once. It appears to come from a central, unchanging sensibility. That this sensibility can seem to change so little is most likely due to the fact that it is a sensibility that accepts change, or flux, as part of its natural method. The quest is for a way to encompass separate aspects (the two rivers) of the self into a unified, and unique, vision. It is difficult to tell poems that were first printed in *West of Your City* from poems that appeared over twenty-five years later in *An Oregon Message.* Both the themes and the methods have remained consistent. Scattered throughout all of his books is a mixture of biographical poems, rooted in his personal life, and other, less factual poems where his imagination has led him to a persona or to the stance of the more distanced observer. Because the poems have this "mix and match" property, they have been variously collected by editors according to theme or chronology or central concern. In each case the collection works as a whole. This study will follow Stafford's major publications as they appear chronologically, attempting to piece together an unfolding understanding (on the part of the reader) of his larger vision.

Stafford was not as young as many of his "generation" when he first published his poetry. His first trade edition came out in 1962, but it must be noted that it won him immediate critical attention and acclaim. At this time Lowell's watershed book, *Life Studies,* had been in print for three years. Stafford and Lowell shared the experience of refusing to fight in the Second World War, but they differed dramatically on how they would use that experience in their poetry. Lowell's militantly defiant stance would seem anathema to Stafford's temperament, with its nearly invisible thrust toward a pacifistic way of thinking. In fact, both thematically and stylistically, Stafford seems to share more with a slightly younger generation; he belongs to the poetic generation that includes James Wright, Robert Bly, Richard Hugo, and Donald Hall, among others. Both his themes and his style place him as a transitional poet, between generations.

Stafford could be characterized as a poet of the ordinary. For him small things often have their own historical significance. What is eventful may be something that is hardly noticed; the poet's task is to notice, and to listen. Out of this listening, several dominant themes emerge in the work; these themes could be characterized as threads which, woven together, make up the intricate tapestry of a lifetime's work. There is his concern with family and home which extends to the past (and therefore time in general). Another thread is that of the West, which is, for him, equated with the wilderness and a communion with nature (and, by extension, his eventual death). Still another concern is technology and the accompanying fear that the nation will fail to put it to its proper uses. These themes, however, are all part of a larger vision. Stafford is not afraid to commit himself to moral values; the poems examine the origin of these values and at the same time apply them to the present and the future. In writing he is learning how to live—and how to die.

It is impossible to look at Stafford's poems and how they work without taking into account some of his statements about the writing process itself. Luckily, he has always been free with these opinions, and his essays have been collected in two volumes for the University of Michigan's Poets on Poetry series. In the most recent collection, *You Must Revise Your Life* (1986), Stafford's introductory essay, entitled "Sources and Resources," states, "For me an artist is someone who lets the material talk back." He goes on to say, "I wanted to disappear as teacher, as writer, as citizen—be 'the quiet of the land,' as we used to designate ourselves in CO camps."[8]

The habit of disappearing, of letting the material speak, led Stafford to an "immediate engagement with the language."[9] Rather than beginning with an idea, Stafford advocates beginning anywhere, with anything, and let-

ting the idea develop through a series of moves, what he terms almost a dance. To do this the poet must be receptive—even passive—so that the ideas or possibilities inherent in the images can assert themselves. "My progressions are perhaps provable after the fact, but I don't progress because I think they're going to be provable. I progress by hunches and echoes."[10] If one writes this way, the writing is the discovery, and the surprise at where the poem has gone is shared by writer and reader alike.

In *Writing the Australian Crawl* (1978) Stafford compares the making of a poem to starting a car on ice. Rather than revving the motor, the driver must ease the car into motion; the same is true for poems:

> If you compose a poem you start without any authority. . . . But a poet—whatever you are saying, and however you are saying it, the only authority you have builds from the immediate performance, or it does not build.
>
> If the reader or listener enters the poem, I want the moves to come from inside the poem, the coercion to be part of the life right there.
>
> Someplace he [Auden] said he feared repeating himself as the years went by, and this fear shocked me, for it undercut a view I have long cherished—that a writer is not trying for a product, but accepting sequential signals and adjustments toward an always-arriving present. To slight that readiness—even in order to avoid repetition—would be to violate the process, would be to make writing into a craft that neglected its contact with the ground of its distinction."[11]

The essay are filled with a pithy wisdom. Lines can be lifted at random to demonstrate how solidly Stafford stands behind the principle of receptivity:

> Poetry is the kind of thing you have to see from the corner of your eye.
>
> A poem is a serious joke, a truth that has learned *jujitsu.*
>
> Literature is not a picture of life, but is a separate experience with its own kind of flow and enhancement.
>
> A person writes by means of that meager but persistent little self he has with him all the time.[12]

Stafford's willingness to accept signals and to listen to his "little self" has resulted in poems that feel their way into their material. What happens inside the poem is often quiet, almost imperceptible. But something happens. The transformations in Stafford's poetry seem to take place off the page but enter the meaning of the poem. For this reason George Lensing and Ronald Moran have included him in their study of poets of "the emotive imagination."[13] They rightly assess this accumulation of associative images, and the leap of imagination that fuses them, as being like similar strategies in Robert Bly and James Wright. For Stafford, though, the truth does not lie in the images themselves, but in the linkage of specific images with an *idea* of the world. And it is always a moment in this world that reveals the other world. As Peter Stitt observes in a review of *A Glass Face in the Rain,* "Stafford's gaze is not turned upon any world other than this one."[14]

In an essay entitled "Some Arguments Against Good Diction," Stafford makes clear that he believes language shapes the event, not the other way around. In fact, he recounts his "distrust" of words, especially as conveyors of "truth." He goes on to say:

> The transaction also begins to enhance the experience because of a weird quality in language: the successive distortions of language have their own kind of cumulative potential, and under certain conditions the distortions of language can reverberate into new experiences more various, more powerful, and more revealing than the experiences that set off language in the first place."[15]

This receptivity to distortion results in interesting verbal constructions ("Under my hat I custom you intricate, Ella"[16]; leaves "numbering along through summer"[17]), occasional striking adjectives ("free-spending sycamores"[18]; "hysterical water"[19]), and somewhat nebulous statements that suggest a meaning beyond explication ("And a world begins under the map"[20]). Synesthesia, or mixing of the senses, is one element of this distortion, as though precise description would somehow miss the "feel" of the moment: "a touch / of light survived in amethyst."[21] Personification, too, allows the poems to try out new modes of perception ("four bicycles / in line unreeling their shadows"[22]; "sunlight stretches out its limbs"[23]). He deliberately slants meaning in order to "get it right." Such openness to these possibilities in language admits contradictory ideas as well. In fact, Stafford is best read by looking for the countless opposites that his poems contain. His basic concerns are doubled and redoubled as he explores the dual nature of language and life.

Light and dark, lake and sky, present and past, sound and sight, near and far, rational and intuitive—all are included, often simultaneously, in the world of his poetry. The polarities of mother and father are explored; he sees two sides of himself—the judgmental, fearful side and the receptive, open side. One poem, **"Vocation,"** seems to sum up this underlying tension:

> This dream the world is having about itself
> includes a trace on the plains of the Oregon trail,
> a groove in the grass my father showed us all
> one day while meadowlarks were trying to tell
> something better about to happen.
>
> I dreamed the trace to the mountains, over the hills,
> and there a girl who belonged wherever she was.
> But then my mother called us back to the car:
> she was afraid; she always blamed the place,
> the time, anything my father planned.

> Now both of my parents, the long line through the plain,
> the meadowlarks, the sky, the world's whole dream
> remain, and I hear him say while I stand between the two,
> helpless, both of them part of me:
> "Your job is to find what the world is trying to be."[24]

Not only does the poem include the contrasting attitudes of the parents, it also characterizes Stafford's representation of time. The trace is ancient, from a history that can't be uncovered except as it leaves its "trace," and it persists in the present. The memory is of a past action when the father "showed" and the mother "called." But the poem itself takes place in the present; the third stanza begins with the word *now.* The world's dream "about itself," as it moves through time, is the larger dream that includes the individual dreams of its inhabitants (in this instance, the speaker's dream of a girl); the writer stands between the dream and the world as it manifests itself, trying to find out what to make of what happens, or is about to happen. The speaker begins in the present, looking back, and then ends in a present tense that is buried within that past. The poem mediates between two times—the intensely felt moment of the poem and the past that persists into the present. He is called in both directions, out into the world and back to the safety of family. The vocation of writing is truly a calling—internal, through personal necessity; external, through listening hard to whatever message is out there.

"Both of them part of me." The mother and father figures permeate Stafford's poetry. There is a side that wants to name, to blame, to speak out, both for and *against.* There is another side that honors his father's essence, wanting to feel its way toward meaning, willing to listen and discover and believe. This internal war is reflected in his language. Every word contains the shadow of its opposite, and this is particularly true in the work of William Stafford.

The willingness to be part of the world and, at the same time, the recognition that the world is a cold, indifferent place to be forces Stafford to find a world of his own. This world is understood by recognizing its specific vocabulary. Some words become symbolic or, at the very least, invested with an overtone of extended meaning. The reader develops a shorthand through which he can read the poems, especially as these words recur in changing patterns and combinations. Common objects begin to function in specific ways: home is associated with self, river with change, snow with the page, wires with communication. Certain verbs take on idiosyncratic meanings: seeing is equated with knowing, listening with understanding. The poems move to the edge of meaning, a quiet brinksmanship. *Edge* becomes one of those charged words. The world creates those edges; people test themselves in the face of the abyss. *Swerve,* too, becomes a word with heightened meaning. It almost always is used in a double sense, a movement in the physical world and a mental motion where the true action of the poem takes place.

This doubleness extends to the land, and for Stafford this is very significant. In a manner reminiscent of Whitman he celebrates the land and its people. Speaking for the earth, he says, "have a place, be what that place / requires."[25] He sees two kinds of lives—the surface, everyday life, on earth, and the life that is evidenced "under" the earth, "deep, the way it is."[26] Subterranean caves, underground streams, animals in their burrows— these are the physical embodiments in the poems that represent this deeper place in the earth (and in the self), where meaningful events take place in isolation and silence. The poet must feel his way back to an original source: "Inside: the universe that happens."[27] The quest for even a glimpse of this interior state is at the heart of most of Stafford's poetry.

In what he later refers to as a "dream vision," the young Stafford had an experience that changed his life. While still in high school, he biked twelve miles to camp on the banks of the Cimarron River. He spent one complete day and night watching the sun fall and rise again. "No person was anywhere, nothing, just space, the solid earth. . . . That encounter with the size and serenity of the earth and its neighbors in the sky has never left me. The earth was my home; I would never feel lost while it held me."[28] In Stafford's poetry there is often an attempt to duplicate, at least in feeling, that original dream vision. Often, when this happens, the "earth" becomes the "world," and a distinction is made between the *place* of living and a larger, natural order which governs all life. **"Starting with Little Things"** begins by admonishing "Love the earth like a mole" and ends with the promise "Tomorrow the world."[29] This subtle but important transformation mirrors the knowledge gained in that one evening on the Cimarron.

Beyond sight, in the realm of the invisible, imagination is possible. In Stafford's poetry this usually takes place under cover of darkness. Imagination is so essential that it leads to a nearly religious experience. Something exists beyond human comprehension; imagination puts man in touch with that larger possibility. Perhaps the most difficult concept to understand in the work of William Stafford is this religious moment. Although Stafford has no formal religion, the poems contain many words associated with the Quaker faith. For example, *witness* is used in all its senses. He is witness *to* injustice, to history as it is being made; and he is witness *for* alternatives, for values, a way of thinking as well as a way of living. The idea of balance is paramount. *Friend,* too, is a common word, extending beyond the personal to a brotherhood of man. The silent communion of the meetinghouse is echoed in Stafford's silent communion with nature. He faces himself, looking inward. All this suggests the religious nature of the work, and a method by which the reader can mine the larger implications in a poem that is, on the surface, somewhat transparent.

The use of the word *God* often parallels his use of the word *dream.* The untitled poem included in the essay, "Whose Tradition?," is a good example. "There is a dream going on while I am awake,"[30] he says. This is the "perpetual dream" in which each individual participates; for want of a better word Stafford sometimes (but not always) refers to this idea as "God" or "prayer" or "truth." He often surrounds the word *dream* with a vocabulary associated with religion. Whatever else, this suggests some sense of an eternal, sustaining force which implies as well an ultimate purpose: the dream persists even after death: "When I die the dream is the only / thing left." When an individual life coincides with that larger, ongoing dream, there is a moment of grace, a "blending / of our chance selves with what sustains / all chance." To embody the dream is to become part of the sublime. In this sense Stafford's work could be called religious, but the religion is highly individual and its tenets can be found only in the body of the work. There is, beyond this sense of the religious, a sense of the mystical, seen most often when the poems hover on the verge of knowing. The poems hesitate, surge forward, circle around something that remains undefined. The world reveals itself; the poem turns, then quietly goes on.

Time, for Stafford, is more a concern than a theme. It is both fluid and fixed. Acutely aware of flux, Stafford finds several ways to recapture the present. The lyric moment becomes his focus—the lived present with its felt emotions and its feeling toward meaning, as opposed to the clarity of hindsight. In the early poems this concern with time shows up in the tense of the poem and a characteristic "slippage" between tenses. Time is seen to be cyclical and layered:

> We stand
> inside a curve, inside long lines
> that make a more secret curve."[31]

It is something to live within. But the later poems address Time as though it were a character in its own right, with its own properties: "Time is back in its cage."[32] In 1988 Stafford published eight poems in *The Ohio Review* under the title "Finding Our Way." In one way or another these poems demonstrate this altered sense of time. Time locks us all within the confines of an individual life, and yet it also hints at a "different country"—possibly an alternative life, certainly something we live *without.* Mesh, calendar squares, prison bars, screen, lace—the matrices of time catch and hold us, while its motion is a "sideways drift." And if only the "now" is real, at least it is now that contains a "then":

It's the country where
you already are, bringing where you have been.[33]

Stafford's poems are often about the process of their own creation. To this end they allow themselves to meander. The language is often simple—even deceptively so. Stafford has been described as a sort of mid-western Robert Frost; the similarities are there, but not in the way the description suggests. Each poet worked hard to create an easy, colloquial speech pattern and to be receptive to the cadences of the spoken word. Stafford often starts a poetry reading by talking and then suddenly moving into a poem. It takes the audience approximately one stanza to recognize that the subtle shift has been made. Like Frost, Stafford looks hard at the world, and often the world comes up wanting. The dark side is explored under the guise of what might seem like innocuous images. Each poet has been misunderstood, thought of as a "nature" poet with simple observations about the world, when actually each of them, from a unique vantage point, has handed his public a bleak, sometimes cruel, picture of the world's indifference. In the moments of grace where men and women find a way to live within their own uncertain times, Stafford's poems, like Frost's, rise to a simple eloquence and offer a message of hope.

The message, for Stafford, is more in the forward motion of the poem than in what the poem ultimately "says." The poet is often likened to a walker, someone leaving prints/tracks/trails/marks on the world. He discovers his own road and makes his own map. Process is so important to Stafford that many of his poems embody his theories of writing—the way poems find out what they are about. The pace is often slow, including what looks like nonsequitur (what he terms "distractions in a positive direction"[34]). This sometimes makes the poem feel "talky," and the reader would like to hurry it to its point. But its point is in its method of discovering itself, and that often involves letting the various elements come together to suggest a deeper connection. These distractions might imply a lack of craft, but the opposite is almost always the case; the craft has been subsumed in favor of the process.

For Stafford craft, in the sense of traditional poetic forms, is simply too easy. It offers him no challenge. It is clear that he has a natural ear and writes easily with a near-perfect rhythmical cadence. His poems have consistently fought against this natural ability, working toward a much more complex sense of rhythm and rhyme than the conventional sonnet would call for. This is partly due to his belief that tradition should also

include the spoken word—its inflections and variations and subtle changes—as well as the "literary" tradition. "Poetry is not a going back, but a going forward."[35] Stafford's sense of craft is one that moves from, and enlarges, literary tradition. He is a master of subliminal rhymes, variations on expected meters, and a syncopation of line which calls attention to specific words—and silences.

Stafford's work has been characterized by critic Jonathan Holden as belonging to a convention he terms the "contemporary conversation poem."[36] There is an easy, even intimate, conversational style, stories to be told, thoughts to be examined. Some poems seem to speak directly to the reader, or audience, often employing the device of direct address. Almost all of them use a colloquial speech pattern. A closer look, though, shows a characteristic distance between writer and reader. Certainly the language invites, but the poems hold the reader off with an abstraction of both image and idea and a curious lack of detail. This resistance is sustained by the use of certain rhetorical and poetic devices, not the least of which is sound. Stafford weaves a dense tapestry, or pattern, of sound throughout his poems, alerting the ear to the formal aspects of his work. In this way he can pretend to let readers directly into his most private thoughts, but the poem itself serves as a sort of mask, fending them off even as it calls out a welcome. To participate one must do more than listen as the story unfolds; one must discover how to enter the imaginative landscape that the sounds, as well as the images, are defining.

In the end, the poems are about love—about daring to love under hard circumstances and in difficult times. They are an acceptance of duty—a duty to "find a place,"[37] a duty to be of, and for, the earth. The reader who follows Stafford through more than a thousand poems, accepting the "signals" as Stafford accepted them, will find insight into the human condition. He will experience the world in all its facets, will face the dark and the light. "A writer is not so much someone who has something to say as he is someone who has found a process that will bring about new things he would not have thought of if he had not started to say them."[38] The "new things" are the poems; in the case of William Stafford the poems make whole new worlds to explore.

STAFFORD AND THE CRITICS

Over the years that William Stafford has been writing, critical fashion has changed. When he attended the Writing Program at the University of Iowa, New Criticism was at its height. By the late 1980s, he has watched the rise (and at least partial fall) of structuralism and various postmodernisms, including deconstruction (an approach broadly based on the skeptical attitude toward language embodied in the work of the French philosopher Jacques Derrida). Throughout this evolution Stafford's own work has remained consistent, but how it has been read by these movements has varied. Under some of these methods of criticism his work cannot receive much critical attention since it does not readily fit the requirements of the movement.

The simple language and the unstrained quality of Stafford's poems have led to misunderstanding. Like Frost before him Stafford has been most interested in a wide audience of sympathetic readers; to gain that audience he has studiedly avoided the appearance of being too esoteric or "difficult." With some critics he may have become the victim of his own quest for a readership of "ordinary" people. The seeming simplicity of his subject matter and his conversational tone have gained the wrong kind of attention from some scholars.

"You see / intricate but fail at simple," says Stafford, in **"Seeing and Perceiving."**[39] He is accusing himself, noting a human failing, but the statement could easily be leveled at some of his critics. It is difficult to write about the simple, and most of his critics have failed at this task. Reviews of his work rely on characteristic phrases such as "unassuming tone" and "natural modesty." It has been easy for reviewers to note the colloquial speech patterns without fully analyzing their effect and, even more, why Stafford is using them. Unfortunately many critics have also equated "simple" with "unimportant." In addition, Stafford's refusal to edit his own work and to limit the amount he publishes has caused critics to take him less seriously than they should. Stephen Corey, writing in the *Virginia Quarterly Review*, warns him of this, saying "Recurrent ideas can become repetitive poems."[40]

Critics have tended to view Stafford in one of two categories: as a poet of place or as a poet of myth. Sanford Pinsker acknowledges Stafford's roots in Kansas, but looks to the imagery and attitudes (even psychology) that make him a "northwestern" poet. Pinsker does not want to call Stafford a regional poet (knowing that Stafford would resist the label), so he cites the Indian myth poems as examples of his identification with the region. In the end Pinsker is forced to read Stafford's poems in a broader context, discovering their universal properties: "Wonder brings him to his poems, and it is there that he has said God's plenty about the light and darkness of our condition, and about the constant amazement and tentative truths we all share."[41]

George Lensing and Ronald Moran emphasize the "mythic" in *Four Poets of the Emotive Imagination.* This particular reading of Stafford looks at the father figure as archetypal, the westward "journey" as Jungian. The emphasis is on the transcendent moment when, in an intuitive leap, the poet discerns in the wilderness what is otherwise concealed. But Lensing and Moran note that Stafford does not quite fit their prescriptive formula. If Stafford can be called mythic, it is in the sense that he creates his *own* mythology, composed of the elements of being (time, space, earth, air, water), and his sense of how personal history fits within human history.

Only one full-length study based solely on Stafford's work has appeared: *The Mark to Turn,* by Jonathan Holden, published in 1976. This is an excellent study of his first five books. Holden was certainly the first, and perhaps only, critic to note what he calls Stafford's "interlocking set of metaphors."[42] In defining for himself the specific vocabulary of the poems, Holden builds a strong case for the coherence of the body of the work and recognizes a similarity with Wallace Stevens.

One contemporary critic, Charles Altieri, uses Stafford as a foil for a larger argument. In *Self and Sensibility in Contemporary American Poetry,* Altieri claims that American poetry of the 70s had been dominated, and enervated, by what he terms "the scenic style."[43] He defines this as poetry characterized by the sensibility of the poet, supposedly present in a specific "real" scene (geographic or emotional or both), in which the poet's insights are allowed to become a sufficient justification for the poem. In such poetry, Altieri argues, craft and sensibility are taken as ultimate values, the reader is manipulated, and the means of poetry remain as unquestioned as its ends. There is no room for a "dialectical thinking" about what Altieri sees as the truly important issues; language is taken for granted in the service of a "smug, self-satisfied lyrical persona constantly transported into visionary states by the poet's apt metaphors or turns of events."[44]

But how well does this fit Stafford? Altieri, choosing one very early Stafford poem (**"Ceremony"** from *West of Your City*), notes in this poem an "imposed congruence" and the "controlling hand of the craftsman." These, he feels, are subtly used to try to express the"inexpressible."The result is, according to Altieri, an artificial "naturalness" used only to convey this "scenic effect." What Altieri would like, however, is a poet who feels the "responsibility to reflect upon the rhetorical figures producing the poem's moment of vision."[45] In other words, Stafford is not enough of a philosopher for Altieri's taste.

This is an example of the damage done by taking a Stafford poem out of its larger context. If Altieri were not intent on making his own arguments, he might have read further only to discover that Stafford is more aware than most of his contemporaries that meaning does lie outside as well as inside language. His poems demonstrate that awareness over and over. The body of Stafford's work is an example of dialectical thinking;

the "controlling hand" that Altieri so dislikes is only one piece of the evidence that Stafford is well aware of the double bind in writing.

In fact, Stafford's intuitive sense of the rift between reality and language may lie at the heart of his refusal to be his own critic. He recognizes the "faker"—the writer of the poem—within himself. His desperate need to protect his writing self from his critical self may well have led him to his controversial theories of nonintervention. This is revealed in a *Northwest Review* discussion with Richard Hugo, who suspected earlier that Stafford was a "shrewd judge" of his own work.[46] Hugo responds to a statement by Stafford that maybe "the world happens three times":

HUGO:

> But when you say things like that, you start leaving the poem. Those are footnotes. . . .

STAFFORD:

> Well, maybe the poem says that, but in my life I really want to say the world happens three times: once what I superficially see, second what I do my best to see, and third what I suspect I'll never be able to see it as.

HUGO:

> Right. Maybe the better way to put it is that the world happens three times; two of them you can use in poems.

STAFFORD:

> Yeah, the third time is when you take the poem apart and say, Here's the faker inside the poem.

HUGO:

> And that third way is the way of the critic.[47]

Stafford goes on in the interview to say that it's "dangerous" to look at poems when they have been completed because "you can out-think yourself." Perhaps Stafford's greatest fear is this ability to out-think himself; to give in to the critic might be to lose the poems before they came to fruition.

Typically, Stafford reveals this fear in a roundabout way throughout his poetry. The "logical ones" that he resists in favor of another way of "knowing" may be the flip side of himself. His wry wit and the way he often turns his poems back on their speaker would indicate that he senses this: "But awaking from awaking, I am a little man myself crying, / 'Faker! Faker!'"[48]; "Last I accuse—/ Myself: my terrible poise."[49] He looks hard, and with suspicion, at his own judgmental nature. The source of the tension that creates the poems may be his desire *not* to judge in the face of his natural inclinations. *Judgment* is, therefore, one more highlighted word in Stafford's linking vocabulary. He notes his own tendency to be a bit didactic about others, and at the same time he manages to be highly self-critical. Often he projects this tendency onto the landscape itself so that the judgment seems to be coming from the large impersonal force of nature. In all this he has been careful to turn his own judgment inward, and there he has found justice as well as accusation—the "silence and the judgment of the sky."[50]

William Stafford's poems are about survival in a complex, even threatening, world. The poems themselves survive in a complicated critical milieu. They will outlast both poetic and critical "fashion" because, in them, Stafford has looked for, and found, the "self which endures." That self may be best described by his own dream of the perfect reading, ending in a unifying vision that is almost, but not quite, an assertion:

> What would be dear to me would be not to enter and make an impression or leave and be forgotten—either of those—but to have it be like something that happens and you don't know what it is and after it's over you still don't know; nevertheless, something has happened.

> I would like the poems to be like that too. Instead of having all the effects of the poem be recognized while I'm there, I would like them just to linger after I've gone, and no one needs to know what happened.[51]

Notes

1. William Stafford, *You Must Revise Your Life* (Ann Arbor: University of Michigan Press, 1986) 11.

2. *You Must Revise Your Life* 13.

3. *You Must Revise Your Life* 19.

4. William Stafford, *Stories That Could Be True: New and Collected Poems* (New York: Harper, 1977) 96-97; *Traveling Through the Dark* (New York: Harper, 1962) 75.

5. William Stafford, *Down in My Heart* (Columbia, SC: The Bench Press, 1985) 3.

6. *You Must Revise Your Life* 12.

7. William Carlos Williams, *Paterson* (New York: New Directions, 1958) 9. "Say it! No ideas but in things."

8. *You Must Revise Your Life* 21.

9. William Stafford, *Writing the Australian Crawl* (Ann Arbor: University of Michigan Press, 1978) 58.

10. *You Must Revise Your Life* 111.

11. *Writing the Australian Crawl* 62, 65, 66.

12. *Writing the Australian Crawl* 3, 12, 27.

13. George Lensing and Ronald Moran, *Four Poets and the Emotive Imagination: Robert Bly, James Wright, Louis Simpson, and William Stafford* (Baton Rouge: Louisiana State University Press, 1976).

14. Peter Stitt, "A Remarkable Diversity," rev. of *A Glass Face in the Rain,* by William Stafford, *The Georgia Review* 36 (1982): 913.

15. *Writing the Australian Crawl* 60.

16. "Homecoming," *Stories That Could Be True* 115; *The Rescued Year* (New York: Harper, 1966) 13.

17. "The Little Lost Orphans," *Stories That Could Be True* 240; *Someday, Maybe* (New York: Harper, 1973) 69.

18. "Fictions," *Stories That Could Be True* 13.

19. "A Survey," *Stories That Could Be True* 35.

20. "A Course in Creative Writing," *A Glass Face in the Rain* (New York: Harper, 1982) 65.

21. "A Cameo of Your Mother," *A Glass Face in the Rain* 83.

22. "What I'll See That Afternoon," *A Glass Face in the Rain* 114.

23. "Looking for Gold," *An Oregon Message* (New York: Harper, 1987) 37.

24. *Stories That Could Be True* 107; *Traveling Through the Dark* 94.

25. "In Response to a Question," *Stories That Could Be True* 75-76; *Traveling Through the Dark* 33.

26. "Bi-Focal," *Stories That Could Be True* 48.

27. "In Fog," *Stories That Could Be True* 194-95; *Allegiances* (New York: Harper, 1970) 75.

28. *You Must Revise Your Life* 9, 8.

29. *An Oregon Message* 72.

30. *Writing the Australian Crawl* 81.

31. "Flowers at an Airport," *Stories That Could Be True* 172-73; *Allegiances* 35.

32. "Whenever It is," *Stories That Could Be True* 22-23.

33. "The Gift," *The Ohio Review* 40 (1988): 26.

34. *You Must Revise Your Life* 62.

35. *Writing the Australian Crawl* 77.

36. Jonathan Holden, *Style and Authenticity in Postmodern Poetry* (Columbia: University of Missouri Press, 1986) 33-44.

37. "In Dear Detail, by Ideal Light," *Stories That Could Be True* 105-06; *Traveling Through the Dark* 91.

38. *Writing the Australian Crawl* 17.

39. *A Glass Face in the Rain* 46.

40. Stephen Corey, "Lives on Leaves," rev. of *Things That Happen Where There Aren't Any People,* by William Stafford, *Virginia Quarterly Review* 57 (1981): 735.

41. Sanford Pinsker, *Three Pacific Northwest Poets: William Stafford, Richard Hugo, and David Wagoner* (Boston: Twayne, 1987) 11.

42. Jonathan Holden, *The Mark to Turn* (Lawrence: University Press of Kansas, 1976) 2.

43. Charles Altieri, *Self and Sensibility in Contemporary American Poetry* (Cambridge: Cambridge University Press, 1984) 11.

44. Altieri 15.

45. Altieri 14.

46. Richard Hugo, "Problems with Landscapes in Early Stafford Poems," *Kansas Quarterly* 2 (1970): 35.

47. "The Third Time the World Happens: A Dialogue on Writing Between Richard Hugo and William Stafford," *Northwest Review,* 13 (1973): 31-32.

48. "The Title Comes Later," *Stories That Could Be True* 99.

49. "Judgments," *Stories That Could Be True* 118; *The Rescued Year* 14.

50. "Willa Cather," *Stories That Could Be True* 40.

51. Stan Sanvel Rubin and Judith Kitchen, "A Conversation with William Stafford," SUNY Brockport, 22 Mar. 1988.

Bibliography

WORKS BY WILLIAM STAFFORD

POETRY

"Winterward." Dissertation. University of Iowa, 1954. Twelve of these poems were subsequently published.

West of Your City. Los Gatos, CA: Talisman Press, 1960.

Traveling Through the Dark. New York: Harper and Row, 1962.

The Rescued Year. New York: Harper and Row, 1966.

Eleven Untitled Poems. Mt. Horeb, WI: Perishable Press, 1968.

Weather: Poems. Mt. Horeb, WI: Perishable Press, 1969.

Allegiances. New York: Harper and Row, 1970.

Temporary Facts. Athens, OH: Duane Schneider Press, 1970.

Poems for Tennessee, with Robert Bly and William Matthews. Martin, TN: Tennessee Poetry Press, 1971.

Someday, Maybe. New York: Harper and Row, 1973.

In the Clock of Reason. Victoria, BC: Soft Press, 1973.

That Other Alone. Mt. Horeb, WI: Perishable Press, 1973.

Going Places: Poems. Reno, NV: West Coast Poetry Review, 1974.

North by West, with John Haines. Seattle: Spring Rain Press, 1975.

Braided Apart, with Kim Robert Stafford. Lewiston, ID: Confluence Press, 1976.

Late, Passing Prairie Farm. Northampton, MA: Main Street, Inc., 1976.

Stories That Could Be True: New and Collected Poems. New York: Harper and Row, 1977; London: Harper and Row, 1980.

The Design on the Oriole. Mt. Horeb, WI: Night Heron Press, 1977.

Two about Music. Knotting, Bedfordshire: The Sceptre Press, 1978.

All about Light. Athens, OH: Croissant, 1978.

Tuned in Late One Night. Northampton, MA: Deerfield Press, 1978; Dublin: The Gallery Press, 1978.

Passing a Creche. Seattle: Sea Pen Press, 1978.

Tuft by Puff. Mt. Horeb, WI: Perishable Press, 1978.

The Quiet of the Land. New York: Nadja Press, 1979.

Around You, Your House & a Catechism. Knotting, Bedfordshire: The Sceptre Press, 1979.

Things That Happen Where There Aren't Any People. Brockport, NY: BOA Editions, 1980.

Absolution. Knotting, Bedfordshire: Martin Booth, 1980.

Passwords. Seattle: Sea Pen Press, 1980.

Wyoming Circuit. Tannersville, NY: Tideline Press, 1980.

Sometimes Like a Legend: Puget Sound Country. Port Townsend, WA: Copper Canyon Press, 1981.

A Glass Face in the Rain: New Poems. New York: Harper and Row, 1982; London: Harper and Row, 1985.

Segues: A Correspondence in Poetry, with Marvin Bell. Boston: Godine, 1983.

Roving across Fields: A Conversation and Uncollected Poems 1942-1982. Ed. Thom Tammaro. Daleville, IN: Barnwood Press Cooperative, 1983.

Smoke's Way: Poems. Port Townsend, WA: Graywolf Press, 1978.

Stories and Storms and Strangers. Rexburg, ID: Honeybrook Press, 1984.

Listening Deep. Great Barrington, MA: Penmaen Press, Chapbook Series 3, 1984.

Wyoming. Bristol, RI: Ampersand Press, 1985.

Brother Wind. Rexburg, ID: Honeybrook Press, 1986.

An Oregon Message. New York: Harper and Row, 1987.

PROSE

Down in My Heart (autobiography). Elgin, IL: Brethren Publishing House, 1947; rpt. Columbia, SC: The Bench Press, 1985.

Writing the Australian Crawl: Views on the Writer's Vocation. Ann Arbor: University of Michigan Press, 1978. This and the following title are part of the University of Michigan's Poets on Poetry series. They contain essays and interviews which were originally published in literary magazines.

You Must Revise Your Life. Ann Arbor: University of Michigan Press, 1986.

SELECTED COMMENTS ON POETRY

Comment on "The Farm on the Great Plains." *Poets Choice.* Ed. Paul Engle and Joseph Langland. New York: Dell, 1962. 142-43.

"No Answer to this Day," on Richard Eberhart's "Am I My Neighbor's Keeper?" *The Contemporary Poet as Artist and Critic.* Ed. Anthony Ostroff. Boston: Little, Brown, 1964. 153-57.

"Brother Antoninus—The World as a Metaphor." Introduction to *The Achievement of Brother Antoninus.* Glenview, IL: Scott, Foresman, 1967. 1-18.

Analysis of "Traveling through the Dark." *Reading Modern Poetry.* Ed. Paul Engle and Warren Carrier. Rev. ed. Glenview, IL: Scott, Foresman, 1968. 56-56.

"Finding the Language." *Naked Poetry.* Ed. Stephen Berg and Robert Mezey. Indianapolis: Bobbs-Merrill, 1969. 82-83.

"Ask Me" *Fifty Contemporary Poets: The Creative Process.* Ed. Alberta T. Turner. New York: McKay, 1977. 290-95.

Thomas E. Benediktsson (essay date 1990)

SOURCE: Benediktsson, Thomas E. "Montana Eclogue: The Pastoral Art of William Stafford." In *World, Self, Poem: Essays on Contemporary Poetry from the*

"Jubilation of Poets," edited by Leonard M. Trawick, pp. 196-206. Kent, Ohio: The Kent State University Press, 1990.

[In the following essay, Benediktsson explores whether Stafford's poetry serves as an example of the "new pastoralism" of the 1960s and 1970s.]

Many critics of contemporary poetry have noted what they call the new pastoralism of the neo-romantic poetry of the 1960s and 1970s. Jonathan Holden's remark is typical: "Even today, when most Americans live in cities, the best American poetry in the Romantic tradition—the work of poets such as Robert Bly, James Dickey, Galway Kinnell, Theodore Roethke, William Stafford and James Wright—is apt to be pastoral" (*Rhetoric* 73). So, for that matter, is Louis Simpson's rather irritable reaction: "To read some American poets, you would think that they lived far away from roads and supermarkets, that they never had thoughts of the people you meet, that they looked with the eyes of the crow and listened with the ears of the beaver. That their habitation was darkness and their house made of earth and stones. That they were pure in thought and deed" (quoted by Holden, *Rhetoric* 73).

But is it accurate to use the term *pastoral* in this way? A strict constructionist would say pastoral as a literary form is tied to certain specific conventions that died sometime before the advent of the romantic movement. Yet most critics allow some latitude beyond the conventional genre of idealized shepherds and shepherdesses derived from classical models and find instances of pastoral into the nineteenth century and beyond. As W. W. Gregg pointed out in 1906, the constant element in all the varied forms of pastoral is the "recognition of a contrast, implied or expressed, between pastoral life and some more complex types of civilization" (4). This recognition gives rise to the pastoral reaction against the sophistication of the court or the city in favor of the simpler life of the country. Heavily imbued with sentiment and nostalgia, pastoral is based on a desire to retreat from the pressures of the present moment into an idealized simplicity—in classical literature an Arcadian or Golden Age; in romantic literature a cult of childhood, an ideal of the noble savage, a myth of an organic society, or an idyll of unspoiled nature. Written by the sophisticated in praise of the unsophisticated, pastoral is a literature of escapism and wish-fulfillment.

Since the pastoral impulse itself arises from the appeal of an illusion, recent writers have shown an interest in exploring the aesthetic and dramatic possibilities of the genre's self-contradictions. Modern theories accordingly stress reflexive or dialectical design in the structure of pastoral works. For William Empson, for example, pastoral design is a way of embodying the complex in the simple—an aesthetic of metonymy. For Leo Marx, pastoral design is metaphoric, an attempt to resolve within the text opposing "kingdoms of force," natural and technological, which are utterly incompatible in the real landscape. For Raymond Williams, the pastoral illusion contrasts with the "counter-pastoral" political reality of exploited peasants, and for J. R. Ebbotson, it must confront the Darwinian antipastoral of violence and natural aggression. Thus, though modern pastorals appeal to the universal desire for simplicity and escape, they also employ a rhetorical strategy that attempts to deal with the contradictions between the "real world" and the world of pastoral fantasy.

It is only in these terms that the neo-romantic American poetry of the 1960s and 1970s can properly be termed pastoral. As Gary Snyder puts it in a famous formulation:

> Class-structured civilized society is a kind of mass ego. To transcend the ego is to go beyond society as well. "Beyond" there lies inwardly, the unconscious. Outwardly, the equivalent of the unconscious is the wilderness: both of these terms meet, one step even further on, as *one*.
>
> (*Earth* 118, 122)

The poetry that establishes this unity springs from a pastoral impulse, but it must employ a conscious and artful rhetoric to convey a sense of primal unconsciousness. In the process it must continually struggle with the traditional aesthetic problems of pastoralism: how through a sophisticated literary form to express the value and wonder of the unsophisticated and unworldly, and how to deal with the sentimentalism associated with the effort, when the awareness sought for is so clearly antisentimental.

Partly because of the strong pull of the pastoral impulse in his work, partly because of his use of highly but subtly rhetorical pastoral design, William Stafford might be the most representative poet in this movement. In Stafford's work we find nearly every element of sentimental pastoral: a poignant nostalgia for his Midwestern childhood; a reverence for American Indians as "noble savages," whose tie with the land was elemental and spiritual and who lived in a kind of Arcadia before the encroachment of white people; a panegyric to unspoiled nature, imaged particularly in idealized versions of the Pacific Northwest. But Stafford modifies the sentimentalism inherent in these stereotypes with a rhetoric that quietly incorporates the surreal and demonic into the pastoral landscape; in fact, one of the special qualities of his poetry rests in its dialectic of the sentimental and the demonic, a dialectic achieved through the use of surrealist metaphor.

THE SURREALIST MODE: SENTIMENTAL
DEMONIC

Surrealist technique, an important rhetorical element in Stafford's poetry, is a way of opening up possibilities of irrational, potentially mystical significance within what might be otherwise rational or merely sentimental. To give a simple example, we might examine the mild surrealism of **"Universe is One Place"** (81), in which a consciously sentimental, even trite pastoral subject—a farm girl bringing water to tired field hands—is opened to larger significance by dislocations in syntax and imagery:

> Crisis they call it?—when
> when the gentle wheat leans at the combine and
> and when the farm girl brings cool jugs wrapped in
>   burlap
> slapping at her legs?
>
> We think—drinking cold water
> water looking at the sky—
> *Sky is home, universe is one place.*
> Crisis? City folks make
>
> make such a stir.
> Farm girl away through the wheat.

Syntactic dislocations—the repetition of "when / when," "and / and," "water / water," "sky / sky," and "make / make,"—open the signification to possibilities of non-coherence. The didactic "universe is one place" may be the coherent center of the poem, but the dislocations of the syntax force the final image away from the merely literal, holding forth the potential of metaphor without exactly establishing what the terms of the metaphor might be.

In other poems, the terms of the controlling metaphor might seem clear, even conventional, but the surrealist movement of the poem strains against that clarity toward more mysterious possibilities. In **"Letter from Oregon"** (123) the poet, watching the salmon fight upstream to return to their home waters to spawn, imagines returning to his own birthplace. The metaphor for this imagined journey is an eastbound train moving through mountains:

> Mother, here there are shadowy salmon;
> ever their sides argue up the falls.
> Watching them plunge with fluttering gills,
> I thought back through Wyoming where I came from.
>
> The gleaming sides of my train glimmered
> up over passes and arrowed through shoals
> of aspen fluttering in a wind of yellow.

To the extent that it provides a conventional rhetorical link between tenor and vehicle, the controlling metaphor is coherent and rational. The train-as-salmon image, in fact, is an example of pastoral design in Leo Marx's sense of the term, in which an object of technology is placed in a harmonious relationship with nature through a metaphor that makes it seem a part of nature. Likewise, the speaker's journey away from home and his imagined return seem by metaphoric extension part of a natural process, as inevitable as the migrations of salmon. But in the middle section of the poem, Stafford casts the comparison literally and figuratively into doubt:

> Only the sky stayed true; I turned,
>
> justifying space through those miles of Wyoming
> till the wave of the land was quelled by the stars;
> then tunnels of shadow led me far
> through doubt, and I was home.
>
> Mother, even home was doubtful;
> many slip into the sea and are gone for years,
> just as I boarded the six-fifteen there.
> Over the bar I have leaped outward.

The salmon's journey into the sea and back has become a metaphor for a migration from another mode of being, a "home" far different from the Midwestern home Stafford left behind. The primal imagery of "tunnels of shadow" and "the wave of the land was quelled by the stars" prepare us for the metamorphosis of the controlling figure in the final stanza, where mystery and doubt are not resolved but are intensified in a surrealist version of the same metaphor:

> Somewhere in the ocean beyond Laramie
> when that grass folded low in the dark
> a lost fin waved, and I felt the beat
> of the old neighborhood stop, on our street.

Reminiscent of the fish in the wheatfield in Chagall's backdrop for *Aleko,* this surrealist image annihilates the rational frame for the poem's controlling metaphor and casts into doubt its ostensibly nostalgic motive, quietly reintroduced in the last line. In place of sentimental nostalgia we are left with a sense of indeterminacy and a suggestion of some primal, unconscious being from which we have migrated and to which we wish to return.

Seen, then, as an element of pastoral design, Stafford's surrealism is a way of introducing a more mystical level, which interacts with the simple surface pastoralism of his poem. In this context Albert Cook's semiotic definition of surrealist metaphor is useful:

> On the one hand the surrealist poem envisions a dream by erasing, or tending to erase, the distinction between tenor and vehicle, floating both the signifier and signified far away from an object single or composite. On the other hand, by according a dream significance to every object and slight event in the waking world, the erasure of distinction operates in the service of a giant reference, a giant referent.

(36)

This technique, Cook maintains, "induces a surrender to primal metaphor." He goes on to distinguish between pastoral and primal: the pastoral vocabulary of some surrealist poets is not really pastoral but "preliterary and ultraliterary." Though he makes this comment regarding the vocabulary of "Mediterranean" poets like W. S. Merwin, the same could be said of Stafford, who uses a pastoral vocabulary to convey his sense of the primal or demonic.

In **"Bi-Focal"** (48), for example, the pastoral realm is the proper landscape for love, but love is "of the earth only." This benign surface is what we often call "nature," but nature's essence, the demonic, is rooted in darkness; it "legends" itself up from subterranean depths, "deep as the mine / the thickest rocks won't tell." By contrast with the chthonic, mythic level of things, the sentimental pastoral is mere illusion:

> So, the world happens twice—
> once what we see it as;
> second, it legends itself
> deep, the way it is.

Poetry could be the "map" of the surface or it could be the "legend" of the depths; many of Stafford's poems are such legends, in which the natural landscape becomes a kind of extended metaphor for the unconscious mind. These poems work not through a contrast of pastoral and demonic, but through a metamorphosis of pastoral into demonic through surrealist metaphor. As Holden has shown in his book *The Mark to Turn*, Stafford employs an extensive and surprisingly consistent series of conventions in many of his poems. Darkness, for example, is the realm of the irrational or demonic self; hearing and touch, not sight, are linked to the power of the imagination to contact that realm. Light, even moonlight, is the enemy of the revitalizing imagination (24-27).

Any number of poems might serve as models of this rhetorical technique, but **"In the Deep Channel"** (31) is representative:

> Setting a trotline after sundown
> if we went far enough away in the night
> sometimes up out of deep water
> would come a secret-headed channel cat,
>
> Eyes that were still eyes in the rush of darkness,
> flowing feelers noncommittal and black,
> and hidden in the fins those rasping bone daggers,
> with one spiking upward on its back.
>
> We would come at daylight and find the line sag,
> the fishbelly gleam and the rush on the tether:
> to feel the swerve and the deep current
> which tugged at the tree roots below the river.

This poem owes its resonance to a careful choice of metaphors. The "secret-headed" catfish is the emblem of the irrational and demonic within nature and within the self. Its mode of sight ("eyes that were still eyes in the rush of darkness") is denied us; but pulling the line, we can feel "the swerve and the deep current" in which it has its secret life.

In terms of the dualism of **"Bi-Focal," "In the Deep Channel"** would have to be considered an antipastoral poem, moving from the idyllic imagination into the demonic. But in another sense, it is a version of pastoral, written out of the pressure to escape poetically from the banality and moral turpitude of everyday existence. For Stafford is very much a poet of suburban academic life, whose rejection of that familiar world is as characteristically a literary gesture as was the Renaissance courtly poet's pastoral rejection of the court. The "literariness" of the enterprise is evident through Stafford's frequent use of a set of "deep image" conventions as artificial in their way as the conventions of traditional pastoral were for the Renaissance poet. It would be an error, however, to see this use of artifice as an artistic flaw; it is part of a conscious pastoral design, an effort to achieve within the literary text a unity that is denied in ordinary life.

THE DIDACTIC MODE

In pastoral terms, separation from nature is the fall of "man," and romantic pastoral elegy both mourns that separation and tries to heal it. In Stafford's poetry, separation is often represented by antipastoral winter landscapes that suggest nature in its most hostile and inhuman aspect. In **"Doubt on the Great Divide"** (126), for example, when we discover that one of the lies we have been taught is the lie of transcendence, "that God grips boards by thought into Plato's table," we find ourselves isolated in a desolate landscape: "Mountains that thundered promises now say something small—/ wire in the wind, and snow beginning to fall." And in **"Winterward"** (127), doubt has become terror, infecting all of life. Stafford's campers who have "pitched this fact of a life in dust" cannot bear the hazards of living without certainty. Even summer was a "green alarm," and in autumn "threatenings flared." Now they look to winter as a refuge from fear and a fulfillment of what they most fear: "Oh winter, oh snowy interior, / rocks and hurt birds, we come."

This theme is the subject of many poems like **"Walking the Wilderness"** (138), one of a number of elegies about Stafford's mother:

> My mother in a dream dreamed
> this place, where storms drown
> down or where God makes it arch to mountains,
> flood with winter, stare upward at His
> eye that freezes people, His zero breath
> their death.

Even though it is possible to see individual deaths as part of a hidden pattern—"snowflake designs lock; they clasp in the sky"—there is no consolation in the thought. And yet, facing winter in the right way can be ennobling, an occasion to move toward what is most elemental and authentic in life, and a final test of courage and solitude:

> Warm human representatives may vote and
> manage man; but at last the blizzard will dignify
> the walker, the storm hack trees to cyclone
> groves, he catch the snow, his brave eye
> become command, the whole night howl against
> his ear, till found by dawn he
> reach out to God no trembling hand.

By occurring to us, by the mere fact of our imagining them, these winter landscapes have a power over us, demonic in their capacity to revitalize us. They stand for the death that seems to be our ultimate separation from nature, but which is actually the promise of our reunion. The fact that they are unvisited, only imagined, is crucial to their idealization; and it is the poet's task to help us imagine them, thus serving as an intermediary between our dull warmth and their vital cold.

Stafford never moves far from this role. He sees himself as a teacher; and didacticism, rare in contemporary poetry, is fundamental to his aesthetics. Many poems could be cited to demonstrate this sense of vocation. In **"Representing Far Places"** (96), for example, Stafford establishes a radical contrast between the "canoe wilderness," where "fish in the lake leap arcs of realization," and "society where the talk turns witty." But standing in the room, listening to the talk, the wilderness "fans in your head / canyon by canyon." Stafford represents far places; as a poet he is important because he can imagine the weather we are all sheltered from.

The didactic mode in Stafford's pastoralism is presented quite directly in **"Montana Eclogue"** (166), a poem in three parts (longer than most of his lyrics, which tend to be less than 30 lines.) Here he presents a major role of the transforming literary imagination and explicitly links it with the pastoral tradition.

The opening section of the poem presents us with a sentimental, stereotyped Western landscape: a high cattle camp in a remote valley of the Montana Rockies. It is after the trail drive, and only one man—Logue—remains to close down the camp. The setting is a "remote, stone cathedral" with highly generalized names: "High Valley," "Stone Creek," "Clear Lake," "Winter Peak." As Logue goes about his chores, the approaching winter begins to flood the country; the aspens feel its current, and above them, "high miles of pine tops bend." A significance attaches to the aptly named Logue, who "by being there, suddenly / carries for us everything that we can load on him." We have "stepped indoors" and have forgotten "how storms come"; Logue faces winter for us.

The title of this poem and its echo in "Logue" remind us of the literary tradition of pastoral at the same time that we are asked to observe nature in its inhuman aspect, a perception contrary to the pastoral tradition. Our Arcadia is Montana in the grip of the approaching winter, and our Thyrsis is the cattleman Logue. But Logue's name reminds us that he is made only of words; he is a literary invention no more substantial than Thyrsis. Logue is a repository of poetic value, and the movement of the poem through his point of view does not point to a reality beyond language. We experience winter through words, by inventing Logue, whom we imagine living in what we avoided when we "stepped indoors."

It is through Logue that we catch a glimpse of "those ranches our trees hardly hear of." Stafford moves into a more didactic and visionary mode as he describes a landscape even Logue cannot see, "the clear-cut miles the marmots own" near the timberline, high above the aspen valley and pine ridges of Logue's camp. We "citizens" who are "gripped in a job" or "aimed steady at a page" need to imagine through Logue the coldness of these high places, because they remind us of death. Stafford's language grows apocalyptic as he describes an ultimate winter:

> We glimpse that last storm when the wolves
> get the mountains back, when our homes will flicker
> bright, then dull, then old; and the trees
> will advance, knuckling their roots or lying in
> windows to match the years. We glimpse
>
> a crack that begins to run down the wall,
> and like a blanket over the window at night
> that world is with us and those wolves are here.

Through the pastoral design of the poem, death has become part of the beauty of this unvisited landscape, and we can be revitalized by the thought of it. The grandeur of Montana has shed grandeur on death, and the discovery of our own insignificance is liberating: "things can come so great / that your part is too small to count, / if winter can come."

It should by now be evident that Stafford's art is pastoral in more than a superficial way; he directs the sentimental impulse toward pastoral simplicity into a more profound literary encounter with the demonic and with the necessity to use the imagination to gain the strength to face death. The pastoral setting, then, is the boundary of the human; the inhuman world can only be imagined, but in the act of imagining it, we can transform it into an unvisited pastoral landscape, as in **"In Dear Detail, by Ideal Light"** (105):

> There, for the rest of the years,
> by not going there, a person could believe
> some porch looking south,
> and steady in the shade—maybe you,
>
> Rescued by how the hills
> happened to arrive where they are,

depending on that wire
going to an imagined place

Where finally the way the world feels
really means how things are,
in dear detail,
by ideal light all around us.

By "not going there" we can be "rescued" by our belief
in an imagined place, and the pastoral cycle will be
complete: Prospero can return from his island, the Duke
from the forest of Arden. And we can face the rest of
our lives "deep in a story strongly told."

Works Cited

Gregg, Walter Wilson. *Pastoral Poetry and Pastoral Drama.* London: A. H. Bullen, 1906.

Holden, Jonathan. *The Mark to Turn.* Lawrence, KS: UP of Kansas, 1976.

————. "Poetry and Commitment." *Ohio Review* 29 (1982): 15-30.

————. *The Rhetoric of the Contemporary Lyric.* Bloomington: Indiana UP, 1980.

Snyder, Gary. *Earth House Hold.* New York: New Directions, 1969.

Erland G. Anderson (essay date spring 1996)

SOURCE: Anderson, Erland G. "Stafford's 'Ask Me.'" *Explicator* 54, no. 3 (spring 1996): 175-77.

[*In the following essay, Anderson discusses the influence of other writers and poets on Stafford's poetic persona as articulated in the poem "Ask Me."*]

William Stafford's **"Ask Me,"** which first appeared in *The New Yorker* in 1975 and was included in his major collection ***Stories That Could Be True*** in 1977, has as a central theme the degree of influence "others" have had on the life of the speaker (the "I" of the poem). Although the speaker's homespun diction suggests that "others" refers to anyone with whom he has come in contact, other living writers and/or writers frequently anthologized in the traditional "canon" of poets are not excluded as possible references.

Some time when the river is ice ask me
mistakes I have made. Ask me whether
what I have done is my life. Others
have come in their slow way into
my thought, and some have tried to help
or to hurt: ask me what difference
their strongest love or hate has made.

I will listen to what you say.
You and I can turn and look

at the silent river and wait. We know
the current is there, hidden; and there
are comings and goings from miles away
that hold the stillness exactly before us.
What the river says, that is what I say.

—*William Stafford*

For one thing, **"Ask Me"** is about as close as Stafford comes in his best poems to a formal sonnet of fourteen lines. From a purely formal point of view, Stafford obviously does not share many traditional poets' ideas concerning meter and regular end rhymes, but the poem *is* a sonnet full of internal (and a few end) rhymes poking their way up to the surface. Repetition of various kinds is a key element in Stafford's sustained discourse, emphasized most strongly when he repeats the words "ask me" three times in the first half of the sonnet.

Stafford clearly seeks his own form, but not without strong echoes from other more formal writers. As in many of the more traditional poems by, for example, Robert Frost, Stafford places himself (or his poetic persona) in a winter landscape. This approach is typical of Stafford, who often hypothesizes a "conversation" in an imagined landscape, where the "I" and the "you" of the poem delve below the words they exchange (or come to the limits of those words) to "turn and look / at the silent river" and "wait" for answers or better understanding.

But it is not inappropriate for the reader to ask what kind of conversation these two personae might be having, and why it was necessary, in the first place, for the speaker of the poem to defer questions about "mistakes I have made" until a time when "the river is ice." In fact, questions arise about the meaning of the "slow way" people come "into / my thought," as well as what "difference," exactly, "their strongest love or hate has made."

As in a formal sonnet, questions have been raised in the first half of the poem which the reader expects to be answered (or at least resolved) in the second half. But what is learned from looking at the "silent river" of ice, and why in the end does the poet, in effect, choose silence by identifying the speaker's answer with what the river "says" in the cold of winter?

The questions deferred in the first line of **"Ask Me"** seem to involve some ultimate judgment about the speaker of the poem; and I think we are also to take the clause "when the river is ice" in a metaphorical way. That is, in this reading, the "you" is asked to wait until a crucial moment of frozen resistance, or to a moment when the "I" is faced with hatred, or profound criticism, or disagreement over "what I have done" in life. (Certainly the hostility Stafford experienced when he chose to be a conscientious objector during World War

II qualifies him as an expert on these encounters.) In moments of hardening positions between opposing points of view, time might be said to have frozen. People are at odds with each other, and the strength of their convictions is put to the ultimate test. Paradoxically, they also may be approaching a time when they might be ready to "listen."

The "you" addressed, however, may not be an antagonist; rather, he or she is placed in a large (river-like) continuum of "others" who have judged or tried to influence the "I" of the poem with "their strongest love or hate." But these outsiders are said to "come in their slow way into / my thought," suggesting that the "I" has found an equivalently calm (or "frozen"?) center from which to perceive, then accept and/or reject those influences. In any case, the speaker in Stafford's poem will not discuss "whether / what I have done is my life" until "the river is ice."

Another possible reading of "ice" may relate to Stafford's technique of less-formal, but equally meaningful, writing. Stafford may be seen as trying to get his poems to *jell,* to achieve a place in the canon of English poets despite his lack of adherence to traditional forms; but the intensity of his statement suggests much more.

In fact, the metaphor of "ice" expands further in the second half of the poem, becoming a protective mask (of "stillness" or emotional equilibrium) that hides "the current" below, or in the face of hatred and opposition, permits the life-sustaining waters to come and go "from miles away" despite appearances to the contrary. Instead of simply resigning himself to a recognition of the potentially destructive power of outside forces, Stafford lets "what the river says" answer all deep questions concerning actions and influences. The speaker of the poem seems to have found a way to resist, passively, all antagonisms and distractions with silence and at the same time to affirm the hope of an eventual, life-sustaining thaw that the covering ice obscures. In terms of the potential weight of tradition, Stafford has also found a way to transform that tradition into support for his own style of writing.

Perhaps in the end, no final judgment can be made about the "I" of the poem, nor about Stafford's place in any literary canon. Life is too ambiguous; social values are changeable. Nature, through the voice of the "silent river," always has the last word. But on the frozen surface of the poem, despite its chill, Stafford has managed to "hold" parts of the current of art and of life in "the stillness exactly before us." And he has done so by maintaining a strong sense of his own identity while still acknowledging the fluid complexities likely to be discovered beneath his smooth surface.

Work Cited

Stafford, William. "Ask Me." *Stories That Could Be True.* New York: Harper and Row, 1977.

William Young (essay date winter 1998)

SOURCE: Young, William. "*Traveling through the Dark*: The Wilderness Surrealism of the Far West." *Midwest Quarterly* 39, no. 2 (winter 1998): 187-201.

[*In the following essay, Young compares the wilderness poetry of Stafford, Richard Hugo, and Gregory Corso.*]

"I am following a process that leads wildly and originally into new territory. . . ."

William Stafford

In the last three decades, as an outgrowth of the Sixties and in response to the influx of people and translations from all corners of the world, a particular kind of symbolist literature became prominent, the surreal. Some form of surrealist literature has found a home in all regions of the country. Yet an American surrealism, or, more accurately, "near surrealism," has primarily been developed in the West, where the stark juxtaposition of nature and machine as well as the juxtapositions of a wide range of subcultures creates an art of dreamlike displacement.

The spectacular and desolate curve of sky and land, of mountain and plain, and of high plains and desert has long contributed to making western American literature somewhat more otherworldly than the literatures of the eastern, central, and southern United States. Western American literature is derived from the sun and moon as much as it is from the earth and society: the cosmic or metaphysical dimension is strong, and a rootless, solitary, and reticent attitude prevails. The recent massive growth of the western U.S. has led to a confrontation between frontier attitudes and the necessities of a highly complex technological and multicultural society. This conflict encourages a derealization in the way the world is experienced and described, even in a writer such as William Stafford, who, as Robert Bly writes in an introduction to *The Darkness Around Us Is Deep,* "looks to the palpable and hearable" (x).

Poets as unlike as Stafford and Gregory Corso, whom I use here as parameters of Sixties poetry styles in the West, inherit and develop a new geography. A brief listing of some of the West's more interesting poets— Robert Duncan, Thom Gunn, Charles Bukowski, Ishmael Reed, Ed Dorn, John Haines, Diane Wakoski, Sandra McPherson, Norman Dubie—indicates the importance of a near-surrealist/neoromantic strain. There is a strong sense of the "wild" in all of these poets, and a strong sense of the significance of "wilderness" in most of them.

In discussing the early Sixties work of three Western poets—Corso, Richard Hugo, and, in particular, Stafford—I proceed from a discussion of an urban,

"Beat" tradition, which is largely a product of New York and California, to a discussion of a wilderness, "Deep Image" tradition, which is largely a product of the Midwest and Northwest.

Finally, by projecting forward a little beyond the Sixties, I argue that Stafford emerges as the poet of wilderness surrealism most thoroughly in the American grain by virtue of his continuing faith in the open road and his sense of being "at home" no matter where he is. In Stafford, outsiderness receives a new twist: there is no such thing as a permanent home and yet we are never disconnected nor displaced. This is a distinctly postmodern attitude and links Stafford to the future in ways unavailable to either Beat or Deep Image poets. Stafford's postmodernism belies Charles Altieri's notion, in *Self and sensibility in contemporary American poetry*, that Stafford is a poet trapped in scenic mode of contemporary poetry in which a "reticent, plain-speaking, and self-reflective speaker within a narratively presented scene" evokes "a sense of loss" (10).

I. GREGORY CORSO: BEAT SURREALIST

Many of the urban surrealists of the late Fifties and early Sixties who had gathered in New York found it necessary and profitable to shift the focus of their concerns to the "Wild West," finding a center of activity in San Francisco. Although some stayed home—O'Hara, Ashbery—others, especially those associated with the Beat movement, headed west.

In *The Dharma Bums,* Jack Kerouac describes what they found.

> It took exactly the entire twenty-five miles to get out of the smog of Los Angeles; the sun was clear in Riverside. I exulted to see a beautiful dry riverbottom with white sand and just a trickle river in the middle as we rolled over the bridge into Riverside. I was looking for my first chance to camp out for the night and try out my new ideas. But at the hot bus station a Negro saw me with my pack and came over and said he was part Mohawk and when I told him I was going back up the road to sleep in that riverbottom he said "No sir, you can't do that, cops in this town are the toughest in the state. . . ."

> "This ain't no India, is it," I said, sore, and walked off anyway to try it. . . . I laughed thinking what would happen if I was Fuke the Chinese sage of the ninth century who wandered around China constantly ringing his bell. The only alternative to sleeping out, hopping freights, and doing what I wanted, I saw in a vision would be to just sit with a hundred other patients in front of a nice television set in a madhouse, where we could be "supervised." . . . I saw many cop cruising cars and they were looking for me suspiciously: sleek, well-paid cops in brand-new cars with all that expensive radio equipment to see that no bhikku slept in his grove tonight.

(95-96)

Essential characteristics of the Beat surreal are revealed in this passage. Surrealism, generally defined, is the juxtaposition of elements from different space-times. Here Kerouac interfaces the open landscape of the vast west with efficient, and malevolent, machines of the new world. We also have references to several cultures, ancient and modern. The traditional American images of the "machine in the garden" and the "melting pot" are incorporated, but the emphasis is on the fear and loathing they represent and produce on the last frontier. Kerouac's swift-moving style enhances the effect of all these elements, here juxtaposed, passing before one's eyes as though part of a strange, unholy, dream. And finally, Kerouac's odd yet touching sense of humor—the Negro claiming that he is part Mohawk, the reference to Fuke the Chinese sage—gives the scene, however unholy, the feeling of surprising, wide-eyed joy that only the deepest melancholy can generate. Like other surrealists, Kerouac has decided to "dig" rather than lament the strange and lonesome world he has come across.

The myth of the Beat hero is well described by Dorothy Van Ghent.

> The hero is the "angelheaded hipster." He comes of anonymous parentage, parents who he denies in correct mythological fashion. He has received a mysterious call—to the road, the freights, the jazz dens, the "negro streets." . . . His tortures—the heroic "ordeals" of myth—send him into ecstasy and he bursts into song, song filled with metaphors of destruction, an ironic invertedly apocalyptic Mollie Bloom paean of accent.

(213)

If Allen Ginsberg, in "Howl," wrote the quintessential poem of this myth as romantic anguish, Corso's "Marriage" has most clearly married the myth to the metaphysical tradition. And surprisingly, it is the relative impersonality (and impersonating) strategies of the latter tradition which prefigures surrealism. The (necessary) element of romantic agony is transformed, when clothed in metaphysical wit and flights of fancy, into modern surrealism.

"Marriage" leans toward the poetic practice of Donne, Marvell, et al., as well as Eliot in our own time. Corso's poem, it seems to me, is a direct take-off on "The Love Song of J. Alfred Prufrock": "Should I get married? Should I be good?" like Prufrock's "Do I dare" or "And how should I presume?" (26) But whereas Prufrock is at the mercy of his questions and his introspectiveness, the speaker in "Marriage" moves toward exclamations:

>   . . . and I get up from
>   by big papa chair
> saying Christmas teeth! Radiant brains! Apple deaf!
> God what a husband I'd make! Yes, I should get married!

(*SP*[*Selected Poems*], 38)

Yet the appeal of Corso's poem rests not so much with its outrageousness, but in its remarkable mix of outrageous and sublime. The inventive conceits of the poem as well as the swift shifts in tone recall the metaphysical poets. Marvell's "To His Coy Mistress" beautifully incorporates and juxtaposes such stunningly different tones as "But at my back I always hear / Time's winged chariot hurrying near" and "The grave's a fine and private place, / But none, I think do there embrace" (*CP* [*The Complete Poems*], 51); in similar fashion Corso shifts from a weird but sonorous opening stanza—"Don't take her to movies but to cemeteries / tell all about werewolf bathtubs and forked clarinets / then desire her and kiss her and all the preliminaries" (36)—to the awkward, sardonic, yet touching questions of stanza two and three—"After tea and homemade cookies they ask What you do for / a living?" (37) to, in stanza four, exclamations like those above. Stanza five again picks up the melodic, sentimental vision of stanza one, shifting rather rapidly back to exclamations once again.

Corso's poem proclaims the inability of the poet/ outsider to embrace the suburban social world, using the extended figure of marriage as a dramatic metaphor for acting out the allegory. The surrealist (and metaphysical) joy in assuming masks is central to the movement of the poem. Whereas Kerouac imagines himself and his friends as "holy goofs," like Fuke the Chinese sage, and Ginsburg, in "A Supermarket in California," from *Howl,* imagines himself walking through supermarkets with Walt Whitman as Whitman asks, "Who killed the pork chops? What price bananas? Are you my angel?" (23), Corso often takes the next step and *becomes* another person and another voice— one that plays off of and against Beatness (both in terms of "beatific" and "beaten down"). Both Corso and Ginsburg refer to ancient cultures in the last line of their respective poems, "Marriage" and "A Supermarket in California," indicating, perhaps, what Van Ghent calls the "authentic archaic lines" (213) of the Beat myth. Yet the Beat myth has tended to obscure significant differences among Beat poets. Ginsberg works out of a tradition of exhortation and lament, Biblical in its orientation (despite the inversions of traditional good and evil), while Corso often becomes more of a clown than a seer, tending toward an "objective" presentation of the bare metaphysical facts that, more often that not, overwhelm man, Buster Keaton fashion.

Corso, much like his fellow New Yorker O'Hara, explores an urban wilderness, concentrating on social organization. Yet Corso's move to San Francisco signifies an important difference between the two poets. Corso, as is the case with other Beats, is usually in flight from something. Whereas O'Hara, in postmodern fashion, is more accepting of modern city life—and indeed delights in it—Corso remains more of an outsider. O'Hara, in *Selected Poems,* asks is his laconic and domestic manner, "Oh Jane, is there no more frontier?" (25) while Corso, an apocalyptic comedian, states his misgivings more forcibly in a poem from *Mindfield*:

> I am a great American
> I am almost nationalistic about it!
> I love America like a madness!
> But I am afraid to return to America
> I'm even afraid to go into the American Express—
>
> (144)

II. RICHARD HUGO: DEEP IMAGE SURREALIST

Richard Hugo, a native Westerner, has perhaps gone the furthest in terms of emphasizing the lonesome quality of the West, especially his own Northwest. This lonesomeness is a product of, and ever leads Hugo to, remote places.

Yet before turning to Hugo, I'd like to make a few brief comments on the work of Gary Snyder, often labeled a "Beat" as well as a nature poet, as a way of showing some of the connections and differences between Corso and Hugo.

In Snyder's poetry an attention to the natural order of the universe produces a contemplative approach to the world and leads, ultimately, to a reticence which has an effect quite similar to Corso's urban wildness. Although Corso employs a far wider range of tones than Snyder (Snyder is more transcendentalist than surrealist), both poets usually suppress the links in the chain, i.e., connecting and explanatory matter. The things themselves are permitted to speak for themselves which creates (at least the impression of) a more objective presentation, beyond personal anguish and lamentation. In *Standing Still and Walking in New York,* O'Hara was the first to point out the central "brevity" of Corso's work (83). However, in Snyder as in Hugo, the world is not so much the lunatic world Corso describes as a kind of ancient, pastoral dream world. Snyder's reticence—his unwillingness to level too much blame, his acceptance of the rule of nature, his willingness to let the old gods speak to our time—is all in keeping with the code of mystics and poets of both Asia and the United States.

In "Stafford Country" Hugo also points to an element of reticence in the American—especially western American—tradition:

> Where land is flat, words are far apart.
> Each word is seen, coming from far off,
> a calm storm almost familiar, across
> the plain. The word floats by, alive.
>
> (*SP,* 92)

This is indeed Stafford country; Hugo's own landscape is farther north, less open, darker, nearer to the sea. It is peopled by derelicts, seafarers, Indians, and common laborers, all of whom move, often courageously, within the ruins of their lives. Hugo is the Northwest's Russian poet, battling forces of the early dark and melancholy, though believing, finally, in the possibilities of dignity and transformation. Hugo's strong identification with the many-voiced world of common life produces a kind of ventriloquism, with Hugo speaking *for* the lost. In his poems one life leads, like a river, toward other waters; one word merges with another. Hugo seeks to subsume, within himself, the rise and fall and rise again of lives caught in the waves of a certain place and time. And these lives can do little more than talk about what has happened to them, or didn't happen, as in "Port Townsend":

> A novel fakes a start in every bar,
> gives way to gin and talk. The talk gives way
> to memories of elk, and elk was never here.
> Freighters never give this town a second look.
> The dead are buried as an afterthought
> and when the tide comes glittering with smelt
> the grebes have gone to look for meaty ports.
>
> (*SP*, 93)

Strangeness and unreality is central to Hugo's poetry, as if we are only passing through toward some unknown other side.

This unknown other side has been labeled, in our time, the "unconscious." In a discussion of the surrealist element in James Wright's poetry, James E. B. Breslin writes:

> Wright does not present the clean, hard-edge perception of physical surface that we get in much of imagism; instead, his images, carrying suggestions of invisible, magical realities beyond the literal world, seem to float up out of the unconscious at the moment when the boundaries between self and world are crossed. They are *deep* images.
>
> (194)

Like Wright, Hugo often fuses two disparate words or images, drawing from the "unconscious" a marriage of self and world. "The Blond Road" illustrates how Hugo's impressionistic and melancholy images and tones animate landscapes, until the landscape itself begins to speak for him. Hugo's ventriloquism is not only a product of the multiple personalities of the self, often released by the dark and drink, it is also an outgrowth of the multiple non-human presences of the self, often released when traveling along on an "empty" road.

> This road dips and climbs but never bends.
> The line it finally is strings far beyond
> my sight, still the color of useless dirt.
> Trees are a hundred greens in varying light
> as sky breaks black on silver over and in
> the sea. Not one home or car. No shacks

> abandoned to the storm. On one side,
> miles of high grass; on the other, weather
> and the sea reflecting tons of a wild day.
>
> (*SP*, 98)

In the following stanza Hugo makes a deft transition from "wild day" to "The wind is from Malay," but it is the sentence which follows that which really causes the twist or torque in our apprehension of the scene: "Tigers in the wind / makes lovers claw each other orange." From this point on the poem is inhabited by many varieties of 'wildlife'; there is a strange merging, a synergy of the great chain of being—although angels remain just outside the frame. Or they do until, perhaps, the last line of the poem, when "stone birds" go "climbing to their names" (in a dream unrealizable). Again I find Breslin's comments applicable:

> It is this distance between the two terms of his metaphors that has prompted many critics to describe Wright as surrealist; yet this label disguises the crucial fact that Wright's images (like Bly's) embody a vision that is closer to that of Walt Whitman than that of André Breton.
>
> (181)

Breslin finds a Whitmanesque natural harmony in Wright's use of images.

But while there is a leap of joy and lyrical transmutation in the last line of "The Blond Road"—both dear to surrealism—there is throughout an underlying grotesquery and sadness, which perhaps evokes a world more Naturalistic than harmonious. Rarely are crises in Hugo enlivened by a Kerouac-like humor, wild and joyful, digging the world. Hugo's sardonic humor grows out the black tangle of the thwarted lives and ruined landscape that held him in thrall—often to the point of confessional-like despair. In "The Art of Poetry," he writes:

>   And think,
> sad Raymond, of the wrong way maturation came.
> Wanting only those women you despised, imitating
> the voice of every man you envied. The slow walk
> home alone. Pause at the door. The screaming kitchen.
> And every day this window, loathing the real horizon.
>
> (*SP*, 272)

III. WILLIAM STAFFORD: SURREALIST IN THE AMERICAN GRAIN

William Stafford hails from Kansas. His poems employ a flatter, more common, clean-eyed diction than anyone mentioned so far: the Midwest is the language of prose. Yet Stafford's poems often display surrealist tendencies—his inclination for deep images and reticence transmuting common-voice materials.

Midwest poets, especially of so-called Iowa School, resist oratorical flourishes, preferring deep images to exclamations, cries, chants, etc. With Stafford, we have traveled a long way from the performance tendencies of Corso. But in Stafford's work a gentle, quiet near-surrealism emerges, derived from the earth and common life, although it is often confrontations with urban life which provoke the surrealist response. Stafford's work is akin to that of Stephen Crane, who is perhaps the first surrealist in the American grain. John Berryman wrote in *Stephen Crane*: "His work is wrung as clear (of the documentary burden') as Poe's or Hawthorne's; and unlike theirs his revolt did not drive him into fantasy or allegory. His eyes remained open on the world" (4). Stafford, like Crane, keeps his eyes on the "real" world, but he seems to also believe that realism is not equipped (or no longer equipped) to describe its affective colors and structures.

In Stafford's *Traveling Through the Dark* we can see this. The book reveals a clean yet impressionistic style we associate with midwesterners like Hemingway, Cather, and Weldon Kees, but at times the poems also verge on surrealism. In the famous title poem (*NCP* [*Stories That Could Be True: New and Collected Poems*], 61), for instance, a doe, carrying her unborn fawn, is found dead on the edge of a narrow road by a driver of a car. His headlights provide the only illumination, white and red, in the darkness; and the only sound is the "purr" of the "steady engine." It is a frozen, nearly silent scene—"she had stiffened already, almost cold"—although the doe is also warm because "her fawn lay waiting / alive, still, never to be born." The most audible presences in the poem are the ruminations of the speaker and the wilderness itself, which "listens" (the steady five-beat line which runs through most of the poem contributes to the sense that the wilderness is alive—pulsing). The speaker concludes the poem: "I thought hard for us all—my only swerving—, / then pushed her over the edge into the river." The word "swerve," repeated in the poem (in two forms), is central to the way a Stafford poem moves, i.e., by swerving away from a clearly seen object (the deer in the road) toward the apprehension of that object in the curve of space and light, as well as in one's own thoughts ("I stood in the glare of the warm exhaust turning red;"), until we once more see the object in relation to its swirling environment, and often, moving within the stream of the place's consciousness.

The activity of the poem—the movement of the speaker's mind through the dark—can be seen in the tonal shifts of the successive stanzas, four quatrains and a closing two-line verse unit. The first of these five stanzas details, in a matter of fact manner, the stark picture of the dead deer and speaker's thought that it "is usually best to roll them into the canyon." After dragging the doe off the road—stanza two ends with the detail that she "was large in the belly"—we discover in stanza three, as the speaker touches the side of the doe, that there is yet-to-be-born life within death. So the

mood of the poem is gently yet radically altered, as one's responsibility to human life—other cars that will be traveling through the dark—is coupled with one's responsibility to the unborn, "never to be born." The stanza ends: "Beside that mountain I hesitated."

In stanza four we have the juxtaposition of machine and wilderness, complicated by the animal "purr" of the motor and the human listening of the wilderness. In the final two-line stanza the speaker's thoughts "for us all," which is a kind of false "swerving" away from necessity as well as one's own solitariness, are dissolved in action, the doe and her fawn "pushed . . . over the edge into the river." This river of thought and action is, of course, the river of life and death, but more importantly it is the river of the poem itself, its process.

The impressionistic rendering of light and of movement with stasis in **"Traveling Through the Dark"** nicely dovetails into the opening lines of the book's second poem, **"In Medias Res."**

> On Main one night when they sounded the chimes
> my father was ahead in shadow, my son
> behind coming into the streetlight. . . .
>
> (*NCP*, 61)

The urban and historical details of this second poem, and their power to alter and distort vision, as well as the simple juxtaposition of the two poems, increases the sense that we are in world more surreal than realistic or impressionistic.

In the beginning of the poem we find ourselves in the midst of a family history, a "one-stride God." The chimes of death and heaven have sounded for the speaker's father and will sound for them all. A synesthesia of sound and light creates an otherworldly atmosphere; and each new line blends another family figure (or figures) into the celestial scene. At the end of the first stanza they are "all walkers in a cloud." But a significant shift in tone and imagery occurs in the second stanza, one that remakes the poem as a whole into a kaleidoscopic vision of betrayal:

> I saw pictures, windows taking shoppers
> where the city went, a great shield hammering out,
> my wife loving the stations on that shield
> and following into the shades calling back.
> I had not thought to know the hero quite so well.
> "Aeneas," I cried, "just man, defender!"
> And our town burned and burned.
>
> (*NCP*, 62)

In the brilliant image of the (store?) windows we have, once again, the characteristic surrealistic movement from impressionistic blending to leaping, curving, superimposed images which destroy individual compositions in favor of fiery juxtapositions of distantly related space-times and distantly related peoples. The "town" burns and burns in the light cast by the city. The contrast of natural town life and unnatural city life, a version of the conflict between open landscape and machine, is made clear (though rather indirectly).

However, in this poem we have little sense of Beat joy, noticeable in Kerouac, Corso, and to some degree in Snyder, or even the delicious northern melancholy of Theodore Roethke and Hugo. Stafford's is a quieter, more even-handed approach, and Charles Altieri, in *Self and sensibility,* commenting on Stafford's early poem **"Ceremony,"** is right when he warns of the limitations of such a modest and, for Altieri, controlled style:

> Naturalness in Stafford is so elaborately controlled, one wonders how any feelings not certified as "poetic" can flow on or how any humble self can swim such a river. The poem itself utterly lacks fluidity because we are never allowed to forget how each detail must perform the symbolic chore of preparing for the "surprising" visionary consummation.
>
> (3)

But even as far back as *Traveling Through the Dark,* and certainly after that time, Stafford's imagistic wit provides grounds for what Judith Kitchen, in response to Altieri, describes as Stafford's "intuitive sense of the rift between reality and language" (33). Stafford rarely calls attention to such a rift in a manner that might satisfy the dialectically-minded Altieri, but it is difficult to read Stafford very long without an awareness of slippage in both language and the poet's persona. The deep-image heritage of image and revelation is given the slip by this singularly elusive poet precisely because he, unlike Corso or Hugo, but like Whitman, is everywhere the same. At home everywhere (and yes, perhaps nowhere).

The third poem in *Traveling Through the Dark,* **"Elegy,"** opens with a witty, metaphysical, and mildly ironic image of common life: "The responsible sound of the lawnmower / puts a new under the afternoon" (*NCP,* 62). One might call this a surrealist image, but Stafford's repartee is often so gentle it has the effect of softening and undercutting the surrealist edge—yet this is just what frees up the poem from any sort of controlled, mannered, and/or heavily political tone (which *does* mar, as Altieri points out in *Enlarging the Temple,* some of Robert Bly's deep image work). Dislocation is neither unexpected nor memorialized in Stafford. He does not turn any certain place into an object-fetish, as (too oversimplify) O'Hara makes of New York, or Corso makes of the Beat world, or Hugo makes of lonely places. Nothing is particularly exotic to Stafford; all is part of an extended network.

"Elegy" continues the surrealistic, oneiric movement of the book as a whole:

> Remember in the Southwest going down the canyons?
> We turned off the engine, the tires went hoarse
> picking up sound out of turned away mountains;
> We felt the secret sky lean down.
>
> (*NCP,* 63)

The landscape of the west imbues this surrealism with something that goes beyond, I believe, traditional, and rather passive, appeals to the unconscious, or to the lyrical, or to some sort of dissociation of sensibility—or some "immanentist" revelation, which Altieri discounts as ahistorical. Landscape provides for the possibility of action in the objective world. The curving sounds and sights of the poem give us the feeling (best known from Westerns) that most anything could happen here, including revelation—"At the sight of angels or anything unusual / you are to mark the spot with a cross. . . ." (*NCP,* 63)—(although the "anything unusual" provides a characteristic Stafford disclaimer). Furthermore, the tableau of machine and landscape reminds us that, however static and scenic the description, new conjunctions of time and space have taken place. There is still an open road, and no matter what happens, or doesn't happen, Stafford is ready, and at home, living in the present. He writes in a late poem, **"The Dream of Now,"** from *Passwords*:

> When you wake to the dream of now
> from night and its other dream,
> you carry day out of the dark
> like a flame.
>
> When spring comes north, and flowers
> unfold from earth and its even sleep,
> you lift summer on with your breath
> lest it be lost ever so deep.
>
> Your life you live by the light you find
> and follow it on as well as you can,
> carrying through the darkness wherever you go
> your one little fire that will start again.
>
> (26)

Stafford is as one of the representative poets of the Information Age despite his being a product of the Depression and the late Industrial Age; and no doubt the ahistorical nature of the Information Age will inevitably leave a critic such as Altieri (and myself, for that matter) somewhat disappointed in the poetry of our time. Here it is perhaps enough to say that wilderness surrealism, especially as handled by Stafford, provides grounds for reorienting modern consciousness toward a connectedness between all peoples and places, and toward a poetics that is not so much personal as planetary.

Bibliography

Altieri, Charles. *Enlarging the Temple.* Lewisburg: Bucknell University Press, 1979.

————. *Self and sensibility in contemporary American poetry.* Cambridge: Cambridge University, 1984.

Berryman, John. *Stephen Crane.* New York: Farrar, Straus, Giroux, 1962.

Breslin, James E. B. *From Modern to Contemporary: American Poetry 1945-1965.* Chicago: University of Chicago Press, 1984.

Corso, Gregory. *Mindfield.* New York: Thunder's Mouth, 1989.

Eliot, T. S. *The Complete Poems and Plays.* London: Faber and Faber, 1969.

Ginsburg, Allen. *Howl.* San Francisco: City Lights, 1956.

Hugo, Richard. *Making Certain It Goes On: Collected Poems.* New York: W. W. Norton, 1984.

Kerouac, Jack. *The Dharma Bums.* New York: Viking, 1959.

Marvell, Andrew. *The Complete Poems.* Ed. Elizabeth Story Donno. Middlesex, England: Penguin, 1972.

O'Hara, Frank. *Selected Poems.* Ed. Donald Allen. New York: Random House, 1974.

————. *Standing Still and Walking in New York.* Bolinas, California: Grey Fox, 1975.

Van Ghent, Dorothy. "Comment." *A Casebook on the Beat.* Ed. Thomas Parkinson. New York: Thomas Y. Crowell, 1961.

Stafford, William. *The Darkness Around Us Is Deep: Selected Poems.* Ed. Robert Bly. New York: Harper and Row, 1993.

————. *Passwords.* New York: Harper and Row, 1991.

Judith Kitchen (essay date 1999)

SOURCE: Kitchen, Judith. "World Please Note: *Passwords,* Other Collections, *The Methow River Poems, The Way It Is.*" In *Writing the World: Understanding William Stafford,* pp. 87-100. Corvallis, Oreg.: Oregon State University Press, 1999.

[*In the following excerpt, Kitchen provides an overview of the poetry in Stafford's later collections from the 1990s.*]

PASSWORDS

Passwords, Stafford's ninth major collection, reveals a growing tension between opposing impulses toward the public and the private. The book opens with a series of "public" poems, many of them reflections on general

themes, most of them told as "stories" the poet has heard. One early poem, however, is a personal story. **"Reading with Little Sister: A Recollection"** demonstrates how the act of reading makes the reader enter the story. The poem unfolds as though the story were theirs:

> The stars have died overhead in their great cold.
> Beneath us the sled whispers along. Back there
> our mother is gone. They tell us, "If you hold on
> the dogs will take you home." And they tell us never
> to cry. We'll die too, they say, if we
> are ever afraid. All night we hold on.
> The stars go down. We are never afraid.[1]

Stafford's revisions of this poem are recorded in the videotape, "The Life of the Poem," filmed by Michael Markee and Vincent Wixon. On the tape, its changing form is recorded, showing a gradual realignment of the basic sentences. The result is a kind of geographical location within the poem—overhead, beneath, back there—until the reader is centered on the sled, in the middle of the poem's emotional geography. Once again, the familiar "chimes" of sound carry the motion of the poem from "overhead/sled" through "cry/die" to "gone/on/down." And again, the ending is enigmatic, flies in the face of readerly experience by boasting that "we are never afraid" (what Stafford termed a kind of "nervous vaunting"). The title, however, suggests that they may be learning courage not through braggadocio, but through the imaginative act of reading.

"The Day Millicent Found the World" follows a girl into the forest until she becomes lost: "She had achieved a mysterious world / where any direction would yield only surprise" (9, *233*). This is the state of the poet as he enters the poem, and to learn to lose yourself in the larger world is the ultimate goal. "That time she returned," but the poem hints that there will be a time when she simply becomes a part of the unknown.

The final poem of the first section, **"An Archival Print,"** asks the reader to imagine that God "snaps your picture." As Stafford cautions the reader—"don't look away"—his observation becomes intensely personal: he's speaking outward, but he's making a private discovery at the same time. Stafford exposes the "self" here as a "partial disguise you call your character" (20, *236*). There are influences and reasons behind what we are, he suggests, but

> The camera, wide open
> stands ready; the exposure is thirty-five years
> or so—after that you have become
> whatever the veneer is, all the way through.

The second section contains an important new poem. **"The Summer We Didn't Die"** speaks of a collective experience ("we played out there in the cottonwood") but is, perhaps, the most private of poems. Remembering a specific time in his past—"that year, that summer, that vacation"—Stafford recreates the emotions of the children climbing out on fragile limbs above adults who call them back in fear. A variation of a villanelle, **"The Summer We Didn't Die,"** ends with the repeated phrase: "We were young. We had to be brave" (30). The title, however, adds hindsight; reader and poet alike face the dangerous implication that bravery is not always sufficient.

Throughout the book, a complex of words and phrases reveals a new thematic element for Stafford. "Scarier," "afraid," "never afraid," "scared," "brave," "fears," "shivers," "afraid even now"—the words occur in that order, leading inevitably to one of the later poems and the phrase "if you survive." This hints at a temporal urgency in *Passwords*; its "moment" (or time sense) contains an instance of personal loss and the various fears that surround such a loss. If Stafford seemed to come to terms with death in his two previous books (*A Glass Face in the Rain* and *An Oregon Message*), *Passwords* demonstrates otherwise. Stafford's oldest son, Bret, had recently died. The fourth section, entitled **"Elegies,"** explores private grief by attempting to give it a larger and more universal context. **"For a Lost Child"** tries to fuse loss with the abstraction of time, but fails: "You are a memory / too strong to leave this world that slips away / even as its precious time goes on" (60, *244*).

The section's title is in the plural—and Stafford mourns many other losses, along with that of his son. The sequence mirrors the process of grieving; just when the poems seem to have found a resolution, Stafford undermines them with doubt or fresh pain. Such titles as **"Going On," "Consolations," "Security," "Rescue,"** and **"Yes"** imply a way to deal with loss. Many of the poems end with phrases such as "go on" or "let go", but often the poems do not let go, rather, they fly in the face of their titles, piling doubt upon doubt. **"Going On"** looks hard at the evidence of his son's death: "Then, the stillest / way a hand can be and still be, / it lies there in mine" (61). The final stanza seems, on the surface, to have found a degree of acceptance:

> Easy world, you gave it once—
> please quietly welcome it back,
> that hand.

But the word "easy" betrays an underlying skepticism. There is nothing easy about the world or death as Stafford represents them. Both require a kind of inward attentiveness. A sense of mortality drives the poet to examine the self as when **"Your Life"** takes a long look (in the second person) at the idea of death where you will be "more real, more true, at the last" (70, *247*). Stafford says, "You learn what you are, but slowly,"

and then, in a line that certainly includes himself, he discovers "a self often shattered"—a self that is essentially effaced in the glass, become no more than its past.

Stafford may have failed to conquer fear or accept death, but *Passwords* culminates with a powerful final section, **"Vita."** Here, in thirteen pieces clearly dominated by the first-person singular, he retraces his life, touching on old themes and finding once more the source of his poetry—and possibly his "self." **"What's in My Journal"** is especially telling for it lists several things that matter to him but also includes such items as "clues that lead nowhere" and "deliberate obfuscation, the kind / that takes genius" (75, *248*).

Central to this section is a significant poem. **"Life Work"** is reminiscent of Stafford's most famous poem, **"Traveling Through the Dark,"** but whereas in the earlier poem the speaker had to confront the harsh reality of animal life and death before traveling on, in **"Life Work"** he is more closely identified with the physical self and, by extension, with death. As in his earlier poem, Stafford calls up a specific time and place:

> Even now in my hands the feel of the shovel comes
>   back,
> the shock of gravel or sand. Sun-scorch on my
>   shoulders
> bears down. The boss is walking around barking.
> All the cement mixers rattle and jolt.
>
> That day the trench we are digging goes deeper
> and deeper, over my head; then the earth heaves
> in one giant coffin gulp. They keep
> digging and pulling and haul me out still breathing.
>
> The sky, right there, was a precious cobalt dome
> so near it pressed on my face. Beside me my hands
> lay twitching and begging at the end of my arms.
> Nothing is far anymore, after that trench, the
>   stones. . . .
>
> Oh near, and blessing again and again: my breath.
> And the sky, and steady against my back, the earth.
>
>   (80, *250*)

The recounted accident allows him to experience his body in a new relationship to earth and sky: "Nothing is far anymore." This is not the willed mobility of **"Traveling Through the Dark,"** where the speaker goes on with his life in the face of nature, but a stasis, an almost mystical acceptance of the interrelationship of life and death. In the final couplet, this acceptance is seen as a blessing which contains a kind of rehearsal for death. But the poem is called **"Life Work."** He has been revived, brought up from within the ground to lie flat on it—and earth's the right place for love, though he'd never go so far as to say that.

"Life Work" is more formal than many of Stafford's poems, looking, on the page, more like one by Frost.

Fourteen lines here almost equals a sonnet. And the alternating slant rhymes (back/barking, shoulders/jolt, deeper/keep, heaves/breathing, etc.) both cement the form and disrupt its expectations. The closest rhymes are found in the couplet (breath/earth), fusing the two so that they are virtually inseparable.

If there is one word that dominates this collection, it is "breath." Everything breathes—breezes, early morning, mountains. Words or thoughts go "on your breath out into the dark." Even the land was "invented by breath." Finally, death itself is imagined as a universal "breath" saying the names of his children. But breathing is both physical and individualized. Thus **"The Size of a Fist"** links survival to the heartbeat that pumps steadily through the lines, taking the man from infancy through schoolyard fights to work and family—and finally to old age ("who is this old guy?"): "beat, beat, engine cruising, day, night, / beat and away" (86, 252).

For all his public invitation, Stafford has remained intensely private. Though his poems embrace the reader, what greets us is not so much the man as the reflection he wants us to see. Reconciled briefly, the public and private coexist in the final poem **"Vita."** Stafford makes a distinction between *the* life and *a* life:

> God guided my hand
> and it wrote,
> "Forget my name."
>
> World, please note—
> a life went by, just
> a life, no claims,
>
> A stutter in the millions
> of stars that pass,
> a voice that lulled—
>
> A glance
> and a world
> and a hand.
>
> (88, 252)

But where can the world take note, if not in the poems themselves? With supreme economy, the final stanza moves from individual vision outward and then back again to Stafford's recognizably symbolic gesture.

If his essential disguise (the one his character has hardened into) had been the "universal" self of the earlier poems, perhaps this book's new tension came from a burgeoning need to assert (and share?) the private self. Each of Stafford's books brought with it subtle shifts in perspective; now *Passwords* threatened to crack the "veneer" of the created self and release an even more powerful voice.

OTHER COLLECTIONS, *THE METHOW RIVER POEMS*

In 1992, Confluence Press collected the poems from five previous chapbooks and published them under the title *My Name Is William Tell,* which subsequently won the 1992 Western States Book Award in Poetry. In citing Stafford's work, the judges stated:

> His way of writing and of offering his work stands in silent rebuke to all that is loud, strident, assertive and shallow. Yet close readers of Stafford's poetry know that there is a wildness at its center, by turns as gentle or tough as an undomesticated animal in an indifferent wilderness. He of course, presents his poems and himself as if they should be taken for granted. We would like to say on this occasion that we do not.[2]

This statement may be, in some measure, a response to Stafford's own somewhat defensive prose statement at the beginning of the book. Clearly smarting at some remarks that had classified him as a "regional" poet, he begins: "Being tagged a regional artist doesn't hurt much" (xiii). He goes on to say that art itself is regional, that it takes a kind of "sniffing along," that the artist can't look up to find a critic's approval or to discern the public's taste. The trail is "one-person wide." The artist is individual.

In a paper delivered at the Flint Hills Literary Festival in 1997, Stan Sanvel Rubin noted the "hurdles" of the front matter in Stafford's later books. In place of Stafford's usual gestures of greeting, Rubin found what he termed a "strategy of exclusion." Looking at **"You, Reader,"** the final poem in the book (the last full-length book to be published while Stafford was alive), Rubin notes the challenging tone—"the land rolls out its own / magnificence, and you inherit whatever your eyes / can prove by their glance that they're worthy of" (74)—and its concomitant question:

> Stafford was a habitual walker, but considering his method of composition in a state of physical stasis, the dynamic picture here raises a further question: is the reader in fact meant to be a companion—*sharing* the poet's journey by retracing the metaphoric "route" he already has taken towards inspiration—or is the poet metaphorically sending the reader away, abolishing the reader, so that he will remain in possession of (and possessed by) his own "world"?[3]

He goes on to compare Stafford's final stanza with Whitman's gesture of leave-taking at the end of "Song of Myself." Where Whitman says, "I stop some where waiting for you," Stafford commands, "Now, go back and begin again." The figure of the poet is decidedly different in each case. Stafford seems to have reversed not only the place of the poet, but the place of the reader. Whether this is a dismissive gesture or one that hands the reader more responsibility could be debated.

In 1996, three years after Stafford's death, a similar collection, **Even in Quiet Places,** was published by Confluence Press. This book also collects poems previously published only in chapbooks and has an extensive afterword by the poet's son Kim. It, too, contains an opening prose statement by the poet, but this statement, entitled "Another Language,"[4] is less defensive than in the previous collection. Defining the new language as one that "courteously gives credit to the needs but also to the dignity of the person addressed," as a language that refuses to distort or become self-serving, Stafford makes a quiet declaration of independence for "freedom in speech."

The opening poem, **"Deep Light,"** reiterates the veiled challenge of the final poem in *My Name is William Tell* by suggesting that there are some people who, if they are not unworthy, are at least unaware, and therefore may not be able to enter the "far place" of the poem. The faint light hovering out there in the "deep night" is all the imaginative person will need:

> From far a light, maybe a hill ranch
> remote and unvisited, beams on the horizon
> when we pass; then it is gone.
> For the rest of our lives that far place
> waits; it's an increment, one more
> hollow that slips by out there, almost
> a gift, an acquaintance taken away.
>
> Still, beyond all ranches the deep
> night waits, breathing when we breathe,
> always ready to offer new light,
> over and over, so long as we search
> for something so faint most people
> won't know, even when it is found.
>
> (4)

Here Stafford deliberately equates the "dark" with the "deep." The pronoun is plural—*we*; the poem speaks *for* as well as *to* us. There is a kind of linguistic transformation; the night of the poem becomes the light of the title. The darkness remains wholly outside, yet it breathes when we breathe. It contains new light, available to those capable of recognizing it, those who can participate in the dream. By now, the farm light has become another recurring image, but here it takes on the added dimension of something new.

The attitude in **"Deep Light"** is perhaps more skeptical than is usually associated with Stafford. Darker, less hopeful than Frost's great poem, "Directive," **"Deep Light"** echoes its speculative emphasis on a lost place, a chosen recipient who must by definition be "lost enough to find yourself."[5] Frost's quest for an attainable grail becomes, for Stafford, a continuous search. In Frost, the cup is hidden so the "wrong ones" won't find it. In Stafford's view, they probably wouldn't recognize it if they did. Stafford does not offer Frost's optimistic possibility of drinking and becoming whole "beyond confusion"—he simply asserts that these faint lights do exist, deep and ineffable, one more "far place" within the breathing night.

Even in Quiet Places also contains a few poems that allude—somewhat obliquely—to the Gulf War. Stafford's pacifism is inherent in the poems—"Play like you had a war. Hardly anyone / got killed except thousands of the enemy" (**"Pretend You Live in a Room,"** 42) and "Back of history, leading afar / when the armies marched / on the heads of the people, / was there a way too fine / for the blundering stumbling multitude?" (**"Browser,"** 85)—but he refuses to make the specific war the point of the poem; instead he reminds the reader that overhead the stars keep telling their stories, that this is only one small piece of history in a longer history of violence that is "loose again."

The book culminates with a sequence of nineteen poems, called *The Methow River Poems,* written over a fairly brief period of time at the request of two forest rangers who wanted poetry road signs to place along a hundred-mile stretch along the Methow River. Six of these poems, along with **"Ask Me,"** have since been etched and mounted along the roadway. The only truly distinguished poem in this series is **"Ask Me"** which had, by that time, become recognized as one of Stafford's most important poems. The rest have a conversational tone, seem less formal and more relaxed than most of his other poems, either digress or else end abruptly. In the "Afterword," Kim Stafford describes them:

> Some poems seem quickly made, hit or miss, almost random things, but with deft nuggets of insight. I think of Edward Weston's last photograph, that image of scattered rocks and sand at Point Lobos, a kind of reduction of universal spin to the elements of its original making. . . . I think also here of Joan Miro's late paintings from Majorca, the large, open canvases with a few bold strokes.
>
> (111)

The first of this sequence, **"Being a Person,"** speaks directly to anyone who might stand by the river. "Be a person here," it urges. The idea of the shared dream is made explicit. If you listen hard enough, everything will converge: "Suddenly this dream you are having matches / everyone's dream, and the result is the world" (89). Stafford wants to embrace a unified country, a democratic place where all dreams converge to one dream. This desire is recapitulated in **"Is This Feeling About the West Real?"** where the speaker moves from a particularly regional outlook (where people know they live in a hemisphere beyond what Columbus discovered) to a more inclusive view of history. You can deny this world, the poem implies, but what happens outside—"whole mountain ranges, history, the holocaust, / sainthood, Crazy Horse" (93, *176*)—demands your attention. There is an "other world" and the individual who can discover that place will have a vision to bring back to this one.

Perhaps the oddest of this sequence is **"Emily, This Place, and You."** The poem recounts how a woman named Emily got out of the car one day to watch the snow fill up the world. "It was quiet, you know" (101, *35*). The reader, too, can remember this place, "just being part of things, getting used to being a person, / taking it easy, you know." Often spoken informally to the reader, often referring to a specific place or sound or animal or tree in the immediate setting, the *Methow River Poems* focus on the world even as they seem to let it go. They hold the reader to the particulars of the landscape even as they demand the reader's attention with a series of informal instructions: "Nobody cares if you stop here"; "How you stand here is important"; "Please think about this as you go on"; "Hey, let's hurry down and forget this." At the same time, with all their enigmatic power, they proclaim a kind of poetic independence: "You see, there is something / beyond music"; "Stand here till all that / you were can wander away and come back slowly"; "What the river says, that is what I say." If these poems are regional, they are regional in its best sense; they speak of the place itself and of the interior space it generates. They embody every contradictory impulse Stafford ever felt—public and private, dark and light, physical and spiritual—and reconcile those impulses; the sound of the water becomes the sound of the poem. In this particular project, Stafford was able to realize a longstanding dream: "Instead of having all the effects of the poem be recognized while I'm there, I would like them just to linger after I'm gone, and no one needs to know what happened."[6]

THE WAY IT IS

In 1998, Graywolf Press published Stafford's new and selected poems in a collection entitled *The Way It Is*—a title taken directly from one of Stafford's late poems, but echoing the ending of **"Bi-Focal"** where the world legends itself "deep, the way it is." The book itself is comprehensive, including all of Stafford's most significant poems and a number of representative poems from each stage of his career. The poems were selected by Kim Stafford, with help from the staff of the William Stafford archives as well as poets and critics across the country. The book opens with two sections of "new" poems—a selection entitled **"Sometimes I Breathe"** (written in 1992) from a book manuscript intended for publication, and one called **"There's a Thread You Follow,"** written between January 1993 and his death in August.

These opening sections contain seventy-one poems and together they exhibit the same uneven quality seen in almost all of Stafford's books. Elegant and complex poems are accompanied by ones that feel slight in comparison; one might call this a lack of quality control, but this time it was not the poet himself who made the selections. This leads to the conclusion that Stafford's way of writing produced so many ideas, not all of which came to aesthetic fruition, that it is nearly impossible to create a tightly structured book. The strong poems that follow these sections further confirm this: they make a strong statement about the importance of Stafford's vision through careful selection of the best from over three thousand published poems.

There are few surprises in the new poems. They fit rather comfortably into the overall oeuvre—a combination of memories, observations, pithy statements, and tentative meanderings. Interestingly, many return to early themes. **"Clash"** revives the dormant duality of father and mother, unexpectedly rhyming the first and third lines of each four-line stanza, thus creating a "clash" of its own. The penultimate stanza steps back to take another look at the speaker's relationship with his mother:

> I won before too late,
> *and—adult before she died—*
> I had traveled from love to hate,
> and partway back again.[7]

The ending of the prose poem, **"Something That Happens Right Now,"** reiterates the visionary concept of death found at the end of **"The Farm on the Great Plains"**:

> Then my feet would come loose from Earth and rise by the power of longing. I wouldn't let the others know about this, but I would be everywhere, as I am right now, a thin tone like the wind, a sip of blue light—no source, no end, no horizon.
>
> (8)

Nor had Stafford changed his attitude toward war, but the overtly antiwar poems are more strident, almost accusatory. **"Right to Die"** sets the tone: "God takes care of it for / everyone, once. And armies / figure it out, wholesale, / for others, in the air, on the ground, / at sea" (*12*). It is hard not to read the specificities of the Gulf War into some of the explicit contemporary allusions. **"Entering History"** ends with just such a note:

> Where was your money when the tanks
> grumbled past? Which bombs did you buy
> for the death rain that fell? Which year's
> taxes put that fire to the town
> where the screaming began?
>
> (10)

One noticeable change, however, is the open naming of Bret, Stafford's oldest son who had committed suicide. In *Passwords*, Stafford had relegated poems about his death to the category of "elegy" and had softened any specific references to generality. With the distance of time, he was able to come closer to the event. Written in 1992, **"Third Street"** looks back to a time when the poet had been ill as a child, thinking he might die. He remembers his father's look. Time is conflated as he concludes: "Years later my son will die and that look / will return. Something will break in the sky that was welded / and forged back home by a thousand pledges of truth" (5). His steady world was shaken. **"A Memorial: Son Bret"** begins "In the way you went you were important" (16) and then reveals regret over what they would not experience together. Still, the poem ends with a question—"remember?"—tying father and son to a time and a place they had shared. More disturbing is **"Crossing Our Campground"** where the opening ("Part of the time when I move it's for / Bret") is tinged with an implied reproach:

> This is for you, Bret, I think; this
> is the way an old man walks who still
> stays vigorous and strong, firm, alert,
> holding on through the years for you—
>
> The kind of old man you could be,
>   or could have been.
>
> (37)

Although he had used his mother and father as symbolic dualities, with rare exceptions Stafford had not written so specifically about his immediate family. **"Retirement"** suggests that when the children have left, the rest of life is like driving into a snowstorm, "the soft / careful sound of little worlds falling" (28). For young readers who might not understand this sensation, the speaker states, "there will be time."

A large percentage of the new poems hark back to the beginnings—the farm on the great plains with its expanse of sky. These are the most fully realized of the late poems, often orchestrated in regular stanzas and emphasizing a web of sound. **"Haycutters"** invokes an almost idyllic (though not perfected) past. **"One Evening"** stills the remembered moment, almost like the "frozen pond a mile north of Liberal," where sixty years ago he skated "wild circles." The final stanza is urgent with longing:

> I would go home, confront all my years, the tangled
>   events to come, and never know more than I did
>   that evening waving my arms in the lemon-colored
>   light.
>
> (11)

"Living on the Plains" also resurrects a specific time and place—"If you come back years later your name / will be there carved on the windowsill / in the hayloft"—even as it also connects us to the American mythology—"If you ever climb the map again / you could stop there and whisper a few hymns, / the ones that civilized Dodge, Cody, Abilene" (41).

"Slow News from Our Place," catches up several of Stafford's abiding themes, creating an informal summa-

tion. Speaking directly to some of the influential American poets who had preceded him, he weighs their words in contrast to the permanence of the land:

> It isn't that the blossoms fall, Ezra.
> It isn't that certain vagueness, Wallace.
> It isn't even how those flies buzz,
> either, Emily. It's only the plains
> out here, how they take it all and wait,
> morning, evening, night, forever;
> how they don't move, no matter what
> Galileo says, or The Church, or God himself.
>
> We stand on the ground, out here. Go ahead, speakers;
> tell us your theories, your judgments, the latest assess-
>   ments
> from the centers of power, any styles or truths you
>   like.
> We're out by The Platte, The Missouri,
> The Smoky Hill. We're quiet on this slow scanner
> The Earth, under its arch of sky.
> Go ahead. Tell us. We're listening.
>
> (34)

Inclusive (written in first person plural), but highly individualized in its particularities, the poem is strikingly full of doubt and defiance. Underneath its surface is a core of darkness. What does poetry mean in the vastness of forever? The answer, the poem suggests, is not to be found in theories, judgments, science, or religion, but in the active act of listening, of being receptive to whatever the world wants to tell us under its wide arch of sky. The late poems come full circle, back to their origins; to quote a line from Frost's "West-Running Brook," they are the "current paying tribute to the source."

Notes

1. William Stafford, *Passwords* (New York: Harper, 1991), 7. Page numbers of quotations from this volume are noted parenthetically. Also in *The Way It Is*, 233. Italic page numbers indicate poems found in *The Way It Is*. Revisions of the poem are reprinted in *Crossing Unmarked Snow* (Ann Arbor: University of Michigan Press, 1998), 36-37.

2. Stafford, *My Name is William Tell* (Lewiston, ID: Confluence Press, 1992). Page numbers of quoted material from this volume appear in parentheses. Reprinted in *On William Stafford: The Worth of Local Things*, edited by Tom Andrews (Ann Arbor: University of Michigan Press, 1993), 271.

3. Stan Sanvel Rubin, "A Trail 'One Person Wide'," Flint Hills Literary Festival, Kansas State University, 1997.

4. Stafford, *Even in Quiet Places* (Lewiston, ID: Confluence Press, 1996), 3. Page numbers of quoted material from this volume are listed in parentheses. Italic page numbers indicate poems found in *The Way It Is*.

5. Robert Frost, *The Poetry of Robert Frost: The Collected Poems, Complete and Unabridged,* edited by Edward Connery Lathem (NY: Henry Holt and Company, Owl Books Edition, 1979), 377-79.

6. Stan Sanvel Rubin and Judith Kitchen, "A Conversation with William Stafford," SUNY Brockport, 22 March 1988.

7. William Stafford, *The Way It Is* (St. Paul: Graywolf, 1998), 8-9. Page numbers of quotations from this volume are noted parenthetically.

Bibliography

WORKS BY WILLIAM STAFFORD

POETRY

Traveling through the Dark. New York: Harper & Row, 1962. Reprinted by Weatherlight Press, Bristol, England, 1997.

Passwords. Seattle: Sea Pen Press, 1980.

A Glass Face in the Rain: New Poems. New York: Harper & Row, 1982. London: Harper & Row, 1985.

An Oregon Message. New York: Harper & Row, 1987.

The Methow River Poems. Lewiston, ID: Confluence Press, 1995.

Even In Quiet Places. Lewiston, ID: Confluence Press, 1996.

The Way It Is: New and Selected Poems. Introduction by Naomi Shihab Nye. St. Paul, MN: Graywolf Press, 1998.

PROSE

Crossing Unmarked Snow: Further Views on the Writer's Vocation, edited by Paul Merchant and Vincent Wixon. Ann Arbor: University of Michigan Press, 1998.

VIDEOTAPES

William Stafford: The Life of the Poem. A video by Vincent Wixon and Michael Markee, TTTD Productions, Ashland, OR. 29 min.

BOOKS

Andrews, Tom. *On William Stafford: The Worth of Local Things.* Ann Arbor: The University of Michigan Press, 1993.

Sally Bishop Shigley (essay date fall 2000)

SOURCE: Shigley, Sally Bishop. "Pax Femina: Women in William Stafford's West." *Rocky Mountain Review* 54, no. 2 (fall 2000): 77-84.

[*In the following essay, Shigley examines Stafford's ambivalent treatment of women in his poetry.*]

In **"Things That Come,"** a poem in *A Glass Face in the Rain,* William Stafford's speaker questions a critic: "You think that my poems are soft? That there isn't a wolf in them? Listen." In these brief lines, Stafford provides a synecdoche for an interesting problem in his poetry: a problem, that is, for the reader sympathetic to the concerns of women. Lacking the political, experimental edginess of many of his post-modernist contemporaries and confessing openly in print that trust in one's poetic voice is more important than rigorous poetic discipline, Stafford was often viewed by critics and colleagues as a soft, perhaps minor, poetic voice. This sense is compounded by other traditionally feminine archetypes that Stafford embraces. His pacifism as a conscientious objector in World War II, his ambivalence about the effects of technology and industrialism on the earth, his environmentalism, and his tender concern for his children combine to form an image that a contemporary cultural feminist would feel very much at home with. Yet Stafford's creation of women characters and voices is troubling. Having accessed his so-called feminine side in his politics, Stafford demonstrates great ambivalence when dealing poetically with women. The women who populate Stafford's poems are very limited, one-dimensional figures: fearful, pathologically timid mothers; slow, promiscuous or otherwise impaired romantic teens; or small-town sirens whose soft voices linger liquidly in the memories of male speakers. In all cases, Stafford's personae use the female figure to cathect or catalyze the anger of the male speaker or to illustrate the kindness and virtue of the speaker to the less fortunate woman. Stafford's defensive insistence on the existence of the wild "wolf" in his poetry is a symbol of how Stafford's so-called feminine sensibilities about nature and culture are embedded with a personal ambivalence about women. Stafford's speakers insist on *man's* peaceful coexistence with his fellow *men* and with nature, but cannot seem to make peace with the women around them.

Although a modern psychoanalytic critic might go spelunking in the dark recesses of Stafford's psychosexual past to find clues to this paradox, the answer lies in a much more boundaried geographical terrain. From his first book *Down in My Heart* (1947), a series of poignant vignettes of his life in a camp for conscientious objectors to World War II, through his last book, Stafford thoughtfully interrogates an American man's relationship with the land, God, and family, as well as with development, violence, and technology, very often speaking specifically about the Rockies and the Pacific Northwest. Using the West as a backdrop, Stafford skillfully embraces the troubling binaries of the twentieth century and reminds us that the grey areas show the most promise for resolving these seemingly black and white dilemmas. In this respect, Stafford is what Jane Tompkins would consider a classic Western man. In her book *West of Everything,* Tompkins describes the Western man as one who strives to

> depict a world of clear alternatives—independence vs. connection, anarchy vs. law, town vs. desert—but [he is] just as compulsively driven to destroy these opposites and make them contain one another.

(48)

Aided by what biographical critic Judith Kitchen calls a high "sense of moral and spiritual responsibility" (3), Stafford is an environmentalist, a pacifist, and a believer in free and democratic communication. He is tolerant of the failings of himself and others as poets, and an exuberant and patient coach to beginning writers. So why does he seem uninterested in or unwilling to investigate one of the most obvious questions facing the liberal modern thinker of either gender: the sometimes difficult relationship between men and women? Stafford is not anti-female or anti-feminist by any means, yet his general yearning to close the gaps between men and wilderness, men and their fathers, men and their history, and men and technology does not seem to extend specifically to the gap between men and women.

Feminist critic Nina Baym ("Melodramas of Beset Manhood") suggests that one of the primary paradoxes facing male American writers, especially writers of the West, is the dual role in which they cast the female sensibility: on the one hand, women are associated with the hearth and the stultifying effects of society that men are escaping West to avoid, while on the other women are allegorically associated with the beckoning virgin land that these men are journeying toward (75). Women are either bossy mothers or seductive, passive virgins awaiting the cultivation of the Adamic explorer. Speaking specifically of the Western as film, Tompkins enlarges on this point. She suggests:

> There are two choices [for the Western man]: either you can remain in the world of illusions, by which is understood religion, culture, and class distinctions, a world of fancy words and pretty actions, of "manners for the parlor" . . . or you can face life as it really is—blood, death, a cold wind blowing, and a gun in the hand.

(48)

The interior, fussy female space that limits by its trivial, constructed rules or the law of the gunfight: these are the only alternatives within this genre, which is not surprising considering the obviously mythic quality of Westerns. Yet despite his otherwise progressive, liberal, environmentalist philosophy, Stafford seems caught in the same kind of dilemma.

This is nowhere more evident than in the poems in which he actually discusses mothers and their relationship with their children. Writing about Stafford's early life, Kitchen suggests that Stafford derived his personal sense of justice from his father and his sense of fairness from his mother (4), a statement that falls along fairly traditional gender and cultural stereotypes. Yet the mothers in Stafford's poetry would suggest something different. In his first book, *West of Your City* (1960),[1] mothers are conspicuous by their absence. There are several fathers in this book but no mothers. **"Circle of Breath"** details the speaker's despondency at the death of his wise father. The speaker recalls a childhood lesson in which the father took him off into a dark field to show him that calm was possible even when alone in the dark if he had a good sense of himself and where he belonged. **"A Visit Home"** expresses a similar nostalgia as the speaker hopes to capture the security of youth by buying a hat and wearing it "as my father did. / At the corner of Central and Main." The poem **"Listening"** associates the father again with wisdom, this time adding prescience as the father hears more "from the soft wild night / than came to our porch for us on the wind." These fathers are wise and strong and almost mythic Western men, seeing and hearing and knowing things that the young speakers cannot.

The first image we have of a mother paints a very different picture. In the poem **"In Fear and Valor"** from *Traveling Through the Dark* (1962), the speaker tells us "My mother was afraid / and in my life her fear has hid." While the speaker resists this fear with images of wildness and strength associated with the previous poetic fathers, the mother is "vanquished and trembling" and "cringes." Even more insidious, the mother has "claimed a place in my every limb," handicapping the speaker with fear that he will spend his life trying to overcome. **"Vocation,"** from the same book, makes the speaker's dilemma even more explicit as the father shows the family a path westward, "a groove in the grass" that represents the Oregon Trail, while the mother "called us back to the car: / she was afraid; she always blamed the place, / the time, anything my father planned." The speaker in this poem is literally standing between his parents, "both of them a part of me," while his mother tries to hold him back with her fear and the father wisely points out a path and intones, "Your job is to find what the world is trying to be."

This pattern of weak, emotionally crippled mothers and wise and wild fathers, a trend noted by critic David Carpenter, continues in subsequent books. **"Vacation Trip,"** from the significantly titled *Allegiances* (1970), tells us "the loudest sound in our car / was Mother being glum." Her sullenness is associated metaphorically with the sound of the "chiding valves" in the car, the "deep chaos" of the internal combustion engine, and the huge, metaphoric trailing balloon slowing the car's progress, filled with the words "I wish I hadn't come." The mother's sullenness is deeply embedded, literally a part of the engine that moves, or in this case impedes the family. From the book *A Glass Face in the Rain* (1982) come even more didactic statements. **"Our Kind"** tells us "Our mother knew our worth—/ not much. To her success / was not being noticed at all." Again, the focus on withdrawal and creating obstacles is associated with the mother. This is amplified in the ironically titled **"My Mother Was A Soldier"**: "'No harm in being quiet' / my mother said: 'that's the sound that finally wins.'" The anxiety of the earlier poems, it seems, has produced a sort of agoraphobia in which safety is associated with staying home and silent. If you are not out in the world and you never speak, nothing can threaten or harm you. Yet the word "wins" implies a subversive, passive-aggressive power in all of this insular silence.

An Oregon Message (1987) attempts to make an uneasy peace with the mother figure, but the speaker's ambivalence wins out. **"A Memorial for My Mother"** connects the speaker with the mother directly as the speaker returns home at his mother's death and says,

> We knew if they knew our hearts they would blame.
> We knew we deserved nothing. I go along
> now being no one, and remembering this—
> how alien we were from others, how hard we chewed
> on our town's tough rind. How we loved its flavor.

The "we" in this poem represents the speaker's bonding with the mother figure in their common lack of self-esteem, their fear of discovery and censure. They are tenuously connected in their mutual sense of alienation and their greedy consumption of the social scraps flung at them by an unsympathetic town, but this is an ambivalent connection at best. The speaker wants to make peace with the memory, but the mother's legacy of fear and insecurity intrudes. This is magnified by the other two poems in this volume that deal directly with mothers. **"Mother's Day"** presents two small children who pick out a hideous candy jar as a gift for their mother. It stands for them on a table as a symbol of their love for her, which seems an uncharacteristically positive treatment of the mother by Stafford, at least until the poem's ending.

> Now Peg says, "Remember that candy jar?"
> She smooths the silver. "Mother
> hated it." I am left standing
> Alone by the counter, ready to buy what
> will hold Mother by its magic, so
> she will never be mad at us again.

This sad childhood memory of the mother's lack of "motherly" appreciation obviates the uneasy truce the speaker attempts in the earlier poem. Construction paper turkeys, hand-prints in clay, or even adult extravagances have no power to mollify the mother's slow-burning anger. This sense of maternal doom is cemented in **"My Mother Said,"** in which the mother is metaphorically associated with a miner's canary who willfully "withholds its song," sending the miners to stumble and crawl their way to safety. Only a small leap is required to see the scrambling miners as the children, young and old, in the previous poem, crawling and scraping to try to break the sullen silence of the perpetually disappointed mother. In the symbolic universe of this poem, motherly love and attention is like oxygen to the children buried alive by the mother's indifference.

The non-maternal women in Stafford's poetry don't receive the unsympathetic treatment that the mothers do, but they are similarly limited. The young women in Stafford's canon are either slow, pitiable girls that the speakers treat with a sort of pathetic nostalgia, or friendly, sensual idols that the speakers remember with palpable erotic nostalgia. **"Thinking for Berky"** from *Traveling Through the Dark* presents us with Berky, a character from the pitiable category, a girl whose poverty and cruel parents kept her "looking out / for the rescue that—surely, some day—would have to come." Associated with crises and sirens and disaster, Berky, in the speaker's mind, is doomed. She is ominously unfocused, untamed, and has "terrible things to do." He says,

> Windiest nights, Berky, I have thought for you,
> and no matter how lucky I've been I've touched wood.
> There are things not solved in our town though tomor-
>   row came:
> there are things time passing can never make come
>   true.

The speaker obviously has sympathy for Berky's past and her limited future, but his concern is tinged with a patronizing arrogance. He does not think *of* Berky, he thinks *for* her. She is associated with wildness and sexuality and the body, and he implicitly deems her unable to think for herself. He superstitiously knocks wood and ominously warns in the final stanza that "justice will take us millions of intricate moves" before the Berkys of the world get the opportunities they deserve. He is safely distant from her predicament, however, looking down with moral and intellectual authority and going through the rote and abstract action of thinking for her. The girl in **"Back Home"** from *The Rescued Year* (1966) receives similar treatment. She is a girl who used to sing in the church choir and who "had a slow shadow on dependable walls." She is slow where Berky is wild but they are both seen as handicapped by their respective speakers. Unlike the enlightened speaker, the people of the town are able to know only "a kind of Now." They represent a danger to this girl, symbolized by the insane, insistent song of the insects as the speaker and the girl pass, as well as by the deep darkness that is only partially quelled by the lights of the town. When the speaker returns to the town after a life apart from its limitations, he imagines the girl as "broke into jagged purple glass," shattered by the narrowness of the town and their intolerance for her slow-ness. The image of the purple glass suggests not only the speaker's romantic, and therefore distanced opinion about this girl, but also the "colored" lens through which he evaluates both her and the people of the town. In **"A Gesture Toward an Unfound Renaissance,"** "the slow girl in art class / less able to say where our lessons led," yet romantic in her "rich distress, knowing almost enough / to find a better art inside the lesson" is given much same treatment. Again, there is sympathy in these speakers, and they are ostensibly more enlightened than the small town denizens they are describing, but their poignant nostalgia is marred by their disdain and their pity.

A trio of poems in *Allegiances* provides a foil to the pitiable girls of the previous poems, but these idealized portraits are in their own way just as limited. In **"Remembering Althea,"** the speaker tells of a girl so genuine and unaffected that she radiates light: "After the others / asserted, claimed their place, posed for / every storm, your true beam found all." She is above the trivialities of the schoolyard and the parlor and knows "delicately, through amber" the truth behind pretense. The image of amber echoes the purple shards of glass of the earlier poem and again suggests the tinted, if not distorted, perspective that colors the speaker's memory. **"Bess"** is the poetic sister of the previous girl, a woman whose bravery and cheerfulness in the face of fatal cancer make her similarly ideal.

> Pain moved where she moved. She walked
> ahead; it came. She hid; it found her.
> No one ever served another so truly;
> no enemy ever meant so strong a hate.
> It was almost as if there was no room
> left for her on earth. But she remembered
> where joy used to live. She straightened its flowers;
> she did not weep when she passed its houses;
> and when she finally pulled into a tiny corner
> and slipped from pain, her hand opened
> again, and the streets opened, and she wished all well.

This is noble behavior, but it is presented from the outside in much the same way as the frailties of the pitiable girls. Idealizing this woman's forbearance and cheerfulness tells us nothing about her. She represents a moral ideal that is congruent with the speaker's moral universe and he approves of her, but he never empathizes with her pain or enters her world to show her coping with the pain. Similarly, in **"Monuments for a Friendly Girl at a Tenth Grade Party,"** the speaker crystalizes a moment in which he locks eyes with a girl at a party and "we found each other alive / by our glances never to accept our town's / ways, torture for advancement, / nor ever again be prisoners by choice." They never speak. Later, the speaker hears that the woman, a community activist and volunteer, has died and decides to remember her with this poem: "May

[your friends] never / forsake you, nor you need monuments / other than this I make." The memory is idealized, but it is as much about the speaker's liberal ideals being confirmed then and now as it is about the girl herself. She is a vehicle for the realization of the consistency of the speaker's ideals.

In his book *Writing the Australian Crawl,* Stafford says,

> When you enter art, you may be allowing a self you have only partly, to enjoy its best choices. The action of writing, for instance, is the successive discovery of cumulative epiphanies in the self's encounter with the world. It would be too much to claim that art, the practice of it, will establish a "good," a serene, a superior self. No. But art will, if pursued for itself and not for adventitious reasons or by spurious ways, bring into sustained realization the self most centrally yours. . . .
>
> (51)

The self that Stafford discovers through his male personae speaking about women is a self plagued by serious ambivalence on the subject of women. Normally, Stafford embraces ambivalence. Nature and the pastoral are never a perfect alternative to technology. Man is never completely comfortable with the decisions he makes. The speaker in **"Traveling Through the Dark"** hesitates, ponders, listens and still isn't sure that pushing the dead pregnant doe into the ravine is the best solution for all concerned. Yet this willingness to explore the deep and complicated darkness of the human condition does not seem to extend to women.

Stafford's Native American heritage and its resulting pantheism and his personification of the land throughout his poetry aptly prepare us for the benign way that Stafford looks at the traditionally female figure of nature. Stafford is very comfortable writing poems in which speakers figuratively shield and explore the curving landscape and the womb-like darkness we connotatively read as feminine. Going back to Baym's metaphors, he is comfortable with a static portrait of the passive virgin landscape symbolized by the various young women in the poems, but he is unwilling or unable to create a sympathetic portrait of the other half of that feminine metaphor: the mother, associated with the hearth and society. It is ultimately futile to question why Stafford couldn't write about women with the same empathy with which he viewed Native Americans, soldiers or nature, but it is curious that a poet skilled enough to translate for us what the river said cannot hear and record the voices that are much closer to home.

Notes

1. In 1977, Harper and Row published the book *Stories That Could Be True: New and Collected Poems.* This volume included *West of Your City, Traveling Through the Dark, The Rescued Year,*

Allegiances, Someday, Maybe, as well as the title volume. When I quote poems from these books, this is the compilation to which I am referring. This book, although out of print, is much easier to obtain than the previous volumes. I have included the year of publication for the individual volumes for purposes of maintaining a sense of the chronology of Stafford's work.

Works Cited

Baym, Nina. "Melodramas of Beset Manhood: How Theories of American Fiction Exclude Women Authors." *The New Feminist Criticism: Essays on Women, Literature, and Theory.* Ed. Elaine Showalter. NY: Pantheon, 1985. 63-80.

Carpenter, David A. *William Stafford.* Boise: Boise State University Western Writers Series no. 72, 1986.

Kitchen, Judith. *Understanding William Stafford.* Columbia: University of South Carolina Press, 1989.

Stafford, William. *Down in My Heart.* Elgin, IL: Brethren Publishing House, 1947.

———. *A Glass Face in the Rain.* NY: Harper and Row, 1982.

———. *An Oregon Message.* NY: Harper and Row, 1987.

———. *Stories That Could Be True: New and Collected Poems.* NY: Harper and Row, 1977.

———. *Writing the Australian Crawl: Views on the Writer's Vocation.* Ann Arbor: University of Michigan Press, 1978.

Tompkins, Jane. *West of Everything: The Inner Life of Westerns.* NY: Oxford University Press, 1992.

Erland G. Anderson (essay date fall 2003)

SOURCE: Anderson, Erland G. "Stafford's 'Aunt Mabel.'" *Explicator* 62, no. 1 (fall 2003): 44-7.

[*In the following essay, Anderson examines the strong, "aggressive" language in Stafford's poem "Aunt Mabel."*]

The problem with William Stafford's **"Aunt Mabel,"** from **The Rescued Year** (1966), is the poem's strong, even aggressive, language. Although most readers understand at first reading that the speaker in the poem means to praise her, few can describe clearly how the portrait of Aunt Mabel can be emphatically positive despite the negative charge of many of the similes and

metaphors used by Stafford in the poem. Identifying the tone, or more precisely the countertone, of that language, more than a few confused (or perverse?) readers have concluded that Aunt Mabel was simply a troublemaker who got what she deserved: just another of the many "graves in the rain."

When challenged by such an obviously erroneous reading, I have to admit that, from the start, Stafford has stacked a few weighty words against the good, old girl. The speaker speaks, for example, of the town being "haunted":

> This town is haunted by some good deed
> that reappears like a country cousin, or truth
> when language falters these days trying to lie,
> because Aunt Mabel, an old lady gone now, would
> accost even strangers to give bright flowers
> away, quick as a striking snake. It's deeds like this
> have weakened me, shaken by intermittent trust,
> stricken with friendliness.
>
> (1-8)

Of course, the first explication here requires an awareness of indirect ironies and paradoxes. Naturally such a small-town speaker might use the common hyperbole of being "haunted" to convey the idea of a pleasant memory. Without any more fanfare than "some good deed," Stafford has managed to invoke other uses of "haunt," such as returning to one's old or favorite "haunts." But the poet does not mind letting the more literal-minded reader wonder about towns haunted by ghosts and witches. After all, small towns, as well as big cities, can be noted for their gruesome events as easily as their friendly or lively hospitality. The whole poem requires the reader to put on bifocals.

If "good deeds" can haunt a town, they also can reappear "like country cousins." In small towns such relatives do drop in unexpectedly and perhaps uninvited, but also not too often. The speaker in the poem may like or dislike these country cousins, and may be ambivalent about the frequency or infrequency of their appearance. Clearly the reader is still a bit haunted enough not to be able to pin down these paradoxes yet. And when a new simile emerges to say that "some good deed" reappears like "truth / when language falters these days trying to lie," the tissue of deception may grow more sinister. Has a taste for indirect irony brought the speaker into the perception that his or her small-town life is based on a pattern of lies that most people accept as common truth? Has society found a language that seems true until it ever-so-rarely falters faced with undeniable realities? And if so, what on earth does Aunt Mabel have to do with it? Is she not part of the conspiracy?

Well, no, most readers will respond. In the very next line Stafford has the speaker discuss how she gave flowers away to strangers! Certainly these are her deeds of kindness, but then why does the speaker use the word "accost" and say she gives these flowers away "quick as a striking snake"? There is some violence in this action, even if it is only in the shock to the stranger who does not expect an "aloha greeting" in the great Middle West.

But the speaker goes further to generalize from Mabel's gesture a psychologically lasting effect. Deeds like that "have weakened me, shaken by intermittent trust, / stricken with friendliness." Something about these ablatives is absolute. These kinds of unexpected acts of kindness have been an assault on something in the speaker that has not been entirely pleasant. He or she is both "shaken" and, even worse, "stricken." The condition, though intermittent, has become a chronic one. What is the matter with the speaker? Is he or she making a mountain out of a mole hill?

The arrival of the senator does much to focus the poem:

> Our Senator talked like war, and Aunt Mabel said,
> "He's a brilliant man, but we didn't elect him that
> much."
>
> (10-11)

Again, however, some explication is needed to clarify what may be going on here. If the senator "talked like war," we may wonder about the content as well as the style of his speech. Does the simile merely stand for the force of his rhetoric as in the cliché: "he gave a fiery speech"? Or does the speaker mean to suggest that the senator "talked like [he wanted to take us into] war" or advocated some other militant political stance? Whether the focus is on the effect of the rhetoric or the topic of the senator's speech, there is something both leveling and reductive about Aunt Mabel's response.

Legal logic might insist on a simple either/or condition here: either the senator was elected or he was not. But Aunt Mabel stumbles into an important nuance: how far can an elected senator go with his or her mandate from the voters? There are, or should be, gradations of power and authority.

If we are inclined to see assertiveness or even aggression in Aunt Mabel, readers understand how her respect for the senator's brilliance, either from his education or charisma, does not negate the truth she needs to utter here about the relationship between the people and their elected representatives in a democracy. Aunt Mabel may not be able to explain why she does not agree with whatever the senator is proposing, and Stafford is care-

ful not to give us the opportunity to take sides on what is at issue. Aunt Mabel's reaction is as intuitive as it is immediate and final.

And maybe that is the problem that haunts the town and shocks the speaker out of his complacency of "white" lies:

> Everyone's resolve weakens toward evening
> or in a flash when a face melds—a stranger's even—
> reminded for an instant between menace and fear:
> There are Aunt Mabels all over the world,
> or their graves in the rain.
>
> (12-16)

The speaker has resolved, like everyone else, to get on with life as it is. To be a realist is to accept a world that one needs to fight in, to establish clear boundaries and defenses against strangers, country cousins, one's immediate family members—even one's inner self.

Yet the speaker acknowledges times when that resolve "weakens," and it is in the "evening / or in a flash when a face melds—a stranger's even." To "meld" is another interesting word for the speaker to use here. It both denotes merged images and connotes, by association with "melding" in the game of pinochle, a card game commonly played after dinner in the Midwest. The image is comfortably homey and blindingly instantaneous.

Whatever the effect, the normal life of the speaker exists between "menace and fear." Being caught in a vice between two words that seem two sides of the same coin, or a cycle of action and reaction, produces yet another paradox, oxymoron, and hyperbole all in one breath. "[M]enace" and "fear" were revealed with lightning clarity to the speaker by "some good deed" Aunt Mabel did or some off-handed comment she made that was the equivalent of the proverbial statement, "The Emperor has no clothes!" She may have made people like the speaker in that town feel a bit more uncomfortable than they preferred to be, but she played an important part in allowing the speaker and the town to have wider visions of truth, the world, and greater realities than those touted by visiting senators and people of social importance.

Aunt Mabel is in fact one of millions of common people with finely tuned intuition who know no geographical, ethnic, or other human barriers. Without perhaps being able to elaborate on their reactions, they have a natural skepticism when it comes to charisma and media hype. The speaker is forced to acknowledge, perhaps against his or her own assumptions and convictions, that such people are found everywhere on the planet—even, say, in Baghdad. They live, or they have died, but not without leaving something memorable and ordinary, such as the glistening rain on grave stones.

Work Cited

Stafford, William E. "Aunt Mabel." *Stories That Could Be True: New and Collected Poems.* New York: Harper and Row, 1977, 120.

Kim Stafford (essay date 2003)

SOURCE: Stafford, Kim. "What Is Left for Us: An Introduction." In *Every War Has Two Losers: William Stafford on Peace and War,* edited by Kim Stafford, pp. 5-12. Minneapolis, Minn.: Milkweed Editions, 2003.

[*In the following excerpt, Stafford recalls his father's pacifist beliefs and the poetry that grew out of those convictions.*]

Is it naive to seek for national and international security through poetry? My father believed it is naive to seek with weapons of steel. Behind the strife of nations, there is another way. This way is individual, collective, and universal. This way feels the wounds of any war, but looks beyond.

> And what is left, for us, between the sky and the earth
> is a scar.
>
> —*from* **"These Mornings"**

When my father, the poet William Stafford, wrote **"These Mornings"** it was January of 1944. He had just turned thirty, and he was living in a camp for conscientious objectors in the mountains of California. He and his pacifist companions were fighting forest fires instead of killing and being killed by the young men of Germany, Italy, or Japan. This was before the big Allied bombing campaigns—Berlin, Dresden, Tokyo, and finally Hiroshima and Nagasaki—but already my father saw the scar that would be left for us. His poem is eerily relevant to what was left at Ground Zero in New York City in September 2001—the scar in the ground left by the death of thousands on the wrong side of someone's anger, and the scar in our national psyche with all its military consequences of reprisal. It is relevant also to the scars left among the people of distant lands where our own bombs have fallen.

What would it be like for a thoughtful member of the Taliban to write a poem of compassion for the victims of the attack on the World Trade Center and the Pentagon? What would it be like for American poets to write of their compassion for the families of the fanatics—or the families under the rain of bombs intended for the Taliban or Saddam Hussein? In his published and unpublished writings my father showed it is possible—and crucial—to think independently when fanatics act, and to speak for reconciliation when nations take sides.

All his life William Stafford was witness for a comprehensive view. He believed in the fragile but essential community of the world, and he wrote on behalf of what he called "the unknown good in our enemies." In his view, such a life of witness was both compassionate and profoundly practical—in the long term, wars simply don't work as well as reconciliation. So every day of his life, from those years in World War II until his death in 1993, William Stafford would rise before first light to remember, to ponder, and to write—often writing about peace and reconciliation.

It would be difficult to overestimate the unusual importance of William Stafford's daily writing practice. Most of us read or hear the daily news, beginning each day with a dose of another person's truth. My father had a different way: to *create* the news of our common life by writing your own. This act is true freedom and constructive citizenship. It is available to all of us.

From Stafford's morning writings, and from poems, statements, and interviews that grew from his thinking about reconciliation as it developed in those mornings, I with others have assembled this book ten years after his death. My father's pacifist writings speak to us directly—including both published poems and many passages from his daily writings not previously published.

Every country needs generous conversation among differing views. This book provides an alternative approach to a nation's military habit, our government's aggressive instincts, and our legacy of armed ventures in Europe, the Pacific, Korea, Vietnam, the Persian Gulf, Afghanistan, and beyond.

What is the place of writing, and a life of witness, in national affairs? Our nation has a founding document, the Declaration of Independence. In our first war, we defended the sentiments of that document with a military revolution. We killed for those self-evident words. Some of those who did not join the killing were called traitors, and were shunned. Thus, our beginning.

My family, by contrast, has a founding story. Sometime around 1920, the young William Stafford came home from school and told his mother that two new students had been surrounded on the playground and taunted by the others because they were black.

"And what did you do, Billy?" said his mother.

"I went and stood by them," Billy said.

No one knows how my father got to be that way. His brother became a bomber pilot in World War II. His sister married a navy man. But as a child my father somehow arrived at the idea that one does not need to fight; nor does one need to run away. Both those actions are failures of imagination. Instead of fighting or running you can stand by the oppressed, the frightened, or even "the enemy." You can witness for connection, even when many around you react with fury, or with fear.

In this belief, Stafford wrote each day, and often his writing included specific considerations of human connection. His daily writing included instructive dreams:

> I am in an army and we are in a place like a stadium and are supposed to start fighting; but we look at each other and somehow just don't quite get started. Then we realize that maybe we won't have the war. I am aware of the chancy nature of things—if we can keep from frightening each other, maybe it all won't start.

He had personal experience with the chancy nature of human interaction. Such experience made him thoughtful, and in his early morning writing he often began with a single sentence, one he never made part of a poem or otherwise published. We call these his aphorisms:

> Every war has two losers.

> The wars we haven't had saved many lives.

> You may win a war you are sorry to have started.

When I come upon these lines in the archive of my father's work, I wonder why he never gathered them himself. (He called his unpublished work his compost pile.) Sometimes these isolated statements show a quirky humor:

> Children of heroes have glory for breakfast.

> The Militarist's Farewell: Good-bye, Boomerang, see you later.

> Children playing with knives.
> Children swearing. Children
> running a country.

For the most part, his writing is not accusatory, but inclusive. He knows he is caught in our great human charade, and he struggles to step outside and see things in an independent way:

> Fool that I am, I keep thinking things will work out, that we can coast along while injustice prevails, and somehow it will change.

> It began to dawn on me how weak and fallible people are, how habits and limited environments had fostered institutionalized smugness and vainglory: when saber-toothed tigers died out bravery began to be possible;

lack of association with superior sensibilities allows the assumption that we apprehend all that is around us; success at customary activities enables us to assume that we are in control of anything we put our minds to. This mirror that we admire will shatter if touched by any of the real rocks around us.

As he continues writing every morning, his words might begin to gather momentum as a poem:

> If you don't know the kind of person I am
> and I don't know the kind of person you are
> a pattern that others made may prevail in the world
> and following the wrong god home we may miss our
>   star.
>
> —*from* **"A Ritual to Read to Each Other"**

If my father achieved his most lasting and public utterance in his poems, I believe the cradle of those poems was his habit of living apart from narrow patriotism in a way made possible by his pacifism. This book shows what it is like to live in a mind where pacifism prevails, where mother country is the world.

Every War Has Two Losers is a collection of considerations that step outside the confines of nationality, politics, narrow patriotism, and other ways of life that imprison the imagination. If you live outside, on your own, you do not see the people of the world as loyal citizens or as enemies. You see them as individuals, as parents, neighbors, and friends—or potential friends. You begin to ask absolute questions:

> Save the world by torturing one innocent child?
> Which innocent child?

Standing outside the frenzy of your country's ways, you inquire about the complexities behind the news of winning, as in this statement Stafford published in the summer of 1991, at the conclusion of the Gulf War:

> Is there a quiet way, a helpful way, to question what has been won in a war that the victors are still cheering? Can questions be asked without slighting that need to celebrate the relief of a war quickly ended?

> Or does the winning itself close out questions about it? Might failing to question it make it easier to try a war again?

> Maybe a successful performance that kills tens of thousands, that results in the greatest pollution in history, that devastates a nation, that helps confirm governments in the reliance on weapons for security—maybe such an action deserves a cautious assessment? Maybe some people might be forgiven a few thoughtful moments amid the cheering?

Much of my father's oblique view of American history, policy, and militarism was formed in the unusual company of the CO camps during World War II. In selections from interviews gathered here, Stafford talks about his friends in the camps who taught him new ways to consider the military decisions being made quickly in the wake of Pearl Harbor:

> There was a fellow named Hidarro Herrera from Coyote, New Mexico, and he could speak a little English, and I asked him about his draft board. He said they asked him, "Why are you refusing to go to war?" And he said, "God don't like war." So, where do you go from there? What could you ask next?

Included in this book is a chapter from my father's account of life in those camps, his 1947 book *Down in My Heart,* with its report of his near hanging at the hands of American patriots. But even about such an adventure, my father is thoughtful, and a student of human process:

> It takes such an intricate succession of misfortunes and blunders to get mobbed by your own countrymen—and such a close balancing of good fortune to survive—that I consider myself a rarity, in this respect, in being able to tell the story, from the subject's point of view; but just how we began to be mobbed and just where the blunders and misfortunes began, it is hard to say.

Toward the end of his life my father wrote of the quiet heroes of his world—the champions not of war but of reconciliation—in words that I take to describe his own presence:

> In the center of human life are those who hold it together. They make home what it is. They listen to "leaders," receive, decide. Whatever country is, whatever a profession, a town—they establish that.

With much help, I have shaped this book to sustain people who hold life together. As a father, as a teacher, as a citizen of the world, I intend to do what I can to raise up a generation in the spirit of peace. All around us, it's war, terror, reprisal. But we may step aside, invited to join each other on the path of peace by my father's words before dawn.

FURTHER READING

Criticism

Barnes, Dick. "The Absence of the Artist." In *On William Stafford: The Worth of Local Things,* edited by Tom Andrews, pp. 154-64. Ann Arbor: The University of Michigan Press, 1993.

> Examines issues of voice, poetic persona, and the pathetic fallacy in Stafford's poetry.

Giles, Ronald K. "Stafford's *Traveling through the Dark.*" *Explicator* 43, no. 3 (spring 1985): 44-5.

> Brief analysis of the theme of Stafford's most famous poem, "Traveling through the Dark."

Holden, Jonathan. "Landscape Poems." *Denver Quarterly* 20-21, nos. 4-1 (spring-summer 1986): 159-76.

> Discussion of the landscape poetry of Emily Dickinson, Richard Hugo, and William Stafford.

Lynch, Dennis Daley. "Journeys in Search of Oneself: The Metaphor of the Road in William Stafford's *Traveling through the Dark* and *The Rescued Year.*" *Modern Poetry Studies* 7, no. 2 (autumn 1976): 122-31.

> Examination of Stafford's use of journeys of remembrance, quest, and experience throughout his poetry.

Stafford, William, and Michael J. Bugeja, et al. "An Interview with William Stafford." *Cimarron Review* 72 (July 1985): 41-7.

> Interview dealing with Stafford's theories on writing poetry and the difficulties faced by poets who are not well known.

———, and David M. Cicotello. "The Art of Writing: An Interview with William Stafford." *College Composition and Communication* 34, no. 2 (May 1983): 173-77.

> Interview covering the principles and problems of teaching writing in the classroom.

———, and Claire Cooperstein. "Postmark: Lake Oswego—A Mail Interview with William Stafford." *Northwest Review* 26, no. 3 (1988): 25-32.

> Stafford discusses the pessimism apparent in some of his later poems.

———, and William Young. "The Art of Poetry: *The Paris Review* Interview with William Young." In *William Stafford: The Answers Are Inside the Mountains: Meditations on the Writing Life,* edited by Paul Merchant and Vincent Wixon, pp. 22-41. Ann Arbor: University of Michigan Press, 2003.

> Interview conducted in the winter of 1993 in which Stafford discusses the creative process and his relationship to other poets of the past and present.

Stitt, Peter. "William Stafford's Wilderness Quest." In *On William Stafford: The Worth of Local Things,* edited by Tom Andrews, pp. 165-202. Ann Arbor: The University of Michigan Press, 1993.

> Contends that Stafford is an unusual poet in that he refuses to analyze his own poetry, thereby resisting the urge to dominate the material intellectually.

Wagner, Linda W. "William Stafford's Plain-Style." *Modern Poetry Studies* 6, no. 1 (spring 1975): 19-30.

Compares Stafford's use of everyday language and plain style to Walt Whitman's.

Additional coverage of Stafford's life and career is contained in the following sources published by Thomson Gale: *American Writers Supplement,* **Vol. 11;** *Contemporary Authors,* **Vols. 5-8R;** *Contemporary Authors Autobiography Series,* **Vol. 3;** *Contemporary Authors New Revision Series,* **Vols. 5 and 22;** *Contemporary Authors—Obituary,* **Vol. 142;** *Contemporary Literary Criticism,* **Vols. 4, 7, and 29;** *Contemporary Poets,* **Eds. 1, 2, 3, and 4;** *Dictionary of Literary Biography,* **Vols. 5 and 206;** *DISCovering Authors Modules: Poets; Exploring Poetry; Literature Resource Center; Modern American Literature,* **Ed. 5;** *Poetry for Students,* **Vols. 2, 8, and 16;** *Reference Guide to American Literature,* **Ed. 4; and** *World Poets.*

How to Use This Index

The main references

Calvino, Italo
1923-1985 .... CLC 5, 8, 11, 22, 33, 39,
73; SSC 3, 48

list all author entries in the following Thomson Gale Literary Criticism series:

AAL = *Asian American Literature*
BG = *The Beat Generation: A Gale Critical Companion*
BLC = *Black Literature Criticism*
BLCS = *Black Literature Criticism Supplement*
CLC = *Contemporary Literary Criticism*
CLR = *Children's Literature Review*
CMLC = *Classical and Medieval Literature Criticism*
DC = *Drama Criticism*
FL = *Feminism in Literature: A Gale Critical Companion*
GL = *Gothic Literature: A Gale Critical Companion*
HLC = *Hispanic Literature Criticism*
HLCS = *Hispanic Literature Criticism Supplement*
HR = *Harlem Renaissance: A Gale Critical Companion*
LC = *Literature Criticism from 1400 to 1800*
NCLC = *Nineteenth-Century Literature Criticism*
NNAL = *Native North American Literature*
PC = *Poetry Criticism*
SSC = *Short Story Criticism*
TCLC = *Twentieth-Century Literary Criticism*
WLC = *World Literature Criticism, 1500 to the Present*
WLCS = *World Literature Criticism Supplement*

The cross-references

See also CA 85-88, 116; CANR 23, 61;
DAM NOV; DLB 196; EW 13; MTCW 1, 2;
RGSF 2; RGWL 2; SFW 4; SSFS 12

list all author entries in the following Thomson Gale biographical and literary sources:

AAYA = *Authors & Artists for Young Adults*
AFAW = *African American Writers*
AFW = *African Writers*
AITN = *Authors in the News*
AMW = *American Writers*
AMWR = *American Writers Retrospective Supplement*
AMWS = *American Writers Supplement*
ANW = *American Nature Writers*
AW = *Ancient Writers*
BEST = *Bestsellers*
BPFB = *Beacham's Encyclopedia of Popular Fiction: Biography and Resources*
BRW = *British Writers*
BRWS = *British Writers Supplement*
BW = *Black Writers*
BYA = *Beacham's Guide to Literature for Young Adults*
CA = *Contemporary Authors*
CAAS = *Contemporary Authors Autobiography Series*
CABS = *Contemporary Authors Bibliographical Series*
CAD = *Contemporary American Dramatists*
CANR = *Contemporary Authors New Revision Series*
CAP = *Contemporary Authors Permanent Series*
CBD = *Contemporary British Dramatists*
CCA = *Contemporary Canadian Authors*
CD = *Contemporary Dramatists*
CDALB = *Concise Dictionary of American Literary Biography*

CDALBS = *Concise Dictionary of American Literary Biography Supplement*

CDBLB = *Concise Dictionary of British Literary Biography*

CMW = *St. James Guide to Crime & Mystery Writers*

CN = *Contemporary Novelists*

CP = *Contemporary Poets*

CPW = *Contemporary Popular Writers*

CSW = *Contemporary Southern Writers*

CWD = *Contemporary Women Dramatists*

CWP = *Contemporary Women Poets*

CWRI = *St. James Guide to Children's Writers*

CWW = *Contemporary World Writers*

DA = *DISCovering Authors*

DA3 = *DISCovering Authors 3.0*

DAB = *DISCovering Authors: British Edition*

DAC = *DISCovering Authors: Canadian Edition*

DAM = *DISCovering Authors: Modules*

   DRAM: *Dramatists Module;* **MST:** *Most-studied Authors Module;*

   MULT: *Multicultural Authors Module;* **NOV:** *Novelists Module;*

   POET: *Poets Module;* **POP:** *Popular Fiction and Genre Authors Module*

DFS = *Drama for Students*

DLB = *Dictionary of Literary Biography*

DLBD = *Dictionary of Literary Biography Documentary Series*

DLBY = *Dictionary of Literary Biography Yearbook*

DNFS = *Literature of Developing Nations for Students*

EFS = *Epics for Students*

EXPN = *Exploring Novels*

EXPP = *Exploring Poetry*

EXPS = *Exploring Short Stories*

EW = *European Writers*

FANT = *St. James Guide to Fantasy Writers*

FW = *Feminist Writers*

GFL = *Guide to French Literature,* Beginnings to 1789, 1798 to the Present

GLL = *Gay and Lesbian Literature*

HGG = *St. James Guide to Horror, Ghost & Gothic Writers*

HW = *Hispanic Writers*

IDFW = *International Dictionary of Films and Filmmakers: Writers and Production Artists*

IDTP = *International Dictionary of Theatre: Playwrights*

LAIT = *Literature and Its Times*

LAW = *Latin American Writers*

JRDA = *Junior DISCovering Authors*

MAICYA = *Major Authors and Illustrators for Children and Young Adults*

MAICYAS = *Major Authors and Illustrators for Children and Young Adults Supplement*

MAWW = *Modern American Women Writers*

MJW = *Modern Japanese Writers*

MTCW = *Major 20th-Century Writers*

NCFS = *Nonfiction Classics for Students*

NFS = *Novels for Students*

PAB = *Poets: American and British*

PFS = *Poetry for Students*

RGAL = *Reference Guide to American Literature*

RGEL = *Reference Guide to English Literature*

RGSF = *Reference Guide to Short Fiction*

RGWL = *Reference Guide to World Literature*

RHW = *Twentieth-Century Romance and Historical Writers*

SAAS = *Something about the Author Autobiography Series*

SATA = *Something about the Author*

SFW = *St. James Guide to Science Fiction Writers*

SSFS = *Short Stories for Students*

TCWW = *Twentieth-Century Western Writers*

WLIT = *World Literature and Its Times*

WP = *World Poets*

YABC = *Yesterday's Authors of Books for Children*

YAW = *St. James Guide to Young Adult Writers*

Literary Criticism Series
Cumulative Author Index

Africa, Ben
See Bosman, Herman Charles

Afton, Effie
See Harper, Frances Ellen Watkins

Agapida, Fray Antonio
See Irving, Washington

Agee, James (Rufus) 1909-1955 ...... **TCLC 1, 19**
See also AAYA 44; AITN 1; AMW; CA 108; 148; CANR 131; CDALB 1941-1968; DAM NOV; DLB 2, 26, 152; DLBY 1989; EWL 3; LAIT 3; LATS 1:2; MAL 5; MTCW 2; MTFW 2005; NFS 22; RGAL 4; TUS

Aghill, Gordon
See Silverberg, Robert

Agnon, S(hmuel) Y(osef Halevi) 1888-1970 .... **CLC 4, 8, 14; SSC 30; TCLC 151**
See also CA 17-18; 25-28R; CANR 60, 102; CAP 2; EWL 3; MTCW 1, 2; RGSF 2; RGWL 2, 3; WLIT 6

Agrippa von Nettesheim, Henry Cornelius 1486-1535 .... **LC 27**

Aguilera Malta, Demetrio 1909-1981 .... **HLCS 1**
See also CA 111; 124; CANR 87; DAM MULT, NOV; DLB 145; EWL 3; HW 1; RGWL 3

Agustini, Delmira 1886-1914 .... **HLCS 1**
See also CA 166; DLB 290; HW 1, 2; LAW

Aherne, Owen
See Cassill, R(onald) V(erlin)

Ai 1947- .... **CLC 4, 14, 69**
See also CA 85-88; CAAS 13; CANR 70; DLB 120; PFS 16

Aickman, Robert (Fordyce) 1914-1981 .... **CLC 57**
See also CA 5-8R; CANR 3, 72, 100; DLB 261; HGG; SUFW 1, 2

Aidoo, (Christina) Ama Ata 1942- .... **BLCS; CLC 177**
See also AFW; BW 1; CA 101; CANR 62, 144; CD 5, 6; CDWLB 3; CN 6, 7; CWD; CWP; DLB 117; DNFS 1, 2; EWL 3; FW; WLIT 2

Aiken, Conrad (Potter) 1889-1973 .... **CLC 1, 3, 5, 10, 52; PC 26; SSC 9**
See also AMW; CA 5-8R; 45-48; CANR 4, 60; CDALB 1929-1941; CN 1; CP 1; DAM NOV, POET; DLB 9, 45, 102; EWL 3; EXPS; HGG; MAL 5; MTCW 1, 2; MTFW 2005; RGAL 4; RGSF 2; SATA 3, 30; SSFS 8; TUS

Aiken, Joan (Delano) 1924-2004 ...... **CLC 35**
See also AAYA 1, 25; CA 9-12R; 182; 223; CAAE 182; CANR 4, 23, 34, 64, 121; CLR 1, 19, 90; DLB 161; FANT; HGG; JRDA; MAICYA 1, 2; MTCW 1; RHW; SAAS 1; SATA 2, 30, 73; SATA-Essay 109; SATA-Obit 152; SUFW 2; WYA; YAW

Ainsworth, William Harrison 1805-1882 .... **NCLC 13**
See also DLB 21; HGG; RGEL 2; SATA 24; SUFW 1

Aitmatov, Chingiz (Torekulovich) 1928- .... **CLC 71**
See Aytmatov, Chingiz
See also CA 103; CANR 38; CWW 2; DLB 302; MTCW 1; RGSF 2; SATA 56

Akers, Floyd
See Baum, L(yman) Frank

Akhmadulina, Bella Akhatovna 1937- .... **CLC 53; PC 43**
See also CA 65-68; CWP; CWW 2; DAM POET; EWL 3

Akhmatova, Anna 1888-1966 ..... **CLC 11, 25, 64, 126; PC 2, 55**
See also CA 19-20; 25-28R; CANR 35; CAP 1; DA3; DAM POET; DLB 295; EW 10; EWL 3; FL 1:5; MTCW 1, 2; PFS 18; RGWL 2, 3

Aksakov, Sergei Timofeyvich 1791-1859 .... **NCLC 2**
See also DLB 198

Aksenov, Vasilii (Pavlovich)
See Aksyonov, Vassily (Pavlovich)
See also CWW 2

Aksenov, Vassily
See Aksyonov, Vassily (Pavlovich)

Akst, Daniel 1956- .... **CLC 109**
See also CA 161; CANR 110

Aksyonov, Vassily (Pavlovich) 1932- .... **CLC 22, 37, 101**
See Aksenov, Vasilii (Pavlovich)
See also CA 53-56; CANR 12, 48, 77; DLB 302; EWL 3

Akutagawa Ryunosuke 1892-1927 ... **SSC 44; TCLC 16**
See also CA 117; 154; DLB 180; EWL 3; MJW; RGSF 2; RGWL 2, 3

Alabaster, William 1568-1640 .... **LC 90**
See also DLB 132; RGEL 2

Alain 1868-1951 .... **TCLC 41**
See also CA 163; EWL 3; GFL 1789 to the Present

Alain de Lille c. 1116-c. 1203 .... **CMLC 53**
See also DLB 208

Alain-Fournier .... **TCLC 6**
See Fournier, Henri-Alban
See also DLB 65; EWL 3; GFL 1789 to the Present; RGWL 2, 3

Al-Amin, Jamil Abdullah 1943- .... **BLC 1**
See also BW 1, 3; CA 112; 125; CANR 82; DAM MULT

Alanus de Insluis
See Alain de Lille

Alarcon, Pedro Antonio de 1833-1891 .... **NCLC 1; SSC 64**

Alas (y Urena), Leopoldo (Enrique Garcia) 1852-1901 .... **TCLC 29**
See also CA 113; 131; HW 1; RGSF 2

Albee, Edward (Franklin) (III) 1928- .. **CLC 1, 2, 3, 5, 9, 11, 13, 25, 53, 86, 113; DC 11; WLC**
See also AAYA 51; AITN 1; AMW; CA 5-8R; CABS 3; CAD; CANR 8, 54, 74, 124; CD 5, 6; CDALB 1941-1968; DA; DA3; DAB; DAC; DAM DRAM, MST; DFS 2, 3, 8, 10, 13, 14; DLB 7, 266; EWL 3; INT CANR-8; LAIT 4; LMFS 2; MAL 5; MTCW 1, 2; MTFW 2005; RGAL 4; TUS

Alberti (Merello), Rafael
See Alberti, Rafael
See also CWW 2

Alberti, Rafael 1902-1999 .... **CLC 7**
See Alberti (Merello), Rafael
See also CA 85-88; 185; CANR 81; DLB 108; EWL 3; HW 2; RGWL 2, 3

Albert the Great 1193(?)-1280 ...... **CMLC 16**
See also DLB 115

Alcaeus c. 620B.C.- .... **CMLC 65**
See also DLB 176

Alcala-Galiano, Juan Valera y
See Valera y Alcala-Galiano, Juan

Alcayaga, Lucila Godoy
See Godoy Alcayaga, Lucila

Alciato, Andrea 1492-1550 .... **LC 116**

Alcott, Amos Bronson 1799-1888 ... **NCLC 1, 167**
See also DLB 1, 223

Alcott, Louisa May 1832-1888 . **NCLC 6, 58, 83; SSC 27; WLC**
See also AAYA 20; AMWS 1; BPFB 1; BYA 2; CDALB 1865-1917; CLR 1, 38; DA; DA3; DAB; DAC; DAM MST, NOV; DLB 1, 42, 79, 223, 239, 242; DLBD 14; FL 1:2; FW; JRDA; LAIT 2; MAICYA 1, 2; NFS 12; RGAL 4; SATA 100; TUS; WCH; WYA; YABC 1; YAW

Alcuin c. 730-804 .... **CMLC 69**
See also DLB 148

Aldanov, M. A.
See Aldanov, Mark (Alexandrovich)

Aldanov, Mark (Alexandrovich) 1886-1957 .... **TCLC 23**
See also CA 118; 181; DLB 317

Aldington, Richard 1892-1962 .... **CLC 49**
See also CA 85-88; CANR 45; DLB 20, 36, 100, 149; LMFS 2; RGEL 2

Aldiss, Brian W(ilson) 1925- . **CLC 5, 14, 40; SSC 36**
See also AAYA 42; CA 5-8R, 190; CAAE 190; CAAS 2; CANR 5, 28, 64, 121; CN 1, 2, 3, 4, 5, 6, 7; DAM NOV; DLB 14, 261, 271; MTCW 1, 2; MTFW 2005; SATA 34; SCFW 1, 2; SFW 4

Aldrich, Bess Streeter 1881-1954 .... **TCLC 125**
See also CLR 70; TCWW 2

Alegria, Claribel
See Alegria, Claribel (Joy)
See also CWW 2; DLB 145, 283

Alegria, Claribel (Joy) 1924- .... **CLC 75; HLCS 1; PC 26**
See Alegria, Claribel
See also CA 131; CAAS 15; CANR 66, 94, 134; DAM MULT; EWL 3; HW 1; MTCW 2; MTFW 2005; PFS 21

Alegria, Fernando 1918- .... **CLC 57**
See also CA 9-12R; CANR 5, 32, 72; EWL 3; HW 1, 2

Aleichem, Sholom .... **SSC 33; TCLC 1, 35**
See Rabinovitch, Sholem
See also TWA

Aleixandre, Vicente 1898-1984 .... **HLCS 1; TCLC 113**
See also CANR 81; DLB 108; EWL 3; HW 2; MTCW 1, 2; RGWL 2, 3

Aleman, Mateo 1547-1615(?) .... **LC 81**

Alencar, Jose de 1829-1877 .... **NCLC 157**
See also DLB 307; LAW; WLIT 1

Alencon, Marguerite d'
See de Navarre, Marguerite

Alepoudelis, Odysseus
See Elytis, Odysseus
See also CWW 2

Aleshkovsky, Joseph 1929-
See Aleshkovsky, Yuz
See also CA 121; 128

Aleshkovsky, Yuz .... **CLC 44**
See Aleshkovsky, Joseph
See also DLB 317

Alexander, Lloyd (Chudley) 1924- ... **CLC 35**
See also AAYA 1, 27; BPFB 1; BYA 5, 6, 7, 9, 10, 11; CA 1-4R; CANR 1, 24, 38, 55, 113; CLR 1, 5, 48; CWRI 5; DLB 52; FANT; JRDA; MAICYA 1, 2; MAICYAS 1; MTCW 1; SAAS 19; SATA 3, 49, 81, 129, 135; SUFW; TUS; WYA; YAW

Alexander, Meena 1951- .... **CLC 121**
See also CA 115; CANR 38, 70, 146; CP 7; CWP; FW

Alexander, Samuel 1859-1938 .... **TCLC 77**

Alexeyev, Constantin (Sergeivich)
See Stanislavsky, Konstantin (Sergeivich)

Alexie, Sherman (Joseph, Jr.)
1966- .... **CLC 96, 154; NNAL; PC 53**
See also AAYA 28; BYA 15; CA 138;
CANR 65, 95, 133; CN 7; DA3; DAM
MULT; DLB 175, 206, 278; LATS 1:2;
MTCW 2; MTFW 2005; NFS 17; SSFS
18

al-Farabi 870(?)-950 .... **CMLC 58**
See also DLB 115

Alfau, Felipe 1902-1999 .... **CLC 66**
See also CA 137

Alfieri, Vittorio 1749-1803 .... **NCLC 101**
See also EW 4; RGWL 2, 3; WLIT 7

Alfonso X 1221-1284 .... **CMLC 78**

Alfred, Jean Gaston
See Ponge, Francis

Alger, Horatio, Jr. 1832-1899 .... **NCLC 8, 83**
See also CLR 87; DLB 42; LAIT 2; RGAL
4; SATA 16; TUS

Al-Ghazali, Muhammad ibn Muhammad
1058-1111 .... **CMLC 50**
See also DLB 115

Algren, Nelson 1909-1981 ..... **CLC 4, 10, 33;
SSC 33**
See also AMWS 9; BPFB 1; CA 13-16R;
103; CANR 20, 61; CDALB 1941-1968;
CN 1, 2; DLB 9; DLBY 1981, 1982,
2000; EWL 3; MAL 5; MTCW 1, 2;
MTFW 2005; RGAL 4; RGSF 2

**al-Hariri, al-Qasim ibn 'Ali Abu
Muhammad al-Basri**
1054-1122 .... **CMLC 63**
See also RGWL 3

Ali, Ahmed 1908-1998 .... **CLC 69**
See also CA 25-28R; CANR 15, 34; CN 1,
2, 3, 4, 5; EWL 3

Ali, Tariq 1943- .... **CLC 173**
See also CA 25-28R; CANR 10, 99

Alighieri, Dante
See Dante
See also WLIT 7

al-Kindi, Abu Yusuf Ya'qub ibn Ishaq c.
801-c. 873 .... **CMLC 80**

Allan, John B.
See Westlake, Donald E(dwin)

Allan, Sidney
See Hartmann, Sadakichi

Allan, Sydney
See Hartmann, Sadakichi

Allard, Janet .... **CLC 59**

Allen, Edward 1948- .... **CLC 59**

Allen, Fred 1894-1956 .... **TCLC 87**

Allen, Paula Gunn 1939- .... **CLC 84, 202;
NNAL**
See also AMWS 4; CA 112; 143; CANR
63, 130; CWP; DA3; DAM MULT; DLB
175; FW; MTCW 2; MTFW 2005; RGAL
4; TCWW 2

Allen, Roland
See Ayckbourn, Alan

Allen, Sarah A.
See Hopkins, Pauline Elizabeth

Allen, Sidney H.
See Hartmann, Sadakichi

Allen, Woody 1935- .... **CLC 16, 52, 195**
See also AAYA 10, 51; AMWS 15; CA 33-
36R; CANR 27, 38, 63, 128; DAM POP;
DLB 44; MTCW 1; SSFS 21

Allende, Isabel 1942- ... **CLC 39, 57, 97, 170;
HLC 1; SSC 65; WLCS**
See also AAYA 18; CA 125; 130; CANR
51, 74, 129; CDWLB 3; CLR 99; CWW
2; DA3; DAM MULT, NOV; DLB 145;
DNFS 1; EWL 3; FL 1:5; FW; HW 1, 2;
INT CA-130; LAIT 5; LAWS 1; LMFS 2;
MTCW 1, 2; MTFW 2005; NCFS 1; NFS
6, 18; RGSF 2; RGWL 3; SATA 163;
SSFS 11, 16; WLIT 1

Alleyn, Ellen
See Rossetti, Christina

Alleyne, Carla D. .... **CLC 65**

Allingham, Margery (Louise)
1904-1966 .... **CLC 19**
See also CA 5-8R; 25-28R; CANR 4, 58;
CMW 4; DLB 77; MSW; MTCW 1, 2

Allingham, William 1824-1889 ...... **NCLC 25**
See also DLB 35; RGEL 2

Allison, Dorothy E. 1949- .... **CLC 78, 153**
See also AAYA 53; CA 140; CANR 66, 107;
CN 7; CSW; DA3; FW; MTCW 2; MTFW
2005; NFS 11; RGAL 4

Alloula, Malek .... **CLC 65**

Allston, Washington 1779-1843 .... **NCLC 2**
See also DLB 1, 235

Almedingen, E. M. .... **CLC 12**
See Almedingen, Martha Edith von
See also SATA 3

Almedingen, Martha Edith von 1898-1971
See Almedingen, E. M.
See also CA 1-4R; CANR 1

Almodovar, Pedro 1949(?)- .... **CLC 114;
HLCS 1**
See also CA 133; CANR 72; HW 2

Almqvist, Carl Jonas Love
1793-1866 .... **NCLC 42**

**al-Mutanabbi, Ahmad ibn al-Husayn Abu
al-Tayyib al-Jufi al-Kindi**
915-965 .... **CMLC 66**
See Mutanabbi, Al-
See also RGWL 3

Alonso, Damaso 1898-1990 .... **CLC 14**
See also CA 110; 131; 130; CANR 72; DLB
108; EWL 3; HW 1, 2

Alov
See Gogol, Nikolai (Vasilyevich)

al'Sadaawi, Nawal
See El Saadawi, Nawal
See also FW

al-Shaykh, Hanan 1945- .... **CLC 218**
See also CA 135; CANR 111; WLIT 6

Al Siddik
See Rolfe, Frederick (William Serafino
Austin Lewis Mary)
See also GLL 1; RGEL 2

Alta 1942- .... **CLC 19**
See also CA 57-60

Alter, Robert B(ernard) 1935- .... **CLC 34**
See also CA 49-52; CANR 1, 47, 100

Alther, Lisa 1944- .... **CLC 7, 41**
See also BPFB 1; CA 65-68; CAAS 30;
CANR 12, 30, 51; CN 4, 5, 6, 7; CSW;
GLL 2; MTCW 1

Althusser, L.
See Althusser, Louis

Althusser, Louis 1918-1990 .... **CLC 106**
See also CA 131; 132; CANR 102; DLB
242

Altman, Robert 1925- .... **CLC 16, 116**
See also CA 73-76; CANR 43

Alurista .... **HLCS 1; PC 34**
See Urista (Heredia), Alberto (Baltazar)
See also CA 45-48R; DLB 82; LLW

Alvarez, A(lfred) 1929- .... **CLC 5, 13**
See also CA 1-4R; CANR 3, 33, 63, 101,
134; CN 3, 4, 5, 6; CP 1, 2, 3, 4, 5, 6, 7;
DLB 14, 40; MTFW 2005

Alvarez, Alejandro Rodriguez 1903-1965
See Casona, Alejandro
See also CA 131; 93-96; HW 1

Alvarez, Julia 1950- .... **CLC 93; HLCS 1**
See also AAYA 25; AMWS 7; CA 147;
CANR 69, 101, 133; DA3; DLB 282;
LATS 1:2; LLW; MTCW 2; MTFW 2005;
NFS 5, 9; SATA 129; WLIT 1

Alvaro, Corrado 1896-1956 .... **TCLC 60**
See also CA 163; DLB 264; EWL 3

Amado, Jorge 1912-2001 ... **CLC 13, 40, 106;
HLC 1**
See also CA 77-80; 201; CANR 35, 74, 135;
CWW 2; DAM MULT, NOV; DLB 113,
307; EWL 3; HW 2; LAW; LAWS 1;
MTCW 1, 2; MTFW 2005; RGWL 2, 3;
TWA; WLIT 1

Ambler, Eric 1909-1998 .... **CLC 4, 6, 9**
See also BRWS 4; CA 9-12R; 171; CANR
7, 38, 74; CMW 4; CN 1, 2, 3, 4, 5, 6;
DLB 77; MSW; MTCW 1, 2; TEA

Ambrose, Stephen E(dward)
1936-2002 .... **CLC 145**
See also AAYA 44; CA 1-4R; 209; CANR
3, 43, 57, 83, 105; MTFW 2005; NCFS 2;
SATA 40, 138

Amichai, Yehuda 1924-2000 .. **CLC 9, 22, 57,
116; PC 38**
See also CA 85-88; 189; CANR 46, 60, 99,
132; CWW 2; EWL 3; MTCW 1, 2;
MTFW 2005; WLIT 6

Amichai, Yehudah
See Amichai, Yehuda

Amiel, Henri Frederic 1821-1881 .... **NCLC 4**
See also DLB 217

Amis, Kingsley (William)
1922-1995 ...... **CLC 1, 2, 3, 5, 8, 13, 40,
44, 129**
See also AITN 2; BPFB 1; BRWS 2; CA
9-12R; 150; CANR 8, 28, 54; CDBLB
1945-1960; CN 1, 2, 3, 4, 5; CP 1, 2,
3, 4; DA; DA3; DAB; DAC; DAM MST,
NOV; DLB 15, 27, 100, 139; DLBY 1996;
EWL 3; HGG; INT CANR-8; MTCW 1,
2; MTFW 2005; RGEL 2; RGSF 2; SFW
4

Amis, Martin (Louis) 1949- .... **CLC 4, 9, 38,
62, 101, 213**
See also BEST 90:3; BRWS 4; CA 65-68;
CANR 8, 27, 54, 73, 95, 132; CN 5, 6, 7;
DA3; DLB 14, 194; EWL 3; INT CANR-
27; MTCW 2; MTFW 2005

Ammianus Marcellinus c. 330-c.
395 .... **CMLC 60**
See also AW 2; DLB 211

Ammons, A(rchie) R(andolph)
1926-2001 ...... **CLC 2, 3, 5, 8, 9, 25, 57,
108; PC 16**
See also AITN 1; AMWS 7; CA 9-12R;
193; CANR 6, 36, 51, 73, 107; CP 1, 2,
3, 4, 5, 6, 7; CSW; DAM POET; DLB 5,
165; EWL 3; MAL 5; MTCW 1, 2; PFS
19; RGAL 4; TCLE 1:1

Amo, Tauraatua i
See Adams, Henry (Brooks)

Amory, Thomas 1691(?)-1788 .... **LC 48**
See also DLB 39

Anand, Mulk Raj 1905-2004 ...... **CLC 23, 93**
See also CA 65-68; 231; CANR 32, 64; CN
1, 2, 3, 4, 5, 6, 7; DAM NOV; EWL 3;
MTCW 1, 2; MTFW 2005; RGSF 2

Anatol
See Schnitzler, Arthur

Anaximander c. 611B.C.-c.
546B.C. .... **CMLC 22**

Anaya, Rudolfo A(lfonso) 1937- ...... **CLC 23,
148; HLC 1**
See also AAYA 20; BYA 13; CA 45-48;
CAAS 4; CANR 1, 32, 51, 124; CN 4, 5,
6, 7; DAM MULT, NOV; DLB 82, 206,
278; HW 1; LAIT 4; LLW; MAL 5;
MTCW 1, 2; MTFW 2005; NFS 12;
RGAL 4; RGSF 2; TCWW 2; WLIT 1

Andersen, Hans Christian
1805-1875 .... **NCLC 7, 79; SSC 6, 56;
WLC**
See also AAYA 57; CLR 6; DA; DA3;
DAB; DAC; DAM MST, POP; EW 6;
MAICYA 1, 2; RGSF 2; RGWL 2, 3;
SATA 100; TWA; WCH; YABC 1

Behrman, S(amuel) N(athaniel)
1893-1973 .... **CLC 40**
See also CA 13-16; 45-48; CAD; CAP 1;
DLB 7, 44; IDFW 3; MAL 5; RGAL 4

Bekederemo, J. P. Clark
See Clark Bekederemo, J(ohnson) P(epper)
See also CD 6

Belasco, David 1853-1931 .... **TCLC 3**
See also CA 104; 168; DLB 7; MAL 5;
RGAL 4

Belcheva, Elisaveta Lyubomirova
1893-1991 .... **CLC 10**
See Bagryana, Elisaveta

Beldone, Phil ''Cheech''
See Ellison, Harlan (Jay)

Beleno
See Azuela, Mariano

Belinski, Vissarion Grigoryevich
1811-1848 .... **NCLC 5**
See also DLB 198

Belitt, Ben 1911- .... **CLC 22**
See also CA 13-16R; CAAS 4; CANR 7,
77; CP 1, 2, 3, 4; DLB 5

Belknap, Jeremy 1744-1798 .... **LC 115**
See also DLB 30, 37

Bell, Gertrude (Margaret Lowthian)
1868-1926 .... **TCLC 67**
See also CA 167; CANR 110; DLB 174

Bell, J. Freeman
See Zangwill, Israel

Bell, James Madison 1826-1902 .... **BLC 1;
TCLC 43**
See also BW 1; CA 122; 124; DAM MULT;
DLB 50

Bell, Madison Smartt 1957- ...... **CLC 41, 102**
See also AMWS 10; BPFB 1; CA 111, 183;
CAAE 183; CANR 28, 54, 73, 134; CN
5, 6, 7; CSW; DLB 218, 278; MTCW 2;
MTFW 2005

Bell, Marvin (Hartley) 1937- .... **CLC 8, 31**
See also CA 21-24R; CAAS 14; CANR 59,
102; CP 1, 2, 3, 4, 5, 6, 7; DAM POET;
DLB 5; MAL 5; MTCW 1

Bell, W. L. D.
See Mencken, H(enry) L(ouis)

Bellamy, Atwood C.
See Mencken, H(enry) L(ouis)

Bellamy, Edward 1850-1898 ..... **NCLC 4, 86,
147**
See also DLB 12; NFS 15; RGAL 4; SFW
4

Belli, Gioconda 1948- .... **HLCS 1**
See also CA 152; CANR 143; CWW 2;
DLB 290; EWL 3; RGWL 3

Bellin, Edward J.
See Kuttner, Henry

Bello, Andres 1781-1865 .... **NCLC 131**
See also LAW

**Belloc, (Joseph) Hilaire (Pierre Sebastien
Rene Swanton)** 1870-1953 .... **PC 24;
TCLC 7, 18**
See also CA 106; 152; CLR 102; CWRI 5;
DAM POET; DLB 19, 100, 141, 174;
EWL 3; MTCW 2; MTFW 2005; SATA
112; WCH; YABC 1

Belloc, Joseph Peter Rene Hilaire
See Belloc, (Joseph) Hilaire (Pierre Sebastien Rene Swanton)

Belloc, Joseph Pierre Hilaire
See Belloc, (Joseph) Hilaire (Pierre Sebastien Rene Swanton)

Belloc, M. A.
See Lowndes, Marie Adelaide (Belloc)

Belloc-Lowndes, Mrs.
See Lowndes, Marie Adelaide (Belloc)

Bellow, Saul 1915-2005 ...... **CLC 1, 2, 3, 6, 8,
10, 13, 15, 25, 33, 34, 63, 79, 190, 200;
SSC 14; WLC**
See also AITN 2; AMW; AMWC 2; AMWR
2; BEST 89:3; BPFB 1; CA 5-8R; 238;
CABS 1; CANR 29, 53, 95, 132; CDALB
1941-1968; CN 1, 2, 3, 4, 5, 6, 7; DA;
DA3; DAB; DAC; DAM MST, NOV,
POP; DLB 2, 28, 299; DLBD 3; DLBY
1982; EWL 3; MAL 5; MTCW 1, 2;
MTFW 2005; NFS 4, 14; RGAL 4; RGSF
2; SSFS 12; TUS

Belser, Reimond Karel Maria de 1929-
See Ruyslinck, Ward
See also CA 152

Bely, Andrey .... **PC 11; TCLC 7**
See Bugayev, Boris Nikolayevich
See also DLB 295; EW 9; EWL 3

Belyi, Andrei
See Bugayev, Boris Nikolayevich
See also RGWL 2, 3

Bembo, Pietro 1470-1547 .... **LC 79**
See also RGWL 2, 3

Benary, Margot
See Benary-Isbert, Margot

Benary-Isbert, Margot 1889-1979 .... **CLC 12**
See also CA 5-8R; 89-92; CANR 4, 72;
CLR 12; MAICYA 1, 2; SATA 2; SATA-
Obit 21

Benavente (y Martinez), Jacinto
1866-1954 .... **DC 26; HLCS 1; TCLC 3**
See also CA 106; 131; CANR 81; DAM
DRAM, MULT; EWL 3; GLL 2; HW 1,
2; MTCW 1, 2

Benchley, Peter 1940- .... **CLC 4, 8**
See also AAYA 14; AITN 2; BPFB 1; CA
17-20R; CANR 12, 35, 66, 115; CPW;
DAM NOV, POP; HGG; MTCW 1, 2;
MTFW 2005; SATA 3, 89, 164

Benchley, Peter Bradford
See Benchley, Peter

Benchley, Robert (Charles)
1889-1945 .... **TCLC 1, 55**
See also CA 105; 153; DLB 11; MAL 5;
RGAL 4

Benda, Julien 1867-1956 .... **TCLC 60**
See also CA 120; 154; GFL 1789 to the
Present

Benedict, Ruth (Fulton)
1887-1948 .... **TCLC 60**
See also CA 158; DLB 246

Benedikt, Michael 1935- .... **CLC 4, 14**
See also CA 13-16R; CANR 7; CP 1, 2, 3,
4, 5, 6, 7; DLB 5

Benet, Juan 1927-1993 .... **CLC 28**
See also CA 143; EWL 3

Benet, Stephen Vincent 1898-1943 ..... **PC 64;
SSC 10, 86; TCLC 7**
See also AMWS 11; CA 104; 152; DA3;
DAM POET; DLB 4, 48, 102, 249, 284;
DLBY 1997; EWL 3; HGG; MAL 5;
MTCW 2; MTFW 2005; RGAL 4; RGSF
2; SUFW; WP; YABC 1

Benet, William Rose 1886-1950 ..... **TCLC 28**
See also CA 118; 152; DAM POET; DLB
45; RGAL 4

Benford, Gregory (Albert) 1941- ..... **CLC 52**
See also BPFB 1; CA 69-72, 175; CAAE
175; CAAS 27; CANR 12, 24, 49, 95,
134; CN 7; CSW; DLBY 1982; MTFW
2005; SCFW 2; SFW 4

Bengtsson, Frans (Gunnar)
1894-1954 .... **TCLC 48**
See also CA 170; EWL 3

Benjamin, David
See Slavitt, David R(ytman)

Benjamin, Lois
See Gould, Lois

Benjamin, Walter 1892-1940 .... **TCLC 39**
See also CA 164; DLB 242; EW 11; EWL
3

Ben Jelloun, Tahar 1944-
See Jelloun, Tahar ben
See also CA 135; CWW 2; EWL 3; RGWL
3; WLIT 2

Benn, Gottfried 1886-1956 .. **PC 35; TCLC 3**
See also CA 106; 153; DLB 56; EWL 3;
RGWL 2, 3

Bennett, Alan 1934- .... **CLC 45, 77**
See also BRWS 8; CA 103; CANR 35, 55,
106; CBD; CD 5, 6; DAB; DAM MST;
DLB 310; MTCW 1, 2; MTFW 2005

Bennett, (Enoch) Arnold
1867-1931 .... **TCLC 5, 20**
See also BRW 6; CA 106; 155; CDBLB
1890-1914; DLB 10, 34, 98, 135; EWL 3;
MTCW 2

Bennett, Elizabeth
See Mitchell, Margaret (Munnerlyn)

Bennett, George Harold 1930-
See Bennett, Hal
See also BW 1; CA 97-100; CANR 87

Bennett, Gwendolyn B. 1902-1981 .... **HR 1:2**
See also BW 1; CA 125; DLB 51; WP

Bennett, Hal .... **CLC 5**
See Bennett, George Harold
See also DLB 33

Bennett, Jay 1912- .... **CLC 35**
See also AAYA 10; CA 69-72; CANR 11,
42, 79; JRDA; SAAS 4; SATA 41, 87;
SATA-Brief 27; WYA; YAW

Bennett, Louise (Simone) 1919- .... **BLC 1;
CLC 28**
See also BW 2, 3; CA 151; CDWLB 3; CP
1, 2, 3, 4, 5, 6, 7; DAM MULT; DLB 117;
EWL 3

Benson, A. C. 1862-1925 .... **TCLC 123**
See also DLB 98

Benson, E(dward) F(rederic)
1867-1940 .... **TCLC 27**
See also CA 114; 157; DLB 135, 153;
HGG; SUFW 1

Benson, Jackson J. 1930- .... **CLC 34**
See also CA 25-28R; DLB 111

Benson, Sally 1900-1972 .... **CLC 17**
See also CA 19-20; 37-40R; CAP 1; SATA
1, 35; SATA-Obit 27

Benson, Stella 1892-1933 .... **TCLC 17**
See also CA 117; 154, 155; DLB 36, 162;
FANT; TEA

Bentham, Jeremy 1748-1832 .... **NCLC 38**
See also DLB 107, 158, 252

Bentley, E(dmund) C(lerihew)
1875-1956 .... **TCLC 12**
See also CA 108; 232; DLB 70; MSW

Bentley, Eric (Russell) 1916- .... **CLC 24**
See also CA 5-8R; CAD; CANR 6, 67;
CBD; CD 5, 6; INT CANR-6

ben Uzair, Salem
See Horne, Richard Henry Hengist

Beranger, Pierre Jean de
1780-1857 .... **NCLC 34**

Berdyaev, Nicolas
See Berdyaev, Nikolai (Aleksandrovich)

Berdyaev, Nikolai (Aleksandrovich)
1874-1948 .... **TCLC 67**
See also CA 120; 157

Berdyayev, Nikolai (Aleksandrovich)
See Berdyaev, Nikolai (Aleksandrovich)

Berendt, John (Lawrence) 1939- ...... **CLC 86**
See also CA 146; CANR 75, 93; DA3;
MTCW 2; MTFW 2005

Beresford, J(ohn) D(avys)
1873-1947 .... **TCLC 81**
See also CA 112; 155; DLB 162, 178, 197;
SFW 4; SUFW 1

Bishop, John Peale 1892-1944 ..... **TCLC 103**
See also CA 107; 155; DLB 4, 9, 45; MAL 5; RGAL 4

Bissett, Bill 1939- .... **CLC 18; PC 14**
See also CA 69-72; CAAS 19; CANR 15; CCA 1; CP 1, 2, 3, 4, 5, 6, 7; DLB 53; MTCW 1

Bissoondath, Neil (Devindra)
1955- .... **CLC 120**
See also CA 136; CANR 123; CN 6, 7; DAC

Bitov, Andrei (Georgievich) 1937- ... **CLC 57**
See also CA 142; DLB 302

Biyidi, Alexandre 1932-
See Beti, Mongo
See also BW 1, 3; CA 114; 124; CANR 81; DA3; MTCW 1, 2

Bjarme, Brynjolf
See Ibsen, Henrik (Johan)

Bjoernson, Bjoernstjerne (Martinius)
1832-1910 .... **TCLC 7, 37**
See also CA 104

Black, Robert
See Holdstock, Robert P.

Blackburn, Paul 1926-1971 .... **CLC 9, 43**
See also BG 1:2; CA 81-84; 33-36R; CANR 34; CP 1; DLB 16; DLBY 1981

Black Elk 1863-1950 .... **NNAL; TCLC 33**
See also CA 144; DAM MULT; MTCW 2; MTFW 2005; WP

Black Hawk 1767-1838 .... **NNAL**

Black Hobart
See Sanders, (James) Ed(ward)

Blacklin, Malcolm
See Chambers, Aidan

Blackmore, R(ichard) D(oddridge)
1825-1900 .... **TCLC 27**
See also CA 120; DLB 18; RGEL 2

Blackmur, R(ichard) P(almer)
1904-1965 .... **CLC 2, 24**
See also AMWS 2; CA 11-12; 25-28R; CANR 71; CAP 1; DLB 63; EWL 3; MAL 5

Black Tarantula
See Acker, Kathy

Blackwood, Algernon (Henry)
1869-1951 .... **TCLC 5**
See also CA 105; 150; DLB 153, 156, 178; HGG; SUFW 1

Blackwood, Caroline (Maureen)
1931-1996 .... **CLC 6, 9, 100**
See also BRWS 9; CA 85-88; 151; CANR 32, 61, 65; CN 3, 4, 5, 6; DLB 14, 207; HGG; MTCW 1

Blade, Alexander
See Hamilton, Edmond; Silverberg, Robert

Blaga, Lucian 1895-1961 .... **CLC 75**
See also CA 157; DLB 220; EWL 3

Blair, Eric (Arthur) 1903-1950 .... **TCLC 123**
See Orwell, George
See also CA 104; 132; DA; DA3; DAB; DAC; DAM MST, NOV; MTCW 1, 2; MTFW 2005; SATA 29

Blair, Hugh 1718-1800 .... **NCLC 75**

Blais, Marie-Claire 1939- .... **CLC 2, 4, 6, 13, 22**
See also CA 21-24R; CAAS 4; CANR 38, 75, 93; CWW 2; DAC; DAM MST; DLB 53; EWL 3; FW; MTCW 1, 2; MTFW 2005; TWA

Blaise, Clark 1940- .... **CLC 29**
See also AITN 2; CA 53-56, 231; CAAE 231; CAAS 3; CANR 5, 66, 106; CN 4, 5, 6, 7; DLB 53; RGSF 2

Blake, Fairley
See De Voto, Bernard (Augustine)

Blake, Nicholas
See Day Lewis, C(ecil)
See also DLB 77; MSW

Blake, Sterling
See Benford, Gregory (Albert)

Blake, William 1757-1827 . **NCLC 13, 37, 57, 127; PC 12, 63; WLC**
See also AAYA 47; BRW 3; BRWR 1; CD-BLB 1789-1832; CLR 52; DA; DA3; DAB; DAC; DAM MST, POET; DLB 93, 163; EXPP; LATS 1:1; LMFS 1; MAICYA 1, 2; PAB; PFS 2, 12; SATA 30; TEA; WCH; WLIT 3; WP

Blanchot, Maurice 1907-2003 .... **CLC 135**
See also CA 117; 144; 213; CANR 138; DLB 72, 296; EWL 3

Blasco Ibanez, Vicente 1867-1928 . **TCLC 12**
See Ibanez, Vicente Blasco
See also BPFB 1; CA 110; 131; CANR 81; DA3; DAM NOV; EW 8; EWL 3; HW 1, 2; MTCW 1

Blatty, William Peter 1928- .... **CLC 2**
See also CA 5-8R; CANR 9, 124; DAM POP; HGG

Bleeck, Oliver
See Thomas, Ross (Elmore)

Blessing, Lee (Knowlton) 1949- .... **CLC 54**
See also CA 236; CAD; CD 5, 6

Blight, Rose
See Greer, Germaine

Blish, James (Benjamin) 1921-1975 . **CLC 14**
See also BPFB 1; CA 1-4R; 57-60; CANR 3; CN 2; DLB 8; MTCW 1; SATA 66; SCFW 1, 2; SFW 4

Bliss, Frederick
See Card, Orson Scott

Bliss, Reginald
See Wells, H(erbert) G(eorge)

Blixen, Karen (Christentze Dinesen)
1885-1962
See Dinesen, Isak
See also CA 25-28; CANR 22, 50; CAP 2; DA3; DLB 214; LMFS 1; MTCW 1, 2; SATA 44; SSFS 20

Bloch, Robert (Albert) 1917-1994 .... **CLC 33**
See also AAYA 29; CA 5-8R, 179; 146; CAAE 179; CAAS 20; CANR 5, 78; DA3; DLB 44; HGG; INT CANR-5; MTCW 2; SATA 12; SATA-Obit 82; SFW 4; SUFW 1, 2

Blok, Alexander (Alexandrovich)
1880-1921 .... **PC 21; TCLC 5**
See also CA 104; 183; DLB 295; EW 9; EWL 3; LMFS 2; RGWL 2, 3

Blom, Jan
See Breytenbach, Breyten

Bloom, Harold 1930- .... **CLC 24, 103, 221**
See also CA 13-16R; CANR 39, 75, 92, 133; DLB 67; EWL 3; MTCW 2; MTFW 2005; RGAL 4

Bloomfield, Aurelius
See Bourne, Randolph S(illiman)

Bloomfield, Robert 1766-1823 ..... **NCLC 145**
See also DLB 93

Blount, Roy (Alton), Jr. 1941- .... **CLC 38**
See also CA 53-56; CANR 10, 28, 61, 125; CSW; INT CANR-28; MTCW 1, 2; MTFW 2005

Blowsnake, Sam 1875-(?) .... **NNAL**

Bloy, Leon 1846-1917 .... **TCLC 22**
See also CA 121; 183; DLB 123; GFL 1789 to the Present

Blue Cloud, Peter (Aroniawenrate)
1933- .... **NNAL**
See also CA 117; CANR 40; DAM MULT

Bluggage, Oranthy
See Alcott, Louisa May

Blume, Judy (Sussman) 1938- .... **CLC 12, 30**
See also AAYA 3, 26; BYA 1, 8, 12; CA 29-32R; CANR 13, 37, 66, 124; CLR 2, 15, 69; CPW; DA3; DAM NOV, POP; DLB 52; JRDA; MAICYA 1, 2; MAICYAS 1; MTCW 1, 2; MTFW 2005; SATA 2, 31, 79, 142; WYA; YAW

Blunden, Edmund (Charles)
1896-1974 .... **CLC 2, 56; PC 66**
See also BRW 6; BRWS 11; CA 17-18; 45-48; CANR 54; CAP 2; CP 1, 2; DLB 20, 100, 155; MTCW 1; PAB

Bly, Robert (Elwood) 1926- .... **CLC 1, 2, 5, 10, 15, 38, 128; PC 39**
See also AMWS 4; CA 5-8R; CANR 41, 73, 125; CP 1, 2, 3, 4, 5, 6, 7; DA3; DAM POET; DLB 5; EWL 3; MAL 5; MTCW 1, 2; MTFW 2005; PFS 6, 17; RGAL 4

Boas, Franz 1858-1942 .... **TCLC 56**
See also CA 115; 181

Bobette
See Simenon, Georges (Jacques Christian)

Boccaccio, Giovanni 1313-1375 ... **CMLC 13, 57; SSC 10, 87**
See also EW 2; RGSF 2; RGWL 2, 3; TWA; WLIT 7

Bochco, Steven 1943- .... **CLC 35**
See also AAYA 11; CA 124; 138

Bode, Sigmund
See O'Doherty, Brian

Bodel, Jean 1167(?)-1210 .... **CMLC 28**

Bodenheim, Maxwell 1892-1954 .... **TCLC 44**
See also CA 110; 187; DLB 9, 45; MAL 5; RGAL 4

Bodenheimer, Maxwell
See Bodenheim, Maxwell

Bodker, Cecil 1927-
See Bodker, Cecil

Bodker, Cecil 1927- .... **CLC 21**
See also CA 73-76; CANR 13, 44, 111; CLR 23; MAICYA 1, 2; SATA 14, 133

Boell, Heinrich (Theodor)
1917-1985 ..... **CLC 2, 3, 6, 9, 11, 15, 27, 32, 72; SSC 23; WLC**
See Boll, Heinrich (Theodor)
See also CA 21-24R; 116; CANR 24; DA; DA3; DAB; DAC; DAM MST, NOV; DLB 69; DLBY 1985; MTCW 1, 2; MTFW 2005; SSFS 20; TWA

Boerne, Alfred
See Doeblin, Alfred

Boethius c. 480-c. 524 .... **CMLC 15**
See also DLB 115; RGWL 2, 3

Boff, Leonardo (Genezio Darci)
1938- .... **CLC 70; HLC 1**
See also CA 150; DAM MULT; HW 2

Bogan, Louise 1897-1970 .... **CLC 4, 39, 46, 93; PC 12**
See also AMWS 3; CA 73-76; 25-28R; CANR 33, 82; CP 1; DAM POET; DLB 45, 169; EWL 3; MAL 5; MAWW; MTCW 1, 2; PFS 21; RGAL 4

Bogarde, Dirk
See Van Den Bogarde, Derek Jules Gaspard Ulric Niven
See also DLB 14

Bogosian, Eric 1953- .... **CLC 45, 141**
See also CA 138; CAD; CANR 102; CD 5, 6

Bograd, Larry 1953- .... **CLC 35**
See also CA 93-96; CANR 57; SAAS 21; SATA 33, 89; WYA

Boiardo, Matteo Maria 1441-1494 .... **LC 6**

Boileau-Despreaux, Nicolas 1636-1711 . **LC 3**
See also DLB 268; EW 3; GFL Beginnings to 1789; RGWL 2, 3

Boissard, Maurice
See Leautaud, Paul

Bojer, Johan 1872-1959 .... **TCLC 64**
See also CA 189; EWL 3

Bok, Edward W(illiam)
1863-1930 .... **TCLC 101**
See also CA 217; DLB 91; DLBD 16

Boker, George Henry 1823-1890 . **NCLC 125**
See also RGAL 4

Boland, Eavan (Aisling) 1944- .. **CLC 40, 67, 113; PC 58**
See also BRWS 5; CA 143, 207; CAAE 207; CANR 61; CP 1, 7; CWP; DAM POET; DLB 40; FW; MTCW 2; MTFW 2005; PFS 12, 22

Boll, Heinrich (Theodor)
See Boell, Heinrich (Theodor)
See also BPFB 1; CDWLB 2; EW 13; EWL 3; RGSF 2; RGWL 2, 3

Bolt, Lee
See Faust, Frederick (Schiller)

Bolt, Robert (Oxton) 1924-1995 ...... **CLC 14; TCLC 175**
See also CA 17-20R; 147; CANR 35, 67; CBD; DAM DRAM; DFS 2; DLB 13, 233; EWL 3; LAIT 1; MTCW 1

Bombal, Maria Luisa 1910-1980 .... **HLCS 1; SSC 37**
See also CA 127; CANR 72; EWL 3; HW 1; LAW; RGSF 2

Bombet, Louis-Alexandre-Cesar
See Stendhal

Bomkauf
See Kaufman, Bob (Garnell)

Bonaventura .... **NCLC 35**
See also DLB 90

Bonaventure 1217(?)-1274 .... **CMLC 79**
See also DLB 115; LMFS 1

Bond, Edward 1934- .... **CLC 4, 6, 13, 23**
See also AAYA 50; BRWS 1; CA 25-28R; CANR 38, 67, 106; CBD; CD 5, 6; DAM DRAM; DFS 3, 8; DLB 13, 310; EWL 3; MTCW 1

Bonham, Frank 1914-1989 .... **CLC 12**
See also AAYA 1; BYA 1, 3; CA 9-12R; CANR 4, 36; JRDA; MAICYA 1, 2; SAAS 3; SATA 1, 49; SATA-Obit 62; TCWW 1, 2; YAW

Bonnefoy, Yves 1923- . **CLC 9, 15, 58; PC 58**
See also CA 85-88; CANR 33, 75, 97, 136; CWW 2; DAM MST, POET; DLB 258; EWL 3; GFL 1789 to the Present; MTCW 1, 2; MTFW 2005

Bonner, Marita .... **HR 1:2**
See Occomy, Marita (Odette) Bonner

Bonnin, Gertrude 1876-1938 .... **NNAL**
See Zitkala-Sa
See also CA 150; DAM MULT

Bontemps, Arna(ud Wendell)
1902-1973 .. **BLC 1; CLC 1, 18; HR 1:2**
See also BW 1; CA 1-4R; 41-44R; CANR 4, 35; CLR 6; CP 1; CWRI 5; DA3; DAM MULT, NOV, POET; DLB 48, 51; JRDA; MAICYA 1, 2; MAL 5; MTCW 1, 2; SATA 2, 44; SATA-Obit 24; WCH; WP

Boot, William
See Stoppard, Tom

Booth, Martin 1944-2004 .... **CLC 13**
See also CA 93-96, 188; 223; CAAE 188; CAAS 2; CANR 92; CP 1, 2, 3, 4

Booth, Philip 1925- .... **CLC 23**
See also CA 5-8R; CANR 5, 88; CP 1, 2, 3, 4, 5, 6, 7; DLBY 1982

Booth, Wayne C(layson) 1921-2005 . **CLC 24**
See also CA 1-4R; CAAS 5; CANR 3, 43, 117; DLB 67

Borchert, Wolfgang 1921-1947 .... **TCLC 5**
See also CA 104; 188; DLB 69, 124; EWL 3

Borel, Petrus 1809-1859 .... **NCLC 41**
See also DLB 119; GFL 1789 to the Present

Borges, Jorge Luis 1899-1986 ... **CLC 1, 2, 3, 4, 6, 8, 9, 10, 13, 19, 44, 48, 83; HLC 1; PC 22, 32; SSC 4, 41; TCLC 109; WLC**
See also AAYA 26; BPFB 1; CA 21-24R; CANR 19, 33, 75, 105, 133; CDWLB 3; DA; DA3; DAB; DAC; DAM MST,

MULT; DLB 113, 283; DLBY 1986; DNFS 1, 2; EWL 3; HW 1, 2; LAW; LMFS 2; MSW; MTCW 1, 2; MTFW 2005; RGSF 2; RGWL 2, 3; SFW 4; SSFS 17; TWA; WLIT 1

Borowski, Tadeusz 1922-1951 .... **SSC 48; TCLC 9**
See also CA 106; 154; CDWLB 4; DLB 215; EWL 3; RGSF 2; RGWL 3; SSFS 13

Borrow, George (Henry)
1803-1881 .... **NCLC 9**
See also DLB 21, 55, 166

Bosch (Gavino), Juan 1909-2001 ..... **HLCS 1**
See also CA 151; 204; DAM MST, MULT; DLB 145; HW 1, 2

Bosman, Herman Charles
1905-1951 .... **TCLC 49**
See Malan, Herman
See also CA 160; DLB 225; RGSF 2

Bosschere, Jean de 1878(?)-1953 ... **TCLC 19**
See also CA 115; 186

Boswell, James 1740-1795 ... **LC 4, 50; WLC**
See also BRW 3; CDBLB 1660-1789; DA; DAB; DAC; DAM MST; DLB 104, 142; TEA; WLIT 3

Bottomley, Gordon 1874-1948 ..... **TCLC 107**
See also CA 120; 192; DLB 10

Bottoms, David 1949- .... **CLC 53**
See also CA 105; CANR 22; CSW; DLB 120; DLBY 1983

Boucicault, Dion 1820-1890 .... **NCLC 41**

Boucolon, Maryse
See Conde, Maryse

Bourdieu, Pierre 1930-2002 .... **CLC 198**
See also CA 130; 204

Bourget, Paul (Charles Joseph)
1852-1935 .... **TCLC 12**
See also CA 107; 196; DLB 123; GFL 1789 to the Present

Bourjaily, Vance (Nye) 1922- .... **CLC 8, 62**
See also CA 1-4R; CAAS 1; CANR 2, 72; CN 1, 2, 3, 4, 5, 6, 7; DLB 2, 143; MAL 5

Bourne, Randolph S(illiman)
1886-1918 .... **TCLC 16**
See also AMW; CA 117; 155; DLB 63; MAL 5

Bova, Ben(jamin William) 1932- ...... **CLC 45**
See also AAYA 16; CA 5-8R; CAAS 18; CANR 11, 56, 94, 111; CLR 3, 96; DLBY 1981; INT CANR-11; MAICYA 1, 2; MTCW 1; SATA 6, 68, 133; SFW 4

Bowen, Elizabeth (Dorothea Cole)
1899-1973 . **CLC 1, 3, 6, 11, 15, 22, 118; SSC 3, 28, 66; TCLC 148**
See also BRWS 2; CA 17-18; 41-44R; CANR 35, 105; CAP 2; CDBLB 1945-1960; CN 1; DA3; DAM NOV; DLB 15, 162; EWL 3; EXPS; FW; HGG; MTCW 1, 2; MTFW 2005; NFS 13; RGSF 2; SSFS 5; SUFW 1; TEA; WLIT 4

Bowering, George 1935- .... **CLC 15, 47**
See also CA 21-24R; CAAS 16; CANR 10; CN 7; CP 1, 2, 3, 4, 5, 6, 7; DLB 53

Bowering, Marilyn R(uthe) 1949- .... **CLC 32**
See also CA 101; CANR 49; CP 4, 5, 6, 7; CWP

Bowers, Edgar 1924-2000 .... **CLC 9**
See also CA 5-8R; 188; CANR 24; CP 1, 2, 3, 4, 5, 6, 7; CSW; DLB 5

Bowers, Mrs. J. Milton 1842-1914
See Bierce, Ambrose (Gwinett)

Bowie, David .... **CLC 17**
See Jones, David Robert

Bowles, Jane (Sydney) 1917-1973 ..... **CLC 3, 68**
See Bowles, Jane Auer
See also CA 19-20; 41-44R; CAP 2; CN 1; MAL 5

Bowles, Jane Auer
See Bowles, Jane (Sydney)
See also EWL 3

Bowles, Paul (Frederick) 1910-1999 . **CLC 1, 2, 19, 53; SSC 3**
See also AMWS 4; CA 1-4R; 186; CAAS 1; CANR 1, 19, 50, 75; CN 1, 2, 3, 4, 5, 6; DA3; DLB 5, 6, 218; EWL 3; MAL 5; MTCW 1, 2; MTFW 2005; RGAL 4; SSFS 17

Bowles, William Lisle 1762-1850 . **NCLC 103**
See also DLB 93

Box, Edgar
See Vidal, (Eugene Luther) Gore
See also GLL 1

Boyd, James 1888-1944 .... **TCLC 115**
See also CA 186; DLB 9; DLBD 16; RGAL 4; RHW

Boyd, Nancy
See Millay, Edna St. Vincent
See also GLL 1

Boyd, Thomas (Alexander)
1898-1935 .... **TCLC 111**
See also CA 111; 183; DLB 9; DLBD 16, 316

Boyd, William (Andrew Murray)
1952- .... **CLC 28, 53, 70**
See also CA 114; 120; CANR 51, 71, 131; CN 4, 5, 6, 7; DLB 231

Boyesen, Hjalmar Hjorth
1848-1895 .... **NCLC 135**
See also DLB 12, 71; DLBD 13; RGAL 4

Boyle, Kay 1902-1992 .... **CLC 1, 5, 19, 58, 121; SSC 5**
See also CA 13-16R; 140; CAAS 1; CANR 29, 61, 110; CN 1, 2, 3, 4, 5; CP 1, 2, 3, 4; DLB 4, 9, 48, 86; DLBY 1993; EWL 3; MAL 5; MTCW 1, 2; MTFW 2005; RGAL 4; RGSF 2; SSFS 10, 13, 14

Boyle, Mark
See Kienzle, William X(avier)

Boyle, Patrick 1905-1982 .... **CLC 19**
See also CA 127

Boyle, T. C.
See Boyle, T(homas) Coraghessan
See also AMWS 8

Boyle, T(homas) Coraghessan
1948- .... **CLC 36, 55, 90; SSC 16**
See Boyle, T. C.
See also AAYA 47; BEST 90:4; BPFB 1; CA 120; CANR 44, 76, 89, 132; CN 6, 7; CPW; DA3; DAM POP; DLB 218, 278; DLBY 1986; EWL 3; MAL 5; MTCW 2; MTFW 2005; SSFS 13, 19

Boz
See Dickens, Charles (John Huffam)

Brackenridge, Hugh Henry
1748-1816 .... **NCLC 7**
See also DLB 11, 37; RGAL 4

Bradbury, Edward P.
See Moorcock, Michael (John)
See also MTCW 2

Bradbury, Malcolm (Stanley)
1932-2000 .... **CLC 32, 61**
See also CA 1-4R; CANR 1, 33, 91, 98, 137; CN 1, 2, 3, 4, 5, 6, 7; CP 1; DA3; DAM NOV; DLB 14, 207; EWL 3; MTCW 1, 2; MTFW 2005

Bradbury, Ray (Douglas) 1920- .... **CLC 1, 3, 10, 15, 42, 98; SSC 29, 53; WLC**
See also AAYA 15; AITN 1, 2; AMWS 4; BPFB 1; BYA 4, 5, 11; CA 1-4R; CANR 2, 30, 75, 125; CDALB 1968-1988; CN 1, 2, 3, 4, 5, 6, 7; CPW; DA; DA3; DAB; DAC; DAM MST, NOV, POP; DLB 2, 8;

EXPN; EXPS; HGG; LAIT 3, 5; LATS
1:2; MAL 5; MTCW 1, 2;
MTFW 2005; NFS 1, 22; RGAL 4; RGSF
2; SATA 11, 64, 123; SCFW 1, 2; SFW 4;
SSFS 1, 20; SUFW 1, 2; TUS; YAW

Braddon, Mary Elizabeth
1837-1915 .... **TCLC 111**
See also BRWS 8; CA 108; 179; CMW 4;
DLB 18, 70, 156; HGG

Bradfield, Scott (Michael) 1955- .... **SSC 65**
See also CA 147; CANR 90; HGG; SUFW
2

Bradford, Gamaliel 1863-1932 .... **TCLC 36**
See also CA 160; DLB 17

Bradford, William 1590-1657 .... **LC 64**
See also DLB 24, 30; RGAL 4

Bradley, David (Henry), Jr. 1950- .... **BLC 1;
CLC 23, 118**
See also BW 1, 3; CA 104; CANR 26, 81;
CN 4, 5, 6, 7; DAM MULT; DLB 33

Bradley, John Ed(mund, Jr.) 1958- . **CLC 55**
See also CA 139; CANR 99; CN 6, 7; CSW

Bradley, Marion Zimmer
1930-1999 .... **CLC 30**
See Chapman, Lee; Dexter, John; Gardner,
Miriam; Ives, Morgan; Rivers, Elfrida
See also AAYA 40; BPFB 1; CA 57-60; 185;
CAAS 10; CANR 7, 31, 51, 75, 107;
CPW; DA3; DAM POP; DLB 8; FANT;
FW; MTCW 1, 2; MTFW 2005; SATA 90,
139; SATA-Obit 116; SFW 4; SUFW 2;
YAW

Bradshaw, John 1933- .... **CLC 70**
See also CA 138; CANR 61

Bradstreet, Anne 1612(?)-1672 ...... **LC 4, 30;
PC 10**
See also AMWS 1; CDALB 1640-1865;
DA; DA3; DAC; DAM MST, POET; DLB
24; EXPP; FW; PFS 6; RGAL 4; TUS;
WP

Brady, Joan 1939- .... **CLC 86**
See also CA 141

Bragg, Melvyn 1939- .... **CLC 10**
See also BEST 89:3; CA 57-60; CANR 10,
48, 89; CN 1, 2, 3, 4, 5, 6, 7; DLB 14,
271; RHW

Brahe, Tycho 1546-1601 .... **LC 45**
See also DLB 300

Braine, John (Gerard) 1922-1986 . **CLC 1, 3,
41**
See also CA 1-4R; 120; CANR 1, 33; CD-
BLB 1945-1960; CN 1, 2, 3, 4; DLB 15;
DLBY 1986; EWL 3; MTCW 1

Braithwaite, William Stanley (Beaumont)
1878-1962 .... **BLC 1; HR 1:2; PC 52**
See also BW 1; CA 125; DAM MULT; DLB
50, 54; MAL 5

Bramah, Ernest 1868-1942 .... **TCLC 72**
See also CA 156; CMW 4; DLB 70; FANT

Brammer, Billy Lee
See Brammer, William

Brammer, William 1929-1978 .... **CLC 31**
See also CA 235; 77-80

Brancati, Vitaliano 1907-1954 .... **TCLC 12**
See also CA 109; DLB 264; EWL 3

Brancato, Robin F(idler) 1936- .... **CLC 35**
See also AAYA 9, 68; BYA 6; CA 69-72;
CANR 11, 45; CLR 32; JRDA; MAICYA
2; MAICYAS 1; SAAS 9; SATA 97;
WYA; YAW

Brand, Dionne 1953- .... **CLC 192**
See also BW 2; CA 143; CANR 143; CWP

Brand, Max
See Faust, Frederick (Schiller)
See also BPFB 1; TCWW 1, 2

Brand, Millen 1906-1980 .... **CLC 7**
See also CA 21-24R; 97-100; CANR 72

Branden, Barbara .... **CLC 44**
See also CA 148

Brandes, Georg (Morris Cohen)
1842-1927 .... **TCLC 10**
See also CA 105; 189; DLB 300

Brandys, Kazimierz 1916-2000 .... **CLC 62**
See also CA 239; EWL 3

Branley, Franklyn M(ansfield)
1915-2002 .... **CLC 21**
See also CA 33-36R; 207; CANR 14, 39;
CLR 13; MAICYA 1, 2; SAAS 16; SATA
4, 68, 136

Brant, Beth (E.) 1941- .... **NNAL**
See also CA 144; FW

Brant, Sebastian 1457-1521 .... **LC 112**
See also DLB 179; RGWL 2, 3

Brathwaite, Edward Kamau
1930- .... **BLCS; CLC 11; PC 56**
See also BW 2, 3; CA 25-28R; CANR 11,
26, 47, 107; CDWLB 3; CP 1, 2, 3, 4, 5,
6, 7; DAM POET; DLB 125; EWL 3

Brathwaite, Kamau
See Brathwaite, Edward Kamau

Brautigan, Richard (Gary)
1935-1984 .... **CLC 1, 3, 5, 9, 12, 34, 42;
TCLC 133**
See also BPFB 1; CA 53-56; 113; CANR
34; CN 1, 2, 3, 4; CP 1, 2, 3, 4; DA3; DAM
NOV; DLB 2, 5, 206; DLBY 1980, 1984;
FANT; MAL 5; MTCW 1; RGAL 4;
SATA 56

Brave Bird, Mary .... **NNAL**
See Crow Dog, Mary (Ellen)

Braverman, Kate 1950- .... **CLC 67**
See also CA 89-92; CANR 141

Brecht, (Eugen) Bertolt (Friedrich)
1898-1956 ..... **DC 3; TCLC 1, 6, 13, 35,
169; WLC**
See also CA 104; 133; CANR 62; CDWLB
2; DA; DA3; DAB; DAC; DAM DRAM,
MST; DFS 4, 5, 9; DLB 56, 124; EW 11;
EWL 3; IDTP; MTCW 1, 2; MTFW 2005;
RGWL 2, 3; TWA

Brecht, Eugen Berthold Friedrich
See Brecht, (Eugen) Bertolt (Friedrich)

Bremer, Fredrika 1801-1865 .... **NCLC 11**
See also DLB 254

Brennan, Christopher John
1870-1932 .... **TCLC 17**
See also CA 117; 188; DLB 230; EWL 3

Brennan, Maeve 1917-1993 ... **CLC 5; TCLC
124**
See also CA 81-84; CANR 72, 100

Brenner, Jozef 1887-1919
See Csath, Geza
See also CA 240

Brent, Linda
See Jacobs, Harriet A(nn)

Brentano, Clemens (Maria)
1778-1842 .... **NCLC 1**
See also DLB 90; RGWL 2, 3

Brent of Bin Bin
See Franklin, (Stella Maria Sarah) Miles
(Lampe)

Brenton, Howard 1942- .... **CLC 31**
See also CA 69-72; CANR 33, 67; CBD;
CD 5, 6; DLB 13; MTCW 1

Breslin, James 1930-
See Breslin, Jimmy
See also CA 73-76; CANR 31, 75, 139;
DAM NOV; MTCW 1, 2; MTFW 2005

Breslin, Jimmy .... **CLC 4, 43**
See Breslin, James
See also AITN 1; DLB 185; MTCW 2

Bresson, Robert 1901(?)-1999 .... **CLC 16**
See also CA 110; 187; CANR 49

Breton, Andre 1896-1966 .. **CLC 2, 9, 15, 54;
PC 15**
See also CA 19-20; 25-28R; CANR 40, 60;
CAP 2; DLB 65, 258; EW 11; EWL 3;
GFL 1789 to the Present; LMFS 2;
MTCW 1, 2; MTFW 2005; RGWL 2, 3;
TWA; WP

Breytenbach, Breyten 1939(?)- .. **CLC 23, 37,
126**
See also CA 113; 129; CANR 61, 122;
CWW 2; DAM POET; DLB 225; EWL 3

Bridgers, Sue Ellen 1942- .... **CLC 26**
See also AAYA 8, 49; BYA 7, 8; CA 65-68;
CANR 11, 36; CLR 18; DLB 52; JRDA;
MAICYA 1, 2; SAAS 1; SATA 22, 90;
SATA-Essay 109; WYA; YAW

Bridges, Robert (Seymour)
1844-1930 .... **PC 28; TCLC 1**
See also BRW 6; CA 104; 152; CDBLB
1890-1914; DAM POET; DLB 19, 98

Bridie, James .... **TCLC 3**
See Mavor, Osborne Henry
See also DLB 10; EWL 3

Brin, David 1950- .... **CLC 34**
See also AAYA 21; CA 102; CANR 24, 70,
125, 127; INT CANR-24; SATA 65;
SCFW 2; SFW 4

Brink, Andre (Philippus) 1935- . **CLC 18, 36,
106**
See also AFW; BRWS 6; CA 104; CANR
39, 62, 109, 133; CN 4, 5, 6, 7; DLB 225;
EWL 3; INT CA-103; LATS 1:2; MTCW
1, 2; MTFW 2005; WLIT 2

Brinsmead, H. F(ay)
See Brinsmead, H(esba) F(ay)

Brinsmead, H. F.
See Brinsmead, H(esba) F(ay)

Brinsmead, H(esba) F(ay) 1922- ...... **CLC 21**
See also CA 21-24R; CANR 10; CLR 47;
CWRI 5; MAICYA 1, 2; SAAS 5; SATA
18, 78

Brittain, Vera (Mary) 1893(?)-1970 . **CLC 23**
See also BRWS 10; CA 13-16; 25-28R;
CANR 58; CAP 1; DLB 191; FW; MTCW
1, 2

Broch, Hermann 1886-1951 .... **TCLC 20**
See also CA 117; 211; CDWLB 2; DLB 85,
124; EW 10; EWL 3; RGWL 2, 3

Brock, Rose
See Hansen, Joseph
See also GLL 1

Brod, Max 1884-1968 .... **TCLC 115**
See also CA 5-8R; 25-28R; CANR 7; DLB
81; EWL 3

Brodkey, Harold (Roy) 1930-1996 .. **CLC 56;
TCLC 123**
See also CA 111; 151; CANR 71; CN 4, 5,
6; DLB 130

Brodsky, Iosif Alexandrovich 1940-1996
See Brodsky, Joseph
See also AITN 1; CA 41-44R; 151; CANR
37, 106; DA3; DAM POET; MTCW 1, 2;
MTFW 2005; RGWL 2, 3

Brodsky, Joseph . **CLC 4, 6, 13, 36, 100; PC
9**
See Brodsky, Iosif Alexandrovich
See also AMWS 8; CWW 2; DLB 285;
EWL 3; MTCW 1

Brodsky, Michael (Mark) 1948- .... **CLC 19**
See also CA 102; CANR 18, 41, 58; DLB
244

Brodzki, Bella ed. .... **CLC 65**

Brome, Richard 1590(?)-1652 .... **LC 61**
See also BRWS 10; DLB 58

Bromell, Henry 1947- .... **CLC 5**
See also CA 53-56; CANR 9, 115, 116

Bryant, William Cullen 1794-1878 . NCLC 6, 46; PC 20
   See also AMWS 1; CDALB 1640-1865; DA; DAB; DAC; DAM MST, POET; DLB 3, 43, 59, 189, 250; EXPP; PAB; RGAL 4; TUS

Bryusov, Valery Yakovlevich 1873-1924 .... TCLC 10
   See also CA 107; 155; EWL 3; SFW 4

Buchan, John 1875-1940 .... TCLC 41
   See also CA 108; 145; CMW 4; DAB; DAM POP; DLB 34, 70, 156; HGG; MSW; MTCW 2; RGEL 2; RHW; YABC 2

Buchanan, George 1506-1582 .... LC 4
   See also DLB 132

Buchanan, Robert 1841-1901 .... TCLC 107
   See also CA 179; DLB 18, 35

Buchheim, Lothar-Guenther 1918- .... CLC 6
   See also CA 85-88

Buchner, (Karl) Georg 1813-1837 .... NCLC 26, 146
   See also CDWLB 2; DLB 133; EW 6; RGSF 2; RGWL 2, 3; TWA

Buchwald, Art(hur) 1925- .... CLC 33
   See also AITN 1; CA 5-8R; CANR 21, 67, 107; MTCW 1, 2; SATA 10

Buck, Pearl S(ydenstricker) 1892-1973 .... CLC 7, 11, 18, 127
   See also AAYA 42; AITN 1; AMWS 2; BPFB 1; CA 1-4R; 41-44R; CANR 1, 34; CDALBS; CN 1; DA; DA3; DAB; DAC; DAM MST, NOV; DLB 9, 102; EWL 3; LAIT 3; MAL 5; MTCW 1, 2; MTFW 2005; RGAL 4; RHW; SATA 1, 25; TUS

Buckler, Ernest 1908-1984 .... CLC 13
   See also CA 11-12; 114; CAP 1; CCA 1; CN 1, 2, 3; DAC; DAM MST; DLB 68; SATA 47

Buckley, Christopher (Taylor) 1952- .... CLC 165
   See also CA 139; CANR 119

Buckley, Vincent (Thomas) 1925-1988 .... CLC 57
   See also CA 101; CP 1, 2, 3, 4; DLB 289

Buckley, William F(rank), Jr. 1925- . CLC 7, 18, 37
   See also AITN 1; BPFB 1; CA 1-4R; CANR 1, 24, 53, 93, 133; CMW 4; CPW; DA3; DAM POP; DLB 137; DLBY 1980; INT CANR-24; MTCW 1, 2; MTFW 2005; TUS

Buechner, (Carl) Frederick 1926- . CLC 2, 4, 6, 9
   See also AMWS 12; BPFB 1; CA 13-16R; CANR 11, 39, 64, 114, 138; CN 1, 2, 3, 4, 5, 6, 7; DAM NOV; DLBY 1980; INT CANR-11; MAL 5; MTCW 1, 2; MTFW 2005; TCLE 1:1

Buell, John (Edward) 1927- .... CLC 10
   See also CA 1-4R; CANR 71; DLB 53

Buero Vallejo, Antonio 1916-2000 ... CLC 15, 46, 139; DC 18
   See also CA 106; 189; CANR 24, 49, 75; CWW 2; DFS 11; EWL 3; HW 1; MTCW 1, 2

Bufalino, Gesualdo 1920-1996 .... CLC 74
   See also CA 209; CWW 2; DLB 196

Bugayev, Boris Nikolayevich 1880-1934 .... PC 11; TCLC 7
   See Bely, Andrey; Belyi, Andrei
   See also CA 104; 165; MTCW 2; MTFW 2005

Bukowski, Charles 1920-1994 ... CLC 2, 5, 9, 41, 82, 108; PC 18; SSC 45
   See also CA 17-20R; 144; CANR 40, 62, 105; CN 4, 5; CP 1, 2, 3, 4; CPW; DA3; DAM NOV, POET; DLB 5, 130, 169; EWL 3; MAL 5; MTCW 1, 2; MTFW 2005

Bulgakov, Mikhail (Afanas'evich) 1891-1940 ..... SSC 18; TCLC 2, 16, 159
   See also BPFB 1; CA 105; 152; DAM DRAM, NOV; DLB 272; EWL 3; MTCW 2; MTFW 2005; NFS 8; RGSF 2; RGWL 2, 3; SFW 4; TWA

Bulgya, Alexander Alexandrovich 1901-1956 .... TCLC 53
   See Fadeev, Aleksandr Aleksandrovich; Fadeev, Alexandr Alexandrovich; Fadeyev, Alexander
   See also CA 117; 181

Bullins, Ed 1935- ... BLC 1; CLC 1, 5, 7; DC 6
   See also BW 2, 3; CA 49-52; CAAS 16; CAD; CANR 24, 46, 73, 134; CD 5, 6; DAM DRAM, MULT; DLB 7, 38, 249; EWL 3; MAL 5; MTCW 1, 2; MTFW 2005; RGAL 4

Bulosan, Carlos 1911-1956 .... AAL
   See also CA 216; DLB 312; RGAL 4

Bulwer-Lytton, Edward (George Earle Lytton) 1803-1873 .... NCLC 1, 45
   See also DLB 21; RGEL 2; SFW 4; SUFW 1; TEA

Bunin, Ivan Alexeyevich 1870-1953 ... SSC 5; TCLC 6
   See also CA 104; DLB 317; EWL 3; RGSF 2; RGWL 2, 3; TWA

Bunting, Basil 1900-1985 ...... CLC 10, 39, 47
   See also BRWS 7; CA 53-56; 115; CANR 7; CP 1, 2, 3, 4; DAM POET; DLB 20; EWL 3; RGEL 2

Bunuel, Luis 1900-1983 ... CLC 16, 80; HLC 1
   See also CA 101; 110; CANR 32, 77; DAM MULT; HW 1

Bunyan, John 1628-1688 ..... LC 4, 69; WLC
   See also BRW 2; BYA 5; CDBLB 1660-1789; DA; DAB; DAC; DAM MST; DLB 39; RGEL 2; TEA; WCH; WLIT 3

Buravsky, Alexander .... CLC 59

Burckhardt, Jacob (Christoph) 1818-1897 .... NCLC 49
   See also EW 6

Burford, Eleanor
   See Hibbert, Eleanor Alice Burford

Burgess, Anthony . CLC 1, 2, 4, 5, 8, 10, 13, 15, 22, 40, 62, 81, 94
   See Wilson, John (Anthony) Burgess
   See also AAYA 25; AITN 1; BRWS 1; CD-BLB 1960 to Present; CN 1, 2, 3, 4, 5; DAB; DLB 14, 194, 261; DLBY 1998; EWL 3; RGEL 2; RHW; SFW 4; YAW

Burke, Edmund 1729(?)-1797 .... LC 7, 36; WLC
   See also BRW 3; DA; DA3; DAB; DAC; DAM MST; DLB 104, 252; RGEL 2; TEA

Burke, Kenneth (Duva) 1897-1993 ... CLC 2, 24
   See also AMW; CA 5-8R; 143; CANR 39, 74, 136; CN 1, 2; CP 1, 2, 3, 4; DLB 45, 63; EWL 3; MAL 5; MTCW 1, 2; MTFW 2005; RGAL 4

Burke, Leda
   See Garnett, David

Burke, Ralph
   See Silverberg, Robert

Burke, Thomas 1886-1945 .... TCLC 63
   See also CA 113; 155; CMW 4; DLB 197

Burney, Fanny 1752-1840 .... NCLC 12, 54, 107
   See also BRWS 3; DLB 39; FL 1:2; NFS 16; RGEL 2; TEA

Burney, Frances
   See Burney, Fanny

Burns, Robert 1759-1796 ... LC 3, 29, 40; PC 6; WLC
   See also AAYA 51; BRW 3; CDBLB 1789-1832; DA; DA3; DAB; DAC; DAM MST, POET; DLB 109; EXPP; PAB; RGEL 2; TEA; WP

Burns, Tex
   See L'Amour, Louis (Dearborn)

Burnshaw, Stanley 1906- .... CLC 3, 13, 44
   See also CA 9-12R; CP 1, 2, 3, 4, 5, 6, 7; DLB 48; DLBY 1997

Burr, Anne 1937- .... CLC 6
   See also CA 25-28R

Burroughs, Edgar Rice 1875-1950 . TCLC 2, 32
   See also AAYA 11; BPFB 1; BYA 4, 9; CA 104; 132; CANR 131; DA3; DAM NOV; DLB 8; FANT; MTCW 1, 2; MTFW 2005; RGAL 4; SATA 41; SCFW 1, 2; SFW 4; TCWW 1, 2; TUS; YAW

Burroughs, William S(eward) 1914-1997 .. CLC 1, 2, 5, 15, 22, 42, 75, 109; TCLC 121; WLC
   See Lee, William; Lee, Willy
   See also AAYA 60; AITN 2; AMWS 3; BG 1:2; BPFB 1; CA 9-12R; 160; CANR 20, 52, 104; CN 1, 2, 3, 4, 5, 6; CPW; DA; DA3; DAB; DAC; DAM MST, NOV, POP; DLB 2, 8, 16, 152, 237; DLBY 1981, 1997; EWL 3; HGG; LMFS 2; MAL 5; MTCW 1, 2; MTFW 2005; RGAL 4; SFW 4

Burton, Sir Richard F(rancis) 1821-1890 .... NCLC 42
   See also DLB 55, 166, 184; SSFS 21

Burton, Robert 1577-1640 .... LC 74
   See also DLB 151; RGEL 2

Buruma, Ian 1951- .... CLC 163
   See also CA 128; CANR 65, 141

Busch, Frederick 1941- ... CLC 7, 10, 18, 47, 166
   See also CA 33-36R; CAAS 1; CANR 45, 73, 92; CN 1, 2, 3, 4, 5, 6, 7; DLB 6, 218

Bush, Barney (Furman) 1946- .... NNAL
   See also CA 145

Bush, Ronald 1946- .... CLC 34
   See also CA 136

Bustos, F(rancisco)
   See Borges, Jorge Luis

Bustos Domecq, H(onorio)
   See Bioy Casares, Adolfo; Borges, Jorge Luis

Butler, Octavia E(stelle) 1947- .. BLCS; CLC 38, 121
   See also AAYA 18, 48; AFAW 2; AMWS 13; BPFB 1; BW 2, 3; CA 73-76; CANR 12, 24, 38, 73, 145; CLR 65; CN 7; CPW; DA3; DAM MULT, POP; DLB 33; LATS 1:2; MTCW 1, 2; MTFW 2005; NFS 8, 21; SATA 84; SCFW 2; SFW 4; SSFS 6; TCLE 1:1; YAW

Butler, Robert Olen, (Jr.) 1945- ...... CLC 81, 162
   See also AMWS 12; BPFB 1; CA 112; CANR 66, 138; CN 7; CSW; DAM POP; DLB 173; INT CA-112; MAL 5; MTCW 2; MTFW 2005; SSFS 11

Butler, Samuel 1612-1680 .... LC 16, 43
   See also DLB 101, 126; RGEL 2

Butler, Samuel 1835-1902 .... TCLC 1, 33; WLC
   See also BRWS 2; CA 143; CDBLB 1890-1914; DA; DA3; DAB; DAC; DAM MST, NOV; DLB 18, 57, 174; RGEL 2; SFW 4; TEA

Butler, Walter C.
   See Faust, Frederick (Schiller)

Canfield, Dorothea F.
   See Fisher, Dorothy (Frances) Canfield
Canfield, Dorothea Frances
   See Fisher, Dorothy (Frances) Canfield
Canfield, Dorothy
   See Fisher, Dorothy (Frances) Canfield
Canin, Ethan 1960- .... **CLC 55; SSC 70**
   See also CA 131; 135; MAL 5
Cankar, Ivan 1876-1918 .... **TCLC 105**
   See also CDWLB 4; DLB 147; EWL 3
Cannon, Curt
   See Hunter, Evan
Cao, Lan 1961- .... **CLC 109**
   See also CA 165
Cape, Judith
   See Page, P(atricia) K(athleen)
   See also CCA 1
Capek, Karel 1890-1938 .... **DC 1; SSC 36;**
   TCLC 6, 37; WLC
   See also CA 104; 140; CDWLB 4; DA;
   DA3; DAB; DAC; DAM DRAM, MST,
   NOV; DFS 7, 11; DLB 215; EW 10; EWL
   3; MTCW 2; MTFW 2005; RGSF 2;
   RGWL 2, 3; SCFW 1, 2; SFW 4
Capote, Truman 1924-1984 . **CLC 1, 3, 8, 13,**
   19, 34, 38, 58; SSC 2, 47; TCLC 164;
   WLC
   See also AAYA 61; AMWS 3; BPFB 1; CA
   5-8R; 113; CANR 18, 62; CDALB 1941-
   1968; CN 1, 2, 3; CPW; DA; DA3; DAB;
   DAC; DAM MST, NOV, POP; DLB 2,
   185, 227; DLBY 1980, 1984; EWL 3;
   EXPS; GLL 1; LAIT 3; MAL 5; MTCW
   1, 2; MTFW 2005; NCFS 2; RGAL 4;
   RGSF 2; SATA 91; SSFS 2; TUS
Capra, Frank 1897-1991 .... **CLC 16**
   See also AAYA 52; CA 61-64; 135
Caputo, Philip 1941- .... **CLC 32**
   See also AAYA 60; CA 73-76; CANR 40,
   135; YAW
Caragiale, Ion Luca 1852-1912 ...... **TCLC 76**
   See also CA 157
Card, Orson Scott 1951- .... **CLC 44, 47, 50**
   See also AAYA 11, 42; BPFB 1; BYA 5, 8;
   CA 102; CANR 27, 47, 73, 102, 106, 133;
   CPW; DA3; DAM POP; FANT; INT
   CANR-27; MTCW 1, 2; MTFW 2005;
   NFS 5; SATA 83, 127; SCFW 2; SFW 4;
   SUFW 2; YAW
Cardenal, Ernesto 1925- .... **CLC 31, 161;**
   HLC 1; PC 22
   See also CA 49-52; CANR 2, 32, 66, 138;
   CWW 2; DAM MULT, POET; DLB 290;
   EWL 3; HW 1, 2; LAWS 1; MTCW 1, 2;
   MTFW 2005; RGWL 2, 3
Cardinal, Marie 1929-2001 .... **CLC 189**
   See also CA 177; CWW 2; DLB 83; FW
Cardozo, Benjamin N(athan)
   1870-1938 .... **TCLC 65**
   See also CA 117; 164
Carducci, Giosue (Alessandro Giuseppe)
   1835-1907 .... **PC 46; TCLC 32**
   See also CA 163; EW 7; RGWL 2, 3
Carew, Thomas 1595(?)-1640 . **LC 13; PC 29**
   See also BRW 2; DLB 126; PAB; RGEL 2
Carey, Ernestine Gilbreth 1908- ...... **CLC 17**
   See also CA 5-8R; CANR 71; SATA 2
Carey, Peter 1943- .... **CLC 40, 55, 96, 183**
   See also CA 123; 127; CANR 53, 76, 117;
   CN 4, 5, 6, 7; DLB 289; EWL 3; INT CA-
   127; MTCW 1, 2; MTFW 2005; RGSF 2;
   SATA 94
Carleton, William 1794-1869 .... **NCLC 3**
   See also DLB 159; RGEL 2; RGSF 2
Carlisle, Henry (Coffin) 1926- .... **CLC 33**
   See also CA 13-16R; CANR 15, 85
Carlsen, Chris
   See Holdstock, Robert P.

Carlson, Ron(ald F.) 1947- .... **CLC 54**
   See also CA 105, 189; CAAE 189; CANR
   27; DLB 244
Carlyle, Thomas 1795-1881 ..... **NCLC 22, 70**
   See also BRW 4; CDBLB 1789-1832; DA;
   DAB; DAC; DAM MST; DLB 55, 144,
   254; RGEL 2; TEA
Carman, (William) Bliss 1861-1929 ... **PC 34;**
   TCLC 7
   See also CA 104; 152; DAC; DLB 92;
   RGEL 2
Carnegie, Dale 1888-1955 .... **TCLC 53**
   See also CA 218
Carossa, Hans 1878-1956 .... **TCLC 48**
   See also CA 170; DLB 66; EWL 3
Carpenter, Don(ald Richard)
   1931-1995 .... **CLC 41**
   See also CA 45-48; 149; CANR 1, 71
Carpenter, Edward 1844-1929 .... **TCLC 88**
   See also CA 163; GLL 1
Carpenter, John (Howard) 1948- ... **CLC 161**
   See also AAYA 2; CA 134; SATA 58
Carpenter, Johnny
   See Carpenter, John (Howard)
Carpentier (y Valmont), Alejo
   1904-1980 . **CLC 8, 11, 38, 110; HLC 1;**
   SSC 35
   See also CA 65-68; 97-100; CANR 11, 70;
   CDWLB 3; DAM MULT; DLB 113; EWL
   3; HW 1, 2; LAW; LMFS 2; RGSF 2;
   RGWL 2, 3; WLIT 1
Carr, Caleb 1955- .... **CLC 86**
   See also CA 147; CANR 73, 134; DA3
Carr, Emily 1871-1945 .... **TCLC 32**
   See also CA 159; DLB 68; FW; GLL 2
Carr, John Dickson 1906-1977 .... **CLC 3**
   See Fairbairn, Roger
   See also CA 49-52; 69-72; CANR 3, 33,
   60; CMW 4; DLB 306; MSW; MTCW 1,
   2
Carr, Philippa
   See Hibbert, Eleanor Alice Burford
Carr, Virginia Spencer 1929- .... **CLC 34**
   See also CA 61-64; DLB 111
Carrere, Emmanuel 1957- .... **CLC 89**
   See also CA 200
Carrier, Roch 1937- .... **CLC 13, 78**
   See also CA 130; CANR 61; CCA 1; DAC;
   DAM MST; DLB 53; SATA 105
Carroll, James Dennis
   See Carroll, Jim
Carroll, James P. 1943(?)- .... **CLC 38**
   See also CA 81-84; CANR 73, 139; MTCW
   2; MTFW 2005
Carroll, Jim 1951- .... **CLC 35, 143**
   See also AAYA 17; CA 45-48; CANR 42,
   115; NCFS 5
Carroll, Lewis ..... **NCLC 2, 53, 139; PC 18;**
   WLC
   See Dodgson, Charles L(utwidge)
   See also AAYA 39; BRW 5; BYA 5, 13; CD-
   BLB 1832-1890; CLR 2, 18; DLB 18,
   163, 178; DLBY 1998; EXPN; EXPP;
   FANT; JRDA; LAIT 1; NFS 7; PFS 11;
   RGEL 2; SUFW 1; TEA; WCH
Carroll, Paul Vincent 1900-1968 ...... **CLC 10**
   See also CA 9-12R; 25-28R; DLB 10; EWL
   3; RGEL 2
Carruth, Hayden 1921- ..... **CLC 4, 7, 10, 18,**
   84; PC 10
   See also CA 9-12R; CANR 4, 38, 59, 110;
   CP 1, 2, 3, 4, 5, 6, 7; DLB 5, 165; INT
   CANR-4; MTCW 1, 2; MTFW 2005;
   SATA 47
Carson, Anne 1950- .... **CLC 185; PC 64**
   See also AMWS 12; CA 203; DLB 193;
   PFS 18; TCLE 1:1
Carson, Ciaran 1948- .... **CLC 201**
   See also CA 112; 153; CANR 113; CP 7

Carson, Rachel
   See Carson, Rachel Louise
   See also AAYA 49; DLB 275
Carson, Rachel Louise 1907-1964 .... **CLC 71**
   See Carson, Rachel
   See also AMWS 9; ANW; CA 77-80; CANR
   35; DA3; DAM POP; FW; LAIT 4; MAL
   5; MTCW 1, 2; MTFW 2005; NCFS 1;
   SATA 23
Carter, Angela (Olive) 1940-1992 ...... **CLC 5,**
   41, 76; SSC 13, 85; TCLC 139
   See also BRWS 3; CA 53-56; 136; CANR
   12, 36, 61, 106; CN 3, 4, 5; DA3; DLB
   14, 207, 261, 319; EXPS; FANT; FW; GL
   2; MTCW 1, 2; MTFW 2005; RGSF 2;
   SATA 66; SATA-Obit 70; SFW 4; SSFS
   4, 12; SUFW 2; WLIT 4
Carter, Nick
   See Smith, Martin Cruz
Carver, Raymond 1938-1988 ..... **CLC 22, 36,**
   53, 55, 126; PC 54; SSC 8, 51
   See also AAYA 44; AMWS 3; BPFB 1; CA
   33-36R; 126; CANR 17, 34, 61, 103; CN
   4; CPW; DA3; DAM NOV; DLB 130;
   DLBY 1984, 1988; EWL 3; MAL 5;
   MTCW 1, 2; MTFW 2005; PFS 17;
   RGAL 4; RGSF 2; SSFS 3, 6, 12, 13;
   TCLE 1:1; TCWW 2; TUS
Cary, Elizabeth, Lady Falkland
   1585-1639 .... **LC 30**
Cary, (Arthur) Joyce (Lunel)
   1888-1957 .... **TCLC 1, 29**
   See also BRW 7; CA 104; 164; CDBLB
   1914-1945; DLB 15, 100; EWL 3; MTCW
   2; RGEL 2; TEA
Casal, Julian del 1863-1893 .... **NCLC 131**
   See also DLB 283; LAW
Casanova, Giacomo
   See Casanova de Seingalt, Giovanni Jacopo
   See also WLIT 7
Casanova de Seingalt, Giovanni Jacopo
   1725-1798 .... **LC 13**
   See Casanova, Giacomo
Casares, Adolfo Bioy
   See Bioy Casares, Adolfo
   See also RGSF 2
Casas, Bartolome de las 1474-1566
   See Las Casas, Bartolome de
   See also WLIT 1
Casely-Hayford, J(oseph) E(phraim)
   1866-1903 .... **BLC 1; TCLC 24**
   See also BW 2; CA 123; 152; DAM MULT
Casey, John (Dudley) 1939- .... **CLC 59**
   See also BEST 90:2; CA 69-72; CANR 23,
   100
Casey, Michael 1947- .... **CLC 2**
   See also CA 65-68; CANR 109; CP 2, 3;
   DLB 5
Casey, Patrick
   See Thurman, Wallace (Henry)
Casey, Warren (Peter) 1935-1988 .... **CLC 12**
   See also CA 101; 127; INT CA-101
Casona, Alejandro .... **CLC 49**
   See Alvarez, Alejandro Rodriguez
   See also EWL 3
Cassavetes, John 1929-1989 .... **CLC 20**
   See also CA 85-88; 127; CANR 82
Cassian, Nina 1924- .... **PC 17**
   See also CWP; CWW 2
Cassill, R(onald) V(erlin)
   1919-2002 .... **CLC 4, 23**
   See also CA 9-12R; 208; CAAS 1; CANR
   7, 45; CN 1, 2, 3, 4, 5, 6, 7; DLB 6, 218;
   DLBY 2002
Cassiodorus, Flavius Magnus c. 490(?)-c.
   583(?) .... **CMLC 43**
Cassirer, Ernst 1874-1945 .... **TCLC 61**
   See also CA 157

DA3; DAM MULT, POET; DLB 5, 41;
EXPP; MAICYA 1, 2; MTCW 1, 2;
MTFW 2005; PFS 1, 14; SATA 20, 69,
128; WP

Clinton, Dirk
See Silverberg, Robert

Clough, Arthur Hugh 1819-1861 .. **NCLC 27,
163**
See also BRW 5; DLB 32; RGEL 2

Clutha, Janet Paterson Frame 1924-2004
See Frame, Janet
See also CA 1-4R; 224; CANR 2, 36, 76,
135; MTCW 1, 2; SATA 119

Clyne, Terence
See Blatty, William Peter

Cobalt, Martin
See Mayne, William (James Carter)

Cobb, Irvin S(hrewsbury)
1876-1944 .... **TCLC 77**
See also CA 175; DLB 11, 25, 86

Cobbett, William 1763-1835 .... **NCLC 49**
See also DLB 43, 107, 158; RGEL 2

Coburn, D(onald) L(ee) 1938- .... **CLC 10**
See also CA 89-92

Cocteau, Jean (Maurice Eugene Clement)
1889-1963 ...... **CLC 1, 8, 15, 16, 43; DC
17; TCLC 119; WLC**
See also CA 25-28; CANR 40; CAP 2; DA;
DA3; DAB; DAC; DAM DRAM, MST,
NOV; DLB 65, 258, 321; EW 10; EWL
3; GFL 1789 to the Present; MTCW 1, 2;
RGWL 2, 3; TWA

Codrescu, Andrei 1946- .... **CLC 46, 121**
See also CA 33-36R; CAAS 19; CANR 13,
34, 53, 76, 125; CN 7; DA3; DAM POET;
MAL 5; MTCW 2; MTFW 2005

Coe, Max
See Bourne, Randolph S(illiman)

Coe, Tucker
See Westlake, Donald E(dwin)

Coen, Ethan 1958- .... **CLC 108**
See also AAYA 54; CA 126; CANR 85

Coen, Joel 1955- .... **CLC 108**
See also AAYA 54; CA 126; CANR 119

The Coen Brothers
See Coen, Ethan; Coen, Joel

Coetzee, J(ohn) M(axwell) 1940- ..... **CLC 23,
33, 66, 117, 161, 162**
See also AAYA 37; AFW; BRWS 6; CA 77-
80; CANR 41, 54, 74, 114, 133; CN 4, 5,
6, 7; DA3; DAM NOV; DLB 225; EWL
3; LMFS 2; MTCW 1, 2; MTFW 2005;
NFS 21; WLIT 2; WWE 1

Coffey, Brian
See Koontz, Dean R.

Coffin, Robert P(eter) Tristram
1892-1955 .... **TCLC 95**
See also CA 123; 169; DLB 45

Cohan, George M(ichael)
1878-1942 .... **TCLC 60**
See also CA 157; DLB 249; RGAL 4

Cohen, Arthur A(llen) 1928-1986 ...... **CLC 7,
31**
See also CA 1-4R; 120; CANR 1, 17, 42;
DLB 28

Cohen, Leonard (Norman) 1934- ...... **CLC 3,
38**
See also CA 21-24R; CANR 14, 69; CN 1,
2, 3, 4, 5, 6; CP 1, 2, 3, 4, 5, 6, 7; DAC;
DAM MST; DLB 53; EWL 3; MTCW 1

Cohen, Matt(hew) 1942-1999 .... **CLC 19**
See also CA 61-64; 187; CAAS 18; CANR
40; CN 1, 2, 3, 4, 5, 6; DAC; DLB 53

Cohen-Solal, Annie 1948- .... **CLC 50**
See also CA 239

Colegate, Isabel 1931- .... **CLC 36**
See also CA 17-20R; CANR 8, 22, 74; CN
4, 5, 6, 7; DLB 14, 231; INT CANR-22;
MTCW 1

Coleman, Emmett
See Reed, Ishmael (Scott)

Coleridge, Hartley 1796-1849 .... **NCLC 90**
See also DLB 96

Coleridge, M. E.
See Coleridge, Mary E(lizabeth)

Coleridge, Mary E(lizabeth)
1861-1907 .... **TCLC 73**
See also CA 116; 166; DLB 19, 98

Coleridge, Samuel Taylor
1772-1834 ...... **NCLC 9, 54, 99, 111; PC
11, 39, 67; WLC**
See also AAYA 66; BRW 4; BRWR 2; BYA
4; CDBLB 1789-1832; DA; DA3; DAB;
DAC; DAM MST, POET; DLB 93, 107;
EXPP; LATS 1:1; LMFS 1; PAB; PFS 4,
5; RGEL 2; TEA; WLIT 3; WP

Coleridge, Sara 1802-1852 .... **NCLC 31**
See also DLB 199

Coles, Don 1928- .... **CLC 46**
See also CA 115; CANR 38; CP 7

Coles, Robert (Martin) 1929- .... **CLC 108**
See also CA 45-48; CANR 3, 32, 66, 70,
135; INT CANR-32; SATA 23

Colette, (Sidonie-Gabrielle)
1873-1954 .... **SSC 10; TCLC 1, 5, 16**
See Willy, Colette
See also CA 104; 131; DA3; DAM NOV;
DLB 65; EW 9; EWL 3; GFL 1789 to the
Present; MTCW 1, 2; MTFW 2005;
RGWL 2, 3; TWA

Collett, (Jacobine) Camilla (Wergeland)
1813-1895 .... **NCLC 22**

Collier, Christopher 1930- .... **CLC 30**
See also AAYA 13; BYA 2; CA 33-36R;
CANR 13, 33, 102; JRDA; MAICYA 1,
2; SATA 16, 70; WYA; YAW 1

Collier, James Lincoln 1928- .... **CLC 30**
See also AAYA 13; BYA 2; CA 9-12R;
CANR 4, 33, 60, 102; CLR 3; DAM POP;
JRDA; MAICYA 1, 2; SAAS 21; SATA 8,
70; WYA; YAW 1

Collier, Jeremy 1650-1726 .... **LC 6**

Collier, John 1901-1980 . **SSC 19; TCLC 127**
See also CA 65-68; 97-100; CANR 10; CN
1, 2; DLB 77, 255; FANT; SUFW 1

Collier, Mary 1690-1762 .... **LC 86**
See also DLB 95

Collingwood, R(obin) G(eorge)
1889(?)-1943 .... **TCLC 67**
See also CA 117; 155; DLB 262

Collins, Billy 1941- .... **PC 68**
See also AAYA 64; CA 151; CANR 92;
MTFW 2005; PFS 18

Collins, Hunt
See Hunter, Evan

Collins, Linda 1931- .... **CLC 44**
See also CA 125

Collins, Tom
See Furphy, Joseph
See also RGEL 2

Collins, (William) Wilkie
1824-1889 .... **NCLC 1, 18, 93**
See also BRWS 6; CDBLB 1832-1890;
CMW 4; DLB 18, 70, 159; GL 2; MSW;
RGEL 2; RGSF 2; SUFW 1; WLIT 4

Collins, William 1721-1759 .... **LC 4, 40**
See also BRW 3; DAM POET; DLB 109;
RGEL 2

Collodi, Carlo .... **NCLC 54**
See Lorenzini, Carlo
See also CLR 5; WCH; WLIT 7

Colman, George
See Glassco, John

Colman, George, the Elder
1732-1794 .... **LC 98**
See also RGEL 2

Colonna, Vittoria 1492-1547 .... **LC 71**
See also RGWL 2, 3

Colt, Winchester Remington
See Hubbard, L(afayette) Ron(ald)

Colter, Cyrus J. 1910-2002 .... **CLC 58**
See also BW 1; CA 65-68; 205; CANR 10,
66; CN 2, 3, 4, 5, 6; DLB 33

Colton, James
See Hansen, Joseph
See also GLL 1

Colum, Padraic 1881-1972 .... **CLC 28**
See also BYA 4; CA 73-76; 33-36R; CANR
35; CLR 36; CP 1; CWRI 5; DLB 19;
MAICYA 1, 2; MTCW 1; RGEL 2; SATA
15; WCH

Colvin, James
See Moorcock, Michael (John)

Colwin, Laurie (E.) 1944-1992 .... **CLC 5, 13,
23, 84**
See also CA 89-92; 139; CANR 20, 46;
DLB 218; DLBY 1980; MTCW 1

Comfort, Alex(ander) 1920-2000 .... **CLC 7**
See also CA 1-4R; 190; CANR 1, 45; CN
1, 2, 3, 4; CP 1, 2, 3, 4, 5, 6, 7; DAM
POP; MTCW 2

Comfort, Montgomery
See Campbell, (John) Ramsey

Compton-Burnett, I(vy)
1892(?)-1969 .... **CLC 1, 3, 10, 15, 34**
See also BRW 7; CA 1-4R; 25-28R; CANR
4; DAM NOV; DLB 36; EWL 3; MTCW
1, 2; RGEL 2

Comstock, Anthony 1844-1915 ...... **TCLC 13**
See also CA 110; 169

Comte, Auguste 1798-1857 .... **NCLC 54**

Conan Doyle, Arthur
See Doyle, Sir Arthur Conan
See also BPFB 1; BYA 4, 5, 11

Conde (Abellan), Carmen
1901-1996 .... **HLCS 1**
See also CA 177; CWW 2; DLB 108; EWL
3; HW 2

Conde, Maryse 1937- .... **BLCS; CLC 52, 92**
See also BW 2, 3; CA 110, 190; CAAE 190;
CANR 30, 53, 76; CWW 2; DAM MULT;
EWL 3; MTCW 2; MTFW 2005

Condillac, Etienne Bonnot de
1714-1780 .... **LC 26**
See also DLB 313

Condon, Richard (Thomas)
1915-1996 .... **CLC 4, 6, 8, 10, 45, 100**
See also BEST 90:3; BPFB 1; CA 1-4R;
151; CAAS 1; CANR 2, 23; CMW 4; CN
1, 2, 3, 4, 5, 6; DAM NOV; INT CANR-
23; MAL 5; MTCW 1, 2

Condorcet .... **LC 104**
See Condorcet, marquis de Marie-Jean-
Antoine-Nicolas Caritat
See also GFL Beginnings to 1789

**Condorcet, marquis de
Marie-Jean-Antoine-Nicolas Caritat**
1743-1794
See Condorcet
See also DLB 313

Confucius 551B.C.-479B.C. .... **CMLC 19, 65;
WLCS**
See also DA; DA3; DAB; DAC; DAM
MST

Congreve, William 1670-1729 ... **DC 2; LC 5,
21; WLC**
See also BRW 2; CDBLB 1660-1789; DA;
DAB; DAC; DAM DRAM, MST, POET;
DFS 15; DLB 39, 84; RGEL 2; WLIT 3

Conley, Robert J(ackson) 1940- .... **NNAL**
See also CA 41-44R; CANR 15, 34, 45, 96;
DAM MULT; TCWW 2

Connell, Evan S(helby), Jr. 1924- . **CLC 4, 6,
45**
See also AAYA 7; AMWS 14; CA 1-4R;
CAAS 2; CANR 2, 39, 76, 97, 140; CN
1, 2, 3, 4, 5, 6; DAM NOV; DLB 2;
DLBY 1981; MAL 5; MTCW 1, 2;
MTFW 2005

Dillard, R(ichard) H(enry) W(ilde)
1937- .... **CLC 5**
See also CA 21-24R; CAAS 7; CANR 10;
CP 2, 3, 4, 5, 6, 7; CSW; DLB 5, 244

Dillon, Eilis 1920-1994 .... **CLC 17**
See also CA 9-12R, 182; 147; CAAE 182;
CAAS 3; CANR 4, 38, 78; CLR 26; MAI-
CYA 1, 2; MAICYAS 1; SATA 2, 74;
SATA-Essay 105; SATA-Obit 83; YAW

Dimont, Penelope
See Mortimer, Penelope (Ruth)

Dinesen, Isak ..... **CLC 10, 29, 95; SSC 7, 75**
See Blixen, Karen (Christentze Dinesen)
See also EW 10; EWL 3; EXPS; FW; GL
2; HGG; LAIT 3; MTCW 1; NCFS 2;
NFS 9; RGSF 2; RGWL 2, 3; SSFS 3, 6,
13; WLIT 2

Ding Ling .... **CLC 68**
See Chiang, Pin-chin
See also RGWL 3

Diphusa, Patty
See Almodovar, Pedro

Disch, Thomas M(ichael) 1940- ... **CLC 7, 36**
See Disch, Tom
See also AAYA 17; BPFB 1; CA 21-24R;
CAAS 4; CANR 17, 36, 54, 89; CLR 18;
CP 7; DA3; DLB 8; HGG; MAICYA 1, 2;
MTCW 1, 2; MTFW 2005; SAAS 15;
SATA 92; SCFW 1, 2; SFW 4; SUFW 2

Disch, Tom
See Disch, Thomas M(ichael)
See also DLB 282

d'Isly, Georges
See Simenon, Georges (Jacques Christian)

Disraeli, Benjamin 1804-1881 ... **NCLC 2, 39, 79**
See also BRW 4; DLB 21, 55; RGEL 2

Ditcum, Steve
See Crumb, R(obert)

Dixon, Paige
See Corcoran, Barbara (Asenath)

Dixon, Stephen 1936- .... **CLC 52; SSC 16**
See also AMWS 12; CA 89-92; CANR 17,
40, 54, 91; CN 4, 5, 6, 7; DLB 130; MAL
5

Dixon, Thomas, Jr. 1864-1946 ..... **TCLC 163**
See also RHW

Djebar, Assia 1936- .... **CLC 182**
See also CA 188; EWL 3; RGWL 3; WLIT
2

Doak, Annie
See Dillard, Annie

Dobell, Sydney Thompson
1824-1874 .... **NCLC 43**
See also DLB 32; RGEL 2

Doblin, Alfred .... **TCLC 13**
See Doeblin, Alfred
See also CDWLB 2; EWL 3; RGWL 2, 3

Dobroliubov, Nikolai Aleksandrovich
See Dobrolyubov, Nikolai Alexandrovich
See also DLB 277

Dobrolyubov, Nikolai Alexandrovich
1836-1861 .... **NCLC 5**
See Dobroliubov, Nikolai Aleksandrovich

Dobson, Austin 1840-1921 .... **TCLC 79**
See also DLB 35, 144

Dobyns, Stephen 1941- .... **CLC 37**
See also AMWS 13; CA 45-48; CANR 2,
18, 99; CMW 4; CP 4, 5, 6, 7; PFS 23

Doctorow, E(dgar) L(aurence)
1931- .... **CLC 6, 11, 15, 18, 37, 44, 65, 113, 214**
See also AAYA 22; AITN 2; AMWS 4;
BEST 89:3; BPFB 1; CA 45-48; CANR
2, 33, 51, 76, 97, 133; CDALB 1968-
1988; CN 3, 4, 5, 6, 7; CPW; DA3; DAM
NOV, POP; DLB 2, 28, 173; DLBY 1980;

EWL 3; LAIT 3; MAL 5; MTCW 1, 2;
MTFW 2005; NFS 6; RGAL 4; RHW;
TCLE 1:1; TCWW 1, 2; TUS

Dodgson, Charles L(utwidge) 1832-1898
See Carroll, Lewis
See also CLR 2; DA; DA3; DAB; DAC;
DAM MST, NOV, POET; MAICYA 1, 2;
SATA 100; YABC 2

Dodsley, Robert 1703-1764 .... **LC 97**
See also DLB 95; RGEL 2

Dodson, Owen (Vincent) 1914-1983 .. **BLC 1; CLC 79**
See also BW 1; CA 65-68; 110; CANR 24;
DAM MULT; DLB 76

Doeblin, Alfred 1878-1957 .... **TCLC 13**
See Doblin, Alfred
See also CA 110; 141; DLB 66

Doerr, Harriet 1910-2002 .... **CLC 34**
See also CA 117; 122; 213; CANR 47; INT
CA-122; LATS 1:2

Domecq, H(onorio Bustos)
See Bioy Casares, Adolfo

Domecq, H(onorio) Bustos
See Bioy Casares, Adolfo; Borges, Jorge
Luis

Domini, Rey
See Lorde, Audre (Geraldine)
See also GLL 1

Dominique
See Proust, (Valentin-Louis-George-Eugene)
Marcel

Don, A
See Stephen, Sir Leslie

Donaldson, Stephen R(eeder)
1947- .... **CLC 46, 138**
See also AAYA 36; BPFB 1; CA 89-92;
CANR 13, 55, 99; CPW; DAM POP;
FANT; INT CANR-13; SATA 121; SFW
4; SUFW 1, 2

Donleavy, J(ames) P(atrick) 1926- .... **CLC 1, 4, 6, 10, 45**
See also AITN 2; BPFB 1; CA 9-12R;
CANR 24, 49, 62, 80, 124; CBD; CD 5,
6; CN 1, 2, 3, 4, 5, 6, 7; DLB 6, 173; INT
CANR-24; MAL 5; MTCW 1, 2; MTFW
2005; RGAL 4

Donnadieu, Marguerite
See Duras, Marguerite

Donne, John 1572-1631 ... **LC 10, 24, 91; PC 1, 43; WLC**
See also AAYA 67; BRW 1; BRWC 1;
BRWR 2; CDBLB Before 1660; DA;
DAB; DAC; DAM MST, POET; DLB
121, 151; EXPP; PAB; PFS 2, 11; RGEL
3; TEA; WLIT 3; WP

Donnell, David 1939(?)- .... **CLC 34**
See also CA 197

Donoghue, Denis 1928- .... **CLC 209**
See also CA 17-20R; CANR 16, 102

Donoghue, P. S.
See Hunt, E(verette) Howard, (Jr.)

Donoso (Yanez), Jose 1924-1996 .... **CLC 4, 8, 11, 32, 99; HLC 1; SSC 34; TCLC 133**
See also CA 81-84; 155; CANR 32, 73; CD-
WLB 3; CWW 2; DAM MULT; DLB 113;
EWL 3; HW 1, 2; LAW; LAWS 1; MTCW
1, 2; MTFW 2005; RGSF 2; WLIT 1

Donovan, John 1928-1992 .... **CLC 35**
See also AAYA 20; CA 97-100; 137; CLR
3; MAICYA 1, 2; SATA 72; SATA-Brief
29; YAW

Don Roberto
See Cunninghame Graham, Robert
(Gallnigad) Bontine

Doolittle, Hilda 1886-1961 . **CLC 3, 8, 14, 31, 34, 73; PC 5; WLC**
See H. D.
See also AAYA 66; AMWS 1; CA 97-100;
CANR 35, 131; DA; DAC; DAM MST,

POET; DLB 4, 45; EWL 3; FW; GLL 1;
LMFS 2; MAL 5; MAWW; MTCW 1, 2;
MTFW 2005; PFS 6; RGAL 4

Doppo, Kunikida .... **TCLC 99**
See Kunikida Doppo

Dorfman, Ariel 1942- .... **CLC 48, 77, 189; HLC 1**
See also CA 124; 130; CANR 67, 70, 135;
CWW 2; DAM MULT; DFS 4; EWL 3;
HW 1, 2; INT CA-130; WLIT 1

Dorn, Edward (Merton)
1929-1999 .... **CLC 10, 18**
See also CA 93-96; 187; CANR 42, 79; CP
1, 2, 3, 4, 5, 6, 7; DLB 5; INT CA-93-96;
WP

Dor-Ner, Zvi .... **CLC 70**

Dorris, Michael (Anthony)
1945-1997 .... **CLC 109; NNAL**
See also AAYA 20; BEST 90:1; BYA 12;
CA 102; 157; CANR 19, 46, 75; CLR 58;
DA3; DAM MULT, NOV; DLB 175;
LAIT 5; MTCW 2; MTFW 2005; NFS 3;
RGAL 4; SATA 75; SATA-Obit 94;
TCWW 2; YAW

Dorris, Michael A.
See Dorris, Michael (Anthony)

Dorsan, Luc
See Simenon, Georges (Jacques Christian)

Dorsange, Jean
See Simenon, Georges (Jacques Christian)

Dorset
See Sackville, Thomas

Dos Passos, John (Roderigo)
1896-1970 ... **CLC 1, 4, 8, 11, 15, 25, 34, 82; WLC**
See also AMW; BPFB 1; CA 1-4R; 29-32R;
CANR 3; CDALB 1929-1941; DA; DA3;
DAB; DAC; DAM MST, NOV; DLB 4,
9, 274, 316; DLBD 1, 15; DLBY 1996;
EWL 3; MAL 5; MTCW 1, 2; MTFW
2005; NFS 14; RGAL 4; TUS

Dossage, Jean
See Simenon, Georges (Jacques Christian)

Dostoevsky, Fedor Mikhailovich
1821-1881 .. **NCLC 2, 7, 21, 33, 43, 119, 167; SSC 2, 33, 44; WLC**
See Dostoevsky, Fyodor
See also AAYA 40; DA; DA3; DAB; DAC;
DAM MST, NOV; EW 7; EXPN; NFS 3,
8; RGSF 2; RGWL 2, 3; SSFS 8; TWA

Dostoevsky, Fyodor
See Dostoevsky, Fedor Mikhailovich
See also DLB 238; LATS 1:1; LMFS 1, 2

Doty, M. R.
See Doty, Mark (Alan)

Doty, Mark
See Doty, Mark (Alan)

Doty, Mark (Alan) 1953(?)- .... **CLC 176; PC 53**
See also AMWS 11; CA 161, 183; CAAE
183; CANR 110

Doty, Mark A.
See Doty, Mark (Alan)

Doughty, Charles M(ontagu)
1843-1926 .... **TCLC 27**
See also CA 115; 178; DLB 19, 57, 174

Douglas, Ellen .... **CLC 73**
See Haxton, Josephine Ayres; Williamson,
Ellen Douglas
See also CN 5, 6, 7; CSW; DLB 292

Douglas, Gavin 1475(?)-1522 .... **LC 20**
See also DLB 132; RGEL 2

Douglas, George
See Brown, George Douglas
See also RGEL 2

Douglas, Keith (Castellain)
1920-1944 .... **TCLC 40**
See also BRW 7; CA 160; DLB 27; EWL
3; PAB; RGEL 2

Douglas, Leonard
See Bradbury, Ray (Douglas)
Douglas, Michael
See Crichton, (John) Michael
Douglas, (George) Norman
1868-1952 .... **TCLC 68**
See also BRW 6; CA 119; 157; DLB 34,
195; RGEL 2
Douglas, William
See Brown, George Douglas
Douglass, Frederick 1817(?)-1895 ..... **BLC 1;**
NCLC 7, 55, 141; WLC
See also AAYA 48; AFAW 1, 2; AMWC 1;
AMWS 3; CDALB 1640-1865; DA; DA3;
DAC; DAM MST, MULT; DLB 1, 43, 50,
79, 243; FW; LAIT 2; NCFS 2; RGAL 4;
SATA 29
Dourado, (Waldomiro Freitas) Autran
1926- .... **CLC 23, 60**
See also CA 25-28R; 179; CANR 34, 81;
DLB 145, 307; HW 2
Dourado, Waldomiro Freitas Autran
See Dourado, (Waldomiro Freitas) Autran
Dove, Rita (Frances) 1952- . **BLCS; CLC 50,**
81; PC 6
See also AAYA 46; AMWS 4; BW 2; CA
109; CAAS 19; CANR 27, 42, 68, 76, 97,
132; CDALBS; CP 7; CSW; CWP; DA3;
DAM MULT, POET; DLB 120; EWL 3;
EXPP; MAL 5; MTCW 2; MTFW 2005;
PFS 1, 15; RGAL 4
Doveglion
See Villa, Jose Garcia
Dowell, Coleman 1925-1985 .... **CLC 60**
See also CA 25-28R; 117; CANR 10; DLB
130; GLL 2
Dowson, Ernest (Christopher)
1867-1900 .... **TCLC 4**
See also CA 105; 150; DLB 19, 135; RGEL
2
Doyle, A. Conan
See Doyle, Sir Arthur Conan
Doyle, Sir Arthur Conan
1859-1930 . **SSC 12, 83; TCLC 7; WLC**
See Conan Doyle, Arthur
See also AAYA 14; BRWS 2; CA 104; 122;
CANR 131; CDBLB 1890-1914; CMW
4; DA; DA3; DAB; DAC; DAM MST,
NOV; DLB 18, 70, 156, 178; EXPS;
HGG; LAIT 2; MSW; MTCW 1, 2;
MTFW 2005; RGEL 2; RGSF 2; RHW;
SATA 24; SCFW 1, 2; SFW 4; SSFS 2;
TEA; WCH; WLIT 4; WYA; YAW
Doyle, Conan
See Doyle, Sir Arthur Conan
Doyle, John
See Graves, Robert (von Ranke)
Doyle, Roddy 1958- .... **CLC 81, 178**
See also AAYA 14; BRWS 5; CA 143;
CANR 73, 128; CN 6, 7; DA3; DLB 194;
MTCW 2; MTFW 2005
Doyle, Sir A. Conan
See Doyle, Sir Arthur Conan
Dr. A
See Asimov, Isaac; Silverstein, Alvin; Sil-
verstein, Virginia B(arbara Opshelor)
Drabble, Margaret 1939- ...... **CLC 2, 3, 5, 8,**
10, 22, 53, 129
See also BRWS 4; CA 13-16R; CANR 18,
35, 63, 112, 131; CDBLB 1960 to Present;
CN 1, 2, 3, 4, 5, 6, 7; CPW; DA3; DAB;
DAC; DAM MST, NOV, POP; DLB 14,
155, 231; EWL 3; FW; MTCW 1, 2;
MTFW 2005; RGEL 2; SATA 48; TEA
Drakulic, Slavenka 1949- .... **CLC 173**
See also CA 144; CANR 92
Drakulic-Ilic, Slavenka
See Drakulic, Slavenka

Drapier, M. B.
See Swift, Jonathan
Drayham, James
See Mencken, H(enry) L(ouis)
Drayton, Michael 1563-1631 .... **LC 8**
See also DAM POET; DLB 121; RGEL 2
Dreadstone, Carl
See Campbell, (John) Ramsey
Dreiser, Theodore (Herman Albert)
1871-1945 .... **SSC 30; TCLC 10, 18, 35,**
83; WLC
See also AMW; AMWC 2; AMWR 2; BYA
15, 16; CA 106; 132; CDALB 1865-1917;
DA; DA3; DAC; DAM MST, NOV; DLB
9, 12, 102, 137; DLBD 1; EWL 3; LAIT
2; LMFS 2; MAL 5; MTCW 1, 2; MTFW
2005; NFS 8, 17; RGAL 4; TUS
Drexler, Rosalyn 1926- .... **CLC 2, 6**
See also CA 81-84; CAD; CANR 68, 124;
CD 5, 6; CWD; MAL 5
Dreyer, Carl Theodor 1889-1968 ...... **CLC 16**
See also CA 116
Drieu la Rochelle, Pierre(-Eugene)
1893-1945 .... **TCLC 21**
See also CA 117; DLB 72; EWL 3; GFL
1789 to the Present
Drinkwater, John 1882-1937 .... **TCLC 57**
See also CA 109; 149; DLB 10, 19, 149;
RGEL 2
Drop Shot
See Cable, George Washington
Droste-Hulshoff, Annette Freiin von
1797-1848 .... **NCLC 3, 133**
See also CDWLB 2; DLB 133; RGSF 2;
RGWL 2, 3
Drummond, Walter
See Silverberg, Robert
Drummond, William Henry
1854-1907 .... **TCLC 25**
See also CA 160; DLB 92
Drummond de Andrade, Carlos
1902-1987 .... **CLC 18; TCLC 139**
See Andrade, Carlos Drummond de
See also CA 132; 123; DLB 307; LAW
Drummond of Hawthornden, William
1585-1649 .... **LC 83**
See also DLB 121, 213; RGEL 2
Drury, Allen (Stuart) 1918-1998 .... **CLC 37**
See also CA 57-60; 170; CANR 18, 52; CN
1, 2, 3, 4, 5, 6; INT CANR-18
Druse, Eleanor
See King, Stephen
Dryden, John 1631-1700 ..... **DC 3; LC 3, 21,**
115; PC 25; WLC
See also BRW 2; CDBLB 1660-1789; DA;
DAB; DAC; DAM DRAM, MST, POET;
DLB 80, 101, 131; EXPP; IDTP; LMFS
1; RGEL 2; TEA; WLIT 3
du Bellay, Joachim 1524-1560 .... **LC 92**
See also GFL Beginnings to 1789; RGWL
2, 3
Duberman, Martin (Bauml) 1930- ..... **CLC 8**
See also CA 1-4R; CAD; CANR 2, 63, 137;
CD 5, 6
Dubie, Norman (Evans) 1945- .... **CLC 36**
See also CA 69-72; CANR 12, 115; CP 3,
4, 5, 6, 7; DLB 120; PFS 12
Du Bois, W(illiam) E(dward) B(urghardt)
1868-1963 ..... **BLC 1; CLC 1, 2, 13, 64,**
96; HR 1:2; TCLC 169; WLC
See also AAYA 40; AFAW 1, 2; AMWC 1;
AMWS 2; BW 1, 3; CA 85-88; CANR
34, 82, 132; CDALB 1865-1917; DA;
DA3; DAC; DAM MST, MULT, NOV;
DLB 47, 50, 91, 246, 284; EWL 3; EXPP;
LAIT 2; LMFS 2; MAL 5; MTCW 1, 2;
MTFW 2005; NCFS 1; PFS 13; RGAL 4;
SATA 42

Dubus, Andre 1936-1999 ..... **CLC 13, 36, 97;**
SSC 15
See also AMWS 7; CA 21-24R; 177; CANR
17; CN 5, 6; CSW; DLB 130; INT CANR-
17; RGAL 4; SSFS 10; TCLE 1:1
Duca Minimo
See D'Annunzio, Gabriele
Ducharme, Rejean 1941- .... **CLC 74**
See also CA 165; DLB 60
du Chatelet, Emilie 1706-1749 .... **LC 96**
See Chatelet, Gabrielle-Emilie Du
Duchen, Claire .... **CLC 65**
Duclos, Charles Pinot- 1704-1772 .... **LC 1**
See also GFL Beginnings to 1789
Dudek, Louis 1918-2001 .... **CLC 11, 19**
See also CA 45-48; 215; CAAS 14; CANR
1; CP 1, 2, 3, 4, 5, 6, 7; DLB 88
Duerrenmatt, Friedrich 1921-1990 ... **CLC 1,**
4, 8, 11, 15, 43, 102
See Durrenmatt, Friedrich
See also CA 17-20R; CANR 33; CMW 4;
DAM DRAM; DLB 69, 124; MTCW 1, 2
Duffy, Bruce 1953(?)- .... **CLC 50**
See also CA 172
Duffy, Maureen (Patricia) 1933- ...... **CLC 37**
See also CA 25-28R; CANR 33, 68; CBD;
CN 1, 2, 3, 4, 5, 6, 7; CP 7; CWD; CWP;
DFS 15; DLB 14, 310; FW; MTCW 1
Du Fu
See Tu Fu
See also RGWL 2, 3
Dugan, Alan 1923-2003 .... **CLC 2, 6**
See also CA 81-84; 220; CANR 119; CP 1,
2, 3, 4, 5, 6, 7; DLB 5; MAL 5; PFS 10
du Gard, Roger Martin
See Martin du Gard, Roger
Duhamel, Georges 1884-1966 .... **CLC 8**
See also CA 81-84; 25-28R; CANR 35;
DLB 65; EWL 3; GFL 1789 to the
Present; MTCW 1
Dujardin, Edouard (Emile Louis)
1861-1949 .... **TCLC 13**
See also CA 109; DLB 123
Duke, Raoul
See Thompson, Hunter S(tockton)
Dulles, John Foster 1888-1959 .... **TCLC 72**
See also CA 115; 149
Dumas, Alexandre (pere)
1802-1870 .... **NCLC 11, 71; WLC**
See also AAYA 22; BYA 3; DA; DA3;
DAB; DAC; DAM MST, NOV; DLB 119,
192; EW 6; GFL 1789 to the Present;
LAIT 1, 2; NFS 14, 19; RGWL 2, 3;
SATA 18; TWA; WCH
Dumas, Alexandre (fils) 1824-1895 ...... **DC 1;**
NCLC 9
See also DLB 192; GFL 1789 to the Present;
RGWL 2, 3
Dumas, Claudine
See Malzberg, Barry N(athaniel)
Dumas, Henry L. 1934-1968 .... **CLC 6, 62**
See also BW 1; CA 85-88; DLB 41; RGAL
4
du Maurier, Daphne 1907-1989 .. **CLC 6, 11,**
59; SSC 18
See also AAYA 37; BPFB 1; BRWS 3; CA
5-8R; 128; CANR 6, 55; CMW 4; CN 1,
2, 3, 4; CPW; DA3; DAB; DAC; DAM
MST, POP; DLB 191; GL 2; HGG; LAIT
3; MSW; MTCW 1, 2; NFS 12; RGEL 2;
RGSF 2; RHW; SATA 27; SATA-Obit 60;
SSFS 14, 16; TEA
Du Maurier, George 1834-1896 ..... **NCLC 86**
See also DLB 153, 178; RGEL 2
Dunbar, Paul Laurence 1872-1906 ... **BLC 1;**
PC 5; SSC 8; TCLC 2, 12; WLC
See also AFAW 1, 2; AMWS 2; BW 1, 3;
CA 104; 124; CANR 79; CDALB 1865-
1917; DA; DA3; DAC; DAM MST,
MULT, POET; DLB 50, 54, 78; EXPP;
MAL 5; RGAL 4; SATA 34

Dunbar, William 1460(?)-1520(?) .... **LC 20; PC 67**
See also BRWS 8; DLB 132, 146; RGEL 2

Dunbar-Nelson, Alice .... **HR 1:2**
See Nelson, Alice Ruth Moore Dunbar

Duncan, Dora Angela
See Duncan, Isadora

Duncan, Isadora 1877(?)-1927 .... **TCLC 68**
See also CA 118; 149

Duncan, Lois 1934- .... **CLC 26**
See also AAYA 4, 34; BYA 6, 8; CA 1-4R;
CANR 2, 23, 36, 111; CLR 29; JRDA;
MAICYA 1, 2; MAICYAS 1; MTFW
2005; SAAS 2; SATA 1, 36, 75, 133, 141;
SATA-Essay 141; WYA; YAW

Duncan, Robert (Edward)
1919-1988 .... **CLC 1, 2, 4, 7, 15, 41, 55;
PC 2**
See also BG 1:2; CA 9-12R; 124; CANR
28, 62; CP 1, 2, 3, 4; DAM POET; DLB
5, 16, 193; EWL 3; MAL 5; MTCW 1, 2;
MTFW 2005; PFS 13; RGAL 4; WP

Duncan, Sara Jeannette
1861-1922 .... **TCLC 60**
See also CA 157; DLB 92

Dunlap, William 1766-1839 .... **NCLC 2**
See also DLB 30, 37, 59; RGAL 4

Dunn, Douglas (Eaglesham) 1942- .... **CLC 6, 40**
See also BRWS 10; CA 45-48; CANR 2,
33, 126; CP 1, 2, 3, 4, 5, 6, 7; DLB 40;
MTCW 1

Dunn, Katherine (Karen) 1945- .... **CLC 71**
See also CA 33-36R; CANR 72; HGG;
MTCW 2; MTFW 2005

Dunn, Stephen (Elliott) 1939- .. **CLC 36, 206**
See also AMWS 11; CA 33-36R; CANR
12, 48, 53, 105; CP 3, 4, 5, 6, 7; DLB
105; PFS 21

Dunne, Finley Peter 1867-1936 ...... **TCLC 28**
See also CA 108; 178; DLB 11, 23; RGAL
4

Dunne, John Gregory 1932-2003 ..... **CLC 28**
See also CA 25-28R; 222; CANR 14, 50;
CN 5, 6, 7; DLBY 1980

Dunsany, Lord .... **TCLC 2, 59**
See Dunsany, Edward John Moreton Drax
Plunkett
See also DLB 77, 153, 156, 255; FANT;
IDTP; RGEL 2; SFW 4; SUFW 1

**Dunsany, Edward John Moreton Drax
Plunkett** 1878-1957
See Dunsany, Lord
See also CA 104; 148; DLB 10; MTCW 2

Duns Scotus, John 1266(?)-1308 ... **CMLC 59**
See also DLB 115

du Perry, Jean
See Simenon, Georges (Jacques Christian)

Durang, Christopher (Ferdinand)
1949- .... **CLC 27, 38**
See also CA 105; CAD; CANR 50, 76, 130;
CD 5, 6; MTCW 2; MTFW 2005

Duras, Claire de 1777-1832 .... **NCLC 154**

Duras, Marguerite 1914-1996 . **CLC 3, 6, 11, 20, 34, 40, 68, 100; SSC 40**
See also BPFB 1; CA 25-28R; 151; CANR
50; CWW 2; DFS 21; DLB 83, 321; EWL
3; FL 1:5; GFL 1789 to the Present; IDFW
4; MTCW 1, 2; RGWL 2, 3; TWA

Durban, (Rosa) Pam 1947- .... **CLC 39**
See also CA 123; CANR 98; CSW

Durcan, Paul 1944- .... **CLC 43, 70**
See also CA 134; CANR 123; CP 1, 7;
DAM POET; EWL 3

Durfey, Thomas 1653-1723 .... **LC 94**
See also DLB 80; RGEL 2

Durkheim, Emile 1858-1917 .... **TCLC 55**

Durrell, Lawrence (George)
1912-1990 ..... **CLC 1, 4, 6, 8, 13, 27, 41**
See also BPFB 1; BRWS 1; CA 9-12R; 132;
CANR 40, 77; CDBLB 1945-1960; CN 1,
2, 3, 4; CP 1, 2, 3, 4; DAM NOV; DLB
15, 27, 204; DLBY 1990; EWL 3; MTCW
1, 2; RGEL 2; SFW 4; TEA

Durrenmatt, Friedrich
See Duerrenmatt, Friedrich
See also CDWLB 2; EW 13; EWL 3;
RGWL 2, 3

Dutt, Michael Madhusudan
1824-1873 .... **NCLC 118**

Dutt, Toru 1856-1877 .... **NCLC 29**
See also DLB 240

Dwight, Timothy 1752-1817 .... **NCLC 13**
See also DLB 37; RGAL 4

Dworkin, Andrea 1946-2005 ..... **CLC 43, 123**
See also CA 77-80; 238; CAAS 21; CANR
16, 39, 76, 96; FL 1:5; FW; GLL 1; INT
CANR-16; MTCW 1, 2; MTFW 2005

Dwyer, Deanna
See Koontz, Dean R.

Dwyer, K. R.
See Koontz, Dean R.

Dybek, Stuart 1942- .... **CLC 114; SSC 55**
See also CA 97-100; CANR 39; DLB 130

Dye, Richard
See De Voto, Bernard (Augustine)

Dyer, Geoff 1958- .... **CLC 149**
See also CA 125; CANR 88

Dyer, George 1755-1841 .... **NCLC 129**
See also DLB 93

Dylan, Bob 1941- .... **CLC 3, 4, 6, 12, 77; PC 37**
See also CA 41-44R; CANR 108; CP 1, 2,
3, 4, 5, 6, 7; DLB 16

Dyson, John 1943- .... **CLC 70**
See also CA 144

Dzyubin, Eduard Georgievich 1895-1934
See Bagritsky, Eduard
See also CA 170

E. V. L.
See Lucas, E(dward) V(errall)

Eagleton, Terence (Francis) 1943- .. **CLC 63, 132**
See also CA 57-60; CANR 7, 23, 68, 115;
DLB 242; LMFS 2; MTCW 1, 2; MTFW
2005

Eagleton, Terry
See Eagleton, Terence (Francis)

Early, Jack
See Scoppettone, Sandra
See also GLL 1

East, Michael
See West, Morris L(anglo)

Eastaway, Edward
See Thomas, (Philip) Edward

Eastlake, William (Derry)
1917-1997 .... **CLC 8**
See also CA 5-8R; 158; CAAS 1; CANR 5,
63; CN 1, 2, 3, 4, 5, 6; DLB 6, 206; INT
CANR-5; MAL 5; TCWW 1, 2

Eastman, Charles A(lexander)
1858-1939 .... **NNAL; TCLC 55**
See also CA 179; CANR 91; DAM MULT;
DLB 175; YABC 1

Eaton, Edith Maude 1865-1914 .... **AAL**
See Far, Sui Sin
See also CA 154; DLB 221, 312; FW

Eaton, (Lillie) Winnifred 1875-1954 ...... **AAL**
See also CA 217; DLB 221, 312; RGAL 4

Eberhart, Richard 1904-2005 ...... **CLC 3, 11, 19, 56**
See also AMW; CA 1-4R; 240; CANR 2,
125; CDALB 1941-1968; CP 1, 2, 3, 4, 5,
6, 7; DAM POET; DLB 48; MAL 5;
MTCW 1; RGAL 4

Eberhart, Richard Ghormley
See Eberhart, Richard

Eberstadt, Fernanda 1960- .... **CLC 39**
See also CA 136; CANR 69, 128

**Echegaray (y Eizaguirre), Jose (Maria
Waldo)** 1832-1916 .... **HLCS 1; TCLC 4**
See also CA 104; CANR 32; EWL 3; HW
1; MTCW 1

Echeverria, (Jose) Esteban (Antonino)
1805-1851 .... **NCLC 18**
See also LAW

Echo
See Proust, (Valentin-Louis-George-Eugene)
Marcel

Eckert, Allan W. 1931- .... **CLC 17**
See also AAYA 18; BYA 2; CA 13-16R;
CANR 14, 45; INT CANR-14; MAICYA
2; MAICYAS 1; SAAS 21; SATA 29, 91;
SATA-Brief 27

Eckhart, Meister 1260(?)-1327(?) .. **CMLC 9, 80**
See also DLB 115; LMFS 1

Eckmar, F. R.
See de Hartog, Jan

Eco, Umberto 1932- .... **CLC 28, 60, 142**
See also BEST 90:1; BPFB 1; CA 77-80;
CANR 12, 33, 55, 110, 131; CPW; CWW
2; DA3; DAM NOV, POP; DLB 196, 242;
EWL 3; MSW; MTCW 1, 2; MTFW
2005; NFS 22; RGWL 3; WLIT 7

Eddison, E(ric) R(ucker)
1882-1945 .... **TCLC 15**
See also CA 109; 156; DLB 255; FANT;
SFW 4; SUFW 1

Eddy, Mary (Ann Morse) Baker
1821-1910 .... **TCLC 71**
See also CA 113; 174

Edel, (Joseph) Leon 1907-1997 .. **CLC 29, 34**
See also CA 1-4R; 161; CANR 1, 22, 112;
DLB 103; INT CANR-22

Eden, Emily 1797-1869 .... **NCLC 10**

Edgar, David 1948- .... **CLC 42**
See also CA 57-60; CANR 12, 61, 112;
CBD; CD 5, 6; DAM DRAM; DFS 15;
DLB 13, 233; MTCW 1

Edgerton, Clyde (Carlyle) 1944- ...... **CLC 39**
See also AAYA 17; CA 118; 134; CANR
64, 125; CN 7; CSW; DLB 278; INT CA-
134; TCLE 1:1; YAW

Edgeworth, Maria 1768-1849 ... **NCLC 1, 51, 158; SSC 86**
See also BRWS 3; DLB 116, 159, 163; FL
1:3; FW; RGEL 2; SATA 21; TEA; WLIT
3

Edmonds, Paul
See Kuttner, Henry

Edmonds, Walter D(umaux)
1903-1998 .... **CLC 35**
See also BYA 2; CA 5-8R; CANR 2; CWRI
5; DLB 9; LAIT 1; MAICYA 1, 2; MAL
5; RHW; SAAS 4; SATA 1, 27; SATA-
Obit 99

Edmondson, Wallace
See Ellison, Harlan (Jay)

Edson, Margaret 1961- ...... **CLC 199; DC 24**
See also CA 190; DFS 13; DLB 266

Edson, Russell 1935- .... **CLC 13**
See also CA 33-36R; CANR 115; CP 2, 3,
4, 5, 6, 7; DLB 244; WP

Edwards, Bronwen Elizabeth
See Rose, Wendy

Edwards, G(erald) B(asil)
1899-1976 .... **CLC 25**
See also CA 201; 110

Edwards, Gus 1939- .... **CLC 43**
See also CA 108; INT CA-108

Edwards, Jonathan 1703-1758 ..... **LC 7, 54**
See also AMW; DA; DAC; DAM MST;
DLB 24, 270; RGAL 4; TUS

Ford, Jack
See Ford, John
Ford, John 1586-1639 .... **DC 8; LC 68**
See also BRW 2; CDBLB Before 1660;
DA3; DAM DRAM; DFS 7; DLB 58;
IDTP; RGEL 2
Ford, John 1895-1973 .... **CLC 16**
See also CA 187; 45-48
Ford, Richard 1944- .... **CLC 46, 99, 205**
See also AMWS 5; CA 69-72; CANR 11,
47, 86, 128; CN 5, 6, 7; CSW; DLB 227;
EWL 3; MAL 5; MTCW 2; MTFW 2005;
RGAL 4; RGSF 2
Ford, Webster
See Masters, Edgar Lee
Foreman, Richard 1937- .... **CLC 50**
See also CA 65-68; CAD; CANR 32, 63,
143; CD 5, 6
Forester, C(ecil) S(cott) 1899-1966 . **CLC 35;
TCLC 152**
See also CA 73-76; 25-28R; CANR 83;
DLB 191; RGEL 2; RHW; SATA 13
Forez
See Mauriac, Francois (Charles)
Forman, James
See Forman, James D(ouglas)
Forman, James D(ouglas) 1932- .... **CLC 21**
See also AAYA 17; CA 9-12R; CANR 4,
19, 42; JRDA; MAICYA 1, 2; SATA 8,
70; YAW
Forman, Milos 1932- .... **CLC 164**
See also AAYA 63; CA 109
Fornes, Maria Irene 1930- .... **CLC 39, 61,
187; DC 10; HLCS 1**
See also CA 25-28R; CAD; CANR 28, 81;
CD 5, 6; CWD; DLB 7; HW 1, 2; INT
CANR-28; LLW; MAL 5; MTCW 1;
RGAL 4
Forrest, Leon (Richard)
1937-1997 .... **BLCS; CLC 4**
See also AFAW 2; BW 2; CA 89-92; 162;
CAAS 7; CANR 25, 52, 87; CN 4, 5, 6;
DLB 33
Forster, E(dward) M(organ)
1879-1970 ...... **CLC 1, 2, 3, 4, 9, 10, 13,
15, 22, 45, 77; SSC 27; TCLC 125;
WLC**
See also AAYA 2, 37; BRW 6; BRWR 2;
BYA 12; CA 13-14; 25-28R; CANR 45;
CAP 1; CDBLB 1914-1945; DA; DA3;
DAB; DAC; DAM MST, NOV; DLB 34,
98, 162, 178, 195; DLBD 10; EWL 3;
EXPN; LAIT 3; LMFS 1; MTCW 1, 2;
MTFW 2005; NCFS 1; NFS 3, 10, 11;
RGEL 2; RGSF 2; SATA 57; SUFW 1;
TEA; WLIT 4
Forster, John 1812-1876 .... **NCLC 11**
See also DLB 144, 184
Forster, Margaret 1938- .... **CLC 149**
See also CA 133; CANR 62, 115; CN 4, 5,
6, 7; DLB 155, 271
Forsyth, Frederick 1938- .... **CLC 2, 5, 36**
See also BEST 89:4; CA 85-88; CANR 38,
62, 115, 137; CMW 4; CN 3, 4, 5, 6, 7;
CPW; DAM NOV, POP; DLB 87; MTCW
1, 2; MTFW 2005
Forten, Charlotte L. 1837-1914 .... **BLC 2;
TCLC 16**
See Grimke, Charlotte L(ottie) Forten
See also DLB 50, 239
Fortinbras
See Grieg, (Johan) Nordahl (Brun)
Foscolo, Ugo 1778-1827 .... **NCLC 8, 97**
See also EW 5; WLIT 7
Fosse, Bob .... **CLC 20**
See Fosse, Robert Louis
Fosse, Robert Louis 1927-1987
See Fosse, Bob
See also CA 110; 123

Foster, Hannah Webster
1758-1840 .... **NCLC 99**
See also DLB 37, 200; RGAL 4
Foster, Stephen Collins
1826-1864 .... **NCLC 26**
See also RGAL 4
Foucault, Michel 1926-1984 . **CLC 31, 34, 69**
See also CA 105; 113; CANR 34; DLB 242;
EW 13; EWL 3; GFL 1789 to the Present;
GLL 1; LMFS 2; MTCW 1, 2; TWA
**Fouque, Friedrich (Heinrich Karl) de la
Motte** 1777-1843 .... **NCLC 2**
See also DLB 90; RGWL 2, 3; SUFW 1
Fourier, Charles 1772-1837 .... **NCLC 51**
Fournier, Henri-Alban 1886-1914
See Alain-Fournier
See also CA 104; 179
Fournier, Pierre 1916-1997 .... **CLC 11**
See Gascar, Pierre
See also CA 89-92; CANR 16, 40
Fowles, John (Robert) 1926- . **CLC 1, 2, 3, 4,
6, 9, 10, 15, 33, 87; SSC 33**
See also BPFB 1; BRWS 1; CA 5-8R;
CANR 25, 71, 103; CDBLB 1960 to
Present; CN 1, 2, 3, 4, 5, 6, 7; DA3; DAB;
DAC; DAM MST; DLB 14, 139, 207;
EWL 3; HGG; MTCW 1, 2; MTFW 2005;
NFS 21; RGEL 2; RHW; SATA 22; TEA;
WLIT 4
Fox, Paula 1923- .... **CLC 2, 8, 121**
See also AAYA 3, 37; BYA 3, 8; CA 73-76;
CANR 20, 36, 62, 105; CLR 1, 44, 96;
DLB 52; JRDA; MAICYA 1, 2; MTCW
1; NFS 12; SATA 17, 60, 120; WYA;
YAW
Fox, William Price (Jr.) 1926- .... **CLC 22**
See also CA 17-20R; CAAS 19; CANR 11,
142; CSW; DLB 2; DLBY 1981
Foxe, John 1517(?)-1587 .... **LC 14**
See also DLB 132
Frame, Janet .. **CLC 2, 3, 6, 22, 66, 96; SSC
29**
See Clutha, Janet Paterson Frame
See also CN 1, 2, 3, 4, 5, 6, 7; CP 2, 3, 4;
CWP; EWL 3; RGEL 2; RGSF 2; TWA
France, Anatole .... **TCLC 9**
See Thibault, Jacques Anatole Francois
See also DLB 123; EWL 3; GFL 1789 to
the Present; RGWL 2, 3; SUFW 1
Francis, Claude .... **CLC 50**
See also CA 192
Francis, Dick
See Francis, Richard Stanley
See also CN 2, 3, 4, 5, 6
Francis, Richard Stanley 1920- ... **CLC 2, 22,
42, 102**
See Francis, Dick
See also AAYA 5, 21; BEST 89:3; BPFB 1;
CA 5-8R; CANR 9, 42, 68, 100, 141; CD-
BLB 1960 to Present; CMW 4; CN 7;
DA3; DAM POP; DLB 87; INT CANR-9;
MSW; MTCW 1, 2; MTFW 2005
Francis, Robert (Churchill)
1901-1987 .... **CLC 15; PC 34**
See also AMWS 9; CA 1-4R; 123; CANR
1; CP 1, 2, 3, 4; EXPP; PFS 12; TCLE
1:1
Francis, Lord Jeffrey
See Jeffrey, Francis
See also DLB 107
Frank, Anne(lies Marie)
1929-1945 .... **TCLC 17; WLC**
See also AAYA 12; BYA 1; CA 113; 133;
CANR 68; CLR 101; DA; DA3; DAB;
DAC; DAM MST; LAIT 4; MAICYA 2;
MAICYAS 1; MTCW 1, 2; MTFW 2005;
NCFS 2; SATA 87; SATA-Brief 42; WYA;
YAW
Frank, Bruno 1887-1945 .... **TCLC 81**
See also CA 189; DLB 118; EWL 3

Frank, Elizabeth 1945- .... **CLC 39**
See also CA 121; 126; CANR 78; INT CA-
126
Frankl, Viktor E(mil) 1905-1997 ...... **CLC 93**
See also CA 65-68; 161
Franklin, Benjamin
See Hasek, Jaroslav (Matej Frantisek)
Franklin, Benjamin 1706-1790 .... **LC 25;
WLCS**
See also AMW; CDALB 1640-1865; DA;
DA3; DAB; DAC; DAM MST; DLB 24,
43, 73, 183; LAIT 1; RGAL 4; TUS
**Franklin, (Stella Maria Sarah) Miles
(Lampe)** 1879-1954 .... **TCLC 7**
See also CA 104; 164; DLB 230; FW;
MTCW 2; RGEL 2; TWA
Franzen, Jonathan 1959- .... **CLC 202**
See also AAYA 65; CA 129; CANR 105
Fraser, Antonia (Pakenham) 1932- . **CLC 32,
107**
See also AAYA 57; CA 85-88; CANR 44,
65, 119; CMW; DLB 276; MTCW 1, 2;
MTFW 2005; SATA-Brief 32
Fraser, George MacDonald 1925- ...... **CLC 7**
See also AAYA 48; CA 45-48, 180; CAAE
180; CANR 2, 48, 74; MTCW 2; RHW
Fraser, Sylvia 1935- .... **CLC 64**
See also CA 45-48; CANR 1, 16, 60; CCA
1
Frayn, Michael 1933- .... **CLC 3, 7, 31, 47,
176; DC 27**
See also BRWC 2; BRWS 7; CA 5-8R;
CANR 30, 69, 114, 133; CBD; CD 5, 6;
CN 1, 2, 3, 4, 5, 6, 7; DAM DRAM,
NOV; DFS 22; DLB 13, 14, 194, 245;
FANT; MTCW 1, 2; MTFW 2005; SFW
4
Fraze, Candida (Merrill) 1945- .... **CLC 50**
See also CA 126
Frazer, Andrew
See Marlowe, Stephen
Frazer, J(ames) G(eorge)
1854-1941 .... **TCLC 32**
See also BRWS 3; CA 118; NCFS 5
Frazer, Robert Caine
See Creasey, John
Frazer, Sir James George
See Frazer, J(ames) G(eorge)
Frazier, Charles 1950- .... **CLC 109**
See also AAYA 34; CA 161; CANR 126;
CSW; DLB 292; MTFW 2005
Frazier, Ian 1951- .... **CLC 46**
See also CA 130; CANR 54, 93
Frederic, Harold 1856-1898 .... **NCLC 10**
See also AMW; DLB 12, 23; DLBD 13;
MAL 5; NFS 22; RGAL 4
Frederick, John
See Faust, Frederick (Schiller)
See also TCWW 2
Frederick the Great 1712-1786 .... **LC 14**
Fredro, Aleksander 1793-1876 .... **NCLC 8**
Freeling, Nicolas 1927-2003 .... **CLC 38**
See also CA 49-52; 218; CAAS 12; CANR
1, 17, 50, 84; CMW 4; CN 1, 2, 3, 4, 5,
6; DLB 87
Freeman, Douglas Southall
1886-1953 .... **TCLC 11**
See also CA 109; 195; DLB 17; DLBD 17
Freeman, Judith 1946- .... **CLC 55**
See also CA 148; CANR 120; DLB 256
Freeman, Mary E(leanor) Wilkins
1852-1930 .... **SSC 1, 47; TCLC 9**
See also CA 106; 177; DLB 12, 78, 221;
EXPS; FW; HGG; MAWW; RGAL 4;
RGSF 2; SSFS 4, 8; SUFW 1; TUS
Freeman, R(ichard) Austin
1862-1943 .... **TCLC 21**
See also CA 113; CANR 84; CMW 4; DLB
70

Gent, Peter 1942- .... CLC 29
See also AITN 1; CA 89-92; DLBY 1982

Gentile, Giovanni 1875-1944 .... TCLC 96
See also CA 119

Gentlewoman in New England, A
. See Bradstreet, Anne

Gentlewoman in Those Parts, A
See Bradstreet, Anne

Geoffrey of Monmouth c.
1100-1155 .... CMLC 44
See also DLB 146; TEA

George, Jean
See George, Jean Craighead

George, Jean Craighead 1919- .... CLC 35
See also AAYA 8; BYA 2, 4; CA 5-8R;
CANR 25; CLR 1; 80; DLB 52; JRDA;
MAICYA 1, 2; SATA 2, 68, 124; WYA;
YAW

George, Stefan (Anton) 1868-1933 . TCLC 2,
14
See also CA 104; 193; EW 8; EWL 3

Georges, Georges Martin
See Simenon, Georges (Jacques Christian)

Gerald of Wales c. 1146-c. 1223 ... CMLC 60

Gerhardi, William Alexander
See Gerhardie, William Alexander

Gerhardie, William Alexander
1895-1977 .... CLC 5
See also CA 25-28R; 73-76; CANR 18; CN
1, 2; DLB 36; RGEL 2

Gerson, Jean 1363-1429 .... LC 77
See also DLB 208

Gersonides 1288-1344 .... CMLC 49
See also DLB 115

Gerstler, Amy 1956- .... CLC 70
See also CA 146; CANR 99

Gertler, T. .... CLC 34
See also CA 116; 121

Gertsen, Aleksandr Ivanovich
See Herzen, Aleksandr Ivanovich

Ghalib .... NCLC 39, 78
See Ghalib, Asadullah Khan

Ghalib, Asadullah Khan 1797-1869
See Ghalib
See also DAM POET; RGWL 2, 3

Ghelderode, Michel de 1898-1962 ..... CLC 6,
11; DC 15
See also CA 85-88; CANR 40, 77; DAM
DRAM; DLB 321; EW 11; EWL 3; TWA

Ghiselin, Brewster 1903-2001 .... CLC 23
See also CA 13-16R; CAAS 10; CANR 13;
CP 1, 2, 3, 4, 5, 6, 7

Ghose, Aurabinda 1872-1950 .... TCLC 63
See Ghose, Aurobindo
See also CA 163

Ghose, Aurobindo
See Ghose, Aurabinda
See also EWL 3

Ghose, Zulfikar 1935- .... CLC 42, 200
See also CA 65-68; CANR 67; CN 1, 2, 3,
4, 5, 6, 7; CP 1, 2, 3, 4, 5, 6, 7; EWL 3

Ghosh, Amitav 1956- .... CLC 44, 153
See also CA 147; CANR 80; CN 6, 7;
WWE 1

Giacosa, Giuseppe 1847-1906 .... TCLC 7
See also CA 104

Gibb, Lee
See Waterhouse, Keith (Spencer)

Gibbon, Edward 1737-1794 .... LC 97
See also BRW 3; DLB 104; RGEL 2

Gibbon, Lewis Grassic .... TCLC 4
See Mitchell, James Leslie
See also RGEL 2

Gibbons, Kaye 1960- .... CLC 50, 88, 145
See also AAYA 34; AMWS 10; CA 151;
CANR 75, 127; CN 7; CSW; DA3; DAM
POP; DLB 292; MTCW 2; MTFW 2005;
NFS 3; RGAL 4; SATA 117

Gibran, Kahlil 1883-1931 . PC 9; TCLC 1, 9
See also CA 104; 150; DA3; DAM POET,
POP; EWL 3; MTCW 2; WLIT 6

Gibran, Khalil
See Gibran, Kahlil

Gibson, Mel 1956- .... CLC 215

Gibson, William 1914- .... CLC 23
See also CA 9-12R; CAD; CANR 9, 42, 75,
125; CD 5, 6; DA; DAB; DAC; DAM
DRAM, MST; DFS 2; DLB 7; LAIT 2;
MAL 5; MTCW 2; MTFW 2005; SATA
66; YAW

Gibson, William (Ford) 1948- ... CLC 39, 63,
186, 192; SSC 52
See also AAYA 12, 59; BPFB 2; CA 126;
133; CANR 52, 90, 106; CN 6, 7; CPW;
DA3; DAM POP; DLB 251; MTCW 2;
MTFW 2005; SCFW 2; SFW 4

Gide, Andre (Paul Guillaume)
1869-1951 ..... SSC 13; TCLC 5, 12, 36;
WLC
See also CA 104; 124; DA; DA3; DAB;
DAC; DAM MST, NOV; DLB 65, 321;
EW 8; EWL 3; GFL 1789 to the Present;
MTCW 1, 2; MTFW 2005; NFS 21;
RGSF 2; RGWL 2, 3; TWA

Gifford, Barry (Colby) 1946- .... CLC 34
See also CA 65-68; CANR 9, 30, 40, 90

Gilbert, Frank
See De Voto, Bernard (Augustine)

Gilbert, W(illiam) S(chwenck)
1836-1911 .... TCLC 3
See also CA 104; 173; DAM DRAM, POET;
RGEL 2; SATA 36

Gilbreth, Frank B(unker), Jr.
1911-2001 .... CLC 17
See also CA 9-12R; SATA 2

Gilchrist, Ellen (Louise) 1935- .. CLC 34, 48,
143; SSC 14, 63
See also BPFB 2; CA 113; 116; CANR 41,
61, 104; CN 4, 5, 6, 7; CPW; CSW; DAM
POP; DLB 130; EWL 3; EXPS; MTCW
1, 2; MTFW 2005; RGAL 4; RGSF 2;
SSFS 9

Giles, Molly 1942- .... CLC 39
See also CA 126; CANR 98

Gill, Eric .... TCLC 85
See Gill, (Arthur) Eric (Rowton Peter
Joseph)

Gill, (Arthur) Eric (Rowton Peter Joseph)
1882-1940
See Gill, Eric
See also CA 120; DLB 98

Gill, Patrick
See Creasey, John

Gillette, Douglas .... CLC 70

Gilliam, Terry (Vance) 1940- .... CLC 21, 141
See Monty Python
See also AAYA 19, 59; CA 108; 113; CANR
35; INT CA-113

Gillian, Jerry
See Gilliam, Terry (Vance)

Gilliatt, Penelope (Ann Douglass)
1932-1993 .... CLC 2, 10, 13, 53
See also AITN 2; CA 13-16R; 141; CANR
49; CN 1, 2, 3, 4, 5; DLB 14

Gilligan, Carol 1936- .... CLC 208
See also CA 142; CANR 121; FW

Gilman, Charlotte (Anna) Perkins (Stetson)
1860-1935 ...... SSC 13, 62; TCLC 9, 37,
117
See also AMWS 11; BYA 11; CA 106; 150;
DLB 221; EXPS; FL 1:5; FW; HGG;
LAIT 2; MAWW; MTCW 2; MTFW
2005; RGAL 4; RGSF 2; SFW 4; SSFS 1,
18

Gilmour, David 1946- .... CLC 35

Gilpin, William 1724-1804 .... NCLC 30

Gilray, J. D.
See Mencken, H(enry) L(ouis)

Gilroy, Frank D(aniel) 1925- .... CLC 2
See also CA 81-84; CAD; CANR 32, 64,
86; CD 5, 6; DFS 17; DLB 7

Gilstrap, John 1957(?)- .... CLC 99
See also AAYA 67; CA 160; CANR 101

Ginsberg, Allen 1926-1997 .... CLC 1, 2, 3, 4,
6, 13, 36, 69, 109; PC 4, 47; TCLC
120; WLC
See also AAYA 33; AITN 1; AMWC 1;
AMWS 2; BG 1:2; CA 1-4R; 157; CANR
2, 41, 63, 95; CDALB 1941-1968; CP 1,
2, 3, 4, 5, 6; DA; DA3; DAB; DAC; DAM
MST, POET; DLB 5, 16, 169, 237; EWL
3; GLL 1; LMFS 2; MAL 5; MTCW 1, 2;
MTFW 2005; PAB; PFS 5; RGAL 4;
TUS; WP

Ginzburg, Eugenia .... CLC 59
See Ginzburg, Evgeniia

Ginzburg, Evgeniia 1904-1977
See Ginzburg, Eugenia
See also DLB 302

Ginzburg, Natalia 1916-1991 .... CLC 5, 11,
54, 70; SSC 65; TCLC 156
See also CA 85-88; 135; CANR 33; DFS
14; DLB 177; EW 13; EWL 3; MTCW 1,
2; MTFW 2005; RGWL 2, 3

Giono, Jean 1895-1970 .... CLC 4, 11; TCLC
124
See also CA 45-48; 29-32R; CANR 2, 35;
DLB 72, 321; EWL 3; GFL 1789 to the
Present; MTCW 1; RGWL 2, 3

Giovanni, Nikki 1943- ...... BLC 2; CLC 2, 4,
19, 64, 117; PC 19; WLCS
See also AAYA 22; AITN 1; BW 2, 3; CA
29-32R; CAAS 6; CANR 18, 41, 60, 91,
130; CDALBS; CLR 6, 73; CP 2, 3, 4, 5,
6, 7; CSW; CWP; CWRI 5; DA; DA3;
DAB; DAC; DAM MST, MULT, POET;
DLB 5, 41; EWL 3; EXPP; INT CANR-
18; MAICYA 1, 2; MAL 5; MTCW 1, 2;
MTFW 2005; PFS 17; RGAL 4; SATA
24, 107; TUS; YAW

Giovene, Andrea 1904-1998 .... CLC 7
See also CA 85-88

Gippius, Zinaida (Nikolaevna) 1869-1945
See Hippius, Zinaida (Nikolaevna)
See also CA 106; 212

Giraudoux, Jean(-Hippolyte)
1882-1944 .... TCLC 2, 7
See also CA 104; 196; DAM DRAM; DLB
65, 321; EW 9; EWL 3; GFL 1789 to the
Present; RGWL 2, 3; TWA

Gironella, Jose Maria (Pous)
1917-2003 .... CLC 11
See also CA 101; 212; EWL 3; RGWL 2, 3

Gissing, George (Robert)
1857-1903 .... SSC 37; TCLC 3, 24, 47
See also BRW 5; CA 105; 167; DLB 18,
135, 184; RGEL 2; TEA

Gitlin, Todd 1943- .... CLC 201
See also CA 29-32R; CANR 25, 50, 88

Giurlani, Aldo
See Palazzeschi, Aldo

Gladkov, Fedor Vasil'evich
See Gladkov, Fyodor (Vasilyevich)
See also DLB 272

Gladkov, Fyodor (Vasilyevich)
1883-1958 .... TCLC 27
See Gladkov, Fedor Vasil'evich
See also CA 170; EWL 3

Glancy, Diane 1941- .... CLC 210; NNAL
See also CA 136; 225; CAAE 225; CAAS
24; CANR 87; DLB 175

Gordone, Charles 1925-1995 .. **CLC 1, 4; DC 8**
See also BW 1, 3; CA 93-96, 180; 150; CAAE 180; CAD; CANR 55; DAM DRAM; DLB 7; INT CA-93-96; MTCW 1

Gore, Catherine 1800-1861 .... **NCLC 65**
See also DLB 116; RGEL 2

Gorenko, Anna Andreevna
See Akhmatova, Anna

Gorky, Maxim .... **SSC 28; TCLC 8; WLC**
See Peshkov, Alexei Maximovich
See also DAB; DFS 9; DLB 295; EW 8; EWL 3; TWA

Goryan, Sirak
See Saroyan, William

Gosse, Edmund (William)
1849-1928 .... **TCLC 28**
See also CA 117; DLB 57, 144, 184; RGEL 2

Gotlieb, Phyllis (Fay Bloom) 1926- .. **CLC 18**
See also CA 13-16R; CANR 7, 135; CN 7; CP 1, 2, 3, 4; DLB 88, 251; SFW 4

Gottesman, S. D.
See Kornbluth, C(yril) M.; Pohl, Frederik

Gottfried von Strassburg fl. c.
1170-1215 .... **CMLC 10**
See also CDWLB 2; DLB 138; EW 1; RGWL 2, 3

Gotthelf, Jeremias 1797-1854 .... **NCLC 117**
See also DLB 133; RGWL 2, 3

Gottschalk, Laura Riding
See Jackson, Laura (Riding)

Gould, Lois 1932(?)-2002 .... **CLC 4, 10**
See also CA 77-80; 208; CANR 29; MTCW 1

Gould, Stephen Jay 1941-2002 .... **CLC 163**
See also AAYA 26; BEST 90:2; CA 77-80; 205; CANR 10, 27, 56, 75, 125; CPW; INT CANR-27; MTCW 1, 2; MTFW 2005

Gourmont, Remy(-Marie-Charles) de
1858-1915 .... **TCLC 17**
See also CA 109; 150; GFL 1789 to the Present; MTCW 2

Gournay, Marie le Jars de
See de Gournay, Marie le Jars

Govier, Katherine 1948- .... **CLC 51**
See also CA 101; CANR 18, 40, 128; CCA 1

Gower, John c. 1330-1408 .... **LC 76; PC 59**
See also BRW 1; DLB 146; RGEL 2

Goyen, (Charles) William
1915-1983 .... **CLC 5, 8, 14, 40**
See also AITN 2; CA 5-8R; 110; CANR 6, 71; CN 1, 2, 3; DLB 2, 218; DLBY 1983; EWL 3; INT CANR-6; MAL 5

Goytisolo, Juan 1931- .... **CLC 5, 10, 23, 133; HLC 1**
See also CA 85-88; CANR 32, 61, 131; CWW 2; DAM MULT; DLB 322; EWL 3; GLL 2; HW 1, 2; MTCW 1, 2; MTFW 2005

Gozzano, Guido 1883-1916 .... **PC 10**
See also CA 154; DLB 114; EWL 3

Gozzi, (Conte) Carlo 1720-1806 .... **NCLC 23**

Grabbe, Christian Dietrich
1801-1836 .... **NCLC 2**
See also DLB 133; RGWL 2, 3

Grace, Patricia Frances 1937- .... **CLC 56**
See also CA 176; CANR 118; CN 4, 5, 6, 7; EWL 3; RGSF 2

Gracian y Morales, Baltasar
1601-1658 .... **LC 15**

Gracq, Julien .... **CLC 11, 48**
See Poirier, Louis
See also CWW 2; DLB 83; GFL 1789 to the Present

Grade, Chaim 1910-1982 .... **CLC 10**
See also CA 93-96; 107; EWL 3

Graduate of Oxford, A
See Ruskin, John

Grafton, Garth
See Duncan, Sara Jeannette

Grafton, Sue 1940- .... **CLC 163**
See also AAYA 11, 49; BEST 90:3; CA 108; CANR 31, 55, 111, 134; CMW 4; CPW; CSW; DA3; DAM POP; DLB 226; FW; MSW; MTFW 2005

Graham, John
See Phillips, David Graham

Graham, Jorie 1950- .... **CLC 48, 118; PC 59**
See also AAYA 67; CA 111; CANR 63, 118; CP 4, 5, 6, 7; CWP; DLB 120; EWL 3; MTFW 2005; PFS 10, 17; TCLE 1:1

Graham, R(obert) B(ontine) Cunninghame
See Cunninghame Graham, Robert (Gallnigad) Bontine
See also DLB 98, 135, 174; RGEL 2; RGSF 2

Graham, Robert
See Haldeman, Joe (William)

Graham, Tom
See Lewis, (Harry) Sinclair

Graham, W(illiam) S(idney)
1918-1986 .... **CLC 29**
See also BRWS 7; CA 73-76; 118; CP 1, 2, 3, 4; DLB 20; RGEL 2

Graham, Winston (Mawdsley)
1910-2003 .... **CLC 23**
See also CA 49-52; 218; CANR 2, 22, 45, 66; CMW 4; CN 1, 2, 3, 4, 5, 6, 7; DLB 77; RHW

Grahame, Kenneth 1859-1932 ...... **TCLC 64, 136**
See also BYA 5; CA 108; 136; CANR 80; CLR 5; CWRI 5; DA3; DAB; DLB 34, 141, 178; FANT; MAICYA 1, 2; MTCW 2; NFS 20; RGEL 2; SATA 100; TEA; WCH; YABC 1

Granger, Darius John
See Marlowe, Stephen

Granin, Daniil 1918- .... **CLC 59**
See also DLB 302

Granovsky, Timofei Nikolaevich
1813-1855 .... **NCLC 75**
See also DLB 198

Grant, Skeeter
See Spiegelman, Art

Granville-Barker, Harley
1877-1946 .... **TCLC 2**
See Barker, Harley Granville
See also CA 104; 204; DAM DRAM; RGEL 2

Granzotto, Gianni
See Granzotto, Giovanni Battista

Granzotto, Giovanni Battista
1914-1985 .... **CLC 70**
See also CA 166

Grass, Guenter (Wilhelm) 1927- ... **CLC 1, 2, 4, 6, 11, 15, 22, 32, 49, 88, 207; WLC**
See Grass, Gunter (Wilhelm)
See also BPFB 2; CA 13-16R; CANR 20, 75, 93, 133; CDWLB 2; DA; DA3; DAB; DAC; DAM MST, NOV; DLB 75, 124; EW 13; EWL 3; MTCW 1, 2; MTFW 2005; RGWL 2, 3; TWA

Grass, Gunter (Wilhelm)
See Grass, Guenter (Wilhelm)
See also CWW 2

Gratton, Thomas
See Hulme, T(homas) E(rnest)

Grau, Shirley Ann 1929- .... **CLC 4, 9, 146; SSC 15**
See also CA 89-92; CANR 22, 69; CN 1, 2, 3, 4, 5, 6, 7; CSW; DLB 2, 218; INT CA-89-92; CANR-22; MTCW 1

Gravel, Fern
See Hall, James Norman

Graver, Elizabeth 1964- .... **CLC 70**
See also CA 135; CANR 71, 129

Graves, Richard Perceval
1895-1985 .... **CLC 44**
See also CA 65-68; CANR 9, 26, 51

Graves, Robert (von Ranke)
1895-1985 .. **CLC 1, 2, 6, 11, 39, 44, 45; PC 6**
See also BPFB 2; BRW 7; BYA 4; CA 5-8R; 117; CANR 5, 36; CDBLB 1914-1945; CN 1, 2, 3; CP 1, 2, 3, 4; DA3; DAB; DAC; DAM MST, POET; DLB 20, 100, 191; DLBD 18; DLBY 1985; EWL 3; LATS 1:1; MTCW 1, 2; MTFW 2005; NCFS 2; NFS 21; RGEL 2; RHW; SATA 45; TEA

Graves, Valerie
See Bradley, Marion Zimmer

Gray, Alasdair (James) 1934- .... **CLC 41**
See also BRWS 9; CA 126; CANR 47, 69, 106, 140; CN 4, 5, 6, 7; DLB 194, 261, 319; HGG; INT CA-126; MTCW 1, 2; MTFW 2005; RGSF 2; SUFW 2

Gray, Amlin 1946- .... **CLC 29**
See also CA 138

Gray, Francine du Plessix 1930- ..... **CLC 22, 153**
See also BEST 90:3; CA 61-64; CAAS 2; CANR 11, 33, 75, 81; DAM NOV; INT CANR-11; MTCW 1, 2; MTFW 2005

Gray, John (Henry) 1866-1934 ...... **TCLC 19**
See also CA 119; 162; RGEL 2

Gray, John Lee
See Jakes, John (William)

Gray, Simon (James Holliday)
1936- .... **CLC 9, 14, 36**
See also AITN 1; CA 21-24R; CAAS 3; CANR 32, 69; CBD; CD 5, 6; CN 1, 2, 3; DLB 13; EWL 3; MTCW 1; RGEL 2

Gray, Spalding 1941-2004 .... **CLC 49, 112; DC 7**
See also AAYA 62; CA 128; 225; CAD; CANR 74, 138; CD 5, 6; CPW; DAM POP; MTCW 2; MTFW 2005

Gray, Thomas 1716-1771 .... **LC 4, 40; PC 2; WLC**
See also BRW 3; CDBLB 1660-1789; DA; DA3; DAB; DAC; DAM MST; DLB 109; EXPP; PAB; PFS 9; RGEL 2; TEA; WP

Grayson, David
See Baker, Ray Stannard

Grayson, Richard (A.) 1951- .... **CLC 38**
See also CA 85-88; 210; CAAE 210; CANR 14, 31, 57; DLB 234

Greeley, Andrew M(oran) 1928- ...... **CLC 28**
See also BPFB 2; CA 5-8R; CAAS 7; CANR 7, 43, 69, 104, 136; CMW 4; CPW; DA3; DAM POP; MTCW 1, 2; MTFW 2005

Green, Anna Katharine
1846-1935 .... **TCLC 63**
See also CA 112; 159; CMW 4; DLB 202, 221; MSW

Green, Brian
See Card, Orson Scott

Green, Hannah
See Greenberg, Joanne (Goldenberg)

Green, Hannah 1927(?)-1996 .... **CLC 3**
See also CA 73-76; CANR 59, 93; NFS 10

Green, Henry .... **CLC 2, 13, 97**
See Yorke, Henry Vincent
See also BRWS 2; CA 175; DLB 15; EWL 3; RGEL 2

Green, Julian .... **CLC 3, 11, 77**
See Green, Julien (Hartridge)
See also EWL 3; GFL 1789 to the Present; MTCW 2

Harrison, Elizabeth (Allen) Cavanna
1909-2001
See Cavanna, Betty
See also CA 9-12R; 200; CANR 6, 27, 85, 104, 121; MAICYA 2; SATA 142; YAW

Harrison, Harry (Max) 1925- .... **CLC 42**
See also CA 1-4R; CANR 5, 21, 84; DLB 8; SATA 4; SCFW 2; SFW 4

Harrison, James (Thomas) 1937- ...... **CLC 6, 14, 33, 66, 143; SSC 19**
See Harrison, Jim
See also CA 13-16R; CANR 8, 51, 79, 142; DLBY 1982; INT CANR-8

Harrison, Jim
See Harrison, James (Thomas)
See also AMWS 8; CN 5, 6; CP 1, 2, 3, 4, 5, 6, 7; RGAL 4; TCWW 2; TUS

Harrison, Kathryn 1961- .... **CLC 70, 151**
See also CA 144; CANR 68, 122

Harrison, Tony 1937- .... **CLC 43, 129**
See also BRWS 5; CA 65-68; CANR 44, 98; CBD; CD 5, 6; CP 2, 3, 4, 5, 6, 7; DLB 40, 245; MTCW 1; RGEL 2

Harriss, Will(ard Irvin) 1922- .... **CLC 34**
See also CA 111

Hart, Ellis
See Ellison, Harlan (Jay)

Hart, Josephine 1942(?)- .... **CLC 70**
See also CA 138; CANR 70; CPW; DAM POP

Hart, Moss 1904-1961 .... **CLC 66**
See also CA 109; 89-92; CANR 84; DAM DRAM; DFS 1; DLB 7, 266; RGAL 4

Harte, (Francis) Bret(t)
1836(?)-1902 ... **SSC 8, 59; TCLC 1, 25; WLC**
See also AMWS 2; CA 104; 140; CANR 80; CDALB 1865-1917; DA; DA3; DAC; DAM MST; DLB 12, 64, 74, 79, 186; EXPS; LAIT 2; RGAL 4; RGSF 2; SATA 26; SSFS 3; TUS

Hartley, L(eslie) P(oles) 1895-1972 ... **CLC 2, 22**
See also BRWS 7; CA 45-48; 37-40R; CANR 33; CN 1; DLB 15, 139; EWL 3; HGG; MTCW 1, 2; MTFW 2005; RGEL 2; RGSF 2; SUFW 1

Hartman, Geoffrey H. 1929- .... **CLC 27**
See also CA 117; 125; CANR 79; DLB 67

Hartmann, Sadakichi 1869-1944 ... **TCLC 73**
See also CA 157; DLB 54

Hartmann von Aue c. 1170-c.
1210 .... **CMLC 15**
See also CDWLB 2; DLB 138; RGWL 2, 3

Hartog, Jan de
See de Hartog, Jan

Haruf, Kent 1943- .... **CLC 34**
See also AAYA 44; CA 149; CANR 91, 131

Harvey, Caroline
See Trollope, Joanna

Harvey, Gabriel 1550(?)-1631 .... **LC 88**
See also DLB 167, 213, 281

Harwood, Ronald 1934- .... **CLC 32**
See also CA 1-4R; CANR 4, 55; CBD; CD 5, 6; DAM DRAM, MST; DLB 13

Hasegawa Tatsunosuke
See Futabatei, Shimei

Hasek, Jaroslav (Matej Frantisek)
1883-1923 .... **SSC 69; TCLC 4**
See also CA 104; 129; CDWLB 4; DLB 215; EW 9; EWL 3; MTCW 1, 2; RGSF 2; RGWL 2, 3

Hass, Robert 1941- ... **CLC 18, 39, 99; PC 16**
See also AMWS 6; CA 111; CANR 30, 50, 71; CP 3, 4, 5, 6, 7; DLB 105, 206; EWL 3; MAL 5; MTFW 2005; RGAL 4; SATA 94; TCLE 1:1

Hastings, Hudson
See Kuttner, Henry

Hastings, Selina .... **CLC 44**
Hathorne, John 1641-1717 .... **LC 38**
Hatteras, Amelia
See Mencken, H(enry) L(ouis)

Hatteras, Owen .... **TCLC 18**
See Mencken, H(enry) L(ouis); Nathan, George Jean

Hauptmann, Gerhart (Johann Robert)
1862-1946 .... **SSC 37; TCLC 4**
See also CA 104; 153; CDWLB 2; DAM DRAM; DLB 66, 118; EW 8; EWL 3; RGSF 2; RGWL 2, 3; TWA

Havel, Vaclav 1936- ..... **CLC 25, 58, 65, 123; DC 6**
See also CA 104; CANR 36, 63, 124; CD-WLB 4; CWW 2; DA3; DAM DRAM; DFS 10; DLB 232; EWL 3; LMFS 2; MTCW 1, 2; MTFW 2005; RGWL 3

Haviaras, Stratis .... **CLC 33**
See Chaviaras, Strates

Hawes, Stephen 1475(?)-1529(?) .... **LC 17**
See also DLB 132; RGEL 2

Hawkes, John (Clendennin Burne, Jr.)
1925-1998 .. **CLC 1, 2, 3, 4, 7, 9, 14, 15, 27, 49**
See also BPFB 2; CA 1-4R; 167; CANR 2, 47, 64; CN 1, 2, 3, 4, 5, 6; DLB 2, 7, 227; DLBY 1980, 1998; EWL 3; MAL 5; MTCW 1, 2; MTFW 2005; RGAL 4

Hawking, S. W.
See Hawking, Stephen W(illiam)

Hawking, Stephen W(illiam) 1942- . **CLC 63, 105**
See also AAYA 13; BEST 89:1; CA 126; 129; CANR 48, 115; CPW; DA3; MTCW 2; MTFW 2005

Hawkins, Anthony Hope
See Hope, Anthony

Hawthorne, Julian 1846-1934 .... **TCLC 25**
See also CA 165; HGG

Hawthorne, Nathaniel 1804-1864 ... **NCLC 2, 10, 17, 23, 39, 79, 95, 158; SSC 3, 29, 39, 89; WLC**
See also AAYA 18; AMW; AMWC 1; AMWR 1; BPFB 2; BYA 3; CDALB 1640-1865; CLR 103; DA; DA3; DAB; DAC; DAM MST, NOV; DLB 1, 74, 183, 223, 269; EXPN; EXPS; GL 2; HGG; LAIT 1; NFS 1, 20; RGAL 4; RGSF 2; SSFS 1, 7, 11, 15; SUFW 1; TUS; WCH; YABC 2

Hawthorne, Sophia Peabody
1809-1871 .... **NCLC 150**
See also DLB 183, 239

Haxton, Josephine Ayres 1921-
See Douglas, Ellen
See also CA 115; CANR 41, 83

Hayaseca y Eizaguirre, Jorge
See Echegaray (y Eizaguirre), Jose (Maria Waldo)

Hayashi, Fumiko 1904-1951 .... **TCLC 27**
See Hayashi Fumiko
See also CA 161

Hayashi Fumiko
See Hayashi, Fumiko
See also DLB 180; EWL 3

Haycraft, Anna (Margaret) 1932-2005
See Ellis, Alice Thomas
See also CA 122; 237; CANR 90, 141; MTCW 2; MTFW 2005

Hayden, Robert E(arl) 1913-1980 ..... **BLC 2; CLC 5, 9, 14, 37; PC 6**
See also AFAW 1, 2; AMWS 2; BW 1, 3; CA 69-72; 97-100; CABS 2; CANR 24, 75, 82; CDALB 1941-1968; CP 1, 2, 3; DA; DAC; DAM MST, MULT, POET; DLB 5, 76; EWL 3; EXPP; MAL 5; MTCW 1, 2; PFS 1; RGAL 4; SATA 19; SATA-Obit 26; WP

Haydon, Benjamin Robert
1786-1846 .... **NCLC 146**
See also DLB 110

Hayek, F(riedrich) A(ugust von)
1899-1992 .... **TCLC 109**
See also CA 93-96; 137; CANR 20; MTCW 1, 2

Hayford, J(oseph) E(phraim) Casely
See Casely-Hayford, J(oseph) E(phraim)

Hayman, Ronald 1932- .... **CLC 44**
See also CA 25-28R; CANR 18, 50, 88; CD 5, 6; DLB 155

Hayne, Paul Hamilton 1830-1886 . **NCLC 94**
See also DLB 3, 64, 79, 248; RGAL 4

Hays, Mary 1760-1843 .... **NCLC 114**
See also DLB 142, 158; RGEL 2

Haywood, Eliza (Fowler)
1693(?)-1756 .... **LC 1, 44**
See also DLB 39; RGEL 2

Hazlitt, William 1778-1830 ...... **NCLC 29, 82**
See also BRW 4; DLB 110, 158; RGEL 2; TEA

Hazzard, Shirley 1931- .... **CLC 18, 218**
See also CA 9-12R; CANR 4, 70, 127; CN 1, 2, 3, 4, 5, 6, 7; DLB 289; DLBY 1982; MTCW 1

Head, Bessie 1937-1986 ...... **BLC 2; CLC 25, 67; SSC 52**
See also AFW; BW 2, 3; CA 29-32R; 119; CANR 25, 82; CDWLB 3; CN 1, 2, 3, 4; DA3; DAM MULT; DLB 117, 225; EWL 3; EXPS; FL 1:6; FW; MTCW 1, 2; MTFW 2005; RGSF 2; SSFS 5, 13; WLIT 2; WWE 1

Headon, (Nicky) Topper 1956(?)- ..... **CLC 30**

Heaney, Seamus (Justin) 1939- ..... **CLC 5, 7, 14, 25, 37, 74, 91, 171; PC 18; WLCS**
See also AAYA 61; BRWR 1; BRWS 2; CA 85-88; CANR 25, 48, 75, 91, 128; CD-BLB 1960 to Present; CP 1, 2, 3, 4, 5, 6, 7; DA3; DAB; DAM POET; DLB 40; DLBY 1995; EWL 3; EXPP; MTCW 1, 2; MTFW 2005; PAB; PFS 2, 5, 8, 17; RGEL 2; TEA; WLIT 4

Hearn, (Patricio) Lafcadio (Tessima Carlos)
1850-1904 .... **TCLC 9**
See also CA 105; 166; DLB 12, 78, 189; HGG; MAL 5; RGAL 4

Hearne, Samuel 1745-1792 .... **LC 95**
See also DLB 99

Hearne, Vicki 1946-2001 .... **CLC 56**
See also CA 139; 201

Hearon, Shelby 1931- .... **CLC 63**
See also AITN 2; AMWS 8; CA 25-28R; CANR 18, 48, 103, 146; CSW

Heat-Moon, William Least .... **CLC 29**
See Trogdon, William (Lewis)
See also AAYA 9

Hebbel, Friedrich 1813-1863 . **DC 21; NCLC 43**
See also CDWLB 2; DAM DRAM; DLB 129; EW 6; RGWL 2, 3

Hebert, Anne 1916-2000 .... **CLC 4, 13, 29**
See also CA 85-88; 187; CANR 69, 126; CCA 1; CWP; CWW 2; DA3; DAC; DAM MST, POET; DLB 68; EWL 3; GFL 1789 to the Present; MTCW 1, 2; MTFW 2005; PFS 20

Hecht, Anthony (Evan) 1923-2004 .... **CLC 8, 13, 19; PC 70**
See also AMWS 10; CA 9-12R; 232; CANR 6, 108; CP 1, 2, 3, 4, 5, 6, 7; DAM POET; DLB 5, 169; EWL 3; PFS 6; WP

Hecht, Ben 1894-1964 ..... **CLC 8; TCLC 101**
See also CA 85-88; DFS 9; DLB 7, 9, 25, 26, 28, 86; FANT; IDFW 3, 4; RGAL 4

Hedayat, Sadeq 1903-1951 .... **TCLC 21**
See also CA 120; EWL 3; RGSF 2

Hewes, Cady
See De Voto, Bernard (Augustine)

Heyen, William 1940- .... **CLC 13, 18**
See also CA 33-36R, 220; CAAE 220;
CAAS 9; CANR 98; CP 3, 4, 5, 6, 7; DLB
5

Heyerdahl, Thor 1914-2002 .... **CLC 26**
See also CA 5-8R; 207; CANR 5, 22, 66,
73; LAIT 4; MTCW 1, 2; MTFW 2005;
SATA 2, 52

Heym, Georg (Theodor Franz Arthur)
1887-1912 .... **TCLC 9**
See also CA 106; 181

Heym, Stefan 1913-2001 .... **CLC 41**
See also CA 9-12R; 203; CANR 4; CWW
2; DLB 69; EWL 3

Heyse, Paul (Johann Ludwig von)
1830-1914 .... **TCLC 8**
See also CA 104; 209; DLB 129

Heyward, (Edwin) DuBose
1885-1940 .... **HR 1:2; TCLC 59**
See also CA 108; 157; DLB 7, 9, 45, 249;
MAL 5; SATA 21

Heywood, John 1497(?)-1580(?) .... **LC 65**
See also DLB 136; RGEL 2

Heywood, Thomas 1573(?)-1641 .... **LC 111**
See also DAM DRAM; DLB 62; LMFS 1;
RGEL 2; TEA

Hibbert, Eleanor Alice Burford
1906-1993 .... **CLC 7**
See Holt, Victoria
See also BEST 90:4; CA 17-20R; 140;
CANR 9, 28, 59; CMW 4; CPW; DAM
POP; MTCW 2; MTFW 2005; RHW;
SATA 2; SATA-Obit 74

Hichens, Robert (Smythe)
1864-1950 .... **TCLC 64**
See also CA 162; DLB 153; HGG; RHW;
SUFW

Higgins, Aidan 1927- .... **SSC 68**
See also CA 9-12R; CANR 70, 115; CN 1,
2, 3, 4, 5, 6, 7; DLB 14

Higgins, George V(incent)
1939-1999 .... **CLC 4, 7, 10, 18**
See also BPFB 2; CA 77-80; 186; CAAS 5;
CANR 17, 51, 89, 96; CMW 4; CN 2, 3,
4, 5, 6; DLB 2; DLBY 1981, 1998; INT
CANR-17; MSW; MTCW 1

Higginson, Thomas Wentworth
1823-1911 .... **TCLC 36**
See also CA 162; DLB 1, 64, 243

Higgonet, Margaret ed. .... **CLC 65**

Highet, Helen
See MacInnes, Helen (Clark)

Highsmith, (Mary) Patricia
1921-1995 .... **CLC 2, 4, 14, 42, 102**
See Morgan, Claire
See also AAYA 48; BRWS 5; CA 1-4R; 147;
CANR 1, 20, 48, 62, 108; CMW 4; CN 1,
2, 3, 4, 5; CPW; DA3; DAM NOV, POP;
DLB 306; MSW; MTCW 1, 2; MTFW
2005

Highwater, Jamake (Mamake)
1942(?)-2001 .... **CLC 12**
See also AAYA 7; BPFB 2; BYA 4; CA 65-
68; 199; CAAS 7; CANR 10, 34, 84; CLR
17; CWRI 5; DLB 52; DLBY 1985;
JRDA; MAICYA 1, 2; SATA 32, 69;
SATA-Brief 30

Highway, Tomson 1951- ...... **CLC 92; NNAL**
See also CA 151; CANR 75; CCA 1; CD 5,
6; CN 7; DAC; DAM MULT; DFS 2;
MTCW 2

Hijuelos, Oscar 1951- .... **CLC 65; HLC 1**
See also AAYA 25; AMWS 8; BEST 90:1;
CA 123; CANR 50, 75, 125; CPW; DA3;
DAM MULT, POP; DLB 145; HW 1, 2;
LLW; MAL 5; MTCW 2; MTFW 2005;
NFS 17; RGAL 4; WLIT 1

Hikmet, Nazim 1902-1963 .... **CLC 40**
See Nizami of Ganja
See also CA 141; 93-96; EWL 3; WLIT 6

Hildegard von Bingen 1098-1179 . **CMLC 20**
See also DLB 148

Hildesheimer, Wolfgang 1916-1991 .. **CLC 49**
See also CA 101; 135; DLB 69, 124; EWL
3

Hill, Geoffrey (William) 1932- ...... **CLC 5, 8,**
18, 45
See also BRWS 5; CA 81-84; CANR 21,
89; CDBLB 1960 to Present; CP 1, 2, 3,
4, 5, 6, 7; DAM POET; DLB 40; EWL 3;
MTCW 1; RGEL 2

Hill, George Roy 1921-2002 .... **CLC 26**
See also CA 110; 122; 213

Hill, John
See Koontz, Dean R.

Hill, Susan (Elizabeth) 1942- ...... **CLC 4, 113**
See also CA 33-36R; CANR 29, 69, 129;
CN 2, 3, 4, 5, 6, 7; DAB; DAM MST,
NOV; DLB 14, 139; HGG; MTCW 1;
RHW

Hillard, Asa G. III .... **CLC 70**

Hillerman, Tony 1925- .... **CLC 62, 170**
See also AAYA 40; BEST 89:1; BPFB 2;
CA 29-32R; CANR 21, 42, 65, 97, 134;
CMW 4; CPW; DA3; DAM POP; DLB
206, 306; MAL 5; MSW; MTCW 2;
MTFW 2005; RGAL 4; SATA 6; TCWW
2; YAW

Hillesum, Etty 1914-1943 .... **TCLC 49**
See also CA 137

Hilliard, Noel (Harvey) 1929-1996 ... **CLC 15**
See also CA 9-12R; CANR 7, 69; CN 1, 2,
3, 4, 5, 6

Hillis, Rick 1956- .... **CLC 66**
See also CA 134

Hilton, James 1900-1954 .... **TCLC 21**
See also CA 108; 169; DLB 34, 77; FANT;
SATA 34

Hilton, Walter (?)-1396 .... **CMLC 58**
See also DLB 146; RGEL 2

Himes, Chester (Bomar) 1909-1984 .. **BLC 2;**
CLC 2, 4, 7, 18, 58, 108; TCLC 139
See also AFAW 2; BPFB 2; BW 2; CA 25-
28R; 114; CANR 22, 89; CMW 4; CN 1,
2, 3; DAM MULT; DLB 2, 76, 143, 226;
EWL 3; MAL 5; MSW; MTCW 1, 2;
MTFW 2005; RGAL 4

Himmelfarb, Gertrude 1922- .... **CLC 202**
See also CA 49-52; CANR 28, 66, 102

Hinde, Thomas .... **CLC 6, 11**
See Chitty, Thomas Willes
See also CN 1, 2, 3, 4, 5, 6; EWL 3

Hine, (William) Daryl 1936- .... **CLC 15**
See also CA 1-4R; CAAS 15; CANR 1, 20;
CP 1, 2, 3, 4, 5, 6, 7; DLB 60

Hinkson, Katharine Tynan
See Tynan, Katharine

Hinojosa(-Smith), Rolando (R.)
1929- .... **HLC 1**
See Hinojosa-Smith, Rolando
See also CA 131; CAAS 16; CANR 62;
DAM MULT; DLB 82; HW 1, 2; LLW;
MTCW 2; MTFW 2005; RGAL 4

Hinton, S(usan) E(loise) 1950- .. **CLC 30, 111**
See also AAYA 2, 33; BPFB 2; BYA 2, 3;
CA 81-84; CANR 32, 62, 92, 133;
CDALBS; CLR 3, 23; CPW; DA; DA3;
DAB; DAC; DAM MST, NOV; JRDA;
LAIT 5; MAICYA 1, 2; MTCW 1, 2;
MTFW 2005 !**; NFS 5, 9, 15, 16; SATA
19, 58, 115, 160; WYA; YAW

Hippius, Zinaida (Nikolaevna) .... **TCLC 9**
See Gippius, Zinaida (Nikolaevna)
See also DLB 295; EWL 3

Hiraoka, Kimitake 1925-1970
See Mishima, Yukio
See also CA 97-100; 29-32R; DA3; DAM
DRAM; GLL 1; MTCW 1, 2

Hirsch, E(ric) D(onald), Jr. 1928- .... **CLC 79**
See also CA 25-28R; CANR 27, 51; DLB
67; INT CANR-27; MTCW 1

Hirsch, Edward 1950- .... **CLC 31, 50**
See also CA 104; CANR 20, 42, 102; CP 7;
DLB 120; PFS 22

Hitchcock, Alfred (Joseph)
1899-1980 .... **CLC 16**
See also AAYA 22; CA 159; 97-100; SATA
27; SATA-Obit 24

Hitchens, Christopher (Eric)
1949- .... **CLC 157**
See also CA 152; CANR 89

Hitler, Adolf 1889-1945 .... **TCLC 53**
See also CA 117; 147

Hoagland, Edward (Morley) 1932- .. **CLC 28**
See also ANW; CA 1-4R; CANR 2, 31, 57,
107; CN 1, 2, 3, 4, 5, 6, 7; DLB 6; SATA
51; TCWW 2

Hoban, Russell (Conwell) 1925- ... **CLC 7, 25**
See also BPFB 2; CA 5-8R; CANR 23, 37,
66, 114, 138; CLR 3, 69; CN 4, 5, 6, 7;
CWRI 5; DAM NOV; DLB 52; FANT;
MAICYA 1, 2; MTCW 1, 2; MTFW 2005;
SATA 1, 40, 78, 136; SFW 4; SUFW 2;
TCLE 1:1

Hobbes, Thomas 1588-1679 .... **LC 36**
See also DLB 151, 252, 281; RGEL 2

Hobbs, Perry
See Blackmur, R(ichard) P(almer)

Hobson, Laura Z(ametkin)
1900-1986 .... **CLC 7, 25**
See also BPFB 2; CA 17-20R; 118; CANR
55; CN 1, 2, 3, 4; DLB 28; SATA 52

Hoccleve, Thomas c. 1368-c. 1437 ...... **LC 75**
See also DLB 146; RGEL 2

Hoch, Edward D(entinger) 1930-
See Queen, Ellery
See also CA 29-32R; CANR 11, 27, 51, 97;
CMW 4; DLB 306; SFW 4

Hochhuth, Rolf 1931- .... **CLC 4, 11, 18**
See also CA 5-8R; CANR 33, 75, 136;
CWW 2; DAM DRAM; DLB 124; EWL
3; MTCW 1, 2; MTFW 2005

Hochman, Sandra 1936- .... **CLC 3, 8**
See also CA 5-8R; CP 1, 2, 3, 4; DLB 5

Hochwaelder, Fritz 1911-1986 .... **CLC 36**
See Hochwalder, Fritz
See also CA 29-32R; 120; CANR 42; DAM
DRAM; MTCW 1; RGWL 3

Hochwalder, Fritz
See Hochwaelder, Fritz
See also EWL 3; RGWL 2

Hocking, Mary (Eunice) 1921- .... **CLC 13**
See also CA 101; CANR 18, 40

Hodgins, Jack 1938- .... **CLC 23**
See also CA 93-96; CN 4, 5, 6, 7; DLB 60

Hodgson, William Hope
1877(?)-1918 .... **TCLC 13**
See also CA 111; 164; CMW 4; DLB 70,
153, 156, 178; HGG; MTCW 2; SFW 4;
SUFW 1

Hoeg, Peter 1957- .... **CLC 95, 156**
See also CA 151; CANR 75; CMW 4; DA3;
DLB 214; EWL 3; MTCW 2; MTFW
2005; NFS 17; RGWL 3; SSFS 18

Hoffman, Alice 1952- .... **CLC 51**
See also AAYA 37; AMWS 10; CA 77-80;
CANR 34, 66, 100, 138; CN 4, 5, 6, 7;
CPW; DAM NOV; DLB 292; MAL 5;
MTCW 1, 2; MTFW 2005; TCLE 1:1

Hoffman, Daniel (Gerard) 1923- . **CLC 6, 13,**
23
See also CA 1-4R; CANR 4, 142; CP 1, 2,
3, 4, 5, 6, 7; DLB 5; TCLE 1:1

Hoffman, Eva 1945- .... **CLC 182**
See also CA 132; CANR 146

Hoffman, Stanley 1944- .... **CLC 5**
See also CA 77-80

Hoffman, William 1925- .... **CLC 141**
See also CA 21-24R; CANR 9, 103; CSW;
DLB 234; TCLE 1:1

Hoffman, William M.
See Hoffman, William M(oses)
See also CAD; CD 5, 6

Hoffman, William M(oses) 1939- ..... **CLC 40**
See Hoffman, William M.
See also CA 57-60; CANR 11, 71

Hoffmann, E(rnst) T(heodor) A(madeus)
1776-1822 .... **NCLC 2; SSC 13**
See also CDWLB 2; DLB 90; EW 5; GL 2;
RGSF 2; RGWL 2, 3; SATA 27; SUFW
1; WCH

Hofmann, Gert 1931-1993 .... **CLC 54**
See also CA 128; CANR 145; EWL 3

Hofmannsthal, Hugo von 1874-1929 ... **DC 4;**
TCLC 11
See also CA 106; 153; CDWLB 2; DAM
DRAM; DFS 17; DLB 81, 118; EW 9;
EWL 3; RGWL 2, 3

Hogan, Linda 1947- ..... **CLC 73; NNAL; PC**
35
See also AMWS 4; ANW; BYA 12; CA 120,
226; CAAE 226; CANR 45, 73, 129;
CWP; DAM MULT; DLB 175; SATA
132; TCWW 2

Hogarth, Charles
See Creasey, John

Hogarth, Emmett
See Polonsky, Abraham (Lincoln)

Hogarth, William 1697-1764 .... **LC 112**
See also AAYA 56

Hogg, James 1770-1835 .... **NCLC 4, 109**
See also BRWS 10; DLB 93, 116, 159; GL
2; HGG; RGEL 2; SUFW 1

Holbach, Paul-Henri Thiry
1723-1789 .... **LC 14**
See also DLB 313

Holberg, Ludvig 1684-1754 .... **LC 6**
See also DLB 300; RGWL 2, 3

Holcroft, Thomas 1745-1809 .... **NCLC 85**
See also DLB 39, 89, 158; RGEL 2

Holden, Ursula 1921- .... **CLC 18**
See also CA 101; CAAS 8; CANR 22

Holderlin, (Johann Christian) Friedrich
1770-1843 .... **NCLC 16; PC 4**
See also CDWLB 2; DLB 90; EW 5; RGWL
2, 3

Holdstock, Robert
See Holdstock, Robert P.

Holdstock, Robert P. 1948- .... **CLC 39**
See also CA 131; CANR 81; DLB 261;
FANT; HGG; SFW 4; SUFW 2

Holinshed, Raphael fl. 1580- .... **LC 69**
See also DLB 167; RGEL 2

Holland, Isabelle (Christian)
1920-2002 .... **CLC 21**
See also AAYA 11, 64; CA 21-24R; 205;
CAAE 181; CANR 10, 25, 47; CLR 57;
CWRI 5; JRDA; LAIT 4; MAICYA 1, 2;
SATA 8, 70; SATA-Essay 103; SATA-Obit
132; WYA

Holland, Marcus
See Caldwell, (Janet Miriam) Taylor
(Holland)

Hollander, John 1929- .... **CLC 2, 5, 8, 14**
See also CA 1-4R; CANR 1, 52, 136; CP 1,
2, 3, 4, 5, 6, 7; DLB 5; MAL 5; SATA 13

Hollander, Paul
See Silverberg, Robert

Holleran, Andrew .... **CLC 38**
See Garber, Eric
See also CA 144; GLL 1

Holley, Marietta 1836(?)-1926 .... **TCLC 99**
See also CA 118; DLB 11; FL 1:3

Hollinghurst, Alan 1954- .... **CLC 55, 91**
See also BRWS 10; CA 114; CN 5, 6, 7;
DLB 207; GLL 1

Hollis, Jim
See Summers, Hollis (Spurgeon, Jr.)

Holly, Buddy 1936-1959 .... **TCLC 65**
See also CA 213

Holmes, Gordon
See Shiel, M(atthew) P(hipps)

Holmes, John
See Souster, (Holmes) Raymond

Holmes, John Clellon 1926-1988 ...... **CLC 56**
See also BG 1:2; CA 9-12R; 125; CANR 4;
CN 1, 2, 3, 4; DLB 16, 237

Holmes, Oliver Wendell, Jr.
1841-1935 .... **TCLC 77**
See also CA 114; 186

Holmes, Oliver Wendell
1809-1894 .... **NCLC 14, 81; PC 71**
See also AMWS 1; CDALB 1640-1865;
DLB 1, 189, 235; EXPP; RGAL 4; SATA
34

Holmes, Raymond
See Souster, (Holmes) Raymond

Holt, Victoria
See Hibbert, Eleanor Alice Burford
See also BPFB 2

Holub, Miroslav 1923-1998 .... **CLC 4**
See also CA 21-24R; 169; CANR 10; CD-
WLB 4; CWW 2; DLB 232; EWL 3;
RGWL 3

Holz, Detlev
See Benjamin, Walter

Homer c. 8th cent. B.C.- .... **CMLC 1, 16, 61;**
PC 23; WLCS
See also AW 1; CDWLB 1; DA; DA3;
DAB; DAC; DAM MST, POET; DLB
176; EFS 1; LAIT 1; LMFS 1; RGWL 2,
3; TWA; WP

Hongo, Garrett Kaoru 1951- .... **PC 23**
See also CA 133; CAAS 22; CP 7; DLB
120, 312; EWL 3; EXPP; RGAL 4

Honig, Edwin 1919- .... **CLC 33**
See also CA 5-8R; CAAS 8; CANR 4, 45,
144; CP 1, 2, 3, 4, 5, 6, 7; DLB 5

Hood, Hugh (John Blagdon) 1928- . **CLC 15,**
28; SSC 42
See also CA 49-52; CAAS 17; CANR 1,
33, 87; CN 1, 2, 3, 4, 5, 6, 7; DLB 53;
RGSF 2

Hood, Thomas 1799-1845 .... **NCLC 16**
See also BRW 4; DLB 96; RGEL 2

Hooker, (Peter) Jeremy 1941- .... **CLC 43**
See also CA 77-80; CANR 22; CP 2, 3, 4,
5, 6, 7; DLB 40

Hooker, Richard 1554-1600 .... **LC 95**
See also BRW 1; DLB 132; RGEL 2

hooks, bell
See Watkins, Gloria Jean

Hope, A(lec) D(erwent) 1907-2000 .... **CLC 3,**
51; PC 56
See also BRWS 7; CA 21-24R; 188; CANR
33, 74; CP 1, 2, 3, 4; DLB 289; EWL 3;
MTCW 1, 2; MTFW 2005; PFS 8; RGEL
2

Hope, Anthony 1863-1933 .... **TCLC 83**
See also CA 157; DLB 153, 156; RGEL 2;
RHW

Hope, Brian
See Creasey, John

Hope, Christopher (David Tully)
1944- .... **CLC 52**
See also AFW; CA 106; CANR 47, 101;
CN 4, 5, 6, 7; DLB 225; SATA 62

Hopkins, Gerard Manley
1844-1889 .... **NCLC 17; PC 15; WLC**
See also BRW 5; BRWR 2; CDBLB 1890-
1914; DA; DA3; DAB; DAC; DAM MST,
POET; DLB 35, 57; EXPP; PAB; RGEL
2; TEA; WP

Hopkins, John (Richard) 1931-1998 .. **CLC 4**
See also CA 85-88; 169; CBD; CD 5, 6

Hopkins, Pauline Elizabeth
1859-1930 .... **BLC 2; TCLC 28**
See also AFAW 2; BW 2, 3; CA 141; CANR
82; DAM MULT; DLB 50

Hopkinson, Francis 1737-1791 .... **LC 25**
See also DLB 31; RGAL 4

Hopley-Woolrich, Cornell George 1903-1968
See Woolrich, Cornell
See also CA 13-14; CANR 58; CAP 1;
CMW 4; DLB 226; MTCW 2

Horace 65B.C.-8B.C. .... **CMLC 39; PC 46**
See also AW 2; CDWLB 1; DLB 211;
RGWL 2, 3

Horatio
See Proust, (Valentin-Louis-George-Eugene)
Marcel

Horgan, Paul (George Vincent
O'Shaughnessy) 1903-1995 .. **CLC 9, 53**
See also BPFB 2; CA 13-16R; 147; CANR
9, 35; CN 1, 2, 3, 4, 5; DAM NOV; DLB
102, 212; DLBY 1985; INT CANR-9;
MTCW 1, 2; MTFW 2005; SATA 13;
SATA-Obit 84; TCWW 1, 2

Horkheimer, Max 1895-1973 .... **TCLC 132**
See also CA 216; 41-44R; DLB 296

Horn, Peter
See Kuttner, Henry

Horne, Frank (Smith) 1899-1974 ...... **HR 1:2**
See also BW 1; CA 125; 53-56; DLB 51;
WP

Horne, Richard Henry Hengist
1802(?)-1884 .... **NCLC 127**
See also DLB 32; SATA 29

Hornem, Horace Esq.
See Byron, George Gordon (Noel)

Horney, Karen (Clementine Theodore
Danielsen) 1885-1952 .... **TCLC 71**
See also CA 114; 165; DLB 246; FW

Hornung, E(rnest) W(illiam)
1866-1921 .... **TCLC 59**
See also CA 108; 160; CMW 4; DLB 70

Horovitz, Israel (Arthur) 1939- .... **CLC 56**
See also CA 33-36R; CAD; CANR 46, 59;
CD 5, 6; DAM DRAM; DLB 7; MAL 5

Horton, George Moses
1797(?)-1883(?) .... **NCLC 87**
See also DLB 50

Horvath, odon von 1901-1938
See von Horvath, Odon
See also EWL 3

Horvath, Oedoen von -1938
See von Horvath, Odon

Horwitz, Julius 1920-1986 .... **CLC 14**
See also CA 9-12R; 119; CANR 12

Hospital, Janette Turner 1942- .... **CLC 42,**
145
See also CA 108; CANR 48; CN 5, 6, 7;
DLBY 2002; RGSF 2

Hostos, E. M. de
See Hostos (y Bonilla), Eugenio Maria de

Hostos, Eugenio M. de
See Hostos (y Bonilla), Eugenio Maria de

Hostos, Eugenio Maria
See Hostos (y Bonilla), Eugenio Maria de

Hostos (y Bonilla), Eugenio Maria de
1839-1903 .... **TCLC 24**
See also CA 123; 131; HW 1

Houdini
See Lovecraft, H(oward) P(hillips)

Houellebecq, Michel 1958- .... **CLC 179**
See also CA 185; CANR 140; MTFW 2005

Ivask, Ivar Vidrik 1927-1992 .... **CLC 14**
See also CA 37-40R; 139; CANR 24
Ives, Morgan
See Bradley, Marion Zimmer
See also GLL 1
Izumi Shikibu c. 973-c. 1034 .... **CMLC 33**
J. R. S.
See Gogarty, Oliver St. John
Jabran, Kahlil
See Gibran, Kahlil
Jabran, Khalil
See Gibran, Kahlil
Jackson, Daniel
See Wingrove, David (John)
Jackson, Helen Hunt 1830-1885 .... **NCLC 90**
See also DLB 42, 47, 186, 189; RGAL 4
Jackson, Jesse 1908-1983 .... **CLC 12**
See also BW 1; CA 25-28R; 109; CANR
27; CLR 28; CWRI 5; MAICYA 1, 2;
SATA 2, 29; SATA-Obit 48
Jackson, Laura (Riding) 1901-1991 .... **PC 44**
See Riding, Laura
See also CA 65-68; 135; CANR 28, 89;
DLB 48
Jackson, Sam
See Trumbo, Dalton
Jackson, Sara
See Wingrove, David (John)
Jackson, Shirley 1919-1965 . **CLC 11, 60, 87;
SSC 9, 39; WLC**
See also AAYA 9; AMWS 9; BPFB 2; CA
1-4R; 25-28R; CANR 4, 52; CDALB
1941-1968; DA; DA3; DAC; DAM MST;
DLB 6, 234; EXPS; HGG; LAIT 4; MAL
5; MTCW 2; MTFW 2005; RGAL 4;
RGSF 2; SATA 2; SSFS 1; SUFW 1, 2
Jacob, (Cyprien-)Max 1876-1944 .... **TCLC 6**
See also CA 104; 193; DLB 258; EWL 3;
GFL 1789 to the Present; GLL 2; RGWL
2, 3
Jacobs, Harriet A(nn)
1813(?)-1897 .... **NCLC 67, 162**
See also AFAW 1, 2; DLB 239; FL 1:3; FW;
LAIT 2; RGAL 4
Jacobs, Jim 1942- .... **CLC 12**
See also CA 97-100; INT CA-97-100
Jacobs, W(illiam) W(ymark)
1863-1943 .... **SSC 73; TCLC 22**
See also CA 121; 167; DLB 135; EXPS;
HGG; RGEL 2; RGSF 2; SSFS 2; SUFW
1
Jacobsen, Jens Peter 1847-1885 .... **NCLC 34**
Jacobsen, Josephine (Winder)
1908-2003 .... **CLC 48, 102; PC 62**
See also CA 33-36R; 218; CAAS 18; CANR
23, 48; CCA 1; CP 2, 3, 4, 5, 6, 7; DLB
244; PFS 23; TCLE 1:1
Jacobson, Dan 1929- .... **CLC 4, 14**
See also AFW; CA 1-4R; CANR 2, 25, 66;
CN 1, 2, 3, 4, 5, 6, 7; DLB 14, 207, 225,
319; EWL 3; MTCW 1; RGSF 2
Jacqueline
See Carpentier (y Valmont), Alejo
Jacques de Vitry c. 1160-1240 ...... **CMLC 63**
See also DLB 208
Jagger, Michael Philip
See Jagger, Mick
Jagger, Mick 1943- .... **CLC 17**
See also CA 239
Jahiz, al- c. 780-c. 869 .... **CMLC 25**
See also DLB 311
Jakes, John (William) 1932- .... **CLC 29**
See also AAYA 32; BEST 89:4; BPFB 2;
CA 57-60, 214; CAAE 214; CANR 10,
43, 66, 111, 142; CPW; CSW; DA3; DAM
NOV, POP; DLB 278; DLBY 1983;
FANT; INT CANR-10; MTCW 1, 2;
MTFW 2005; RHW; SATA 62; SFW 4;
TCWW 1, 2

James I 1394-1437 .... **LC 20**
See also RGEL 2
James, Andrew
See Kirkup, James
James, C(yril) L(ionel) R(obert)
1901-1989 .... **BLCS; CLC 33**
See also BW 2; CA 117; 125; 128; CANR
62; CN 1, 2, 3, 4; DLB 125; MTCW 1
James, Daniel (Lewis) 1911-1988
See Santiago, Danny
See also CA 174; 125
James, Dynely
See Mayne, William (James Carter)
James, Henry Sr. 1811-1882 .... **NCLC 53**
James, Henry 1843-1916 .... **SSC 8, 32, 47;
TCLC 2, 11, 24, 40, 47, 64, 171; WLC**
See also AMW; AMWC 1; AMWR 1; BPFB
2; BRW 6; CA 104; 132; CDALB 1865-
1917; DA; DA3; DAB; DAC; DAM MST,
NOV; DLB 12, 71, 74, 189; DLBD 13;
EWL 3; EXPS; GL 2; HGG; LAIT 2;
MAL 5; MTCW 1, 2; MTFW 2005; NFS
12, 16, 19; RGAL 4; RGEL 2; RGSF 2;
SSFS 9; SUFW 1; TUS
James, M. R.
See James, Montague (Rhodes)
See also DLB 156, 201
James, Montague (Rhodes)
1862-1936 .... **SSC 16; TCLC 6**
See James, M. R.
See also CA 104; 203; HGG; RGEL 2;
RGSF 2; SUFW 1
James, P. D. .... **CLC 18, 46, 122**
See White, Phyllis Dorothy James
See also BEST 90:2; BPFB 2; BRWS 4;
CDBLB 1960 to Present; CN 4, 5, 6; DLB
87, 276; DLBD 17; MSW
James, Philip
See Moorcock, Michael (John)
James, Samuel
See Stephens, James
James, Seumas
See Stephens, James
James, Stephen
See Stephens, James
James, William 1842-1910 .... **TCLC 15, 32**
See also AMW; CA 109; 193; DLB 270,
284; MAL 5; NCFS 5; RGAL 4
Jameson, Anna 1794-1860 .... **NCLC 43**
See also DLB 99, 166
Jameson, Fredric (R.) 1934- .... **CLC 142**
See also CA 196; DLB 67; LMFS 2
James VI of Scotland 1566-1625 .... **LC 109**
See also DLB 151, 172
Jami, Nur al-Din 'Abd al-Rahman
1414-1492 .... **LC 9**
Jammes, Francis 1868-1938 .... **TCLC 75**
See also CA 198; EWL 3; GFL 1789 to the
Present
Jandl, Ernst 1925-2000 .... **CLC 34**
See also CA 200; EWL 3
Janowitz, Tama 1957- .... **CLC 43, 145**
See also CA 106; CANR 52, 89, 129; CN
5, 6, 7; CPW; DAM POP; DLB 292;
MTFW 2005
Japrisot, Sebastien 1931- .... **CLC 90**
See Rossi, Jean-Baptiste
See also CMW 4; NFS 18
Jarrell, Randall 1914-1965 .... **CLC 1, 2, 6, 9,
13, 49; PC 41**
See also AMW; BYA 5; CA 5-8R; 25-28R;
CABS 2; CANR 6, 34; CDALB 1941-
1968; CLR 6; CWRI 5; DAM POET;
DLB 48, 52; EWL 3; EXPP; MAICYA 1,
2; MAL 5; MTCW 1, 2; PAB; PFS 2;
RGAL 4; SATA 7

Jarry, Alfred 1873-1907 .... **SSC 20; TCLC 2,
14, 147**
See also CA 104; 153; DA3; DAM DRAM;
DFS 8; DLB 192, 258; EW 9; EWL 3;
GFL 1789 to the Present; RGWL 2, 3;
TWA
Jarvis, E. K.
See Ellison, Harlan (Jay)
Jawien, Andrzej
See John Paul II, Pope
Jaynes, Roderick
See Coen, Ethan
Jeake, Samuel, Jr.
See Aiken, Conrad (Potter)
Jean Paul 1763-1825 .... **NCLC 7**
Jefferies, (John) Richard
1848-1887 .... **NCLC 47**
See also DLB 98, 141; RGEL 2; SATA 16;
SFW 4
Jeffers, (John) Robinson 1887-1962 .. **CLC 2,
3, 11, 15, 54; PC 17; WLC**
See also AMWS 2; CA 85-88; CANR 35;
CDALB 1917-1929; DA; DAC; DAM
MST, POET; DLB 45, 212; EWL 3; MAL
5; MTCW 1, 2; MTFW 2005; PAB; PFS
3, 4; RGAL 4
Jefferson, Janet
See Mencken, H(enry) L(ouis)
Jefferson, Thomas 1743-1826 . **NCLC 11, 103**
See also AAYA 54; ANW; CDALB 1640-
1865; DA3; DLB 31, 183; LAIT 1; RGAL
4
Jeffrey, Francis 1773-1850 .... **NCLC 33**
See Francis, Lord Jeffrey
Jelakowitch, Ivan
See Heijermans, Herman
Jelinek, Elfriede 1946- .... **CLC 169**
See also AAYA 68; CA 154; DLB 85; FW
Jellicoe, (Patricia) Ann 1927- .... **CLC 27**
See also CA 85-88; CBD; CD 5, 6; CWD;
CWRI 5; DLB 13, 233; FW
Jelloun, Tahar ben 1944- .... **CLC 180**
See Ben Jelloun, Tahar
See also CA 162; CANR 100
Jemyma
See Holley, Marietta
Jen, Gish .... **AAL; CLC 70, 198**
See Jen, Lillian
See also AMWC 2; CN 7; DLB 312
Jen, Lillian 1955-
See Jen, Gish
See also CA 135; CANR 89, 130
Jenkins, (John) Robin 1912- .... **CLC 52**
See also CA 1-4R; CANR 1, 135; CN 1, 2,
3, 4, 5, 6, 7; DLB 14, 271
Jennings, Elizabeth (Joan)
1926-2001 .... **CLC 5, 14, 131**
See also BRWS 5; CA 61-64; 200; CAAS
5; CANR 8, 39, 66, 127; CP 1, 2, 3, 4, 5,
6, 7; CWP; DLB 27; EWL 3; MTCW 1;
SATA 66
Jennings, Waylon 1937-2002 .... **CLC 21**
Jensen, Johannes V(ilhelm)
1873-1950 .... **TCLC 41**
See also CA 170; DLB 214; EWL 3; RGWL
3
Jensen, Laura (Linnea) 1948- .... **CLC 37**
See also CA 103
Jerome, Saint 345-420 .... **CMLC 30**
See also RGWL 3
Jerome, Jerome K(lapka)
1859-1927 .... **TCLC 23**
See also CA 119; 177; DLB 10, 34, 135;
RGEL 2
Jerrold, Douglas William
1803-1857 .... **NCLC 2**
See also DLB 158, 159; RGEL 2

Jewett, (Theodora) Sarah Orne
    1849-1909 .... SSC 6, 44; TCLC 1, 22
    See also AMW; AMWC 2; AMWR 2; CA
        108; 127; CANR 71; DLB 12, 74, 221;
        EXPS; FL 1:3; FW; MAL 5; MAWW;
        NFS 15; RGAL 4; RGSF 2; SATA 15;
        SSFS 4

Jewsbury, Geraldine (Endsor)
    1812-1880 .... NCLC 22
    See also DLB 21

Jhabvala, Ruth Prawer 1927- . CLC 4, 8, 29,
        94, 138
    See also BRWS 5; CA 1-4R; CANR 2, 29,
        51, 74, 91, 128; CN 1, 2, 3, 4, 5, 6, 7;
        DAB; DAM NOV; DLB 139, 194; EWL
        3; IDFW 3, 4; INT CANR-29; MTCW 1,
        2; MTFW 2005; RGSF 2; RGWL 2;
        RHW; TEA

Jibran, Kahlil
    See Gibran, Kahlil

Jibran, Khalil
    See Gibran, Kahlil

Jiles, Paulette 1943- .... CLC 13, 58
    See also CA 101; CANR 70, 124; CWP

Jimenez (Mantecon), Juan Ramon
    1881-1958 .... HLC 1; PC 7; TCLC 4
    See also CA 104; 131; CANR 74; DAM
        MULT, POET; DLB 134; EW 9; EWL 3;
        HW 1; MTCW 1, 2; MTFW 2005; RGWL
        2, 3

Jimenez, Ramon
    See Jimenez (Mantecon), Juan Ramon

Jimenez Mantecon, Juan
    See Jimenez (Mantecon), Juan Ramon

Jin, Ha .... CLC 109
    See Jin, Xuefei
    See also CA 152; DLB 244, 292; SSFS 17

Jin, Xuefei 1956-
    See Jin, Ha
    See also CANR 91, 130; MTFW 2005;
        SSFS 17

Jodelle, Etienne 1532-1573 .... LC 119
    See also GFL Beginnings to 1789

Joel, Billy .... CLC 26
    See Joel, William Martin

Joel, William Martin 1949-
    See Joel, Billy
    See also CA 108

John, Saint 10(?)-100 .... CMLC 27, 63

John of Salisbury c. 1115-1180 ..... CMLC 63

John of the Cross, St. 1542-1591 .... LC 18
    See also RGWL 2, 3

John Paul II, Pope 1920-2005 .... CLC 128
    See also CA 106; 133; 238

Johnson, B(ryan) S(tanley William)
    1933-1973 .... CLC 6, 9
    See also CA 9-12R; 53-56; CANR 9; CN 1;
        CP 1, 2; DLB 14, 40; EWL 3; RGEL 2

Johnson, Benjamin F., of Boone
    See Riley, James Whitcomb

Johnson, Charles (Richard) 1948- .... BLC 2;
        CLC 7, 51, 65, 163
    See also AFAW 2; AMWS 6; BW 2, 3; CA
        116; CAAS 18; CANR 42, 66, 82, 129;
        CN 5, 6, 7; DAM MULT; DLB 33, 278;
        MAL 5; MTCW 2; MTFW 2005; RGAL
        4; SSFS 16

Johnson, Charles S(purgeon)
    1893-1956 .... HR 1:3
    See also BW 1, 3; CA 125; CANR 82; DLB
        51, 91

Johnson, Denis 1949- . CLC 52, 160; SSC 56
    See also CA 117; 121; CANR 71, 99; CN
        4, 5, 6, 7; DLB 120

Johnson, Diane 1934- .... CLC 5, 13, 48
    See also BPFB 2; CA 41-44R; CANR 17,
        40, 62, 95; CN 4, 5, 6, 7; DLBY 1980;
        INT CANR-17; MTCW 1

Johnson, E(mily) Pauline 1861-1913 . NNAL
    See also CA 150; CCA 1; DAC; DAM
        MULT; DLB 92, 175; TCWW 2

Johnson, Eyvind (Olof Verner)
    1900-1976 .... CLC 14
    See also CA 73-76; 69-72; CANR 34, 101;
        DLB 259; EW 12; EWL 3

Johnson, Fenton 1888-1958 .... BLC 2
    See also BW 1; CA 118; 124; DAM MULT;
        DLB 45, 50

Johnson, Georgia Douglas (Camp)
    1880-1966 .... HR 1:3
    See also BW 1; CA 125; DLB 51, 249; WP

Johnson, Helene 1907-1995 .... HR 1:3
    See also CA 181; DLB 51; WP

Johnson, J. R.
    See James, C(yril) L(ionel) R(obert)

Johnson, James Weldon 1871-1938 .. BLC 2;
        HR 1:3; PC 24; TCLC 3, 19, 175
    See also AFAW 1, 2; BW 1, 3; CA 104;
        125; CANR 82; CDALB 1917-1929; CLR
        32; DA3; DAM MULT, POET; DLB 51;
        EWL 3; EXPP; LMFS 2; MAL 5; MTCW
        1, 2; MTFW 2005; NFS 22; PFS 1; RGAL
        4; SATA 31; TUS

Johnson, Joyce 1935- .... CLC 58
    See also BG 1:3; CA 125; 129; CANR 102

Johnson, Judith (Emlyn) 1936- .... CLC 7, 15
    See Sherwin, Judith Johnson
    See also CA 25-28R; 153; CANR 34; CP 7

Johnson, Lionel (Pigot)
    1867-1902 .... TCLC 19
    See also CA 117; 209; DLB 19; RGEL 2

Johnson, Marguerite Annie
    See Angelou, Maya

Johnson, Mel
    See Malzberg, Barry N(athaniel)

Johnson, Pamela Hansford
    1912-1981 .... CLC 1, 7, 27
    See also CA 1-4R; 104; CANR 2, 28; CN
        1, 2, 3; DLB 15; MTCW 1, 2; MTFW
        2005; RGEL 2

Johnson, Paul (Bede) 1928- .... CLC 147
    See also BEST 89:4; CA 17-20R; CANR
        34, 62, 100

Johnson, Robert .... CLC 70

Johnson, Robert 1911(?)-1938 .... TCLC 69
    See also BW 3; CA 174

Johnson, Samuel 1709-1784 .... LC 15, 52;
        WLC
    See also BRW 3; BRWR 1; CDBLB 1660-
        1789; DA; DAB; DAC; DAM MST; DLB
        39, 95, 104, 142, 213; LMFS 1; RGEL 2;
        TEA

Johnson, Uwe 1934-1984 .. CLC 5, 10, 15, 40
    See also CA 1-4R; 112; CANR 1, 39; CD-
        WLB 2; DLB 75; EWL 3; MTCW 1;
        RGWL 2, 3

Johnston, Basil H. 1929- .... NNAL
    See also CA 69-72; CANR 11, 28, 66;
        DAC; DAM MULT; DLB 60

Johnston, George (Benson) 1913- .... CLC 51
    See also CA 1-4R; CANR 5, 20; CP 1, 2, 3,
        4, 5, 6, 7; DLB 88

Johnston, Jennifer (Prudence)
    1930- .... CLC 7, 150
    See also CA 85-88; CANR 92; CN 4, 5, 6,
        7; DLB 14

Joinville, Jean de 1224(?)-1317 ..... CMLC 38

Jolley, (Monica) Elizabeth 1923- ..... CLC 46;
        SSC 19
    See also CA 127; CAAS 13; CANR 59; CN
        4, 5, 6, 7; EWL 3; RGSF 2

Jones, Arthur Llewellyn 1863-1947
    See Machen, Arthur
    See also CA 104; 179; HGG

Jones, D(ouglas) G(ordon) 1929- ..... CLC 10
    See also CA 29-32R; CANR 13, 90; CP 1,
        2, 3, 4, 5, 6, 7; DLB 53

Jones, David (Michael) 1895-1974 .... CLC 2,
        4, 7, 13, 42
    See also BRW 6; BRWS 7; CA 9-12R; 53-
        56; CANR 28; CDBLB 1945-1960; CP 1,
        2; DLB 20, 100; EWL 3; MTCW 1; PAB;
        RGEL 2

Jones, David Robert 1947-
    See Bowie, David
    See also CA 103; CANR 104

Jones, Diana Wynne 1934- .... CLC 26
    See also AAYA 12; BYA 6, 7, 9, 11, 13, 16;
        CA 49-52; CANR 4, 26, 56, 120; CLR
        23; DLB 161; FANT; JRDA; MAICYA 1,
        2; MTFW 2005; SAAS 7; SATA 9, 70,
        108, 160; SFW 4; SUFW 2; YAW

Jones, Edward P. 1950- .... CLC 76
    See also BW 2, 3; CA 142; CANR 79, 134;
        CSW; MTFW 2005

Jones, Gayl 1949- ..... BLC 2; CLC 6, 9, 131
    See also AFAW 1, 2; BW 2, 3; CA 77-80;
        CANR 27, 66, 122; CN 4, 5, 6, 7; CSW;
        DA3; DAM MULT; DLB 33, 278; MAL
        5; MTCW 1, 2; MTFW 2005; RGAL 4

Jones, James 1921-1977 ...... CLC 1, 3, 10, 39
    See also AITN 1, 2; AMWS 11; BPFB 2;
        CA 1-4R; 69-72; CANR 6; CN 1, 2; DLB
        2, 143; DLBD 17; DLBY 1998; EWL 3;
        MAL 5; MTCW 1; RGAL 4

Jones, John J.
    See Lovecraft, H(oward) P(hillips)

Jones, LeRoi .... CLC 1, 2, 3, 5, 10, 14
    See Baraka, Amiri
    See also CN 1, 2; CP 1, 2, 3; MTCW 2

Jones, Louis B. 1953- .... CLC 65
    See also CA 141; CANR 73

Jones, Madison (Percy, Jr.) 1925- ...... CLC 4
    See also CA 13-16R; CAAS 11; CANR 7,
        54, 83; CN 1, 2, 3, 4, 5, 6, 7; CSW; DLB
        152

Jones, Mervyn 1922- .... CLC 10, 52
    See also CA 45-48; CAAS 5; CANR 1, 91;
        CN 1, 2, 3, 4, 5, 6, 7; MTCW 1

Jones, Mick 1956(?)- .... CLC 30

Jones, Nettie (Pearl) 1941- .... CLC 34
    See also BW 2; CA 137; CAAS 20; CANR
        88

Jones, Peter 1802-1856 .... NNAL

Jones, Preston 1936-1979 .... CLC 10
    See also CA 73-76; 89-92; DLB 7

Jones, Robert F(rancis) 1934-2003 .... CLC 7
    See also CA 49-52; CANR 2, 61, 118

Jones, Rod 1953- .... CLC 50
    See also CA 128

Jones, Terence Graham Parry
    1942- .... CLC 21
    See Jones, Terry; Monty Python
    See also CA 112; 116; CANR 35, 93; INT
        CA-116; SATA 127

Jones, Terry
    See Jones, Terence Graham Parry
    See also SATA 67; SATA-Brief 51

Jones, Thom (Douglas) 1945(?)- ..... CLC 81;
        SSC 56
    See also CA 157; CANR 88; DLB 244

Jong, Erica 1942- .... CLC 4, 6, 8, 18, 83
    See also AITN 1; AMWS 5; BEST 90:2;
        BPFB 2; CA 73-76; CANR 26, 52, 75,
        132; CN 3, 4, 5, 6, 7; CP 2, 3, 4, 5, 6, 7;
        CPW; DA3; DAM NOV, POP; DLB 2, 5,
        28, 152; FW; INT CANR-26; MAL 5;
        MTCW 1, 2; MTFW 2005

Jonson, Ben(jamin) 1572(?)-1637 . DC 4; LC
        6, 33, 110; PC 17; WLC
    See also BRW 1; BRWC 1; BRWR 1; CD-
        BLB Before 1660; DA; DAB; DAC;
        DAM DRAM, MST, POET; DFS 4, 10;
        DLB 62, 121; LMFS 1; PFS 23; RGEL 2;
        TEA; WLIT 3

Keynes, John Maynard
1883-1946 .... **TCLC 64**
See also CA 114; 162, 163; DLBD 10;
MTCW 2; MTFW 2005

Khanshendel, Chiron
See Rose, Wendy

Khayyam, Omar 1048-1131 ... **CMLC 11; PC 8**
See Omar Khayyam
See also DA3; DAM POET; WLIT 6

Kherdian, David 1931- .... **CLC 6, 9**
See also AAYA 42; CA 21-24R, 192; CAAE
192; CAAS 2; CANR 39, 78; CLR 24;
JRDA; LAIT 3; MAICYA 1, 2; SATA 16,
74; SATA-Essay 125

Khlebnikov, Velimir .... **TCLC 20**
See Khlebnikov, Viktor Vladimirovich
See also DLB 295; EW 10; EWL 3; RGWL
2, 3

Khlebnikov, Viktor Vladimirovich 1885-1922
See Khlebnikov, Velimir
See also CA 117; 217

Khodasevich, Vladislav (Felitsianovich)
1886-1939 .... **TCLC 15**
See also CA 115; DLB 317; EWL 3

Kielland, Alexander Lange
1849-1906 .... **TCLC 5**
See also CA 104

Kiely, Benedict 1919- ... **CLC 23, 43; SSC 58**
See also CA 1-4R; CANR 2, 84; CN 1, 2,
3, 4, 5, 6, 7; DLB 15, 319; TCLE 1:1

Kienzle, William X(avier)
1928-2001 .... **CLC 25**
See also CA 93-96; 203; CAAS 1; CANR
9, 31, 59, 111; CMW 4; DA3; DAM POP;
INT CANR-31; MSW; MTCW 1, 2;
MTFW 2005

Kierkegaard, Soren 1813-1855 ..... **NCLC 34, 78, 125**
See also DLB 300; EW 6; LMFS 2; RGWL
3; TWA

Kieslowski, Krzysztof 1941-1996 .... **CLC 120**
See also CA 147; 151

Killens, John Oliver 1916-1987 .... **CLC 10**
See also BW 2; CA 77-80; 123; CAAS 2;
CANR 26; CN 1, 2, 3, 4; DLB 33; EWL
3

Killigrew, Anne 1660-1685 .... **LC 4, 73**
See also DLB 131

Killigrew, Thomas 1612-1683 .... **LC 57**
See also DLB 58; RGEL 2

Kim
See Simenon, Georges (Jacques Christian)

Kincaid, Jamaica 1949- ...... **BLC 2; CLC 43, 68, 137; SSC 72**
See also AAYA 13, 56; AFAW 2; AMWS 7;
BRWS 7; BW 2, 3; CA 125; CANR 47,
59, 95, 133; CDALBS; CDWLB 3; CLR
63; CN 4, 5, 6, 7; DA3; DAM MULT,
NOV; DLB 157, 227; DNFS 1; EWL 3;
EXPS; FW; LATS 1:2; LMFS 2; MAL 5;
MTCW 2; MTFW 2005; NCFS 1; NFS 3;
SSFS 5, 7; TUS; WWE 1; YAW

King, Francis (Henry) 1923- ...... **CLC 8, 53, 145**
See also CA 1-4R; CANR 1, 33, 86; CN 1,
2, 3, 4, 5, 6, 7; DAM NOV; DLB 15, 139;
MTCW 1

King, Kennedy
See Brown, George Douglas

King, Martin Luther, Jr. 1929-1968 . **BLC 2; CLC 83; WLCS**
See also BW 2, 3; CA 25-28; CANR 27,
44; CAP 2; DA; DA3; DAB; DAC; DAM
MST, MULT; LAIT 5; LATS 1:2; MTCW
1, 2; MTFW 2005; SATA 14

King, Stephen 1947- .... **CLC 12, 26, 37, 61, 113; SSC 17, 55**
See also AAYA 1, 17; AMWS 5; BEST
90:1; BPFB 2; CA 61-64; CANR 1, 30,
52, 76, 119, 134; CN 7; CPW; DA3; DAM
NOV, POP; DLB 143; DLBY 1980; HGG;
JRDA; LAIT 5; MTCW 1, 2; MTFW
2005; RGAL 4; SATA 9, 55, 161; SUFW
1, 2; WYAS 1; YAW

King, Stephen Edwin
See King, Stephen

King, Steve
See King, Stephen

King, Thomas 1943- .... **CLC 89, 171; NNAL**
See also CA 144; CANR 95; CCA 1; CN 6,
7; DAC; DAM MULT; DLB 175; SATA
96

Kingman, Lee .... **CLC 17**
See Natti, (Mary) Lee
See also CWRI 5; SAAS 3; SATA 1, 67

Kingsley, Charles 1819-1875 .... **NCLC 35**
See also CLR 77; DLB 21, 32, 163, 178,
190; FANT; MAICYA 2; MAICYAS 1;
RGEL 2; WCH; YABC 2

Kingsley, Henry 1830-1876 .... **NCLC 107**
See also DLB 21, 230; RGEL 2

Kingsley, Sidney 1906-1995 .... **CLC 44**
See also CA 85-88; 147; CAD; DFS 14, 19;
DLB 7; MAL 5; RGAL 4

Kingsolver, Barbara 1955- .... **CLC 55, 81, 130, 216**
See also AAYA 15; AMWS 7; CA 129; 134;
CANR 60, 96, 133; CDALBS; CN 7;
CPW; CSW; DA3; DAM POP; DLB 206;
INT CA-134; LAIT 5; MTCW 2; MTFW
2005; NFS 5, 10, 12; RGAL 4; TCLE 1:1

Kingston, Maxine (Ting Ting) Hong
1940- .... **AAL; CLC 12, 19, 58, 121; WLCS**
See also AAYA 8, 55; AMWS 5; BPFB 2;
CA 69-72; CANR 13, 38, 74, 87, 128;
CDALBS; CN 6, 7; DA3; DAM MULT,
NOV; DLB 173, 212, 312; DLBY 1980;
EWL 3; FL 1:6; FW; INT CANR-13;
LAIT 5; MAL 5; MAWW; MTCW 1, 2;
MTFW 2005; NFS 6; RGAL 4; SATA 53;
SSFS 3; TCWW 2

Kinnell, Galway 1927- ..... **CLC 1, 2, 3, 5, 13, 29, 129; PC 26**
See also AMWS 3; CA 9-12R; CANR 10,
34, 66, 116, 138; CP 1, 2, 3, 4, 5, 6, 7;
DLB 5; DLBY 1987; EWL 3; INT CANR-
34; MAL 5; MTCW 1, 2; MTFW 2005;
PAB; PFS 9; RGAL 4; TCLE 1:1; WP

Kinsella, Thomas 1928- .... **CLC 4, 19, 138; PC 69**
See also BRWS 5; CA 17-20R; CANR 15,
122; CP 1, 2, 3, 4, 5, 6, 7; DLB 27; EWL
3; MTCW 1, 2; MTFW 2005; RGEL 2;
TEA

Kinsella, W(illiam) P(atrick) 1935- . **CLC 27, 43, 166**
See also AAYA 7, 60; BPFB 2; CA 97-100,
222; CAAE 222; CAAS 7; CANR 21, 35,
66, 75, 129; CN 4, 5, 6, 7; CPW; DAC;
DAM NOV, POP; FANT; INT CANR-21;
LAIT 5; MTCW 1, 2; MTFW 2005; NFS
15; RGSF 2

Kinsey, Alfred C(harles)
1894-1956 .... **TCLC 91**
See also CA 115; 170; MTCW 2

Kipling, (Joseph) Rudyard 1865-1936 . **PC 3; SSC 5, 54; TCLC 8, 17, 167; WLC**
See also AAYA 32; BRW 6; BRWC 1, 2;
BYA 4; CA 105; 120; CANR 33; CDBLB
1890-1914; CLR 39, 65; CWRI 5; DA;
DA3; DAB; DAC; DAM MST, POET;
DLB 19, 34, 141, 156; EWL 3; EXPS;
FANT; LAIT 3; LMFS 1; MAICYA 1, 2;

MTCW 1, 2; MTFW 2005; NFS 21; PFS
22; RGEL 2; RGSF 2; SATA 100; SFW
4; SSFS 8, 21; SUFW 1; TEA; WCH;
WLIT 4; YABC 2

Kircher, Athanasius 1602-1680 .... **LC 121**
See also DLB 164

Kirk, Russell (Amos) 1918-1994 .. **TCLC 119**
See also AITN 1; CA 1-4R; 145; CAAS 9;
CANR 1, 20, 60; HGG; INT CANR-20;
MTCW 1, 2

Kirkham, Dinah
See Card, Orson Scott

Kirkland, Caroline M. 1801-1864 . **NCLC 85**
See also DLB 3, 73, 74, 250, 254; DLBD
13

Kirkup, James 1918- .... **CLC 1**
See also CA 1-4R; CAAS 4; CANR 2; CP
1, 2, 3, 4, 5, 6, 7; DLB 27; SATA 12

Kirkwood, James 1930(?)-1989 .... **CLC 9**
See also AITN 2; CA 1-4R; 128; CANR 6,
40; GLL 2

Kirsch, Sarah 1935- .... **CLC 176**
See also CA 178; CWW 2; DLB 75; EWL
3

Kirshner, Sidney
See Kingsley, Sidney

Kis, Danilo 1935-1989 .... **CLC 57**
See also CA 109; 118; 129; CANR 61; CD-
WLB 4; DLB 181; EWL 3; MTCW 1;
RGSF 2; RGWL 2, 3

Kissinger, Henry A(lfred) 1923- ..... **CLC 137**
See also CA 1-4R; CANR 2, 33, 66, 109;
MTCW 1

Kivi, Aleksis 1834-1872 .... **NCLC 30**

Kizer, Carolyn (Ashley) 1925- ... **CLC 15, 39, 80; PC 66**
See also CA 65-68; CAAS 5; CANR 24,
70, 134; CP 1, 2, 3, 4, 5, 6, 7; CWP; DAM
POET; DLB 5, 169; EWL 3; MAL 5;
MTCW 2; MTFW 2005; PFS 18; TCLE
1:1

Klabund 1890-1928 .... **TCLC 44**
See also CA 162; DLB 66

Klappert, Peter 1942- .... **CLC 57**
See also CA 33-36R; CSW; DLB 5

Klein, A(braham) M(oses)
1909-1972 .... **CLC 19**
See also CA 101; 37-40R; CP 1; DAB;
DAC; DAM MST; DLB 68; EWL 3;
RGEL 2

Klein, Joe
See Klein, Joseph

Klein, Joseph 1946- .... **CLC 154**
See also CA 85-88; CANR 55

Klein, Norma 1938-1989 .... **CLC 30**
See also AAYA 2, 35; BPFB 2; BYA 6, 7,
8; CA 41-44R; 128; CANR 15, 37; CLR
2, 19; INT CANR-15; JRDA; MAICYA
1, 2; SAAS 1; SATA 7, 57; WYA; YAW

Klein, T(heodore) E(ibon) D(onald)
1947- .... **CLC 34**
See also CA 119; CANR 44, 75; HGG

Kleist, Heinrich von 1777-1811 ...... **NCLC 2, 37; SSC 22**
See also CDWLB 2; DAM DRAM; DLB
90; EW 5; RGSF 2; RGWL 2, 3

Klima, Ivan 1931- .... **CLC 56, 172**
See also CA 25-28R; CANR 17, 50, 91;
CDWLB 4; CWW 2; DAM NOV; DLB
232; EWL 3; RGWL 3

Klimentov, Andrei Platonovich
See Klimentov, Andrei Platonovich

Klimentov, Andrei Platonovich
1899-1951 .... **SSC 42; TCLC 14**
See Platonov, Andrei Platonovich; Platonov,
Andrey Platonovich
See also CA 108; 232

Kubrick, Stanley 1928-1999 .... **CLC 16; TCLC 112**
See also AAYA 30; CA 81-84; 177; CANR 33; DLB 26

Kumin, Maxine (Winokur) 1925- ..... **CLC 5, 13, 28, 164; PC 15**
See also AITN 2; AMWS 4; ANW; CA 1-4R; CAAS 8; CANR 1, 21, 69, 115, 140; CP 2, 3, 4, 5, 6, 7; CWP; DA3; DAM POET; DLB 5; EWL 3; EXPP; MTCW 1, 2; MTFW 2005; PAB; PFS 18; SATA 12

Kundera, Milan 1929- . **CLC 4, 9, 19, 32, 68, 115, 135; SSC 24**
See also AAYA 2, 62; BPFB 2; CA 85-88; CANR 19, 52, 74, 144; CDWLB 4; CWW 2; DA3; DAM NOV; DLB 232; EW 13; EWL 3; MTCW 1, 2; MTFW 2005; NFS 18; RGSF 2; RGWL 3; SSFS 10

Kunene, Mazisi (Raymond) 1930- ... **CLC 85**
See also BW 1, 3; CA 125; CANR 81; CP 1, 7; DLB 117

Kung, Hans .... **CLC 130**
See Kung, Hans

Kung, Hans 1928-
See Kung, Hans
See also CA 53-56; CANR 66, 134; MTCW 1, 2; MTFW 2005

Kunikida Doppo 1869(?)-1908
See Doppo, Kunikida
See also DLB 180; EWL 3

Kunitz, Stanley (Jasspon) 1905- .. **CLC 6, 11, 14, 148; PC 19**
See also AMWS 3; CA 41-44R; CANR 26, 57, 98; CP 1, 2, 3, 4, 5, 6, 7; DA3; DLB 48; INT CANR-26; MAL 5; MTCW 1, 2; MTFW 2005; PFS 11; RGAL 4

Kunze, Reiner 1933- .... **CLC 10**
See also CA 93-96; CWW 2; DLB 75; EWL 3

Kuprin, Aleksander Ivanovich 1870-1938 .... **TCLC 5**
See Kuprin, Aleksandr Ivanovich; Kuprin, Alexandr Ivanovich
See also CA 104; 182

Kuprin, Aleksandr Ivanovich
See Kuprin, Aleksander Ivanovich
See also DLB 295

Kuprin, Alexandr Ivanovich
See Kuprin, Aleksander Ivanovich
See also EWL 3

Kureishi, Hanif 1954- .. **CLC 64, 135; DC 26**
See also BRWS 11; CA 139; CANR 113; CBD; CD 5, 6; CN 6, 7; DLB 194, 245; GLL 2; IDFW 4; WLIT 4; WWE 1

Kurosawa, Akira 1910-1998 ..... **CLC 16, 119**
See also AAYA 11, 64; CA 101; 170; CANR 46; DAM MULT

Kushner, Tony 1956- .... **CLC 81, 203; DC 10**
See also AAYA 61; AMWS 9; CA 144; CAD; CANR 74, 130; CD 5, 6; DA3; DAM DRAM; DFS 5; DLB 228; EWL 3; GLL 1; LAIT 5; MAL 5; MTCW 2; MTFW 2005; RGAL 4; SATA 160

Kuttner, Henry 1915-1958 .... **TCLC 10**
See also CA 107; 157; DLB 8; FANT; SCFW 1, 2; SFW 4

Kutty, Madhavi
See Das, Kamala

Kuzma, Greg 1944- .... **CLC 7**
See also CA 33-36R; CANR 70

Kuzmin, Mikhail (Alekseevich) 1872(?)-1936 .... **TCLC 40**
See also CA 170; DLB 295; EWL 3

Kyd, Thomas 1558-1594 .. **DC 3; LC 22, 125**
See also BRW 1; DAM DRAM; DFS 21; DLB 62; IDTP; LMFS 1; RGEL 2; TEA; WLIT 3

Kyprianos, Iossif
See Samarakis, Antonis

L. S.
See Stephen, Sir Leslie

Laȝamon
See Layamon
See also DLB 146

Labe, Louise 1521-1566 .... **LC 120**

Labrunie, Gerard
See Nerval, Gerard de

La Bruyere, Jean de 1645-1696 .... **LC 17**
See also DLB 268; EW 3; GFL Beginnings to 1789

Lacan, Jacques (Marie Emile) 1901-1981 .... **CLC 75**
See also CA 121; 104; DLB 296; EWL 3; TWA

Laclos, Pierre-Ambroise Francois 1741-1803 .... **NCLC 4, 87**
See also DLB 313; EW 4; GFL Beginnings to 1789; RGWL 2, 3

Lacolere, Francois
See Aragon, Louis

La Colere, Francois
See Aragon, Louis

La Deshabilleuse
See Simenon, Georges (Jacques Christian)

Lady Gregory
See Gregory, Lady Isabella Augusta (Persse)

Lady of Quality, A
See Bagnold, Enid

La Fayette, Marie-(Madelaine Pioche de la Vergne) 1634-1693 .... **LC 2**
See Lafayette, Marie-Madeleine
See also GFL Beginnings to 1789; RGWL 2, 3

Lafayette, Marie-Madeleine
See La Fayette, Marie-(Madelaine Pioche de la Vergne)
See also DLB 268

Lafayette, Rene
See Hubbard, L(afayette) Ron(ald)

La Flesche, Francis 1857(?)-1932 ...... **NNAL**
See also CA 144; CANR 83; DLB 175

La Fontaine, Jean de 1621-1695 .... **LC 50**
See also DLB 268; EW 3; GFL Beginnings to 1789; MAICYA 1, 2; RGWL 2, 3; SATA 18

Laforet, Carmen 1921-2004 .... **CLC 219**
See also CWW 2; DLB 322; EWL 3

Laforgue, Jules 1860-1887 . **NCLC 5, 53; PC 14; SSC 20**
See also DLB 217; EW 7; GFL 1789 to the Present; RGWL 2, 3

Lagerkvist, Paer (Fabian) 1891-1974 ..... **CLC 7, 10, 13, 54; TCLC 144**
See Lagerkvist, Par
See also CA 85-88; 49-52; DA3; DAM DRAM, NOV; MTCW 1, 2; MTFW 2005; TWA

Lagerkvist, Par .... **SSC 12**
See Lagerkvist, Paer (Fabian)
See also DLB 259; EW 10; EWL 3; RGSF 2; RGWL 2, 3

Lagerloef, Selma (Ottiliana Lovisa) .... **TCLC 4, 36**
See Lagerlof, Selma (Ottiliana Lovisa)
See also CA 108; MTCW 2

Lagerlof, Selma (Ottiliana Lovisa) 1858-1940
See Lagerloef, Selma (Ottiliana Lovisa)
See also CA 188; CLR 7; DLB 259; RGWL 2, 3; SATA 15; SSFS 18

La Guma, (Justin) Alex(ander) 1925-1985 . **BLCS; CLC 19; TCLC 140**
See also AFW; BW 1, 3; CA 49-52; 118; CANR 25, 81; CDWLB 3; CN 1, 2, 3; CP 1; DAM NOV; DLB 117, 225; EWL 3; MTCW 1, 2; MTFW 2005; WLIT 2; WWE 1

Laidlaw, A. K.
See Grieve, C(hristopher) M(urray)

Lainez, Manuel Mujica
See Mujica Lainez, Manuel
See also HW 1

Laing, R(onald) D(avid) 1927-1989 . **CLC 95**
See also CA 107; 129; CANR 34; MTCW 1

Laishley, Alex
See Booth, Martin

Lamartine, Alphonse (Marie Louis Prat) de 1790-1869 .... **NCLC 11; PC 16**
See also DAM POET; DLB 217; GFL 1789 to the Present; RGWL 2, 3

Lamb, Charles 1775-1834 ..... **NCLC 10, 113; WLC**
See also BRW 4; CDBLB 1789-1832; DA; DAB; DAC; DAM MST; DLB 93, 107, 163; RGEL 2; SATA 17; TEA

Lamb, Lady Caroline 1785-1828 ... **NCLC 38**
See also DLB 116

Lamb, Mary Ann 1764-1847 .... **NCLC 125**
See also DLB 163; SATA 17

Lame Deer 1903(?)-1976 .... **NNAL**
See also CA 69-72

Lamming, George (William) 1927- ... **BLC 2; CLC 2, 4, 66, 144**
See also BW 2, 3; CA 85-88; CANR 26, 76; CDWLB 3; CN 1, 2, 3, 4, 5, 6, 7; CP 1; DAM MULT; DLB 125; EWL 3; MTCW 1, 2; MTFW 2005; NFS 15; RGEL 2

L'Amour, Louis (Dearborn) 1908-1988 .... **CLC 25, 55**
See also AAYA 16; AITN 2; BEST 89:2; BPFB 2; CA 1-4R; 125; CANR 3, 25, 40; CPW; DA3; DAM NOV, POP; DLB 206; DLBY 1980; MTCW 1, 2; MTFW 2005; RGAL 4; TCWW 1, 2

Lampedusa, Giuseppe (Tomasi) di .... **TCLC 13**
See Tomasi di Lampedusa, Giuseppe
See also CA 164; EW 11; MTCW 2; MTFW 2005; RGWL 2, 3

Lampman, Archibald 1861-1899 ... **NCLC 25**
See also DLB 92; RGEL 2; TWA

Lancaster, Bruce 1896-1963 .... **CLC 36**
See also CA 9-10; CANR 70; CAP 1; SATA 9

Lanchester, John 1962- .... **CLC 99**
See also CA 194; DLB 267

Landau, Mark Alexandrovich
See Aldanov, Mark (Alexandrovich)

Landau-Aldanov, Mark Alexandrovich
See Aldanov, Mark (Alexandrovich)

Landis, Jerry
See Simon, Paul (Frederick)

Landis, John 1950- .... **CLC 26**
See also CA 112; 122; CANR 128

Landolfi, Tommaso 1908-1979 .... **CLC 11, 49**
See also CA 127; 117; DLB 177; EWL 3

Landon, Letitia Elizabeth 1802-1838 .... **NCLC 15**
See also DLB 96

Landor, Walter Savage 1775-1864 .... **NCLC 14**
See also BRW 4; DLB 93, 107; RGEL 2

Landwirth, Heinz 1927-
See Lind, Jakov
See also CA 9-12R; CANR 7

Lane, Patrick 1939- .... **CLC 25**
See also CA 97-100; CANR 54; CP 3, 4, 5, 6, 7; DAM POET; DLB 53; INT CA-97-100

Lang, Andrew 1844-1912 .... **TCLC 16**
See also CA 114; 137; CANR 85; CLR 101; DLB 98, 141, 184; FANT; MAICYA 1, 2; RGEL 2; SATA 16; WCH

Leavitt, David 1961- .... **CLC 34**
See also CA 116; 122; CANR 50, 62, 101, 134; CPW; DA3; DAM POP; DLB 130; GLL 1; INT CA-122; MAL 5; MTCW 2; MTFW 2005

Leblanc, Maurice (Marie Emile) 1864-1941 .... **TCLC 49**
See also CA 110; CMW 4

Lebowitz, Fran(ces Ann) 1951(?)- ... **CLC 11, 36**
See also CA 81-84; CANR 14, 60, 70; INT CANR-14; MTCW 1

Lebrecht, Peter
See Tieck, (Johann) Ludwig

le Carré, John .... **CLC 3, 5, 9, 15, 28, 220**
See Cornwell, David John Moore
See also AAYA 42; BEST 89:4; BPFB 2; BRWS 2; CDBLB 1960 to Present; CMW 4; CN 1, 2, 3, 4, 5, 6, 7; CPW; DLB 87; EWL 3; MSW; MTCW 2; RGEL 2; TEA

Le Clezio, J(ean) M(arie) G(ustave) 1940- .... **CLC 31, 155**
See also CA 116; 128; CWW 2; DLB 83; EWL 3; GFL 1789 to the Present; RGSF 2

Leconte de Lisle, Charles-Marie-Rene 1818-1894 .... **NCLC 29**
See also DLB 217; EW 6; GFL 1789 to the Present

Le Coq, Monsieur
See Simenon, Georges (Jacques Christian)

Leduc, Violette 1907-1972 .... **CLC 22**
See also CA 13-14; 33-36R; CANR 69; CAP 1; EWL 3; GFL 1789 to the Present; GLL 1

Ledwidge, Francis 1887(?)-1917 .... **TCLC 23**
See also CA 123; 203; DLB 20

Lee, Andrea 1953- .... **BLC 2; CLC 36**
See also BW 1, 3; CA 125; CANR 82; DAM MULT

Lee, Andrew
See Auchincloss, Louis (Stanton)

Lee, Chang-rae 1965- .... **CLC 91**
See also CA 148; CANR 89; CN 7; DLB 312; LATS 1:2

Lee, Don L. .... **CLC 2**
See Madhubuti, Haki R.
See also CP 2, 3, 4

Lee, George W(ashington) 1894-1976 .... **BLC 2; CLC 52**
See also BW 1; CA 125; CANR 83; DAM MULT; DLB 51

Lee, (Nelle) Harper 1926- . **CLC 12, 60, 194; WLC**
See also AAYA 13; AMWS 8; BPFB 2; BYA 3; CA 13-16R; CANR 51, 128; CDALB 1941-1968; CSW; DA; DA3; DAB; DAC; DAM MST, NOV; DLB 6; EXPN; LAIT 3; MAL 5; MTCW 1, 2; MTFW 2005; NFS 2; SATA 11; WYA; YAW

Lee, Helen Elaine 1959(?)- .... **CLC 86**
See also CA 148

Lee, John .... **CLC 70**

Lee, Julian
See Latham, Jean Lee

Lee, Larry
See Lee, Lawrence

Lee, Laurie 1914-1997 .... **CLC 90**
See also CA 77-80; 158; CANR 33, 73; CP 1, 2, 3, 4; CPW; DAB; DAM POP; DLB 27; MTCW 1; RGEL 2

Lee, Lawrence 1941-1990 .... **CLC 34**
See also CA 131; CANR 43

Lee, Li-Young 1957- .... **CLC 164; PC 24**
See also AMWS 15; CA 153; CANR 118; CP 7; DLB 165, 312; LMFS 2; PFS 11, 15, 17

Lee, Manfred B(ennington) 1905-1971 .... **CLC 11**
See Queen, Ellery
See also CA 1-4R; 29-32R; CANR 2; CMW 4; DLB 137

Lee, Nathaniel 1645(?)-1692 .... **LC 103**
See also DLB 80; RGEL 2

Lee, Shelton Jackson 1957(?)- .. **BLCS; CLC 105**
See Lee, Spike
See also BW 2, 3; CA 125; CANR 42; DAM MULT

Lee, Spike
See Lee, Shelton Jackson
See also AAYA 4, 29

Lee, Stan 1922- .... **CLC 17**
See also AAYA 5, 49; CA 108; 111; CANR 129; INT CA-111; MTFW 2005

Lee, Tanith 1947- .... **CLC 46**
See also AAYA 15; CA 37-40R; CANR 53, 102, 145; DLB 261; FANT; SATA 8, 88, 134; SFW 4; SUFW 1, 2; YAW

Lee, Vernon .... **SSC 33; TCLC 5**
See Paget, Violet
See also DLB 57, 153, 156, 174, 178; GLL 1; SUFW 1

Lee, William
See Burroughs, William S(eward)
See also GLL 1

Lee, Willy
See Burroughs, William S(eward)
See also GLL 1

Lee-Hamilton, Eugene (Jacob) 1845-1907 .... **TCLC 22**
See also CA 117; 234

Leet, Judith 1935- .... **CLC 11**
See also CA 187

Le Fanu, Joseph Sheridan 1814-1873 .... **NCLC 9, 58; SSC 14, 84**
See also CMW 4; DA3; DAM POP; DLB 21, 70, 159, 178; GL 3; HGG; RGEL 2; RGSF 2; SUFW 1

Leffland, Ella 1931- .... **CLC 19**
See also CA 29-32R; CANR 35, 78, 82; DLBY 1984; INT CANR-35; SATA 65

Leger, Alexis
See Leger, (Marie-Rene Auguste) Alexis Saint-Leger

Leger, (Marie-Rene Auguste) Alexis Saint-Leger 1887-1975 .. **CLC 4, 11, 46; PC 23**
See Perse, Saint-John; Saint-John Perse
See also CA 13-16R; 61-64; CANR 43; DAM POET; MTCW 1

Leger, Saintleger
See Leger, (Marie-Rene Auguste) Alexis Saint-Leger

Le Guin, Ursula K(roeber) 1929- ..... **CLC 8, 13, 22, 45, 71, 136; SSC 12, 69**
See also AAYA 9, 27; AITN 1; BPFB 2; BYA 5, 8, 11, 14; CA 21-24R; CANR 9, 32, 52, 74, 132; CDALB 1968-1988; CLR 3, 28, 91; CN 2, 3, 4, 5, 6, 7; CPW; DA3; DAB; DAC; DAM MST, POP; DLB 8, 52, 256, 275; EXPS; FANT; FW; INT CANR-32; JRDA; LAIT 5; MAICYA 1, 2; MAL 5; MTCW 1, 2; MTFW 2005; NFS 6, 9; SATA 4, 52, 99, 149; SCFW 1, 2; SFW 4; SSFS 2; SUFW 1, 2; WYA; YAW

Lehmann, Rosamond (Nina) 1901-1990 .... **CLC 5**
See also CA 77-80; 131; CANR 8, 73; CN 1, 2, 3, 4; DLB 15; MTCW 2; RGEL 2; RHW

Leiber, Fritz (Reuter, Jr.) 1910-1992 .... **CLC 25**
See also AAYA 65; BPFB 2; CA 45-48; 139; CANR 2, 40, 86; CN 2, 3, 4, 5; DLB 8;

FANT; HGG; MTCW 1, 2; MTFW 2005; SATA 45; SATA-Obit 73; SCFW 1, 2; SFW 4; SUFW 1, 2

Leibniz, Gottfried Wilhelm von 1646-1716 .... **LC 35**
See also DLB 168

Leimbach, Martha 1963-
See Leimbach, Marti
See also CA 130

Leimbach, Marti .... **CLC 65**
See Leimbach, Martha

Leino, Eino .... **TCLC 24**
See Lonnbohm, Armas Eino Leopold
See also EWL 3

Leiris, Michel (Julien) 1901-1990 ..... **CLC 61**
See also CA 119; 128; 132; EWL 3; GFL 1789 to the Present

Leithauser, Brad 1953- .... **CLC 27**
See also CA 107; CANR 27, 81; CP 7; DLB 120, 282

le Jars de Gournay, Marie
See de Gournay, Marie le Jars

Lelchuk, Alan 1938- .... **CLC 5**
See also CA 45-48; CAAS 20; CANR 1, 70; CN 3, 4, 5, 6, 7

Lem, Stanislaw 1921- ...... **CLC 8, 15, 40, 149**
See also CA 105; CAAS 1; CANR 32; CWW 2; MTCW 1; SCFW 1, 2; SFW 4

Lemann, Nancy (Elise) 1956- .... **CLC 39**
See also CA 118; 136; CANR 121

Lemonnier, (Antoine Louis) Camille 1844-1913 .... **TCLC 22**
See also CA 121

Lenau, Nikolaus 1802-1850 .... **NCLC 16**

L'Engle, Madeleine (Camp Franklin) 1918- .... **CLC 12**
See also AAYA 28; AITN 2; BPFB 2; BYA 2, 4, 5, 7; CA 1-4R; CANR 3, 21, 39, 66, 107; CLR 1, 14, 57; CPW; CWRI 5; DA3; DAM POP; DLB 52; JRDA; MAICYA 1, 2; MTCW 1, 2; MTFW 2005; SAAS 15; SATA 1, 27, 75, 128; SFW 4; WYA; YAW

Lengyel, Jozsef 1896-1975 .... **CLC 7**
See also CA 85-88; 57-60; CANR 71; RGSF 2

Lenin 1870-1924
See Lenin, V. I.
See also CA 121; 168

Lenin, V. I. .... **TCLC 67**
See Lenin

Lennon, John (Ono) 1940-1980 .. **CLC 12, 35**
See also CA 102; SATA 114

Lennox, Charlotte Ramsay 1729(?)-1804 .... **NCLC 23, 134**
See also DLB 39; RGEL 2

Lentricchia, Frank, (Jr.) 1940- .... **CLC 34**
See also CA 25-28R; CANR 19, 106; DLB 246

Lenz, Gunter .... **CLC 65**

Lenz, Jakob Michael Reinhold 1751-1792 .... **LC 100**
See also DLB 94; RGWL 2, 3

Lenz, Siegfried 1926- .... **CLC 27; SSC 33**
See also CA 89-92; CANR 80; CWW 2; DLB 75; EWL 3; RGSF 2; RGWL 2, 3

Leon, David
See Jacob, (Cyprien-)Max

Leonard, Elmore (John, Jr.) 1925- . **CLC 28, 34, 71, 120**
See also AAYA 22, 59; AITN 1; BEST 89:1, 90:4; BPFB 2; CA 81-84; CANR 12, 28, 53, 76, 96, 133; CMW 4; CN 5, 6, 7; CPW; DA3; DAM POP; DLB 173, 226; INT CANR-28; MSW; MTCW 1, 2; MTFW 2005; RGAL 4; SATA 163; TCWW 1, 2

Leonard, Hugh .... **CLC 19**
See Byrne, John Keyes
See also CBD; CD 5, 6; DFS 13; DLB 13

Leonov, Leonid (Maximovich)
1899-1994 .... CLC 92
See Leonov, Leonid Maksimovich
See also CA 129; CANR 76; DAM NOV;
EWL 3; MTCW 1, 2; MTFW 2005

Leonov, Leonid Maksimovich
See Leonov, Leonid (Maximovich)
See also DLB 272

Leopardi, (Conte) Giacomo
1798-1837 .... NCLC 22, 129; PC 37
See also EW 5; RGWL 2, 3; WLIT 7; WP

Le Reveler
See Artaud, Antonin (Marie Joseph)

Lerman, Eleanor 1952- .... CLC 9
See also CA 85-88; CANR 69, 124

Lerman, Rhoda 1936- .... CLC 56
See also CA 49-52; CANR 70

Lermontov, Mikhail Iur'evich
See Lermontov, Mikhail Yuryevich
See also DLB 205

Lermontov, Mikhail Yuryevich
1814-1841 .... NCLC 5, 47, 126; PC 18
See Lermontov, Mikhail Iur'evich
See also EW 6; RGWL 2, 3; TWA

Leroux, Gaston 1868-1927 .... TCLC 25
See also CA 108; 136; CANR 69; CMW 4;
MTFW 2005; NFS 20; SATA 65

Lesage, Alain-Rene 1668-1747 .... LC 2, 28
See also DLB 313; EW 3; GFL Beginnings
to 1789; RGWL 2, 3

Leskov, N(ikolai) S(emenovich) 1831-1895
See Leskov, Nikolai (Semyonovich)

Leskov, Nikolai (Semyonovich)
1831-1895 .... NCLC 25; SSC 34
See Leskov, Nikolai Semenovich

Leskov, Nikolai Semenovich
See Leskov, Nikolai (Semyonovich)
See also DLB 238

Lesser, Milton
See Marlowe, Stephen

Lessing, Doris (May) 1919- ... CLC 1, 2, 3, 6,
10, 15, 22, 40, 94, 170; SSC 6, 61;
WLCS
See also AAYA 57; AFW; BRWS 1; CA
9-12R; CAAS 14; CANR 33, 54, 76, 122;
CBD; CD 5, 6; CDBLB 1960 to Present;
CN 1, 2, 3, 4, 5, 6, 7; CWD; DA; DA3;
DAB; DAC; DAM MST, NOV; DFS 20;
DLB 15, 139; DLBY 1985; EWL 3;
EXPS; FL 1:6; FW; LAIT 4; MTCW 1, 2;
MTFW 2005; RGEL 2; RGSF 2; SFW 4;
SSFS 1, 12, 20; TEA; WLIT 2, 4

Lessing, Gotthold Ephraim
1729-1781 .... DC 26; LC 8, 124
See also CDWLB 2; DLB 97; EW 4; RGWL
2, 3

Lester, Richard 1932- .... CLC 20

Levenson, Jay .... CLC 70

Lever, Charles (James)
1806-1872 .... NCLC 23
See also DLB 21; RGEL 2

Leverson, Ada Esther
1862(?)-1933(?) .... TCLC 18
See Elaine
See also CA 117; 202; DLB 153; RGEL 2

Levertov, Denise 1923-1997 .. CLC 1, 2, 3, 5,
8, 15, 28, 66; PC 11
See also AMWS 3; CA 1-4R, 178; 163;
CAAE 178; CAAS 19; CANR 3, 29, 50,
108; CDALBS; CP 1, 2, 3, 4, 5, 6; CWP;
DAM POET; DLB 5, 165; EWL 3; EXPP;
FW; INT CANR-29; MAL 5; MTCW 1,
2; PAB; PFS 7, 17; RGAL 4; TUS; WP

Levi, Carlo 1902-1975 .... TCLC 125
See also CA 65-68; 53-56; CANR 10; EWL
3; RGWL 2, 3

Levi, Jonathan .... CLC 76
See also CA 197

Levi, Peter (Chad Tigar)
1931-2000 .... CLC 41
See also CA 5-8R; 187; CANR 34, 80; CP
1, 2, 3, 4, 5, 6, 7; DLB 40

Levi, Primo 1919-1987 ...... CLC 37, 50; SSC
12; TCLC 109
See also CA 13-16R; 122; CANR 12, 33,
61, 70, 132; DLB 177, 299; EWL 3;
MTCW 1, 2; MTFW 2005; RGWL 2, 3;
WLIT 7

Levin, Ira 1929- .... CLC 3, 6
See also CA 21-24R; CANR 17, 44, 74,
139; CMW 4; CN 1, 2, 3, 4, 5, 6, 7; CPW;
DA3; DAM POP; HGG; MTCW 1, 2;
MTFW 2005; SATA 66; SFW 4

Levin, Meyer 1905-1981 .... CLC 7
See also AITN 1; CA 9-12R; 104; CANR
15; CN 1, 2, 3; DAM POP; DLB 9, 28;
DLBY 1981; MAL 5; SATA 21; SATA-
Obit 27

Levine, Norman 1923-2005 .... CLC 54
See also CA 73-76; 240; CAAS 23; CANR
14, 70; CN 1, 2, 3, 4, 5, 6; CP 1; DLB 88

Levine, Norman Albert
See Levine, Norman

Levine, Philip 1928- .. CLC 2, 4, 5, 9, 14, 33,
118; PC 22
See also AMWS 5; CA 9-12R; CANR 9,
37, 52, 116; CP 1, 2, 3, 4, 5, 6, 7; DAM
POET; DLB 5; EWL 3; MAL 5; PFS 8

Levinson, Deirdre 1931- .... CLC 49
See also CA 73-76; CANR 70

Levi-Strauss, Claude 1908- .... CLC 38
See also CA 1-4R; CANR 6, 32, 57; DLB
242; EWL 3; GFL 1789 to the Present;
MTCW 1, 2; TWA

Levitin, Sonia (Wolff) 1934- .... CLC 17
See also AAYA 13, 48; CA 29-32R; CANR
14, 32, 79; CLR 53; JRDA; MAICYA 1,
2; SAAS 2; SATA 4, 68, 119, 131; SATA-
Essay 131; YAW

Levon, O. U.
See Kesey, Ken (Elton)

Levy, Amy 1861-1889 .... NCLC 59
See also DLB 156, 240

Lewes, George Henry 1817-1878 ... NCLC 25
See also DLB 55, 144

Lewis, Alun 1915-1944 .... SSC 40; TCLC 3
See also BRW 7; CA 104; 188; DLB 20,
162; PAB; RGEL 2

Lewis, C. Day
See Day Lewis, C(ecil)
See also CN 1

Lewis, C(live) S(taples) 1898-1963 .... CLC 1,
3, 6, 14, 27, 124; WLC
See also AAYA 3, 39; BPFB 2; BRWS 3;
BYA 15, 16; CA 81-84; CANR 33, 71,
132; CDBLB 1945-1960; CLR 3, 27;
CWRI 5; DA; DA3; DAB; DAC; DAM
MST, NOV, POP; DLB 15, 100, 160, 255;
EWL 3; FANT; JRDA; LMFS 2; MAI-
CYA 1, 2; MTCW 1, 2; MTFW 2005;
RGEL 2; SATA 13, 100; SCFW 1, 2; SFW
4; SUFW 1; TEA; WCH; WYA; YAW

Lewis, Cecil Day
See Day Lewis, C(ecil)

Lewis, Janet 1899-1998 .... CLC 41
See Winters, Janet Lewis
See also CA 9-12R; 172; CANR 29, 63;
CAP 1; CN 1, 2, 3, 4, 5, 6; DLBY 1987;
RHW; TCWW 2

Lewis, Matthew Gregory
1775-1818 .... NCLC 11, 62
See also DLB 39, 158, 178; GL 3; HGG;
LMFS 1; RGEL 2; SUFW

Lewis, (Harry) Sinclair 1885-1951 . TCLC 4,
13, 23, 39; WLC
See also AMW; AMWC 1; BPFB 2; CA
104; 133; CANR 132; CDALB 1917-
1929; DA; DA3; DAB; DAC; DAM MST,
NOV; DLB 9, 102, 284; DLBD 1; EWL
3; LAIT 3; MTCW 1, 2; MTFW 2005;
NFS 15, 19, 22; RGAL 4; TUS

Lewis, (Percy) Wyndham
1884(?)-1957 .. SSC 34; TCLC 2, 9, 104
See also BRW 7; CA 104; 157; DLB 15;
EWL 3; FANT; MTCW 2; MTFW 2005;
RGEL 2

Lewisohn, Ludwig 1883-1955 .... TCLC 19
See also CA 107; 203; DLB 4, 9, 28, 102;
MAL 5

Lewton, Val 1904-1951 .... TCLC 76
See also CA 199; IDFW 3, 4

Leyner, Mark 1956- .... CLC 92
See also CA 110; CANR 28, 53; DA3; DLB
292; MTCW 2; MTFW 2005

Lezama Lima, Jose 1910-1976 .... CLC 4, 10,
101; HLCS 2
See also CA 77-80; CANR 71; DAM
MULT; DLB 113, 283; EWL 3; HW 1, 2;
LAW; RGWL 2, 3

L'Heureux, John (Clarke) 1934- ...... CLC 52
See also CA 13-16R; CANR 23, 45, 88; CP
1, 2, 3, 4; DLB 244

Li Ch'ing-chao 1081(?)-1141(?) .... CMLC 71

Liddell, C. H.
See Kuttner, Henry

Lie, Jonas (Lauritz Idemil)
1833-1908(?) .... TCLC 5
See also CA 115

Lieber, Joel 1937-1971 .... CLC 6
See also CA 73-76; 29-32R

Lieber, Stanley Martin
See Lee, Stan

Lieberman, Laurence (James)
1935- .... CLC 4, 36
See also CA 17-20R; CANR 8, 36, 89; CP
1, 2, 3, 4, 5, 6, 7

Lieh Tzu fl. 7th cent. B.C.-5th cent.
B.C. .... CMLC 27

Lieksman, Anders
See Haavikko, Paavo Juhani

Li Fei-kan 1904-
See Pa Chin
See also CA 105; TWA

Lifton, Robert Jay 1926- .... CLC 67
See also CA 17-20R; CANR 27, 78; INT
CANR-27; SATA 66

Lightfoot, Gordon 1938- .... CLC 26
See also CA 109

Lightman, Alan P(aige) 1948- .... CLC 81
See also CA 141; CANR 63, 105, 138;
MTFW 2005

Ligotti, Thomas (Robert) 1953- ...... CLC 44;
SSC 16
See also CA 123; CANR 49, 135; HGG;
SUFW 2

Li Ho 791-817 .... PC 13

Li Ju-chen c. 1763-c. 1830 .... NCLC 137

Lilar, Francoise
See Mallet-Joris, Francoise

Liliencron, (Friedrich Adolf Axel) Detlev
von 1844-1909 .... TCLC 18
See also CA 117

Lille, Alain de
See Alain de Lille

Lilly, William 1602-1681 .... LC 27

Lima, Jose Lezama
See Lezama Lima, Jose

Lima Barreto, Afonso Henrique de
1881-1922 .... TCLC 23
See Lima Barreto, Afonso Henriques de
See also CA 117; 181; LAW

Lima Barreto, Afonso Henriques de
See Lima Barreto, Afonso Henrique de
See also DLB 307

McGinley, Patrick (Anthony) 1937- . **CLC 41**
See also CA 120; 127; CANR 56; INT CA-127

McGinley, Phyllis 1905-1978 .... **CLC 14**
See also CA 9-12R; 77-80; CANR 19; CP 1, 2; CWRI 5; DLB 11, 48; MAL 5; PFS 9, 13; SATA 2, 44; SATA-Obit 24

McGinniss, Joe 1942- .... **CLC 32**
See also AITN 2; BEST 89:2; CA 25-28R; CANR 26, 70; CPW; DLB 185; INT CANR-26

McGivern, Maureen Daly
See Daly, Maureen

McGrath, Patrick 1950- .... **CLC 55**
See also CA 136; CANR 65; CN 5, 6, 7; DLB 231; HGG; SUFW 2

McGrath, Thomas (Matthew)
1916-1990 .... **CLC 28, 59**
See also AMWS 10; CA 9-12R; 132; CANR 6, 33, 95; CP 1, 2, 3, 4; DAM POET; MAL 5; MTCW 1; SATA 41; SATA-Obit 66

McGuane, Thomas (Francis III)
1939- .... **CLC 3, 7, 18, 45, 127**
See also AITN 2; BPFB 2; CA 49-52; CANR 5, 24, 49, 94; CN 2, 3, 4, 5, 6, 7; DLB 2, 212; DLBY 1980; EWL 3; INT CANR-24; MAL 5; MTCW 1; MTFW 2005; TCWW 1, 2

McGuckian, Medbh 1950- .... **CLC 48, 174; PC 27**
See also BRWS 5; CA 143; CP 4, 5, 6, 7; CWP; DAM POET; DLB 40

McHale, Tom 1942(?)-1982 .... **CLC 3, 5**
See also AITN 1; CA 77-80; 106; CN 1, 2, 3

McHugh, Heather 1948- .... **PC 61**
See also CA 69-72; CANR 11, 28, 55, 92; CP 4, 5, 6, 7; CWP

McIlvanney, William 1936- .... **CLC 42**
See also CA 25-28R; CANR 61; CMW 4; DLB 14, 207

McIlwraith, Maureen Mollie Hunter
See Hunter, Mollie
See also SATA 2

McInerney, Jay 1955- .... **CLC 34, 112**
See also AAYA 18; BPFB 2; CA 116; 123; CANR 45, 68, 116; CN 5, 6, 7; CPW; DA3; DAM POP; DLB 292; INT CA-123; MAL 5; MTCW 2; MTFW 2005

McIntyre, Vonda N(eel) 1948- .... **CLC 18**
See also CA 81-84; CANR 17, 34, 69; MTCW 1; SFW 4; YAW

McKay, Claude .... **BLC 3; HR 1:3; PC 2; TCLC 7, 41; WLC**
See McKay, Festus Claudius
See also AFAW 1, 2; AMWS 10; DAB; DLB 4, 45, 51, 117; EWL 3; EXPP; GLL 2; LAIT 3; LMFS 2; MAL 5; PAB; PFS 4; RGAL 4; WP

McKay, Festus Claudius 1889-1948
See McKay, Claude
See also BW 1, 3; CA 104; 124; CANR 73; DA; DAC; DAM MST, MULT, NOV, POET; MTCW 1, 2; MTFW 2005; TUS

McKuen, Rod 1933- .... **CLC 1, 3**
See also AITN 1; CA 41-44R; CANR 40; CP 1

McLoughlin, R. B.
See Mencken, H(enry) L(ouis)

McLuhan, (Herbert) Marshall
1911-1980 .... **CLC 37, 83**
See also CA 9-12R; 102; CANR 12, 34, 61; DLB 88; INT CANR-12; MTCW 1, 2; MTFW 2005

McManus, Declan Patrick Aloysius
See Costello, Elvis

McMillan, Terry (L.) 1951- . **BLCS; CLC 50, 61, 112**
See also AAYA 21; AMWS 13; BPFB 2; BW 2, 3; CA 140; CANR 60, 104, 131; CN 7; CPW; DA3; DAM MULT, NOV, POP; MAL 5; MTCW 2; MTFW 2005; RGAL 4; YAW

McMurtry, Larry 1936- .... **CLC 2, 3, 7, 11, 27, 44, 127**
See also AAYA 15; AITN 2; AMWS 5; BEST 89:2; BPFB 2; CA 5-8R; CANR 19, 43, 64, 103; CDALB 1968-1988; CN 2, 3, 4, 5, 6, 7; CPW; CSW; DA3; DAM NOV, POP; DLB 2, 143, 256; DLBY 1980, 1987; EWL 3; MAL 5; MTCW 1, 2; MTFW 2005; RGAL 4; TCWW 1, 2

McNally, T. M. 1961- .... **CLC 82**

McNally, Terrence 1939- ... **CLC 4, 7, 41, 91; DC 27**
See also AAYA 62; AMWS 13; CA 45-48; CAD; CANR 2, 56, 116; CD 5, 6; DA3; DAM DRAM; DFS 16, 19; DLB 7, 249; EWL 3; GLL 1; MTCW 2; MTFW 2005

McNamer, Deirdre 1950- .... **CLC 70**

McNeal, Tom .... **CLC 119**

McNeile, Herman Cyril 1888-1937
See Sapper
See also CA 184; CMW 4; DLB 77

McNickle, (William) D'Arcy
1904-1977 .... **CLC 89; NNAL**
See also CA 9-12R; 85-88; CANR 5, 45; DAM MULT; DLB 175, 212; RGAL 4; SATA-Obit 22; TCWW 1, 2

McPhee, John (Angus) 1931- .... **CLC 36**
See also AAYA 61; AMWS 3; ANW; BEST 90:1; CA 65-68; CANR 20, 46, 64, 69, 121; CPW; DLB 185, 275; MTCW 1, 2; MTFW 2005; TUS

McPherson, James Alan 1943- . **BLCS; CLC 19, 77**
See also BW 1, 3; CA 25-28R; CAAS 17; CANR 24, 74, 140; CN 3, 4, 5, 6; CSW; DLB 38, 244; EWL 3; MTCW 1, 2; MTFW 2005; RGAL 4; RGSF 2

McPherson, William (Alexander)
1933- .... **CLC 34**
See also CA 69-72; CANR 28; INT CANR-28

McTaggart, J. McT. Ellis
See McTaggart, John McTaggart Ellis

McTaggart, John McTaggart Ellis
1866-1925 .... **TCLC 105**
See also CA 120; DLB 262

Mead, George Herbert 1863-1931 . **TCLC 89**
See also CA 212; DLB 270

Mead, Margaret 1901-1978 .... **CLC 37**
See also AITN 1; CA 1-4R; 81-84; CANR 4; DA3; FW; MTCW 1, 2; SATA-Obit 20

Meaker, Marijane (Agnes) 1927-
See Kerr, M. E.
See also CA 107; CANR 37, 63, 145; INT CA-107; JRDA; MAICYA 1, 2; MAIC-YAS 1; MTCW 1; SATA 20, 61, 99, 160; SATA-Essay 111; YAW

Medoff, Mark (Howard) 1940- .... **CLC 6, 23**
See also AITN 1; CA 53-56; CAD; CANR 5; CD 5, 6; DAM DRAM; DFS 4; DLB 7; INT CANR-5

Medvedev, P. N.
See Bakhtin, Mikhail Mikhailovich

Meged, Aharon
See Megged, Aharon

Meged, Aron
See Megged, Aharon

Megged, Aharon 1920- .... **CLC 9**
See also CA 49-52; CAAS 13; CANR 1, 140; EWL 3

Mehta, Deepa 1950- .... **CLC 208**

Mehta, Gita 1943- .... **CLC 179**
See also CA 225; CN 7; DNFS 2

Mehta, Ved (Parkash) 1934- .... **CLC 37**
See also CA 1-4R, 212; CAAE 212; CANR 2, 23, 69; MTCW 1; MTFW 2005

Melanchthon, Philipp 1497-1560 .... **LC 90**
See also DLB 179

Melanter
See Blackmore, R(ichard) D(oddridge)

Meleager c. 140B.C.-c. 70B.C. ...... **CMLC 53**

Melies, Georges 1861-1938 .... **TCLC 81**

Melikow, Loris
See Hofmannsthal, Hugo von

Melmoth, Sebastian
See Wilde, Oscar (Fingal O'Flahertie Wills)

Melo Neto, Joao Cabral de
See Cabral de Melo Neto, Joao
See also CWW 2; EWL 3

Meltzer, Milton 1915- .... **CLC 26**
See also AAYA 8, 45; BYA 2, 6; CA 13-16R; CANR 38, 92, 107; CLR 13; DLB 61; JRDA; MAICYA 1, 2; SAAS 1; SATA 1, 50, 80, 128; SATA-Essay 124; WYA; YAW

Melville, Herman 1819-1891 ..... **NCLC 3, 12, 29, 45, 49, 91, 93, 123, 157; SSC 1, 17, 46; WLC**
See also AAYA 25; AMW; AMWR 1; CDALB 1640-1865; DA; DA3; DAB; DAC; DAM MST, NOV; DLB 3, 74, 250, 254; EXPN; EXPS; GL 3; LAIT 1, 2; NFS 7, 9; RGAL 4; RGSF 2; SATA 59; SSFS 3; TUS

Members, Mark
See Powell, Anthony (Dymoke)

Membreno, Alejandro .... **CLC 59**

Menand, Louis 1952- .... **CLC 208**
See also CA 200

Menander c. 342B.C.-c. 293B.C. .... **CMLC 9, 51; DC 3**
See also AW 1; CDWLB 1; DAM DRAM; DLB 176; LMFS 1; RGWL 2, 3

Menchu, Rigoberta 1959- .. **CLC 160; HLCS 2**
See also CA 175; CANR 135; DNFS 1; WLIT 1

Mencken, H(enry) L(ouis)
1880-1956 .... **TCLC 13**
See also AMW; CA 105; 125; CDALB 1917-1929; DLB 11, 29, 63, 137, 222; EWL 3; MAL 5; MTCW 1, 2; MTFW 2005; NCFS 4; RGAL 4; TUS

Mendelsohn, Jane 1965- .... **CLC 99**
See also CA 154; CANR 94

Mendoza, Inigo Lopez de
See Santillana, Inigo Lopez de Mendoza, Marques de

Menton, Francisco de
See Chin, Frank (Chew, Jr.)

Mercer, David 1928-1980 .... **CLC 5**
See also CA 9-12R; 102; CANR 23; CBD; DAM DRAM; DLB 13, 310; MTCW 1; RGEL 2

Merchant, Paul
See Ellison, Harlan (Jay)

Meredith, George 1828-1909 .. **PC 60; TCLC 17, 43**
See also CA 117; 153; CANR 80; CDBLB 1832-1890; DAM POET; DLB 18, 35, 57, 159; RGEL 2; TEA

Meredith, William (Morris) 1919- .... **CLC 4, 13, 22, 55; PC 28**
See also CA 9-12R; CAAS 14; CANR 6, 40, 129; CP 1, 2, 3, 4, 5, 6, 7; DAM POET; DLB 5; MAL 5

Merezhkovsky, Dmitrii Sergeevich
See Merezhkovsky, Dmitry Sergeyevich
See also DLB 295

Mourning Dove 1885(?)-1936 .... **NNAL**
See also CA 144; CANR 90; DAM MULT; DLB 175, 221

Mowat, Farley (McGill) 1921- .... **CLC 26**
See also AAYA 1, 50; BYA 2; CA 1-4R; CANR 4, 24, 42, 68, 108; CLR 20; CPW; DAC; DAM MST; DLB 68; INT CANR-24; JRDA; MAICYA 1, 2; MTCW 1, 2; MTFW 2005; SATA 3, 55; YAW

Mowatt, Anna Cora 1819-1870 ..... **NCLC 74**
See also RGAL 4

Moyers, Bill 1934- .... **CLC 74**
See also AITN 2; CA 61-64; CANR 31, 52

Mphahlele, Es'kia
See Mphahlele, Ezekiel
See also AFW; CDWLB 3; CN 4, 5, 6; DLB 125, 225; RGSF 2; SSFS 11

Mphahlele, Ezekiel 1919- .... **BLC 3; CLC 25, 133**
See Mphahlele, Es'kia
See also BW 2, 3; CA 81-84; CANR 26, 76; CN 1, 2, 3; DA3; DAM MULT; EWL 3; MTCW 2; MTFW 2005; SATA 119

Mqhayi, S(amuel) E(dward) K(rune Loliwe) 1875-1945 .... **BLC 3; TCLC 25**
See also CA 153; CANR 87; DAM MULT

Mrozek, Slawomir 1930- .... **CLC 3, 13**
See also CA 13-16R; CAAS 10; CANR 29; CDWLB 4; CWW 2; DLB 232; EWL 3; MTCW 1

Mrs. Belloc-Lowndes
See Lowndes, Marie Adelaide (Belloc)

Mrs. Fairstar
See Horne, Richard Henry Hengist

M'Taggart, John M'Taggart Ellis
See McTaggart, John McTaggart Ellis

Mtwa, Percy (?)- .... **CLC 47**
See also CD 6

Mueller, Lisel 1924- .... **CLC 13, 51; PC 33**
See also CA 93-96; CP 7; DLB 105; PFS 9, 13

Muggeridge, Malcolm (Thomas) 1903-1990 .... **TCLC 120**
See also AITN 1; CA 101; CANR 33, 63; MTCW 1, 2

Muhammad 570-632 .... **WLCS**
See also DA; DAB; DAC; DAM MST; DLB 311

Muir, Edwin 1887-1959 . **PC 49; TCLC 2, 87**
See Moore, Edward
See also BRWS 6; CA 104; 193; DLB 20, 100, 191; EWL 3; RGEL 2

Muir, John 1838-1914 .... **TCLC 28**
See also AMWS 9; ANW; CA 165; DLB 186, 275

Mujica Lainez, Manuel 1910-1984 ... **CLC 31**
See Lainez, Manuel Mujica
See also CA 81-84; 112; CANR 32; EWL 3; HW 1

Mukherjee, Bharati 1940- ..... **AAL; CLC 53, 115; SSC 38**
See also AAYA 46; BEST 89:2; CA 107, 232; CAAE 232; CANR 45, 72, 128; CN 5, 6, 7; DAM NOV; DLB 60, 218; DNFS 1, 2; EWL 3; FW; MAL 5; MTCW 1, 2; MTFW 2005; RGAL 4; RGSF 2; SSFS 7; TUS; WWE 1

Muldoon, Paul 1951- .... **CLC 32, 72, 166**
See also BRWS 4; CA 113; 129; CANR 52, 91; CP 2, 3, 4, 5, 6, 7; DAM POET; DLB 40; INT CA-129; PFS 7, 22; TCLE 1:2

Mulisch, Harry (Kurt Victor) 1927- .... **CLC 42**
See also CA 9-12R; CANR 6, 26, 56, 110; CWW 2; DLB 299; EWL 3

Mull, Martin 1943- .... **CLC 17**
See also CA 105

Muller, Wilhelm .... **NCLC 73**

Mulock, Dinah Maria
See Craik, Dinah Maria (Mulock)
See also RGEL 2

Multatuli 1820-1887 .... **NCLC 165**
See also RGWL 2, 3

Munday, Anthony 1560-1633 .... **LC 87**
See also DLB 62, 172; RGEL 2

Munford, Robert 1737(?)-1783 .... **LC 5**
See also DLB 31

Mungo, Raymond 1946- .... **CLC 72**
See also CA 49-52; CANR 2

Munro, Alice (Anne) 1931- .... **CLC 6, 10, 19, 50, 95; SSC 3; WLCS**
See also AITN 2; BPFB 2; CA 33-36R; CANR 33, 53, 75, 114; CCA 1; CN 1, 2, 3, 4, 5, 6, 7; DA3; DAC; DAM MST, NOV; DLB 53; EWL 3; MTCW 1, 2; MTFW 2005; RGEL 2; RGSF 2; SATA 29; SSFS 5, 13, 19; TCLE 1:2; WWE 1

Munro, H(ector) H(ugh) 1870-1916 .... **WLC**
See Saki
See also AAYA 56; CA 104; 130; CANR 104; CDBLB 1890-1914; DA; DA3; DAB; DAC; DAM MST, NOV; DLB 34, 162; EXPS; MTCW 1, 2; MTFW 2005; RGEL 2; SSFS 15

Murakami, Haruki 1949- .... **CLC 150**
See Murakami Haruki
See also CA 165; CANR 102, 146; MJW; RGWL 3; SFW 4

Murakami Haruki
See Murakami, Haruki
See also CWW 2; DLB 182; EWL 3

Murasaki, Lady
See Murasaki Shikibu

Murasaki Shikibu 978(?)-1026(?) .. **CMLC 1, 79**
See also EFS 2; LATS 1:1; RGWL 2, 3

Murdoch, (Jean) Iris 1919-1999 ... **CLC 1, 2, 3, 4, 6, 8, 11, 15, 22, 31, 51; TCLC 171**
See also BRWS 1; CA 13-16R; 179; CANR 8, 43, 68, 103, 142; CBD; CDBLB 1960 to Present; CN 1, 2, 3, 4, 5, 6; CWD; DA3; DAB; DAC; DAM MST, NOV; DLB 14, 194, 233; EWL 3; INT CANR-8; MTCW 1, 2; MTFW 2005; NFS 18; RGEL 2; TCLE 1:2; TEA; WLIT 4

Murfree, Mary Noailles 1850-1922 .. **SSC 22; TCLC 135**
See also CA 122; 176; DLB 12, 74; RGAL 4

Murnau, Friedrich Wilhelm
See Plumpe, Friedrich Wilhelm

Murphy, Richard 1927- .... **CLC 41**
See also BRWS 5; CA 29-32R; CP 1, 2, 3, 4, 5, 6, 7; DLB 40; EWL 3

Murphy, Sylvia 1937- .... **CLC 34**
See also CA 121

Murphy, Thomas (Bernard) 1935- ... **CLC 51**
See Murphy, Tom
See also CA 101

Murphy, Tom
See Murphy, Thomas (Bernard)
See also DLB 310

Murray, Albert L. 1916- .... **CLC 73**
See also BW 2; CA 49-52; CANR 26, 52, 78; CN 7; CSW; DLB 38; MTFW 2005

Murray, James Augustus Henry 1837-1915 .... **TCLC 117**

Murray, Judith Sargent 1751-1820 .... **NCLC 63**
See also DLB 37, 200

Murray, Les(lie Allan) 1938- .... **CLC 40**
See also BRWS 7; CA 21-24R; CANR 11, 27, 56, 103; CP 1, 2, 3, 4, 5, 6, 7; DAM POET; DLB 289; DLBY 2001; EWL 3; RGEL 2

Murry, J. Middleton
See Murry, John Middleton

Murry, John Middleton 1889-1957 .... **TCLC 16**
See also CA 118; 217; DLB 149

Musgrave, Susan 1951- .... **CLC 13, 54**
See also CA 69-72; CANR 45, 84; CCA 1; CP 2, 3, 4, 5, 6, 7; CWP

Musil, Robert (Edler von) 1880-1942 .... **SSC 18; TCLC 12, 68**
See also CA 109; CANR 55, 84; CDWLB 2; DLB 81, 124; EW 9; EWL 3; MTCW 2; RGSF 2; RGWL 2, 3

Muske, Carol .... **CLC 90**
See Muske-Dukes, Carol (Anne)

Muske-Dukes, Carol (Anne) 1945-
See Muske, Carol
See also CA 65-68, 203; CAAE 203; CANR 32, 70; CWP

Musset, (Louis Charles) Alfred de 1810-1857 .... **DC 27; NCLC 7, 150**
See also DLB 192, 217; EW 6; GFL 1789 to the Present; RGWL 2, 3; TWA

Mussolini, Benito (Amilcare Andrea) 1883-1945 .... **TCLC 96**
See also CA 116

Mutanabbi, Al-
See al-Mutanabbi, Ahmad ibn al-Husayn Abu al-Tayyib al-Jufi al-Kindi
See also WLIT 6

My Brother's Brother
See Chekhov, Anton (Pavlovich)

Myers, L(eopold) H(amilton) 1881-1944 .... **TCLC 59**
See also CA 157; DLB 15; EWL 3; RGEL 2

Myers, Walter Dean 1937- .. **BLC 3; CLC 35**
See also AAYA 4, 23; BW 2; BYA 6, 8, 11; CA 33-36R; CANR 20, 42, 67, 108; CLR 4, 16, 35; DAM MULT, NOV; DLB 33; INT CANR-20; JRDA; LAIT 5; MAICYA 1, 2; MAICYAS 1; MTCW 2; MTFW 2005; SAAS 2; SATA 41, 71, 109, 157; SATA-Brief 27; WYA; YAW

Myers, Walter M.
See Myers, Walter Dean

Myles, Symon
See Follett, Ken(neth Martin)

Nabokov, Vladimir (Vladimirovich) 1899-1977 .... **CLC 1, 2, 3, 6, 8, 11, 15, 23, 44, 46, 64; SSC 11, 86; TCLC 108; WLC**
See also AAYA 45; AMW; AMWC 1; AMWR 1; BPFB 2; CA 5-8R; 69-72; CANR 20, 102; CDALB 1941-1968; CN 1, 2; CP 2; DA; DA3; DAB; DAC; DAM MST, NOV; DLB 2, 244, 278, 317; DLBD 3; DLBY 1980, 1991; EWL 3; EXPS; LATS 1:2; MAL 5; MTCW 1, 2; MTFW 2005; NCFS 4; NFS 9; RGAL 4; RGSF 2; SSFS 6, 15; TUS

Naevius c. 265B.C.-201B.C. .... **CMLC 37**
See also DLB 211

Nagai, Kafu .... **TCLC 51**
See Nagai, Sokichi
See also DLB 180

Nagai, Sokichi 1879-1959
See Nagai, Kafu
See also CA 117

Nagy, Laszlo 1925-1978 .... **CLC 7**
See also CA 129; 112

Naidu, Sarojini 1879-1949 .... **TCLC 80**
See also EWL 3; RGEL 2

Naipaul, Shiva(dhar Srinivasa) 1945-1985 .... **CLC 32, 39; TCLC 153**
See also CA 110; 112; 116; CANR 33; CN 2, 3; DA3; DAM NOV; DLB 157; DLBY 1985; EWL 3; MTCW 1, 2; MTFW 2005

Pepys, Samuel 1633-1703 ... **LC 11, 58; WLC**
See also BRW 2; CDBLB 1660-1789; DA;
DA3; DAB; DAC; DAM MST; DLB 101,
213; NCFS 4; RGEL 2; TEA; WLIT 3

Percy, Thomas 1729-1811 .... **NCLC 95**
See also DLB 104

Percy, Walker 1916-1990 .... **CLC 2, 3, 6, 8,
14, 18, 47, 65**
See also AMWS 3; BPFB 3; CA 1-4R; 131;
CANR 1, 23, 64; CN 1, 2, 3, 4; CPW;
CSW; DA3; DAM NOV, POP; DLB 2;
DLBY 1980, 1990; EWL 3; MAL 5;
MTCW 1, 2; MTFW 2005; RGAL 4; TUS

Percy, William Alexander
1885-1942 .... **TCLC 84**
See also CA 163; MTCW 2

Perec, Georges 1936-1982 .... **CLC 56, 116**
See also CA 141; DLB 83, 299; EWL 3;
GFL 1789 to the Present; RGWL 3

**Pereda (y Sanchez de Porrua), Jose Maria
de** 1833-1906 .... **TCLC 16**
See also CA 117

Pereda y Porrua, Jose Maria de
See Pereda (y Sanchez de Porrua), Jose
Maria de

Peregoy, George Weems
See Mencken, H(enry) L(ouis)

Perelman, S(idney) J(oseph)
1904-1979 .. **CLC 3, 5, 9, 15, 23, 44, 49;
SSC 32**
See also AITN 1, 2; BPFB 3; CA 73-76;
89-92; CANR 18; DAM DRAM; DLB 11,
44; MTCW 1, 2; MTFW 2005; RGAL 4

Peret, Benjamin 1899-1959 .... **PC 33; TCLC
20**
See also CA 117; 186; GFL 1789 to the
Present

Peretz, Isaac Leib
See Peretz, Isaac Loeb
See also CA 201

Peretz, Isaac Loeb 1851(?)-1915 .... **SSC 26;
TCLC 16**
See Peretz, Isaac Leib
See also CA 109

Peretz, Yitzkhok Leibush
See Peretz, Isaac Loeb

Perez Galdos, Benito 1843-1920 ..... **HLCS 2;
TCLC 27**
See Galdos, Benito Perez
See also CA 125; 153; EWL 3; HW 1;
RGWL 2, 3

Peri Rossi, Cristina 1941- .. **CLC 156; HLCS
2**
See also CA 131; CANR 59, 81; CWW 2;
DLB 145, 290; EWL 3; HW 1, 2

Perlata
See Peret, Benjamin

Perloff, Marjorie G(abrielle)
1931- .... **CLC 137**
See also CA 57-60; CANR 7, 22, 49, 104

Perrault, Charles 1628-1703 .... **LC 2, 56**
See also BYA 4; CLR 79; DLB 268; GFL
Beginnings to 1789; MAICYA 1, 2;
RGWL 2, 3; SATA 25; WCH

Perry, Anne 1938- .... **CLC 126**
See also CA 101; CANR 22, 50, 84; CMW
4; CN 6, 7; CPW; DLB 276

Perry, Brighton
See Sherwood, Robert E(mmet)

Perse, St.-John
See Leger, (Marie-Rene Auguste) Alexis
Saint-Leger

Perse, Saint-John
See Leger, (Marie-Rene Auguste) Alexis
Saint-Leger
See also DLB 258; RGWL 3

Persius 34-62 .... **CMLC 74**
See also AW 2; DLB 211; RGWL 2, 3

Perutz, Leo(pold) 1882-1957 .... **TCLC 60**
See also CA 147; DLB 81

Peseenz, Tulio F.
See Lopez y Fuentes, Gregorio

Pesetsky, Bette 1932- .... **CLC 28**
See also CA 133; DLB 130

Peshkov, Alexei Maximovich 1868-1936
See Gorky, Maxim
See also CA 105; 141; CANR 83; DA;
DAC; DAM DRAM, MST, NOV; MTCW
2; MTFW 2005

Pessoa, Fernando (Antonio Nogueira)
1888-1935 ..... **HLC 2; PC 20; TCLC 27**
See also CA 125; 183; DAM MULT; DLB
287; EW 10; EWL 3; RGWL 2, 3; WP

Peterkin, Julia Mood 1880-1961 ...... **CLC 31**
See also CA 102; DLB 9

Peters, Joan K(aren) 1945- .... **CLC 39**
See also CA 158; CANR 109

Peters, Robert L(ouis) 1924- .... **CLC 7**
See also CA 13-16R; CAAS 8; CP 1, 7;
DLB 105

Petofi, Sandor 1823-1849 .... **NCLC 21**
See also RGWL 2, 3

Petrakis, Harry Mark 1923- .... **CLC 3**
See also CA 9-12R; CANR 4, 30, 85; CN
1, 2, 3, 4, 5, 6, 7

Petrarch 1304-1374 .... **CMLC 20; PC 8**
See also DA3; DAM POET; EW 2; LMFS
1; RGWL 2, 3; WLIT 7

Petronius c. 20-66 .... **CMLC 34**
See also AW 2; CDWLB 1; DLB 211;
RGWL 2, 3

Petrov, Evgeny .... **TCLC 21**
See Kataev, Evgeny Petrovich

Petry, Ann (Lane) 1908-1997 .. **CLC 1, 7, 18;
TCLC 112**
See also AFAW 1, 2; BPFB 3; BW 1, 3;
BYA 2; CA 5-8R; 157; CAAS 6; CANR
4, 46; CLR 12; CN 1, 2, 3, 4, 5, 6; DLB
76; EWL 3; JRDA; LAIT 1; MAICYA 1,
2; MAICYAS 1; MTCW 1; RGAL 4;
SATA 5; SATA-Obit 94; TUS

Petursson, Halligrimur 1614-1674 .... **LC 8**

Peychinovich
See Vazov, Ivan (Minchov)

Phaedrus c. 15B.C.-c. 50 .... **CMLC 25**
See also DLB 211

Phelps (Ward), Elizabeth Stuart
See Phelps, Elizabeth Stuart
See also FW

Phelps, Elizabeth Stuart
1844-1911 .... **TCLC 113**
See Phelps (Ward), Elizabeth Stuart
See also DLB 74

Philips, Katherine 1632-1664 . **LC 30; PC 40**
See also DLB 131; RGEL 2

Philipson, Morris H. 1926- .... **CLC 53**
See also CA 1-4R; CANR 4

Phillips, Caryl 1958- .... **BLCS; CLC 96**
See also BRWS 5; BW 2; CA 141; CANR
63, 104, 140; CBD; CD 5, 6; CN 5, 6, 7;
DA3; DAM MULT; DLB 157; EWL 3;
MTCW 2; MTFW 2005; WLIT 4; WWE
1

Phillips, David Graham
1867-1911 .... **TCLC 44**
See also CA 108; 176; DLB 9, 12, 303;
RGAL 4

Phillips, Jack
See Sandburg, Carl (August)

Phillips, Jayne Anne 1952- .... **CLC 15, 33,
139; SSC 16**
See also AAYA 57; BPFB 3; CA 101;
CANR 24, 50, 96; CN 4, 5, 6, 7; CSW;
DLBY 1980; INT CANR-24; MTCW 1,
2; MTFW 2005; RGAL 4; RGSF 2; SSFS
4

Phillips, Richard
See Dick, Philip K(indred)

Phillips, Robert (Schaeffer) 1938- .... **CLC 28**
See also CA 17-20R; CAAS 13; CANR 8;
DLB 105

Phillips, Ward
See Lovecraft, H(oward) P(hillips)

Philostratus, Flavius c. 179-c.
244 .... **CMLC 62**

Piccolo, Lucio 1901-1969 .... **CLC 13**
See also CA 97-100; DLB 114; EWL 3

Pickthall, Marjorie L(owry) C(hristie)
1883-1922 .... **TCLC 21**
See also CA 107; DLB 92

Pico della Mirandola, Giovanni
1463-1494 .... **LC 15**
See also LMFS 1

Piercy, Marge 1936- .... **CLC 3, 6, 14, 18, 27,
62, 128; PC 29**
See also BPFB 3; CA 21-24R; 187; CAAE
187; CAAS 1; CANR 13, 43, 66, 111; CN
3, 4, 5, 6, 7; CP 1, 2, 3, 4, 5, 6, 7; CWP;
DLB 120, 227; EXPP; FW; MAL 5;
MTCW 1, 2; MTFW 2005; PFS 9, 22;
SFW 4

Piers, Robert
See Anthony, Piers

Pieyre de Mandiargues, Andre 1909-1991
See Mandiargues, Andre Pieyre de
See also CA 103; 136; CANR 22, 82; EWL
3; GFL 1789 to the Present

Pilnyak, Boris 1894-1938 . **SSC 48; TCLC 23**
See Vogau, Boris Andreyevich
See also EWL 3

Pinchback, Eugene
See Toomer, Jean

Pincherle, Alberto 1907-1990 ...... **CLC 11, 18**
See Moravia, Alberto
See also CA 25-28R; 132; CANR 33, 63,
142; DAM NOV; MTCW 1; MTFW 2005

Pinckney, Darryl 1953- .... **CLC 76**
See also BW 2, 3; CA 143; CANR 79

Pindar 518(?)B.C.-438(?)B.C. .... **CMLC 12;
PC 19**
See also AW 1; CDWLB 1; DLB 176;
RGWL 2

Pineda, Cecile 1942- .... **CLC 39**
See also CA 118; DLB 209

Pinero, Arthur Wing 1855-1934 .... **TCLC 32**
See also CA 110; 153; DAM DRAM; DLB
10; RGEL 2

Pinero, Miguel (Antonio Gomez)
1946-1988 .... **CLC 4, 55**
See also CA 61-64; 125; CAD; CANR 29,
90; DLB 266; HW 1; LLW

Pinget, Robert 1919-1997 .... **CLC 7, 13, 37**
See also CA 85-88; 160; CWW 2; DLB 83;
EWL 3; GFL 1789 to the Present

Pink Floyd
See Barrett, (Roger) Syd; Gilmour, David;
Mason, Nick; Waters, Roger; Wright, Rick

Pinkney, Edward 1802-1828 .... **NCLC 31**
See also DLB 248

Pinkwater, D. Manus
See Pinkwater, Daniel Manus

Pinkwater, Daniel
See Pinkwater, Daniel Manus

Pinkwater, Daniel M.
See Pinkwater, Daniel Manus

Pinkwater, Daniel Manus 1941- .... **CLC 35**
See also AAYA 1, 46; BYA 9; CA 29-32R;
CANR 12, 38, 89, 143; CLR 4; CSW;
FANT; JRDA; MAICYA 1, 2; SAAS 3;
SATA 8, 46, 76, 114, 158; SFW 4; YAW

Pinkwater, Manus
See Pinkwater, Daniel Manus

Ralegh, Sir Walter
See Raleigh, Sir Walter
See also BRW 1; RGEL 2; WP

Raleigh, Richard
See Lovecraft, H(oward) P(hillips)

Raleigh, Sir Walter 1554(?)-1618 .... **LC 31, 39; PC 31**
See Ralegh, Sir Walter
See also CDBLB Before 1660; DLB 172; EXPP; PFS 14; TEA

Rallentando, H. P.
See Sayers, Dorothy L(eigh)

Ramal, Walter
See de la Mare, Walter (John)

Ramana Maharshi 1879-1950 .... **TCLC 84**

Ramoacn y Cajal, Santiago 1852-1934 .... **TCLC 93**

Ramon, Juan
See Jimenez (Mantecon), Juan Ramon

Ramos, Graciliano 1892-1953 .... **TCLC 32**
See also CA 167; DLB 307; EWL 3; HW 2; LAW; WLIT 1

Rampersad, Arnold 1941- .... **CLC 44**
See also BW 2, 3; CA 127; 133; CANR 81; DLB 111; INT CA-133

Rampling, Anne
See Rice, Anne
See also GLL 2

Ramsay, Allan 1686(?)-1758 .... **LC 29**
See also DLB 95; RGEL 2

Ramsay, Jay
See Campbell, (John) Ramsey

Ramuz, Charles-Ferdinand 1878-1947 .... **TCLC 33**
See also CA 165; EWL 3

Rand, Ayn 1905-1982 ...... **CLC 3, 30, 44, 79; WLC**
See also AAYA 10; AMWS 4; BPFB 3; BYA 12; CA 13-16R; 105; CANR 27, 73; CDALBS; CN 1, 2, 3; CPW; DA; DA3; DAC; DAM MST, NOV, POP; DLB 227, 279; MTCW 1, 2; MTFW 2005; NFS 10, 16; RGAL 4; SFW 4; TUS; YAW

Randall, Dudley (Felker) 1914-2000 . **BLC 3; CLC 1, 135**
See also BW 1, 3; CA 25-28R; 189; CANR 23, 82; CP 1, 2, 3, 4; DAM MULT; DLB 41; PFS 5

Randall, Robert
See Silverberg, Robert

Ranger, Ken
See Creasey, John

Rank, Otto 1884-1939 .... **TCLC 115**

Ransom, John Crowe 1888-1974 .. **CLC 2, 4, 5, 11, 24; PC 61**
See also AMW; CA 5-8R; 49-52; CANR 6, 34; CDALBS; CP 1, 2; DA3; DAM POET; DLB 45, 63; EWL 3; EXPP; MAL 5; MTCW 1, 2; MTFW 2005; RGAL 4; TUS

Rao, Raja 1909- .... **CLC 25, 56**
See also CA 73-76; CANR 51; CN 1, 2, 3, 4, 5, 6; DAM NOV; EWL 3; MTCW 1, 2; MTFW 2005; RGEL 2; RGSF 2

Raphael, Frederic (Michael) 1931- ... **CLC 2, 14**
See also CA 1-4R; CANR 1, 86; CN 1, 2, 3, 4, 5, 6, 7; DLB 14, 319; TCLE 1:2

Ratcliffe, James P.
See Mencken, H(enry) L(ouis)

Rathbone, Julian 1935- .... **CLC 41**
See also CA 101; CANR 34, 73

Rattigan, Terence (Mervyn) 1911-1977 .... **CLC 7; DC 18**
See also BRWS 7; CA 85-88; 73-76; CBD; CDBLB 1945-1960; DAM DRAM; DFS 8; DLB 13; IDFW 3, 4; MTCW 1, 2; MTFW 2005; RGEL 2

Ratushinskaya, Irina 1954- .... **CLC 54**
See also CA 129; CANR 68; CWW 2

Raven, Simon (Arthur Noel) 1927-2001 .... **CLC 14**
See also CA 81-84; 197; CANR 86; CN 1, 2, 3, 4, 5, 6; DLB 271

Ravenna, Michael
See Welty, Eudora (Alice)

Rawley, Callman 1903-2004
See Rakosi, Carl
See also CA 21-24R; 228; CANR 12, 32, 91

Rawlings, Marjorie Kinnan 1896-1953 .... **TCLC 4**
See also AAYA 20; AMWS 10; ANW; BPFB 3; BYA 3; CA 104; 137; CANR 74; CLR 63; DLB 9, 22, 102; DLBD 17; JRDA; MAICYA 1, 2; MAL 5; MTCW 2; MTFW 2005; RGAL 4; SATA 100; WCH; YABC 1; YAW

Ray, Satyajit 1921-1992 .... **CLC 16, 76**
See also CA 114; 137; DAM MULT

Read, Herbert Edward 1893-1968 ..... **CLC 4**
See also BRW 6; CA 85-88; 25-28R; DLB 20, 149; EWL 3; PAB; RGEL 2

Read, Piers Paul 1941- ...... **CLC 4, 10, 25**
See also CA 21-24R; CANR 38, 86; CN 2, 3, 4, 5, 6, 7; DLB 14; SATA 21

Reade, Charles 1814-1884 .... **NCLC 2, 74**
See also DLB 21; RGEL 2

Reade, Hamish
See Gray, Simon (James Holliday)

Reading, Peter 1946- .... **CLC 47**
See also BRWS 8; CA 103; CANR 46, 96; CP 7; DLB 40

Reaney, James 1926- .... **CLC 13**
See also CA 41-44R; CAAS 15; CANR 42; CD 5, 6; CP 1, 2, 3, 4, 5, 6, 7; DAC; DAM MST; DLB 68; RGEL 2; SATA 43

Rebreanu, Liviu 1885-1944 .... **TCLC 28**
See also CA 165; DLB 220; EWL 3

Rechy, John (Francisco) 1934- ...... **CLC 1, 7, 14, 18, 107; HLC 2**
See also CA 5-8R, 195; CAAE 195; CAAS 4; CANR 6, 32, 64; CN 1, 2, 3, 4, 5, 6, 7; DAM MULT; DLB 122, 278; DLBY 1982; HW 1, 2; INT CANR-6; LLW; MAL 5; RGAL 4

Redcam, Tom 1870-1933 .... **TCLC 25**

Reddin, Keith 1956- .... **CLC 67**
See also CAD; CD 6

Redgrove, Peter (William) 1932-2003 .... **CLC 6, 41**
See also BRWS 6; CA 1-4R; 217; CANR 3, 39, 77; CP 1, 2, 3, 4, 5, 6, 7; DLB 40; TCLE 1:2

Redmon, Anne .... **CLC 22**
See Nightingale, Anne Redmon
See also DLBY 1986

Reed, Eliot
See Ambler, Eric

Reed, Ishmael (Scott) 1938- . **BLC 3; CLC 2, 3, 5, 6, 13, 32, 60, 174; PC 68**
See also AFAW 1, 2; AMWS 10; BPFB 3; BW 2, 3; CA 21-24R; CANR 25, 48, 74, 128; CN 1, 2, 3, 4, 5, 6, 7; CP 1, 2, 3, 4, 5, 6, 7; CSW; DA3; DAM MULT; DLB 2, 5, 33, 169, 227; DLBD 8; EWL 3; LMFS 2; MAL 5; MSW; MTCW 1, 2; MTFW 2005; PFS 6; RGAL 4; TCWW 2

Reed, John (Silas) 1887-1920 .... **TCLC 9**
See also CA 106; 195; MAL 5; TUS

Reed, Lou .... **CLC 21**
See Firbank, Louis

Reese, Lizette Woodworth 1856-1935 . **PC 29**
See also CA 180; DLB 54

Reeve, Clara 1729-1807 .... **NCLC 19**
See also DLB 39; RGEL 2

Reich, Wilhelm 1897-1957 .... **TCLC 57**
See also CA 199

Reid, Christopher (John) 1949- .... **CLC 33**
See also CA 140; CANR 89; CP 4, 5, 6, 7; DLB 40; EWL 3

Reid, Desmond
See Moorcock, Michael (John)

Reid Banks, Lynne 1929-
See Banks, Lynne Reid
See also AAYA 49; CA 1-4R; CANR 6, 22, 38, 87; CLR 24; CN 1, 2, 3, 7; JRDA; MAICYA 1, 2; SATA 22, 75, 111, 165; YAW

Reilly, William K.
See Creasey, John

Reiner, Max
See Caldwell, (Janet Miriam) Taylor (Holland)

Reis, Ricardo
See Pessoa, Fernando (Antonio Nogueira)

Reizenstein, Elmer Leopold
See Rice, Elmer (Leopold)
See also EWL 3

Remarque, Erich Maria 1898-1970 . **CLC 21**
See also AAYA 27; BPFB 3; CA 77-80; 29-32R; CDWLB 2; DA; DA3; DAB; DAC; DAM MST, NOV; DLB 56; EWL 3; EXPN; LAIT 3; MTCW 1, 2; MTFW 2005; NFS 4; RGWL 2, 3

Remington, Frederic S(ackrider) 1861-1909 .... **TCLC 89**
See also CA 108; 169; DLB 12, 186, 188; SATA 41; TCWW 2

Remizov, A.
See Remizov, Aleksei (Mikhailovich)

Remizov, A. M.
See Remizov, Aleksei (Mikhailovich)

Remizov, Aleksei (Mikhailovich) 1877-1957 .... **TCLC 27**
See Remizov, Alexey Mikhaylovich
See also CA 125; 133; DLB 295

Remizov, Alexey Mikhaylovich
See Remizov, Aleksei (Mikhailovich)
See also EWL 3

Renan, Joseph Ernest 1823-1892 . **NCLC 26, 145**
See also GFL 1789 to the Present

Renard, Jules(-Pierre) 1864-1910 .. **TCLC 17**
See also CA 117; 202; GFL 1789 to the Present

Renault, Mary .... **CLC 3, 11, 17**
See Challans, Mary
See also BPFB 3; BYA 2; CN 1, 2, 3; DLBY 1983; EWL 3; GLL 1; LAIT 1; RGEL 2; RHW

Rendell, Ruth (Barbara) 1930- .. **CLC 28, 48**
See Vine, Barbara
See also BPFB 3; BRWS 9; CA 109; CANR 32, 52, 74, 127; CN 5, 6, 7; CPW; DAM POP; DLB 87, 276; INT CANR-32; MSW; MTCW 1, 2; MTFW 2005

Renoir, Jean 1894-1979 .... **CLC 20**
See also CA 129; 85-88

Resnais, Alain 1922- .... **CLC 16**

Revard, Carter (Curtis) 1931- .... **NNAL**
See also CA 144; CANR 81; PFS 5

Reverdy, Pierre 1889-1960 .... **CLC 53**
See also CA 97-100; 89-92; DLB 258; EWL 3; GFL 1789 to the Present

Rexroth, Kenneth 1905-1982 .... **CLC 1, 2, 6, 11, 22, 49, 112; PC 20**
See also BG 1:3; CA 5-8R; 107; CANR 14, 34, 63; CDALB 1941-1968; CP 1, 2, 3; DAM POET; DLB 16, 48, 165, 212; DLBY 1982; EWL 3; INT CANR-14; MAL 5; MTCW 1, 2; MTFW 2005; RGAL 4

Reyes, Alfonso 1889-1959 .... **HLCS 2; TCLC 33**
See also CA 131; EWL 3; HW 1; LAW

Robbins, Tom .... CLC 9, 32, 64
  See Robbins, Thomas Eugene
  See also AAYA 32; AMWS 10; BEST 90:3;
  BPFB 3; CN 3, 4, 5, 6, 7; DLBY 1980

Robbins, Trina 1938- .... CLC 21
  See also AAYA 61; CA 128

Roberts, Charles G(eorge) D(ouglas)
  1860-1943 .... TCLC 8
  See also CA 105; 188; CLR 33; CWRI 5;
  DLB 92; RGEL 2; RGSF 2; SATA 88;
  SATA-Brief 29

Roberts, Elizabeth Madox
  1886-1941 .... TCLC 68
  See also CA 111; 166; CLR 100; CWRI 5;
  DLB 9, 54, 102; RGAL 4; RHW; SATA
  33; SATA-Brief 27; TCWW 2; WCH

Roberts, Kate 1891-1985 .... CLC 15
  See also CA 107; 116; DLB 319

Roberts, Keith (John Kingston)
  1935-2000 .... CLC 14
  See also BRWS 10; CA 25-28R; CANR 46;
  DLB 261; SFW 4

Roberts, Kenneth (Lewis)
  1885-1957 .... TCLC 23
  See also CA 109; 199; DLB 9; MAL 5;
  RGAL 4; RHW

Roberts, Michele (Brigitte) 1949- .... CLC 48,
  178
  See also CA 115; CANR 58, 120; CN 6, 7;
  DLB 231; FW

Robertson, Ellis
  See Ellison, Harlan (Jay); Silverberg, Robert

Robertson, Thomas William
  1829-1871 .... NCLC 35
  See Robertson, Tom
  See also DAM DRAM

Robertson, Tom
  See Robertson, Thomas William
  See also RGEL 2

Robeson, Kenneth
  See Dent, Lester

Robinson, Edwin Arlington
  1869-1935 .... PC 1, 35; TCLC 5, 101
  See also AMW; CA 104; 133; CDALB
  1865-1917; DA; DAC; DAM MST,
  POET; DLB 54; EWL 3; EXPP; MAL 5;
  MTCW 1, 2; MTFW 2005; PAB; PFS 4;
  RGAL 4; WP

Robinson, Henry Crabb
  1775-1867 .... NCLC 15
  See also DLB 107

Robinson, Jill 1936- .... CLC 10
  See also CA 102; CANR 120; INT CA-102

Robinson, Kim Stanley 1952- .... CLC 34
  See also AAYA 26; CA 126; CANR 113,
  139; CN 6, 7; MTFW 2005; SATA 109;
  SCFW 2; SFW 4

Robinson, Lloyd
  See Silverberg, Robert

Robinson, Marilynne 1944- ...... CLC 25, 180
  See also CA 116; CANR 80, 140; CN 4, 5,
  6, 7; DLB 206; MTFW 2005

Robinson, Mary 1758-1800 .... NCLC 142
  See also DLB 158; FW

Robinson, Smokey .... CLC 21
  See Robinson, William, Jr.

Robinson, William, Jr. 1940-
  See Robinson, Smokey
  See also CA 116

Robison, Mary 1949- .... CLC 42, 98
  See also CA 113; 116; CANR 87; CN 4, 5,
  6, 7; DLB 130; INT CA-116; RGSF 2

Roches, Catherine des 1542-1587 ...... LC 117

Rochester
  See Wilmot, John
  See also RGEL 2

Rod, Edouard 1857-1910 .... TCLC 52

Roddenberry, Eugene Wesley 1921-1991
  See Roddenberry, Gene
  See also CA 110; 135; CANR 37; SATA 45;
  SATA-Obit 69

Roddenberry, Gene .... CLC 17
  See Roddenberry, Eugene Wesley
  See also AAYA 5; SATA-Obit 69

Rodgers, Mary 1931- .... CLC 12
  See also BYA 5; CA 49-52; CANR 8, 55,
  90; CLR 20; CWRI 5; INT CANR-8;
  JRDA; MAICYA 1, 2; SATA 8, 130

Rodgers, W(illiam) R(obert)
  1909-1969 .... CLC 7
  See also CA 85-88; DLB 20; RGEL 2

Rodman, Eric
  See Silverberg, Robert

Rodman, Howard 1920(?)-1985 .... CLC 65
  See also CA 118

Rodman, Maia
  See Wojciechowska, Maia (Teresa)

Rodo, Jose Enrique 1871(?)-1917 .... HLCS 2
  See also CA 178; EWL 3; HW 2; LAW

Rodolph, Utto
  See Ouologuem, Yambo

Rodriguez, Claudio 1934-1999 .... CLC 10
  See also CA 188; DLB 134

Rodriguez, Richard 1944- .... CLC 155; HLC 2
  See also AMWS 14; CA 110; CANR 66,
  116; DAM MULT; DLB 82, 256; HW 1,
  2; LAIT 5; LLW; MTFW 2005; NCFS 3;
  WLIT 1

Roelvaag, O(le) E(dvart) 1876-1931
  See Rolvaag, O(le) E(dvart)
  See also CA 117; 171

Roethke, Theodore (Huebner)
  1908-1963 .... CLC 1, 3, 8, 11, 19, 46,
  101; PC 15
  See also AMW; CA 81-84; CABS 2;
  CDALB 1941-1968; DA3; DAM POET;
  DLB 5, 206; EWL 3; EXPP; MAL 5;
  MTCW 1, 2; PAB; PFS 3; RGAL 4; WP

Rogers, Carl R(ansom)
  1902-1987 .... TCLC 125
  See also CA 1-4R; 121; CANR 1, 18;
  MTCW 1

Rogers, Samuel 1763-1855 .... NCLC 69
  See also DLB 93; RGEL 2

Rogers, Thomas Hunton 1927- .... CLC 57
  See also CA 89-92; INT CA-89-92

Rogers, Will(iam Penn Adair)
  1879-1935 .... NNAL; TCLC 8, 71
  See also CA 105; 144; DA3; DAM MULT;
  DLB 11; MTCW 2

Rogin, Gilbert 1929- .... CLC 18
  See also CA 65-68; CANR 15

Rohan, Koda
  See Koda Shigeyuki

Rohlfs, Anna Katharine Green
  See Green, Anna Katharine

Rohmer, Eric .... CLC 16
  See Scherer, Jean-Marie Maurice

Rohmer, Sax .... TCLC 28
  See Ward, Arthur Henry Sarsfield
  See also DLB 70; MSW; SUFW

Roiphe, Anne (Richardson) 1935- .. CLC 3, 9
  See also CA 89-92; CANR 45, 73, 138;
  DLBY 1980; INT CA-89-92

Rojas, Fernando de 1475-1541 ... HLCS 1, 2;
  LC 23
  See also DLB 286; RGWL 2, 3

Rojas, Gonzalo 1917- .... HLCS 2
  See also CA 178; HW 2; LAWS 1

Roland (de la Platiere), Marie-Jeanne
  1754-1793 .... LC 98
  See also DLB 314

**Rolfe, Frederick (William Serafino Austin
  Lewis Mary)** 1860-1913 .... TCLC 12
  See Al Siddik
  See also CA 107; 210; DLB 34, 156; RGEL
  2

Rolland, Romain 1866-1944 .... TCLC 23
  See also CA 118; 197; DLB 65, 284; EWL
  3; GFL 1789 to the Present; RGWL 2, 3

Rolle, Richard c. 1300-c. 1349 ...... CMLC 21
  See also DLB 146; LMFS 1; RGEL 2

Rolvaag, O(le) E(dvart) .... TCLC 17
  See Roelvaag, O(le) E(dvart)
  See also DLB 9, 212; MAL 5; NFS 5;
  RGAL 4

Romain Arnaud, Saint
  See Aragon, Louis

Romains, Jules 1885-1972 .... CLC 7
  See also CA 85-88; CANR 34; DLB 65,
  321; EWL 3; GFL 1789 to the Present;
  MTCW 1

Romero, Jose Ruben 1890-1952 .... TCLC 14
  See also CA 114; 131; EWL 3; HW 1; LAW

Ronsard, Pierre de 1524-1585 . LC 6, 54; PC
  11
  See also EW 2; GFL Beginnings to 1789;
  RGWL 2, 3; TWA

Rooke, Leon 1934- .... CLC 25, 34
  See also CA 25-28R; CANR 23, 53; CCA
  1; CPW; DAM POP

Roosevelt, Franklin Delano
  1882-1945 .... TCLC 93
  See also CA 116; 173; LAIT 3

Roosevelt, Theodore 1858-1919 ..... TCLC 69
  See also CA 115; 170; DLB 47, 186, 275

Roper, William 1498-1578 .... LC 10

Roquelaure, A. N.
  See Rice, Anne

Rosa, Joao Guimaraes 1908-1967 ... CLC 23;
  HLCS 1
  See Guimaraes Rosa, Joao
  See also CA 89-92; DLB 113, 307; EWL 3;
  WLIT 1

Rose, Wendy 1948- . CLC 85; NNAL; PC 13
  See also CA 53-56; CANR 5, 51; CWP;
  DAM MULT; DLB 175; PFS 13; RGAL
  4; SATA 12

Rosen, R. D.
  See Rosen, Richard (Dean)

Rosen, Richard (Dean) 1949- .... CLC 39
  See also CA 77-80; CANR 62, 120; CMW
  4; INT CANR-30

Rosenberg, Isaac 1890-1918 .... TCLC 12
  See also BRW 6; CA 107; 188; DLB 20,
  216; EWL 3; PAB; RGEL 2

Rosenblatt, Joe .... CLC 15
  See Rosenblatt, Joseph
  See also CP 3, 4, 5, 6, 7

Rosenblatt, Joseph 1933-
  See Rosenblatt, Joe
  See also CA 89-92; CP 1, 2; INT CA-89-92

Rosenfeld, Samuel
  See Tzara, Tristan

Rosenstock, Sami
  See Tzara, Tristan

Rosenstock, Samuel
  See Tzara, Tristan

Rosenthal, M(acha) L(ouis)
  1917-1996 .... CLC 28
  See also CA 1-4R; 152; CAAS 6; CANR 4,
  51; CP 1, 2, 3, 4; DLB 5; SATA 59

Ross, Barnaby
  See Dannay, Frederic

Ross, Bernard L.
  See Follett, Ken(neth Martin)

Ross, J. H.
  See Lawrence, T(homas) E(dward)

Ross, John Hume
  See Lawrence, T(homas) E(dward)

Ross, Martin 1862-1915
See Martin, Violet Florence
See also DLB 135; GLL 2; RGEL 2; RGSF 2

Ross, (James) Sinclair 1908-1996 ... **CLC 13; SSC 24**
See also CA 73-76; CANR 81; CN 1, 2, 3, 4, 5, 6; DAC; DAM MST; DLB 88; RGEL 2; RGSF 2; TCWW 1, 2

Rossetti, Christina 1830-1894 ... **NCLC 2, 50, 66; PC 7; WLC**
See also AAYA 51; BRW 5; BYA 4; DA; DA3; DAB; DAC; DAM MST, POET; DLB 35, 163, 240; EXPP; FL 1:3; LATS 1:1; MAICYA 1, 2; PFS 10, 14; RGEL 2; SATA 20; TEA; WCH

Rossetti, Christina Georgina
See Rossetti, Christina

Rossetti, Dante Gabriel 1828-1882 . **NCLC 4, 77; PC 44; WLC**
See also AAYA 51; BRW 5; CDBLB 1832-1890; DA; DAB; DAC; DAM MST, POET; DLB 35; EXPP; RGEL 2; TEA

Rossi, Cristina Peri
See Peri Rossi, Cristina

Rossi, Jean-Baptiste 1931-2003
See Japrisot, Sebastien
See also CA 201; 215

Rossner, Judith (Perelman) 1935- . **CLC 6, 9, 29**
See also AITN 2; BEST 90:3; BPFB 3; CA 17-20R; CANR 18, 51, 73; CN 4, 5, 6, 7; DLB 6; INT CANR-18; MAL 5; MTCW 1, 2; MTFW 2005

Rostand, Edmond (Eugene Alexis) 1868-1918 .... **DC 10; TCLC 6, 37**
See also CA 104; 126; DA; DA3; DAB; DAC; DAM DRAM, MST; DFS 1; DLB 192; LAIT 1; MTCW 1; RGWL 2, 3; TWA

Roth, Henry 1906-1995 ..... **CLC 2, 6, 11, 104**
See also AMWS 9; CA 11-12; 149; CANR 38, 63; CAP 1; CN 1, 2, 3, 4, 5, 6; DA3; DLB 28; EWL 3; MAL 5; MTCW 1, 2; MTFW 2005; RGAL 4

Roth, (Moses) Joseph 1894-1939 ... **TCLC 33**
See also CA 160; DLB 85; EWL 3; RGWL 2, 3

Roth, Philip (Milton) 1933- ... **CLC 1, 2, 3, 4, 6, 9, 15, 22, 31, 47, 66, 86, 119, 201; SSC 26; WLC**
See also AAYA 67; AMWR 2; AMWS 3; BEST 90:3; BPFB 3; CA 1-4R; CANR 1, 22, 36, 55, 89, 132; CDALB 1968-1988; CN 3, 4, 5, 6, 7; CPW 1; DA; DA3; DAB; DAC; DAM MST, NOV, POP; DLB 2, 28, 173; DLBY 1982; EWL 3; MAL 5; MTCW 1, 2; MTFW 2005; RGAL 4; RGSF 2; SSFS 12, 18; TUS

Rothenberg, Jerome 1931- .... **CLC 6, 57**
See also CA 45-48; CANR 1, 106; CP 1, 2, 3, 4, 5, 6, 7; DLB 5, 193

Rotter, Pat ed. .... **CLC 65**

Roumain, Jacques (Jean Baptiste) 1907-1944 .... **BLC 3; TCLC 19**
See also BW 1; CA 117; 125; DAM MULT; EWL 3

Rourke, Constance Mayfield 1885-1941 .... **TCLC 12**
See also CA 107; 200; MAL 5; YABC 1

Rousseau, Jean-Baptiste 1671-1741 ...... **LC 9**

Rousseau, Jean-Jacques 1712-1778 .... **LC 14, 36, 122; WLC**
See also DA; DA3; DAB; DAC; DAM MST; DLB 314; EW 4; GFL Beginnings to 1789; LMFS 1; RGWL 2, 3; TWA

Roussel, Raymond 1877-1933 .... **TCLC 20**
See also CA 117; 201; EWL 3; GFL 1789 to the Present

Rovit, Earl (Herbert) 1927- .... **CLC 7**
See also CA 5-8R; CANR 12

Rowe, Elizabeth Singer 1674-1737 ..... **LC 44**
See also DLB 39, 95

Rowe, Nicholas 1674-1718 .... **LC 8**
See also DLB 84; RGEL 2

Rowlandson, Mary 1637(?)-1678 .... **LC 66**
See also DLB 24, 200; RGAL 4

Rowley, Ames Dorrance
See Lovecraft, H(oward) P(hillips)

Rowley, William 1585(?)-1626 ... **LC 100, 123**
See also DFS 22; DLB 58; RGEL 2

Rowling, J. K. 1966- .... **CLC 137, 217**
See also AAYA 34; BYA 11, 13, 14; CA 173; CANR 128; CLR 66, 80; MAICYA 2; MTFW 2005; SATA 109; SUFW 2

Rowling, Joanne Kathleen
See Rowling, J.K.

Rowson, Susanna Haswell 1762(?)-1824 .... **NCLC 5, 69**
See also AMWS 15; DLB 37, 200; RGAL 4

Roy, Arundhati 1960(?)- .... **CLC 109, 210**
See also CA 163; CANR 90, 126; CN 7; DLBY 1997; EWL 3; LATS 1:2; MTFW 2005; NFS 22; WWE 1

Roy, Gabrielle 1909-1983 .... **CLC 10, 14**
See also CA 53-56; 110; CANR 5, 61; CCA 1; DAB; DAC; DAM MST; DLB 68; EWL 3; MTCW 1; RGWL 2, 3; SATA 104; TCLE 1:2

Royko, Mike 1932-1997 .... **CLC 109**
See also CA 89-92; 157; CANR 26, 111; CPW

Rozanov, Vasilii Vasil'evich
See Rozanov, Vassili
See also DLB 295

Rozanov, Vasily Vasilyevich
See Rozanov, Vassili
See also EWL 3

Rozanov, Vassili 1856-1919 .... **TCLC 104**
See also Rozanov, Vasilii Vasil'evich; Rozanov, Vasily Vasilyevich

Rozewicz, Tadeusz 1921- ...... **CLC 9, 23, 139**
See also CA 108; CANR 36, 66; CWW 2; DA3; DAM POET; DLB 232; EWL 3; MTCW 1, 2; MTFW 2005; RGWL 3

Ruark, Gibbons 1941- .... **CLC 3**
See also CA 33-36R; CAAS 23; CANR 14, 31, 57; DLB 120

Rubens, Bernice (Ruth) 1923-2004 . **CLC 19, 31**
See also CA 25-28R; 232; CANR 33, 65, 128; CN 1, 2, 3, 4, 5, 6, 7; DLB 14, 207; MTCW 1

Rubin, Harold
See Robbins, Harold

Rudkin, (James) David 1936- .... **CLC 14**
See also CA 89-92; CBD; CD 5, 6; DLB 13

Rudnik, Raphael 1933- .... **CLC 7**
See also CA 29-32R

Ruffian, M.
See Hasek, Jaroslav (Matej Frantisek)

Ruiz, Jose Martinez .... **CLC 11**
See Martinez Ruiz, Jose

Ruiz, Juan c. 1283-c. 1350 .... **CMLC 66**

Rukeyser, Muriel 1913-1980 . **CLC 6, 10, 15, 27; PC 12**
See also AMWS 6; CA 5-8R; 93-96; CANR 26, 60; CP 1, 2, 3; DA3; DAM POET; DLB 48; EWL 3; FW; GLL 2; MAL 5; MTCW 1, 2; PFS 10; RGAL 4; SATA-Obit 22

Rule, Jane (Vance) 1931- .... **CLC 27**
See also CA 25-28R; CAAS 18; CANR 12, 87; CN 4, 5, 6, 7; DLB 60; FW

Rulfo, Juan 1918-1986 .. **CLC 8, 80; HLC 2; SSC 25**
See also CA 85-88; 118; CANR 26; CD-WLB 3; DAM MULT; DLB 113; EWL 3; HW 1, 2; LAW; MTCW 1, 2; RGSF 2; RGWL 2, 3; WLIT 1

Rumi, Jalal al-Din 1207-1273 ...... **CMLC 20; PC 45**
See also AAYA 64; RGWL 2, 3; WLIT 6; WP

Runeberg, Johan 1804-1877 .... **NCLC 41**

Runyon, (Alfred) Damon 1884(?)-1946 .... **TCLC 10**
See also CA 107; 165; DLB 11, 86, 171; MAL 5; MTCW 2; RGAL 4

Rush, Norman 1933- .... **CLC 44**
See also CA 121; 126; CANR 130; INT CA-126

Rushdie, (Ahmed) Salman 1947- .... **CLC 23, 31, 55, 100, 191; SSC 83; WLCS**
See also AAYA 65; BEST 89:3; BPFB 3; BRWS 4; CA 108; 111; CANR 33, 56, 108, 133; CN 4, 5, 6, 7; CPW 1; DA3; DAB; DAC; DAM MST, NOV, POP; DLB 194; EWL 3; FANT; INT CA-111; LATS 1:2; LMFS 2; MTCW 1, 2; MTFW 2005; NFS 22; RGEL 2; RGSF 2; TEA; WLIT 4

Rushforth, Peter (Scott) 1945- .... **CLC 19**
See also CA 101

Ruskin, John 1819-1900 .... **TCLC 63**
See also BRW 5; BYA 5; CA 114; 129; CD-BLB 1832-1890; DLB 55, 163, 190; RGEL 2; SATA 24; TEA; WCH

Russ, Joanna 1937- .... **CLC 15**
See also BPFB 3; CA 25-28; CANR 11, 31, 65; CN 4, 5, 6, 7; DLB 8; FW; GLL 1; MTCW 1; SCFW 1, 2; SFW 4

Russ, Richard Patrick
See O'Brian, Patrick

Russell, George William 1867-1935
See A.E.; Baker, Jean H.
See also BRWS 8; CA 104; 153; CDBLB 1890-1914; DAM POET; EWL 3; RGEL 2

Russell, Jeffrey Burton 1934- .... **CLC 70**
See also CA 25-28R; CANR 11, 28, 52

Russell, (Henry) Ken(neth Alfred) 1927- .... **CLC 16**
See also CA 105

Russell, William Martin 1947-
See Russell, Willy
See also CA 164; CANR 107

Russell, Willy .... **CLC 60**
See Russell, William Martin
See also CBD; CD 5, 6; DLB 233

Russo, Richard 1949- .... **CLC 181**
See also AMWS 12; CA 127; 133; CANR 87, 114

Rutherford, Mark .... **TCLC 25**
See White, William Hale
See also DLB 18; RGEL 2

Ruyslinck, Ward .... **CLC 14**
See Belser, Reimond Karel Maria de

Ryan, Cornelius (John) 1920-1974 ..... **CLC 7**
See also CA 69-72; 53-56; CANR 38

Ryan, Michael 1946- .... **CLC 65**
See also CA 49-52; CANR 109; DLBY 1982

Ryan, Tim
See Dent, Lester

Rybakov, Anatoli (Naumovich) 1911-1998 .... **CLC 23, 53**
See Rybakov, Anatolii (Naumovich)
See also CA 126; 135; 172; SATA 79; SATA-Obit 108

Rybakov, Anatolii (Naumovich)
See Rybakov, Anatoli (Naumovich)
See also DLB 302

Schnitzler, Arthur 1862-1931 ..... **DC 17; SSC 15, 61; TCLC 4**
See also CA 104; CDWLB 2; DLB 81, 118; EW 8; EWL 3; RGSF 2; RGWL 2, 3

Schoenberg, Arnold Franz Walter 1874-1951 .... **TCLC 75**
See also CA 109; 188

Schonberg, Arnold
See Schoenberg, Arnold Franz Walter

Schopenhauer, Arthur 1788-1860 . **NCLC 51, 157**
See also DLB 90; EW 5

Schor, Sandra (M.) 1932(?)-1990 ..... **CLC 65**
See also CA 132

Schorer, Mark 1908-1977 .... **CLC 9**
See also CA 5-8R; 73-76; CANR 7; CN 1, 2; DLB 103

Schrader, Paul (Joseph) 1946- . **CLC 26, 212**
See also CA 37-40R; CANR 41; DLB 44

Schreber, Daniel 1842-1911 .... **TCLC 123**

Schreiner, Olive (Emilie Albertina) 1855-1920 .... **TCLC 9**
See also AFW; BRWS 2; CA 105; 154; DLB 18, 156, 190, 225; EWL 3; FW; RGEL 2; TWA; WLIT 2; WWE 1

Schulberg, Budd (Wilson) 1914- .. **CLC 7, 48**
See also BPFB 3; CA 25-28R; CANR 19, 87; CN 1, 2, 3, 4, 5, 6, 7; DLB 6, 26, 28; DLBY 1981, 2001; MAL 5

Schulman, Arnold
See Trumbo, Dalton

Schulz, Bruno 1892-1942 .. **SSC 13; TCLC 5, 51**
See also CA 115; 123; CANR 86; CDWLB 4; DLB 215; EWL 3; MTCW 2; MTFW 2005; RGSF 2; RGWL 2, 3

Schulz, Charles M. 1922-2000 .... **CLC 12**
See also AAYA 39; CA 9-12R; 187; CANR 6, 132; INT CANR-6; MTFW 2005; SATA 10; SATA-Obit 118

Schulz, Charles Monroe
See Schulz, Charles M.

Schumacher, E(rnst) F(riedrich) 1911-1977 .... **CLC 80**
See also CA 81-84; 73-76; CANR 34, 85

Schumann, Robert 1810-1856 ...... **NCLC 143**

Schuyler, George Samuel 1895-1977 . **HR 1:3**
See also BW 2; CA 81-84; 73-76; CANR 42; DLB 29, 51

Schuyler, James Marcus 1923-1991 .. **CLC 5, 23**
See also CA 101; 134; CP 1, 2, 3, 4; DAM POET; DLB 5, 169; EWL 3; INT CA-101; MAL 5; WP

Schwartz, Delmore (David) 1913-1966 ... **CLC 2, 4, 10, 45, 87; PC 8**
See also AMWS 2; CA 17-18; 25-28R; CANR 35; CAP 2; DLB 28, 48; EWL 3; MAL 5; MTCW 1, 2; MTFW 2005; PAB; RGAL 4; TUS

Schwartz, Ernst
See Ozu, Yasujiro

Schwartz, John Burnham 1965- .... **CLC 59**
See also CA 132; CANR 116

Schwartz, Lynne Sharon 1939- .... **CLC 31**
See also CA 103; CANR 44, 89; DLB 218; MTCW 2; MTFW 2005

Schwartz, Muriel A.
See Eliot, T(homas) S(tearns)

Schwarz-Bart, Andre 1928- .... **CLC 2, 4**
See also CA 89-92; CANR 109; DLB 299

Schwarz-Bart, Simone 1938- . **BLCS; CLC 7**
See also BW 2; CA 97-100; CANR 117; EWL 3

Schwerner, Armand 1927-1999 .... **PC 42**
See also CA 9-12R; 179; CANR 50, 85; CP 2, 3, 4; DLB 165

Schwitters, Kurt (Hermann Edward Karl Julius) 1887-1948 .... **TCLC 95**
See also CA 158

Schwob, Marcel (Mayer Andre) 1867-1905 .... **TCLC 20**
See also CA 117; 168; DLB 123; GFL 1789 to the Present

Sciascia, Leonardo 1921-1989 .. **CLC 8, 9, 41**
See also CA 85-88; 130; CANR 35; DLB 177; EWL 3; MTCW 1; RGWL 2, 3

Scoppettone, Sandra 1936- .... **CLC 26**
See Early, Jack
See also AAYA 11, 65; BYA 8; CA 5-8R; CANR 41, 73; GLL 1; MAICYA 2; MAICYAS 1; SATA 9, 92; WYA; YAW

Scorsese, Martin 1942- .... **CLC 20, 89, 207**
See also AAYA 38; CA 110; 114; CANR 46, 85

Scotland, Jay
See Jakes, John (William)

Scott, Duncan Campbell 1862-1947 .... **TCLC 6**
See also CA 104; 153; DAC; DLB 92; RGEL 2

Scott, Evelyn 1893-1963 .... **CLC 43**
See also CA 104; 112; CANR 64; DLB 9, 48; RHW

Scott, F(rancis) R(eginald) 1899-1985 .... **CLC 22**
See also CA 101; 114; CANR 87; CP 1, 2, 3, 4; DLB 88; INT CA-101; RGEL 2

Scott, Frank
See Scott, F(rancis) R(eginald)

Scott, Joan .... **CLC 65**

Scott, Joanna 1960- .... **CLC 50**
See also CA 126; CANR 53, 92

Scott, Paul (Mark) 1920-1978 .... **CLC 9, 60**
See also BRWS 1; CA 81-84; 77-80; CANR 33; CN 1, 2; DLB 14, 207; EWL 3; MTCW 1; RGEL 2; RHW; WWE 1

Scott, Ridley 1937- .... **CLC 183**
See also AAYA 13, 43

Scott, Sarah 1723-1795 .... **LC 44**
See also DLB 39

Scott, Sir Walter 1771-1832 .... **NCLC 15, 69, 110; PC 13; SSC 32; WLC**
See also AAYA 22; BRW 4; BYA 2; CD-BLB 1789-1832; DA; DAB; DAC; DAM MST, NOV, POET; DLB 93, 107, 116, 144, 159; GL 3; HGG; LAIT 1; RGEL 2; RGSF 2; SSFS 10; SUFW 1; TEA; WLIT 3; YABC 2

Scribe, (Augustin) Eugene 1791-1861 . **DC 5; NCLC 16**
See also DAM DRAM; DLB 192; GFL 1789 to the Present; RGWL 2, 3

Scrum, R.
See Crumb, R(obert)

Scudery, Georges de 1601-1667 .... **LC 75**
See also GFL Beginnings to 1789

Scudery, Madeleine de 1607-1701 .. **LC 2, 58**
See also DLB 268; GFL Beginnings to 1789

Scum
See Crumb, R(obert)

Scumbag, Little Bobby
See Crumb, R(obert)

Seabrook, John
See Hubbard, L(afayette) Ron(ald)

Seacole, Mary Jane Grant 1805-1881 .... **NCLC 147**
See also DLB 166

Sealy, I(rwin) Allan 1951- .... **CLC 55**
See also CA 136; CN 6, 7

Search, Alexander
See Pessoa, Fernando (Antonio Nogueira)

Sebald, W(infried) G(eorg) 1944-2001 .... **CLC 194**
See also BRWS 8; CA 159; 202; CANR 98; MTFW 2005

Sebastian, Lee
See Silverberg, Robert

Sebastian Owl
See Thompson, Hunter S(tockton)

Sebestyen, Igen
See Sebestyen, Ouida

Sebestyen, Ouida 1924- .... **CLC 30**
See also AAYA 8; BYA 7; CA 107; CANR 40, 114; CLR 17; JRDA; MAICYA 1, 2; SAAS 10; SATA 39, 140; WYA; YAW

Sebold, Alice 1963(?)- .... **CLC 193**
See also AAYA 56; CA 203; MTFW 2005

Second Duke of Buckingham
See Villiers, George

Secundus, H. Scriblerus
See Fielding, Henry

Sedges, John
See Buck, Pearl S(ydenstricker)

Sedgwick, Catharine Maria 1789-1867 .... **NCLC 19, 98**
See also DLB 1, 74, 183, 239, 243, 254; FL 1:3; RGAL 4

Seelye, John (Douglas) 1931- .... **CLC 7**
See also CA 97-100; CANR 70; INT CA-97-100; TCWW 1, 2

Seferiades, Giorgos Stylianou 1900-1971
See Seferis, George
See also CA 5-8R; 33-36R; CANR 5, 36; MTCW 1

Seferis, George .... **CLC 5, 11; PC 66**
See Seferiades, Giorgos Stylianou
See also EW 12; EWL 3; RGWL 2, 3

Segal, Erich (Wolf) 1937- .... **CLC 3, 10**
See also BEST 89:1; BPFB 3; CA 25-28R; CANR 20, 36, 65, 113; CPW; DAM POP; DLBY 1986; INT CANR-20; MTCW 1

Seger, Bob 1945- .... **CLC 35**

Seghers, Anna .... **CLC 7**
See Radvanyi, Netty
See also CDWLB 2; DLB 69; EWL 3

Seidel, Frederick (Lewis) 1936- .... **CLC 18**
See also CA 13-16R; CANR 8, 99; CP 1, 2, 3, 4, 5, 6, 7; DLBY 1984

Seifert, Jaroslav 1901-1986 . **CLC 34, 44, 93; PC 47**
See also CA 127; CDWLB 4; DLB 215; EWL 3; MTCW 1, 2

Sei Shonagon c. 966-1017(?) .... **CMLC 6**

Sejour, Victor 1817-1874 .... **DC 10**
See also DLB 50

Sejour Marcou et Ferrand, Juan Victor
See Sejour, Victor

Selby, Hubert, Jr. 1928-2004 ..... **CLC 1, 2, 4, 8; SSC 20**
See also CA 13-16R; 226; CANR 33, 85; CN 1, 2, 3, 4, 5, 6, 7; DLB 2, 227; MAL 5

Selzer, Richard 1928- .... **CLC 74**
See also CA 65-68; CANR 14, 106

Sembene, Ousmane
See Ousmane, Sembene
See also AFW; EWL 3; WLIT 2

Senancour, Etienne Pivert de 1770-1846 .... **NCLC 16**
See also DLB 119; GFL 1789 to the Present

Sender, Ramon (Jose) 1902-1982 ...... **CLC 8; HLC 2; TCLC 136**
See also CA 5-8R; 105; CANR 8; DAM MULT; DLB 322; EWL 3; HW 1; MTCW 1; RGWL 2, 3

Seneca, Lucius Annaeus c. 4B.C.-c. 65 .... **CMLC 6; DC 5**
See also AW 2; CDWLB 1; DAM DRAM; DLB 211; RGWL 2, 3; TWA

Simmons, Charles (Paul) 1924- .... **CLC 57**
   See also CA 89-92; INT CA-89-92

Simmons, Dan 1948- .... **CLC 44**
   See also AAYA 16, 54; CA 138; CANR 53, 81, 126; CPW; DAM POP; HGG; SUFW 2

Simmons, James (Stewart Alexander) 1933- .... **CLC 43**
   See also CA 105; CAAS 21; CP 1, 2, 3, 4, 5, 6, 7; DLB 40

Simms, William Gilmore 1806-1870 .... **NCLC 3**
   See also DLB 3, 30, 59, 73, 248, 254; RGAL 4

Simon, Carly 1945- .... **CLC 26**
   See also CA 105

Simon, Claude 1913-2005 ... **CLC 4, 9, 15, 39**
   See also CA 89-92; 241; CANR 33, 117; CWW 2; DAM NOV; DLB 83; EW 13; EWL 3; GFL 1789 to the Present; MTCW 1

Simon, Claude Eugene Henri
   See Simon, Claude

Simon, Claude Henri Eugene
   See Simon, Claude

Simon, Myles
   See Follett, Ken(neth Martin)

Simon, (Marvin) Neil 1927- ... **CLC 6, 11, 31, 39, 70; DC 14**
   See also AAYA 32; AITN 1; AMWS 4; CA 21-24R; CAD; CANR 26, 54, 87, 126; CD 5, 6; DA3; DAM DRAM; DFS 2, 6, 12, 18; DLB 7, 266; LAIT 4; MAL 5; MTCW 1, 2; MTFW 2005; RGAL 4; TUS

Simon, Paul (Frederick) 1941(?)- ..... **CLC 17**
   See also CA 116; 153

Simonon, Paul 1956(?)- .... **CLC 30**

Simonson, Rick ed. .... **CLC 70**

Simpson, Harriette
   See Arnow, Harriette (Louisa) Simpson

Simpson, Louis (Aston Marantz) 1923- .... **CLC 4, 7, 9, 32, 149**
   See also AMWS 9; CA 1-4R; CAAS 4; CANR 1, 61, 140; CP 1, 2, 3, 4, 5, 6, 7; DAM POET; DLB 5; MAL 5; MTCW 1, 2; MTFW 2005; PFS 7, 11, 14; RGAL 4

Simpson, Mona (Elizabeth) 1957- ... **CLC 44, 146**
   See also CA 122; 135; CANR 68, 103; CN 6, 7; EWL 3

Simpson, N(orman) F(rederick) 1919- .... **CLC 29**
   See also CA 13-16R; CBD; DLB 13; RGEL 2

Sinclair, Andrew (Annandale) 1935- . **CLC 2, 14**
   See also CA 9-12R; CAAS 5; CANR 14, 38, 91; CN 1, 2, 3, 4, 5, 6, 7; DLB 14; FANT; MTCW 1

Sinclair, Emil
   See Hesse, Hermann

Sinclair, Iain 1943- .... **CLC 76**
   See also CA 132; CANR 81; CP 7; HGG

Sinclair, Iain MacGregor
   See Sinclair, Iain

Sinclair, Irene
   See Griffith, D(avid Lewelyn) W(ark)

Sinclair, Mary Amelia St. Clair 1865(?)-1946
   See Sinclair, May
   See also CA 104; HGG; RHW

Sinclair, May .... **TCLC 3, 11**
   See Sinclair, Mary Amelia St. Clair
   See also CA 166; DLB 36, 135; EWL 3; RGEL 2; SUFW

Sinclair, Roy
   See Griffith, D(avid Lewelyn) W(ark)

Sinclair, Upton (Beall) 1878-1968 ..... **CLC 1, 11, 15, 63; TCLC 160; WLC**
   See also AAYA 63; AMWS 5; BPFB 3; BYA 2; CA 5-8R; 25-28R; CANR 7; CDALB 1929-1941; DA; DA3; DAB; DAC; DAM MST, NOV; DLB 9; EWL 3; INT CANR-7; LAIT 3; MAL 5; MTCW 1, 2; MTFW 2005; NFS 6; RGAL 4; SATA 9; TUS; YAW

Singe, (Edmund) J(ohn) M(illington) 1871-1909 .... **WLC**

Singer, Isaac
   See Singer, Isaac Bashevis

Singer, Isaac Bashevis 1904-1991 .. **CLC 1, 3, 6, 9, 11, 15, 23, 38, 69, 111; SSC 3, 53, 80; WLC**
   See also AAYA 32; AITN 1, 2; AMW; AMWR 2; BPFB 3; BYA 1, 4; CA 1-4R; 134; CANR 1, 39, 106; CDALB 1941-1968; CLR 1; CN 1, 2, 3, 4; CWRI 5; DA; DA3; DAB; DAC; DAM MST, NOV; DLB 6, 28, 52, 278; DLBY 1991; EWL 3; EXPS; HGG; JRDA; LAIT 3; MAI-CYA 1, 2; MAL 5; MTCW 1, 2; MTFW 2005; RGAL 4; RGSF 2; SATA 3, 27; SATA-Obit 68; SSFS 2, 12, 16; TUS; TWA

Singer, Israel Joshua 1893-1944 .... **TCLC 33**
   See also CA 169; EWL 3

Singh, Khushwant 1915- .... **CLC 11**
   See also CA 9-12R; CAAS 9; CANR 6, 84; CN 1, 2, 3, 4, 5, 6, 7; EWL 3; RGEL 2

Singleton, Ann
   See Benedict, Ruth (Fulton)

Singleton, John 1968(?)- .... **CLC 156**
   See also AAYA 50; BW 2, 3; CA 138; CANR 67, 82; DAM MULT

Siniavskii, Andrei
   See Sinyavsky, Andrei (Donatevich)
   See also CWW 2

Sinjohn, John
   See Galsworthy, John

Sinyavsky, Andrei (Donatevich) 1925-1997 .... **CLC 8**
   See Siniavskii, Andrei; Sinyavsky, Andrey Donatovich; Tertz, Abram
   See also CA 85-88; 159

Sinyavsky, Andrey Donatovich
   See Sinyavsky, Andrei (Donatevich)
   See also EWL 3

Sirin, V.
   See Nabokov, Vladimir (Vladimirovich)

Sissman, L(ouis) E(dward) 1928-1976 .... **CLC 9, 18**
   See also CA 21-24R; 65-68; CANR 13; CP 2; DLB 5

Sisson, C(harles) H(ubert) 1914-2003 .... **CLC 8**
   See also BRWS 11; CA 1-4R; 220; CAAS 3; CANR 3, 48, 84; CP 1, 2, 3, 4, 5, 6, 7; DLB 27

Sitting Bull 1831(?)-1890 .... **NNAL**
   See also DA3; DAM MULT

Sitwell, Dame Edith 1887-1964 ..... **CLC 2, 9, 67; PC 3**
   See also BRW 7; CA 9-12R; CANR 35; CDBLB 1945-1960; DAM POET; DLB 20; EWL 3; MTCW 1, 2; MTFW 2005; RGEL 2; TEA

Siwaarmill, H. P.
   See Sharp, William

Sjoewall, Maj 1935- .... **CLC 7**
   See Sjowall, Maj
   See also CA 65-68; CANR 73

Sjowall, Maj
   See Sjoewall, Maj
   See also BPFB 3; CMW 4; MSW

Skelton, John 1460(?)-1529 ..... **LC 71; PC 25**
   See also BRW 1; DLB 136; RGEL 2

Skelton, Robin 1925-1997 .... **CLC 13**
   See Zuk, Georges
   See also AITN 2; CA 5-8R; 160; CAAS 5; CANR 28, 89; CCA 1; CP 1, 2, 3, 4; DLB 27, 53

Skolimowski, Jerzy 1938- .... **CLC 20**
   See also CA 128

Skram, Amalie (Bertha) 1847-1905 .... **TCLC 25**
   See also CA 165

Skvorecky, Josef (Vaclav) 1924- ...... **CLC 15, 39, 69, 152**
   See also CA 61-64; CAAS 1; CANR 10, 34, 63, 108; CDWLB 4; CWW 2; DA3; DAC; DAM NOV; DLB 232; EWL 3; MTCW 1, 2; MTFW 2005

Slade, Bernard 1930- .... **CLC 11, 46**
   See Newbound, Bernard Slade
   See also CAAS 9; CCA 1; CD 6; DLB 53

Slaughter, Carolyn 1946- .... **CLC 56**
   See also CA 85-88; CANR 85; CN 5, 6, 7

Slaughter, Frank G(ill) 1908-2001 ... **CLC 29**
   See also AITN 2; CA 5-8R; 197; CANR 5, 85; INT CANR-5; RHW

Slavitt, David R(ytman) 1935- ..... **CLC 5, 14**
   See also CA 21-24R; CAAS 3; CANR 41, 83; CN 1, 2; CP 1, 2, 3, 4, 5, 6, 7; DLB 5, 6

Slesinger, Tess 1905-1945 .... **TCLC 10**
   See also CA 107; 199; DLB 102

Slessor, Kenneth 1901-1971 .... **CLC 14**
   See also CA 102; 89-92; DLB 260; RGEL 2

Slowacki, Juliusz 1809-1849 .... **NCLC 15**
   See also RGWL 3

Smart, Christopher 1722-1771 . **LC 3; PC 13**
   See also DAM POET; DLB 109; RGEL 2

Smart, Elizabeth 1913-1986 .... **CLC 54**
   See also CA 81-84; 118; CN 4; DLB 88

Smiley, Jane (Graves) 1949- ...... **CLC 53, 76, 144**
   See also AAYA 66; AMWS 6; BPFB 3; CA 104; CANR 30, 50, 74, 96; CN 6, 7; CPW 1; DA3; DAM POP; DLB 227, 234; EWL 3; INT CANR-30; MAL 5; MTFW 2005; SSFS 19

Smith, A(rthur) J(ames) M(arshall) 1902-1980 .... **CLC 15**
   See also CA 1-4R; 102; CANR 4; CP 1, 2, 3; DAC; DLB 88; RGEL 2

Smith, Adam 1723(?)-1790 .... **LC 36**
   See also DLB 104, 252; RGEL 2

Smith, Alexander 1829-1867 .... **NCLC 59**
   See also DLB 32, 55

Smith, Anna Deavere 1950- .... **CLC 86**
   See also CA 133; CANR 103; CD 5, 6; DFS 2, 22

Smith, Betty (Wehner) 1904-1972 .... **CLC 19**
   See also BPFB 3; BYA 3; CA 5-8R; 33-36R; DLBY 1982; LAIT 3; RGAL 4; SATA 6

Smith, Charlotte (Turner) 1749-1806 .... **NCLC 23, 115**
   See also DLB 39, 109; RGEL 2; TEA

Smith, Clark Ashton 1893-1961 .... **CLC 43**
   See also CA 143; CANR 81; FANT; HGG; MTCW 2; SCFW 1, 2; SFW 4; SUFW

Smith, Dave .... **CLC 22, 42**
   See Smith, David (Jeddie)
   See also CAAS 7; CP 3, 4, 5, 6, 7; DLB 5

Smith, David (Jeddie) 1942-
   See Smith, Dave
   See also CA 49-52; CANR 1, 59, 120; CSW; DAM POET

Smith, Florence Margaret 1902-1971
   See Smith, Stevie
   See also CA 17-18; 29-32R; CANR 35; CAP 2; DAM POET; MTCW 1, 2; TEA

Stephen, Adeline Virginia
　　See Woolf, (Adeline) Virginia

Stephen, Sir Leslie 1832-1904 .... **TCLC 23**
　　See also BRW 5; CA 123; DLB 57, 144, 190

Stephen, Sir Leslie
　　See Stephen, Sir Leslie

Stephen, Virginia
　　See Woolf, (Adeline) Virginia

Stephens, James 1882(?)-1950 .... **SSC 50; TCLC 4**
　　See also CA 104; 192; DLB 19, 153, 162; EWL 3; FANT; RGEL 2; SUFW

Stephens, Reed
　　See Donaldson, Stephen R(eeder)

Stephenson, Neal 1959- .... **CLC 220**
　　See also AAYA 38; CA 122; CANR 88, 138; CN 7; MTCW 2005; SFW 4

Steptoe, Lydia
　　See Barnes, Djuna
　　See also GLL 1

Sterchi, Beat 1949- .... **CLC 65**
　　See also CA 203

Sterling, Brett
　　See Bradbury, Ray (Douglas); Hamilton, Edmond

Sterling, Bruce 1954- .... **CLC 72**
　　See also CA 119; CANR 44, 135; CN 7; MTFW 2005; SCFW 2; SFW 4

Sterling, George 1869-1926 .... **TCLC 20**
　　See also CA 117; 165; DLB 54

Stern, Gerald 1925- .... **CLC 40, 100**
　　See also AMWS 9; CA 81-84; CANR 28, 94; CP 3, 4, 5, 6, 7; DLB 105; RGAL 4

Stern, Richard (Gustave) 1928- ... **CLC 4, 39**
　　See also CA 1-4R; CANR 1, 25, 52, 120; CN 1, 2, 3, 4, 5, 6, 7; DLB 218; DLBY 1987; INT CANR-25

Sternberg, Josef von 1894-1969 .... **CLC 20**
　　See also CA 81-84

Sterne, Laurence 1713-1768 .... **LC 2, 48; WLC**
　　See also BRW 3; BRWC 1; CDBLB 1660-1789; DA; DAB; DAC; DAM MST, NOV; DLB 39; RGEL 2; TEA

Sternheim, (William Adolf) Carl 1878-1942 .... **TCLC 8**
　　See also CA 105; 193; DLB 56, 118; EWL 3; IDTP; RGWL 2, 3

Stevens, Margaret Dean
　　See Aldrich, Bess Streeter

Stevens, Mark 1951- .... **CLC 34**
　　See also CA 122

Stevens, Wallace 1879-1955 . **PC 6; TCLC 3, 12, 45; WLC**
　　See also AMW; AMWR 1; CA 104; 124; CDALB 1929-1941; DA; DA3; DAB; DAC; DAM MST, POET; DLB 54; EWL 3; EXPP; MAL 5; MTCW 1, 2; PAB; PFS 13, 16; RGAL 4; TUS; WP

Stevenson, Anne (Katharine) 1933- .. **CLC 7, 33**
　　See also BRWS 6; CA 17-20R; CAAS 9; CANR 9, 33, 123; CP 3, 4, 5, 6, 7; CWP; DLB 40; MTCW 1; RHW

Stevenson, Robert Louis (Balfour) 1850-1894 ...... **NCLC 5, 14, 63; SSC 11, 51; WLC**
　　See also AAYA 24; BPFB 3; BRW 5; BRWC 1; BRWR 1; BYA 1, 2, 4, 13; CD-BLB 1890-1914; CLR 10, 11; DA; DA3; DAB; DAC; DAM MST, NOV; DLB 18, 57, 141, 156, 174; DLBD 13; GL 3; HGG; JRDA; LAIT 1, 3; MAICYA 1, 2; NFS 11, 20; RGEL 2; RGSF 2; SATA 100; SUFW; TEA; WCH; WLIT 4; WYA; YABC 2; YAW

Stewart, J(ohn) I(nnes) M(ackintosh) 1906-1994 .... **CLC 7, 14, 32**
　　See Innes, Michael
　　See also CA 85-88; 147; CAAS 3; CANR 47; CMW 4; CN 1, 2, 3, 4, 5; MTCW 1, 2

Stewart, Mary (Florence Elinor) 1916- .... **CLC 7, 35, 117**
　　See also AAYA 29; BPFB 3; CA 1-4R; CANR 1, 59, 130; CMW 4; CPW; DAB; FANT; RHW; SATA 12; YAW

Stewart, Mary Rainbow
　　See Stewart, Mary (Florence Elinor)

Stifle, June
　　See Campbell, Maria

Stifter, Adalbert 1805-1868 .. **NCLC 41; SSC 28**
　　See also CDWLB 2; DLB 133; RGSF 2; RGWL 2, 3

Still, James 1906-2001 .... **CLC 49**
　　See also CA 65-68; 195; CAAS 17; CANR 10, 26; CSW; DLB 9; DLBY 01; SATA 29; SATA-Obit 127

Sting 1951-
　　See Sumner, Gordon Matthew
　　See also CA 167

Stirling, Arthur
　　See Sinclair, Upton (Beall)

Stitt, Milan 1941- .... **CLC 29**
　　See also CA 69-72

Stockton, Francis Richard 1834-1902
　　See Stockton, Frank R.
　　See also AAYA 68; CA 108; 137; MAICYA 1, 2; SATA 44; SFW 4

Stockton, Frank R. .... **TCLC 47**
　　See Stockton, Francis Richard
　　See also BYA 4, 13; DLB 42, 74; DLBD 13; EXPS; SATA-Brief 32; SSFS 3; SUFW; WCH

Stoddard, Charles
　　See Kuttner, Henry

Stoker, Abraham 1847-1912
　　See Stoker, Bram
　　See also CA 105; 150; DA; DA3; DAC; DAM MST, NOV; HGG; MTFW 2005; SATA 29

Stoker, Bram .. **SSC 62; TCLC 8, 144; WLC**
　　See Stoker, Abraham
　　See also AAYA 23; BPFB 3; BRWS 3; BYA 5; CDBLB 1890-1914; DAB; DLB 304; GL 3; LATS 1:1; NFS 18; RGEL 2; SUFW; TEA; WLIT 4

Stolz, Mary (Slattery) 1920- .... **CLC 12**
　　See also AAYA 8; AITN 1; CA 5-8R; CANR 13, 41, 112; JRDA; MAICYA 1, 2; SAAS 3; SATA 10, 71, 133; YAW

Stone, Irving 1903-1989 .... **CLC 7**
　　See also AITN 1; BPFB 3; CA 1-4R; 129; CAAS 3; CANR 1, 23; CN 1, 2, 3, 4; CPW; DA3; DAM POP; INT CANR-23; MTCW 1, 2; MTFW 2005; RHW; SATA 3; SATA-Obit 64

Stone, Oliver (William) 1946- .... **CLC 73**
　　See also AAYA 15, 64; CA 110; CANR 55, 125

Stone, Robert (Anthony) 1937- ... **CLC 5, 23, 42, 175**
　　See also AMWS 5; BPFB 3; CA 85-88; CANR 23, 66, 95; CN 4, 5, 6, 7; DLB 152; EWL 3; INT CANR-23; MAL 5; MTCW 1; MTFW 2005

Stone, Ruth 1915- .... **PC 53**
　　See also CA 45-48; CANR 2, 91; CP 7; CSW; DLB 105; PFS 19

Stone, Zachary
　　See Follett, Ken(neth Martin)

Stoppard, Tom 1937- ... **CLC 1, 3, 4, 5, 8, 15, 29, 34, 63, 91; DC 6; WLC**
　　See also AAYA 63; BRWC 1; BRWR 2; BRWS 1; CA 81-84; CANR 39, 67, 125; CBD; CD 5, 6; CDBLB 1960 to Present; DA; DA3; DAB; DAC; DAM DRAM, MST; DFS 2, 5, 8, 11, 13, 16; DLB 13, 233; DLBY 1985; EWL 3; LATS 1:2; MTCW 1, 2; MTFW 2005; RGEL 2; TEA; WLIT 4

Storey, David (Malcolm) 1933- . **CLC 2, 4, 5, 8**
　　See also BRWS 1; CA 81-84; CANR 36; CBD; CD 5, 6; CN 1, 2, 3, 4, 5, 6; DAM DRAM; DLB 13, 14, 207, 245; EWL 3; MTCW 1; RGEL 2

Storm, Hyemeyohsts 1935- ... **CLC 3; NNAL**
　　See also CA 81-84; CANR 45; DAM MULT

Storm, (Hans) Theodor (Woldsen) 1817-1888 .... **NCLC 1; SSC 27**
　　See also CDWLB 2; DLB 129; EW; RGSF 2; RGWL 2, 3

Storni, Alfonsina 1892-1938 . **HLC 2; PC 33; TCLC 5**
　　See also CA 104; 131; DAM MULT; DLB 283; HW 1; LAW

Stoughton, William 1631-1701 .... **LC 38**
　　See also DLB 24

Stout, Rex (Todhunter) 1886-1975 ..... **CLC 3**
　　See also AITN 2; BPFB 3; CA 61-64; CANR 71; CMW 4; CN 2; DLB 306; MSW; RGAL 4

Stow, (Julian) Randolph 1935- ... **CLC 23, 48**
　　See also CA 13-16R; CANR 33; CN 1, 2, 3, 4, 5, 6, 7; CP 1, 2, 3, 4; DLB 260; MTCW 1; RGEL 2

Stowe, Harriet (Elizabeth) Beecher 1811-1896 .... **NCLC 3, 50, 133; WLC**
　　See also AAYA 53; AMWS 1; CDALB 1865-1917; DA; DA3; DAB; DAC; DAM MST, NOV; DLB 1, 12, 42, 74, 189, 239, 243; EXPN; FL 1:3; JRDA; LAIT 2; MAICYA 1, 2; NFS 6; RGAL 4; TUS; YABC 1

Strabo c. 64B.C.-c. 25 .... **CMLC 37**
　　See also DLB 176

Strachey, (Giles) Lytton 1880-1932 .... **TCLC 12**
　　See also BRWS 2; CA 110; 178; DLB 149; DLBD 10; EWL 3; MTCW 2; NCFS 4

Stramm, August 1874-1915 .... **PC 50**
　　See also CA 195; EWL 3

Strand, Mark 1934- .. **CLC 6, 18, 41, 71; PC 63**
　　See also AMWS 4; CA 21-24R; CANR 40, 65, 100; CP 1, 2, 3, 4, 5, 6, 7; DAM POET; DLB 5; EWL 3; MAL 5; PAB; PFS 9, 18; RGAL 4; SATA 41; TCLE 1:2

Stratton-Porter, Gene(va Grace) 1863-1924
　　See Porter, Gene(va Grace) Stratton
　　See also ANW; CA 137; CLR 87; DLB 221; DLBD 14; MAICYA 1, 2; SATA 15

Straub, Peter (Francis) 1943- ... **CLC 28, 107**
　　See also BEST 89:1; BPFB 3; CA 85-88; CANR 28, 65, 109; CPW; DAM POP; DLBY 1984; HGG; MTCW 1, 2; MTFW 2005; SUFW 2

Strauss, Botho 1944- .... **CLC 22**
　　See also CA 157; CWW 2; DLB 124

Strauss, Leo 1899-1973 .... **TCLC 141**
　　See also CA 101; 45-48; CANR 122

Streatfeild, (Mary) Noel 1897(?)-1986 .... **CLC 21**
　　See also CA 81-84; 120; CANR 31; CLR 17, 83; CWRI 5; DLB 160; MAICYA 1, 2; SATA 20; SATA-Obit 48

Stribling, T(homas) S(igismund) 1881-1965 .... **CLC 23**
　　See also CA 189; 107; CMW 4; DLB 9; RGAL 4

Synge, (Edmund) J(ohn) M(illington)
1871-1909 .... **DC 2; TCLC 6, 37**
See also BRW 6; BRWR 1; CA 104; 141;
CDBLB 1890-1914; DAM DRAM; DFS
18; DLB 10, 19; EWL 3; RGEL 2; TEA;
WLIT 4

Syruc, J.
See Milosz, Czeslaw

Szirtes, George 1948- .... **CLC 46; PC 51**
See also CA 109; CANR 27, 61, 117; CP 4,
5, 6, 7

Szymborska, Wislawa 1923- ... **CLC 99, 190;**
PC 44
See also CA 154; CANR 91, 133; CDWLB
4; CWP; CWW 2; DA3; DLB 232; DLBY
1996; EWL 3; MTCW 2; MTFW 2005;
PFS 15; RGWL 3

T. O., Nik
See Annensky, Innokenty (Fyodorovich)

Tabori, George 1914- .... **CLC 19**
See also CA 49-52; CANR 4, 69; CBD; CD
5, 6; DLB 245

Tacitus c. 55-c. 117 .... **CMLC 56**
See also AW 2; CDWLB 1; DLB 211;
RGWL 2, 3

Tagore, Rabindranath 1861-1941 .... **PC 8;**
SSC 48; TCLC 3, 53
See also CA 104; 120; DA3; DAM DRAM,
POET; EWL 3; MTCW 1, 2; MTFW
2005; PFS 18; RGEL 2; RGSF 2; RGWL
2, 3; TWA

Taine, Hippolyte Adolphe
1828-1893 .... **NCLC 15**
See also EW 7; GFL 1789 to the Present

Talayesva, Don C. 1890-(?) .... **NNAL**

Talese, Gay 1932- .... **CLC 37**
See also AITN 1; CA 1-4R; CANR 9, 58,
137; DLB 185; INT CANR-9; MTCW 1,
2; MTFW 2005

Tallent, Elizabeth (Ann) 1954- .... **CLC 45**
See also CA 117; CANR 72; DLB 130

Tallmountain, Mary 1918-1997 .... **NNAL**
See also CA 146; 161; DLB 193

Tally, Ted 1952- .... **CLC 42**
See also CA 120; 124; CAD; CANR 125;
CD 5, 6; INT CA-124

Talvik, Heiti 1904-1947 .... **TCLC 87**
See also EWL 3

Tamayo y Baus, Manuel
1829-1898 .... **NCLC 1**

Tammsaare, A(nton) H(ansen)
1878-1940 .... **TCLC 27**
See also CA 164; CDWLB 4; DLB 220;
EWL 3

Tam'si, Tchicaya U
See Tchicaya, Gerald Felix

Tan, Amy (Ruth) 1952- . **AAL; CLC 59, 120,**
151
See also AAYA 9, 48; AMWS 10; BEST
89:3; BPFB 3; CA 136; CANR 54, 105,
132; CDALBS; CN 6, 7; CPW 1; DA3;
DAM MULT, NOV, POP; DLB 173, 312;
EXPN; FL 1:6; FW; LAIT 3, 5; MAL 5;
MTCW 2; MTFW 2005; NFS 1, 13, 16;
RGAL 4; SATA 75; SSFS 9; YAW

Tandem, Felix
See Spitteler, Carl (Friedrich Georg)

Tanizaki, Jun'ichiro 1886-1965 ... **CLC 8, 14,**
28; SSC 21
See Tanizaki Jun'ichiro
See also CA 93-96; 25-28R; MJW; MTCW
2; MTFW 2005; RGSF 2; RGWL 2

Tanizaki Jun'ichiro
See Tanizaki, Jun'ichiro
See also DLB 180; EWL 3

Tannen, Deborah F(rances) 1945- .. **CLC 206**
See also CA 118; CANR 95

Tanner, William
See Amis, Kingsley (William)

Tao Lao
See Storni, Alfonsina

Tapahonso, Luci 1953- .... **NNAL; PC 65**
See also CA 145; CANR 72, 127; DLB 175

Tarantino, Quentin (Jerome)
1963- .... **CLC 125**
See also AAYA 58; CA 171; CANR 125

Tarassoff, Lev
See Troyat, Henri

Tarbell, Ida M(inerva) 1857-1944 . **TCLC 40**
See also CA 122; 181; DLB 47

Tarkington, (Newton) Booth
1869-1946 .... **TCLC 9**
See also BPFB 3; BYA 3; CA 110; 143;
CWRI 5; DLB 9, 102; MAL 5; MTCW 2;
RGAL 4; SATA 17

Tarkovskii, Andrei Arsen'evich
See Tarkovsky, Andrei (Arsenyevich)

Tarkovsky, Andrei (Arsenyevich)
1932-1986 .... **CLC 75**
See also CA 127

Tartt, Donna 1964(?)- .... **CLC 76**
See also AAYA 56; CA 142; CANR 135;
MTFW 2005

Tasso, Torquato 1544-1595 .... **LC 5, 94**
See also EFS 2; EW 2; RGWL 2, 3; WLIT
7

Tate, (John Orley) Allen 1899-1979 .. **CLC 2,**
4, 6, 9, 11, 14, 24; PC 50
See also AMW; CA 5-8R; 85-88; CANR
32, 108; CN 1, 2; CP 1; DLB 4, 45, 63;
DLBD 17; EWL 3; MAL 5; MTCW 1, 2;
MTFW 2005; RGAL 4; RHW

Tate, Ellalice
See Hibbert, Eleanor Alice Burford

Tate, James (Vincent) 1943- ...... **CLC 2, 6, 25**
See also CA 21-24R; CANR 29, 57, 114;
CP 1, 2, 3, 4, 5, 6, 7; DLB 5, 169; EWL
3; PFS 10, 15; RGAL 4; WP

Tate, Nahum 1652(?)-1715 .... **LC 109**
See also DLB 80; RGEL 2

Tauler, Johannes c. 1300-1361 ...... **CMLC 37**
See also DLB 179; LMFS 1

Tavel, Ronald 1940- .... **CLC 6**
See also CA 21-24R; CAD; CANR 33; CD
5, 6

Taviani, Paolo 1931- .... **CLC 70**
See also CA 153

Taylor, Bayard 1825-1878 .... **NCLC 89**
See also DLB 3, 189, 250, 254; RGAL 4

Taylor, C(ecil) P(hilip) 1929-1981 .... **CLC 27**
See also CA 25-28R; 105; CANR 47; CBD

Taylor, Edward 1642(?)-1729 . **LC 11; PC 63**
See also AMW; DA; DAB; DAC; DAM
MST, POET; DLB 24; EXPP; RGAL 4;
TUS

Taylor, Eleanor Ross 1920- .... **CLC 5**
See also CA 81-84; CANR 70

Taylor, Elizabeth 1912-1975 ...... **CLC 2, 4, 29**
See also CA 13-16R; CANR 9, 70; CN 1,
2; DLB 139; MTCW 1; RGEL 2; SATA
13

Taylor, Frederick Winslow
1856-1915 .... **TCLC 76**
See also CA 188

Taylor, Henry (Splawn) 1942- .... **CLC 44**
See also CA 33-36R; CAAS 7; CANR 31;
CP 7; DLB 5; PFS 10

Taylor, Kamala (Purnaiya) 1924-2004
See Markandaya, Kamala
See also CA 77-80; 227; MTFW 2005; NFS
13

Taylor, Mildred D(elois) 1943- .... **CLC 21**
See also AAYA 10, 47; BW 1; BYA 3, 8;
CA 85-88; CANR 25, 115, 136; CLR 9,
59, 90; CSW; DLB 52; JRDA; LAIT 3;
MAICYA 1, 2; MTFW 2005; SAAS 5;
SATA 135; WYA; YAW

Taylor, Peter (Hillsman) 1917-1994 .. **CLC 1,**
4, 18, 37, 44, 50, 71; SSC 10, 84
See also AMWS 5; BPFB 3; CA 13-16R;
147; CANR 9, 50; CN 1, 2, 3, 4, 5; CSW;
DLB 218, 278; DLBY 1981, 1994; EWL
3; EXPS; INT CANR-9; MAL 5; MTCW
1, 2; MTFW 2005; RGSF 2; SSFS 9; TUS

Taylor, Robert Lewis 1912-1998 .... **CLC 14**
See also CA 1-4R; 170; CANR 3, 64; CN
1, 2; SATA 10; TCWW 1, 2

Tchekhov, Anton
See Chekhov, Anton (Pavlovich)

Tchicaya, Gerald Felix 1931-1988 .. **CLC 101**
See Tchicaya U Tam'si
See also CA 129; 125; CANR 81

Tchicaya U Tam'si
See Tchicaya, Gerald Felix
See also EWL 3

Teasdale, Sara 1884-1933 .... **PC 31; TCLC 4**
See also CA 104; 163; DLB 45; GLL 1;
PFS 14; RGAL 4; SATA 32; TUS

Tecumseh 1768-1813 .... **NNAL**
See also DAM MULT

Tegner, Esaias 1782-1846 .... **NCLC 2**

Teilhard de Chardin, (Marie Joseph) Pierre
1881-1955 .... **TCLC 9**
See also CA 105; 210; GFL 1789 to the
Present

Temple, Ann
See Mortimer, Penelope (Ruth)

Tennant, Emma (Christina) 1937- .. **CLC 13,**
52
See also BRWS 9; CA 65-68; CAAS 9;
CANR 10, 38, 59, 88; CN 3, 4, 5, 6, 7;
DLB 14; EWL 3; SFW 4

Tenneshaw, S. M.
See Silverberg, Robert

Tenney, Tabitha Gilman
1762-1837 .... **NCLC 122**
See also DLB 37, 200

Tennyson, Alfred 1809-1892 ... **NCLC 30, 65,**
115; PC 6; WLC
See also AAYA 50; BRW 4; CDBLB 1832-
1890; DA; DA3; DAB; DAC; DAM MST,
POET; DLB 32; EXPP; PAB; PFS 1, 2, 4,
11, 15, 19; RGEL 2; TEA; WLIT 4; WP

Teran, Lisa St. Aubin de .... **CLC 36**
See St. Aubin de Teran, Lisa

Terence c. 184B.C.-c. 159B.C. .... **CMLC 14;**
DC 7
See also AW 1; CDWLB 1; DLB 211;
RGWL 2, 3; TWA

Teresa de Jesus, St. 1515-1582 .... **LC 18**

Teresa of Avila, St.
See Teresa de Jesus, St.

Terkel, Louis 1912-
See Terkel, Studs
See also CA 57-60; CANR 18, 45, 67, 132;
DA3; MTCW 1, 2; MTFW 2005

Terkel, Studs .... **CLC 38**
See Terkel, Louis
See also AAYA 32; AITN 1; MTCW 2; TUS

Terry, C. V.
See Slaughter, Frank G(ill)

Terry, Megan 1932- .... **CLC 19; DC 13**
See also CA 77-80; CABS 3; CAD; CANR
43; CD 5, 6; CWD; DFS 18; DLB 7, 249;
GLL 2

Tertullian c. 155-c. 245 .... **CMLC 29**

Tertz, Abram
See Sinyavsky, Andrei (Donatevich)
See also RGSF 2

Tesich, Steve 1943(?)-1996 .... **CLC 40, 69**
See also CA 105; 152; CAD; DLBY 1983

Tesla, Nikola 1856-1943 .... **TCLC 88**

Teternikov, Fyodor Kuzmich 1863-1927
See Sologub, Fyodor
See also CA 104

Trogdon, William (Lewis) 1939-
See Heat-Moon, William Least
See also AAYA 66; CA 115; 119; CANR
47, 89; CPW; INT CA-119

Trollope, Anthony 1815-1882 .... **NCLC 6, 33, 101; SSC 28; WLC**
See also BRW 5; CDBLB 1832-1890; DA;
DA3; DAB; DAC; DAM MST, NOV;
DLB 21, 57, 159; RGEL 2; RGSF 2;
SATA 22

Trollope, Frances 1779-1863 .... **NCLC 30**
See also DLB 21, 166

Trollope, Joanna 1943- .... **CLC 186**
See also CA 101; CANR 58, 95; CN 7;
CPW; DLB 207; RHW

Trotsky, Leon 1879-1940 .... **TCLC 22**
See also CA 118; 167

Trotter (Cockburn), Catharine
1679-1749 .... **LC 8**
See also DLB 84, 252

Trotter, Wilfred 1872-1939 .... **TCLC 97**

Trout, Kilgore
See Farmer, Philip Jose

Trow, George W. S. 1943- .... **CLC 52**
See also CA 126; CANR 91

Troyat, Henri 1911- .... **CLC 23**
See also CA 45-48; CANR 2, 33, 67, 117;
GFL 1789 to the Present; MTCW 1

Trudeau, G(arretson) B(eekman) 1948-
See Trudeau, Garry B.
See also AAYA 60; CA 81-84; CANR 31;
SATA 35

Trudeau, Garry B. .... **CLC 12**
See Trudeau, G(arretson) B(eekman)
See also AAYA 10; AITN 2

Truffaut, Francois 1932-1984 ... **CLC 20, 101**
See also CA 81-84; 113; CANR 34

Trumbo, Dalton 1905-1976 .... **CLC 19**
See also CA 21-24R; 69-72; CANR 10; CN
1, 2; DLB 26; IDFW 3, 4; YAW

Trumbull, John 1750-1831 .... **NCLC 30**
See also DLB 31; RGAL 4

Trundlett, Helen B.
See Eliot, T(homas) S(tearns)

Truth, Sojourner 1797(?)-1883 ...... **NCLC 94**
See also DLB 239; FW; LAIT 2

Tryon, Thomas 1926-1991 .... **CLC 3, 11**
See also AITN 1; BPFB 3; CA 29-32R; 135;
CANR 32, 77; CPW; DA3; DAM POP;
HGG; MTCW 1

Tryon, Tom
See Tryon, Thomas

Ts'ao Hsueh-ch'in 1715(?)-1763 .... **LC 1**

Tsushima, Shuji 1909-1948
See Dazai Osamu
See also CA 107

Tsvetaeva (Efron), Marina (Ivanovna)
1892-1941 .... **PC 14; TCLC 7, 35**
See also CA 104; 128; CANR 73; DLB 295;
EW 11; MTCW 1, 2; RGWL 2, 3

Tuck, Lily 1938- .... **CLC 70**
See also CA 139; CANR 90

Tu Fu 712-770 .... **PC 9**
See Du Fu
See also DAM MULT; TWA; WP

Tunis, John R(oberts) 1889-1975 ..... **CLC 12**
See also BYA 1; CA 61-64; CANR 62; DLB
22, 171; JRDA; MAICYA 1, 2; SATA 37;
SATA-Brief 30; YAW

Tuohy, Frank .... **CLC 37**
See Tuohy, John Francis
See also CN 1, 2, 3, 4, 5, 6, 7; DLB 14,
139

Tuohy, John Francis 1925-
See Tuohy, Frank
See also CA 5-8R; 178; CANR 3, 47

Turco, Lewis (Putnam) 1934- ..... **CLC 11, 63**
See also CA 13-16R; CAAS 22; CANR 24,
51; CP 1, 2, 3, 4, 5, 6, 7; DLBY 1984;
TCLE 1:2

Turgenev, Ivan (Sergeevich)
1818-1883 ..... **DC 7; NCLC 21, 37, 122;
SSC 7, 57; WLC**
See also AAYA 58; DA; DAB; DAC; DAM
MST, NOV; DFS 6; DLB 238, 284; EW
6; LATS 1:1; NFS 16; RGSF 2; RGWL 2,
3; TWA

Turgot, Anne-Robert-Jacques
1727-1781 .... **LC 26**
See also DLB 314

Turner, Frederick 1943- .... **CLC 48**
See also CA 73-76, 227; CAAE 227; CAAS
10; CANR 12, 30, 56; DLB 40, 282

Turton, James
See Crace, Jim

Tutu, Desmond M(pilo) 1931- .. **BLC 3; CLC
80**
See also BW 1, 3; CA 125; CANR 67, 81;
DAM MULT

Tutuola, Amos 1920-1997 ..... **BLC 3; CLC 5,
14, 29**
See also AFW; BW 2, 3; CA 9-12R; 159;
CANR 27, 66; CDWLB 3; CN 1, 2, 3, 4,
5, 6; DA3; DAM MULT; DLB 125; DNFS
2; EWL 3; MTCW 1, 2; MTFW 2005;
RGEL 2; WLIT 2

Twain, Mark .... **SSC 6, 26, 34, 87; TCLC 6,
12, 19, 36, 48, 59, 161; WLC**
See Clemens, Samuel Langhorne
See also AAYA 20; AMW; AMWC 1; BPFB
3; BYA 2, 3, 11, 14; CLR 58, 60, 66; DLB
11; EXPN; EXPS; FANT; LAIT 2; MAL
5; NCFS 4; NFS 1, 6; RGAL 4; RGSF 2;
SFW 4; SSFS 1, 7, 16, 21; SUFW; TUS;
WCH; WYA; YAW

Tyler, Anne 1941- . **CLC 7, 11, 18, 28, 44, 59,
103, 205**
See also AAYA 18, 60; AMWS 4; BEST
89:1; BPFB 3; BYA 12; CA 9-12R; CANR
11, 33, 53, 109, 132; CDALBS; CN 1, 2,
3, 4, 5, 6, 7; CPW; CSW; DAM NOV,
POP; DLB 6, 143; DLBY 1982; EWL 3;
EXPN; LATS 1:2; MAL 5; MAWW;
MTCW 1, 2; MTFW 2005; NFS 2, 7, 10;
RGAL 4; SATA 7, 90; SSFS 17; TCLE
1:2; TUS; YAW

Tyler, Royall 1757-1826 .... **NCLC 3**
See also DLB 37; RGAL 4

Tynan, Katharine 1861-1931 .... **TCLC 3**
See also CA 104; 167; DLB 153, 240; FW

Tyndale, William c. 1484-1536 .... **LC 103**
See also DLB 132

Tyutchev, Fyodor 1803-1873 .... **NCLC 34**

Tzara, Tristan 1896-1963 .... **CLC 47; PC 27;
TCLC 168**
See also CA 153; 89-92; DAM POET; EWL
3; MTCW 2

Uchida, Yoshiko 1921-1992 .... **AAL**
See also AAYA 16; BYA 2, 3; CA 13-16R;
139; CANR 6, 22, 47, 61; CDALBS; CLR
6, 56; CWRI 5; DLB 312; JRDA; MAI-
CYA 1, 2; MTCW 1, 2; MTFW 2005;
SAAS 1; SATA 1, 53; SATA-Obit 72

Udall, Nicholas 1504-1556 .... **LC 84**
See also DLB 62; RGEL 2

Ueda Akinari 1734-1809 .... **NCLC 131**

Uhry, Alfred 1936- .... **CLC 55**
See also CA 127; 133; CAD; CANR 112;
CD 5, 6; CSW; DA3; DAM DRAM, POP;
DFS 11, 15; INT CA-133; MTFW 2005

Ulf, Haerved
See Strindberg, (Johan) August

Ulf, Harved
See Strindberg, (Johan) August

Ulibarri, Sabine R(eyes)
1919-2003 .... **CLC 83; HLCS 2**
See also CA 131; 214; CANR 81; DAM
MULT; DLB 82; HW 1, 2; RGSF 2

Unamuno (y Jugo), Miguel de
1864-1936 .. **HLC 2; SSC 11, 69; TCLC
2, 9, 148**
See also CA 104; 131; CANR 81; DAM
MULT, NOV; DLB 108, 322; EW 8; EWL
3; HW 1, 2; MTCW 1, 2; MTFW 2005;
RGSF 2; RGWL 2, 3; SSFS 20; TWA

Uncle Shelby
See Silverstein, Shel(don Allan)

Undercliffe, Errol
See Campbell, (John) Ramsey

Underwood, Miles
See Glassco, John

Undset, Sigrid 1882-1949 ..... **TCLC 3; WLC**
See also CA 104; 129; DA; DA3; DAB;
DAC; DAM MST, NOV; DLB 293; EW
9; EWL 3; FW; MTCW 1, 2; MTFW
2005; RGWL 2, 3

Ungaretti, Giuseppe 1888-1970 ... **CLC 7, 11,
15; PC 57**
See also CA 19-20; 25-28R; CAP 2; DLB
114; EW 10; EWL 3; PFS 20; RGWL 2,
3; WLIT 7

Unger, Douglas 1952- .... **CLC 34**
See also CA 130; CANR 94

Unsworth, Barry (Forster) 1930- .... **CLC 76,
127**
See also BRWS 7; CA 25-28R; CANR 30,
54, 125; CN 6, 7; DLB 194

Updike, John (Hoyer) 1932- . **CLC 1, 2, 3, 5,
7, 9, 13, 15, 23, 34, 43, 70, 139, 214;
SSC 13, 27; WLC**
See also AAYA 36; AMW; AMWC 1;
AMWR 1; BPFB 3; BYA 12; CA 1-4R;
CABS 1; CANR 4, 33, 51, 94, 133;
CDALB 1968-1988; CN 1, 2, 3, 4, 5, 6,
7; CP 1, 2, 3, 4, 5, 6, 7; CPW 1; DA;
DA3; DAB; DAC; DAM MST, NOV,
POET, POP; DLB 2, 5, 143, 218, 227;
DLBD 3; DLBY 1980, 1982, 1997; EWL
3; EXPP; HGG; MAL 5; MTCW 1, 2;
MTFW 2005; NFS 12; RGAL 4; RGSF 2;
SSFS 3, 19; TUS

Upshaw, Margaret Mitchell
See Mitchell, Margaret (Munnerlyn)

Upton, Mark
See Sanders, Lawrence

Upward, Allen 1863-1926 .... **TCLC 85**
See also CA 117; 187; DLB 36

Urdang, Constance (Henriette)
1922-1996 .... **CLC 47**
See also CA 21-24R; CANR 9, 24; CP 1, 2,
3, 4; CWP

Uriel, Henry
See Faust, Frederick (Schiller)

Uris, Leon (Marcus) 1924-2003 ... **CLC 7, 32**
See also AITN 1, 2; BEST 89:2; BPFB 3;
CA 1-4R; 217; CANR 1, 40, 65, 123; CN
1, 2, 3, 4, 5, 6; CPW 1; DA3; DAM NOV,
POP; MTCW 1, 2; MTFW 2005; SATA
49; SATA-Obit 146

Urista (Heredia), Alberto (Baltazar)
1947- .... **HLCS 1**
See Alurista
See also CA 182; CANR 2, 32; HW 1

Urmuz
See Codrescu, Andrei

Urquhart, Guy
See McAlmon, Robert (Menzies)

Urquhart, Jane 1949- .... **CLC 90**
See also CA 113; CANR 32, 68, 116; CCA
1; DAC

Usigli, Rodolfo 1905-1979 .... **HLCS 1**
See also CA 131; DLB 305; EWL 3; HW 1;
LAW

Zangwill, Israel 1864-1926 ... **SSC 44; TCLC 16**
See also CA 109; 167; CMW 4; DLB 10, 135, 197; RGEL 2

Zanzotto, Andrea 1921- .... **PC 65**
See also CA 208; CWW 2; DLB 128; EWL 3

Zappa, Francis Vincent, Jr. 1940-1993
See Zappa, Frank
See also CA 108; 143; CANR 57

Zappa, Frank .... **CLC 17**
See Zappa, Francis Vincent, Jr.

Zaturenska, Marya 1902-1982 ..... **CLC 6, 11**
See also CA 13-16R; 105; CANR 22; CP 1, 2, 3

Zayas y Sotomayor, Maria de 1590-c. 1661 .... **LC 102**
See also RGSF 2

Zeami 1363-1443 .... **DC 7; LC 86**
See also DLB 203; RGWL 2, 3

Zelazny, Roger (Joseph) 1937-1995 . **CLC 21**
See also AAYA 7, 68; BPFB 3; CA 21-24R; 148; CANR 26, 60; CN 6; DLB 8; FANT; MTCW 1, 2; MTFW 2005; SATA 57; SATA-Brief 39; SCFW 1, 2; SFW 4; SUFW 1, 2

Zhang Ailing
See Chang, Eileen
See also CWW 2; RGSF 2

Zhdanov, Andrei Alexandrovich
1896-1948 .... **TCLC 18**
See also CA 117; 167

Zhukovsky, Vasilii Andreevich
See Zhukovsky, Vasily (Andreevich)
See also DLB 205

Zhukovsky, Vasily (Andreevich)
1783-1852 .... **NCLC 35**
See Zhukovsky, Vasilii Andreevich

Ziegenhagen, Eric .... **CLC 55**

Zimmer, Jill Schary
See Robinson, Jill

Zimmerman, Robert
See Dylan, Bob

Zindel, Paul 1936-2003 ...... **CLC 6, 26; DC 5**
See also AAYA 2, 37; BYA 2, 3, 8, 11, 14; CA 73-76; 213; CAD; CANR 31, 65, 108; CD 5, 6; CDALBS; CLR 3, 45, 85; DA; DA3; DAB; DAC; DAM DRAM, MST, NOV; DFS 12; DLB 7, 52; JRDA; LAIT 5; MAICYA 1, 2; MTCW 1, 2; MTFW 2005; NFS 14; SATA 16, 58, 102; SATA-Obit 142; WYA; YAW

Zinn, Howard 1922- .... **CLC 199**
See also CA 1-4R; CANR 2, 33, 90

Zinov'Ev, A. A.
See Zinoviev, Alexander (Aleksandrovich)

Zinov'ev, Aleksandr (Aleksandrovich)
See Zinoviev, Alexander (Aleksandrovich)
See also DLB 302

Zinoviev, Alexander (Aleksandrovich)
1922- .... **CLC 19**
See Zinov'ev, Aleksandr (Aleksandrovich)
See also CA 116; 133; CAAS 10

Zizek, Slavoj 1949- .... **CLC 188**
See also CA 201; MTFW 2005

Zoilus
See Lovecraft, H(oward) P(hillips)

Zola, Emile (Edouard Charles Antoine)
1840-1902 ...... **TCLC 1, 6, 21, 41; WLC**
See also CA 104; 138; DA; DA3; DAB; DAC; DAM MST, NOV; DLB 123; EW 7; GFL 1789 to the Present; IDTP; LMFS 1, 2; RGWL 2; TWA

Zoline, Pamela 1941- .... **CLC 62**
See also CA 161; SFW 4

Zoroaster 628(?)B.C.-551(?)B.C. ... **CMLC 40**

Zorrilla y Moral, Jose 1817-1893 .... **NCLC 6**

Zoshchenko, Mikhail (Mikhailovich)
1895-1958 .... **SSC 15; TCLC 15**
See also CA 115; 160; EWL 3; RGSF 2; RGWL 3

Zuckmayer, Carl 1896-1977 .... **CLC 18**
See also CA 69-72; DLB 56, 124; EWL 3; RGWL 2, 3

Zuk, Georges
See Skelton, Robin
See also CCA 1

Zukofsky, Louis 1904-1978 ... **CLC 1, 2, 4, 7, 11, 18; PC 11**
See also AMWS 3; CA 9-12R; 77-80; CANR 39; CP 1, 2; DAM POET; DLB 5, 165; EWL 3; MAL 5; MTCW 1; RGAL 4

Zweig, Paul 1935-1984 .... **CLC 34, 42**
See also CA 85-88; 113

Zweig, Stefan 1881-1942 .... **TCLC 17**
See also CA 112; 170; DLB 81, 118; EWL 3

Zwingli, Huldreich 1484-1531 .... **LC 37**
See also DLB 179

PC Cumulative Nationality Index

AMERICAN

Aiken, Conrad (Potter) **26**
Alexie, Sherman **53**
Ammons, A(rchie) R(andolph) **16**
Angelou, Maya **32**
Ashbery, John (Lawrence) **26**
Auden, W(ystan) H(ugh) **1**
Baca, Jimmy Santiago **41**
Baraka, Amiri **4**
Benét, Stephen Vincent **64**
Berry, Wendell (Erdman) **28**
Berryman, John **64**
Bishop, Elizabeth **3, 34**
Bly, Robert (Elwood) **39**
Bogan, Louise **12**
Bradstreet, Anne **10**
Braithwaite, William **52**
Brodsky, Joseph **9**
Brooks, Gwendolyn (Elizabeth) **7**
Brown, Sterling Allen **55**
Bryant, William Cullen **20**
Bukowski, Charles **18**
Cage, John **58**
Carruth, Hayden **10**
Carver, Raymond **54**
Cervantes, Lorna Dee **35**
Chin, Marilyn (Mei Ling) **40**
Ciardi, John **69**
Cisneros, Sandra **52**
Clampitt, Amy **19**
Clifton, (Thelma) Lucille **17**
Collins, Billy **68**
Corso, (Nunzio) Gregory **33**
Crane, (Harold) Hart **3**
Cullen, Countée **20**
Cummings, E(dward) E(stlin) **5**
Dickey, James (Lafayette) **40**
Dickinson, Emily (Elizabeth) **1**
Doolittle, Hilda **5**
Doty, Mark **53**
Dove, Rita (Frances) **6**
Dunbar, Paul Laurence **5**
Duncan, Robert (Edward) **2**
Dylan, Bob **37**
Eliot, T(homas) S(tearns) **5, 31**
Emerson, Ralph Waldo **18**
Erdrich, Louise **52**
Ferlinghetti, Lawrence (Monsanto) **1**
Forché, Carolyn (Louise) **10**
Francis, Robert (Churchill) **34**
Frost, Robert (Lee) **1, 39, 71**
Gallagher, Tess **9**
Ginsberg, Allen **4, 47**
Giovanni, Nikki **19**
Glück, Louise (Elisabeth) **16**
Graham, Jorie **59**

Guest, Barbara **55**
Hacker, Marilyn **47**
Hall, Donald **70**
Hammon, Jupiter **16**
Harjo, Joy **27**
Harper, Frances Ellen Watkins **21**
Hass, Robert **16**
Hayden, Robert E(arl) **6**
H. D. **5**
Hecht, Anthony **70**
Hogan, Linda **35**
Holmes, Oliver Wendell **71**
Hongo, Garrett Kaoru **23**
Howe, Susan **54**
Hughes, (James) Langston **1, 53**
Hugo, Richard **68**
Ignatow, David **34**
Jackson, Laura (Riding) **44**
Jacobsen, Josephine **62**
Jarrell, Randall **41**
Jeffers, (John) Robinson **17**
Johnson, James Weldon **24**
Jordan, June **38**
Justice, Donald **64**
Kenyon, Jane **57**
Kinnell, Galway **26**
Kizer, Carolyn **66**
Knight, Etheridge **14**
Komunyakaa, Yusef **51**
Kumin, Maxine (Winokur) **15**
Kunitz, Stanley (Jasspon) **19**
Lanier, Sidney **50**
Levertov, Denise **11**
Levine, Philip **22**
Lindsay, (Nicholas) Vachel **23**
Longfellow, Henry Wadsworth **30**
Lorde, Audre (Geraldine) **12**
Lowell, Amy **13**
Lowell, Robert (Traill Spence Jr.) **3**
Loy, Mina **16**
MacLeish, Archibald **47**
Mackey, Nathaniel **49**
Madhubuti, Haki R. **5**
Masters, Edgar Lee **1, 36**
McHugh, Heather **61**
Meredith, William (Morris) **28**
Merrill, James (Ingram) **28**
Merton, Thomas **10**
Merwin, W. S. **45**
Millay, Edna St. Vincent **6, 61**
Momaday, N(avarre) Scott **25**
Moore, Marianne (Craig) **4, 49**
Mueller, Lisel **33**
Nash, (Frediric) Ogden **21**
Nemerov, Howard (Stanley) **24**
Niedecker, Lorine **42**

O'Hara, Frank **45**
Olds, Sharon **22**
Olson, Charles (John) **19**
Oppen, George **35**
Ortiz, Simon J(oseph) **17**
Parker, Dorothy (Rothschild) **28**
Piercy, Marge **29**
Pinsky, Robert **27**
Plath, Sylvia **1, 37**
Poe, Edgar Allan **1, 54**
Pound, Ezra (Weston Loomis) **4**
Quintana, Leroy V. **36**
Ransom, John Crowe **61**
Reed, Ishmael **68**
Reese, Lizette Woodworth **29**
Rexroth, Kenneth **20**
Rich, Adrienne (Cecile) **5**
Riley, James Whitcomb **48**
Ríos, Alberto **57**
Robinson, Edwin Arlington **1, 35**
Roethke, Theodore (Huebner) **15**
Rose, Wendy **13**
Rukeyser, Muriel **12**
Sanchez, Sonia **9**
Sandburg, Carl (August) **2, 41**
Sarton, (Eleanor) May **39**
Schwartz, Delmore (David) **8**
Schnackenberg, Gjertrud **45**
Schwerner, Armand **42**
Sexton, Anne (Harvey) **2**
Shapiro, Karl (Jay) **25**
Silverstein, Shel **49**
Simic, Charles **69**
Snyder, Gary (Sherman) **21**
Song, Cathy **21**
Soto, Gary **28**
Stafford, William **71**
Stein, Gertrude **18**
Stevens, Wallace **6**
Stone, Ruth **53**
Strand, Mark **63**
Stryk, Lucien **27**
Swenson, May **14**
Tapahonso, Luci **65**
Tate, Allen **50**
Taylor, Edward **63**
Teasdale, Sara **31**
Thoreau, Henry David **30**
Toomer, Jean **7**
Urista, Alberto H. **34**
Viereck, Peter (Robert Edwin) **27**
Wagoner, David (Russell) **33**
Wakoski, Diane **15**
Walker, Alice (Malsenior) **30**
Walker, Margaret (Abigail) **20**
Warren, Robert Penn **37**

ITALIAN

Ariosto, Ludovico **42**
Carducci, Giosue **46**
Dante **21**
Gozzano, Guido **10**
Leopardi, Giacomo **37**
Martial **10**
Montale, Eugenio **13**
Pasolini, Pier Paolo **17**
Pavese, Cesare **13**
Petrarch **8**
Quasimodo, Salvatore **47**
Stampa, Gaspara **43**
Ungaretti, Giuseppe **57**
Zanzotto, Andrea **65**

JAMAICAN

Goodison, Lorna **36**

JAPANESE

Hagiwara, Sakutaro **18**
Ishikawa, Takuboku **10**
Matsuo Basho **3**
Nishiwaki, Junzaburō **15**
Yosano Akiko **11**

LEBANESE

Gibran, Kahlil **9**

MARTINICAN

Césaire, Aimé (Fernand) **25**

MEXICAN

Juana Inés de la Cruz **24**
Paz, Octavio **1**, **48**
Urista, Alberto H. **34**

NEW ZEALAND

Curnow, (Thomas) Allen (Monro) **48**

NICARAGUAN

Alegria, Claribel **26**
Cardenal, Ernesto **22**
Darío, Rubén **15**

NIGERIAN

Okigbo, Christopher (Ifenayichukwu) **7**

PERSIAN

Khayyam, Omar **8**
Rumi, Jalâl al-Din **45**

POLISH

Herbert, Zbigniew **50**
Mickiewicz, Adam **38**
Milosz, Czeslaw **8**
Szymborska, Wisława **44**
Zagajewski, Adam **27**

PORTUGUESE

Camões, Luís de **31**
Pessoa, Fernando (António Nogueira) **20**

PUERTO RICAN

Cruz, Victor Hernández **37**

ROMAN

Horace **46**
Martial **10**
Ovid **2**
Vergil **12**

ROMANIAN

Cassian, Nina **17**
Celan, Paul **10**
Tzara, Tristan **27**

RUSSIAN

Akhmadulina, Bella **43**
Akhmatova, Anna **2**, **55**
Bely, Andrey **11**
Blok, Alexander (Alexandrovich) **21**
Brodsky, Joseph **9**
Lermontov, Mikhail Yuryevich **18**
Mandelstam, Osip (Emilievich) **14**
Pasternak, Boris (Leonidovich) **6**
Pushkin, Alexander (Sergeyevich) **10**
Shvarts, Elena **50**

Tsvetaeva (Efron), Marina (Ivanovna) **14**
Yevtushenko, Yevgeny (Alexandrovich) **40**

SALVADORAN

Alegria, Claribel **26**
Dalton, Roque **36**

SCOTTISH

Burns, Robert **6**
Dunbar, William **67**
Henryson, Robert **65**
Muir, Edwin **49**
Scott, Walter **13**

SENEGALESE

Senghor, Léopold Sédar **25**

SINGAPORAN

Thumboo, Edwin Nadason **30**

SOUTH AFRICAN

Brutus, Dennis **24**

SPANISH

Castro, Rosalia de **41**
Cernuda, Luis **62**
Fuertes, Gloria **27**
García Lorca, Federico **3**
Guillén, Jorge **35**
Jiménez (Mantecón), Juan Ramón **7**

ST. LUCIAN

Walcott, Derek **46**

SWEDISH

Ekeloef, (Bengt) Gunnar **23**

SYRIAN

Gibran, Kahlil **9**

WELSH

Abse, Dannie **41**
Dafydd ap Gwilym **56**
Thomas, Dylan (Marlais) **2**, **52**

PC-71 Title Index

ISBN 0-7876-8705-7

90000